HIPPOCRENE STANDARD DICTIONARY

PERSIAN-ENGLISH DICTIONARY

HIPPOCRENE STANDARD DICTIONARY

PERSIAN-ENGLISH DICTIONARY

S. Haim

Introduction translated by Iraj Anvar

HIPPOCRENE BOOKS
New York

Originally published in 1989 by Farhang Moaser, Tehran.

Hippocrene paperback edition 1993.

Fourth printing, 2002.

For information, please address:
HIPPOCRENE BOOKS, INC.
171 Madison Avenue
New York, NY 10016

ISBN 0-7818-0055-2

Printed in the United States of America.

اکحل - بدوح - بضعه - تدویر - چشم سفید - خطیط - رسیل - زقوم -
حمدل - خضارت - داشخار - درواخ - دندین - راحل -
شیاع - ظافر - عواد - غافر - فرغند - قاص - کعب الاحبد - لقلقیات

have been left out of the Compact Haim Persian-English Dictionary.

Acknowledgments

It is obvious that one individual cannot, by himself, author a dictionary and any such effort will run into numerous difficulties, inevitably resulting in omissions and mistakes. On the other hand, getting together a group at one time presents its own difficulties and one person, using his own taste and techniques, may be able to do a better and faster job. To achieve both results, I had no choice but to seek the assistance of my knowledgeable friends and now is the time to thank them all for their help. I would especially like to mention Mr. Jamshid Sirous, one of the best teachers of English language and literature who extended tremendous assistance in finding English equivalents for many Persian slang words and phrases, and Mr. Ali-Ashraf Sheybani, the Persian language scholar, who assisted me in finding the origins and etymology of Persian words. I wish them both health and success.

S. Haim

which is a derivative of " انگل "; then you see the colloquial word " انگلک ". Also the word " کمد ", of French origin, comes between " کم‌خونی " and " کم‌دل ", while it is not etymologically related to either. In another place, you see an animal called " گوگردانک " has separated the word " گوگرد " from its adjective form " گوگردی ". The only exception to this rule are compound verbs with " کردن " and " شدن " which appear immediately after the word they are derived from. This is also true for compound words and idioms such as " انگل‌کردن " which appears after " انگل " and not after " انگل‌شناسی " and " گوگردزدن " or " جوهرگوگرد " which come under " گوگرد " in smaller typeface. In other words, such words and idioms are not part of the main body of the dictionary which is printed in bold.

2- Grammatical Points - Various grammatical forms of a word give different meanings to it. For example, if the word " درست " is used as an adjective, the English words "correct", "right" and "honest" can be used for it, while in its adverbial form, it is equivalent to "correctly" or "properly". Therefore, before attempting to find the meaning for a word, one has to recognize its grammatical role in the sentence, otherwise much time will be lost finding the right meaning.

3- Finding the Unknown Through the Known - Many devices have been employed for the sake of brevity and it has been left to the intelligence and creativity of the student to find the meanings of terms not included here through the ones included.

Example:

Bleeder; Phlebotomist رگ‌زن
Bloodletting, bleeding رگ‌زنی

These two examples show that "bloodletter" can be used for " رگ‌زن " because "bloodletting" has been listed for " رگ‌زنی " and it is also possible to use "phlebotomy" for " رگ‌زنی " because "phlebotomist" is listed for " رگ‌زن ". (Of course, this may be more useful for native English speakers who know what words are available in their language).

The following is also another example of brevity:

[کُتُب] A. کُتّاب
[ریز] ریختن

The first one shows that " کُتُب " is the Arabic plural of " کُتّاب " and the second example shows that " ریز " is derived from the verb " ریختن ", but no explanation is given as to the plurality of the first or the imperative form of the second.

4- Unreasonable Expectations - An 800-page dictionary cannot be expected to contain as many terms as a 2000-page one. Therefore, obscure terms such as :

the fact that the "Farhangestân"[2] has coined Persian equivalents for them. Of this type are terms such as:

تداخل امواج - غلبه خون - تصعید - قرع و انبیق - تفرق و اتصال -
باروت پنبه - تقدمة المعرفه - جنین کاذب - جوع البقری - حجر الیهود -
حس لمس - رداءت مزاج

and many others. There also numerous technical terms coined by people, sellers of technical items and even drivers, that are either completely fabricated or borrowed and adapted from other languages, such as:

پارازیت انداختن - چکش برق - کلید روکار - ساسات - کنتور
ساعت دار - سرفنتیل - شاتون - ضد ضربه - عایق کاری - گرفتن یا
ول کردن کلاچ

There was no choice but to accept and include them.

Pronunciation of Persian Words

Since this dictionary is primarily aimed at native Persian users, no transliteration is included because it would only have contributed to the size of the book. I have only transliterated difficult words and those easy to mispronounce, such as:

حیز - hayez　　مطلع - motale'　　مطلع - matla'

Using the Dictionary

As I mentioned in the introduction to the first printing, using a dictionary efficiently and finding the desired words and meanings is a science in itself which, unfortunately, is known only to those who have had extensive exposure to various dictionaries. Therefore, I feel some guidelines should be given.

1- Similarity of Words In some monolingual dictionaries, a method called grouping is used, meaning that all derivatives of a word and all words of the same root are grouped together in one place, while in bilingual dictionaries (including this one) the order of words, of either simple or compound nature, are merely alphabetical. Thus the word " انگلستان " immediately follows " انگل " and then comes " انگل‌شناسی "

[2]Iranian Academy of Languages and Literature.

In the Name of God

Introduction

In our age, when cultural exchanges among countries have become so much a part of life, learning foreign languages is a vital part of anyone's education. Fortunately, facilities for foreign language study are abundantly available in Iran and it would be wrong for students, authors and publishers to neglect what is expected of them by society.

Good text books, experienced teachers and appropriate methods are the tools required for the study of any science. For foreign language study, however, a good bilingual dictionary undoubtedly must be added to the above ingredients.

Evolution of Language and Culture

I have been preparing various Persian-English and English-Persian dictionaries for a quarter of a century now and have, every now and then, asked my publishers to put out a new, improved version with fewer errors[1]. A bilingual dictionary is in constant need of revision - more so than any other book, since the language of any developed nation changes and evolves constantly and dictionaries also must be updated constantly to meet the needs of translators.

Usefulness and Brevity

In recent years, large groups of people have discovered a need for small and inexpensive dictionaries. Nevertheless, I personally believe that even a compact dictionary should contain a certain number of idioms and even scientific and technical terms; otherwise, it would not be very useful and would, in many cases, just disappoint the user. Now that I have the chance to present the new compact version of Haim Persian-English Dictionary to my fellow citizens, I thank God for having given me the opportunity to achieve this goal and I have tried to include words in various categories, from literary and obsolete words to colloquial and slang ones, to the extent the scope of this book would permit.

In scientific and technical categories, in which some claim Persian is lacking, it would have been a pity not to include some older terms and to lose those valuable nuggets in spite of

---

[1] I would like to take this opportunity to thank all my publishers for the time and capital they have invested for this purpose.

HIPPOCRENE STANDARD DICTIONARY

PERSIAN-ENGLISH DICTIONARY

Hints on the pronunciation and transliteration of Persian.

The present work is not supposed to be a pronouncing dictionary. Occasionally, however, the vowel-points (َ), (ِ), and (ُ), which will be explained below, have been used, or else resort has been made to transliteration. These exceptions were especially necessary when two words were written alike but pronounced differently, as آبرو and آبرو (-row), or مُبیّن and مبیَن (*mobayen*), or when it was very difficult, even for Iranian students, to guess the pronunciation of a word like حیز (*hayez*)

The Persian vowels and consonants are explained below, and English equivalents are given so far as possible:

I. The Vowels.

(a) The literal vowels.

ا *alef* corresponds to "*a*" in "*far*", and has been represented by the Roman "a" (in contradistinction with the italic *a*).

و *vaw* corresponds to "*oo*" in "*loop*", and has been represented by *u:*.

ی *yeh* corresponds to "*i*" in "*prestige*", or to "*ee*" in "*fleet*", and has been represented by *i:*

(b) The vowel-points.

(َ) *zebar* corresponds to *a* in the French word "blasé"

( ) *zi:r* corresponds to *e* in "*petrol*".

( ) *pi:sh* corresponds to *o* in *omit*.

The above three vowel-points are usually left out in print except when it is intended to avoid confusion.

II. The Consonants.

(a) The 'hard' consonants.

Only the following 'hard' consonants need to be commented on

خ is pronounced as "ch" in the Scotch word "loch", or as "gh" in the word "ugh". In transliteration it has been represented by *kh*.

ژ is pronounced as "s" in "measure", and has been represented in transliteration by *zh*.

غ & ق have a guttural sound which is produced by pressing together the muscles of the pharyngeal passage and allowing the breath to pass through.

گ is pronounced as the hard *g* in *go*

و (which was before enlisted among vowels) is here introduced as a consonant, being pronounced as *v*.

ی is pronounced as *y* in *young*. (It is also a vowel corresponding to *ee*, as was explained before).

(b) *Hamzeh*, the 'consonant *alef*'

It is a Persian grammatical theory that a true vowel is one that follows a consonant, not one that i followed by it. Accordingly, the English people should admit that *a* is a vowel in *ha*, but a consonant in *apt*, and also that *i* is a vowel in *tin*, but a consonant in *in*.

Hamzeh represents all those English vowels that begin a syllable, as in *apt*; *into*, *onward*, *elf*, etc. At the beginning of a word it always appears as ا (which may well be called a 'consonant *alef*'), and may be followed by any of the six vowels. Ex. از *az*, from; اِسم *esm*, name;. اُلاغ *olagh*, donkey; اورمزد *u:rmozd*, Ormuzd; ایمان *i:man*, faith; آب (originally اااب) *ab*, water.

A quiescent *hamzeh*, i. e. one which is not followed by a vowel, is represented in transliteration by an apostrophe ('), which indicates a hiatus. Such a *hamzeh* assumes different shapes as follows

(a) the shape of an *alef*, marked by the sign (ٔ)

when the preceding vowel is *a*, as in رافت *ra'fat*

(b) the shape of a ی , marked by (ء) , when the preceding vowel is *e*. Ex. ذِئب *ze'b*.

(c) the shape of a و , marked by (ء) , if the preceding vowel is *o*. Ex. لؤلؤ *lo'lo'*.

(d) the shape (ء) alone when preceded by a long vowel. Ex. آراء *ara'*.

(c) The letter ع

ع is originally a guttural consonant , but is usually pronounced as the consonant *alef* (ا) or *hamzeh*, already treated above. Thus عاری and آری would both be pronounced (*ari:*).

Abbreviations اختصارات

A.	Arabic	عربی
a.; *adj.*	adjective	صفت
ad.	adverb	قید
Anat.	Anatomy	کالبد شناسی
a. p.	Arabic elements combined in the Persian fashion.	دو جزء عربی که بقاعده فارسی با هم ترکیب شده‌اند
Arith.	Arithmetic	علم حساب
Astr.	Astronomy	هیئت
Bot.	Botany	گیاه شناسی
By e.	By extension	با تعمیم معنی ، توسعاً
C. E.	Customary error	غلط مشهور
Cf.	*Confer* = Compare	مقایسه کنید با
Chem.	Chemistry	شیمی
comb.	combination (ترکیب) ; i. e. compound words	
comp.	comparative	درجه تفضیلی
conj.	conjunction	حرف عطف
Cont.	Contraction	مختصر
C. P.	Card-playing	ورق بازی
D.	Dual	تثنیه
Dim.	Diminutive	مصغر ، تصغیر
E.	English	انگلیسی
ep.	epithet	صفت
esp.	especially	بویژه
etc.	et cætera ; and so forth	وغیره
Ex.	Example	مثال
f.	from	از
F.	Figuratively	مجازاً
Fem	Feminine	مؤنث
Fr.	French	فرانسه
G.	Greek	یونانی
Geog.	Geography	جغرافیا
Geom.	Geometry	هندسه
Gr.	Grammar	دستور زبان
H.	Hindoostani	هندوستانی
Heb.	Hebrew	عبری
H. t.	Honorific title	لقب
i. e.	*id est* = that is	یعنی
Imp.	Imperative	امر
int.	interjection	حرف ندا
inter.	interrogative	استفهامی
It.	Italian	ایتالیائی
L.	Loosely	با مسامحه ، اگر زیاد دقیق نشویم
Lat.	Latin	لاتین
M.	Machines ; also mechanics	ماشین یا مکانیك
Mas.	Masculine	مذکر
Math.	Mathematics	ریاضیات
Med.	Medicine	طب ، پزشکی
Met.	Metaphorically	بطریق استعاره
Mil.	Military	نظام
Mus.	Music	موسیقی
n.	noun	اسم
Obs.	Obsolete	مهجور
Orig.	Originally	در اصل
OS.	Original sense(s)	معنی یا معانی اصلی
P.	Persian	فارسی
p. c.	polite conversation	مکالمات آمیخته به ادب و تعارف
Per.	Perhaps	شاید
Phys.	Physics	فیزیك
Pl ; pl	plural	جمع

P. P.	**past participle**	اسم‌مفعول
pr.	**proper**	خاص
prep.	**preposition**	حرف اضافه
pron.	**pronoun**	ضمیر
q. v.	*quod vide* = **which see**	که باید بدان مراجعه شود
R.	**Russian**	روسی
rel.	**relative**	موصول [در ضمیر]
s.	**singular**	مفرد
S. a.	*See also*	نیز مراجعه شود به
s. **o.**	**some one**	کسی
s. **t.**	**something**	چیزی
S. u.	*See under*	زیر (فلان لغت) آمده است
Suf.	**Suffix**	پس وند، لفظ الحاقی
sup.	**superlative**	درجه عالی
syl.	**syllable**	هجا ، سیلاب
T.	**Turkish**	ترکی
U. S.	United States	کشور های متحد امریکا
usu.	**usually**	معمولاً
vi.	**intransitive verb**	فعل لازم
vt.	**transitive verb**	فعل متعدی
Z.	Zoology	جانور شناسی
1st.	**first**	اول
2nd.	**second**	دوم
&	and	وَ

Conventional Signs علامات قراردادی

○	Rare	کمیاب
•	Poetic(al)	شاعرانه
+	1) Colloquial	محاوره‌ای
	2) Colloquially	در محاوره
×	Slang	عامیانه باحرفه ای
:	(For) example	مثال ـ مثلا
?	Origin unknown to the author	مأخذ آن برای مؤلف مجهول ماند

آ - ا

آ *or* آی [In p. of آمدن] Come thou [usu. بیا]

آب Water. Juice. Humour. — آب افتادن To water, as the mouth. — آب انداختن To stale; make w.: said of beasts. [*With* در] To supply or fill with w. — آب بآب شدن To travel for health improvement purposes. *F.* To go west: die. — آب برداشتن To be equivocal. — آب پس دادن To leak. — آب جوش = **آبجوش** ‖ آب خوردن To drink w. *F.* To crop up; originate. — آبِ خوردن Drinking w. — آب خوش از گلویش پایین نرفت He was never happy; he led a dog's life. — آب دادن To give a drink (to). To water. To plate; coat with silver, gold, etc. To temper or anneal. — آب درگوش کسی کردن To throw dust in some one's eyes. — آب در هاون ساییدن To carry water in a sieve; flog a dead horse. — آب دردست داری نخور Don't let the grass grow under your feet. — آبِ دهان Saliva. Spittle. — آب زدن To moisten. To water; add w. to. — آب زیپو ×Wishy-washy drink, soup, etc.; mere wash. — آب زیر کاه Sly (person); deep or shrewd (p.); snake in the grass. — آب در چیزی کردن To adulterate s. t. — آبِ سبز *or* آبِ سیاه Glaucoma. — آبِ سفید *or* آبِ مروارید Cataract (in the eye). — آب شدن To melt or thaw. To be dissolved. *F.* To be sold off. — آب طلا Gold plating. Rolled gold. — آب کردن To m. To dissolve. To sell off trade off. — آب کشیدن To rinse. To swill (out). — آب لیمو = آبِ لیمو ‖ **آبلیمو** آب نقره Silver plating; electroplating. — آبِ یخ Ice water. — از آب در آمدن To prove (to be). — به آ. انداختن To launch.

آباد Habitable; populous; cultivated. — آ. کردن To make habitable. To improve.

آبادانی Development; improvement. Populousness.

آبادی 1) Village. 2) آبادانی

آباژور *Fr.* Lamp-shade.

آبان *Eighth month having 30 days.*

آب انبار (Underground) water tank or cistern.

آب باز Swimmer. Diver.

آب بازی Diving. Swimming.
آب بندی Stopping a leak. *M.* Valve grinding.
آب بها Water-rate.
آب پا Water supervisor.
آب پاش Watering-can. – اتوموبیل آ. Watering-cart.
آب پاشی Sprinkling of water.
آب پز Boiled (in water).
آبتنی (Cold) bath. – آ. کردن To take a b.
آبجو Beer.
آبجو سازی Beer-brewing.
آبجوش Boiling water.
آب خشك كن Blotting-paper.
آبخور Irrigable area. [*Of a ship*] Draught.
آبخوری Drinking-cup; tankard. – دهنهٔ آ. Snaffle or halter; also, bit. – لیوان آ. Glass; tumbler.
آبخیز Aquiferous.
آبدار Juicy. Hydrous. *F.* Lustrous. Gross; deep; full.
آبدار Butler.
آبدارخانه Butler's pantry.
آبدان Bladder; vesica.
آبدانك Vescicle.
آبدزدك Syringe. Squirt. Mole-cricket.
آبدست (Water for) ablution.
آبدوغ Yogurt diluted with water.
آبدیده Damaged by water. – آهك آ. Slaked lime.
آبراهه Floodway; flood-channel.
آبرسان *M.* Injector.
آبرسانی Water supply.
آبرُفت Alluvium.
آبرنگ Water-colour.
آبِرو Honour; reputation; credit. – آبروی کسیرا ریختن To disgrace s. o.
[Gutter.
آبرو (*-row*) Watercourse.
آبرود (یا آبلود) کردن To soak, as a chicken, for plucking.
آبرودار ‖ آبرومند (1 2) Who maintains a respectable appearance; genteel.
آبرومند Respectable.
آبرومندانه Respectably. —*a*. Respectable.
آبریز Water-closet. W.-shed.
آبریزش *Med.* Epiphora.
آبزی Marine; aqueous.

آبستن Pregnant. – آ. بودن To expect a baby. – آ. شدن To conceive. – آ. کردن To make p.; impregnate. – آبستن ششماهه Six months gone with child.
آبستنی Pregnancy.
آبشار Waterfall.
[Destiny.
آبشخور Watering-trough. *F.*
آبشی *or* آبشیر Sink.
آبغوره Verjuice.
آبفشان Geyser.
[tiller.
آبكار Plater (of metals). Dis-
آبكاری Plating (of metals).
آبكش Strainer. Water-carrier.
آبكشی Rinsing. – آ. کردن To

rinse. To swill (out).
آبکشیده Rinsed. Infected. — موش آ. Drowned rat.
آبکی Liquid. Watery; washy.
آبگاه Hypochondrium. Pond ○.
آبگذر Watercourse.
آبگردان (Large) ladle. Dipper.
آب‌گرم‌کن Geyser.
آبگوشت Broth.
آبگونه Liquid.
آبگیر River-basin. Tankage. —*a.* Submergible.
آبگیری Supplying with water. Tankage; tonnage. — آ. کردن To supply or refill with water.
آبگین Aqueous.
آبگینه 1) شیشه 2) آئینه
آبلمبو کردن + To soften by squeezing, as a pomegranate.
آبله Small-pox. Blister. — آ. کردن or آ. درآوردن To be affected with s.-p.—آبلهٔ گاوی Cowpox.— آبلهٔ کسیرا کوبیدن To vaccinate s. o. against s. -p.
آبله‌رو With a pockmarked face.
آبله‌کوب Vaccinator.
آبله‌کوبی Vaccination against small-pox.
آبله مرغان Chicken-pox.
آبلیمو Lemon-juice.
آبلیموگیر Lemon-squeezer.
آب نارنج Orange-juice.
آب‌نبات Sweet(s). Barley-sugar.
آبنما Water-view.

آبنوس *A.* Ebony.
ابنوس‌کار *A. P.* Ebonist; cabinet-maker.
آب و تاب Bombastic style; grandiloquence.
آب و رنگ Rosy complexion.
آبونمان *Fr.* Subscription.
آبونه *Fr.* Subscriber. — آ. شدن To subscribe to.
آب وهوا Climate.
آبی Blue. Aquatic.
آبی ○ Quince [به].
آبیار Water-distributor. Person employed in irrigation.
آبیاری Irrigation. — آ. کردن To irrigate.
آپارات کردن *R.P.* To vulcanize.
آپارتمان *Fr.* Flat; apartment.
آتش Fire. — آ. زدن To set f. to; set on f. To light. *F.* To enrage. To squander. — آ. کردن To start, a a bus. To stoke. — آ. گرفتن To catch f. To explode. *F.* To be enraged.— آ. به اختیار *Mil.* Ready! — آتش: شروع *Mil.* Open fire! — آتشِ گرسنگی Flames of hunger
آتشبار Artillery. -*a.* Flaming.
آتشبازی Fireworks.
آتش بس Cease fire.
آتش پاره Fire-brand. Spark. *F.* (1) Quarrelsome person; (2) naughty child.
آتش پرست Fire-worshipper.
آتش پرستی Fire-worship.
آتشدان 1) منقل 2) Hearth;

fireplace.
آتش سوزی Fire.
آتش فشان Volcano [usu. کوه آ.].
آتش فشانی Volcanic (action).
آتشك Mild charcre.
آتشکده Fire-temple.
آتشگیر Inflammable.
آتشی مزاج *P.A.* Of a fiery temper; irascible.
آتش نشان Fireman.
آتش نشانی Fire-fighting. — ادارهٔ آ. Fire station.
آتشی Fiery. Fire-red. Igneous. *F.* Enraged. — آ. شدن To fire up. — آ. کردن To enrage.
آتشین Fiery. Ardent.
آتن *Fr.* Athens.
آتی *A.* Coming; future. *Cf. the fem.* آتیه
اتیه *A.* The future [آینده]. [*Orig. fem. of* آتی]
آثار *A.* Traces. Relics; monuments. Traditions. *Cf. the s.* اثر ‖ آثار ادبی Literary works. [elevations.
آج Rough surface; small
آجدار Granulated. Having a rough surface. [brick.
آجر Brick. — آجر نسوز Fire-
آجرپز Brick-burner.
آجرپزی Brick-burning. — کورهٔ آ. Brick-kiln.
آجرسازی Brick-making. — کارخانهٔ آ. Brickworks.
آجرفرش *P. A.* Brick pavement.*
آجری Of brick; b.-made. Brick-red.
آجل *A.* Ultimate.
آجلاً *A.* Ultimately.
اجودان *Fr.* Aide-de-camp.
آجیده Quilted. —*n. Kind of* گیوه *with a quilted sole.*
آجیل Dried nuts or seeds; dried fruit.
آچار *T.* Screw-driver. Wrench. Spanner. Pickles. — آجیل آ. Nuts or seeds seasoned with vinegar. — آچار بوکس Box wrench; socket spanner. — آچار پیچ گوشتی Screw-driver. — آچار دوسر Double-end spanner. — آچارشلاقی Stillson w. — آچار چکش Monkey-w. — آچار زنجیری Chain-w. — آچارفرانسه Adjustable spanner. — آچار قاشقی Ring s.
آحاد [Pl. of احد]
آخ + Ah! Alas! Ouch! — آخ و واخ کردن To moan with pain. [sheathe.
آختن ٥ [آز] To draw or un-
آخر *A.* Last. —*n.* [Pl. اواخر] End. *ad.* At last. — آخرِسر & آخرکار In the end. At l. — یکی به آ. مانده L. but one; penultimate.
آخرالامر *A.* At last.
آخربین *A. P.* Provident.
آخرت *A.* Futurity; future life.
آخری *or* آخرین *A. P.* (The) last.
آخور Manger; crib.
آخورك Collar-bone.

آخوند Theologian. Tutor.
آخوندك Praying mantis.
آداب *A.* Ceremonies; formalities. Rules. Manners. *Cf. the s.* ادب [*Adams* brand.
آدامس *E.* Chewing-gum
آدم *A.* Adam. Human; mankind. Man of consequence. — آدم جنگلی Orang-outang or other anthropoid. — آ. نمیداند چه بکند One does not know what to do.
آدم خوار *or* **آدم خور** *A. P.* Man-eating. *—n.* M.-eater.
آدمك *A. P.* Toy-man. Automaton. Pupil of the eye.
آدم کش *A. P.* Homicide; assassin.
آدمکشی *A. P.* Homicide.
آدم نما *or* **آدم‌وار** Anthropoid.
آدمی *A. P.* Human(ity). Man.
آدمیت *A.* Humanity.
آدمیزاد(ه) *A.P.* Human (being).
آدینه Friday.
آذر 1) آتش 2) *Ninth month having 30 days.*
آذرخش *or* **آزرخش** Lightning.
آذرین Igneous.
آذوقه Provisions.
آذین Decoration. — آ. بستن To decorate: شهر را آ. بستند
آر = * **آور**
آر *Fr.* Are.
آرا *or* **آرای** [Imp. of آراستن]
آراء [Pl. of رای] [ment.
آراستگی Arrangement; adorn-
آراستن [آرای] To adorn or decorate. To arrange; put in order.
آراسته Decorated. Arranged.
آرام Quiet. *—n.* Tranquillity; rest.— آ. شدن To quiet down; become q. — آ. کردن To q. or pacify. — آ. گرفتن To q. (down). To find comfort.
آرام بخش *a.* Tranquillizing. Comforting.
آرام ده Soothing; calmative.
آرامش Peace. Tranquillity; repose.
آرامگاه Resting-place. Tomb.
آرامی Calmness. *S. a.* آرامش
آرای *S. u.* **آرا**
آرایش Decoration. Adornment. Toilet; dressing-up. — آ. دادن To dress up. To adorn. — آ. کردن To d. up.
آرایشگاه Hairdressing saloon; barber's shop. [dresser ○.
آرایشگر Decorator. Hair-
آرتیست *Fr.* Artist. (Female) dancer or singer+.
آرد Flour. — آرد برنج Ground rice.— آرد خود را بیخته است He's had his fling. He has sown his wild oats.
آرد بیز ○ Sieve.
آردی Floury. Farinaceous.
آرزو Wish; desire. Aspiration Ideal. Hope. — آ. بردن To aspire (for). — آ. * پختن To nourish a h. — آ. کردن To wish; aspire for. To

آزادی Freedom; liberty. — آزادی عقیده L. of conscience. — آزادی عمل Free hand; elbow-room. — آزادی مطبوعات L. of the press.
آزادیخواه Freedom-loving. Liberal.
آزادیخواهی Love of freedom.
آزار Injury; harm. Persecution. — آ. کردن *or* آ. دادن To torment. To persecute. — آ. دیدن To be hurt or injured.
آزار [Imp. of آزردن]
آزاله *Fr.* Azalea.
آزرخش *S. u.* آذرخش
آزردگی 1) State of being vexed; annoyment. 2) آزار
آزردن [آزار] To annoy; vex. To afflict. To torment. To oppress.
آزرده Annoyed; offended; vexed. Harmed. Lacerated.
آزرده‌خاطر *P. A.* & آزرده دل Offended; annoyed. Distressed.
آزرم * Shame. Modesty.
آزرمجو ○ Modest. Mild.
آزرمیدن ○ To feel ashamed.
آزما(ی) [Imp. of آزمودن]
آزمایش Test; experiment. Temptation. — آ.کردن To test or e. To try. To tempt.
آزمایشگاه Laboratory.
آزمایشگاهی Laboratorial.
آزمایشی Tentative. Probational; probationary.
آزمند Greedy.
آزمودگی Experience.

covet. — آ. بگور بردن To die frustrated in one's w.
آرزومند Desirous. Hopeful. — توفیق شما را آرزومندم I wish you success.
آرژانتین *Fr.* Argentine.
آرشه *Fr.* (Violin's) bow.
آرشیو *Fr.* = بایگانی & ضبط
آرم *Fr.* Arms; armorial bearings.
آرمان Ideal. Aim. Desire.
آرمیدن * [آرام] = **آرام** گرفتن
آرنج Elbow. — استخوان آ. Crazy-bone.
آرواره Jaw.
آروغ زدن To belch.
آره + = آری & بله
آری Yes. Yea.
آریایی Aryan.
آز Greed; avidity.
آزاد Free. Exempt. Optional. *Mil.* Stand at ease! — آ. شدن To obtain liberty; be released. — آ. کردن To set at l. To release. To lift the ban on. — در هوای آ. In the open air. — ماهی آ. Salmon-trout.
آزادانه Freely. Frankly.
آزاد (درخت) Azedarach.
آزادگان [Pl. of آزاده].
آزادگی Freedom. Frankness. Broad-mindedness.
آزاد ماهی Salmon-trout.
آزاده Free (-born). Noble. Broad-minded. F. from care. —*n.* [Pl. آزادگان] Freeman. B.-m. person.

آزمودن [آزمای] To test. To experience.
آزموده Experienced. Tried.
آزمون Test; experiment.
آزوقه = **آذوقه** [خبرگزاری
آژانس *Fr.* 1) نمایندگی *or* نماینده 2)
آژنگ ο Wrinkle.
آژور *Fr.* Open-work ; also ; open work. —*a.* Up-to-date.
آژیر Alarm; tocsin. [*poker.*
آس Ace. *Game similar to*
آسا *or* **آسای** [Imp. of آسودن]
آسان Easy. -*ad**. Easily.— آ.کردن To render easy; facilitate.— آ. گرفتن To take e. To be lenient.
آسانی Easy. — به آ. Easily.
آسایش Rest. Tranquillity. — آسایش خاطر Peace of mind.
آسایشگاه Sanatorium. Rest-house.
آستان 1) * Threshold; sill. 2) *F.* Audience.
آستانه Sill; threshold.
آستر Lining. Priming ; first coat.— آ کردن To line.— آ.زدن To prime ; put the first coat on. To line ο.
آستردوز Liner.
آستین Sleeve.— باد در آ. انداختن To put on airs. — آ. بالا زدن To turn up one's sleeve. *F.* To gird up one's loins. — آ. برافشاندن * To dance.
آستین سرخود (With a) raglan sleeve.
آسمان Sky; heaven.— آ. وریسمان Chalk and cheese; cock-and-bull story.
آسمان خراش Sky-scraper.
آسمان غُرغُره + = رعد - تندر
آسمانه Canopy ; baldachin ; tester. [*Of an aircraft*] Visibility; ceiling.
آسمانی Heavenly ; divine. [For آبی آ.] Sky-blue.
آسودگی Tranquillity; peace. Ease. Comfort.
آسودن * [آسای] To repose; rest. To obtain peace of mind.
آسوده Tranquil; quiet. Peaceful. Well-to-do. — آ. شدن To get q.; be relieved.— آ. کردن To q. To relieve; give peace of mind. To disembarrass.
آسوده حال *P. A.* Well-to-do; well off. Tranquil.
آسوده خاطر *P. A.* Enjoying peace of mind; tranquil.
آسوری Assyrian.
آسه Axis or axle.
آسیا Asia. — آسیای صغیر A. Minor.
آسیا *or* **آسیاب** (Water-) mill.— آ. کردن To grind ; mill. — آسیای بادی Windmill.— دندان آ. Molar tooth; grinder.— سنگ آ. Millstone.
آسیابان Miller.
آسیابانك Ant-lion.
آسیاسنگ * Millstone.
آسیائی Asiatic.
آسیب Injury. Damage.— آ. دیدن To sustain an injury ; be hurt.— آ. رساندن To injure ;

harm.– آسیب‌دیدگانِ زلزله Earthquake victims.

آش *T*.(Sour) pottage or soup. Starch for stiffening. – آش کردن To impregnate with infusions for tanning or tawing. – آش دهن سوزی نیست It is nothing to write home (*or* shout) about ; it isn't particularly good (*or* pleasant).– آ. برای کسی پختن To cook some one's goose.

آشام 1) [Imp. of آشامیدن]. 2) Absorption.

آشامیدن [آشام] To drink. To absorb. [Beverage.

آشامیدنی Drinkable. –*n*.

آشپز *T*. *P*. Cook.

آشپزخانه *T*. *P*. Kitchen.

آشپزی *T*.*P*. Cooking; cookery. آ.کردن To be a cook.

آشتی Peace. Reconciliation. – آ. دادن To reconcile.– آ.کردن To make it up; m. peace.

آشغال Rubbish; refuse; litter. Garbage.

آشفتگی Agitation; disturbance; unrest. Amazement.

آشُفتن [آشوب] To be disturbed or agitated. To get excited.– *vt*. To disturb. To amaze.

آشُفته Disturbed. Distressed. Amazed. Dishevelled*.

آشکار Manifest; evident. Open; public. –*ad*. Openly.– آ. شدن To become manifest. To be revealed. – آ.کردن To reveal; divulge. To detect.

آشکارا Openly; frankly.

آشکوب *S*. *u*. اُشکوب

آشنا Acquainted; familiar. –*n*. [Pl. آشنایان] Acquaintance ; friend. – آ. شدن To get acquainted ; become familiar. To get used. – آ.کردن To familiarize; acquaint. To intimate. To initiate.

آشنائی Acquaintance.

آشوب Riot; disturbance; revolt. Confusion. – آ. کردن To riot ; cause a d.

آشوب انگیز Seditious or revolutionary (person).

آشوب طلب *P*. *A*. Riotous.

آشوبگر Agitator.

آشوبی Revolutionary : حرکت آ.

آشور(ی) Assyria(n).

آشیان* Nest. آ. بستن– To build a nest.– آ.کردن To live, as in a n.– آ.گرفتن To choose one's n. in. To build a n.– آشیانِ مسلسل *Mil*. Pill-box.

آشیانه Nest. Hangar.

آغا *T*. Eunuch. [Fem. of آقا used in pr. names: انیس‌آغا].

آغاز Beginning. – آ. کردن To begin; start.

آغازگر Starter [*in races*].

آغازیان The Protista.

آغشتن ٥ [آغر *or* آغار] To macerate. To impregnate. To pollute.

آغشته Mixed. Soaked.ـ آ. بخون Weltering in one's blood.

آغل *T*. Fold ; sheep-cote.

آغوز *T*. Beestings; colostrum.

آغوش Bosom; breast.ـ در آ. کشیدن *or* در آ. گرفتن To embrace.

آفات [Pl. of آفت].

آفاق *A*. [Pl. of افق] Horizons. *By e*. (Quarters of) the world.

آفت *A*. [آفات] Calamity. Plague; pest; vermin.

آفتاب Sun(shine). ـ آ. شد The sun shone *or* is shining again. ـ آفتابِ لبِ بام Person having one foot in the grave.

آفتاب پرست Sun-worshipper. Chameleon [also آفتاب‌کردك].

آفتاب پرستی Sun-worship.

آفتاب‌رو Exposed to the sun ; sunlit.

آفتاب زدگی Sunburn.

آفتاب زده Sun-stricken.

آفتاب زردی Sunset.

آفتاب غروب *P. A*. Sunset.

آفتاب‌گردان Visor. Sun-shade. Sun-protector. ـ گل آ. Sunflower.

آفتاب‌گرفتگی Sun-eclipse.

آفتاب گیر Parasol.—*a*. = آفتاب‌رو

آفتابه Ewer; aiguière.ـ آ. خرج لحیم است It's not worth powder and shot. The game is not worth the candle.

آفتابی Sunny ; fair ; fine. Solar. ـ آ. شدن To appear on the surface. *F*. To be published or noised abroad.

آفتامات *R*. Cutout; current and voltage regulator.

آفت زده *A. P*. Damaged. Calamity-stricken.

آفریدگار Creator.

آفریدن [آفرین] To create.

آفریده Created. —*n*. [Pl. آفریدگان] C. being.

آفرین 1) Praise ; applause. 2) —*int*. Well done !ـ آ. خواندن To praise or extol. To applaud. [Also آ. کردن].

آفرین [Imp. of آفریدن]

آفرینش Creation.

آفریننده Creator.

آقا *T*. Gentleman. Sir. ـ آقای ... Mr. (Mister) ... ـ آقای دکتر میر Dr. Mir. ـ آقا و مهندس میر Engineer Mir.ـ آقا و بانو میر Mr. & Mrs. Mir.

آقاجان *T. P*. (Dear) papa ; daddy. Dear fellow. *Mas. pr. name*.

آقازاده *T. P*. Son or daughter of a gentleman. [*In p. c*.] Your son (or d.) .

آقامنش *T. P*. Gentlemanly.

آقایی *T. P*. Character of a gentleman. Generosity. Mastership.

آك ○ = عیب Defect; blemish.

آکتر *Fr*. = هنرپیشه Actor.

آکتریس *Fr*. Actress.

آکله *A*. Phagedenic ulcer.
آگندن = آکندن
آگاه Aware. — آ. کردن To inform. [warn.
آگاهانیدن To inform. To
آگاهی Information. Advice; notice. — ادارهٔ آ. Criminal Investigation Department. — آ. دادن To inform; advise. — آ. یافتن To be informed; come to know; understand.
آگندن ○ [آکن] To stuff or fill.
آگه * [Cont. of آگاه]
آگهی 1) آگاهی 2) Notice; advertisement. [with.
آگین *Suf*. Full of. Mixed
آگینی Connective : بافتهٔ آ.
آل *A*. Descendants; posterity; also, people. Dynasty or house.
آلا *or* آلای [Imp. of آلودن]
آلات [Pl. of آلت].
آلاچیق *T*. Arbour; bower. *OS*. Tent covered with felt.
آلاگارسن *Fr*. Eton crop.
آلاله Buttercup.
آلام [Pl. of الم]
آلایش Contamination. Taint. Corruption. Alloy.
آلبوم *Fr*. Album.
آلت *A*. [آلات]. Tool. Instrument. (Genital) organ. Glazing bar. *F*. Tool; cat's-paw. — نقره‌آلات Silverware. — آ. کردن To use as one's tool.
آلتر *Fr*. Dumb-bell.
آلش Beech. [Germans.
المان *Fr*. Germany. — آ. ها The
آلمانی German.
آلو Plum. — آلوی بخارا Prune.
آلوبالو Black cherry.
آلوبالوئی Ox-blood (red); puce.
آلوچه Damson. Prunella.
آلودگی Contamination. Implication. Embarrassment.
آلودن [آلای] To contaminate. To taint.
آلوده Contaminated. Implicated. Embarrassed. — آ. شدن To be c. To get involved. — آ. کردن To contaminate. To implicate; involve.
آلوزرد Mirabelle.
آلومینیوم *Fr*. Aluminium.
آلونك Hut; hovel.
آماتور *Fr*. Amateur.
آماج * Target.
آمادگاه Depot; training centre.
آمادگی Readiness. Fitness.
آماده Ready; prepared. Fit. Equipped. — آ. شدن To get ready. — آ. کردن To make r. To equip. — برگِ آ. بخدمت R.-for-service certificate.
آمار Statistics.
آمارشناس Statistician.
آماری Statistical.
آماس Swelling; inflammation. — آ. کردن To swell.
آمال [Pl. of امل].
آمبولانس *Fr*. Ambulance.

آمپر *Fr*. Ampere.
آمپرسنج *Fr. P*. Ammeter.
آمپول *Fr*. Ampoule.
آمد + Luck [f. آمدن]. آ. کردن ـ To bring good luck.
آمدن [آی *or* آ]. 1) To come. 2) To become; suit; match. 3) * To become. بیائید بازی کنیم ـ Let us play.
آمدنی Coming; sure to come.
آمد و رفت Traffic. Frequentation. ـ آ. کردن To come and go; ply to and fro; traffic.
آمدوشد = آمد و رفت
آمده [P.P. of آمدن] Come.
آمر *A*. Commanding; imperious. —*n*. One who gives an order ○. دلال و آمر وی ـ The broker and his principal.
آمرانه *A. P*. Imperiously; in a commanding tone. — *a*. Imperious.
آمرز [Imp. of آمرزیدن].
آمرزش Forgiveness; absolution.
آمرزنده (One) who forgives.
آمرزیدگی Absolution; salvation.
آمرزیدن [آمرز] To forgive.
آمرزیده Forgiven. — *n*. [Pl. آمرزیدگان] One who has found salvation.
آمله Emblic myrobalan.
آموختگی Tameness. Addiction.
آموختن [آموز] To learn. To teach*.
آموخته Tame. Accustomed; used; addicted.
آمودریا Amudarya; Oxus.
آموز [Imp. of آموختن]
آموزانیدن ○ To teach.
آموزش Instruction; training. ـ آ. وپرورش Education.
آموزشگاه School.
آموزگار Teacher.
آموزگاری Teaching.
آموزنده Learner. Instructor. —*a*. Instructive.
آمیختگی Mixture.
آمیختن [آمیز] To mix. To associate.
آمیخته Mixed.
آمیز [Imp. of آمیختن]
آمیزش Intercourse. Association. ـ آ. کردن To associate.
آمیزشی Venereal: ناخوشی آ.
آمیزه ○ Alligation.
آمین *A*. Amen!
آن That. The former *. ـ آنکه That which. He who ـ دوم آنکه Secondly. ـ بر آنم که 1) I am determined to. 2) I maintain that.
آن *A*. [آوان] Instant; moment. ـ آ. بآن At every m.
آناً *A*. Instantaneously.
آنان [Pl. of آن] They. Those. ـ آنانکه They who; those who.
آناناس *Lat*. Pineapple.
آنتن *Fr*. Aerial.
آنتیل *Fr*. Antilles. ـ جزایر آنتیل

West Indies.
آنجا There ; (in) that place.— از آنجائی که Since ; inasmuch as. — که از آ. Whence.
آنچنان So. Such.
آنچه What; that which. — هرآ. Whatever.
آنژین *Fr*. Angina.
آنسان (In) that manner.
آنفلوانزا *Fr*. Influenza.
آنقدر *S. u.* قدر
آنکه = • **آنکو** & **آنك** آن ، **نکه** *S. u.*
آنگاه Then; afterwards.
آنگه • [Cont. of آنگاه]
آنورس *Fr*. Antwerp.
آنها [Pl. of آن] Those; they [*for persons, animals, or things*]. — آنهایی که *or* آنهاکه They who. Those which.
آنی *A*. Instantaneous.
آوا • [Cont. of آواز]
آوار Load; pressure; weight. Debris. *By e*. Collapse. — زیر آ. ماند He was buried under the d.
آوارگی Vagrancy; homelessness.
آواره Vagrant ; homeless ; wandering (about). — آ. شدن To go vagrant; wander.— آوارگان *n*. Refugees; h. persons.
آواری Detrital.
آواز Voice. Tune or melody (not limited in time by notes) Call. Fame. — آ. دادن • To c. out. — آ. خواندن To sing (a m.) «آوازِ . . .» (Sung) by . . .
آوازه 1) آواز 2) Fame.
آوازه‌خوان (Professional) singer.
آوان ○ *A*. [Pl. of آن] Moments. Time(s). [Usu. written اَوان]
آوخ • Ah ! Alas !
آوَر [Imp. of آوردن]
آورُتا *G*. Aorta.
آوردن [آور] To bring. *F*. To produce. To occasion. To embrace : اسلام آورد ‖ آورده‌اند It is related.
آوَرده [P. P. of آوردن] Brought.
آوَرنده Bringer. Bearer.
آوریل *Fr*. April.
آوند Vessel; vasculum.
آوندی Vascular.
آونس *E*. Ounce.
آونگ 1) Pendulum. 2) آویزان
آویختن [آویز] To hang ; suspend. To cling •.
آویخته Suspended; hanging.
آویز 1) [Imp. of آویختن]. 2) Pendant. — گل آ. Fuschia.
آویزان Hanging ; suspended.— آ. کردن & آ. شدن To hang.
آویزه (Earring with a) pendant. Vermiform appendix.
آویزه بند Suspensor.
آه Sigh. —*int*. Ah ! Alas ! — آه‌سرد Bitter (*or* discouraged sigh. — آه‌کشیدن To s. ; utter a s. — آه ندارد که با ناله سوداکند He has not a penny to bless himself with.

آها + Aha ! I see !
آهار Starch. Stiffness. ـ آ. زدن To starch. ـ گل آ. Zinnia.
آهاردار Starched; stiff.
آهاری Starched ; starchy.
آهستگی Slowness . ـ به آ. Slowly. Softly.
آهسته Slow(ly). Soft(ly). Gradual(ly).
آهك Lime . ـ آهكِ آبديده or آهك كشته Slaked lime. ـ آهك آب نديده Quicklime. ـ سنگ آ. Limestone.
آهك پز Lime-burner.
آهك پزی Lime-burning. ـ كورهٔ آ. Lime-kiln. [calcify.
آهكی Calcareous. ـ آ. كردن To
آهن Iron. ـ آهن سفيد Galvanized iron. ـ آهن سرد كوبيدن To flog a dead horse.
آهن آلات P. A. Ironware.
آهن بُر Iron-cutter o ـ ارهٔ آ. Hacksaw.
آهن پاره Scrap iron.
آهن جامه Iron bands or fastenings. Ironwork
آهن رُبا Magnet.
آهن ربایی Magnetic.
اهن ريزی Iron-foundry.
آهن ساز Iron-worker. White cooper.
آهنكوب Tin-roofer ; tinman.
آهنگ Tune. Music; setting; air. Intention ; attempt •. ـ آهنگ رفتن كردن To intend (or be about) to go.

آهنگر Blacksmith ; ironsmith.
آهنگری Blacksmith's trade or craft ; blacksmithing.
آهنگ ساز Composer.
آهنی (Made of) iron.
آهنين Iron. Hard, as iron.
آهو Gazelle. ـ آهوی ختايی Musk-deer. ـ گوشت آ. Venison.
آهو بره Fawn.
آهيانه Parietal bone.
آی S. u. آ
آيا 1) *inter. particle. Ex.* آ. او آمد؟ Did he come ? آ. خواهيد رفت؟ Will you go ? 2) *conj.* Whether.
آيات [Pl. of آيت & آيه].
آيت *A.* [آيات] Sign; miracle.
آيش Fallow (land).
آمد و رفت = آيندو رَوَند
آينده Coming; future. -*n.* The f. Comer [pl. آيندگان].
آينه [Cont. of آئينه]
آيه *A.* [آيات] Verse.
آيين or آئين Custom. Rule. Religion. Formality. Decoration.
آئين نامه Regulation(s).
آئينه Looking-glass; mirror. ـ آ. كردن X To plank down.
اَب o *A.* [آباء] = پدر
اِباء *A.* Refusal . ـ از رفتن ا. كرد He refused to go.
اباطيل [Pl. of باطل]
اَباًعن جدً *A.* (*aban-anja d en*) From generation to g.
اِبتداء *A.* Beginning.
اِبتدائی *A.* Primary; elemen-

tary.— . کتاب ا Primer.

اِبتکار A. Initiative. Originative faculty.

اِبتلاء A. Suffering (from a disease). Addiction.

اِبتهاج A. = خوشی

اِبتیاع A. Buying. — ا. کردن To buy [خریدن]. To redeem.

ابخره [Pl. of بخار].

اَبد A. [آباد]Eternity (without end) . — . تا ا Forever.

ابداً A. At all. Never.

اِبداع A. Innovation; creation.

ابدالآباد A. Eternity of eternities. — . تا ا Forever.

ابدالدهر A. (To) eternity.

ابدان [Pl. of بدن].

ابدی A. Eternal; everlasting.

ابدیت A. Eternity.

اَبر Cloud. Sponge.— هوا ا. است The weather is cloudy.

اِبراز A. Divulging. Expressing. — ا. کردن To divulge. To express.

اِبرام A. Insisting.Importunity. Confirmation. — ا. کردن To confirm. To insist (on).

ابرص ٥ A. Leprous.

اَبرو Eyebrow. Brace. — ا. درهم کشیدن To knit the brow.

ابروگشاده * Cheerful. Genial. Generous. *OS*. Open-browed.

اَبره ٥ = رویه The outside (of a cloth).

ابره‌ای Variegated.

ابری Cloudy. — . شیشهٔ ا Granulated glass.

ابریشم Silk. — ابریشم مصنوعی Rayon.— . کرم ا Silkworm.

ابریشمی Silken. — . گل ا Silk-tasseled acacia.

اِبریق ٥ A. 1) آفتابه 2) کوزه

ابزار Tool(s). Seasoning.

ابزارمند = افزارمند

اِبطال A. Making void.

اَبعاد A. [Pl. of بُعد] Dimensions.

اِبقاء A. Retaining. — ا. کردن To retain. To preserve.

اِبلاغ A. Communication. — ا. کردن To communicate.

ابلاغیه A. Communique.

اَبلق A. Parti-coloured; piebald.

اَبله A. Silly. [Silly.

ابلهانه A. P. Foolishly. —*a*.

ابلهی A. P. Silliness.

اِبلیس A. Satan.

اِبن ٥ A. = پسر. Son. [Pl. اَبناء].

ابناء [Pl. of ابن].

اِبن‌الوقت A. Time-server.

اُبنه A. Itching in the fundament; prurience.

ابنیه [Pl. of بناء]

ابواب [Pl. of باب]

اَبواب جمع *a. p.* Put in one's charge and responsibility.

ابواب جمعی *a. p.* Property in one's charge. Financial responsibility.

ابوالزوجه A. = پدر زن

بوالملیح ٥ا A. = چکاوك

ابوالهول A. Sphinx.

اُبوّت ٥ A. = پدری

ابوعلی‌سینا A. Avicenna.

اَبوی A. My father [پدرم]

Father + .
اِبهام A. Ambiguity. Thumb or great toe.
اُبّهت (obahat) A. Imposing presence ; dignity.
اَبهر A. Aorta. Jugular vein.
اُبهل Juniper-berries. Savin.
ابی A. Paternal. Consanguine.
اَیا Woodcock.
اَبیات A. [Pl. of بیت] Distiches; couplets. By e. Verses.
ابیض A. = سفید
اپیقوری A.G. Epicurean.
اَت Thy [affixed to a word ending in mute ه : خانه‌ات].
اتابك T. Lord father : title of former premiers.
اتازونی Fr. The United States.
اَتباع A. [Pl. of تبع] Followers. Subjects.
اِتحاد A. Union. — ا. کردن To form a u. To be united.
اتحادیه A. Union : اتحادیهٔ اصناف
اِتخاذ A. Adopting. — ا. کردن To adopt. — اتخاذ سند کردن To take note.
اتر Fr. Ether. [citron.
اُترج A. Large variety of
اِتساع A. Dilatation.
اِتصال A. Connection. Contiguity. — ا. دادن To connect; join. To put through [in the telephone].
اتصالاً A. = دائماً
اتصالی A. P. Short circuit.
اِتفاق A. Alliance. Agreement. Event; accident — افتادن To happen. — باتفاق In company with each other. By joint action. Unanimously [usu. بر حسب ا. — .] باتفاق آراء By chance.
اتفاقاً A. By chance. Occasionally. — ا. اورا دیدم I happened to see him.
اتفاقی A. Casual ; occasional. Accidental.
اِتکاء A. Reliance. OS. Leaning. — ا. بنفس Self-reliance. — ا. کردن To rely. — نقطهٔ ا. Fulcrum. Point d'appui. — باتکاء Relying on ; on the strength of. — بیمه اتکائی Reinsurance.
اِتلاف A. Wasting; losing; loss. Prodigality. Destruction. — ا. کردن To waste. To destroy.
اتلال ٥ A. [Pl. of تل] Hills. Ruins. [اطلس
اتلس G. Atlas (bone). S. a.
اَتم ٥ [Comp. of تمام]
اتم Fr. Atom.
اِتمام A. Completion. — به ا. رساندن To complete; finish. — به ا. رسیدن To be finished.
اتمی Fr. P. Atomic. — بمب ا. A. bomb; A-bomb.
اَتو Fr (C P) Trump
اُتو etc. = اطو etc.
اتوبوس Fr. Bus; omnibus.
اتوشویی Fr. P. Service station [for ا. جایگاه].
اتوموبیل Fr. Motor car. ; automobile. — اتوموبیل شماره ۱۱ Shanks's mare.
اتوموبیل رانی Fr. P. Motoring.
اِتهام A. [اتهامات] Accusation ;

خانه اجاره‌ای House to r.
اجاره‌بندی *A.P*. Rent assessment.
اجاره بها *A.P*. Rent.
اجاره‌دار *A.P*. Tenant. Farmer.
اجاره داری *A.P*. Leasehold. Farming (operations).
اجاره‌کار *A.P*. Revenue farmer.
اجاره‌نامه *A.P*. Lease contract.
اجاره نشین *A.P*. Tenant.
اِجازه *A*. Permission; leave. – ا. خواستن To ask permission. – ا. دادن To give p. (to); permit; allow; authorize. – اجازهٔ or باجازهٔ By permission of.
اُجاق *T*. Fireplace used for cooking purposes; oven. – اجاقش کور است He is issueless.
اجامر *A*. Ragtag.
اجانب [Pl. of اجنبی]
اِجبار *A*. Compulsion. [force.
اجباراً *A*. Compulsorily; by
اجباری *A*. Compulsory.
اِجتماع *A*. [اجتماعات]. Gathering; reunion. Society; social life.
اجتماعی *A*. Social. Gregarious.
اِجتناب *A*. Avoiding; shunning. – از . . . . ا. کردن To avoid or shun.... – غیرقابل ا. Inevitable; unavoidable.
اِجتهاد *A*. Exegesis of divine law on matters of theology and law. *OS*. Striving hard. – ا. کردن To practise religious jurisprudence.
اِجحاف *A*. Overcharging; extortion. – ا. کردن To overcharge.

charge. – باتهامِ On c. of.
اَثاث *A*. Furniture. Chattels.
اثاث‌البیت *A*. House furniture.
اثاثه *A*. Equipment. Household furniture.
اثاثیه *C. E.* = **اثاثه**
اِثبات *A*. Proving. – ا. کردن To prove; demonstrate. To affirm. – برای اثباتِ In order to prove. In proof of.
اَثر *A*. [آثار] Effect. Impression. Trace. Mark. Literary work. – اثرانگشت Fingerprint. – اثرِ پا Footprint. – اثرِ زخم Scar; cicatrice. – ا. کردن To produce an effect or result. To make an impression. To be efficacious [also ا. بخشیدن]. – بر اثرِ In consequence of; as the r. of. – در اثرِ As the r. of.
اثقال See ثقل & جرّ اثقال
اِثم o *A*. [آثام] = گناه
اثمار [Pl. of ثمر]
اَثناء *A*. Middle o. Interval. – در این ا. In the meantime.
اِثناعشر *A*. = دوازدهه Duodenum [for رودهٔ ا.].
اَثیر *A*. Ethereal atmosphere.
اثیم o *A*. = **گناهکار**
اِجابت *A*. Accepting; granting (a prayer). – ا. کردن To accept; grant. To respond to.
اِجاره *A*. Rent. – ا. دادن To (put out to) lease. To farm out. – ا. کردن To rent; also, hire. – در اجاره On lease. – مورداجاره *Law*. Object of l. –

اجداد [Pl. of جد & جده]
اَجدادی *A. P.* Ancestral. Traditional.
اَجر *A.* [اُجور] Reward.
اِجراء *A.* Execution ; performance. Enforcement. — ا.کردن To execute ; carry out. — بموقع ا. گذاشتن To put into force ; enforce. To e. ; carry out. — قابل ا. Enforceable. Practicable.
اجرام *A.* *See* جرم
اجرائی *A.* Executive. [Fem. قوهٔ ا. : اجرائیه e. power].
اجرائیه *A.* 1) *S. u.* اجرائی 2) Executive order. 3) E. power.
اُجرت *A.* = دستمزد & مزد
اجرت المثل *A.* Fair equivalent remuneration.
اجرت المسمی *A.* Specified rent; r. proper.
اَجزاء *A.* [Pl. of جزء] Ingredients. Components. Parts. Members ○ .
اجساد [Pl. of جسد]
اجسام [Pl. of جسم]
اَجل *A.* Death; end. *OS.* Fixed term or period. — اجلش فرا رسید Fate overtook him; his hour was come.
اَجلّ *A.* [Comp. of جليل]
اِجلاس *A.* Causing to sit. (Holding a) session. — ا.کردن To hold a meeting.
اجلاسیه *A.* [f. اجلاس] Designating a (parliamentary) session. Ex. دورهٔ ا. P. session. — دورهٔ اجلاسیه دوم The 2nd. Parliament.
اجلاف [Pl. of جلف]
اِجلال *A.* Glory ; honour.
اجله *A.* [Pl. of جليل] . — او از اجلهٔ علما است He is one of the greatest learned men.
اِجماع *A.* Gathering. Consensus (of opinions). — ا.کردن To gather together.
اجماعاً *A.* In company.
اِجمال *A.* Brevity. Compendium.
اجمالاً *A.* Briefly.
اجمالی *A.* Brief; summary. — نظر اجمالی Glance.
اَجناس *A.* [Pl. of جنس] Goods; commodities.
اَجنبی *A.* [اجانب] Foreigner.
اجنه *A.* [Pl. of جنی]
اَجوِبه ○ [Pl. of جواب]
اُجور [Pl. of اجر]
اَجوَف ○ *A.* Hollow. —[For ورید اجوف] Vena cava.
اَجیر *A.* Hired (worker). Mercenary. — ا. کردن To hire ; employ for wages. — ا. شدن To be hired.
احادیث [Pl. of حديث & احدوثه]
اِحاطه *A.* Surrounding. *F.* Full knowledge. — ا. داشتن بر To be conversant with. — ا.کردن To surround.
اِحاله *A.* Turning over; transfer. — ا. بمحال Reduction to absurdity. — ا. کردن To turn over; leave (to another).
احباء [Pl. of حبيب]

احباب [Pl. of حبیب]
اِحتجاب *A.* Being hidden. *F.* Privation; scale. *Astr.* Immersion.
اِحتراز *A.* Avoiding; shunning. — ا. کردن از To avoid or shun. To abstain from. — غیر قابل ا. Unavoidable.
اِحتراق *A.* Burning; combustion. Oxidation. Explosion.
اِحترام *A.* [احترامات] Respect; honour. — ا. کردن *or* ا. گزاردن To respect or h.; do h. to. — باتقدیمِ احترامات بیکران Assuring you of our highest esteem.
احتراماً *A.* Respectfully.
احترام‌گزار *A. P.* Respectful.
احتساب *A.* Calculating. — ا. کردن To calculate.
اِحتشام *A.* Glory; pomp.
اِحتضار *A.* Being at the point of death. — در حال ا. بودن To be at the p. of death.
اِحتقان *A.* (*Med.*) Congestion.
اِحتکار *A.* Hoarding. — ا. کردن To hoard (up).
اِحتمال *A.* [احتمالات] Probability. Eventuality. — ا. دادن To consider probable. — ا. میرود *or* ا. دارد It is p. — باحتمالِ قریب به یقین In all probability.
احتمالاً *A.* Probably. Eventually.
احتمالی *A.* Probable. Contingent. Eventual.
اِحتواء ٥ *A.* Containing.
اِحتیاج *A.* [احتیاجات] Need; necessity. Requirement. — ا. داشتن To need; be in n. (of); require. — احتیاجی بخدمات او نیست There is no n. for his services. — مورد احتیاج Required; needed.
اِحتیاط *A.* Precaution. Reservation. — ا. کردن To be precautious. — با ا. Precautiously. — بقیدِ ا. With reserve; with a grain of salt. — صندوق ا. Provident fund.
احتیاطاً *A.* By way of precaution.
احتیاطی *A. P.* Precautionary. — سرمایه ا. Reserve fund.
احجار [Pl. of حجر]
اَحد *A.* [آحاد] One. Unit. احدی نرفت No one went.
اِحداث *A.* Innovation. Erection; construction. Establishment. — ا. کردن To erect; establish. To create.
اُحدوثه ٥ *A.* [احادیث] Narrative.
اَحدیت *A.* Oneness By. e. The one God.
اَحرار *A.* [Pl. of حُرّ] Freemen. Broad-minded persons.
اِحراز *A.* Obtaining. Holding. — ا. کردن To obtain. To attain. To hold. To retain.
احرام *A.* Pilgrim's garb.
احزاب [Pl. of حزب]
احزان [Pl. of حزن]
اِحساس *A.* [احساسات] Feeling; sentiment. — ا. کردن To feel.
احساساتی *A. P.* Sentimental. Emotional.
اِحسان *A.* Favour. Beneficence. — ا. کردن To do favour; do good.
اَحسن *A.* [Comp. of حَسَن]

Better or best.ـ تبدیل به ا. کردن To change for the better.
اَحسنت *A.* Well done!
احشاء *A.* [Pl. of حشا] = **اندرونه**
احشام [Pl. of حشم]
اِحصان *A.* Continence.
اِحصائیه *A.* = **آمار**
اِحضار *A.* Summoning. Recalling.ـ ا. کردن To summon; call up. To recall.
احضاریه *A.* Summons; subpœna [often ا. برگ].
احفاد *A.* [Pl. of حفید] Grandchildren. *By e* Posterity.
اِحقاق *A.* Adjudication [usu. احقاق حق].ـ [احقاقِ حق کردن] To administer justice.
احکام [Pl. of حُکم] [penis.
اِحلیل *A.* (Orifice of the)
اَحمد (*A.*) *Mas. pr. name. OS.* More or most praiseworthy. [Comp. of حمید].
احمر *A.* = **سرخ** & **قرمز**
اَحمق *A.* Silly; foolish. —*n.* Fool. [Foolish.
احمقانه *A. P.* Foolishly. —*a.*
اَحوال *A.* [Pl. of حال] Condition(s). Circumstances. ـ احوال شما چطور است How are you? ـ ا. کسی را پرسیدن To inquire after a person's health; ask after him. ـ احوال شخصی Personal status.
اَحوَل ○ *A.* = **لوچ**
اِحیاء *A.* Restoring to life. Revival. Spending the night awake [usu. احیاء لیل]. ـ ا.کردن To revive. To rehabilitate. To reclaim or improve (land).
اَحیاناً *A.* Occasionally.
اَخ ○ *A.* = **برادر**
اَخاذی *A. P.* Extortion.
اِخافه ○ *A.* Intimidation.
اَخبار [Pl. of خبر]
اِخبار *A.* Informing.
اِخباری *A.* (*Gr.*) Indicative.
اِختتام *A.* Being finished. End; conclusion. ـ ا. پذیرفتن *or* ا. یافتن To come to an end.
اختر Star. *Fem. pr. name.*ـ گل ا Canna; Indian shot.
اِختراع *A.* [اختراعات] Invention. ـ ا.کردن To invent.
اخترشناس ○ Astronomer. Astrologer.
اِختصار *A.* Brevity. Abbreviation[اختصارات].ـ به ا. = اختصاراً ‖ به ا. کوشیدن To be brief.
اختصاراً *A.* Briefly; summarily.
اختصاری *A.* Summary: محاکمهٔ ا. ‖ Abbreviated; brief.
اِختصاص *A.* Allocation.ـ ا.دادن To allocate; earmark.
اختصاصاً *A.* Specially. Exclusively. [Special.
اختصاصی *A.P.* Allocated.
اختفاء *A.* Concealment.
اختلاج ○ *A.* Nictitation. Convulsion. ـ اختلاج ماهیچه Tic.
اختلاس *A.* Embezzlement. ـ ا. کردن To embezzle; misappropriate.
اختلاط *A.* Mixture. Intercourse. Free interchange of jokes; symposium. ـ ا. کردن To i. jokes. To talk familiarly.
اِختلاف *A.* [اختلافات] Differ-

ence. Dispute. Discrepancy. Diversity of opinions. — با مال من ا. دارد It differs from mine.

اِختلال A. Disorder; derangement.

اختناق A. Strangulation.

اَخته Castrated. — اسب ا. Gelding. — خروس ا. Capon. — قوچ ا. Wether. — ا. کردن To castrate.

اِختیار A. [اختیارات] Authority; power(s). Option. Choice. Control. Free will. — ا. دادن To empower; authorize. — ا. کردن To choose or adopt. To take, as a wife. — ا. با شما است As you wish.

اختیار داری A. P. Exercise of control. Ruling the roast. — ا. کردن To exercise c. To lord it. To rule the roast.

اختیاری A. Facultative; optional.

اَخذ A. Taking. Receipt. Seizure. Imitation; adoption. — ا. کردن To take. To collect. To imitate.

اِخراج A. Sending out; expulsion. — ا. کردن To send out; discharge; dismiss; expel.

اُخرَوی A. Otherworldly.

اُخری A. -ra [For گِل ا.] Ochre.

اَخصّ A. [Comp. of خاص]. More particular. — بالاَخص More particularly.

اَخضر A. = سبز Green.

اِخطار A. Notice; warning. — بکسی ا. کردن To notify or warn s. o. — اخطار کم مدت Short notice.

اخطاریه A. (Written) notice.

اِخفاء A. Concealing.

اِخ کردن × To plank down.

اَخگر 1) Embers. 2) جرقه

اِخلاص A. Devotion. Sincerity.

اخلاط [Pl. of خِلط].

اخلاف [Pl. of خلف *khalaf*]

اَخلاق A. [Pl. of خُلق] Morals; morality. — علم ا. Ethics.

اخلاقاً A. Morally.

اخلاقی A. Moral. Ethical.

اِخلال A. Deranging; spoiling. (Causing) trouble. Intrigue. — در کاری ا. کردن To spoil or derange an affair.

اخلالگر A. P. Trouble-causer; agitator. Intrigant.

اَخم Frowning. — ا. کردن To frown.

اَخمو + Frowning; surly.

اخوالزوجه A. = برادر زن

اخوان A. (*akha-*) Two brothers. [D. of اَخ].

اخوان ○ A. (*ekh-*)* Brothers.

اُخوت A. Brotherhood; fraternity.

اَخ و تُف + Hawking and spitting. Expectoration.

اَخوی A. (My) brother.

اَخیار A. [Pl. of خیر] Good men.

اَخیر A. Recent.

اخیراً A. Recently.

اخیرالذکر A. Latter; last-mentioned.

اَخیه Rope or stake to which a horse's tether is fastened. Enclosure. — کسیرا زیر اخیه کشیدن To keep one's nose to the grindstone.

اَداء *A*. Payment. Discharge (of a duty). Utterance. — ا. و اصول Grimace ; mimic. — ا. درآوردن To pull a wry face. To imitate; mimic. — ا.کردن To pay. To enunciate; pronounce. To discharge.

ادات *S. u.* ادوات

ادارات [Pl. of اداره]

اِداره *A*. Administration ; department ; office [ادارات]. Management . — اُ. کردن To manage ; run.

اداری *A*. Administrative. — محکمهٔ ا. Disciplinary court.— هزینهٔ ا. Overhead expenses.

اَدام‌الله *A*. (*-ma*lah) May God prolong. [To continue.

اِدامه *A*. Continuation.— ا. دادن

ادانی *A*. [Pl. of ادنی] Inferiors.

اَدب *A*. Politeness. [For. علم ا.] Letters ; literature. — ا. کردن To correct; chastise. — شرط ا. نبود It was not polite.— اهل ا. Men of letters.

ادباء [Pl. of ادیب]

ادبار *A*. Adversity.

اَدبی *A*. Literary. [Fem. ادبیه]

ادبیات *A*. Literature. [tion.

اِدخال *A*. Insertion. Introduc-

اِدرار *A*. Urine. — ادرار خونی Haematuria. — ا. کردن To make water ; urinate.

اِدراك *A*. Perception. Understanding. — درك کردن = ا. کردن

اِدریس *A*. Enoch.

اِدّعا *A*. Claim. Pretension. — ا.کردن To c. To pretend.

ادّعانامه *A. P.* = کیفر خواست

ادعائی *A.P.* Claimed. Alleged.

ادعیه [Pl. of دعا]

ادکلن (*Fr.*) *Eau de Cologne*.

ادله [A pl. of دلیل]

اَدنی *A*. (*-na*) [Comp. of دنی] Lower or lowest ; inferior. Less ; least. *See* ادانی

اَدوات *A*. [Pl. of ادات] Instruments. Tools. *Gr*. Particles.

ادوار *A*. [Pl. of دور] Periods; ages ; times. [Spice(s).

ادویه *A*. [Pl. of دوا] Drugs.

اَدهم ٥ *A*. Black (horse).

ادیان [Pl. of دین *di:n*]

اَدیب *A*. [اُدبا] Man of letters; literary man ; critic. Tutor. [Fem. ادیبه]

ادیبانه *A. P.* In a literary style. —*a*. Literary. [bane.

اذاراقی *A*. Nux vomica. Dog's-

اذان *A*. Call to prayer.

اِذعان *A*. Acknowledging. — ا. کردن To acknowledge; admit.

اِذن *A*. = اجازه

اُذن‌الفار *A*. Wallwort.

اذهان [Pl. of ذهن]

اَذیت *A*. Harm ; injury. Annoyance ; inconvenience. — ا.کردن To tease; annoy ; vex. To harm or hurt.

ار * [Cont. of اگر]

ارابه Cart. [False rumours.

اراجیف *A*. [Pl. of اُرجوفه ٥]

اِرادت *A*. Devotion ; attachment. Admiration.

ارادت‌کیش *A.P.* = ارادتمند

ارادتمند *A.P.* Devoted.—ارادتمند شما Yours sincerely ; your

devoted friend.
اِراده *A*. Will; determination; resolution. ا. کردن — To determine ; will ; resolve.
اَرّاده 1) Landing-gear; under-carriage. 2) ارابه
اِرادی *A*. Voluntary. غیرِ ا. — Involuntary. [Rascals.
اراذل *A*. [Pl. of اردل o]
اراضی [Pl of ارض]
ارامل o *A*. [Pl. of ارمله]Widows.
ارامنه [Pl. of ارمنی]
اِرائه *A*. Presentation. Production : ارائهٔ سند ǁ ا. دادن To show ; produce. — ارائهٔ طریق راهنمائی کردن = کردن
ارباب *A*. [Pl. of رب] Master(s). Landlord(s). Employer. Mr. [with Zoroastrian names]. Those endowed (with) : ارباب دانش the learned (people). — ارباب انواع Gods [pl. of رب النوع]. — ارباب رجوع Clients. Customers.
اربابی *A. P*. Privately-owned.
اَرَبیان *A*. Sea-locust.
اربه Water-germander.
اِرتباط *A*. [ارتباطات] Connection ; relation. Communication. — ا. دادن To connect.
اِرتجاجی *A*. Clonic : تشنج ا.
اِرتجاع *A*. Reaction. Elasticity. — قابل ا. Elastic.
ارتجاعی *A*. Reactionary.
اِرتجال o *A*. Improvisation.
ارتجالاً *A*. Extemporaneously.
اِرتداد *A*. Apostasy.
اِرتزاق *A*. Obtaining one's daily bread. — ا. کردن To obtain one's daily b. To feed.
اَرتش Army.
اِرتشاء *A*. Receiving a bribe.
ارتشتار & **ارتشدار** o = **سرباز**
ارتش کشی *Mil*. Expedition.
ارتشی Belonging to the army.
اِرتعاش *A*. Trembling.— ا. کردن To tremble.
اِرتفاع *A*. [ارتفاعات] Height ; altitude. Elevation. *Astr*. Apparent celestial latitude.
ارتفاع سنج *A. P*. Altimeter.
ارتفاعی *A*. Altitudinal. Vertical.
اِرتفاق *A*. 1) o = همراهی 2) Symphysis.— حق ا. Right of easement.
اِرتقاء *A*. Promotion. — ا. دادن To promote.— ا. یافتن To be promoted.
اِرتکاب *A*. Commission; perpetration.— (در) حین ا. In the very act.
اُرتودوکس *Fr*. Orthodox.
اِرث *A*. Inheritance. — مالیات بر ارث I. tax ; death duties. — به ا. بردن To inherit. — به ا. رسیدن To come down by inheritance. — به ا. گذاشتن To bequeath or devise. — از ارث محروم کردن To disinherit; cut off with a shilling.
ارثاً *A*. By inheritance.
اِرثی *A.P*. = **موروثی**
اَرج 1) Worth ; esteem. 2) o Swan [قو].
اِرجاع *A*. Referring. Turning over. — ا. کردن To turn o

To refer . ـ ارجاع شغل بکسی کردن
To appoint s. o. to duty.
اَرجح *A.* [Comp. of راجح]
(More) preferable.
اَرجمند Honourable. Dear.
اَردج Juniper.ـ تخم ا. J.-berry.
اردشیر *Mas. Pr. name.*
اُردَك *T.* Duck. ـ اردك نر
Drake. ـ جوجه ا. Duckling.
اردك ماهی Pike (*fish*).
اُردُن *A.* Jordan.
اُردو *T.* Camp.ـ ا. زدن To c.
اردوگاه *T.P.* Camp(ing-place);
encampment.
اَرده Ground sesame.
اردهای Beige.
اُردی بهشت *Second month having 31 days.*
اَرز Foreign exchange (*or* currency) . ـ معاملات **ارزی**
F. e. transactions.
ارز Cedar.
اَرزاق *A.* [Pl. of رزق] Provision; foodstuffs.
اَرزان Cheap. ـ ا. کردن To make cheap ; cheapen.
ارزانی Cheapness. ـ ا. داشتن *or* ا. فرمودن To give ; grant.
اَرزش Value; worth. ـ ا. ندارد
It is not w. while.
اَرزن Millet ـ ارزن خوشهای
Broomcorn millet.ـ ارزن هندی
Indian m. ; durra. ـ ارزن
جوگندمی Sorghum.
ارزنده That is worth (a specified price). W. the trouble.
ارزنی Miliary.
ارزیاب Assessor ; appraisor.
ارزیابی Assessment. ـ ا. کردن
To assess (the value of); appraise ; evaluate.
ارزیافت Assessed value.
ارزیدن [ارز]. To be worth ; cost. ـ دو ریال می ارزد It is w. two *rials*. ـ بزحمتش نمی ارزد
It is not w. the trouble.
ارژن Oriental almond. Wild a.
اِرسال *A.* Despatch. Remittance. ـ ا. داشتن *or* ا. کردن
[= فرستادن] To remit. To despatch or send.
ارسالی *A. P* (That is to be) sent. —*n.* Remittance.
ارسطو *A-G.* Aristotle.
اَرسلان (*T.*) *Mas. pr. name.*
OS. = شیر Lion.
اَرَش ○ Forearm. Cubit.
اِرشاد *A.* Showing the right way; guidance. Orthodoxy.ـ
ا. کردن To show the r. w.
اَرشد *A.* [Comp. of رشید]
Elder. Senior. [ship.
ارشدیت *A.* Seniority. Eldership.
ارشمیدس *A-G.* Archimedes.
ارض *A.* [اراضی] Land Territory. ـ کرهٔ ا. The earth.
اِرضاء *A.* Satisfying.
اِرضاع ○ *A.* Giving suck (to)
اَرضی *A.* = **زمینی**
اِرعاب ○ *A.* = **تخویف**
اَرغنون *A-G.* Organ. *Mus.*
اَرغوان Judas-tree. Purple.
ارغوانی Purple.
اِرفاق *A.* Leniency. Assistance.
Compassion. ـ با کسی ا. کردن
To assist, or be compassionate with, s. o. [grounds.
ارفاقاً *A.* On compassionate
ارفاقی *A.* Done on compas-

sionate grounds.
ارفع [Comp. of رفیع]
ارقام [Pl. of رقم]
ارقه × Crafty. —*n*. Cheat.
ارکان [Pl. of رکن]
ارکستر *Fr*. Orchestra.
اَرگ Small citadel.
اُرگ *Fr*. Organ. *Mus*.
اُرگان *Fr*. Organ.
ارگاندی *Fr*. Organdie.
اِرم *A*. Earthly paradise.
اَرمغان Souvenir; present.
اُرمك Cheap grey stuff used for making school uniform (for girls).
ارمنی [A. pl. ارامنه] Armenian.
اَرَن بیژ Sapan-wood; brazil-w.
ارواح [Pl. of روح] Spirits. — ارواحنا فدا May our souls be sacrificed to him.
اروپا(یی) Europe(an).
ارّه Saw. — ا. کردن To saw.
اره کش Sawyer.
اره کشی Sawing; sawyer's trade.
اَریب *A*. Sagacious; shrewd.
اُریب *A*. Diagonal; oblique.
اریسا *A-G*. Rushgrass.
اریکه ○ *A*. = تخت
اُریون *Fr*. Mumps.
از 1) From. 2) Of: یکی از آنها 3) Since. 4) Than. 5) Out of; ex. 6) Belonging to: کتاب از من است The book belongs to me. 7) On account of; due to. 8) With: پر از آب Filled with, or full of, water. 9) For: از خوشی ‖ از بی کفشی For lack of shoes.
اِزاء *A*. Lieu; stead. Exchange.— در ازاء In lieu of. In exchange for. In recognition of; in acknowledgment of.
اِزاره *A*. Plinth (-course).
اِزاله *A*. Removal. — ا. کردن To remove. — ازالهٔ بکارت Defloration. — ازالهٔ بکارت کردن [with از] To deflower.
ازت *Fr*. Nitrogen; azote.
از خود راضی *P*. *A*. Selfish. Self-satisfied; self-important; overweening.
از خود گذشتگی Self-denial; abnegation.
اِزدحام *A*. Crowd(ing).— ا. کردن To crowd. To press on one another. To swarm.
ازدو *or* زدو Gum (of wild almond).
اِزدواج *A*. Marriage. — ا. کردن [To marry.
اِزدیاد *A*. Being increased; increase. — رو به ا. گذاشتن To begin to be increased.
ازرق *A*. = کبود
از کار افتادگی Disablement.
از کار افتاده Disabled. Laid-up.
اَزگیل Medlar.
ازل *A*. Eternity without beginning.
ازلی *A*. Eternal; preexistent.
ازمن داری Blindman's-buff.
ازمنه [Pl. of زمان]
ازن *Fr*. Ozone.
ازواج ○ *A*. Pairs, couples. [Pl. of زوج]. — ازواج دماغی Cranial nerves.
اژدر 1) Torpedo. 2) = اژدها
اژدر افگن Torpedo-boat.
اژدر انداز Torpedo-tube.
اژدرمار ○ Boa.

اژدها *or* اژدرها Dragon.
اُسّ *A*. Basic element; basis.
اساتید [Pl. of استاد]
اِسارت *A*. Captivity. — به ا. بردن To lead into c. [bacca.
اُسارون *A-G*. Asarum ; asara-
اَساس *A*. Basis ; foundation. Base. — براساس On the basis of. — ا. ندارد It is unfounded.
اساساً *A*. Fundamentally. Substantially.
اساس نامه *A. P*. Articles of association. Constitution.
اساسی *A*. Fundamental; constitutional. Basic. Radical.
اساطیر *A-G*. [Pl. of اُسطوره] Myths; fables. Mythology.
اسافل [Pl. of اسفل]
اسامی [Pl. of اسم] [elevator.
اسانسور *Fr*. Lift ; [*U. S*.]
اسائهٔ ادب *a. p*. = بی ادبی
اسب Horse. *Chess*. Knight. — اسب آبی Hipppopotamus. — اسب کوهی Zebra.
اَسباب *A*. [Pl. of سبب]Things; effects; chattels. Equipment. Instrument; tool; apparatus. Utensil. *F*. Means. Cause. — اسباب بازی Toy ; plaything. — اسبابِ خانه House furniture. — اسبابِ کار Tools; kit. Materials. — اسباب زحمت خواهد شد It will cause inconvenience.
اسباب چینی *A. P*. Intrigue. — ا. کردن To form (*or* weave) a plot ; make an intrigue.

اسباب کشی *A. P*. Moving (to a new place). *O S*. M. the furniture. — ا. کردن To move to a new p.
اسباط [Pl. of سبط]
اسب‌دوانی Horse-race. — میدان ا. Racecourse. [woman.
اسب سوار Horseman or horse-
اسب سواری Horsemanship ; riding.
اسبق *A*. [Comp. of سابق] More or most previous (.*or* ancient). Last but one.
اسبی Horse-drawn. Equine.
اِسپانیا Spain. [(Language).
اسپانیولی Spaniard. Spanish
اِسپرت *E*. Sport.
اِسپرز Spleen. [Sainfoin.
اسپرس [*Per. f. Fr*. esparcette]
اِسپرك Dyer's-weed ; dyer's rocket. [In a hoe or spade] Footrest.
اسپریس Racecourse.
اسفناج = اسپناج
اسفند = اسپند
اسفندیار = اسپندیار
است Is. — خوب است It is good. We should better... *Cf*. هست
استاپ o Dimmer switch.
استاخی *A-It*. Eustachian.
استاد [A. pl. اساتید]. Professor. Master. Head-artisan ; master - workman [used before a pr. name: ا. حسن]. —[*Used as an a*.] Skilled ; expert.
استادانه Skilfully. —*a*. Workmanlike.
استادی Professorship. Mastership. Cleverness.
استارت *E*. Self-starter ; starting motor; cranking m.

استاژ *Fr*. Probation. — ا. دادن To serve on p.

استامپ *Fr*. Ink-pad ; stamp-pad.

اُستان (Large) province.— دادگاه استان Court of appeal.

استاندار Governor-general.

اِستبداد *A*. Despotism.

استبدادی *A. P*. Despotic.

اِستبعاد *A*. Unlikelihood ; improbability.— استبعادی ندارد It is not unlikely ; it is possible.

اِستتار *A*. Concealment. *Mil*. Camouflage.

اِستثمار *A*. Exploitation.— ا. کردن To exploit (unfairly).

اِستثناء *A*. Exception.— باستثنایِ With the e. of.— ا. کردن To make an e. of; exclude.

استثناءً *A*. Exceptionally.

استثنائی *A*. Exceptional.

اِستجابت *A*. Granting (a prayer).

استجاره ○ *A*. Renting.

استجازه *A*. Asking permission.— ا. کردن To ask p.

استحاله *A*. Transformation ; transmutation.

اِستحداث *A*. Producing something new. — ا. کردن To reclaim from the sea.

اِستحسان *A*. Praising. Approving.

اِستحصال *A*. Seeking to acquire ; acquisition. Production.

اِستحضار *A*. Information. — ا. داشتن To be informed or aware.— محترماً باستحضار عالی میرساند I beg to inform you.

اِستحقار *A*. Contempt.

اِستحقاق *A*. Merit. Right or title.— بچیزی ا. داشتن To merit s. t.; be entitled to it.

اِستحکام *A*. Firmness; solidity.

استحکامات *A*. Fortification(s). *Cf. the s.* استحکام

اِستحمام *A*. Taking a (hot) bath.— ا. کردن To take a b.

اِستخاره *A*. Consulting a book (or bidding beads) at random in order to decide one's procedure. — ا. کردن To consult a book. To bid beads.

اِستخدام *A*. Recruitment ; engagement. Service.— ا. کردن To recruit; engage.— دراستخدامِ In the employ of.

اِستخر Pond. Pool : استخر شنا

اِستخراج *A*. Extraction ; production: استخراج نفت ‖ Working (of a mine). Decipherment.— استخراج جذر *Math*. Evolution.— استخراج آراء Counting votes.— استخراج سنگ Quarry of stone.— ا. کردن To work or exploit. To decipher.

اِستخلاص *A*. Delivery; release. — ا. کردن To save or release. To recover ; reclaim.

اُستخوان Bone.— ا. لای زخم گذاشتن *Met*. To abstain from a radical cure ; dally with an illness or other case.

استخوان بندی Skeleton. *F*. Framework.

استخوان تراش Scalping-iron.

استخوان چه Ossicle.

استخوانخوار ○ Bone-eating. — مرغ ا. Osprey.

استخوان شناسی Osteology.

استخوانی Bony; osseous. — تب ا.

Hectic fever. — سل ا. Tubercular osteomyelitis.

اِستدعاء *A*. Request; prayer. — ا. كردن To request or ask.

اِستدلال *A*. Reasoning. — ا. كردن To reason.

استدلالی *A*. Based on reasoning; deductive.

استدن [ستان] = **گرفتن**

اَستر Mule.

اِستراحت *A*. Rest. — ا. كردن To rest.

استراق ○ *A*. Stealing [دزدیدن]. — استراق سمع Eavesdropping. — استراق سمع كردن To eavesdrop.

استراك *G*. Styrax; storax.

استرالیا(ئی) Australia(n).

اِسترحام *A*. Imploration for mercy.

اِسترداد *A*. 1) Reclamation. 2) *C.E.* Restoration; restitution. — ا. كردن To reclaim; ask restitution of. To (cause to) restore.

استرلاب *or* **اسطرلاب** *G*. Astrolabe.

اُستره ○ Razor [تیغ].

اِستسقاء *A*. Dropsy. — استسقاء خایه Hydrocele. — استسقاء رحم Hydrometra. — استسقاء سر Hydrocephalus. — استسقاء سینه Hydrothorax. — استسقاء عمومی Anasarca. — استسقاء مشیمه Hydramnios. — استسقاء مفصل Hydrarthrosis.

استسقائی *A*. Dropsical.

اِستسناد ○ *A*. Seeking to support oneself by a document.

اِستشاره *A*. Consulting.

اِستشمام *A*. Smelling. — ا. كردن To smell.

اِستشهاد *A*. Summoning or producing a witness. Citation. — از كسی ا. كردن To call s. o. to witness; c. him in evidence. — ورقهٔ ا. Documentary evidence signed by witnesses.

استصواب *A*. Approbation.

استطاعت *A*. (Pecuniary) ability or means. — استطاعت خرید آنرا ندارم I cannot afford to buy that.

استطاله *A*. (*Med.*) Process.

اِستطلاع ○ *A*. = **استفسار**

اِستظهار *A*. Trust; confidence. *OS*. (Seeking) support. — ا كردن به To trust; rely on.

اِستعاره *A*. Metaphor.

اِستعانت *A*. Seeking help. — ا. كردن To seek h.

اِستعجاب ○ *A*. Wonder; admiration.

اِستعداد *A*. Talent; parts. Aptitude. Predisposition; suscebtibility; liability (to a disease; etc.).

اِستعفاء *A*. Resignation. — ا. دادن To resign (one's office); send in one's papers. — ا. دادن از *or* ا. كردن از To resign *vt*.

استعلاج ○ *A*. Seeking a remedy. — مرخصی **استعلاجی** Sick leave.

اِستعلام *A*. Asking for information; inquiry. — از كسی ا. كردن To call upon s. o. to give information.

استعلامیه *A*. Inquiry.

اِستعمار *A*. Colonization. — ا. كردن To colonize.

اِستعمال *A*. Using; application. — ا. كردن To use; apply. — استعمال دخانیات Smoking.

اِستغاثه *A*. Supplication. Imploration for help. — ا.کردن To implore for h. ; supplicate.

اِستغفار A. Asking forgiveness.— ا.کردن To ask f.

اَستغفرالله A. God forbid! Not at all. OS. I ask G. to forgive me.

اِستغناء A. Showing ability to do without. Independence. Disdain. Magnanimity [usu. استغنای طبع].

اِستفاده A. (Making) use; utilization. Profit +. — ا.کردن از To make use of ; utilize. To p. by.— مورد استفاده قراردادن To utilize. — از حسابی ا. کردن To operate an account. — سوء ا. کردن از To abuse. To take advantage of. — قابل ا. Utilizable. — غیرقابل ا. Unutilizable ; useless. — مرخصی با ا. از حقوق Leave with pay.

استفاده جو A.P. Profiteer.

استفاده چی A.T. = استفاده جو

اِستفتاء A. Seeking advice on a legal or religious matter.

اِستفراغ A. Vomiting. — ا.کردن To vomit.

اِستفسار A. Inquiry; questioning. — ا. کردن To make enquiries; ask questions; [with از] to ask; inquire of.

اِستفهام A. Interrogation.

استفهامی A. Interrogative.

اِستقامت A. Perseverance. — ا.کردن To persevere ; keep or hold on. To be constant.

اِستقبال A. Going to meet. — ا. کردن (از) To welcome; receive gladly.— باستقبال کسی رفتن To go to meet s. o.

اِستقراء A. Inductive reasoning. a posteriori r.

اِستقرار A. Settlement. Rehabilitation.

اِستقراض A. Receiving a loan.— بانک استقراضی Loan bank. — سهم استقراضی Bond; debenture.

اِستقراع A. Balloting. S. a. قرعه کشی

اِستقرائی A. Inductive.

استقصاء A. Deep investigation.

اِستقطاب A. Polarization.

اِستقلال A. Independence.

استکان R. Small glass (for tea).— گل ا. Campanula; bell-flower.

اِستکتاب A. Asking (a person) to write with a view to verifying his handwriting.

اِستکشاف ○ A. Exploration ; discovery.

اِستلقاء A. (Dorsal) decubitus.

اِستماع A. Hearing.

استمالت A. = دلجویی

اِستمداد A. Seeking help. — ا.کردن To seek h.

اِستقرار A. Continuation.

استمراری A. Progressive : ماضی ا.

اِستمزاج A. Sounding some one's inclination or consulting his opinion.— ازکسی ا.کردن To ask some one's opinion; sound him; take his sense.

اِستملاک A. Acquisition of property.

اِستمناء A. Masturbation.

استمهال *A*. Asking for a respite. **استمهالی** معاملات Credit transactions.

استن *Fr*. Aceton.

اِستناد *A*. Supporting oneself (by a document). ـ ا. کردن به To rely on. To invoke : باستنادِ ‖ بمادهٔ دوم ا. کردند On the strength of.

اِستنباط *A*. Inference; presumption. ـ ا. کردن To infer ; gather; deduce.

اِستنتاج *A*. Drawing a conclusion. ـ ا.کردن To draw a c. ; conclude.

اِستنساخ *A*. Transcription Multiplication of copies. ـ ا. کردن از To copy. To make copies of.

اِستنشاق *A*. Inhalation. Snuffing; drawing up through the nostrils. ـ ا.کردن To inhale ; breathe in. To smell.

اِستنطاق *A*. Interrogation; cross-examination . ـ ا. کردن To interrogate.

اِستنکاف *A*. Refusal. ـ از رفتن ا.کرد He refused to go.

اِستواء *A*. [For خط ا.] Equator.

اُستوار Firm; solid. -*n*. Warrant officer. ـ ا. کردن To make firm or s.

استوارنامه Credentials.

اُستوانه Cylinder.

استوانه‌ای Cylindrical.

استودیو *Fr*. Studio.

استهزاء *A*. Derision. ـ ا.کردن To mock; scorn.

اِستهلاك *A*. Amortization. Depreciation.

اِستجاری *A. P*. (That is to be) rented.

اِستیصال *A*. Extreme poverty.

اِستیضاح *A*. Interpellatron. ـ ا.کردن از To interpellate.

اِسیفاء *A*. Demanding the fulfilment of a promise or the settlement of a debt. ـ استیفای حقوق Vindication of rights.

اِستیلاء *A*. Domination; ascendency.

استیلن *Fr*. Acetylene.

اِستیناف *A*. Appeal. ـ ا. دادن To go to a.; a. to a higher court. ـ محکمهٔ ا. Court of A.

استینافی *A*. Appellate.

اَسد *A*. Lion [شیر]. The Leo.

اَسدالله (*A*.) *Mas. pr. name. OS*. Lion of God.

اسراء [Pl. of اسیر].

اَسرار *A*. [Pl. of سرّ] Secrets.

اسرارآمیز *A.P*. Mysterious.

اِسراف *A*. Lavishment; prodigality. ـ ا.. کردن To lavish; be wasteful or prodigal.

اسرائیل *A*. Israel.

اسرائیلی *A*. Israeli. Israelite.

اَسرع ○ *A*. [Comp. of سریع] Quicker. ـ باسرع اوقات At the earliest possible time.

استخر = اسطخر

اسطو خودوس *or* **اسطخودوس** *A-G*. Spike lavender.

استرلاب اُسطرلاب *S.u*.

اُسطقس *A-G*. Element○. Temperature○. Stoutness+.

اسطوانه etc. = **استوانه** etc.

اَسعار A. =ارز Foreign exchange. [Pl. of سِعر price].
اَسعد ○ A. [Comp. of سعید]
اَسف A. Regret; sorrow.
اسفالت Fr. Asphalt. ـا.کردن To asphalt ; lay with a.
اسف‌آور A. P. = **اسفناك**
اسفار [Pl. of سفر]
اسفرزه or **اسپرزه** Fleawort.
اَسفل ○ A. [Comp. of سفیل; pl. اسافل ; fem. سُفلی -la] Lower or lowest; inferior. ـاسافل ناس The dregs of society ; the low classes.
اِسفناج Spinach ; spinage. ـ اسفناج کوهی or اسفناج رومی Mountain spinach. ـ اسفناج صحرائی Wild spinach ; good-henry. [rettable.
اسفناك A. P. Deplorable. Reg-
اِسفنج A-G. Sponge.
اِسفنجی A. Spongy.
اسفند 1) *Twelfth month having 29 or 30 days*. 2) Wild rue.
اسفندیار *Mas. pr. name.*
اِسقاء A. Giving a drink to○. Impregnation. ـا.کردن To impregnate. To give a d. to.
اِسقاط A. Waiving; relinquishing. ـ ا. کردن To waive. ـ اسقاط جنین Abortion. ـ اسقاط حق *Law*. Waiver.
اِسقاط + Scrapped. Dilapidated.
اُسقف A-G. [اساقفه]. Bishop.
اُسقفی A. Episcopal. —n. Bishopry.
اِسکات A. Silencing. Convincing.
اِسکان A. Settling.
اِسکلت Fr. = **استخوان بندی**
اِسکله [f. It. origin] Jetty.
اِسکناس R-Fr. Bank-note.
اِسکندر Alexander.
اِسکندریّه Alexandria.
اِسکنه (Mortise) chisel.
اِسکنه‌ای Chisel-like ; scalpriform. ـ پیوند اسکنه‌ای Chink-grafting ; cleft-grafting.
اسکی Fr. Ski.
اسکیت E. Roller skate.
اسلاف [Pl. of سلف].
اِسلام A. Islam; Mohammedanism. [OS.] Submitting to God's will.
اَسلحه A. [Pl. of سلاح but used also as s.] Weapon(s); arm(s). ـ اسلحهٔ گرم Firearms. ـ اسلحهٔ سرد Weapons other than f. ـ اسلحهٔ کمری Sidearms.
اسلحه ساز A. P. Armourer.
اُسلوب A. [اسالیب] Method.
اِسم A. [اسامی & اسماء] Name. Gr. Noun. ـ ا. بردن To name; mention. ـ اسم‌شب Watchword.
اَسماء [Pl. of **اسم**].
اِسماً A. Nominally.
اِسمعیلیه A. The Assassins.
اِسم‌گذاری A. P. Christening; giving a name to (a child).
اسمنجونی ○ Hyacinth.
اسم نویسی A. P. = **نام نویسی**
اِسموکینگ Fr-E. Dinner-jacket; tuxedo [U. S.].
اِسمی A. 1) Nominal. ـ بهای ا. N. value; face v. 2) Substantive. 3) + Famous.
اَسناد [Pl. of سند]
اِسناد A. Attribution; ascrip-

اشپل = اِشپیل
اشپیل *R*. Split pin.
اشتالنگ Astragalus.
اِشتباه *A*. [اشتباهات] Error; mistake. — ا. است It is a m.; it is wrong. — در اشتباه انداختن To lead into a ne. — ۵۰ ریال اشتباه حساب دارم I am 50 Rials out. — ا. کردن To make a m.; err.
اشتباهاً *A*. By mistake; erroneously. [tation.
اشتباه کاری *A. P*. Misrepresen-
اشتباهی *A. P*. Erroneous.
اشتداد ○ *A*. Aggravation.
اُشتر • = شتر
اِشتراء ○ *A*. = خریداری
اِشتراك *A*. Participation. Partnership. Subscription. — اشتراك مساعی Cooperation. — بالاشتراك = اشتراکاً [in partnership.
اشتراکاً *A*. In common; jointly;
اشتراکی *A*. Held in common. Communal. Communistic. —*n* ○. Communist.
اِشتعال *A*. Inflammation. *F*. Enthusiasm ; ardour.
اِشتغال *A*. Employment; occupation. — ا. به تحصیل دارد He is studying. — ا. ورزیدن به To occupy oneself with ; address oneself to.
اِشتقاق *A*. Derivation.
اُشتلم ○ = زور Violence; force.
اِشتهاء *A*. Appetite. — به ا. آوردن To give an appetite to. — ا. صاف کردن + To whet the a.
اشتهاآور *A. P*. Appetizing. —*n*. Appetizer.

tion. Imputation. — ا. کردن To attribute or ascribe.
اَسنادی *A. P*. Documentary.
اَسواران *Mil*. Troop.
اَسوَد ○ *A*. = سیاه
اِسهال *A*. Diarrhoea. — اسهال خونی Bloody flux; dysentery.
اسهالی *A. P*. Diarrhetic.
اَسهام *A*. = سهام
اَسهل ○ *A*. [Comp. of سهل]
اسید *Fr*. Acid.
اسید فنیك *Fr*. Carbolic acid.
اَسیر *A*. [اُسراء] Captive. — ا. شدن To be taken c. — ا. کردن To take c.; reduce to captivity.
اسیری *A. P*. = اسارت
اَش His; her; its [affixed to a word ending in mute ه. Ex. خانه‌اش]
اِشارات [Pl. of اشارت or اشاره]
اِشارپ *Fr*. Scarf.
اشارت • *A*. = اشاره
اِشاره *A*. Pointing with the finger. Beckon. Hint; allusion. Sign; indication. Reference. [Pl. اشارات]. — ا. کردن To point. To make a s. To b. To h.; allude. To refer. — ضمیر ا. Demonstrative pronoun — صفت ا. D. adjective.
اِشاعه *A*. Publication; propagation. — ا. کردن To propagate; spread about. To divulge.
اشباح [Pl. of شبح]
اِشباع *A*. Saturation. — ا. کردن To saturate. To impregnate. — بحدّ اشباع To satiety; fully.
اُشبل *or* اشپل Caviar(e).

اِشتهار *A.* Renown; notoriety. Publicity. — بچیزی ا. داشتن To be famous or notorious for s. t.

اِشتیاق *A.* Eagerness ; anxiousness ; ardent desire.

اشجار [Pl. of شجر]

اشخاص [Pl. of شخص]

اشدّ [Comp. of شدید]

اَشرار *A.* [Pl. of شریر] Insurgent people.

اَشراف [Pl. of شریف] Nobles. Aristocrats.— ا. حکومت Aristocracy.

اشرافی *A. P.* Aristocratic.

اِشراق *A.* Illumination. Intuition.

اَشرف [Comp. of شریف] Nobler or noblest. — *n. Fem. pr. name.*— جناب ا. His (or Your) Excellency.

اشرفی (*A. P.*) *Gold coin orig. worth* 10 *'rials'.* — گل ا. Calendula.

اَشعار [Pl. of شعر]

اِشعار *A.* Stating. — ا. داشتن To state or advise.

اشعه [Pl. of شعاع]

اِشغال *A.* Occupation.— ا. کردن To occupy. — ارتش **اشغالی** Army of occupation.

اشفاق *A.* Pitying. Sympathy.

اُشق *A.* Persian ammoniac ; gum a. [f. P. اشه]

اَشقیاء [Pl. of شقی]

اَشك Tear(s).

اِشکاف *R.* Wardrobe.

اَشکال [Pl. of شکل]

اِشکال *A.* [اشکالات] Difficulty.— ا. تراشیدن To make difficulties ; obstruct. — ا. کردن To make, or point out, d.

اشکال تراشی *A. P.* Creating or making difficulties.

اشك آور Lachrymatory. — گاز اشك آور L. gas; tear g.

اشك ریز & **اشك بار** Shedding tears; tearful.

اشکلک Pilliwinks; thumbscrew.— ا. کردن *or* ا. دادن To torture by pilliwinks or the like.

اِشکنه Broth with eggs.

آشکوب-اُشکوب Storey; floor.— اشکوب اول Ground f.— اشکوب دوم First floor. [*OS.* Shrink.

اِشمئزاز *A.* Disgust ; horror.

اُشنان Common soda-plant ; Salsola soda.

اُشنه Treemoss..

اشهد بالله *A.* I call God to witness. Indeed.

اشیاء [Pl. of شیئی]

اِصابت *A.* Hitting. Falling. Attack (of a disease).— ا. کردن به To hit. To attack. — قرعه بنام من ا. کرد The lot fell upon me.

اِصالت *A.* Genuineness. Noble birth. (Acting on) one's own behalf.

اِصالةً *A.* In one's own right; on one's own behalf.

اَصحاب *A.* [Pl. of صاحب] Possessors.— اصحاب ِ Those endowed with. — اصحاب دانش Learned men.— اصحاب کهف *S.u.* کهف ‖ اصحاب دعوی Parties to a dispute.

اِصرار *A.* Insistence; urging.— بمن ا. کرد He insisted on me.

ا.کردن To amend. To correct. To improve. To reform. To adjust ; clear up. To make peace ; m. it up. To shave. To cut (another's) hair or to have one's hair cut. — اصلاح پذیر = قابل ا. ‖ اصلاح ناپذیر = غیر قابل ا.

اصلاح پذیر *A. P.* Corrigible. Amendable. Reformable. Adjustable. Reconcilable.

اصلاح طلب *a. p.* Reformist. —*a.* Who seeks to reform.

اصلاح ناپذیر *A. P.* Incorrigible. Irreconcilable.

اصلاحی *A. P.* Amendatory. Reformatory.

اَصلح ० *A.* [Comp. of صالح] Better. More advisable.

اَصله ० *A.* Single root. [Used only in counting trees and the like. Ex. سه ا. درخت 3 trees].

اصلی *A.* Original. Fundamental; basic. Main. *Gr.* Cardinal : عدد اصلی [Surd. جذر اصم — [کر] Deaf *A.* ० **اَصمّ**

اصناف [Pl. of صنف]

اصنام [Pl. of صنم]

اصوات [Pl. of صوت]

اُصول *A.* [Pl. of اصل] Elements; principles. Doctrines. Method(s). Basic principles of jurisprudence. — موافقتِ اصولی Agreement in principle.

اصولاً *A.* In principle.

اَصیل *A.* Of noble birth; trueborn. Full-blooded.

اصطبل *A-G.* = **طویله**

اِصطخر = **استخر**

اصطرلاب *A-G.* = **استرلاب**

اِصطکاک *A.* Friction. Conflict. Clash.

اِصطلاح *A.* [اصطلاحات] Term. Terminology. Idiom; collocation. Acceptation. — ا. کردن To accept or use conventionally. — به ا. میخواست زرنگی کند He wished to be what we call clever. — مجلسِ به ا. ملی The so-called National Assembly.

اصطلاحاً *A.* In (technical) terminology. Idiomatically.

اِصغاء *A.* Listening. — ا. کردن To listen [گوش کردن].

اَصغر *A.* Smaller ; minor. [Comp. of صغیر] —*n.* *Mas. pr. name.*

اَصفر *A.* = **زرد**

اَصل *A.* [اصول] Origin. Element. Principal. Basis. Original (copy). *OS.* Root. [*As an a.*] Genuine ; real . Original. — از اصل Originally. To begin with. — اصلِ حقوق Basic salary. — ایرانی‌الاصل Of Iranian extraction or origin.

اصلاً *A.* Originally. At all : ا. خوب نیست ‖ To begin with.

اصل‌السوس *A.* Liquorice root.

اِصلاح *A.* [اصلاحات] Amendment. Correction. Improvement. Reform. Adjustment. Redressing. Reconciliation. Haircut or shave ; also, dressing the hair or shaving the beard.—

اِضاعه *A*. Wasting; spoiling.

اِضافه *A*. [اضافات] Addition. Annexation. Excess. *Gr*. 1) Relation of a noun to the genitive case or the adjective following it. 2) The sign(ِ) which expresses such relation. – ا.کردن To add; annex. To increase. To connect (to the genitive case or to an adjective). – ا. بر In addition to; on top of. In excess of.– باضافهٔ Plus; in addition to.– حالت ا. The case of a noun governing the genitive; the possessive c.

اضافه بار *A.P*. Excess luggage.

اضافه حقوق *a. p*. Salary increment.

اضافه کار(ی) *A. P*. Overtime [work.

اضافی *A*. Additional.

اَضحی (-*h*a) *A*. = قربانی Sacrifice. – عید اضحی = **عید قربان**

اضداد [Pl. of ضد]

اِضطراب *A*. Agitation. Disturbance of mind.

اِضطرار *A*. Distress. Constraint Helplessness. Emergency.

اضطراراً *A*. Under necessity.

اضطراری *A*. Compulsory; constrained. Motivated by indigence or necessity.

اضلاع [Pl. of ضلع]

اِضمحلال *A*. Overthrow.

اِطاعت *A*. Obedience. – ا.کردن To obey.

اُطاق *T*. Room. Chamber. Body (of a bus or motor car).

اِطاله ٥ *A*. Stretching. – زبان درازی = اطالهٔ لسان

اطباء [Pl. of طبیب]

اِطر or **اتر** *Fr*. Ether.

اَطراف *A*. [Pl. of طرف] Sides. Suburbs. – دراطرافِ Around. *F*. About. – ملاحظهٔ اطراف کار Circumspection. – اطراف سافله Lower extremities. – اطراف عالیه Upper e.

اطرافی *A. P*. Outsider. Bystander. [Pl. اطرافیان Associates].

اُطریش *Fr*. Austria.

اطریشی *Fr. P*. Austrian.

اِطعام *A*. Feeding.– ا.کردن To feed.

اطعمه [Pl. of طعام]

اِطفاء *A*. Extinguishing. – ا. کردن = **خاموش** کردن

اطفال [Pl. of طفل]

اطفائیه *A*. Fire station. Fire-fighting. [Fem. of اطفائی f. اطفاء]. *See* آتش نشانی

اِطلاع *A*. [اطلاعات] Information; news. –(به) ا. دادن To inform; advise. – ا. یافتن To be informed; come to know. – باطلاع کسی رساندن To bring to the notice of s. o. – بدین وسیله باطلاع عموم میرساند The public are hereby notified. – بقرارِ اطلاع We understand that.

اطلاعاً *A*. For (your, his, etc.) information.

اطلاع نا *A. P*. Prospectus.

اِطلاق *A*. Release. (General) application. Relaxation. Diarrhoea. – اطلاق بی اندازه از مسهل –

laration. — ا. کردن *or* ا. داشتن To state. To declare. To express.

اظهار کننده *A. P.* Declarer.

اظهارنامه *A. P.* Declaration; d. form.

اظهاریه *A.* Statement (of claim). Declaration.

اظهر من الشمس *A.* Too obvious or clear. *OS.* Clearer than the sun.

اِعاده *A.* Giving back; returning. Reestablishment. — اعادهٔ اعتبار Rehabilitation (of a discredited person or of a bankrupt). — اعادهٔ ذکر = **تکرار**.

اعاشه *A.* Providing means of subsistence for; sustaining. — ا. کردن To provide with m. of subsistence; support.

اعاظم [Pl. of اعظم] [اعانه

اعانت *A.* 1) Assistance. 2) ○ =

اعانه *A.* Relief fund ; charitable contribution.

اعتاق ○ *A.* Emancipation ; redemption.

اِعتبار *A.* Credit [اعتبارات] . Solvency ; good standing. Esteem; weight. Validity. Example ; lesson. — باعتبارِ On the strength of ; relying on. In respect of. — بهای **اعتباری** Nominal *or* face value.

اعتبار نامه *A. P.* 1) Letter of credit. 2) = استوار نامه

اعتدال *A.* Temperance. Equinox. — به ا. Moderately.

اعتدالی *A.* Moderate (politician). [Pl. اعتدالیون]

اعتدالین *A.* [D. of اعتدال] The

Superpurgation. — ا. کردن To apply (generally or absolutely). To loosen ; release. To relax. — علی الاطلاق Absolutely; generally. — قادرعلی الاطلاق The Almighty or Omnipotent.

اطلس *A.* Satin.

اطلس *A-G.* Atlas. — اقیانوس ا. The Atlantic Ocean.

اطلسی *A.* (Made of) satin. Satin-like. — گل ا. Petunia.

اِطمینان *A.* Confidence. Assurance. Safety. — دریچهٔ ا. S.-valve. — ا. دادن (به) To assure; warrant. — ا. داشتن To be sure; [with به] have c. on; trust. — قابل ا. Reliable. — غیر قابل ا. Unreliable.

اطناب *A.* Prolixity; verbosity. — ا. کردن To be verbose.

اطو *or* **اتو** [Per. f. T. اوتی] Iron ; flatiron; press iron. — ا. کشیدن *or* ا. کردن To iron. To press. — از اطو افتاده است It needs ironing or pressing. — ازاطو انداختن To crumple.

اطوار *A.* [Pl. of طور]. Manners. Mannerism. Coquettish moods. — +ا. درآوردن To grimace. To act coquettishly. To put on an act. To tease.

اطواری *A. P.* Who has coquettish moods or makes a wry face. *See* اطوار

اطوکش Presser.

اطوکشی Pressing and ironing. — ماشین ا. Hoffman's press.

اظهار *A.* [اظهارات] Expressing; manifesting. Statement. Dec-

two equinoxes.

اعتذار o *A*. = **عذرخواهی**

اِعتراض *A*. [اعتراضات] Objection. Protest. — ا. کردن To object ; take exception. To protest.

اعتراف *A*. [اعترافات] Confession. — ا. کردن To confess ; admit; acknowledge. — از کسی ا. گرفتن To c. a person.

اعتزاز o *A*. = **بزرگی & عزت**

اعتزال *A*. Schism. Abdication.

اعتزالی *A*. Schismatic(al).

اِعتصاب *A*. Strike.— ا.کردن To strike; go on s.

اعتقاد *A*. Belief. — بکسی ا.آوردن To believe in s. o. — ا. کردن To b.

اعتقادنامه *A*. *P*. Credo ; creed.

اعتکاف o *A*. = **گوشه نشینی**

اعتلاء o *A*. Exaltation.

اِعتماد *A*. Confidence; trust ; reliance. — ا. بنفس Self-r. — بکسی ا. کردن To rely on s. o. — قابل ا. Reliable ; trustworthy. — غیر قابل ا. Unreliable. — عدم ا Lack of confidence; distrust.

اِعتنا *A*. Heed ; attention. — بکسی ا.کردن To take notice of, or pay a. to, a person.

اعتیاد *A*. Addiction.

اعجاب *A*. Admiration.

اِعجاز *A*. Miracle.— ا.کردن To work a miracle.

اَعجب o *A*. [Comp. of عجیب]

اعجم o *A*. Who does not speak or write Arabic idiomatically; barbarian.

اُعجوبه *A*. Prodigy (of a specified thing).

اعداء [Pl. of عدو]

اعداد [Pl. of عدد]

اِعدام *A*. Execution. — ا. کردن To execute ; put to death.

اَعراب [Pl. of اعرابی]

اِعراب *A*. (Change in) the final vowel of an Arabic word.

اَعرابی *A*. [اعراب] Nomadic Arab; bedouin.

اَعراض *A*. [Pl. of عَرَض]

اِعراض *A*. Turning away the face o. Opposition. Worry. — ا. کردن To turn away the f. To worry (oneself).

اعراف (*A*.) *Wall between hell and paradise*. Purgatory.

اعرج o *A*. = لنگ Lame.

اعزاز *A*. Honour. Holding dear.

اِعزام *A*. Despatch.— ا. داشتن To d. or send. [be d.

اعزامی *A*. *P*. Despatched. To

اِعسار *A*. Insolvency.

اَعشار *A*. [Pl. of عشر] Decimals.

اعشاری *A*. *P*. Decimal.

اعصاب [Pl. of عصب]

اعصار [Pl. of عصر]

اعضاء *A*. [Pl. of عضو]

اِعطاء *A*. Granting. — ا. کردن To grant. To award. To invest with.

اعطائی *A*. Granted. Dative.

اَعظم *A*. [Comp. of عظیم] Greater or greatest. Grand. [Pl. اعاظم—fem. عظمی *ozma*]

اعقاب *A*. [Pl. of عقب] Posterity; descendants.

اعقل o [Comp. of عاقل]

اعلا *S. u.* اعلی

اِعلاء ○ *A.* Exalting.

اِعلام *A.* Announcement; proclamation. — ا.کردن *or* ا. داشتن To announce; proclaim.

اَعلام *A.* [Pl. of علم] Standards; flags ○. — علمای ا. The distinguished Ulema.

اعلامیه *A.* Manifesto; statement. Advice.

اعلان *A.* [اعلانات] Notice; advertisement. Proclamation. — ا. کردن To advertise. To publish a n. (for); notify.

اعلم ○ *A.* More or most learned. [Comp. of عالم].

اعلی *A.* (*a'l*a) [Comp. of عالی] Of superior quality; extra; super; champion [often written اعلا].

اعلیحضرت *A.* His Majesty. — اعلیحضرت اقدس همایونی H. M. the Shah.

اعلیحضرتین *A.* [D. of اعلیحضرت] Their Majesties.

اَعمّ *A.* [Comp. of عام] More or most common. General; generic: ا. از مرد و ‖ معنی ا. زن Both men and women.

اعماق [Pl. of عمق] [deeds.

اَعمال *A.* [Pl. of عمل] Acts;

اِعمال *A.* Exercising; using: اعمال زور u. force; exertion of f. — اعمال نظر Showing partial views. — ا. کردن To use. To exert.

اعمام *A.* [Pl. of عم]

اعمی *A.* (*a'm*a) = **کور**

اعوان [Pl. of عون]

اعوَج ○ *A.* = **کج**

اعوِجاج ○ *A.* = **کجی** — پیچ وخم

اَعوذُ بالله *A.* (-*be*lah) I take refuge in God. [For usage see استغفرالله]

اَعوَر *A.* One-eyed. —*n.* Blind gut; cœcum. — ضمیمهٔ ا. Vermiform appendix.

اعیاد [Pl. of عید]

اَعیان *A.* [Pl. of عین] Nobles; dignitaries. [Also اعیانی] Standing property; superstructure. — مجلس ا. House of Lords.

اعیانی *A. P.* Luxurious; aristocratic +. —*n.* 1) L. life. 2) *S. u.* **اعیان**

اغبرار ○ *A.* Dustiness. — اغبرار خاطر = **رنجش**

اِغتشاش *A.* Disturbance; disorder; riot. — ا.کردن To cause a disturbance or r.

اغتنام *A.* Seizing. Regarding as a booty ○. — اغتنام فرصت S. an opportunity.

اغذیه [Pl. of غذا]

اغراض [Pl. of غرض]

اغراق *A.* Exaggeration. — ا.گفتن To exaggerate.

اغراق آمیز *A. P.* Exaggerated. — ا.کردن To exaggerate; magnify

اغشیه [Pl. of غشاء]

اِغضاب *A.* Provocation.

اغفال کردن *A.P.* To take advantage of the inadvertence of; delude.

اغلاط [Pl. of [illegible]]

اَغلب *A.* [Comp. of غالب

Most; the most part. — اغلب اوقات M. of the time; very often.

اِغماء *A.* Coma; swooning.

اِغماض *A.* Connivance. Indulgence. — ا. کردن To connive at; tolerate. — قابل ا. Tolerable; negligible.

اغنیاء [Pl. of غنی]

اِغوا *A.* Temptation. Persuasion. — ا. کردن To tempt or seduce. To persuade.

اغیار [Pl. of غیر]

اُف * Fie ! [ing).

افادت *A.* Conveying (a mean-

افاده *A.* Conveying : افادهٔ معنی ‖ Explanation. Expression. Causing to benefit. Pride or vainglory+. — با ا. Haughty; *-ad*. haughtily. — ا. کردن To convey; express *. To boast; give oneself airs.

افاضل [Pl. of افضل]

افاضه *A.* Diffusion. Effusion. Pouring out.

افاعی [Pl. of افعی]

افاغنه [A. pl. of افغان]

اِفاقه *A.* Improvement in health ; convalescence. Margin of hope. — افاقه‌ای نمی‌بخشد It doesn't do much good.

افانین ○ *A.* [Pl. of افنان pl. of فنّ] Branches. *F.* Ways.

افت Fall(ing) ○. *S. a. under* افتادن ‖ *F.* Subsidence. (Shortage on account of) impurities: افت کندم

افتادگی Humility. Omission.

اُفتادن [افت] To fall. To be omitted. To happen ; h. to be *. — افتان و خیزان Falling and rising. In violent trepidation ○.

افتاده [P. P. of افتادن] Fallen. Omitted. *F.* Humble; prostrate; meek. — *n.* H. or oppressed person; underdog [pl. افتادگان].

اِفتتاح *A.* Opening; inauguration. — ا. کردن To inaugurate.

افتتاحی *A.* Inaugural.

افتخار *A.* [افتخارات] Honour.— ا. کردن به To pride oneself on ; be proud of ; glory in. — بافتخارِ In honour of.

افتخاراً *A.* Honorarily.

افتخاری *A.* Honorary.

افتراء *A.* Calumny; slander. — ا. زدن به To calumniate.

افترا آمیز *A. P.* Calumniatory; scandalous.

اِفتضاح *A.* Disgrace; scandal.— ا. در آوردن To cause a disgrace. To bring d. on oneself.

افتضاح آمیز *or* **افتضاح آور** *A.P.* Disgraceful; shameful.

افتکاك *A.* Separation.

افخم [Comp. of فخیم]

اَفرا Maple.

افراختن etc. = **افراشتن** etc.

افراد [Pl. of فرد]

اِفراد ○ *A.* Using in the singular.— ا. و جمع *Gr.* Number.

اَفراز [Imp. of افراشتن]

اِفراز *A.* Separating ; partition. — ا. کردن To divide ;

partition. — قابل ا. Partible.
افراسیاب *Mas. pr. name.*
افراشتگی *or* **افراختگی** Exaltation
افراشتن [افراز] To elevate; exalt. To hoist.
افراشته Exalted. Hoisted. — نیمه ا. At half-mast
اِفراط *A.* Extravagance. Excessiveness. — ا. کردن To be extravagant. To take an extreme course. — ا. وتفریط Going to extremes. — بحد افراط رساندن To carry to excess.
افراطکار *A. P.* Wasteful.
افراطی *A. P.* Extremist.
افروختگی Blaze; being aflame. *F.* Excitement.
افروختن [افروز] To kindle. To burn. *F.* To provoke.
افروخته [P. P. of افروختن]
افروز [Imp. of افروختن].
افروزش Ignition.
افریقا(ئی) Africa(n).
افزا *or* **افزای** [Imp of افزودن]
افزار = 1) ابزار 2) Spices.
افزارمند Artisan.
افزایش Addition. Increase. — ا. یافتن To be increased.
افزاینده Increasing. Crescent. —*n.* ○ Augmenter.
افزودن [(افزا(ی)] To add To increase; augment. —*vi.* To be increased. To grow.
افزوده Increased. Added.
افزون Increased ○. More * : ا. از More than; exceeding. — ا.شدن To be increased; grow; with از] exceed.
افزونی Excess.
افساد *A.* Corrupting. Demoralizing. Doing mischief.
اَفسار Bridle. — ا. کردن To b.
افسارگسیخته Unrestrained; libertine.
افسانه Fable; myth. By-word.
افسد *A.* [Comp. of فاسد] More corrupt. Worse. — دفع فاسد به ا. Elimination of an evil by a worse e.
اَفسر Officer. Crown *
افسردگی Dejection; depression. *OS.* Congelation.
افسردن ○ To freeze; congeal. *F.* To be depressed.
افسرده Dejected; depressed. Disappointed. *OS.* Frozen.
افسرده خاطر *P. A.* & افسرده دل Downhearted; depressed.
افسری Officer's rank. — دانشکدهٔ ا. Officers' college.
افسنطین *A.-G.* Wormwood. — عرق ا. Absinth(ium).
افسوس Regret —*int.* Alas! — ا. خوردن To regret. — ا. که It is to be regretted that.
افسون Incantation; charm. — ا. خواندن To utter a spell. — ا. کردن To enchant; conjure.
افسونگر Enchanter. Magician.
اِفشاء *A.* Revealing; disclosing. — ا. شدن To be disclosed; leak out. — ا. کردن To disclose.
افشار [Imp. of افشردن]
افشان [Imp. of افشاندن]
افشاندن [افشان] To scatter. To sow. To sprinkle. To shake

off. To brandish.
افشانده Scattered. Sown.
افشردن [افشار] To press. To squeeze (out). [Squeezed.
افشرده [P. P. of افشردن] Pressed
افشره Expressed juice ; also, (lemon) squash, or the like.
افصح o [Comp. of فصیح]
افضل *A.* [Comp. of فاضل] More learned. Better. Predominant. — ا. از Better than ; superior to. —*n*. [Only in the pl. افاضل learned men].
افضلیت *A.* Superiority ; preference.
افطار *A.* Breaking one's fast.— ا. کردن To break one's f.
اَفعال [Pl. of فعل] Verbs. Deeds ; acts; actions.
افعی *A.* [افاعی] Viper.
افغان Groan(ing). Wail(ing).
افغان [A. pl. افاغنه] Afghan.
افغانستان Afghanistan.
اُفق *A.* Horizon [usu. خط ا.] *Cf. the pl.* آفاق ‖ افق حسی or افق مرئی Sensible horizon.— افق حقیقی Rational h.
افقا *A.* Horizontally.
افقی *A.* Horizontal.
افکار *A.* [Pl. of فکر] Thoughts. Opinion(s).—افکارعمومی Public opinion . — مراجعه بافکارِ عمومی Referendum.
افکن [Imp. of افکندن]
افکندگی State of being (over)thrown. Abjection.
افکندن [افکن] To throw. To overthrow. To project.
افکنده (Over)thrown. Humiliated; abject. [flicted.
افگار * Wounded; galled. Af-
افگانه o Abortive child.
افگنده - افگندن - افگندگی = **افکندگی** etc.
اِفلاس *A.* 1) = **ورشکستگی** 2) = **تهیدستی**
افلاطون *A-G.* Plato.
افلاطونی *A.* Platonic.
افلاك [Pl. of فلك]
اِفلیج *A.* = **فالج** [tion.
افناء *A.* Annihilation; destruc-
افندی *T-G.* Effendi.
افواج [Pl. of فوج]
افواه *A.* [Pl. of فم] = دهن‌ها Mouths. — در افواه است که There is a rumour that.
افواها *A.* By hearsay.
افواهی *A. P.* Rumoured.
اُفول *A.* Setting (of stars). — ا. کردن To set.
افیون [f. G. origin] Opium.
اقارب *A.* [Pl. of اقرب] Relatives.
اقاقیا *A-Lat.* False acacia ; common locust-tree.
اقاله *A.* Rescission. Cancellation.— ا. کردن To cancel.
اِقامت *A.* Residing; staying. — محل ا. Residence. — پروانهٔ ا. R. permit. [Domicile.
اقامتگاه *A. P.* Residence.
اقامه *A.* Adducing. Producing.— ا. کردن To adduce ; raise. To produce. — برعلیه کسی اقامهٔ دعوی کردن To bring an action, or lodge a complaint, against s. o.

اقانیم [Pl. of اقنوم]
اقباض o *A*. Delivering; giving delivery. [Facing.
اِقبال *A*. Fortune; luck. *OS*.
اقبح o. [Comp. of قبیح]
اقتباس *A*. Borrowing. Acquiring. Extract(ion). – ا. کردن To borrow. To extract; excerpt. To acquire. To cite.
اقتداء *A*. Following an example. – ا. کردن To follow *or* imitate [*with* به].
اقتدار *A*. Power; authority.
اقتراب o *A*. = نزدیکی
اقتراح o *A*. Improvisation.
اقتران *A*. Conjunction (of stars). Association.
اِقتصاد *A*. Economy.– مقرون به ا. Economical.
اقتصادی *A*. Economic.
اقتصادیات *A*. Economics.
اقتصار *A*. Confining oneself to little. Abridgment.
اِقتضاء *A*. Exigency; necessity; occasion. Advisability. – ا. کردن To necessitate; demand. To be expedient. – لدی‌الاقتضاء (*ladul-eghteza'*) When occasion arises; on occasion; as circumstances may allow. – باقتضای وقت On the spur of the moment. – باقتضای دوستی As friendship requires.
اَقدام [Pl. of قدم]
اِقدام *A*. [اقدامات] Action; measure; steps. – ا. کردن To take action.– ا. لازم بعمل آوردن To take necessary action.

اقدس *A*. [Comp. of قدوس]. – *Fem. pr. name*.
اِقرار *A*. Confession.– ا. بگناهان C. of one's sins. – ا. بکسی آوردن To believe in s. o.– ا. کردن To confess.– از کسی ا. گرفتن To c. a person.
اقرار نامه *A. P.* Affidavit.
اقران [Pl. of قرین]
اقرب o [Comp. of قریب]
اقرباء *A*. Kinsmen. *Cf. the s.* قریب
اقساط [Pl. of قسط]
اقساطی + *A. P.* = قسطی
اقسام [Pl. of قِسم]
اقصاء *A*. [Pl. of قصی o] Remote parts; extremities.
اقصر [Comp. of قصیر]. Shorter or shortest. – اقصر طرق Shortest way; bee-line.
اقصی *A*. [Comp. of قاصی o] Farther or farthest.
اقطار *A*. [Pl. of قطر] Regions.
اَقطی (-*ta*) *A-G*. Common elder. Elder-berry.
اقلّ *A*. [Comp. of قلیل] Less or least. – حد اقل Minimum.
اقلاً *A*. At least.
اقلام *A*. Pl. of قلم] [tion.
اقلت *A*. Minority. The opposi-
اِقلیدس *A-G*. Euclid.
اِقلیم *A-G*. [اقالیم] Climate o. Region; country. Continent.
اقمار [Pl. of قمر]
اقمشه [Pl. of قماش]
اِقناع *A*. Satisfying; convincing.
اقنوم *A-G*. [اقانیم] Hypostasis.
اقوال [Pl. of قول]

اقوام [Pl. of قوم]
اَقوی (-va) [Comp. of قوی]
اقویاء *A.* [Pl. of قوی] The strong or powerful.
اقیانوس *A-G.* Ocean.
اقیانوسی *A.* Oceanic.
اقیانوسیه *A.* Oceanea; Oceanica.
اکابر *A.* Adults. Great men; nobles. *Cf. the s.* اکبر
اکاذیب *A.* [Pl. of اکذوبه o]
اکارم [Pl. of اکرم]
اکال o *A.* [Fem. اکاله] Corrosive. Caustic. — مادهٔ اکاله Corrosive.
اکالیپتوس *Fr.* Eucalyptus.
اکالیت *A.* Corrosiveness.
اکباتان *Fr.* Ecbatana.
اکبر *A.* [Comp. of کبیر] Greater or greatest. *—n. Mas. pr. name. Cf. the pl.* اکابر
اِکبیر × Mangy appearance. Nasty fellow. [lousy.
اکبیری × Nasty. Mangy ;
اکتبر *Fr.* October.
اِکتساب *A.* Acquisition.—ا. کردن To acquire.
اکتسابی *A.* Acquired.
اِکتشاف *A.* [اکتشافات] Discovery. Exploration. — ا. کردن To discover. To explore.
اکتشافی *A.* Exploratory. — عملیات ا. Reconnaissance.
اِکتفاء *A.* Contenting oneself.— بچیزی ا. کردن To content oneself with s. t.
اکثر *A.* [Comp. of کثیر] More or most. More or most numerous. Greater or greatest. *S. a.* اکثراً — *n.* Most ; the m. part. — اکثر اوقات M. of the time.—حداکثر Maximum.
اکثراً *A.* Mostly [often اکثر].
اکثریت *A.* Majority.—باکثریت آراء By a m. vote.—ازاکثریت انداختن To cause (an assembly) to lose its quorum.
اکراد [A. pl. of کُرد]
اِکرام *A.* Honour(ing).—ا. کردن To honour.
اِکراه *A.* Reluctance. Dislike. Duress. — باکراه = **اکراهاً**
اکراهاً *A.* Reluctantly ; under duress.
اکر دو کر Hopscotch.
اکردئون *Fr.* Accordion.
اکرم *A.* [Comp. of کریم —pl. اکارم] More or most generous. Great ; honourable. *—n. Fem. pr. name.*
اکزما *Fr.* Eczema.
اکسید *Fr.* Oxide.
اکسیر *A.* Elixir.
اکسیژن *Fr.* Oxygen.
اکسیژنه o *Fr.* Oxygenated. — آب ا. Hydrogen peroxide.
اکل *A.* Eating o. — ا. ازقفا Doing a thing in a roundabout way.
اِکلیل *A.* Bronze powder. Diadem. Garland. — ا. زدن To apply bronze p. (to) — اکلیلِ جنوبی Corona Australis.—اکلیل شمالی C. Borealis. — اکلیل کروی Sector of a sphere.—اکلیل کوهی Common rosemary.
اکلیلی *A.* Coronary. — درز اکلیلی C. suture.

اکمل A. [Comp. of کامل] More or most perfect.
اکناف A. Parts; regions; borders. *Cf. the s.* کنف
اکنون Now. [Ravenous.
اکول ○ A. = پرخور Gluttonous.
اَکید A. Strict; emphatic.
اکیداً A. Strictly.
اگر If. Though * . — ا. نه Otherwise; or else; if not. — ا. هم Even if; even though.
اگرچه Although.
اگیر T. [usu. اگیر ترکی] Common sweet-flag; Asiatic calamus.
اَلا * O! Beware! Behold! Ah!
الا A. (el'a) Except; save. — ا. اینکه E. that. Only. — والا Otherwise; or.
الان A. Just now. Presently +.
اُلاغ Donkey.
الاکلنگ Spanish fly. See-saw.
الباب ○ A. [Pl. of لُب] Hearts; minds. *See* الوالالباب
الباقی A. = (باقی) مانده
البته A. Certainly; of course.
اَلبرز Elburz.
البسه [Pl. of لباس]
التجاء A. Taking refuge.
التذاذ ○ A. Taking relish.
اِلتزام A. Being bound (over). Recognizance; undertaking. — ا. دادن To give an u. To be bound over. — ا. گرفتن از To bind over.
التزامی A. (*Gr.*) Potential.
التصاق A. Adhesion. Cohesion. Being affixed.
اِلتفات A. Favour. Attention. *OS.* Turning the face toward another. — التفات شما زیاد Thank you. — ا. فرمودن [*In p. c.*] To give; grant. To be good enough to . . . . — ا. کردن To do or show favour. [*In p. c.*] To give.
التقاء ○ A. Conjunction; meeting.
اِلتماس A. Entreaty; supplication. — ا. کردن To entreat.
التواء ○ A. Twisting; contortion. — التواءِ قدم Clubfoot.
التهاب A. Inflammation.
التهاب‌آور A. P. Inflammatory.
اِلتیام A. Healing up; cicatrization. *F.* Conciliation. — ا. پذیرفتن To be reconciled. To heal up. — ا. دادن To conciliate. To consolidate. To cause to h. up.
التیام پذیر A. P. Reconcilable. *OS.* That can heal up.
التیام ناپذیر A. P. Irreconcilable.
الجزایر Algeria. Algiers.
الچی S. u. ایلچی [nately.
اِلحاح A. Insisting importu-
الحاد ○ A. Atheism.
الحاصل ○ A. To sum up.
اِلحاق A. Joining. Annexation.
اَلحاقی A. Annexed. Supplemental.
الحال * A. = اکنون
الحان [Pl. of لحن]
الحذر * A. Beware! [Indeed.
الحق A. Justly. [*Ironically*].
الحمدلله A. (*alham'dolelah*) Praise be to God. *L.*

Thank you.
الخی *S. u.* **ایلخی**
الدنگ × Clown. Unfeeling person. Blockhead. Coward.
اِلزام *A.* [الزامات] Obligation.
الزام‌آور *A. P.* Binding *a.*
الزامی *A. P.* Obligatory.
الزم ○ *A.* [Comp. of لازم]
الساعه *A.* Just now. In a moment.
السنه [Pl. of لسان]
الشجاع *A.* (*Astr.*) The Hydra.
اِلصاق *A.* Affixing. Attaching. - ا. کردن To affix. To pin.
الطاف [Pl. of لطف]
اِلغاء *A.* Cancellation. Annulment. - ا. کردن To cancel; annul.
الغرض * *A.* Anyhow; at any rate. In a word.
الغیاث * *A.* Cry for help. —*int.* Help! Justice!
الف ○ *A.* = هزار Thousand.
الفاظ [Pl. of لفظ]
اِلفباء *A.* Alphabet. - بترتیب ا. Alphabetically.
الفبائی *A. P.* Alphabetic(al).
الفت *A.* Familiarity. Friendship. - ا. گرفتن To become familiar. *S. a.* انس گرفتن
اِلقاء *A.* Suggestion. Infusion. *Ph.* Induction. - ا. کردن To suggest. To inspire.
القائی *A.* (*Ph.*) Inductive.
القاب [Pl. of لقب]
اِلقاح *A.* Impregnation; fecundation. Pollination.
القصه * *A.* Briefly stating; to make a long story short.
اَلَك *T.* Hairsieve. - ا. کردن To sift.
الکترون *Fr.* Electron.
الکتریك *Fr.* Electric light *or* current. - چراغ ا. E. lamp.
لکتریکی *Fr. P.* Electric(al). Electrically-driven.
الکل Alcohol [f. *A.* الکحل collyrium] - الکل چوب Wood alcohol; wood spirit; methyl a. - الکل تقلیبی Denatured a. - الکل صنعتی Industrial a.
الکل سنج *or* **الکل نما** Alcoholometer. *See* الکل
الکلی Alcoholic. Addicted to drinking alcoholic liquors. - تراز الکلی Spirit level.
الکن * *A.* Stammering *a.*
اُلگو *T.* Pattern.
الله *A.* (*a*llah) = خدا God.
الله الله *A.* (a*la'ha*la*h*) For God's sake. Good God!
الله بختی *A. P.* At random; haphazard.
اللهیار (*A. P.*) *Mas. pr. name. See.* الله & یار
الم *A.* [آلام] Pain. Grief.
الماس *A—Lat.* Diamond.
المپیك *Fr.* Olympic.
المثنی *A.* Duplicate (copy).
النسق *A.* (*anasagh*) Orion.
النگو (Ring) bracelet; bangle.
الو + [f. الاو] Flame.
الواح [Pl. of لوح]
الوار Lumber.
الوار [A. pl. of لر] The *Lurs*;

the inhabitants of *Luristan*.
الواط *A*. [Pl. of لوطی but properly of لوط]. Lewd person(s). Clown(s).
الوان *A*. [Pl. of لون] Colours. —*a*. + Coloured.
الوداع *A*. Farewell!
الوهیت *A*. Divinity.
الویه [Pl. of لواء].
اله *A*. (*e*lah) A god. God.
اِلهام *A*. [الهامات] Inspiration.— ا. کردن To reveal by inspiration; inspire.
الهام‌بخش *A*. *P*. Inspiring *a*.— قوهٔ ا. Muse.
الهامی *A*. Inspired.
اللهم o *A*. (*a*la*ho*m'*a*)=خدایا O God!
الهه *A*. [Fem. of اله] Goddess.
الهی *A*. (*e*la*hi:'*) Divine.
الهی *A*. (*e*la'*hi:*) My God!— ا. شفا یابد May he be cured.
الهیات *A*. Divine matters. Theology.
الی *A*. (*e'*la) = تا Until; to; [(up) to.
الیاس *A*. Elijah.
الیق o [Comp. of لایق]
الیاف [Pl. of لیف]
الیکائی Wren.
الیم o *A*. Painful; excruciating.
الیه o *A*. To him.
الیها o *A*. To her.
الیهم o *A*. = بایشان To them.
ام *Pron. affixed to a word ending in mute* ه. 1) My. Ex. خانه ام ‖ 2)= هستم I am. رفته‌ام I have gone; I am g.

اُمّ o *A*. [امهات]=مادر Mother. *F*. Source; parent.
اما *A*. But. — و اما (B.) as to. Now [*introductory word*].
اماثل o *A*. [Pl. of امثل] Equals; peers.
اُماج *T*. Pottage with flour.
اماجد [Pl. of امجد]
امارت *A*. [امارات] Indication; sign [also اماره]. Circumstantial evidence. — امارهٔ قضائی Judge-made law.
اِمارت *A*. Emirate; principality.
اماره *A*. (*a*ma*reh*) Leading one by force into sin [only in نفس ا. spirit of lasciviousness]. *OS*. Imperious.
اماکن [A pl. of مکان]
ام‌الصبیان o *A*. (*o*m'*o*se*b*y*a*n) Elf. Hydrocephalus of newborn children.
اِماله *A*. Enema; injection. Clyster. — امالهٔ فرنگی Clysopump; i.-pump. — ا. کردن To give e. to. To inject.
امام *A*. [ائمه] Imam; pontiff.
امامت *A*. Imamate; leadership.
امامزاده *A*. *P*. Offspring of an Imam. Shrine.
اَمان *A*. Security. Safety. (Cry for) quarter. Respite. — ا. خواستن To seek q. — بامانِ حق Good luck to you! — ا. ازدستِ Who can help ...?
امانات [Pl. of امانت]
اَمانت *A*. Honesty. Trusteeship. Deposit. Parcel. Consignment. [Pl. امانات] — نزد کسی

ا.گذاردن To d. with s. o. – ا.نگاه داشتن To hold in trust.– دفتر امانات پستی Parcel post.

امانت‌دار *A. P.* Depositary.

امانت فروش *A. P.* Commission-merchant ; broker on commission.

امانت فروشی *A. P.* Sale on commission ; consignment s.

امانت‌گذار *A. P.* Depositor.

امانةً *A.* In trust; as a deposit.

امانتی *A. P.* Given in trust ; deposited. —*n.* Deposit. – وجوه ا. T. funds.

امانی *A. P.* Based on trusteeship. Operated direct (by the Government) Meant for sale on commission ; on consignment s.

امپراطور *Lat.* Emperor.

امپراطوری *Lat. P.* Empire.

اُمت *A.* [امم] Nation; people ; body of believers.

اِمتثال *A.* Complying with.

امتثالاً *A.* Conformably.

اِمتحان *A.* Examination. Test. Temptation. Proof. – ا. دادن To take an examination; sit for an e. – ا.کردن To test ; try. To examine. To try on. – بشرط ا. On trial.

امتحاناً *A.* Tentatively; by way of experiment or trial.

امتحانی *A.* Experimental. – کاغذِ ا. Examination paper.

اِمتداد *A.* Prolongation; extension. – ا. دادن To extend ; prolong. – ا. یافتن To be extended. – در امتدادِ Along.

اِمتزاج *A.* Being mixed ; mixture. *F.* Compatibility.

امتعه [Pl. of متاع]

اِمتلاء *A.* Fulness. Surfeit. – امتلاء معده Surfeited stomach ; cropsickness.

اِمتناع *A.* Refusal. Abstention. – ا. ورزیدن *or* ا. کردن To abstain : او از رأی دادن ا. ورزید He abstained from voting.

اِمتنان *A.* Gratefulness. Indebtedness ; obligation. – اظهارِ ا.کردن To express (one's) thanks.– موجب ا. خواهد بوداگر... I shall be grateful if . . .

امتیاز *A.* [امتیازات] Distinction. Privilege . Concession . Licence. – صاحب ا. Concessionaire. Licence-owner.

امتیازنامه *A. P.* Concessionary agreement ; concession.

امتیازی *A.* Concessionary.

امثال [Pl. of مثل *masal & mesl*]

امثله [Pl. of مثال]

امجد *A.* [Comp. of مجید] More or most glorious. Nobler or noblest. [Pl. اَماجِد]

اِمحاء *A.* Wiping out; effacement. *F.* Annihilation.

اِمداد *A.* Assistance. Relief. – ا.کردن To assist ; help.

امدادی *A.* Tending to assist or relieve. Reenforcing. – مسابقهٔ ا. ‖ تیمارگاه = پست ا. Relay event.

اَمر *A.* [امور] Affair; matter.– وزارت امور خارجه *S. u.* خارجه

اَمر *A.* [اوامر] Order; command. *Gr.* Imperative. — (به) ا کردن To order or c. [Construed also with دادن].
امراء [Pl. of امیر]
اِمرار *A.* Passing. — امرار وقت کردن To pass, or idle away, one's time. — امرار معاش کردن To earn one's livelihood.
امراض [Pl. of مرض]
امربر *A. P.* (*Mil.*) Orderly.
امرد * *A.* [اَمارِد] Beardless (youth).
امرداد = مرداد
امرود 1) ○ = گلابی ‖ 2) Fusee of a watch.
امروز To-day. [امروزی
امروزه Nowadays. *—a.* =
امروزی Of to-day; modern.
امری *A.* Imperative: وجه ا.
امریکا(یی) America(n).
امزجه [Pl. of مزاج]
امزیك *T.* Cigarette-holder.
اِمساك *A.* Thrift; also, parsimony. — ا. کردن To be thrifty. To restrict oneself.
امسال This year.
امشب To-night. [sprayer.
اِمشی *A.* Imshi. — تلمبه ا. Imshi-
اِمضاء *A.* Signature. — ا. کردن To sign; execute. — صاحب ا. Signatory. — بامضا رساندن To have signed. — نامه ای بامضایِ A letter s. by. — امضاکنندهٔ زیر The undersinged.
امضاء سازی *A. P.* Forgery. *OS.* Forging signatures.
امعاء *A.* [Pl. of معاء] Bowels.
اِمعان *A.* [Also امعان نظر] Looking attentively.
امکان [امکانات] *A.* Possibility. — ا. داشتن To be possible. — بقدر امکان As far (*or* so f.) as possible; as much as p. — درحدودامکان Within p. limits. — در صورت ا. If p. — عدم ا. Impossibility.
امکان پذیر *A. P.* Possible.
امکان ناپذیر *A. P.* Impossible.
امکنه [A pl. of مکان]
اَمل ○ *A.* [آمال] = آرزو
اُمّل × Fogyish.
اِملاء *A.* Spelling. Dictation.
املاح [Pl. of ملح]
اِملاك [Pl. of مُلك]
املائی *A.* Orthographic.
املح ○ [Comp. of ملیح]
املیك *T.* Newly-born lamb.
امم [Pl. of امت]
اَمن *A.* Security ○. *-a.* + Secure; safe; peaceful.
امنا [Pl. of امین]
امنیت *A.* Security.
امنیه *A.* Gendarmerie.
اموات [Pl. of میت]
امواج [Pl. of موج]
اموال [Pl. of مال]
امور (*A.*) *S*, *u*, امر [monia.
امونیاك *Fr.* (Solution of) am-
امونیوم *Fr.* Ammonium.
امهات [Pl. of اُم]
اِمهال ○ *A.* Giving a respite.
اُمّی *A.* Illiterate. Uterine.
امیال [Pl. of میل]
امید Hope. — ا. بستن To rely. —

ا. بریدن * To lose hope ; despair. — ا. داشتن To h. — ا. است که It is hoped that. — بامیدِ In the hope of. — بامیدشما هستم I count on you.
امیدبخش Promising; inspiring hope; hope-giving; hopeful.
امیدوار Hopeful ; expectant. — امیدوارم کامیاب شوید I hope you will succeed.
امیدواری Hopefulness.
امیر *A.* [امراء] Emir ; prince.
امیرالبحر *A.* = **دریاسالار**
امیرالحج *A.* Leader of a caravan going on pilgrimage.
امیرالمؤمنین *A.* Commander of the Faithful : title of the Caliphs, esp. of Ali.
امیر نشین *A. P.* Emirate.
اَمین *A.* Honest. *-n.* [Pl. اُمَناء] Trustee. — امین‌صلح Justice of the Peace.
اَن [*Indecent*] Shit.
اِناء o *A.* = **ظرف**
انابت *A.* = **توبه**
اِناث *A.* [Pl. of انثی *onsa*] Females ; women.
اِناثی o *A.* [Fem. اناثیه] Female. Girls' ; women's.
اناجیل [Pl. of انجیل]
انار Pomegranate.
انام * *A.* Mankind. Creatures.
اَنانیت *A.* Egotism.
انبار 1) Warehouse ; depot. [*Of a lamp*] Reservoir. [*For grains*] Granary. — انبارصحرائی *or* انبار کاه Barn. — انبار گمرکی Bonded warehouse. — ا. کردن To store. To hoard. 2) o [*Imp. of* انباشتن]
انباردار Storekeeper ; warehouseman.
انبارداری Warehousing.
انبارگردانی Stock-taking.
انباره Accumulator.
انباز * = شریك Partner. Companion.
انبازی * = شریك Partnership. Companionship.
انباشتگی Ful(l)ness; repletion.
انباشتن [انبار] To store. To fill up. To hoard.
انباشته [P. P. of انباشتن]
انبان Scrip ; leathern bag. — انبان شناور Life-buoy.
انبانچه *Anat.* Utricle.
انبر (*ambor*) Tongs. — انبر جراحی & انبر قابلگی Forceps.
انبر دست Pliers.
انبرك Pincers. Forceps. Nippers. Bodkin.
اِنبساط *A.* Expansion. *F.* Exhilaration. Cheerfulness [usu. انبساط خاطر] . — قابل ا. Expansible.
انبوه (*ambu:h*) Crowded. Numerous. Thick. Bushy : ریش ا. ‖ *-n.* Multitude. Large number. — ا. شدن To crowd. To become thick. To luxuriate.
انبوهی Abundance. Bushiness. Thickness. Congestion.
انبه (*ambeh*) Mango.
انبیاء [Pl. of نبی]
انبیق *A-G.* Alembic.
انتباه o *A.* Waking. Vigilance.
انتحار *A.* = **خودکشی**
انتحال *A.* Plagiarism.

اِنتخاب *A.* Selection; choice. Election. — ا. کردن To select or choose. To elect.

انتخابات *A.* [Pl. of انتخاب] General elections.

انتخابی *A.P.* Elective. Elected. [Fem. انتخابیه]. — حوزهٔ انتخابیه Electorate; constituency.

انتزاع *A.* Wresting. Separation. Abstraction.

انتزاعی *A.* Abstract.

انتساب *A.* Relation. Descent.

اِنتشار *A.* Spreading. abroad; publication. Circulation: انتشار اسکناس ‖ Rumour. [Pl. انتشارات Publications; also, information]. — ا. دادن To spread or noise abroad. To give publicity to. To divulge. To circulate or issue. — ا. یافتن To be published. To be spread abroad. — ا. دارد که There is a rumour that.

اِنتصاب *A.* Appointment. — حکم انتصابِ امین ترکه *Law.* Letters of administration.

انتصابی *A.* Appointed. Dative.

اِنتظار *A.* Waiting. Expectation. Anticipation. [Pl. انتظارات]. — اطاق ا. W. room. — انتظار خدمت Status of an employee who is on the waiting list. — ا. داشتن To expect; anticipate. — ا. کشیدن To be w. — درانتظارِ کسی بودن To be w. for s. o. — درانتظار گذاشتن To keep w. — ازانتظار در آوردن To relieve from waiting.

اِنتظام *A.* [انتظامات] Order; discipline. — ا. دادن To put in order. To arrange (methodically).

انتظامی *A. P.* Disciplinary. Pertaining to the police.

انتفاع *A.* Profit(ing); benefit(ing). — عمل انتفاعی Exploitation.

اِنتقاد *A.* [انتقادات] Criticism. [For فنّ ا.] Critique; critic. ا. کردن To criticize.

انتقادی *A.* Critical; based on criticism.

اِنتقال *A.* Transfer. Transmission. Change-over; switch-over. — انتقال بانکی Clearing. — انتقال خون Transfusion of blood. — ا. دادن To transfer; make over. To transmit. — ا. یافتن To be transferred. — قابل ا. = انتقال پذیر ‖ انتقال ناپذیر = غیرقابل ا.

انتقال پذیر *A. P.* Transferable.

انتقال دهنده *A. P.* Transferor.

انتقال گیرنده *A. P.* Transferee; assignee.

انتقال ناپذیر *A. P.* Not to be transferred. Inalienable.

انتقال نامه *A. P.* Conveyance; deed of transfer. [Ceded

انتقالی *A. P.* Transferred.

انتقام *A.* Vengeance; revenge. — ا. گرفتن *or* ا. کشیدن To take vengeance. — انتقام خود را از کسی کشیدن To r. oneself on s. o. — انتقام مرا از او بگیرید Avenge me on him.

اِنتهاء *A*. End ; extremity. — در انتهایِ At the end of.
انتیك *E*. & *Fr*. Antique ; ancient relic.
انتیمون *A-Lat*. Antimony. — انتیمون مقی Tartar emetic.
انجبار *S. u*. **انگبار**
انجدان *S. u*. **انگدان**
انجام Conclusion; end. Accomplishment . — ا. دادن To accomplish ; do; perform. To complete. To fulfil. To comply with; grant: خواهشِ ا. یافتن *or* ا. گرفتن ‖ مرا ا. داد To be accomplished or achieved. To be fulfilled. To come to an end. — به ا. رساندن To bring to a conclusion. To accomplish. — به ا. انجام وظیفه ‖ ا. گرفتن = رسیدن کردن To perform or discharge one's duty. — حین انجام وظیفه While on d.; in the harness. — امر انجام شده Accomplished act; *fait accompli*.
انجامیدن [o انجام] To (come to an) end. To be accomplished. To lead *vi*. — بطول ا. To take a long time. To be prolonged.
انجره Male nettle.
انجم [A pl. of نجم]
انجماد *A*. Freezing. Concretion.
اَنجمن Society ; association. Meeting . — انجمن شهر(داری) Town council ; municipal c. — ا. کردن To hold a meeting. To gather together.
انجیر Fig. — انجیر بابا آدم Adam's fig. — انجیر هندی Indian f. ; cactus.
انجیر خور [For مرغ ا.] 1) Beccafico. 2) Oriole.
انجیل *A-G*. [اناجیل] Gospel.
انچوچك (Dried) pear seeds. Kind of prune (*Prunus Syriaca*).
انحاء [Pl. of نحو]
اِنحراف *A*. Deviation. Digression. — ا. ورزیدن To deviate. — زاویهٔ ا. *Ph*. Declination.
اِنحصار *A*. Monopoly. Restriction. — ا. داشتن به . . . To be a monopoly of . . . ; be confined to . . . — گواهی نامهٔ انحصارِ وراثت Probate.
انحصاراً = **منحصراً**
انحصاری *A*. Exclusive. Monopolistic.
انحطاط *A*. Decline. Decadence. — رو به ا. گذاردن To begin to decline. — انحطاط افق Depression of the horizon.
اِنحلال *A*. Dissolution ; disorganization. Winding up.
انحناء *A*. Curvature. — قابل ا. Flexible. — غیرقابل ا. Inflexible.
اَند o Small number ; fraction. — دو سال و اندی Something over 2 years. — دو هزار و اندی Two-thousand odd.
اندا(ی) [Imp. of اندودن]
انداختن [انداز] To throw; cast. To fell. To omit. To lay low: force to stay in bed.
انداخته [P. P. of انداختن] Thrown. Omitted.
انداز [Imp. of انداختن]

اَندازه Size. Measure. Gauge. — ا. گرفتن ا. کردن To measure. — To m.; take m. To dip. — ا. نگهداشتن To keep within bounds. — باندازه Of the required s. Moderate(ly). — بهمان ا. To the same extent. Proportionately. — تا یك ا. To some e.

اندازه‌گیری Measurement.

اَندام Limb. Organ. Body. Figure. — عرض ا. کردن To put oneself forward; attract attention.

اَندر * In(to).

اَندرز (Piece of) advice.

اندرزا *Same as* گاو دارو

اندرون Interior. Women's apartment. Bowels. Heart.

اندرونه Viscera.

اندرونی Internal. Middle. —*n* Women's apartment.

اندك Few; little. Short: درمدت اندکی نان ‖ اندکی A l. bread.

اندك اندك Little by little.

اندك رنج = زود رنج

اَندوختن [اندوز] To amass; accumulate; heap up. To save. To acquire.

اندوخته [P. P. of اندوختن] Amassed. Saved. — *n*. Saving(s). Reserve (fund). Amassed wealth.

اندود Plaster. Coating. — ا. کردن = اندودن [Inlayer.

اندودگر *or* **اندودکار** Plasterer.

اَندودن [اندای ○] To plaster. To plate; coat. To inlay.

اندوده [P. P. of اندودن]

اندوز [Imp. of اندوختن]

اندونزی *Fr.* Indonesia.

اَندوه Grief; sorrow.

اندوهناك *or* **اندوهگین** Sad.

اندیش [Imp. of اندیشیدن]

اندیشناك Apprehensive. Mistrustful.

اندیشه Thought; reflection. Fear; apprehensiveness. — ا. کردن * To think; reflect. To fear.

اندیشیدن * [اندیش] To reflect; think. To fear.

انذار ○ *A.* Prognosis.

اِنزال *A.* Seminal effusion; ejaculation of sperm. — سرعت ا. Hasty discharge of s.

اِنزجار *A.* Aversion; repulsion.

انزروت Sarcocolla.

انزوا *A.* = گوشه نشینی

اِنس ○ *A.* Human being.

اُنس *A.* Familiarity. Tameness. Sociability. — ا. گرفتن To become familiar. To (come to) feel at home. To associate. — انجمن ا. Social party.

اِنسان *A.* Man; human.

انسان‌شناسی *A.P.* Anthropology.

انسانی *A.* Human.

انسانیت *A.* Humanity.

انسب *A.* Fitter or fittest. — بقای ا. Survival of the f.

انسداد *A.* Obstruction.

انسولین *Fr.* Insulin.

اِنشاء *A.* Style. Composition. Letter-writing. *OS.* Creation. — ا. کردن To compose; write; indite.

انشاءالله (*ensh*a-*a*llah) *A*. God willing; D.V. (Deo volenti). May (it please G. that). I hope so.
انشاد *A*. Reciting verses.
انشائی *A*. Creative ; originative. Epistolary.
اِنشعاب *A*. Branching out. Service line; extension.
انشقاق *A*. Being split.
انصار *A*. [Pl. of ناصر].
اِنصاف *A*. Equity ; justice. — ا. دادن To judge fairly.
انصافاً *A*. Justly; indeed.
اِنصراف *A*. Dispensing (with).— ا. ورزیدن از To dispense with.
اِنضباط *A*. Discipline; order.— ا. دادن To put in o. To bring under control.
انضباطی *A*. Disciplinary.
اِنضجار *A*. Disgust.
اِنضمام *A*. Being annexed. — بانضمام Including.
اِنطباع *A*. Being printed. Publication [pl. انطباعات].
اِنطباق *A*. Conformity. Applicability. Coincidence. *Geom*. Superposition.
اَنظار *A*. [Pl. of نظر] Looks. Views. — در انظار عموم In the sight of the public ; to the p. view; openly. [Camels.
اَنعام o *A*. [Pl. of نَعم] Cattle.
اِنعام *A*. Prize; bonus; gratuity.
اِنعدام *A*. Annihilation.
اِنعطاف *A*. Inflection. Inclination. — قابل ا Flexible — غیرقابل ا. Inflexible.
انعقاد *A*. 1) Conclusion : انعقاد قرارداد ‖ 2) Holding : انعقاد جلسه ‖ 3) Coagulation.
اِنعکاس *A*. Reflection. Reaction.— ا. پیدا کردن To have a reaction. — انعکاس صدا Echo.— عمل ا. Reflex action. — قابل ا. Reflexible.
اَنف o *A*. = بینی Nose.— انفش معیوب است + He is not right in his upper storey.
انفاذ o *A*. = **اجرا**
انفاس [Pl. of نفس *nafas*]
اِنفاق *A*. Spending money. Nourishing. — ا. کردن To sustain; nourish.
اِنفجار *A*. Explosion; detonation. Eruption. *OS*. Bursting. — قابل ا. Explosive.
اِنفراد *A*. Singleness. Isolation.
انفراداً = بالانفراد
انفراداً *A*. Individually. Singly. Alone.
اِنفصال *A*. Discharge; dismissal. Separation.
اِنفعال *A*. Reaction. Passion. Shame. [tion.
انفکاک *A*. Separation. Redemp-
انفیه *A*. Snuff.
انفیه‌دان *A*. *P*. Snuff-box.
اِنقباض *A*. Contraction. Condensation.— انقباض‌حدقه Myosis.— انقباض قلب و شرائین Systole. — انقباض‌ماهیچه Muscular contraction ; myonicity. — حجرهٔ ا. Condenser. —قوهٔ ا. Contractile force.
انقدر *S*. *u*. **قدر**
اِنقراض *A*. Overthrow; decline; extinction; fall. — تا انقراض

عالم Forever. [division.
انقسام o *A*. Being divided;
اِنقضاء *A*. Expiry; termination.
انقطاع *A*. Being cut off; separation. Cessation.
انقلاب *A*. [انقلابات] Revolution. Sudden or radical change. *Astr*. Solstice. *Med*. Nausea; revolt. — ا.کردن To revolt. — انقلابات زمان Vicissitudes of time. — انقلاب رحم Retroversion of the womb.
انقلابی *A*. Revolutionary. —*n*. Revolutionist. [Pl. انقلابیون]
انقوزه Asaf(o)etida.
اِنقیاد *A*. Submission; obedience. — تحت ا. در آوردن To reduce to submission.
اِنکار *A*. Denial. — ا.کردن To deny. To renounce. — قابل ا. Deniable. — غیر قابل ا. Undeniable. Indisputable.
انکاری *A*. Based on denial. Negative. — استفهام ا. Positive interrogation with a negative implication.
اِنکسار *A*. Despondency. Contrition. — انکسار نور Refraction of light. [the sun.
انکساف *A*. Being eclipsed, as
اِنکشاف *A*. Being discovered. Discovery [انکشافات].
انگ Hall-mark; brand.
اَنگار [Imp. of انگاشتن]
انگار Supposition; imagination. [*Used as an ad.*] As if; you'd think... — ا. کردن To suppose. — انکار چیزی را کردن To consider as if one has never had (*or* owned) s. t; forget about it.
انگاره Rough dimension. R. draft. Measure. Dose.
انگاشتن o [انگار] To suppose. To consider as if.
انگبار *or* **انجبار** Bistort.
انگدان *or* **انجدان** Sweet asa. — انجدان رومی Lavage.
انگشت (*angosht*) Finger. — انگشت پا Toe. — ا.کردن To put one's finger. — در انگشت کردن To wear, as a ring. — اثر انگشت F.-print. — * ا. بدندان گزیدن To bite one's f.; regret or repent. — ا. توی شیر کردن To queer some one's pitch; put a spoke in his wheel.
اَنگشت (*angesht*) o = **زغال**
انگشتانه Thimble.
انگشتر(ی) Ring. — انگشترخاتم Signet-ring.
انگشت شمار To be counted on one's fingers; few.
انگشت نگاری Dactyloscopy. — ادارهٔ ا. Fingerprint Department.
انگشت نما Flagrant; notorious. — ا. شدن To become a by-word. خود را انگشت نما کردن To make an exhibition of oneself.
انگشتانه (2 سنراب (1 **انگشتواله**
اَنگل Parasite; hanger-on. — انگلِ کسی شدن To hang on a person; sponge on him.
انگلستان England; Great Britain.
انگل شناسی Parasitology.
انگلک × Slight touch with the finger. — ا.کردن To fool

or mess about with.
انگل کش Parasiticide.
انگلی Parasitism. —*a*. Parasitical.
انگلیس Great Britain.— دولت ا. The British Government. — ا. ها The B. people.
انگلیسی British. English. —*n*. Britisher. Englishman ; Englishwoman.— زبان ا. English; the E. language.
انگلیسی زبان English-speaking.
انگم (Cherry-tree) gum.
اِنگنار Artichoke.
انگور Grape.— انگور جنگلی Fox-grape; wild wine.— انگورروباه *or* انگور سگ = **تاجریزی** — انگور فرنگی Gooseberry. Red currants.
انگورچینی Vintage.
انگوری Vinaceous. Grape-like.. باغ ا. = **تاکستان**
انگیختن [انگیز] To rouse ; provoke. To excite ; stimulate. To instigate. To cause ○.
انگیخته [P. P. of انگیختن]
انگیز [Imp. of انگیختن]
انگیزش Exciting; provocation.
انگیزنده Exciter. Instigator.
انگیزه Motive. Stimulant.
انموذج ○ *A*. Model; exemplar. [f. P. نمونه]
انوار [Pl. of نور]
انواع [Pl. of نوع]
انوَر *A*. Luminous.
انوری *(A.) Anvari : a Persian poet*.
انوریسما *A-G*. Aneurism.
انوشیروان *Iranian king in whose reign the Prophet was born*.
انهار [Pl. of نهر]
اِنهدام *A*. Destruction; demolition. Overthrow. [feat.
انهزام ○ *A*. Being routed ; de-
انی (e*ni* :) *A*. Inductive ; *a posteriori*.
انیاب [Pl. of ناب]
اَنیس *A*. Companion; associate; comrade. *Fem. pr. name*. —*a*. Familar; friendly.
او He. She. [*Governed by a prep.*] Him. Her.
اواخر *A*. [Pl. of آخر] Last part(s); last days.—دراواخرسال At (*or* toward) the end of the year.— در این ا. Recently.
اواسط *A*. [Pl. of اوسط] Middle part(s) : در اواِسط سال
اوامر *A*. [Pl. of امر]. Orders; commands.
اوائل *A*. [Pl. of اول] Early part; beginning : در اوائل سال at the b. of the year.
اوباش *A*. Ruffians; rogues. [Pl. of ○ وبش]. —*a*. + Ruffianly.
اوت *Fr*. August.
اوتاد [Pl. of وتد]
اوتار [Pl. of وتر]
اوتو etc. = **اطو** etc.
اوج *A*. Culmination; highest point; zenith; peak; pinnacle. *Astr*. Apogee. [*Of an aircraft*] Ceiling. *Mus*. Highest pitch.

اوجا ○ = **نارون** Elm.
واجب ○ [Comp. of واجب]
اوچ وپس *T.* (*C. P.*) Full hand.
اوخ + Ouch!
اوراد [Pl. of وِرد]
اوراق *A.* [Pl. of ورق] Documents; papers. *OS.* Leaves.— این کتاب ا. است The leaves of this book have come off (*or* apart). — ا. کردن To dismantle.
اورانوس *Fr.* Uranus.
اورانیوم *Fr.* Uranium.
اورشلیم *A.* Jerusalem.
اورُمزد Ormuzd.
اورنگ = تخت Throne.
اوزان [Pl. of وزن]
اوزوم *T.* = انگور Grape. [Only in ا. و انگور Six of one and half a dozen of the other].
اوِستا Avesta.
اوَسط *A.* [Fem. وسطی *vosta*; pl. اواسط] Median. Intermediate. Osculant.
اوشن + = **اویشن**
اوصاف [Pl. of وصف]
اوضاع *A.* [Pl. of وضع] Conditions. Situation ; state of affairs. — اوضاع و احوال Circumstances.
اوطان [Pl. of وطن]
اوطراق ○ *T.* Halting. — ا. کردن To halt or rest.
اوف Ah ! Ouch !
اوقات *A.* [Pl. of وقت] Times. Hours. — اوقات شما تلخ است You are upset; you seem to be angry. — اوقاتم تلخ شد I was upset. I got angry.
اوقات َتلخی *A. P.* Anger ; indignation. Ill humour. — باکسی ا. کردن To speak angrily to s. o.
اوقاف [Pl. of وقف]
اوکالیپتوس *Fr.* Eucalyptus.
اوّل *A.* First. *F.* Foremost. (Of) superior quality ; first-rate. — عدد اول Prime number. — عدد غیر اول Composite n. —*ad.* First(ly). —*n.* Beginning.
اولاً *A.* In the first place ; first(ly). To begin with.
اولاد *A.* [Pl. of ولد] Children; offspring ; descendants. *OS.* Sons. —*Note.* اولاد is also construed as singular, meaning 'child.'
اولتیماتوم *Fr.* Ultimatum.
اولوالابصار ○ *A.* Those having foresight.
اولوالالباب ○ *A.* Men of mind; intelligent people.
اولوالامر ○ *A.* = **فرمانروا**
اولوالعزم *A.* Resolute (men).— پیغمبر اولوالعزم Arch (*or* prominent) prophet.
اولویت *A.* Priority; preference.— ا. داشتن بر To be prior to.
اولی *u:la* [Fem. of اول]
اولی *A. P. ava-* (The) first or former. Initial. Primary. [Fem. اولیه]. — حقایق اولیه P. truths. — کمك های اولیه First aid. — مواد اولیه Raw materials.
اولی *A.* (*owla*) [Comp. of ولی] Prior ; superior ; better. —

بطریق ا. All the more ; *a fortiori*.

اولیتر *A. P.* (*ow*la-) Better. Preferable. [Double comp. of ولی]

اولیاء *A.* [Pl. of ولی] Guardians. Saints. – اولیای امور Authorities of the State.

اولین *A. P.* First ; foremost [used before a noun].

اوهام [Pl. of وهم] [joram.

اَویشن Origan(um). Wild mar-

اویون *T.* Psora.

اَه [*Interjection expressing disgust*] Ugh !

اهالی *A.* [Pl. of اهل] Inhabitants.

اِهانت *A.* Contempt. Insolence.– ا. کردن (به) To affront; treat with insolence.

اهانت آمیز *A. P.* Insolent. Contemptuous.

اِهتزاز *A.* Shaking ; oscillation. Pulsation. *F.* Joy ; mirth. – برچمی را به ا. درآوردن To fly a flag.

اِهتمام *A.* Effort. – باهتمامِ By the good offices of.

اِهداء *A.* Dedication. – ا. کردن To dedicate ; offer.

اهرام [Pl. of هرم]

اهرُم Lever. Crow-bar. – ا. کردن To raise with a lever. – اهرم نوع اول L. of the first order.

اهریمن The Evil Principle (in the Zoroastrian religion) The Devil.

اهریمنی Devilish ; fiendish.

اهل *A.* Native(s) ; citizen(s) ; inhabitant(s). One who is (*or* those who are) endowed with , or possessed of , a specified quality , belief , etc.). –*a.* Capable ; fit. Tractable ; docile. – اهل ایمان Believer(s).– خانواده = اهل بیت || اهل حال Pleasure-seeking ; jovial. – اهل حرفه Professional (man). Craftsman. – اهل دنیا Cosmopolitan. Worldly (persons). – اهل فن Technician(s). – اهل قلم Literary person(s). – اهل کتاب Those possessing bibles.– اهل وعیال Wife and children; family. – اهل هنر Those who possess virtues o. Artists or technicians.

اهلی *A.* Domestic . – ا کردن To domesticate.

اهلیت *A.* Legal capacity.

اهلیلجی *A. P.* Elliptical.

اهمّ *A.* [Comp. of مهم]

اِهمال *A.* Negligence; remissness. – ا کردن در To neglect. To delay through r.

اهمال کار *A. P* Negligent ; careless.

اهمیت *A.* Importance. – ا. دادن [with به] To attach i. to. To emphasize; lay stress on. To mind.– ا. داشتن To be important.– ا. ندارد It doesn't matter.

اهور مزدا = **اورمزد**

اِی O ! Ex. ای پادشاه O king !– ای وای Oh ! Alas !

ایا (*ay'*a) O !

اياب *A.* Returning. — ا. و ذهاب Going and r. Traffic.
ايادى [Pl. of يد]
ايار (*A.*) *Jewish and Syriac month* (April-May).
اياز *Mas. pr. name.*
اياغ ○ = **كاسه - پياله**
ايالت *A.* [ايالات] State. (Large) province. — ايالات متحده امريكا The United States of America.
ايالتى *A. P.* Provincial.
ايام *A.* [Pl. of يوم] Days.
ايتاليا *or* **ايطاليا** Italy.
ايتاليايى Italian.
ايتام [Pl. of يتيم]
ائتلاف *A.* Coalition. — ا. كردن To coalesce.
ايثار *A.* Giving in abundance ○. Excessive generosity.
ايجاب *A.* Necessitating. Affirmation. Exigency. Compliance. — ا. كردن To necessitate. To occasion.
ايجابى *A.* Affirmative.
ايجاد *A.* Creation. Invention. Establishment. — ا. كردن To create. To establish.
ايجاز *A.* Brevity; conciseness.
ايدآل *Fr.* Ideal; aim.
ايدرات *Fr.* Hydrate
ايدروژن *Fr.* Hydrogen.
ايدروژنى *Fr. P.* Hydrogenated. — بمب ا. Hydrogen bomb ; H-bomb.
ايدروكاربور *Fr.* Hydrocarbon.
ايذاء *A.* Molestation.
ايراد *A.* Objection [ايرادات]. Adducement. Delivery: ايراد نطق ‖ Inflicting. Citing ; mentioning. — ا. كردن To deliver. To adduce. To cavil. — بكسى ا. گرفتن To find fault with s. o.; object to, or pick on, him. — ايرادى ندارد It is in order ; it will meet with no objection.
ايرادگير *A. P.* Of cavilling or nagging habits.
ايران Persia; Iran.
ايرانى Iranian; Persian.
ايرانيت *A.* Iranian nationality. Iranianism.
ايرَج *Mas. pr. name.*
ايرسا *A-G.* Iris-root.
ايرلندى *Fr. P.* Irish.
ايزد = خدا God.
ايزدى Divine.
ايست Halt; stoppage. — ا. كردن To halt; stay. To last ○. — ا. دادن To order (s. o.) to h.
ايست [Imp. of ايستادن]
ايستادگى Resistance. Steadfastness. — ا. كردن To persevere. — در برابر كسى ا. كردن To resist or withstand s. o.
ايستادَن [ايست] To stand. To stop ; halt. To cease. To wait. — سر قول خود ايستادن To abide by one's word.
ايستاده 1) Standing. 2) Stood. —*ad.* In a standing posture.
ايستاندَن To cause to stand ; halt. To set up.
ايستگاه Station: ايستگاه راه‌آهن ‖ ايستگاه اتوبوس Bus stop.
ايشان They. [*In p. c.*] He or

she. [*Governed by a prep.*] Them. [warding.

ایصال *A.* Remittance. Onfor-

ایضاً *A.* Ditto. Also.

ایضاح *A.* Explaining.

ایفاء *A.* Fulfilment; discharge. Satisfaction. Payment. — ا. کردن To fulfil or d. To satisfy. To pay. To perform. To play (a part).

ایفاد *A.* Despatch. — ا کردن To despatch or send.

ایقاع *A.* Unilateral obligation. Cadence o.

ایقان *A.* Certitude. Conviction.

ایل *T* [A. pl. ایلات] Tribe.

ایلاتی *T. A. P.* Tribal.

ایلاووس *A-G.* Ileus; iliac passion [usu. قولنج ا.].

ایلچی *or* **الچی** *T.* = **سفیر**

ایلخان *T.* Tribal chief; chieftain.

ایلخی *or* **الخی** *T.* Stud.

ایلغار o *T.* Expedition. Invasion.

ایلول (*A.*) *Jewish and Syriac month* (Aug. -Sept.).

ایلیات *T. A.* Tribes(men).

ایلیاتی *T. A. P.* Tribesman.

ایماء *A.* Sign. Hint. Allusion.

ایمان *A.* Faith; belief. — بکسی ا. آوردن To believe in s. o.

ایمن *A.* Secure; safe. Void of care *.

ائمه [Pl. of امام]

این [اینها - اینان] This. The latter *. — این زنان These women. — اینکه The fact that. — خبر دوم اینکه The second news is that. — ا. به آن در Tit for tat. — *Note.* این است is often contracted in writing to اینست

اینجا Here. *OS.* This place.

اینجانب *P. A.* I [in formal usage]. — ا. امضاء کنندهٔ زیر I, the undersigned.

اینچ *E.* Inch.

اینچنین Such (a). [manner.

اینسان *or* **بدینسان** In this

اینست *S. u.* **این**

اینقدر *S. u.* قدر

اینك Behold! Now.

این نه‌آنی Diversity.

این همانی Identity.

ایواللّه *P. A.* 1) Well-done! 2) Hear! H.! — ا. آمدن To fall at one's feet; admit one's failure or inability. Also, to take off one's hat (to s. o.). [Palace.

ایوان Veranda; portico. *By e.*

ایوب *A.* Job (*mas. pr. name*).

ایهام *A.* Amphibology or ambiguity; quibble; equivocation [tion.

ایهام گویی *A. P.* Equivoca-

اَیهقان *A.* Wild mustard.

به *S. u.* بِ

با With. By (means of). In spite of; notwithstanding. — با آنکه *or* با اینکه In s. of the fact that. — با شما است که It is up to you to. [proved

با اجازه *P. A.* Authorized. Ap-

با ادب *P. A.* Polite. [gifted.

با استعداد *P. A.* Talented;

با اسم *P. A.* Registered: سهام ب.

با اطلاع *P. A.* = آگاه & بصیر

باب = بابا *or* پدر

باب + Fashionable. Suitable. — باب من نیست It does not suit me.

باب *A.* [ابواب] Door; gate ○. Strait. Chapter; section. Matter; subject. — در باب ِ Concerning; on the s. of; regarding.

بابا Papa; daddy. Grandpa.

باباآدم *P. A.* (Father) Adam. — انجیر بابا آدم Adam's fig. — ریشهٔ ب. Burdock-root.

باباقوری Onyx. Staphyloma.

باب المعده *A.* Pylorus.

بابانوئل *P. Fr.* Santa Claus.

بابت *A.* Concern; matter. Account; score. Behalf. — ازچه ب. On what account? — بابت ِ *or* از بابت ِ On a. of. — ۲۰۰ ریال بابت بهای کتاب 200 *rials*, being cost of books; [*in account statements*] to cost of books 200 *rials*.

بابونه Matricaria. — بابونه شیرازی Camomile. — بابونه گاوی Motherwort.

بابیت *Fr.* White metal; babbit.

باتجربه *P. A.* = آزموده & مجرّب

باتری *or* **باطری** *Fr.* Battery; cell. — باتری تر (Rechargeable) battery. — باتری خشك Dry c.

باتلاق [f. T. باطلاق] Swamp.

باتلاقی *T. P.* Swampy; marshy.

باتماشا *P. A.* = **تماشائی**

با تمیز *P. A.* Discerning *a.*

باتُن *Fr.* Truncheon.

باتیست *Fr.* Batiste; French lawn.

باج Tribute; toll; tax. — باج سبیل Blackmail.

با جرأت *P. A.* Courageous.

باجگیر ○ Tax-gatherer.

باجناغ *T.* Brother-in-law: husband of the wife's sister.

باجه Box-office; ticket-office.

باجی *T.* Female servant. *O. S.* Sister. [چشمان ب.

با حالت *P. A.* Expressive

با حرارت *P. A.* Enthusiastic; fervent.

باحقوق *P. A.* Grateful. Paid. — مرخصی ب. Leave with pay.

باحیاء *P. A.* Modest; decent.

با خبر *P. A.* = **آگاه** [game.

باخت Loss. Amount lost in a

باختر West.

باختری Western.

باختن [باز] To lose [in a game]. *F*. To give away. To play*.

باخته [P. P. of باختن] Lost. —*n*. Amount lost.

با خدا Pious; godly.

با خرد = خردمند

باد Wind. Swelling. *F* Pride. Elation.— بادسرخ Erysipelas.— باد فتق Hernia. — باد مفاصل Articular rheumatism.— ب.خوردن To be exposed to wind; dry. *F*. To be discontinued. — ب. بزخمش خورد His enthusiasm cooled down.— ب.دادن To air.— ب. زدن To fan. — ب. کردن To swell (with pride). To blow up; distend. To elate.— ب. گرفتن To have a sudden pain. — ب. درسر داشتن To be proud or haughty. — بر باد دادن To dissipate.

باد *or* **بادا** May... be. — زنده باد Long live! — (هرچه) بادا باد Come what may.

باد افشان Winnower.

بادام Almond. — بادام زمینی Peanut; earthnut. — روغن ب. A.-oil. — مغز بادام Shelled almond.

بادامك Tonsil.

بادامه Chrysalis.

بادامی Oval. Containing almonds.

بادآورد Blessed thistle.

بادآورده Brought by the wind. —*n*. Windfall.— ب. را باد میبرد Light come; light go.

بادبادك Kite.

بادبان Sail.

بادبزن Fan.

باد پا Fleet-footed. —*n*.* Swift horse; fleet courser.

بادخور Vent. *F*. Interruption; intermission; discontinuance.

باد خورده Rancid. Blasted.

بادخیز Windy : ناحیهٔ ب.

باد دار Inflated. Inflamed. Windy. Flatulent. Causing flatulence. *F*. Haughty.

باد در سر Haughty. Empty-headed.

بادرنجبویه *S. u.* بادرنگبویه

بادرنگ 1) Cedrate. 2) *Variety of cucumber*.

بادرنگبویه *or* **بادرنجبویه** Moldavic calamint; Moldavian balm; b.-mint.

بادزن [usu. بادبزن] Fan.

بادزهره Quinsy.

باد سُرخ Erysipelas.

باد سنج Wind-gauge; anemometer.

باد شکن Carminative.

باد کرده Swollen; inflamed.

بادکش Dry cupping. Vent-hole. Shaft (of a mine). —*a*. × Tediously long. Who buttonholes one. — ب. کردن To dry-cup.

بادکنك Bladder. Air-chamber.

بادگیر Ventilation-shaft. Air trap. Vent(-hole). Louver.

بادنجان Brinjal; aubergine; egg-plant.

بادنجان دور قاب چین *P. A.* + Pickthank; sycophant.

بادنجانی Blue-red. Solanaceous.

بادنما Weather-cock; vane; air-cock. Wind-gauge.

بادوام *P. A.* Durable; lasting.

باده • Wine. *Cf.* شراب & می

بادی Windy. — سازهای ب. Wind instruments. — آسیای ب. Windmill. — چراغ ب. Hurricane lantern.

بادی ० *A.* = آغاز & ابتدا

بادیان Anise. — بادیان ختائی Star-anise. — تخم‌ب. Aniseed. — نقل‌ب. Comfits.

با دیانت *P. A.* Pious; honest.

بادیه *A.* = بیابان

بادیه [Erroneous form of باطیه]

باذوق *P.A.* Possessing a literary or artistic gift or understanding; elegant.

بار Load; burden; weight; [*of a ship*] cargo. Yield; fruit. Alloy. Coat (of the tongue). Audience. Time; turn. — بار دیگر Next time. — دوبار Twice. — ب. ها Many a time; frequently. — ب. آمدن To be brought up (in a specified way). — ب. آوردن To bear fruit. To bring up (in a specified way). — ب. دادن To grant audience. To fructify. — ب. یافتن To have the a. (of s. o.). — بار عام دادن To hold a levee. — ب. گرفتن&ب. برداشتن To conceive; become pregnant. — بارخودرا بستن To feather one's nest. — ب. کردن To load. — چیزی را بار کامیون کردن To load s. t. on to a truck; l. a truck with s. t. — فحش بار کسی کردن To heap insults on s. o. — زیر بارِ چیزی نرفتن To be intolerant of s. t. — بار دل *or* بار خاطر Sorrow; heartache.

بار *E.* Bar(room).

باران Rain. — ب.می آید *or* ب. میبارد It rains; it is raining. — مرغ ب. Plover.

بارانداز Landing-place; wharf; [dock.

باران سنج Rain-gauge.

باران‌گیر Shelter from rain; penthouse. Hut.

بارانی Rainy. —*n*. Rain-coat.

بارانیدن To cause to rain.

بارآوَر Fruit-bearing; productive.

باربر Porter.

باربردار • Load-carrying.

باربری Porterage; handling charges.

باربندی Packing. — ب. کردن To [pack (up).

بارپیچ Pack-cloth.

بارپیچی = باربندی

بار خدا • God [usu. in بارخدایا O G.!].

بارخیز Fertile; productive.

بارِد ० *A.* = سرد

باردار Fruit-bearing. Pregnant.

بارده Fructiferous.

بارِز *A.* 1) آشکار 2) برجسته

بارش + = باران

بارفتن [*f. Fr.* barbotine] Semi-vitrified porcelaine.

بارقه ० *A.* Lightning. — بارقهٔ امید Flash or ray of hope.

بارکاس *R.* Barque.

بارک‌الله *A.* Well done *OS.* May God bless thee.

بارکش Truck ; lorry. Cart. —*a*. Load-carrying. Pains-taking. — اسب ب. Draught-horse.

بارکشی Transport.

بارگاه Hall of audience; court.

بارگی * Pack-horse. [burden.

بارگیر Ship's tonnage. Beast of

بارگیری Loading. Handling a ship's cargo.—ب. کردن To load.

بارُن or بارون *Fr*. Baron.

بارنامه Way-bill ; road-bill ; [*of cargo*] bill of lading.

بارَندگی Rainfall. [or cargo.

بارنویس Tally clerk for bales

بارو Rampart; wall.

باروت [f. G. origin and per. through T.] Gunpowder. — مخزن ب. Powder magazine.

باروت پنبه Gun-cotton.

باروح *P. A*. Full of life. Vivacious. [*Of a house*] Bright and cheerful.

باروَر Fruitful.

باره Regard. — در بارهٔ On the subject of ; concerning; regarding.

باره ο Coat of the tongue. Tartar of the teeth.

باره = بارو [tain.

بارهنگ or بارتنگ ο Plan-

باری Load-carrying. — حیوان ب. Pack-animal; beast of burden.— اتومبیل ب. Lorry; truck.

باری *A*. = آفریدگار

باری (*ba'ri:*) Anyhow ; in any case. Well. Now. In short. At least*

باریجه Galbanum.

باریدن [بار] To rain. — (باران) میبارد It rains ; it is raining. —*vt*. To shed : اشك ب.

باریك Narrow. Slender. *F*. Delicate ; subtle . — ب. شدن To become narrow. To taper. To look with subtlety. — ب. کردن To make n. or slender.— رودهٔ ب. Small intestine.

باریك بین Subtle (observer).

باریك بینی Subtlety; fineness.

باریکه Strip. [ness.

باریکی Narrowness. Slender-

باز Open. Clear, as a road. *Geom*. Obtuse. — ب. شدن To open. To clear up.— ب. کردن To o. To establish or start. To break, as a fast.— از تاه ب. کردن To unfold. — + از سر باز کردن To play or put off; evade. To bungle. To give a stand-off (to).

باز Hawk; also, falcon.

باز Again. Still. Yet. Nevertheless. Further.

باز [Imp. of باختن]

باز * [Prefix meaning "back", "again", "re-" , etc.]. — ب. آمدن To come b. — ب. ایستادن To stop. — ب. خریدن To buy back; redeem. — ب. داشتن To prevent. To dissuade. To detain. To hold back. — ب. گرداندن To return. To refund. To cancel. — ب. گرفتن To take back. To withdraw. To requisition. — ب. گشتن To return. — ب. ماندن

To be detained or hindered. To remain or lag behind. — ب. یافتن To recover.

بازار Market(-place) ; bazaar.

بازارگرمی Skill in making one's customers interested in commodities presented for sale; sales talk.

بازاری Belonging to the market. Ready-made. — سگ ب. Street-dog ; cur. — مردم ب. Business men.

بازبین Controller. [control.

بازبینی Control. — ب. کردن To

بازپُرس Examining magistrate; interrogator.

بازپُرسی Interrogation ; cross-examination. — از کسی ب. کردن To interrogate s. o.

بازپَسین ○ Last [آخر] — روزِ ب. The last day ; the d. of judgment.

بازتاب Reflex.

بازتابی & بازتابِش Reflexion.

بازجو Investigator.

بازجویی Investigation; inquiry. — ب. کردن از To inquire.— ب. کردن در To investigate.

بازچینی Turn over.

بازخاست Resurrection.

بازخواست Calling to account.— ب. کردن از To call to a.; take to task. — روز بازخواست Day of judgment.

بازدار Falconer.

بازداری Faconry.

بازداشت Detention ; arrest. — ب. کردن To a. or detain.

بازداشتگاه House of detention. Concentration camp. *Mil.* Detention barrack.

بازدانه Gymnospermous.

بازدم Expiration.

بازده Output. [*Of machinery*] Efficiency.

بازدید Return-visit. Survey. Audit. Control. — ب. کردن To return a visit (to). To survey.

بازرس Inspector. [inspect.

بازرسی Inspection. — ب. کردن To

بازرگان Merchant.

بازرگانی Commerce ; trade. —*a.* (*C. E.*) Commercial. — قانون ب C. code. [tion.

بازستانی Recovery ; reclama-

بازکرد Opening (of an account).

بازگشت Return. Cancellation.— ب. کردن To return. To refer.

بازگو کردن To repeat.

بازگیری *Mil.* Requisition.

بازمان Residual magnetism.

بازمانده Remaining. Surviving. Hindered. Tired out. —*n.* [usu. in بازماندگان survivors]

بازنده Loser.

بازنشستگی Retirement. Pension. — حقوق ب. Old age pension; retiring p.— سنّ ب. Pensionable age.

بازنشسته Retired; superannuated. — ب. کردن To pension off; superannuate.

بازو (Upper) arm. Crank. — سعی ب. * Manual labour. — ب. زدن To jostle or elbow.

بازوبند Armlet. Amulet. Curtain-loop.
بازه Span (of an aircraft).
بازی Game. Sport. Play(ing). – ب. کردن To play. – ب. درآوردن +To grimace. To start monkey-business. To dodge. To back out. – ب. دادن To amuse deceitfully. – به ب. نگرفتن To take no account of.
باز یافتی & باز یافت Thing recovered; salvage; hit.
بازیچه Toy; plaything.
بازیکن Player. Gambler.
بازیگر Buffoon.
بازیگوش Playful; wanton.
باستان Ancient. –*n*. A. tin es.
باستان شناس Archaeologist.
باستان شناسی Archaeology.
باستانی Ancient. Traditional.
باسترك Thrush.
باسق ∘ *A*. Lofty [بلند]. [taste.
با سلیقه *P. A.* Having a good
با سواد *P. A.* Literate.
باسیل *Fr*. Bacillus.
باش [Imp. of بودن] Be thou. – میباشم-میباشی-میباشد etc. • I am; thou art; he is; etc.
با شرف *P. A.* Honourable.
با شعور *P. A.* Intelligent; of sense; having common s.
باشکوه Splendid; magnificent.
باشگاه Club. Club-house.
باشلق *T*. Hood; cowl.
باشلیه *Fr*. Bachelor.
باشه Sparrow-hawk.
باشی *T*. Head or chief [in comb.]. Ex. حکیم باشی H.-physician. [vantageous.
باصرفه *P. A.* Economical; ad-
باصره *A*. = بینایی Sight. – عصب ب Optic nerve.
با صفا *P. A.* Pleasant: باغ ب.
باصمه or باسمه *T*. Type; also, block. Stamp. Printed calico. – ب. زدن To s. To print.
باطری *S. u.* باتری
باطل *A*. Null; void. Vain; false. Useless; futile –*n*. [Pl. اباطیل: اباطیل دنیا Vanities of the world]. – ب. کردن To render null. To cancel. To counteract.
باطله [For دفتر باطله] *A*. Waste-book. Day-book. Minute-book [Orig. fem. of باطل]
باطن *A*. Interior. Heart; mind. Conscience. – باطناً = درباطن
باطناً *A*. Inwardly. In actual truth. At heart. [Esoteric.
باطنی *A*. Inward. Heartfelt.
باطیه *A*. Bowl; cup.
با ظرف *P. A.* Packed; sold in containers. – نفت ب. P. oil.
باعاطفه *P. A.* Sentimental; feeling.
باعث *A*. Cause; motive. – ب. شدن To c. or occasion.
با عزم *P. A.* Resolute.
باعظمت *P. A.* Great; glorious.
باغ [A. pl. باغات] Garden. – باغ میوه Orchard. – باغ وحش Zoo.
باغبان Gardener.

باغبانی Gardening. [bed.
باغچه Little garden. Flower-
باغچه بندی Layout of flower-beds or of a garden.
باغی o *A.* 1) = یاغی 2) = ستمگر
با غیرت *P. A.* Zealous.
باف [Imp. of بافتن]
با فایده *P. A.* = مفید
بافت Texture. Tissue.
بافت برداری Biopsy.
بافت شناس Histologist.
بافت شناسی Histology.
بافتن [باف] To weave. To knit. To braid. To plait. *F.* To fabricate.
بافتنی Textile. *—n.* Knitting.
بافته Woven. Braided. Knitted. *—n.* Textile. Tissue.
بافراست *P. A.* Keen; sagacious.
بافرهنگ Cultured; educated.
با فکر *P. A.* = فکور & با کله
بافندگی Weaving. Knitting.
بافنده Weaver. Knitter.
بافه Sheaf. [Erudite.
باقر (*A.*) *Mas. pr. name. OS.*
با قرقره Grouse. [Lupine.
باقلا (Broad) bean. — باقلای مصری
باقلوا (*T.*) *Kind of pastry usu. cut out in lozenges.*
باقی *A.* Remainder; balance; difference. Rest. Arrear [بقایا]. *— a.* Remaining; left. Immortal. — ب. آوردن To have a deficit. — ب. گذاردن To leave. — ب. ماندن To be left (over).
باقی‌دار *A. P.* Having a deficit or debt; owing a balance.
باقی مانده *A. P.* Remainder. Residue. *—a.* Remaining.
باک Fear. Anxiety. Care.
باک *R.* Petrol tank; gas t. — درِ باك Tank cap.
باکارا *Fr.* Baccarat.
باکتری *Fr.* Bacteria.
باکرگی *A. P.* = بکارت
باکره *A.* Virgin; maid [used also as an adjective].
باکفایت. *P. A.* Capable; efficient.
باکله Able-minded.
باکمال *P. A.* Accomplished; educated.
باگذشت Easy to forgive; placable; forbearing. Indulgent.
بال Wing. — ب. زدن To flap (the wings). — بال و پر Plumage.
بال *or* وال Whale.
بال *A.* Mind [*usu. in comb.*].
بالا Up. Upwards. *—n.* Upper part; top. Height*. Stature*. *—a.* High; superior. Upper. — ب. آمدن To come up. To be trained or brought up (in a specified way). To cost (a s. sum). To swell. — ب. آوردن To bring up; train. To throw up; vomit. — ب. بردن To carry up. To raise (the price of). To promote. — ب. رفتن To go up. To rise (in price). [Of a curtain] To r. —

از کوهی ب. رفتن To climb a mountain. ـ ب. زدن To tuck up. To do up, as one's hair. To lift. ـ ب. کردن To raise. To carry up. ـ ب. کشیدن To draw, carry, or lift up. To embezzle +. To improve or prosper +. ـ بینی ب. کشیدن To sniff; snivel. ـ ب. گرفتن To hold up. To p. or thrive. ـ ب. و پایین رفتن To fluctuate.

بالابان *T.* Lanner(et).

بالا َبر o Lift; elevator [U.S.].

بالا بلند Tall. [to boot.

بالا بود Excess. Amount paid

بالا پوش Overcoat. Quilt.

بالاتفاق *A.* = متفقاً

بالا َتنه Upper part of the body; trunk. Body (of a dress); corsage.

بالاخانه (House in the) upper storey; u. chamber.

بالاخره *A.* At last.

بالاخص (*A.*) *See* اخص

بالا دست Something superior to another thing. Superior position. —*a.* Upper. S. ـ بالا دستِ S. to. Above.

بالارُتبه *P. A.* Senior.

بالاستقلال *A.* = مستقلاً

بالاقتضا *A.* As occasion arises.

بالاکراه *A.* = اکراهاً

بالانس *Fr.* Handstand. ـ ب. زدن To do a handstand.

بالا نشین Occupying the seat of honour.

بالایِ Above; over. On. On account of. For the sake of. ـ بالای سرِ ما Above us.

بالایی Upper.

بالبداهه *A.* Extemporaneously.

بالت *Fr.* Ballet.

بالتمام *A.* = تماماً

بالجمله *A.* To sum up. Totally.

بالدار Winged.

بالدست Cheiropteran.

بالذات *A.* By nature.

بالسویه *A.* Equally.

بالش Pillow; bolster.

بالشت + = **بالش**

بالِشتک Small pillow; cushion. Pad. [*For rails*] Tie-plate. [*In automobiles*] Coil. ـ بالشتك مار Kind of carpet beetle.

بالصراحه *A.* = صراحةً

بالضروره *A.* Of necessity.

بالطبع & بالطبیعه Naturally.

بالعکس *A.* Vice versa. On the contrary.

بالغ *A.* Adult; of age. Amounting. ـ ب. شدن To come of age. [*With* به *or* بر] To amount to.

بالفرض *A.* = فرضاً

بالفعل *A.* Actually.

بالقوه *A.* With all one's power. Potential(ly).

بالکل *A.* = کلیةً

بالکن *Fr.* Balcony.

بالله *A.* By God.

بالمرّه *A.* All at once. At all.

بالمشافهه *A.* Mouth to m. Face to f.
بالمعاينه *A.* Ocularly.
بالمناصفه *A.* Half and half.
بالمواجهه *A.* Face to face.
بالن *or* بالون *Fr.* Balloon.
بالنتيجه *A.* As a result.
بالنسبه *A.* Comparatively.
بالنگ Cedrate. (*Variety of*) cucumber.
بالَنگو (Seeds of) calaminth.
بالوراثه *A.* By inheritance.
بالیدن [بال] To boast ; pride oneself [usu. بخود بالیدن].
بالین 1) Bed-side. 2) بالش
بالینی Clinical : طب ب.
بام 1) House-top; roof. 2) + Thump on the head.
بام [Cont. of بامداد]
بام ول × Humbug. ـ ب. در آوردن To (behave like a) humbug.
با محبت *P. A.* Affectionate ; kind; loving.
بامداد = صبح Morning.
بامدادان * In the morning.
با مروّت *P. A.* Humane. Generous.
با مزه Tasty. *F.* Interesting.
با مسمی *P. A.* Worthy of its name; bearing out its n.
با معنی *P. A.* Significant; expressive.
بام غلتان Roller used on [house-tops.
با ملاحظه *P. A.* Circumspective. Regardful.
بامیه Okra. Confectionery resembling okra.
بان *Suf. meaning* keeper.
بان *A.* 1) Myrobalan. 2)بیدمشك
با نام = با اسم
باند *Fr.* Clique; coterie; band. Landing-strip; runway.
باندازه *S. u.* اندازه
بانژو *Fr.* Banjo.
با نفوذ *P. A.* Influential ; of consequence.
بانک *Fr.* Bank. ـ معاملات بانکی B. transactions.
بانکدار *Fr. P.* Banker.
بانکداری *Fr. P.* Banking.
بانگ Clamour ; cry. Cock's crow. ـ ب. بر آوردن To exclaim. ـ ب. زدن To cry. To e.; call out.
بانو Lady . ـ آقای سیروس و بانو Mr. and Mrs. Siroos.
بانی *A.* Founder; author.
با وُجود *P. A.* Of personality. Efficient.
با وُجودِ *S. u.* وجود
باور Believing as true○. ـ ب. کردن To believe. ـ باورم نیست I do not b. [dible.
باورکردنی Believable ; credible.
باور نکردنی Incredible.
باوفا *P. A.* Loyal; faithful ; constant.
باوقار *P. A.* Graceful; stately.
باه *A.* Virility ; generative power.
باهِر *A.* Manifest. Splendid.
با هم *S. u.* هم
با هنر Ingenious; skilled.

باهو *or* **بائو** Stile (of a door).
باهوش Intelligent; clever.
باید Must ; ought to. *OS.* (It) is necessary [f. بایستن *q. v.*]. — ب بروم I must go. — نباید بروید You m. not go.— ب. رفت It is necessary to go. [زمین ب.
بائر *A.* *or* **بایر** Unutilized :
بایست *or* **بایستی** = **باید**
—*Note.* بایست is sometimes regarded as the past of باید
بایستن [بای ○] To be necessary.
بایسته ○ Necessary. Proper.
بایستی *S. u.* **بایست**
بایع *A.* = **فروشنده**
بایقوش *T.* Screech-owl.
بایگان Archivist; file-keeper.
بایگانی Records. File-keeping.— ب. کردن *C. E.* To keep on file.
ببر Tiger. — ببر بیان Armour made of (tiger) skin.
بُت Idol.
بتاوی *or* **بتابی** Pomelo.
بت پرست Idolater.
بت پرستی Idolatry. [pagoda.
بتخانه *or* **بتکده** Idol-temple ;
بتر * = بدتر Worse.
بترک * *P. A.* = **بدرود**
بِتن *Fr.* Concrete. [concrete.
بتن آرمه *Fr.* Reinforced
بتن ساز *Fr. P.* Concrete-mixer.
بتول (*A.*) *Fem. pr. name. OS.* Virgin [باکره].
بُته Bush. Shrub. Brushwood. Kindling. Goat's thorn.— بتهٔ سریش Asphodel; king's spear.— گل وبته Flower design.
بته مرده + Good-for-nothing ; inefficient. Dull; stiff; inelegant. *OS.* Grown on a stunted bush.
بثورات *A.* Pustules.— بثورات سلی Tubercles. — بثورات گوشتی Proud flesh.
بجا Opportune; proper.
بجز *S. u.* جُز
بجمال * *P. A.* = **جمیل**
بُجول Astragalus; ankle-bone.
بچشم *S. u.* چشم
بچگان [Pl. of بچه]
بچگانه Childish. Children's : لباس ب ‖ *-ad.* Childishly.
بچگی Childhood. Childish act.
بچه [بچگان & بچه ها] Child. Young (of an animal). — ب. گذاشتن *or* ب. کردن [*Of animals*] To produce a young.
بچه بازی Pederasty; active sodomy. Child's play +.
بچه خوره Polypus of the womb. [children.
بچه‌دار Having a child or
بچه‌داری Mothercraft.
بچه‌زا Viviparous.
بچه شاخ Tine.
بچه‌کشی & **بچه‌کش** Infanticide.
بحار [Pl. of بحر]
بُحبوحه *A.* Middle part ○. — بحبوحهٔ جوانی Flower of youth.— در بحبوحهٔ جنگ In the thick of the fight.
بحث *A.* Argument ; debate.

Discussion. ـ ب. کردن To argue. To debate or dispute. To discuss; treat. ـ کتابِ موضوع ب. The book in question. ـ قابل ب. Disputable; questionable. ـ غیرقابل ب. Indisputable; incontestable.

بحر *A*. Sea [pl. بحار]. Poetical metre [pl. بحور]. ـ ماوراء بحار Overseas.

بحرالجزایر *A*. Archipelago.

بُحران *A*. Crisis.

بحرانی *A. P*. Critical.

بحر پیما *A. P*. = دریانورد

بحری *A*. = دریایی

بحریه *A*. [*Orig. fem. of* بحری] Navy [now نیروی دریایی].

بحل *P. A*. Pardon(ed). ـ ب. کردن To pardon; absolve.

بحمدالله *A*. = الحمدلله

بحور *S. u*. بحر

بخار *A*. [ابخره]. Steam; vapour. ـ ماشین ب. S. engine.

بخارزا *A. P*. Steam-generating.

بخارسنج *A. P*. Vaporimeter.

بخاری *A. P*. Heater; stove. Fireplace; grate. -*a*. Cooked by steam. ـ ترمزِ بخاری Steam-brake. [owoopor.

بخاری پاك کن *A. P*. Chimney-

بخت Luck; fortune.

بخت آزمایی Lottery.

بخت برگشته Unlucky.

بختك Nightmare. [camel.

بُختی ० Two-humped Bactrian

بختیار • Lucky.

بِخرد • = خردمند

بَخس *A*. Very low [only in ثمن ب. very low price].

بخش 1) Portion; part; share. Division. Distribution [usu. بخش]. District. Squadron. Ward: بخش چهار تهران ‖ ب. کردن To divide. To distribute. ـ دادگاه ب. Peace court. 2) [Imp. of بخشیدن].

بخشایش Forgiveness. Mercy. *Cf*. بخشش

بخشایندگی (Quality of) mercy.

بخشاینده Merciful; forgiving.

بخش پذیر Divisible.

بخشدار Governor of a district; deputy-g.; lieutenant-g.

بخشش Munificence. Gift. Pardon; remission. ـ ب کردن To bestow gifts. *Cf*. بخشیدن

بخش ناپذیر Indivisible.

بخشنامه Circular (letter). ـ به ادارات ب. کردند They circularized the departments.

بخشندگی Liberality; generosity. Quality of mercy.

بخشنده Merciful. Liberal.

بخشودگی Exemption.

بخشودن 1) To exempt. 2) بخشیدن

بخشوده Exempt.

بخشی *Arith*. Dividend.

بخش یاب Divisor.

بخشیدن [بخش] To forgive or pardon. To excuse. To give; grant; bestow. ـ ببخشید Excuse me; I beg your pardon.; I am sorry. ـ تنمه شمارا بمن بخشید

He spared me your punishment.

بخصوص *S. u.* خصوص

بُخل *A.* Jealousy. Stinginess.— ب. کردن To be parsimonious (in). To be sparing (of).

بخو [f. T. بُخاو] Manacle(s); handcuff.

بخود بسته Affected; assumed.

بُخور Incense. *Med.* Inhalant. *OS.* Anything which diffuses a fragrance, as aloes, frankincense, etc. Dark grey. — بخور مریم Cyclamen; sow-bread.— ب. دادن To administer an inhalant to. *F.* To play the gallant; flirt. [*Obsolete*].

بخور سوز *A. P.* Censer.

بخولق *T.* Pastern.

بخیل *A.* Jealous. Miserly. —*n.* J. person. Miser.

بخیه Stitch. — ب. کردن or ب. زدن To stitch.

بد Bad. Of poor quality. Ill. Evil. Base : پول بد ‖ —*n.* Evil. Adversity. Foul language; insult. —*ad.* Badly : ب. نمیخواند He sings well enough.— ب. کردن To do evil.— ب. گذراندن To have a rough time; be ill at ease. To live in straitened circumstances.— بکسی ب. گفتن To insult s. o. — ب. گفتن از To slander or backbite. — از او بدم می آید I hate him.

بُد * = بود Was.

بدآب وهوا Of a bad climate; unhealthy; insalubrious.

بداحوال *P. A.* = **بیمار - بدحال**

بد اختر * Ill-starred.

بد اخلاق *P. A.* Immoral.

بد اخلاقی *P. A.* Immorality.

بد اخم Surly; morose. [frown.

بداخمی Moroseness.— ب. کردن To

بد ادا *P. A.* Of ungraceful manners.

بد اصل *P. A.* Low-born.

بداعت *A.* Something new or strange.

بُداغ Guelder-rose.

بدان = بآن To that. [fully.

بدانجام Turning out unsuccess-

بد اندیش Malevolent; malicious.

بداندیشی Malevolence; malice.

بداهت *A.* Improvisation.

بداههً *A.* = **بالبداهه**

بدایت *A.* Beginning.— محکمهٔ ب. = Court of First Instance [now دادگاه شهرستان].

بدایع *A.* [Pl. of بدیعه] New things; rarities.

بدایةً *A.* Preliminarily.

بدائی ○ *A.* Preliminary; primary.

بد آئین * Irreligious; impious.

بد باطن *P. A.* Inwardly bad; ill-intentioned.

بدبخت Unlucky.

بدبختانه Unfortunately.

بدبختی Bad luck. Adversity.

بد بدرقه Inconstant.

بَدبَدك or **بد بده** Quail.

بَد ِبده Not prompt in paying one's dues.— آدم ب. ایست He

is a poor pay.
بدبو Of a bad odour ; fetid.
بد بیاری + Bad luck, esp. in gambling. [Pessimist.
بدبین Pessimistic. — آدم ب.
بدبینی Pessimism.
بدتبار Low-born.
بدترکیب *P. A.* Ugly.
بدجنس *P. A.* Malicious ; bad-hearted.
بدجنسی *P. A.* Maliciousness.— بد جنسی خود را بروز دادن To show the cloven hoof.
بد چشم Evil-eyed or jealous.
بد چشمی Envy. Evil eye.
بد حال *P. A.* (Very) ill.
بدحالت *P. A.* 1) بدحال 2) بدخو
بد حرفی *P. A.* Insult ; bad language ; railing.
بد حساب *P. A.* = بد ِبده
بد خط *P. A.* (Whose writing is) illegible.
بدُخلق *P. A.* Ill-humoured.
بد ُخلقی *P. A.* Ill humour.
بد خو *or* بد خوی Ill-natured.
بد خواه Malevolent.
بدخواهانه Maliciously.
بد خواهی Malevolence.
بد خوراك Disagreeable to the taste. Off one's food *or* feed.
بدخویی Ill nature; ill. humour; bad temper.
بددماغ Proud. Hard to please.
بد دهن Scurrilous; abusive.
بد دهنه Hard-mouthed.
بدذات *P. A.* Roguish. Mischievous. Base. Malicious.

بد ذاتی *P. A.* Roguishness. Meanness. Mischievousness.
بدر َ *A.* = ماه ُبر Full moon.
بد راه Perverted. — ب. کردن To pervert or misguide.
بد رفتار Misbehaving; ill-treating.
بد رفتاری Ill-treatment ; bad conduct. — باکسی ب. کردن To ill treat or abuse s. o.
بدر َقه Escort; guard. Convoy.— بدرقهٔ کسی رفتن To see a person off. [اسب ب.
بدرکاب *P. A.* Hard to mount.
بد رگ Of bad stock.
ِبدرود Farewell. — ب. گفتن To bid farewell.
بدروزگار * Wicked. Miserable.
بدره * Bag of gold (money).
بد ریخت Of an ugly figure.
بد دهن = بد زبان
بد روزگار = * بد زندگانی
بد سابقه *P. A.* Having a bad record. Notorious (for immorality).
بد ساخت Of poor workmanship; badly manufactured.
بد سرشت Ill-set.
بد ِسگال * Malevolent.
بد سلوکی *P. A.* = بد رفتاری
بد سلیقه *P. A.* = کج سلیقه
بد سیرت *P. A.* Of a bad character ; immoral.
بدشکل *P. A.* Deformed ; disfigured. Ugly.
بد طبع *P. A.* Ill-natured.
بدطینت *P. A.* Bad-hearted; ill-

intentioned. Ill-natured.

بدعادت *P. A.* Having acquired a bad habit; spoiled.

بدعت *A.* Innovation. Heresy.— ب.گذاردن To introduce something new or heretical.

بدعت‌گذار *A. P.* Innovator. Heretic.

بد عمل *P. A.* = **بدکردار**

بد عنق *P. A.* × Surly ; ill-humoured and proud.

بد عهد *P. A.* Unfaithful to one's promise.

بد عهدی *P. A.* Infidelity ; unfaithfulness. Breach of one's promise. — ب کردن To be untrue to one's p.

بد انجام = **بد فرجام**

بد قدم *P. A.* Bringing bad luck ; unlucky. — آدم ب. Stormy petrel. *Met.*

بدقلب *P. A.* Bad-hearted ; malevolent. [malevolence.

بد قلبی *P. A.* Bad feeling ;

بد قلق + *P. T.* Moody. Ill-tempered.

بد قمار *P. A.* One who gets nervous or backs out in gambling; bad loser. [Used also as an adjective].

بد قول *P. A.* Unfaithful to one's promise.

بد قولی *P. A.* Breach of one's promise. — ب. کردن To break one's p.; forfeit one's word.

بد قیافه *P. A.* Sinister. Ugly.

بدکار *or* **بدکردار** * Evil-doing; wicked.

بد آئین = **بدکیش**

بدگذران Living on scanty means ; indigent.

بدگل Ugly ; plain.

بدگلی Ugliness.

بدگمان Suspicious.

بدگمانی Suspicion; mistrust.

بدگو Slanderous; ill-speaking. —*n.* Slanderer. Backbiter.

بدگوهر * Base; low-born.

بدگویی Ill-speaking; vilification; backbiting. — ب. کردن از To backbite or slander.

بدل *A.* [ابدال]. Substitute. Exchange. *Gr.* Apposition ; appositive. —*a.* False. — الماس بدل Imitation diamond. — بدل ما یتحلل S. for what is worn out ; i. e. food.

بدل چینی *A. P.* Crockery.

بدل سنا *a. p.* Coronilla.

بد لقا *P. A.* Ugly. Sinister.

بد دهنه = **بد لجام** & **بد لگام**

بد مذهب *P. A.* Irreligious. [Often used as an insult].

بد مزاج ○ *P. A.* Cachectic. Peevish.

بدمزه Disagreeable to the taste.

بدمست Drunk and disorderly.— **بدمستی** کردن To be drunk and disorderly ; also, brawl, as a drunkard.

بد معامله *P. A.* Dishonest or irregular in one's dealings.

بد منش Fastidious.

بدن *A.* [ابدان] Body. *Cf.* تن

بد نام Infamous; ignominious.— ب. کردن To defame; disgrace.
بد نامی Infamy ; ill repute ; ill fame.
بد نقش *P. A.* Unlucky.
بد نقشی *P. A.* Bad luck.
بد نما Unsightly. Indecent.
بدنه *A. P.* Trunk. Hull. Frame. [*Of a plane*] Fuselage. [*Of a column*] Shaft.
بد نهاد * Ill-set ; ill-natured.
بدنی *A.* Bodily; physical. Flesh-coloured.
بد نیت *P. A.* Having a sly meaning ; ill-intentioned.
بدو *A.* (*badv*) Beginning.
بدو *. = باو To him or her.
بدون *S. u.* دون
بدوی *A.* Primary.
بدوی *A.* (*bada-*) Bedouin. Rude; embryonic.
بده + = بدهی & بدهکاری ‖ ب. و بستان Transaction. *OS.* Give-and-take.
بد هضمی *P. A.* Dyspepsia.
بدهکار Debtor. — دو ریال بمن ب. است He owes me 2 *rials*. — برگ ب. Debit note. — ب. کردن To debit.
بدهکاری Debt. Indebtedness.
بد هوا Badly ventilated. Of a bad weather or climate.—
بدهی (Sum) due; debt. Liability. — دو ریال بمن ب. دارد He owes me 2 *rials*.
بد هیئت *P. A.* = **بد قیافه**
بدی Badness. Evil. Wicked - ness. Wrong. — ب. کردن To do evil.— بکسی ب. کردن To do an ill turn to s. o.
بدیع *A.* New. Strange. —*n.* Figures of speech. — صنایع بدیعی Rhetorical f. ; f. of s.
بدیع الجمال *A.* = **بدیع شمایل**
بدیع شمایل * *a. p.* Of rare beauty.
بدیعه *A.* [بدایع] Rarity. Novelty.
بدُیمن *P. A.* Inauspicious.
بدین * = باین To this.
بدیهه *A.* Improvisation. — بالبدیهه Extemporaneously.
بدیهه‌گو *A. P.* Improvisator.
بدیهه‌گویی *A.P.* Improvisation.
بدیهی *A.* Evident. — ب. است Evidently; of course.
بدیهیات *A.* Self-evident truths ; axioms.
بذر *A.* [بذور] Seed.
بذر افشان *A. P.* Seeder ; corn-drill.
بذرالبنگ *A. P.* Henbane seeds.
بذرك *A. P.* = **بزرك** or **برزك**
بذل *A.* Giving generously; munificence. — ب. کردن To give generously. — بذل مساعی کردن To make an effort. — بذل مساعدت کردن To give (*or* lend) one's assistance.
بذله *A.* Wit. Witty jest.
بذله‌گو *A. P.* Witty (person).
بذله‌گویی *A. P.* Witticism.
بَر (*prep.*) Upon; on. Over. — برآن بودن * To be determined. To be planning. — برآن داشتن * To persuade. — بر آن شدن *. To determine. To plan.

بَر (*ad.*) [Used as a prefix]. Up; above. Over. Back. Away. Ex. برداشتن-برچیدن etc.

بَر (*n.*) Side. Bosom. — از بر خواندن To recite from memory. — از بردانستن To know by heart. — در بر داشتن To comprise. To entail. To wear; have on*. — *در بر کردن To put on. — در بر گرفتن To embrace.

بَر* Fruit. *F*. Result; profit. — برخوردن از To enjoy.

بَر [Imp. of بردن].

بُر [Imp. of بریدن].

بُر *C. P.* Shuffling. — بر زدن To shuffle.

بَرّ *A*. Land. Continent. — برّ قدیم The Old World.

بُرّا Cutting; sharp.

برابر Equal; on a par. Tantamount. Opposite.—*ad*. Equally. —*n*. O. side; front. Equivalent.—ب. کردن To compare; place s. by s. To bring on the same level. — برابرِ Equal to. Opposed to. According to. — ب. با E., equivalent, or tantamount to.— دربرابرِ In front of; before. Against. As compared with (*or* to). — دو برابرِ Twice as much, or as many, as.

برابری Equality. — ب. کردن با To be equal or equivalent to. To oppose. To compare with.

بَرات [بَرَوات] Draft; bill of exchange [f. A. برائت *q.v.*]— ب.کردن To make a d. for. — ب. بر شاخ آهو دادن To send s. o. on a wild-goose chase. *O.S.* To draw a cheque on a gazelle's horn.

براتکش Drawer (of a cheque).

براتگیر Drawee.

برادر Brother.

برادرانه Brotherly. —*ad*. In a b. manner.

برادرخوانده Adopted brother.

برادر زاده Brother's son or daughter.

برادر زن Wife's brother; b.-in-law.

برادرشوهر Husband's brother; b.-in-law.

برادرکشی & برادرکش Fratricide.

برادر وار Brotherly. —*ad*. In a b. manner.

برادری Brotherhood; fraternity.

بُراده *A*. Filings: برادهٔ آهن

بُراز *A*. Feces; excrement.

برازندگی Comeliness; grace.

برازنده Comely; becoming; graceful.

برازیدن [بَراز] To become; suit; befit.

برآشفتن [Emphatic for آشفتن].

بر افروختن [Emphatic for افروختن].

برانداختن & افگندن = برافگندن

بَرّاق *A*. Shining; glittering.— ب.کردن To polish; shine.

بُراق *Designating a cat* with bristling hair and attacking aspect.

برآمد Issue; outcome. Expenditure ○.

برآمدگی Projection. Knob. Outgrowth. Swelling.

برآمدن * To come up. To cope. To be inferred. To be accomplished. To elapse. – دروغ گفتن از من برنمی‌آید I am incapable of lying; I cannot lie.

برامکه *S. u.* برمکی

بُرّان Cutting; trenchant.

بر انداختن To abolish. To overthrow. To dissipate *.

برانداز کردن To look up and down. To take stock of.

برانکار *Fr.* Stretcher.

برانگیختن = انگیختن

برآورد Estimate. – ب. کردن To estimate. – هزینهٔ آنرا هزار ریال ب. کردند The expenses were estimated at 1000 *rials*.

برآوردن * To grant; comply with. To meet. To supply.

براهین [Pl. of برهان]

برایِ (*bara'ye*) For. For the sake of. For the purpose of. – (از) برای *or* (از) برای اینکه آنکه Because. In order that. – برای چه Why? What for?

برائت *A.* Acquittance. Exemption. – برائت ذمه Acquittal; clearance from obligation.

برایند Resultant. [barian.

بربر (Native of) Barbary. Bar-

بربری Native of Barbary. --*a.* Rude; savage; barbarian.

بربریت *A.* Barbarity; savagery.

بربط Harp; also, lyre.

بربط زن Harper.

برتر [Comp. of بر] Higher. Superior. Perferable.

برتری Preference; superiority. – ب. داشتن بر To have preference over; be superior to; be better than.

برج + Minor or secondary expenses.

بُرج *A.* [بروج] Tower. Sign of the zodiac. *By e.* Solar month. – برج کبوتر Columbarium. – برج زهرمار *Met.* Sore as a boil. – برج ناقوس Belfry. – برج نور Lighthouse. – برج و بارو Ramparts. [Prominence.

برجستگی Relief. Saliency. *F.*

برجسته Relief; embossed. Salient. *F.* Outstanding; prominent; distinguished; of distinction. – ب. کردن To raise in relief. To emboss.

برجسته کاری Embossed work.

بُرجی *A.* Zodiacal. Solar.

برجیس Jupiter. *Cf.* مشتری

برچسب Label.

برچه *Bot.* Carpel.

برچیدن To pick up. To gather. To remove. To wind up. – سفره را برچیدن To clear the table; draw the cloth.

برحق *F. A.* True!

برخاستن [برخیز] To rise; get up. To adjourn a meeting ○. To disappear ○. *Cf.* خاستن

برخورد Encounter. Contact. Conjunction. Attitude. – ب. کردن با To encounter; come in contact with.

برخوردار Enjoying. Success-

ful. Prosperous. — ب. شدن از To enjoy (the fruits of).
برخورداری Enjoyment. Fruition. Success.
برخوردگی Wounded feelings; [offence.
برخوردن *S. u.* خوردن
برخورنده Hurting the feelings; irritating *a*.
برخه Fraction. Portion.
برخه شُمار Numerator.
برخه نام Denominator.
بَرخی ○ Offering; ransom.
برخی (*bar'-*) Some (of); part of [f. برخ ○].
برخیزانیدن To cause to rise.
بَرد ○ *A.* = سرما
بُرد Winning. Amount won. Range. *F.* Advantage.— ب. کردن To be better off; have an advantage.
بُرد Striped cloth from Yemen [usu. بُرد یمانی].
بَردار [Imp. of برداشتن]
بُردار 1) Vector. 2) = برنده
بردارو برمال *S. u.* وردارو ورمال
برداشت Withdrawal; taking(s). Deduction in advance. Off-take. Lifting. Harvest. — ب. کردن از To withdraw from; draw on.
برداشتن [بردار] To take (up); pick up. To remove. To t. off : کلاه خود را بردار ‖ To run away (with). To take the bit between one's teeth. To permit of : تعبیر بردار نیست ‖ To raise. To shoot, as a film. — دست ب. To desist.
بُردبار Meek; forbearing.
بُردباری Forbearance; fortitude; patience; meekness.
بردست Aid; mate.
بردگان Pl. of [برده]
بَردگی Slavery.
بُردن [بَر] To carry; take. To steal. To take to wife; marry. To lead. To win.— کلاهش را باد برد His hat blew off.
بَرده [بردگان] Slave; bondman.
بُرده [P. P. of بردن] Carried. Stolen. Won. —*n*. Amount w.
بَرده فروشی Dealing in slaves.
بردی ○ Papyrus.
بررسی Study(ing). — ب. کردن To study; consider.
بَرز ○ = 1) تخم 2) کشاورزی
بُرز * Tallness; stature.
برزخ Isthmus. *F.* Perilous or awkward situation; rough time +. Connecting link.— ب. شدن To be upset.
برزك Linseed. Flax.
برزگر Agriculturist; farmer.
برزگری Farming.
برزن Municipal division (of a town); quarter.
بَرسام Diaphragm(at)itis.
برزنت *R.* Tarpaulin.
بُرش *R.* Borsch. [ochre.
بَرش [For گِل ب.] Yellow
بُرِش Cut(ting). Slice. Section. Coupon.

برشته Torrefied. Toasted. Roasted. — ب. کردن To torrefy; parch. [شمردن

برشمردن * To enumerate. *S. a.*

برص *A.* Leprosy.

برطرف *S. u.* طرف

برعکس *S. u.* عکس

برعلیه *S. u.* علیه

برف Snow. — ب. میبارد *or* ب. میآید It snows. — زیر برف ماندن To be snowed under. — گل ب. Snow-berry.

برفاب Snow-water. Slush.

برف انباز Heaped up (like snow). —*n*. Snow-drift.

برف پاک‌کن Snow-sweeper. Snow-plough. Windscreen wiper. [rain.

برف خوره Small drizzling

برف‌روب Snow-sweeper. Snow-plough.

برف روبی Cleaning the snow.

برف ریزه Hoar-frost. Sleet.

برفك Thrush; aphtha.

برفی Snowy : روز برفی ‖ Of snow. — آدم ب. Snowman.

برق *A.* Lightning. Electricity. Flash. Lustre. Polish. — ب. انداختن To p.; cause to glitter. — ب. زدن To g.; scintillate; shine. — چراغ ب. Electric light. — کارخانه‌ب. Power station. — مهندس ب. Electrical engineer.

برق آسا *A. P.* Flashlike. Sudden. —*ad*. Suddenly.

برق بین *A. P.* Electroscope.

برق‌زا *A. P.* Electromotive.

برقرار *P. A.* Confirmed; established. In working order. — ب. کردن To institute. To instal. To commission.

برقراری *P. A.* Establishment. Working order. Installation. Appointment. [shock.

برق زدگی *A. P.* Electrical

بُرقَع * *A.* Veil. Mask.

برق‌گیر *A. P.* Lightning-rod; lightning-conductor. Fuse.

بُرقو Reamer. — ب. زدن To ream.

برقی *A. P.* Electric(al). Electrically-driven. Quick and sudden; foudroyant; galloping+. —*ad*.+Like a shot. — چرم ب. Patent leather. — موتور برقی Electromotor.

بَرَك Cloth made of camel's hair.

برکات [Pl. of برکت]

برکت *A.* [برکات]. Blessing. Abundance. Prosperous effect. — ب. دادن (به) To bless. — ب. کردن To be multiplied (as if by blessing).

برکنار Discharged; dismissed. — ب. شدن To be d. — ب. کردن To dismiss; discharge.

برکناری Dismissal; discharge.

برکه *A.* Pool. Pond. Lake.

بَرگ Leaf. Sheet. Form. Document; certificate. — برگ سبز Widow's mite. — برگ‌عطر Stork's-bill. — گلبرگ = برگ‌گل

بَرگ بال Neuropteran.

برگچه Foliole; leaflet.
برگدُم Petiole; footstalk.
برگذار کردن To make shift. To dispose of. To carry on. To content oneself ; get along. To g. over. — ب. شدن To be disposed of. To pass off : مهمانی خوب ب. شد
برگرد Turndown : یخهٔ ب.
برگردان Refrain ; burden. Lapel. Echo.— عکس ب. Transfer picture. — یخه ب Turndown collar.
برگرداندن To return : send (*or* give) back. To turn ; change ; reverse. To turn off. To throw up : vomit. To reduce. To invert.
برگ ریز Deciduous.
برگ ریزان Fall; autumn.
برگزیدن To choose; select.
برگزیده Chosen; selected.
برگشت Return. Decline. Revocation. Reflection. Difference; deduction. — قابل ب. *or* برگشت پذیر Revocable. — غیر قابل ب. *or* برگشت ناپذیر Irrevocable : اعتبار غیر قابل ب.
برگشت پذیر *S. u.* برگشت
برگشتن [برگرد]. To return ; come back ; go b. To be changed. *Cf.* گشتن ‖ اورادر برگشتن ملاقات کردم I met him on my way back.
برگشت ناپذیر *S. u.* برگشت
برگشته Turned up *or* down. Changed. Converted. — یقهٔ ب. Turndown collar.
برگشته‌حال * *P. A.* Unhappy; afflicted.
برگشته روزگار * Unfortunate.
برگماشتن [Emphatic for گماشتن]
برگ و نوا * *or* برگ و ساز Means ; riches.
برگه Fly (on a coat, etc.) ; flap (of a pocket) ; tongue (of a boot). Index card ; slip. Clue : part of stolen goods discovered in a person's possession. Dried peaches or apricots.
برگه‌دان Card-index file or [cabinet.
برگی Leaf-shaped ; foliaceous.
برلیان *Fr.* [Also الماس ب.] Brilliant.
برمکی [A. pl. برامکه] Barmecide.
برملاء *P. A.* Public. Flagrant; notorious. — ب شدن To be divulged or published. — ب. کردن To divulge; make public.
برنا * = جوان Young (person).
برنامه Programme ; schedule. Time-table. *By e.* Plan.
برنج Rice. Brass. — خط ب. Column-rule.
برنجاسف Common mugwort.
برنجزار & برنج کاری Rice-field.
برنجی (Made of) brass ; brazen. Of rice.
بَرنده Winner. [In an auction] Highest bidder. Bearer. Carrier. —*a.* Winning. — خال ب. *C. P.* Trump.
بُرنده Cutting ; sharp. Inci-

sive. Digestive+.

برنز *Fr.* Bronze. [set up.

برنشاندن To cause to sit up;

برانشیت *Fr.* Bronchitis.

ِبرنگِ کاُبلی Chebulic myrobalan.

ِبرنو Bruno; Brno. — تفنگ ب. Bruno gun; Bren g.

بروات [Pl. of برات]

ُبروت o = سبیل Moustache. — باد بروت Airs; conceit.

بروج [Pl. of برج]

برودت *A.* = سردی Cold. *F.* Indifference.

برودری *Fr.* Embroidery.

برودری دوزی *Fr. P.* Embroidery. — ب.کردن To embroider.

َبرو رو + Good looks.

بروز *A.* Appearing. — ب. دادن To divulge. — ب. کردن To appear. To leak out.

بروس *Fr.* (*bros*) Brush. — بروس مو Hairbrush.

بروکسل *Fr.* Brussels.

برومند Fruitful.

برومور or برمور *Fr.* Bromide.

ُبرون * [Cont. of بیرون]

ُبرون‌رو(ی) Exogenous.

برون شامه Exterior membrane. [*Of the heart*] Pericardium.

برون مرزی Extraterritorial.

برّه Lamb.

بره *Fr.* Beret.

ُبرهان *A.* [براهین] Demonstration; logical reason. Theorem. — برهان موجز Enthymeme. — برهان انّی *A priori* reasoning. — برهان لمی *A posteriori* r. — براهین جمجمه Phrenology.

برهم *S. u.* هم

برهمن Brahman. [A. pl. براهمه]

برهنگی Nakedness.

برهنه Naked; bare. — ب.کردن To make n.; strip of clothing.

برهنه پا Barefoot(ed).

برهنه خوشحال + *P. A.* Happy in spite of poverty.

بری *A.* Exempt. (De)void. Weary; disgusted +.

برّی *A.* = 1) زمینی 2) وحشی

بری‌الذمه *A.* Clear from obligation; quit; discharged. — ب.کردن To acquit from o.; discharge.

بریان Roasted (whole). Grilled. — گندم ب. Parched corn. — ب.کردن To dress or roast w.; barbecue. To parch.

بریانی Liver prepared for food.

بریتانیا Britain.

َبرید = 1) چاپار 2) قاصد

بریدگی Cut; incision. Notch. *F.* Separation

بریدن [ُبر] To cut. To pick. ‖ *F.* جیب‌کسیرا بریدن To settle; decide. To sever; separate. — *vi.* To be c. To turn or change: شیر برید

ُبریده [P. P. of بریدن] Cut. Separated. [*Of milk*] Turned. — ب. ب. In snatches.

َبرین * Highest. Eternal.

بُز Goat. — بز کوهی Wild goat; chamois ; ibex. — بز ماده She-g. — بز نر He-g. — ب.گیر آوردن To have (a thing) a great bargain.
بَزادی Beryl.
بزّاز *A*. Cloth-dealer; draper.
بزازی *A. P*. Dealing in cloth; drapery; mercery. [Diastase.
بُزاق *A*. Saliva. — جوهر بزاق
بُزاقی *A. P*. Salivary.
بَز باز Mace; nutmeg's cover.
بُز چران Goatherd.
بزخو Goatish. —*n*. Ambuscade.
بز دل Chicken-hearted. [dity.
بز دلی Pusillanimity ; timi-
بَزَرك Linseed. Flax.
بُزرگ Large ; big. Great. Grown up; adult. —*n*. [pl. بزرگان] Person of distinc - tion. — ب. شدن To grow up.— ب کردن To enlarge. To bring up. To magnify.
بزرگ ارتشتاران فرمانده Commander-in-Chief of the Army.
بُزرگتر Elder. Guardian. —*a*. E. or older. [Orig. , comp. of بزرگ] [birth.
بزرگ زاده Person of noble
بزرگ سیاهرگ Vena cava.
بزرگ طبع *P. A. or* **بزرگمنش** Magnanimous. [بزرگ & مِهر
بزرگمهر *Mas. pr. name. See*
بزرگوار Great. Magnanimous. —*n*. (The G.) God.
بزرگواری Greatness. Magna - nimity. Generosity.
بزرگی Largeness. Greatness. Size. Adult age.
بزغاله Kid.
بُز غُنج Galls of pistachio.
بزك *T*. Toilet; make-up; dress-(ing). — ب کردن To make one's toilet; dress (up).
بزل *A*. Trepanning.
بَزم = مهمانی & سور
بُزمجه Lizard.
بِزن بهادر + Sturdy; valiant. —*n*. Rowdy; tough guy.
بزنگاه Proper moment ; nick of time. — سر بزنگاه In the n. of t. ; at the right m.
بزودی *S. u*. زودی
بزه Misdemeanour. Sin *.
بزهکار 1) گناهکار 2) Misdemeanant or criminal.
بُزی Of or like a goat. — ریش ب Vandyke-beard; goatee.
بژ *Fr*. Beige; natural-coloured.
بَس Enough. Sufficient. Many a *. — بس‌است That is enough; t. will do. — بس‌کردن To stop; cease. — از خدا میترسم و بس I fear God alone. — (از) بسکه گریه کرد ناخوش شد He wept so much that he fell ill.— همینقدر بس که Suffice it to say that.
بسا (*ba'sa*) Many (a) ; much. —*ad*. Many a time; often.— ای ب. * *or* چه ب. How many! H. much! H. o.!
بساتین [A. pl. of بُستان]

بساط *A*. (Place for) goods exposed for sale [esp. by one who has no shop]. Stand. Layout. Carpet.

بساك Anther.

بسامد *Ph*. Frequency.

بسان *S. u.* سان

بساوایی (Sense of) touch.

بسباس & بسباسه *A-P*. = بز باز

بسپایك Polypody.

بست Fastening. Brace. Clamp. Sanctuary; inviolable place of refuge. — ب. نشستن To take (r. in a) sanctuary.

بُستان [Cont. of بوستان] 1) Garden. 2) جالیز [A. pl.بساتین]

بِستانکار Creditor. — مبلغی را به بستانکار حساب کسی گذاشتن To credit s. o. with a sum ; credit a sum to s. o.

بُستانکار Horticulturist.

بِستانکاری Credit(orship) ; amount due to a person.

بُستانکاری Horticulture.

بستر Bed.— بستر رود River-bed.

بستری Confined to bed; bedridden. — ب. شدن To be confined to bed.

بستگان *S. u* بسته

بستگاه Place of refuge; sanctuary.

بستگی Relation ; connection. Dependence. Relationship.— ب. دارد با It depends on.

بستن [بند] To close; shut. To tie. To bind ; fasten. To pack. To dress, as a wound. To turn off. To shut off. To conclude : قرارداد بستن ‖ To levy : مالیات ب. ‖ To lay at the door (of) + . —*vi*. To freeze; also, coagulate. [*S. a.* شرط ب.] — بخود بستن To affect; assume.

بستنی Ice-cream.

بستو Earthenware pitcher. *Bot*. Conceptacle; follicle.

بست و بند Fastening. Bracing. Spanner (of a bridge). *S. a.* بند و بست

بسته [P.P. of بستن] Closed. Fastened; tied. Barred. Frozen. Coagulated. Related. Crossed: چك‌ب. ‖ *F*. Knotty. Dependent or depending. — ب. است به مقتضیات It depends on circumstances. —*n*. Package ; parcel. Paper (of pins ; et c.). Captive or prisoner. Dose of medicine enclosed in paper. Relative [usu. in the pl. بستگان]. [To pack.

بسته بندی Packing. — ب کردن

بسد (*bosad*) * = مرجان

بسزا *S. u.* سزا

بس‌شماری Multiplication.

بس‌شمر Multiplier

بس‌شمرده Multiplicand.

بسط *A*. Expansion. Amplification. Explanation. — ب. دادن To expand ; enlarge upon ; develop ; amplify.

بسفر *Fr*. Bosporus.

بسکه *S. u.* بس

بسم‌الله *A*. In the name of God.

[Used to mean (1) Help yourself; (2) Please come, sit, say, etc.].

بسنده ○ = کافی Sufficient.

بسوی *S. u.* سو

بسی * (*bas'i:*) Many. Much. —*ad*. Very. Often.

بسیار Many; numerous. Much. —*ad*. Very: ب. خوب

بسیارخوار * = پرخور

بسیاری * Numerousness; excessiveness از بسیاری غصه from excessive grief.

بسیج or **بسیچ** Mobilization. Intention ○. — ب. دادن To mobilize.

بسیجیدن ○ To intend. To prepare. To mobilize.

بسیط *A*. Extensive; vast. Simple. —*n*. Extent; stretch. — جسم ب. or **سیطه** *A*. Element.

بسیم *A*. Smiling *a*.

بشارت *A*. [بشارات] = مژده Good (*or* glad) tidings.

بشاش *A*. Cheerful; smiling.

بشاشت Cheerfulness.

بشر *A*. Mankind.

بشردوست *A. P*. Philanthropic. —*n*. Philanthropist.

بشر دوستی *A. P*. Philanthropy.

بشره *A*. Complexion. Cuticle.

بشری *A*. = انسانی

بشریت *A*. Human nature. Humanity; humanism.

بشقاب *T*. Plate; dish.

بشقابی *T. P*. Placoid.

بشکن Snapping one's fingers (to follow the tempo). — ب. زدن To snap one's f.

بشکه *R*. Barrel.

بشیر *A*. Harbinger of good news.

بشیز = پشیز

بصر *A*. [ابصار] Sight. Eye.

بصری *A*. Optical. Visual.

بصل‌النخاع *A*. = پیازمغز

بصیر *A*. Well-informed. Discerning; clear-sighted.

بصیرت *A*. Insight. Intelligence. Expert knowledge.

بضاعت *A*. Financial ability. *OS*. Goods or capital.

بَط * = اردك & مرغابی

بطالت *A*. Vanity. Idleness. — وقت خود را به ب. گذراندن To idle away one's time.

بطانه *A*. Putty; filler. — بطانهٔ روسی Glaziers' putty. — ب. کردن To p. or seal (up).

بَطَر * *A*. Insolence. Petulance.

بُطری [Per. f. E. or R.] Bottle. — بطری لید Leyden jar. —*Note*. لید is a *Fr*. word.

بطش * *A*. Attack. Violence.

بطلان *A*. Falseness; invalidity.

بطلمیوس *A-G*. Ptolemy.

بطلمیوسی *A*. Ptolemaic. — هیئت ب. P. system.

بطن *A*. [بُطون] Abdomen; belly. Womb. Ventricle. *F*. Interior. — بطن پیچیدهٔ گوش Labyrinth of the ear.

بطنی *A*. Uterine. Abdominal.

بطوء *A*. (*bot'*) Slowness.

بطون *A*. [Pl. of بطن] Interior or secret part; bedrock.

بطی *A*. Slow. [prehension.

بطی الانتقال *A*. Dull of ap-
بطی السیر *A*. = کندرو
بطی الهضم *A*. Indigestible.
بع بع + Baa; bleating.— ب.کردن To bleat or baa.
بعثت *A*. Prophetic mission.
بعد *A*. Then; afterwards. —*a*. Next: از .ب ‖ روز بعد After. — از این بیعد *or* ب. از این Hereafter.— ب. از این وکیل + Would-be deputy. — ب. از آن *or* از آن بیعد Thereafter. — ب. از آنکه او رفت A. (*or* when) he had gone. — ب. ازظهر After-noon. — دو ساعت ب. ازظهر (At) 2 p. m.— یکی ب. از دیگری One after another. — ب. ها Later (on); at a later period.
بعد *A*. Remoteness; distance. Dimension [ابعاد]. *Astr*. Celestial longitude.
بعداً *A*. Afterwards. Subsequently. Later.
بعدی *A. P*. Subsequent. Next.
بعض ० *A*. Part; few; some.
بعضاً *A*. Partly; partially.
بعضی *A. P*. (*ba''-*) Some. — ب. اوقات Sometimes. — ب. از ایشان Some (*or* a few) of them.
بعلاوه *S. u*. علاوه
بعلبك Heliopolis.
بعید *A*. Far ; remote. *F*. Improbable; unlikely.— از من ب. است It is inconsistent of me.— ب. نمیدانم که I should not be surprised if.
بعینه *A*. Exactly; just. *See* عین

بغاز *T*. Strait; channel.
بغبغو Cooing. — ب.کردن To coo.
بغتة = ناگهان [cloth wrapper.
بغچه *T*. Bundle; pack. Square
بغداد Bagdad.
بغرنج Complicated; intricate.
بغض *A*. Spite; grudge.— ب.گلوی اورا گرفت He was choked with tears. — بغضش ترکید He burst into t. — بغضش گرفت He felt a lump in his throat.
بغل Arm(-pit). Bosom. Side; edge. Armful. — ب.کردن To carry in the arms. To hug; cuddle; embrace [usu. در بغل گرفتن]. — بغل کسی خوابیدن To lie with, or by the side of, s. o. — ب. خالی کردن To buck, as a horse. — جیب ب. Inside breast-pocket.
بغل خوابی Sexual intercourse.
بغلی Carried in arms : بچهٔ ب child in a. —*n*. Flask. — کیف ب. *S. u*. کیف
بغی ० *A*. (*bagh-y*) Revolt; rebellion. Injustice.
بقاء *A*. Duration. Permanence. Eternity.
بقاع [Pl. of بقعه]
بقال *A* Grocer [selling cereals].
بقالی *A. P*. Grocery.
بقایا *A*. [Pl. of باقی] Remains. Arrears; dues.
بقچه = بغچه
بقدری *S. u*. قدر
بقر ० *A*. = گاو
بقراط *A-G*. Hippocrates.
بقعه *A*. [بقاع] Mausoleum.

بقم Logwood [بقم بنفش]. Sapan-wood [بقم قرمز].

بُقول *or* **بُقولات** *A.* [Pl. of بقل or بقله] Cereals; vegetables.

بقیت *S. u.* بقیه.

بقیه Remainder; rest; balance. [f. A. بقیة *or* بقیت].

بقیةالسیف *A.* Remnant(s). *OS.* What has escaped the sword.

بکارت *A.* Virginity. ـ بکارتِ دختری را برداشتن To deflower a maiden ـ پردهٔ ب. Hymen.

بکر *A.* Virgin. Intact. Original. —*ad.* ×Completely; categorically: ب. حاشا کرد He made a flat denial.

بُکسل [f. R. بوکسیر] Towing; tug. ـ ب. کردن To tow; take in tow. ـ زنجیر بکسل Towing attachment; towline.

بکلی *A.* Entirely. *See* کل

بُکم o *A.* Dumb (person).

بگو نگو + Words; argument.ـ ب. کردن To have (*or* bandy) words with each other; altercate.

بل *A.* = **بلکه**

بلا *A.* [بلایا] Calamity; misfortune. Nuisance. ـ ب. برای جان خود خریدن To make a rod for one's own back.

بِلا *A.* Without [used in the following model phrases]: ب. استفاده Useless. ـ ب. تخلف Without fail. ـ ب. تردید Doubtless(ly).ـ تصدیق ب. تصور Prejudgment. ـ ب. درنگ Immediately. ـ ب. شرط Unconditional(ly).ـ ب. عوض *See in the vocab.*ـ ب. فاصله Immediately. ـ ب. متصدی Vacant: تصرف ب. معارض ‖ محل ب. Usucaption. ـ ب. واسطه = بیواسطه ‖ ب. نسبت Incomparably [*Used as an int.*] Saving your reverence.

بلاد [Pl. of بلد or بلده]

بلادت *A.* Stupidity.

بلادُر Marking-nut.

بلادن *Fr.* Belladonna; deadly nightshade.

بلاعزل *A.* Irrevocable: وکیل ب.

بلاعوض *A.* Gratuitous(ly); ex gratia.

بلاغ *A.* Delivery of a message.

بلاغت *A.* Eloquence.

بلافصل *A.* Immediate: وارث ب.

بلاکش *A. P.* Afflicted. Suffering. Miserable.

بلال (Roasted) maize.

بلبل Nightingale. ـ بلبل زرد Canary [قناری]

بلد *A.* [بلاد *or* بلدان] City [شهر]. Region or country. Guide; escort +.ـ ب. نیستم + I do not know (such and s. a place or subject).

بلدان [A pl. of بلد]

بلدرچین *T.* Quail.

بلدی *A.* Municipal. Urban.

بلدیه *A.* = **شهرداری**

بلژیك *Fr.* Belgium.

بلژیکی *Fr. P.* Belgian.

بلسان *A.* Balsam; balm. ـ بلسان اسرائیل Balm of Gilead.ـ

بلسان مکی B. of Mecca. — بلسان هندی B. of Peru. — روغن ب. Balsam oil.
بلشویك R. Bolshevik.
بلع A. Swallowing; ingestion.— ب. کردن To swallow.
بُلعجب P-A. Wonder. Buffoon. —a. Wonderful.
بلعیدن A. P. [بلع] To swallow. To devour.
بلغاء [Pl. of بلیغ]
بُلغار Bulgaria. Russian leather.
بلغارستان Bulgaria.
بلغار(ی) Bulgarian.
بلغم [A-G.] Phlegm; lymph.
بلغمی A. Phlegmatic.
بلغور T. Groats.
بلفضول S. u. بوالفضول
بُلقیس A. Fem. pr. name.
بلکه A. P. 1) Perhaps. — ب. خواب باشد P. he is asleep. 2) But ; rather ; on the contrary. 3) Suppose . . .
بُل گرفتن + To take advantage of a (specified) situation ; seize an opportunity. OS. To catch a fly.
بلم Small rowing boat.
بُلند 1) Tall : درخت ب. ‖ High: کوه ب. ‖ Long : ریسمان ب. ‖ Loud : صدای ب. ‖ F. Exalted, eminent. 2) —ad. Aloud ; loudly. — ب. شدن To rise ; get up. — ب. کردن 1) To lift; raise. 2) To remove. 3) × (a) To embezzle. (b) To pick up, as a woman.
بلند بالا 1) Tall. 2) + Long; detailed : عریضه ب.
بلند پرواز High-flying. F. Of extravagant ambitions or opinions.
بلند قد P. A. Tall : پهلوان ب.
بلندگو Loud speaker.
بلند نظر P. A. High-minded.
بلند همت P. A. Of high aspirations. Of a lofty purpose. Magnanimous.
بلندی Height ; elevation. Highness. Tallness. Loudness. F. Eminence.
بلوا Riot ; disturbance. — ب. کردن To raise a d.
بُلور Crystal. Cut-glass; flint-g. — بلور کوهی Rock crystal. — کارخانهٔ بلورسازی Glassworks ; glass factory.
بلور شناسی Crystallography.
بلور لایه Crystallophylian.
بلوری or بلورین Crystalline. Made of (cut) glass.
بلوز Fr. Blouse; shirt-blouse.— بلوز نظامی Tunic. [Oak.
بلوط A. Acorn. — درخت ب.
بلوط آور A. P. Glandiferous.
بلوغ A. Maturity ; puberty.— بسن ب رسیدن To attain p. ; come of age.
بُلوك T. District; civil parish.
بلوك Fr. (blok) Bloc.
بلوکه Fr. Frozen ; blocked. — ب. کردن To freeze, as a capital.
بله + Yes. See بلی
بله A. (bolh) Stupidity.
بله‌بله‌چی + P. T. Yes-man.
بلهوس or بوالهوس P. A.

Capricious; whimsical; freakish. Sensual.
بلهوسی or **بوالهوسی** *P. A.* Capriciousness; vagary. Sensuality.
بلی * Yes. *See* بله
بلیات [Pl. of بلیه]
بلید *A.* Stupid; doltish. —*n.* S. person; dunce.
بلیط *R.* Ticket.
بلیطفروش *R. P.* Ticket-seller. Conductor (of a bus, etc.).
بلیغ *A.* [بلغاء] Eloquent. — سعی ب. Great effort.
بلیله Belleric myrobalan.
بلیه *A.* [بلیات] Calamity; misfortune. *Cf.* بلا
بم Bass (voice).
بمب *Fr.* Bomb.
بمباران *Fr. P.* Bombardment. — ب. کردن To bombard.
بمباسی + Blackamoor; negro.
بمب افگن or **بمب‌انداز** *Fr. P.* Bomber.
بمبئی Bombay. — گل ب. Hybrid tea-rose.
بمراتب *S. u.* مراتب
بمرور *S. u.* مرور
بمل *Fr.* (*Mus.*) Flat.
بموقع *P. A.* [*See* موقع] 1) *a.* Opportune; well-timed. 2) *ad.* In time; in season.
بن *A.* [Cont. of ابن] = **پسر**
بن Root. Bottom. *F.* Foundation. [layer.
بنا *A.* (*ba*na) Builder; brick-
بناء *A.* [ابنیه] Building; construction. — ب. کردن To build; erect. To begin : ب. کرد بخوردن He began to eat. — ب. گذاشتن To lay the foundation (of). — ب. است امروز برسد He is due to arrive to-day. — ب. شد باهم بروند They agreed to go together. — ب. بر According to.
بنا براین *A. P.* Therefore.
بنات [Pl. of بنت]
بنات‌النعش *A.* The Bear. *Astr.*
بنادر [A. pl. of بندر]
بناگوش Cavity behind the ear. — غدهٔ **بناگوشی** Parotid gland. — آماس غده بنا گوشی Parotitis; mumps.
بنام = **نامی** & **معروف**
بنان *A.* = **سرانگشت**
بنائی *A.P.* Builder's profession; building.
بن بست Blind. — کوچهٔ ب. B. alley; cul-de-sac. ‖ —*n.* Deadlock.
بنت ○ *A.* [بنات] = **دختر**
بنجل × Unsalable or dead stock; drug in the market.
بنچاق Original document or title-deed.
بند Band. Rope; cord. Fastening; clamp; brace. Cramp-iron. Chains*. Dam. Joint. Stanza. Strophe. Paragraph. Kanck; trick; sleight. Ream (of paper). — بند انگشت Phalanx; knuckle-joint. — بند تفنگ ‖ تسمه پروانه = پروانه Sling of a rifle. — بند تنبان The string of drawers. — بند جوراب Garters; suspenders. — بند رکاب Stirrup-leather. — بند ساعت Watch-ribbon. — بند شلوار Pair of braces or suspen-

ders. — بند شمشیر Sword-belt; baldrick. — بند کفش Shoe-lace. — ب. آمدن To stop; cease to flow. To be blocked, as a road. — ب آوردن To s. or staunch. To block. — ب. زدن To tinker; mend. — نکسی ب شدن + To hang or sponge on s. o. — ب. کشیدن 1) To point. 2) To string. — در بند نهادن To put in chains.

بَند [Imp. of بستن]

بندباز Rope-dancing; acrobat.

بند بازی Rope-dancer; acrobatics. Also, skipping the rope.

بند پائیان The Arthropoda.

بندِ تنبانی × Doggerel.

بندر [A. pl. بنادر] Port.

بندرگاه Harbour.

بند زن Tinker.

بند فنگ *Mil.* Sling arms!

بندکش Pointer. Bodkin.

بندکشی Pointing. *See* بند کشیدن ‖ ب. کردن To point.

بندگان [Pl. of بنده]

بندگی Slavery. Servitude. Worship; devotion. — ب. کردن [In p. c.] To give.

بندوبست Collusion. *Cf.* بست؛ بند

بنده [بندگان] Slave. Servant. [*In p. c.*] I. — ب. و سرکار You and I.

بنده‌زاده My child; my son. *OS.* Son o your slave.

بنده پروری = بنده نوازی

بنده نواز Kind to inferiors.

بنده نوازی Kindness to inferiors.

بندی 1) Prisoner; captive. 2) —*a.* Laced: کفش ب.

بنزین *Fr.* Motor spirit; gasoline; petrol; gas; benzene. — بنزین هواپیمائی Aviation s. — ب. گرفتن To fuel up.

بُنشن Cereals; legumes; pulse.

بنصر o *A.* Ring-finger.

بنفسه *A.* In (his) person; personally. *See* نفس

بنفش Violet (colour).

بنفشه Violet. — ب. فرنگی Pansy.

بنقد *S. u.* نقد

بنکدار Wholesale dealer.

بنگ Bhang; henbane.

بنگاه Institution; establishment.

بنگالی Bengalese.

بنگی (One) who is addicted to the use of bhang.

بُنلاد o Layer.

بنوّت o *A.* Affiliation.

بُنه Baggage; luggage.

بَنه Persian turpentine tree.

بنه‌کن + For good (and all).

بنی *A.* [Pl. of ابن] Sons [*in comb.*]: ب. آدم S. of Adam; mankind. — ب. اسرائیل Children of Israel; Jews. — ب. عمّ Cousins.

بنیاد Foundation. Origin. — ب نهادن To lay the f. of; found. To begin.

بنیامین *A-Heb.* Benjamin.

بنیان *A.* Structure; building.

بنیان‌کن *A. P.* Destructive. — سیل ب. Sweeping flood.

بنیچه Quota of troops or of taxes in lieu thereof; matricula.

بنیه *A.* Physical condition; health. *F.* Ability.

بو *or* **بوی** Smell; odour. — بو بردن از To suspect or scent; get wind of. — بو دادن To give out a smell. To stink. To roast or parch. — بو کردن To smell. — بو گرفتن To contract a s.; turn fetid. — بوی . . . از آن می‌آید It savours, or smacks, of. . .

بوآ *Fr.* Boa (constrictor).

بوّاب ○ *A.* = دربان

بواجب • *P. A.* Condine; fitting

بواسطه *P. A.* (*Gr.*) Indirect.

بواسطهٔ *S. u.* واسطه

بواسیر *A.* [Pl. of باسور ○] Piles; hemorrhoids. Polypus.

بواسیری *A. P.* Hemorrhoidal.

بوالعجب = **بلعجب** [Meddler.

بوالفضول *or* **بلفضول** *A.*

بوالهوس = **بلهوس**

بوته Crucible; melting pot. — در بوتهٔ اجمال افتاد It fell into abeyance. — گل ب. C.-earth; fire-clay.

بوتیمار *A. P.* Bittern.

بوجار Sifter and cleaner of rice or wheat. — بوجار لنجان Vicar of Bray; time-server; trimmer.

بوجاری Sifting and cleaning (rice or wheat).

بود 1) Existence. 2) Was [P. of بودن].

بُوَد • =(می)باشد He, she, it is.

بودا Buddha.

بودایی Buddhist.

بودباش Dwelling-place.

بودجه *Fr.* Budget.

بودجه‌ای *Fr.* Budgetary.

بودن [باش] To be. To exist. — او به . . . مایل است He is fond of . . . . — خدا هست God is; G. exists. — کسی اینجا نیست There is no one here. — اگر من جای شما بودم If I were you. — رفته بود He had gone.

بوده Been. — ب. ام I have b.

بور Blond.

بور + Baffled (in one's plans). — ب. شدن To look foolish *or* blank; draw a blank; fail disgracefully. — ب. کردن To embarrass. To trick.

بوراق *A. P.* Borax. Nitre.

بوران Sleet. Squall. [nach.

بورانی *or* **بُرانی** Dish of spi-

بورس *Fr.* Stock exchange. Scholarship.

بور مور + = **برومور**

بوره Nitre. Borax. Tincal.

بوری Blow-pipe.

بوریا Mat. Rush-mat. — نی ب. Marsh-reed. Wicker.

بوریا باف Mat-weaver.

بوریاپوش Cased in wicker [only in قرابه ب. demijohn].

بوزک Barm.

بوزه = 1) بوزك 2) آبجو

بوزینه Monkey; ape.

بوس 1) [Imp. of بوسیدن]. 2) = بوسه ‖ ب. کردن To kiss.

بوستان Garden. [A. pl. بساتین]

بوسه Kiss. — ب. دادن To allow

to be kissed. — ب. زدن بر To kiss.
بوسیدن [بوس] To kiss.
بوسیر Mullein; Aaron's rod.
بوش *E.* Bush(ing). *M.*
بوشن *Fr.* (Reducing) socket; reducer; also, union.
بوف Owl. *See* بوم & جغد
بوفه *Fr.* Buffet. Side-board. Refreshments.
بوق Horn. Bugle. — بوق الکتریکی Klaxon. — ب. زدن To blow the horn. — تا بوق سگ Till the small *or* early hours of the morning.
بوقت *P. A.* In time. *See* وقت
بوقلمون *A.* Turkey. Chameleon. — بوقلمون ماده T.-hen. — بوقلمون نر T.-cock; gobbler. — گل ب. Sweet-william; bearded pink. — ایام ب. * Fickleness of fortune.
بوکس *Fr-E.* [Also بوکس بازی] Boxing. — بکسی ب. زدن To box s. o.
بوگرفته Stinking; fetid.
بول *A.* = **پیشاب**
بولاغ اودی *T.* Water-cress.
بولدوگ *Fr-E.* Bulldog.
بولدوگوم *Fr.* Jujube.
بوم Region. Country.
بوم *A.* (Stone-)owl.
بومادران Milfoil; yarrow.
بومی Native. Vernacular.
بویا Odoriferous.
بویایی Sense of smell.
بویژه *S. u.* ویژه [snuff.
بوییدن [بوی] To smell. To

بَه [Usu. به به] 1) Well done! 2) How nice! H. lovely! Oh! Wow!
به *beh* [Usu. contracted to ب] To : آنرا بمن داد ‖ At : بمن نگاه کرد ‖ By : بساعت من ‖ In : بنام عدالت ‖ With : به آسانی with ease; easily. ‖ Against پشت بدیوار with one's back against the wall.
به *beh* Quince. — به میدهد ده بگیرد He throws a sprat to catch a herring *or* mackerel.
به ,, [Comp. of خوب] = **بهتر**
بها Price; cost. — از روی ب. *Ad valorem.*
بهاء *A.* Beauty. Elegance.
بهادار Valuable. Negotiable.
بهادُر Valiant. Warlike.
بهار Spring. Blossom ○. — بهارعمر Prime of life. — بهار نارنج Orange flower.
بهاران Springtide. [porch.
بهارخواب Terrace; sleeping-
بهاره 1) = بهاری 2) (Wool) produced in the spring.
بهاری Vernal.
بها گذاری Costing. — ب. کردن To cost.
بهانه Pretext. Excuse. — به بهانه Under the p. of. — ب. آوردن To make an excuse or p. — ب. کردن To pretend. — مستی ب. کرد He pretended to be drunk. — ب. گرفتن To pick quarrels. To nag. To be finical or finicking.
بهانه جویی Seeking excuses. Picking quarrels.

بهانه‌گیر = ایرادگیر
بهائم [Pl. of بهیمه]
بهبود Well-being ; welfare. Health. Amelioration ; improvement. Recovery — ب. یافتن To gain (in health).
به به *S. u.* بَه [ment.
بهت *A.* Consternation ; amazement.
بهتان *A.* Calumny ; false accusation. — ب. زدن به To calumniate; accuse falsely.
بهت آور *A. P.* Astonishing.
بهتر [Comp. of خوب] Better : این ب. از آنست This is b. than that. — این از همه ب. است This is the best of all. — بهترِ شما So much the better for you. — ب. شدن To improve. To gain in health. — ب. کردن To improve ; ameliorate ; make b. — از ما بهتران Fairies; also, the fair sex. [ment.
بهتری Preference. Improvement.
بهترین [Sup. of خوب] Best.
بهجت *A.* Cheerfulness. *Fem. pr. name.*
بهدار 1) Hygienist. 2) Sub-assistant surgeon.
بهداری Public health.
بهداشت Hygiene.
بهداشتی Hygienic.
بهدانه Quince-seeds.
بهر *Unit of length* = 1.28 inches. *L.* Inch. ‖ Portion; share. Quotient. Sake ; account. — از بهرِ For (the sake of) . — (از) بهر چه ? What for ? Why ?
بهرام 1) *Astr.* Mars. 2) *Mas. pr. name.* [name.
بهروز Prosperous. *Mas. pr.*
بهره Portion; share. Interest. Profit. — از چیزی ب. بردن To enjoy s. t. To profit by s. t. — به ب. گذاشتن To put out to interest.
بهره برداری Revenue operation; exploitation. — ب. کردن از To exploit or operate. — آمادهٔ ب. کردن To develop , as a mine.
بهره مند Enjoying ; having a share. *F.* Fortunate. — از چیزی ب. شدن To enjoy s. t. To profit by s. t.
بهره ور = بهره مند
بهریار Assistant scout commissioner.
بهشت Paradise; heaven.
بهشتی Paradisaical; heavenly. — مرغ ب. Bird of paradise ; lyre-bird. — نان ب. *Kind of pastry.* [chalant.
بهل بشو + Easy-going. Non-
بهل بشویی + Non-chalance ; laissez-aller.
بهله Falconer's glove.
بهم *S. u.* هم
بهمان *S. u.* فلان
بهم خوردگی Indisposition. Derangement. [ranged.
بهم خورده Indisposed. Deranged.
بهمن Avalanche. *Eleventh month having 30 days. Mas. pr. name.*

بهنجار Normal. *See* هنجار
بهنگام Opportune; well-timed.
بهوش Conscious. *See* هوش
بهی * = خوبی & بهبود.
بهیمه ○ *A.* [بهائم] Beast; quadruped.
بهین ○ Best ; also, better.
بهینه ○ Best.
بهیه *A.* [Fem. of بهی ○] Bright. *Fem. pr. name.*
بی Without. *Prefix* = -less ; im-; in-; ir-; dis-; un-.
بیابان Desert. Wilderness.
بیابانی Pertaining to the desert. Wild. Nomadic.
بی آب Dry. Dehydrate. — ب. کردن To dehydrate.
بی آبرو Disgraced. Impudent. — ب. کردن To disgrace ; dishonour. [dence.
بی آبرویی Disgrace. Impudence.
بی آبی Drought; dryness.
بی آزار Harmless; inoffensive.
بیات *A.* Stale : نان ب.
بی اثر *P. A.* Ineffective. Null.
بی اجاره *P. A.* Rent-free.
بی اجازه *P. A.* Unauthorized.
بی احترامی *P. A.* Disrespect ; dishonour. — بکسی ب. کردن To d. or insult s. o. — ب. بمقدسات Profanity.
بی احتیاط *P. A.* Incautious ; careless; imprudent.
بی احتیاطی *P. A.* Want of precaution; improvidence. — ب. کردن To be incautious, careless, or imprudent.
بی اختیار *P. A.* Involuntary. —*ad.* Involuntarily.
بی ادب *P. A.* Impolite; rude; unmannerly.
بی ادبانه *P. A.* Impolitely.
بی ادبی *P. A.* Impoliteness. — ب. کردن To be impolite ; act rudely.
بی اذیت *P. A.* = **بی آزار**
بی ارتباط *P. A.* Disconnected. Irrelevant. Incoherent.
بی اساس *P. A.* Unfounded.
بی اسباب *P. A.* Free-hand.
بی استعداد *P. A.* Untalented.
بی استطاعت *P. A.* Lacking pecuniary ability.
بی اسلحه *P. A.* Unarmed. — چشم ب. The naked eye.
بی اسم *P. A.* Nameless. Obscure. — سهام ب. Bearer shares.
بی اشتها *P. A.* Lacking appetite.
بی اشتهایی *P. A.* Lack of appetite; inappetence.
بی اصل *P. A.* = **بی اساس**
بی اُصول *P. A.* Immethodical.
بیاض ○ *A.* Whiteness. Blank book. — بیاض مرجان Madrepore. — در بیاض افتادن To be written fair.
بیاض البیضی *A.* Albuminous. — پیشاب ب. Bright's disease. — مادهٔ ب. Proteid. [norant.
بی اطلاع *P. A.* Unaware. Ignorant.
بی اطلاعی *P. A.* Lack of information. Ignorance.

بی اعتبار *P. A.* Unreliable. Creditless. Disreputable.
بی اعتباری *P. A.* Unreliability. Invalidity. Lack of credit.
بی اعتدال *P. A.* Immoderate.
بی اعتدالی *P. A.* Immoderateness. Intemperance. Injustice. — ب. کردن To be intemperate or immoderate.
بی اعتقاد *P. A.* 1) = بی ایمان 2) Incredulous.
بی اعتقادی *P. A.* Unbelief. Incredulity.
بی اعتنا *P. A.* Heedless; taking no notice; inattentive.
بی اعتنایی *P. A.* Heedlessness. Defiance. Disrespect. — بکسی ب. کردن To be regardless of, or pay no attention to, s. o.
بی آلایش Pure; immaculate.
بی التفات *P. A.* Unkind.
بی التفاتی *P. A.* Unkindness; disobliging treatment.
بیان *A.* Statement. Explanation. — ب. کردن To state; set forth. To explain.
بی انتظام *P. A.* Disorderly.
بی انتظامی *P. A.* Disorder; want of discipline [less.
بی انتها *P. A.* Endless. Bound-
بی اندازه Out of size; out of measure. Extreme. —*ad.* Extremely. Immeasurably.
بی انصاف *P. A.* Unfair; unjust.
بی انصافی *P. A.* Unfair dealing; injustice. — ب. کردن To be unjust; act unfairly.
بی انضباط *P. A.* Lacking discipline; disorderly; confused.
بی انضباطی *P. A.* Absence of discipline.
بیانیه *A.* Statement; manifesto.
بی اولاد *P. A.* Childless.
بی اهمیت *P. A.* Unimportant.
بی ایمان *P. A.* Unbelieving; unfaithful.
بی ایمانی *P. A.* Unbelief.
بی بار Fruitless. Infecund.
بی باک Dauntless; intrepid.
بی باکانه Fearlessly.
بی باکی Intrepidity.
بی بال Wingless; apterous. — بی بالان The Aptera.
بی پر و بال = بی بال و پر
بی بدل *P.A.* Peerless; matchless.
بی بخار × *P. A.* Good-for-nothing. *S. a.* بیعرضه & بیدبست وپا ‖ *OS.* Vapourless.
بی بَر Fruitless. Sterile.
بی برگشت Irrevocable.
بی بصر *P. A.* Deprived of vision. Lacking foresight.
بی بصیرت *P. A.* Undiscerning.
بی بقا *P. A.* Transient.
بی بندو بار Unrestrained.
بی بنیاد Unfounded. [atony.
بی بنیگی *P. A.* Weakness;
بی بنیه *P. A.* Weak.
بی بو Odourless. — بی بو و بی خاصیت + Good-for-nothing; useless.

بی بها Worthless. [nate.
بی بهره Portionless. Unfortu-
بی بی Matron. Venerable lady. Grandmother.
بی بی طوطی Poll(-parrot).
بی پا Footless. *F*. Impoverished.
بی پایان Endless. Infinite.
بی پدر و مادر Base-born.
بی پرده Frankly. —*a*. Frank.
بی پروا Dauntless; reckless.
بی پر و بال Unfledged. *F*. Helpless; defenceless.
بی پروپا Unfounded.
بی پشتوانه Without cover; wild-cat.
بی پناه Shelterless. Bleak; exposed. *F*. Defenceless.
بی پول Moneyless; penniless.
بی پیر Unaccompanied by a spiritual guide.
بی پیرایه Unadorned. Simple.
بیت *A*. [ابیات] Distich; verse; also, couplet.
بیت ○ *A*. [بُیوت] = خانه
بیتاب Impatient. Restless.
بی تاریخ *P*. *A*. Undated.
بیت الحزن * *A*. House of grief [cp. of Jacob's house]
بیت اللحم *A*. Bethlehem.
بیت الله *A*. House of God.
بیت المال *A*. = خزانه
بیت المقدس *A*. Jerusalem.
بی تأمل *P*. *A*. Inconsiderately; rashly. Unhesitatingly.
بی تجربگی *P*. *A*. Inexperience.
بی تجربه *P*. *A*. Inexperienced.
بی تدبیر *P*. *A*. Imprudent. Shiftless.
بی تربیت *P*. *A*. Ill-bred; rude; impolite. [politeness.
بی تربیتی *P*. *A*. Rudeness; im-
بی ترتیب *P*. *A*. Irregular.
بی ترتیبی *P*. *A*. Lack of order or method.
بی تزویر *P*. *A*. Guileless.
بی تشریفات *P*.*A*. Unceremonious. Requiring no formalities.
بی تعارف *P*. *A*. Unceremonious. *OS*. Without compliments.
بی تعصب *P*. *A*. Open-minded; unprejudiced. [nocent.
بی تقصیر *P*. *A*. Guiltless; in-
بی تقصیری *P*. *A*. Guiltlessness; innocence.
بی تکلف *P*. *A*. Unaffected(ly). Unceremonious(ly). Free and easy.
بی تکلیف *P*. *A*. At a loss what course to pursue; in suspense; at a loose end.
بی تکلیفی *P*. *A*. Suspense; undecided state of affairs. Abeyance.
بی تلبیس *P*. *A*. Guileless.
بی تمیز *P*. *A*. Undiscerning.
بی تمیزی *P*. *A*. Lack of discernment.
بی تناسب *P*. *A*. Disproportionate. Incongruous.
بی توان Weak. Inert.

بیتوته • *A.* Passing the night.— ب.کردن To stay during the n.
بی توجه *P. A.* Inattentive ; careless.
بی توجهی *P. A.* Inattention. Carelessness. Want of care.
بی تهیه *P. A.* Offhand.
بی ثبات *P. A.* Inconstant.
بی ثباتی *P. A.* Instability.
بی ثمر *P. A.* Fruitless. Futile.
بیجا Inopportune; improper.
بیجاده Amber. *Kind of ruby.*
بیجان Lifeless ; inanimate. — ب.کردن To deprive of life.
بی جرأت *P. A.* Courageless.
بیجک Bill; invoice.
بی جلا *P. A.* Lustreless.
بیجمال ○ *P. A.* Plain; ugly.
بیجمالی ○ *P. A.* Want of beauty.
بی جنس *P. A.* Sexless; neuter.
بی جواب *P. A.* Unable to reply ; speechless. Unanswered. Indisputable. [answer.
بی جوابی *P. A.* Inability to
بی جهت *P. A.* Undue. —*ad.* For no reason; unduly.
بیچارگی Helplessness. Need.
بیچاره Helpless. Remediless. Poor. [*As an int.*] P. fellow ! P. thing ! —*n.* [Pl. بیچارگان] The helpless ; the poor. — ب.کردن To make h. poor. To bring to bay. To harass.
بیچون Incomparable. Ineffable —*ad.* Indisputably.
بیچون و چرا Indisputable.
بیچیز Poor; indigent.
بیچیزی Poverty; indigence.
بیحاصل *P. A.* Unproductive. *F.* Useless. [listless.
بیحال *P. A.* Faint. Languid ;
بیحالت *P. A.* Inexpressive ; expressionless ; glassy : چشمانش ب. بود
بیحالی *P. A.* Faintness. Listlessness. Bad health.
بیحجاب *P. A.* Unveiled. *F.* Immodest. [Excessively.
بیحد *P. A.* Boundless. —*ad.*
بیحرف *P. A.* Dumb. Indisputable. —*ad.* Indisputably. —*int.* Quiet !
بیحرکت *P. A.* Motionless; still.
بیحرمت *P. A.* Disgraced . — ب. کردن To dishonour or disgrace. To profane.
بیحرمتی *P. A.* Disgrace. Outrage. Profanity.
بیحس *P.A.* Insensible. *F.* Unfeeling. — ب. کردن To render insensible ; anaesthetize (locally). [gular.
بیحساب *P. A.* Countless. Irre-
بیحسی *P. A.* Insensibility. Torpidity. Unfeelingness.
بیحصر • *a. P. A.* = بیحد
بیحضور • *P. A.* Inattentive. Abstracted. [Naked.
بی حفاظ *P. A.* Unprotected.
بی حقوق *P. A.* Ungrateful. Unpaid. — مرخصی ب. Leave without pay.
بی حقوقی *P. A.* Ingratitude.

بی حقیقت *P. A.* False. Insincere. Hollow-hearted.

بی حمیت *P. A.* Cowardly. Cold-hearted.

بی حواس *P. A.* Absent-minded. Out of spirits; in bad s.

بیحواسی *P. A.* Absence of mind or of good spirits.

بی حوصلگی *P. A.* Impatience. Irritability. [Irritable.

بی حوصله *P. A.* Impatient.

بی حیا *P. A.* Impudent; shameless; immodest.

بی حیائی *P. A.* Impudence; immodesty.

بیخ Root. Bottom. — از بیخ درآوردن (یا کندن) To root up; eradicate. — بیخ شب بو Herb bennet. — بیخ کبر رومی Scolopendrium.

بیخار Thornless.

بی خاصیت *P. A.* Useless; never-do-well; good-for-nothing. *OS.* Virtueless.

بیخان Smoothbore(d). — تفنگ ب. Smoothbore(d gun).

بی خانمان Homeless. Ruined.

بیخبر *P, A,* Unaware. Ignorant. —*ad.* Suddenly; without (giving) notice; unawares.

بیخبری *P. A.* Ignorance.

بیختن [بیز] To sift; bolt. — آرد خود را بیخته است He's had his fling. [Inexpensive.

بیخرج *P. A.* Free of charge.

بیخرد Foolish; imprudent.

بیخردی Lack of wisdom; folly. Injudiciousness.

بی خزان Evergreen. Perennial.

بی خطا *P. A.* Unerring. Innocent.

بی خطر *P. A.* Dangerless. Harm less; safe. *Med.* Benign.

بیخکن Uprooted. — ب. کردن To eradicate. *F.* To cure fundamentally.

بی خلوص *P. A.* Insincere.

بیخواب Sleepless. Napless.

بیخوابی Sleeplessness.

بیخود 1) Ecstasized. Out of one's senses. 2) + Unwarranted; undue. Motiveless. —*ad.* + Without a good cause. To no purpose. Unduly.

بیخودی Ecstasy; rapture.

بی خیال *P. A.* Thoughtless. Unintentional. — بی خیالش باش × Nevermind; don't bother about that; I don't care a fig.

بی خیر *P. A.* Uncharitable; not useful to others.

بید Willow. — بید, بید خشتی Common crack-willow; brittle willow. — بیدبید خشتی = بید تافته ‖ بیدسبدی Osier. — بید مجنون Weeping w. — جوهر بید Salicin.

بید Moth; clothes'-moth.

بیداد Oppression; injustice.

بیدادگر Oppressor; —*a.* Cruel.

بیدادگری Oppression.

بیدار Awake. *F.* Enlightened. — ب. شدن To wake up. — ب. کردن To w. or awaken. To enlighten. — ب. ماندن To stay up; keep awake; k. vigil.

بیداری Wakefulness. Awakening. Vigilance. — شیپور بیداری *Mil.* Reveille.

بید انجیر Castor(-oil plant). — بید انجیر هندی *or* بید انجیر ختایی Pavana wood; croton.— روغن ب. Castor-oil. [rant.

بیدانش Void of learning; ignorant.

بیدانشی Ignorance. Foolish act*.

بیدانه Seedless.

بید خشت (Manna of) common crack-willow.

بید خورده Moth-eaten.

بیدرد Painless. Indolent. Callous; unfeeling.

بی‌دردسر Convenient; easy.

بی‌دررو Adiabatic.

بیدرمان Irremediable.

بیدرنگ Immediately.

بیدریغ Unsparing(ly); without stint. Immense *.

بید خورده = **بید زده**

بیدستر o Beaver; castor.

بی‌دست و پا Shiftless; gawky.

بید سُرخ *Kind of willow.*

بی‌دغدغه *P.A.* Without mental unrest. —*a.* Tranquil.

بیدل Enamoured of love. Impatient. Poor-spirited.

بیدلی Impatience; lack of self-possession. Poor spirits.

بیدماغ + Out of spirits; in a bad humour. Displeased.

بیدمشک Pussy willow. Catkin.

بیدوا *P. A.* = **بی‌درمان**

بیدوام *P. A.* Not lasting long; flimsy. Short-lived; transient.

بی دیانت *P. A.* Impious. Dishonest. [Impiety.

بی دیانتی *P. A.* Dishonesty.

بیدین *P. A.* Irreligious. [ety.

بیدینی *P. A.* Irreligion; impi-

بی‌ذوق *P. A.* Inelegant; void of (literary) taste.

بیراه Deviated. Astray. Misleading. Indecent. —*n.* = **بیراهه**

بیراهه Deviated path. By-way.

بیربط *P. A.* Irrelevant.

بیرحم *P. A.* Cruel. [Cruel.

بیرحمانه *P. A.* Cruelly. —*a.*

بیرحمی *P. A.* Cruelty.

بی‌رخنه Water-tight. Air-tight.

بیرضایتی *P. A.* 1). Unwilligness. 2) نارضایتی

بیرغبت *P. A.* Having no relish; nauseating. Reluctant.

بیرغبتی *P. A.* Want of relish; inappetence. Unwillingness.

بیرق *T.* = **پرچم**

بیرگ Nerveless. Effeminate.

بیرنگ Colourless; achromatic.

بیروت Beirut; Beyrouth.

بیروح *P. A.* Inanimate; lifeless. *F.* Prosaic.

بیروزی Deprived of one's daily bread

بیرون *ad.* Out(side).—*n.* Outside; external part.—*a.* = **بیرونی** ‖ ب. آمدن To come out. — ب. رفتن To go o. To ease nature. [*With* از] To leave. — ب. کردن To send o.; dismiss. —

از بیرون From without.
بیرون افتادگی Prolapsus.
بیرون بر ○ Exporter.
بیرونق *P. A.* Lustreless. Dull; unsuccessful, as a business.
بیرونی Outer; external; exterior. *—n.* Men's apartment.
بیرویه *P. A.* Irregular. Immethodical. Impolitic.
بیریا *P. A.* Sincere; candid.
بیریایی *P. A.* Lack of hypocrisy; sincerity.
بدریخت = + بی‌ریخت
بی‌ریش Beardless (youth). Catamite.
بیز [Imp. of بیختن]
بیزار Weary; disgusted; fed up.— ب.کردن To weary; make d.
بیزاری Disgust. Estrangement.
بیزبان Dumb; speechless.
بیزحمت *P. A.* Easy; convenient. — ب. در را به‌بندید Please close the door.
بیزر * Moneyless; penniless; empty-handed. *—ad.* Without money.
بیزَوال *P. A.* Imperishable. [Eternal.
بیزور Weak; powerless.
بی‌سامان Homeless; unsettled.
بی‌سبب *P. A.* = **بیجهت**
بیست Twenty.
بیستم Twentieth.
بیستمی (The) twentieth.
بیستمین The twentieth.
بیستون *Behistun.*
بیسر Headless. Acephalous.
بی‌سروپا Worthless. Rustic. Vulgar; low.
بی‌سروته Incoherent. Silly.
بی‌سروصدا Quiet; serene; insidious. Hush-hush.
بیسکویت *R.-Fr.* Biscuit.
بی‌سلیقه *P. A.* Lacking taste or tact. Awkward; inexpert.
بیسموت *Fr.* Bismuth.
بیسواد *P. A.* Illiterate.
بیسوادی *P. A.* Illiteracy. — برنامه های مبارزه با بیسوادی Literacy programs.
بی‌سیرت *P. A.* Having a bad character; characterless. — ب.کردن To ravish; violate. [Also vulgarly بیصورت کردن]
بیسیم Wireless. *—n.* W. (telegraph); radio.
بیش 1) More [comp. of زیاد *or* خیلی]. — ب. از پیش M. than ever. 2) Much.— ب. وکم *or* کم یا بیش More or less.
بی‌شائبه *P. A.* Unmixed; pure; taintless.
بی‌شبهه *P. A.* = **بیشک**
بیشتر More [comp. of بیش in the sense of خیلی & زیاد]. M. often; oftener. Rather. Longer [*in time*]. *—n.* M. or most; greater or greatest part. — بیشتر اوقات Most of the time.
بیشتری Excess.
بیشترین Most [sup. of بیش in the sense of خیلی & زیاد]. *—n.* (The) most; the greatest

(*or* greater) part.
بیشرف *P. A.* Knavish; roguish; dishonourable.
بیشرفانه *P. A.* Dishonourably.
بیشرفی *P. A.* Disgraceful act; outrage. Knavishness.
بیشرم Shameless; impudent.
بیشرمانه Shamelessly. [desty.
بیشرمی Impudence; immo-
بی‌شعور *P. A.* Lacking common sense; foolish; silly.
بی‌شعوری *P. A.* Lack of common sense. Idiocy; folly.
بیشك *P. A.* Undoubtedly.
بی‌شکل *P. A.* Amorphous.
بی‌شکیب Impatient.
بیشمار Innumerable; countless.
بیشه Thicket; coppice; grove.
بیشینه = حداکثر Maximum.
بی‌صبر *P. A.* Impatient.
بی‌صبری *P. A.* Impatience.
بیصدا Noiseless; quiet. Dumb. Mute; silent.
بی‌صرفه *P. A.* Unprofitable. Disadvantageous.
بی‌صفا *P. A.* Not pleasant or cheerful. *F.* Insincere.
بی‌صفت *P. A.* Ungrateful.
بیضاء o *A.* White. Clear.
بی‌ضرر *P. A.* Harmless; inoffensive. Involving no loss.
بیضتین *S. u.* بیضه
بیضه *A.* = تخم Egg. Testicle. [D. بیضتین] ـ ورم ب. Orchitis
بیضه بند *A. P.* Suspensory.
بیضی *A.* Elliptical. —*n.* Ellipse. — بیضیِ مجسم Ellipsoid.
بیضیت *A.* Ellipticity.
بیطار *A.* = دام پزشك
بیطاری *A. P.* Veterinary.
بیطاقت *P. A.* Impatient. Unable to bear pain; susceptible to p. Wanting fortitude. — ب. شدن To lose patience.
بیطاقتی *P. A.* Impatience. Inability to bear pain.
بی‌طالع *P. A.* Ill-starred.
بیطرف *P. A.* Impartial. Neutral.
بیطرفانه *P. A.* Impartially. —*a.* Impartial. [Neutrality.
بیطرفی *P. A.* Impartiality.
بی‌طعم *P. A.* Flavourless.
بی‌طمع *P. A.* Disinterested. Not covetous.
بی‌ظرافت *P. A.* Inelegant.
بیظرف *P. A.* Unpacked. — نفت ب. Bulk oil.
بیع *A.* 1) Selling; sale [فروش]. 2)+ = بیعانه ‖ بیع‌شرط Revocable s. — بیع قطع Irrevocable s.
بیعار *P. A.* Profligate; shameless. [wantonness.
بیعاری *P. A.* Profligacy;
بی‌عاطفه *P. A.* Unfeeling; heartless; cold-hearted.
بیعانه *A. P.* Earnest-money.
بیعت *A.* (Oath of) allegiance; fealty. — ب. کردن To swear a.
بیعد • *P. A.* = بیشمار
بیعدالت *P. A.* Unjust.
بیعدالتی *P. A.* Injustice.

بیعدیل • *P. A.* Peerless.
بیعرضگی *P. A.* Inefficiency; incapability. [ficient.
بیعرضه *P. A.* Incapable; inef-
بیعزتی ○ *P. A.* Dishonour; disrespect. Disgrace.
بی‌عصمت *P. A.* Unchaste.
بی‌عفت *P. A.* Unchaste.
بی‌عفتی *P. A.* Unchastity.
بی‌عقل *P. A.* = بیخرد [ness.
بیعلاقگی *P. A.* Disinterested-
بی‌علاقه *P. A.* Disinterested.
بی‌علت *P. A.* 1) Causeless. 2) بی‌عیب [ignorant.
بیعلم *P. A.* Void of learning;
بیعلمی *P. A.* Lack of learning; ignorance. [of sale.
بیع نامه *P. A.* Bill (*or* deed)
بیعوض *P. A.* Irreplaceable.
بی‌عیب *P. A.* Faultless; sound; in perfect condition.
بی‌غرض *P. A.* Having no private motive; disinterested.
بیغرضانه *P. A.* Without private motive or interest.
بیغرضی *P. A.* Lack of private motive; disinterestedness.
بیغل و غش *or* بیغش *P. A.* Unalloyed; pure. Sincere.
بیغم Worriless.
بیغوله Cave. —*a.* Lonely.
بیغیرت *P. A.* Spiritless; cowardly; zealless. Callous.
بیغیرتی *P. A.* Lack of zeal or spirit; dastardliness.
بیف + Stupid; beef-headed.

بیفایده *P. A.* Useless. Unprofitable. Futile. — کوشش ب. Lost labour; useless effort.
بیفتك *Fr.* (Beef)steak.
بی‌فراست *P. A.* Unintelligent.
بی‌فرزند Childless; issueless.
بی‌فرهنگ Void of culture; uneducated.
بی‌فروغ Lustreless.
بی‌فکر *P. A.* Mindless; thoughtless. Giddy. Rash. —*ad.* Rashly. Offhand.
بی‌قابلیت *P. A.* = ناقابل
بیقاعدگی *P. A.* Irregularity.
بیقاعده *P. A.* Irregular.
بیقدر *P. A.* Of no value.
بیقرار *P. A.* Restless; uneasy. Fidgety. Irregular. Unstable.
بیقراری *P. A.* Uneasiness. Impatience. Instability. — ب. کردن To be uneasy. [less.
بی‌قرین *P. A.* Matchless; peer-
بیقصد *P. A.* Unintentional(ly).
بی‌قرینه *P. A.* Unsymmetrical.
بیقوت *P. A.* Having no nourishment. [powerless.
بی‌قوه & بیقوت *P. A.* Weak;
بیقیاس • *P. A.* Immeasurable; immense.
بیقید *P. A.* Unrestrained. Easygoing; careless. Unconditional [also بیقید و شرط].
بیقیدی *P. A.* = لاقیدی
بی‌قیمت *P. A.* Invaluable. Priceless.
بیکار Unemployed; out of

employment. Idle. Not busy. بیکارالدوله (*Humorous*) (Title of a) gentleman at large.
بیکاری Unemployment. Idleness. Leisure.
بیکران * Boundless. Immense.
بی کردار * Not practising what one preaches. Ungrateful.
بیکس Having no relatives or friends; forlorn.
بی کفایت *P. A.* Incapable ; inefficient.
بی کفایتی *P. A.* Inefficiency.
بی کله Brainless; weak-minded.
بی کمال *P. A.* Void of accomplishments; uneducated.
بی کمالی *P. A.* Lack of education or civility.
بی کم و زیاد *P. A.* Exactly ; neither more nor less.
بی کم و کاست Entirely. Exactly.
بیگ o *T.* Lord or prince.
بیگار(ی) Forced labour ; unpaid l.; statute l.
بیگانگی Foreignness; alienation.
بیگانه Foreign. —*n.* [pl. بیگانگان] Foreigner ; stranger.
بیگانه پرست Xenophilous. —*n.* Xenophile.
بیگانه پرستی Xenophilism.
بیگاه Ill-timed ; untimely. — گاه و بیگاه Now and then.
بیگدار Fordless. —*ad.* Inconsiderately. — ب. به آب زدن To be rash (in a specified act) ; leap before one looks.

بی گزند Harmless; inoffensive.
بی گلبرگ Apetalous.
بیگم o *T.* Lady of rank.
بیگمان Undoubtedly.
بیگناه Innocent. Sinless.
بیگناهی Innocence.
بیگودی *Fr.* Hair-curler.
بیل 1) Spade; shovel. 2) خیش ‖ ب. زدن To turn up with a s.— بیلش خیلی گل برمیدارد × He carries a lot of weight.
بیلان *Fr.* = ترازنامه
بی لبه Edgeless. — واگن ب. Platform car.
بی لپه Acotyledonous.
بیلچه Small shovel. Dibble ; trowel.
بیل زن Labourer with a shovel.
بی لطافت *P. A.* Ungainly. *S. a.* بی لطف
بی لطف *P. A.* Unkind. Insipid. Bald.
بی لطفی *P. A.* Unkindness.
بی لفاف *P. A.* Uncovered. Unpacked. *F.* Frank(ly).
بی لگام Unbridled. *F.* Dissolute.
بی لیاقت *P. A.* Incapable. Undeserving. [Lack of merit.
بی لیاقتی *P. A.* Incapability.
بیلیون *Fr.* Billion.
بیم Fear. Danger. — ب. داشتن To fear.— بیم آن میرود که It is to be feared that. — از بیم جان For one's life.
بیمار Ill; sick. —*n.* S. person; patient. — بیمار عشق Love-

sick. — ب. شدن To fall sick.
بیمارداری Attendance on the sick.
بیمارستان Hospital. Infirmary.
بیماری Illness. Disease.
بی‌مانند Unparalleled. [less.
بی‌ماوا or بی‌ماوی P. A. Home-
بیمایگی Superficial knowledge. Indigence.
بیمایه Fundless. Indigent. Having no yeast (or leaven). F. Having a superficial knowledge. — شعر بیمایه Doggerel.
بی‌مبالات P. A. Careless.
بی‌مبالاتی P. A. Carelessness.
بیمثال P. A. Unparalleled.
بی مِثل P. A. — بی‌مانند
بی مُحابا P. A. Dauntless(ly). Unsparing(ly). Regardless(ly).
بی‌محبت P. A. Unaffectionate; unkind.
بی‌محل P. A. Untimely. Not provided for (in the budget) ; unallocated. — چك ب. Dud cheque : c. for which (sufficient) funds are not available in the bank.
بی‌مرحمت P. A. Unkind.
بیمروّت P. A. Ungenerous. Unjust. [Injustice.
بیمروتی P. A. Inhumanity.
بیمزگی Insipidity. Flat joke.
بیمزه Insipid; tasteless. F. Uninteresting. Flat: شوخی ب.
بی‌مسلک P. A. Unprincipled.
بی‌مسمی P. A. Not answering to its significance. — اسم ب. Name which does not answer to its meaning; misnomer. Abstract term.
بی‌مصرف P. A. Useless.
بی‌مطالعه P. A. Offhand.
بی‌معرفت P. A. = نادان ـ بیدانش
بی‌معطلی P. A. Prompt(ly). Quick(ly).
بی‌معنی P. A. Meaningless. Good-for-nothing.
بی‌مغز Pithless. Deaf, as a nut. F. Brainless; giddy. Hollow.
بی‌مقدار * P. A. Unworthy.
بی‌مقدمه P. A. Abrupt(ly) . Suddenly. OS. Without preamble.
بی‌ملاحظه P. A. Regardless (of others) ; careless. Rash.
بی‌مناسبت P. A. Irrelevant. Unwarranted. Unsuitable.
بیمناک Apprehensive. Afraid.
بی‌منت P. A. Freely and without reproach.
بی‌مورد P. A. Out of place ; amiss; inopportune.
بیموقع P. A. Untimely ; unseasonable , inopportune.
بیمه Insurance. — ب. کردن To insure. To guarantee +. — بیمهٔ اتکائی Reinsurance.— بیمهٔ عمر Life i. or assurance. — حق ب. Premium.— سند بیمه I. policy.
بی مهارت P. A. Unskilful ; inexpert.
بی مُهره Invertebrate.
بی‌مِهری Unkindness.

بیمه‌گر Insurer.
بیمه‌گزار The insured.
بیمه شده Insured. —*n*. The i.
بیمه نامه Insurance policy.
بیمیل *P. A.* Unwilling.
بیمیلی *P. A.* Unwillingness.
بین [Imp. of دیدن]
بَین *A.* Distance between; interval. Middle. — در بین In the m. Between the parties. — دراین ب. In the meantime. — در بین نهادن To set forth (for discussion). — بینِ *or* در بینِ Between. In the middle of.
بین *A.* o (*bayen*) = آشکار
بینا That can see; not blind. *F.* Clear-sighted.
بیناب Spectrum.
بینابَین *A. P.* Halfway. In the middle.
بَینِ اثنین *A.* Mutual.
بین‌السطور *A.* Interlinear.
بین‌المدارین *A.* Intertropical (regions).
بین‌الملل *A.* Between the nations. *S. a.* بین‌المللی
بین‌المللی *A. P.* International.
بین‌النهرین *A.* Mesopotamia.
بی نام Anonymous. — سهام ب. Bearer shares.
بی ناموس *P. A.* Unprincipled. Unchaste.
بی (نام و) نشان Untraceable; traceless.
بینایی (Sense of) sight. *F.* Clear-sightedness.
بی نتیجه *P. A.* Futile; abortive. Inconclusive; indeterminate. — ب. گذاردن To frustrate.
بینِ راهی *A. P.* In transit.
بی نزاکت Inelegant; rude.
بینش Insight; perspicacity.
بی نشاط *P.A.* Joyless; mirthless.
بی نشان Traceless.
بی نصیب *P. A.* Portionless.
بی نظم *P. A.* Disorderly.
بی نظمی *P. A.* Disorder; confusion.
بی نظیر *P. A.* Unparalleled; incomparable.
بی نماز (Disqualified for saying her prayers on account of being) menstruous.
بی نمک Saltless. Insipid. *F.* Inattractive; plain. Flat, as a joke.
بیننده 1) Seer; spectator. 2)* The eye [pl. بینندگان].
بی ننگ Shameless.
بینوا Indigent. Helpless.
بینوایی Indigence; poverty.
بینور *P. A.* Lustreless. Blind.
بینوری *P. A.* Dimness. Stupidity.
بینه Dressing-room in a bath-house.
بینه *A.* (*baye-*) Clear proof or evidence.
بی نهایت *P. A.* Extreme(ly). Infinite(ly). —*n*. Infinite quantity.
بینی Nose. — آماس ب. Rhinitis. — ب. گرفتن To blow the nose.
بی نیاز [*With* از] Able to do without or dispense with;

independent of. ب. کردن — To free from want.

بی‌نیازی Ability to do without; independence. Freedom from want.

بیواسطه *P. A.* Direct. Immediate.

بی‌وجود *P. A.* Good-for-nothing; worthless.

بیوَر ○ Ten-thousand; myriad.

بی‌وصیت *P. A.* Intestate.

بی‌وعده *P. A.* Payable at sight.

بیوفا *P. A.* Unfaithful. Inconstant. [Inconstancy.

بی‌وفائی *P. A.* Unfaithfulness.

بی‌وقار *P. A.* Ungraceful; undignified.

بیوقت *P. A.* = **بیموقع**

بی‌وقوف *P. A.* Ignorant. Unaware.

بیوک *T.* 1) بزرگ 2) *Mas. pr. name.*

بیوگی Widowhood.

بیوه Widow(ed). — زن ب. Widow. — مرد بیوه Widower.

بیهده * [Cont. of بیهوده].

بی‌هراس Fearless(ly).

بی‌نظیر & **بی‌مانند** = **بیهمال**

بی‌همت *P. A.* Spiritless. Lacking good ambition.

بی همتی *P. A.* Lack of ambition or spirit. [of God.

بی‌همتا Matchless; unique: ep

بی‌همه چیز + Unscrupulous unprincipled.

بی‌هنر Void of any art or virtue. Unskilful. Good-for-nothing.

بی‌هنگام Untimely.

بیهوا + Suddenly. Rashly.

بیهودگی Vanity. Futility.

بیهوده Vain; useless; futile. Absurd. Empty. —*ad.* In v.

بیهوش Unconscious. Slow-witted; dull. — ب. شدن To become u.; swoon. — ب. کردن To anæsthetize. To make u.

بیهوشی Unconsciousness. Anæsthesia. [For داروی ب.] Anæsthetic (agent). — بیهوشیِ اعصاب Narcolepsy.

بی‌یار Friendless. Love-lorn.

پا or پای Foot. Leg. *F*. Foundation. Support.— پا خوردن + To be cheated.— پا دادن + To happen.— پا زدن + To kick away. To keep step.— بکسی پا زدن + To cheat s. o.— پا بیخت خود زدن + To forfeit one's chance.— پا خوردن + To be cheated.— پا شدن + To get up; rise.— پا کردن To put on or wear (on the feet).— از پا انداختن To walk (s. o.) off his legs. To undo; break down; overwhelm. *S. a.* از پا درآمدن ‖ از پا درآوردن To collapse; succumb. To be ruined. To be undone.— از پا درآوردن To ruin; impoverish.— مشروب او را از پا در آورد Drink was his undoing.— پا برای کسی انداختن + To involve s. o. in a difficulty.— پایش توی ۲۰ (سال) است He is going on for the age of 20.— پای کار On site.— بپاکردن To start. To excite. *S. a.* پا کردن ‖ باپیاکردن To barter; clear; adjust.— برپا کردن To erect. To establish. To set afoot.— دو ریال پای من حساب کرد He charged me *2 rials* for it.— او هم یك پا دروغگو است He, too, is somewhat of a liar.— پای کمی از دزدی ندارد It is next door to, or nothing less than, theft.

پا or پای [Imp. of پاییدن]

پاافزار or پای‌افزار ○ Footwear.

پا انداز Foot-cloth. Pimp×.

پا برجا Firm. Established or regular. Confirmed.

پا برچین + Softly; slowly.

پا برسر Cephalopod.

پا برهنه Barefoot(ed).

پا بست or پای بست Bound. Encumbered.—*n*. * Foundation.

پا بلند Long-legged.

پا بماه Near her time.

پا بمهر Duly sealed.

پابند Fetters. *F*. Hindrance.— پابندِ Encumbered by. Particular about.

پابوس * Presence; audience.

پابوسی (Honour of being given) audience.

پاپ *Fr*. Pope.

پاپا *Fr*. Papa; daddy. Grandpa.

پاپوش Slipper. *F*. Difficulty.

پاپیتال English ivy.

پاپیته St. Ignatius's bean.

پاپیچ Puttee.

پاپیروس *Fr*. = بردی Papyrus.

پاپی شدن To hound or persecute. To insist or urge on.

پاپیون *Fr*. Bowtie.

پاتابه or پاتاوه Leggings.

پا تخته Footboard. Treadle.

پا تختی (Feast on) the day following the consummation of a marriage. —*a*. : میز پاتختی Bedside table.

پاتوق *P. T.* Haunt ; resort ; hangout ; joint. [drunk.

پاتیل Cauldron. —*a*. × Dead

پاچنبری Club-footed ; bow-legged.

پاچه (Sheep's) trotters.

پاچه بند [usu. پاچه بند قوش] Jess.

پاچه ورمالیده × Light-fingered (person) ; old rogue.

پاچین Skirt [*now usu*. دامن].

پادار کردن To provide for. To allocate a budget for.

پاداش Reward; remuneration.— پ. دادن (به) To reward ; re-munerate. [sive.

پا دراز Long-legged. *F*. Intru-

پا درازی Intrusion. Trespass-ing.—پ. کردن To be intrusive.

پا درهوا Unconfirmed. (Quite) in the air. Illusive.—پ. حرف زدن Not to have a leg to stand on.

پادری Door-mat.

پادزهر Bezoar-stone. Antitoxin.— گیاه پ. Milkweed.

پادشاه King.

پادشاهی Reign. Sovereignty ; kingship. —*a*. Royal. King-ly. — حکومت پ. Monarchy. — پ. کردن To reign.

پادشه * [Cont. of بادشاه].

پادگان Garrison.

پادگانه Terrace on a slope.

پادنگ Threshing instrument worked by foot. Anchor escapement.— ساعت پ. Lever watch; w. with an anchor e.

پادو Footboy ; errand boy. Footman attending a person on horseback.

پار ○ * Past; last : سال پ.

پارابلوم *Ger*. Parabellum.

پارازیت *Fr*. = انگل & طفیلی ‖ پ. انداختن در [*In wireless*] To jam. [To initial.

پاراف *Fr*. Initials. — پ. کردن

پارافین *Fr*. Paraffin.

پارالل *Fr*. Parallel bars.

پاراوان *Fr*. Folding screen.

پارت *Fr*. Parthia.

پارتی *Fr*. (Single) consign-ment; lot. Friend at court.

پارچ Kind of jar.

پارچه Cloth; stuff. Plot : یك پ. زمین ‖ Piece. Block. — دو پارچه آبادی Two villages.

پارچه باف Cloth-weaver.

پارچه بافی Cloth-weaving. — کارخانهٔ پ. C.-w. factory.

پارچه کاری Piece-work.— بطورِ پ. By the piece.

پاردسو *Fr*. Overcoat.

پاردُم Crupper.

پاردم ساییده Cunning as a fox.

پارس = 1) فارس 2) ایران

پارس Barking. — پ کردن To bark.

پارس Panther.

پارسا Devout or abstemious (person). Pious (person)..

پارسال Last year. [voutness.

پارسایی Abstemiousness ; de-
پارسنگ Tare : allowance for tare. Counterweight.
پارسی Persian. Parsee. Fire-worshipper. —*a*. Of Fars. Persian [usu. فارسی].
پارک *E*. & *Fr*. Park. — پ. کردن To park.
پارلمان *Fr*. Parliament.
پارلمانی *Fr*. *P*. Parliamentary.
پارو(ب) Snow-shovel. Oar. — پ. زدن To row. — پ. کردن To clean with a shovel.
پاروزن Oarsman; rower.
پاره Piece. Part. Rag; patch. Bribe ○. —*a*. Torn; ragged. — پ. شدن To be torn. To go to pieces. — پ. کردن To tear; rend. To break or cut, as bread. To devour. To wear out : در ششماه دو جفت کفش پ. کرد
پاره آجر Brickbat.
پاره آهن Piece of iron; scrap.
پاره‌پاره Torn to piece ; ragged.
پاره‌دوز Botcher ; patcher.
پاریا [f. Tamil origin] Pariah.
پاریس *Fr*. & *E*. Paris.
پاریسی *Fr*. *P*. Parisian.
پارینه & پارین Last year's. Old.
پارینه سنگی Paleolithic.
پازند *Pazand*: commentary on the زند *q. v.*
پاس Watch (of the night). Guard . — بپاسِ In consideration (*or* recognition) of; in acknowledgment of.
پاسار [*In a door*] Rail.
پاساژ *Fr*. Arcade.
پاساوان *Fr*. Passavant.
پاسبان Policeman. Watchman.
پاسبانی Guardianship; policeman's duty. — پ. کردن To guard. To serve as a policeman.
پاس بخش Relief of sentry.
پاستوریزه *Fr*. Pasteurized.
پاسخ Answer; reply. — پ. دادن To a. or r. — درپاسخِ In r. to.
پاسدار Sentry; picket.
پاسگاه Post of duty; sentry p.
پاسیار Colonel [in the Police Department].
پاش [Imp. of پاشیدن].
پاشا *T*. Pasha; Pacha.
پاشام [Usu. پاشام مغز] Meninges.
پاشاندن + To scatter about.
پاشنه Heel. Trigger. Stern (of a ship) . — پ. را ورکشیدن To take to one's heels. — در روی چه پ. می‌گردد ؟ How does the wind blow? What quarter is the w. in? Which way does the cat jump?
پاشنه بلند High-heeled.
پاشنه ساییده + Down at heel. *F*. Roguishly cunning.
پاشنه‌کش Shoe-horn.
پاشویه Foot-bath. — پ. کردن To give a foot-bath to.
پاشیدن [باش] To sprinkle. To scatter +. — از هم پ. + To be scattered. To break up.
پاشیده [P. P. of پاشیدن]
پا فِشاری Persistence. — پ. کردن

Innocence. Acquittal.— آب پاکی روی دست کسی ریختن To give a flat refusal or a disappointing reply to s. o.
پاکیزگی Cleanliness.
پاکیزه Neat. Clean. Proper.
پاگرد Landing(-place); ramp.
پاگن *R.* سردوشی
پاگیر *or* پایگیر Encumbrance; impediment. Obstruction.
پالا *or* پالای [Imp. of پالودن]
پالان Pack-saddle.— پالان خردجال Penelope's winding-sheet. *See under* خردجال ‖ دجال پالانش کج است She is loose in the hilts; she is a lightskirts ; she is a woman of easy virtue.
پالاندوز Pack-saddle maker.
پالایش Filtration. Refining.
پالایشگاه Refinery.
پالتو *Fr.* (Over)coat ; (great) coat; (top-) coat.
پالگانه ○ = بالکن Balcony.
پالگی Litter. Palanquin.
پالودن [پالا(ی)] To filter. To strain. To refine.
پالوده Filtered. Refined —*n.* Sweet beverage containing thin fibres of starch jelly.
پالونه ○ Colander. Strainer. Filter. *See* صافی
پالهنگ Halter. Bridle. Leash.
پالیز Kitchen-garden. Melon-bed.
پامال etc. = پایمال etc.
پامچال Primrose.
پا ملخ Cylinder escapement. — To persist.
پافنگ *Mil.* Order arms !
پاک Clean. Pure. *F.* Chaste. —*ad.* Absolutely. Entirely. — پ. شدن To be cleaned or purified. To be obliterated. To be settled; as a debt. — پ. کردن To cleanse. To erase; delete. To purge. To settle; clear up. — بینی پ. کردن To blow one's nose. — گل پ. Alumina.
پاک *Fr.* Passover. Easter.
پاکار = دشتبان
پاکباز *a.* Risking all in gambling. Playing fairly.
پاکت Envelope. Paper bag. [f. Fr. *paquet*].
پاکدامن Chaste ; continent.
پاکدامنی Chastity; continence.
پاکدوزی Overcast stitch ; whipstitch.
پاکرو * = خوب رو
پاکرو ○ *-row* Dealing honestly.
پاکزاد Of noble birth.
پاکسرشت Of noble extraction.
پاک طینت *P. A.* Of a pure nature. Well-intentioned.
پاک طینتی *P.A.* Noble disposition. Pure nature.
پاک کن Eraser. Rubber.
پاک نژاد Of a pure race.
پاکنویس Fair copy. — پ. کردن To write fair ; make a f. copy of; also, type f.
پاکی Cleanliness. Purity.

ساعت پ. Watch with a cylinder e.

پاندول *Fr.* Pendulum.

پانزده Fifteen.

پانزدهم Fifteen.

پانزدهمین The fifteenth.

پانسمان *Fr.* Dressing of a wound.

پانسیون *Fr.* Boarding-house.

پانصد Five-hundred.

پانصدم Five-hundredth.

پانما Flesh-coloured : جوراب پ.

پاورقی *P. A.* Serial story; feuilleton.

پای *S. u.* پا & پایستن

پایا Permanent.

پایاب Shallow.

پایاپای Clearing; compensation. Barter. *Cf.* با پیاکردن

پایان End. Conclusion. — به پ. رساندن To bring to an end.— به پ. رسیدن To come to an e.

پایان نامه Thesis.

پای افزار *S. u.* پا افزار

پای انداز = پا انداز

پای بست *S. u.* پا بست

پای بند = • پا بند

پای بوس etc. = پابوس etc.

پایتخت Capital; metropolis.

پایدار Permanent. Constant; faithful. Firm. *Ph.* Stable.

پایداری Stability; durability. Constancy. — پ. کردن To be constant; stand fast.

پایستن ○ [پای] To last (long); be permanent. To be constant •.

پایک Peduncle.

پایگاه *Mil.* Base. *F.* Degree.

پایگیر *S. u.* پاگیر

پایمال Trampled (upon); trodden. *F.* Disregarded. Violated. — پ. کردن To trample upon. To devastate. To suppress; disregard. To violate.

پایمالی Trampling. Suppression. Violation.

پایمردی Assistance. Intercession.

پایمزد (Doctor's) fees; honorarium. [*See* ضامن

پایندان Surety; guarantor.

پاینده Lasting; permanent.

پایوَر Police officer.

پایه Leg (of a chair, etc.). Pillar; pile. Stand; rest; bracket. Pedestal. [*In grafting*] Stock. [*Of a drill*] Drill-stock. *F.* Foundation; basis; grounding. Scale; degree; rank. [*Of a logarithm*] Base.

پایه‌بلند Having tall supports.— مخزن پ. Overhead tank.

پله پله = ○ پایه پایه

پایه‌دار Legged. Provided with a stand, pillar, etc. Graded.

پایی Worked by the feet.

پاییدن [پای] 1) = پایستن 2) To watch; fix one's eyes on.

پائیز *or* پاییز Autumn; fall.

پائیزه Autumnal (product). (Wool) obtained in the autumn.

پائین *ad.* Down. —*a.* Low(er). —*n.* Lower part.— پ. آمدن To come down(stairs). To descend. *F*. To fall, as prices.– پ. آوردن To bring down. To lower. – پ. رفتن To go d. To descend. To sink. To fall. – پ. کردن To drop : put down. To lower. To pull d. – پ. تر Farther d.

پایین تنه 1) Lower part of the body. 2) × Privates.

پائین دست Lower part.–پائین‌دست رودخانه Down the river.

پایین رتبه *P. A.* Junior; of a low grade.

پائینی Lower. Inferior.

پپسین *Fr.* Pepsin.

پپلین *Fr.* Poplin.

پَت Papilla.

پُتک Sledge : smith's hammer.

پتو Blanket.

پته Permit. تهٔ طلب Promissory note. – پتهٔ کسیرا روی آب انداختن To show up s. o.; expose him.

پتی Bare : با پای پ. Barefoot.

پتیاره Quarrelsome; termagant. –*n*. Shrew. [chatter.

پچ پچ + Chatter. – پ. کردن To

پچل × Slatternly.

پَخ Bevel. Chamfer. – پخ دادن To bevel or chamfer.

پُخت (Manner of) cooking or baking. Batch.

پختگی Ripeness. Experience.

پُختن [پَز] To cook. To bake. *F*. To talk into doing s. t. To nourish in the mind. –*vi*. To be cooked or baked. To ripen.

پختنی Culinary.

پُخته [P.P. of پُختن] Cooked. Baked. Ripe. Mellow. Experienced.– پ. کردن To settle (once and for all).

پَخته Metalled, as a road.

پَخ‌دار Beveled; chamfered.

پخش Distribution. Broadcast. Scattering about. –*a*. Scattered a. – پ. کردن To scatter. To distribute. To broadcast.

پخمه + Shiftless. Stupid.

پدال *Fr.* Pedal. – پدالِ گاز *M.* Accelerator.

پدر Father. – پدر کسیرا درآوردن + To serve one out ; give it to him hot.

پدر اندر ○ Step-father.

پدرانه Fatherly ; paternal. –*ad*. In a f. manner.

پدر بزرگ Grandfather.

پدرجد *P. A.* Great grandfather.

پدر زن Father-in-law.

پدرسوخته + Knavish; roguish.

پدر شوهر Father-in-law.

پدرکشی & پدرکش Patricide.

پدروار – **پدرانه**

پدری Fatherhood. –*a*. Paternal.

پدید Visible. – پ. آمدن To come in sight; appear. To happen. To originate. – پ. آوردن To cause to a. or h.

پدیدار Visible. Manifest. – پ.شدن To appear; become v.

پدیده Phenomenon.
پذیر [Imp. of پذیرفتن
پذیرا Accepting. —*n*. Acceptor.
پذیرانیدن To cause to accept. To make acceptable.
پذیرایی Entertainment; reception. — پ. کردن از To entertain or receive. — اطاق پ. Drawing-room.
پذیرش Acceptance. Agrément. Admittance.
پذیرفتار Acceptor.
پذیرُفتن [پذیر] To accept. To admit. To adopt. To listen to.
پذیرُفته [P. P. of پذیرفتن] Accepted.
پذیرنده Acceptor.
پذیره ○ Accepting. Obedience.
پذیره نویسی Subscription.
پَر Feather. — پر درآوردن To be fledge. *F*. To show signs of strength or boldness. — پر ریختن To shed off one's feathers; moult. — پر زدن To flap (the wings); fly. To flutter. — پ. کندن To pluck.— پرِ قو Swan-feather. Eider-down. — پرِ کلاه Plume (in a hat). — پرِ نرم Down.
پَر [Imp. of پریدن]
پِر etc. *S. u.* فِر etc.
پُر Full: پر از آب f. of water; filled with water. ‖ Loaded; charged. —*ad*. Too (much).— پر خوردن To eat too m.; overeat (oneself). —پر کردن To fill. To load, as a gun. To stop, as a tooth. To poison the mind of; infect with an opinion +. — ماه امشب پر میشود The moon fulls to-night.
پرآب Juicy.
پرآب و تاب Grandiloquent; bombastic; high-flown.
پرآشوب Confused; turbulent.
پرافتخار *P. A*. Glorious; honourable.
پراکندگی State of being scattered. Dispersion.
پراکندن [پراکن ○] To scatter; disperse. To broadcast.
پراکنده [P. P. of پراکندن] Scattered. Dispersed. *F*. Disturbed. Scanty. — پ. شدن To be scattered.— پ. کردن To scatter.
پراکنده حال *P. A*. = پریشان‌حال
پراکنش Dispersion.
پَران [Imp. of پراندن]
پَرّان Flying; on the wing.
پرانطز *Fr*. Parentheses *or* -sis; bracket(s).
پراندن & پرانیدن [پران] To cause to fly. To blow out. *F*. To blunder out; blurt.
پربار Laden with fruit. Prolific.
پُربرگ Many-leaved; multifoliate.
پُربسامد *Ph*. High-frequency.
پربلا *P. A*. Calamitous. Fateful.
پُرپَر Double; many-leaved.
پَرپَر زدن To flutter; hover.
پِرپِری 1) = فرفری 2) Thin; flimsy.

پرتو نگار Radiographer.
پرتو نگاری Radiography.
پرتوه Ray.
پرتوی *Bot*. Radiant.
پُرجثه *P. A.* Huge; bulky.
پرجرأت *P. A.* Courageous.
پرجمعیت *P. A.* Thickly populated; populous.
پَرچ Rivetting; rivet. — پ. کردن To rivet. To clench. — میخ پ. Rivet.
پرچانه = پرگو & پرحرف
پَرچم Flag. *Bot*. Stamen. — خدمت زیر پ. Military service.
پرچم دار Standard-bearer. *F*. Leader; pioneer.
پرچمی Flag-like o. *Bot*. Staminal. — پارچهٔ پ. Bunting.
پَرچین Fence; hedge. Paling. —*a*. Riveted; bent. — پ. کردن To rivet. To clinch. To enclose with a fence or h.
پُرچین Full of curls; curly. F. of wrinkles. Puckered.
پرحادثه *P. A.* Eventful; adventurous.
پرحرف *P. A.* = پرگو & وراج
پرحرفی *P. A.* = پرگویی
پَرخاش Quarrel. — پ. کردن To q.
پرخاش‌جو Quarrelsome.
پُرخرج *P.A.* Costly; expensive.
پرخطر *P. A.* = خطرناك
پُرخور Gluttonous.
پرخوری Gluttony.
پَرداخت Payment. Polish(ing). — پ. کردن To pay. To give a

پُرپشت Luxuriant; lush; exuberant.
پَرت Flung; thrown down. Outlying; straggling. Out-of-the-way. Deviated (from the main subject); digressed. — پ. شدن To be thrown; fall down. To digress; deviate from the main s. — پ. کردن To throw; hurl To cause to digress. — پ. گفتن To talk nonsense. — از حساب پ. Out in one's reckoning. — ازموضوع پ. Wide of the subject; off the track. *S. a.* مرحله ‖ + پ و پلا Scattered about. —*n*. Nonsense; irrelevant talk.
پرتاب Hurled. Shot. —*n*. Hurling. — پرتاب وزنه Putting the shot. — پ. کردن To fling; throw. To shoot.
پرت سعید *Geog*. Port Said.
پرتقال Portugal. Orange.
پرتقالی Orange. Portugese.
پرتکل *Fr*. Protocol.
پرتگاه Cliff; precipice. F. Abyss
پرتو Ray(s). — پ. افکندن To radiate. — پرتومجهول X-rays. — معالجه با پرتو مجهول Radiotherapy; treatment by X-rays. — در پرتو حمایتِ Under the protection or auspices of.
پرتوافگن Radiant. —*n*. Projector.
پرتو افگنی Radiation.
پرتو بینی Radioscopy.
پرتو شناس Radiologist.
پرتو شناسی Radiology.

finish to. — قابل پ. Payable.— مأمور پرداخت Paymaster. — سرمایهٔ پ. شده Paid-in capital.
پرداخت‌گر Polisher; furbisher.
پرداختن [پرداز] To pay; settle. To polish; furbish. To give a finish to. To proceed. — اکنون بپردازیم به . . . Let us now turn to. . . . — از کاری پ. To get through a business*.
پرداختنی Payable. Due; mature.
پرداخته [P. P. of پرداختن] Paid. Polished . Accomplished Cleared.
پردار Winged; flying : ماهیِ پ.
پرداز 1) [Imp. of پرداختن]. 2) Stump [as used in drawing].
پردگی Chaste and secluded woman ; odalisque ০. *Z.* Pupa ; nymph.
پُردل Courageous.
پردوام *P. A.* = **بادوام**
پَرده Curtain. Screen. Veil. Mantle. Membrane. Layer ; coating. Film. Act (*division of a play*). Painting; tableau. *Mus.* 1) Note. 2) Scale. 3) Fret. *F.* Reserve. Modesty. — پردهٔ دل Pericardium. Midriff ; diaphragm. — پردهٔ صماخ Tympanum of the ear. *See* صماخ ‖ پردهٔ عنبی Iris of the eye. — پردهٔ عنکبوت Cobweb. — پ. از روی کار برداشتن To divulge a secret ; unveil a matter. — پ. برکسی دریدن * To disgrace s. o. by divulging his secrets. — پارچهٔ پرده ای Drapery. [statue , etc.
پرده برداری Unveiling a
پرده پال Hymenopterous.
پرده پوشی Glossing over a fault. Keeping a secret.
پرده دار Chamberlain. Doorkeeper. —*a*. Webbed.
پرده دَری Betrayal of secrets.
پُر رنگ Richly coloured. Strong : چای پ.
پُر رو Cheeky or saucy: بچهٔ پ.
پُرروئی Cheekiness. — پ. کردن To be cheeky. To brazen it out.
پُرز Villosity. Nap; pile.
پُرزا Multiparous; prolific.
پُرزور Powerful. Violent.
پرزحمت *P. A.* Laborious.
پُرس [Imp. of پرسیدن]
پُرس *R.* Helping.
پرست [Imp. of پرستیدن]
پرستار Nurse. Baby-sitter.
پرستارخانه Infirmary.
پرستاری Nursing. Attendance.— پ. کردن To nurse; attend.
پرستش Worship. — پ. کردن To w.
پرستش‌گاه House of worship.
پرستنده [پرستندگان] Worshipper.
پرستو(ک) Swallow.
پرستیدن [پرست] To worship. To adore. [To q. or ask.
پُرسش Question. — پ. کردن از
پرسش نامه Questionnaire.

پُرسنل *Fr.* = کارکنان Personnel; staff.

پرسه‌زدن + To prowl or moon; [hang round.

پرِ سیاوش Maidenhair; adianthum.

پُرسیدن [پرس] To ask: ازاو بپرسید Ask him. — پرسان‌پرسان Always asking (one's way).

پَرش Jumping; leap. Flight. — پرش به ارتفاع High jump. — پرش بطول Long or broad j.

پرشگاه Take-off.

پُرصدا Noisy. Sonorous.

پرطاقت *P. A* Hardy. Patient.

پر طاوسی Chatoyant; shot; pavonine. — گل پ. Broom.

پرطمع *P. A.* = طماع

پرفایده *P. A.* = پرمنفعت

پر فتوح *P. A.* Bestowed with God's grace [only in پ ‍دوح].

پرفشار High-pressure. High-tension.

پرك Fin. *OS.* Small feather. — پرك هندی (Seeds of) *Butea frondosa.*

پُرکار Elaborate. Durable.

پَرکنده Plucked: مرغ پ.

پَرگار (Pair of) compasses. — پرگار بازودار Beam-compass. — پرگار تقسیم Dividers.

پَرگرد ○ Paragraph. Section.

پُرگو Talkative; loquacious.

پرگویی Talkativeness.

پرمایه Strong, as tea. Rich. Pithy. [Loquacious.

پرمدعا *P. A.* Pretentious.

پرمشت ○ Decoy(-bird).

پرمعنی *P. A.* Full of meaning; pithy; significant.

پرمغز Pithy. [profitable.

پرمنفعت *P. A.* Lucrative;

پرمنگنات *Fr.* Permanganate.

پُرمو Hairy; shaggy.

پرند * Plain or painted silk.

پرنده [پرندگان] Bird [مرغ]. — *a.* Flying. — بشقاب پ. F. saucer.

پرنده شناس Ornithologist.

پرنده شناسی Ornithology.

پرنیان * Shot silk.

پرو *R.* (*prov*) Fitting(on). — پ. کردن To have *or* give a fitting; fit (*or* try) on.

پروا Care. Fear. Concern. — پ. داشتن To be concerned or anxious. To fear.

پَروار Fattened (animal).

پرواری Stall-fed; fattened.

پَرواز Flight. — پ. کردن To fly. [*Of a plane*] To take off. — قابل پ. Airworthy.

پرواز خوبی Aerobatics.

پرواس ○ Feel; touch.

پروانه Butterfly. Moth. Licence; permit. *M.* 1) Fan (of a radiator). 2) Propeller. 3) Governor.

پروبال Plumage. — پ. درآوردن To fledge. *F.* To grow strong or bold; also, go too far.

پروپا + Foundation. — پروپایی ندارد It is unfounded.

پروپاقرص + *P. A.* Firm;

پُرهنر Skilled in arts; ingenious.

پرهیختن ○ [پرهیز] = پرهیز کردن

پرهیز Abstinence. Austerity. Regimen; diet. — پ. داشتن To be on d. — پ. کردن To abstain; keep away.

پرهیزکار or پرهیزگار Abstemious. Virtuous. Chaste.

پرهیزگاری Abstemiousness. Virtuousness. Continence.

پَری Fairy. *Fem. pr. name.*

پُری Fullness.

پری پیکر * Delicate in body, as a fairy.

پریچهر Fairy-faced. *Fem. pr. [name.*

پریدخت *Fem. pr. name.* *OS.* Fairy's daughter.

پَریدن [پَر] To fly. To jump. *F.* To pass away suddenly.

پریرو or پریرُخ Fairy-faced; beautiful. *Cf.* پریچهر

پریروز Day before yesterday.

پریز *Fr.* Wall-plug; point.

پریزاد Fairy(-born).

پریشان = * پریش

پری شاهرخ Oriole.

پریشان Distressed. Distracted. Disturbed. Dishevelled. — پ. کردن To dishevel. To distress. To agitate. — پ. گفتن To speak incoherently.

پریشان حال *P.A.* & پریشانروزگار Distressed. [condition.

پریشان حالی *P. A.* Distressed

پریشانی Distress. (Mental) dis-

confimed. Regular مشتری پ.

پروتست *Fr.* = واخواهی

پروتستان *Fr.* Protestant.

پرور [Imp. of پروردن]

پروردن = پروراندن

پَروردگار Providence; God. *OS.* The Nourisher.

پَروردن [پرور] To foster; rear; cherish. To develop. To preserve in sugar.

پرورده [P. P. of پروردن]. — زنجبیل پ. Preserved ginger.

پَرورِش Nourishment; nurture. Training. — پ. دادن To train. To foster; cherish. To develop. — پ. یافتن To be trained or fostered.

پرورشگاه Nursery. Crèche. — پرورشگاه یتیمان Orphan asylum; orphanage. — پرورشگاه آزادی Nurse of freedom.

پَروَزن *P. A.* Feather-weight.

پروژکتور *Fr.* Projector.

پروژه *Fr.* = طرح Project.

پروس *Fr.* Prussia.

پروفسور *Fr.* Professor [استاد].

پروَنده File; dossier. *By e.* Case

پرونده سازی Frame-up.

پرویز *Mas. pr. name.*

پرویزَن ○ = الك & غربال

پرویزنی Ethmoid : استخوان پ.

پروین Pleiades. *Fem. pr. name.*

پَرّه Paddle. Blade. Sail (of a windmill). Spoke (of a wheel). Wing (of the nose).

turbance; agitation.
پریشب Night before last.
پریموس *Fr.* Primus (stove).
پریوَش Fairy-like. *Fem. pr. name.*
پَز [Imp. of پختن]
پُز *Fr.* Posture. — پز دادن To show off. To strike an attitude. — پز عالی جیب خالی Great boast little toast.
پزا Not tough; easily cooked.
پزشک Physician; doctor.
پزشک خانه Dispensary.
پزشکی Medical profession. —*a.* Medical.
پزشک یار Medical assistant.
پزنده (One) who cooks or bakes
پژمان ○ Dejected.
پژمردگی Withered state. Dejection.
پژمردن To fade; wither.
پژمرده Faded; withered. Pale. *F.* Sad; dejected.
پژوه [Imp. of پژوهیدن]
پژوهش Search; investigation. Appeal.
پژوهش خواسته Object of appeal.
پژوهش خوانده Appellee ; respondent.
پژوهش خواه Appellant.
پژوهیدن [پژوه] To search ; investigate. To inquire.
پُژه Moss.
پَس *ad.* Then. So. Afterwards. Behind. —*n.* Back (part). — ازپس... برآمدن To come back. — پس آمدن + کسی برآمدن To cope with s. o.; manage s. o. — پس آوردن To bring back (for resale to the seller). — پس از After. — پس از این A. this; hereafter. — پس از آن Afterwards ; thereafter. — پس از آنکه او رفت After (*or* when) he had gone. — ازاین پس Hereafter. — پس افتادن To fall behind. To f. in arrears. — پس انداختن To delay the payment of. To postpone. To give birth to X. — پس دادن To give back ; return. To refund. To recite, as a lesson. — آب پس دادن To leak. — پس رفتن To go b. To get out of the way. To decline. — پس زدن To draw b. To flow b. To displace. — پس گرفتن To take b. ; retake. To retract. To buy back. — حرف خودرا پس گرفتن To go b. on one's word; r. one's w. ; also, eat one's words. — پس نشستن To recoil. To retreat.
پساب Weakest water. Hog-wash.
پسادست Credit transaction.
پس افت Back rent.
پس افتاده Arreared; in arrears; outstanding.
پس انداز Savings. — پ. کردن To save.
پس اندازی Saving.
پس پریروز Three days ago.
پَست Low. Mean. Humble. Of inferior quality. — پ. باد Down with ! — پ. کردن To

lower. To weaken.

پُست *Fr.* Post; mail. P. (of duty). — با اولین پست (آینده) By next m.; by return of post. — فراش پ. Postman. — به پ. دادن To post or mail. — پول پ. Postage.

پستا 1) = نوبت 2) Preparation.

پستائی Prepared; kept as reserve. Cut out: tailor's word.

پِستان Breast. [*Of a cow*] Udder. — غدهٔ پ. Mammary gland. — نوك پ. Nipple.

پستان بند Brassière. [Mammal.

پستاندار Mammiferous. —*n.*

پستانک Nipple.

پستچی *Fr. T.* Postman. Member of the Post Office.

پستخانه *Fr. P.* Post Office.

پَست فطرت *P. A.* Mean; base.

پست فطرتی *P. A.* Meanness.

پست قد Short; dwarfish.

پَستو Closet. Back part of a shop.

پِسته Pistachio. — پستهٔ زمینی Peanut.

پَستی Meanness. Lowness. — پستی و بلندی روزگار Ups and downs.

پُستی *Fr. P.* Postal.

پس درد Afterpains.

پس دوزی Overcast stitch on the wrong side of a cloth.

پِسر Son. Boy. Baby boy.

پسر بچه Boy.

پسر خاله *P. A.* Cousin: son of a maternal aunt.

پسر خوانده Adopted son.

پسر دایی Cousin: son of a maternal uncle.

پسرعمو *or* **پسرعم** *P. A.* Cousin: son of a paternal uncle.

پسرعمه *P. A.* Cousin: son of a paternal aunt.

پَسرو Retrograde.

پس فردا Day after to-morrow.

پس قراول *P. T.* Rearguard.

پس کرایه *P. A.* Balance of freight (paid on taking delivery of goods).

پس کوچه By-lane; by-road.

پس گردنی + Slap on the neck.

پسله + Behind one's back; on the sly; underhand.

پس مانده Refuse; leavings; residue.

پَسند 1) Selection. Admiration. Approval. — پ. آمدن To be admired or selected. To please. — پ. کردن To select. To admire. 2) [Imp. of پسندیدن]

پسندیدن [پسند] To admire. To select; choose.

پسندیده Praiseworthy; acceptable; admirable. Pleasing.

پس و پیش Back and forth; to and fro. — پ. کردن To change the places of. To adjust.

پس وَند Suffix.

پسین Last. Latest. Posterior.

پسین فردا + Three days hence. *Cf.* پس فردا

پُشت Back. B. part. [*Of a cloth*] Wrong side. [*Of leather*] Flesh (side). *F.* Support. Continuation. Generation. — پشتِ Behind ; at the b. of. — پشت بام House-top ; flat roof. — پ. بدیوار With one's back against the wall. — پشت پا Instep. — پشتِ پا زدن به To recalcitrate against (*or* at). To trip (up). — پشت سکه Verso ; reverse of a coin. — پشت سرِ Behind. In the absence of. — پشت سر کسی حرف زدن To backbite s. o. — پشتِ گردن Nape of the neck. — پشت خود را بستن To feather one's nest. — پ. کردن To turn one's b. To repose *. — بخت بما پشت کرده است. We are down on our luck. — پشت هم انداختن To pack, as cards. *—vi.* + To shoot a line.

پشت‌بند Fastening; brace; clamp. [In railways] Fish-plate. *F* + Continuation; sequel.

پشت پوش Opaque. [to g.

پشت در پشت From generation

پشت درد Backache.

پشت شیشه‌ای *or* **پشتِ دری** Half net curtain.

پشت رو Turned inside out. — پ. کردن To turn i. out.

پشتک Somersault. — پ. زدن To turn a s.

پشتِ کار Perseverance.

پشت کاردار Perseverant.

پشت‌گرمی Assurance. Encouragement. Support.

پشتِ گلی Light red.

پشتِ گوش فراخ Neglectful ; nonchalant.

پشت مازه *or* **پشت مازو** Fillet; undercut; also, chine.

پشتِ میزنشین + White-collar.

نشت نویس Endorsed. *—n.* Endorser.

پشت نویسی Endorsement. — پ. کردن To endorse; back.

پشتواره Knapsack. [bullion.

پشتوانه Cover (for banknotes);

پشته Mound; eminence.

پشتِ هم انداز Charlatan. Blusterer.

پشتی Cushion (for the back). *F.* + Support. — پ. کردن To support ; back ; give a knee to. *See* پشتیبانی

پشتیبان Supporter. Buttress. Pillar. [*In football*] Back.

پشتیبانی Support. — پ. کردن To support or back. To second. To assist.

پشکِ Lot. — پ. انداختن To cast lots.

پشکل Orbicular dung.

پشم Wool. Fleece. — پ. چیدن To shear (a sheep). — کلاهش پشم ندارد He is a mere figurehead; he is feared by none. — پشمش بدان ×To hell (*or* heck) with it ; take it easy.

پشمالو(د) Shaggy; woolly.

پشم چینی Sheep-shearing.

پشم ریسی Wool-spinning.

پشمک *Kind of sweets.*

پشمین *or* **پشمی** Woollen.

پشمینه Woollen (garment).
پشه Gnat. Mosquito.— پشهٔ خاکی Sandfly.— پشه را در هوا نعل کردن To break fly on wheel.
پشه بند Mosquito-net.
پشه پران Fly-net; fly-flap.
پشه خوار Goatsucker; fern-owl.
پشیز Copper or nickel coinage.
پشیمان Sorry; regretful; penitent; remorseful. — پ. شدن To repent; regret; rue (it).
پشیمانی Regret; remorse.
پطر کبیر *G A*. Peter the Great.
پفک Pea-shooter. Puff (paste).
پُف کردن To blow out To puff (up); inflate.
پفیوز × Sullen. Good-for-nothing.
پُک Puff; draught. — پك بچپق زدن To puff a pipe.
پکر + Gloomy; disappointed.— پ. شدن To be d.; pull a long face.
پکیدن + [پك] = ترکیدن
پگاه ○ = سپیده دم
پُل Bridge. [In trousers, etc.] Loop; keeper. — پل دره ای Viaduct. — پل دماغ Pons varolii.— پل کشتی Deck.— پل متحرك Drawbridge. — پل معلق Suspension bridge.— روی رودخانه ای پ. زدن To b. a river; construct a b. over it.
پلاتین or پلاطین *Fr*. Platinum. *M*. Contact point.
پلاس Sackcloth.— درجائی پ. شدن + To outstay one's welcome; plant oneself in a place.
پلاسیدن = پژمرده شدن
پلاسیده = پژمرده
پلاک *Fr*. Plate; plaque; tag.
پلخنگ Aqueduct.
پل سازی Construction of [bridges.
پلشت بر Antiseptic.
پلک Eye-lid.
پلکی Palpebral.
پلکیدن × To scratch along. To hang around.
پلکان [Pl. of پله] Stairs; steps. [Staircase.
پلمب *Fr*. (*plomb*) Lead seal.— پ. کردن To s.; stamp or plumb with lead.
پلمه ○ Slate.
پلمه سنگ Schist.
پلنگ Leopard. — پلنگ ماده Leopardess.
پلو *T*. Pilaw: dish of rice, chopped meat, vegetables, and spices.
پله Stair; step. Round of a ladder. *F*. Degree. Stage. *Cf. the pl.* پلکان
پله پله By degrees; step by s.— پ. رفتن To ricochet.
پلید * Unclean. — پ. کردن To defile.
پلیدی Uncleanness. Abomination.
پُلیس *Fr*. Police(man).
پلی کپی کردن *Fr. P*. To duplicate; stencil; manifold.
پناه Shelter. Refuge; asylum. *F*. Protection. — بچیزی پ. بردن

To take (*or* seek) refuge in s t. — پ. برخدا *See* اعوذبالله *and* استغفرالله ‖ در پناه Under the protection (*or* cover) of.

پناه‌گاه Refuge; shelter; asylum.

پناهنده Refugee. — پ. شدن To seek refuge. To resort.

پنبه Cotton. C.-wool. — پنبهٔ روی Zinc oxide; flowers of zinc.— پنبه فرنگی Sterilized cotton.— پنبهٔ ناسوز Asbestos.— پنبهٔ هیدروفیل Absorbent cotton-wool — پ. در گوش گذاشتن To turn a deaf ear (to s. o.).

پنبه آب Whitewash.

پنبه ای (Made of) cotton. Resembling c. *F*. Soft; mild.

پنبه پاك كن Cotton-gin. Willow(ing-machine).

پنبه دانه Cotton-seed. [blower.

پنبه زن Cotton-beater; c.

پنج Five.

پنج *or* **فنج** *H-P*. Punch

پنج انگشت Five-leaved chaste-tree.

پنجاه Fifty.

پنجاهم Fiftieth.

پنجاهمین The fiftieth.

پنج برگ Cinquefoil; five-leaved.

پنج پر 1) = پنج برگ 2) Pentapetalous.

پنج پهلو Pentagon(al).

پنج تیر Five-loader; five-cartridge magazine rifle.

پنجره Window. Grating.

پنج سطحی *P. A.* = پنج وجهی

پنج شنبه Thursday.

پنج ضلعی *P. A.* = **پنج پهلو**

پنجگانه (The) five . . .

پنجگی Toe-cap.

پنج گوش *or* **پنج گوشه** Five-angled; pentagonal. —*n*. Pentagon.

پنجم Fifth.

پنجمی (The) fifth.

پنجمین The fifth.

پنج وجهی *P. A.* Pentahedral.— جسم پ. Pentahedron.

پنجول زدن + To scratch.

پنجه The hand; the five fingers. Claw; paw. Cross-arm.— پ. انداختن To gripe.— دست و پنجه نرم کردن To break a lance; cross swords.

پنجه‌ای Palmate; digitate.

پنجه بوکس *P E* Knuckle-duster. *See* بوکس

پنجه کلاغ Wild bryony; wild grape.

پنجه‌گرگی Lycopodium; wolf's-claw; clubmoss.

پنجه مریم *P. A.* Cyclamen.

پنج یك Fifth part.

پند Counsel; piece of advice. Maxim. — پ. گرفتن To take counsel. — پندی بصدتومان Good a. beyond all price.

پندار 1) Thought. Imagination. Self-conceit. 2) *Imp.* of پنداشتن [imagine.

پنداشتن [پندار] To suppose;

پَنس *Fr*. Forceps ; pincers. Hairpin.
پِنس *E*. Pence.
پنکه *H*. Punka(h); fan.
پنهان Hidden; secret. — پ. شدن To hide (oneself). — پ کردن or پ. داشتن To h.; conceal.
پنهانی Concealment.
پنیر Cheese. — کرم پ. C.-mite.
پنیر تراش Grater.
پنیرك Fairy-cheeses.
پنیرکی Malvaceous. — پنیر کیان *npl*. The Malvaceae.
پنیر مایه Rennet.
پنی‌سیلین *Fr*. Penicillin.
پو or پوی [Imp. of پوییدن]
پوت *S. u.* پود
پوتین Boot [f. Fr. *bottine*].
پوچ Vain ; futile. Empty ; hollow. Blank. Null; void.— پ. کشیدن To draw a blank.
پود Woof; weft. *Cf*. تار
پود or پوت *R*. Pood.
پودر *Fr*. Powder. *Cf*. گرد
پودردان *Fr*. *P*. Vanity(-box) ; compact. Puff-box.
پودنه or پونه Pennyroyal.
پور = پسر Son.
پوره *Fr*. Purée ; mash. — پورهٔ سیب زمینی Mashed potatoes.
پوز or پوزه Snout.
پوز بند or پوزه بند Muzzle.
پوزخند [Derogatory for لبخند]
پوزش Apology ; excuse. *Cf*. عذر ‖ پ. خواستن To offer an apology ; apologize.
پوزش پذیر Forgiving *a*.
پوساندن or پوسانیدن To cause to decay or rot. To wear out.
پوست Skin. Hide. Rind. Hull. Peel. Shell. Crust. Bark. Parchment. — پ. انداختن To moult. *F*. To have a hard time of it.— پ. بستن To skin over; scab.— پ. کندن To peel To strip of the bark. To flay. To husk. *F*. To fleece. To punish severely. — پوست بخارا Astrakhan. — پوست خام Raw hide; pelt.— پوست زخم Scab.— پوست سر Scalp. — پوست کنه‌کنه Peruvian bark. — پوست مار Slough (of a snake). — پ. و استخوان Skinny; bare-bone. — از خوشی در پوست نمی‌گنجید He could not contain himself for joy; he seemed to tread on air.
پوست تراش Hide-dresser.
پوست رفته Galled ; chafed ; raw; excoriated.
پوست فروش Peltmonger; furrier.
پوست فروشی Furriery.
پوستک (Small) pelt. Cuticle.
پوست کلفت Thick-skinned ; pachydermous. *F*. Impassive.
پوست کلفتی Impassiveness ; insensibility.
پوست کن Flayer. Fleecer.
پوست کنده Peeled ; shelled. Flayed. *F*. + Frank(ly).
پوسته Crust. Scale. Pellicle. —

پ. پ. شدن To s. To exfoliate ; fall away in flakes.

پوستی Made of, or like, skin. — کاغذ پ. Parchment paper.

پوستین Fur cloak ; pelisse. — در پوستین کسی افتادن * To backbite s. o.

پوسیدگی Decay. Rottenness. — پوسیدگی استخوان Caries.

پوسیدن [پوس] To decay; rot. To wear out.

پوسیده [P. P. of پوسیدن] Decayed. Rotten. Putrefied. Worn out. Flimsy; undurable. Carious.

پوش 1) *Imp. of* پوشیدن 2) Tarpaulin. [stuff.

پوشاک Clothing ; wearing

پوشال Stuffing or packing (material); straw; dunnage.

پوشالی Made of straw or dunnage. *F.* Fragile; flimsy. — دولت پ. Puppet government ; g. of s.

پوشاندن *or* **پوشانیدن** [پوشان] To cause to wear ; clothe. To cover. To conceal.

پوشش Covering. Mantle.

پوشنده Wearer. Concealer.

پوشه Folder ; flat file.

پوشیدن [پوش]. To wear. To put on. To cover; conceal.

پوشیده [P.P. of پوشیدن]Covered. Concealed. Clothed. Secret ; occult. — پ. داشتن To keep secret; conceal.

پوشینه Capsule.

پوطاس *Fr.* Potash.

پوطاسیوم *Fr.* Potassium.

پوک Hollow. Deaf, as a nut. — پ. کردن To hollow. To cave.

پوکه Cartridge-shell; cartridge-case. — پوکهٔ زغال سنگ Coke.

پول Money. — پول چای Tip ; drink-money. — پول کاغذ Paper m. — پولش‌را باید بدهید You must pay for it.

پولاد *or* **فولاد** Steel.

پولادگر Steel manufacturer.

پولادسازی Steel manufacture. [For کارخانهٔ پ.] S.-works.

پولادی *or* **پولادین** (Made of) steel. *F.* Hard; irresistible.

پولدار Wealthy : آدم پ.

پولک Sequin; spangle. Fish-scale. Disc. Washer. Confetti. — پولك فنری Lock washer; spring w.

پولکی + Venal : آدم پ.

پولوور *E.* (*-lover*) Pull-over.

پولی Monetary. Pecuniary. Purchasable.

پوماد *Fr.* Pomade; pomatum; ointment. *Cf.* مرهم

پوند *E.* (*pond*) Pound ; sterling

پونز *Fr.* Drawing-pin.

پونط *R.* Point: حروف ۸ پ. 8-point type.

پونه *S. u.* پودنه

پویا Searching. — پ. شدن To search; run (after).

پوینده Searcher. [run for s.

پوییدن [پوی] To search. To

پَه Fie! Phew! Fudge!
پَهلو Side. Flank.— پ. به پ. S. by s. — (در) پهلوی . . . نشستن To sit by the side of . . . — از پهلوی کسی رد شدن To go past s. o. — پ. زدن به * To emulate. — پ. گرفتن To berth, as a ship.
پهلوان Hero; champion. Athlete. —*a*. Very strong. Heroic.
پهلوانانه Like a champion. Heroically.
پهلوان پنبه Cardboard cavalier; man of straw.
پهلوان کچل Punchinello. — نمایش پ. Punch and Judy show.
پهلوانی Athletic strength or game. —*a*. Athletic. Heroic.
پهلوشکن o Flanking (party).
پهلوی Pahlavi language. P. dynasty. *Name of a gold coin*. [Lateral.
پهلویی Next; situated next.
پهله = **بهله**
پَهن Wide; broad. Flat. — پ.شدن To widen or flatten *vi*. *F*. To spread; get about. [*Of colour*] To run. — پ. کردن To s. To f. or widen *vt*.
پِهِن (*pehen*) Dung. — پ. پا زدن To hang about; twiddle one's thumbs.
پهنا Width; breadth. Expanse.
پهناوَر Extensive; wide.
پهنك Tape. *Bot*. Limb.
پهنه Area. Race ground o.
پهنی Width; breadth.
پی (*pey*) Nerve. Sinew. Heel. Foot. *F*. Track; trace. Foundation; groundwork. — پی بردن به To trace. To penetrate into. To realize. — پی ریختن To lay the f. — پی کردن To pursue.— پیِ . . . . راگرفتن To pursue or follow . . . To apply oneself assiduously to. — پی گم کردن To lose the track. — پی بگر به گم کردن To lead s. o. off the track; mislead him.— پی کسی فرستادن To send for s. o.— درپیِ After; on the track of.— (در) پی چیزی گشتن To look for s. t.; search after it.
پی (*pi:*) *Fr*. Pi. (*Math.*)
پی در پی = **پیاپی**
پیاده On foot. — *n*. Pedestrian. [*At chess*] Pawn. — سرباز پیاده Infantryman. — پ. شدن To dismount; alight. To land. To disembark. To get off.— پ. شو باهم راه برویم Come off the high horse. — پ. کردن To l. To unship. To put down; drop : راننده کجا شمارا پیاده کرد ‖ To dismantle. To lay down, as the plan of a building.
پیاده پا On foot. — سرباز پیاده پا Foot-soldier. [footpath.
پیاده‌رو Pavement; sidewalk;

پیاده نظام *P. A.* Infantry. — سرباز پ. I.-man; foot-soldier.
پیاز Onion. Bulb. — پیاز مغز Medulla oblongata.
پیازچه Spring onion. [Goblet.
پیاله [f. G. origin] Cup. Bowl.
پیامبر *See* **پیمبر** & **پیغمبر**
پی بر Horse winning any other prize than the first; placed horse.
پی بندی Underpinning. — پ. کردن To underpin (a wall).
پیپ *Fr.* Pipe.
پیت Large tin.
پیجامه *E-P.* Pyjamah(s).
پی جویی Search. — پ. کردن To s.
پیچ Twist; turn. Curl. Curve. Involution. Twining plant; vine. Screw. Bolt. ‖ *Mus.* Peg or pin [also پیچ کوك] *See* گوشك or گوشی ‖ *F.* Complication; intricacy. — پیچ امین‌الدوله Honeysuckle. — پیچ درِ بشکه Bung. — پیچِ سر بطری Cork-screw. — پیچ شبدر Dodder. — پیچ لامپا Wick-winder. — پیچ‌وخم Meanders. — پ. ومهره. Bolt and nut. — پ. خوردن To turn (the corner). — از چپ پ. میخورد It screws to the left. — پ. دادن To twist. To wind. To turn. To screw.
پیچ [Imp. of پیچیدن].
پیچاپیچ Meandrous. Winding. Spiral. Intricate.
پیچازی Plaid; checkered.
پیچان 1) Winding; twisting. 2) [*Imp. of* پیچاندن].
پیچاندن or **پیچانیدن** To twist. To wind. To distort.
پیچاپیچ = **پیچ پیچ** [Strain.
پیچ خوردگی Contortion. Twist.
پیچ خورده Contorted. Twisted. Strained. [Complicated.
پیچدار Twisted. Screwed. *F.*
پیچ درپیچ * Intricate; complicated.
پیچش Gripes; tenesmus.
پیچک Bobbin. Ivy. Bindweed. Tendril. Scroll; volute.
پیچ و تاب Kinks and twists. Curls and plaits.
پیچ و دنده Endless screw.
پیچه Black veil used by Moslem women wishing to cover their faces from men's views. — پ زدن To put on a veil; cover one's face.
پیچیدگی Contortion; twist. Warp. *F.* Knottiness; intricacy
پیچیدن [پیچ] To wind. To wrap. To twist. To roll up. To set, as the hair. To coil To compound or fill ; نسخه پ. ‖ To turn. To turn the corner. — بخود پیچیدن To struggle; show signs of uneasiness.
پیچیده [P. P. of پیچیدن] Wrapped. Rolled. Twisted. Crooked. *F.* Intricate; complex; knotty; abstruse.

پیخال ○ Fecal matter.
پیخاله Fecaloid.
پیدا Visible ; apparent. Evident. — پ. شدن To be found. To become visible.—پ. کردن To find. To earn. —عاقبت پیداش شد + He turned up at last.
پیدازا Phanerogamous. — گیاه پ. Phanerogam. [genesis.
پیدایش Coming into existence;
پی درپی Successive(ly). Continuous(ly).
پیر Old; aged. —*n*. O. person. Nestor; wise, old counsellor. Spiritual guide ; saint. — پ. شدن To grow old.
پیرا *or* پیرای [Imp. of پیراستن].
پیرارسال Year before last.
پیراستن [(ی)پیرا] To trim (off); dress up. Also, to decorate.
پیراسته Trimmed. Decorated.
پیرامون Perimeter. Skirt. Environs. — درپیرامونِ *or* پیرامونِ About; on the subject of. — در پیرامون چیزی گشتن To search for (*or* after) s.t. *F*. To seek to do a thing ; also, approach it.
پیرانه سَر (In) old age ○.
پیراهن Shirt. — پیراهن خواب Night shirt; n. gown.— پیراهن عثمان کردن To make capital, or a faked evidence, of — پ. قبا کردن * To rend one's s.
پیراهن دوز Shirt-maker.
پیراهنی Shirting.
پیرایش 1) Trimming. 2)آرایش
پیرایه Ornament; decoration.— بچیزی پ. بستن To ornament or embellish s. t.
پیر زن Old woman.
پیر سـ. داری Bean-capers.
پیر مرد Old man.
پیرو Follower; disciple.
پیروز Victorious.— پ شدن بر To gain a victory over; defeat.
پیروزمند Victorious.
فیروزه = پیروزه
پیروزی Victory. — پ. یافتن To gain a victory.
پیرَوی (Act of) following. — پ.کردن To follow; [*with* از] go by; observe.
پیره زن *C. E.* = پیرزن
پیرهن etc. = پیراهن etc.
پیری Old age.
پیریزی Foundation work. — پ.کردن To lay the f. (of).
پیزُر Rush. Padding; dunnage.— پ. لای پالان کسی گذاشتن To load (*or* stuff) s. o. with flattery.
پیزُری +Rushy. Flimsy; frail.
پیس *Fr*. = نمایش نامه
پی‌سپر *or* پی‌سپار * Travelling; proceeding on a journey.
پیستون *Fr*. Piston. *Cf*. سنبه
پیسه *or* پیسی Alphosis. Leprosy. Spot. —پ.سر کسی در آوردن ×To give s. o. a hard time; ballyrag s. o.
پیش *n*. Front. Presence. —*ad*. Forward ; ahead. Before ;

formerly. In advance. —*a*. Ago : یك ماه پ. a month ago. ‖ Before : شب پ. the night before. ‖ Of old; ancient.—پ.از این B. this; previous to this; formerly. — پ. از آنکه او برود B. he goes. — پ. آمدن To come forward. [*Of the stomach*] To stick out. *F*. To come up ; happen ; arise ; develop.— پ. آوردن To bring f.; present; put forth; offer.— پ.افتادن To advance; progress. To get the start. [*With* از] To leave behind ; outrun. — پ. بردن To win. — پ. رفتن To advance. To make way. — پ.کردن To shoo (a cat). — در را پیش‌کنید Push the door to. — پ.گرفتن To set oneself to ; take up; choose. —از پیش From old. — از پیش بردن To succeed in doing.— از پیش رفتن To be accomplished.—پیش‌خود By oneself. Within o. — دندان پ. Incisor; chisel tooth.—

پیش *prep*. Before ; in the presence of. Beside. With : کتابرا پیش او گذاشتم

پیش *The vowel-point* (').

پیشاب Urine.

پیشاب‌آور Uretic. — داروی پ. Diuretic.

پیشاب‌دان Urinal; urinary.

پیشاب راه Urethra.

پیشاب سنج Urinometer.

پیشاب شناسی Urinology.

پیشابی Urinous; urinary; uric.

پیشاپیش Beforehand ; in anticipation. (Far) before.

پیش‌آگهی (Previous) notice. Forewarning.

پیشامد Circumstance(s); event. Emergency. Occurrence. Development . — پ. کردن To occur ; arise. To develop. — دستخوش پ Adrift ; at the mercy of circumstances. — کار ها را به پ. واگذار کردن To let things drift.

پیشامدگی Projection. Saliency.—پ. داشتن To project; jut.

پیشامده Projecting. Salient. Sticking out.

پیش اندیش Provident.

پیش اندیشی Forethought.

پیشانی Forehead.

پیشانی‌بند Fillet.

پیشانی‌گشاده Candid ; ingenuous.

پیشانی نوشت Predestination.

پیشاهنگ Leader of a flock , file, etc. Pioneer. Scout.

پیشاهنگی Scouting. Scout training. — پیشاهنگی پسران Boy scouts. — پیشاهنگی دختران Girl guides.

پیش بخاری Mantle-piece cloth. [For آهن پ.] Fender ; fireguard.

پیش بَر First winner.—سه‌دست‌پ. Rubber [*at backgammons*].

پیش بند Apron. Pinafore; bib.

پیش بندی Prevention ; providing against.

پیش بها Earnest(-money).

پیش بین Provident: آدم پ.

پیش بینی Foresight ; forecast ; anticipation. — پ. کردن To foresee; anticipate. To provide for. — پ. نشده Unforeseen.

پیش‌پا افتاده Commonplace.

پیش پرداخت Advance (money); payment in advance.

پیش‌پرده Interlude; entresmès.

پیشاپیش = پیش پیش

پیشتاب [*Per. f. E.* pistol] Pistol.

پیشخوان = پیش تخته

پیشتر Formerly. Farther ahead.

پیشخدمت *P. A.* Waiter; garcon; also, ferash.

پیش خرید Forward purchasing. — پ. کردن To buy in advance.

پیشخوان Counter.

پیشخور Received or used up in advance. — پ. کردن To anticipate; use up in a.

پیشدامن Apron. Pinafore.

پیشدرآمد Prelude; overture.

پیشدستی Anticipation. Dessert-plate; bread-and-butter p.; tea-plate. — بر کسی پ کردن To steal a march on s. o. To anticipate or outreach s. o.

پیشرس Early; precocious.

پیشرفت Progress ; advance ; headway. — پ. کردن To make h. ; progress. To proceed.

پیشرفتگی Projection ; jut. Advanced state ; advancement.

پیشرفته Advanced. Jutting.

پیشرو Forerunner. Pioneer. [*In football*] Forward.

پیشرَوی Advance. — پ. کردن To advance.

پیش ساحل *P. A.* Foreshore.

پیش‌سینه Shirt-front; plastron.

پیش فاکتور *P. Fr.* Pro forma invoice.

پیش فروش Forward sale; short sale. — پ. کردن To sell in advance; s. short.

پیش فنگ Present arms!

پیشقدم *P. A.* Leader; initiator; pioneer. — پ. شدن To take the lead; l. the way.

پیش قراول *P. T.* Advance-guard; vanguard.

پیش قسط *P. A.* First instalment.

پیش قطار *P. A.* (*Mil.*) Limber.

پیشکار Agent. Steward. Majordomo.

پیش‌کرایه *P. A.* Advance(d) freight.

پیشکش Given as a present. Making a p. of. — پ. کردن To make a p. of.

پیشکشی Present ; gift. Also, presented or offered.

پیشکی In advance.

پیشگاه Presence. — در پیشگاهِ

Before. To : در پیشگاه وزیر مسئول است

پیش‌گفتار Foreword.

پیشگو Foreteller; predictor.

پیشگویی Prediction. — پ. کردن To foretell ; predict.

پیشگیر Pinafore; bib. Napkin.

پیشگیری Prevention. Prophylaxis.

پیشدامن = پیش لنگی

پیش مرگ Dying before another [only in پیش‌مرگ کسی شدن to die before s. o.]

پیش مزد Advance wage(s).

پیش نماز Chaplain ; officiant.

پیش نویس Draft (of a letter).

پیشنهاد Proposal. Motion. Bid; offer. — پ. کردن To propose. To offer — پ. برای چیزی دادن To b. , or make a tender for, s. t.

پیشنهادی (That is to be) proposed or offered.

پیشوا Leader. Pontiff; Imam.

پیشواز Going out to meet one (returning from a journey).— (به) پیشواز کسی رفتن To go to meet s. o. — پیشواز گرگ رفتن × To m. one's death ; ask for it.

پیشوایی Leadership. Imamate.

پیش وَند Prefix.

پیشه Calling ; profession ; trade. — پیشهٔ خود or پ. کردن قرار دادن To choose as one's p.

پیشه‌وَر Tradesman; craftsman.

پیشه‌ای Professional.

پیشی Precedence. Priority. — پ.گرفتن To take the lead.

پیشی or پیشین (The) former.

پیشی Pussy; puss.

پیشین Old; ancient; early. Former; previous. Anterior ; front. — دندان پ. Incisor.

پیشینه Antecedent. Record.

پیشینیان The ancients.

پیغام Message.

پیغام‌آور Messenger.

پیغمبر & پیغام‌آور = پیغام بَر

پیغمبر Prophet.

پیغمبری Prophethood. Prophet's mission.

پیف Pooh ! Ugh !

پیک Courier. Messenger.

پیکاپ *E*. Pick-up.

پیکار Battle.

پیکان Arrow-head. Point of a spear; fluke. *By e*. Arrow.

پیکر Figure. Effigy. Body *

پی کرد Prosecution.

پیکرنگار Portraitist; painter.

پیکره Framework.

پیکنیک *E*. Picnic.

پی گرد Explorer.

پی گردی Exploration.

پیل Elephant. *S. a.* فیل

پیل *Fr*. Battery.

پیلبان Elephant-driver.

پیلتن * Of a huge body.

پیله Cocoon. Gumboil. Eyelid+. — پ. بستن To pass the

pupal stage in a cocoon. — پ. کردن To produce a gumboil. *F*. To persist; importune. Also, to be obstinate.

پیله‌ور Pedlar *or* pedler.

پیله‌وری Peddling.

پیما *or* **پیمای** [Imp. of پیمودن]

پیمان Contract; agreement. Treaty; pact. Promise. *S. a.* پیمانه ‖ پ. بستن To conclude a contract, treaty, etc.

پیمان شکن Guilty of perjury.

پیمان شکنی Breach of promise; perjury. Violation of a treaty or contract.

پیمان کار Contractor.

پیمان کاری Contract (work).

پیمان نامه Written contract or agreement. Treaty.

پیمانه Measure. — پ. کردن To measure. — پ. اش پر شد (*or* پیمانه عمرش پرشد His days are numbered. — پیمانه صبرش لبریز شد His patience was exhausted; he was out of p. with it.

پیمای *S. u.* پیما

پیمایش Measurement.

پیمایش پذیر Measurable.

پیمایش ناپذیر Immeasurable.

پیماینده Measurer.

پیمبر [Cont. of پیامبر & پیغمبر].

پیمودن [پیما (ی)] To measure. To travel; traverse; go. To drink * — راه درازی پیمودیم We went a long way.

پیموده [P. P. of پیمودن] Measured. Traversed.

پی نوشت Recommendatory note; footnote.

پینکی Slumber; drowse; nap. — پ. زدن To slumber.

پینگ پونگ *E*. Ping-pong.

پینه Patch. Hard skin. Callosity. — پ. خوردن To become callous; indurate; harden *vi*. — پ. زدن To patch up.

پینه خورده Hardened. Callous.

پینه دوز Cobbler. Ladybug.

پینه دوزی Cobbling.

پیوره *Fr*. Pyorrhea.

پیوست Connected. —*n*. Union. Enclosure.

پیوستگی Connection. Adherence.

پیوستن [پیوند]. To join; connect [usu. بهم پ.].

پیوسته [P. P. of پیوستن] Connected. Continuous. Associate. Versified. —*ad*. Continually; consistently. — جریان پ. Direct current.

پیوسته گلبرگ *or* **پیوسته جام** Gamopetalous.

پیوک Guineaworm.

پیوند 1) Graft; scion. Grafting. Union (by marriage). Relationship. Link. Ligament. Joint. — پ. زدن To graft. To join. — آنرا بدرخت دیگری پ. زدند It was engrafted into (*or*

پیه Suet. Fat. — پیه آب کرده Tallow. — پیه خوك Lard. — پیه چیزیرا بخود مالیدن To anticipate, or be prepared for, s. t.; also, risk it.

پیه سوز Tallow-burner.

پیه مالی Tallowing; greasing with tallow.

upon) another tree. — پ. کردن To unite in marriage; get spliced. — پیوندِ مریم Mahaleb cherry. 2) [Imp. of پیوستن].

پیوندکار Grafter.

پیوندگاه Joint. Commisure.

پیوندی Grafted. Produced by grafting. Crossbred; mongrel.

ت 1) Thy : نامت thy name: 2) Thee : دیدمت I saw t.

تا *prep.* Till. Ex. تافردا ‖ To. Ex. از تهران تا اصفهان ‖ —*conj.* Till ; until. Ex. بمانید تا من بیایم ‖ So that; in order t. Ex. بخوانید تامن یاد بگیرم ‖ As much as. As long as. As far as. Ex. تاصفحهٔ ۳ خواندیم ‖ 3 Since*. [*With a negative context*] Unless. Ex. تا نکوشید کامیاب نخواهید شد U. you try, you will not succeed.— تا ابد Forever. — تاآنکه *or* تا اینکه Until. So that. — تا بحال *or* تاکنون Hitherto. (As) yet. — تاکی *or* تا بکی How long ? - Until what time ? — تاچند How l. ? — تابتوان So far as possible.—تابه بینیم We will see what we can do. It remains to be seen. — تا چه رسد Still less ; much l.

تا Fold *or* crease [also تاه]. Match; peer.—تازدن To fold.— تا کردن To f. *F.* To get on. To put up. To agree. — من دو کتاب دارم ، شما چند تادارید ؟ I have 2 books: how many do you h. ?

تاب [Imp. of تابیدن]

تاب Twist. Curl. Swing. Glow. Lustre. Resistance. Power to stand hardship ; fortitude. — تاب گرسنگی Patience of hunger.—بتاب آمدن *or* ت. آمدن To glow ; become redhot. — ت. آوردن To stand ; endure ; resist. — در تاب و تب بودن To glow (with passion). — ت. خوردن To swing. To be twisted. — ت. دادن To s. To twist; twirl. To curl.

تابان Shining; luminous.

تاباندن *or* تابانیدن To cause to shine. To set in a glow.

تا بتا Odd : کفشهای ت.

تابداده Twisted. Curled.

تابدار Curled. Twisted.

تابستان Summer.

تابستانی Belonging to summer; aestival. — لباس ت. S. wear.— ت. شدن To get sick, as children, from summer heat.

تابش Radiation. Radiancy. Shining. Glow. Heat.

تابع *A.* Subject; citizen. Follower ; dependant. *Math.* Function. *Cf. the plurals* توابع & تبعه ‖ تابع اولیه Integral. — تابع چیزی بودن To be subject to, or governed by, s. t.

تابعیت *A.* Citizenship; nationa-

lity. Dependence. Allegiance. [picture.
تابلو *Fr*. Sign(board). Tableau;
تابلو ساز *Fr. P*. Sign-painter.
تابلو نویس *Fr. P*. Sign-writer.
تابناک * Luminous; shining.
تابندگی Luminousness.
تابنده Luminous. Glowing.
تابوت Bier; coffin.
تابه or تاوه Frying-pan.
تابیدن [تاب] To shine. To glow. To twist. To spin. To throw (silk).
تابین *Mil*. Private. [jar.
تاپو Earthen vessel; earthen
تاتار Tartar. Tartary.
تاتاری or تتری Of Tartary.
تآتر *Fr*. = تماشاخانه
تآتری *Fr. P*. Theatrical.
تاتوره + = داتوره
تاتی کردن + To toddle.
تأثر *A*. Being impressed or touched. Passion. Sadness.
تأثیر *A*. Effect. Impression. Influence. — ت. کردن در or تحت ت. قرار دادن To touch; impress; leave an impression on.— بی ت. نیست or ت. دارد It has its effect.
تاج Crown. *Z*. Crest; comb. — تاج گل Garland; wreath of flowers. — تاج ستون Chapiter.
تاج‌الملوك *A*. Aconite; monkshood; also, columbine.
تاج خروس 1) Amaranth. 2) Cockscomb.

تاجدار Crowned. *Z*. Crested.— پدر تاجدار The Crowned Father; i. e. the king.
تاجر *A*. [تجار] Merchant.
تاجریزی Nightshade.
تاجگذاری Coronation.— ت. کردن To crown; coronate.
تاجور *a*. Wearing a crown.
تاجیك Iranian [as opposed to a Turk].
تاخت Gallop. Invasion. —ت. کردن To gallop. — ت. آوردن To make an invasion.
تاختن [تاز] To rush; make an inroad. — ت. آب o = شاشیدن
تاخت و تاز Invasion; inroad.
تأخر *A*. Coming next.
تأخیر *A*. Delay. — ت. کردن To d. To be late.— تأخیرورود Tardiness; l. arrival. — به ت. افتادن To be delayed.— به ت. انداختن To delay. To postpone.
تأدیب *A*. Chastisement; correction. — ت. کردن To chastise; correct.
تأدیبی *A*. Correctional: حبس ت.
تأدیه *A*. Payment. — ت. کردن To pay. [Annoyance.
تأذی *A*. Being injured.
تار Cord. Wire. Fibre; staple. Warp. *Tar:* Iranian musical instrument of the guitar class.— تارآوا Vocal cord. — تار عنکبوت Spider's web; cobweb. — تار مو (Single) hair. — ت. زدن To play on the *tar*.— تار و پود Warp and

woof. *F*. Texture; structure; constitution.

تار Somewhat dark. Dim. Tarnished. [*Of the eye*] Dim; weak. — شیشهٔ ت. Focusing-screen.

تاراج Plunder — ت. کردن *or* به ت. بردن To plunder.

تاراندن To put to flight.

تاراجگر Plunderer.

تار زن "Tarist": one who can play the "tar".

تارک Crown of the head. Vertex.

تارِک *A*. Forsaker o.— تارك دنیا Anchorite. — زن تارك دنیا Nun.

تارکش Wire-drawer. Heddles.

تارُمی = **طارمی**

تارومار Routed. Scattered. Confused.— ت. کردن To rout; put to flight. To scatter.

تاری Dimness. Darkness.

تاریخ *A*. [تواریخ] Date. History. Era. — از تاریخِ (With effect) from. — ت. گذاشتن To date.— به ترتیب ت. In chronological order.

تاریخچه *A*. *P*. Diary. *OS*. Short history. — تاریخچهٔ زندگی — Biography.

تاریخ نویس *A*. *P*. Historian.

تاریخی *A*. Historic(al).

تاریک Dark. — ت. شدن To get dark; grow d. — ت. کردن To darken. To dim.— ت. وروشن کردن To flicker the lights.

تاریک خانه Dark room.

تاریک دل • Dark-hearted; benighted.

تاریکی Darkness; dark.— درتاریکی In the d.

تاز [Imp. of تاختن]

تازاندن To cause to gallop.

تازش Attack(ing). *Mus*. Syncopation.

تازگی Freshness. Novelty. — ت. ندارد It is nothing new; that is no news to me. — بتازگی Recently.

تازنده Galloper. Invader.

تازه *a*. Fresh. New. Recent. —*n*. News [often خبرِ تازه]. —*ad*. Just. Recently. Newly. After all (this business)+.— ت. شدن To be refreshed. To be renewed. — ت. کردن To make fresh. To renew. To refresh.

تازه بدولت رسیده *P*. *A*. = **نو کیسه**

تازه ساز *or* **تازه ساخت** New-[built.

تازه کار Fresh; green; inexperienced.

تازه نفس *P*. *A*. Fresh; of a fresh vigour; untired.

تازه وارد *P*. *A*. Newly arrived. —*n*. New comer.

تازی Greyhound [usu. سگ ت.]. Arabic. Arabian: اسب ت.

تازیانه Scourge. — ت. خوردن To receive a scourge. — ت. زدن To s. or whip.

تازی بان Master of the hounds.

تازیدن = **تاختن**

تأکید *A.* Emphasis ; stress. — ت.کردن To recommend emphatically. To emphasize ; lay stress on. To impress; i. on.
تالاب Pond. Pool.
تالار Hall; saloon; parlour.
تالان *T.* = **دزدی** & **غارت**
تألم *A.* [تألمات] Suffering ; pain. Sorrow.
تألم آور *A.P.* Sad : خبر تالم آور
تالی *A a.* Following. Second. Similar. —*n.* Consequent.
تألیف *A.* Compilation. Literary work [pl. تالیفات]. — تألیفِ آقای . . . (Compiled) by Mr . . . — ت. کردن To compile.
تام *A.* Complete; full.
تام الاختیار *A.* Fully authorized.
تامپن *Fr.* (-*pon*) (Stamp-)pad.
تأمل *A.* Deliberation ; reflection. Hesitation. — ت. کردن To deliberate. To hesitate. To wait +.
تأمین *A.* Securing ; safeguarding. Security ; guarantee.— ت. کردن To secure , give security for. To provide for ; meet; cover. — تأمین آتیه کردن To p. for one's future; [*in a bad sense*] feather one's nest. — ادارهٔ تأمینات = ادارهٔ **آگاهی**
تأمینی *A.* Reserved for secu-

تاس *S. u.* **طاس**
تأسف *A.* Regret. — ت. داشتن *or* ت. خوردن To regret. — جای ت. است It is to be regretted. — باکمال ت. Most regretfully. — مایهٔ ت. Regrettable.
تأسف آور *A. P.* Regrettable.
تاسوعا *A. The ninth day of Moharram.*
تأسی *A.* Following; imitating; taking model. — بکسی ت.کردن To follow s. o.
تاسی Cuboid : استخوان ت.
تأسیس *A.* Establishment. — ت.کردن To establish; found.
تأسیسات *A.* Installations. *Cf. the s.* تأسیس
تاشو *or* **تاه شو** That can be folded. Collapsible.— صندلی ت. Folding chair.
تاغ A tree of the goosefoot family resembling the tamarisk and yielding a wood which has a long-enduring fire.
تافتن [تاب] To cause to glow; make redhot. To twist. To shine. To become r.— روی ت. To turn away one's face, as by displeasure.
تافته *a.* Twisted; spun. Set in a glow. —*n.* Taffeta.
تاقدیس Anticline.
تاک Vine.
تاکستان Vineyard.
تاکسی *Fr.* Taxi; cab; taxi-cab.
تاکسیمتر *Fr.* Taximeter.

rity purposes. [Fem. تامینیه Ex. قوای تأمینیه S. forces].
تان 1) Your. Ex. پسرتان 2) You [*Objective*]. Ex. دیدمتان
تانک *Fr.* (*Mil.*) Tank.
تانگو *Fr.* Tango.
تأنی *A.* Acting slowly. Delay. – ت.کردن To d.; act slowly.
تأنیث *A.* Regarding as feminine o. *S. a. under* تذکیر
تاوان Indemnity; damages. Penalty. – ت. دادن To make good; compensate. [With به] To indemnify.
تاوانگاه [*In football*] Penalty area.
تاول Blister. – ت. زدن To b.
تاوه *S. u.* تابه
تأویل *A.* Paraphrase. Interpretation. – ت. کردن To paraphrase. To explain (away).
تاه *S. u.* تا
تاه شو *S. u.* تاشو
تأهل *A.* Marriage. Married life. – ت. (اختیار) کردن To marry.
تائب o *A.* = توبه‌کار
تایر *E.* Tire; tyre.
تأیید *A.* Confirmation. Assistance; grace; aid [pl. تاییدات]. – ت.کردن To confirm.
تَب Fever. – تب داشتن To have fever; be ill with f.; be feverish. – تب کردن To be attacked by f.; get a f. – (درجه) تبِ کسیرا گرفتن To take a person's temperature.

تبادُر o *A.* Making haste. – ت. بذهن Springing to the mind first. *See* متبادر
تبادُل *A.* Interchange. Alternation. – تبادل نظر Exchange of views.
تبار * Family. Extraction; origin.
تَبار * *A.* Destruction; ruin.
تبارك *A.* (*taba':rakah*) May... be blessed. – ت. وتعالی *-rak-va-ta-ala* Blessed and exalted.
تباشیر Chalk o. – تباشیر فرنگی Magnesia.
تباعد *A.* Divergence. – ت. از مرکز Eccentricity.
تبانی *A.* Collusion. – ت. (باهم) کردن To collude.
تَباه Corrupt; spoiled. – ت.کردن To c. To spoil. To corrode.
تباه‌کار Corrupt. *S. a.* تبه‌کار
تباهی Corruption. Destruction.
تبایُن *A.* Marked difference; contrast.
تب‌بُر Febrifuge; antipyretic.
تبت Tibet.
تبحر *A.* Erudition; profound knowledge; mastery.
تبخال Cold sore; *herpes labialis*.
تبختر o *A.* Walking proudly or with airs; strutting.
تبخیر *A.* Evaporation. – ت. شدن & ت.کردن To evaporate.
تب‌دار Feverish.
تبدیل *A.* Changing. Conversion. Reduction. Permutation. – تبدیل شکل Transformation. –

تبدیل قیافه یا لباس Disguise. ـ ت. دادن or ت. کردن To change or reduce. ـ ت. یافتن To be changed or reduced. ـ قابل ت. Reducible. Convertible. ـ غیر قابل ت. Irreducible. In-convertible. ـ کلید تبدیل Two-way switch.

تبذیر ○ *A.* Dissipation.

تبر Large axe; hatchet.

تبرخون ○ = عناب Jujube.

تبردار Halberdier. Sapper.

تبرزد ○ White sugar. Rock salt.

تبرزین Battle-axe; halberd.

تبرّع ○ *A.* Doing a thing voluntarily. Donation.

تبرعاً *A.* Voluntarily. Gratuitously.

تبرّک *A.* (Receiving or making a) gift looked upon as bringing good luck. ـ برای ت. For luck.

توبره = تُبره

تبرّی *A.* Immunity. Exoneration. ـ ت. جستن از To renounce or deny.

تبریدکردن *A. P.* To cool ○. To eat or drink refrigerants.

تبریزی [For درخت ت.] Poplar.

تبریک *A.* [تبریکات] Congratulation. Good wishes.ـ ت.گفتن To congratulate. To wish.ـ سال نورا بهمه ت. میگویم (I w. all a) Happy New Year.

تبرئه *A.* Acquittal; exoneration; exculpation. ـ ت.کردن To exonerate; acquit.

تبسم *A.* Smile. *Cf.* لبخند & خنده ‖ ت.کردن To smile.

تبشیر ○ *A.* Giving good tidings.

تبصبص ○ *A.* Flattery. *OS.* Wagging the tail.

تبصره *A.* Note. *Nota bene.*

تبعه *A.* [A pl. of تابع] Subjects : تبعهٔ ایران Iranian subjects or nationals.

تبعی *A.* (*Gr.*) Subordinate.

تبعیت *A.* Following; imitating.ـ ت. کردن از To follow (the example of); imitate.

تبعید *A.* Banishment; exile.. ـ ت.کردن To banish; exile.

تبعیض *A.* (Unjust) discrimination. ـ نسبت بکسی ت. کردن To discriminate against s. o.

تب‌گیر Clinical thermometer.

تبلبل ○ *A.* Confusion; disorder.

تبلور *A.* Crystallization.

تبلیغ *A.* [تبلیغات] Propaganda; propagandism. ـ ادارهٔ تبلیغات Department of Propaganda.ـ ت. کردن To propagandize. To (try to) convert to another religion.

تبلیغاتی *A. P.* Propagandistic.ـ فیلم های ت. Publicity films.

تبلیه *Fr.* Apron. *Cf.* پیش دامن

تبنی *A.* Adoption of a child.

تبه [Cont. of تباه] Corrupt; spoiled. [تباه‌کار

تبه‌کار Criminal; felon. *S. a.*

تبه‌کاری Felony; crime.

تبیان ○ *A.* Manifestation.

تبیین ○ *A.* Making clear.

تپاله Cow-dung dried for fuel.
تپانیدن + To stuff; cram.
تپانچه Pistol. Slap ; box on the ear. — کسیرا تپانچه زدن To slap s. o. To shoot s. o. with a pistol.
تپ‌تپ کردن +To go pit-a-pat; beat or throb. To patter.
تپش Palpitation : تپش قلب
تپق زدن *T. P.* [*Of horses*] To interfere.
تپه Hill.— تپهٔ گل Flower-bed. — تپهٔ دریایی Reef.
تپیدن [تپ]+To beat; palpitate.
تتار [Cont. of **تاتار**]
تتری [Cont. of **تاتاری**]
تتری o = **سماق**
تتبع *A.* [تتبعات] Research.
تتق o = **چادر** – **پرده**
تتمه *A.* Balance. Supplement; complement.
تثبیت *A.* Stabilization.— ت کردن To stabilize.
تثلیث *A.* Trinity.
تثنیه *A.* Dual (number).—سفر تثنیه Deuteronomy.
تجار [Pl. of تاجر]
تجارب [Pl. of تجربه]
تجارت *A.* Commerce. — ت.کردن To trade; be a merchant.
تجارتخانه *A. P.* Commercial firm. [*Cf.* بازرگانی
تجارتی *A. P.* Commercial.
تجاری *A.* = **تجارتی**
تجاسر *A.* Insurgence.
تجانس *A.* Homegeneity.
تجاوز *A.* Transgression. Aggression. Violation. — ت. کردن از To exceed; be more than.— ت.کردن به To encroach on. To trespass against; violate.
تجاوزکار *A. P.* Aggressive. —*n.* Aggressor. Trespasser.
تجاوزکارانه *A. P.* Aggressively. —*a.* Aggressive : عملیات ت.
تجاوزی *A.* Aggressive ; offensive.
تجاهل *A.* Feigning ignorance.— ت. کردن To feign i.
تجدّد *A.* Revival; renaissance. Modernity.
تجددخواه *A.P.* Modern-minded. —*n.* Advocate of revival.
تجدید *A.* Renewal. — تجدید چاپ Reprint; revision.— تجدیدروابط *Rapprochement*. — تجدید عهد Renewal of friendly relations .— تجدید فراش Remarrying. — تجدید قوا Reenforcement. Refreshment.—تجدید نظر Revision. Rehearing.—تجدیدهوا Ventilation. — ت. کردن To renew. To revise. To repeat.— تجدید نظر کردن (در) To revise. To rehear.
تجدیدی *A. P.* (That is to be) renewed. Having to sit for another examination ; conditioned. — امتحان ت. Resitting.
تجربه *A.* [تجارب] Experience. Experiment. — اصالت ت. Empiricism.— ت.کردن *or* به‌ت.رسانیدن To (prove by) experience.
تجربی *A.* Experimental. Empi-

ric(al). — طب ت. Empiricism.
تجربیات *A.* Experiences. Experiments.
تجرّد *A.* Single life. Solitude.
تجرّی *A.* Insolence. Boldness.
تجرید *A.* Abstraction.
تجزیه *A.* Analysis; breakdown.— ت. کردن To analyze.
تجزیه طلب *a. p.* Separatist.
تجسس *A.* [تجسسات] Search; investigation.— ت. کردن To s.
تجسم *A.* Incarnation.
تجلی *A.* [تجلیات] Manifestation. Appearing with glory or brightness; transfiguation,
تجلید o *A.* Binding; furnishing with a cover.
تجلیل *A.* Glorification.— ت. کردن To glorify; honour.
تجلیلی *A.* Honorific.
تجمع *A.* Gathering. — تجمع خون Hyperemia.
تجمل *A.* [تجملات] Luxury. Articles of luxury; *articles de luxe.* [tuous.
تجملی *A, P. De luxe.* Sump-
تجنب o *A.* = احتراز & دوری
تجنیس *A.* Playing on words. Reduction of a mixed number to an improper fraction.
تجویز *A.* Declaring permissible; approving (of). Recommending; advising. — ت. کردن To recommend; advise; order.
تجهیز *A.* Mobilizing. — ت کردن To mobilize. To equip.
تجهیزات *A.* Mobilizations; equipment. *Cf. the s.* تجهیز
تجیر Tent-walling. Folding screen. [To abstain.
تحاشی *A.* Abstaining. — ت. کردن
تحبیب *A.* Causing to love or be loved.
تحت o *A.* = زیر Under or lower part.— تحتِ or درتحتِ U.— درتحتِ توجهاتِ U. the auspices of.
تحت الارضی *A.* = زیر زمینی
تحت البحری *A.* = زیر دریایی
تحت الحفظ *A.* Under arrest.
تحت الحمایه *A.* Under protection. — کشور تحت الحمایه Protectorate; protégé.
تحت الجلدی *A.* = زیر پوستی
تحت الحنك o *A.* Fold of the turban passed under the chin.
تحت السلاح *A.* Under arms. — خدمت ت. Military service [now خدمت زیر پرچم].
تحت الشعاع *A.* Eclipsed (by the rays of a specified object).— ت. قرار دادن To outshine; eclipse; surpass.
تحت اللفظی *A. a.* Interlinear; literal. —*ad.* Word for w.
تحتانی *A.* = زیری Lower.
تحجر *A.* Petrifaction.
تحدّب *A.* Convexity. [*Of the brain*] Convolution.
تحدید *A.* Limitation. — ت. کردن To limit. To define.— تحدیدِ حدود کردن To delimit.

تحدیدی *A*. Limitative.
تحذیر *A*. Caution; warning.
تحرّی *A*. Research. Selection of the most worthy.
تحریر *A*. Writing (out). Kind of trill in singing. [Pl. تحریرات writings]. — ت. دادن To trill (one's voice). — ماشین ت. ‖ نوشتن = ت. کردن Typewriter. — میز تحریر Desk. — از حال ت. From the present date.
تحریری *A*. *P*. Used for writing : کاغذ تحریری w. paper.
تحریص *A*. Making greedy or eager. — ت. کردن To make e. To exhort. To excite.
تحریف *A*. [تحریفات] Alteration. Tampering with (s. t.). — ت. کردن To tamper with.
تحریک *A*. [تحریکات] Instigation. Stimulation. — ت کردن To instigate. To stimulate.
تحریم *A*. Declaring as unlawful. — ت. کردن To ban or boycott. To prohibit.
تحسر *A*. Regret(ting).
تحسین *A*. Applause; praise. Admiration. — ت کردن To admire. To applaud or p. — قابل ت. Admirable; praiseworthy.
تحسین آمیز *A*. *P*. Applausive.
تحصن *A*. Taking refuge in a sanctuary. — بست نشستن = ت. کردن
تحصنگاه *A*. *P*. Place of refuge; sanctuary.
تحصیل *A*. Acquisition. Studying. Training. [Pl. تحصیلات studies; education]. — ت. کردن To acquire; obtain. To study; receive training. — تحصیل‌حاصل Effort to acquire what is already acquired; vain effort.
تحصیلدار *A*. *P*. Collector.
تحصیل کرده *A*. *P*. Educated.
تحصیلی *A*. *P*. Educational. Academic; scholastic: سال ت.
تحف [Pl. of تحفه]
تُحفه *A*. [تحف *tohaf*] (Rare object given as a) present; gift. Object of curiosity.
تحقق *A*. Certainty. Proving to be true. — ت. پیدا کردن To prove to be true.
تحقیر *A*. Despising. Contempt. — ت کردن To despise; belittle.
تحقیر آمیز *A*. *P*. Contemptuous; derogatory: سخنان ت.
تحقیراً *A*. Despisingly.
تحقیق *A*. [تحقیقات] Inquiry; investigation; research. — ت. کردن To inquire; investigate. — از من ت. کرد He inquired me about it.
تحقیقاً *A*. Certainly. Exactly. Through, or as a result of, inquiries.
تحکم *A*. Commanding; domineering. — بر کسی ت. کردن To order s. o. about; domineer over him. [haughty.
تحکم‌آمیز *A*. *P*. Domineering;
تحکیم *A*. Strengthening. —

ت. کردن To strengthen.

تحلیف *A.* Administering an oath; swearing (in).

تحلیل *A.* Analysis. Absorption. Dissolving. Decomposition. Corrosion. Resolution (of a tumour). Wasting; loss. — ت. بردن To digest or assimilate. To resolve.— ت. رفتن To be digested. To be resolved. To be wasted or exhausted.— اوخیلی ت. رفته است He is much reduced. — جذب وتحلیل غذا Assimilation of food.

تحلیلی *A.* Analytic : هندسهٔ ت.

تحمل *A.* Supporting; bearing. Forbearance; tolerance. Patience. — ت. کردن To tolerate; endure; forbear. To support; sustain. — قابل ت. etc. — تحمل پذیر etc.

تحمل پذیر *A. P.* Tolerable; endurable. [insupportable.

تحمل ناپذیر *A. P.* Intolerable;

تحمیل *A.* [تحمیلات] Imposition.— ت. کردن To impose.

تحمیلی *A. P.* Imposed. Forced.

تحوّل *A.* Change. Transformation. Transition. Take-over; (taking) delivery. *Cf.* تحویل

تحویل *A.* Delivery. Reduction. — ت. دادن To deliver; hand over. — تحویل پاسبان دادن To give in charge; turn over to the police — ت. گرفتن To take delivery of. To collect. To take over. — قابل ت. Reducible. — غیرقابل ت. Irreducible.— تحویل سال Transition to the new year.

تحویل خانه *A. P.* Cash-office.

تحویلدار *A. P.* Cashier.

تحویلداری *A. P.* Function of a cashier.

تحیات [Pl. of تحیت]

تحیت *or* تحیه *A.* [تحیات] Salutation. Benediction.

تحیر *A.* Astonishment.

تحیرآور *A. P.* — شگفت آور Astonishing; surprising.

تخالف *A.* Disagreeing with each other.

تخت *n.* Throne. Elevated seat. Couch. [*Of a shoe*] Sole. —*a.*+Flat. Even; level.— تخت جمشید Persepolis. — تخت روان Litter; palanquin. تخت عمل Operating table. — ت. کردن To level. To fill to the brim. — بر تخت نشستن To ascend to the throne.

تختخواب Bed(stead). [For a child] Cot.— بیمارستان صد تختخوابی 100-bedded hospital.

تخته Board. Slab. Sheet; layer. Width: سه ت. آستری ‖ تختهٔ شطرنج Chessboard. — تخته شکسته بندی Splint. — ت. کردن + To close (a shop) —*vi.* To c. up shop. To quit.

تخته ای Made of boards or planks; wooden.

تخته بندی Boarding; planking. Splintering. — ت کردن To

board or plank. To splinter.
تخته بید Wall-louse.
تخته پل Pontoon-bridge.
تخته پوست Wool-felt.
تخته پهن Hotbed.
تخته چکش *P. T.*(Proof)planer.
تخته سنگ Slate. Slab.
تخته سیاه Blackboard.
تخته شستی Pallette ; pallet.
تخته شنا Push-up board.
تخته قاپو کردن *P. T.* To settle (a tribe).
تخته کوبی Wainscot ; panelling. – ت. کردن To panel or wainscot. To board up.
تخته نرد Backgammon(-board).
تخدیر *A.* Stupefying (with a narcotic).
تخرّش *A.* Irritation.
تخریب *A.* Demolition.– ت. کردن To demolish ; destroy. To ruin ; spoil.
تخریبی *A. P.* Destructive. – عملیات ت. Sabotage.
تُخس + Naughty. Intractable.
تخشایی [For ادارهٔ ت.] Army's Industrial Department.
تخشب ○ *A.* Lignification. *Med.* Catalepsy.
تخصص *A.* Expert knowledge.– ت. داشتن To be specialized or skilled.
تخصصی *A. P.* Specialized.
تخصیص *A.* Allocation.– ت. دادن To allocate; appropriate.
تخطی *A.* Offending. Aggression. – ت. کردن از To offend against.
تخطیط ○ *A.* Delineation. Survey. – تخطیط اراضی Topography.
تخطئه کردن *A. P.* To charge with a fault. To condemn; proscribe.
تخفیف *A.* Reduction. Mitigation. – ت. دادن To give a r.
تخلخل *A.* Porosity.
تخلص *A.* Pen-name ; *nom de plume*.– این شاعر سعدی ت. می کرد This poet adopted "Sa'di" as his nom de p.
تخلف *A.* Offending ; violation. – ت. کردن از To offend against ; infringe.
تخلیص *A.* Delivering.
تخلیه *A.* Evacuation. Offloading. – ت. کردن To evacuate. To offload.
تُخم Seed. Egg. Sperm. Balls; testicle. – تخم جاروب Crowfoot. – تخم چشم Eye-ball ; globe of the eye. – تخم حرام Illegitimate child.– تخم درمنه Wormseed. – بارهنگ = تخم سئید ‖ تخم مرغ Egg. – تخم سگ ماهی Caviare– ت. ریختن To spawn. To go to seeds. – ت. گذاشتن To lay (*or* deposit) an egg [also ت. کردن]..– از تخم در آوردن To hatch.– تخم چیزیرا برانداختن To annihilate s. t. ; root it out; leave no trace of it.
تخماق *T.* Beetle; rammer.
تخم پاش Seeder; seed-drill.

تخمچه Ovule. [plant.
تخمدار Seedy. — گیاه ت. Seed-
تخمدان Ovary. [to seeds.
تخم ریزی Spawning. Running
تخمک Ovule. *OS*. Little seed.
تخم کاری Cultivation. *OS*. Sowing seeds. — فصل ت. Seed-time.
تخم کشی Breeding.
تخم کن Egg-laying. — مرغ ت. E.-laying bird ; layer.
تخم گذار Oviparous.
تخم گذاری Laying eggs ; oviposition.
تخم مرغ Egg.
تخم مرغی Egg-shaped; oval. — شکل بمبئی = گل ت.
تخمه Roasted seed (of melons, etc.). Ovum ; ovule. *F*. Stock ; origin. [gestion.
تخمه (*tokh-* ; *tokha-*) Indi
تخمی Seedy ; going to seeds. Male ; used for breeding purposes. — آدم ت. × Odd person; freak (of nature). Also, sloppy p.
تخمیر *A*. Fermentation. — ت کردن & ت. شدن To ferment.
تخمین *A*. Estimating. (Rough) estimate. Conjecture. — ت.زدن To e. (roughly). [roughly.
تخمیناً *A*. Approximately ;
تخمینی *A*. Approximate.
تخویف o *A*. Intimidation.
تخیل *A*. [تخیلات] Imagination.
تدابیر [Pl. of تدبیر].
تداخل *A*. Eating between meals ; eating piecemeal. *Ph*. Interference : تداخل امواج
تداخلی *A*. Interferential.
تدارک *A*. [تدارکات] Preparation. Provision. — ت. دیدن To make preparations. To prepare ; provide. — اداره تدارکات Supplies Department.
تداعی *A*. Calling (*or* challenging) each other o. — تداعی معانی Association of ideas.
تدافع *A*. Defense. Repulsion.
تدافعی *A*. Defensive.
تداول *A*. Usage. Circulation.
تداوی *A*. (*—va*) Medical treatment (of oneself).
تدبیر *A*. [تدابیر] Plan. Policy ; expedient. Prudence. Management. — باتدبیر Prudent(ly). — ت.کردن To contrive a plan. To manage. — تدبیرمنزل Domestic economy; household management. — حسن ت. Good m. or policy. تدابیر احتیاطی Precaution precautionary measures. — تدابیر جنگی *Mil*. Tactics.
تدخین o *A*. Fumigation.
تدریج *A*. Graduation o. — بتدریج Gradually. — بتدریجی که As and when.
تدریجا *A*. Gradually.
تدریجی *A*. Gradual.
تدریس *A*. Teaching. — ت. کردن To teach ; give lessons.
تدفین *A*. Burial.
تدقیق *A*. Scrutinizing. — ت. کردن

To scrutinize : examine minutely.

تدقیقا *A*. Minutely.

تدلیس *A*. Guile ; hypocrisy.— ت.کردن To play the hypocrite.

تدوین *A*. Collection (into a book); compilation.— ت.کردن To compile; collect. To draw up. To codify.

تدهین *A*. Anointment. —ت.کردن To anoint; embrocate.

تدین *A*. Religiousness.

تذبذب ○ *A*. Hesitation; perplexity.

تذرو ○ * (*tazarv*) = **قرقاول**

تذکار *A*. Remembrance. Token.

تذکاریه *A*. Reminder.

تذکر *A*. Reminding. Pointing out. Commemoration. —مجلس ت. Memorial service. — ت. دادن To point out. [With به] To remind. To notify.

تذکراً *A*. By way of reminding.

تذکره *A*. 1) = گذرنامه 2) Biography. 3) Memento.

تذکیر *A*. Masculinity ○. Regarding as masculine ○. — ت. و تأنیث *Gr*. Gender.

تذهیب *A*. Gilding. Illumination (of a book). — ت. کردن To illuminate. To gild.

تذییل ○ *A*. Furnishing with an appendix. *S. a*. ذیل

تَر Wet. — تر کردن To wet ; make w. —تروتازه Fresh and green. Flush.—ترو ُخشك *Met*. The good with the bad. — تر و خشك کردن + To look after or nurse.

تَر *Suffix forming the comparative degree*.

تُرا = **تورا** Thee.

تُراب ○ *A*. = **خاک**

ترابالقی *A*. = **تریاكبرگردان**

ترادُف *A*. Succession. Synonymity.

تراز Level. Balance. Adornment. — ترازآبی Water level.— تراز الکلی Spirit l. — ت.کردن To l. To (cause to) balance.

ترازدار Leveller ; instrumentman.

ترازمند Equilibrated; balanced.

ترازنامه Balance-sheet.

ترازو Balance; scale. — يك ت. A pair of balances. — ترازوی ماشینی Weighing-machine.

ترازودار Weigher ; salesman.۹

ترازی Horizontal [افقی].

تراژدی *Fr*. Tragedy.

تراش 1) [*Imp. of* تراشیدن] 2) *n*. Shave : يك تراش پاکیزه ‖ Shaving; lop. Paring. Curettage. Cut (of a diamond, etc.). — ت. دادن To cut. To grind, as a lens. To turn in the lathe. — ت. کردن To prune; trim; lop. To grind.— چرخ ت. Lathe.

تراشدار (Diamond-) cut.

تراشکار(ی) Turner(y).

تراشنده Shaver. Cutter. Parer.

تراشه *or* **تریشه** Shaving(s); excelsior. Splint; chip. — تریشهٔ

همان کنده Chip of the old block.

تراشیدگی Erasure.

تراشیدن [تراش] To shave. To scrape. To sharpen. To cut or hew, as a gem. To sculpture. To erase. To pare. To grate. *F.* To forge. To create.

تراشیده [P. P. of تراشیدن]. Shaven. Hewn. Cut. Sculptured. Erased.

تراضی *A.* Mutual consent.

تراک Fissure. *Cf.* ترك

تراکم *A.* Accumulation. Heaping up. Compression. – تراکمِ خون Blood congestion.

تراکمِ *Fr.* Trachoma.

تراکمه [A. pl. of ترکمان]

تراموای *Fr.* Tramway.

ترانزیت *Fr.* Transit.

ترانگبین *S. u.* ترنجبین

ترانه Song. Trill.

تراورس *Fr.* Sleeper ; tie.

تراوش Oozing ; exudation ; leakage ; seepage. Osmosis. – تراوش فکر(ی) Reflection(s) ; thought. – ت. کردن To exude; ooze. *F.* To flow.

تراویدن = **تراوش کردن**

تربت *A.* Dust o. *Met.* Ashes ; tomb.

تربچه *or* **ترب** Radish.

تربد Turpeth.

تربیت *A.* Training ; education. Nurture. Civility.– ت. کردن To train; educate. To manage, as a horse. – تربیت کرمِ ابریشم Sericulture. [Manageable.

تربیت پذیر *A. P.* Educable.

تربیع *A.* Quarter of the moon. Quadrature. – قوس ت. Quadratrix.

ترتیب *A.* [ترتیبات] Arrangement ; order. Manner ; system. Formula. – ترتیب اثردادن To give effect (to) ; g. a follow-up (to); entertain (an application, etc.). – ت. دادن To arrange ; make arrangements (for). To manage.– بچه ت. In what manner ? How ? – به ترتیب الفباء Alphabetically.

ترتیبی *A.* Serial. Systematic.

ترتیزک *or* **تره تیزک** (Garden) cress, peppergrass. – ترتیزك آبی Water-cress ; brooklime.

ترتیل *A.* Chanting (the Koran).

ترجمان *A.* 1) Interpreter ; dragoman. – ترجمانِ . . بودن To manifest, or be expressive of, s. t. 2) Fine[جریمه]. [Per. Corruption of تجرمان].

ترجمه *A.* [تراجم] Translation. ترجمهٔ حال Biography. – ت. کردن To translate. To interpret.

ترجیح *A.* Preference.– ت. داشتن بر To have preference to; be preferable (*or* bettr) than.– ت. دادن بر To prefer to. *Note.* بر may be replaced by به

ترجیع بند *A. P.* Strophe-poem; return-tie.
ترحم *A.* Pity ; compassion. — بر کسی ت.کردن To pity, or have mercy on, s. o.
ترحیم *A.* Wishing God's mercy for a deceased person ○ [مجلس ت. Funeral service held for this purpose].
ترخص *A.* Being permitted ○.— حد ترخص [also حد ترخیص] Tolerance ; allowance; margin of difference of weight in coins.
ترخون Tarragon.
ترخیص *A.* Releasing (from a custom-house). — حد ترخیص *S. u.* ترخص
ترخیم *A.* Curtailing ○. Apocope.
تُرد Brittle.
تر دامن ○ Unchaste.
تردّد *A.* Traffic. Going back and forth. — ت.کردن To ply (*or* travel) b. and forth.
تردست Dexterous. [hand.
تردستی Dexterity. Sleight-of-
تُردی Brittleness; fragility.
تَردید *A.* Doubt. Hesitation.— ت. داشتن To have doubts ; be doubtful ; be in two minds. — تردید رأی Irresolution ; indecision. — ت. کردن To doubt.— قابل ت. Dubitable; questionable. — غیر قابل ت. Unquestionable.
ترذیلی *A.* Degrading : مجازات ت.
ترس 1) *n.* Fear ; dread. — ت. داشتن To fear; be afraid.— ت.کردن To be shocked with f. — از ترسِ For fear of. 2) *Imp. of* ترسیدن
ترسا ○ = **مسیحی**
ترسان Afraid.
ترساندن *or* **ترسانیدن** To frighten.
ترسناک Dreadful; frightening.
ترسنده (One) who fears.
ترسو Timid.— ترسویی Timidity.
ترسیدن [ترس] To fear ; be afraid. — او از دزد میترسد He is a. of a thief.
ترسیده [P. P. of ترسیدن].
ترسیم *A.* Drawing; tracing. — ت.کردن To draw ; describe.
ترسیمی *A.* Descriptive: هندسهٔ ت.
تُرش Sour.— گلِ ت. Bisulphate of lime. — ت. سدن To turn acid; become sour.— ت.کردن To make s. To suffer from acidity . — شیر دارد ترش میشود The milk is on the turn.
ترشح *A.* Oozing ; excretion ; secretion [ترشحات]. Splash. — ت. کردن To exude ; be secreted. To splash. [tory.
ترشحی *A. P.* Secretory; excre-
ترشرو Sour-faced; peevish.
ترشرویی Moroseness; sourness.
ترشک Sorrel.— جوهر ترشك Oxalic acid. [flavour.
ترش مزه Sour ; of an acid
ترشی Sourness. Acidity. Pickles (made with vinegar).

ترشیدگی Rancidity. Fermented state.
ترشیدن To become sour; turn acid. To get rancid. [acid.
ترشیده Rancid. (Having) turned
ترصد ○ *A*. Lying in wait. Observation. Expectation.
ترصیع *A*. Inlaying with gems. Using words which correspond in measure and rime.
ترضیه *A*. Securing satisfaction of; gratification. — برای ترضیهٔ او In order to secure his satisfaction (*or* to please him). — ت. خواستن To ask pardon. — ترضیهٔ نفس Indulgence in one's wishes.
ترعه *A*. Canal : ترعهٔ سوئز
ترغیب *A*. Persuasion. — ت. کردن To persuade or encourage.
ترفیع *A*. [ترفیعات] Promotion. *OS*. Elevating. — ت دادن (به) To promote. [welfare.
ترفیه ○ *A*. (Causing to have)
ترق [usu. ترق وتروق] Cracking (noise).
ترقوه *A*. Clavicle.
ترقوی *A*. Clavicular.
ترقه Firecracker.
ترقی *A*. Progress; improvement. Rise. — ت. دادن To cause to progress. To promote. To raise the price of. — ت. کردن To make progress; improve. To rise in price. — ترقی معکوس Retrogradation. — رو به ت. On the rise. On the progress.
ترقی خواه *A. P*. Progressive.
ترقیة *A*. Dilution.
ترک *A*. Abandonment. — ت. کردن To abandon; forsake [also ت. گفتن]. To renounce; relinquish. — ترك ادب Impoliteness. — ترك اولی Failure to do the better thing: considereed as a venial sin. — ت. دادن To cause to abandon. — ترك دعوا Relinquishment of a claim; disclaimer. — ترك دعوا کردن To relinquish a c. — ترك وظیفه Lapse from duty. — ترك سلاح کردن To lay down arms. — ترك عادت دادن To wean from a (specified) habit.
ترک Back. Pillion.
ترک + Crevice; crack. — ت. خوردن *or* ت. برداشتن To c.; (be) split; craze.
ترک Turk(ish).
ترکاندن To (cause to) burst. To blast; explode.
ترك بند 1) Carrier (of a bicycle). 2) Pillion.
ترکتازی Incursion. Depradation.
ترکتور *Fr*. Tractor.
ترکش Quiver. — آخرین تیر در ترکش را انداخت He shot his last bolt; he had no arrow left in his quiver.
ترکمان [A. pl. تراکمه] Turkoman.

ترکمانی Turkoman : قالیچه ت.

تَرکه Twig.

تَرِکه A. [ترکات]. Legacy ; patrimony ; heirloom. — مدیر ترکه Administrator (*law term*).

تُرکی Turkish. Selvage.

تَرکیب A. [ترکیبات]. Composition. Combination. Mixture. Compound. Syntax. Manner; form+.—ت.کردن To compound or compose. To combine. — بچه ت. In what m.? How?

ترکیب بند A. P. Poem of several stanzas of equal size; "composite-tie". [pound.

ترکیبی A. Synthetic. Com-

تَرکیدن [ترك] To burst. To split ; crack. [whipstitch.

تُرکی دوزی Overcast-stitch ;

ترکیده [P. P. of ترکیدن]

تُرکیه *Geog*. Turkey.

ترمبون *Fr*. Trombone.

ترمپت *Fr*. Trumpet.

ترمتای Merlin.

تُرمز *R*. Brake. — ترمز بادی Air-brake.— ترمزدستی Hand-brake.— ترمز روغنی Hydraulic brake.— ت. کردن To put on the brakes; pull up.

ترمس *Fr*. Thermos flask ; vacuum f.

تُرمس Lupine.

ترمه Cashmere.

تَرمیم A. Reparation. Amendment. — ترمیم کابینه Cabinet reshuffle. — ت. کردن To r. To amend.

ترمیمی A. Plastic : جراحی ت.

ترن *Fr*. = قطار [a whip.

ترنا o Cloth twisted into

تُرنج Citron.

ترنجبین (Manna of) Hedysarum.

ترنم A. Singing melodiously.— ت.کردن To sing m.; trill.

ترور *Fr*. Terror o. — ت. کردن To assassinate; shoot up.

تروریست *Fr*. Terrorist.

تَرویج A. Advancement; promotion; propagation. Circulating. — ت. کردن To propagate ; promote ; advance. To give currency to.

ترّه (Kind of) leek.

ترّهات A. Idle talks. Trifles.

تره بار Fresh fruit and vegetables.

ترهیبی A. Afflictive: مجازات ت.

تَری Wetness. Freshness.

تریاق *A-G*. Antidote.—تریاق‌فاروق Thebaic electuary.

تریاک [*f*. *G*. theriaca] Opium.

تریاک برگردان Emetic resin.

تریاکی *a*. Addicted to smoking opium. Opium-coloured. —*n*. Opium-smoker; o.-fiend.

تریبون *Fr*. Rostrum. — پشتِ ت. رفتن To mount the r.

تَرید Broth in which pieces of bread have been dipped; sop.—تریدروغن *Met*. Buttered on both sides

تراشه = تریشه
تریلیون *Fr.* Trillion.
ترین *Suf. forming the superlative degree.*
تزاید *A.* Augmentation ; growth. — رو به ت.گذاردن To begin to increase.
تزریق *A.* [تزریقات] Injection; shot. — ت.کردن To inject. *F.* To infuse.
تزکیه *A.* Purification:تزکیهٔ نفس
تزلزل *A.* Shaking. Instability. *F.* Agitation. [shaky.
تزلزل پذیر *A. P.* Unstable ;
تزلزل ناپذیر *A. P.* Firm.
تزویج *A.* Giving in marriage. *OS.* Coupling. — ت. کردن To join in m. To couple.
تزویر *A.* Dissimulation; guile; hypocrisy. — ت کردن To act hypocritically.
تزیید *A.* Increasing. — ت.کردن To increase; augment.
تزیین *A.* [تزیینات] Decoration. — ت.کردن To decorate.
تزئینی *A.* Decorative. Ornamental.
تسامح *A.* Negligence. — ت. کردن To act negligently.
تساوی *A.* Equality [برابری]. — بتساوی Equally.
تساهلo *A.* = مساهله
تسبیح *A.* Rosary; chaplet. Praise (to God) ; doxology [تسبیحات]. — ت. خواندن To praise (God) in hymns. — ت. گرداندن To tell (*or* bid) beads. — دانهٔ ت. Bead.
تسبیح‌خوان * *A.P.* Who praises God in hymns.
تستُ [*Cont. of* تواست].
تسجیع o *A.* Giving rime or cadence to.
تسجیل *A.* Confirmation.
تسحیر o *A.* Enchanting.
تسخر *A.* Mockery.
تسخیر *A.* Conquering. — ت.کردن To conquer; subjugate.
تسخیر ناپذیر *A. P.* Unconquerable ; invincible.
تسخیری *A.* Conquered o. — وکیل ت. Counsel briefed by the Government.
تسریع *A.* Acceleration.—ت.کردن [*usu. with*در] To accelerate; expedite.
تسطیح *A.* Levelling. Surfacing. — ت. کردن To level. To surface. [To convert.
تسعیر *A.* Conversion.— ت.کردن
تسکین *A.* Quieting. Appeasing; pacification. Alleviation. — ت. دادن To quiet; soothe; allay. To comfort. — ت. یافتن To become q. To be appeased. To find c.
تسلسل *A.* Interconnection ; concatenation. Continuity ; succession. Infinite series.— دورتسلسل The vicious circle.
تسلط *A.* Domination. *F.* Mastery; proficiency.— ت. داشتن بر

To dominate over.— ت. کردن To d. or rule.

تسلی *A*. Consolation. — ت. دادن To console; comfort. *Cf*. تسلیت

تسلی‌بخش *A. P*. Consolatory.— جایزهٔ ت. Booby prize.

تسلی پذیر *A. P*. Consolable.

تسلی ناپذیر *A. P*. Inconsolable.

تسلیت *A*. Condolence. — ت. گفتن To offer one's condolences to; condole with.

تسلیت نامه *A. P*. Letter of condolence.

تسلیح *A*. Arming. [*s*. تسلیح

تسلیحات *A*. Armaments. *Cf. the*

تسلیم *A*. Delivery. Surrendering. Submission; resignation. — ت. شدن To surrender. To submit; yield; resign oneself. — ت. کردن To surrender; give up (*or* over). To deliver. — سرِ تسلیم فرود آوردن به To bow or submit to; abide by.

تسمه *T*. Belt; leather band. — تسمهٔ پروانه *M*. Fan-belt. — آهن ت. Hoop-iron; band i.

تسمیه *A*. Denomination; giving a name. — وجه تسمیهٔ آن اینست که It is so called because.

تسنن *A*. Professing to be a sunnite. — اهل ت. Sunnite(s).

تسوید ० *A*. Making a rough draft of.

تسویه *A*. Liquidation. *OS*. Equalization. — ت. کردن To settle; liquidate.

تسهیل *A*. Facilitating.—ت. کردن To facilitate. [*s*. تسهیل

تسهیلات *A*. Facilities. *Cf. the*

تسهیم *A*. Sharing; dividing.

تشابه *A*. Similarity.

تشاله Jolly - boat.

تشبث *A*. Resort(ing). Recourse. Enterprise. — ت. کردن To have recourse.— اهل ت. Adventurer; one who resorts to irregular means. [Pl. تشبثات Hole-and-corner methods; irregular means.

تشبیه *A*. Likening. Comparison. Simile. Image. — ت. کردن To liken; compare.

تشت *or* **طشت** Flat wash-tub.

تشتت *A*. Diversity. Dispersion.

تشتک Small tub or basin. Ewer-stand.

تشجیع *A*. Emboldening. Encouragement. — ت. کردن To brave. To encourage.

تشخص *A*. Personification. Distinction. Overbearing mien.

تشخیص *A*. Distinction. Discretion. Discernment. Assessment (of tax, income, etc.). *Law*. Finding. *Med*. Diagnosis. — ت. دادن To distinguish; tell. To find. To assess. To determine. To diagnose. — ازهم ت. دادن To know apart; tell one from the other.— ت. دادیم که فوریت ندارد

We found that it was not urgent.

تشدّد *A*. Severity ; harshness. Violence. — ت.کردن To speak harshly.

تشدید *A*. Aggravation. Corroboration. The mark (ّ) put over a letter to indicate that it is to be pronounced hard, as if it were two letters. — ت.کردن To aggravate; intensify.

تشرزدن [*With* به] To tell (*or* tick) off loudly ; snap (a person's) head (*or* nose) off.

تشرّف *A*. Being honoured (by visiting a dignitary or a holy place).

تشریح *A*. Description. Anatomy. — ت. کردن To describe or analyse. To dissect.

تشریحدان *A*. *P*. = **کالبد شناس**

تشریحی *A*. Descriptive. Anatomical.

تشریف *A*. Honouring. — ت.آوردن [*In p. c.*] To come or arrive. — ت. بردن [*In p. c.*] To go. — ت. داشتن [*In p. c.*] To be or stay. *Cf.* تشریفات

تشریفات *A*. Ceremonies. Formalities. Circumstance. *Cf. the s.* تشریف [Formal.

تشریفاتی *A*. *P*. Ceremonial.

تشریف فرما شدن *A*. *P*. [*In p. c.*] To come or attend.

تشریکِ مساعی *a*. *p*. [*Better say* توحید مساعی] Cooperation.

تشرین *A*. *Either of two Jewish and Syriac months:* تشرین‌اول September - October and تشرین ثانی O.-November.

تشعشع *A*. Radiation. Brilliancy.

تشفی خاطر *a*. *p*. Cooling (after anger).

تشک [f. T. دوشك] Mattress. [*In a motor car*] Seat. — تشك بیمار Air-cushion.

تشك چه *T*. *P*. Small mattress. Pad. Seat.

تشکر *A*. Thanking. [Pl. تشکرات thanks]. — ت. کردن To thank : اززحمات او تشکر کردم I thanked him for his troubles.

تشکل *A*. Formation. Being organized.

تشکی *A*. Complaining.

تشکیل *A*. Formation. Framing. Organizing. — ت. دادن To form. To call, as a meeting. To organize. — ت. یافتن To be formed. To be held.

تشکیلات *A*. = **سازمان** Organization. *Cf. the s.* تشکیل

تشمس o *A*. Insolation.

تشمع *A*. Inceration. Cirrhosis.

تشنج *A*. Convulsion; spasm [usu. تشنج موضعی]. *F*. Confusion. — تشنج آبستنی Eclampsy. — تشنج آرواره Lockjaw [usu. کزاز]. — تشنج زهدان Uterine spasm.

تشنجی *A*. Spasmodic.

تشنکَ (*–nak*) Fontanel.
تشنک (*tashanak*) Sage. *Bot.*
تشنگی Thirst.
تشنه Thirsty. *F.* Eager. Greedy. — ت. بخون Bloodthirsty. — ت.کردن To make thirsty. — تشنهٔ Thirsty or eager for.
تشویر o *A.* Confusion. Shame.
تشویش *A.* Anxiety ; uneasiness; agitation. — تشویش خاطر Fear; apprehension. — ت.کردن To be disturbed. To have a fear or apprehension.
تشویق *A.* Encouragement. — ت.کردن To encourage.
تشی Porcupine.
تشیع *A.* Professing to be a shiite. — اهل ت. Shiite(s).
تشیید *A.* Strengthening.
تشییعِ جنازه *a. p.* Escorting a funeral ; f. ceremonies ; exequies.
تصاحب کردن *A. P.* To take possession of ; make oneself the owner of.
تصادف *A.* Coincidence. Collision. — ت.کردن To arrive by chance. To collide. — در راه با من ت.کرد He happened to meet me on the way. — نوروز با قتل ت.کرد The New Year fell on the Martyrdom Day. — حسنِ ت. Happy chance or hit.
تصادفاً *A.* By chance.
تصادم *A.* Collision. *Med.* Concussion. — ت.کردن To collide.

To strike.
تصاعد *A.* Progression.
تصاعدی *A. P.* Progressive.
تصانیف [Pl. of تصنیف]
تصاویر [Pl. of تصویر]
تصحیح *A.* [تصحیحات] Correction. — ت.کردن To correct. To read (a proof).
تصحیف *A.* (Making an) error in reading or writing. Changing the diacritical points of words.
تصحیف خوانی *A. P.* Misreading.
تصدّق *A.* Almsgiving. Alms (supposed to avert calamities) ; ransom. — ت. کردن To give (away as) alms. — تصدقت گردم May I be sacrificed to thee. [Form of addressing the Shah or other dignitaries].
تصدی *A.* Being in charge ; tenure of office ; incumbency. — دورهٔ ت. Period of o.
تصدیع *A.* (Causing) inconvenience. — ت. دادن To trouble or i. To importune.
تصدیق *A.* Confirmation ; certification. Attestation. Legalization : تصدیق امضاء ‖ ت.کردن To confirm. To certify. To admit. To legalize. — تصدیقِ بلاتصوّر Prejudgment.
تصدیق نامه *A. P.* = **گواهی نامه**
تصرف *A.* [تصرفات] Possession. — تصرف بلامعارض Usucaption. — ت. کردن To take possession

of ; possess. To deflower.— درچیزی تصرفات کردن To bring about changes in the condition of s. t.

تصریح *A*. Specifying. Stipulating ; also, stipulation [تصریحات]. — ت. کردن To stipulate. To specify.

تصریف *A*. [تصریفات]. Conjugation. Declension. *Med*. Revulsion.

تصعید *A*. Sublimation.— ت. کردن To sublimate.

تصغیر *A*. Diminution. — اسم ت. Diminutive (noun).

تصفیه *A*. Filtration. Refining; refinement. *F*. Settlement.— ت. کردن To refine. To filter. To settle; liquidate.— تصفیهٔ هوا Air-conditioning. — مدیر تصفیه Liquidator.

تصفیه خانه *A. P.* = **پالایشگاه**

تصلب *A*. Induration.— تصلب انساج Scleroma. — تصلب پوست Scleroderma. — تصلب پیله Tylosis.

تصمیم *A*. Decision; resolution; determination. Ruling. — ت. اتخاذ کردن or ت. گرفتن To take a decision ; arrive at a conclusion. To determine.

تصنع *A*. Affectation ; artificiality.

تصنیف *A*. Composition (of a book, etc.). Musical composition; popular song; ditty [pl. تصانیف or تصنیفات].— ت. کردن To compose or write.

تصنیف ساز *A. P*. Composer of popular songs ; sonneteer.

تصوّر *A*.[تصورات] Imagination; conception. Idea. — اصالت ت. Idealism. — تصورات اولیه First intentions [*in logic*].— ت. کردن To imagine ; conceive. To suppose ; think. — بتصورِ اینکه Thinking or supposing that.— قابل ت. Conceivable ; imaginable. — غیر قابل ت. Inconceivable; unthinkable.

تصوّف *A*. Sufism.

تصویب *A*. Approval ; sanction ; ratification. — ت. کردن To approve ; pass ; ratify ; sanction. — بتصویب رساندن To have approved.— بتصویب رسیدن To be a. ; meet approval.

تصویب نامه *A. P*. Decree (of the Council of Ministers).

تصویر *A*. [تصاویر] Picture ; effigy. Image. Description. Painting ; drawing. — ت. کردن To draw ; paint. — خط تصویری Hieroglyph.

تضادّ *A*. Contrast; contrariety. Antilogy.

تضامن *A*. Standing surety for each other. Joint and several responsibility.

تضامنی *A. P*. [*Of liabilities*] Joint and several — شرکت ت. General partnership.

تضرع *A*. Supplication; entreaty. ـ ت.کردن To entreat.

تضعیف *A*. Doubling. Weakening. ـ ت.کردن To double. To weaken. [tion.

تضمن *A*. Inclusion. Implica-

تضمین *A*. [تضمینات] Guarantee; security. Giving a s. Insertion of another's verses in one's own poem. ـ ت. کردن To guarantee.

تضییع *A*. Spoiling. Wasting. ـ ت. کردن To spoil. To waste.

تضییق *A*. Restraining; restriction [تضییقات]. *Med*. Stricture. [ment.

تطابق *A*. Conformity. Agree-

تطاول *A*. Trespassing. Usurpation. Arrogance.

تطبیق *A*. Comparing. Checking; verification. Collation. Application : تطبیق قانون باموارد A. of the law to instances. ـ ت.کردن To compare; collate. To check. To adapt; apply. *–vi*. To conform.

تطبیقی *A*. Comparative.

تطمیع *A*. Alluring. Corruption. ـ ت.کردن To allure. To corrupt.

تطوّر *A*. Gradual change; development; evolution.

تطویل *A*. Prolongation.

تطهیر *A*. Purification.

تطیر o *A*. Ornithomancy. Regarding as a bad omen.

تظاهر *A*. Affectation. Demonstration [pl. تظاهرات]. Eyewash. ـ ت. کردن To act; make a show; demonstrate.

تظلم *A*. Complaining against an injustice. Grievance [pl. تظلمات]. ـ ت.کردن To complain against an i.

تعادل *A*. Equilibrium. Par. ـ بحالت.در آوردن To equilibrate. ـ مسابقهٔ تعادلی Handicap race.

تعارف *A*. [تعارفات]. Compliment(s). Ceremony. Offer. Present. ـ ت.کردن To offer. To stand on ceremony. To make a present of. ـ تعارفِ آب‌حمام Worthless or insincere compliment. [tary.

تعارف‌امیز *A. P*. Complimen-

تعارفی *a*. *A.P*. Offered; made a present of. Ceremonious. *–n*. +Present.

تعاطی *A*. Exchange : تعاطی افکار

تعاقب *A*. Pursuing. ـ ت.کردن To pursue; chase; follow.

تعالی *A*. Elevation; rise.

تعالی *A*. (-1a) *OS*. May he be exalted. [*Used as an a*.] Exalted; Most High : خدای ت.

تعالیم [Pl. of تعلیم]

تعاوُن *A*. Cooperation; mutual assistance. ـ صندوق ت. Aid fund.

تعاونی *A. P*. Cooperative. ـ شرکت ت. C. society.

تعب • *A*. Toil. Fatigue.

تعبد *A*. Devoutedness; (obligatory) obedience.

تعبداً *A*. For mere obedience.

تعبیر *A*. [تعبیرات] Explanation ; interpretation : تعبیر خواب ‖ Expression. Phrase. — حسن ت. Euphemism.— ت.کردن To interpret. To construe.

تعبیه *A*. Preparation. Arrangement. — ت.کردن To prepare or arrange.

تعجب *A*. Surprise ; wonder. — ت.کردن To be surprised ; wonder. — جای تعجب است It is surprising.

تعجب آور *A. P*. Surprising.

تعجیل *A*. Haste; hurry . — ت.کردن To haste; make h.

تعداد *A*. Number. [Polygamy.

تعدّد *A*. Plurality. — تعدد زوجات

تعدی *A*. [تعدیات]Encroachment. Injustice. — ت. کردن به To oppress; do injustice to. To wrong.

تعدیل *A*. Adjustment.— ت.کردن To adjust. — قابل ت. Adjustable.

تعرّض *A*. Aggression. Molestation. Expostulation.— ت.کردن To make an attack. To molest. To object. To expostulate.

تعرضی *A. P*. Aggressive ; offensive.

تعرفه *A*. Tariff.

تعرفه بندی *A.P*. Tariff classification.

تعریض *A*. Widening. Exposition. — ت. کردن To widen.

تعریف *A*. Definition. Commendation. Description. — تعریف امراض Nosography. — ت. کردن To define. To speak highly [with از]. To give an account of ; narrate. — حرفِ ت. (Definite) article.

تعریفی + *A.P*. Commendable.

تعریق *A*. Causing to perspire.

تعزیت *A*. Condolence. Mourning. — ت.گرفتن To mourn.

تعزیم *A*. o Exorcism.

تعزیه *A*. Passion-play; miracle-play. *OS*. = تعزیت

تعزیه گردان *A. P*. Stage-manager (in a passion-play). *F*. Ringleader.

تعشق *A*. Showing love; amorousness.— ت ورزیدن To show l.

تعصب *A*. Fanaticism; bigotry. Intolerance. Prejudice. Party-spirit.

تعصبی + *A. P*. Jealously sensitive. Arising from fanaticism. *Cf*. متعصب

تعطیل *A*. [تعطیلات]. Cessation or suspension of work . Standstill. [For روز تعطیل] Holiday ; vacation. — ت. شدن To be closed or shut down.— ت.کردن To suspend or stop. To close (*or* shut) down. —*vi*. To cease to w. — یك روز تعطیل کردم I took a day off.

تعظیم *A*. Homage; reverence. Bowing down. — ت.کردن To

bow d. To do homage (to).

تعفن *A*. Fetidness. Putrefaction. — بوی ت. Fetid smell.

تعفین *A*. Tincture.

تعقل *A*. Reasoning ; intellection. — ت.کردن To reason.

تعقیب *A*. Pursuance ; following. Prosecution. — ت. کردن To pursue; follow. To continue. To sue; prosecute. — در تعقیبِ In pursuance of ; further to ; following. — در تعقیب کسی بودن To be on some one's track. — قابل ت. Suable; indictable. Liable to prosecution. Traceable.

تعقید *A*. Abstruseness. Obscurity of meaning.

تعلق *A*. Belonging. Attachment. Dependence. Connection. Possession. — ت. داشتن To belong. To depend. — ت.گرفتن To be chargeable or payable. To accrue. To be incumbent. To go or fall (to). — مبالغی بمن ت. میگیرد I am entitled to certain sums.

تعلل *A*. Making excuses. Procrastination. — ت. کردن or ت. ورزیدن To make e. To procrastinate.

تعلم *A*. Learning; being taught.

تعلیف *A*. Putting to grass. — ت.کردن To put to grass; graze.

تعلیق *A*. Suspension. Abeyance. — ت. بمحال Stipulation of a condition which is impossible of realisation.

تعلیل o *A*. Explaining the causes of. — حسن ت. Poetical aetiology.

تعلیم *A*. [تعلیمات & تعالیم] Teaching. Instruction. — ت. دادن To teach ; instruct. To train. — ت. گرفتن To train ; receive training. — علم ت. Pedagogy; art of teaching.

تعلیم بردار or **تعلیم پذیر** *A. P.* Teachable ; disciplinable.

تعلیمی *A*. Didactic.

تعلیمی *A*. Martingale. Switch. Walking stick o.

تعمد *A*. Acting intentionally. Intention ; design. — ت.کردن To act intentionally.

تعمداً *A*. = **دانسته** & **قصداً**

تعمدی *A. P*. Intentional.

تعمق *A*. Deep thinking. — در چیزی ت. کردن To go deep into s. t.

تعمید *A*. Baptism. — ت. دادن To baptize.

تعمیدی o *A*. Baptismal.

تعمیر *A*. [تعمیرات] Repair. Building. — ت.کردن To repair; mend.

تعمیرگاه *A. P*. Repair shop ; workshop. [Of a ship] Dock.

تعمیری *A. P*. Under repair. Requiring repairs.

تعمیق *A*. Sounding. *OS*. Deepening. — ت.کودن To sound.

تعمیم *A*. Generalization. — ت. کردن To generalize. To

extend (the meaning of).

تعنت * *A*. Faultfinding.

تعویذ *A*. Amulet.

تعویض *A*. Replacement. — ت. کردن To replace.

تعویق *A*. Putting off. — بتعویق انداختن To put off; postpone. — بعهدهٔ ت. افتادن To be postponed or delayed.

تعهد *A*. [تعهدات] Undertaking; guarantee. Commitment. Engagement. — ت. کردن To undertake; agree. To g. To subscribe.

تعیش *A*. Seeking means of livelihood. Living in pleasure +.

تعیین *A*. Appointment. Fixing. Ascertainment. — ت. کردن To appoint; fix. To ascertain. To determine.

تغابن *A*. Being cheated.

تغار *T*. Kneading-trough. Deep earthen pan. Bin. Large e. flower-pot. Wash-tub.

تغافل *A*. (Feigning) negligence. — ت.کردن To feign n.

تغ تغ Knock ; tap ; rap. — ت. در زدن To knock repeatedly at the door.

تغ تغ Knocking or rattling noise. — ت. کردن To rattle or knock.

تغذی *A*. Nourishment.

تغذیه *A*. Nourishing. — ت.کردن To feed ; nourish.

تغزل *A*. Singing love poems.

تغلق o *A*. Invagination ; intussusception.

تغنی o *A*. = خواندن Singing.

تغوّط *A*. Relieving the bowels.

تغّ و لغّ *or* **تق و لق** × Slack; not confirmed. Irregular. — مدرسه ت. است The school is not yet confirmed.

تغیر *A*. Getting angry. Indignation. Harshness. — ت. کردن To speak angrily or harshly.

تغییر *A*. [تغییرات] Change; alteration. — ت. دادن To change; alter; modify. — ت.کردن To change. To vary. — ت. یافتن To undergo a c. — تغییر رویه Change-over.

تغییر پذیر *A. P*. Changeable ; variable. [able.

تغییر ناپذیر *A, P*. Unchange-

تُف + Spittle; sputum. — تف‌خونی Haemoptysis. — بکسی تف انداختن To spit at (*or* upon) s. o. — تف کردن To s. out. — تف بر Shame or fie on. . .

تفاخر *A*. Vying with each other in glory. Self-glorification.

تفاریق *A*. = دفعات & اقساط *Cf. the s.* تفریق

تفاسیر [Pl. of تفسیر]

تفاصیل [Pl. of تفصیل]

تفاضل *A*. Difference. Differential. Fluxion. — تفاضل قطرین Ellipticity.

تفاضلی *A*. Differential.

تفأل *A*. Divination ; augury.– ت. زدن To augur. To divine. ت. با کتاب Bibliomancy.

تفاله Refuse. – تفالهٔ آهن Dross.– تفالهٔ قهوه Coffee-grounds. – تفالهٔ معدنی Scoria. – تفالهٔ نیشکر Megass.

تفاوت *A*. Difference. – تفاوتی نمیکند It does not make any difference. – این با آن ت. دارد This is different from that.

تفاهم *A*. Mutual understanding. – حسن ت. Good u.– سوء ت. Misunderstanding.

تفت Gardener's wicker basket; frail.

تفته [Cont. of تافته *a*.]

تفتیش *A*. = بازرسی Inspection.– ت. کردن To inspect. To search.

تفتین *A. P*. Exciting a sedition. – ت. کردن To excite a s. ; make mischief.

تفحص *A*. Minute research. – ت. کردن To make a minute research.

تفخیم o *A*. Honouring.

تفدان Spittoon.

تفرج *A*. Walking for pleasure. Recreation. – ت. کردن To take a walk.

تفرجگاه *A. P*. Place for recreation ; promenade ; public walk.

تفرس o *A*. Judgment by physiognomy. Perspicacity.

تفرعن *A*. Haughtiness. Vanity.

تفرق *A*. Separation ; dissipation ; dispersion. – تفرق اتصال Solution of continuity. *Med*. Dialysis.

تفرقه *A*. Disunion; dispersion. – تفرقه حواس Aprosexia. – بین دو نفر تفرقه انداختن To cause disunion between two persons ; separate them from each other.

تفریح *A*. Recreation ; diversion. Fun; sport.– ت. کردن To take recreation ; recreate. To amuse (*or* divert) oneself. To act in sport ; jest. – زنگ ت. Recess.

تفریحی *A. P*. Intended for fun. Recreative.

تفریط *A*. Wasting ; dissipation. Falling below a perfect state or limit. – ت. کردن To waste. – افراط و تفریط کردن To go to extremes.

تفریغ *A*. Liquidation. – ت. کردن To settle ; liquidate.

تفریق *A*. Subtraction. *Cf*. کاهش ‖ ت. کردن To subtract.

تفسیر *A*. [تفاسیر] Comment(ary). Exegesis. Interpretation. – تفسیر قضائی Judge-made law. – ت. کردن To comment on. To explain or interpret.

تفصیل *A*. [تفاصیل] Detailed account; detail.– بتفصیل In d.– با این تفاصیل + In spite of all this.

تفصیلا *A*. In detail.

تفصیلی *A. P*. Detailed.

تفضل *A*. Favour ; grace.

تفضلاً *A*. As a favour.
تفضیلی *A*. (*Gr.*) Comparative.
تفقد *A*. Sympathy; kindness. — از کسی ت. کردن To (be kind enough to) remember s. o. or inquire after his health. To speak kindly to s. o.
تفک Pea-shooter; blow-tube.
تفکر *A*. [تفکرات] Meditation; reflection. — ت. کردن To meditate; reflect.
تفکیک *A*. Separation. Analysis; breakdown. — ت. کردن To separate; segregate.
تفکیکاً *A*. Separately.
تفنگ *T*. Rifle; gun.
تفنگچی *T*. Rifleman. Watchman.
تفنگدار *T. P.* Rifleman.
تفنگ ساز *T. P.* Gunsmith.
تفنگ سازی *T. P.* Gunsmithing. Gunsmithery.
تفنن *A*. Diversion; amusement. Fancy.
تفنناً *A*. For fun; not seriously or regularly. Fancifully.
تفننی *A. P.* Fanciful; fancy *a*.
تفو * Fie! — ت. بر F. upon.
تفوق *A*. Supremacy; superiority. — بر کسی ت. جستن To gain s. over s. o.; surpass him.
تفویض *A*. Handing over. Abdication. Submission; resignation. — ت. کردن To give or turn over. To entrust.
تفهم *A*. Understanding.
تفهیم *A*. Causing to understand.

تقابل *A*. Oppositeness. Encounter. Reciprocity. *Astr*. Syzygy. — قابل ت. Opposable.
تقادیر [Pl. of تقدیر]
تقارُب *A*. Convergence [now همگرائی]. *Name of a metre*.
تقارن *A*. Conjunction. Simultaneity. Symmetry.
تقاص *A*. Vengeance. — ت. دادن To suffer v. — ت. گرفتن To take v.
تقاصیر [Pl. of تقصیر]
تقاضا *A*. Demand. Application. Request. Exigency. — ت. کردن To demand; solicit [usu. with از]. To apply for: برحسبِ تقاضایِ ‖ تقاضای کار کردن At the request of; at the instance of. [plication.
تقاضا نامه *A. P.* Written application.
تقاطع *A*. Intersection. — ت. کردن To intersect.
تقاعد *A*. = 1) بازنشستگی 2) مسامحه
تقاویم [Pl. of تقویم]
تقبل کردن *A. P.* To accept; undertake.
تقبیح *A*. Disapproval; condemning. — ت. کردن To disapprove or condemn. To decry or denounce.
تقدّس *A*. Holiness; sanctity.
تقدّم *A*. Priority; precedence. — برچیزی ت. داشتن To be prior to s. t. — حق ت. Priority.
تقدمةالمعرفه *A*. Prognosis.
تقدیر *A*. Destiny; fate [تقادیر]. Appreciation. — قابل ت. Wor-

thy of appreciation. — غیر قابل ت. Inappreciable. — ت. کردن To appreciate. To predestinate. — بهر تقدیر In any case.

تقدیراً *A.* Virtually.

تقدیر نامه *A. P.* Letter of commendation. *OS.* L. of appreciation.

تقدیری *A.* Virtual. *S. a.* مقدّر

تقدیس *A.* Sanctification. — ت. کردن To sanctify. To appreciate greatly ; praise +

تقدیم *A.* Presentation ; offering. Giving precedence (to). — ت. کردن To offer ; present ; make a p. of. [*In p. c.*] To give or pay. — با تقدیم احترامات بیکران Assuring you of our highest esteem . . . — تقدیم اعتدالین Precession of equinoxes.

تقدیمی *n. A. P.* Present; gift. — *a.* Offered. Dedicatory. — نسخهٔ ت. Presentation copy.

تقرّب *A.* Access ; approach. Favour.

تقرّح *A.* Ulcer o. — تقرح استخوان Caries ; cariosity.

تقریب *A.* Approximation. — بطور تقریب = **تقریباً**

تقریباً *A.* Nearly ; almost.

تقریبی *A. P.* Approximate.

تقریر *A.* Utterance. Recital. — ت. کردن To speak out ; utter. To assert. To recite.

تقریظ *A.* Commendation ; foreword.

تقسیط *A.* Arrangement for payment by instalments.

تقسیم *A.* Division. Distribution. Share ; portion + [pl. تقسیمات]. — ت. کردن To divide or share. To distribute. — قابل ت. Divisible.

تقصیر *A.* Guilt ; fault. Shortcoming. — تقصیر اواست *or* تقصیر با اوست It is his f. ; he is to blame. — ت. کردن To commit a f. To be guilty of a shortcoming.

تقصیر کار + *A. P.* = **مقصر**

تقطیر *A.* Distillation. — ت. کردن To distil. — کارخانهٔ ت. Distillery.

تقطیرالبول *A.* Strangury.

تقطیع *A.* Scansion. — ت. کردن To scan.

تقلا *A.* Struggle ; effort. — ت. کردن To struggle; make e.

تقلب *A.* [تقلبات] Dishonesty ; fraud. — ت کردن To cheat ; use trickery.

تقلبی *A.P.* Counterfeit. Fraudulent ; fraudulous.

تقلی′ Lamb from six months to one year old.

تقلیب o *A.* Inversion. Transformation. — الکل **تقلیبی** Denatured alcohol.

تقلید *A.* Imitation. Following (a religious leader). Mimicry. — ت. کردن To imitate. — ت. در آوردن To mime. To play the buffoon. To mock.

تقلیدی *A*. Imitation [*used as an a*.]. Counterfeit. Mimic; mimetic. Adopted or embraced by imitation. مذهب ت. ‖ تسمیهٔ ت. Onomatopoeia.

تقلیل *A*. = کاهش Diminution; reduction — ت. دادن To reduce. To diminish.

تقنین *A*. Legislation.

تقنینی *A*. Legislative. [Fem. تقنینیه Ex. دورهٔ تقنینیهٔ پانزدهم the Fifteenth Parliament].

تق و لق *S. u*. **تغ و لغ**

تقوی *A*. Virtue; piety.

تقویت *A*. Strengthening; fortification. Reinforcement. Support. — ت. کردن To strengthen. To support. To reinforce. — تقویت مزاج کردن To establish one's health. — تلمبهٔ تقویت فشار Boosting-pump.

تقویم *A*. Calendar. Evaluation; appraisal. — ت. کردن To appraise; evaluate; assess.

تقی (*A*.) *Mas. pr. name. OS*. Virtuous or pure. [Pl. اتقیاء]

تقیه *A*. Dissimulation — ت. کردن To dissimulate. To be cautious in religious matters.

تَک *or* **تَگ** Running; run.

تَک *T*. Single; lone. Unique.

تَک o = **ته** Bottom.

تک + = **نوك**

تکاپو Search. Running about. — ت. کردن To run a.; cast a.

تکاثر o *A*. Being numerous.

تکادو = **تکاپو** [parture.

تك آغاز Start: point of de-

تکاسل *A*. Indolence.

تکافو *A*. Sufficiency. — ت. کردن To meet; cover. To be sufficient (for).

تکالیف [Pl. of تکلیف].

تکامل *A*. Gradual perfection or development. Evolution.

تکاملی *A*. Evolutional.

تکان Shake. Movement; motion. Jerk. Shock. — ت. خوردن To shake; move. To be shocked. — ت. دادن To shake or m. To wag: دُم ت. دادن

تک الجام Winning-post.

تکایا [Pl. of تکیه]

تکاندن [تکان] To shake (down or off). To cause to s.

تکاهل o *A*. Indolence.

تکبد o *A*. Culmination.

تکبد نما *A. P*. Transit-instrument.

تکبر *A*. Pride; haughtiness.

تکبر آمیز *A. P*. Proud; arrogant: سخنان ت.

تک برگ Monophyllous.

تك تك One by one; separately. Insular. Sporadic.

تکثر o *A*. Abounding; being increased.

تکثیر *A*. Increasing. — ت. کردن To increase; multiply.

تکثیف o *A*. Condensing. Thickening.

تک خال *C. P*. Ace.

تک خوان Soloist.

تک‌خوانی Solo; vocal recital.

تک دانه Monospermous.
تکدّر *A*. Being offended; offence.
تکدی *A*. = **گدایی**
تکدیر o *A*. Causing offence. *OS*. Making turbid. — مجازات **تکدیری** Punishment of a minor offence.
تکذیب *A*. Denial. — ت.کردن To deny ; refute.
تکرار *A*. Repetition.— تکرار جرم Recidivism. — ت. کردن To repeat.
تکرّر *A*. Being repeated. Repetition. Frequency.
تکریم *A*. Honour(ing).
تک‌زا Uniparous.
تکسر o *A*. = 1) شکستگی 2) شکسته نفسی
تک سُم Soliped.
تکفل *A*. Guaranteeing ; undertaking. Supporting — تحت تکفل من بود I supported him ; he was dependent on me for support. — ت.کردن To support. To guarantee.
تکفیر *A*. Excommunication. — ت.کردن To accuse of heresy.
تکلان o *A*. = **اعتماد & توکل**
تک لپه Monocotyledonous.
تکلتو *T*. Saddle-pad ; panel.
تکلف *A*. (Taking) pains ; trouble. Ceremony [تکلفات].
تکلم *A*. Speaking ; conversation. — تکلم صدری Pectoriloquy. — ت.کردن To speak.
تکلیس *A*. Calcination.
تکلیف *A*. [تکالیف] Duty. School exercise. Suggestion. Imposition. — ت.کردن To suggest; propose. To impose. To require. — ت. چیست ؟ What is the proper course to pursue? How shall we proceed ? — بحد تکلیف رسیدن To come of age.
تکمل *A*. Completion.
تکمله o *A*. Complement ; supplement. Codicil.
تکمید o *A*. Fomentation.
تکمیل *A*. Completion. — ت.کردن To complete ; finish.
تکمیلی *A*. Complementary.
تك نواز Soloist.
تک نوازی Solo; recital.
تك و توك + Sporadic; few ; here and there.
تکوّن *A*. Coming into existence.
تکوین *A*. Bringing into existence ; creation ; genesis.
تکه *T*. (*tekeh*) or تیکه Piece. Morsel. — ت کردن To cut to pieces.— تکه تکه 1) *a*. Torn to pieces ; ragged. Broken into p. 2) *ad*. A piece at a time. Piecemeal. — ت. ت. کردن To tear (to pieces). To break into pieces. — ت. سرچیزی دادن To piece out s. t.
تکه *T*. (*takeh*) He-goat. Ibex.
تکی *T*, *P*. 1) Odd : جلد تکی 2) Single.
تك یاخته Unicellular.
تکیه *A*. Leaning. Support ;

prop. *F*. Reliance. Stress. — Theatre for passion-plays [pl. تکایا]. ت. دادن — To (cause to) lean. — برچیزی ت. کردن To lean on s. t. — تکیه کلام Habitual phrase or word.

تکیه‌گاه *A. P.* Support. Resting-place. Refuge. Fulcrum.

تگرگ Hail. — دانهٔ ت. Hailstone. — ت. میبارد It hails.

تگرگی Dotted ; spotted. — نمای ت. Stippling finish. — شیشهٔ ت. Ground glass.

تَل *A.* [تلال & اتلال] Hill [تپه]. *By e.* Heap. — تل شدن + To be heaped.

تِل *T.* Aigrette ; plume.

تلاش Search. Struggle. ت. کردن To struggle.

تلاشی *A.* Dispersion. Disappearance.

تلاطم *A.* Dashing : تلاطم امواج ‖ Collision. — ت. کردن To dash. To collide together.

تلافی *A.* Retaliation ; vengeance. Recompense. — ت. کردن To recompense. To retaliate. To make up for. — ت. برسر کسی درآوردن To take v. on s. o.

تلاقی *A.* Confluence ; meeting. — تلاقی رگها Inosculation of blood-vessels.

تلال ○ [A pl. of تل]

تلألؤ *A.* Sparkle. Shining.

تلامذه or **تلامید** [Pl. of تلمید]

تلان تلان + In a stately manner. — ت. رفتن To sail.

تل انبار *A. P.* Heap ; accumulation.

تلاوَت *A.* Reading or chanting (the Koran). — ت کردن To chant or read.

تلبیس *A.* Imposture. Disguise. Hypocrisy. — ت. کردن To use guile ; dissemble.

تلحین *A.* Modulation.

تلخ Bitter. *F.* Acrimonious. — ت. کردن To embitter. — اوقاتِ کسی را تلخ کردن To make s. o. angry ; upset him. — اوقاتش ت. شد He was u. He got a.

تلخ کام Disappointed ; sad ; afflicted.

تلخ کامی Disappointment ; sadness ; affliction.

تلخه Darnel ; tare.

تلخی Bitterness. *F.* Hardship.

تلخیص *A.* Summarisation. — ت. کردن To summarize ; make a resumé of.

تلذّذ *A.* (Taking) pleasure.

تلسکپ *Fr.* Telescope. *Cf.* دوربین

تلطف *A.* Kindness ; favour. — ت. کردن To show kindness.

تلطیف *A.* Making fine or pure.

تلغ تلغ کردن + To jolt. To rattle. To rumble.

تلف *A.* [تلفات] Loss; casualty. Wasting. Perishing. — ت. کردن To waste. To perish. — ت. شدن To p. or die. To be wasted.

تلفظ *A.* Pronunciation. — ت. کردن To pronounce.

تلفن *Fr.* Telephone. — ت. زدن or ت. کردن To telephone. — بکسی ت. کردن To telephone (to), or ring up, s. o. — پای ت. شمارا میخواهند You are wanted on the telephone.

تلفن‌چی *Fr. T.* Telephone operator. [message.

تلفن‌گرم *Fr.* Telephonic

تلفنی *Fr. P.* Telephonic.

تلفیق *A.* Putting together; composing. — ت. کردن To compose.

تلقی کردن *A. P.* To receive or meet. — فوری ت. کردن To treat as urgent. — خوب ت. کردن To take in good part. To greet. — با تردید تلقی کردن To take with a grain of salt; regard as doubtful. — حسن ت. Embracement.

تلقیح *A.* Fecundation. Pollination. Inoculation.

تلقین *A.* [تلقینات] Suggestion. Inculcation. Inspiration. Prompting. — ت. کردن To suggest. To inculcate. To instruct. To dictate.

تلکه کردن + To touch for.

تلگراف *Fr. & E.* Telegraph. Telegram. — ت. کردن To telegraph; wire: به شیراز تلگراف کردیم We telegraphed Shiraz. — بوسیلهٔ ت. By telegram; telegraphically.

تلگرافاً *Fr. A.* (*C. E.*) By telegram; telegraphically.

تلگرافچی *Fr. T.* Telegraph operator.

تلگراف خانه *Fr. P.* Telegraph office.

تلگرافی *a. Fr. P.* Telegraphic. — گل ت. Periwinkle. — مخابرهٔ ت. Telegram. *-ad.* (*C.E.*) Telegraphically. [sery.

تلمبار or **تلیبار** Silkworm nur-

تلمبه *T.* Pump. — ت. زدن To pump.

تلمبه چی *T.* Pumpman.

تلمبه خانه *T. P.* Pump-house.

تلمذ *A.* Discipleship. Pupilship. — نزد که ت. میکرد؟ Whose pupil was he?

تلمیح *A.* Allusion.

تلمیذ o *A.* = شاگرد [تلامیذ & تلامذه] Pupil. Disciple.

تلنگر + Flick; fillip. — ت. زدن To f.

تلوآ *A.* = لفاً [staging.

تلواره o Small scaffold or

تلواسه o Struggle. Agitation.

تلوتلو خوردن + To stagger. To totter.

تلوّن *A.* Versatility; capriciousness; fickleness [usu. تلون مزاج].

تلویح *A.* (Making a) hint.

تلویحاً *A.* Implicitly. — ت. بمن گفت که He as good as told me that.

تلویزیون *Fr.* Television. — با تلویزیون فرستادن To televise.

تله Trap. *Cf.* دام ‖ در تله انداختن

To trap.

تله موش Mouse-trap.

تلیسه Two-year-old heifer.

تلئلوء [Erroneous for تلألوء]

تمّ ٥ (*tam'a*) *A.* Finis ; end. *OS.* It has been finished. [Fem. تمت]

تماثیل [Pl. of تمثال]

تمادی ٥ *A.* Protraction.

تمارض *A.* Feigning illness. — ت.کردن To feign i.; malinger.

تماس *A.* Contact. Impact. Tangency. — ت. داشتن To be in contact or touch.— ت. پیدا کردن *or* ت.گرفتن To c.; get into c.

تماشا *A.* Sightseeing. Spectacle; show. — ت. دارد It is worth seeing ; it has much to see.— ت.کردن To watch ; see.

تماشاچی *A. T.* Spectator ; looker-on.

تماشاخانه *A. P.* Theatre.

تماشایی *A. P.* Worth seeing ; spectacular ; as good as a play.

تمام *a. A.* Whole. Complete. Full. Round, as a number.— وقت ت. است Time is over (*or* up). —*n.* The whole. All: تمام دخترها all (of the) girls.— ت. وکمال In full (amount). — ت. شدن To be finished; come to an end. To be consumed. To full, as the moon. To go out of print.— صد ریال برای من ت. شد It cost me (*or* I spent for it) 100 *rials*.— صبرم ت. شد My patience has been tried; I am (*or* was) out of p. — ت. کردن 1) *vt.* To finish ; complete; bring to an end; have done with; get through w. To waste ; dissipate. — کار را تمام کرده اند They have left nothing undone or undiscovered. 2) *vi.* To expire; die. — بزودی هرچه تمامتر As quickly as possible.

تماماً *A.* Entirely; completely; fully ; all.

تمام اهنگی *A. P.* Wholly musical.

تمام رسمی *A. P.* Full : لباس ت. f. dress.

تمام رنگی *A. P.* Coloured by Technicolor.

تمام عیار *A. P.* Of standard purity ; sterling.

تمام قد *A. P.* Full-length ; life-size(d).

تمامی *A. P.* The whole ; all.

تمامیت *A.* Entirety; integrity.

تمایل *A.* [تمایلات .Pl] Inclination.— ت. داشتن To be inclined. — رای ت. Vote of intent or inclination.

تمبر *Fr.* Stamp. — ت. خوردن To be stamped. — ت. زدن To stamp. — کسر تمبر داشتن To be understamped. — ۵۰ دینار کسر تمبر '50 *dinars* postage due'.

تمبر جمع کن *Fr. A. P.* Philatelist.

تمتع *A*. Enjoyment. Fruition. — ازچیزی ت. یافتن To enjoy s. t.
تمثال *A*. [تماثیل] Portrait; effigy; image. Picture.
تمثل *A*. Citing a proverb.
تمثیل *A*. Allegory. Proverb.
تمجید *A*. Praise. — ت. کردن To p. — ت. شایان Praiseworthy.
تمدّد *A*. Stretching oneself. Tension. — تمدد اعصاب Relaxation or recreation. — تمددِ ماهیچه Muscular tonicity. — قوهٔ ت. Tensile force.
تمدن *A*. Civilization.
تمدید *A*. Extension; prolongation. — ت. کردن *or* ت. دادن To extend; prolong. — ت. یافتن To be extended.
تمر *A*. Tamarind. [This is properly تمر هندی]. — تمرگجرات Red tamarind.
تمرّد *A*. Disobedience. Rebellion. — ت. کردن To rebel. — از فرمان کسی ت. کردن To disobey s. o.
تمرکز *A*. Centralization. Concentration. — ت. دادن To centralize. To concentrate. — ت. یافتن To be centralized.
تمرین *A*. [تمارین *or* تمرینات] Exercise; drill. Rehearsal. — ت. کردن To d. or exercise; take exercises. To go over and o. (again).
تمساح *A*. Crocodile..
تمسخر *A*. Ridicule. — ت. کردن To ridicule; mock.
تمسک *A*. Obligation; bond. — ت. کردن To take hold of. To resort to.
تمشک Raspberry.
تمشیت *A*. Managing. Promoting. — ت. کردن To manage. To promote. [Power.
تمکن *A*. Financial ability.
تمکین *A*. 1) • Sedateness; gravity; dignity. 2) + Submission or obedience; also, non-resistance. — ت. کردن [With از] To submit to; obey; also, condescend to.
تملق *A*. Flattery. — ت. گفتن To flatter [*with* از *or* به].
تملک *A*. Taking possession. — ت. کردن To take p. of.
تملیک *A*. Giving (in) possession o. (Door-)latch.
تملیکی *A*. [*Of a will*] Directive; vesting possessory rights.
تمنا *or* **تمنی** *A*. Desire; wish. Request. — ت. کردن از To request. To demand.
تموّج *A*. Undulation. Fluctuation.
تموز *Jewish and Syriac month* (June-July).
تموّل *A*. = ثروت - دولت
تمهید *A*. Arrangement; preparation. Manœuvre. Skill.
تمهیدی *A*. Interlocutory. Preparatory.

تمیز *n. A.* Discernment. Distinction. Appeal to the Supreme Court of Justice.—*a.*+ Neat; clean. Proper. — دیوانِ عالی ت. Supreme Court; High C. of Cassation. — ت. دادن To distinguish; tell. To appeal to the Supreme Court. — ت. کردن To clean. To dust. To clear.

تمیزی + *A. P.* Cleanliness.

تَن Body. Person. — دو تن ازایشان Two of them. تن بتن *See in the vocab.* — تن (در) دادن To yield; submit. To cave in. To give in. — تن بکار دادن To put one's shoulder to the wheel. — تن کردن + To put on; wear. — تن کسی کردن To cause s. o. to wear; help him with (his clothes). — تنش میخارد He is itching for trouble; he asks for it. He is eager for the fray.

تَن [Imp. of تنیدن]

تُن *Fr.* Ton. — کشتی ۲۰۰۰ تنی Two-thousand tonner.

تنازع *A* (Mutual) struggle. — تنازع بقاء S. for existence.

تن آسا(ی) • Self-indulgent.

تن آسایی *or* تن آسانی • Self-indulgence.

تناسب *A.* Proportion. — بتناسب Proportionately; proportionally. — تناسب اندام Symmetry.

تناسخ *A.* Metempsychosis.

تناسخی *A.* Metempsychosist.

تناسل *A.* Reproduction. — آلت ت. Genital organ.

تناسلی *A.* [Fem. تناسلیه] Genital: آلات تناسلیه

تنافر *A.* Mutual aversion. — تنافر اصوات Dissonance. — تنافرحروف Cacophony.

تناقض *A.* Contradiction. — با چیزی ت. داشتن To be contradictory to s. t.

تناقض گویی *A. P.* Self-contradiction.

تناوُب *A.* Alternation. Intermittence. — به ت. Alternately. Intermittently.

تناور Corpulent; big.

تناول کردن • *A. P.* = خوردن To eat.

تنباکو Tobacco.

تنبان Loose breeches. Loose skirt formerly worn by women.

تن بتن. Carried on between two persons. — جنگ ت. Duel.

تنبک One-headed long (orchestral) drum. — ت. زدن To play on the *tombak.*

تنبل Lazy. [be lazy.

تنبلی Laziness. — ت. کردن To

تنبور (Kind of) guitar or lute.

تنبوشه (Clay) waterpipe.

تنبول Betel.

تنبه *A.* Being roused. *F.* Notice. Admonition.

تنبیه *A.* Punishment. Note;

remark. — ت. کردن To punish.
تن پرست Self-indulgent. Lazy.
تن پرور Self - indulgent. Voluptuous.
تن پروری Self-indulgence.
تن پیمایی Anthropometry.
تنخواه Funds; capital. — تنخواهِ گردان Imprest.
تُند *a*. Quick ; rapid ; express. Fast : ساعت ت. است ‖ Rash. Harsh. Abrupt. Steep. Hot-tempered. Pungent. Strong : قهوهٔ ت. ‖ Deep; also, bright as a colour. *Geom*. Acute. —*ad*. Fast; quickly. Rashly. Hastily. Harshly. — ت. رفتن To go (*or* walk) fast. *F*. To come it rather strong. To take an extreme course ; go to great lengths. — ت. شدن To quicken. To become strong. To get angry. — ت. کردن To q. ; accelerate. To set f. To make pungent. — ت. کارکردن [*Of a watch*] To gain ; go too f. — تند وکند کردن To regulate (the speed of).
تند باد Hurricane.
تند خو Hot-tempered.
تندخویی Hot temper; fiery t.
تندر = رعد Thunder.
تندرست Healthy.
تندرستی Good health.
تندرو Swift (in walking). *F*. Extravagant. Ultraprogressive. [*Of a train*] Express.
تندرَوی Excessive progressiveness. Extravagance.
تند مزاج & تند طبع *P. A*. Hot-tempered.
تندکن Accelerator.
تند مزاجی *P. A*. Hot temper.
تند و تیز Pungent. *F*. Hot-tempered; harsh.
تند وکندکن Speed-regulator.
تنده *n*. Steep slope; escarpment. Swift stream. —*a*. Steep.
تندی Rapidity ; speed. Steepness. Abruptness. Harshness. *See* تند ‖ باکسی ت. کردن To speak harshly to s. o.
تندیس Image.
تنزل *A*. Decline. Retrogradation. Fall.— ت. کردن To decline. To fall; be reduced (in price). To retrograde. To be degraded. — ت. دادن To degrade. To reduce in price. — تنزل رتبه Degradation; demotion[*U.S.*].
تنزیب Tanjib ; netting.
تنزیل *A*. Discount. Interest. — Revelation o. — ت. کردن To discount. To borrow on interest.
تنزیه *A*. Purifying. Considering inviolable. Transcendence.
تنسیق *A*. Regulating; arranging.
تنشوی Bath(ing-tub).
تنصیف *A*. Bisection. Dividing in halves.
تنطق *A*. Speaking.

تنتور - تنطور *Fr*. Tincture.

تنظيف *A*. Cleaning; cleansing.– ت.کردن To clean, To deterge.

تنظيم *A*. Putting in order; regulating. [Pl. تنظيمات arrangements; regulations]. – ت. کردن To regulate. To compose. To draw up.

تنعم *A*. Living luxuriously.

تنفخ *A*. Inflation o. – تنفخ ريه Emphysema.

تنفر *A*. Aversion; dislike. – تنفر طبيعى Antipathy.– ت. داشتن To d. or hate [*with* از].

تنفرآميز & تنفر آور *A. P.* Disgusting. Repugnant.

تنفس *A*. Breathing; respiration. Break; recess. – ت.کردن To breathe.

تنفسی *A*. Respiratory. – تلمبهٔ ت. Suction-pump.

تنفيذ *A*. Authorization. Confirmation. Affirmation. – ت.کردن To authorize. To confirm.

تنقل *A*. Dessert; junket [usu. in the pl. تنقلات].

تنقيح *A*. Expurgation.

تنقيد *A*. = انتقاد

تنقيه *A*. Purging. Dredging. Enema; injection. – ت.کردن To dredge. To purge. To give an enema or i. to.

تنک Thinly scattered.

تنکاب Shallow. *F*. Raw; green.

تنکار [*Per. f. Fr.* tincal] Borax.

تنکه Knickers; panties. Shorts. Panel (of a door). Flake. Metal sheet. – ت. کردن To make into sheets. To slab.

تنگ *a*. Narrow. Tight: لباس ت. ‖ [*Of breath*] Short. *See* تنگ نفس ‖ Barren or hard, as a year. –*n*. Girth. Strap. –*ad*. Closely. – ت.کردن To make narrow. To tighten. – (به) ت. آمدن To be made helpless. To be driven to extremities. To be fed up.– (به) ت. آوردن To render h.; drive to e.– خودرا از تنگ وتا نينداختن + To save one's face; join in the laugh. – تنگِ هم Close(ly); compact(ly). – خلقش ت. است He is in a bad mood.– دلم ت.است I feel lonely.

تنگ Water-bottle; carafe. Decanter. Flagon.– تنگ آزمايشگاه Flask. – تنگ کوچك Cruet; castor.

تنگاب Concentrated; strong. – آبگوشت ت. Consommé.

تنگ بست All-in; everything included.

تنگ‌چشم Insatiable. Avaricious.

تنگ حوصله *P. A.* Impatient. Testy; peevish.

تنگدست Indigent.

تنگدستی Indigence; poverty.

تنگدل Heartsick. Despondent. Lonely; homesick.

تنگدلی Heartsickness. Loneliness.

تنگنا(ی) Narrow pass. Strait. *F*. Tight corner. Straitened circumstances.
تنگ نفس *P*. *A*. Asthmatic.
تنگ نظر etc. = نظر تنگ etc.
تنگه Strait. Isthmus.
تنگه نفس *P*. *A*. Asthma.
تنگی Narrowness. Tightness. *F*. Scarcity. Difficulty; pinch.
تندویی Arachnoid.
تنور Oven.
تنوّع *A*. Variety; relief.
تنومند Corpulent; big.
تنومندی Corpulence.
تنویر *A*. Illumination. — تنویرِ افکار Enlightenment. — ت. کردن To (en)ligten.
تنه Trunk. [*Of a plane*] Fuselage. — ت. خوردن To be brushed against; be hustled. — ت. زدن به To hustle or jostle; brush or push against.
تنها Alone. Solitary. Sole; only. — ت. کسیکه The o. person who.
تنهایی Solitude. — بتنهایی Alone.
تنه‌دار Bulky; corpulent.
تنی Of full blood: برادر تنی
تنیدن o [تن] To spin or weave. *See* ریستن & بافتن
تنین *A*. (*Astr*.) The Dragon.
تو (*to*) Thou. [*Governed by a prep*.] Thee. [*Preceded by an 'ezafah'*] Thy : کتابِ تو
تو (*tu:*) *ad*.1) In : بفرمائید تو Come in, please. 2) Within. —*n*. Interior; inside. — توی *prep*. In; into. — تو بردن To retract. — تو کردن + To take in; enter; cause to enter. — تو گذاشتن To take in. To hem.
توابع *A*. [Pl. of تابع] Dependencies *Math*. Functions.
تواتر *A*. (Successive) hearsay. Tradition related by successive witnesses. — به ت. رسیدن To be handed down (by tradition).
تواتراً *A*. By successive hearsay.
توارث *A*. Inheritance. — از راه ت. By i.
تواری *A*. Lying hid. Fleeing.
تواریخ [Pl. of تاریخ].
توازن *A*. Equilibrium; balance.
توازی *A*. Parallelism.
تواضع *A*. Humility. Curtsy. — ت. کردن To show humility.
توافق *A*. Mutual agreement; m. consent. Harmony. — به توافق آراء By a unanimous vote; unanimously. — ت. کردن To agree (with each other).
توالت *Fr*. Toilet; dress(ing). *Cf*. بزك&آرایش ‖ ت. کردن To make one's toilet; dress (up).
توالد *A*. Reproduction.
توالی *A*. Succession. — بتوالی *or* علی‌التوالی Successively; consecutively. Continuously.
توام *A*. Twin. *F*. Linked; joint. — ت. کردن To twin. To join or link together.
تواماً *A*. (Both) together.

توان 1) *n*. Power. Ability.— توانِ دوم 2nd. power ; square. توان سوم Third p. ; cube. 2) [Imp. of توانستن]. — آیا میتوان آنرا دید Can one see it? Is it possible to see it? — تا بتوان or تامیتوان So far as p.

توانا Powerful.

توانایی Power; ability.

توانستن [توان] To be able : من میتوانم بروم I can go; I am able to go. — خواهم توانست I shall be a. — شما می‌توانید بروید یا بمانید You may (choose to) go or stay.

توانگر • Rich (person).

توانگری • Wealth; riches.

توبره or **تبره** Nose-bag.

توبه *A*. Repentance. — ت. کردن To repent. [Regretful.

توبه‌کار *A. P.* Penitent.

توبیخ *A*. = **سرزنش** Reprimand; reproach. — ت. کردن To reprimand or reproach.

توپ *T*. Cannon ; gun. Ball. Piece : يك ت. چلوار ‖ Paper يك ت. سنجاق ‖ *C.P.* 1) Bid. 2) Bluff — توپ سلام انداختن To fire a salute. — بتوپ بستن To bombard; cannonade. — ت. زدن To kick a ball. *C. P.* To (raise the) bid. To bluff.

توپ بازی *T. P.* Game of ball.

توپچی *T*. Artillery-man.

توپخانه *T. P.* Artillery (department).

توپدار *T. P.* Gun-boat.

توپُر Solid : not hollow.

توپوز *T*. (*topoz*) Mace. Knobstick.

توپوزی *T. P.* Mace-like ; clublike. — خال ت. *C. P.* Spade. [hub.

توپی Plug ; spigot. Nave ;

توت or **تود** Mulberry.

توت انجیر Sycamore.

توت فرنگی Strawberry.

توتون *T*. (Pipe) tobacco.

توتیاء *A*. Tutty; vitriol. — توتیای روی Sulphate of zinc; white v. — توتیای سبز Green v. — توتیای قرمز Oxide of copper. — توتیای کبود Sulphate of c. — توتیای چشم = **سرمه**

توتیاءالبحر *A*. Sea-urchin.

توجه *A*. Attention. Care. Favour. Concentration. [Pl. توجهات Auspices ; good offices]. — ت. کردن (از) To take care of; look after. — شخصِ مورد توجه طرف ت. Favourite. — ت. قرار دادن To consider. To give attention to. — قابل ت. Worthy of a. Considerable. — غیر قابل ت. Not worthy of a. Insignificant. — باتوجه به With due a. to.

توجیه *A*. Explaining (away). Explanation [pl. توجیهات]. — ت. کردن To account for ; explain (away). To justify.

توحش *A*. Horror. Unsociableness. Savagery.

توحید *A*. Unification. Monotheism. — توحید مساعی Cooperation; also, team-work.

تود *S. u.* **توت**

تودار Deep; reserved.

تودرتو Allowing free passage to one another. *F*. Intricate.

تودلبرو + Of attractive features or manners; charming.

تودماغی *a*. Nasal. *–ad*. Nasally; with a twang. — ت. حرف زدن To twang; speak through the nose.

توده Heap; pile. Mass. The (great) mass. The rabble. — ت.کردن To heap up; stack.

توده شناسی Folk-lore.

تودهنی + Rebuff.—بکسیت. زدن To rebuff or snub s. o.

تودیع A. (Bidding) farewell; valediction. Depositing. — باکسی ت.کردن To bid farewell to s. o.

تور [f. Fr. *tulle*] Net. Lace. Tulle.—تورسیمی Wire screen.— تور صورت Veil.— تورگیس Snood.

تورات *or* **تورية** *A*. (*towrat*) Mosaic Law. Old Testament.

توران Transoxania. *Fem. pr. name*.

تورّب *A*. Obliquity.

توربین *Fr*. Turbine.

تورّق *A*.Lamination; scaliness.

تورّم *A*. Swelling. Inflation.— ت.کردن To swell. To inflate.

تورن سل *Fr*. Litmus.

توری [f. تور *q. v.*]Net. Lace. Trimming. Veil. (Incandescent)mantle.— چراغت M.-lamp.

توریه *A*. Dissimulation.

توزیع *A*. Distribution. — ت.کردن To distribute.

توُسرخ Shaddock.

توسط *A*. Intermediation. Agency. — ت. کردن To mediate.— توسطِ *or* بتوسطِ By; by means of; by the intermediation of. Through. Care of (C/O).

توسعاً *A*. By extension.

توسعه *A*. Expansion; extension, development. — ت. دادن To expand; extend; develop. — ت. یافتن To be expanded, extended, or developed.

توسعه طلب *a. p*. Expansionist.

توسل *A*. Resorting. — ت. کردن To resort. To betake oneself.

توسن Unmanageable (horse).

توسه (Russian) alder.

توشه Provisions for a journey.

توشه‌دان Wallet; knapsack.

توشیح *A*. Acrostic. Double riming. — بتوشیح همایونی رسید It received royal assent; it was signed by His Majesty the Shah.

توصیف *A*. Description. Commendation. — ت.کردن To describe; qualify.

توصیفی *A. P*. Descriptive.

توصیه *A*. Recommendation. —

ت.کردن To recommend. To advise.

توضیح A. [توضیحات] Explanation. — ت. دادن To explain.

توضیحی A. P. Explanatory.

توطن A. Settling, as in one's own country. — در کشوری ت. کردن To choose a country as one's home; settle in a c.

توطئه A. Plot; conspiracy. — ت. چیدن To weave a plot; conspire.

توفال Lath. — توفال بهن Shingle.

توفال‌کوب Lather.

توفان etc. = طوفان etc.

توف بار (Rain) storm.

توفیر A. Difference. Increased revenues ○.

توفیق A. Success. Grace. — توفیق اجباری Blessing in disguise. — ت. یافتن To succeed.

توقع A. [توقعات] Expectation. Request. Begging. — ت. داشتن از To expect. — ت.کردن To request or ask. To beg.

توقف A. Staying Halting. Pause. Insolvency; suspension of payment. — ت. کردن To stay; stop. To pause.

توقف‌گاه A. P. Halting-place.

توقیر A.P. Honouring. Honour; respect. — با کمال ت. Most respectfully. [3) فرمان

توقیع ○ A. = 1) امضا 2) مُهر

توقیف A. Arrest; confinement. Attachment; confiscation. Custody. Ban. — ت.کردن To arrest; confine. To confiscate. or attach; sequester. To suppress; (place under the) ban. — توقیف کشتی در بندر Embargo.

توکا Ortolan.

توکار Built-in; tailed in.

توکل A. Reliance; trust. Resignation. — بخدا توکل کردن To rely on God; trust in God.

توکیل A. Appointing as one's attorney. Keeping in custody. — وکیل در توکیل Attorney with right of substitution.

تولد A. [تولدات] Birth. — ت.کردن To give birth to; bring forth. Cf. زاییدن

تولک رفتن To moult.

توله Young [of certain animals]. Hunting-dog; hound. — تولهٔ خرس Whelp, cub. — تولهٔ سگ Pup. — تولهٔ شیر Whelp. — تولهٔ مار Young of a serpent.

تولی A. (*tava*la) Taking as a friend. Friendship.

تولیت A Custodianship (of a pious foundation). — تحت ت. In ward.

تولید A. Generation. Production. — ت. کردن To beget. To generate. To produce.

تون Stove or furnace (of a bathhouse).

تونل Fr. Tunnel.

توهم A. [توهمات] Imagination. Misgiving; also; groundless fear. — ت. کردن To imagine. To suspect.

توهین *A.* Insult. — بکسی ت. کردن To insult s. o. To disgrace s.o.; offer an affront to him.

توهین امیز *A. P.* Disgracing; aspersive; affrontive; humiliating.

توی *S. u.* **تو**

تویی + Inner; inward.

تَه Bottom. Base. [*Of a rifle*] Breech. [*Of a chair*] Seat. — از ته دل From the depth of one's heart; heartily. — تا ته To the bottom or end. — ته رفتن To sink. — ته کشیدن To run out; draw to an end. — ته چیزیرا بالا آوردن To consume a thing entirely; exhaust it. — ته وتو + The ins and outs.

تهاتر *A.* Clearing; adjustment; compensation.

تهاتری *A.* = **پایاپای**

تهاجم A. Invasion. Offence. — ت. کردن To make an attack.

تهاجمی *A. P.* Offensive ; aggressive.

تهاون *A.* Negligence; slackness.

ته بندی *or* **ته گیری** Snack.

ته پُر Breech-loading. — تفنگ ت Breech-loader.

ته پیاله + A half ; heel-tap.

تهجی *A.* Spelling. — حروف ت. The alphabet.

ته چك *P. E.* Counterfoil or stub (of a cheque).

ته دوزی Taping. Stapling.

تهدید *A.* Threat ; menace. — ت. کردن To threat : او را تهدید باخراج کردند They threatened to discharge him.

تهدیدآمیز *A. P.* Threatening.

تهذیب *A.* Refining; polishing. — ت. کردن To refine; edify.

تهلیل *A.* Praising God o. Chorus. Antiphon.

ته مانده Leavings.

تهمت *A.* Accusation. — بکسی ت. زدن To accuse s. o. ; bring a charge against him. — تهمت دروغ Calumny; false accusation.

تهمت آمیز *A. P.* Accusatory.

تهمتن *Title of Rostam. OS.* Stout or valiant.

ته نشست *n.* Sediment; deposit. —*a.* Settled; deposited.

ته نشسته Sedimentary.

ته نشین شدن To settle.

ته نقش *P. A.* Watermark.

تهنیت *A.* Congratulation. — بکسی ت. گفتن To congratulate or felicitate s. o.

تهنیت آمیز *A. P.* Congratulatory.

تهوّر A. Impetuosity; rashness. *L.* Courage.

تهوّع *A.* Nausea.

تهویه *A.* Ventilation. — ت. کردن To ventilate.

تهی * Empty. Bare.

تهیدست Indigent.

تهیدستی Indigence.

تهیگاه Hypochondrium; flank

تهی‌مغز Empty-headed.

تهیه *A*. Preparation. Supply.— ت. دیدن To make preparations. — ت. کردن To prepare; supply; provide. To procure.

تهییج *A*. Exciting; stimulation.— ت. کردن To stimulate.

تیار کردن To prepare. To equip.

تیاری Preparation. Manipulation: تیاری تریاك

تیان Cauldron. [set ; rank.

تیپ *n*. Brigade —*a*. Closely

تیپچه Bird-call. [*For a quail*] Quail-pipe.

تیر Arrow. Beam; girder. Post; pole. Pile. Shaft. Shot. Shooting pain ; twinge. *Fourth month having 31 days*. *Astr*. Mercury. — ت. انداختن To shoot. — ت. خوردن To be shot. — ت. زدن To shoot. — ت. کردن To edge, or set, on.— ت. کشیدن To shoot, as a pain. To twinge with p.

تیر انداز Shooter. Archer.

تیر اندازی Shooting. Archery.— ت. کردن To shoot.

تیرباران کردن To shoot down ; execute by shooting.— اورا به تهمت جاسوسی تیرباران کردند She was shot for a spy.

تیر رس Rifle-shot. Gunreach.

تیرک Rolling-pin. — ت. زدن To roll out, as dough.

تیرکوب Pile-driver.

تیرکوبی Pile-driving. Staking.

تیرگی Darkness; dullness. Turbidity. — تیرگی روابط Strained relations.

تیره Dark; dull. Turbid. *F*. Gloomy. Strained: روابط ت. ‖ ت. کردن To darken. To disturb. To tarnish.

تیره Sect. *Z*. & *Bot*. Family.— تیرهٔ پشت Vertebral column.

تیره بخت * etc. = بدبخت etc.

تیره‌دل * Obscure-minded. Ignorant.

تیره روز(گار) * = بدبخت

تیز *a*. Sharp. Pungent. Shrill. —*ad*. Quickly ; swiftly. — ت. کردن To sharpen ; whet.

تیزاب Nitric acid.— تیزاب تیز کرده Pure nitric a. — تیزاب سلطانی Aqua regia. — تیزاب شوره و نمك Nitro-muriatic acid. — تیزابِ صابون پزی Lye. — تیزاب [illegible] Impure nitric a. — نمك ت. Nitrate.— بچیزی ت. زدن To nitrate or nitrify s. t.

تیزابی Nitrated; nitrified.

تیزبین Sharp-sighted.

تیز بینی Sharp-sightedness.

تیز پا Swift-footed.

تیز پر(واز) * Swift-winged.

تیز چشم = تیز بین

تیزچنگ * Having sharp claws.

تیزدندان * Sharp-toothed. Fierce.

تیزرو & **تیزرفتار** * Quick-paced; walking swiftly.

تیزکن Grinder. Sharpener.

تیزگر * = چاقو تیزکن

تیزگوش Sharp of hearing.
باهوش = * تیز هوش
تیزی Sharpness. Shrillness. Pungency. Swiftness.
تیشه Chip-axe; adze. ــ ت. بریشهٔ خودزدن To be self-destructive. ــ سرِ تیشه or نوك ت. Met. The thin end of the wedge.
تیغ Razor. Thorn. Sword *. ــ ت. زدن To strike with a sword. To make an incision into. To touch for ×.
تیغ تیزکن Grinder. [For سنگ ت] Whetstone; hone.
شمشیرزن = * تیغ زن
تیغه Blade. Partition-wall. Bulk-head. ــ استخوان تیغه‌ای Vomer.
تیفوس *Fr*. Typhus.
تیفوئید *Fr*. Typhoid.
تیک تیک Click; tick.
تیکه *S. u.* تکه
تیله Marble; taw. Potsherd.
تیم *E*. Team.
تیماج Goat leather.
تیمار * Care; attendance. Sorrow *. ــ ت. کردن 1) To groom. 2) To attend; care for; look after; also, nurse.
تیمارستان Lunatic asylum.
تیمارگاه First-aid station.
تیمچه Arcade.
تیمسار *Word meaning* آقا *and preceding titles of brigadiers and higher ranks.*
تیمم *A*. Ablution with earth or sand.
تیمور *Mas. pr. name.*
تیهو Dull-yellow partridge.
تیول Fief; feud.

ثابت *A.* Fixed. Firm ; immovable; steady ; constant. Proved. *Math.* Invariable. *Cf. the fem.* ثابته ‖ حقوق ث. Basic salary.— رنگ ث Fast colour. — روغن ث. Fixed oil.— ث.کردن To prove ; demonstrate. To fix, as a colour. To make steady.

ثابت قدم *a. p.* Resolute ; steadfast.

ثابته * *A.* [ثوابت] Fixed star. [Orig. fem. of ثابت]

ثاقب *A.* Penetrating ○. Shooting.— شهاب ث. S.-star; meteor.

ثالث *A.* = سوم Third. — عنس ث. T. party.

ثالثاً *A.* = سوم آنکه Thirdly; in the third place.

ثامن ○ *A.* = **هشتم**

ثانوی *A.* Second ○. *Cf.* دوم & تا اخطار ثانوی ‖ دومی Until further notice.

ثانی *A.* = دوم Second.

ثانیاً *A.* = دوم آنکه Secondly ; in the second place.

ثانیه *A.* Second. [Orig. fem. of ثانی].

ثانیه شمار *A. P.* [*In a timepiece*] Second hand.

ثَبات *A.* Constancy; firmness. Perseverance. Resoluteness.

ثبات *A.* (*sabat*) Registrar.

ثبت *A.* Registration. Register; record. Inscription. Entry (in a book). — ث.کردن To register ; enter ; record ; write down. To patent.—به ثبت عمومی گذاردن To bring under general registration.

ثبتی *A.P.* Registered. Notarial.

ثبوت *A.* Demonstration. Proof. به ث. رساندن To prove ; demonstrate.—به ث. رسیدن To be proved.— محلول ث. Fixing-bath.

ثرب *A.* Omentum.

ثَروَت *A.* Wealth.—ثروت اقتصادی Political economy.

ثروت مند *A. P.* = دولتمند

ثری ○ *A.* (*sara*) *or* ثرا = **خاك**

ثریا *A.* = **پروین**

ثعلب *A.* Salep; male orchis.

ثُغور *A.* [Pl. of ثَغر ○.] = حدود Frontiers; borders.

ثُفل *A.* Apple-core. Dregs.

ثُقبه ○ *A.* = **سوراخ**

ثقل *A.* [اثقال] Weight . Gravity. Surfeited stomach. — ثقل سرد Sporadic cholera.

ثقل سنج *A. P.* Gravimeter.

ثَقیل *A.* Heavy [سنگین]. Indigestible. — جرّ ثقیل *S. u.* جرّ

ثلاث *A.* = سه Three.
ثلاثه o*A.* = سه گانه The three.
ثُلث *A.* 1) Third [سوم]. 2) T. portion of a person's property which may be bequeathed to persons other than his heir.
ثمر *A.* [اثمار] Fruit [میوه] *F.* Result.
ثمر بخش *A.P.* Fruitful. Useful.
ثمره *A.* [ثمرات] (Single) Fruit. *F.* Offspring.
ثمن *A.* (*saman*) [اَثمان] = بها
ثُمن *A.* 1) o Eighth [هشتم]. 2) E. portion of a man's estate which is inherited by his widow in case she has children.
ثمین *A.* = **گرانبها & قیمتی**
ثناء *A.* Eulogy; praise.
ثنا خوان *A. P.* Panegyrist.
ثنایا *A.* Incisors; chisel-teeth. [Pl. of ثنیه o]
ثنیه *S. u.* **ثنایا**
ثواب *A.* 1) (Spiritual) reward. 2) + Good deed.— ث. دارد There is a spiritual r. for it. — ث. کردن To do a pious or good act.
ثوابت *S. u.* ثابته
ثوب o *A.* [ثیاب] Garment. Suit.
ثور *A.* = گاو نر Bull; ox o. *Astr.* Taurus. *Old name of* اردی بهشت *q. v.*

جا *or* **جای** Place. Seat. Room; space. *F*. Occasion; cause ; ground. Margin. — جا دارد که It is proper or befitting to. — جای شماسبز بود *or* جای شماخالی بود We thought of you ; we missed you. — بجای *or* جای ِ Instead of. In place of. For; in behalf of. — جاافتادن To be set or reduced, as a bone. — جا انداختن To set or reduce. — جا بجا کردن To displace; dislocate. To dispose of or allocate (prudently)+. To rearrange. To put in shape. — جابجاشدن‌درد *Med*. Revulsion. — جای اعتراض Ground for objection. — جا خالی کردن To give way. To sidestep (a rush or attack). To duck. — جاخوردن+ = یکه خوردن ‖ جا دادن To accommodate , house. To seat, place. To insert. — جازدن To fake; adulterate. — جاکردن+ To get a firm footing. To make oneself popular. To curry favour. — جا گذاردن To leave out. — جاگرفتن To hold. To take room. — از جا در رفتن To lose one's temper. — خلقش بجا آمد He resumed his spirits; he cheered up. — بجاآوردن To do ; execute. To comply with ; grant. To recognize. — سرکار بنده را می شناسید ولی بنده سرکار را بجا نمیآورم You have the advantage of me. — بجایی نرسیدن To fail ; come to nothing. — بجا رساندن To do; achieve. — درجا زدن To mark time. — کسیرا سرجای‌خود نشاندن To show one his seat ; put him in his place ; settle his hash. — جایی که *or* آنجا که Where. — از آنجایی که Since ; in view of the fact that.

جاا ُفتاده Well-matured. Mellow.

جا انگشتی Keyboard. Fingerboard.

جا بجا 1) *S. u.* جا 2) [With the stress on the first syl.] On the spot. Right away.

As the case may be.

جابر *u. A.* [Fem. جابره] Oppressive ; despotic. Coercive. —*n*. Oppressor. Despot. قوهٔ جابره ○ Force majeure.

جابرانه *A. P*. Forcibly. Extortionately.

جا پا Footprint. Foothold.

جا پاکتی Paper-rack. *See* پاکت

جاجیم *T*. Coarse, loosely-woven woollen cloth.

جادار Roomy ; spacious ; commodious.

جادو Magic(ian). — ج. کردن To exercise magic. To bewitch.

جادو(گر) Magician.

جادوگری Sorcery; magic.

جادویی Magic(al).

جادّه *A.* Path ; road.

جاده صاف کن *A. P.* Road-roller ; steam-roller.

جاذب *A.* Attractive. Absorbent. *Cf. the fem.* جاذبه

جاذبه *A.* [Orig. fem. of جاذب] Attractive force. Allure. [*Of the earth*] Gravity. — جاذبهٔ جنسی Sex appeal.

جاذبیت *A.* Attractiveness.

جار *T.* Proclamation ; public crying. — ج زدن *or* ج. کشیدن To cry ; proclaim.

جار Chandelier.

جار ° *A.* [جیران] = همسایه

جارچی *T.* Town crier.

جارختی Coat-hanger ; dress-hanger. *Cf.* چوب رخت

جاروب *or* **جارو** +. Broom. — ج. کردن To sweep. — ج. کشیدن To s. To be a sweeper. — تخم ج. Crowfoot.

جاروکش Sweeper.

جاروکشی Sweeping.

جاری *A.* Flowing ; running. Current : حساب ج. ‖ سوم ماه ج. The third instant (or 3 d. inst.). — ج. شدن To flow ; run. — ج. کردن To cause to f. To execute : صیغهٔ عقد را جاری کردند ‖ [Fem. : جاریه مقررات جاریه Regulations in force].

جاری *A.* Sister-in-law [wife of the brother of one's husband].

جاز *E.* Jazz(-band).

جازغالی Bin (for coal.). Coal-hod.

جازده Adulterated ; buse ; faked.

جازم ° *A. a.* Resolving.

جاسوس *A.* Spy.

جاسوسی *A. P.* Espionage ; spying. — ج. کردن To spy.

جاشو Member of ship's crew. [Pl. جاشویان ship's c.]

جاشیر *S. u.* جاوشیر

جا صابونی (*See* صابون) Soap-tray.

جا کاغذی Paper-rack.

جاکش Pimp; panderer.

جاکشی Panderism. — ج. کردن To pander or pimp.

جاگیر *S. u.* جایگیر

جالب *A.* Attractive. — جالب‌توجه Interesting.

جا لباسی *P. A.* = جارختی

جالیز Kitchen-garden. Melon ground.

جالینوس *A.-G.* Galen.

جالینوسی *A.* Galenic. — طب ج. Galenism.

جام Cup. *Bot.* Corolla. — جامِ پنجره Window-pane. — جام‌پیروزی Cup. — ج. انداختن To glaze [*with* به].

جامد *A.* Solid. — اسم ج. Pri -

mitive noun.

جامع *A.* Comprehensive; full. Catholic. —*n.* (Principal) mosque [pl. جوامع]. [sive.

جامع الاطراف *A.* Comprehen-

جامع الشرایط *A.* Fully qualified.

جامعه *n. A.* [جوامع] Society. Community. —*a.* ○ [Fem. of جامع]. — حساب ج. Integral calculus. کتاب ج. Ecclesiastes.

جامعه شناسی *A. P.* Sociology.

جامعیت *A.* Comprehensiveness. Universality.

جامه * Garment; clothing[لباس]. Cloth ○. — جامهٔ عمل پوشیدن To materialize.

جامه بر ○ = **مقراض** & **قیچی**

جامه دار One who keeps the clothes in a public bath-house.

جامه دان *or* **چمدان** + Suitcase.

جان Life ; soul. — ج. دادن To give up one's life. To give life (to). To be very suitable +. — ج. تسلیم کردن *or* ج.سپردن To give up one's life; give up the ghost. —ج. کندن To be in the agony of death. *F.*+ To drudge or fag [usu. جان مفت کندن] — جان بدر بردن To have a narrow escape. — از دل و جان Most heartily or willingly. —جانش راروی آن گذاشت It cost him his life. —پدرجان Dear father. [Said also by a man to his child]. — جانم My dear fellow! Darling! — جان من 1) = جانم 2) For my life's sake. — بجان خودم 'pon my life. — جان من است و او He is all the world to me.

جانّ *A.* [More fully جانِ بن ج.] *Name of the first jinnee.*— از دور جانِ بن ج. From immemorial times.

جان آزار *or* **جان خراش** • *a.* Tormenting ; vexing.

جان آفرین * Creator (of the soul).

جانان * Sweetheart [also جانانه].

جانانه Lovely. *S. a.* جانان

جانب *A.* [جوانب] Side ; direction. Quarter. — ملاحظه اطراف وجوانب کار Circumspection. — بجانبِ In the d. of; toward.— از جانبِ من On my part (*or* behalf). From me.—جانب کسیرا نگاه داشتن To take the p. of s. o. — اینجانب *See in the vocab.*

جانبازی Risking one's life. Dangerous calling. Self-sacrifice.

جان بخش • Life-bestowing.

جانبدار(ی) *A. P.* = **طرفدار(ی)**

جانبین *A.* Both parties. [D. of جانب). *Cf.* طرفین

جان پرور • Animating.

جان پناه Parapet. Life-line. Trench.

جانِ جانی + Very dear or

close. *Cf.* جان در یك قالب

جاندار *a.* Animate. Living. Durable or tough ×. *–n.* L. creature; animal. *Cf.* جانور

جان دارو o Antidote. Theriac.

جان در یك قالب + *P. A.* [Cont. of دو جان در یك قالب] United as two kernels in one shell; very dear, close, or intimate.

جان سخت Die-hard.

جان سوز • Doleful; heart-rending.

جانشین Successor; locum tenens; substitute. Replacement. – جانشینِ . . . شدن To succeed. . . To replace . . . – جانشین خود کردن To declare one's successor.

جانشینی Succession. Replacment.

جان فشانی Self-sacrifice; devotion.

جانکاه • = جان آزار

جان کن + Drudge; fagger.

جان کنی Drudgery; fag.

جانگداز • = جانسوز

جان نثار *P. A.* Ready to sacrifice one's life. – این بندهٔ ج. Your devoted servant; i. e. I.

جانماز Prayer-carpet. – ج. آب کشیدن *Met.* To be prudish or hypocritical.

جانوَر Animal. Monster. Vermin.

جانور شناس Zoologist.

جانور شناسی Zoology.

جانی Sincerely devoted. – دشمن ج. Bitter enemy. – دوست ج. Bosom friend.

جانی *A.* Criminal. Murderer.

جانی خانی *Obs.* Hair-sack.

جاودان *Same as* جاوید(ان)

جاودانی Eternal.

جاوَرس *A-P.* = گاورس

جاوشیر *A.* [f. P. گاو شیر] Opoponax.

جاوید(ان) *a.* Eternal. Immortal. *–n.* Eternity.

جاه Rank; dignity.

جاهد *A.* Diligent; industrious.

جاه طلب *P. A.* Ambitious [used in an ill sense]. Greedy of honours.

جاه طلبانه *P. A.* Ambitiously.

جاه طلبی *P. A.* Greed for honours; ambitiousness.

جاهل *A.* Ignorant. [Pl. جهال or جهلاء the ignorant].

جاهلانه *A .P.* Ignorantly.

جاهلیت *A.* The pagan state of the Arabs before Mohammed.

جای etc. = جا etc.

جایز [f. *A.* جائِز] Permissible; allowable. Revocable; voidable: عقد جایز ‖ ج. دانستن To allow; consider lawful.

جایز الخطا *A.* Peccable; liable to sin or make a mistake.

جایزه *A.* [جوائز] Prize. Premium. Award.

جایزه‌دار *A. P.* Who has won a prize; laureate.

جایگاه Place; centre; station.— جایگاه فروش بنزین Filling-s.

جای گزین شدن To supersede or replace . . .

جایگیر *or* **جاگیر** Fixed; established. Impressed. — ج. کردن To fix. To impress.

جایی (*Indecent*) = مستراح

جبار *A*. Powerful. Tyrannical. Almighty. —*n*. Tyrant. Oppressor. *Astr*. The Orion.

جبال [Pl. of جبل].

جبان *A*. = ترسو Timid; cowardly.

جبر *A*. Constraint. Oppression. Fatalism. Algebra [usu. جبر ومقابله]. *Med*. Reduction.— خاصیب ج. Inertia. — ج. کردن To use force. [*With* بر] To oppress.

جبراً *A*. By force; compulsorily.

جبران *A*. Compensation; amends. — ج. کردن To make good; compensate; make amends for. To cover.

جبران پذیر *A. P*. That can be compensated; indemnifiable.

جبران ناپذیر *A. P*. Irreparable.

جبروت • *A*, Almightiness. — عالم ج. Celestial kingdom.

جبری *a*. *A*. Forced. Algebraic. —*n*. Fatalist [pl. جبریون].

جبرئیل *or* **جبرائیل** *A-Heb*. Gabriel.

جبل o *A*. [جبال] = کوه• Mountain.

جبل الطارق *A*. Gibraltar.

جبلت o *A*. Natural disposition.

جبلی *A*. Natural; inborn.

جبن *A*. = ترس & ترسویی

جبون [Erroneous for جبان]

جبه *A*. Tall gown; cloak.

جبه o = زره

جبهه *A*. Front. *OS*. = پیشانی ‖ خدمت در جبهه Active service.

جبیره o *A*. [جبائر] Splint.

جبین • *A*. Forehead; brow. — ج. درهم کشیدن To knit the b.— ج. کشادن To smooth the b.

جت *E*. Jet(-propelled plane).

جثه *A*. Bulk(iness). Body +.

جثه‌دار *A. P*. Bulky; huge.

جحد o *A*. Denial. Negation.— ج. کردن To deny. To abjure one's faith.

جحیم *A*. = دوزخ & جهنم

جخت + (Only) just. — ج. اگر ۳ سال داشته باشد He is scarcely 3 years old.

جد *A*. [اجداد] = نیا Grandfather; ancestor. — جدّ اعلی Great grandfather.

جد *A*. Endeavour. — جد کردن To try hard. To be dogmatic. — جدو جهد Great effort.— بجد. Seriously; in earnest.

جدا *a*. Separate. Isolated. Loose. —*ad*. Separately. — ج. ج. S.; one by o.— ج. شدن To be separated. — ازهم ج. شدن To part with each other. — ج. کردن To separate. To detach. To select.

جداً *A*. Seriously; in earnest.—

ج. میکوئید؟ Do you mean what you say?

جدا برگ *a*. Loose-leaf.

جدار *A*. Wall. Partition. Casing [also ج. لولهٔ].

جداری *A*. Parietal : استخوان ج. ‖ لولهٔ ج. Casing.

جدا شدنی Separable.

جداگانه Separate(ly).

جدا نشدنی Inseparable.

جدال *A*. Dispute ; debate. Quarrel. — ج. کردن To dispute or quarrel.

جداول [Pl. of جدول]

جدایی Separation. Departure. Parting.

جدل *A*. Dispute ; debate. — ج. کردن To d. To polemize.

جدلی *A*. Polemic. Given to controversy.

جدوار *A-P*. = **زدوار**

جدوگاه Withers.

جَدوَل *A*. [جداوِل] Table ; schedule ; list. Kerb. [For جدول معمائی] Crossword puzzle. *OS*. Brook.

جدول بندی *A. P*. Tabulation.

جدّه *A*. [Fem. of جد] Ancestress ; grandmother.

جدّی *A*. Serious. Earnest. Bona fide. Energetic. Conscientious. — شوخی را بدرجهٔ ج. رسانید He carried the joke too far.

جدی *A*. (*jad'y*) 1) ○ = بزغاله 2) *Astr*. The Capricorn.

جُدَی *A*. The Pole Star. *OS*. Small kid.

جدیت *A*. Effort ; endeavour. — ج. کردن To e.

جَدید *A*. New. Modern. *Cf*. تازه

جدیداً *A*. Newly Recently.

جدیدالاحداث *A*. = **نوبنیاد**

جدیدالاسلام *A*. New convert to Islam.

جدیدالبناء *A*. = تازه ساز *or* تازه ساخت New-built.

جدیدالنسق *A*. Newly cultivated.

جدیدالورود *A*. Newly-arrived.

جدیدالولاده *A*. = **نوزاد**

جذاب *A*. (Very) attractive.

جذابیت *A*. Attractiveness.

جُذام *A*. Black leprosy.

جذامی *A*. Leprous.

جَذب *A*. Attraction. Absorption. — ج. کردن To attract. To absorb.

جذبه *A*. Rapture.

جذر *A*. [جُذور] Square root. — جذر اصم Surd ; irrational. — جذر مُنطق Rational root. — جذر مکعب Cube r.

جذری *Math*. Radical.

جَرّ *A*. Dragging ; hauling. *See* جر ثقیل *or* جرّ اثقال ‖ جریه Crane. — جرثقیل کابلی Winch. *See* کابل

جِر + Fissure. Foul play ; backing out. — جر آمدن To play the woman. — جر آوردن To infuriate ; make mad. —

جر دادن To tear with a noise. — جر زدن To back out (*in a game*); cheat. — جرم می گیرد It gets on my nerves; it gets my goat.

جُرأت *A.* Courage. — ج. دادن To give courage to; embolden. — بخود جرأت دادن To muster (up) one's courage. — ج. کردن To dare. — به ج. میتوان گفت I daresay.

جرّاح *A.* Surgeon.

جراحت *A.* [جراحات] 1) = زخم 2) Pus [چرك] — تولید جراحت Suppuration.

جرّاحی *A. P.* Surgery. — عمل جراحی Surgical operation.

جرّار * *A.* Numerous. Warlike.

جرائد [Pl. of جریده]

جرائم [Pl. of جریمه]

جَرَب *A.* (Dry) scab; mange.— کرم ج Acarus.

جربز *A.* [f. P. گربز] Sly or deceitful (person).

جُربُزه Slyness. Capability+.

جرثومه ○ *A.* Germ. Origin.

جِرجیس *A.* St. George.

جَرح *A.* Wound(ing).— جرح و تعدیل کردن To modify or adapt.

جِرز Pier; pillar.

جرس * *A.* = زنگ Bell.

جرعه * *A.* Drink; draught; gulp; sip.

جرقه Spark.

جَرگه Circle; ring. — ج. زدن To form a circle.

جِرم *A.* [اَجرام] Body [جسم]. Incrustation. Mass.— جرم آسمانی Celestial body; orb. — جرم دماغ Cerebrum. — جرم دماغ کبیر Encephalon. — ج. گرفتن To be covered with incrustation.

جُرم *A.* Crime; offence. Fine.— ج. کردن To commit a crime. To fine. — اعلام ج. برعلیه کسی کردن To lay an information against s. o.

جرمانه *A. P.* = جریمه

جرم شناسی *A. P.* Criminology.

جرنگ Jingling sound; clangour.

جرنگی × [For پول ج.] Hard [cash.

جُرّه Of medium size. — قوش ج. Male falcon.— مرغابی ج. Teal.

جَری *A.* Bold.

جَریان *A.* Flow(ing). Course. Current; draft. Circulation. *Med.* Flux. *F.* 1) Progress; conduct : جریان امتحانات ‖ 2) Proceeding.— ج. داشتن To take place; come to pass. To be in circulation. — در جریان بودن To be under way. To be in circulation. — در جریان اوضاع بودن To be acquainted with what is going on; be up to date in affairs; keep a breast of the times.

جریانات *A.* [Pl. of جریان]. Incidents; circumstances.

جریب *A.* (Iranian) acre.

جریبا ○ North-west wind

جریحه *A*. Wound.

جریحه‌دار *A. P*. Wounded.

جریدبازی *A. P*. Mock combat with lances. Jousting.

جریده *A*. [جرائد] Newspaper. *Cf*. روزنامه

جریده نگار *A. P*. Journalist.

جریده‌نگاری *A. P*. Journalism.

جَریمه *A*. [جرائم] Fine; penalty. — ج. کردن To fine.

جرّیه *A*. Traction Service. *See* جرّ

جُز *or* بجز Except. Other than. — ج. اینکه E. that. Unless.

جِز + Sizzling; frizz.

جزء *A*. [اجزاء] Part; portion. — ذکر جزء واراده کل Metonymy. — صورت ج. Detailed statement. — بجزء In detail. — جزء ترکیبی Ingredient [mostly in the pl. form اجزاء]

جزا *A*. Retribution; punishment. Reward. — روزجزا Day of judgment. — جزای‌شرط *Gr*. Apodosis. — ج. دادن (به) To reward. To punish.

جزائر [Pl. of جزیره]

جزائی *A*. = کیفری Penal

جِزجِز + Sizzling. Skirl (in the pan). — ج. کردن To sizzle.

جُزدان *A. P*. Wallet. Pocket-book.

جَزر *A*. Ebb-tide.

جزر و مدّ *a. p*. Tide; flow and ebb. *See* مدّ

جزع *A*. (*jaz'*) Onyx. Anxiety o.

جزع o *A*. (*jaza'*) Grief. Complaint.

جزغال Dripping; fried fat.

جزغاله 1) = جزغال 2) Burnt; fried.

جزم *A*. (Taking a) definite decision; resolution. — عزم‌خود را جزم‌کردن To resolve (upon doing s. t.)

جزمی o *A*. Dogmatic. — فلسفهٔ ج. Dogmatism.

جزو *A*. (*jozv*) Part; ingredient. — درجزوِ *or* جزوِ Among.

جزوجمع *a. p*. (Tax) rolls.

جزو وز + Sizzle.

جُزوه *A.P*. Fascicle. Section. — ج. ج. In numbers. In pamphlets.

جزوه‌دان *A. P*. Box-file.

جزیره *A*. [جَزائر] Island.

جزیرة‌العرب *A*. The Arabian Peninsula.

جزیل o *A*. = زیاد & فراوان

جزیه *A*. Poll-tax anciently paid in lieu of conversion to Islam. Tribute o.

جُزئی *A*. Slight; little. Trivial; petty; insignificant. — کسوف‌ج. Partial eclipse.

جزئیات *A*. Details.

جسارت *A*. Boldness; presumption. — ج. کردن *or* ج. ورزیدن To venture. To presume. To take (the) liberty.

جسارت آمیز *A. P*. Bold; presumptuous: جواب ج.

جسارةً *A*. Venturingly ; presumptuously.

جساست ο *A*. Bulkiness.

جِست Leap ; jump. — ج. زدن To j. or leap.

جستجو Search. — ج. كردن To search; make investigations. To look for. — در جستجوىِ In s. of.

جستن (*jas*–; *jes*–) [جِه] To jump ; leap. *F*. To escape [*with* از]. — بيخ گلو جستن [*Of food in the mouth*] To go the wrong way. — مفت جست He had a narrow e.

جُستن [جو(ى)] To search ; seek. To find.

جست وخيز Leaping. Caper. — ج. كردن To leap.

جسته [P. P. of جستن]

جسته جسته Little by little. At odd moments. By catches.

جسته(و)گريخته Desultory. Fragmentary. Here and there.

جسد *A*. [اَجساد] Body. Corpse.

جِسر *A*. Bridge. Ferry-boat. *Cf*. پل

جِسم *A*. [اَجسام]. Body. Flesh. *Geom*. Solid. [ally.

جسماً *A*. Physically. Corpore-

جسمانى *A*. Corporeal. Bodily. Material; worldly.

جسمى *A*. Corporeal. Bodily.

جسميت *A*. Corporeality. Substance ο.

جِسور *A*. Bold; daring. Pert ; saucy. Presumptuous.

جسورانه *A.P. ad*. Boldly. Pertly. — *a*. Bold; presumptuous.

جسيم * *A*. Bulky; huge ; massive. Corpulent.

جَشن Celebration. Festival. — ج. گرفتن To hold a celebration. To celebrate.

جعبه *A*. Box.

جعبه آئينه *A. P*. Showcase.

جعبه تقسيم *a. p*. Junction box; also, distribution-box [also جعبة تقسيم]

جعبه خزانه *a. p*. [In a rifle] Magazine.

جعبه دنده *A. P*. Gear-box.

جعد * *A*. Curl ; lock of hair; ringlet.

جعفر (*A*.) *Mas. pr. name. OS*. Small river.

جعفرى *A*. Parsley. [For گل ج.] French marigold. — زر جعفرى Pure variety of gold. — مارجعفرى Adder; green viper.

جعل *A*. 1) Forging. — جعل اسناد Forgery. 2) Making ; creating. — ج. كردن To forge; counterfeit.

جعلق × Loutish, lumpish, or stupid (fellow).

جَعلى *A*. Forged. Fictitious.

جغتايى *Jaghatai* : old language of Central Asia— a branch of Turkish.

جِغ جِغ + Rattling noise.

جغجغه Rattle(-box). Ratchet. — متهٔ ج. R. brace.

جغد Owl.
جغرافی etc. = جغرافیا etc.
جغرافیا *A.G.* Geography.
جغرافیادان Geographer.
جغرافیائی Geographical.
جِغله + Tiny child.
جغور بغور + Roasted pluck.
جغه = جقه
جفا *A.* 1) Oppression or persecution. 2) * Unkindness or unfaithfulness*.– بر کسی ج. کردن To oppress s. o. To treat s. o. unkindly.– رضا بجفای معشوق Masochism.
جفاپیشه *A. P.* = ستمگر
جفّ القلم *A.* The pen (that wrote the words of Fate) has dried up ; i. e. fate is unchangeable.
جفاکار * *A. P.* = ستمگر
جَفت Tan-bark.
جُفت *n.* Pair. Even number. Mate; fellow. [For جفت جنین] Placenta. –*a.* Even. Double. Associate. – ج. آوردن To throw doublets. – ج. زدن To leap. – ج. شدن To pair. To fit. [*With* با] To match ; go with. – ج. کردن To couple or p. To fit together. *F.* To fabricate. To compose.– ج. ج. In pairs; two by t.
جفتک Fling(ing). – ج. زدن *or* ج. انداختن To fling. To caper. *F.* To kick or recalcitrate against (*or* at) rules, etc.
جفتك چارکش Leapfrog.
جفته ○ = 1) جفتك 2) کفل
جفتی *a.* Double. – *ad.* + Two by two; in doubles.
جفت گیری Pairing; coupling. – ج. کردن To pair; couple.
جفر *A.* Arithmomancy.
جفن *A.* [اجفان] = پلك چشم
جفنگ + *n.* Nonsense; rubbish. –*a.* Nonsensical.
جفنی *A.* Palpebral.
جقه *T P.* Aigrette; tuft.
جک *E.* Jack. *Cf.* خرك
جکر *or* جوکر *E.* (*C. P.*) Joker. *Cf.* شوخ
جگر Liver. *F.* Courage; pluck; guts. – جگر سفید Lung(s). – جگر سیاه Liver.– جگرم کباب شد+ I felt great sorrow (for him).
جگربند * The liver, the heart, and the lungs. – ج. پیش زاغ نهادن * To choose misery for oneself.
جگرگوشه *or* جگر پاره Lobe of the ear. *F.* (Dear) child.
جگردار Plucky; courageous.
جگرسوز Heart-rending. Painful.
جگرکی + Crimson.
جگری Hepatic. Crimson.
جگن Osier. (Bul)rush.
جلّ *A.* (*jal'a*) May he be glorified. [*Used as an a.*] Glorious : حق جلّ و علا The G. and Most High God.
جُل Horse-cloth ; housing. –

جل وَزَغ Frogspawn. Moss. — جل و پلاس × Things ; chattels ; outfit.

جلاَ *A.* Emigration; exile. — جلای وطن کردن To go into e.; emigrate.

جلاَ *A.* Polish. Lustre.— روغن ج. French polish; varnish. — ج. دادن To p.

جلاب *A.* [f. P. گلاب] Julep.

جلاجل ० *A.* [Pl. of جلجل] Bells hung to an animal's neck. — مار جلاجل Rattle-snake [= مار زنگی].

جلاد *A.* Executioner.

جلاگر *A. P.* Polisher.

جلال *A.* Glory. *Mas. pr. name.*

جلالت *A.* Dignity; glory.

جل الخالق *A.* May the Creator be glorified : said while admiring God's wonderful works.

جلَب *A.* Arrest. Procuring. — ج. کردن To arrest. To attract. To summon. To acquire. — توجه کسیرا جلب کردن To draw a person's attention.

جلب × (*jalab*) Base. Deceitful. *See* زن جلب

جلب *or* **جلپ** (,,) Jalap.

جُلبک Alga; seaweed.

جلت × Rascal. Trickish.

جلَد *A.* Quick(ly). — کبوتر جلد Homing pigeon; homer.

جِلد *A.* Skin ०. Cover ; binding. Volume. Copy : یك ج. آنرا شش ج. کتاب ‖ فروخت 6 books.— جلد دوم ... است He is the dead image (*or* spit) of ...— ج. کردن To bind ; furnish with a cover. To encase. — در جلد نمی گنجد He seems to tread in the air.

جلدگر *A. P.* صحاف

جلدیَ Quickness ; agility.

جِلدی *A.* Cutaneous.— بیماریهای ج. Skin diseases.

جلزو ولز × Frizz(le).

جلساء [Pl. of جلیس]

جلسات [Pl. of جلسه]

جلسه *A.* [جلسات] Session. sitting; meeting.

جلف *a.* 1) *A.* Frivolous. Rude. 2)+Gay; gaudy. -*n.* F. or rude person. Dandy. [Pl. اَجلاف].

جلق *or* **جرق** Masturbation. — ج. زدن To masturbate.

جُلگه Plain.

جلنار •. *A-P.* = گلنار

جلنگ+Clink(ing noise). [Usu. ج. ج.] — ج. کردن To clink.

جِلو *n.* Front (part). Bridle. —*ad.* Forward. —*a.* Ahead ; advance(d) . Fast : ساعت ج. است ‖ پول ج. Advance money.— جلوِ In front of ; before. — از کسی ج. افتادن To get ahead of s. o. ; get the start of s. o. ; leave s. o. behind ; get the upper hand of s. o. — ج. انداختن To push forward. To promote. — ج. آوردن To set f., as a clock. — ج. زدن [*Of a watch*] To gain. [*With* از] 1) To outpace. 2) [*Of a vehicle*] To overtake. — جلو کسیرا گرفتن — To restrain or control s. o. — ج. بردن To carry or push forward. To advance. — جلوش ول شده است He is unrestrained or lewd. — خوب از جلوش در آمدم I treated him well. I gave him hot; I gave it to him hard.

جلو خان Frontage; bay. Forecourt.

جلودار Postillion. Outrider. Herald. Van(guard).

جلوس *A.* Accession (to the throne). — بتخت ج. کردن To come to, or ascend, the throne.

جلوگرد Single-breasted.

جلوگیری Prevention. Anticipation. Restraint; repression. — ج. از آبستنی Birth-control. — ج. کردن از To prevent. To repress; stop. To control. داروی ج. Prophylactic or preventive medicine.

جلوه *A.* (*jel-*) Manifestation. Airs. — ج. کردن To show off; set off. To display. To make a parade of. To cut a figure; show; have a s.

جلوه‌گاه * *A. P.* Place where beauties are displayed. *S. a.* حجله

جلوه‌گر *A. P.* Appearing in full beauty. Showy.

جلوی Situated in front. — اطاق ج. The f. room.

جلی *A.* Manifest; clear. — بخط ج In bold characters.

جلیتقه *R.* Waistcoat; vest.

جلیس * *A.* [جلسا ○] = همنشین

جلیدیه *A.* = زجاجیه

جلیل *A.* Great; glorious; honourable. *See the pl.* اجله

جلیل‌القدر *A.* (Very) great or honourable.

جم [Cont. of جمشید]

جم ○ *A.* = گروه & جمعیت

جماجم [Pl. of جمجمه]

جماد *A.* [جمادات] Inanimate object. Solid body.

جمادی *A.* Inanimate; solid.

جمادی‌الاخری (*A.*) *6 th. month of the A. lunar year.*

جمادی‌الاولی (*A.*) *5th. month of the A. lunar year.*

جماز *A.* Swift-footed: شترجماز

جمازه *A.* Dromedary.

جماع *A.* Sexual intercourse. — ج. کردن To unite in sexual intercourse; lie.

جماعت *A.* [جماعات] Congregation; assembly. Community.

جمال *A.* Beauty. *Mas. pr. name.*

جماهیر [Pl. of جمهور]

جمجمه *A.* [جماجم] Skull; cranium. — براهین ج. *S. u.* برهان

جمجمه‌شناسی *A.P.* Craniology.

جمشید *Mas. pr. name.*

جَمع *A. n.* Crowd. Number (of people). Conjunction. Receipt(s). *Arith.* (1)Addition; (2) sum, total. *Gr.* Plural. —*a.* Collected. Compact. — حواسش ج. نیست He is absent-minded; he cannot concentrate.— ج. آوردن • To gather together; rally. — ج. بستن *or* ج زدن To add up; count up. To do (*or* work) a sum.— ج. شدن To gather together. To assemble. To accumulate. To shrink. — ج. کردن To g.; assemble. To rally. To collect. To amass. To g. up. To add. To withdraw from circulation.— بجمع... گذاشتن To credit (a sum) to ...— ج. تر بنشینید Close up. — جمع کل Grand total.— اسم ج. Collective noun.— شیپور جمع *Mil.* Assembly call.

جمعاً *A.* In all; totally.

جمع المال *A.* Having things in common. Intercommunal.

جمع آوری *A. P.* Collecting; gathering. — ج. کردن To collect. To levy; muster. To rally.

جمع بندی *A. P.* Adding up. — ج. کردن To add up; totalize.

جمعه *A.* = آدینه Friday.

جمعی *A. P.* Collective. Cumulative.— رای ج. Scrutin-de-liste; voting for several members (out of a list).

جمعیت *A.* Crowd; mob. Population. Association. — جمعیتِ خاطر • Peace of mind; composure.

جَمل o *A.* = شتر

جُمل [Pl. of جمله] [crowd.

جملگی *A. P.* All; the whole

جُمله *A.* The whole; all. *Gr.* Sentence. *Math.* Term. [Pl. جمل *jomal*]. — ج. خریدن To buy in a lump. — ج. فروختن To deal (by) wholesale. — ج. ازآن Among them.— ج. کردن To integrate. To consolidate.

جمله بندی *A. P.* Phrasing; wording; phraseology.

جُمود *A.* Stiffness. Congelation. — جمود مفصل Stiffness of a joint. Ankylosis.— جمود نعش Rigor mortis.

جمهور *A.* [جماهیر] The public. Republic. — جمهور اهل ادب R. of letters. — رئیس ج. President of a republic.

جمهوری *A. P.* Republic.

جمهوریت *A* Republicanism.

جمهوریخواه *A.P.* Republican.

جمیع *A.* (The) whole; all. *Cf.* همه ‖ جمیع مردم All people; everybody.

جمیعاً *A.* All. *Cf.* همه & تماماً

جمیل *A.* Handsome; beautiful. Good; reputable.

جمیله (*A.*) *Fem. pr. name.*

[*Orig. fem. of* جمیل]

جنّ *A.* The genii or fairies. [Collective for جنی].

جناب *A.* Excellency. – جناب آقای His E.

جنابَت *A.* Pollution.

جنابعالی *a. p.* Your Excellency. [*In p. c.*] = شما

جنات [Pl. of جنت]

جناح *A.* [اجنحه o] 1) o = بال Wing. 2) *Mil.* Flank.

جناحی *A.* Lateral. Pertaining to the wing of an army. Alar; wing-shaped.

جنازه *A.* Corpse. Funeral.

جناس *A.* Play on words; pun.

جناغ Wishing-bone. – جناغ سینه Sternum. [zigzag.

جناغی Herring-bone; Forked :

جنان *A.* [A pl. of جنت]

جنایت *A.* Felony ; crime.

جنایت‌آمیز *A. P.* Felonious.

جنایتکار *A. P.* Criminal.

جنایتکارانه *A. P.* Feloniously.

جنائی *A.* Criminal.

جنب *A.* (*jamb*) Side; flank. – در جنبِ or جنبِ Next to. – غشاء جنب ریه Pleura.

جنب (*jomb*) [Imp. of جنبیدن]. – ج. خوردن + To move.

جنب *A.* (*jonob*) Polluted ; ceremonially unclean.

جنباندن [جنبان] To move. To shake. To wag. To nod.

جنبش Movement ; motion. Oscillation. – ج دادن To move. – ج. کردن To start a movement. – به ج. در آوردن To set moving. To shake.

جنبش پذیر Movable. Unstable.

جنبش شناسی Kinematics.

جنبش ناپذیر Unshakable ; stable.

جنبنده *a.* Moving. Oscillating. Creeping. –*n.* [Pl. جنبندگان] C. animal; reptile.

جَنبه *A.* Aspect; nature.

جنبی *A.* Lateral.

جُنبیدن [جنب] To move; shake. To oscillate. To get a move on ; stir one's stump; buck up [usu. in the imp. بجنب].

جنت *A.* [جنات & جنان] = 1) o باغ 2) بهشت

جنت‌مکان * *a.* (*a.p.*) Dwelling in paradise.

جنجال Tumult; jangle; brawl. – ج. راه انداختن + To kick up a row.

جُنحه *A.* Misdemeanour.

جُند Castoreum.

جِنده Prostitute ; harlot.

جنده باز Whoremonger. [tion.

جنده بازی Whoring ; fornica-

جنده خانه = فاحشه خانه

جِنس *A.* Kind. Genus. Sex. Stamp; quality. Goods; commodity or commodities [pl. اَجناس] . – جنسِ آن بد است It is of an inferior quality.

جنساً *A.* In kind. With regard

to quality. By nature.
جنسی A. Sexual. Generic. — مالیات ج. Taxes in kind. — جاذبهٔ ج. Sex appeal.
جنسیت A. Sexuality.
جنطیانا A-Lat. Gentian.
جنکه Bull-calf from 1 year to 3 years old.
جَنگ 1) War. Quarrel. — جنگ تن بتن Duel. — ج. کردن To fight; wage (or make) war. 2) Imp. of جنگیدن
جُنگ (Literary) miscellany or miscellania. [warfare.
جنگ آزموده Experienced in
جنگاوَر Warlike.
جنگجو Warlike; quarrelsome.
جَنگل Forest; wood; jungle.— جنگل مولی Incongruous community. Thickset growth of hairs; wild tangled mass. — علم احداث ج. Forestry.
جنگلبان Forester; woodman.
جنگل بُری Deforestation.
جنگلبان = جنگلدار
جنگلبانی or جنگلداری Forestry.
جنگل نشین Woodsman.
جنگلی Living, or growing in, the forest; wild. — چوب ج. Hardwood. — درخت ج. Forest-tree. — آدم ج. Orang-outang.
جنگنده Fighter.
جنقولك بازی or جنگولك بازی × Monkey-business; dodging.

جنگی Martial. Warlike. — کشتیِ ج. Warship; man-of-war.
جنگیدن [جنگ] To fight; wage war. To quarrel.
جِن گیر A. P. Exorcist.
جنم + Stamp; type. — جنم آنرا ندارد He is not of that stamp (or type).
جنوب A. South. — درجنوبِ On the s. of. In the southern part of. — جنوب شرق South-east. — جنوب غرب Southwest.
جنوباً A. On the south.
جنوبشرقی a. p. South-eastern.
جنوبغربی a. p. South-western.
جنوبی A. Southern.— افریقای ج. South Africa.
جنود ○ A. [Pl. of (جند)ی] Soldiers; host. See ربالجنود
جُنون A. Insanity; lunacy. Mania.— جنونالکلی Dipsomania.— جنونخمری Delirium tremens.— جنونشهوانیزن Nymphomania.— جنون شهوانی مرد Satyriasis. — جنون عشق Frenzy of love.
جنی n. A. [۱&۲] Jinnee; genus; fairy. —a. Demoniac; possessed of an evil spirit
جنیبت ○ A. [جنائب] = اسب یدك Led horse.
جنین A. Fœtus. — اسقاط ج. Abortion. — جنین ساقط Abortive foetus. — جنین کاذب Mola.
جنینشناسی A. P. Embryology.
جنینکشی A. P. Foeticide.
جنینی A. Fœtal.

جو *or* **جوی** Brook ; stream.– بقیمت آب جو Dirt-cheap.
جو *or* **جوی** [Imp. of جُستن].
جو (*jow*) Barley. B.-corn. *F.* Particle ; grain. – جو برهنه & جو صحرائی & جو دو سر Oats.
جو (*jow*) [Imp. of جَویدن]
جوّ *A.* Atmosphere. *Cf.* هوا ‖ هوا شناسی = علم کائنات ج.
جَواب *A.* = پاسخ Answer; reply.– جواب‌سرجواب Rejoinder.– ج.دادن To answer ; reply to. To meet.– ج.کردن To dismiss. To condemn; pronounce hopeless.– در جوابِ In reply to.
جواباً *A.* In reply. [مسئول
جواب‌گو & جواب ده *A. P.* =
جواب‌گویی *A. P.* = مسئولیت
جوابی *A.* Responsive. [Fem. جوابیه] [*OS.* Generous.
جواد (*A.*) *Mas. pr. name.*
جَوار *A.* Neighbourhood; vicinity. – در جوارِ In the v. or neighbourhood of ; near.
جوارح *A.* Members ; limbs. [Pl. of جارِحه ٥]
جواز *A.* = پروانه Permit; licence.
جوال Large woollen sack. – ج. رفتن × To grapple; fight. To cope. – باخرس درجوال رفتن To catch a Tartar.
جوالدوز Sack-maker. [For سوزن ج.] Packing needle.
جَوان *a.* Young. –*n.* Y. person; youth.– ج.کردن & ج. شدن To ج. ماندن To wear one's years well.
جوانب [Pl. of جانب]
جوانبخت Fortunate ; promising.
جوانک Youngster; lad.
جوانمرد Generous or brave youth.
جوانمردانه Generously. Bravely. Gentlemanly. [ness.
جوانمردی Generosity. Manli-
جوانمرگ *a.* Dying in youth.
جوان نما *a.* Looking young.
جوانه Sprout ; bud. – ج. زدن To b. or sprout; germinate.
جوانی Youth. – ج. از سرگرفتن To rejuvenize.
جواهر *A.* [Pl. of جوهر]. Jewels; gems.
جواهرآلات *a. p.* Jewelled articles. *L.* Jewels.
جواهرساز & جواهر تراش *A. P.* Lapidary; jeweller.
جواهر نشان *A. P.* = **گوهر نشان**
جواهری *A. P.* Jeweller.
جوائز [Pl. of جایزه]
جوجو = **ساس**
جوجو (*jowjow*) Grain by grain ; little by little.
جوجه Chicken.
جوجه تیغی Porcupine.
جوجه خروس Young cock ; cockerel.
جوجه‌کشی *or* **جوجه سازی** Incubation.– اسباب ج. Incubator.
جوخه *Mil* Section.

جوخه یار Assistant patrol leader.

جود A. = بخشش & بخشندگی

جودانه Barley-corn. [For کافور جودانه] Purified camphor.

جودت o A. Good qualities; excellence. Bounty.

جور n. Sort; kind. Mate; pair; fellow. —a. Alike; similar. Assorted. Harmonious.— ج شدن To be assorted. To become alike. To harmonize vi. — ج کردن To assort; classify. To harmonize. To pack, as cards. — صندلی با پرده ج. نیست The chair does not match the curtain. — چه ج. What k. (of)? How? In what manner? Like hell! — چه ج. پرنده‌ایست What k. of a bird is it? — اینجور! Thus! In this m.— اینجوراشخاص Such people. همه ج. All sorts (of). In every way. — ج. بجور Of all kinds; various.—وچه‌ج.هم With a vengeance; and no mistake.

جور A. (jowr) Oppression. — ج. کردن بر To oppress.—جورهمه را میکشم I will stand treat all round.

جوراب Sock or stocking; hose.—جوراب‌ساقه بلند Stocking.

جوراب باف Knitter (of socks and stockings).

جوراب‌بافی Knitting (of socks and stockings).

جوراب فروش Dealer in socks and stockings; hosier.

جور بجور S. u. جور.

جوری Assortment. Similarity.

جوز A. Nut(s). Walnut [گردو]. — جوز هندی or جوزبویا Nutmeg.— گل‌جوزبویا or پوست‌جوز بویا Mace. جوهر جوز بویا Myristic acid.— جوز سرو Cypress-cone. — جوز کلاغ Pine-cone. — جوز کوئل Gardenia. — جوز مائل Stramonium.

جوزاء A. 1) = دوپیکر 2) Old name for خرداد.

جوز(ا)غند A. P. Dried apricots or peaches stuffed with pulverized walnut and sugar.

جوزالقی A. Nux vomica.

جوزآور A. P. Coniferous.

جوزق A-P. Cotton-pod.

جوزک A. P. Adam's apple.

جوش Boiling. Fermentation. Cinder; slag; scoria. Welding. Skin eruption. Granulation. — جوش اکسیژن Oxygen-acetylene welding.—جوش ترش Tartaric acid.—جوش زغال‌سنگ Clinker. — جوش شیرین Sodium bicarbonate; soda.—جوش صورت Acne; pimple. — جوش و خروش Fermentation; foam(ing); effervescence. — (به) ج. آمدن To boil.— خونش بجوش آمده است His blood is up. — (به) ج. آوردن To cause to boil.—خون‌کسیرا بجوش آوردن To stir one's blood. — ج. دادن To weld. To cause to heal up. To conciliate. To boil.— ج. خوردن To weld. To heal up. To grow together. F. To be settled or conciliated. — ج. زدن To boil. To effervesce. F. To fret ; (roar with) worry.— ازجوش افتادن To cease boiling. — آبِ ج. Boiling water.

جوش [Imp. of جوشیدن].

جوشان 1) a. Boiling. 2) Imp. of جوشاندن

جوشاندن [جوشان] To boil.

جوشانده 1) Ptisan ; decoction. 2) [P. P. of جوشاندن]

جوشش Enthusiasm ; effort.

جوشکار or **جوشگر** Welder.

جوشکاری or **جوشگری** Welding.

جوشن * Cuirass. [etc.

جوّ شناس etc. A.P. = هوا شناس

جوشیدن [جوش] To boil. To gush. F. To be agitated. S. a. جوش زدن

جوشیده [P. P. of جوشیدن] Boiled : آب ج.

جوع A. = گرسنگی Hunger. — جوع بقری or جوع‌کلبی Bulimia; polyphagia.

جوف A. Cavity ; hollow. Interior. — در جوفِ Inside ; enclosed with.— ورم جوف دهان Stomatitis.

جوفاً A. (Herewith) enclosed.

جوفروش Barley-dealer [esp. in جو فروش گندم نما Who cries wine and sells vinegar].

جوقه A.P. 1) = جوخه 2) Crowd.

جوکر E. Joker. See شوخ

جوکی + Stingy [خسیس].

جوگندمی Half-grey : ریش ج.

جولان A. Flaunt ; parade ; career. — ج. دادن To c. To run across a race course. To show off. [podrome.

جولانگاه ○ A. P. Circus. Hip-

جولاه Weaver. Knitter.

جونده a. Chewing. —n. Rodent [pl. جوندگان].

جونه گاو [Originally جوانه‌گاو] Young ox.

جوهر A. [f. P. گوهر] Essence; substance . Nature. Dye-stuff. Ink (containing a coloring matter). F. Efficiency; natural ability. — جوهر آبلیمو Citric acid.— جوهر بزاق Diastase. — جوهر فرد 1) Monad ; 2) atom. — جوهر مخدر افیون Narcotine. — جوهر مسکن افیون Codeine. — جوهر منوّم افیون Morphine. [گوهری

جوهری A. P. Aniline. S. a.

جوی S. u. جو [oric.

جوّی A. Atmospheric. Mete-

جویا شدن To inquire; i. about [usu. with از].

جویبار Place abounding in streams. Brook ○.

جویدن [جو] To chew. To gnaw.

جویده [P.P. of جویدن] Chewed.— ج. حرف زدن To mutter or

mumble.

جوین * Made of barley. — نانِ ج. Barley bread.

جوینده [جویندگان]. Seeker. — ج. یابنده است Who seeks will find; he that seeketh findeth.

جه [Imp. of جهیدن]

جهات [Pl. of جهت].

جهاد A. Holy war.

جهاز A. [جهازات] Ship [کشتی]. Apparatus Dowry; dower. Rigging. [*Of a camel*] Saddle. *Anat.* 1) Organ; 2) system.

جهال [A pl. of جاهل]

جهالت A. Ignorance.

جهان * World [دنیا].

جهان * Leaping. *F.* Transient.

جهان‌آفرین * Creator of the world.

جهانتاب * *a.* Illuminating the world : آفتاب ج.

جهاندیده (One) who has travelled very much. Experienced (tourist).

جهانگرد Tourist.

جهانگردی Travelling over the world [obeyed

جهان‌مطاع * *P. A.* Universally

جهان‌نما Cosmorama. Stereoscope. Planisphere.

جهانی World-wide : شهرت ج. ‖ Worldly ○. Mortal ○.

جهانیان Inhabitants of the world; mortals. *Cf.* جهانی

جهاندن or جهانیدن [جهان] To cause to leap or escape.

جهت A. [جهات] Direction; side. Cause. Respect. — جهاتِ چهارگانه The four cardinal points. — بچه ج. For what reason? Why? — (به) جهتِ For; for the sake of. — از این ج. For this r.; therefore. — از این ج. که or بجهت اینکه Because. — از جهتِ For. With regard to. — بجهاتی For certain reasons. — بهر جهت At any rate; anyhow. — از هر جهت In every respect.

جهد A. = کوشش Effort; endeavour. — ج. کردن To e.

جهراً A. Publicly; openly.

جهره Reel; skein-winder.

جهش Leap(ing); jump. [*In biology*] Mutation.

جهل A. = نادانی Ignorance.

جهلاء [A pl. of جاهل]

جهندگی Resilience. Elasticity.

جهنده Jumping. Resilient. Elastic. Salient.

جهنم *A-Heb.* Hell! به ج. H. with it! Nevermind. I don't care a fig. — سر به ج. زدن +To come to an exorbitant amount. — سنگ ج. Silver nitrate. — سنگ جهنم قلمی Pencil of silver nitrate; lunar caustic. — ج. شو H. with you! Go to h.! Get off!

جهنمی *A. P.* Infernal. *Met.* Damned.

جهود = یهودی

جهودانه o Sausage.

جهول o *A*. Very ignorant.

جهیدن [جه] To leap ; jump. [*With* از] To escape.

جهیز *or* **جهیزیه** *A*. Dowry ; dower. *Cf*. جهاز

جیب Pocket. Opening in the collar. *Geom*. Sine. [In the last two senses pronounced *jeyb*]. — جیب بغل *S*. *u*. بغل ‖ جیب‌ساعتی Watch pocket; also, fob. — جیب تمام Cosine. — جیب مقلوب Reversed sine. — بجیب زدن × To pocket or appropriate. — پول **جیبی** P.-money.

جیب‌بر *A*. *P*. Pickpocket.

جیپ *E*. Jeep.

جیحون *A*. = آمودریا

جید *A*. (*jayed*) Benign.

جیر Suède; chamois or shammy; wash-leather.

جیرجیر Chirp. Chirr. — ج. کردن To chirp or chirr.

جیرجیرك Cricket. — جیرجیرك دشتی Cicada.

جیرو *It*. = پشت‌نویسی

جیره Ration. — (به) ج. دادن To ration.

جیره‌بندی Rationing (system).

جیش o *A*. [جیوش] = لشکر

جیغ Scream. — ج. زدن *or* ج. کشیدن To scream. To squeak.

جیفه *A*. Carcase. — جیفهٔ دنیا Mammon; pelf; yellow dirt.

جیك + Peep or chirp [usu. جیك‌جیك *q*. *v*.]. — ج. زدن To dare to speak ; breathe. — دیگر حالا جیك نمی‌زند He sings small now.

جیك‌جیك + Chirp. Peep. — ج. کردن To chirp. To peep.

جیک‌وبک The two larger surfaces of the astragalus. *F*. Ins and outs ; secrets.

جیم شدن × To sneak out.

جین [Cont. of دوجین 'dozen'- now often = ten].

جیوش [Pl. of جیش]

جیوه Mercury; quicksilver. — (به) ج. زدن To silver, as a mirror.

جیوه‌ای Mercurial. Hydrargyric.

چابُک Nimble; agile ; quick.
چابک‌دست Clever; dexterous.
سوارکار = چابک‌سوار
چابُکی Agility ; nimbleness.
چاپ T. (f. Chinese) Impression; print. Edition: چاپ دوم ‖ چ. خوردن To be printed. — سه چ. خورد It ran into three editions. — چ. زدن To print. F. To fabricate ; invent. — چ. کردن To print or publish. To print off.— چاپ سربی Typography. — چاپ سنگی Lithography. — حروف چ. Type; print. —زیر چاپ In the press ; in print. — ماشین چ. Printing machine; press.
چاپار T. Courier.
چاپچی + T. Impostor. Charlatan. [press.
چاپخانه T. P. Printing-house;
چاپلوس Flatterer.
چاپلوسانه Flatteringly.
چاپلوسی Flattery. — چ. کردن To flatter.
چاپی Printed. —موادچاپی P. or printing material; print.
چاپیدن [چاپ] To plunder.
چاتمه T. Stack ; pile (of arms). —چ. زدن To p. arms.
چاچول باز Quack ; charlatan.
چاچول بازی Charlatanry.
چاخان × Boasting ; bragging. Braggart ; quack. —چ. کردن To play the q. To flatter. To draw the long bow.
چادُر Tent. Awning. Large veil worn by a woman to cover her body and dress.— چادر قلندری Bell-tent ; gypsy-tent. — چ. زدن To pitch a tent.
چادرشب Wrapper for bed-clothes. [mad.
چادرنشین Tent-dweller ; no-
چادرنماز Veil worn by women when they are indoors, especially when they say their prayers.
چار = چهار [mostly in comb.].
چارآئینه Caparison..
چارَبر Quadrilateral.
چاربند The hips.
چارپا [چارپایان] Quadruped.
چارپادار Driver of beasts of burden ; carrier ; sumpter.
چارپاره Lead ball ; buckshot.
چارپایه Stool. — دندان چ. Molar tooth.
چارپر Case-bottle. [lateral.
چارپهلو Four-sided ; quadri-
چارترک or چهارترک Four-sided.— شیروانی چ. Mansard roof.

چارچار Period of 8 days in midwinter.
چارچوب (Wooden) frame.
چار دانگ o Of medium size. *OS*. Two - thirds. — قوش چ. Tercel ; male falcon.
چهاردیواری *S. u.* **چاردیواری**
چارراه *or* **چهارراه** Crossroads.
چارزانو With legs crossed.
چارسو Crossroads.
چارشانه Square-shouldered.
چارشکاف *or* **چهارشکاف** Crucial incision. — چ. کردن To make a crucial i. in.
چارطاق Flung open. Wide o.
چارطاقی Pent-house; lean-to.
چارطبع * o *P. A.* The four temperaments.
چارغ *or* **چارق** = **چاروغ** etc.
چارك = **چهاريك** Quarter. *Old weight = 750 grammes.*
چارگوش & **چارگوشه** *a.* Quadrangular. —*n*. Quadrangle ; also, square.
چارمیخ Cross. — بهچ. کشیدن To crucify . — چ. کردن + To confirm or corroborate. To silence or refute. [To g.
چارنعل *P. A.* Gallop. — چ. رفتن
چارپادار = + **چارواادار**
چاروغ *or* **چاروق** Shoe consisting of a piece of hide and a few thongs.
چارناچار & **چاروناچار** Of necessity ; nolens volens.
چاره Remedy. Cure. — چ. کردن To remedy. — چ. ای نیست *or* چ. ندارد It cannot be helped; there is no alternative. — چ. اش نمیشود + He is incorrigible.
چاره‌پذیر Remediable.
چاره‌جوئی Seeking a remedy.— چ. کردن To seek a r.
چاره‌ناپذیر Irremediable. Inevitable. [one-fourth.
چاريك *or* **چهار يك** Quarter ;
چاشت Middle hour of the forenoon. Early lunch o.
چاشنی Percussion-cap. Detonator. Sauce. (Fore)taste. Relish. — چ. زدن To season with a sauce.
چاق *T*. Fat. — چ. شدن To grow fat ; put on weight. To be cured +. — چ. کردن To fatten. To cure. To prepare for smoking +. — چ. وچله + Plump.
چاقو *T*. Knife . — چ. دسته کردن To squat (oneself) down. *OS*. To shut a knife o. — چ. کشیدن To (threaten to) knife s. o.; stab at s. o.
چاقو تیز کن *T.P.* Knife-grinder.
چاقو کش *T. P.* Ruffian (armed with a knife); *Cf*. Cosh-boy.
چاقو کشی *T. P.* (Hooligan's practice of) knifing or stabbing.
چاقی *T. P.* Fatness. Obesity.
چاک Rent. Slit. Cleft ; fissure. — چاك نای *or* چاك صوت

Glottis.— ج. زدن & ج. کردن & ج. دادن To tear. To slit. — بچاك جاده زدن × To tramp it; pad the hoof.— بزن بچاك × Buzz off! Hop it! Scram!

چاك چاك * Full of slits.

چاکر Servant. [*In p. c.*] Your obedient servant, i. e. I.

چاکری Servitude o. Devotion.

چال Hollow; pit. — ج. کردن (*Derogatory*) To bury.

چالاک * Nimble; quick.

چالاکی Nimbleness; agility.

چاله Hollow; pit.

چانه Chin. — ج. زدن To haggle; bargain.

چاودار *T.* Rye.

چاووش *or* **چاوُش** *T.* Herald. Mace-bearer. Leader of a caravan.

چاه Well. Pit. — چاه زنخدان Dimple. — چاه مستراح Cesspool. — چاه هوائی Air-pocket. — ج. کندن To sink, drill, or dig a well.

چاهك Soak-away-pit. Sink. Sump.

چاه کن Well-digger; sinker.

چاه کنی Well-drilling.

چای [*Of Chinese origin*] Tea [usu. چائی].— گل ج. Tea-rose.

چای خوری [For فنجان ج.] Teacup. — روزی دو فنجان ج. 2 teacupfuls a day.

چای دان (Tea-)caddy.

چای صاف کن *P.A.* Tea-strainer.

چائیدن [چای] To catch cold. To cool.

چائیمان Chill; cold.

چپ Left. [Of eyes] Squint. — دست چپ بروید Keep to the left. — بچپ چپ! Left face! — چپ نگاه کردن To look daggers (at). — باکسی چپ افتادن + To fall out, or be at loggerheads, with s. o. — از دندهٔ چپ پاشدن To get out of bed on the wrong side.

چپانیدن To cram; jam; thrust.

چپاول *T.* & **چپو** + — غارت

چپ چپی Cornel; dogwood.

چپ چشم Squint-eyed.

چپ دست Left-handed.

چپر 1) Wattle; also, hurdle of wattled twigs. 2) = چاپار

چپراس *or* **چپراست** Clasp. Buckle.

چپق [f. T. چبوق] Pipe with a long stem.

چپه + Capsized. — ج. شدن & ج. کردن To capsize.

چپیدن [چپ] To be crammed or packed into a small space. To press together. To thrust.

چتائی *H.* Jute.

چتر Umbrella. Parachute [also چتر نجات]. — چتر زلف Bang. — چتر زنانه Parasol. — ج. انداختن *or* ج. زدن To strut, as a peacock.

چترباز Parachutist.

چترك Umbellule. Spleenwort

چتری *Bot.* Umbelliferous. —

ضمیمهٔ ج. — Umbel. آرایش ج. Umbraculum.

چتکه *R.* Abacus.

چخماق [f. T. چقماق] Steel for striking a light. Hammer or cock of a gun. — سنگ ج. Flint; silex. — تفنگ چخماقی Flintgun.

چُدن Cast iron.

چدن ریزی Foundry.

چدنی Made of cast iron.

چر [Imp. of چریدن]

چرا 1) Why? 2) Yes [affirmative reply to a negative question]. — زیراکه = ج. که —

چَرا Grazing. — چریدن = ج. کردن —

چراغ Lamp; light. — چراغ جلو Headlight. — چراغ خطر Stop-light. — چراغ راهنما 1) Traffic light; 2) indicator. — چراغ عقب Taillight. — چراغ موشی Lampion. — روغن ج. (Unclarified) castor-oil.

چراغان کردن To illuminate.

چراغ آویز Lustre.

چراغ روشن + At dusk.

چراگاه Pasture; pasturage.

چراندن *or* چرانیدن To (cause to) graze or pasture.

چَرب Fat. Oily; greasy. — ج. کردن To oil; lubricate. To anoint. To make rich, as food. To allow to exceed the due weight; give the baker's dozen [usu. چربش کن].

چرب زبان Glib-tongued.

چرب و چیل × Fat; rich in fat.

چرب و نرم Honeyed; glib. Sleek.

چربه Tracing-paper; oil-paper.

چربی Fatness. Fat; grease.

چربیدن [چرب] To exceed the due weight; preponderate; turn the scale. — زورش بمن میچربد He prevails over me in force.

چرت *or* چرت و پرت × Irrelevant talk; nonsense.

چُرت Nap; slumber; forty winks. — ج. زدن To take a nap. To doze off; nod; drowse. — چرت کسیرا پاره کردن + To give one a start; interrupt his day-dream.

چرتنه ○ Octopus.

چرتی + Given to dozing.

چَرخ Wheel. Machine. Vehicle. Cart. Turn; whirl. *L.* Bicycle. *F.* Firmament. Fate; fortune. — چرخ خیاطی Sewing-machine. — چرخ دستی 1) Trolley. 2) Wheel-barrow [also چرخ خاك كشی]. — ج. كردن To mince. To sew in a sewing-machine. To burr, as a tooth [also ج. گذاشتن]. — ج. خوردن To turn round and r.; whirl; spin. — ج. زدن ‖ چرخاندن = ج. دادن To turn or s. To w. — چرخ وفلك 1) Girandole; sun-and-planet wheel. 2) Merry-go-round. —

چهار چرخه Four-wheeled.
چرخ [Imp. of چرخیدن]
چرخاندن To turn round. To spin. To rotate.
چرخچي *P. T.* Carter.
چرخ دار Wheeled. — صندلی چ. or صندلی گردنده 1) Wheel-chair; 2) swivel-chair. — میز چرخدار Trolley.
چرخ ریسك Titmouse.
چرخ ساز Wheelwright.
چرخ سواری Cycling.
چرخش Rotation.
چرخشت Wine-press.
چرخک Reel. Rowel. Trundle.
چرخ کار Machine-operator. Turner.
چرخه Reel. Rotation.
چرخی +*a*. Machine-made. Circular. Churned. —*n*. Carter.
چرخیدن [چرخ] To rotate. To spin. To turn. To whirl.
چرس Indian hemp-juice.
چرغ Lanner(et). Kestrel.
چِرک *n.* Dirt. Pus. —*a*. Dirty.— چرك گوش Ear-wax; cerumen. *Med*. Otorrhea.— چ. شدن To get dirty. — چ. کردن To soil; make d. — چ. کردن or چ. نشستن To suppurate. — چ. گرفتن = چرکِ ... را گرفتن ‖ چ. شدن To clean; dry-clean; remove the dirt of ...
چرك تاب Of a colour that does not show the dirt.
چرك نویس Rough copy; draft.
چرکه [Erroneous for چتکه]
چرکین * Dirty. — چ. کردن To make dirty. *F*. To disgrace.
چَرم Leather. Hide.
چرم ساز Currier.
چرم سازی Curriery.
چرمی Leathern; of leather.
چرمین * = چرمی
چرند + or چرند و پرند × Nonsense; balderdash. — چ. گفتن To talk nonsense.
چرنده Grazing (animal); beast [pl. چرندگان].
چریدن [چر] To graze; pasture.
چریک *T*. Irregular troops.
چزیدن + To burn. *F*. To implore earnestly.
چِسان * = چگونه & چطور
چسان فسان کردن × To tog oneself up (*or* out).
چَسب 1) Paste; gum; glue; mucilage. Sticking-plaster. 2) *Imp. of* چسبیدن
چسبان 1) چسبیده 2) Close-fitting. 3) *Imp. of* چسباندن
چسبانده [P.P. of چسباندن].
چسباندن To stick. To cause to adhere. To sew on, as a button. — بدیوار چسباندن To paste up.
چسبناک Sticky.
چسبندگی Adhesiveness. Tenacity.
چسبنده Sticky; adhesive. Tenacious.

چسبیدن [چسب] To stick. To cling. To adhere.– باو نمی‌چسبد I can't see him having done it ; his withers are unwrung.

چسبیده [P. P. of چسبیدن].

چست * Quick ; nimble.

چسِ فیل Pop-corn ; puffed maize.

چشان [Imp. of چشانیدن]

چشانیدن To cause to taste.

چشایی Sense of taste.

چشته o Food given to hunting animals. Whet ; little food as a taste.

چشته خوار * (Person) spoiled by too much kindness (orig. by being fed too much or too often).

چشم *n*. Eye. *F*. Expectation; hope. –*int*. [Also بچشم] Right oh ! very well. – چ. پوشیدن از To renounce. – To connive at ; tolerate. – چ. داشتن To expect or hope.– چ. زدن To influence by an evil eye. – چشم کسی را بستن To blindfold s. o. –بادوچشم دیدن To make a difference between . – چ. چیدن To counteract (the effect of) an evil eye.–چشم‌خوش باز نکردن To lead a dog's life. – چشمش بدست شما است He is looking forward to you.چشمم آب نمیخورد I have little hope in that ; I doubt it very much ; I wonder. چشم *or* چشم بد دور ! شیطان کور ! Touch wood. – چشمم بدست او است I depend on him. – چشم شما روشن [also چشم‌ماروشن] I congratulate you (for the arrival of such a one).– چ. برهم‌زدن To wink (the eyes); bat an eyelid.– بیك چ. برهم زدن In the twinkling of an eye. – تا چشمش هم کور شود That serves him right. – تا چشم کار میکند As far as the eye can reach.

چشم انداز View ; perspective. [Outlook.

چشم براه Waiting impatiently; kept waiting.

چشم بسته Blindfold(ed). *Cf*. چشم و گوش بسته

چشم بند Conjuror ; juggler. Blinkers.

چشم بندی Conjuring.

چشم پزشک Oculist ; ophthalmologist.

چشم پوشی Connivance. Renouncement.

چشم ترسیده Scared ; deterred; also, discouraged.

چشم چرانی Gloating (from lust). [of the eye.

چشمخانه * Eye-socket ; orbit

چشمِ خروس Indian licorice.

چشم داشت Prospect ; hope.

چشم درد Sore eyes ; ophthalmia.

چشم درشت Ox-eyed.

چشم دریده Impudent.

چشم رس Purview ; eyeshot.
چشم روشنی Present.
چشم زخم Injury caused by an evil eye.
چشم غرّه + Glaring; glare. — بکسی چ. رفتن To g. at s. o.; look at him menacingly.
چشمک Wink ; twinkling. — چ. زدن To wink; twinkle.
چشم و گوش باز Sophisticated.
چشم و گوش بسته Unsophisticated.
چشم و همچشمی = هم چشمی
چشمه Spring; fountain. Source. Opening. Span (of a bridge). Eyelet; mesh. — چشمهٔ آب گرم Thermal spring.
چشمه دوزی Meshwork.
چشیدن [چش] To taste.
چطور S. u. طور
چغر + Tough.
چُغلی Tale-bearing. — چ. کردن To tell tales.
چغندر or چقندر Beetroot.
چفیدن ○ To breathe.
چِفت Hasp. — چ. کردن To hasp; fasten by a h.
چفته Trellis ; vine-prop.
چقدر S. u. قدر
چقماق S. u. چخماق
چَک Slap; box on the ear.
چَک 1) [Imp. of چکیدن] 2) Drop [چکه].
چِک (f. E. or Fr.) Cheque.— چك كشيدن To draw (a cheque).
چَکاچاک * Clank(ing noise).
چکامه * = قصیده
چکان [Imp. of چکاندن].
چکاندن or چکانیدن To cause to drop or trickle.
چکاوك Lark.
چک چک Drop by drop. — چ. کردن To fall in drops.
چَکچکی Stone-chat.
چکر E. Chequers ; draughts.
چکش T. Hammer. — چکش چوبی Mallet. — چکش در Knocker.— چکش برق Distributor rotor. — چکش دوشاخ Claw-hammer. — چکش دق Med. Plexor. — چ. خوردن To be hammered. — چ. زدن To hammer. To malleate.
چکش خور T. P. Malleable.
چکشی 1) a. Hammer-hardened.— نبض چ. Dicrotic pulse. — چ. کردن To hack; dress with a hammer. — جواب چ. + Harsh answer. 2) ad. Harshly ; in a stiff manner.
چکمه T. High boots ; riding b. ; Wellingtons.
چکمه دوز T. P. Bootmaker .
چك و چانه × Chops or jaws. Haggling.
چکمیزك Strangury.
چِکه Drop. — چ. کردن To leak.— سقف چ. کرده است The rain has

seeped (*or* soaked) through the roof.

چکی By the job.

چکیدن [چك] To drip. To trickle. — آب از دستش نمی‌چکد He is close-fisted.

چکیده *a*. Distilled. Dropped. —*n*. Extract. Distillate.

چگال Dense.

چگالی Density.

چگونگی Quality. Circumstance. — چگونگی امر Fact(s).

چگونه How? *See* گونه

چل + Half-witted.

چلاق Crippled; lame. — چ. کردن To cripple; maim.

چلاندن [چلان] + To squeeze; press.

چلپاسه Small lizard.

چلتوك *T*. Paddy.

چلچراغ Chandelier.

چلچله = پرستوك

چلچلی × Youthful and wild acts. — چلچلی خود را کردن To sow one's wild oats.

چلر (*chelar*) Beech.

چلمن × Nincompoop.

چلنگر *T*. Locksmith.

چلو Plain boiled rice.

چلوار Longcloth; also, white cambric. [f. چل40 + وار corruption of «yard»].

چلو صاف کن *A. P*. Strainer.

چله Period of 40 days, esp. of retirement and asceticism or of fasting. Bowstring Selvage.

چلیپا [f. A. صلیب] Cross.

چلیپائی *Bot*. Cruciferous.

چلیک Drum; also, cask.

چم [Imp. of چمیدن]

چماق *T*. Club; mace.

چمچه Ladle; scoop.

چمدان Suit-case; trunk. [Corruption of جامه دان]

چمن Lawn; grass.

چمن‌بر Lawn-mower.

چمن‌زار Grass-plot; lawn.

چمنی Grass-green.

چم و خم × Coquettish elegance. Knack; trick.

چموش Mulish; vicious.

چمیدن * [چم] To strut. To flaunt.

چنار Plane-tree.

چنان *a*. Such (as that). —*ad*. Such; so; thus. —*prep*. Like.

چنانچه 1) In the event that; if. 2) = چنانکه

چنانکه = بطوریکه As.

چنباتمه *T*. Squatting posture. — چ. زدن To squat.

چنبر Hoop. Loop. Circle. Dog's collar. *Anat*. Clavicle. — چرخ کسیرا چنبر کردن To queer some one's pitch; also, harass or worry him.

چنبره Circle. Coil. Bend. Pad (used by porters). Air-cushion. [Of the ear] Helix. — چ. زدن To wreathe oneself.

چنبری Circular. Curved.

چنته *T*. Satchel; bag. — ج . اش خالی شد He is (*or* was) at the end of his tether.

چَند Some; several; a few. How many? H. much? [*only for money*]. H. long?* — ج. تا H. many? [used as a pron]. — چندی For some time. A little while. — چندی است که For some time past. — یك ج. * For a w. A few. — ج، وقت پیش * تا چند H. long? — *or* چندی‌پیش Some time ago. — ج. وقت است که؟ H. long is it since . . ? — ج. درصد *or* ج. صدی H. many per cent?

چندان So: ج. سرد نیست It is not so (very) cold. ‖ So many. So much. — ده ج. Ten times as many (*or* as much). — نه ج Not so very. Not so m. (*or* many). — ج. که؟ * As m. as; as many as.

چند برابر Manifold; several times as much (*or* as many).

چند جمله‌ای *P. A.* Polynomial.

چند درصد Percentage.

چند روزه Of short duration; short-lived; precarious.

چندش Horripilation; goose-flesh.

چندك زدن + To squat; crouch.

چند گوشه Many-cornered; polygonal.

چند سطحی *or* **چند وجهی** *P. A.* Polyhedral. — جسم ج. Polyhedron.

چندی Quantity.

چندین Many. So many. So much.

چَنگ Claw. Grip. Clutch. *Mus.* 1) Harp or lyre; 2) quaver. — ج. زدن To play on the harp. [With به] To grip; grapple; clutch at. — بچنگ آوردن To seize or obtain. — چنگی بدل نمیزند It does not appeal to one.

چنگار *Med.* Cancer.

چنگال Fork. Claws. Clutches. — چنگال مرگ The jaws of death.

چنگ زَن Harpist.

چنگک Hook; grappling-iron. — پیوند چنگکی Claw-coupling.

چنگیز *Mas. pr. name.*

چنین Such . . . . as this. So; thus. — ج. کتابی Such a book (as this).

چو (*cho*) * [*Cont. of* چون]

چو × (*c'how*) Rumour. — چو انداختن To spread a rumour.

چوب Wood. Stick. Staff. *By e.* Cane; rod; i. e. beating. — چوب بیلیارد Cue. — چوب پاسبان Truncheon. — چوب پرده Curtain-rod. — چوب چپق Pipe-stem. — چوب ذرت Corn-cob. — چوبِ طبل Drumstick. — چوب زیر بغل Crutch(es). — چوب سفید Deal. — ج. خوردن To be beaten. — چوبِ چیزیرا خوردن To suffer the evil consequences, or pay the price, of s. t.— چوب دیگری را خوردن To be a whipping-boy or scapegoat.— چ. زدن To beat.— چوبش توی آب است We have a rod in pickle for him.

چوب بست Scaffolding; staging.

چوب پا Stilt.

چوب پنبه Cork.

چوب پنبه کش Corkscrew.

چوب ساب Float-cut. — چ. سوهان Float-cut file ; rasp. — چوب ساب نرم Bastard f.

چوبخط *P. A.* Tally ; notch ; score. — چ. زدن To tally.

چوبدار Cattle-man; drover.

چوبدستی Walking-stick; cane.

چوب رخت Hat-rack; clothes-rack; hat-and-coat r.

چوب شدگی Lignification. Stiffness.

چوب شکاف = گوه Wedge.

چوبک *Kind of soapy root - per.* amole: *the root of the soap plant.*

چوبکاری Beating o.—چ. کردن To give a (good) beating to. *F.* To make one blush.

چوبه Shaft. Staff. Rolling-pin.— چوبهٔ دار Gallows-tree.

چوبی Wooden. Coach-built, as the body of a bus.

چوپان etc. = **شبان** etc

چوروک *or* **چروک** Shrink-age. — چ. دادن *or* چ. کردن To wrinkle ; shrink ; shrivel. — چ. شدن *or* چ. خوردن To shrink; shrivel (up) ; pucker.

چوگان Polo-stick. Bat. — جفتِ **چوگانی** Battledore placenta.

چوگان بازی Game of polo.

چوله *or* **چاوله** + Crooked.

چون Since; as. When. *—prep.* Like; (such) as. *—ad.* How ? چون و چرا کردن To dispute.

چونکه Because. Since.

چونه Cake of dough; pat. — چانه زدن = + چ. زدن

چونی Quality.

چه * (*chah*) [*Cont. of* چاه]

چه (*che*) *pr.* What?—چه خبر است W. is up? W. is going on?— چه شده است W. has happened?— من چه میدانم How do I know ? *—conj.* [*Repeated*] Whether . . . or. Ex. چه بیاید چه نیاید من خواهم رفت ‖ As; because. *—ad.* = چقدر How: چه خوش است H. pleasant (it) is . . . — چه پسر خوبی است ! There's (*or* that's) a good boy ! — چه بهتر So much the better. — چه وقت ؟ When? — بشماچه What is that to you ; that is none of your business.

چهار Four. *—Note.* چهار پا - چهارچوب - چهار پایه - چهار پاره - چهار شانه - چهار سو - چهار زانو چهارگوش - چهار طبع - چهار طاقی etc. may be looked up un-

der the variants چارپا etc.
چهار برابر Fourfold; quadruple.
چهارجانبی *P.A.* Quadripartite.
چهار جمله‌ای *P. A.* Quadrinomial.
چهارچرخه *a.* Four-wheeled. —*n.* F.-w. vehicle.
چهار حرفی *P.A.* Quadriliteral.
چهاردست Four-handed; quadrumanous.
چهار دست و پا On all fours. — چ. رفتن To crawl.
چهاردکمه(ای) [*Of a jacket*] Double-breasted.
چهارده Fourteen.
چهاردهم Fourteenth.
چهاردهمی (The) fourteenth.
چهاردهمین The fourteenth.
چاردیواری or چهار دیواری Enclosure within four walls. One's private house. *F.* Framework; limits.
چهار راه *S. u.* چار راه
چهار سر *C. P.* Double-pair royal. *OS.* Four-headed.
چهار شنبه Wednesday.
چهار صد(م) Four-hundred(th).
چهارطاق *P. A. See* چارطاق
چهارگانه The four . . .
چهارلا Four-fold. Four-ply.
چهارلا چنگ Sixty-fourth note.
چهارم Fourth.
چهارمی (The) fourth.
چهارمین The fourth.
چهچه Warbling; twittering. — چ. زدن To twitter; trill; warble.
چهره = چهر
چهره * Face. Cheek. Countenance.
چهره‌ای Rose-coloured. Pink.
چهل Forty.
چهلم Fortieth.
چهلمی (The) fortieth.
چهلمین The fortieth.
چیت *H.* Chintz; printed calico (*or* cotton).
چیت سازی *H.P.* Chintz-making (factory).
چیدن [چین] To pick (off); pluck. To mow To clip; cut; shear [قیچی کردن]. To pare. To arrange; put in order. To lay, as a table. To set, as type.
چیرگی * Victory. Valour. Violence.
چیره Prevailing; victorious. — چ. شدن بر To prevail over.
چیز Thing. Matter. Effects. — (یك) چیزی Something. — هرچیز Everything. Anything. — هیچ چ. ‖ هرچه = هر چیز یکه Nothing. — چیزی نیست It is nothing serious. It doesn't matter. — چیزی که هست Only; the thing is. — هزار ریال(و) چیزی بالا Something over 1000 *rials*.
چیزخورکردن + To poison.
چیزدار Well-to-do; wealthy.
چیست [Cont. of چه است] What is (it)?

چیستان * = معما Riddle; enigma.

چیله Small piece of firewood; chat.

چین Wrinkle. Pleat. Crease. Fold. Math; crop. — چین دوم Aftermath. — چین طاقی Anticline. — ج. خوردن To be wrinkled. To be puckered (up). — ج. دادن To wrinkle. To plait. To curl. To knit, as the brow. To purse, as the lips.

چین [Imp. of چیدن]

چین China. — جنگ چین و ژاپن The Sino-Japanese War.

چین چین Full of wrinkles or folds

چین چینی Trimming.

چین خوردگی Fold. Wrinkle. Rugosity.

چین خورده Wrinkled. Puckered. Rugose.

چین‌دار Wrinkled Puckered. Creasy. Curly. Currugated.

چیننده Picker; plucker. Mower. Shearer. Cutter. *See* چیدن

چینه Clay-wall; pisé-wall. Stratum; layer. Grain (for birds). — ج. کشیدن To build, or enclose in, a clay-wall.

چینه‌دان Crop; maw.

چینی *a.* Chinese. —*n.* C. language. Chinaman. China; porcelaine. — چوب ج. China-root. — خاك ج. Kaolin.

چینی‌آلات *P. A.* Chinaware.

چینی بندزن Mender of chinaware; tinker(er).

ح

حاجّ *A.* [حجاج] Pilgrim (to Mecca). [Used before the name of a man. *Fem.* حاجیه]
حاجات [Pl. of حاجت]
حاجب ○ *A.* Doorkeeper; chamberlain. Curtain. Eyebrow.— حاجب ماوراء Opa que.
حاجت *A.* [حوائج & حاجات] Need ; want. — بچیزی ح . داشتن To need or want s. t.— ح.خواستن To pray for one's needs. — حاجت کسیرا برآوردن To grant a person's request. — چه ح. به No need of. — قضای ح.کردن To ease nature.
حاجتمند *A.P.* = محتاج & نیازمند
حاجز *a. A.* Hindering. Separating. — حجاب ح. Diaphragm.
حاجزی *A.* Phrenic.
حاجی = + حاجّ
حاجی فیروز *A. P.* × Nigger minstrel.
حاجیه [Fem. of حاجی or حاجّ]
حادّ *A*. Acute. *OS.* = تیز Sharp. [Fem. حادّه] . — زاویهٔ حاده A. angle.
حادِث *A.* New [تازه]. Created; not eternal.— ح. شدن To happen; occur.
حادثه *A.* [حوادث & حادثات] Accident. Event. Phenomenon.
حاذق *A.* Proficient; ingenious.
حارّ *A.* = گرم Hot ; torrid. [Fem. حارّه]
حارس ○ *A.* Guardian.
حاسد ○ *A.* [حُسّاد]=حسود
حاسه *S. u.* حواس
حاشا (*A.*) *n.* Denial. —*int* . [*with the stress on the 1st syl.*] Far from it ! God forbid! [also ح.که *]. — ح کردن To deny.
حاش لله • *A.* God forbid that.
حاشیه *A.* Margin. Marginal note. Edge; border. List; selvage. *Astr.* & *Bot.* Limb.— ح. رفتن+ To make an indirect remark.
حاشیه‌دار *A P* Having a margin. Hemmed. Rimmed.
حاشیه نشین *A. P.* (One) who sits on the outskirts of an assembly. *S. a.* فضول
حاصل (*A.*)*n.* Crop; produce. *F.* Result. —*a.* Obtained. [Fem. حاصله]. — مزایای حاصله از Benefits accruing on.— حاصل جمع Sum; total. — حاصل ضرب Product. — ح.کردن To obtain ; get. To grant *. To fulfil *.— مارا از آن چه ح. ؟ What will it profit us?
حاصلخیز *A. P.* Fertile.
حاصلخیزی *A. P.* Fertility.
حاضر *A.* Ready ; prepared.

[*fem.* حاکمه Ex. هیئت حاکمه the ruling or g. class].

حاکم نشین *A. P.* Chief town or residence; governor's seat.

حاکمیت *A.* Sovereignty [often حق ح·]. Jurisdiction.

حاکی (*A.*) *a.* Indicating; stating. — ح· بودن از To indicate. To state. To forebode.

حال (*A.*) *n.* [احوال] Condition (of health). State ; circumstance. Natural disposition. Ecstasy. [For زمان ح·] Present tense. —*ad.* Now. —*a.* Due.— ح·شدن To fall due; mature.— حالِ شما چطوراست How are you? H. is your health? — ح· ندارم I do not feel well.— حالِ کردن کاری را داشتن To be in a mood to do s. t. ; feel like doing it. — حال دعوا کردن Mood to fight. — حالش جاآمد + He came round; he came to his senses. He recovered. — حال کسیرا جا آوردن To bring s. o. to his senses. *F.* To give it to s. o. hot; serve him out.— تابحال Hitherto; up to now.— بهرحال or در هر حال In any case. — از حال رفتن To faint.— بحال آمدن To come to one's senses ; c. round.— بحال آمدن = (1 + ح· آمدن 2) To put on weight or flesh.— بحال آوردن To bring r.; b. to one's senses. To make fat.— علی ای ح ّ (*al*a-*a*y*o*-) In any case. — اهل ح· Pleasure-seeking

Present. Willing. —*n.* [pl. حاضرین & حضار those present ; the audience] . — در حال ح· At present. — ح· شدن To get ready. To appear. — ح· شد برود He agreed (*or* was prepared) to go. — ح· کردن To prepare ; make ready.— حاضرخدمت Complaisant ; obliging. — حاضر و غایب کردن To call the rolls.

حاضر الذهن *A.* Ready-witted. Having presence of mind.

حاضر جواب *a. p.* Quick at repartee.

حاضر جوابی *a. p.* Readiness to answer or retort ; power of repartee.

حاضری + *A.P.* Hastily prepared (or frugal) food; simple dish.

حاضر یراق + *A. T.* Ready for service ; equipped and prepared.

حافظ (*A.*) *n.* Keeper; preserver. —*a.* Retaining; retentive [usu. in the fem. حافظه *q. v.*] — خدا حافظِ *or* خدا حافظ شما Good-bye !

حافظ الصحه o *A.* Preservative.

حافظه *A.* [For قوهٔ ح·] Retentive faculty ; memory . [*Orig. fem. of* حافظ *q. v.*].

حاق الفخذ *A.* Acetabulum.

حاکم *A.* [حکام] Governor [*now* فرماندار] . Magistrate. Judge *. Winning party. — *a.* Ruling ; governing

or jovial (person). — ح. کردن To be in an ecstasy o. To go pleasuring; have fun×. — ح. زبان Mute language. — وحال آنکه Whereas.

حالا *A. P.* Now; at present. In a moment+. — از حالا ببعد From now on; henceforth; hereafter. تاحالا Up to now; hitherto. — ح. که + Now that; seeing that; since.

حالاً *A.* With regard to health. — ح. چطور به How is your health?

حالات [Pl. of حالت]

حالب *A.* Ureter.

حالت *A.* [حالات] State; condition. Condition of health. Rapture; ecstasy. *Gr.* Case. *Mus.* Expression.

حال ندار + *A. P.* = ناخوش Sick; ill [used mostly attributively].

حالی + *A. P.* Explained. Coming to understand. — حالیم نشد I did not get it into my head. — چیزی حالیش نیست He is unconscious. — ح. کردن To explain; bring home. To cause to understand. [circumstances.

حالیا • *A. P.* In the present

حالی بحالی شدن *A. P.* To go to ecstasies. To have a funny feeling ×. To undergo an emotional change.

حالیه *A.* At present.

حامض *A.* Acid. *See* ترش

حامِل *A.* Bearer. *Mus.* Stave; staff. [For خط ح.] Vector. — شعاع ح. Radius vector. *Cf. the fem.* حامله

حاملگی *A. P.* = آبستنی

حامله *A.* = آبستن Pregnant; expectant. [*Orig. fem. of* حامل *q. v.*] — ح. شدن To conceive; become pregnant.

حامی *A.* Protector. Defender; supporter. Patron.

حانوت o *A.* = دکان

حاوی *A.* Containing. — ح. بودن To contain; comprise.

حاویه *A.* = روده بند Mesentery.

حائز *A.* Possessing. Holding. — حائز اهمیت Important. — حائزِ مقامی شدن To (come to) hold a position. — حائز حداکثر بودن To be the highest bidder.

حائل *A.* 1) *a.* Intervening; standing between. Guarding. Retaining: دیوار حائل ‖ 2) *n.* Screen. Guard. Fender.

حَبّ *A.* Pill. Berry. Grain [only in the pl. حبوب o or the double pl. حبوبات]. — حب خوردن To take a pill or pills. — حب کردن To pill; form into pills.

حُبّ *A.* = دوستی Love. — حب جاه Ambitiousness. — حب نفس Self-love. — حب وطن Patriotism. — حب و بغض Bias; likes and dislikes. — حب ولد Love of offspring. [shade.

حُباب A. Bubble. Globe. Lamp-
حبّ الاثل A. Gall of the tamarisk.
حبّ الآس A. Myrtle-berry.
حبّ الغار A. Laurel-berry.
حبّ القرع A. = کرم کدو or کدودانه
حبّ المشك A. Abelmosk.
حبّ النیل A. Blue water-lily seeds.
حباله ○ A. Trap.— زنی را بحبالهٔ نکاح درآوردن To marry a woman.
حبذا• (habaza) = زهی
حَبس A. Imprisonment. *Law*. Entailment; tail. *Med*. Retention; suppression.— حبس ابد I. for life. — ح. با اعمال شاقه S. u. شاق ‖ حق حبس کالا Lién on goods. — حبس مجرد Solitary confinement. — ح. شدن To be imprisoned.— ح. کردن To imprison. To suppress. To record, as a sound. *Law*. To tie up; entail.
حبسی + A. P. 1) = زندانی 2) Imprisonment. — حبسی خود را گذراندن To serve one's term of imprisonment.
حبش A. Abyssinia; Ethiopia.
حبشی A. Abyssinian; Ethiopian.
حبل الورید A. Jugular vein.
حبوب S. u. حَب
حُبوبات A. Grains. Cereals. [Pl. of حبوب pl. of حَب]
حَبه A. Grain; seed. Berry.— حبهٔ انگور A single grape.

حَبیب A. [اَحباب & احباء] n. Friend. Lover. *Cf*. دوست ‖ *Mas. pr. name.*—*a*. Beloved.
حبیب الله A. Beloved one of God. *Mas. pr. name.*
حبیبه A. [Fem. of حبیب]Sweetheart. *Fem. pr. name.*
حَتم A. Making up one's mind○. [*Used as an a.*] Obligatory; necessary; incumbent. — بر من ح. است که بروم It is incumbent on me to go. —*ad*. = حتماً ‖ ح. داشتن To be sure or positive. — ح کردن To make s. To resolve.
حتماً A. By all means; certainly. Inevitably. — ح. بیائید Do not fail to come.
حتمی A. Sure; certain. — رفتنِ وی ح. است He is sure to go.
حتمی الوقوع A. Sure to happen; unavoidable.
حتی A. (hat'a) Even.— ح. اینکه Not only that but... Moreover.
حتی الامکان A. (hatal-em-) As far as possible.
حتی القوه A. To the best of one's ability.
حتی المقدور A. = حتی الامکان
حجّ A. Pilgrimage to Mecca.
حِجاب A. Veil. Curtain○. *F*. Modesty. — حجاب حاجز S. u. حاجز
حجاج [Pl. of حاج]
حَجار A. Stonecutter; mason.
حجاری A. P. Stone-cutting.—

ح. كردن To carve (stones).
حجاز ِ A. Arabia. Petrae.
حجام ० A. = **رگزن**
حجامت A. Cupping; phlebotomy. ـ ح. كردن To bleed; cup. ـ شاخ ح. Cupping-glass.
حُجب A. Modesty; shyness.
حُجت A. [حجج] Argument; reason. Proof. Plea. ـ ح. آوردن To raise an argument. ـ اتمام ح. Ultimatum. ـ اتمام ح. كردن To pronounce an u. [With به] To deliver an u. to; present with an u. ـ حضرت ح. See **صاحب‌الزمان**
حجت‌الاسلام A. (His) Eminence or Reverence.
حجج [Pl. of حجت]
حجر (*hajar*) A. [اَحجار] = سنگ Stone. ـ احجار كريمه Precious stones. ـ حجر رملی Sandstone.
حجر ० A. (*hajr*) Protection. Prohibition. Interdiction.
حجرالاسود A. The Black Stone which pilgrims kiss at Mecca.
حجرالبرق A. Aventurine.
حجرالدم A. Bloodstone.
حجرالرحمن A. Lapis divinus.
حجرالقمر A. Moonstone.
حجرالنور A. Marcasite. [Also حجرالطور].
حجرالولاده A. Eaglestone.
حجراليهود A. Lapis judaicus.
حُجرَوی A. Cellular.
حُجره A. [حُجر or حجرات] Cell. Chamber. Commercial office.
حجری ० A. = سنگی Petrous.
حَجله A. Bridal chamber.
حَجم A. Volume. Bulk.
حَجيم A. Voluminous; huge.
حدّ A. [حدود] Limit; boundary. Extent. ـ حدّاقل Minimum. ـ حدّ اكثر Maximum. ـ بحدّ بلوغ رسيدن To come of age; attain the age of puberty. ـ حدّ ِ متوسط or حدّ وسط Average; mean. ـ حد زدن To penance by the lash. ـ تا چه حد To what extent? ـ تا حديكه To the e. that. ـ از حد بيرون است It knows no bounds. ـ از حد گذشتن vi. & از حد گذرانيدن vt. To exceed b. ـ بحدّ امكان As far as possible.
حداثت ० A. = **جوانی - تازگی**
حدّاد A. = **آهنگر**
حدبه ० A. Convexity. Gibbosity. Protuberance.
حدّت A. Acuteness. Force. Vehemence. ـ حدت مرض or شدت مرض Paroxysm.
حَدَث ० A. = **حادثه - حداثت**
حَدس A. Guess. ـ ح. زدن To guess (at). ـ درست ح. زدن To g. right; hit the mark.
حدساً A. By guess. Roughly.
حدسی A. P. Based on guesswork; rough.
حدشكنی A. P. Encroachment; trespass.
حدقه A. 1) Pupil of the eye [مردمك]. 2) + Eye-socket.
حدوث A. Occurrence; taking place.
حُدود A. [Pl. of حد] Limits;

boundaries. Extent. Regions. Neighbourhood. — در حدود In the neighourhood (or region) of ; about . Within the limits of.

حَدیث A. [اَحادیث] Tradition. Discourse*.

حدید A. = آهن

حدیده A. Die. Cf. قلاویز

حدیقه ○ A. [حَدایق] = باغ

حذاقت A. Ingenuity.

حَذَر A. Avoiding. Caution. Warning. — ح.کردن از To beware; avoid. — برحذر بودن To be on one's guard; beware.

حَذف A. Omission. Elimination.— ح.کردن = انداختن To omit. To eliminate. — مسابقهٔ حذفی Knockout competition.

حُر ○ A. = آزاد(ه)

حراج A. or هراج (Sale by) auction. — ح . کردن To sell by a.; put up to a. — چوبِ ح. خوردن To come under the hammer.

حرارت A. = گرما Heat. Temperature. F. Enthusiasm. Dash.— حرارت ذوب و تبخیر Latent heat.— حرارتش خوابید He lost his enthusiasm ; he cooled down ; also, he lost interest.

حراست A. = نگهداری Guarding. Custody.— ح.کردن To protect.

حرّاف A. Talkative . Glib - tongued; eloquent.

حرام A. Unlawful ; religiously prohibited. Ceremonially unclean ; unlawful to eat [usu. حرام‌گوشت]. Illegal; illegitimate. — ح.کردن To declare unlawful. To forbid (the eating or drinking of). — چیزیرا برخود حرام‌کردن To deny oneself s. t. — خواب بمن ح. شد Sleep was lost to me.

حرام خور A. P. Usurer. Bribee. Profiteer.

حرامزادگی A. P. Illegitimacy. F. Roguery. Slyness +.

حرامزاده A. P. Illegitimate ; bastard. F. Roguish. Sly +. گلِ ح. Mixture of clay, sand, and lime; puddle.

حرام‌گوشت A. P. S. u. حرام

حرام لقمه a. p. = حرامزاده

حرامی * A. = دزد & غارتگر

حرب ○ A. See جنگ & جنگیدن ‖ Fight(ing) . — ارکان ح. See ستاد ‖ دیوان ح. Court martial.

حرباء ○ A. = بوقلمون Chameleon.

حَربه A. Weapon.

حَربی A. Pertaining to war. [Fem. حَربیه] . — تدابیر حربیه Tactics. — کافر حربی Infidel deserving to be fought with.

حَرَج A. Fault; sin ○.— بر او حرجی نیست He is not guilty on that account.

حِرز ○ A. [احراز] Amulet.

حِرص A. Greed; avidity [آز].— ح. زدن To be greedy. To eat greedily ; guzzle.

حَرف *A.* [حُروف] Letter. Talk; speech. Saying. — حرف اضافه Preposition. — حرف بد Bad language. — حرف تعریف (Definite) article. — حرف ربط or حرف عطف Conjunction. — حرف ندا Interjection. — ح. زدن To speak; talk. — با من ح. نمی زند He is not on speaking terms with me. — حرف معترضه زدن To throw in a remark. — حرف مفت Idle talk. Bad language. — اسباب ح. شدن To cause trouble. To meet with an objection. — حرفشان شد They had words. — حرفش دوتا شد He contradicted himself. — یك کلمه با شما حرف دارم I have a word with you.

حرف (*heraf*) [Pl. of حرفه]

حرف گوش کن or **حرف شنو** *A. P.* Obedient.

حرف نشنو *A. P.* Disobedient.

حِرفه *A.* [حِرَف] Profession; trade. Craft. — اهل ح. Professional man; craftsman.

حرفه‌ای *A. P.* Professional. Occupational: بیماری ح.

حرفی *A.* 1) Literal. 2) + On speaking terms.

حرقت‌البول *A.* Blennorrhoea; gleet.

حرقفی *A.* Iliac.

حرکات [Pl. of حرکت]

حَرکت *A.* [حرکات] Motion; movement [جنبش]. Act; gesture. Start(ing); departure. Stimulation. Erection. — حرکت انقلابی Revolution. — حرکت وضعی Rotation. — ح. دادن To move [تکان دادن]. — ح. کردن To m. To s. To proceed; leave.

حرم *A.* 1) Harem; women's apartment [also حرم سرا]. 2) Sanctuary.

حِرمان *A.* Privation. Disappointment.

حُرمت *A.* Reverence; respect. Inviolability. — ح. کردن To regard with reverence.

حرمت گزار *A. P.* Respectful; deferential.

حرمسرا *A. P. S. u.* حرم

حرمین *A.* [D. of حرم] The Two Sanctuaries at Mecca and Medinah.

حروف *A.* [Pl. of حرف] Letters. Type(s). *Gr.* Particles.

حروف چین *A. P.* Typesetter; compositor.

حروف چینی *A. P.* Type setting; typesetter's profession.

حروف ریزی *A. P.* Type-foundry.

حروفی *A. P.* Literal. — قفل ح. Combination-lock; letter-lock.

حُرّیت *A.* = آزادی

حَریر *A.* (Fine) silk. Silk cloth.

حریر باف *A. P.* Silk-weaver.

حریر بافی *A. P.* Silk-weaving.

حریر نما *A. P.* Silk-like. Mercerized.

حریره *A. Kind of pap.*

حریری (*A.*) *a.* Silk(en). Very thin. —*n.* Silk merchant o+.

حَریص *A.* Greedy.

حریصانه *A. P.* Greedily.

حَریف *A.* Rival. Opponent. Match ; partner. — حریف من نیست He is not a match for me. He cannot cope with me. — حریف او نشدم که برود I couldn't get him to go ; I could not prevail on him to go.

حَریق *A.* = آتش‌سوزی Fire.

حریق زده *A. P.* [حریق زدگان] Victim of, or sufferer by, a fire.

حَریم *A.* 1) Limits; frontage; 2) * = حرم

حِزب *A.* [اَحزاب] Party. — حزب کارگر The Labour P.

حزبی *A.* Pertaining to a (political) party. — تعصب ح. Party spirit.

حَزم *A.* Prudence; sound judgment. Resolution.

حُزمه *A.* Corymb.

حُزن *A.* = اندوه & غصه

حزن انگیز & حزن آور *A. P.* Sorrowful ; sad.

حزیران (*A.*) *Jewish and Syriac month* (May-June).

حزین *A.* = 1) غمگین 2) غم‌انگیز

حِسّ *A.* [Pl. حَواس properly pl. of حاسه] Sense. Feeling. Go; energy+. — حس پیش از وقوع Presentiment. — حس تشخیص Sensibility; scent. — حس مشترك Common sense. — حس کردن To feel. To perceive.

حِساب *A.* Account. [For علم ح.] Arithmetic. *F.* Number ; limit. — ح. پس دادن To render an account. — ازکسی ح. خواستن To call s. o. to account. — ح. کردن To calculate ; compute; reckon. — بد حساب کردن To miscalculate. — بحساب آوردن To take into a. — بحساب خودم On my own a. — مبلغی را بحساب بدهی کسی گذاشتن To charge a sum to (*or* against) s. o.; debit it to him; d. him with it. — چقدر بای‌شما ح. کرد How much did he charge you for it? — مبلغی‌را به بستانکار حساب کسی گذاشتن To credit a sum to s. o.; credit him with a sum. — از حساب پرت است He is out in his reckoning. — از کسی ح. بردن To hold s. o. in reverence ; think much of him ; look up to him. — حرف حساب زدن To talk sense. — صورت ح. Account (statement). Invoice; debit note. — حسابی نداریم *or* ح. بی ح. + We are quits.

حسابدار *A. P.* Accountant.

حسابداری *A. P.* Accountancy ;

accounting. [For ادارهٔ ح.] Accounts Department.

حسابدان *A. P.* Arithmetician.

حساب رس *A. P.* Auditor.

حسابرسی *A. P.* Audit(ing). Auditorship.

حساب سازی *A. P.* Manipulation of accounts.

حساب‌گر *A. P.* Arithmomancer.

حسابی *A.* Arithmetical. Tenable ; logical. — یك آشپز حسابی A regular cook. — یك كتك ح. A good beating

حسادت *A.* Jealousy. — ح. كردن To be jealous; act jealously.

حسادت‌آمیز *A. P.* Jealous ; envious : نگاه ح.

حسّاس *A.* Sensitive; quick. Feeling ; sentimental. Delicate. Precise. Susceptible. Essential.

حساسیت *A.* Sensitiveness. Susceptibility.

حسام‌الدین *A.* *Hesamedin* : mas. pr. name. *OS.* Sword of religion.

حَسب *A.* (Sufficient) quantity or measure o. *S. a. the next entry.* — بر حسبِ According to. In proportion to. In terms of. — برحسب اینکه A. as.

حسب *A.* (*hasab*) (Noble) descent. Personal merit. Quantity; proportion. Manner. — *S. a. the preceding entry.* — ح. و نسب Descent or lineage. — برحسبِ According to. In proportion to. In terms of. —

حسب‌الامر *A.* According to your, his, etc. order.

حسب‌المعمول *A.* As usual.

حسب‌الوظیفه *A.* In view of one's duty.

حَسبی *A.* Non-litigious. — قانون امور حسبی N.-l. jurisdiction act.

حَسد *A.* Envy; jealousy. — بكسی ح. بردن To be jealous of s.o.

حسرت *A.* Regret; rue. — حسرتِ مال دیگرا را خوردن To begrudge others' wealth. — ح. بردن [With به] To begrudge. To envy. — گل ح. Snowdrop.

حسرت بدل + *A. P.* Hope-sick.

حسرت خور *A. P.* Green-eyed.

حَسک Star-thistle.

حَسن *A. Hasan: mas. pr. name. OS.* = نیکو. [Fem. حسنه].

حُسن *A.* Beauty. Goodness. Advantage. Virtue. — از حسنِ اتفاق By some lucky chance.

حسنات *A.* Good acts. [Pl. of حسنه *q. v. under* حَسن]

حسن لبه *A. P.* Benzoin ; gum benjamin. — جوهر حسن لبه Benzoic acid.

حسود *A.* Jealous; envious.

حسودی + *A. P.* Jealousy. — ح. كردن To be jealous. [*With* به] To envy.

حِسی *A.* Felt (by the senses); palpable. — ح. است It is a

حصات A. = ریگ Calculus;
حِصاد A. Harvest.
حصار A. Fence; wall. S. a. دور آن ح. بکشید ‖ محاصره Enclose it with a fence.
حَصبه A. Typhoid fever; enteric f.
حَصر A. Restriction; limit. — حصر وراثت See انحصار وراثت under انحصار
حصری o A. Limitative.
حصص [Pl. of حصه]
حِصن A. Fortress. Cf. دژ & قلعه ‖ Fortification.
حُصول A. Acquisition. Attainment. — قابل ح. Obtainable. — غیر قابل ح. Unobtainable.
حِصه A. [حصص] Share; portion.
حَصیر A. = بوریا Mat.
حصیرباف A. P. Mat-weaver.
حصیری A. P. Mat-like. — صندلی ح. Cane-seated chair. — کلاه ح. Straw hat.
حَصین A. Well-fortified.
حضار S. u. حاضر [sidence.
حَضر A. (Being at) home. Residence.
حضرات A. [Pl. of حضرت]. Excellencies. Gentlemen. They; these gentlemen.
حَضرت A. 1) = حضور 2) Excellency; Highness; Majesty, etc. — حضرت اشرف His (or Your) E. — حضرت والا . . . His Excellency Prince . . .
حضرتعالی a. p. You [in p. c.].
حُضور A. Presence. Attendance. Appearance. — حضور

matter of common sense; it is (too) obvious +.
حُسین A. *Hosein: mas. pr. name.* OS. = نیکو
حشاء S. u. احشا
حَشر A. Assembling o. — روزِ ح. Resurrection day.
حشرات [Pl. of حشره].
حشره A. [حشرات] Insect.
حشره خوار A. P. Insectivorous.
حشره شناسی A. P. Entomology.
حشره کش A. P. Insecticide.
حشفه A. (Glans) penis.
حشل + Awkward or dangerous situation.
حشم A. [احشام] Retinue.
حِشمت A. Retinue; pomp. *Fem. pr. name.*
حَشو A. Redundant word(s); pleonasm. Marginal note. — حشو قبیح Cacopleonasm; also, tautology. — حشو ملیح Eupleonasm.
حشیش (A.) *Hashish*: narcotic preparation from Indian hemp.
حشیشةالبرص A. Buckhorn plantain.
حشیشةالبرق A. Star-of-Bethlehem. [scabious.
حشیشةالجرب A. Common field
حشیشةالطحال A. Spleenwort.
حشیشیون A. The Assassins. OS. Those addicted to the use of hashish. [gravel.

ذهن P. of mind.— عدم ح. Non-attendance. Non-appearance.— ح. داشتن To be present; [with در] attend. — ح. بهم ح. یافتن or رساندن To be p.; come; [with در] attend.

حضوراً A. In (your, etc.) presence; verbally.

حضوری A. P. Performed in one's presence. Verbal.

حضیض A. Perigee. [*Of the sun*] Perihelion. F. Abyss.

حطام o A. Vanities of the world; mammon [in full حطام دنیا].

حطب o A. = **هیزم**

حظ A. Delight; enjoyment; delectation. — حظ نفس Sensual gratification or pleasure. — حظ بردن از To enjoy or like very much. — حظ کردم I enjoyed it very m.; I loved it.

حفار A. Digger; excavator.

حفاری A. P. Excavation.

حفاظ A. Fence. Protection. Guard(ing) F. Modesty. Reserve.

حفاظت A. = نگهداری Guardianship; custody. Keeping; safeguarding. — ح. کردن To keep.

حفاظی A. Protective.

حفر A. Digging; excavation. — ح. کردن = کندن To dig.

حفره A. Pit. Ditch. Socket. *Anat*. Fossa; cavity.

حفریات A. Excavations.

حفظ A. Protection; preservation. — ازحفظ خواندن To recite from memory. — ح. کردن To protect; preserve. To memorize; learn by heart.— از حفظ داشتن or بودن To know by h. — حفظ ظاهر کردن To save (*or* keep up) appearances.

حفظ الصحه A. = **بهداشت**

حفظ الغیب A. Sticking up for s. o.

حفظی A. P. Memory work.

حفید o A. — **نواده** & **نوه**

حق (A.) *n*. [حقوق] Right; title. Fee. Duty; moral obligation. Truth. God. —*a*. Just; true. Legitimate. [Fem. حقه : دعاوی حقه L. or rightful claims]. — حق ارشدیت Birthright. — حق تقدم Priority. — حق رأی Right to vote; suffrage. — حق شارع Right of way. — حق همسایگی Tie of neighbourhood. — حق با شما or حق دارید You are right. — او حق است بگردن شما دارد You are indebted to him. — حق دادن به To consider rightful; justify. To entitle. — حق دوستی را بجا آوردن To do what friendship requires. حق مطلب‌را اداکردن— To do justice to the subject.— بحق Justly. — بحق By [*in oaths*]; in the name of.— برخلاف حق Unjustly.— حق‌وحساب × Bribe. — پاروی حق گذاشتن + To be unfair;

turn away from justice.— بحق دانستن To justify ; consider rightful.— مرغ حق Screechowl.

حقاً *A.* Justly ; rightfully ; by rights.— حقا که (*hagh'ake*) Indeed ! Forsooth !

حقابه *A. P.* Right of water.

حقارت *A.* Contempt. — بچشم ح. نگریستن To regard with contempt ; think little of ; despise.

حق الارض *A.* Land-right.

حق الامتیاز *A.* Royalty.

حق التألیف *A.* Compiling fees; author's f.

حق التحریر *A.* Notary public's fees (for drawing up documents).

حق التعلیم *A.* Tuition fees.

حق الثبت *A.* Registration fees.

حق الحفاظه *A.* Interest on money loaned by pawnshops (disguised under the phrase " fees for protection of the object pawned").

حق الحکومه *A.* (*Humorous*) Parson's nose. *OS.* Fees going to the governor('s office); governor's share [also حق حاکم].

حق الزحمه *A.* Fees ; remuneration.

حق السعی *A.* = کارمزد

حق السکوت *A.* Hush-money.

حق الشرب *A.* = آب بها

حق الضرب *A.* Seignorage; mintage.

حق العبور *A.* Passage (-money). [*Of goods*] Transit duty.

حق العمل *A.* = کارمزد

حق العمل کار *A. P.* Commission agent ; factor.

حق العمل کاری *A. P.* Commission ; factorage.

حق القدم *A.* = پایمزد

حق الله *A.* What is due to God. Sin against G.

حق الناس *A.* What is due to men. Sin against mankind.

حق الورود *A.* = ورودیه

حق الوکاله *A.* Lawyer's fees ; honorarium.

حقانی *A.* True. Rightful.

حقانیت *A.* Truth. Rightfulness ; legitimacy.

حقایق [Pl. of حقیقت].

حق بجانب *A. P.* Specious ; plausible. Pitiable: صورت ح.

حق بین *A. P.* Just ; fair.

حق بینی *A. P.* Justice; equity.

حق پرست *A. P.* = خدا پرست

حق پرستی *A. P.* = خدا پرستی

حق تعالی *A.* The Most High God.

حق جو *A. P.* Truth-seeking.

حقد *A.* = کینه

حقدار ○ *A.P.* Rightful (person); entitled (party). *Cf.* ذیحق

حق شناس *A. P.* Grateful.

حق شناسی *A. P.* Gratitude.

حق کشی *A. P.* Unjust attitude.

tude; partiality.
حق گو *A. P.* Just; impartial. Truthful ○.
حق گویی *A.P.* Impartial judgment. Truthfulness ○.
حق ناشناس *A. P.* Ungrateful.
حق ناشناسی *A. P.* Ingratitude.
حقنه *A.* = **اماله**
حق نیوش * *A. P.* Who listens to what is right.
حقوق *A.* [Pl. of حق] Rights. Fees. Dues. Salary; pay. [For علم ح.] Law : دانشکدهٔ ح. ‖ دکتر در حقوق Doctor of laws. حقوق گمرکی Customs duties.
حقوق بگیر *A. P.* Salaried.
حقوق دان *A. P.* Lawyer. Jurist.
حقوقی *A. P.* Legal. Civil. — آئین دادرسی ح. Civil procedure. — شخص ح. Legal person.
حَقه *S. u.* حق
حُقه *A.* Bowl (of an opium-smoker's pipe). Capsule. Calyx. Trick(y person) +. — بکسی ح. زدن To play a trick on s. o.
حُقه باز *A. P.* Conjuror. Impostor.
حُقه بازی *A. P.* Conjuring (tricks); also, jugglery. — ح. کردن To conjure; juggle. To play tricks +.
حَقیر *A.* Humble; despised. [*In p. c.*] Your h. servant; i. e. I. — ح. شمردن To despise.
حقیقت *A.* [حقایق] = درستی Truth. Reality. Fact [usu. حقیقت امر]. — در حقیقت In fact; indeed. — ح. ندارد There is no truth in it.
حقیقةً *A.* Truly; in truth.
حقیقی *A.* Real; true.
حک *A.* Rubbing. Erasing; obliteration. — پاك کردن = حك کردن To erase. — حك و اصلاح کردن To alter; modify.
حکاک *A.* Engraver. Polisher of gems.
حکاکی *A. P.* Engraving. Polishing of jewels. — ح. کردن To engrave.
حکام [Pl. of حاکم]
حکایات [Pl. of حکایت]
حکایت *A.* [حکایات] Story; anecdote. — ح. کردن To narrate; tell (a story). — ح. می کنند که The story goes that. — عجب حکایتی است + It is strange indeed.
حُکم *A.* [اَحکام] Order; commandment. Sentence; judgment; verdict. Control ○. *Geom.* 1) Axiom; 2) theorem. *C. P.* a) Trump; b) whisk. — حکم اعدام Death sentence. — حکم توقیف Writ of attachment. — احکام دینی Religious commandments or precepts. — ح. دادن To issue an order. To pass a j. — ح. کردن To judge. — بحکم آنکه Inasmuch as. — بحکمِ ضرورت Of necessity. — در حکمِ Tantamount to.
حَکم *A.* (*hakam*) Arbitrator. *Cf.* داور

حِکَم (*hekam*) [Pl. of حکمت]

حُکماً A. Without fail. Certainly. Peremptorily.

حکماء [Pl. of حکیم]

حکم انداز o A. P. Marksman ; sharpshooter.

حِکمت A. Wisdom. Philosophy. Metaphysics. Wise saying; motto [*pl.* حکم *hekam*]. — حکمت ایقور Epicurean philosophy ; p. of the Garden. — حکمت ارسطو P. of the Lyceum. — حکمت افلاطون P. of the Academy ; Platonism. — حکمت الهی Theology. — حکمت رواقیون Philosophy of the Porch ; stoic philosophy. — حکمتِ طبیعی Physics o. — ح. کلِ Lute.

حکمت آمیز A. P. Wise: ح. سخنان

حکمران A.P. Ruler. Governor.

حکمرانی A. P. Rule. Governorship. — ح. کردن [*With* بر] To govern ; rule over.

حکمفرما A. P. Ruling ; dominant. Prevailing.

حُکمی A. Peremptory. Incorporeal. Appointed or engaged by an official order.

حکمیت A. Arbitration. *Cf.* داوری

حُکومت A. Government. Governorship. Small province. — ح. کردن To govern ; rule.

حکومت نشین A. P. Governor's seat.

حِکّه A. Itching. Prurience.

حَکیم A. [حکماء] Sage. Philosopher. Doctor ; physician [پزشك]. — حکیم الهی Theologian.

حکیمانه A. P. *ad*. Wisely ; philosophically. —*a*. Wise.

حکیم فرموده + A. P. Prescribed by a physician. *F*. Indispensable. — ح. است It is doctor's orders. It is very essential.

حَل A. Dissolving ; melting; solution. — حل و عقد Management. — حل وفصل Settlement. — حل کردن To dissolve ; melt. To solve. — حل شدن To be dissolved or melted. — راه حل Solution. — قابل حل Dissolvable ; soluble. — غیرقابل حل Insoluble.

حِل o Absolution; pardon. — *See* (کردن) بحل

حلاج A. = پنبه زن

حلاجی A. P. Cotton-blowing; cotton-beating. *F*. Analysis; discussion. — ح. کردن To beat cotton. To analyze; discuss; in detail.

حلال A. Lawful. Ceremonially clean ; lawful to eat [usu. حلال گوشت] . — ح. کردن To declare l. To absolve. To waive. — بول ح. درآوردن To turn an honest penny.

حلال A. (*ha*lal) Dissolver. Solvent. *F*. Resolver.

حلال زاده A. P. Legitimate (child).

حلال گوشت A. P. *S.u.* حلال

حل المسائل A. Key to solutions.

حلاوَت A. Sweetness [شیرینی]. Flavour.

حلَب A. Tin. *Geog.* Aleppo.— نفت ح. Packed oil.

حلب پرکن A. P. Tin-filler.

حلبی A. P. Tin-plate.

حلبی‌ساز A. P. Tinman.

حلزون A. Snail. [*Of the ear*] Cochlea.— حلزون بی‌صدف Slug.

حلزونی A. Limacine. Spiral.— منحنی ح. Helix.

حلَق A. Throat[گلو]. Pharynx.— آماس ح. — از حلق Gutturally. Pharyngitis . — علم امراض ح. Pharyngology. — حلق و جلق و دلق Creature comforts.

حلق‌بین A. P. Pharyngoscope.

حلقوم A. = حلق [nelid.

حلقوی A. Ring-shaped, An-

حلقَه A. Ring. Hoop. *Bot.* Whorl. *Z.* Segment. *F.* Circle (of men); assembly. — حلقهٔ زلف * Ringlet. —حلقهٔ زنجیر Link. — حلقهٔ گل Wreath. — ح گره Bowling-knot [also * ح. بر در زدن — [گره خرگوشی To knock at a door.— ح. زدن To form a ring or circle. — ح. درگوش کسی کردن To reduce s. o. to slavery.

حلقه بگوش A. P. Bondman ; slave. *OS.* (One) who wears the earring (of slavery).

حلقه حلقه *a. p.* Annulated ; annular. *Z.* Segmentary.

حلقی A. Guttural. Pharyngeal.

حِلم A. Meekness; forbearance.

حلوا (*A.*) *Kind of sweetmeat or sweet paste.* — حلوای قدرت o Manna.— ح. ماهی Sole.

حلوا ماهی A. P. *or* ماهیِ حلوا Sole.

حُلول A. Penetration. Coming; approach. *Ph.* Osmosis — ح. کردن To penetrate. To enter. To a.

حلول پذیر A. P. Penetrable.

حلول ناپذیر A. P. Impenetrable.

حلویات A. Sweets ; sweet pastes. *Cf.* شیرینی

حُله * A. Robe. Priestly vestment.

حلیت o A. Pardon. Leave.

حَلیم A. Meek ; forbearing.

حلیم *S. u.* هلیم

حلیه A. Ornament . External appearance.

حما *S. u.* حمی

حمار A. = خر Ass.

حماری A. Asinine. [Fem. حماریه]. — قضیهٔ حماریه The asses' bridge, *pons asinorum.*

حماسه A. Epic poem.

حماسی A. Epic.

حماقت A. Silliness ; foolishness . — ح. کردن To act foolishly. [سخنان ح.

حماقت‌آمیز A.P. Silly; foolish:

حمال A. (*ha*mal) = باربر Porter.

By e. **Fagger.**— تیرِ حمال **Girder.**

حمالی *A.P.* **Porterage.**— ح. کردن **To be a porter; carry loads.** *F.* **To drudge or fag.**

حمام *A.* = گرمابه **Turkish bath(-house); hammam.**

حمامی *A. P.* **Bath-keeper.**

حمایت *A.* **Protection; support.** — ح. کردن از **To s. or protect. To take the part of. To patronize.** — حمایت از خویشاوندان *or* حمایت اقرباء **Nepotism.**

حمایل *A.* **Shoulder-belt. Sword belt. Baldrick.** — ح. کردن **To hold or carry about diagonally.**

حمایل فنگ *A. P.* **Position of a rifle slung diagonally across the back.**

حمد A. **Praise; eulogy.** — ح کردن **To praise (God); also, thank (God).**

حمراء [**Fem. of** احمر]

حُمره ο *A.* = 1) سرخی 2) بادسرخ

حمزه (*A.*) *Mas. pr. name.*

حمل *A.* **Transport. Shipment. Forwarding. Pregnancy.** — ح. کردن **To carry. To ship; forward.** [**With** بر] **To interpret as; attribute to** — ح. برداشتن **To conceive.**— حمل و نقل **Transport.** — قابل ح. **Portable.** — متصدی حمل و نقل **Forwarding agent; carrier.** — حمل کاذب **Pseudo-pregnancy.**

حمل *A.* (*hamal*) **Aries.** *Old name of* فروردین

حمله *A.* [حملات] **Attack; rush. Epilepsy; falling sickness.**— ح. کردن.— ح. آوردن بر* **To attack.** **To make an attack;** [**with** بر] **to a. To fall into a fit of epilepsy.**

حمله‌دار *A. P.* **Courier.**

حمله‌ور (*A. P.*) *a.* **Attacking.**— ح. شدن **To make an attack.**

حموضت *A.* = ترشی **Acidity.**

حمی *A.* (*homa*) *or* حما = **تب**

حمیت *A.* **Ardour; enthusiasm. Zeal.**

حمید *A.* 1) *a.* **Praiseworthy.** [**Fem.** حمیده **Ex.** اخلاق حمیده]. 2) *n. Mas. pr. name.*

حنا *A.* **Henna; (Egyptian) privet.**— دست کسیرا توی ح. گذاشتن **To leave s. o. holding the baby; l. him in a muddle.** — حنایش پیش من رنگ ندارد **I know him too well to think much of him; his words have no weight with me.** — گل ح. **Garden balsam.**

حنان ο *A.* **Compassionate: ep. of God.**

حنائی *A. P.* **Reddish-brown; russet; henna.**

حنجره *A.* = خشك نای **Larynx.**

حنجری *A.* **Laryngeal.**

حنظل * *A.* **Colocynth.**

حُنوط *A*. Embalmment. — ح. کردن To embalm.
حنیف *A*. Orthodox (Moslem).
حوّا *A*. Eve (*pr. name*).
حواجب [Pl. of حاجب].
حوادث [Pl. of حادثه]
حواری *A*. [حواریون] Disciple. Apostle.
حواس *A*. [Pl. of حاسه o] Senses. — ح. ندارم I am not in the mood. — حواسش پرت است He is out of his mind; he is absent-minded. He is all abroad. — حواسِ خودرا جمع کردن To focus one's attention; concentrate. To collect one's wits. — حواس پنجگانه *or* حواس ظاهره The five (external) senses.
حواس پرت *A. P.* Absent-minded. [mindedness.
حواس‌پرتی *A. P.* Absent-
حواشی [Pl. of حاشیه]
حواصل *A. or* **حواصیل** = **ماهیخوار**
حوالت o *A*. Leaving (an affair to another's care).
حوالجات [Pl. of حواله]
حواله *A*. [حوالجات] (Money-) order; draft. Transfer. Assignment. — ح. کردن To order (the payment of); draw a cheque for. To delegate; refer. — ح. اش باخدا + I refer his case to God; I leave it to God to judge him.
حواله‌کرد *A. P.* Order. — به حواله کردِ To the order of.
حوالیَ *A*. Environs; neighbourhood. Suburbs.
حوائج [A pl. of حاجت].
حوت *A*. Large fish. *Astr*. Pisces. *Old name of* اسفند
حور *A*. Houris of Paradise.
حور پیکر * *A. P.* Like a fairy in body or figure.
حوری *A*. Houri; nymph.
حوزه *A*. Area. Domain; realm; extent. Range of influence.— حوزهٔ انتخابیه Constituency.
حوش o *A*. Enclosure. Courtyard [per. only in حول‌وحوش *q. v.*]
حوصله *A*. Crop; maw*. *F*. 1) Compass; scope; comprehension. 2) Patience. 3) Mood.— ح. کردن To have or use patience.— حوصلهٔ نامه نویسی ندارم I am not in the mood to write, or I don't feel like writing, a letter. — ح. ام سر رفت *or* ح. ام تنگ شد 1) I was (*or* am) fed up. 2) I lost p.
حوض *A*. Tank; pond. Basin.— حوض تعمیر(گاه) Dock.
حوض چه *A. P.* Little pool. Small basin.
حوضه *A*. (River) basin.
حول o (*howl*) *A*. = **قوه**
حول o (*haval*) *A*. = **لوچی**
حول وحوش *a. p.* Environs;

suburbs; outskirts.

حوله (?) Towel. — پارچهٔ حوله ای Towelling.

حومه *A.* Outskirts; environs.

حیَ *A.* [احیاء] *a.* Alive or living [زنده]. —*n.* ○ Tribe; family. — حیّ وحاضر Ready; accessible.— خودش حی وحاضر است There he is; i. e. you may ask himself.

حیا *or* **حیاء** *A.* Pudency; modesty; modest reserve. — ح. کردن To feel ashamed. To be coy. — حیاش را (با نان وماست) خورده است + He has swallowed shame and drunk after it.

حیات *A.* Life [زندگی]. Lifetime.— در حیات بودن To be living. — ترك ِح. گفتن To pass away; die.— اگر حیاتم باقی باشد If my life should not fail me.

حیاتی *A.* Vital; of vital importance. — اندامهای ح. V. organs; vitals.— موضوع ح. و مماتی Matter of life and death.

حیازت *A.* Possession.

حیاط *A.* Court-yard; compound.— حیاط خلوت Backyard; back-court. — حیاط طویله (Stable) yard. Outhouse.

حیث *A.* Respect. — ازحیث ِ With respect to; in regard to.

حیثیت *A.* Prestige. Respect.

حیدر (*A.*) *Mas. pr. name.* *OS.* Lion [شیر].

حیران *A.* Perplexed; astonished. — ح. شدن To be perplexed or a. — ح. کردن To preplex; astonish.

حیرانی *A. P.* = حیرت

حیرت *A.* Perplexity; amazement. *Cf.* شگفت ‖ ح. کردن To be astonished.

حیرت انگیز *A. P.* = شگفت انگیز Wonderful; astonishing.

حیرت زده *A. P.* Astonished.

حیز *A.* (*hayez*) Space. Extension. Limit; reach. — از حیز ِ امکان بیرون است It is impossible. [plexity.

حیص بیص *A.* Dilemma. Per-

حیض *A. n.* Menstrual discharge. —*a.* (*C. E.*) Menstruous. — ح. شدن To Menstruate.

حیطه *A.* Reach; compass; range. *OS.* Enclosure. — بحیطهٔ تصرف درآوردن To take possession of.

حیف *A. n.** Injustice; oppression. —*int.* (What a) pity! — برای اینکار حیف است It is too good for this purpose; an inferior quality will do. — ح. کردن To do injustice ○. — حیف ومیل Embezzlement. — حیف و میل کردن To embezzle.— ح. که نمیتوانم او را به بینم If I could only meet him; pity I can't meet him.

حیل [Pl. of حیله]

حیله *A.* [حیل *hial*] Trick.

Deceit.— بکسی ح. زدن To play a trick on s. o. — ح اندیشیدن To think of a trick or artifice. — حیلهٔ جنگی Stratagem.

حیله باز & حیله گر *A. P.* Cunning; artful.

حیله بازی *A. P.* Trickery.

حین *A.* [احیان] Time. Moment.— درحینِ At the moment of ; during [هنگامِ].

حیوان *A.* [حیوانات] 1) = جانور Animal. 2) ○ Life.

حیوان‌شناس *A.P.* = جانور شناس

حیوان شناسی *A. P.* = جانور شناسی

حیوانی *A.* Animal *a.* Brutal.— جغرافیای ح. Zoogeography. — غذای ح. Animal food.

حیوانیت *A.* Animal nature. Brutality.

حیوة *A.* (*hayat*) = **حیات**

حیه ○ *A.* = 1) مار 2) کرمك

خ

خا *or* **خای** [Imp. of خاییدن].
خاتَم *A*. [خواتم&خواتیم]. Signet; seal. Inlaid work; mosaic. — انگشترِ خ. Signet-ring.
خاتِم *A*. Finisher; the last.
خاتَم ساز *or* **خاتم کار** *A*. *P*. Inlayer.
خاتم کاری *A*. *P*. Inlaying; inlaid work. — خ. کردن To inlay with mosaic, etc.
خاتمه *A*. [خواتیم ○]. End; conclusion [پایان]. Adjournment. — بچیزی خ. دادن To put an end to s. t.; bring it to a c. To settle s. t. — خ. پذیرفتن *or* خ. یافتن To be finished; come to a conclusion. To be settled. — درخاتمه Finally; in c.
خاتمةً *A*. Finally; in conclusion
خاتون ○ [A. pl. خواتین] (Noble) lady; matron.
خاج [f. Armenian خاچ] 1) *C*. *P*. Club. 2) Cross. *See* صلیب & چلیپا
خاجدیس Cruciform.
خاجشویان Epiphany. *OS*. Baptizing the Cross. [Sacrum.
خاجی Cross-shaped. — استخوانخ.
خاچ *S*. *u*. خاج
خادِم *A*. [خَدَمه & خدام] = نوکر Servant. [Fem. خادِمه female servant; housemaid].

خار *n*. Thistle. Thorn. Pin. [*Of a scale*] Tongue. [*In machines*] Key. — خار بولوس Half shaft key. —*a*. Neat and tidy, as the hair. — خار ماهی Fish-bone. — بتهٔ خ. Bramble; teasel. — خ. زدن To tease.
خارا Granite. Moire: watered silk.
خاراگوش Common wormwood.
خاراندن [خاران] To scratch: فرصت سر خاراندن ‖ سر خاراندن Breathing-gap.
خارایی Granitic.
خاربست Hedge of thorns.
خاربُن Bramble; heath(er).
خارپشت Porcupine. Hedgehog.
خارپوست Echinodermatous.
خارتوت (Spiny) gooseberry.
خارِج (*A*.) *n*. 1) Outside. — ازخارج From abroad. — درخارج Abroad; outside. 2) Foreign destination(s). —*a*. = خارجی ‖ خ. شدن To go or come out. — خ. کردن To send out; discharge; expel. To emit. — خ. از ضرب *Mus*. Out of tempo or rythm. — خ. ازمقام *Mus*. Off key; out of tune. — خ. ازموضوع Not to the point; irrelevant. — خ. از قاعده Irregular. — خ. از وصف Beyond

description . — خارجِ قسمت Quotient.

خارج‌الارضی *A*. Extraterritorial [now برونمرزی].

خارجه (*A*.) *a*. Foreign [fem. of خارج]. —*n*. F. destinations or countries. — وزارت امور خارجه Ministry of F. Affairs ; F. Office. — وزیر امور خارجه Secretary of State for Foreign A. ; Minister of F. A. — درخارجه Abroad ; in foreign countries.

خارجی (*A*.) *a*. External; outer; exterior. —*n*. Foreigner.

خارخسك Star-thistle; caltrop.

خاردار Thorny ; prickly; spinous. — سیم خ. Barbed wire. — ماهی خ. Perch.

خارِش Itching. Mange.— خ. کردن To itch. *Cf*. خاریدن

خار شتر Camel's-thorn , alhaghi ; also, hedysarum.

خارق‌العاده *A*. Unusual. Supernatural. Wonderful.

خارکن *or* **خارکش** One who digs up prickly bushes.

خارماهی Sword-fish.

خاره 1) Rock [صخره] . 2) *Med*. Papula. *S*. *a*. خارا

خاریدن [خار] 1) To itch : دستم میخارد 2) = خاراندن

خازن *A*. 1) = خزانه‌دار 2) Condenser.

خاستگاه o = مبدأ Origin.

خاستن [خیز] = برخاستن

خاسته Risen [in comb.].

خاشاك • Motes ; chips. Brushwood.

خاشع *A*. = خاضع & فروتن

خاص *A*. Special ; particular [ویژه]. Private. Sacred. *Logic*. Subaltern. *Gr*. Proper: اسم خ. ‖ خاص وعام People of all classes. *Cf*. *the fem*. خاصه

خاصره *A*. Flank ; hypocondrium. — لگن خ. Pelvis.

خاصّه (*A*.) *a*. [*fem*. *of* خاص]. *ad*. Especially [بویژه].

خاصه‌خرجی *or* خاصه‌وخرجی *a*. *p*. Unjust discrimination, (esp. in serving dinner to guests).

خاصه ململ *A*. *P*. Cheese-cloth; also, mull.

خاصیت *A*. [خصائص *but s. a.* خواص]. Virtue. Property. Use(fulness) +. — خ. بخشیدن To be efficacious.

خاضع *A*. = فروتن Humble.

خاطر *A*. [خواطر] Mind; heart. Memory. Sake : برای‌خاطرشما ‖ Behalf. — بخاطر آوردن To remember ; call to mind. — بخاطر کسی آوردن To remind s. o. of. — بخاطرداشتن To remember. — بخاطرم رسید It occurred to me. — خاطر کسیرا خواستن + To be sweet on, or fond of s. o. *See* خاطرخواه ‖ خاطر عالی مستحضر است You are aware [*in formal style*]. — خاطرم جمع است I am sure.

خاطرجمع *a*. *p*. Sure ; certain.

Tranquil ; composed *. — خ.بودن To feel or be sure. — خ.شدن To be assured.—خ.کردن To assure.

خاطرجمعی *A. P.* Assurance ; sureness. *S. a.* جمعیت خاطر

خاطرخواه (*A. P.*) *a.* Loving ; fond. —*n.* Lover. [love.

خاطر خواهی *A. P.* Fondness ;

خاطر نشان کردن *A.P.* To point out ; notify. *OS.* To fix in the mind.

خاطره *A.* [خاطرات] Reminiscence ; remembrance.

خاطی *A.* = **خطاکار**

خاقان *T. Emperor of China or of Chinese Torkestan.*

خاک Earth. Dust. Soil. *By e.* Land. Territory. *Met.* Ashes. Tomb. — خاك آهك‌دار Marl. — خاك اره Sawdust. — خاك چینی Kaolin. — خاك رُس *or* خاك رُست Clay; argil. — خاك زغال Charcoal dust.— خاك‌زغال سنگ Coal-dust ; also , breeze. — خاك سرخ Ferrous oxide. — خاك‌گلدانی Loam. — خ. برسرش Shame on him! Damn him!— خاك(عالم) برسرم Alas for me!— چه خاکی بسر کنم What on earth can I do? How can I help it?— خ. شدن To be reduced to powder. *F.* * To humble oneself. — در خاك *or* بخاك سپردن بخاك‌سیاه نشاندن To bury.— نهادن To ruin utterly. — بخاکپای اعلیحضرت To His Majesty.

خاك آلود Soiled; dusty.

خاك انداز Dust-pan.

خاك برداری Excavation.

خاك دان Dust-bin.

خاکروبه Sweepings ; rubbish.

خاکروبه بر Dustman.

خاکروبه‌دان Dust-bin.

خاکریز Embankment. Earth-work.

خاکریزی Earthfilling ; earth-work. — خ. کردن (در) To fill (in). To embank.

خاکزاد * Earth-born ; human.

خاکزی *Z.* Terrestrial.

خاکسار Humble.

خاکستر Ashes. — طلای زیر خاکستر *Met.* Dark horse.

خاکستردان Ash-tray ; ash-hole.

خاکستری Grey. — روغن خ. G. unguent ; mercurial u.

خاکشو Gold-washer.

خاکشی London rocket-seeds [also خاکشیر +]. [dust.

خاك صفت * *P. A.* Humble as

خاك‌کش Barrow. Navvy. [For کامیون خ.] Dump truck.

خاك و خُل + Dust and dirt; d. and refuse.

خاکه Dust ; powder.

خاکی *a.* Dusty. Earthly. Terrestrial. Earth-coloured; khaki. *F.* * Mortal. Humble.— جادهٔ خ. Dirt-road. —*n.* [Pl. خاکیان * mortals].

خاگینه (*Kind of*) omelet or

scrambled eggs.
خال *A*. Spot ; speckle. Mole. Beauty-spot. Freckle. *C*. *F*. Suit. – خال سوزنی Tattoo. – خال‌مادرزاد Mother's mark; birth-mark. – خ. کوبیدن To tattoo the skin.
خال ० *A*. = دایی [ted.
خال‌خال *a*. *p*. Speckled ; spot-
خالد *A*. 1) = جاودانی 2) *Mas. pr. name*.
خالدار *A*. *P*. Spotted. Having a beauty-spot or mother's mark.
خالص *A*. Pure ; unmixed. Net [ویژه]. – غیر خالص Gross.
خالصاً *A*. Sincerely.
خالصانه *ad*. *A*. *P*. Sincerely. —*a*. Sincere : ادعیهٔ خ.
خالصجات [Pl. of خالصه]
خالصه *A*. [خالصجات] Public domain ; crown land. [Orig. fem. of خالص].
خالق *A*. = آفریننده Creator.
خالقیت *A*. Creative power.
خالکوبی *A*. *P*. Tattooing.
خالو *A*. *P*. – خال & دایی
خاله *A*. (Maternal) aunt.
خالی *A*. Empty [تهی]. Vacant. Void. – خ. کردن To empty. To evacuate. To unload. To discharge; fire off. – جا خالی کردن To give way. To side-step. – جای شما خالی بود We missed you ; we thought of you. – دستش خ. نیست He is busy ; he is not through with his work. – نان خ. Mere bread (*i*. *e*. without any other food). – خ. از همه چیز To leave all jokes aside.
خام *a*. Raw. Crude. *F*. Green; fresh. Vain : خیال خ. ‖ —*n*. R. hide. – خیالات خ. پختن To build castles in the air.
خام‌دست Unskilful; awkward.
خامس *A*. = پنجم Fifth.
خامساً *A*. Fifthly.
خامسوز Raw hide ; pelt.
خامش • [Cont. of خاموش]
خام‌طمع *P*. *A*. (One) who has vain hopes. [horse.
خاموت *R*. Collar of a draught
خاموش *a*. Silent. Extinct. Off. —*int*. Hush ! – خ. کردن To extinguish. To put out ; blow out. To switch off, as an engine. To silence. – خ. شدن To keep silent. To go out : چراغ خ. شد ‖ وادیِ خاموشان *Met*. Necropolis ; cemetery.
خاموشی Silence. – شیپور خاموشی *Mil*. Last post ; taps.
خامه Pen •. Cream. Raw silk. *Bot*. Style.
خامه‌ای Containing or resembling cream. – نان خ. Cream-puff.
خامه‌گیر Cream separator.
خامی Rawness ; crudeness. *F*. Greenness. [groove.
خان Caravanserai ; inn. Rifle;

خان [*Of Mongolian origin*]. Khan : obsolescent title.
خاندار Rifled : تفنگ خ.
خاندان House(hold) ; family.
خانقاه Monastery. Convent.
خانگی Domestic. House-made ; home-baked. Internal; civil.
خانُم [*Of Mongolian origin and fem. of* خان] Lady. Wife. Mistress. Mother +. *Title placed after the first name of a lady. Ex.* اشرف خ.
خانمان House. Family. Household goods.
خانمان برانداز Ruinous ; destructive.
خانوادگی Pertaining to a family. — پزشك خ F. doctor.
خانواده Family. Tribe.
خانوار Family ; house.
خانه House. Home. *OS.* Room. [*In a backgammon board*] Point. [*In a chessboard*] Square. *Anat.* 1) Alveolus. 2) Socket. — آنرا بردم (به) خ. I took it home. — خ. روشن کرده است This is only a lightening before death.
خانه بدوش Vagabond ; homeless (person) ; nomad(ic).
خانه پرورد(ه) Homebred.
خانه تکانی Spring-cleaning.
خانه‌خانه Chequered. Cellular. Honeycombed.
خانه ُخدا • = صاحبخانه
خانه خراب *P. A.* Ruined. — خ. شدن To be ruined. — خ. کردن To ruin ; impoverish.
خانه خواه Familiar ; intimate.
خانه‌دار *a.* Economical ; thrifty. —*n.* Housekeeper. Good manager.
خانه داری Housekeeping. — خ. کردن To keep house.
خانه‌زاد 1) *a.* Home-born. 2) *n.* Child of a slave.
خانه شاگرد Servant-boy.
خانه‌کش Drawer.
خانه نشین Stay-at-home. Confined at home ; retired.
خاوَر East. *Fem. pr. name.*
خاور شناس Orientalist.
خاور شناسی Orientalism.
خاوری Eastern.
خاویار [Fr. f. It. f. T.] Caviare.
خائف *A.* = 1) ترسان 2) ترسو
خائن (*A.*) 1) *a.* Treacherous. 2) *n.* Traitor. — خائنِ کشور Traitor to the country.
خائنانه *A. P.* Treacherously.
خایه 1) Testicle. 2) ○ Egg. — خایهٔ غول را شکستن To perform a Herculean task.
خایه مالی Cringing ; servile flattery. (*Indecent*).
خاییدن • [خای] = جویدن
خباثت *A.* Malice. Villainy.
خباز *A.* = نانوا
خبائث [Pl. of خبیثه]
خُبث *A.* Malice. Villainy. Impurity.
خَبر *A.* [اخبار] News ; information. Announcement. Notice. Tradition. *Gr.* Predi-

cate. — خبر خوش Good news. — خ. دادن To inform; let know. To announce. To send word. To warn. — از من خ. ندارد He has not heard from me. — خ. کردن To call; invite. To give notice. — خ. شدن To come to know; become aware. — خ. گرفتن To obtain information. [*With* از] To inquire after. — چه خ. است What is going on? W. is up? — خبری نیست 1) There is nothing going on. 2) Nothing doing. — خ. رسید که Word came that. — شیپور خبر *Mil.* First post. — لولهٔ خ. Overflow pipe.

خبر بر *A. P.* Tale-bearer.

خبرت * = **خبرگی** & **دانایی**

خَبردار *A. P.* Aware o. — خ. کردن To inform. To warn.

!خبردار *A. P.* (*Mil.*) Attention. [*With the stress on the 1st. syl.*] Look out! — بحال خ. ایستادن To stand at attention.

خبرگزار *A. P.* News-agent.

خبرگزاری *A. P.* News agency.

خبرگی *A. P.* = **کارشناسی**

خبرگیری *A. P.* Inquiry. *S. a.* جاسوسی

خبرنگار *A. P.* (Newspaper) correspondent. Annalist.

خُبرَویت *A.* = **خبرگی** & **کارشناسی**

خُبره *A.* Expert. *Cf.* کارشناس

خَبری *A.* Predicative o. Containing news. — فیلم خ. or فیلم اخباری News-reel.

خَبط *A.* Mistake. — خ. کردن To make a mistake. — خبط دماغ Mental alienation; aberration.

خبیث *A.* Malicious. Malignant; evil. Impure.

خبیثه *A.* [خبیثات or خَبائث] Impure thing. Evil. [Orig. fem. of خبیث]. [niscient.

خبیر *A.* Well-informed. Omniscient.

خپل & **خپله** + Squab or squat.

ختا Cathay.

خِتام * *A.* = پایان End; conclusion. — حسن خ. Happy c.

ختائی Of Cathay. — آجر ختایی Kind of brick 25 cm. by 25 cm.

خَتم *A.* Finishing. Adjournment. (Reading the whole of the Koran in the) days of mourning. — خ. کردن To finish. To settle. — خ. گزاردن To commemorate the dead by reading the whole of the K. — مجلس خ. Service held for this purpose.

خَتنه *A.* Circumcision. — خ. کردن To circumcize. [party.

ختنه سوران *A.P.* Circumcision party.

خجالت *A.* Shame. — خ. دادن To put to shame. To cause to blush. — خ. کشیدن To blush; feel (*or* be) ashamed. — خجالتم ندهید Spare my blushes.

خجالت آور *A. P.* Shameful.
خجالت زده *A. P.* Put to shame; disgraced.
خجالت کش *A.P.* Bashful; shy.
خجستگی Auspiciousness.
خُجسته * Happy; auspicious.
خَجِل *A.* Ashamed. *Cf.* شرمنده ‖ خ. شدن To feel ashamed. — خ. کردن To put to shame; p. to the blush.
خجلت *A.* = خجالت
خجند * = خجسته [ful.
خَجول *A.* Shamefaced; bashful.
خَدّ *A.* = گونه Cheek.
خدا God. — خ. را * For God's sake. — خ کند I hope or God grant that. — خ. نکند Heaven forbid! — بخدا By God. — شمارا بخدا For God's sake. I swear you by God. — خ. حافظ *or* خدا حافظ شما Good-bye! Farewell! — خ. بدور + Devil take him! — خ. میکرد که Would to God that. — از خدا می‌خواست که ... He was too glad to ...
خدا بیامرز + Of blessed memory.
خدابین Who discerns the truth. Godly. [Godliness.
خدابینی Discerning the truth.
خدا پرست *a.* Pious; godly —*n.* Theist.
خدا پرستی Theism. Godliness.
خدا پسندانه Pious; godly.
خدا ترس God-fearing.
خدا ترسی Fear of God; piety;
خدا حافظی *P. A.* Good-bye; farewell. — خ. کردن [*With* با *or* از] To say good-bye to; take one's f. of.
خداداد *Mas. pr. name. OS.* Granted by God; Theodore.
خدا داده Granted by God; gifted. [Theist.
خدا شناس Pious; godly.
خدا شناسی Piety. Theism.
خدام [A pl. of خادم]
خدانشناس Impious. Irreligious.
خُداوَند Lord. God. Master. Possessor (of a specified thing or quality).
خداوندگار Lord. Master.
خداوندی Lordship.
خدایا [*Stress on the 2nd. syl.*] O God!
خدایار *Mas. pr. name. See* خدا & یار
خدایگان (Powerful) monarch.
خدایی *a.* Divine. Providential. —*n.* Godship; divinity.
خَدَر *A.* Torpidity.
خَدِر *A.* Torpid; benumbed.
خدشه *A.* Scratch; (mark of) alteration. — خدشهٔ خاطر Inquietude; anxiety. [فریب
خُدعه *A.* Deceit. *See* حیله &
خدعه آمیز *A. P.* Deceitful.
خدم *A.* [A pl. of خادم] Servants. — خدم و حشم Retinue; suite.
خدمات [Pl. of خدمت]

خدمت ِ *A*. [َخد َمات] Service.— او ده سال (سابقه) خ. دارد He has 10 years service.—خ.کردن To do s.; serve. — در خدمت کسی بودن To be in the employ of s. o.; also, be in his presence.—(به) خدمت ِکسی رسیدن To go to see s. o.; be admitted to his p. — (به) خدمتش خواهم رسید I will serve him out. —(در) سرخدمت On duty. — در حین انجام خ. While on d. — برگ خاتمه خ. Discharge certificate. — خدمت شما عرض کنم [*In p. c.*] Allow me to say.

خدمتانه *A. P.* Tip; drink-money.

خدمتگار *A. P.* Servant.

خدمت گزار *n. A. P.* Servant. *a.* Serving; willing to serve.

خدمت گزاری *A. P.* Service. Willingness to serve.

خدمه *A.* [A pl. of خادم]

خدنگ • (Arrow from) white poplar.

ُخدو ○ = **خیو**

خدیجه (*A.*) *Fem. pr. name.*

خدیو Khedive.

خذلان ○ *A.* = **ترک & واگذاری**

َخر Ass. *F.* Fool; silly person. [*Used as an a.*] Silly; stupid.—خرخاکی Woodlouse.— خر ماده She-ass. — خر شدن + To be(come) silly. To be fooled or cajoled. — خر نشو Don't be silly. —خرخودرا راندن To look after one's own business; also, be regardless of others. — خر خود را از پل گذراندن To get over one's difficulties; hit the right nail on the head. —یاسین بگوش خر خواندن To play a lyre in vain to an ass. — خرم بگل نخوابیده است I am not so hard up as to. — خر َکردن To fool; cajole. —خرش میرود × He is a big shot or bug; he carries much weight.

َخر [Imp. of خریدن].

خراب *A.* (*C. E.*) Ruined; demolished. Desolate. In bad repair; out of r.; impaired. Decayed; spoiled. —*n.* ○ Ruin; destruction — خ. شدن To be demolished or ruined; collapse. To be decayed; go bad; go off, as meat. To be impaired. — خانه‌اش خ. شود The devil take him! May he be ruined! — در این شهر خراب شده In this blooming city. — خ.کردن To demolish; destroy. To impair. To spoil.

خرابات • *A. P.* Pot house; tavern.

خرابآباد *A. P.* Desolate place. *Met.* The world.

خرابکاری *A. P.* Sabotage.

خرابه *A. P.* Ruined place.

خرابی *A.P.* Ruined condition. Impairment. — خرابی اوضاع

Bad state of affairs.
خراتین o Earthworm [کرم خاکی].
خَراج * A. Tax; tribute. Revenue.
خَرّاج A. Lavish.
خُراج A. Anthrax.
خَراج گزار A. P. Tributary.
خرّازی A. P. Haberdashery.
خرّازی‌فروش A. P. Haberdasher.
خرّازی فروشی A. P. Haberdashery; haberdasher's trade.
خراس o Ass-mill.
خراش 1) [Imp. of خراشیدن]. 2) Scratch. Slight wound.
خراشه Filings. Chips.
خراشیدگی Abrasion. Scratch. Slight wound.
خراشیدن [خراش] To scratch; scrape.
خراشیده [P. P. of خراشیدن] Scratched; scraped.
خرّاط A. Turner.
خرّاطی A. P. Turnery; turning. — دستگاه خ. Lathe.
خُرافات A. Extravagant talks. Ridiculous stories. *By e.* Superstitions.
خرافاتی A. P. Superstitious.
خرام 1) [Imp. of خرامیدن] 2) Graceful gait.
خرامان Strutting. Of a graceful gait.
خرامیدن [خرام] To strut. To walk gracefully.
خَرَبط Goose [غاز]. *See* بط.
خربق Hellebore.
خربزه *or* خربوزه Melon. — خربوزه کوتور o Musk-melon.
خرپا Roof-truss.
خرپُشت Convex.
خرپشته Ridge. Sharp roof.
خرپوزکی Hinny.
خرپول + Stinking of money. — آدم خ. Money-bags.
خِرت وپرت + Trumpery; frippery; pedlary. Lumber.
خَرتوخر + Higgledy-piggledy. Rough-and-tumble. Chaotic.
خَرج A. Expenditure; expense. Costs. *Cf.* مخارج ‖ [*In a firearm.*] Priming; amorce. — خرج سفر Travelling e. — خ. شدن To be spent. — خ. کردن To spend [*only in connection with money*]. — بخرج دادن To display or show; pass off. — بندِ من بخرجش نمیرفت He was impervious, or he would not listen, to my advice.
خرج بیار + A. P. Purveyor.
خرج در رفته A. P. After deduction of expenses; net.
خرجی A. P. Money for expenditure. Subsistence. Alimony.
خُرجین A. Saddle-bag; carpet-b. Satchel. (Beggar's) wallet.
خرچُسنه Blaps; churchyard beetle.
خرچنگال *or* خرچنگ Crab or [lobster.
خرچنگ قورباغه‌ای × Crabbed: خط خ.
خرچنگی Crustacean.

خرحمالی + P. A. Drudgery.
خِرخِر Ruckle. – خ. کردن To ruckle. To rattle.
خُرخُر Snoring. Purring. Growl(ing); snarl(ing). – خ. کردن To snore. To purr. To growl. To grunt.
خِرخِره + = خشک نای
خُرخُره Snore. Ruckle; death-rattle.
خِرخِری Hoarse: صدای خ.
خرخشه Ado. Disturbance. Dispute. Anxiety.
خرخیار Wild cucumber.
خُرد Little; small; young. Minute. – خ. کردن To break to pieces; shatter. To crush. To grind. To change, as money. *F.* To suppress. – پول خ. Small c.
خِرَد Wisdom; intellect.
خُرداد *Third month having 31 days.*
خُرد خُرد Little by little. Gradually. Piecemeal.
خرد سال Of tender years.
خرد سالی Childhood.
خُرد سنج Micrometer.
خَردل Mustard – ریشهٔ خ. Horse-radish. – ضماد خردل Sinapism. – مشمع خ. Mustard-plaster or sinapism. – خردل پارسی Penny-cress.
خِردمند * Wise.
خردمندی Wisdom.
خردمندانه *ad.* Wisely. –*a.* Wise.

خُرد نگاری Micrography.
خُرده *n.* Bit; fragment. Minute point. –*a.* 1) = خُرد 2) Retail. – خرده استخوان پا Tarsus. – خرده استخوان دست Carpus. – خ. الماس Diamond-dust. – خ. گرفتن [*With* از or بر] To find fault with; cavil. – بیست و خرده‌ای کتاب 20 odd books.
خرده بین Critical. Cavilling.
خرده بینی Critical or acute observation; scrutiny.
خرده حساب P. A. Small accounts (to settle).
خرده ریز Sundries. Trumpery. Trinkets.
خرده سنگ Gravel. Aggregate.
خرده سیاره P. A. Planetoid; asteroid.
خرده شیشه Glass-dust.
خرده فرمایش + Sundry orders. – خ بکسی دادن To order one about.
خرده‌فروش Retailer. Huckster.
خرده‌فروشی Retail (dealing). – خ. کردن To sell by retail. To peddle.
خرده کاری Minor repairs.
خرده گیر *a.* Cavilling; of c. habits. –*n.* Caviller.
خرده گیری Cavilling.
خرده مالک P. A. (Owned by) petty landowners.
خرده نان Crumbs.
خُردی Littleness. Minuteness. Childhood; infancy.

خر رنگ کن +*n*. Impostor. —*a*. Showy but worthless.

خرزه Glass bead. False pearl.

خرزهره Oleander.

خرس Bear.— خرس ماده She-bear.

خرسک Bear's cub ; whelp. Badger o. Kind of children's game o. Thick-napped or piled carpet.

خرسند Satisfied; content. Glad.

خرسندی Satisfaction. Contentment. Gladness.

خرسواری Riding an ass.

خرشف Squama.

خرطوم *A*. (Elephant's) trunk.

خرطومدار *A.P*. Proboscidian.— خوك خ. o Tapir.

خرطومی *A*. Trunk-like. Flexible. — لولهٔ خ. Hose (pipe).

خرف *A*. (*-raf*) Dotage; anility.

خرف *A*. (*-ref*) Stupid ; weak-minded. Anile.

خرفه *A*. Purslane.

خرفهم کردن *P*. *A*. To demonstrate (s. t.) so that even the fool can understand it. To inculcate (on or upon). [Not to be used in p. c.].

خرق *A*. Rending o. — خرق عادت Supernatural thing or act.

خرقه [*Obsolete*] *A*. Robe ; gown. Wadded cloak. Pelisse.— خ. تهی کردن * *Met*. To resign one's life.

خرقه پوش *A*. *P*. (Dervish) wearing a wadded (*or* tattered) robe.

خرک Little ass ; foal. Jack. *Mus*. Bridge. — خرك پرش Vaulting-horse. — خرك چوب بری Saw-horse ; saw-buck. — شوخی

خرکی Horse-play.— بار خرکی کردن × To make a pig of oneself; overeat (o.)

خرکچی *P*. *T*. Ass-driver.

خرکی *S*. *u*. خرك

خرگاه *Shed. Pavilion. Cottage.

خرگوش Hare. — خرگوش خانگی Rabbit.— خرگوش فرنگی = خرگوش خانگی ‖ خرگوش ماده Doe-rabbit.

خرگه * [Cont. of خرگاه]

خرم Fresh; green. Pleasant. Cheerful.

خرم *R*. Chrome. Box-calf.

خرما Date. — درخت خ. D.-palm.

خرماخارك *or* خرما خرك Kind of astringent date. Unripe dried date.

خرمالو Persimmon. [tree.

خرماندو Date-plum ; ebony-

خرمایی (Reddish) brown.

خرمقدس *P*. *A*. Foolishly pious or religious.

خرمگس Gad-fly ; horse-fly. — خرمگس معرکه *Met*. Kill-joy.

خرمن Stack ; heap. Harvest. [*Of the moon*] Halo. — خ. کردن To stack ; h. up. To gather in.

خرمن سوخته * Ruined ; impoverished.

خرمن کوب Thresher ; flail.

خرمن‌کوبی Thrashing corn.
خَرمُهره Glass bead ; cowrie.
خرّمی Freshness. Cheerfulness. *See* خرّم
خُرناس *or* خرنش Snoring. — خ. کشیدن To snore.
خرند Walk ; footpath ; apron. Parapet (of a gallery).
خَرنوب Carob (bean) ; St. John's bread.
خَروار Ass-load (roughly = 300 kilogrammes).
خُروج *A.* Going out. Exit. Egress. Exodus. *Med.* Prolapse ; prolapsus. — خروج چشم Exophthalmus.
خروجی *P. A.* Balcony.
خِرّوخر + Death-rattle.
خُروس Cock. — جوجه‌خ. [*As compound word*] Young cock; cockerel. — خروس اخته Capon. — خروس‌جنگی Game-cock.
خروسک Cockerel. [*In a rifle*] Hammer. *Med.* Croup.
خروس‌کولی Black cock. Lapwing.
خروس‌وزن *P. A.* Bantam weight.
خُروش 1) Clamour. Roaring. — خ. برآوردن To clamour; roar. 2) *Imp. of* خروشیدن
خروشان Roaring ; shouting.
خروشیدن [خروش] To shout ; roar ; clamour.
خَرّه ○ = لجن Mud sticking to the bottom of a tank.

خرناس = خُرّه
خَری Silliness ; asininity.
خریت *P. A.* (*C. E.*) = خری
خرید Purchase. Shopping. — خ. کردن To make a purchase. To shop. *Cf.* خریدن
خریدار Purchaser ; buyer. — خ. ندارد There is no demand for it.
خریداری *n.* Act of buying; purchase. —*a.* Purchased. — بچشم خ. نگاه‌کردن To make eyes at. — خ. کردن = خریدن
خریدن [خر] To buy; purchase.
خریده [P. P. of خریدن] Bought; purchased.
خریطه ○ *A.* Chart. Leathern bag.
خَریف *A.* = پائیز
خریفی *A.* = پائیزی Autumnal. — اعتدال خ. A. equinox.
خَز Fur. F. coat. — خز دست Muff. — خزگردن Tippet ; fur necklet; boa. — خزسمور Sable.
خَز [Imp. of خزیدن].
خَزان Fall ; autumn. — خ. شدن To turn yellow ; as trees.
خَزان Creeping ; crawling.
خِزانه *A.* [خَزائن] Treasury. Rifle-magazine. Silkworm nursery. — خ. کردن To store up.
خزانه‌دار *A. P.* Treasurer. — تفنگ خ. Magazine-rifle.
خزانه‌داری *A. P.* Treasury. — خزانه‌داری کل T. General.
خزانی Autumnal.

خزائن [Pl. of خزانه]
خزر *Khazar:* tribe formerly inhabiting the Caspian littoral. — بحر خزر The C. Sea.
خزف *A.* Pottery. — خزف ریزه Potsherd.
خز فروش Furrier ; dealer in fur coats.
خز فروشی Furriery.
خزندگان [Pl. of خزنده]
خزَنده *a.* Creeping. —*n.* Reptile [pl. خزندگان].
خزنده شناسی Herpetology.
خزوک 1) = سوسك 2) Cicada.
خزه Moss. — شبه خ. Muscoid.
خزه شناس Muscologist.
خزه‌شناسی Muscology; bryology.
خزیدن [خز] To creep ; crawl.
خزیده [P.P. of خزیدن] Crept. Lying hid.
خزینه *A.* [خزائن] Treasury. Reservoir of a Turkish bath.
خس Small chip of wood ; mote. Thorn. *F.* Mean fellow.
خسارت *A.* Damage(s). Loss. — [*In maritime insurance*] Average. — خ. دیدن To sustain a loss or damage. — خ. وارد آوردن بر To d. — عرضحال خ. دادن To sue for damages.
خسارت‌آمیز *A. P.* Prejudicial.
خساست *A.* = خست
خسبیدن ○ [خسب] = خوابیدن
خس پرور * Cherishing the mean : ep. of the world.
خست *A.* Meanness ; miserliness. Stinginess.
خستگی Fatigue ; weariness.
خستگی ناپذیر Indefatigable.
خستن * [خل] To gall or wound. To tire.
خستو شدن ○ To confess.
خسته Tired. Weary. Wounded; galled ○. — خ. شدن To get tired. — خ. کردن To weary. To make tired ; tire out.
خسته خاطر * *P. A.* & خسته دل Wounded at heart or in spirit.
خسته‌کننده Tiresome ; tedious.
خسخس Râle; rattle. — خ. کردن To r. To wheeze.
خسران *A.* = خسارت & زیان
خسرو *Mas. pr. name. Name of a king. By e.* King *.
خسک Small thorn or chip. *S. a.* حسك
خسوف *A.* Lunar eclipse.
خسیس *A.* Stingy. Mean.
خسیسی *A. P.* = خست
خشاب Loader (of a magazine-rifle).
خشایارشا Xerxes.
خشت Sun-dried brick. — خشت‌زر Ingot of gold. — خ. زدن *or* خ. مالیدن To make (*or* mould) bricks. — خ. برآب زدن * To carry water in a sieve ; also, throw stones on the sea.
خشت خشتی Chequered.
خشت زن = خشتمال
خشتک Seat (of trousers).
خشتمال Maker of sun-dried

bricks.
خشتی Brick-shaped. Made of sun-dried bricks. — خال خ. C. P. Diamond.
خشخاش Poppy. — تخم خ. Maw-seed. — گل خ. Corn-poppy.
خشخاشی Papaverous. Flavoured with poppy-seeds.
خشخش & خش و خش Rustle ; frou-frou. — خ. کردن To rustle.
خشک Dry. Dried. *F.* Brainless ; hollow. Lifeless ; prosaic. Strict ; severe. — خ. افتادن To run dry ; d. up. — خ. انداختن To d. up ; drain. — خ. شدن To (become) dry. To freeze (to death). — در جای خود خشك شد He was astounded ; he was transfixed in his place. — خ. کردن To (make) dry. To wipe. To parch. — خ. و تر *or* تر وخشك The good and the bad. — خشك و خالی Empty ; nonsensical. Outward; lukewarm; left-handed. Mere.
خشکاندن To (cause to) dry. To desiccate. To drain.
خشکبار *or* خشکه بار Dried fruits.
خشك دست Close-fisted.
خشك ریشه Eschar ; slough.
خشکسال Year of drought.
خشك سالی Drought ; dearth.
خشك کن Blotter ; blotting-paper ; blotting-pad. Drier.
خشك مغز • Crack-brained ; rattle-brained; rattle-pated.
خشك مقدس *P. A.* Sanctimonious ; pharisaical.
خشك نای Larynx.
خشکه Everything included ; all-in ; as a fixed sum. In (hard) cash.
خشکه Tool steel; cast steel.
خشکی Dryness. Drought. Land. Stinginess. Severity. Stiffness. — خ. شدن *or* خ. زدن + To chap.
خشکیدن [خشك] To dry (up) ; drain. To freeze (to death).
خشکیده [P. P. of خشکیدن] Dried; withered up. Frozen. Shrivelled; skinny.
خشل ० = مقل Bdellium.
خشم Anger ; indignation. — خ. بخشم آوردن ‖ خشمگین‌شدن = گرفتن To make angry ; provoke.
خشمگین = خشم‌آلود
خشمگین *or* خشمناک Angry. — خ. شدن To get angry. — خ. کردن To make a. ; provoke.
خشن *A.* Rough ; rude. Coarse. Harsh.
خشنود Glad. Satisfied ; content. — ازکسی خ. بودن To be satisfied or pleased with s. o.
خشنودی Satisfaction. Gladness.
خشوع *A.* = خضوع & فروتنی
خشونت *A.* Rudeness; harshness. — خ. کردن To speak harshly. To be rude.
خصال [Pl. of خصلت]
خصائص *A.* [Pl. of خاصیت]

Properties. Special qualities. S. features ; characteristics.

خصائل َ A. [Pl. of خصیلت o] Qualities. Habits.

خصلت ِ A. [خصال] Quality. Character. Virtue. Habit.

خصم َ A. = دشمن Enemy.

خصمانه A. P. *ad*. Hostilely. —*a*. Hostile.

خصوص ُ A. Regard; concern.— درخصوص On the subject of; concerning ; about ; regarding. — بخصوص & علی‌الخصوص Especially. Particularly; in particular.

خصوصا A.=بویژه Especially; particularly.

خصوصی A. Private. Special.

خصوصیات A. Particulars ; specifications. *Cf.* خصوصیت

خصوصیت A. Close acquaintance+. *Cf. the pl.* خصوصیات

خصومت A. = **دشمنی**

خصومت‌آمیز A. P. Hostile.

خصی o (A.) *a*. Castrated. —*n*. Eunuch.

خصیب o A. = **آباد - حاصلخیز**

خصیه ُ A. = **خایه** Testicle.

خصیتین A. The two testicles. [D. of خصیه]

خضاب ِ A. Henna used for tinging the beard and the hands.

خضراء َ [Fem. of اخضر]

خضوع ُ A. = فروتنی Humility.

خط َ A. [خطوط] Line. (Hand) writing; character. Streak.— خط آهن Railway (track). — خط استوا Equator. — خط افق Horizon. — خط اتحاد *or* خط اتصال *Mus*. Slur. — خط برنج Column-rule. — خط جامع المیاه Thalweg. — خط دو راهی Siding. — خط سبز • The down on the cheek of a young man.— خط سیر Route ; itinerary. — خط فرعی Side-track ; siding; branch line. — خطمشی Policy. — خطمصور Projection of a point — خط مماس Tangent. — خط ناظم Normal. — خط زدن To cross out ; write off. — خط کشیدن To draw a line. To cross out.— خط و نشان کشیدن To prewarn s. o. ; make a point (of).— زیر چیزی خط کشیدن To underline s. t.— از خط بیرون افتادن To be derailed ; get off the track.

خطا َ A. Sin. Mistake; error. Wrong. — خ. رفتن To go the wrong way ; make a mistake. — خ. کردن To make a mistake. To slip. To miss (a mark).

خطاب ِ A. Address. Speech. — خ. کردن To address. To speak.— خ. بمن Addressed to me. — خطاب من به اوست I am addressing him.

خطا بخش • A. P. Forgiving ; merciful.

خطا پوش • A.P. Who glosses

over men's faults.
خطابه A. Oration ; lecture; sermon. Cf. نطق & وعظ
خطاط A. Penman; calligraphist. — خ. سرقلم Relief pen-nib.
خطاکار A.P. a. Sinful; guilty —n. Sinner ; wrongdoer.
خطاکاری A. P. Sinfulness.
خطام o A. Rope. Mooring.
خطایا [Pl. of خطیه]
خطبا [Pl. of خطیب]
خطبان A. P. Linesman.
خطبه A. Public homily ; sermon. Cf. خطابه & نطق
خط تراش A. P. Scraper.
خط خط + a. p. Streaky. Scratchy.
خطدار A. P. Striped. Ruled.
خطر A. Danger. Peril.— درخطر انداختن To endanger. To peril. To stake. — در معرض خ. Exposed to danger. At s.
خطرناك A. P. Dangerous.
خط زده A. P. Crossed out.
خطکش A. P. Rule(r).
خطکشی A. P. Ruling. Drawing lines. — خ.کردن To rule.
خطمی A. Marsh mallow; rose-mallow. — خطمی درختی Syrian mallow. — خطمی صحرائی Abutilon. — خطمی فرنگی Hollyhock.— خطمی مجلسی China rose.
خطور A. Occurring (to the mind). — بخاطرش خ.کرد که It occurred to him that.
خطوط [Pl. of خط]
خطه A. Territory ; country.
خطی A.P. Handwritten; manuscript. Linear. [cher.
خطیب A. [خطباء] Orator. Preacher.
خطیر A. Serious; momentous.
خطیه A. [خطایا] = خطا
خف + Stuffy : هواخفاست
خفا A. Concealment. — در خفا Secretly.
خفاش A. = شبپره Bat.
خفت Abscissa. OS. Sleeping.
خفت n. Running noose. Tight necklace. —a. Tight. —ad. Tightly. — گره يك خفتی Half-hitch. — گره دو خفتی Two half-hitches.
خفت A. (khefat) Lightness . Disgrace. — خ. دادن To d.— خفت عقل Light-mindedness.— خفت‌مزاج Flightiness; caprice.
خفت‌آمیز A. P. Disgraceful ; derogatory.
خفتان o Caftan ; under-tunic.
خفتن * [خواب] To sleep.
خفته a. Asleep. Slept. —n. Sleeping person.
خفجه or خفچه Haw(thorn).
خفض خناح A. Humility. OS. Lowering the wing.
خفقان A. Palpitation; throbbing.
خفگی Stuffiness; closeness. Hoarseness. Extinction.
خفه Suffocated; choked. Close; stuffy.— خ. شدن To be suffocated or stifled. To go out.— خ. شو Shut up! — خ.کردن

To choke ; suffocate; strangle. To drown. To damp or extinguish. *F.* To suppress.
خفه کن Damper. Extinguisher. Silencer. *Mus.* Sourdine.
خَفی *A.* Secret. [Fem. خفیه].
خَفیف *A.* Light [سبك]. Slight. Contemptible. Frivolous.
خَفیات *A.* Hidden things.[Pl. of خَفیه fem. of خفیّ]
خُفیه *A.* = پنهانی Concealment.— در خفیه Secretly.
خفیه فروش *A. P.* Smuggler.
خُفیةً *A.* (*-yatan*) Secretly.
خُل + Half-witted.
خَلاء *A.* (*-la'*) Vacuum. [Pronounced *-la*] Water-closet.
خلاص *A. n.* Deliverance. *—a.* (*C. E.*) Delivered ; rid. — خ. شدن To get r. To be released. — خ. کردن To rescue ; save. To despatch; kill. — دندهٔ خ. Neutral gear.
خُلاصه *A.* Resumé; summary. *—ad.* To sum up; in short. — خلاصهٔ مذاکرات Minutes; proceedings. — خ. کردن To summarize.
خلاصی *A. P.* (*C.E.*) = رهایی
خلاف *A.* Minor (*or* petty) offence. Diversity. Contrary ; opposite. — خلاف رویه Irregular (act). — خلاف شرع (Act) contrary to spiritual law. — خلاف قاعده Irregularity ; anomaly. — خ. کردن To commit a minor offence. To do wrong. — خلاف چیزیرا گفتن To contradict a statement. — برخلافِ Contrary to; unlike.— محکمهٔ خ. Court of m. offences ; police-court. [sion.
خَلافت *A.* Caliphate. Succession.
خلاف کار *A. P.* Guilty of a minor offence. Offender.
خلاق *A.* = آفریدگار
خلاقیت *A.* Creative power ; creatorship.
خلال *A.* Interval. Interstice.— درخلال این احوال In the meantime. — در خلال این مدت Since; during this time. — خلال دندان Toothpick. — خلال گوش Ear-pick.— خلال نارنج Orange peel.
خلائق *A.* [Pl. of خلیقه ○] Creatures ○. People.
خَلبان Pilot (of a plane).
خلبانی Pilotage.
خلجان *A.* Agitation. Palpitation of the heart.
خُلد * *A.* [خلود] = بهشت
خلدالله *A.* (*khaladalah*) May God perpetuate. . . .
خُلر (Variety of) green pea.
خَلسه *A.* Ecstasy. *OS.* Seizing.
خلش Prick; prickle. Sting [نیش].
خُلص *A.* Pure; unmixed.
خَلط *A.* Mixing. — خلط مبحث Confused discussion or reasoning. [tum.
خلطِ *A.* [اخلاط] Humour. Sputum.
خُلطه *A.* = آمیزش [form.
خَلطی *A.* Humoral. Plexi-

خَلع *A.* Deposal; removal from an office. Dethronement. — خلع سلاح Disarmament. — خلع سلاح کردن To disarm. — کسیرا از چیزی خلع ید کردن To dispossess a person of s. t. — خ. کردن To depose. — ازسلطنت خ. کردن To dethrone.

خَلعت *A.* Robe of honour.

خُلعی *A.* *Designating a kind of divorce* [طلاق خ.] granted at a woman's request against compensation.

خَلف *A.* = پشت Back; hind part.—برهانخ. Inverse process (in reasoning).

خَلف *A.* (-*laf*) [اخلاف] Successor [جانشین]. — فرزند خلف Son worthy of his father; good son.

خُلف *A.* Breach.— خلف وعده کردن To break one's promise; b. an appointment.

خلفا [Pl. of خلیفه]

خَلفی *A.* Posterior. Retral.

خَلق *A.* Creation. Creature. People [مردم].

خُلق *A.* Humour; temper. [Cf. the pl. اخلاق]. — حسن خ. Good nature; g. humour or t.— خلقش تنگ است He is not in a g. mood. — خلقش تنگ شد He was upset. — سرِ خلق In g. humour or spirits.

خلق الساعه *A.* Spontaneous generation.

خُلقان • *A.* Shabby (garment).

خِلقت *A.* Creation [آفرینش]. Natural disposition.— خ. کردن = آفریدن

خَلل *A.* Disorder. Injury; harm. — خ. رساندن (به) To damage; harm; injure.

خلل پذیر *A. P.* Destructible.

خلل ناپذیر *A. P.* Indestructible. Permanent; constant.

خُلل و فرج *a. p.* Pores.

خلل و فرجدار *A. P.* Porous.

خلنگ ∘ Heath(er).

خلنگزار Heath; moor.

خَلوَت *A. n.* Retired or private place; privacy. Solitude. —*a.* (*C.E.*) Private; retired; lonely. Not crowded.— درخلوت In private.— خ. کردن To retire. To let no one in; clear. [*With* با] To give a private audience to.

خُلود • *A.* 1) [Pl. of خلد]. 2) Eternity.

خُلوص *A.* Sincerity.— باخلوصِ نیت Sincerely.

خَلیج *A.* Gulf. Bay.— خلیج فارس The Persian G.

خلیدن • [خَل] To prick or sting. *Cf.* نیش زدن

خلیع العذار ∘ *A.* Shameless.

خَلیفه *A.* [خُلفاء] Caliph. Successor [جانشین]. Monitor[مبصر].

خلیق *A.* Polite. Moral.

خَلیل *A.* Friend [دوست]. *Mas. pr. name.*

خَم 1) *n.* Curve; bend. —

خم آور تا Arch of the aorta. — خم سینی Sigmoid flexure. — خم به ابرو نیاورد He did not turn a hair. 2) *a*. Bent; curved. — خم شدن To bend; stoop. — خ. کردن To bend; bow. To curve.

خُمره = ○• خُم

خُمار *A*. 1) *n*. Wine-headache; hangover [also خماری]. 2) *a*. Half-drunk. [*Of eyes*] Languishing.

خُماسی ○ *A*. (Word) of five letters.

خمپاره Mortar-shell.

خمپاره‌انداز Mortar. Bombardier.

خَم‌خَم In a stooping posture.

خَمر *A*. = باده & شراب

خُمره Large earthenware jar. [*For dyeing*] Vat. — لیوان خمره‌ای Barrel-glass.

خَمری • *A*. Vinous ○. — جنون خ. Delirium tremens; drunkard's delirium.

خُمس *A*. = (یك) پنجم

خَمسه *A*. Pentad. Quintlet. — خمسهٔ آل عبا The Five Holy Ones: Mohammed, Fatemah, Ali, Hassan, and Hossein.

خمسین *A*. The khamsin. *OS*. = پنجاه

خمود *A*. Going out. Abatement. Torpor.

خَموش etc. = خاموش etc.

خَمیازه Gaping; yawning. — خ. کشیدن To gape; yawn.

F. To aspire.

خمیدگی Curvature.

خمیدن [خم] To bend or stoop.

خمیده [P. P. of خمیدن] Curved. Bent.

خَمیر *A*. 1) *n*. Dough. Paste. — خمیر دندان Tooth paste. — خمیر شیشه Frit. — خمیر کاغذ سازی Pulp. 2) *a*. (*C. E.*) Half-baked; underdone. — خ. کردن To knead; mix with water.

خمیر تُرش *A. P*. Yeast; leaven.

خمیر مایه *A. P*. = خمیر ترش

خمیره *A. P*. Natural disposition; stamp. Mettle; grain.

خمیری *A. P*. Pasty; doughy. Pulpy. Plastic.

خَن Hold (of a ship).

خَنازیر *A*. Scrofula. [Pl. of خنزیر 'pig' = خوك].

خنازیری *A*. Scrofulous.

خُناق *A*. Croup or asphyxia.

خنثی (*khonsa*) *A*. Hermaphrodite; androgynous. *Chem*. Neutral. — خ. کردن To neutralize. *F*. To frustrate.

خَنجر *A*. (Curved) dagger; poniard. — خ. زدن To stab (with a d.)

خنجری *A*. Ensiform; xiphoid.

خَندان Laughing; smiling. — پستهٔ خ. Half-cracked pistachio. *Met*. • Smiling lips.

خنداندن To cause to laugh or smile; make l.

خندق [Arabicized form of کنده]

Moat ; fosse.

خنده Laughter; laugh.—خ. انداختن To cause to l.; set off laughing.— زیرخنده زدن To break into a laugh ; burst out laughing. — خ. راه انداختن To raise a laugh.—خ. کردن&*خ. زدن To smile or laugh.—خ. ام گرفت or خ. ام افتاد It made me l.

خنده آور Provoking laughter ; laughable. Funny.

خنده دار Laughable.

خنده رو Given to smiling. Cheerful.

خندیدن [خند] To smile or laugh.— بچیزی خ. To laugh at s. t.

خنس و فنس ×Pretty kettle of fish ; awkward situation.

خنصر o *A*. The little finger.

خنک Cool. Fresh. *F*. Flat, as a joke. Frigid, as a verse. — خ. شدن To (get) cool.— خ. کردن To c. To refrigerate.

خنک کن Cooling. Refrigerating ; refrigerant.

خنکی Coolness. *Med*. Refrigerant. *F*. Frostiness.

خِنگ o Grey or white (horse). Stupid.

خنیاگر Professional musician ; [minstrel.

خو *or* **خوی** Habit. Disposition. — بچیزی خو گرفتن To get used or accustomed to s. t. To acquire the habit of s. t.

خواب (*khab*) *n*. Sleep. Dream. Pile; nap.—*a*. Asleep.—خ. دیدن To dream. — خواب چیزیرا دیدن To d. of s. t. — خ. رفتن To go to sleep. To get benumbed.—خ. کردن To (put *or* lull to) s. To hypnotize. *F*. To blind the eyes of. — خ. ماندن To oversleep (oneself). — خوابم برد I went off ; I fell asleep. — خوابم نمی برد I can't get to s. — خوابم می آید I feel sleepy. — خود را بخواب زدن To sham sleep ; pretend to be asleep. — بخواب گذراندن To s. away. — اطاق خ. Bedroom. — در عالم خ. دیدم I saw in my dream.

خواب [Imp. of خوابیدن].

خواب آلود Drowsy; sleepy.

خوابانیدن *or* **خواباندن** To cause to sleep (*or* lie down). To lull to s. To lower or strike, as a flag. *F*. To cause to subside. To suppress. To lay up ; put out of commission.. To lay low [*See* انداختن]. To p. by. — مرغ خ. To set eggs.

خوابانده [P. P. of خواباندن]

خواب آور Soporific.

خواب دار Piled; napped.

خواب رفته Benumbed; torpid.

خواب شناس Hypnologist.

خواب شناسی Hypnology.

خوابگاه Bedroom. Dormitory.

خوابیدگی Lying or stooping posture. *F*. Standstill.

خوابیدن [خواب] To sleep. To

lie down. [*Of a watch*] To run down; stop. [*Of a hen*] To brood ; sit. *F*. To subside. To be settled, as dust. To come to a standstill.

خوابیده [P. P. of خوابیدن] Lying. Asleep. Run down. Laid-up. Stagnant.

خوابیده گردی o Sleep-walking.

خواتین [Pl. of خاتون]

خواجه [خواجگان] Eunuch. (Title of a) man of distinction.

خواجه تاش * *P. T.* Fellow-servant.

خواجه سرا Eunuch.

خوار (*khar*) Despised; abject.– خ.شمردن To hold in contempt; despise. – خ. کردن To h. in disrespect; humiliate.

خوار *Suf.* 1) Eater or drinker. 2)-vore; -vorous. Ex. علفخوار herbivorous.

خواربار Foodstuffs; provision; grocery. [sion merchant.

خواربار فروش Grocer ; provi-

خواری Abjectness. Contempt.

خواست Wish; will.

خواستار (*khastar*) *a.* Asking for; soliciting. – خ. شدن to ask for ; solicit. [With از] To request.

خواست برگ Subpœna.

خواستگار Suitor.

خواستگاری Suit. – خ.کردن *vi.* To act as a suitor. –*vt.* To ask for the hand of (a woman) in marriage.

خواستن [خواه] To wish. To want. To intend. To need. [*With* از] To ask ; request.– از من هزار ریال میخواهد I owe him *Rials* 1000. –خواهم رفت- خواهید رفت etc. I shall go, you will go, etc.

خواسته *a.* [P. P. of خواستن] Wished ; wanted . Also , claimed . –*n.* Possessions . Desire. Object of claim.

خواص *A.* [Pl. of خاصه] The (upper *or*) noble classes. *Ph.* Properties.

خواطر [Pl. of خاطر]

خوان * (*khan*) = سفره Table; dinner table. *Cf.* خوانچه

خوان(,,) o Adventure; exploit: هفت خوان رستم

خوان (,,) [Imp. of خواندن]

خوانا Legible.

خوانایی Legibility.

خوانچه Large wooden tray.

خواندن [خوان] *vt.* To read. To sing. To crow: خروس می‌خواند ‖ To study. To call * : (1) invite ; (2) name. –*vi.* To tally or correspond.

خواندنی Interesting to read ; readable.

خوانده [P. P. of خواندن] 1) *a.* Called ; invited. 2) *n.* Defendant.

خوان سالار o Major-domo.

خواندگان [Pl. of خوانده]

خواننده [خوانندگان] *n*. Reader. Singer. —*a*. Singing.
خوانین [A. pl. of خان] The tribal chiefs. The nobility.
خواه (*khah*) 1) Whether. 2) Or [correlative of whether.] : خ. بروم خ. نروم w. I go or not.
خواه (,,) [Imp. of خواستن].
خواهان *a*. Desirous. Willing. Fond. —*n*. Plaintiff.
خواهر (*khahar*) Sister.
خواهر اندر ◦ Half-sister.
خواهرانه Sisterly.
خواهر خوانده Adopted sister.
خواهر زاده Sister's child : nephew or niece. [in-law.
خواهر زن Wife's sister ; s.-
خواهر شوهر Husband's sister; s.-in-law.
خواهری Sisterhood.
خواهش (*khahesh*) Request ; wish. Asking. — خ. کردن To ask or request ; beg [often with از] : از من خ. کرد بمانم He asked me to stay. — خ. دارم بمانید I shall be glad if you will stay; please stay.
خواهشمند بودن To ask or request. — خواهشمندم بمانید I shall be glad if you will stay ; please s.
خواهی نخواهی or **خواه ناخواه** Willy-nilly.
خوب *a*. Good. Nice. Well. Proper.—*ad*. Well Properly. Thoroughly. —*n*. Ex. بدوخوب The g. with the bad ; the g. and the wicked ; also, the rough with the smooth.— خوبان The fair (sex). The g. (people). — بسیار خوب Very well. All right. — خ. کردن + To cure. — خ. شدن + To be cured. To recover.— خ. کرد که رفت He did w. to go.
خوبرو • Fair ; handsome.
خوب سیرت • *P. A*. Of a good character.
خوب صورت • *P. A*. = خوبرو
خوب‌منظر • *P. A*. Good-looking.
خوبی Goodness. Kindness. Beauty •. — خ. کردن To do good. — بخوبی Well. Nicely. Thoroughly. In a good way.
خو پذیر • Apt to acquire a habit; capable of being trained.
خود (*khu:d*) Helmet.
خود (*khod*) *n*. Self : خود من or خودم (I) myself. —*pron*. 1) Oneself : بخود آمدن ‖ 2) Myself ; yourself, etc. [preceded by a personal pron.]. Ex. من خ. ‖ 3) My, your, etc. [according to the verbal pron. following it]. Ex. آیا کتاب خودرا بمن خواهید داد Will *you* give me *your* book؟ کتاب خود را بشما خواهم داد I will give you *my* book.
خودآرا Dandyish ; foppish.
خودآرایی Prinking up oneself ; dandyism.

خود آموز Self-teaching or self-taught. — خود آموز فرانسه 'French self-taught'.
خود بخود Automatic(ally). Spontaneous(ly). — صرافت خ. Spontaneity.
خود بین Self-conceited.
خود بینی Self-conceit.
خود پرست Egotist(ic).
خود پرستی Egotism.
خود پسند Selfish ; egotistic.
خود پسندانه Selfishly.
خود پسندی Selfishness.
خود خواه Egotistic ; selfish.
خود خواهی Selfishness; egotism.
خود خوری Worry.
خوددار Having self-control. Self-possessed.
خودداری Self-control. Forbearance. — خ. کردن To restrain oneself. To abstain ; refrain : از صحبت خ. کرد
خود رأی *P. A.* Obstinate ; opinionated. [obstinacy.
خود رایی *P. A.* Wilfulness ;
خود رنگ Natural-coloured ; beige.
خودرو (*khodru:*) Self-growing; wild. Self-grown.
خودرو (*khodrow*) Self-propelling ; self-propelled.
خودزا Autogenic ; autogenous.
خود ساز Dandyish ; foppy.
خود ستایی Self-praise.

خود سر Headstrong; obstinate.
خود سرانه 1) Wilfully. 2) + Without consulting any one. 3) W. being told.
خود سری Stubbornness; obstinacy.
خود سوز Self-consuming.
خود سوزی Worry. Anguish.
خود شکنی Self-humiliation.
خودشیرینی Officiousness; also, ingratiation. — خ. کردن To be officious; suck up, or make up (to s. o.).
خود فروز Self-luminous.
خود فروش Ostentatious.
خود فروشی Ostentation.
خودکار Automatic.
خودکام Arbitrary. *S. a.* خودسر
خودکشی Suicide. — خ. کردن To commit suicide.
خودمانی Familiar. — زیادخودمانی شدن To take freedoms.
خود مختار *P. A.* Self-determined ; autonomous.
خود مختاری *P. A.* Self-determination ; autonomy.
خود نما Showy. Ostentatious.
خود نمایی Ostentation. Gaudiness. — خ. کردن To show off.
خود نوشت Written by oneself. — خ. وصیت نامه Holograph.
خودنویس Self-writing. Self-recording. — قلم خ. Fountain-pen. — مداد خود نویس Mechanical pencil ; self-propelled

pencil.
خودی *a*. Familiar. —*n*. Relationship. — بخودی خود = خودبخود
خورشید = ° خور
خور Estuary. Narrow gulf.
خوراك Food. Meal. Dish. Course. Dose. — خ. دادن To feed. To board. — خ. ندارد He has no appetite.
آشپز = خوراک پز
خوراک پزی Cookery ; cooking. — چراغ خ. Cook-stove ; cooker ; primus.
خوردنی = خوراکی
خوراندن *or* خورانیدن To cause (*or* give) to eat. To feed.
خورد Eating °. Food °. — خ. دادن To rub in. — بخورد کسی دادن To give s. o. to eat.
خوردن [خور] *vt*. To eat ; also, drink. To take, as a medicine. To gnaw. To corrode ; wear away. To swallow, as one's words. — مبلغی باو قرض دادم و آنرا خورد I lent him a sum, and that was the last I saw of my money. —*vi*. To fit (on) [*With* به] To hit; collide with. — سنگ بدستم خورد The stone touched (*or* hit) my hand. — برخوردن به To hurt the feelings of. To come across. To meet. — بهم خ. To match (with) each other. To be cancelled. To be disbanded. To collide with each other.

خوردنی Eatable; edible.
خورده [P. P. of خوردن].
خورسند etc. = خرسند etc.
خورش *Dish of meat and vegetables served with rice*. — خورش دل ضعفه Barmecide feast.
خورش = + خورشت
خورشید Sun.
خورشیدی Solar.
خورند Suitable ; fit. — خورندما نیست It is not f. for us.
خورنده [خورندگان] Eater.
خوره = 1) آکله 2) جذام
خوش (*khosh*) *a*. Happy. Gay. Well. Pleasant. Good. Lucky; prosperous. — بوی خ. Sweet smell. — خواب خ. Sound or sweet sleep. — زبان خ. Soft words ; sweet tongue. —*ad*. Merrily. Well. Gently ; sweetly. — خ. آمدید You are welcome. — خدا را خوش نمی آید It does not please God. — خ. باشید Have a good time ; enjoy yourself. — شب شما خوش *or* شب بشما خ. G. night. — خ. بحال شما G. for you ! How lucky you are ! — خ. داشتن To p. or like. — خ. گذراندن To live in pleasure. To enjoy oneself. — خ. گذشت We had a good time. — از او خوشم می آید I like him; I am fond of him. — دل خود را خوش کردن To flatter oneself. — آب خوش

از گلویش پائین نرفت He was never happy ; he led a dog's life.
خوش (*khu:sh*) Seton.
خوشا (*khosh'a*) How good (is)! Good for . . . ‖ خ. بحالِ کسیکه Happy (*or* blessed) is he who . . . [Lustrous.
خوش آب Of the first water.
خوشاب Compote.
خوش آتیه *P. A.* Promising to have a good future ; likely. [climate.
خوش آب وهوا Of a healthy
خوش آواز Sweet-singing.
خوشامد Welcome. — بکسی خ. گفتن To welcome s. o.
خوش آهنگ Melodious.
خوش آیند Pleasing. Nice ; decent.
خوش اخلاق *P. A.* 1) Having good morals. 2) خوش خلق
خوش اخلاقی *P. A.* Good morals. G. behaviour.
خوش اقبال *P. A.* = **خوشبخت**
خوش‌الحان * *P. A.* Sweet-singing: مرغان خ.
خوش اندام Of a nice figure.
خوش باطن *P. A.* Inwardly good. [perous.
خوشبخت Lucky. Happy; pros-
خوشبختانه Fortunately.
خوشبختی Prosperity ; happiness. Good luck.
خوش برخورد Sociable. Accessible.
خوش بنیه *P. A.* Physically strong ; robust ; hearty.
خوشبو Sweet-smelling. Perfumed.
خوش بین Optimistic. — شخص خ. Optimist.
خوش بینی Optimism.
خوش ترکیب *P. A.* Good-looking. Of a nice figure ; shapely.
خوش جنس *P. A.* Good-natured ; kind-hearted. [Of a horse] Thoroughbred.
خوشحال *P. A.* Glad; happy.— خ. شدن To become glad. — خ کردن To make h. To give joy or pleasure (to).
خوش حالت *P. A.* Good-natured. Well-disposed.
خوشحالی *P. A.* Gladness. Joy. — خ. کردن To rejoice.
خوش حساب *P. A.* Prompt to pay one's dues. — آدم خ. Good pay.
خوش خبر (*P. A.*) *a.* Bringing good news.
خوش خدمتی *P. A.* Sycophant and supererogatory service.
خوش خط *P. A.* 1) = **خوشنویس** 2) Nicely written.
خوش‌خط و خال *P. A.* Having beautiful stripes and spots. *F.* Outwardly good. [Used in مار خوش خط وخال 'snake in the grass'].
خوش خُلق *P. A.* Good hu-

moured ; good-natured.
خوش ُخلقی *P. A.* Good humour ; good nature.
خوشخو Good-natured ; good humoured.
خوش آواز = خوشخوان
کم‌کم = + خوش خوش
خوشخویی Good nature.
خوش دست Having a lucky hand (*or* touch).
خوشدل Merry; gay; cheerful.
خوشدلی Gaiety; cheerfulness.
خوش‌ذات *P. A.* Inwardly good; good-natured.
خوش رفتار *a.* Behaving well. Walking elegantly *.
خوش رفتاری Good behaviour.
خوش رقصی *P. A.* Supererogatory service. *OS.* Perfect or coquettish dancing.
خوشرنگ Of a pretty colour. Coloury. [smiling.
خوشرو Of a cheerful face;
خوش رَوش Thorough-paced.
خوشرویی Cheerfulness.
خوش ریخت Of a well-cut or nice figure ; well-knit.
خوش زبان Fair-spoken.
خوش‌سابقه *P. A.* Having a clean (*or* good) record. Reputable.
خوش ساخت Of a good make ; of exquisite workmanship.
خوش سخن = خوش صحبت
خوش سلیقه *P.A.* Of an exquisite taste ; of good choice.

خوش سوز Briquette.
خوش صدا Having a good voice ; sweet-singing. Melodious. Euphonious.
خوش صحبت *P. A.* Talking attractively ; conversable.
خوش‌طبع *P. A.* Good-natured. Jocular.
خوش طعم *P. A.* = خوش مزه
خوش‌طینت *P. A.* Good-natured.
خوش ظاهر *P. A.* Outwardly good. – خ. و بد باطن O. good and inwardly bad.
خوش عکس *P. A.* Who photographs well.
خوش قدم *P.A.* Bringing good luck ; lucky.
خوش قلب *P. A.* Kind-hearted; having a good feeling.
خوش قلم *P. A.* 1) = خوشخط 2) Having a good pen or style. 3) Written elegantly.
خوش قواره Nicely cut out. *S. a.* خوش ریخت
خوش‌قول *P. A.* True to one's promise; punctual.
خوش قولی *P. A.* Faithfulness to one's promise ; punctuality.
خوش قیافه *P. A.* Of pleasant features ; personable. *OS.* Of a good physiognomy.
خوش کردار Of good conduct.
خوش‌گذران Who lives in pleasure.
خوش‌گذرانی Living in pleasure; free living. [pretty.

خوشگل + Beautiful; handsome;
خوشگلی Beauty ; handsomeness.
خوش‌گمانی Favourable opinion.
خوش‌گوار Wholesome. Digestible. Agreeable to the taste.
خوش‌گوشت *a*. Giving a delicious meat. Whose wound is easily healed. —*n*.+ Sweetbread. *Cf*. لوزالمعده
خوش‌لباس *P. A.* Well-dressed.
خوش لهجه *P. A.* Having a good accent.
خوش محضر *P. A.* Sociable ; conversable ; accessible.
خوش مزگی Facetiousness ; waggery ; jest. — خ. کردن To j. or joke.
خوش مزه Tasty ; delicious. *F*. Facetious. Interesting.
خوش‌مشرب *P. A.* Good-natured. Sociable. Convivial.
خوش معاشرت *P. A.* Sociable.
خوش معامله *P.A.* Fair in one's dealings.
خوش منظر *P. A.* Good-looking ; comely.
خوش نشین Colonizer ; new settler.
خوش نقش *P. A.* Lucky.
خوش نما Well-seeming. Decent. Glossy.
خوش نمک Savoury ; saltish.
خوش نوا * Sweet-singing.
خوشنود etc. = خشنود etc.

خوشنویس *a*. Who writes elegantly. —*n*. Calligrapher.
خوش نهاد * Good-natured.
خوش نیت *P. A.* Well-intentioned ; well-meaning.
خوش وعده *P.A.* Self-invited; who calls on friends and relatives without waiting to be invited [usu. in خاله خ. (jocular pr. name of a woman of such description)].
خوشوقت *P. A.* Pleased; glad: خوشوقتم که بشما اطلاع دهم که I have pleasure in informing you that.
خوشوقتی *P. A.* Pleasure. — اظهار خوشوقتی کردن To express one's pleasure or joy.
خوشه Ear of corn. Cluster ; bunch (of grapes). Gleanings. — خ. برچیدن To glean.
خوشه‌ای *Bot*. Racemose. — ذرت خ. Giant millet.
خوشه چین Gleaner. *F*. Compiler ; also, plagiary.
خوشه چینی Gleaning. Compilation. Plagiarism.
خوش‌هوا Having a fine weather. Of a good climate.
خوش هیکل *P. A.* Of a nice figure ; well-set; of a handsome stature.
خوشی Happiness. Joy. Pleasure. — خ. کردن To rejoice ; make merry.
خشکیدن = o خوشیدن
خوش یُمن *P. A.* Lucky ; aus-

picious.

خوض ○ *A*. Plunging ; deep consideration.

خوف *A*. = ترس Fear. — خ. داشتن & ترسیدن = خ. کردن To fear ; be afraid.

خوفناك *A. P.* = **ترسان-ترسناك**

خوک Hog ; pig. — خوكِ آبی Seal. — خوك دریایی Sea-hog ; porpoise. — خوك ماده Sow. — چربی خ. Lard. — گوشت خ. Pork.

خوك چران Swine-herd.

خوگرفته & **خوكرده** Accustomed. Addicted. Tame.

خوك ماهی Porpoise ; sea-hog.

خول = زغن Kite.

خولان Buckthorn.

خولنجان Gålingale; galangale.

خون Blood. — از دماغش خ. میاید His nose is bleeding ; he is b. at the n. — خ. افتادن To bleed. — دماغش خ. افتاد His n. began to bleed. — خونش بجوش آمده است His blood is up. — خون کسیرا بجوش آوردن To stir one's b. — خون او از خون من رنگین‌تر نیست He is no better than I am ; a man is a m. ; we should both suffer equally. — خونش بگردن ما His blood be on us. — خون جگر خوردن or خون دل خوردن To eat one's heart out ; suffer very much (in silence). — خون ریختن and خ. کردن + To shed blood ; commit murder. — خون سیاوشان Dragon's-blood.

خونابه Thin transparent blood.

خونبار • *a*. Shedding (tears of) blood.

خون بند Styptic; haemostatic.

خون تاوان or **خون بها** Blood-money.

خونخوار Bloodthirsty; cruel.

خونخواری Atrocity; cruelty.

خونخواه Avenger of murder or bloodshed.

خونخواهی Vengeance for bloodshed.

خون دماغ *a*. Bleeding at the nose. —*n*. Nose-bleed ; epistaxis. — خ. شدن To bleed at the nose.

خون رَوی Haemorrhage.

خونریزی Bloodshed.

خون سرد Cold-blooded. *F*. Calm. Indifferent. Lenient ; easy-going. — خ. بودن To be calm ; keep one's head; k. one's hair on.

خون سردی Cold blood. Coolness ; indifference ; calmness.

خون شناسی Haematology.

خون فشان • Shedding bloody (*i. e.* bitter) tears.

خون‌گرم Warm-blooded. *F*. Warm-hearted.

خون‌گرمی Warm-heartedness ; sympathy.

خون مردگی Ecc yhmosis.

خونی 1) *a*. Bloody ; sanguinary. Haematic. — خلط خ.

Sanguine humour ; also, haemoptysis. 2) *n*. Murderer.

خونین Sanguinary ; bloody. — خ. و مالین × Covered all over with blood ; weltering in one's b.

خوی *S. u.* خو

خوی (*khoy*) Sweat ; perspiration [عرق].

خوی آور Diaphoretic.

خوید Unripe ear of corn.

خویش (*khi:sh*) *n*. Relative ; kinsman. — *pron*. 1) Oneself. 2) [According to the verbal pron. following it] (a) My (own), your (own), etc. : اسب خ. را باودادم ‖ (b) Myself, yourself, etc. [used objectively] : خ. را بدست دشمن سپرد

خویشاوند Relative ; kinsman.

خویشاوندی Relationship.

خویشتن = **خویش** *pron*. —*Note*. خویشتن *and not* خویش is used in comb.

خویشتن‌دار 1) Who takes care of himself. 2) = خوددار

خویشتن نگری Introspection.

خویشی Relationship. — باکسی خ. کردن To ally oneself to s. o. by marriage.

خهی * Bravo! Well done!

خیابان Avenue ; road ; street. Walk ; alley.

خیابان بندی Layout of a garden.

خیار Cucumber. — خیار چنبر Corrugated variety of cucumber. (*Med*.) Cassia fistula ; purging cassia [also خیار شنبر]. — خیار ریز Gherkin.

خیار *A*. Option.

خیارک Bubo. [Groove.

خیاره Fluting ; gadroon.

خیاط *A*. Tailor. — خیاط زنانه Dressmaker.

خیاطه *A*. [Fem. of خیاط]. Tailoress.

خیاطی *A.P*. Tailoring; sewing: نخ خ. s.-needle. — خ. کردن To sew ; be a tailor. — خیاطیِ اتوموبیل Car upholstery.

خیال *A*. [خیالات] Phantom. Hallucination. Thought. Reflection. Intention. — خیالات خام پختن To build castles in the air. — خ. داشتن To intend. — خیال باریدن دارد It threatens to rain. — خ. کردن To reflect. To think. To suppose; take as if. — بخیال افتادن To come to think. — بخیال انداختن To set thinking. — بخیال آنکه On the supposition that. — خ. برش داشت + He was carried off by illusion. He began to think much of himself.

خیالاتی *A. P*. Visionary ; hypochondriac.

خیال باف *A. P*. Visionary.

خیالی *A*. Imaginary ; visionary. Fanciful. Chimerical.

خیام ○ (*khiam*) [Pl. of خیمه]

خیام *A.* *Khayam*: penname of the author of *Robaiyat* or Quatrains. *OS.* Tent-maker.

خیانت *A.* Treachery; perfidy.— خ. در امانت Breach of trust.— خ. کردن To be treacherous.— بمن خ. کرد He was t. to me; he betrayed me.

خیانت‌آمیز *A. P.* Treacherous.

خیانت‌کار or خیانت‌گر *A. P.* *a.* Treacherous. —*n.* Traitor.

خیر *A.* (*kheyr*) 1) *n.* Welfare; benefit; good. Charity. Blessing.— خ. دیدن To have a happy ending; see one's better days. To be blessed. — از اولادش خیری ندید His children brought him no happines.— خیرش را به بینید I wish you joy of it. 2) *a.* Good; charitable. — امر خیر "The good or pious act", i. e. marriage. 3) *ad.* No. [also نه خیر]. — خیرِ مقدم Address of welcome. — خ. کردن To distribute in charity. — خ. و شر کردن To divine by counting beads at random (calling one "good" and the other "evil"). [Pious.

خیر *A.* (*khayer*) Charitable.

خیرات *A.* Charitable deeds; charities. [Pl. of خیره ○]

خیر اندیش *A. P.*= خیرخواه

خیر بده +*A. P.* Charitable; habitually giving alms.

خیرخواه *A. P.* Benevolent. Public-spirited.

خیرخواهانه *A. P.* *ad.* Benevolently. —*a.* Benevolent.

خیرخواهی *A. P.* Benevolence.

خیرگی Impudence.

خیره *a.* Impudent. Bold. Headstrong. Astonished. Dazzled. —*ad.* Staringly.— خ. شدن To be dazzled, as the eye. To act impudently. To stare. — خ. کردن To dazzle. To bewilder. — خ. نگریستن To stare.

خیره چشم * Impudent.

خیره چشمی Impudence.

خیره خیره Staringly.

خیره رای * Stupid. Mean.

خود سر = خیره سر

شب بو - خیری

خیریت *A.* Welfare.

خیریه *A.* Charity institution.

خیز 1) *Imp. of* خواستن 2) *n.* Jump. Swelling. Upheaval. *Arch.* Rise (of an arch); flèche. — خ. گرفتن To jump; leap.

خیزاب ○ = موج Wave; billow.

خیزان Rising.

خیزاندن ○= بلند کردن To cause to rise; raise.

خیزران Bamboo; also, rattan.— عصای خ. B. cane; Malacca c.

خیزیدن ○ [خیز]. = خاستن To rise.

خیس Drenched; wet all over. Soaked in water.— خ. شدن To

become wet all over. — خ. کردن To drench. To soak.

خیساندن To soak; steep.

خیسیدن [خیس] To soak. To become wet all over.

خیسیده Soaked. Macerated.

خیش Ploughshare. Trail of a gun. — خ. زدن To plough.

خیط شدن × *See* بور شدن *under* بور

خیک Skin(-churn). — خیکی بالا آوردن × To make a mess of it; fizzle out; make oneself ridiculous.

خیل o *A*. Army. *See* سپاه & لشکر ‖ Horsdmen. Swarm.

خیلتاش *A. T.* Fellow-soldier.

خیلی *A. P.* [*Stress on the 1st. syl.*] 1) *a*. Many; a lot of: خ. کتاب ‖ Much: خ. باران 2) *ad*. Very: خ. بد ‖ Greatly. — خ. متاسفم که I m. regret that. — خ. خوب Very good; very well; all right. — خ. از مردم A great many people [also خ. ها].

خیم o = خو & خُلق

خیمگی o *A. P.* Officer in charge of tents.

خیمه *A.* [خیام o] Tent. Tabernacle. *Cf.* چادر ‖ Pavilion. — خیمهٔ شب بازی Puppet-show. — خ. زدن To pitch a tent.

خیو Saliva [بزاق].

خیومایه Petiolin.

خیوی Salivary.

داءالاسد *A.* Leontiasis.
داءالثعلب *A.* Alopecia.
داءالحیه *A.* Icthyosis.
داءالخمر *A.* Delirium tremens [usu. جنون خمری].
داءالذقن *A.* Mentagra.
داءالرقص *A.* Chorea ; St. Vitus's dance.
داءالزیبق *A.* Mercurialism.
داءالسبات *A.* Catalepsy.
داءالفیل *A.* Elephantiasis.
داءالکلب *A.* = هاری Rabies.
دأب o *A.* = رسم - عادت
داتوره *or* تاتوره Stramonium; datura.
داخل *A. n.* Inside ; interior. —*a.* 1) = داخلی 2) Mixed. 3) Involved.— در اطاقی د. شدن *or* داخلِ اطاقی شدن To enter (into) a room. — د. کردن To e. ; bring in. To mingle. —ازداخل From within. —داخلِ *prep.* [For درداخلِ] In(side).
داخله *A.* [Fem. of داخل] *a.* Internal. —*n.* Interior.
داخلی *A.* Internal. Inner. Civil: جنگ د. ‖ Local: مصرف د.
داد Justice *. Cry (for j.) ; shout. — د. خواستن To plead for j. — داد سخن دادن * To be most eloquent. — د. زدن To s. — د. کردن 1) To s. 2) To do j. — داد کسیرا دادن To do justice to s. o. — دادِ مرا از او بگیرید Avenge me on him. — بدادم برسید Come to my rescue . — ای د. Mercy ! Good gracious ! Good God ! — داد و قال کردن To kick up a row. To fuss.—داد وبیداد & داد و ستد See *in the vocab.*
دادا o House-maid. Old nurse.
دادار * Just; righteous : ep. of God.
داداش + *T.* = برادر Brother.
دادخواست Petition.
دادخواه One who pleads for justice. Petitioner.
دادخواهی Pleading for justice. — د. کردن To implore, or plead for, justice.
دادرَس Judge.
دادرسی Legal procedure ; trial ; hearing. Judgment. — د. کردن To judge. To try.
دادستان Public prosecutor.
دادسرا Public prosecutor's office.
دادگاه Court of justice.
دادگر * Just; righteous.
دادگستری [For وزارت د.] Ministry of Justice.
دادن [دِه] 1) To give : آنرا

بمن داد He gave it to me. — قدری پول بمن بدهید Give me some money. 2) To pay.
دادنامه (Written) judgment.
دادنی Payable. That must be given.
داد و بیداد Row; brawl.— د. راه انداختن To kick up a row. — د. کردن To shout or uproar.

داد وستد Transaction. — د. کردن To do or carry on business; transact.
داده 1) [P. P. of دادن] Given. Paid. 2) —*n*. Payment(s); amount(s) paid.
دادیار Assistant to the public prosecutor. Counsel for the Crown.
دار o Tree [درخت]. Gallows. Staff (of a flag). — د. زدن *or* بدار آویختن To hang.
دار o *A*. House [خانه]. *Met*. = دنیا World [usu. دار دنیا].
دارا 1) Having; possessing; containing.— دارای سه اطاق است It has 3 rooms. 2) Rich. — د. ها و ندار ها The haves and have-nots.
دارا = داریوش
دارابی *Kind of fruit allied to shaddock.*
داراشکنك — دارکوب
داراشکنه Sublimate.
دارالانشاء *A*. — **دبیرخانه**
دارالایتام *A*. Orphan asylum.
دارالتأدیب *A*. House of correction. See تأدیب
دارالترجمه *A*. Translation office.
دارالحکومه *A*. = **حکومت نشین**
دارالخلافه o *A*. 1) Capital 2) *OS*. Caliphate's seat.
دارالرضاعه *A*. = شیرخوارگاه
دارالسلطنه o *A*. Capital. Royal seat.
دارالشفاء *A*. = **بیمارستان**
دارالشوری *A*. Consultative assembly.
دارالضرب o *A*. = **ضرابخانه**
دارالعجزه *A*. Asylum for invalids.
دارالعلم *A*. Scientific institute.
دارالفنون *A*. 1) Polytechnic institution. 2) = دانشگاه
دارالمجانین *A*. = **تیمارستان**
دارالمساکین *A*. Almshouse; poorhouse.
دارالمعلمین *A*. = **دانش سرا**
دارالوکاله *A*. Lawyer's office.
دارایی Wealth. Assets. — وزارت د. Finance Ministry.
داربست Trellis. Scaffolding.
دارخین *or* **دارخینی** Cinnamon.
داردانل *Fr*. Dardanelles.
دار فلفل Long pepper.
دارکوب Woodpecker.
دارموش White arsenic.
دارندگی Wealth(iness).
دارنده [دارندگان] Possessor. Holder: دارندهٔ گواهی نامه
دارو Medicine; drug.
داروخانه Pharmacy; drugstore.
دارو دسته Gang.

داروساز Druggist; chemist.
داروسازی Pharmacy ; pharmaceutics.
داروشناسی Pharmacology.
داروغه o = 1) کلانتر 2) فرماندار
داروگر o = داروساز [all.
دارو ندار All (one has); one's
دارویی Pharmaceutical.
دارین o A. [D. of دار] The two houses ; i. e. the two worlds.
دازه o Perch; hen-roost.
داس Scythe; sickle. – داس مغز Falx.
داستان Story; tale. Fable.
داستان‌سرا Story-teller.
داسغاله Pruning-knife. Sickle.
داسه Awn.
داسی Falcate ; falciform.
داش × [Per. cont. of داداش] Rowdy; rough; rogue; also, loafer.
داشبورد E. Dashboard.
داشتن [دار] To have. F. To call for : این مژده سور دارد ‖ ندارد He hasn't got; he does not have [U. S.]. – *Notes*. 1) The imp. of داشتن in modern colloquial Persian is داشته باش 2) The present tense of داشتن is دارم not میدارم which is reserved for cases when داشتن occurs in compounds. 3) دارم – دارید etc. before the present, and داشتم – داشتید etc. before the past indicate progressive forms in colloquial Persian. Thus دارم کار میکنم means 'I am working', and داشتم غذا میخوردم means 'I was eating'.
داشته [P. P. of داشتن]
داعی A. Motive; cause. (The) one who prays (for you); i. e. I. Missionary o [دُعاة].
داعیه A. Motive. Desire. Claim.
داغ 1) n. Brand. Scar. F. (Effect of) bereavement. Remorse. – داغ فتیله‌ای Moxa. – داغ نخود Issue-pea. – د. زدن To brand or cauterize. 2) a. Hot. Cf. گرم ‖ د. دیدن To be bereaved (of a relative). – د. شدن To grow hot. – د. کردن To make h.; heat. To cauterize or brand.
داغان Shattered. – د. شدن To be shattered; go to smithereens. – د. کردن To shatter.
داغ‌آهن Cauterizing-iron.
داغدار 1) = داغدیده 2) Branded.
داغدیده Bereaved. See داغ
دافع A. Repulsive. Counteracting ; curing. Expelling. [Fem. دافعه]. – دافع رطوبت Waterproof; impermeable. – قوهٔ دافعه Repellent force.
دال Eagle [عقاب].
دالّ A. [With بر] Suggestive or expressive of. Denoting.
دالان Long passage-way or

entrance-hall. *L*. Vestibule.
دالبر Festoon. Scallop.
دالگوش Lop-eared.
دالیهٔ سودا *a. p.* Clematis.
دام Net. Trap; snare. — بدام انداختن To catch in a net. To trap. *F*. To allure.
دام Domesticated animals.
دام *A*. May... last.
داماد Bridegroom. Son-in-law.— د. کردن To take a wife for.
دامان = **دامن**
دام پرور Animal husbandman.
دام پروری Animal husbandry.
دام پزشک Veterinary surgeon.
دام پزشکی Veterinary.
دامن Lap. Skirt. — یك د هیزم A lapful of firewood. — دامن زیر Petticoat.— د. درکشیدن* To turn aside; keep aloof.— آتش را دامن زدن To add fuel to the fire; fan the fire. *F*. To aggravate the condition. — دست بدامن کسی شدن To appeal to a person for help.— د. کشیدن * To walk mincingly or arrogantly. — دامن (همت) بر کمر زدن To be prepared to serve willingly or to embark on something with a high ambition.
دامن گیر Holding fast. Involving. Chronic. — دامن گیر اوهم شد He, too, was involved in it.
دامنه Slope; skirt. *F*. Extent; scope. — دامنهٔ کوه The foot of a mountain.
دامنه دار Extensive; comprehensive.
دان 1) = دانه 2) Bait; decoy.
دان [Imp. of **دانستن**]
دانا *a*. Learned or wise. —*n*. L. or w. person [pl. دانایان].
دانایی Learning. Sagacity..
دان پاشی Decoying; allurement. — د. کردن To use decoying means. Also, to throw a sprat to catch a herring.
دان دان Granulated; granular. Grained; pebbled. Frosty. — د. کردن To granulate. To pebble or grain, as leather.
دانستگی Knowingness. Knowledge. Intention [only in بدانستگی intentionally].
دانستن [دان] To know. — لازم میدانم I deem it necessary. — آنچه من میدانم From what I k. — من چه میدانم How (on earth) do I k.? —*Note*. The p. form دانستم is rare in colloquial Persian, and should be replaced by میدانستم "I knew"].
دانستنی (Something) worth knowing.
دانسته *a*. Known. —*ad*. Intentionally. [P. P. of دانستن]
دانش Knowledge. Learning.
دانش آموز Pupil. Student.
دانشپایه Class; grade.
دانش پرور Patron of learning.

دانش پژوه * Seeking, seeker of, knowledge.
دانشجو Student. Scholar.
دانش سرا Teachers' college.
دانشکده Faculty; college.
دانشگاه University.
دانشمند *a*. Learned; scholarly. Wise —*n*. L. person; scholar. Sage. *Cf*. دانا
دانش نامه University degree; licence.
دانشور o = **دانشمند**
دانشیار Lecturer.
دانگ Share. Sixth part (of a real state or of the entire pitch of the human voice).
دانگی Shared or paid by all.— سور دانگی Dutch treat.
دانمارک *Fr*. Denmark.
دانمارکی *a*. Danish —*n*. Dane.
دانه Grain. Seed. *Med*. Granulation; small eruption; papula. — د. کردن To break up, as a pomegranate. To get the pips off. — د. بستن To go (*or* run) to seed. دانۀ تسبیح Rosary bead. — دانۀ فلفل Peppercorn. *Note*. دانه is also used after a numeral to mean 'piece.' Ex. سه د. مداد 3 pencils.
دانه آور Gran(ul)iferous.
دانه خوار Gallinaceous.
دانه دانه *a*. Granulated; granular. —*ad*. One by one.

داو Move [in games]. Stake.— د. کردن To increase the stake. To move.
داود *A-Heb*. David.
داودی *A. P*. David's. — گل د. Chrysanthemum; Christmas daisy; ox-eye d.
داور Arbitrator. Judge. Referee.
داوری Arbitration. Judgment.— د. کردن To judge.
داوطلب *P. A*. Candidate. Volunteer. — د. شدن To volunteer; offer voluntarily.
داوطلبانه *P. A*. Voluntarily.
داهیه o *A*. Calamity. Accident.
دایر *A*. In working order (*or* commission).; commissioned.— زمین د. Utilized land. — د. بر Concerning. — د. براینکه To the effect that. — د. کردن To commission; put in w. order. To establish; set up. To set afoot.
دایره *A*. [دوائر] Circle. Section. Tambourine [with or without metal discs.]. — دایرۀ اعتدال Equinoctial line or colure. — دایرۀ انقلاب Solstitial c. — دایرۀ زنگی Timbrel; tambourine. — دایرۀ طول *or* دایرۀ نصف‌النهار Meridian.
دائرةالمعارف *A*. Encyclopedia.
دایره کش *A. P*. = **پرگار**
دایگی Nursing. *See* دایه
دائم *A*. *or* **دائمی** Continual. Permanent. Perpetual.

دائماً *A.* Constantly ; continually; always [همیشه].
دائم غلط *a. p.* (*Med.*) Remittent : تب د.
داین *or* **دائن** *A.* = **بستانکار**
دایه [دایگان] (Wet) nurse. – دایۀ مهربانتر از مادر Nurse kinder to child than its mother; one who is more catholic than the Pope .
دایی *or* **دائی** (Maternal) uncle.
دُبّ o *A.* = خرس Bear. – دب اصغر The Lesser B. ; Ursa Minor. – دب اکبر The Greater B. ; U. Major.
دَباغ *A.* Tanner.
دباغ خانه *A. P.* Tannery.
دباغی *A. P.* Tanning; tannery. – د. کردن To tan.
دبدبه *A.* Pomp.
دُبر o *A.* = 1) عقب 2) مقعد
دَبران *A.* The Aldebaran.
دَبستان *A. P.* Primary school.
دِبش Astringent.
دبور o *A.* West wind.
دبه *A.* Flask: دبۀ باروت powder flask (*or* horn). – د. درآوردن *or* د. کردن To go back on one's bargain; ask for more.
دبیت Satin or percaline (used for lining).
دبیر Secretary. Clerk. Teacher (of a middle school).
دبیرخانه Secretariat(e)
دبیرستان Middle school
دبیری Secretaryship.
دبیقی *A. Kind of damask.*
دِج o [*Of earth*] Solid; hard.
دُجاجه *A.* (*Astr.*) Cygnus ; Swan.
دَجال *A.* The Impostor: ep. of the Islamic Antichrist. – خردجال The monstrous ass on which the Impostor rides before the advent of the Twelfth Imam.
دَجله *A.* Tigris.
دُچار *or* **دوچار** Involved. Encountering ; meeting. – دچارِ Affected with. Involved in. – با چیزی د. شدن *or* دچارِ چیزی شدن To encounter s. t. ; be involved in it. – د کردن To involve.
دخالت *A.* Interference. – د. کردن To interfere. To intervene. To mix; mingle.
دُخانی *A.* [Fem. دخانیه] Used for smoking o. – مواد دخانیه Tobacco products.
دُخانیات *A.* Tobacco products [pl. of دخانیه]. – د. استعمال کردن To smoke. – ادارۀ انحصار دخانیات The Tobacco Monopoly Department.
دخت • = **دختر**
دختر Daughter. Girl. Maid. – دختر خواهر & دختر برادر Niece. – دخترعمو – دختر دایی – دختر خاله – دختر عمه Cousin.
دخترانه Fit for girls. – لباس د.

Girls' dress.
دختر بچه (Little) girl.
دختر خوانده Adopted daughter.
دخترک Little girl.
دَخل A. Earning; drawing. Connection. — بمن دخلی ندارد It does not concern me. — کتاب شما دخلی بکتاب من ندارد Your book cannot be compared to mine. — دخل پول Till; money-drawer. — د. کردن To earn. — دخل و خرج Income and expenditure ; receipts and expenses. — دخلِ کسیرا آوردن × To serve one out; settle his hash ; also, ruin him.
دخمه Tower of silence. Crypt. *By e.* Tomb.
دُخول A. Entrance. — حق د. & اجازهٔ د. Admittance.
دَخیل A. Interfering. Important ; material. Seeking quarter. [*Of words*] Of foreign origin ; introduced.
دَد Wild beasts.
دَدَر [*Childish word*] Out. — د. رفتن × To gad about.
دَدَری × Gadabout.
دده *T.* Negress. Nurse.
دَر Door. Lid. *F.* Topic. — در (بزرگ) خانه Gate. — درِ خانه‌اش همیشه باز است He is open-doored ; i. e. hospitable. — د. زدن To knock at a door. — درش را بگذار × Shut up. Stop it. Hold your tongue (*or* jaw). — دری به تخته خورد + It was a coincidence ; an unexpected occasion offered.
دَر 1) *prep.* In : درشهر ‖ Within: در دو روز ‖ At: در ساعت سه ‖ On: در هر دو طرف ‖ Within the limits of : در صلاحیت اوست ‖ By : یك متر در دو متر ‖ Per : دو در صد two per cent. 2) *ad.* Out : از اطاق درآمد He came out of the room. ‖ In *. Away: درگذشتن To pass away. — این بآن در Tit for tat.
دُرّ A. Pearl [مروارید]. [Collective for دُرّه -pl. درر *dorar*]. — دُرّ کوهی Quartz.
دُراج A. Francolin.
دراز Long. — د. شدن To stretch out. To lie down. — د. کردن To lengthen. To prolong. To s. — د. کشیدن To lie down.
درازا Length. — از درازا Lengthwise. — بدرازا کشیدن To be protracted; become lengthy.
دراز دستی * Aggression. Opression. Violence. *Cf.* دست‌درازی
درازگوش Long-eared : ep. of the ass or of the hare.
دراز نفس *P. A.* Prolix.
دراز نفسی Prolixity.
درازی Length.
در افتادن To engage; grapple.
دَرّاکه *A.* [For قوهٔ د.] Perceptive faculty.
درام *Fr.* Drama ; play.

درآمد Income; revenue. Prelude. — مالیات بردرآمد Income-tax. — د. کردن + To begin. To prelude.

درآمدن To come out. To c. in *. To be earned. To submit of solution. To shine or rise. To shoot; spring. To turn; prove; fall out: خوب درآمد ‖ To work out. — بگریه د. To melt into tears.

درآمیختن = * آمیختن

درانیدن To (cause to) tear or rend.

درآوردن To bring out; take o. To produce. To earn or make: پول د. ‖ To clear (from the Customs). To put forth (leaves, etc.). To work out; solve. To compose+.

درآویختن = * آویختن

دراویش [A. pl. of درویش]

درایت *A.* Intelligence.

دَرب *A.* Gate. *Cf.* در *P. word.*

دَربار Court: وزیر دربار

درباری Courtier.

دَربان Doorkeeper; gatekeeper; porter.

دربانی Porter's office.

دَربچه Shutter. Trap-door.

دَربدر Vagrant; errant; homeless.

دربدری Vagrancy; homelessness.

دَربردن 1) To save: جان ب. ‖ جان سالم بدربردن To save one's hide. 2) To acquire or learn (cleverly). — از راه د. To pervert; lead astray.

دربست Whole. — دربست کرایه کردن To hire (*or* charter) whole. — خانهٔ د. A house in its entirety; a w. house.

دربسته Closed (tightly)

دربند Narrow pass. Canyon. Bolt for a door.

درپوش Bung. Cap.

دَرج *A.* Insertion. — د. کردن To insert.

دُرج *A.* Jewel-box; casket.

درجات *S. u.* درجه

دَرجه *A.* [درجات] Degree; honours. Grade. Rank. — قطارِ درجهٔ اول First-class train. — د. به د. By degrees; gradually. — تا این د. To this extent. — صد درجه‌ای Centigrade *a.* — بدرجات By d. By far. — درجه‌دادن [*With* به] To confer honours on. To promote to a higher rank or degree. — درجهٔ گرما Temperature. — درجهٔ تبِ کسیرا گرفتن To take a person's temperature.

درجه‌بندی *A. P.* Classification. Gradation. — د. کردن To grade. To classify. To rate.

درجه‌دار *A. P.* 1) *a.* Graded. Adjustable. 2) [*Opposed to* پایه دار] Non-graded. —*n.* Non-commissioned officer.

درِخانه باز Hospitable.

دِرَخت Tree.

درختستان Plantation; grove.

دُرد *or* دُردی • Dregs ; lees.

دَردار Lidded. Having a gate.

دردگین • Painful.

دردمند • Ill. Afflicted.

دردناك Painful. Diseased. Sad.

درد نشان Calmative; anodyne.

دِردو × (*-do*) Pert.

دُردی کش • Drinking the very dregs of wine.

درر [Pl. of دُر]

در رسیدن • To overtake. To happen.

در رفتگی Dislocation. Luxation. Leakage. Strain. [*In a stocking*] Ladder.

در رفتن + To run away. To be dislocated. [*Of a gun*] To go off. – از زیرِ . . . د. To dodge or shirk. . . . – حسابش از دستم در رفت I lost count of it. – ازدهنش در رفت He let the cat out of the bag.

در رفته Dislocated.

دررو Outlet. *F*. Effect; result. – کوچهٔ بیدر رو Blind alley.

دَرز *A*. Seam. Suture. Crevice. – د. گرفتن To seam up. *F* × To take in; cut short. – د. کردن × To leak.

درزی(گر) Tailor [خیاط].

دَرس *A*. [دُروس] Lesson. – (به) د. دادن To teach. – د. خواندن To study. – د. گرفتن To take lessons. *F*. To take an example or lesson. – درسش را خوب بلد است + He under-

درخش ○ Lightning. Lustre.

درخشان Bright. *F*. Brilliant.

درخشانیدن ○ To cause to shine.

درخشندگی Luminosity.

درخشنده Shining; luminous.

درخشیدن [درخش] To shine.

درخواست Request. Application. Requisition. – د. کردن از To request ; ask. – درخواستِ شغل کردن To apply for a job.

درخورد *or* درخور Suitable [مناسب]. – در خور من نیست It is not suitable for me.

دَرد Pain ; ache. Ailment. Trouble. Affliction. – درد چشم = چشم دَرد ‖ درد دل کردن To tell out one's grievances ; open out one's heart ; unbosom oneself. – درد زه Pangs of childbirth. – دردسر 1) = سردرد 2) Inconvenience ; trouble. – (به) دردسر دادن To inconvenience; put to trouble. – (به) د. آمدن To become painful; ache. – (به) د. آوردن To give pain to; hurt. – د. کشیدن *or* د. بزدن To suffer p. To travail. – د. کردن To ache, be painful. – سرم د. میکند I have a headache. – همه جای بدنم د. میکند I ache all over. – دست شما درد نکند Thank you for the trouble; also, small thanks to you. – بدرد خوردن To be of use ; serve some purpose.

stands his business very well ; he is in the know.— کتاب درسی Text-book.

دُرست *a*. Correct ; right. Upright ; honest. Proper. Sound. Whole : يك سيب د. a whole apple. —*ad*. Correctly. Properly. Just. [Also درسته+]. Whole: آنرا درست غورت داد ‖ د. کردن To rectify; correct. To adjust. To tidy. To do (one's hair). To make or prepare. To fix. To mend. To forge ; fabricate.

درست پیمان True to one's promise.

درستکار Honest.

درستکارانه Honestly.

درستکاری Honesty; uprightness.

درستی Honesty. Integrity. Truth. Correctness.

درس خوانده *A. P.* Educated.

دُرشت Large. Coarse. Harsh.— د. کردن To magnify.

درشت بافت [Also **درشت باف**] Coarsely woven.

درشت خو(ی) Harsh-tempered.

درشت نی Tibia.

درشتی Coarseness. Largeness. Violence. — د. کردن To act or speak harshly.

درشکه *R.* Carriage. — درشکهٔ بچگانه Pram; perambulator.— درشکهٔ برفی Sledge ; sleigh.

درشکه چی *R. T.* Carriage-driver; cabman.

درشکه‌رو *R. P.* Drive.

درصد Per cent : پنج د.

درفش Awl. Banner *.

درفشیدن o (1 = درخشیدن 2) لرزیدن

دَرقی *A.* Thyroid.— بزرگ شدگی غدهٔ د. Goitre [now usu. گواتر the French word].

دَرک *A.* Perception.— د. کردن = دریافتن To perceive ; understand.

دَرَك *A.* = دوزخ

درکردن+ To fire (off); touch-off. To sift. To deduct. — از راه د. To pervert ; lead astray [also از راه در بردن].

درکشیدن To retract. To swindle out. To pump out. — پول از کسی د. To swindle money out of s. o.

درکه o *A.* [درکات] Abyss. Hell.

درگاه Doorway. [Also کف د.] Sill ; threshold. *Met.* Palace ; court ; audience. — بدرگاه خدا To, before, or in the sight of, Cod.

درگذشت Death.

درگذشتن To pass away. — از چیزی د. To overlook, or connive at, s. t.

درگرفتن To be kindled or spread. To break out, as a war. To overtake *. To overspread *.

درگیر شدن o To break out ; begin. *Cf.* درگرفتن

دِرَم o [*f. G. origin*] *Certain*

unit of weight. Drachm(a).
دَرمان Remedy; cure. *Cf*. چاره.
‖ د. کردن To remedy or c.
درمان پذیر Remediable; curable.
درماندگی Distress. Insolvency.
درماندن To be distressed.
درمانده Helpless. Overpowered. Stuck up. Insolvent.
درمان شناسی Therapeutics.
درمانگاه Clinic.
درمان ناپذیر Irremediable.
درمنه Wormseed; santonica [usu. درمنهٔ ترکی]. — تخم د. Semen contra. — جوهر درمنه Santonin.
دُرنا *T*. Crane (*bird*).
درندگان [Pl. of درنده].
درندگی Fierceness.
درنده [درندگان] Fierce or rapacious (animal).
درنده خو(ی) Of a fierce or brutal nature; fierce.
درنده خویی Fierce nature. Brutality.
درنگ Delay. Hesitation; pause. — د. کردن To delay. To hesitate or p.
درنگیدن ° 1) = درنگ کردن 2) To tinkle or clink; also, tick, as a clock.
درنوردیدن • To fold or roll [up.
درنوشتن • 1) = در نور دیدن 2) To obliterate; set aside.
درو (*derow*) Reaping. — موسم د. Harvest. — درو عرضی *Mil*. Enfilade. — د. کردن To reap.
دَروازه Gate [*See* درب]. Goal.
دروازه‌بان Gate-keeper.
دُرود • Greeting. Praise. — بر کسی د. فرستادن To praise, or send greetings to, s. o.
درودگر Carpenter.
درودگری Carpentry.
دُروس *A*. [Pl. of درس] Lessons. — مدیر دروس Registrar.
دُروغ Falsehood; lie. [*Used as an a*.] False; untrue. — د. درآمدن To prove to be false. To contradict itself. — د. درآوردن To give the lie to; belie. — د. گفتن To lie; tell a lie. — بدروغ Falsely.
دروغ پرداز One who supports a liar. *S. a*. دروغگو
دروغگو *n*. Liar. —*a*. Mendacious. — د. درآمدن To turn out a liar; contradict oneself.
دروغگویی Telling lies.
دروغی *a*. False. Sham. Spurious. —*ad*. + Falsely.
دروگر Reaper.
دَرون • Inside; interior. *F*. Heart; mind.
درونج [often درونج عقربی] Doronicus.
درون رو(ی) Endogenous.
درون ریز Endocrine. [tion.
درون سوز Internal-combus-
درون شامه (دل) Endocardium.
درونی • Inner; internal.
درویدن • [درو] = درو کردن

درویش *n*. Dervish; mendicant. [A. pl. دراویش] —*a*. Poor.

درویش صفت *P. A*. Humble and sociable; hail fellow well met; also, easy-going. *OS*. Possessing the qualities of a dervish.

درویشی Life as a dervish; mendicity. — د. کردن To act or live as a d.; be humble and sociable.

دَرّه Valley. — پل‌دره‌ای Viaduct.

دُرّه *A*. Single pearl. [Pl. دُرَر; collective دُرّ].

دَرهم Confused; mixed up. Interlaced. Intricate. — د. آمیختن To mix together. — د. افتادن To get mixed up. To fall to blows. — د. بافتن To interweave. — د. پیچیدن To wind or twist together. To interlace. — د. شدن • To get angry. To frown. — د. شکستن To break up. — جبین د. کشیدن • To knit the brow. — د. گیر کردن To become entangled or snarled. To mesh.

دِرهم *A-G*. Drachma.

دَرهم‌برهم Higgledy-piggledy; confused. — د. کردن To put in complete disorder. To muddle.

دَری Ancient Persian dialect.

دَریا Sea. — از راه د. By sea. — دریای پر جزیره Archipelago. — دریای روم Mediterranean Sea. — دریای علم Mine of information. — دریای محیط The Ocean. — دریای نیل • The Nile River.

دریابان Vice-admiral.

دریاچه Lake.

دریادار Rear-admiral.

دریاسالار Admiral.

دَریافت Receipt. Perception. — د. کردن To receive; collect.

دریافتن [دریاب] To perceive; understand. To find out.

دریافتی (Amount) received.

دریاکنار Sea-shore.

دریانورد Navigator.

دریانوردی Navigation.

دریایی Marine; maritime. — نیروی د. Navy.

دَریچه Trap-door; hatch. Shutter. Valve [now usu. سوپاپ the French word]. — دریچهٔ نای Epiglottis.

دریدگی Rent. *F*. Impudicity. — دریدگی دهان Rictus.

دَریدن [در] To rend or tear. To devour. To be torn.

دریده [P. P. of دریدن] Rent; torn. *F*. Impudent. [*Of the eyes*] Glaring.

دریغ *n*. Sparing. Refusal. Regret. — د. داشتن از To refuse; withhold from. — د. کردن To w. To spare. — **افسوس** خوردن = د. خوردن

دریغ & دریغا • Alas! Oh!.

دری‌وری + Nonsense. Gossip. — د. گفتن To talk nonsense; tattle.

گدایی = دریوزه
دُزد Thief. دزد دریایی — Pirate.
دزدانه or + دزدکی *ad.* Stealthily. —*a.* Surreptitious. Thievish.
دزد بازار + Disorderly place where every one steals or embezzles.
دزد ریگ Quicksand.
دزدگاه Place infested with thieves.
دزدی Theft; robbery. — د. کردن To commit theft; steal.
دزدیدن [دزد] To steal. — بچه د. To kidnap a child.
دزدیده [P. P. of دزدیدن] *a.* Stolen. Surreptitious. —*ad.* • Surreptitiously.
دِژ Fortress; fort; castle.
دژبان Mititary policeman. *OS.* Keeper of a fortress.
دژبانی [For اداره د.] Military Police Department.
دژپیه Ganglion; also, gland.
دژخیم ○ Executioner.
دژکوب ○ Battering-ram.
افسرده - مست - خشمگین = دژم
دسامبر *Fr.* December.
دسائس [Pl. of دسیسه]
دَست Hand. Arm. *F.* Skill. Authority. Suit: یك د. لباس ‖ Set: سه د. صندلی ‖ Suite (of rooms). Pack (of cards). Connections [*commercial term*]. — دست آخر In the end. Finally. — دستِ بالا At most. — د. بالا کردن To prepare for work. To make preparations (for marriage). — د. به یقه or د بگریبان At close quarters; hand to h. — دست پشت سر ندارد He is born on a bus. — دست کم At least. — دست کمی از . . . ندارد It is nothing short of . . . — د. از جان شستن To despair. — د. انداختن To pull the legs of. — د. بدست رساندن To pass on (from hand to h.) — د. بدست رفتن To change hands. — دست به آب رساندن To ease nature (and purify oneself with water). — د. بدست کردن To procrastinate; dilly-dally; gain time. — د. برداشتن To desist. — د. بسر کردن To put off: get rid of. — د. دادن To shake hands. To afford an opportunity. To take place. — د. خوردن To be touched. To be tampered with. — د. درازکردن To reach out the hand. To beg. — د. زدن To touch. To clap. To set one's hand (to); embark (on). To set (to). — د. کردن To wear on the h. or on the fingers [orig. در دست کردن]. To put or thrust one's h. (in a thing). — دست کسیرا از پشت بستن To make rings round a person. — دست کسیرا گرفتن To give s. o. aid or relief. — د. کشیدن از To leave

off; stop. To desist from. To abandon. — د. نگاه داشتن To hold; forbear. — د. یافتن * To find an opportunity. To acquire skill. — د. یکی کردن To unite; collude. *See* دست‌یکی ‖ از دست دادن To lose ; miss; let slip ; give away ; also, forfeit. — از دست رفتن To be lost or missed. To perish. — از دستش بر نمی‌آید He is not in a position (to do it). — بدست آمدن To come to hand ; be obtained. — آنرا روی‌دست میبرند It sells like hot cakes. — بدست آوردن To obtain. — براش د. گرفتند + They started mocking (*or* flouting) him. — دست و بالش بسته است He is hard up for money. He is tied down. — دستم نمیرسد I find no leisure (to do that). I am not tall enough (to reach that). I have no access (to it). — در دستِ In the course of ; in the process of. — در دست تهیه است It is in preparation. — دست بدست سپرده است One good turn deserves another. — دست خر کوتاه! Hands off! Don't meddle with it. — دستش خوب است He has a lucky touch.

دست ابزار Hand-tool.

دست ارّه *or* **دسترّه** Handsaw.

دستار * = 1) دستمال 2) عمامه

دستاس Hand-mill.

دست‌افشار Hand-pressed.

دست افشانی * Dancing.

دست‌آموز Pet; tame; cade.

دستان * = **داستان**

دست انداز Handrail. Puddle.

دست اندازی Encroachment. Laying hands.

دست اندرکار + Initiated into business. Involved. Exercising influence (in a specified sphere). In practice ; keeping one's hand in s. t.

دستاویز Document. Pretext.

دست باز Liberal. Open-handed.

دست بافت [also دست باف] Hand-woven ; hand-knitted.

دست بدهن + Who lives from hand to mouth.

دستبرد Larceny. Embezzlement. *Mil.* Sneak raid. — بچیزی د. زدن To embezzle s. t.

دستِ برقضا + *P. A.* It happened that ; by chance.

دست بسینه With arms folded (on the breast); cap in hand.

دست بکار *a.* Embarked (on a business). — د. شدن To start (on a) b. To get busy. — دست بکارِ . . . شدن To embark on. . .

دست بیخه *or* **دست بگریبان** At close quarters. Man for m.

دستبند Bracelet. Handcuff.

دستبوس Kissing a superior's hand. *F.* In one's presence

and ready to serve him.
دستبوسی Kissing of hands.
دست پاچگی Hastiness. Excitement. Embarrassment.
دست پاچه Hasty. Excited. Embarrassed. — د. کردن To make excited. To abash. — د. نشوید Don't get excited ; keep cold; k. your hair on.
دست پخت *OS*. Hand-cooked. *F*. Tenderly brought up. — دست پخت کیست ؟ Who has cooked it ?
دست پرورده Pet.
دست پناه Hand-guard.
دستجات Classes. Groups. Numbers. *Cf. the s.* دسته
دست چپ Left-handed.
دست چین Hand-picked ; selected. — د. کردن To hand-pick or select.
دستخط *P. A.* Handwriting. Manuscript.
دستخطی *P. A.* Hand-written ; manuscript.
دست خورده Tampered with. Touched. Violated.
دستخوش Exposed ; subject. — دستخوش اغراض او شدم I fell a victim to his private motives.
دستدانی + Cubby-hole (used) [for storage).
دست درازی Aggression. Violence. *Cf.* دراز دستی
دست دوز Hand-sewn.
دسترس Accessible ; within reach ; available.
دسترسی Access. Resort. Ability.
دسترنج Product of one's làbour.
دست ساز *or* دست ساخت ○ Hand-[made.
دست شکسته Unskilled. Shiftless.
دست شویی Wash-basin. Wash-hand-stand. Lavatory.
دست فروش Pedlar ; hawker.
دست فروشی Pedlary; hawking.
دستک Pad used as a rough day-book. Clapping of hands ○. Prop. Staff. — دستك مساحی Levelling-staff. — د. و دنبك د. زدن To clap ○. — + Details ; enlargement. Difficulties. Monkey business.
دستکاری Minor repairs. Finishing touch. Stroke.— د. کردن To do minor r. (in). To give a finish to.
دستکش Glove(s). [For boxing] Boxing-glove; muffler; mitt.
دستگاه Apparatus. Plant ; machinery. Mechanism. Installation. Organization. Scheme. [In a building] Flat. System: دستگاه تنفس ‖ *F*. Pomp . Power; ability.— دستگاه بافندگی Weaving-loom. — دستگاه بیسیم Wireless set. — سه د. عمارت Three buildings.
دستگیر Arrested. Captured. (One) who gives relief to others *. — د. شدن To be

arrested or captured. To be grasped or understood.— د. کردن To arrest; apprehend; To capture; take prisoner. — مطلب دستگیرش شد He grasped the matter.

دستگیره (Door) handle.

دستگیری Help; aid. Arrest; capture. — ازکسی د. کردن To help s. o.; give him a relief.

دستلاف Handsel; luckpenny.

دَستمال Handkerchief. — دستمال ِ سفره Napkin. — دو دستماله رقصیدن To run with the hare and hunt with the hounds.

دستمالی (Rough) handling. Palpation. — د. کردن To rub with the hand; handle roughly.

دستمزد Wage(s). *Cf.* اجرت & مزد

دستنبو *Variety of small fragrant melon.* [instrument.

دست‌نشانده Satellite. (Mere)

دست و پا + Struggle. Shift; resource. — د. زدن To struggle with twitching limbs; fling one's limbs about; flop. To flounce. — د. کردن To use one's resources; shift.

دست و دل باز Open-hearted. Open-handed.

دَستور Instruction(s); directions. Order. Prescription. — دستور ِ زبان دستور Grammar. — دستور جلسه O. of the day; agenda.— د. دادن To instruct; give instructions (to). To order. To prescribe; advise. — از دستور خارج شدن To lie on the table. — از دستور خارج کردن To lay on the table.

دُستور ○ *A-P*. Minister [وزیر]. Instruction. Rule. Law. *Cf. the pl.* دساتیر

دستورالعمل *A.* Directions. Prescription; recipe.

دستوَرز Handicraftsman.

دستورزی Handicraft.

دستوری Grammatical. Inspired.

دَسته Handle. Party. Faction. Group. [*Of a sword*] Hilt.— *Mil.* Platoon; also, squad. *M.* 1) Starting-handle. 2) Lever. — دستهٔ قلم Penholder.— دستهٔ هاون Pestle. — دستهٔ کاغذ Quire. — یك د. کلید A bunch of keys. — یك د. ماهی A shoal (*or* school) of fish.

دسته بندی Faction. Classification. — د. کردن To classify. To form factions.

دسته جلو Bridle; ribbons.

دسته جمعی *P. A. a.* Collective. Communal. — بمباران د. Mass bombing. *—ad.* All together; in company. Collectively.

دسته‌کوك *a.* Stem-wound. — ساعت د. Stem-winder.

دسته ٔگل Bunch of flowers; bouquet.

دستی *a.* Handmade. Manual. Artificial. Hand-operated. — صنعت د. Manual art; handicraft. *–ad*+. On purpose.– امضای د. Sign manual.– کیف د. Handbag. *See* کیف

دستیار (Technical) assistant ; aid. Accomplice.

دستیاری Assistance.Complicity.

دست یافت * Opportunity. Success. Victory.

دست یکی United.

دِسر *Fr*. Dessert; sweet ; pudding ; after.

داسغاله = دسقاله

دَسیسه *A*. [دسائس] Intrigue ; plot. – د. کردن To intrigue.

دسیسه کار *A. P*. Intriguer ; intrigant.

دسیمتر *Fr*. Decimetre.

دُشبل Gland [غده].

دَشت Plain. Field. First money earned on a business day. Handsel . – د. کردن + To receive (money) for the first time. *By e*. To start selling s. t.

دشتبان Field watchman.

دشتی Pastoral. Wild.

دشوار = o دشخوار

تشک = دشک چه - دشک etc.

دُشمن Enemy. – د. داشتن * To hate : بدگویی را دشمن بدارید

دشمن‌کام *or* دشمن‌شاد * Suffering from a plight such as is wished by one's enemy.

دشمنی Enmity.

دُشنام Insult ; bad language ; abuse. – د. دادن To a. or insult.

دِشنه Short straight poniard ; whinger.

دُشوار Difficult; hard [سخت].

دشوارگیر * Impregnable.

دشواری Difficulty. Hardship.

دُعا *A*. [ادعیه] Prayer. Blessing. Benediction . – د. کردن To pray. To bless. – د. خواندن To p. – دعای سفره Blessing.– ادعیهٔ خالصانه Sincere wishes.

دعا خوان *A. P*. (One) who prays (for others).

دعاگو *A. P*. (One) who prays for another [only in such phrases as د. هستم I (am quite well and) pray for you. – به دعاگویی مشغولم *Same as* دعاگو هستم]

دعا نویس *A. P*. Writer of amulets and benedictions.

دعاة [Pl. of داعی]

دعاوی [Pl. of دعوی]

دَعوا [*f. A.* دعوی] Quarrel. Lawsuit.– د. کردن To quarrel. To go to law ; litigate. [With به] To tell off ; speak angrily to. – میان د. نرخ طی کردن To fish in troubled waters.

دَعوَت *A*. Invitation.– د. کردن To invite; call; summon. – د. داشتن To be invited. – دعوت حق را اجابت کردن To pay the debt of nature ; go the way of all flesh.

دعوت نامه *A. P.* Invitation card.

دَعوی *A.* [دعاوی] Claim. — د. کردن To claim. [Pronounced *da'va*] = دعوا *q. v.*

دَغا * *n.* Deceit(ful person). —*a.* Deceitful. Base.

دغا باز Deceitful (person).

دغا بازی Fraudulousness.

دغدغان Nettle-tree.

دَغدغه *A.* Apprehension. Disturbance. Tickling sensation o. — دغدغهٔ خاطر Mental disturbance.

دَغل *n.* Fraud. Adulteration. —*a.* Fraudulent. Base.

دغل باز etc. = **دغا باز** etc.

دغلی = **دغل** *n.* ‖ د. کردن To cheat. To falsify.

دف * *A.* Tambourine [دایره].

دفاتر [A. pl. of دفتر]

دفاع *A.* Defence.— ازکسی د. کردن To defend s. o.

دفاعی *A.* Defensive.

دفائن [Pl. of دفینه]

دَفتر [A. pl. دَفاتر] Book ; account-book. Blank-book ; note-book. [For اطاق د.] Office. — دفتر باطله Rough day-book. — دفتر جیبی *or* دفتر بغلی — Pocket-(note) book. — دفتر روزنامه *or* دفتر یومیه Day-book or journal. — دفتر کل Ledger.— دفتر مشق Copy-book. — دردفتر واردِ دفتر کردن *or* وارد کردن To enter in a book. To register.— ازدفتر خارج کردن To write off.

دفترچه Blank-book; note-book.— دفترچه چك Cheque - book. — دفترچه انفرادی Regimental-sheet ; company s.

دفترخانه Notary public's office.

دفتردار Book-keeper.

دفترداری Book-keeping.

دفتری Clerical. — کار دفتری C. or office work.

دفتریار Notary public's assistant.

دفتین Weaver's comb.

دفرا [In a ship] Fender.

دَفع *A.* Repelling ; repulse. Warding off ; parrying. — د. کردن To repel. To parry; ward off. To pass off. To fight. To discharge.

دفعات [Pl. of دفعه]

دفع الوقت *A.* Procrastination.— د. کردن To procrastinate. To gain time ; temporize.

دَفعه *A.* [دفعات] Time [بار]. — یك د. Once. — دودفعه Twice. — سه د. Thrice; three times. — دفعهٔ دیگر Next time. Again. — چندین د. Many times. — بدفعات In instalments.

دَفعةً *A.* (*-atan*) All at once. In a lump sum.

دفن *A.* Burial. — د. کردن To bury.

دفینه *A.* [دفائن] Buried treasure.

Cf. گنج & گنجینه

دَقّ *A.* (*Med.*) Percussion. — تختهٔ دق Pleximeter. — چکش دق Plexor.

دِق *A.* Marasmus. — تب دق Hectic fever. — دق کردن To die from hectic fever. To d. of grief. — دق دل را خالی کردن *S. u.* دل

دَق‌الباب کردن *A. P.* To knock at a door.

دقائق [Pl. of دقیقه]

دِقت *A.* Accuracy. Precision. Subtility. Minuteness. Abstruseness — د. کردن To be careful ; take care. — بدقت Carefully.

دقیانوس *A-Lat.* Decius (*a Roman emperor*) — ازعهدِ د. From immemorial times.

دَقیق *A.* Minute; subtle. Punctual ; exact. *Cf. the tem.* دقیقه

دقیقه *A.* [دقائق] Minute. Minute point. Knack * o.

دقیقه شمار *A. P.* Minute-hand.

دکاکین [Pl. of دکان]

دکان *A.* [دکاکین] Shop.

دکاندار *A. P.* Shopkeeper.

دکانداری *A. P.* Shopkeeping. Showmanship.

دکتر *Fr.* Doctor. Physician. — آقای دکتر بلور Dr. Bolour.

دکترا *Fr.* Doctorate.

دکتری *Fr. P.* Medical profession.

دکر *Fr.* (*dekor*) Scenery ; setting; also, stage-effects.

دکرساز *Fr. P.* Stage-designer ; scene-painter.

دَك کردن × To put off; get rid of.

دکلته *Fr.* Low-necked ; décolleté.

دُکمه *T.* Button. *Bot.* 1) Tuber ; 2) stigma; 3) gemma. — دکمهٔ یخه Collar stud. — دکمهٔ چیزیرا انداختن To button s. t. — دکمه چیزیرا بازکردن To unbutton s. t.

دکمه‌ای *T. P.* Button-like o. — کلم د. Brussels sprouts. — گل د. Immortelle; also; bachelor's button.

دکمه‌دار *T. P.* Tuberous. [*Of a pen-nib*] Having a rounded, flaring point. — شمشیر د. Foil.

دك ودهن × Head and mouth. — دك ودهن کسیرا خرد کردن To beat one black and blue.

دکه * *A.* Stone-bench. Shop.

دِگر * [*Cont. of* دیگر]

دك و پوز × Chops. *S. a.* جربزه

دگردیس Metamorphic.

دگرگون Changed. Metamorphosed. — د. کردن To change in form. — ارث د. Mutation.

دگل Mast. — سه دگله Three-masted.

دِل Heart. Stomach +. *F.* Mind. Courage. Patience. Middle. — دل باختن To lose one's heart. — دل بدریا زدن To take a leap in the dark; run the hazard. — دل کسیرا بدست آوردن To humour a person; gratfiy him. — دل بستن به To depend on; let one's heart be won by. — دستت را بگذار روی دلت You need not worry; you may rest assured. — دق دل خودرا خالی کردن To give v. to one's anger or other feelings; get a thing off one's chest. — + دست بدلم نزن Leave me to my sorrows; don't put your finger in my sore. — دل دادن To hearten; encourage. To give one's heart, as to a sweetheart. To pay close attention. — دل کسیرا شکستن To disappoint s. o. — دل ازچیزی کندن To abandon s. t. — دلم بهم میخورد I feel sick. — دلم تمام شد I am (*or* was) out of patience. — دلم تنگ است I am heavy-hearted or depressed. I am homesick. — دلم باز شد I felt light-hearted. I was relieved of my depression. — دلش بهم برآمد * He was moved with compassion. — دلِ خوشی از او ندارم I haven't had a good experience with him. — دلم حال آمد It did my heart good. — دلش خوش است که He flatters himself that. — دلم میخواهد بروم I like (*or* please) to go. I feel like going. — دلم رحم آمد I felt sorry; I was moved with compassion. — دلم برایش میسوزد I pity him. — دلم گرفته است I am depressed. — بدلم افتاد که It occurred to me to; I had a presentiment that. — دلم ریخت پائین I almost had a fit; I was shocked. — با دل و جان With all one's heart. — بدل گرفتن To take to h.; take offence at.

دلار *Fr.-E.* Dollar.

دلارام * *n.* Sweetheart. —*a.* [Lovely.

دل آزار Heart-rending; vexatious.

دل آزرده Offended. Afflicted.

دل آشوب *a.* Nauseating. —*n.* Chaste-tree; *Agnus castus*.

دلافروز * Cheering (the heart); mirthful.

دل افکار * Heartsore; heart-sick.

دلاک *A.* [*In a Turkish bath*] Rubber or masseur; also, barber.

دلاکی *A. P.* Rubber's or barber's craft. *See* دلاك

دلال *A.* Broker; middleman. — دلال معاملات ملکی Real estate broker; land-agent. — دلال خانه House-agent.

دلالت *A.* Guidance. — د. کردن To lead; direct. [With بر] To denote; express.

دلاله *A.* [*Orig. fem. of* دلال]

Procuress. — چرخ د. Idle-wheel.
دلالی *A. P.* Brokerage ; broking. — د. کردن To be a broker.
دلاور Valiant ; brave.
دلاوری Valour ; bravery.
دلاویز * Pleasant ; attractive.
دلائل [A pl. of دلیل]
دل باخته Enamoured of love.
دلباز Bright and cheerful : said of a house.
دل بخواه + Arbitrary ; optional ; done at pleasure.
دل بدریا زن + Adventuresome.
دلبر * *a.* Charming. Coquettish. —*n.* Sweetheart.
دلبری Charm. Coquettishness.
دلبستگی Attachment ; affection. Interest.
دلبسته Attached. Interested.
دلبند * Darling. Attractive.
دلپذیر * Agreeable ; pleasant.
دلپسند Desirable. Agreeable.
دل پیچه Gripes ; tenesmus.
دلتنگ Cheerless. Homesick. — د. شدن To feel homesick. To be annoyed ; take offence.
دلتنگی Homesickness ; nostalgia. Annoyance. Loneliness. — د. برای میهن کردن To pine for home ; feel homesick.
دلجو * Affable. Agreeable.
دلجویی Affability. Encouragement by soft words. Conciliation. — د. کردن از To speak affably to.

دلچسب Desirable. Fit ; meet.
دلخراش * Heart-rending ; harrowing ; grating.
دلخسته * Heart-sore.
دلخواه *n.* Desire. Pleasure ; will. —*a.* Desired. — بدلخواه At pleasure.
دلخور Offended. Annoyed. Indignant. — د. شدن از To be annoyed by ; take offence at. — د. کردن To annoy ; offend.
دلخوری Annoyance ; indignation. Grievance.
دلخوش Happy ; contented.
دل خوش کنك × Object (*or* subject) of self-flattery.
دلخوشی Cheer ; (object of) delight. Satisfaction. — د. بخود دادن To flatter oneself.
دلخون * Heart sore.
دلداده Enamoured of love. — دوعاشق د. Two plighted lovers.
دلدار * Sweetheart.
دلداری Consolation. — د. دادن (به) To console or comfort.
دلدرد Stomachache. [dally.
دلدل کردن To waver ; dilly-
دلربا * Charming. *S. a.* دلکش ‖ سنگ د. Aventurine.
دلربایی * = دلبری
دلریش * Wounded at heart.
دل زنده Enjoying a green old age; hearty and hale [زنده دل]. Genial. Lively.
دل = دل سخت

دلسرد Discouraged; dispirited. — د. شدن To be d. or discouraged. — د. کردن To discourage.

دلسردی Discouragement.

دلسوخته • Bereaved.

دلسوز Compassionate; sympathetic.

دلسوزی Pity; sympathy. — برای کسی د. کردن To feel pity for s. o.

دلشاد Happy.

دلشده • = دلداده [hearted.

دلشکسته Disappointed; broken-

دل ضعفه +P. A. Fainting from hunger; gnawing sensation in the stomach. — خورش د. Barmecide feast.

دلفریب • Charming; attractive.

دَلق A. Coarse woollen garment. *S. a. under* حلق

دلقک A.P. Harlequin; clown; buffoon.

دلکش • Fascinating; winsome; attractive.

دلکو E. Delco : trade-mark. [In a motor car] Distributor.

دلگران Heavy-hearted. Displeased.

دلگرم Confident. Sanguine. — د.کردن To assure. To encourage. [ment.

دلگرمی Assurance. Encourage-

دلگشا Pleasant. Exhilarant.

دلخور = دلگیر [raged.

دل مرده Low-spirited. Discou-

دَلمه Gelatine or jelly. — دلمهٔ غضروفی Chondroma. — د. شدن To coagulate.

دُلمه *T.* Dish of cabbage or other vegetables stuffed with meat-balls and rice.

دلنشین Agreeable. Easily accepted.

دلجو(ئی) = • دلنواز(ی)

دلو *A.* (*dalv*) Bucket. *Astr.* Aquarius. *Old name of* بهمن

دل واپس Anxious; uneasy; worried; concerned.

دل واپسی Anxiety.

دله Marten. *F.* Mean glutton. Pig(gish person).

دله دُزد Pilferer; petty thief.

دِلهره + Apprehension; anxiety. Worry.

دلیجان [f. Fr.] Stage-coach.

دلیر Brave. Intrepid.

دلیرانه Bravely.

دلیری Bravery. Intrepidity.

دَلیل *A.* [دلائل & ادله] Reason. Proof. Guide o [راهنما]. — دلیل غیبت او The reason for his absence. — دلیل اینکه The r. why. — د. ندارد که There is no reason why. — بچه د. Why? For what r.? — بدلیلِ اینکه Because; for the r. that. — د. آوردن To give reasons (for s. t.); adduce an argument.

دَم Breath. Choke-damp. Edge. Bellows. *F.* Instant; moment. — دمِ در At the door.— دم صبح (At) dawn. Early (in the) morning. — دم دست Near at hand. — دم برآوردن * To breathe out. To speak. — دم (فرو) بستن * To hold one's breath.— دم زدن * To breathe. To s. — دم از . . . میزند He talks frequently of, or pretends to advocate. . . ; he boasts of...— دم‌فرو بردن * To inspire . — دم کردن To allow (tea) to draw. To steam or stew. — دم‌کشیدن [*Of tea*] To d. — بادم و دستگاه + With great pomp; in state. — از دم One with the other; without selection.

دَم ○ *A.* = خون

دُم Tail. — دم گاو Yellow mullen.— دمش‌را روی کولش گذاشت. He put his tail between his legs. — پا روی دم کسی گذاشتن To twist a person's tail; pester him.

دمادم * Incessant(ly).

دمار *A.* Perdition.— د. ازروزگارِ کسی برآوردن To take complete vengeance on s. o.

دُم اسبی Like a horse's tail. Equisetaceous.— گیس د. Pony tail.

دماغ *A.* Brain [مخ]. Nose [بینی]. *F.* Mood. Talent. — دماغ صغیر Cerebellum. — دماغ کبیر Cerebrum. — دماغش چاق است + He is well-to-do. — دماغ کسی را سوزاندن To discourage s. o. To snub s. o. — دماغم سوخت I was discouraged. — دماغ خودرا پاك کردن یا گرفتن To blow one's nose.— موی د. Intrusive person; bore.

دماغه Cape. [*Of a door*] Parting bead. [*Of an anvil*] Horn. [*Of a ship*] Nose or prow. *Cf.* سینه

دماغی *A.* Cerebral. Nasal. — کار دماغی Brain work.

دَمان * Blowing. Terrible. — پیل د. Furious elephant.

دمبدم *or* دم‌بدم Every moment; incessantly.

دُم بریده 1) = دُم گل 2) *F.* × Sly; cunning.

دمبلیچه Fat at sheep's coccyx [also دنبلیچه]. Parson's nose.

دَمخور *a.* Congenial. —*n.* C. friend; close associate.

دَم پایی Slippers [also سرپایی].

دَم پخت *Kind of rice dish.*

دُم جنبانک Wagtail.

دَمدار Suffocating; stifling.

دُم دراز Long-tailed.

دمِ دستی + Designated for everyday use: سرویس د. e. set.

دمدمه ○ Redoubt.

دَمدمی Fickle; irresolute.

دمدمی مزاج *P. A.* = دمدمی

دمده [*f. Fr.* démodé] Out of fashion; not fashionable.—

فرومایگی & پستی = .A دنائت

دُنبال Rear. Trail. Tail. — در دنبالِ or دنبالِ Behind . After. — از دنبال (From) b. — د.کردن To follow ; pursue.

دنبالچه Coccyx.

دنباله Trail. Tail. *Astr*. Coma. *F*. Continuation. Cue (of speech).

دنباله‌دار Protracted ; continued. — ستارهٔ د. Comet.

تنبک = دنبک

دُنبلان Lamb's-fry. Truffle.

دُنبه Fat (tail).

دِنج + Cosy ; snug ; tight.

دَندان Tooth. — د. درآوردن To teethe ; cut one's teeth. — د. روی جگر گذاشتن To grin and bear it. — د. زدن To bite with the teeth. — دندان کسیرا شمردن To find the length of one's foot.

o دندان شوی or دندان پاك کن = مسواك

دندان درد Toothache.

دندان ساز Dentist. — جراح د. Dental surgeon. [surgery.

دندان سازی Dentistry; dental

دندان‌شکن Knockdown : جواب د.

دندان قروچه + Gnashing of the teeth. — د.کردن To gnash the teeth.

دندان‌گرد + Covetous. Stingy.

دندان‌گیر + Suitable. Lucrative.

دندان‌موشی Notched. Denticulate.

د. شدن To go out of fashion.

دَمر + Prostrate ; prone.

دُمریز × Off the reel ; uninterruptedly.

دمساز • *n*. Confidant. —*a*. Intimate.

دمشق *A*. Damascus.

دُم فاخته‌ای Dove-tailed.

دَم‌قیچی *P.T.* Snippings; scraps.

دمکرات or دموکرات *Fr*. Democrat.

دُم کل Docktailed ; bobtail.

دُم کلفت × Wealthy and influential. *OS*. Thick-tailed. — د. ها The bigwigs or magnates.

دُمگاه Parson's nose ; rump.

دمگیر Stifling. Sultry.

دُمل Boil ; abscess.

o دُم لابه Fawning.

دَم نگار Pneumograph.

دموکراسی *Fr*. Democracy.

دموی *A*. = خونی Sanguine.

دمه Vapour [بخار].

دمی *Kind of rice dish*.

دمیدن [دَمْ] To blow. To breathe upon (*or* into). To inflate. To appear , as the dawn. To sprout.

دمیر *T*. [For سنگ د.] Lapstone.

دمیر آغاجی *T*. Ironwood.

دمیزون *Fr*. Light overcoat ; spring suitings.

دمینو *Fr*. Domino.

دندانه Tooth ; cog. Jag.
دندانه‌دار Toothed. Serrate. Jagged. — چرخ د. Cogwheel.
دندانی o Dental. Dentate.
دَنده Rib. Gear. — دنده خلاص Neutral gear. — دنده خود کار Automatic shift g. — دنده‌عقب Reverse g. — دنده کمك Auxiliary gear. [*Of the differential*] Double speed rear axle. — دنده یك یا دو First or second g. — بادنده یك رفتن To drive in first g. — با دنده خلاص رفتن To go in neutral. To coast ; freewheel. — دنده عقب زدن To (put into) reverse ; back. — د. عوض کردن To change g. — یك د. اش کم است She is a button short. — د. اش نرم شود That serves him right.
دنده‌ای Costal. Ribbed. — ارگ د. Barrel-organ.
دَنگ Flail ; pestle ; heavy pounder worked by the feet. Fulcrum ; pivot. [In timepieces] Lever escapement. — چرخ د. Escapement wheel.
دنگادنگ o Equipoised.
دنگ و فنگ × Pomp and circumstance.
دنی *A.* = پست Mean.
دُنیا *A.* World. — به د. آمدن To be born. — ازدنیا رفتن To pass away; go to one's last home. — یك د. + Lots of ; tons of. — یك د. با هم فرق دارند They are poles apart. [mammonish.
دنیا پرست *A. P.* Worldly ;
دنیادار *A. P.* Worldly.
دنیا داری *A. P.* Worldliness. Address ; tact.
دنیا دیده *A. P.* = جهاندیده
دنیوی *A.* Mundane. Secular.
دنیی * *A.* (*don-yi:*) = دنیا
دو (*do*) Two. — هر دو Both. — هر دوی ایشان B. of them ; they both.
دو (*dow*) Running; run. Race.
دو ,, [Imp. of دویدن].
دَوا *A.* Medicine. Remedy. *Cf. the pl.* ادویه ‖ د. زدن To apply a medicine to. — د. کردن To cure or treat.
دواب *A.* Beasts of burden ; livestock. [Pl. of دابه o]
دوات *A.* Inkpot ; inkwell.
دوآتشه Overheated; superheated : بخار دوآتشه ‖ Double-distilled. Browned, as bread. *F.* Full-blooded ; hearty.
دوات‌گر *A. P.* = 1) چلنگر 2) میناگر
دواج o = لحاف
دواخانه *A. P.* = داروخانه
دوار *A.* (*davar*) = سرگیجه
دوّار *A.* (*davvar*)*a.* Revolving. —*n.* Capstan.
دَوازده Twelve.
دوازده ضلعی *P. A.* Dodecagon.
دوازده وجهی *P. A.* Dodecahedral.
دوازدهم Twelfth.

دوازدهمی The twelfth (one).
دوازدهمین The twelfth.
دوازدهه Duodenum.
دواساز *A. P.* = داروساز
دوافروش *A. P.* = داروفروش
دوال Thong. Belt. Deceit.
دوال باز Deceitful (person).
دوال پا Bugbear. Octopus.
دواله Treemoss.
دوالی *A.* [Pl. of داليه] Varix.— دوالی صفن Varicocele.
دَوام *A.* Durability; strength.— د. ندارد It does not wear (*or* last) long.
دوان 1) *Imp. of* دوانيدن 2) Running [usu. دوان دوان].
دوانيدن To run *vt.*; cause to r.
دواوين [Pl. of ديوان]
دوائر *A.* Departments. Sections. *Cf. the s.* دائره
دوباره Again ; once more.
دوبال Two-winged. — دو بالان The Diptera.
دو باله Two-winged ; dipterous. — هواپيماى د. Biplane.
دوبدو Two by t. Tête-à-tête.
دو برابر Double ; twice as much; t. as many.— اودوبرابر من سال دارد He is twice as old as I am.
دوبرگه Bifoliate. Bipetalous.
دوبله كردن *Fr. P.* To dub, as a film .
دوبه *T.* Barge.
دوبهمزن Mischief-maker.
دو بهمزنی Mischief-making.
دوبيتی *P. A.* Distich; couplet.
دوبينی Diplopia.
دوپا *n.* Biped. —*a.* Two-footed.
دوپايه Two-legged. Bicuspid.
دوپشته 1) = دو ترکه 2) In two rows.
دوپوسته Two-shelled. Twice-shelled. Of double thickness, as a wall.
دوپهلو Equivocal(ly).
دوپيكر The Gemini.
دوتا [*With the stress on the 1st. syl.*] Two [not before a noun] : من يك نامه دارم او دوتا
دوتا [*With the stress on the 2nd. syl.*] Doubled ; bent.
دوتخمه + Mongrel ; of two breeds.
دوترکه Double : د. سوار شدن
دونه [Of a bicycle] With two horizontal frame tubes.
دوجانبه *P. A.* Reciprocal(ly).
دوجنسه *P. A.* 1) Bisexual. 2) = دوتخمه
دوجمله‌ای *P. A.* Binomial.
دوجين [f. Fr. & E.] Dozen.
دوچار etc. *S. u.* دچار
دوچرخه Bicycle.
دوچرخه سوار Cyclist.
دوچرخه سواری Cycling.
دوچشمه Binocular. — دوربين د. Opera-glass; field-glass.
دوچندان Twofold ; double.

As much again.
دوحرفی *P. A.* Biliteral.
دوحه ○ • *A.* Large tree.
دوخال Double aces; ambsace.
دوخت Sewing. Stitch.— د. گرفتن To sew up; s. together.
دوختن [دوز] To sew. To stitch together. — چشم به چیزی د. To fix one's eyes on s. t.
دوخته [P. P. of دوختن] Sewn. Ready-made.
دوخته فروش Dealer in ready-made clothes.
دود Smoke.— د. از کله‌ام بلند شد I was astounded.—دوددوم Necessaries.— د. دادن *vt.* To smoke. To fum(igat)e. To steam. —*vi.* To emit smoke. — د. شدن To pass off (*or* end) in s. To be dissipated. — د. کردن To (give off) s. To turn to s. — دود چراغ خوردن To burn the midnight oil.
دود ○ *A.* = کرم Worm(s).
دو درجه‌ای *P. A.* Having two classes or degrees.— انتخابات د. Election in two instances.
دو دست Bimanous. — دو دستان The Bimana.
دو دستی Ceremoniously. Willingly. With both hands.
دودکش Chimney. Smoke-stack.
دودل Double-minded; wavering.
دو دلی Irresolution; indecision.
دودم Double-edged. Ancipital.
دودمان • Family. Lineage.
دوده Soot; lamp-black; smut.
دودی Smoky; smoke-coloured. Smoked: عینك د. ‖ ماهی د. S. herring; bloat h.
دودی *A.* Worm-like. — حرکت د. Peristaltic motion; peristalsis.
دودید Bifocal: عینك د.
دور (*du:r*) Far; remote. *F.* Improbable. Inconsistent. Removed.—د. ازمیهن Away from one's home. — از مطلب د. افتادن To digress; deviate from the main subject. — د. انداختن To throw away; discard. — د. شدن To go outo f sight. To keep out of the way. — د. کردن To k. at a distance. To banish. — از دور From the distance.
دور *A.* (*dowr*) [ادوار] Cycle; revolution. Turn. Perimeter. Period; time. Epoch. Orbit. Generation. — دورِ (A)round. — د. زدن To go (*or* turn) round. To turn about. To make a U turn. To make a detour. *F.* To contre. —د. برداشتن + To rev up; gather speed. —دورِ چیزی را گرفتن To surround s. t. — دور گردون • Vicissitudes of time.— دورِ بر *or* دوروبر Entourage; environment. — یك د. + Once.
دورادور From a distance.

دَوَران *A.* = گردش Circulation. Rotation. Vertigo.— د. کردن To circulate. To turn round.
دوران *A.* (*dow-*) Period. Era.
دور اندیش Provident ; far-sighted : شخص د.
دور اندیشی Providence ; fore-sight.
دو راهی Siding ; side-track. *F.* Parting of the ways ; dilemma. — سوزن د. (Railway) switch or point.
دوربر *A. P.* Pericarp.
دوربین *a.* Far-sighted. Presbyopic. —*n.* Field-glass; opera-glass. — دوربین دوچشمه Binoculars; field-glass.— دوربین صحرائی Field - glass. — دوربین عکاسی Camera.— دوربین فیلم برداری Cine-camera.— دوربین نجومی Telescope.— دوربین یك چشمه Spy-glass.
دوربینی Far-sightedness.
دور تادور *A. P.* All round.
دور دست Remote. Outlying.
دور رس Far-reaching.
دور شمار *A. P.* Revolution-counter. *See* دور (*dowr*)
دو رگ *or* دو رگه Mongrel ; half-breed ; cross-bred. Hybrid.
دورگرد *A. P.* Rotating; revolving. — چراغ د. Inspection lamp. [دورو
دو رنگ Bicolour. *S. a. under*
دو رویی = دو رنگی
دورنما Landscape. [*In a photograph*) Background.— دورنمای مسلسل Panorama.
دورنما ساز Landscape painter.
دو رو Double-faced. [*Of fabrics*] Reversible. *F.* Hypocritical; decetiful [often دورو و دو رنگ].
دورویی *n.* Double-dealing.
دوره *A. n.* Period. Cycle. Course. Generation. Set : سه د. فرهنگ ‖ Review ; recapitulation. Perimeter; contour. [*Of a wheel*] ,Rim. دورهٔ تصدی Tenure of office.— دورهٔ زندگی Career. —*a.* Going round; given in turn: د. مهمانی ‖ *ad.* Round : دوره چای دادند They served tea round. — د. کردن To review. *F.* To pull the legs of. To bay.
دوره‌گرد *A. P.* Hawker; pedlar. [pedlary.
دوره‌گردی *A. P.* Hawking ;
دوری Remoteness ; distance. Abstention. Keeping aloof. Separation. — د. کردن از To keep aloof from. To avoid.
دوری *A.* (*dow-*) Periodic(al). *Math.* Recurring.
دوری *A.P.* Paten; patina. Dish.
دوز [Imp. of دوختن]
دوز *T.* Game with marbles and rectangles drawn on paper or on the ground. — دوزوکلك چیدن + To form a complot. To intrigue.
دو زبانه Bilingual.

دو زبانی 1) = دو زبانه 2) Self-contradiction.
دوزخ * Hell [جهنم].
دوزخی (A.) a. Infernal. —n. Dweller of hell.
دوزندگی Sewing ; tailoring.
دوزنده Sewer; tailor.
دو زنه Having two wives. — مرد دو زنه Bigamist.
دوزوکلك S. u. 2 nd. دوز
دوزیست Amphibious.— دوزیستان The Amphibia.
دو ساق یکی P. A. Isoceles.
دوساله 1) Two-year-old من د. بودم ‖ بچهٔ د. I was 2 years old. 2) Biennial.
دوست Friend. — د. داشتن To love; like.— د. تر داشتن To l. more; prefer.— باکسی د. شدن To make friends with s. o.
دوستانه ad. In a friendly manner; amicably. —a. Friendly; amicable.
دوستدار a. Loving. —n. (Your) loving friend.
دوست داشتنی Lovely; nice.
دوست کام Who is as one's friends wish one to be ; fortunate.
دوستگانی Large vessel for wine [also دوستکامی+].
دوستی Friendship. — با کسی د. کردن To contract f. , or make friends, with s. o.
دوسر Two-headed ; bicephalous. — تبر دوسر Double axe. — جو دوسر *or simply* دوسر Oats. — ماهیچهٔ د. Biceps (muscle).
دو سره 1) = دوسر 2) F. Mutual; reciprocal. — بلیط د. Return ticket.— خدمت د. Two-session service. — د. کرایه کردن To pay r. fare for. To freight out and home.
دوش Shoulder. — بدوش گرفتن To carry on one's shoulder or back. — د. بدوش Shoulder to s. — د. بدوش هم کار کردن To collaborate or cooperate.
دوش * = دیشب
دوش [Imp. of دوشیدن].
دوش Fr. Shower-bath — د. گرفتن To take a shower.
دوشا = شیرده Milch.
دوشاب Syrup of grapes.
دوشاخ 1) n. M. Radius rod. 2) a. Two-horned; bicornous.
دوشاخه n. (Contact) plug. Fork. Pitchfork. Tuning-fork. —a. Bifurcate. [*Of a stethoscope*] Binaural.
دوشانیدن To (cause to) milk.
دو ش تبره P. T. Knapsack.
دوشش Double six.
دوش فنگ Shoulder arms !
دوشک = تشک
دوشنبه Monday.
دوشیدن [دوش] To milk, as a cow. To express, as milk. F. To bleed.
دوشیزگان [Pl. of دوشیزه]

دوشیزگی Maidenhood.
دوشیزه [دوشیزگان] Maiden ; girl. Miss : د. پریوش حیم
دوشین * Last night's.
دوشینه = 1) دوشین 2) دیشب
دویست = دوصد
دوطرفه P. A. Bilateral. Mutual ; reciprocal. Double-breasted.
دوطرفی P. A. = دوطرفه
دوغ Churned sour milk; also, yogurt diluted with water.– دوغ و دوشاب پیشش یکیست He can't tell eggs from money.
دوغاب Grout.– د. زدن To grout.
دوفتیله‌ای P. A. Duplex.
دوفلزی P. A. Bimetallism.
دوقاب P. T. Double-cased.
دوقبضه (P. A.) S. u. سفارشی
دو قلی or دو قولو P. T. Twin(s).
دوقولی P. A. Self-contradiction.
دوک Spindle.
دوک Fr. Duke.
دوکپه Bivalve.
دو کرانه *Math.* The two extremes. *Cf.* دومیان
دوکره Having two beakirons. سندان د. Bickern.
دوک مانند Fusiform.
دوکمانه ○ [*Of an arrow*] Rebounding.
دوک نشین Fr. P. Dukedom.
دوکور Double aces; ambsace.
دوکوهانه Two-humped. – شتر دوکوهانه Two-humped or Bactrian camel.
دوگانه *a.* The two. Binary. –*n.* ○ Prayer based on two genuflexions.
دول + (*du:l*) Bucket.
دول (*doval*) [Pl. of دولت]
دولا Of double thickness ; two-ply [also دولایی]. Two-fold.– د. شدن To stoop – د. کردن To d. To bend. To fold d.
دولاب Diabetes.
دولابچه Locker; wall-cupboard.
دولابی ○ Diabetic. Labyrinthine.
دولا پهنا + Of double width.
دولا چنگ *Mus.* Semiquaver.
دولا دولا + In a stooping posture.
دولایی +Of double thickness.
دولپه Dicotyledonous.
دولت A. Wealth. Government ; State [pl. دول *doval*]. – دول بزرگ The great powers. – از دولت سر . . . Thanks to . . .
دولت سرا A. P. Palace. [*In p. c.*] Your house.
دولتمند A. P. Rich; wealthy.
دولتمندی A. P. Wealth(iness).
دولتی A. Governmental ; belonging to the State.– دوائر د. Government departments.
دولچه Small bucket. *See* دول
دولختی Mitral : دریچهٔ د.
دولو Deuce; two.
دولول Double-barrelled.

دو‌ّم Second. — د. آنکه In the second place; secondly.
دوم باره Twice-done. Second. Double.
دو محوره *P. A.* Biaxial.
دو مو(ی) Whose beard is turning grey.
دومی The second (one).— د ندارد + It it s. to none.
دومیان *Math.* The two means. *Cf.* دوکرانه
دومین The second.
دون *A.* Base [پست]. Inferior.— دونِ مقام اوست It is below his position.
دون پرور • *A. P.* Fostering mean people : دنیای د.
دوندگی Chasing ; running about; drive; (special) effort. — د. کردن To run about.
دونده *a.* Running. —*n.* Runner.
دونفره *P. A.* Double ; intended for two persons : رختخواب د. Double bed.
دون همت (*a. p.*) Of low ambition; low-minded.
دونی *A. P.* = دنائت & پستی
دونیم Cut in two halves. — د. کردن To cut in two h.; bisect. — مثل اینکه یك سیب را دو نیم کرده‌اند They are as like as two peas in a pod.
دو هفتگی Biweekly ; fortnightly.
دویدن [دو dow] To run. — چشم و دلش میدود He is greedy.
دویست Two-hundred.
دویستم Two-hundredth.
دوخال & دوکور = ○ دویک
دوئیت + Discord. Enmity. [Comb. of دو and the A. ending یت]
دَه Ten.
دِه or دیه (*dey*h) Village.
دِه [Imp. of دادن]
دهاء ○ *A.* = زیرکی - دانایی
دهات [A. pl. of ده] Villages.
دهاتی *A. P.* = روستایی
دهاقین [Pl. of دهقان]
دَهان or دهن 1) Mouth. 2) دهن بدی خواندن ‖ دهانه = To strike the wrong note. — دستش به دهنش میرسد He can make both ends meet. — دم دهنت را بگذار × Hold your clack or jaw. — • خاکم بدهن May God forgive me for the blasphemy.
. دهان اژدر Ringent ; with ringent corolla : said of certain species of petunia.
دهان بند Muzzle.
ده انگشتی Done by all the ten fingers. — اسلوب د. The touch method [in typing].
دهانه Opening Mouth. Nozzle. [*Of a volcano*] Crater. *S. a.* دهنه
ده برابر Tenfold.— ده برابرِ Ten times as many (*or* as much) as.
ده چندان Ten times as many (*or* as much). Tenfold.

دهخدا o Headman of a village. *Cf.* کدخدا
دهدار Governor of a rural district.
دهدهی Decimal [اعشاری].
دَهر • *A.* [دُهور] Time. World. Fortune.
دهره Reaping-hook ; sickle.
دهری *A.* Materialist(ic). Atheist or atheistic(al).
ده ساله Ten-year-old.
دهستان Rural district.
دِهِش • = بخشش [ment.
دهشت *A.* Fear [ترس]. Amazement.
دهشت زده *A. P.* Frightened. Amazed.
ده ضلعی *P. A.* = ده گوشه
دهقان [دهاقین] Peasant. Farmer. [Arabicized form of دهگان]
دهقانی *A. P.* Rural or rustic.
دهکده Small village; hamlet.
دَهگان *Arit* . Tens.
دِهگان o *S. n.* دهقان
دهگانه The ten : احکام د. the Ten Commandments.
ده گوشه or ده گوش Decagon.
دُهُل Kettledrum. — د. زدن To beat a kettledrum.
دِهلیز 1) = دالان 2) Auricle (of the heart). 3) Labyrinth (of the ear).
دهم Tenth.
دهمست o = غار Laurel.
دهمین & دهمی The tenth.
دَهن etc. = دهان etc.
دُهن o *A.* = روغن Oil. — دهن مصری Balsam oil.
دهن بین Lacking ideas of one's own. Capricious. Irresolute.
دهن دره Yawning; gaping. — د. کردن To yawn or gape.
دهنده *a.* Who gives. *F.* Charitable. —*n.* Giver.
دهن سوز Very hot. [Used in the phrase آش د. q. v. under آش]. *OS.* Burning the mouth.
دهن کجی Grimace; wry mouth.— د. کردن To grimace ; make grimaces ; m. faces.
دَهنه Bit of a bridle ; rein. Opening. Mouth (of a river). Orifice. — د. کردن To b. *F.* To rein or curb.
دَهنی Played by the mouth.— ساز دهنی Mouth-organ ; harmonica.
دُهنی *A.* = روغنی Oily.
دُهینات *A.* Oily substances. [Pl. of دهنیه fem. of دُهنی *q. v.*].
ده نیم Five per cent (dues).
ده وجهی *P. A.* Decahedron.
دهور [Pl. of دهر]
دهه Period of ten days.
ده هزار Ten-thousand.
ده یك One-tenth. Tithe.
دی (*di:*) 1) Last. 2) = دیروز
دی (*dey*) Tenth month having 30 days. *By e.* Winter.
دیاپازُن *Fr.* Tuning-fork.
دیار • *A.* [Pl. of دار] Region. Territory. Country.

دیافرام *Fr.* [*In a gramophone*] 1) Sound-box; 2) diaphragm.

دیاق *T.* [In machines] Bracket.

دیاکلیون *A.G.* Diachylon [usu. مشمع د.].

دیاگنال *Fr.* Diagonal (cloth).

دیان *A.* (*dayan*) Judge or Rewarder : ep. of God.

دیانت *A.* Piety ; honesty. Religion [دین].

دیبا Fine silk or brocade.

دیباچه Preface. [Orig. dim. of دیبا]

دیپلم *Fr.* Diploma.

دیپلمات *Fr.* Diplomat(ist).

دیپلماسی *Fr.* Diplomacy.

دیپلمه *Fr.* Diploma-holder ; graduate.

دیت (*diat*) *or* **دیه** *A.* Mulct ; bloodmoney.

دیجور • Dark ; moonless.

دید Sight. Vision. — د. زدن To estimate or appraise. — دید و بازدید Interchange of, i. e. paying and repaying, visits.

دیدار (Act of) meeting [ملاقات]. View. Sight. [etc.

دیدار بینی Meeting of friends,

دیداری *a.* Sight : payable at sight : برات د. s. draft.

دیدبان Signal-man. Observer. Watchman.— برج د. = **دیدبانگاه**

دیدبانگاه Watch-tower; control-tower [also برج دیدبان].

دیدبانی Look-out. Observation.

دیدسنج Optometer.

دیدگان [Pl. of دیده]

دیدن [بین] To see. To meet. To visit. *F.* To sustain; incur : زیان د. ‖ To go through : دورهٔ طب را دید ‖ To experience ; suffer.— از کسی د. کردن To pay a visit to, or call on, s. o. — بدیدن من آمد He came to see me. — مشکل می بینم I find it difficult...; I don't think...

دیدنی *n.* (Paying a) visit; call. —*a.* Worth seeing. — از کسی د. کردن To pay a visit to s. o.; call on s. o. — دیدنی ها Attractions.

دیده [P. P. of دیدن] Seen. —*n.* • [Pl. دیدگان] Eye [چشم].

دیده‌ور(ی) Scout(ing.)

دیر (*di:r*) Late.— د. رسیدن *or* د. آمدن To come (*or* be) late.— د. کردن To be l. — وقت د. می گذرد Time hangs heavy. — د. شدن To be (*or* get) l. — دیرم شد I was l. — د. زمانی است • It is a long time since. — د. یا زود Sooner or later.

دیر • *A* (*deyr*) Convent. *F.* 1) = میخانه 2) = جهان

دیر آشنا Slow to become sociable ; unsociable.

دیرباز Long time ago.— از دیرباز Since long.

دیر باور Incredulous.

دیر باوری Incredulity.

دیر پای • Lasting long. Cons-

tant.
دیر دیر *or* دیر بدیر At long intervals ; seldom.
دیر رَس Late : میوهٔ د.
دیرغضب * *P. A.* Slow to wrath.
دیر فرست Deferred : تلگراف د.
دیرک Pole. Mast. Rolling pin.
دیر کرد Delay. — جریمهٔ د. Delayed payment penalty.
دیرگاه ○ * Long time. — تا دیرگاه نشستیم We sat (up) late. *Cf.* دیر وقت
دیرگداز Hard to melt. Refractory.
دیرگشا Hard, as a knot.
دیروز Yesterday.
دیر وَقت *P. A.* Late (hour). Long time.
دیر هضم *P. A.* Hard to digest ; indigestible.
دیریاب * Hard to obtain. Rare.
دیرین * Ancient; old. Inveterate.
دیرین شناس Paleontologist.
دیرین شناسی Paleontology.
دیرینگی ○ Long service.
دیرینه Old. Long. Inveterate.
دیز *Fr.* (*diez*) Sharp. *Mus.*
دیز پرده *T. P.* Hammer-cloth.
دیزل *Fr.* Diesel (engine).
دیزه [*Of a horse*] Dark grey ; black. — خر دیزه A kind of ass having a stripe which extends from the head to the tail - proverbial for endangering its life in order to cause a loss to its owner.

دیزی Small earthen pot ; pipkin.
دیژیتال *Fr.* Digitalis.
دیس *Fr.* Dish.
دیسانتری *Fr.* Dysentery.
دیشب Last night.
دیفتری *Fr.* Diphtheria.
دیفرانسیل *Fr.* Differential gear.
دیکتاتور *Fr.* Dictator.
دیکتاتوری *Fr.* Dictatorship.
دیکتافن *Fr.* Dictaphone.
دیکته *Fr.* Dictation; spelling. — د. کردن To dictate.
دیگ Pot. — دیگ بخار (Steam) boiler.
دیگ پایه Trivet [also دیگدان].
دیگچه Small pot; saucepan.
دیگر 1) *a.* Other; another; else. Next. Hence. — دوسال د. Two years h. 2) *ad.* Any longer. Any more. N. time. — چیز(ی) د. Something else. — اشخاص د. Other people; others. — سال د. N. year. — این جمعه نه ، جمعهٔ د. A week from next Friday. — چند کتاب د. Some more books. — بار دیگر N. time. Again. — یك دفعه د. Once m. — جای د. Elsewhere. — طور دیگر In another manner. Otherwise. — د. آنکه Moreover ; furthermore . — د. ندارم I have no m. of that. — هرگز دیگر Never again.
دیگران [Pl. of دیگر used as a

n.] Others; other people.
دیگر بار * Again; next time.
دیگری The other (one); the second (one). [With the stress on the second syl.] Another. — یکی بعد از دیگری One after another.
دیگ ساز Boiler-maker.
دیگه + = دیگر ‖ د. بهتر So much the better.
دیلاغ Year-old camel. Lanky (person); gaunt.
دیلم Crow-bar.
دیلماج *T.* Interpreter. *Obs.*
دیم *A.* (Crop) produced by dry farming.
دیم‌کاری *A. P.* Dry farming.
دیمهاج ○ = **گاوزبان**
دیمی *A. P.* Cultivated by dry farming. *See* دیم ‖ *F.* Not acquired systematically; immethodical.
دین (*di:n*) *A.* [ادیان] Religion.— علم د. *or* علم‌الادیان ○ Theology.
دین *A* (*deyn*) [دُیون] Debt; amount due [بدهی]
دینار *A-Lat.* Dinar: 1) money of account = one-hundredth of a *rial*; 2) Iraqi monetary unit; 3) denarius.
دینار سنج * *A. P.* Assayer of coins.
دینام *Fr.* Dynamo; generator.
دینامیت *Fr.* Dynamite.
دیندار *A. P.* Religious; pious.
دینداری *A. P.* Piety; religiousness.
دینی *A.* Religious.
دیو Demon. Fiend. Devil.
دیوار Wall. د. کشیدن To wall.— دیوار کوتاه *Met.* Person whose meekness is taken for weakness, and who is wronged for that matter. *Cf. the E.* 'low hedge (which is easily leaped over)'. — از در ودیوار From every direction.
دیوارکوب *a.* Fixed on the wall. —*n.* Anything fixed on a wall: a bracket (light), a sampler, etc.— چراغ د. B. candlestick; sconce.
دیواره Parapet (of a bridge). Rim. *Anat.* Septum. *Z.* Paries.
دیواری Wall-type: صندوق د. ‖ Posted on the wall — آگهی د. Poster; placard. — ساعت د. Clock.
دیوان [A. pl. دَواوین] Poetical works. Court; tribunal. — دیوان عالی کشور Supreme C.; High C. of Cassation.
دیوانگی Insanity; lunacy; madness. — د. کردن To behave madly or foolishly.
دیوانه [دیوانگان] Mad(man); insane (person); lunatic. *L.* Fool(ish). د. شدن To run mad. — د. کردن To drive m. To enrage.— دیوانهٔ عشق Frenzied with love.

ديوانه‌وار Madly. Frantically.
ديوانى Governmental.
دَيوث *A*. Cuckold.
ديون [Pl. **of** دين *deyn*].

ديه (*dieh*) *S*. *u*. ديت
ديه (*dey*h) *or* ده + Village.
ديهيم = 1) تاج 2) تخت

ذ

ذات *A.* Substance ; nature. Person(age); individual [pl. ذَوات]. — ذات‌لایزال The Supreme Being. — ذات‌ملوکانه His Majesty the Shah. — اسم ذ. Concrete noun. — حبّ ذ. Self-love. — فی حدّ ذاته In itself ; intrinsically.

ذاتا *A.* By nature. In essence; in substance.

ذات‌البین *A.* Mutual relationship; friendship o. — اصلاح ذ. Reconciliation of two parties.

ذات‌الجنب *A.* Pleurisy.

ذات‌الریه *A.* Pneumonia.

ذات‌الکرسی *A.* Cassiopeia.

ذات‌الکلیه *A.* Nephritis.

ذاتی *A.* Inherent ; natural.

ذائقه *A.* (Sense of) taste.— برای تغییرذائقه For a change.— بذائقه‌اش خوش نیامد It did not suit his t. ; it did not please him.

ذبائح [Pl. of ذبیحه]

ذَبح *A.* Slaughtering. — ذ. کردن To slaughter ; sacrifice.

ذِبح *A.* Slaughtered animal.

ذبذبه = **دو دلی**

ذَبیح *A.* Sacrificed or slaughtered (animal or person).

ذبیح‌الله (*A.*) *Mas. pr. name.* *OS.* Sacrificed for God.

ذبیحه *A.* [ذبائح] Sacrifice ; sacrificed animal.

ذخائر [Pl. of ذخیره].

ذخیره *A.* [ذخائر] Reserve. Store(s).— ذ. کردن To reserve. To put in store.— افسرذخیره & سرباز ذخیره Reservist.

ذرات [Pl. of ذره]

ذُراح *A.* Cantharis ; Spanish fly. [Pl. ذَراریح Cantharides]. — مشمع ذراریح Fly-blister.

ذَراریح *S. u.* ذراح

ذراع *A.* Cubit.

ذُرّت *A.* Maize; Indian corn; sweet c. — ذرّت بو داده Popped c. — ذرت‌جاروبی Guinea-corn.— آرد ذرت Corn-meal.

ذَرع (*A.*) *Obs. unit of length* =41 inches. — ذ کردن To measure (by the *zar'*).

ذروه • *A.* Pinnacle ; apex.

ذرّه *A.* [ذرات] Minute particle; molecule. Corpuscle. Little bit +.

ذره بین *A. P. n.* Magnifying-glass ; burning-glass. *Cf.* میکروسکوب ‖ —*a.*o Meticulous.

ذره بینی *A. P.* Minute; microscopic. Animalcular.

ذره پرور • *A. P.* Kind to

inferiors. *OS.* Fostering particles.

ذره ذره *a. p.* Bit by bit.

ذریعه ○ *A.* = 1) وسیله 2) بهانه 3) نامه

ذُرّیه *A.* Offspring ; seed.

ذغال etc. = **زغال** etc.

ذَقن * *A.* = **چانه** & **زنخدان**

ذکاء & **ذکاوت** *A.* Sagacity. Wit. Intelligence.

ذکر *A.* (*zakar*) Penis. *Cf. the pl.* ذکور

ذکر *A.* (*zekr*) Mention. Memory. Recital. — ذ. کردن To mention. To remember ; commemorate. To cite. — قابل ذ. Worthy of m.; mentionable.

ذُکور *A.* Males; men or boys. *Cf. the s.* ذکر (*zakar*).

ذکوریت ○ *A.* Masculinity ; virility. *Cf.* رجولیت

ذَکی *A.* = باذکاوت Keen. Intelligent. Sagacious.

ذُلّ *A.* = **ذلت** & **خواری**

ذلاقت ○ *A.* Sharpness (of the tongue). Volubility.

ذلت *A.* 1) Abjectness. 2) + Suffering ; hardship.

ذله + Harassed ; wearied.

ذَلیل *A.* Abject. Weak(ened).— ذ. کردن To humiliate. To weaken or overthrow.

ذَمّ *A.* Vilification ; slander. Blaming. Vice [pl. ذُموم].

ذمائم [pl. of ذمیمه]

ذمه *A.* Obligation. Due. — برائت ذ. Clearance from obligation. Acquittal.

ذمه‌دار *A. P. a.* Having an obligation. —*n.* Responsible person. Obligor. Debtor.

ذِمّی ○ *A.* Who pays tribute.

ذَمیم *A.* = نکوهیده Blameworthy. [Fem. ذمیمه]

ذمیمه ○ *A.* [ذمائم] Blameworthy act. Moral imperfection. [Orig. fem. of ذمیم]

ذَنب ○ *A.* (*zamb*) [ذُنوب] Sin.

ذنب *A.* (*zanab*) = دُم Tail.

ذنب‌الدجاجه *A.* (*Astr.*) Deneb.

ذنبی ○ *A.* Caudal.

ذُنوب [pl. of ذنب]

ذوات *A.* 1) [Pl. of ذات] 2) Those endowed with.

ذوات‌الاوتار *A.* = آلات سیمی Stringed instruments.

ذوات‌الضرب *A.* 1) Instruments of percussion. 2) = ذوات‌الاوتار

ذوات‌النفخ *A.* = آلات بادی Wind instruments.

ذو احتمالین ○ *A.* Susceptible of two probabilities. Equivocal.

ذوالاحترام *A.* = **محترم**

ذوالجلال *A.* Glorious.

ذوالفنون ○ *A.* Master of Arts.

ذوالقافیتین *or* **ذوقافیتین** *A.* (Verse) of double rime.

ذوالقربی ○ *A.* [ذوی‌القربی] = **خویشاوند**

ذوالمنن ○ *A.* = **بخشنده**

ذوائب ○ *A.* Hanging ringlets.

[Pl. of ذوابه]

ذوب *A.* Melting. – ذ. شدن *vi.* & ذ. کردن *vt.* To melt. – کارخانهٔ ذوب فلز Foundry.

ذوجسدین *A.* (*Astr.*) Bicorporeal

ذوجنبتین *A.*. = **دوزیست**

ذوحیاتین *A.* = **دوزیست**

ذوحدین *A.* Having two limits or alternatives; dilemmatic. – برهان قاطع ذ Dilemma.

ذوذنب *A.* = ستاره دنباله‌دار Comet.

ذوزنقه *A.* Trapezium. [*In gymnastics*] Trapeze. – شبه ذ. Trapezoid.

ذوق *A.* Taste; elegance; verve; literary talent. Joy +. – توی ذ. ‖ خوشی کردن = ذ.کردن زدن + To be repulsive. – توی‌ذوق کسی زدن + To snub or discourage s. o.

ذوق زده *A. P.* Overwhelmed with joy.

ذوقی *A. P.* Connected with taste or talent.

ذولقی o *A.* = Lingual.

ذوی‌العقول *A.* Rational beings. – غیر ذ. Irrational b.

ذوی‌القربی [Pl. of ذوالقربی]

ذهاب *A.* = رفتن Going [used only in ایاب و ذهاب].

ذَهب o *A.* = **زر** & **طلا**

ذِهن *A.* [اذهان] Mind. Opinion. – در ذهن سپردن To commit to memory. – حضور ذهن Presence of mind.

ذهنی *A.* Mental. Subjective. – ذ. کردن To fix in the mind.

ذهول o *A.* = **فراموشی**

ذهین o *A.* Having a good memory.

ذیحجه or **ذی‌الحجه** *A.* *Twelfth A. lunar month.*

ذیقعده or **ذی‌القعده** *A.* *Eleventh A. lunar month.*

ذیجاه o *A. P.* Of dignity or rank.

ذیحساب *a. p.* Responsible accountant. Financial controller.

ذیحقّ *A.* Rightful (person). (One) having a just claim.

ذی حیات *a. p.* = زنده Living.

ذیروح *A.* Animate; living. – غیر ذیروح Inanimate.

ذیشأن *A.* Of dignity or rank; dignified.

ذی علاقه *A.* Interested; concerned

ذیفقار *A.* Vertebrate. – غیرِ ذ. Invertebrate.

ذیقیمت *A.* = **گرانبها**

ذیل *A.* [اذیال & ذیول] Appendix. Footnote. Bottom. Trail. *OS.* Skirt. – در ذیل Below; hereunder. – در ذیلِ Under. – بشرح ذ. or ازقرار ذیل As follows. – امضا کنندگان ذ. The undersigned. *See* زیر

ذیلاً *A.* Hereunder.

ذینفس *A.* (*zi:nafas*) Breathing (creature). – ذینفسی آنجا نبود There was not a soul there.

ذینفع *A.* Beneficiary. Interested party.

ر

را *Particle serving as a sign of the (definite) direct object, as in* سیب را خورد He ate *the* apple.

رابطه *A. n.* Liaison. Intermediary. *—a.* Communicating. — فعل ر. Copulative (verb).

رابطه *A.* [روابط] Connection; relation. Tie. — رابطهٔ نامشروع Liaison. — روابط دوستی Friendly relations.

رابع *A.* = چهارم

رابعاً *A.* Fourthly.

راتبه ○ *A.* = حقوق - جیره

راتیانج *A-P.* = راتیانه

راتیانه Rosin; colophony.

راج Holly.

راجع *A.* Returning ○. Referring. — تب ر. Relapsing fever. ‖ ر. به Concerning; regarding; on the subject of.

راجه *H.* Raja(h).

راحت *A.* Rest. Comfort. Ease. [*As an a.*] Comfortable. Convenient. Quiet. In easy circumstances. Feeling at home. — ر. شدن To be relieved. To find comfort. — ر. کردن *vi.* To rest. *—vt.* To relieve. To disburden. To give the *coup de grace* to.

راحت الحلقوم *A.* Turkish delight.

راحت باش *A. P.* (*Mil.*) Rest! در جا راحت باش! Stand easy!

راحت بخش *A. P.* Rest-giving. Soothing.

راحت طلب *a. p.* Comfort-loving (person).

راحتی *A. P.* (*C. E.*) = راحت *n.* Rest. Ease. — صندلی ر. Easy chair. — براحتی Easily. Comfortably.

راد • Liberal. Gentlemanlike. Brave.

رادار *Fr.* Radar.

رادع *A. a.* (*Med.*) Revulsive; derivative. *—n.* Obstacle.

رادمرد ○ Liberal man. Gentleman.

راده *A.* Mark of reference.

رادیاتور *Fr.* Radiator. Cooling-system.

رادیان *Fr.* Radian.

رادیو *Fr.* Radio. — در رادیو On the radio.

راز Secret; mystery. — راز و نیاز Silent prayer for one's needs ○. Amorous talks or complaints.

رازدار 1) *n.* Confidant. 2) *a.* Faithful to a secret.

رازدار Green alder.

رازقی *A*. Arabian jasmine.
رازک Hop(-plant). [water.
رازیانه Fennel. — عرق ر. F.
رأس *A*. [رئوس *or* رؤوس] Head [سر]. Headland; cape [دماغه]. Summit; foremost position. — در رأسِ At the head of; presiding over. — سه ر. گوسفند Three head of sheep.
رأساً *A*. Direct(ly) [مستقیماً]. On one's own initiative.
رأس‌الجدی *A*. Capricorn.
رأس‌السرطان *A*. Cancer.
رأس‌المال *A*. Purchase price; cost p. Stock-in-trade.
راست *a*. Straight. Right. True. —*n*. T. remark; truth. —*ad*. Truly. Straight. — دست ر. بروید Turn to the right. — ر. آمدن To come true; be fulfilled. — ر. کردن To straighten. — مو بر بدن انسان ر. میکند It makes one's flesh creep (*or* one's hair stand on end); it freezes one's blood. — ر. گفتن To tell the truth. — براست ر. R. turn! — نظر براست Eyes right! — راست حسینی Fair and square; aboveboard.
راستا Direction.
راست باز • Candid. Dealing (*or* playing) fairly.
راست بال Orthopteran.
راست ساز Rectifier.
راستگو Truthful (person).
راست گوشه *a*. Rectangular. —*n*. Rectangle.
راستگویی Truthfulness.
راسته *n*. Row. Series of shops. Fillet. *Chess* File. *Bot*. Order. —*a*. Round as a sum.
راستی *n*. Truth. Straightness. Uprightness. —*ad*. • Indeed. By the way. — براستی Truly; honestly.
راسخ *A*. = استوار & پابرجا
راسخت Red antimony.
راسن Elecampane.
راسو Weasel.
راشد *A*. Orthodox.
راشی *A*. Briber. *Cf*. مرتشی
راضی *A*. 1) Satisfied; pleased. — ازمن ر. است He is satisfied or p. with me. 2) Content(ed). 3) Willing. — ر. برفتن W. to go. — ر. بمرگ او نیستم I do not wish him dead. — ر. شدن To consent; agree. To be satisfied or p. — ر. کردن To satisfy; consent. To persuade. To please.
راعی o *A*. [رُعاة] = شبان
راغ • Meadow. Mountain-slope.
راغب *A*. Inclined. Desirous. — بچیزی ر. بودن To be fond of s. t.; have a predilection for it.
رأفت *A*. = مهربانی Kindness.
رافد o *A*. Euphrates [فرات]. — رافدان or **رافدین** Tigris

گوشت ر. Gigot.

ران [Imp. of راندن]

راندمان *Fr.* Efficiency.

راندن [ران] To drive. To sail. To propel. *F.* To expel. – بر زبان ر. * To utter; pronounce.

رانده [P. P. of راندن] Driven. D. away. Expelled. Outcast.

رانده وو *Fr.* Rendezvous; appointment; date.

رانش ० Driving; expulsion. Purging effect.

رانکی Crupper. [driver.

رانندگی Driving : being a

راننده [رانندگان] Driver.

رانی Femural.

راوی *A.* [رُواة] Narrator.

راوید Clary.

راه Way. Road; path. Route. *F.* Channel. Method. Cause: در راه فرهنگ for the cause of education. – راه آب Water-course. Gully(-hole).– ر. افتادن To start; set out; move. – پول ر. نیفتاد Money could not be raised (*or* made available).– ر. انداختن To start; put in working order; commission. To raise (money). – ر. بردن To walk *vt.* – ر. بجائی نبرد He did not find his way. He could f. no means.– راه نمی برم (*Provincial dialect*) I don't know (how to do it). – ر. پیمودن To travel: در یکروز ۴۰ کیلو متر راه

and E.

رافع ० *A. a.* Raising. [Fem. رافعه] . – عضلهٔ رافعه Levator.

رافضی *A.* Heretic.

راقم *A.* Writer or painter [used before the name of an artist. Ex. «درویش» راقم : Darvish pinxit].

راقی *A.* [Fem. راقیه] Advancing or advanced : ملل راقیه

راک ० Fighting ram. Drum of battle. Kind of melody.

راکب ० *A.* = سوار

راکد *A.* Stagnant. – بایگانی ر. Dead records. – بازار راکداست The market is dull.

رآلیسم *Fr.* Realism.

رام Tame. Familiar. – ر. شدن To be tamed or managed. – ر. کردن To tame; domesticate. To manage; handle; break in, as a horse.

رامح ० *A.* Lancer. – سماك ر. *Astr.* Arcturus.

رامش * Rest. Cheerfulness.

رام شدنی Tamable; tractable; manageable.

رامشگر Minstrel.

رامنا *R. or* **رانکا** Slip-galley.

رامی ० *A.* 1) = تیرانداز 2) *Astr.* = **قوس**

رامی Tameness. Gentleness.

رامی *E.* (*C. P.*) Rummy.

ران Thigh. [*Of a pig*] Ham. [*Of beef*] Beefsteak. –

G.-post; finger-post. – خط ر. Geom. Directrix. – کتابچهٔ ر. Guide-book ; directory. – کویه = راهنمای شناور Buoy.

راهنمایی Guidance. – ر. کردن To guide ; show the way (to). – ادارهٔ ر. و رانندگی Traffic Department.

راه نورد = **راه پیما**

راهوار or **رهوار** Easy-paced.

راهی ○ About to start. – ر. شدن To proceed (or start) on a journey. – ر. کردن To prepare (one) for proceeding (on his j.).

رای Counsel. Opinion; judgment. Prudence. – ر. زدن * To pronounce a j. ; express one's opinion. To deliberate.

رأی A, [آراء] Vote ; voice. Opinion; judgment. – با رأی مخفی By ballot. – ر. دادن To vote. To pronounce a j. – رأی کسیرا زدن + To dissuade a person (from doing s. t.). – درموضوعی ر. گرفتن To take a v. on a question; put a question to the v. – حق ر. Franchise ; suffrage.

رأی‌العین A. Witness of the eye. – برأی‌العین Ocularly.

رایت * A. [رایات] Banner; flag.

رایج [f. A. رائج] Current.

رایحه A. = بو Odour.

رایزن Counsellor. Advisor.

رایزنی Counsellorship.

ر. دادن ‖ پیمود [With در] To admit to. – ر. رفتن To walk. – ر. یافتن To be admitted. To slip in : اشتباهاتی در آن ر. یافت Certain errors slipped in. – سر راه گذاشتن To expose, as a child. – رفت براه خود He went his way. – از راهِ 1) Via. 2) Through. – دوساعت ر. است تا It is 2 hours' distance from. – در راه خدا For God's sake. By way of charity.

راه‌آهن or **راهِ آهن** Railway.

راه انداز Starter.

راهب A. [رُهبان] Monk.

راه بردار Able to find one's way. F. Having means (of livelihood).

راه بندان Road obstruction.

راهبه A. [Fem. of راهب] Nun. [Pl. رواهب & راهبات]

راه پیما Traveller; wayfarer ○.

راه پیمایی Walking. W. tour.

راهدار Obs. Road-guard.

راهدارخانه Obs. Toll-house.

راه راه Ribbed. Striped.

راهرو Corridor ; passageway.

راهزن Brigand; bandit. – راهزن سواره Highwayman.

راهزنی Highway robbery.

راه سازی Road construction.

راهگذر Passer-by. Wayfarer.

راهن A. Mortgager.

راهنامه Road-book.

راهنما or **رهنما** Guide. Usher. Traffic indicator. – تیر راهنما

رایگان Free (of cost); gratuitous(ly). In vain. — برایگان Gratuitously. [ارباب]

رَبّ *A*. Lord. Master. *Cf*.

رُبّ *A*. Inspissated juice. — رب سوس *S. u.* سوس

رِبا *A*. Usury.

رُبا or **ربای** [Imp. of ربودن]

رُباب *A*. Rebeck; viol.

رُبابه (*A*.) *Fem. pr. name*.

رباخوار *A. P*. Usurer.

رباخواری *A. P*. Usury.

رباط *A*. Inn; caravanserai. Ligament.

رباطی *A*. Ligamentous.

رباعی *A*. [رباعیات] Quatrain.

رب‌الجنود ○ *A*. Lord of Hosts.

رب‌النوع *A*. [ارباب انواع] A god or divinity; *OS*. god of species.

ربانی *A*. Divine. — دعای ر. The Lord's prayer. — عشاء ر. The Lord's Supper.

ربایش ○ Seizure. Attraction.

رباینده Seizing. Attractive. *Z*. Raptorial.

ربح *A*. Interest.

ربدوشامبر *Fr*. Dressing-gown; *robe-de-chambre*.

ربس or **رپس** Reps.

رَبط *A*. Relation; connection. Coherence. — ر. دادن To connect. — ربطی بموضوع ندارد It has no connection, or nothing to do, with the subject on hand. — ر. داشتن از + To be conversant with. — حرف ر. Conjunction.

رُبع *A*. One-fourth. Quarter. — سه و ربع کم or یك ر. مانده بسه A quarter to 3. — سه و ربع or یك ر. ازسه گذشته A q. past 3. — ربع دایره Quadrant. — ربع مسکون Inhabited quarter of the world. — تب ر. Quartan fever. — نوبهٔ ربع معکوس Double quartan f.

ربعی *A. P. a*. Quarto. Quarterly. *—n*. Small bottle of the size of one-fourth of the ordinary b.

ربنا ○ *A*. (*ra*b'*en*a) Our Lord.

رُبودن [ربا(ی)] To seize or snatch; abduct. To ravish.

ربی ○ *A*. My Lord!

ربیع *A*. = بهار Spring.

ربیع‌الثانی or **ربیع‌الاخر** (*A*.) *Fourth A. lunar month*.

ربیع‌الاول (*A*.) *Third A. lunar month*. [تمرین

رپتیسیون *Fr*. Rehearsal. *Cf*.

رپورتاژ *Fr*. (Newspaper) report; reporting. Set of contributed articles on a topical subject.

رُتبه *A*. [رُتَب] Grade; rank. — ر. دادن (به) To promote to a higher grade. — ر. گرفتن To be promoted.

رتق و فتق *a. p*. 1) Managing; handling: رتق و فتق امور 2) *OS*. ○ Closing and opening.

رُجوع *A.* Reference. Returning. — ر. کردن To refer. [With از] To revoke. — ر. شود به Refer to. *Vide*.

رجولیت *A* Virility. — آلت ر. Pudendum virile.

رجه [For بند رجه] Clothes-line.

رجیم *A.* = **ملعون**

رَحل *A.* Book-rack; lectern. Camel's saddle o.—رحل اقامت افکندن • To take abode.

رحلت *A.* Departure. Death.— ر. کردن To pass away; die. To emigrate.

رحم (*rahm*) *A.* Compassion; mercy. — برکسی ر. کردن To have pity (*or* mercy) on s. o. — ر. آوردن • To have p. or mercy. — دلش ر. آمد He was moved with c.

رحم *A.* (*rahem*) = **زهدان** Womb.

رحمانی *A.* Divine.

رَحِم بند *A. P.* Pessary.

رَحمت *A.* Mercy; commiseration. Pardon. Grace; blessing. — برکسی ر. آوردن • To have mercy on, or pity s. o.— برحمت ایزدی پیوستن To go to glory; go the way of all the earth. — ر. فرستادن To invoke God's blessing. — خدافلان را رحمت کند May such a one rest in peace.— ر. به... May . . . be blessed; may... rest in p.

رتوش کردن *Fr.P.* To retouch.

رُتیل *A.* Tarantula. — رتیل باغی Bird-spider; crab-spider.

رثاء o *A.* =1) مرثیه 2) مدیحه

رَج Row. Line. Layer.

رجاء *A.* = امید(واری) Hope.

رجاست *A.* Filth. Crime.

رِجال *A.* [Pl. of رَجُل] Distinguished men; dignitaries.

رجاله *A.* Lackey(s). Vulgar people.

رجب (*A.*) 1) *Seventh A. lunar month*. 2) *Mas. pr. name*.

رج بندی Stacking.

رُجحان *A.* = برتری Preference.— ر. داشتن بر To have preference over; be better than.

رَجز *A.* Name of several poetical metres.·Epic verses.

رجزخوانی *A. P.* Declamation (while defying an enemy). *OS*. Recital of epic verses.

رِجس *A.* Filth(y act).

رَجع *A.* Returning (of a divorced woman to her husband). — طلاق رجعی Revocable or voidable divorce.

رجعت *A.* Returning [برگشت]. Resurrection. — ر. کردن To return [برگشتن].

رجل (*rajol*) *A.* [رِجال] Man (of distinction).

رجل o *A.* (*rejl*) = پا Foot. *See the next two entries*.

رجل الجبار *A.* Rigel. *Astr.*

رجل الغراب *A.* Crowfoot.

رحم دل *A. P.* Compassionate.
رحمن *A.* Clement; merciful.
رحیق o *A.* Pure (wine).
رحیل *A.* Departure. Journey.
رحیم (*A.*) *a.* Merciful. —*n.* *Mas. pr. name.*
رُخ Face. Check. [*At chess*]. Castle. [*Of leather*] Grain side. — ر. دادن To happen. To arise. — برخ کسی کشیدن To cast in a person's teeth.
رخام *A.* = مرمر Marble.
رخاوت *A.* = سستی - نرمی
رخت Clothes. Outfit. — رختِ شستنی Washing; laundry. — ر. (بر)بستن * To pack off; p. away. — ر. کندن To take off, or change, one's clothes. — رخت و بخت × Duds; (old) clothes. [جالباسی
رختآویز = 1) چوب رخت 2)
رختخواب Bedding; *L.* bed.
رختخواب پیچ *Obs.* Wrapper for bedclothes.
رختدار Clothes-keeper.
رخت شو(ی) Washerwoman; laundress; laundry-man.
رختشوی خانه Laundry; wash-house.
رختشوئی Washing; laundry.
رختکن Cloak-room. Dressing-room. Locker.
رُخسار * Cheek; face.
رخساره 1) = رخسار 2) Facies.
رخش *Rakhsh*: name of Rostam's horse.

درخشان = رخشان
درخشنده = رخشنده
درخشیدن = رخشیدن
رُخصت *A.* Leave; permission.— ر. خواستن To ask p. — ر. گرفتن To obtain p.; take leave.
رَخنه Breach; chink. — ر. کردن To leak; ooze out. To penetrate. To make a hole. To slip in.
رِخوَت *A.* = سستی — نرمی
رَدّ *A.* Restitution. Rejection. Track; trace.— حق رد Veto.— رد شدن To be rejected or repealed. To fail. To pass through. To be cleared. — رد شو — Go away. — رد کردن To return or refund. To reject. To turn down, as an offer. To refute; disprove. To defeat, as a bill. To clear (from the customs). To pass (on).— ردّ احسان کردن To rebuff a favour. — رد پای کسیرا گرفتن To follow a person's footprints; track him down. — رد و بدل کردن To (ex)change. To bandy.
رداء *A.* Cloak.
ردالعجز علی الصدر *A.* Anadiplosis; epizeuxis.
ردائت o *A.* Malignity. — ردائت مزاج General bad health; cachexia.
ردخور + *A. P.* Something that is likely to be rejec-

ted. — ر. ندارد It is sure ; it is final.

ردع A. (*Med.*) Revulsion.

ردنگت *Fr*. Frock-coat. Riding-coat.

رده Line. *Bot*. Class. *Mil*. 1) Echelon; 2) array.

رده بندی Classification.

ردیّ A. Malignant. *See* ردائت

رَدیف A. Row. Range; order.— در ردیف چیزی قرار گرفتن To range with s. t.

رذالت A. Meanness; rascality.

رذائل [Pl. of رذیله]

رذل & رذیل A. = پست Mean.

رذیله A. [رذائل] Mean quality. Wicked act. [Orig. fem. of رذیل].

رز Vine. — دختر رز * Wine.

رزّاز A. Rice merchant.

رزّاق A. Provider or supplier : ep. of God.

رزانت A. Firmness. Sedateness.

تاکستان = رزستان

رِزق A. Daily bread. *Cf*. روزی & *the pl*. ارزاق

رَزم Combat. *S. a*. جنگ ‖ ر. کردن To fight.

رزم‌آرا ○ (One) who arrays troops.

رزم‌جو(ی) Warlike.

رزم‌دیده * Experienced in warfare.

رزم‌نامه Book of epic poems.

رزم‌ناو Cruiser.

رزمی Epic(al).

رزه Staple : چفت و رزه

رَزین A. Firm. Sedate.

رِزین *Fr*. Resin.

رژه March past; marching p. ر. رفتن To march p.

رژیم *Fr*. Régime. Regiment. — ر. گرفتن To be on diet. — رژیم لاغری Slimming.

رَس [Imp. of رسیدن].

رُس *S. u.* رُست [sive.

رَسا Audible ; loud. Expressive.

رسالت A. Prophetic mission.

رساله A. [رسائل & رسالات] Epistle. Thesis. Treatise.

رَسام A. Designer. Draftsman. Tracer. — گلولهٔ ر. T. bullet.

رسان [Imp. of رساندن]

رساندن [رسان] To (cause to) reach ; extend. To remit ; send. To deliver : پیغام را نرساندم ‖ To supply : جنس ر. ‖ To communicate. To prompt. To denote; indicate.— بخانه ر. To see or reach home.— بهم ر. To contract ; as a debt. To procure ; obtain. — مقصود را نمیرساند It does not carry the point.

رساننده n. Bearer. Conveyor. Prompter. —a. Expressive.

رسائل [A pl. of رساله]

رسایی Audibility. Range.

رُست or رُس Firm ○. — خاك ر. or گل ر. Clay. — رُس کسی را درآوردن + To sap s. o. ; exhaust his vigour ; also , overpower or overload him.

رُست *Geom.* Ordinate.

رستاخیز Resurrection (Day).

رُستگار Delivered ; saved. — ر. شدن To be s.

رستگاری Deliverance. Salvation.

رستم *Rostam* : mas. pr. name. — رستم درِ حمام *Met.* Man of straw ; cardboard cavalier.

رَستن [رَ ِ] To be delivered. To escape.

رُستن [روی] To grow. To sprout.

رُستنی = گیاه

رستوران *Fr.* Restaurant.

رَسته [P. P. of رستن] Delivered ; saved.

رَسته Class. Guild.

رُسته [P. P. of رُستن]

رُستی Argillaceous. *See* رست ‖ سنگ ر. Shale.

رسد = دسته Platoon.

رسدبان Police lieutenant.

رسدیار Scout-master.

رسل [Pl. of رسول]

رسم *A.* [رسوم] Custom; usage. Rule. Drawing ; design. — ر. نیست که . . . It is not customary to . . . — ر. کردن To draw ; trace ; design. — مِن غیررسم Unofficially. — اسم ورسم Fame. Reputation.

رسماً *A.* Officially. Formally. As a rule. Customarily.

رسم‌الخط *A.* Prescribed form of writing.

رسمانه *A. P.* = 1) رسماً 2) رسمی

رَسمی *A.* Official ; formal. — لباس تمام ر. Full dress. — غیر رسمی Unofficial ; informal. — بطور غیر رسمی Unofficially ; informally.

رسمیت *A.* State of being official. Vogue ; popular acceptation. — ر. پیدا کردن To have a quorum. — رسمیت جلسه را اعلام کردن To open the meeting ; declare it o. — ر. دادن To enable to transact business , as by a quorum. To bring into vogue. — برسمیت شناختن To recognize.

رَسن *A.* = طناب & ریسمان

رُسوا Disgraced. — ر. شدن To be disgraced. — ر. کردن To disgrace or put to shame (publicly)

رسوایی Shame ; disgrace.

رُسوب *A.* Sediment. — ر. کردن = ته نشین شدن

رسوبی *A.* Sedimentary.

رُسوخ *A.* Firmness; constancy. — ر. کردن To be firmly rooted.

رَسول *A.* [مُرسِل] Messenger. Apostle.

رسوم [Pl. of رسم]

رُسومات Excise (on alcoholic liquors). [Double pl. of رسم]

رَسید Arrival. Receipt. — قبض ر. R. (form). — رسید نامه‌ای را

ر. فرنگی Vermicelli or macaroni. — یك ر. دروغ A tissue of lies. — برشتهٔ نظم درآوردن To versify. To compose.

رَشتی (Native) of Resht. — گل ر Brier. — مرغ ر. Variety of guinea-fowl or pintado.

رَشحه * *A*. [رشحات] Exudation. Sweat. Drop.

رُشد *A*. Growth. *F*. Development. Maturity. — ر. کردن To grow up. To attain m.

رَشک * Jealousy. Emulation. — ر. ورزیدن *or* ر. بردن [*With* به] To be jealous of ; envy.

رَشک‌آمیز Envious : نگاه ر.

رِشکک *Bot*. Burnet.

رِشوه *A*. Bribe. Manure. — ر. گرفتن *or* ر. خوردن To receive a bribe. — ر. دادن To give a b. to; corrupt.

رشوه خور *A. P*. Corruptible.

رَشید *A*. Brave. Of an elegant or tall stature. *Law* Mature.

رصد خانه *A. P*. Observatory.

رَصن *A*. Clubmoss.

رِضا *A*. Will ; pleasure. Consent. Resignation. *Mas. pr. name*. — ر. دادن To consent ; agree. [*With* به] To yield or submit. — ر. داشتن To be willing. — محض رضای خدا For God's sake ; to please God.

رضاعی *A*. Foster [*used as an a.*] : برادر رضاعی

اطلاع دادن To acknowledge receipt of a letter.

رَسیدگی Investigation. Audit; verification. Ripeness. — ر. کردن To investigate. To check. To look after ; take care of [often with به]. To handle. To verify.

رسیدن [رَس] To arrive. To be received. To become available. To ripen. To (find a leisure to) attend (to a specified business). [With transitive equivalents through به]. 1) To reach; attain. — دستم به آن نمیرسد I cannot r. it. 2) To overtake. 3) To suffice. — بهمه خواهد رسید It will go round. — بهم ر. To be available; exist. To meet each other (again); reunite. — باشد تا بهم برسیم Thou shalt meet me at Philippi. — تا چه رسد Still less ; much l.

رسیده [P. P. of رسیدن] 1) Imported : کالای ر. 2) Ripe. 3) Mature.

رشادت *A*. Valour ; bravery.

ریستن = رِشتن

رشته [P. P. of رشتن] *a*. Spun. —*n*. Field ; line. String. Range. Series ; train. Tie ; bond. Filament. Fibre. Staple (of wool or cotton). Strip(s) of dough. Ribbon vermicelli. Guinea-worm. —

رضامندی *A. P.* Satisfaction. Good will.

رِضایت *A.* Satisfaction. Consent. Willingness. — از کسی ر. داشتن To be satisfied (*or* pleased) with s. o. — ر. دادن To express one's consent. To give up or relinquish one's claim. — برضایت خاطر Of one's own free will. — عدم ر. Dissatisfaction.

رضایت بخش *A. P.* Satisfactory.

رضایت نامه *A. P.* Letter of satisfaction; testimonial.

رِضوان *A.* = بهشت

رَضَوی *A.* Descended from Imam-Reza.

رَضیع *A.* = شیرخوار

رطب ∘ *A.* (*ratb*) = تر Moist. — جرب ر. M. tetter. — رطب ویابسی را بهم بافتن To fabricate a mixture of truth and fiction.

رطب *A.* (*rotab*) Fresh dates.

رَطل *A.* Rotl; pound. Large cup *.

رُطوبت *A.* Moisture. Humour.

رطوبت نما *A. P.* Hygrometer; psychrometer.

رطوبتی *A. P.* Of a moist and cold temperament.

رُطوبی *A. P.* Moist. Phlegmatic.

رَعاد *A.* [For ماهی ر.] Torpedo or cramp-fish.

رُعاف ∘ *A.* = خون دماغ

رعایا [Pl. of رعیت]

رَعایت *A.* Observance. Regard. Favour. — ر. کردن To observe. To assist or favour. — برای رعایتِ In response to. To a.

رُعب *A.* = بیم [thunder.

رَعد *A.* Thunder. — ر. زدن To

رعد آسا *A. P.* Thunder-like; thunderous.

رَعشه *A.* Tremour; shaking palsy. — رعشهٔ عضلات Dystaxia.

رَعنا * *A.* Of an elegant stature. Elegant. Tender. *OS.* Foolish.

رعنا زیبا *A. P.* China aster.

رعیت *A.* [رُعایا] Peasant; farmer. Subject. — رعایای ایران Iranian subjects or nationals.

رعیت پرور *A. P.* Kind to one's subjects. K. to inferiors.

رعیتی *A. P. n.* Farming. —*a.* Rural.

رغبت *A.* Liking. Delight. Relish. — بچیزی ر. داشتن To have a relish for, or take a delight in, s. t.

رغم *A.* Spite. Reluctance. — علی‌رغمِ (*alaragh'me*) In spite of; in the teeth of; in defiance of.

رَف Built-in shelf or niche in the upper part of a room.

رفاده *A.* Compress. Bandage.

رفاقت *A.* Friendship; companionship. — ر. کردن To make friends; keep company.

رِفاه *or* رفاهیت *A.* Welfare.

Ease ; convenience.
رَفتار Behaviour; act. ر. کردن— To behave ; act.
رُفت‌گر Street-sweeper.
رَفتن [رو *row*] To go. To walk slowly *. To pass (away). To go out = خاموش شدن ‖ این راه بکجا میرود Where does this road lead to ? — به پدرش رفته است He has taken after his father.
رُفتن [روب] To sweep.
رَفتنی About to go. Sure to go. On the point of death.
آمد و رفت = رفت و آمد
رَفته [P. P. of رفتن].—*n*. [Only in the pl. رفتگان the dead].
رفته رفته Gradually; in process of time.
رفراندُم *Fr*. Referendum.
رفری *E*. Referee.
رَفض *A*. Heresy.
رَفع *A*. Raising. Removal. Elimination. *Arith*. Reduction of an improper fraction. Settlement : رفع اختلاف ‖ Supplying or meeting :رفع احتیاجات ‖ رفع حجاب The unveiling of women. — رفع مزاحمت Abatement of nuisance. — ر. کردن To remedy. To remove. To settle; adjust. To abolish. To suppress. — رفع توقیف از چیزی کردن To lift the ban on s. t. — رفع خستگی کردن To rest; refresh oneself. — رفع عطش کردن To quench one's thirst. — رفع و رجوع کردن + To gloss over. To remedy.
رِفعت *A*. High position ; dignity.
رِفق *A*. Leniency ; gentleness.
رفقاء [Pl. of رفیق].
رُفو کردن To darn.
رفوگر Darner.
رفوگری Darning.
رَفیع (*A*.) *a*. = بلند Elevated. —*n*. *Mas*. *pr*. *name*.
رَفیق *A*. [رفقا] Companion ; comrade. Friend.
رفیق باز + *A*. *P*. Faithful to friendship ; constant. Devoted to one's friends.
رقاب *A*. [Pl. of رقبه] Necks. *Met*. * Slaves.
رقابت *A*. Competition.— ر. کردن To compete. To vie.
رَقّاص *A*. (Professional) dancer. Balance-wheel.
رقاص بازی × *A*. *P*. Monkey-business.
رَقّاصه *A*. [Fem. of رقاص] Danceuse ; ballet-girl.
رقّاصی *A P* Dancing.— ر. کردن To be a dancer. To caper.— کسیرا به ر. واداشتن + To lead one a dance. To make a tool of.
رقبا [Pl. of رقیب]
رقبه o *A*. (Nape of the) neck. *Met*. * Slave. [Pl. رقبات] Register of Crown properties].

رُقبی A. (-ba) Right for a prescribed period.

رِقت A. Tenderness. F. Pity or sympathy. – رقت قلب Tender-heartedness; pity. – برکسی ر. آوردن To feel p. for s. o. – برقت آوردن To move (to p.) ; touch.

رقت انگیز - رقت آور - رفت آمیز A. P. Pitiable; pitiful.

رَقص A. Dance ; dancing. – ر. کردن To dance. – رقص محوری Astr. Nutation.

رقصاندن A. P. To cause to dance ; dance vt.

رَقصیدن A. P. [رقص] To dance.

رُقعه A. Letter ; note. Sheet (of paper). Patch (of cloth). Scrap. – کاغذ رقعه ای Letter-paper.

رَقم A. [رقوم & ارقام] Figure ; digit. Character. Writing. Signature *. Kind ; brand ; grade +.

رقم بندی A. P. Sorting ; assortment.

رقمی A. Numerical.

رُقوم [A pl. of رقم]

رقومی A. Numerical. – هندسهٔ ر. Descriptive geometry dealing with one plane of projection.

رَقیب A. [رُقَباء] Rival ; antagonist. Competitor.

رِقیت A. Slavery.

رَقیق A. Dilute ; thin. Soft ; watery. F. Tender. – ر. کردن To dilute. To rarefy.

رقیمه A. = مرقومه & نامه

رقیه A. Fem. pr. name.

رُك Frank(ly). OS. = راست ‖ رك حرف زدن To be frank ; speak frankly.

رِکاب A. Stirrup. Pedal; treadle. Running-board ; coach-step. [In garments] 1) Strap. 2) Brace. – ر. کشیدن To spur and ride full speed ; clap spurs to one's horse. Cf. رکاب کش

رکابدار or رکابی A. P. Strapped.

رکاب کش + A. P. With full speed. OS. Spurring one's horse.

رکرد E. Record. – ر. را شکستن To break the record. [This is not genuine P. , but an imitation of the E.].

رَکعت A. Unit of prayer consisting of three postures.

رُک گو Frank ; outspoken.

رک گویی Outspokenness.

رُکن A. [ارکان] Pillar. (Main) element. – ارکان دولت Dignitaries of the State.

رُکود A. Stagnancy. Standstill.

رُکوع A. Genuflexion.

رَکیك A. Indecent; risqué.

رکین A. Firm. Sedate.

رگ Blood-vessel. Vein. F. Nerve; zeal. Strain ; vein. – رگ زدن To bleed ; phlebo-

رمان نویس *Fr. P.* Novelist.
رُمانی ○ *A.* Ruby-coloured. *OS.* Pomegranate-coloured.
رَمانیدن To rouse. To scare.
رُمبیدن [رمب] To collapse; topple over. To cave in.
رَمد *A.* Ophthalmia. — رمد یابس *or* رمد خشك Xerophthalmia.
رَمز *A.* [رُموز] Mystery. Allusion. Symbol. — تلگراف ر. Ciphered telegram. — کتاب ر. Code.
رمز نویسی *A. P.* Writing of ciphered telegrams. Cryptography. [Allegorical.
رمزی *A.* Mysterious. Cryptic.
رمضان *Ninth A. lunar month. Mas. pr. name.*
رَمق *A.* Last breath of life. — سدّ رمق Bare subsistence.
رَمل *A.* Sand. — ر. انداختن To practise geomancy. — رمل کلیه Renal gravel; renal calculus. [Sandstone.
رملی ○ *A.* Sandy. — سنگ ر.
رموز [Pl. of رمز]
رَموک *or* رمو Skittish.
رَمه Herd; flock. [tion.
رمیدگی Disillusion. Indigna-
رَمیدن [رم] To shy. To startle. To stampede. *F.* To be disillusioned. To be scared.
رمیده [P. P. of رمیدن] Scared. Disillusioned. [carious.
رمیم *A.* = پوسیده Decayed;
رَنج Pains; sufferring. Dis-

tomize. — رگ خواب کسیرا بدست آوردن To get the length of one's foot.
رَگباد Squall.
رَگبار Shower.
رگ َبرگ *Bot.* Vein; rib.
رگ برَگ Sprained. — مچ پایم ر. شد I sprained my ankle.
رگ بندی *Bot.* Venation.
رگزن Bleeder; phlebotomist.
رگزنی Bloodletting; bleeding.
رگ شناسی ○ Angiology.
رگه Vein; nervure. Course. Ledge.
رگه‌دار Veined.
رُل *Fr.* Steering-wheel. Rôle; part [نقش]. — پشت رل نشستن To take the wheel. — رل بازی میکند He is only acting; he is pretending (or playing false)
رل نویسی *Fr. P.* Casting.
رله *Fr.* Relay.
رَم Shying. Stampede. — رم دادن To rouse. To cause to shy. To scare. — ر. کردن To stampede or shy.
رَم [Imp. of رمیدن]
رُم *Fr.* Rome.
رُم *Fr.* Rum.
رَمارم ○ Of an equal footing.
رَمّال *A.* Geomancer.
رَمّالی *A. P.* Geomancy.
رَمان Shy; timid. Scared.
رُمان *Fr.* Novel. — رمان کوچك Novelette.
رُمّان ○ *A.* = انار

ease. — ○ رنج باریك = سلّ ‖ ر.کشیدن or ر. بردن To take pains ; toil ; suffer.

رَنج [Imp. of رنجیدن]

رنجاندن To offend ; annoy. To displease.

رَنجبر Toiling; painstaking. — طبقهٔ ر. The proletariat(e).

رنجش Offence ; umbrage.

رنج کش Painstaking. *S. a.* رنجور

رنجور 1) = بیمار 2) Afflicted.

رنجوری • Illness.

رَنجه • Troubled. Tired. Painful. — ر.کردن To give trouble (*or* pain) to.— قدم ر.فرمودن [In invitation cards] To take the trouble, or be kind enough, to come.

رنجیدگی State of being offended ; indignation.

رنجیدن [رنج] To take offence; be offended. [With از] To take amiss.

رنجیده [P. P. of رنجیدن] Offended. Indignant.

رِند Slyboots. Libertine. Tippler. *Cf.* رُنود

رَنده or رندیدن ر.کردن Plane.— To plane (wood). To grate (cheese).

رَنگ Colour. Dye(stuff). Paint. — نقاشی رنگ وروغنی Oil-painting. — دیوار چه ر. است What c. is the wall ?— رنگ دیوار آبی است The (c. of the) wall is blue. — ر. باختن To turn pale; lose one's colour.— ر.گذاشتن و رنگ برداشتن + To blush.— رنگ وبو Attractive quality. — رنگ و رو Complexion. — ر. ریختن To + work out a scheme. — ر. زدن To paint or c. ; dye. — ر.کردن 1) = ر. زدن 2) + To dupe. 3) To gloss over. — خر رنگ کردن + To deceive a dupe.— از آب ر.گرفتن To skin a flint ; draw blood from a stone.

رِنگ Tune designed for dancing ; dance. *L.* The finale.

رَنگارنگ Variously-coloured ; many-coloured. Various.

رنگ آمیزی Colour-blending.

رنگارنگ = رنگ برنگ

رنگ بندی Colour-scheme.

رنگ پذیر That can be coloured or stained ; chromatine.

رنگ پریده or رنگ رفته Pale.

رنگرز Dyer.- رنگرزی Dyeing.

برگ ریزان = • رنگ ریزان

رنگ زن & رنگ کار Painter.

رنگ شناسی Chromatics.

رنگی 1) Stained : شیشهٔ ر. ‖ 2) Coloured. — « ر. نشوید ». « Wet paint ! »

رنگین Coloured. *F.* Florid.

○ رنگ کمان or رنگین کمان Rainbow [قوس قزح].

رنود [A. pl. of رِند] + Those who are (*or* were) in the know ; also, the interested party. *Cf.* رند

روی *or* **رو** Face. Surface. Right side روی پارچه ‖ Obverse : روی سکه ‖ روی گدایی Audacity to beg. — خیلی رو دارید You have a nerve ! — تو روی من دروغ گفت He lied to my face.— اطاق‌رو بخیابان است The room looks on the street.— روآوردن To proceed. *F.* To resort ; appeal. — پیش‌کسی رو انداختن To stoop to a request.— . . . رویم نمیشود که I don't have the face to...— رو(ی) دادن To happen ; take place. — رو دادن به To make cheeky ; embolden. To indulge. — رو کردن To face or look ○. To l. favourably. *C. P.* To show or declare. — رو(ی) گرداندن To turn away (the face).— روی سخن باشما است The remarks are aimed at you.— روی کسیرا بزمین انداختن To let one down.— روگرفتن To cover one's f; veil oneself.— رو نشان ندادن To abscond.— رو به بهبود گذاشتن To begin to improve.— روی خوش نشان ندادن To give a cold shoulder (to.)— آنروی کسیرا بالا آوردن + To rough one up the wrong way. — رویش سیاه شد He was put to shame. *Cf.* روسیاهی ‖ از رو بردن To f. down ; look d. To put (*or* stare) out of countenance. — **روی**ِ *prep.* On. Over. On top of; in addition to. — روی هم Altogether. — روی هم رفته On the average ; on the whole ○. — از رویِ Over : از روی ماناب ‖ Out of; from : ازروی دشمنی ‖ After the model of. — از چه رو(ی) For what reason ? On w. account. — بروی خود نیاورد He ignored the act. • جانش‌را روی این کارگذاشت It lost him his life.

روی *or* **رو** [Imp. of رویدن]

رو (*row*) [Imp. of رفتن]

رَوا Allowable. Admissible. Lawful. — ر. داشتن To allow; pronounce lawful. To supply; meet •: حاجت وی ر. داشت ‖ در فلان کار غفلت ر. نیست Such a thing does not admit of negligence.

روابط [Pl. of رابطه]:

رَواج *A. n.* Currency; circulation. Good market ; ready sale. *–a.* (*C. E.*) = **رایج** ‖ ر. دادن To propagate. To perform +. — ر. داشتن To be current. To sell well.

رَوادید Visa; visé. [This newly coined word is unsuitable for making a verb, and we use ویزاکردن for "to visé"].

رَواق *A.* = ایوان Porch.

رواقی *A.* [رواقیون] Stoic.— حکمت رواقیون Stoicism ; philosophy of the Porch.

رَوان *a*. Flowing; running. Fluent. *–n*.* Soul; spirit.–روانش شادباد Peace be to his departed spirit. – ر. شدن To flow; run. To learn perfectly. To procced. – ر. کردن To learn; prepare. [Also ر. ساختن] To cause to f. To lubricate.

روا نامه Exequatur.

روان بخش *a*. Animating. *–n*. The Dispenser of the Soul.

روان پزشك Psychotherapist.

روان‌پزشکی Psychic medicine; psychiatry; also, psychotherapy.

روان شناس Psychologist.

روان شناسی Psychology.

روان کاوی Psycho-analysis.

روان نگاری Psychography.

روانه Despatched. (Set) going.– ر. شدن To set out; proceed; launch. –ر. کردن To despatch or send. To dismiss.

روانی Psychic(al). *s. a.* روحی

روانی Fluency. Smoothness.

رواة *or* روات [Pl. of راوی]

روایات [Pl. of روایت]

روایت *A*. [روایات] Narrative. Tradition. – ر. کردن To relate; narrate.

روایح *A*. [Pl. of رایحه]

روب [Imp. of رُفتن]

روباز Uncovered; open; exposed.

روبان *Fr*. Ribbon. [*Of a hat*] Hatband.

روباه Fox. – روباه ماده Vixen; she-fox.

روبراه Ready (to start); prepared.

روبرو Opposite; vis-à-vis. – ر. شدن با To face; confront.– ر. کردن To c. as for cross-examination.

روبکی Rudbeckia; cone-flower. [f. Rudbeck, Swedish botanist].

روبند شدن+To comply with a request from bashfulness.

روبوسی Kissing (each other).

روبه * [Cont. of روباه]

روبه باز * Cunning. *OS*. Playing the fox.

روبه بازی Slyness; cunning.

روبیان = میگو

روبیدن [روب] To sweep.

روپاك ○ = حوله

روپوست Epidermis; cuticle.

روپوش Cover. Bed-sheet.

روپوشی Veiling oneself. Abscondence.

روپیه *H*. Rupee.

روتختخوابی Counterpane; coverlet.

روح *A*. [ارواح] Spirit; soul; ghost. Life. Essence. Zinc [also روی]. – روح توتیا Oil or spirit of vitriol. – ر. بخشیدن To give life to; animate.

روحاً *A*. Spiritually. At heart.

روح افزا *A. P.* Animating;

exhilarating. Cheerful.
روح الاطلس A. Satinet.
روح‌الامین A. (Title of) Gabriel
روح‌القدس A. Holy Spirit.
روح‌الله (A.) *Mas. pr. name.* *OS.* Spirit of God.
روحانی A. Spiritual.
روحانیت A. Spirituality. Purity.
روحانیون A. The clergy [pl. of روحانی used as a n.]
روح پرور A. P. Nourishing the spirit. Animating.
روحی A. Spiritual. Mental.
روحیات [Pl. of روحیه]
روحیه A. Morale. Mentality. [Orig. , fem. of روحی].
رود River. *Kind of harp* o.
رودبار * Place abounding in rivers.
رودخانه River.
رودربایستی Reserve. Delicate situation (preventing the refusal of a request in the presence of him who makes it). Standing on ceremony.— ر. کرد He was too bashful to refuse it).— ر. راکنارگذاشتن To throw off disguise , speak frankly.
رودررو To one's face. Face to face.
رودست خوردن + To be done in.
رودست زدن [*With* به] To play a trick on ; circumvent.
رودل Surfeited stomach; crop-sickness ; foul stomach.

رو دماغی P. A. Nose-band.
روده Intestine ; gut; casing.— رودهٔ باریك Small intestine. — رودهٔ راست Rectum.— رودهٔ فراخ Large i.— آماس ر. Enteritis.— دردروده Enteralgia. — ر. شدن + To tangle ; get snarled. — رودهٔ . . . را درآوردن To disembowel . . . ‖ رودهٔ ماهی را درآوردن To gut a fish.
روده‌ای Intestinal ; enteric.
روده بُرشدن To split one's sides.
روده‌بند Mesentery. — آماس ر. Mesenteritis.
روده دراز Garrulous ; long-winded.
روده درازی Garrulity.— ر. کردن To be garrulous.
روده شناسی Enterology.
روروه Go-cart. Rocker.
روز Day. — روز بد Adversity.— روز خوش Prosperity. — ر. بشما خوش Good day to you ! Good bye !
روزافزون Increasing from day to d. ; ever-increasing.
روزانه *a.* Daily. *ad.* Per day.
روز خیز *Z.* Diurnal.
روزکوری Day-blindedness ; hemeralopia.
روزگار * Time; days. [*In geology*] Age. *F.* Fortune . World. — ر. بردن * To pass one's days; associate.— روزگار کسیرا سیاه‌کردن To ruin s. o.

روزمرّه *P. A. ad.* From day to d. *—a.* Daily.

روزمزد Daily-paid. — کارگر ِ روز مزد Day-worker ; day labourer; daily-wage worker.— کارروزمزد Day-labour.

روزن = روزنه

روزنامه Newspaper; journal. Daybook. — روزنامهٔ رسمی Gazette ; official j.

روزنامه فروش Newsboy.

روزنامه نگار Journalist.

روزنامه نگاری Journalism.

روزن‌دار Foraminate(d.) — روزن داران The Foraminifera.

روزنه Opening. Window. *Z.* Foramen. *Bot.* Stoma. *Mil.* Loophole. [*Of a ship*] Porthole. — روزنهٔ امید Ray of hope ; gleam of h.

روزه Fast ; fasting. — ر. داشتن To be f. — ر. گرفتن To fast ; observe a f. — ر. خوردن *or* ر. شکستن To break one's f.

روزه‌دار Fasting ; who has observed the fast.

روزی Daily bread; sustenance. Man's daily portion fixed by Providence.

روزی خور *a.* Receiving daily food from Providence.

روژ *Fr.* Rouge. *Cf.* سرخاب

روس 1) Russian. 2) = روسیه — جنگ روس و ژاپن ‖ Russo-Japanese war.

رؤسا [Pl. of رئیس]

روکاری & روسازی Superstructure.

روسبی *or* **روسپی** ㅇ Prostitute.

روستا • Village. Rustic.

روستایی *n.* Villager. *—a.* Rural.

روسری Kerchief ; headdress.

روسفید Acquitted. — ر. شدن To prove to be innocent. To be acquitted. — ر. کردن To acquit.

روسی Russian (language).

روسیاه Put to shame ; disgraced. — ر. شدن To be put to s. ; be d.

روسیاهی Shame ; disgrace. — ر. بارآوردن + To d. oneself.

روسیه Russia.

رَوِش Method. Policy; course. Custom. Gait ; walk •.

روشن Bright. Lit ; lighted. On. [Of a person] That can see [بینا]. [Of coal] Live. [Of a furnace] In blast. *F.* Clear. Well-informed. — ر. آبی Light blue. — ر. شدن To light up. To clear up. To be kindled. To be made c. To be enlightened. — ر. کردن To l. (up). To kindle. To switch on. To make c. ; throw l. upon.

روشنایی Light. Luminosity. — چشم کسیرا بهر. انداختن To inveigle and allure s. o.

روشن بین Clear-sighted.

روشن بینی Clear-sightedness.

روشن رای Of a sound or

clear judgment.

روشندل = 1) روشن‌بین 2) روشن‌ضمیر

روشن ضمیر or روشن روان *P. A.* Of an enlightened mind; illumined.

روشن فکر *P. A.* Enlightened; also, broad-minded.

روشنی Brightness. *F.* Clearness.

روشویی Wash-stand.

روضه *A.* (Gathering for the) recital of the tragedies of Karbela. *OS.* = باغ Garden [pl. ریاض]—روضهٔ رضوان = **بهشت**

روضه خوان *A. P.* Professional narrator of the tragedies of Karbela.

روغن Oil. Ghee. Fat. Ointment. — روغن خاکستری *S. u.* روغن ماشین ‖ خاکستری Lubricating-oil. — روغن‌ماهی Cod-liver oil. — روغن مو Bandoline. — روغن ترمز Brake-fluid. — روغن تلخ Mustard oil. — روغن دنده Gear (compound) oil. — روغن موم Cerate. — ر. زدن To lubricate; grease. — ر. گرفتن To extract or press oil. — ر. مالیدن To anoint; embrocate.

روغن داغ کن (Sauce)pan; casserole.

روغن‌دان Oil-can; lubricator. Oil-cruet.

روغن زن Lubricator; oil-can.

روغن سازی or **روغن کشی** Oil-pressing; oil-manufacture. — دستگاه ر. Oil-press.

روغن مالی Unction; embrocation. — ر. کردن To anoint.

روغنی Oily. Dressed with butter. Hydraulic — ترمز روغنی H. brake. — کلید روغنی Oil-immersed switch.

رؤف *S. u.* رووف

روقوری Tea-cosy.

روکار *a.* Built on the surface. —*n.* External part; surface.— کلید روکار Surface-mounting switch.

روکش Plating. Veneer. Slip; pillow-case.— روکش طلا Rolled gold.— ر. کردن To plate; coat. To veneer. *F.* To instigate; use as a tool.

روکفشی Galosh; overshoe.

روکوب Beading; also, moulding.— روکوب چوبی Wainscot.

روگاه Runway. Waterway.

روگردان بودن To abstain; refrain. [*With* از] To reject; refuse.— از هیچ‌چیز روگردان نیست He sticks at nothing; n. is too hot or too heavy for him.

روگیری Partiality [طرفداری]. Veiling oneself. — ر. کردن To be partial.

رولباسی *P. A.* Overall(s).

رولور *Fr.* Revolver.

روله *Fr.* (*roleh*) Relay.

روم Rome.

رومی Roman. Greek ○ [یونانی].—

ر. طاق Semicircular arch.
رومیزی Table-cloth ; cover
رومیه A. = روم
روناس Madder(-root). Alizarine.
روَند Process. Procedure. Also, going. *See* آیند و روند
رونده *n*. [روندگان] Goer. Wayfarer; traveller. —*a*. Going ; about to go.
رونرو Sure-footed, as a horse.
رونق A. Splendour ; brightness. Briskness. ر. یافتن— To brisk up. To flourish.
رونما Present given to a bride unveiling herself for the first time. P. on the occasion of seeing a new-born child for the first time.
رونوشت Copy ر. ازچیزی برداشتن— To copy s. t.
رونویس Copyist. [tion.
رونویسی Copying; transcrip-
رؤوس A. Main topics. *Cf. the s.* رأس
رووف or رؤف A. = مهربان
رویه = + روه
روی S. u. رو
روی S. u. روح
روی S. u. 1st. رو
رَوی A. Last letter of a riming word which remains unchanged throughout a poem.
رویا Growing. [خواب
رؤیا A. Vision ; dream. Cf.
رؤیابین A. P. Visionary.

رویان *Bot*. Embryo.
رویان شناسی Embryology.
رویانیدن To (cause to) grow.
رؤیت A. = دیدار Sight. — ر. کردن To see. To sight, as a bill.— ر. برات Sight-draft.
رویداد Event; incident. Account ; narrative.
روی زرد * Pale. *F*. Disgraced.
رویزردی Paleness. *F*. Shame.
رویگر Zinc-worker. Brazier.
روینده Growing.
رویه Surface. [Of cloth] Outside; right side. [Of a shoe.] Upper; vamp. [Of a pillow] Slip; case. [Of a mattress] Tick.
رویّه A. Policy; method; tack. Reflection ○ [also رویّت].
روی همرفته S. u. رو
رویی Upper. Outer; exterior.
روییدن [رو(ی)] To grow.
روئین * Made of zinc , brass, copper , or iron ; metallic.
روئین تن * Brazen-bodied. *F*. Invulnerable : ep. of *Esfandiar*, a hero of the Shahnameh. [claws.
روئین چنگ * Of brazen
ره [Cont. of راه]
ره [Imp. of رستن or رهیدن].
رَها Loose. Set at liberty.— ر. شدن To be delivered or released. To drop. — ر کردن To set at l.; To d.; let go. To abandon. To divorce ○.

رهان [Imp. of رهانیدن] [save.
رهانیدن [رهان] To deliver ;
ره‌آورد Present brought from a journey.
رَهایی Deliverance. — ر. دادن To deliver ; save. — ر. یافتن To be delivered. [*With* از] To escape.
رهبان *A.* Monk or monks. [Orig. pl. of راهب] [life.
رهبانیت *A.* Monastic or single
رهبر Leader; guide. Conductor.
رَهبری Leadership. Guidance.— ر. کردن To lead ; guide.
رهج‌الغار *A.* Realgar.
رهرو • Wayfarer.
رهسپارشدن To proceed ; set out. To travel.
رهگذر [Cont. of راهگذر] Passer-by. Wayfarer. — از این ر. In this way. On this account.— در هر رهگذر On every hedge; everywhere.
رهن = گرو Mortgage. — ر. دادن *or* ر. گذاشتن To mortgage. To pledge. — ر. کردن To obtain a m. on; take on m.— از رهن درآوردن To redeem.
رهنما [Cont. of راهنما]
رهنمایی etc. = راهنمایی etc.
راهنما *or* رهنما = • رهنمون
رهنورد [Cont. of راه نورد]
رَهنی *A. P.* Hypothecary ; (that is to be) mortgaged. Bonded. — بنگاه ر. Pawnshop.
رهوار *S. u.* راهوار

رَستن = • رهیدن
رَهین *A.* Indebted. — رهین مراحم او I. to his favours.
ری *Rey:* 1) *Obsolete weight = 12 kilogrammes*; 2) the ancient Rages or Rhagae : town south of Tehran.
ریا *A.* Hypocrisy. — ر. کردن To dissimulate.
ریاح [Pl. of ریح]
ریاحین [Pl. of ریحان]
ریاست *A.* Directorship. Chairmanship. Presidentship. — ر. کردن To be (*or* act as) a chief , director , chairman , etc. — کمیسیونی بریاست او A committee presided over by him.— مقامِ محترمِ ریاستِ ... The Honourable, the Director of . . . [position.
ریاست‌طلب *a. p.* Ambitious of
ریاست مآب *a. p.* Who assumes the mien of a chief.
ریاض [Pl. of روضه].
ریاضت *A.* Mortification ; rigour. Self-discipline. Laborious study ; lucubration. — ر. کشیدن To take great pains. To undergo mortification.
ریاضت‌کش *A. P.* Ascetic ; practising strict self-discipline. *L.* Laborious ; painstaking.
ریاضی *A.* Mathematical. [Fem. ریاضیه with the pl. ریاضیات *q. v.*]

ریاضیات *A*. Mathematics. [Orig. pl. of ریاضیه q. v. under ریاضی]

ریاضی‌دان *A.P*. Mathematician.

ریاضیون *A*. [Pl. of ریاضی] Mathematicians.

ریاکار *A. P*. Hypocritical.

ریاکارانه *A. P*. Hypocritically.

ریاکاری *A. P*. Hypocrisy.

ریال *Rial* : monetary unit = 100 *dinars*.

رَیّان ○ *A*. = سیراب

ریائی *A. P*. Hypocritical.

ریب *A*. = تردید [lungs.

ریتین *A*. [D. of ریه] The

ریح ○ *A*. [ریاح] Wind [باد]. Odour [بو]. Breath [نفس]. Flatulency.

ریحان *A*. [ریاحین] Sweet basil. *Mas. pl. name*.

ریخت+ Shape; figure ; cast.

ریختگی Cast. Moulded.

ریختن [ریز] *vt*. To pour. To shed. To spill. To strew. To cast; mould; found. To throw, as dice. To injure : آبرویم را ریخت ‖ To have a rasping effect on : گوشت آدم را میریزد *–vi*. To pour. To be spilt. To fall. – روی هم ر. To click. To get off (with s. o.).

ریخت و پاش Spillage. Waste; extravagance. Profuseness.

ریخته [P. P. of ریختن] Spilt; spilled. Poured. Strewn. Cast ; moulded. – ر. و پاشیده All over the shop. – روغن ر. را نذر امامزاده کردن To make a virtue of necessity.

ریخته‌گر Moulder. Founder.

ریخته‌گری Moulding. [shit.

ریدن [رین] [*Indecent*] To

ریز *a*. Tiny. Fine. – باران ر. Drizzle. *–ad*. In f. grains (*or* drops) ; finely. *– n*. Details. – صورت ر. Detailed statement. – ر. باریدن To drizzle : rain in fine drops.

ریز [Imp. of ریختن]

ریزان *a*. Pouring. Falling.

ریزباف *or* ریزبافت Fine-woven.

ریزبین Microscope.

ریزخوار Microphagous.

ریزخواری Microphagy.

ریز دانه Microlithic.

ریز ریز Minced ; chopped. – ر. کردن To mince. To crumble.

ریزش (Act of) pouring. Effusion. Falling in. Landslip. *Med*. Coryza ; nasal catarrh. – ریزش مو Alopecia. – ریزش برف Snowfall. – ر. کردن To fall in ; collapse. To pour out ; flush.

ریزنده *a*. Falling (off). Flowing.

ریزه *n*. Gleanings. Crumbs. Little bit+. *–a*. Tiny; minute.

ریزه خور *or* ریزه چین Gleaner.

ریزه خوانی Sarcastic slander. Grumbling indirectly.

ریزه ریزه *ad*. Little by little; bit by bit. *–a*. = ریز ریز

ریزه‌کاری Elaborate work ; nicety.

ریزی Minuteness. Tininess.

ریس 1) [Imp. of ریستن]. 2) ○ Soft or liquid food.

ریستن [ریس] To spin.

ریسته [P. P. of ریستن] Spun.

ریسمان String. Rope. Line. — ریسمانِ شاقول ‖ ریسمانِ کار = ماهی گیری Fishing-line.

ریسمان بافی Cotton-spinning.

ریسندگی Spinning.

ریسنده Spinner.

ریسه File ; queue. — ر. کردن To set in a file; cause to stand in a q.

ریش Beard. — ریش وقیچی هر دو در دست شما است I am at your mercy; I am wholly in your power. — ریش بدست کسی دادن To leave a security or credit with s. o. — ر. گذاشتن To grow a b. — بریش کسی خندیدن To snap one's fingers at s. o. — ریشش درآمد His b. started to grow. *F.* 1) He lost his juvenile beauty; 2) it was no more new ; it became commonplace. — ر. گرو گذاشتن To pledge one's honour. — ریش بز *Bot.* Goatsbeard *or* meadowsweet.

ریش 1) *n.* Ulcer; sore. 2) *a.* Wounded. — ر. کردن* To wound.

ریش تراش ○ Barber.

ریشخند Mocking ; derision. Coaxing. — ر. کردن To ridicule. To coax.

ریشدار Bearded.

ریش ریش Lacerated ; wounded. Sore. Unravelled. — ر. ر. کردن To unravel. To ulcerate.

ریش سفید *a.* Grey-bearded. *n.* G.-b. man. Dean; elder.

ریشگی Radical (sign).

ریشو + Having a bushy beard [not in polite use].

ریشه Root. Fringe. Frill. *F.* Origin. [Of a tooth] R. or stump. [Of a word] Stem. — ریشهٔ دوم Square root. — ریشهٔ سوم Cube r. — ریشهٔ ناخن Hangnail. — ر. دواندن *or* ر. کردن To take r. ; strike r. — از ریشه درآوردن To eradicate. — به ر. زدن To strike at the root.

ریشه‌ای Rooty. Radical.

ریشه پایی Rhizopod(an).

ریشه خوار Rhizophagous.

ریشه‌کن کردن To eradicate; extirpate. To cure radically.

ریشه‌گیری *Math.* Evolution.

ریع A. Redundance. Swelling. — ر. کردن To swell.

ریعان *A.* Best part ; choice p. — ریعان جوانی Flower of youth.

ریغ [*Indecent*] Thin excrement; soft stool.

ریغماسی × Weak and sickly.

ریغو × Good-for-nothing;

sluttish.

ریگ Pebble ; shingle. Sand. Gravel. – ریگ روان Moving sand.– ر. درکفش داشتن To have something up one's sleeve. To have a sly meaning. – مثل ر. خرج کردن To spend like water.

ریگ توده & ریگ پشته Sand-hill.

ریگزار Sandy (region).

ریگستان Sandy region.

ریگ شور کردن To scour with sand.

ریگماهی Skink.

ریگی Sandy. – ساعت ر. Sand-glass.

ریل E. Rail. – ر. کشیدن To lay the track.

ریل گذاری E. P. Track-laying.

ریم ○ Pus [چرك]. Dross. Dregs.

ریم آلود Purulent.

ریم آور Suppurative.

ریمل Fr. Eyelash makeup ; mascara.

ریمن ○ Purulent. F. Dirty.

رینگ E. (M.) Ring.

ریو * Deceit; fraud [فریب].

ریواس or ریباس Rhubarb.

ریوند Rhubarb. – ریوند چینی China rhubarb. – رُب ر. Gamboge.

ریوی A. (riavi:) Pulmonary.

ریه A. Lung. [D. ریتین]

ریةالبحر A. Jelly-fish.

رئیس A. [رؤسا] Chief ; head. Director. Manager. [Of a republic] President. [Of a board of directors] Chairman. [Of a police station] Magistrate. [Of a school] Headmaster. [Of a university] Chancellor. [Of a college] Principal. [Of a bank] Governor. – رئیس تشریفات Master of Ceremonies.

رئیس‌الوزراء A. = نخست وزیر

رئیسه A. [Fem. of رئیس] S. a. under هیئت

ز

زا *or* **زای** [Imp. of زائیدن]
زا ○ = **زاییمان** ‖ سر زارفتن ـ To die in labour. [tired.
زاپاس *R. n.* Reserve. — *a.* Re-
زاج *A.* [f. P. زاک] Alum. ـ زاج سبز Sulphate of iron; green vitriol. ـ زاج سفید Alum. ـ زاج کبود Blue or copper v. ـ زاج مکلس Colcothar.
زاد Natality. [In comb.] Child.
زاد *A.* = **توشه**
زاد بوم Birthplace.
زادگان [Pl. of زاده]
زادن * [Cont. of زاییدن]
زادو ولد *P. A.* Reproduction. ـ ز. کردن To procreate.
زاده [P. P. of زادن] Born. —*n.* [pl. زادگان] Child; offspring [*usu. in comb. Ex.* شاهزاده prince].
زار *a.* Deplorable. Bitter. Wounded. ـ کارش ز. است He's done for. — *ad.* Bitterly. Cruelly.
زار [Imp. of زاریدن]
زار *Suf.* = place abounding in. Ex. ریگزار *q. v.*
زار زار Bitterly : ز. گریه کرد
زارع *A.* Farmer. Cultivator.
زارکش کردن To kill cruelly; k. with torture.
زاری Weeping ; lamentation. Beseeching; supplication. ـ ز. کردن To weep.
زاریدن [زار] To weep; lament.
زاستر ○ Transcendent. [Cont. of زانسوتر]
زاغ Raven. ـ زاغ کبود Jay. ـ زاغ سیاه کسیرا چوب زدن To be on some one's track ; shadow him.
زاغ *n.* Alum. Vitriol[زاج]. —*a.* Blue , as an eye. ـ ز. زدن (به) To taw.
زاغ چشم Blue-eyed. [daw.
زاغچه *or* **زاغی** (Mag)pie; jack-
زاغه Cave. Hut.
زاگ ○ *See* زاغ & زاج
زال Very old man (*or* woman). Albino. *Mas. pr. name.*
زالزالك *Kind of wild plum.*
زالو Leech. ـ زالوی اسبی Horse-leech. ـ ز. انداختن To apply a leech.
زاماسکه *R.* Glaziers' putty.
زان Beech.
زان * [Cont. of از آن]
زانکه * [Cont. of از آنکه] Because.
زانگه * [Cont. of از آنگاه] From (*or* since) that time. ـ ز. که Ever since.
زانو Knee. K.-joint ; bend ;

gooseneck [also زانویی]. — ز. انداختن To get baggy at the knees. — ز. زدن To kneel down. — بزانو درآمدن 1) = زانو زدن 2) To yield or surrender. — بزانو درآوردن To cause to yield or s.

زانوبند Shackle for a camel. Kneepiece; knee-cap.

زانو درد Gonalgia.

زانویی Knee-joint; goose-neck.

زانی *A.* Adulterer. [Fem. زانیه Adulteress].

زاویه *A.* [زَوایا]=گوشه Corner; angle. — زاویهٔ مقدسه Shrine — سنگ ز. Cornerstone.

زاویه‌کش *A. P.* = نقاله Protractor. [*S. a.* نقاله

زاویه سنج *A. P.* Goniometer.

زاهد *A.* [زهاد] Devout or ascetic (person).

زاهدانه *A. P.* Devoutly. Ascetically. As a hermit.

زاهدی *A. P.* Devoutness. Abstemiousness.

زای *S. u.* زا [rator.

زایا *a.* Generating. —*n.* Gene-

زایچه Birth certificate. Horoscope ○.

زائد *A.* Superfluous. — ز. بر Surplus to. More than. — سبب ز. Hypermetrical syllable.

زائده *A.* [زَوائد] *Anat.* Process.

زائر *A.* [زوار] Visitor. Pilgrim.

زایش Birth. Production.

زایشگاه Maternity hospital.

زایل *or* **زائل** *A.* Passing away; disappearing. — ز. شدن To disappear. To be forgotten. To lapse. — ز. کردن To cause to d. To remove.

زایمان *or* **زائیمان** Childbirth; childbed; accouchement. — درحال ز. In c.; in labour.

زاینده Giving birth to. *F.* Productive. Self-increasing.

زائو Parturient.

زاییدن [زای] To be delivered of; give birth to To generate. *F.* To originate.

زائیده [P. P. of زائیدن] Born.

زباب ○ *A.* = موش صحرائی

زباد *A.* Civet(-cat); muskcat.

زُباله *A.* Sweepings; rubbish; dirt. — صندوق ز. Orderly bin.

زَبان Tongue. Language. — زبانِ خوش Soft words. — زبان بیزبانی or زبان حال Dumb language; mute l. — زبانش می گیرد He stammers. — زبانِ کوچك Uvula. — ز. نمی‌فهمد He is not amenable to reason. — ز. * زبان بر بستن or درکشیدن To keep silent. — ز زدن To taste or lick. — بزبان آمدن To begin (or learn) to speak. — بزبان آوردن To mention. To cause to s. — زیر زبان کسیرا کشیدن To draw one out. — دو زبان [یا دو زبانه] درآمدن To contradict oneself. — دل برسر زبان‌داشتن To wear one's heart on one's sleeves. — زبان خود را خسته کردن To waste one's breath (*or* words).

زبان آور 1) Eloquent. 2) = چرب زبان

زبان باز Charlatan. Blusterer.

زبان‌بازی Charlatanry. Blustering. Flattery.

زبان‌بُر ○ *n*. Hush-money. —*a*. Silencing.

زبان بریده * Dumb.

زبان بسته Tongue-tied. Dumb.

زباندار Expressive.

زبان‌دان Linguist.

زبان دراز(ی) Abusive(ness).

زبان درقفا *or* زبان پس‌قفا *P.A.* Delphinium.

زبانزد Idiom. Colloquialism ○.

زبانک Uvula. *Bot*. Ligula.

زبان‌گرفتگی Stammering.

زبان‌گنجشک Ash-tree.

زبانه [*Of a bell*] Tongue; clapper. [*Of a scale*] Index. [*Of a lock*] Bolt. [*Of a key*] Bit. [*Of a pipe*] Reed. [*Of fire*] Flame; blaze. — کام و زبانه Mortise and tenon. — ز. کشیدن To spread, as fire; flame.

زبانی *a*. Verbal; oral. Lingual. *F*. Professed. —*ad*. Verbally.

زُبده *A*. Choice part. Compendium; gist. *OS*. Cream.

زِبر Coarse; rough. — زبر و زرنگ + Quick; active.

زبر (*zebar*) 1) * Upper part; top. 2) The vowel-sign (َ).

زبرتنگ Surcingle.

زبرجد Chrysolite. — زبرجد هندی Topaz.

زبردست *a*. Proficient; skilled; clever. —*n*. * Man in power.

زبردستی Proficiency; skill. Superiority; upper hand.

زبره آرد Middlings.

زبره سنگ Trochyte.

زبری Coarseness; roughness.

زبرین * Upper. Superior; higher.

زبل *or* زبیل *A*. Dung.

زَبور *A*. (Book of) Psalms.

زَبون Despicable; humble. Weak. — ز. ساختن To h. To vanquish.

زبیده (*A*.) *Fem. pr. name*.

زبیل *A*. Dung.

زپرتی × Flimsy. Phon(e)y.

زجاج ○ *A*. = شیشه Glass.

زُجاجی *A*. Vitreous. Hyaloid. *Cf. the fem*. زجاجیه

زجاجیت *A*. Vitreosity.

زجاجیه *A*. Crystalline lens. [Orig. fem. of زجاجی *q. v.*] — ورم ز. Crystallitis.

زَجر Torment. Persecution. — ز. کردن *or* ز. دادن To torment. To persecute.

زجرکُش کردن To kill by slow and cruel torture.

زُحل *A*. = کیوان Saturn.

زحمات [Pl. of زحمت]

زَحمت *A.* [زحمات] Trouble ; inconvenience. Pains.— ز. دادن To trouble ; give t. (to). — ز.کشیدن To take pains; take trouble; be at p.—زحمت کسیرا کم کردن To spare one the trouble. — زحمت راکم کنیم Allow us to be excused.

زحمت‌کش *A. P.* Painstaking ; hard-working.

زحیر *A.* Dysentery.

زخارف ○ *A.* [Pl. of زخرف] Allurements or vanities of the world.

زَخم 1) *n.* Wound; sore. — زخم رختخواب Bedsore; decubitus ulcer. — زخم زبان A blow with a word. 2) *a.*+ Sore ; ulcerous. —ز. زدن To wound. To scratch or injure, as a wall. — ز. برداشتن *or* ز. خوردن To be wounded. — ز. کردن To wound. To gall.

زخم‌بند Dresser (of wounds). Dressing; bandage.

زخم‌بندی Dressing (of wounds).

زخم‌خورده Wounded.

زخم‌ناپذیر Invulnerable.

زخمه * = **مضراب**

زخمی Wounded. — ز. شدن To be w. — ز.کردن To wound.

زدا(ی) [Imp. of زُدودن].

زدگی Cancellation. Omission. Hole in a cloth [often زده].

زَدَن [زن] *vt.* To strike; beat; hit. To play (on) : ویولن ز. ‖ To ring : زنگ ز. ‖ To blow : بوق ز. ‖ To knock at. To shoot. To cut (off) ; lop. To blow : پنبه ز. ‖ To cross out; cancel. To cite : مَثل ز. ‖ To inflict. To wear : عینك ز. ‖ To pitch : خیمه ز. ‖ To break into : دکانش را زدند ‖ *—vi.* To beat ; pulsate. To pinch. To rush. To incline: بسفیدی میزند ‖ میزندبرای ریاست جمهوری + He runs for president. — زد بکتاب (خواندن) + He took to books. — بزن بچاك *S. u.* چاك ‖ بآب ز. To splash into water. —اسید به آن میزنند They treat it with acid. — بهم ز. To disturb. To break up. To stir. To procure : ثروت بهم ز. ‖ خود را بدیوانگی زد He pretended to be mad.

زدن‌گاه Tee.

زدو Gum (of wild almonds).

زدوار Zedoary. — زدوار ختائی Z. of China.

زدوبند Collusion. — ز.کردن To collude.

زدوخورد Conflict ; fight. — ز کردن To f. To skirmish.

زدودن [زدای] * To rub off ; file away. To furbish.—زنگ ازدل کسی زدودن * To soothe the heart of s. o.; console him.

زده [P. P. of زدن] *a.* Beaten. Struck. Smitten ; stricken.

Cloyed ; *blasé*. —*n*. Hole [in a cloth]. *See* ذدگی
زَر Gold [طلا]. *F*. Money [پول].
زرّادخانه Arsenal.
زراعت *A*. Tilling ; cultivation.— ز.کردن To do farming.
زراعتی *A. P*. Agricultural. Designed for cultivation.
زرّافه *A*. Giraffe.
زر اندود(ه) Overlaid with gold. — ز.کردن To plate or overlay with g. ; gild.
زراوَند Birthwort.
زربافت *a*. Woven with gold. —*n*. Brocade; g. cloth [often زربفت]
زرپرست Mammonist.
زرپور Roan or sorrel.
زرپوست Chrysalis.
زرتشت Zoroaster.
زرتشتی Zoroastrian.
زرتک Safflower.
زرخرید Bondsman.
زرخیز Auriferous. *By e*. Rich(in natural resources).
زَرد Yellow [also ذرد رنگ] — رنگ زرد فرنگی Chromate of lead. — زردکهربائی Amber. — پول ز. Gold money. — گل ز. Y. rose. — ز. شدن To turn yellow. To grow pale. — ز.کردن To paint y. To make pale.
زرداب Gall ; bile.
زرداب ریز Biliary ; choleric.
زردابی Biliary ; bilious ; choleric.
زردالو Apricot.
زردپی Tendon.
زرد(د) چوبه Turmeric. — گرد زردچوبهٔ هندی Curry powder.
زرد رویی Shame. Paleness o.
زرد زخم Impetigo; ringworm.
زردشت etc. = زرتشت etc.
زرد فام Yellowish.
زردک = هویج Carrot.
زردنبو × Pale.
زرد وره Yellow-hammer.
زر دوزی Gold embroidery.
زرده Yolk (of an egg).
ز.دی Yellowness. Paleness. Chlorosis.
زردیان Jaundice.
زِرزِر +Thrumming or strumming (noise) ; fiddling.
زِرشک Barberry.
زرشکی Maroon.
زَرع *A*. Cultivation; tilling.— قابل ز. Arable. — غیر قابل ز. Barren.
زرفین *Z*. Segment.
زرفینی *Z*. Annelid.
زَرق *A*. Hypocrisy. Deceit.
زرق و برق + *A. P*. Gaudiness.
زرق و برقدار *A. P*. Gaudy ; garish ; tawdry.
زرقوری Crowfoot.
زرقون *or* زرگون Jargon ; zircon ; cinnabar.
زرک = 1) زدورق 2) اکلیل
زرکش Gold-wire drawer. Gold-embroiderer.

طلاکوب = زرکوب
زرگر Goldsmith ; silversmith.
زرگری Goldsmith's or silversmith's trade. — جنگ ز. Sham fight *or* quarrel (between two to deceive a third party).
زرگون *S. u.* زرقون
زُرنا *Kind of oboe.*
زرنباد *A-P.* = زدوار
زرنشان Inlaid with gold.
زِرَنگ Clever. Bright. Smart.
زَرنگار Adorned or overlaid with gold.
زرنگی Cleverness. Smartness.— ز. کردن To (try to) be clever.
زَرنیخ Orpiment. — زرنیخ قرمز Realgar.
زروَرق *P. A.* Gold leaf; gold foil. — زرورق بدل Dutch gold. — از لای زرورق درآمدن To come out of a bandbox.
زرورقی *P. A.* Made of gold leaf. Very thin.— کاغذ زرورقی Tissue paper.
زِرِه Chain mail; coat of m.— زره بازو Brassart. — زره ران Cuisse.— زره ساعد Vambrace.— زره ساق Greave. — زره سینه Cuirass ; breast-plate. — زره شانه Camail.
زره‌باف Manufacturer of chain [mails.
زره پوش Armour-clad ; armoured. — کشتی ز. Iron-clad.
زره‌دار Armour-plated.
زرهی Armour-plated.
زَری Brocaded silk.

زرّین * Golden.
زِشت Ugly. Clumsy. *F.* 1) Not decent or befitting ; indecent. 2) Obscene.
زشتخو(ی) Ill-tempered.
زشتخویی Ill temper.
زشت‌رو(ی) Ugly; ill-favoured.
زشت رویی Ugliness.
زشت‌گویی * = 1) بدگویی 2) بد حرفی
زشت نام * = بد نام
زشتی Ugliness. *F.* Indecency.
زَعفران *A.* Saffron.
زعفران‌الحدید *A.* Crocus of Mars ; C. Martis; colcothar.
زعفرانی *A. P.* Flavoured with saffron. S.-coloured ; pale.
زَعم *A.* Opinion. — بزعمِ In the opinion of ; according to.
زَعیم ○ *A.* [زُعماء] Spokesman ; chief. Feual lord. — زعمای قوم Men of distinction.
زُغال (Char)coal. Carbon. — زغال چوب Charcoal.
زغال اخته Dogberry ; wild cornel.
زغالِ سنگ *or* زغال‌سنگ Coal.— زغال سنگ خالص Anthracite. — زغال سنگ نارس Peat.
زغره *or* زقره Sweat-band.
زغ زغ Clattering ; chirping ; peeping. Throbbing.
زغن Kite (*bird*).
زغنبوت × Gall and wormwood ; very bitter thing. [Used as an abuse].

زِفاف *A*. Consummation of a marriage. *L*. Marriage. *Cf*. عروسی

زِفت Pitch. – زفت رومی Asphalt; Jews'-pitch.

زُفت 1) = ترشرو 2) خسیس

زفره ○ 1) = بوزه 2) Mandibule.

زفیر *A*. Expiration.

زُکام *A*. Cold (in the head); coryza. – ز. شدن To have a cold in the h.

زکریا *A-Heb*. 1) Zachariah; 2) Zacharias.

زَکوة *or* زکاة *A*. Poor-rate as prescribed by Islam.

زَکی ○ *A*. [ازکیاء] Pure. Pious.

زکی × Fudge!

زگیل Wart. – زگیل مقعد و عجان Condyloma.

زَلّ ○ *A*. = لغزش

زِل *S. u.* زیل

زُلال *A*. Limpid (water).

زلالی *A*. [usu. in the fem. زلالیه] Aqueous. Synovial.

زُل‌زل نگاه کردن + To stare or glare.

زِلزله *A*. = زمین لرزه Earthquake. – شرح ز. Seismography.

زلزله زده *A. P.* *a*. Stricken by earthquake. –*n*. Victim of e. [pl. زلزله زدگان].

زلزله سنج *A. P.* Seismometer; also, seismograph.

زلزله‌شناس *A. P.* Seismologist.

زلزله شناسی *A. P.* Seismology.

زُلف Lock of hair; ringlet. *By e*. Hair.

زلوبیا *or* زلیبیا *Kind of* confectionery.

زلیخا *Fem. pr name*.

زماره ○ *A*. Flute; pipe [نی].

زِمام *A*. Rein; bridle. – زمامِ امور را در دست گرفتن To take the reins of government.

زمامدار *A. P.* Statesman in authority; person at the helm; ruler.

زمامداری *A.P.* Statesmanship. Tenure of office.

زَمان *A*. [اَزمنه] Time. Epoch; age. *Gr*. Tense. – در زمانِ In the days of.

زمانه *A. P.* Times; fortune. (Vicissitudes of the) world.

زمانی (*A*.) *a*. Chronological. Temporal. –*n*. [Only in the pl. زمانیان Mortals ○].

زمخت Coarse; gross. Rude.

زمختی Coarseness. Rudeness.

زمرد *A-P*. Emerald.

زمردگیاه ○ = شاهدانه

زمردین * Emerald-coloured.

زُمره *A*. Category; group. – در زمرهٔ Among.

زَمزمه Humming. *F*. Rumour. – ز. کردن To hum; croon.

زِمستان Winter.

زمستانی Hibernal. Suitable for winter. – لباس ز. Winter clothes.

زَمهریر *A*. Intense cold.

زَمین Earth. Land. Ground; floor. Landed property. –

ز. بوسیدن • To do homage. – ز. خوردن [Orig. بزمین خوردن] To fall (down to the ground). *F.* to be overthrown. – ز. زدن [Orig. بزمین زدن] To throw d. To overthrow. – ز. گذاشتن [Orig. بزمین گذاشتن] To lay d. *F.* To abandon.

زمین پیما Land-surveyor. – کرم ز. Geometer.

زمین پیمایی Land-survey; land-measurement.

زمین شناس Geologist.

زمین شناسی Geology.

زمین گیر Paralytic. *OS.* Confined to the ground.

زمین لرزه Earthquake.

زَمینه Background. Ground (work). *F.* Basis. Footing. – در این ز. In this connection. On these lines. – زمینهٔ چیزیرا فراهم کردن To pave the way for s. t.

زمینه سازی Planning. Laying plots; intrigue.

زمینی Terrestrial. Territorial. Overland. – پست ز. Surface mail. – نیروی ز. Land force.– سیب ز. Potato.

زَن Woman. Wife. – کارگر زن Female worker. – ز. دادن To take a wife for; marry. – ز. گرفتن *or* زن بردن To take a w.; m. a woman.

زن [Imp. of زدن].

زِناء *A.* Adultery. – ز. کردن To commit adultery. – ز. دادن To commit a.: said of a woman. – زنای اقرباء Incest.– زنای بعنف Rape. – زنای محصنه Adultery with a married woman.

زنادیق & زنادقه [Pl. of زندیق]

زنار *A-G.* Christian's or Jew's girdle distingushing him from a Moslem.

زنازاده *A. P.* = حرامزاده

زناشویی Matrimony. Marriage. – زندگی ز. Married life.– ز. کردن To join in marriage.

زناکار *A. P.* Adulter-er; -ess.

زناکاری *A. P.* Adultery.

زنانگی (1 = زنانه 2) Femininity. – داروی ز. Nostrum.

زَنانه *a.* Women's; ladies': کفش ز. ‖ Feminine: خوی ز. ‖ علم بیماری های ز. Gynecology. –*n.* Women's apartment.

زنانه دوز Dressmaker.

زن پدر = **زن بابا**

زنبر Hand-barrow.

زن برادر Brother's wife; sister-in-law.

زنبرک Crossbow. Spring ○[فنر].

زنبرکی ○ = فنری Operated by a spring. – کمان ز. Arbalest; crossbow.

زنبق *A.* [f. P. زنبه] Socket of a candlestick; sconce. Iris; lily. – زنبق دشتی White l. – زنبق زرد Day-l.; hemerocallis.

زنبور Bee. Wasp. – زنبور عسل

Bee. ـ زنبور سرخ or زنبور درشت Hornet. ـ زنبور طلائی Cockchafer. ـ زنبور غله Sawfly ; cephus. ـ زنبور عسل نر Drone.ـ چوب در لانهٔ ز. کردن To bring hornets' nest about one's ear.

زنبورخوار [For مرغ ز.] Bee-eater. Titmouse.

زنبورداری Apiculture.

زنبورک 1) زنبرك 2) Falconet.

زنبورکی 1) فنری 2) Alveolar; cellular. 3) Reticular.

زنبوری Cellular ; honey-combed.

زنبه 1) زنبر ‖ 2) *See* زنبق

زنبیل [f. A. زبیل] Basket.

زن پدر Step-mother.

زنجبیل *A*. [f. Sanskrit origin] Ginger. ـ زنجبیل پرورده Preserved ginger. ـ زنجبیل سگ Smartweed ; waterpepper. ـ زنجبیل شامی Elecampane.

زنجره Cricket; grig.

زن جلب × Cuckold.

زنجیر Chain. ـ زنجیر برف Skid-chain. ـ زنجیر خوشبختی Chain-letter. ـ زنجیر راهداری Toll-bar. ـ زنجیر کوچك Chainlet. ـ حلقهٔ ز. Link.ـ مأمور زنجیر Toll-man. ـ پنج ز. فیل ○ Five elephants. ـ ز. کردن To put in chains.

زنجیره Chain mark. C.-work. Milling. Ripple.

زنجیری Chain-like; catenary. Chain-driven. Chained.ـ آچار زنجیری Chain-wrench. ـ پل ز. Chain-bridge. ـ دکمه سردست ز. Sleeve-link.

زنخ (Pit in the) chin.

زنخدان Chin. ـ چاه ز. Dimple (*or* pit) in the chin.

زنخی Genial ; mental.

زند *Zand* : exposition of the *Avest*a. Commentary ○.

زَند *A*. (Bone of the) forearm.ـ زنداعلی Radius. ـ زنداسفل Ulna.

زَندار Married : مرد زندار

زِندان Prison. ـ در زندان افکندن To put in jail ; imprison.

زندانبان Gaoler *or* jailer.

زندانی Prisoner. ـ ز. کردن To imprison.

زند اوستا *Zand-Avest*a : the Avesta and its commentary.

زندایی Wife of one's maternal uncle ; aunt.

زند خوان • Priest chanting the *Zand*. (*See 1st*. زند)
Met. Sweet-singing bird.

زندقه *A*. Dualism. Atheism.

زندگان *S*. *u*. زنده

زِندگانی Life. Living.ـ ز. کردن To live.

زِندگی Life. Living. Life-time. ـ شرح ز. Biography. ـ ز. کردن To live.

زن دوست Philoginous. Uxorious.

زن دوستی Philoginy. Uxoriousness.

زنده *a*. Alive ; living. —*n*. [pl. زندگان the living]. ـ

ز. کردن To restore to life. *F.* To revive. — ز. شدن To be restored to l. To be revived. To be refreshed. — شب ز. داشتن * To spend the night awake. — ز. باد Long live ! — ز. بگور کردن To bury alive. — سر زنده بگور بردن To die a natural death. — سر زنده بگور نخواهد برد He will come to the gallows.

زنده دل Enjoying a green old age; hearty and hale. Lively; vigilant. Pious.

زَندی *A.* Cubital : radial or ulnar. *See 1st.* زند

زندیق *A-P.* [زنادقه & زنادیق] Sadducee. Atheist. Dualist.

زن صفت *P. A.* Effeminate ; womanish.

زن عمو *P. A.* Wife of one's paternal uncle ; aunt.

زن قحبه *P. A.* Cuckold.

زَنگ Bell. [*At school*]Period. Rust. — زنگ آهنی Ferrous oxide. — زنگ سیاه Smut. — زنگ گیاهی Blight; mildew. — زنگ مس Verdigris. — ز. زدن To ring (a b.). To rust.

زنگاب *or* **زنجاب** Stain left after a distemper.

زنگار Verdigris. Rust. — زنگار مس Acetate of copper.

زنگار *or* **زنگال** Leggings.

زنگاری Rust-coloured ; rubiginous.

زنگبال Florican.

زنگ زده Rusty.

زنگ نزن Rustproof. Stainless.

زنگوله Hawkbell ; little bell. — زنگولهٔ پای تابوت *Met.* Little children of an old man. *OS.* Small bells hanging from a coffin.

زَنگی Furnished with a bell; ringing. — ساعت ز. Repeating watch ; repeater. — دایرهٔ ز. Tambourine; timbrel.

زَنگی (Native) of *Z*anzibar. Ethiopian. Blackamoor.

زننده *a.* Repulsive. Shocking. Forbidding. Pungent ; biting; mordant. —*n.* Hitter; beater. Player ; performer [pl. زنندگان].

زِنهار * *n.* Caution. Quarter ; mercy. —*int.* Beware! Take care ! — ز. اگر . . . * God forbid that . . . ; don't you . . . — ز. خواستن To seek quarter or protection.

زنی ○ Womanhood. — بزنی گرفتن To marry; take for a wife.

زنیان Aniseed. — عرق ز. Anisette.

زو * [Cont. of از او]

زوّار *A.* (*zavar*) Pilgrim. : زوار مکه P. to Mecca.

زوار (*zovar*) [Pl. of زائر]

زَوال *A.* Decline. Decadence. — رو بزوال گذاردن To begin to decline or disappear; be on the wane.

زوایا [Pl. of زاویه]

زوائد *A*. Superfluities. *Cf*. [زائده]

زوبین Javelin ; dart.

زوج *A*. [ازواج] Pair ; couple. Even number. Husband.

زوجات [Pl. of زوجه]

زوجه *A*. [زوجات] Wife [زن].

زوجین *A*. [D. of زوج] Married couple ; husband and wife.

زود Quickly. Soon. Early. Easily. — ز. باشید Be quick. Hurry up. — ز. باشد * Before long. — یك روز صبح ز. An early morning. — هرچه ز.تر As e. as possible.

زود آشنا Apt to become sociable or friendly.

زود انداز ० Extemporaneous (speech).

زود باور Credulous; easy of [belief.

زود باوری Credulity.

زود بند Quick-setting : سیمان ز.

زود پَز Easily cooked. — دیگ ز. Pressure-cooker.

زود جوش Apt to mix or become sociable. — آدم ز. A good mixer.

زود خیز Early riser.

زود رنج Touchy ; quick to take offence.

زودرس = **پیشرس**

زود غضب *P. A. or* **زود خشم** Prone to anger ; hot-tempered.

زودگذر Transient.

زودی ० Quickness. — بزودی Soon; shortly; before long. — باین ز. So soon.

زودیاب Easily obtained.

زور Force. Power ; strength ; might. Violence. — حرف ز. Unfair or illogical remark. — ز. آوردن To press. — بکار زور آوردن To work hard ; exert oneself. — ز. دادن To p. upon; push. — ز. زدن + To exert force. — یك زوری زدن + He had a try at it. — بزور By f. — بزور خندیدن To f. a laugh. — راه خود را بزور بازکردن To f. one's way. — بزورگرفتن To extort; exact. — زورم باو نمیرسد I am not a match for him; I cannot cope with him (in strength).

زور آزما ० Athlete.

زور آزمایی Measuring one's strength. — باکسی ز.کردن To measure one's s., or try conclusions, with s. o.

زورآوَر Powerful.

زورچپان کردن *or* **زورتپان کردن** × To cram or thrust with force.

زورخانه Gymanasium; palestra.

زورَق *A*. Boat.

زورقی *A*. Scaphoid [now ناوی].

زورکی + 1) *a*. Forced : خندهٔ ز. ‖ 2) *ad*. Barely.

زورگو (One) who makes illogical remarks or unreason-

able demands.
زورمند Powerful ; strong.
زورمندی (Exercise of) power.
زور وَرزی Exertion of force.
زوزه Howling. — ز. کشیدن To howl ; pule ; yelp.
زوفا Hyssop.
زِه Catgut. Cord. Bowstring. Rim. Chord ; hypotenuse.— زه کردن To string, as a bow. زه زدن × To peter or back out; show the white feather.
زِه Childbirth. —درد زه Pains of childbirth ; labour.
زِه = زهی
زِه Water oozing through a [stream.
زهاد [Pl. of زاهد]
زهار Privy parts. — موی ز. Pubes.
زهتاب Cord-twister.
زُهد *A*. Asceticism; abstemious- [ness.
زِهدان Uterus. — آماس ز. Metritis ; uteritis.
زهد فروش *A. P*. Hypocritical.
زهد فروشی *A. P*. Hypocrisy.
زَهر Poison.—ز. دادن [With به] To poison. — ز. کردن + To make disagreeable or bitter. — زهر مار کردن × [*Contemptuous expression for* خوردن] To eat. — ز. خوردن To p. oneself. — زهر چشم از کسی گرفتن To settle a person's hash ; intimidate him by severe measures. — زهر خود را بمن ریخت + He served me out at last as he had planned.

زَهرا (*A*.) *Fem. pr. name*.
زَهراب Urine [پیشاب].
زهرابه Toxin.
زهرآگین & زهرآلود Poisoned.
زهر باد Quinsy ; tonsillitis.
پادزهر = زهر دارو
زهر شناس Toxicologist.
زهر شناسی Toxicology.
زهرکش ○ *a*. Antidotal; antitoxic. —*n*. Antidote.
زُهروی *A*. Venereal.
زَهره Gall-bladder.— ز. ام ترکید *or* ز. ام آب شد I was frightened to death.
زُهره *A*. = ناهید Venus.
زَهره تراک Frightened to death.— ز. شدن To be frightened to d. ; have one's heart in one's mouth. — ز. کردن To frighten to d. ; freeze one's blood ; make one's b. run cold.
زه قلاب *P. A*. Fishing-line.
زهکش Drain pipe. [drain.
زهکشی Drainage. — ز.کردن To
زِهگیر Archer's thumbstall. Tailpiece of a violin [also سیمگیر].
زُهم *A*. Fetid smell (of meat). Stinking fat.
زِهوار Lace; groove. Rim. — زهوارش در رفت × He pegged out.
زهوار در رفته × Done up ; impotent.

زهی [*With the stress on the 1st. syl.*] Well done!

زی ٥ = سوی Towards; to.

زی *A.* (*ziy*) Garb; appearance.

زیاد *A. P a.* Much: پول ز. ‖ Many: کتاب(های) ز. ‖ Excessive. Great: عدهٔ ز. ‖ Too many: سپکار ها یکی ز. است ‖ —*ad*. Very much or too m.: ز. خورد ‖ Too. ‖ ز. شدن To be increased. To grow. — ز. کردن To increase or multiply. — مرحمت‌سرکارزیاد Thank you (very much).

زیادت *A.* Excess. Increase.

زیادتی *A. P.* Surplus; excess. Abundance.

زیاده *A.* More [بیش or بیشتر]. — ز. از آنست که بتوان شمرد It is (*or* they are) more than can be counted. — ز. از حد Excessively. — ز. بر More than; in excess of.

زیاده رَوی *A.P.* Extravagance. Intemperance. — ز. کردن To go beyond due bounds. To be intemperate.

زیاده ستانی *A. P.* Extortion.

زیادی *A.P. n.* Excess; surplus. —*a*. Extra. Surplus; superfluous. Spare: وقت ز. ‖ —*ad*. Too much; extra.

زیارت *A.* Pilgrimage. — ز. کردن To visit as a pilgrim. [*In p. c.*] To meet. — به ز. رفتن To go on a pilgrimage.

زیارتگاه *A. P.* Sacred place visited by pilgrims.

زیاک = خروس‌کولی

زیان Loss. Detriment. Injury. — ز. دیدن To incur (*or* sustain) a loss. To be injured. — ز. رساندن [With به] To cause to sustain a loss. To injure. To be prejudicial to. — ز. کردن *or* ز. بردن To sustain a l.

زیان‌آور Prejudicial. Injurious.

زیانکار (One) who incurs a loss in whatever he does.

زیب Ornament. Beauty. — ز. دادن To ornament; adorn.

زیبا Beautiful. Handsome. Nice. — مرغ ز. Lapwing; pewit.

زیبایی Beauty. — سالن ز. Beauty-parlour.

زیبائی شناسی Aesthetics.

زیبق *A.* = جیوه & سیماب

زیبندگی Becomingness. Elegance.

زیبنده Becoming. Elegant. Graceful.

زِیبیدن [زیب] To become; suit. To seem beautiful.

زیپ *E.* Zip (fastener); slide f.

زیپلن *Fr.* Zeppelin.

زیپو × Wishy-washy. *See* آب زیپو *under* آب

زیتون *A.* Olive. — زیتون تلخ Margosa-tree; azedarach.

زیتونی *A.* Olivaceous. Olivary. Olive-green. [bles.

زیج *A-P.* Astronomical ta-
زید *(A.) Mas. pr. name.* — یك زیدی Such a one ; a certain person. — زید وعمر Tom, Dick, and Harry.

زیر *n.* Bottom; lower part The vowel-sign (ِ) . *—a.* 1) زیری 2) High-keyed ; shrill. Following ; undermentioned. *—ad.* Below ; underneath.— زیرِ *prep.* Under ; below. — نامبرده در زیر Mentioned b. ; undermentioned. —زیر پا گذاشتن To trample. To repress. — زیر پای کسی نشستن To seduce s. o. — زیر سرش بلند شده است His head has been turned (with the promise of a better position). — زیر سر گرفتن To secure beforehand. — زیر خنده زدن To burst into a laughter. — زیر چیزی زدن + To recalcitrate at (*or* against) s. t. To deny s. t. — زیر گریه خوابیدن To cry oneself to sleep. —بزیر آمدن To come down. To fall. — زیرو زبر کردن To turn upside d. To turn to chaos; destroy completely. — زیرو رو کردن To turn u. d. To ransack ; rummage. — ز. گرفتن To run over. To ride out.

زیرا *or* زیراکه Because.

زیراب Voidance water. Outlet. — زیراب حوضی را کشیدن To drain a pond. — زیراب کسیرا زدن×To do away with s. o. by underhand means; knife him.

زیر انداز ○ Carpet or linen cloth spread under it.

زیر پایی Foothold. Footstool.

زیر پوست Cutis ; derma.

زیر پوستی Hypodermic ; subcutaneous.

زیرپوش Underwear. — زیر پوشِ کشباف Vest.

زیر پیراهنی Undershirt ; vest.

زیر تنگ Belly-band.

زیر جامه 1) زیرشلواری 2) زیرپوش

زیر جلی Clandestine(ly) .

زیر حوله‌ای Towel-horse ; towel-rack ; towel-rail.

زیر خاکی (Relic) dug out of the ground.

زیرخان Ground floor.

زیرخوان Sopranist.

زیر دریایی Submarine.

زیردست Inferior; subordinate.— ز. کردن To subjugate.

زیر دستی Inferiority.

زیر دستی Writing-pad. Blotting-pad. Maulstick.

زیر زبانی Sublingual ; hypoglossal.

زیر زمین Basement. Cellar.

زیر زمینی Subterranean. Underground : ساقهٔ ز. ‖ Subsurface.

زیر سازی Foundation (work) ; substructure. Road-bed. Core.

زیرسوپاپ *or* زیرسوپاپی *P. Fr.*

Tappet. *M.*
زیرسیگاری Ash-tray.
زیر شلواری Pant ; drawers.
زیرفون Linden ; barren jujube tree ; basswood.
زیرك Clever ; smart. Shrewd.
زیرکی Cleverness. Ingenuity. Sagacity. Keenness.
زیرگلدانی Doily. *See* گلدان
زیرگوشی Cushion.
زیر نوشت Sub-title.
زیر نویس *C. E.* = **زیر نوشت**
زیره Cumin or caraway (seed). – زیرهٔ سبز *or* زیرهٔ سفید Cumin-s. – زیرهٔ سیاه Caraway-s. – ز. بکرمان بردن To carry coals to Newcastle.
زیره Outsole (of a shoe).
زیری Lower. Inferior.
زیرین Undermentioned ; following. Lower. Inferior.
زیست Subsistence. Life. – ز. کردن To live.
زیست شناس Biologist.
زیست شناسی Biology.
زیستن [زی] To live; subsist. To exist.
زیغ الشمس *A.* Declination of the sun.
زیل *or* **زِل** (Tailless) sheep. – قوچ ز. Merino s.
زیلو *Kind of pileless carpet.*
زین Saddle. – ز. کردن To saddle. – ز. برگرگ نهادن * To bell the cat.
زین * [Cont. of از این]
زین العابدین (*A.*) *Mas. pr. name. O.S.* The worshippers' beauty.
زینب (*A.*) *Fem. pr. name.*
زین پوش Saddle-cover ; housing.
زینت *A.* Ornament ; decoration. – ز. دادن To decorate or ornament.
زین ساز Saddler.
زین سازی Saddlery.
زینه Degree.
زینه بندی Grad(u)ation.
زنهار = **زینهار**
زیور (Set of) ornaments. *Fem. pr. name.*

ژاپن *Fr.* Japan.

ژاپنی *Fr. P.* Japanese. — گل ژ. Double-cone flower.

ژاژ ० Kind of camelthorn which camels find too tough to chew. — ژ. خائیدن * To babble ; talk nonsense.

ژاژخا(ی) Idle talker; babbler.

ژاژخایی Idle talk ; babbling.

ژاکت *Fr.* Jacket. — ژاکت کشباف Cardigan.

ژاله Dew. Also, hoar-frost.

ژاندارم *Fr.* Gendarme.

ژاندارمری *Fr.* Gendarmerie.

ژانطیانا *Fr.* (Root of the) gentian.

ژانویه *Fr.* January.

ژتن *Fr.* Chip; jeton; counter.

ژرژت *Fr.* Georgette.

ژَرف * Deep. *F.* Hard.

ژرفا *or* ژرفی Depth.

ژرف‌یاب *or* ژرفایاب Sounding-instrument ; sounder.

ژست *Fr.* Gesture ; business. — ژ. گرفتن To strike an attitude ; assume a pose.

ژله *Fr.* Jelly. *Cf.* دلمه &لرزانك

ژلین بیت *Fr.* Gelignite.

ژن *Fr.* Genoa.

ژنده *a.* Shabby ; worn-out. —*n.* Rag; patched garment.

ژنده پوش Clothed in rags.

ژنرال *Fr.* General.

ژنو *Fr.* Geneva.

ژور *Fr.* Open work. — ژ زدن To do open w. —*vt.* To pink; also, hemstitch.

ژولیده Untidy ; ruffled.

ژوئن *Fr.* June.

ژوئیه *Fr.* July.

ژیان Formidable ; devouring : شیرِ ژ.

ژیگلور *Fr.* (Carburettor) jet; (spray) nozzle ; atomizer.

ژیگو *Fr.* Leg of mutton or lamb (when cooked).

ژیگولو *Fr.* Gigolot.

ژیمناستیک *Fr.* Gymnastics. *Cf.* ورزش

س

سا *or* **سای** [Imp. of سائیدن]
سا *or* **سار** *Suf.* = -like.
ساباط *A.* Penthouse ; lean-to.
سابعاً *A.* Seventhly.
سابق *A. a.* Former; previous; old. Preceding. —*n.* Old days; former time. — س. براین Formerly ; in the past.
سابقاً *A.* Formerly; previously; previous to this.
سابق‌الذکر *A.* Aforementioned.
سابقه *A.* [سوابق] Antecedent ; (previous) record. Precedent ; example. Acquaintance. — سابقهٔ خدمت Record of service : او ۲۰ سال سابقهٔ خدمت دارد He has 20 years s. — سوء سابقه Bad record. — عدم سوء سابقه Clean r. — در شهربانی س. دارد He is known to the police.
سابقه‌دار *A. P.* Having (long) service.
سابقی *A. P.* = سابق & پیشین
سابیدن etc. = سائیدن etc.
ساتر ○ *A.* = پوشنده Hider.
ساتگین ○ Bumper ; large cup.
ساج *T.* Teak. Pan used in baking bread. — چوب س. T. wood ; black-wood.
ساچمه *T.* Pellet ; (small) shot. [*In a motor car*] Ball(s). — تفنگ ساچمه‌ای Shotgun. — یاتاقان ساچمه‌ای Ball-bearing.
ساحت *A.* [ساحات] Open space. Square. Area.
ساحر *A.* = جادو(گر) Magician; sorcerer. [Fem. ساحره Sorceress ; witch].
ساحل *A.* [سواحل] Shore. [*Of a river*] Bank.
ساحلی *A. P.* Coastal; littoral. Riparian : حقوق س.
ساخارین *R.* Saccharin.
ساخت Make. — ساخت انگلیس British make; made in England.
ساختگی Artificial. Forged. Feigned ; simulated.
ساختمان Construction. Building. Structure.
ساختمانی Constructional . Structural. — مصالح س. Building materials.
ساختن [ساز] To build ; construct. To make; manufacture. *F.* To forge ; fabricate. —*vi.* 1) To agree : این خوراک بمن نمی‌سازد This food does not a. with me. 2) To put up. 3) To collude. 4) To provide means . *Note.* After an adjective or a concrete noun ساختن means « to make or render ». Ex. (a) او را ناخوش ساخت It made

him sick. (b) او را شاه ساختند They made him king.

ساخت و پاخت + Collusion; covin. — س. کردن To collude.

ساخته [P. P. of ساختن] Manufactured; made. Built. Ready-made. *F*. Forged. Feigned. — کاری ازاو ساخته نیست He is not in a position to do anything. He is incapable of doing a.

ساخلو *T*. = **پادگان**

سادات *A*. The descendants of the Prophet.

سادساً *A*. = ششم آنکه Sixthly.

سادگی Simplicity. Easiness. Simple-mindedness. Austerity.

ساده Simple. Plain. Easy. Artless. Unmixed; pure.

ساده بافت Plain-woven.

ساده دل Simple-hearted.

ساده دلی Simple-heartedness.

ساده‌لوح *P. A*. Simple-minded; credulous. —*n*. Simpleton..

ساده لوحی *P. A*. Credulity. Simpleness.

سار Starling.

سار *Suf*. =1) Place abounding in; 2) full of; 3) -like [also سا].

سارا ० • Pure. Excellent.

ساربان Camel-driver.

ساردین *Fr*. Sardine.

سارِق *A*. = دزد Thief.

سارنگ *or* **سارنج** *Kind of melody. Kind of small bird*.

ساروج Plaster of lime and ashes or sand; mortar. — س. کردن To plaster with m.

ساری ० *A*. Flowing; circulating.

ساز 1) *n*. Musical instrument.— سازدهنی Mouth-organ; harmonicon. 2) *a*. In good condition. Equipped. Tuned. — س. کردن • To tune up; start. To prepare.

ساز [Imp. of ساختن].

ساز زن Musical performer; instrumentalist.

سازِش Composition; arrangement. Agreement. Compatibility. Collusion.—س. کردن To compound. To agree. To put up. To collude.

سازگار Agreeable; wholesome. Sociable. — با هم س. بودن To agree, or be compatible, with each other.

سازگاری Compatibility. Suitability. Agreement.

سازمان Organization. Structure.—سازمان خیریه (Charitable) foundation.

سازندگی Musical performance. M. profession [usu. نوازندگی].

سازنده Maker; manufacturer. Builder. Compositor. Musical performer.

ساز و برگ Equipment; accoutrements.

سازه *Math*. Factor [عامل].

سازی *Mus*. Instrumental.

ساس (Bed)bug.
ساسات *R*. Choke. *M*.
ساطع ○ *A*. Radiant. Clear.
ساطور *A*. Large chopping-knife.
ساعات [Pl. of ساعت].
ساعت *A*. 1) Hour [pl. ساعات]. 2) Watch or clock. — ساعت آبی Clepsydra. — ساعت آفتابی Sun-dial. — ساعت بغلی *or* ساعت جیبی Watch. — ساعت دیواری Clock. — ساعت سیلندر *M*. Dial cylinder gauge. — ساعت مچی Wrist-watch. — چه ساعتی است *or* ساعت چند است What time is it ? — ساعت سه و نیم است It is half past three. — نیم ساعت مانده بظهر It is 11 : 30 a. m. — گل س. *or* گل ساعتی Passion-flower.
ساعت دار *A*. *P*. Timed ○. — کنتور ساعت‌دار Double-acting meter.
ساعت ساز *A*. *P*. Watchmaker.
ساعت سازی *A*. *P*. Horology.
ساعت شمار *A*. *P*. Hour-hand.
ساعد *A*. = ارش Forearm.
ساعدین *A*. [D. of ساعد]. — ساعدین مبدأ نخاع Cerebral peduncles.
ساعی *A*. = کوشا Diligent ; industrious.
ساغر • Cup. *By e*. Wine.
سافل ○ *A*. Low(er). [Fem. سافله]. Ex., اطراف سافله Lower extremities.
ساق *A*. Foreleg. *Geom*. Leg. *Bot*. Stem ; also, stalk. *Z*. Peduncle.
ساقدار *A*. *P*. Pedunculate.
ساقدوش *T*. *P*. Groomsman.
ساقط *A*. Lapsed. Miscarried. *OS*. Fallen or falling. — شعاع س. Incident ray. — س.شدن To lapse. To cease to be valid. — حق وی س. شد He forfeited his right; his r. lapsed. — س. کردن To render null ; invalidate. To deprive or bereave. — از هستی س. کردن To bleed white. — از درجهٔ اعتبار س.است It is no longer valid.
ساقه *A*. *P*. Stem. Stalk. [*Of a flower*] Peduncle. [*Of a leaf*] Petiole ; footstalk. — • ساقهٔ زیر زمینی Rootstock ; rhizome.
ساقه‌دار *A*. *P*. Stemmed. *Bot*. Pediculate ; peduncular. Caulescent.
ساقی • *A*. Cupbearer.
ساقی‌نامه *A*. *P*. (Kind of) bacchanalian verse.
ساک [For آش س.] Pottage or soup with verjuice.
ساکت *A*. Quiet ; silent. *Cf*. ساکن & آرام ‖ س. شدن To keep s. or still. To be calmed or soothed. To subside. — س. کردن To quiet or soothe. To silence.
ساکسوفون *Fr*. Saxophone.
ساکن(*A*.) *a*. Resident; dwelling. Still; motionless [آرام]. *Gr*.

Quiescent. ـ س. اقیانوس Pacific Ocean. –n. [pl. ساکنین or سکنه] Inhabitant; resident. ـ س. شدن To dwell or reside. ـ س. کردن To lodge. To settle.

سال Year. Age. ـ چند سال دارید How old are you? ـ من ٦٠ س. دارم I am 60 years o. ـ ده ریال درسال Rials 10 per annum. ـ س. بسال From year to y.; each y. ـ صد سال به این سالها Many happy returns of the day [cited on festivals, not on birthday occasions]. ـ بچهٔ دو ساله A 2-y.-old child. ـ سال دوازده ماه + Year in year out.

سالاد *Fr.* Salad.

سالانه *S. u.* **سالیانه**

سالار * o Chief; leader.

سالب *A.* [*Fem.* سالبه] Privative; negative.

سالخورده Stricken in years; aged.

سالَک Aleppo boil; A. button.

سالِک *A.* Wayfarer. Disciple.

سالگردش o Anniversary.

سالم *A. a.* Healthy [تندرست]. Safe. Intact. –*n.* *Mas. pr. name.*

سالمند Adult.

سالمندی Adult age.

سالن *Fr.* Hall; saloon.

سالنامه Year-book.

سالن‌دار *Fr. P.* Having a saloon. ـ واکن س. Saloon car.

سالنما Calendar.

سالوس * Hypocrite. Impostor. Hypocrisy.

سالواره Annuity.

سالیان = سالها Years.

سالیانه *or* **سالانه** Yearly; annual(ly).

سام *A.* Pestilential wind [usu. بادسام].

سامان House furniture. Welfare. Order. ـ سرو سامان گرفتن To range oneself; marry and settle down.

سامره *A.* The Samaritans. Samaria [also سامریه].

سامری *A.* Samaritan. ـ گوسالهٔ س. The speaking calf which was raised at the time of Moses.

سامعه *A.* = شنوائی Sense of hearing.

سامی *A.* Semitic.

سامی o *A.* = بلند High; elevated.

سان Parade; also, review. ـ س. دادن To parade. To pass r. ـ س. دیدن To parade (troops); pass in r.

سان *Suf.* = -like; resembling. –*n.* o Manner. ـ اینسان or بدینسان In this manner. ـ بسان * Like. *S. a.* یکسان&چسان

سانتیگراد *Fr.* Centigrade.

سانتیگرم *Fr.* Centigramme.

سانتیم *Fr.* Centime(tre).

سانتیمتر *Fr.* Centimetre.

سانحه *A.* [سوانح] Accident.

ساندویچ *Fr. & E.* Sandwich.

سانسورکردن *Fr. P.* To censor.

سایبان Shady place. Bower. ـ

سایبان کرباسی Awning.

سایر *A*. Rest ; remainder. — سایر کتابها Other books.

سایرین *A*. [Pl. of سایر] = دیگران Others; other people.

سائس *A*. [سائسین] Politician ; diplomat; statesman.

سایش Rubbing. Trituration.

سائل *A*. = گدا

ساینده *n*. Grinder. —*a*. Grinding. Abrading.

سایه Shade. Shadow. *F*. Protection or care. — بسایهٔ شما Under your protection or auspices. — سایه شما کم نشود Thank you for your protection or kindness (which I hope will never cease). — س. گستردن *or* س. افکندن To cast a shadow. — س. زدن To shade or shadow. — درسایهٔ Under the p. of. Thanks to. — س. اش سنگین است He mounts (*or* rides) the high horse; he is inaccessible.

سایه پرورده Reared in indulgence; tenderly brought up.

سایه‌دار Shaded; shady

سایه روشن Light and shade (effect) ; chiaroscuro. Contrast.

سایه‌کوهی [*Of taffetas*] Shot. *OS*. Like a shadow on a mountain.

سایه‌گستر * Adumbrant. *F*. Of a protecting or benevolent nature.

سایه نشین ○ *a*. Sitting in the shade. *F*. Pampered. —*n*. Protégé.

سایدگی Wear. Erosion. Fret.

سائیدن [سای] To pulverize ; grind. To wear (away) ; erode. To rasp. To rub hard.

سائیده [P. P. of سائیدن].

سَبابه *A*. Forefinger ; index.

سُبات *A*. Lethargy. — سبات سنگین Coma. — شریان س. Carotid artery.

سباتی *A*. Lethargic; comatous.

سباط *A*. *Syriac and Jewish month* (Jan.-Feb.).

سباع [Pl. of سبع]

سباعی ○ *A*. Sevensome; heptamerous. Seven-lettered. Heptasyllabic.

سَبب *A*. Cause. Means. *Cf. the pl*. اسباب ‖ س. شدن To cause or occasion. — بچه س. Why ? For what reason ?

سبب ساز *A*. *P*. The Provider of Means; Providence.

سببی *A*. Causative; causal. — خویشاوند سببی Relative in law.

سببیت *A*. Causality.

سَبت *A*. Sabbath. Rest.

سُبحان *A*. Praise; glory. The Glorious God.

سبحان‌الله *A*. Praise be to God. Good God !

سبحه ○ *A*. Rosary [تسبیح]. Prayer.

سَبد Basket. Pannier. Wicker-

work. Side-car. — سبد کاغذ Waste-basket. — گل سر سبد *Met.* Pick of the basket.
سبدی Resembling, or made like, a basket. — کلاه س. Straw-hat.
سَبز *a.* Green. Growing. —*n.* The green colour. — روغن س. Oil of roses. — سبز چمنی Meadow-green. — سبز زیتونی Olive-green. — سرش س. باد * May he be prosperous. — س. شدن To turn green. To germinate; spring. *F.* To appear suddenly+. — س. کردن To colour or paint green. To grow. To confirm +.
سبز فام Green(ish).
سبز قبا *P. A.* Greenfinch.
سبزه *n.* Grass-plot; verdure. Green raisins. —*a.* Of an olive complexion; also, of a dark c.
سبزه‌زار Verdure; meadow; grass-plot.
سبزی 1) (Fresh) vegetables; greens; legume [سبزیجات]. 2) Greenness. — سبزی پختنی Pot-herb. — س. پاك كردن *Met.* To flatter or toady; curry favour with s. o.
سبزی پاك كن Flatterer, fawner.
سبزی‌دار Containing vegetables or greens. — خوراك س. Vegetable diet.
سبزی فروش Green-grocer.
سبزیکاری Market-garden; vegetable g.; kitchen-g.
سبزینه Chlorophyl(l).
سِبط o *A.* [اسباط] Tribe.
سبع *A.* Fierce. —*n.* [only in the pl. سِباع 'f. animals'].
سبعه *A.* = هفتگانه The seven...
سبعیت *A.* Fierceness.
سبق *A.* Precedence. Excellence. Lesson o. — س. بردن To surpass; excel [with از].
سبقت *A.* Precedence. Lead. Overtaking and passing. — س. جستن بر To take precedence of; get the start of. To anticipate. To forestall. — س. گرفتن To overtake and pass [*in driving*].
سبك (*sabk*) *A.* Method. Style.
سبك (*sabok*) Light. Digestible. *Mus.* Gay; quick; lively. *F.* Frivolous; undignified. — خواب من س. است I am a light sleeper. — س. شدن To become l. — س. کردن To lighten. To alleviate. — س. و سنگین کردن To weigh (in one's hand). — س. گرفتن To make light of. To despise. — س. بیا × Draw it mild. Come off the high horse.
سبك اسلحه *P. A.* Light-armed.
سبکبار Disburdened; disencumbered. Free from care.
سبکباری Disencumbrance.
سبکبال *Z.* Passerine.
سبك رفتار Light-footed.

F. Light; undignified.

سبکسر Light-minded. Rash. Stupid. Frivolous. Sober.

سبك مغز Crack-brained; silly.

سبك‌وزن *P. A.* Light(-weight).

سبکی Lightness. *F*. Frivolousness; levity.

سَبل *A*. (*Med.*) Pannus.

سَبو Pitcher. Pot (of wine).

سَبوس Bran; pollard.

سبوسه Dandruff; scurf.

سَبیل *A*. Way ; road [راه]. *F*. Manner. Cause. – برسبیلِ By way of. – چای س. بود + Tea was served free of charge.

سِبیل Moustache. – س. گذاردن To wear a moustache. – سبیل کسیرا چرب کردن To grease the palm of a person. – سبیل کسیرا دود دادن × To give it to s. o. hot. – زیر سبیل در کردن + To pocket, swallow, or brook. – س. به س. × Close together. *OS*. With moustaches close to each other. – سبیلش آویزان شد × He hung his lip; he looked blue.

سپار [Imp. of سپردن]

سپارنده Depositor. Betrayer ○.

سپاس Thanks. – س. گزاردن To give thanks; thank.

سپاس گزاری Thanksgiving. – س. کردن To give thanks. [With از] To thank.

سِپاه Army. Host.

سپتامبر *Fr.* September.

سِپر Shield. *M*. Bumper. – س. انداختن To throw up the sponge.

سپردن [سپار or سپر] To deposit. To (en)trust. – پول در بانك س. To d. money with (*or* in) the bank. – بذهن س. To commit to memory. – بخاك س. To bury. – جان س. To give up the ghost.

سپرده [P. P. of سپردن] *a*. Deposited. *n*. Deposit.

سپرز [Cont. of اسپرز]

سپر ماهی Turbot. Also, brill.

سِپری Elapsed. Finished. – س. شدن To expire.

سپری *Z*. Scutellate; scutiform. *Anat*. Thyroid.

سپس Afterwards; then. – ازاین س. Hereafter.

سپستان Sebestan.

سپلشت "The three unlucky throws" in the game of knuckle-bones. *F*. Bad luck. *Note*. بلشت means 'impure'.

سپنج Three, four, or five; few. *F*. Transient.

سپوختن ○ [سپوز] To pierce or thrust. *Cf*. سوراخ کردن

سپور *T*. = رُفتگر

سپه [Cont. of سپاه]

سِپهبد Lieutenant-general.

سِپهر • Sphere. World. Sky.

سپهسالار [*Old title*] Commander-in-chief.

سپید etc. = سفید etc.

سپیده دم Dawn.
ستا *or* **ستای** [Imp. of ستودن]
ستاد Army staff.
ستار *Kind of cittern played with the nail of the index.*
ستارگان [Pl. of ستاره]
ستاره [ستارگان] Star. — ستارهٔ بامداد Morning-star ; Venus. — ستارهٔ دریایی Star-fish; jelly. — ستارهٔ دنباله دار Comet. — ستارهٔ زمین Talc. — ستارهٔ شام Evening-star ; Hesperus. — س. شمردن* To count sheep.
ستاره‌ای Star-shaped ; stellar. Astral. — گل س. Cosmos.
ستاره پرست Star-worshipper.
ستاره شناس = **اختر شناس**
ستام Harness; trappings.
ستان [Imp. of ستدن *or* ستاندن]
ستاندن = **استدن**
ستاننده One who takes; receiver; recipient [گیرنده].
ستایش Praise. — س. کردن To praise ; pay tribute to. — قابل س. Praiseworthy.
ستبر Thick [کلفت]. Sturdy. Coarse. Big.
ستبرا Thickness.
ستبر پوست Pachydermatous.
ستدن [Cont. of **استدن**] To take.
ستر o Covering. — ستر عورت کردن To cover one's nakedness.
ستر *A*. Veil ; screen; covering. *F*. Modesty.
ستردن * [ستر] To shave. To scrape. To erase. *Cf.* تراشیدن

سترده [P. P. of ستردن]
سترگ * Large. Gross.
سترون Sterile. — س. کردن To sterilize.
سترونی Sterility.
ستل Pail. [*For coal*] Hod. — یك س. آب A pailful of water.
ستم Oppression. — س. کردن بر To oppress; do injustice to.
ستمدیده *a*. Oppressed; injured. —*n*. [pl. ستمدیدگان the oppressed].
ستمکار etc. = **ستمگر** etc.
ستمگر *a*. Oppressive; cruel. —*n*. Oppressor ; tyrant.
ستمگری Oppression.
ستمی o Bill of lading. *See* بارنامه
ستوان Lieutenant. [*In the Air Force*] Flight-lieutenant.
ستوانی Lientenantship.
ستودن [ستا(ی)] To praise.
ستوده 1) Praiseworthy. 2) [P. P. of ستودن]
ستور Quadruped; esp. horse.
ستون Pillar. Column. Army corps. — ستون بدهکار Debit side. — ستون پله *Mil*. Echelon. — ستون فقرات Spinal column. — ستون یك Indian file. — چهار ستون بدن + The whole framework of the body; physical condition. — س. کردن To make a pillar of. To make stiff.
ستون بندی Columniation. *Mil*. Arrangement in échelons.

ستونك *Z.* Columella.

ستونی *a.* Pillar-shaped; columnar. — نمونهٔ س. Galley-proof. —*ad.* : ارقام را ستونی بخوانید Read the figures down.

ستوه Harassment. — بستوه آوردن To harass; put out of patience by harassment.

سته (*seteh*) Berry.

ستیز 1) = ستیزه 2) [Imp. of ستیزیدن]

ستیزگر Quarrelsome. Stubborn.

ستیزه *or* **ستیز** Quarrel; strife. Anger. Obstinacy. — س. کردن = ستیزیدن

ستیزه جو Quarrelsome.

ستیزیدن [ستیز] To quarrel. To be angry. To use violence.

ستیغ Mountain ridge.

سَجاده *A.* Prayer-carpet.

سِجاف False hem; border. — س. کردن To b. — حرف شما بسجاف قبای او برخورد × Your remarks have trodden on his corns.

سجایا [Pl. of سجیه]

سجده *A.* Prostration; bowing down. — س. کردن To bow d.

سَجع *A.* Harmonious cadence. Riming prose.

سجلّ *A.* Register; record.

سِجن ₒ *A.* = زندان

سُجود *A.* Prostration (in prayer); touching the ground with the forehead.

سَجیه *A.* [سجایا] (Natural) disposition or quality.

سحاب *A.* 1) = ابر 2) Nebula.

سحابی *A.* Nebular.

سحر *A.* (*sahar*) (Time just before the) dawn. — مرغ س. Bird of morn: nightingale or cock.

سِحر *A.* (*sehr*) Magic; witchcraft. — س. کردن To practise magic. —*vt.* To fascinate.

سِحر آمیز *A. P.* Magical. *F.* Enchanting.

سحرخیز *A. P. n.* Early riser. —*a.* Rising early.

سحرخیزی *A. P.* Early rising.

سحرگاه *A. P.* Dawn.

سحره [Pl. of ساحر]

سَحری *A. P. a.* Pertaining to the dawn. Matutinal. —*n.* Food eaten before the d. of a fasting day.

سخا(وت) *A.* Generosity.

سَخت *a.* Hard; difficult. *F.* Severe. Rigid. Irresistible. Violent.—*ad.* Hard. Severely. Violently. Terribly. Very.— س. شدن To get hard; harden. To be aggravated. — س. کردن To h. To render difficult. To aggravate. — س. گرفتن To be severe or strict. [*With* بر] To press hard upon.— س. نگیر + Take it easy.

سخت پی Sinewy; strong.

سخت جان Die-hard. Hard-hearted.

سخت دل Hard-hearted.

سخت دلی Cruelty.

سخت شامه Dura mater.
سخت‌گیر Severe ; exacting ; hard ; difficult.
سخت‌گیری Severity ; rigour ; harsh treatment. Exactingness.
سختی Difficulty. Hardship. — س. کشیدن To suffer hardship.
سختیان Morocco leather.
سُخره A. Forced labour. Requisition. — به س. گرفتن To call in requisition; impress.
سُخره A. Derision. Laughing-stock.
سُخریه A. Derision.
سخط o A. Discontent. Anger.
سُخمه T. Rapier. — س. زدن To thrust or stab (with a r.).
سُخن Speech. Word. Remark. — س. راندن To deliver a speech. — س. گفتن To speak ; talk. — که پیشتر از آن س. رفت Which was mentioned before.
سخن پراکنی Broadcasting.
سخن چین Tale-bearer.
سخن چینی Tale-bearing. — س. کردن To tell tales.
سخندان Eloquent.
سخندانی Eloquence ; mastery of words.
سخنران Lecturer. Orator.
سخنرانی Lecture. — س. کردن To give a lecture ; deliver a speech.
سخن رسان Prompter.
سخنگو Spokesman.
سخنوَر a. Eloquent. —n. E. writer or speaker. [gift.
سخنوری Eloquence Poetic
سَخی A. Generous; liberal.
سخیف A. Weak. W.-minded [usu. سخیف‌العقل].
سد One-hundred [usu. صد].
سَدّ A. Dam ; dike. Barrier. Bar. — سد رمق Bare subsistence. — سد بستن To construct a dam. — سد کردن To obstruct ; block. To close. — سدّ سکندر را شکستن To perform a Herculean task; *Lit.* To break Alexander's barrier (which had been erected by him to stem the advance of the Gogs and Magogs).
سُداب Rue. — سداب کوهی = اسپند ‖ سداب کهنه Wall-rue.
سداد A. Obstruction in the nose.
سد بندی A. P. Construction a dam or dams ; barrage.
سِدر A. = کنار Lotus.
سُدس A. = یك ششم Sixth.
سدساله Hundred-year-old Centennial. — جشن س. Centenary.
سدلیس Seidlitz powder.
سدم Hundredth.
سدمی The hundredth (one).
سدمین The hundredth.
سَده Century.
سُدّه A. (*Med.*) Obstruction.
سدی چند Percentage
سدید o = درست A. Right; just.
سَر Head. Top. End; extremity. Chief [usu. in the pl. سران]. Cover ; lid. F.

Intention. — سرِ پا Standing (on foot). — سرِ خُلق In good hurrour. — سرِ دست Over the hand. — سرراه On the way.— سرساعت At the exact time; on t. — سرِ سواری (While) riding.— سرِ بیگناه An innocent or guiltless person.— سرِ پا Standing. *F*. Out and abroad.— سرِ چشمه *See* سرچشمه *in the vocab*. — سرِ شب The first part of the night.— سرشب است The night is young. — سرکار At work; on duty — سرمیز At table. — سرتاپا From head to foot. All over.— سرتاپا غلط است It is all wrong. — سر تا سر Throughout : سرتاسر ایران ‖ All over; across — سرازپا نشناختن • To be utterly confused. — سرآمدن To expire. To excel; attain perfection.— سر باززدن از • To refuse to do; recalcitrate at (*or* against). — سر بردن To ride (*or* run) as if one goes to fetch a midwife. *OS*. To carry away the head of one who has been slain. — سر بسر کسی گذاشتن To tease or annoy s. o.; fool him; be funny with him. — سربلند کردن To rise; attain a (better) social position.— سر بزمین گذاشتن To take one's last sleep; drop (down) dead. — سرِ بی‌شام بزمین گذاشتن To go without supper. — سری توی سرها آوردن

+ To show up in society.— سرپیچیدن از- -ربریدن To behead.— To disobey. To recalcitrate at (*or* against). — سرِحال In good health (*or* spirits). — سرِ خلق In good spirits (*or* humour).— از سر خود *or* سر خود Without permission. Spontaneously. — سرِ دست In labour. Over the hand. — سر خوردن To be disillusioned; look back.— سردادن To free; let go. To set afoot; start : گریه سر دادن ‖ سر درآوردن To make head or tail. To show up new courage. — سر دواندن To put off; p. by.— سرِ دو راهی گیر کردن To be in a dilemma.— سررفتن To boil over. To go over again.— سر رسیدن To arrive unexpectedly. To come to maturity.— سر زدن To be committed. To originate. To drop in. [*With* به] To call on. To run in to; amount to.— سر به جهنم زدن + To come to a fabulous amount. — سر کردن To wear, as a kerchief. To put up. To start. — سرکشیدن To drink off; quaff. To inspect. — بچه ای را سر راه گذاشتن To expose a child. — سرگرداندن To put off; get rid of. — سرگرفتن To be realized. To set in, as rain. — سرِ کسیرا گرم کردن To amuse or beguile s. o.— سرقول خودایستادن To abide by one's word. ــ سروته چیزیرا بهم آوردن To finish ha tily; also, bungle. ــ ازسرو ته یك کرباس Of the same leaven. ــ سر و صورت دادن To settle. To put into shape. ــ سر وعده پرداختن To meet at maturity. ــ سرهم دادن To patch up; also, bungle. ــ از سر From the beginning. Over again. ــ از سرِ From; by way of. ــ از سر باز کردن To rid oneself of. To bungle. ــ ازسر چیزی گذشتن To abandon s. t. To dispense with s. t. ــ دست ازسرکسی برداشتن To leave one alone; cease annoying him. ــ ازسرگرفتن To resume; start again. ــ باسر Head first. ــ بسر آمدن To expire ــ چه بسرش آمد؟ What happened to him? ــ بسرم آمده است I have had the experience. ــ بسر درآمدن • To fall headlong. ــ بسر بردن To pass; spend. To live; get along. To complete •. To succeed ○. ــ سرش بکلاهش می‌ارزد He carries much weight; he is influential. *OS*. His head is worth his hat. ــ سرش نمیشود + He does not know it. ــ محبت سرش نمی‌شود He is blind to kindness. ــ چه درسر دارید؟ What are you intending to do?

سر + Insensible. ــ سر کردن To anaesthetize locally.

سُر Slide. ــ سر خوردن To slide or glide.

سِرّ *A.* [اَسرار] = راز Secret; [mystery.

سَرا or سَرای House. Inn. Commercial warehouse.

سرا or سَرای [Imp. of سرائیدن]

سِرّاً *A.* Secretly.

سراب Mirage.

سراپا All over. ــ س. گوش بودن To be all ears.

سراپرده • (Curtain at the door of a) royal court. Harem. Tent. Enclosure.

سِراج *A.* = چراغ

سَرّاج *A.* = زین ساز

سراجه *A.* Farcy.

سَرّاجی *A. P.* = زین‌سازی

سراچه Small house or palace •. Ventricle of the heart.

سرادق *A.-P.* = سراپرده

سَرازیر Sloping; downhill. ــ س. شدن To slope; slant. To be turned upside down. To come or fall d. ــ کار(م) س. شد I broke the neck of the task; it is nearing completion. ــ س. کردن To turn upside d. To cause to spill.

سرازیری Declivity; slope; downhill.

سرآستین Cuff; wristband.

سراسر *ad*. All over; throughout. Everywhere. —*a*. Quits.

سراسیمگی Confusion. Amazement.

سراسیمه *a*. Confused. Amazed. —*ad*. Headlong.
سرآشپز Head-cook; chef.
سراشیب *a*. Sloping. —*n*. Slope; declivity.
سُراغ *T*. Clue; track. Sign. — س. داشتن To know of. — س. کردن To trace; locate. — ازکسی س. گرفتن To inquire s. o. — سراغ کسیرا گرفتن To i. about s. o.
سرآغاز * Exordium; proem; preamble.
سرافراز Honoured. — س. شدن To be honoured. — س. کردن To honour; exalt.
سرافرازی Honour; credit.
سرافکندگی Shame.
سرافکنده Ashamed.
اسرافیل = سرافیل
سرافین *A-Heb*. Seraphim.
سرآمد Eminent. Perfect.
سرانجام *n*. Conclusion; end. —*ad*. In the long run.
سرانداز Head-carpet.
سُراندن To cause to slide. *F*. To foist.
سراندیپ Ceylon.
سرانگشت Finger-tip.
سَرانه *n*. Share. Head-money. Something given to boot. —*ad*. Per head.
سرای *S. u.* سرا
سرایت *A*. Contagion; transmission. — س. کردن To be communicated by contagion.
سرایدار Custodian; caretaker.
سرایداری Custodianship.
سرائر [Pl. of سریر]
سرایندگی & سرایش Singing.
سراینده [سرایندگان] Singer.
سراییدن [سرای] To sing.
سُرب Lead. — سرب طبیعی *or* سرب معدنی Galena. — سرب مدادی Graphite; plumbago; black lead.
سربار(ی) Small load on top of a heavier one.
سَرباز Soldier. *C. P.* Jack. — سرباز پیاده Infantry-man. — سرباز وظیفه Conscript. — س. گرفتن To recruit for the army.
روباز - باز = سر باز
سربازخانه Barrack.
سربازگیری Conscription; recruitment.
سربازی Military service; soldiering. — س. کردن To serve in the army.
سربالا Ascending; uphill. — جواب س. دادن To give an irrelevant or vague answer.
سربالایی Uphill; acclivity.
سربتو Sly(ly silent); insidious.
سر براه + Manageable; tractable; humble.
سربرگ *C. P.* Elder hand.
سر برهنه Bare-headed.
سر بریده Beheaded.
سر بزیر Humble; tractable.
سربسته *a*. Closed. Water-tight. Air-tight. *F*. Secret. Gene-

ral. —*ad*. Generally.

سر بسر *ad*. Throughout; all over. —*a*. Quits [also سراسر].

سر بطری Stopper ; cork. — سربطری آبجویی or سربطری بهن Cork-screw.

سُرب کار o Artisan working in lead. Plumber.

سر بگم With an untraceable end; tangled. *F*. Intricate. At a loss to understand ; fogged.

سربلند Honoured. Proud.

سربلندی Honour. Pride.

سر بمهر Sealed ; closed up tightly.

سربند o Head-band ; fillet.

سر بهر Captain (in the Police).

سر به نیست کردن + To take on a one-way ride.

سر بهوا Giddy. Careless.

سُربی Leaden. Lead-blue; livid.

سرپاس Brigadier-general (in the Police).

سرپاسبان Sergeant in the Police.

سرپایی Intended for indoor wear. [*Of a visit*] Flying.— [For کفش س.] Slipper. — بیماران س. Outpatients.

سر پُر Muzzle-loading. — تفنگ س. Muzzle-loader.

سرپرست Supervisor; guardian ; person in charge. *Law*. Administrator.

سرپرستی Guardianship; protection ; supervision. — ادارهٔ س. The Administration.

سرپزشک Chief medical officer.

سر پستانک Nipple.

سر پنجه Hand or palm. Claws. *F*. The mailed fist; might.

سرپوش Dish-cover. Lid. Cap. Valve. — سرپوش چاک صوت Epiglottis. — سر پوش معده Pylorus; pyloric valve.

سِرّ پوش *A. P.* = سرّ نگهدار

سرپوشیده *n*. Porch ; covered passage. —*a*. Covered. Lidded. — نهر سرپوشیده Culvert.

سرپیچ Burner (of a lamp). Bung (of a cask). Socket.

سرپیچی Disobedience.— س. کردن To turn away.

سرپیشاهنگ District commissioner ; provincial scout executive.

سرتاسر *S. u.* سر.

سر تا سری Extended from one end to the other end. — راه آهن سر تا سری ایران The Trans-Iranian Railway.

سر تراش Barber. *Cf*. سلمانی

سر تراشی Barbery.

سِر تق × Obstinate. Unreasonable.

سرتیپ Brigadier-general.

سرتیر End of a beam (resting on a girder).

سرتیز *a*. Sharp-pointed. —*n*. o = خار

سرجُنبان + Influential.

سرجوش Froth. Scum. Cream.

سرجوخه *Mil* Corporal.
سرچوق *T.* Bowl of a pipe.
سرچسب Clasp.
سرچشمه Source; fountain-head.– س گرفتن از To originate in; take its rise in.
سرچین Picked; choice.– س. کردن To pick out; select.
سرحان *A.* (*Astr.*) Lupus.
سرحدّ *P. A.* [سرحدات] = مرز Frontier. *F.* Limit.– تاسرحد امکان As far as possible.
سرحدی *P. A.* = مرزی
سر حکم *P. A.* = سرداور
سرحلقه *P. A.* Ringleader.
سُرخ Red. Redhot. – خاك س. Ferrous oxide. – گل س. Red rose. – س شدن To turn red. To be roasted. To blush or flush – س. کردن To redden. To (roast) brown. To fry.
سُرخاب 1) Rouge; paint. 2) *Z.* Barnacle.
سرخالی *P. A.* Light-weight; underweight.
سرخ تیره Roan (horse).
سرخجه *or* سرخك Measles. – سرخجه کاذب Roseola; rose rash.
سُرخدار Yew.
سرِ خر Bore. Gooseberry. – يك سرخرهم کم A good riddance!
سُرخرگ Artery.
سَرخَس Fern.
سُرخ سرك Redbreast.
سرخك = 1) سرخجه 2) ساس
سرخ کرده Browned. Roasted.
سرخ ماهی Gurnard; gurnet.
سرخ نای Oesophagus.
سَرخور Posthumous (child).
سرخوردگی Disillusionment.
سرخوش Slightly intoxicated; on the spree. Gay.
سُرخون Dark grey (horse).
سرخی Redness. Rouge.
سرخیل ○ *P. A.* Commander of a troop.
سَرد Cold.– آه س. Bitter sigh.– سردم هست I feel cold.– س. شدن To get c. *F.* To be disillusioned. – س. کردن To refrigerate; cool. *F.* To discourage.– هوا سرد کرده است It is (getting) cold. – دل کسیرا س کردن To discourage s. o.– سرد وگرم روزگار Vicissitudes of fortune.
سرداب Cellar. Crypt.
سردابه Cellar. Crypt. Catacombs.
سردار [*Old title*] Commander of an army.
سرداری Old-fashioned frock pleated round the waist.
سرداوَر Umpire.
سر دبیر Editor-in-chief. Head-clerk. [Of an embassy] Chancellor.
سَردخانه Refrigerating room; cooler. Cold stores.
سردَر Façade; front. Portal.
سر درپیش = • شرمنده
سر درد Headache.
سر درگم At a loss to understand. *Cf.* سربگم

سر دست Cuff ; wrist-band.
سر دسته Head of a gang. [*In football*] Captain.
سردستی *ad*. Hastily; cursorily; carelessly. —*a*. Cursory.
سرد سیر Cold (region).
سردفتر Notary public.
سردماغ + 1) In good humour. 2) = سرخوش
سر دوزی = پاکدوزی
سردوشی Shoulder-strap.
سردی Coldness. Refrigerant (food or drink). *F*. Disaffection.
سر راست Straightforward. Round, as a sum.
سرِ راهی 1) *a*. Exposed, as a child. — بچهٔ س. Foundling. 2) *n*. Present offered to a person going on a journey.
سر رسید Expiry. Due date. — سررسید پرداخت آن قبض فردا است The bill will mature tomorrow.
سررشته Skill. Clue ; track. — سر رشتهٔ کار را گم کردن To be on the wrong track.
سررشته‌دار Quarter-Master-General; Chief of the Army Supply Department.
سررشته‌داری Commissariat.
سر زده Intruding(ly). — س. آمدن To intrude; come in unexpectedly.
سر زمین Country; territory.
سر زنده Lively; vivaceous.
سرزنش Reproach. — س. کردن To reproach or taunt.
سرژ *Fr*. Serge.
سرسام Delirium.
سرسام آور Delirious. *F*. Dazzling ; stupendous ; astronomical : ارقام س.
سر سبز Prosperous.
سرسپردگی Devotion. [tee.
سرسپرده *a*. Devoted. —*n*. Devotee.
سرستون Capital of a column.
سرسخت Headstrong; obstinate.
سر سختی Obstinacy.
سرسرا Hall; entrance room.
سُرسُره Slide. Slip(way) ; shipway.
سرسره بازی Skating. Skiing.
سَرسَری Perfunctorily.
سرسکه *P. A*. Die.
سرسلامتی *P. A*. Condolence. — بکسی س. گفتن To offer one's condolences to s. o.
سرسلسله *P. A*. Progenitor of a dynasty.
سرسنگین In an angry mood.
سر سیاه و دندان سفید + Raw head and bloody bones. (*Lit*.) He who has a black head and white teeth.
سرسیلندر *P. Fr*. Cylinder-head.
سرسینه Cephalothorax.
سرشاخه Trimmings of a tree; lops; browse.
سرشار • Overfilled. *F*. Overflowing. Enormous.
سرشت Mould; nature.

سرشتن [سریش] To knead; mix; mould. To form.
سرشته [P. P. of سرشتن]
سرشک = * اشك
سرشکستگی Disgrace.
سرشکسته Disgraced; ashamed.
سرشکن کردن To distribute pro rata; prorate.
سرشماری Census. ـ س. کردن To take census. ـ مالیات س. Capitation or poll-tax.
سرشناس Well-known.
سر شیپورچی P. T. Trumpet major.
سرشوی or سرشور + ـ گل س. (Kind of clay consisting principally of) montmorillonite.
سرشیر Cream.
سرصفحه P. A. Title-page. Headline.
سرطاس Scoop.
سرطان A. Cancer. [Old name of تیر] the fourth month of the solar year. ـ سرطان جلدی Cancroid. ـ سرطان جوف دهان Noma. ـ سرطان خایه Sarcocele.
سرطانی A Cancerous; cankeroid. Suffering from cancer. ـ ورم س. Scirrhus. ـ تولید سرطان کردن To cancerate.
سرطویله P. A. Platform in a stable where the groom reposes.
سُرعت A. Speed. Velocity. ـ س. داشتن To exceed the speed-limit. ـ سرعت انتقال Quickness of apprehension. ـ سرعت ‖ انزال S. u. سرعت انزال ـ س. گرفتن نبض Frequent pulse To drive fast(er); step on the gas ـ بسرعت Rapidly; quickly. At once.
سرعت سنج or سرعت پیما A. P. Speedometer; tachometer. [In a ship] Log.
سرعمله P. A. Working foreman.
سرفراز = سر افراز
سرفرمانده Commander in-chief.
سرفتیل P. R. Valve-cap.
سرفصل P. A. Headline; title.
سرفواره P. A. A(d)jutage.
سُرفه Cough(ing). ـ س. کردن To cough.
سرفیدن To cough. S. a. سلفیدن
سرقت A. = دزدی Theft. ـ سرقت س کردن ‖ انتحال = ادبی To commit theft; steal. ـ بسرقت دزدیدن = بردن To s. ـ بسرقت رفتن To be stolen.
سر ُقفلی P. A. Key-money; also, goodwill.
سر قلم P. A. Pen nib.
سرک Furtive look; peep ـ س. کشیدن To p; l. furtively.
سرک Excess; surplus.
سرکاپ P. E. Hub-cap.
سرکار Overseer. [Title used in addressing military ranks up to colonel inclusive, and almost equivalent to] esquire. [In p. c.] You. ـ

بنده و سرکار You and I. — سرکار عالی Your Honour; Y. Fxcellency.

سرکارگر Head workman; foreman; tindal. *Cf.* سرعمله

سرکاغذ Letter-head.

سرکتاب *P. A.* "The top of a book or bible" (regarded as the proper place to touch in bibliomancy). —س. بازکردن To practise b.; divine by means of a book.

سرکج (In)curved.

سرکردگی Command; leadership; generalship.

سرکرده Commander; leader; head.

سرکش Refractory. Unruly.

سرکشی Refractoriness. Mutiny. — س. کردن To rebel.

سرکشی Inspection; visit. — س کردن To inspect or v.

سرکلانتری Central police station.

سرکنگبین *S. u.* **سرکنجبین**.

سرکنسول *P. Fr.* Consul general.

سرکنسولگری *P. Fr.* Consulate-general.

سرکنگبین [f. سرکه vinegar and انگبین honey]. Oxymel. [Usu. سکنجبین *or* سرکنجبین].

سرکوبی Suppression. (Severe) punishment. — س. کردن To punish. To suppress; crush.

سرکوفت Taunt; bitter reproach. — س. دادن To taunt.

سرکه Vinegar — بچهٔ س. Vinegar-plant. — س. ریختن *or* س. انداختن To manufacture vinegar. — جوهرسرکه Acetic acid. — نمکِ جوهر سرکه Acetate.

سرکه با o Pottage made with vinegar.

سرکه شیره Mixture of vinegar and syrup, oxysaccharum.

+**سرو کیسه کردن** *or* **سر کیسه کردن** To fleece (of one's money).

سرگذشت Adventures. Incidents. Narrative.

سرگران = 1) سرسکین 2) سرخوش

سرگرد *Mil.* Major.

سرگردان Wandering; errant. At a loose end. — س. شدن To wander. To go vagrant.— س. کردن To cause to w. To perplex.

سرگردانی Vagrancy. Perplexity. Distress. Suspense.

سرگرم Amused. Intent. Busy.— سرگرم خواندناست He is busy singing. —س. کردن To amuse.

سرگرمی Amusement; pastime; diversion.

سرگشاده Open: نامهٔ س.

سرگشتگی Bewilderment.

سرگشته Bewildered.

سرگل Pick; choice part.

سرگوشی *or* درِگوشی Whisper.— س حرف زدن To whisper in one's ear.

سرگیجه Vertigo.

سرگین Dung; droppings.

سرگین خور Coprophagous.

سرگین غلتان Scarab.
سرلشکر Major-general.
سرلوحه P. A. Epigraph. Title-page; forntispiece. Vignette.
سَرلوله Nozzle.
سرم Fr. Serum.
سَرما Cold (weather).—س. خوردن To catch cold.
سرما خشکه Black frost.
سرماخوردگی Chill(iness); fit of cold. — من س. دارم I have caught cold.
سرما ریزه Hoar-frost.
سرما زدگی Frost-bite. Chilblain.
سرما زده Frost-bitten; nipped by cold.
سرمایه Capital.—سرمایه پرداخته‌شده Paid-in capital. — س. گذاشتن To invest one's c.
سرمایه‌دار Capitalist.
سرمایه‌داری Capitalism.
سرمته Drill-bit; drill-chuck.
سرمد A. Perpetual.
سرمدی A. Eternal.
سرمست = 1) مست 2) Gay.
سرمشق P. A. Copy (slip). Example. — س. شدن To serve as an example.—س. گذاشتن To set an e.—س. گرفتن To take e.
سرمقاله P. A. Leading article; leader; editorial.
سرمنزل P. A. (Last) halting-place. F. Destination; goal.
سُرمه Collyrium. — سنگ س. (Crude) antimony.
سِرمه T. Wire-ribbon; purl.
سُرمه‌ای Dark-blue.
سرمهندس P. A. Engineer-in-chief; chief engineer.
سُرنا Kind of oboe.—س. را از تهِ گشاد(ش) زدن To put the cart before the horse. To get hold of the wrong end of the stick.
سرناچی P. T. or سرنا زن Oboist. L. Piper.
سرناوی Navy corporal.
سُرنج Red lead; minium.
سَرند Riddle; screen. — س. کردن To riddle or s.
سرنشین 1) Member of crew (in an aeroplane). 2) C. E. Passenger of a plane.
سرنگون Head downward; inverted down.—س. شدن To be turned upside d.—س. کردن To turn u. d. — گل س. Crown imperial. [to a secret.
سِرّ نگهدار A. P. Faithful
سرنوشت Predestination; fate.
سرنی [In a hookah] Mouth-piece.
سرنیزه Bayonet. — حکومت س. Sword-law. — بزور سرنیزه At the bayonet-point; by military force.
سرو (sarv) Cypress. — سرو آزاد Cedar (of Lebanon).—سرو کوهی Juniper.
سرو (soru:) Antenna. Z.
سرواد o Verse. Song.
سروان Mil. Captain.
سروته [For سرته] Upside down;

the wrong way. *S. a. under* سر

سُرود Song. Hymn. – سرود ملی National anthem.

سرودن [سَرای] To sing [خواندن]. To compose or recite.

سَروَر * Master. Chief. Leader.

سُرور *A.* Joy; mirth.

سرورآمیز *A. P.* Joyful; glad.

سروسامان *etc. S. u.* سامان

سروستان Cypress-grove.

سُروش * Messenger-angel. Inspiration. Glad tidings.

سروصدا Noise. Fuss. Hue and cry. – سروصدای آنرا در نیاورید Hush it up!

سرو قامت * *or* سرو قد * *P. A.* Of a stature like cypress; of an elegant figure.

سروکار Dealing. Intercourse. Liaison. Concern.

سروکله زدن + To tire out oneself, as in explanations or arguments; talk one's head off.

سروگوش آب دادن + To nose about (or around); smell round; hang about; nose out a secret.

سُرو مُروگنده ×Bursting with health; in rude h.; in full bloom.

سُرون *Z.* Antenna.

سرونك Antennule.

سروهمسر +Equals; fellowmen. *See* همسر

سرویس *Fr.* 1) Set: سرویسِ چای‌خوری ‖ 2) Service.– س. کردن To service, as a motor car.

سَره Pure; unmixed.

سُرّه ○ *A.* = ناف

سرهم بندی کردن + To botch; bungle; nail up; tinker; knock together.

سرهنگ Colonel. *See* هنگ

سرهنگ‌دوم Lieutenant-colonel.

سِری *Fr.* Set; series. *Cf.* دست – رشته – دسته

سِرّی *A.* Mysterious.

سِریانی *A.* Syriac.

سریدن [سُر] To slide or glide.

سریر *A.* = تخت Throne.

سریره ○ *A.* [سرائر] = راز Mystery; secret.

سریش Glue; paste. – بوتهٔ س. Asphodel.

سریشم (Fish-)glue; isinglass.– سریشم پنبه Collodium.

سریشمی Glue-like; viscous. – سرطان س. Colloid cancer. – مشمع س. Court-plaster; sticking plaster.

سَریع *A.* Rapid; quick [تند].

سریعاً *A.* Quickly; very soon; promptly.

سریع‌الاثر *A.* (Very) efficacious.

سریع‌الانتقال *A.* Of quick apprehension.

سریع‌الزوال *A.* = زودگذر

سریع‌السیر *A.* Express; swift.

سریع الهضم A. = زودگوار Easily digested.

سُرین Buttocks. *Anat*. Ilium.

سِزا Retribution. — س. دادن To remunerate or punish duly.— بسزا Just ; well-deserved ; condign.—بسزا رساندن To punish duly.—بسزا رسیدن To receive one's c. punishment.

سزاوار Deserving. Just; right.— سزاوار سرزنش است He deserves to be reprimanded.

سزیدن [سز] To merit; deserve. To be due. To suit o.

سُست *a*. Feeble; weak ; frail. Languid. Slack. Flabby. —*ad*. Slowly. Languidly — س. شدن To grow feeble or w. To droop; flag.— س. کردن To slacken. To relax. To weaken

سست اراده *P. A.* Infirm of purpose.

سست بنیاد Unstable.

سست پی Of weak nerves. Lacking a strong foundation.

سست پیمان Unfaithful to one's promise.

سست پیمانی Unfaithfulness to one's promise.

سست رأی *P. A.* Weak-minded.

سست رغبت • *P. A.* Of blunted passions.

سست رگ Of weak nerves. Impotent. Dastardly.

سست عنصر *P. A.* Void of energy. Unprincipled.

سست کمر Impotent.

سست ِمهر Of a lukewarm affection.

سست‌مهری Lukewarm affection

سست نهاد Weak-natured.

سستی Frailty. Weakness. Remissness. Slackness. — سستی کمر Impotence. — س. کردن To act sluggishly. To be lazy.

سِسك Garden warbler. — سِسك حرامزاده Pipit.

سطبر etc. = ستبر etc.

سَطح *A*. [سُطوح] Surface. Level. — سطح مستوی Plane surface.

سطح پیما *A. P.* Planimeter.

سطحه *A.* = عرشه

سطحی *A. P.* Superficial. *Anat*. Sublime.

سَطر *A* [سُطور] Line.

سطر آرا *A. P.* Rule(r).

سطر بندی *A. P.* Adjustment of lines.

سطل [A. form of ستل]

سَطوَت • *A.* Apalling presence. Reverence. Attack. Power.

سطوح [Pl. of سطح]

سطور [Pl. of سطر]

سَعادت *A.* = خوشبختی Happiness; prosperity. [perous.

سعادتمند *A. P.* Happy; pros-

سعایت *A.* = بدگویی

سعتر ○ *A.* = اویشن

سَعد *A.* Good influence of the stars. *Mas. pr. name*.

[*Used as an a.*] Lucky : سعد اصغر ‖ اختر سعد The lesser lucky star ; i. e. Venus. — سعد اکبر The greater lucky s. ; i. e. Jupiter.

سُعد *A.* Sedge ; galingale [often سعدکوفی].

سَعدین *A.* [D. of سعد] The two lucky stars ; i. e. Jupiter and Venus.

سِعر *A.* [اسعار] = نرخ & بها

سعفه *A.* Frond. *Med.* Ulcer on the head. — سعفهٔ رطبه = سعفهٔ شهدیه ‖ زرد زخم Favus ; honeycomb scall. — سعفهٔ مخاطیه شورهٔ سر = سعفهٔ نخالیه ‖ کچلی = Pityriasis capitis.

سعوط o *A.* 1) = انفیه Snuff. 2) Sternutatory.

سعه or سعت *A.* Amplitude ; extent. Open space. *F.* Easy circumstances. Liberty. — سعهٔ صدر Broadmindedness.

سَعی *A.* Endeavour. Exertion. — س کردن To endeavour; try. — سعی بازو Manual labour.

سَعید *A. a.* Happy; prosperous. Lucky. *—n. Mas. pr. name.*

سفارت *A.* Legation — سفارتِ کبری Embassy : سفارت کبرای ترکیه

سِفارش Recommendation. Enjoinment. Order. — س. کردن To recommend. [*With* به] To enjoin; charge. — س. دادن To order; place an o. for.

سفارش نامه Letter of recommendation. (Written) order.

سفارشی Made to order ; bespoke. [Of clothes] Tailormade ; made-to-measure ; custom [U. S.]. Registered : سفارشی دوقبضه ‖ نامهٔ س. R. with returned receipt ; registered with receipt attached.

سفاک *A.* = خونریز

سفاکی *A. P.* = خونریزی

سِفال Earthenware. Potsherd [often سفال شکسته].

سفالگر(ی) Potter(y).

سفالی or **سفالین** Earthen. — **سفالینه** or ظروف س. Earthenware.

سفاهت *A.* Foolishness. Impudence. — س. کردن To act foolishly.

سفائن [Pl. of سفینه]

سِفت *a.* Tight ; tense. Stiff. Hard. *—ad.* Tightly. Firmly rigidly. Violently. — تخم مرغ س. Hard-boiled eggs. — س. شدن To become hard or stiff. To tighten. To coagulate. To set ; harden. — س. کردن To h. To make tight. To render tough. To thicken. — سفت کن و شل کن درآوردن × To play fast and loose ; veer and haul. *OS.* To repeat saying, "Loosen and tighten."

سفت بافت Of a close texture.

سفت کاری Framework (of a building under construction).

سفتن [سنب] • To pierce ; bore.

سُفته Bored ; pierced.

سفته Promissory note ; also, draft.
سفته بازی Speculation ; stock-jobbery; gambling; agiotage.
سِفتی Hardness. Tightness. Stiffness. Toughness. Solidity.
سفر (*safar*) *A*. Travel(ling). Journey. — سفر دریا Voyage. — در سفر دیگر Next time. — سفر و حضر At home and abroad. — س. کردن To travel ; go on a journey.
سِفر (*sefr*) • *A*. [اسفار] Book; volume.
سفراء [Pl. of سفیر]
سفر کرده *A*. *P*. Travelled. Experienced by travelling.
سفرنامه *A*. *P*. Itinerary; diary.
سفرنگ ○ = تفسیر Commentary.
سُفره *A*. Table-cloth; -linen. (Dinner-) table; food; mess.— سرسفره At t.— شکم کسیرا سفره کردن + To disembowel, or rip up the belly of, a person.
سفره خانه *A*. *P*. Dining-room.
سفره ماهی *A*. *P*. Solo.
سَفری *A*. *P*. 1) *a*. Suitable for use on a journey. — چمدان س. Travelling suitcase. 2) *n*. Expected baby.
سفسطه *A-G*. Sophistry; fallacy.
سفسطه آمیز *A*. *P*. Fallacious ; sophistical.
سفلگی *A*. *P*. Meanness [پستی].
سفله *A*. Mean (person).
سُفلی *A*. (-*la*) [Fem. of اسفل]
سِفلی *A*. Low; inferior.
سفلیس *Fr*. Syphilis.
سفلیسی *Fr*. *P*. Syphilitic.
سفورجنه Viper's-grass.
سفها [Pl. of سفیه]
سفید *a*. White. Blank. Fair. —*n*. (*Mus*.) Minim.— س. شدن To turn white or grey.— س. کردن To whiten. To plaster with "gatch". To tin, as copper vessels. — س. گذاشتن To leave blank. — آهن س. Galvanized iron.—گل س. Whiting; chalk.— ماهی س. W. or whitefish.
سفیداب White powder, ceruse.— سفیداب سرب Ceruse.— سفیداب شیخ Flake white.
سفیدار or سپیدار White poplar.
سفید بخت etc. = خوشبخت etc.
سفید پوست Belonging to the White Race.
سفید چشم • Impudent.
سفیدک Powdery mildew; also, oidiomycosis. Whitish stains on a garment caused by perspiration.
سفیدکاری Gatch-plastering. — س. کردن To plaster with gatch.
سفیدگر Whitesmith.
سفیدگری Whitesmith's trade.
سفیده Albumen; white of the egg. Dawn. — س. دمید The dawn (has) appeared.
سفیدی White(ness). Blank space.
سَفیر *A*. [سفراء] Ambassador

[also سفیر کبیر - pl. سفراء کبار].

سفیل A. 1) ○ = بست 2) + At a loss what to do [often سفیل و سرگردان].

سفینه A. [سفائن] = کشتی Ship.

سفیه A. [سفهاء] Silly (person).

سفیهانه A. P. Foolish(ly).

سق + [Short for (سقف دهان)]

سقا A. Water-carrier.– مرغ س. Pelican.

سقاخانه A. P. Drinking fountain.

سقایت • A. Giving to drink.

سقائك A. P. = دم جنبانك

سقر A. Hell(-fire).

سقراط A.G. Socrates.

سقراطی A. Socratic.

سقز Persian turpentine.– درخت س. Terebinth.

سقط (*saghat*) A. Brick-bat; rubble.– س. شدن 1) To founder, as a horse. 2) × To drop down (*or* stop) dead; break one's neck. – س. گفتن To use bad or opprobrious language.

سقط (*seght*) A. Cast off foetus. Abortion [often سقط جنین]. – س. کردن To miscarry.

سقط آور A. P. Abortifacient.

سقط فروش A. P. Wholesale dealer (of groceries).

سقف A. [سقوف ○] Ceiling. Roof. – سقف دهان R. of the mouth; palate. – س. زدن To roof: cover with a r.

سقلابی T. P. Slavonic; Slavonian.

سقلمه T. Blow with the fist into a person's side.

سقم A. 1) Untruth. 2) ناخوشی

سقنقور A.G. Skink.

سقوط A. Fall(ing). – سقوط جفن Ptosis. – سقوط رحم Prolapsus (*or* prolapse) of the uterus; hysteroptosis. – سقوطِ هواپیما Air crash.– س. کردن = افتادن To fall. To c.

سقیم A. 1) Untrue. 2) ناخوش

سک Goad; prod. – سك زدن To goad.

سکان (*sokan*) A. Rudder. – فرمان س *or* چرخ س. Helm; steering-wheel.

سکان دار A. P. Helmsman; steersman.

سکته A. Stoppage. Pause in a verse. *Med.* Apoplexy. – سکتهٔ قلبی Heart-failure.– سکتهٔ کامل Foudroyant apoplexy.– سکتهٔ ناقص Paralysis; partial a. – س. کردن To fall into a fit of apoplexy. To have a heart-failure.

سکته‌دار A.P. Lame or limping, as a verse.

سکر A. = مستی

سکرات A. Pangs; throes; agony. [Pl. of سکره ○]

سکرآور A. P. Intoxicating.

سکسکه Hiccup. – س. کردن To hiccup.

سکنات A. [Pl. of سکنه ○]. Pauses; inactivities ○. –

حرکات وسکنات What one does and what he does not do.

سکنجبین *or* سرکنکبین Oxymel.

سکنجبینی Subacid.

سکندری Stumbling. — س. خوردن To stumble or trip.

سکنه *A.* [Pl. of ساکن] Inhabitants; residents; dwellers.

سکنی (*sokna*) *A.* Abode; residence. — س. گرفتن To dwell; reside.

سکو (*saku:*) Platform — سکوی تلمبه Pump-island. — سکوی توپ Emplacement. — سکوی مجسمه Entablement.

سُکوت *A.* Silence. Pause. *Mus.* Rest. — س. موجب رضا است Silence gives consent. — س. کردن To remain silent.

سُکون *A.* Calm. Repose. Tranquillity. *Gr.* Quiescence o.

سکونت *A.* Residence; habitation. — س. کردن To dwell; live. — قابل س. Habitable.

سکه *A.* Coin Stamp. *F.* Lustre. Currency. — س خوردن To receive the stamp of a die; be coined. — س زدن To coin; mint.

سکه‌ای *A. P.* Coin-like o. Numismatic o. — تف س. Nummular sputa.

سکه برو + *A. P.* Tin; i. e. money.

سکه شناس *A. P.* Numismatist. *F.* Mammonist.

سکینه (*A.*) *Fem. pr. name.*

سَگ Dog. — سگ آبی Beaver. — سگ تازی Greyhound. — سگ گله Sheep-dog. — سگ ماده Bitch. — سگ زدن + To loaf; idle away one's time. — سگ کیست How dare he?

سگال 1) *Imp. of* سگالیدن 2) o Thought. Word.

سگاله [f. Fr. *seigle*] Spurred rye.

سگالیدن o [سگال] To think. To wish. To speak.

سگ انگور o = **تاجریزی** Night-shade.

سگبینج *A.-P.* Sagapenum.

سگ توله Pup.

سگ جان Used to drudgery; plodding; indefatigable.

سگ خور × Spoiled; wasted.

سگدست Stub-axle; steering-knuckle. Console; prop. Cantilever.

سگک Clasp; small buckle.

سگ کش کردن + To kill cruelly (like a dog).

سگ ماهی Sturgeon. *C.E.* Seal. — تخم س. Caviar(e).

سگی Doggishness.

سِل *A.* Tuberculosis.

سلاح *A.* Armour; arms. *Cf. the pl.* اسلحه

سلاح (بر)دار o *A. P.* Armour-bearer.

سلاخ *A.* Slaughterer; flayer.

سلاخ‌خانه *A. P.* = کشتارگاه

سلاخی *A. P.* Slaughtering (of animals); butchery.

سلاست *A.* Smoothness (of style); ease; fluency.

سلاسل [Pl. of سلسله]

سلاطین [Pl. of سلطان].

سلاله *A.* Progeny. *F.* Essence.

سَلام *A.* Greeting; salutation. Regards. *OS.* Peace. *S. a.* سلام علیکم ‖ سلام عام Public levee.— توپ س. *Mil.* Salute.— س. دادن To greet; salute. — س. کردن (به) To g. — س. گرفتن To take the s. — س. نشستن To hold a levee.— جواب س. دادن To return a greeting.

سلامت *A.* (Good) health. Safety; security. [*Used as an a.*] Healthy. — سلامت عقل Sound mind. — سلامت نفس Simple-heartedness. Peaceableness Good health o. — بسلامت (*response to Good-bye*) Good-bye. Good luck to you! — س. باشید Thank you. — سرشما سلامت باشد Please accept my condolences. *OS.* May you be healthy (yourself).

سلامتی *A. P.* (*C. E*) = سلامت ‖ بسلامتی شما To your health.— بسلامتی کسی نوشیدن To drink some one's h.

سلام علیکم *A.* [Often simply سلام] Good morning. G. afternoon. G. evening. *OS.* Peace be with you!

سلانه (سلانه) + Swaggeringly; struttingly; boastingly.

سَلب *A.* Negation; privation.— س. شدن To be taken away. To lapse. — س. کردن To take a. — سلبِ اختیارات از کسی کردن — To divest (*or* deprive) s. o. of his powers.

سلبی *A.* Negative; privative. [Fem. سلبیه]

سلحشور *A. P.* Gladiator. Knight.

سَلخ *A.* Last day of a lunar month which has 30 days.

سلس‌البول *A.* Diabetes; poluria.

سلسال o *A.* Flowing and limpid water.

سلسبیل *A.* Nectar o. *Name of a fountain in Paradise.*

سلسلهِ *A.* [سلاسل] Chain. Series; train; tissue. C. or range (of mountains). Dynasty. — سلسلهٔ مراتب Hierarchical order; hierarchy.

سلسله جنبان *A. P.* Ringleader. Cause; motive.

سلسله مو • *A. P.* Having ringlets suggestive of the links of a chain.

سُلطان *A.* [سلاطین] Sultan; king. [Old word for سروان]

سلطانی *A. P.* 1) *n.* = سلطنت 2) *a.* Royal.

سَلطنت A. Kingdom. Monarchy. Reign. — س. کردن To reign or rule.
سلطنت طلب a. p. Monarchist.
سلطنتی A. P. Royal.
سلطه A. Rule; sovereignty; sway.
سلعه A. Wen. Sarcoma. Excrescence.— سلعهٔ شحمی Lipoma.
سلف (salaf) A. [اَسلاف] Predecessor. Ancestor. — معاملهٔ س. Forward purchase; short sale; time-bargain; dealing in futures — س. خریدن To buy in advance; make a forward p. — س. فروختن To make a short sale.
سلف (self) Core. [Per. corruption of the A. ثفل q. v.].
سِلف E. (Self-)starter.— س. زدن To press the starter button.
سلف دان Spittoon.
سَلف فروشی A. P. Short sale.
سُلفیدن × To shell out. OS. To cough—vulgar for سرفیدن
سلق (sulugh) [Spurious A. pl. for سلیقه] Tastes. [Used only in the phrase سلق شلق (است) i. e. There is no disputing about tastes; every man to his taste].
سِلک A. Range; category; class. OS. String for pearls.
سَلم n. Advance money. —a. Advanced; forward.
سلماچو Water-cress.

سَلمان Name of an Iranian companion of the Prophet.
سَلمانی A. P. Hairdresser or barber [also استاد سلمانی].
سلمه (تره) Dog's-mercury.
سُلوك A. Behaviour [رفتار].— س. کردن To behave.— حسن س. Good behaviour.
سلول Fr. = یاخته Cell.
سلولوئید Fr. Celluloid.
سلوی or سلبی+[f. Lat. salvia] Salvia; (scarlet) sage.
سَلوی A. (-va) = بلدرچین
سله ٥ A. = سبد
سِلی A. Tubercular.
سلیخه A. Cassia; China cinnamon.
سَلیس A. = روان Fluent; easy.
سلیطه A. Shrew.
سَلیقه A. Good taste; tact.
سلیم A. 1) Meek; humble. 2) Mas. pr. name. — عقل س. Sound judgment.
سلیم الطبع A. Of a meek nature; simple-hearted.
سلیم النفس A. 1) = سلیم‌الطبع 2) Peaceable.
سُلیمان A. Solomon. — خاتم س. or نگین س. Solomon's seal.— شانه بسر = مرغ س.
سلیمانی Of, or like that of, Solomon ٥.— عقیق س. or سنگ س. Onyx; also, carnelian.
سَمّ A. [سُموم] Poison; toxin. Cf. زهر ‖ سم خوردن To take poison. — سم دادن To p.

سُم Hoof [often سنب].
سَماء A. [سموات -ma-] = آسمان
سماجت A. Importunity; repeated urging. — س. کردن To be importunate; press hard.
سماروغ (White) mushroom. Cf. قارچ
سماط A. = سفره
سُماع * A. Singing. Song; music. OS. Hearing.
سماعی A. Founded on usage; irregular; heteroclite.
سُماق A. Sumac. S. a. سماك || ساق کوهی Mountain-ash.
سماق پالان A. P. Colander; cullender.
سماقی Tanned with sumac. — تیماج س. Morocco.
سماك [For سنگ س.] Porphyry.
سمّ الفار A. = مرگ موش
سماور R. Samovar. Urn.
سماوی A. = آسمانی
سم پاش A. P. Poison-sprayer.
سم پاشی A. P. Spraying poison. — س. کردن To spray p. F. To p. the public mind.
سمت (samt) A. Direction; side; way. Astr. 1) Apparent celestial longitude. 2) Azimuth [usu. السمت or سمت الرأس]. — دائره س. Vertical circle. — بسمتِ In the direction of; towards; at. — از سمت مغرب From the west.
سمت (semat) A. Capacity; designation. — بسمتِ In the capacity of; as; like. — سمت برادری بامن دارد He is like a brother to me.
سمت الراس A. Zenith.
سمت القدم A. Nadir.
سُم تراش Butteris.
سِمج A. Importunate: گدای س.
سِمحاق A. Pericranium.
سَمدار A. P. Poisonous.
سُم دار Hoofed; ungulate.
سمر ° A. Story. By-word.
سِمسار Dealer in second-hand goods.
سُم شکافته Cloven-hoofed; fissiped.
سَمع A. Hearing. Ear. — بسمع او رسید He heard it.
سمعاً وطاعةً A. Most willingly. OS. I shall hear and obey.
سمعك A. P. Ear-trumpet.
سَمك A. [سِماك] = ماهی Fish. — سمك رامح Astr. Arcturus.
سمن or یاسمن Jasmine.
سَمناك A. P. = زهردار & سمی
سمنبر * Of a fragrant bosom.
سمنت E. Cement [also سیمان].
سَمند Light-bay; dun-coloured.
سمندر Salamander.
سمنقر Tarlatan.
سَمنو Kind of dish with juice of germinating wheat or malt mixed with flour.
سموّ ° A. = بلندی
سموات [Pl. of سماء]
سموت [Pl. of سمت]
سَمور Sable. Fur from sable. —

سمور آبی Otter.

سَموم A. Simoom ; scorching wind.

سُموم [Pl. of سم]

سموئیل A-Heb. Samuel.

سمی A. Poisonous ; toxic.

سمیت A. Poisonousness.

سمیع ○ A. = شنونده Hearer : ep. of God.

سمین A. = فربه

سِن Kind of June-bug very destructive to wheat.

سن Fr. = صحنه Stage.

سِنّ A. Age : در سن ۵۰ سالگی At the age of 50. — سن شما چقدر است How old are you. — پا بسن گذاشتن To enter upon old age.

سَنا A. Senna. — سنای مکی Cassia lanceolata. — جوهر سنا Cathartic acid.

سِنا Fr. Senate [usu. مجلس س.].

سِنا A. In years; with respect to age.

سناتور Fr. Senator.

سناریو Fr. Scenario.

سنان • A. (Point of a) spear.

سنب (somb) 1) — سُم Hoof. 2) Imp. of سنبیدن or سفتن

سُنباده Emery. — چرخ س. Buff wheel; emery wheel. — سنگ س Corundum. — کاغذ س. Emery-paper; sand-paper. — س. زدن To polish with emery or sand-paper.

سنبل (sombol) A. Hyacinth. (Spike)nard. Met. Ringlet. — سنبل ختائی Angelica; lingwort. — سنبل رومی Celtic nard. — سنبل کوهی Wild hyacinth ; valerian. — سنبل هندی Indian (spike)nard.

سَنبل (sambal) × Bungled work. Bungling. — س. کردن To bungle or botch.

سنبل الطیب A. Valerian.

سنبلک Spikelet.

سنبله A. Ear of corn. Spike. Astr. Virgo. Old name of شهریور

سنبوسه ○ Small pie. Gusset.

سُنبه Ramrod. Pull-through. Punch. Piston. — س. زدن To ram. — + س. اش پر زور است He has a strong piston; i. e. some one to support him.

سنت A. (sonat) [سنن] Sunna(h); tradition. Custom. Circumcision. — اهل س. Sunnite(s).

سنت E. Cent.

سَنتور [f. G. origin] Dulcimer.

سنتوری 1) n. Pediment. Dulcimer-player [usu. سنتورزن]. 2) a. Dulcimer-shaped.

سَنج [Imp. of سنجیدن]

سِنج Cymbal.

سَنجاب Grey squirrel.

سَنجاق T. Pin. — سنجاق زلف Hair-pin. — سنجاق کراوات Brooch. — سنجاق قفلی Safety-pin. — س. زدن To secure by a pin ; p. together; p. up.

سنجاقک T. P. Dragon-fly.

سنجاق گیر T. P. Pin-cushion.

سنجد Kind of tree and its fruit which resembles the

mountain-ash.

سنجش Weighing. Measurement. *F.* Deliberation. Comparison.

سَنجیدن [سنج] To weigh. To measure. *F.* To compare.

سنجیدگی Deliberateness; soberness; judiciousness.

سنجیده [*P. P. of* سنجیدن] Weighed. Measured. Deliberate; reflected; guarded. Judicious.

سِنخ *A.* Class; group; category.

سند (*sanad*) *A.* [اسناد] Document; deed. Promissory note. Bill. — ثبت اسناد Registration of documents. — جعل اسناد Forgery. — سندِ بیمه Insurance policy. — اتخاذ سند کردن To take note.

سند (*send*) The Indus River. — جزایر سند The East Indies.

سِندان *A.* Anvil. *Anat.* Anvil-bone. — سندانِ *or* سندان دو دماغه — دوکرّه Bickern.

سندانچه *A. P.* Hand-anvil.

سندانی *A.P.* Anvil-like; incudal.

سندروس [f. G. origin] Sandarach. — سندروس بلوری Copal resin.

سندس ٥ *A-P.* Silk brocade.

سند ساز *A. P.* Forger of documents.

سند سازی *A. P.* Forgery.

سندل *S. u.* صندل

سِنده [*Indecent*] Thicker part of human excrement.

سنده سلام *P. A.* = گل مژه

سندیان *A-P.* Holm(-oak).

سندیت *A.* Binding force or effect; validity; legal f. Authenticity. — س. داشتن To be valid. To be a binding record.

سندیکا *Fr.* Syndicate.

سنقر Gyrfalcon.

سَنگ Stone. Weight. — سنگ آسمانی Aerolite; aerolith. — سنگ آسیاب Millstone. — سنگ پا Pumice-stone. — سنگ تمام Full weight. *See* سنگ کم *below.* — سنگِ تمام در ترازو گذاشتن To give full measure; go the whole hog. — سنگ چاپ Lithographic stone or slate. — سنگ روی یخ *Met.* One who is played off; also, cat's-paw. — سنگ سفید Ragstone. — سنگ سیاه Sandstone. — سنگ سیاه شیشه گران Manganese. — سنگ کم Short weight. *See* سنگ تمام *above.* — سنگ مثانه Bladder-stone; calculus. — سنگ مزار Gravestone. — معدن س. Quarry. — سرش بسنگ خورد He came to himself (when it was rather too late). — س. زدن To throw a stone (at). — سنگ کسیرا سینه زدن To strike a blow for s. o. — تیرش بسنگ خورد He missed the aim; he failed.

سنگاب Stone-trough.

سنگباران Shower of stones.

سنگ پاره Boulder. Rock.

سنگ پشت Tortoise.— سنگ پشت آبی Turtle.
سنگ پله Ducks and drakes.
سنگتراش Stone-cutter; mason.
سنگتراشی Stone-cutting; masonry.
سنگچین Fence of stones. Stone-revetment. Riprap. —س. کردن To riprap. To revet or fence with stones.
سنگخوار Sand-grouse.
سنگدان Gizzard.
سنگدل Stone-hearted; hard-hearted.
سنگدلی Hard-heartedness.
سنگر Rifle-pit. — سنگر ایستاده Breastwork.
سنگر بندی Intrenchment; fortification.
سنگریزه Gravel(-stone).
سنگساب Grindstone.
سنگستان Rocky or stony place.
سنگسار Stoned to death. — س کردن To stone to d.
سنگ شکن Knapping-hammer.
سنگشناس Petrologist; lithologist.
سنگشناسی Petrology; lithology.
سنگ فرش *P. A.* Stone-pavement; causeway; gravel-walk. — س. کردن To pave with stones; flag.
سنگ قلاب *P. A.* Sling.
سنگک Kind of bread [نان س.] baked on heated pebbles in a furnace.
سنگکار Mason.
سنگلاخ *P. T.* Stony (place).
سنگ لوح *P. A.* = **تخته سنگ**
سنگ نبشته *or* **سنگ نوشته** Petrograph; petroglyph.
سنگ ماسه Sandstone.
سنگی Stony. Of stone.— ساختمان س. S. building; masonry.
سنگواره Fossil.
سنگین 1) *a.* Heavy. Burdensome. Grave. Solemn. Sumptuous. Polite. [*Of food*] Indigestible; hard to digest. [*Of sleep*] Profound. [*Of ears*] Dull. [*Of drinks*] High-proof.— خوابش س. است He is a heavy sleeper. 2) —*ad.* Solemnly. Heavily.— س. کردن To make heavy or burdensome.
سنگین اسلحه *P. A.* Heavy-armed.
سنگین‌دل = **سنگدل**
سنگین قیمت *P. A.* Precious; costly.
سنگینک ο Slowly. Gravely.
سنگین وزن *P. A.* Heavy.
سنگینی Heaviness; weight. Gravity. Dullness.
سنن [Pl. of سنت]
سنوات [Pl. of سنه]
سنواتی *A. P.* = 1) سالیانه 2) معمولی
سَنه *A.* [سنوات & سنین] Year [سال] Era. — سنهٔ جرت منه × (At) some unknown date.
سَنی ο *A.* = بلند - باشکوه
سُنی *A.* Sunnite.
سِنی *A.* Elected (pro tempore) by virtue of his age.
سنین *A.* = سالها [Pl. of سنه] Years. — سنین عمرم ٥٦ سال است

My age is 56.

سو *or* **سوی** Direction; side. — از هرسو From every direction; from all sides.

سو Sight. Light.

سوء *A.* Evil [بدی]. — سوء ادب = سوء استفاده کردن از ‖ بی ادبی To abuse or misuse. To presume upon. To take advantage of. — سوء تعبیر Misinterpretation. — سوء تدبیر Mismanagement; wrong policy. — سوء تفاهم Misunderstanding. — سوء سابقه Bad record. — سوء ظن Suspicion. — سوء ظن داشتن از To suspect. — سوء قصد Attempt (upon some one's life). — سوء نیت Bad intention; bad faith. — سوء هاضمه Indigestion; dyspepsia.

سوا *or* **سوی** *A.* (*seva*) Separate. Different. — س شدن To separate. — ازهم س. شدن To part with each other. To dissolve partnership. — س. کردن To s. To select; pick out.

سَواء o *A.* = **برابر(ی)**

سوابق [Pl. of سابقه]

سواحل [Pl. of ساحل]

سَواد *A.* Literacy; ability to read and write. Copy [رونوشت]. — سواد اعظم o Large city. — س. کردن *or* س. برداشتن از. To make a copy of; transcribe.

سوادالبطن o *A.* = **جگر**

سوادالعین o *A.* = **مردمك چشم**

سَوار *n.* Rider; horseman. —*a.* Riding; mounted. — سوار درشکه Driving in a carriage. — سوار کشتی Embarked in a ship; on board a s. — س. شدن To ride. To mount. — سوار اتوبوس شدن To get in a bus. — سوار کاری شدن To embark upon a business; also, be installed or skilled in it. — سوار کسی شدن + To rule or exploit s. o.; have a hold on him. — سوار کشتی شدن To go on board a ship; embark. — س. شوید! *Mil.* To horse! — س. کردن To cause to ride. To mount. To take on board. To pick up (a passenger). To assemble; erect : ماشین س. کردن

سوار خوبی Trick riding; horsemanship.

سوار کار Jockey. — باشگاه سوار کاران Jockey-club.

سوار کننده Erector (of machinery).

سواره 1) *ad.* On horseback. 2) *a.* Mounted : پلیس س. ‖ Equestrian : مجسمهٔ س. ‖ Galloping : سل س. ‖ 3) *n.* Person on horseback.

سواره‌رو Roadway.

سواره نظام *P. A.* Cavalry.

سواری Riding; horsemanship. — اتوموبیل س. Passenger car. — اسب س. Saddle-horse. — س. کردن To ride. To drive. — س. ازکسی گرفتن + To exploit s. o. *OS.* To ride some one's back. —

س. دادن To allow mounting.— این اسب خوب س. میدهد This horse is a good mount.

سوا سوا *a. p.* Separately; one by one.

سؤال *A.* [سؤالات] Question. Begging — س کردن 1) To ask: س. کرد که آن زن کیست He asked who she was. 2) To beg.

سؤال پیچ کردن *A. P.* To ply with questions.

سوانح [Pl. of سانحه]

سوای *A.P.* [Stress on the 1st. or 2nd. syl.] Except; save.

سوایی *A.P.* Separation. Separate accounts; independent life.

سوبلیمه *Fr.* Sublimate.

سوپ *Fr.* Soup.

سوپاپ *Fr.* Valve.

سوپ خوری *Fr. P.* Tureen. — قاشق س. Tablespoon.— روزی دو قاشق س. Two table-spoonfuls a day.

سوت Whistle. — سوت خطر Siren. — سوت ماشین Steam whistle; hooter; siren. — س. زدن *or* س. کشیدن To (blow a) w.— سوت کردن + To throw (a ball, etc.) out of bounds.

سوت سوتك Whistle.

سوخ *Bot.* Bulb.

سوخاری *R.* Rusk.

سوخت Fuel. — س. شدن To be written off, as a bad debt.

سوخت آما Carburettor.

سوخت پاش Carburettor-jet.

سوخت رسان Feeder. *OS.* Supplier of fuel.

سوختگی Burn; scald.

سوخت گیری (Re)fuelling. [Of a ship] Bunkering — س. کردن To fuel up or refuel. To bunker.

سوختن [سوز] To burn *vi.* & *vt.* To be consumed. [*Of a bulb*] To burn out. [*Of a fuse*] To blow out. *F.* To fret or worry —دلم بحالش میسوزد I pity him.

سوخت و ساز Metabolism.

سوخته Burnt. Scorched. Dark: بوی س. Empyreuma. ‖ قهوه‌ای س.

دل سوخته = سوخته دل

سوختی 1) Fit for fuel: نفت س. Fuel oil. 2) Bad or irrecoverable, as a debt.

سود Profit. Benefit. Advantage. Interest.— حساب سودوزیان Profit-and-loss account. — سود سهام Dividend. — س. بردن To make a profit. To derive a benefit.— س. کردن To make a p.

سود *Fr.* Soda, Sodium.

سودا (*soda*) *or* سُدا *Fr.* Soda.

سودا (*sow-*) Transaction. Trade.

سوداء *A.* Black bile. Melancholy. Tetter; *L.* Eczema. — سودای خام پختن *Met.* To build castles in the air.

سودابه *Fem. pr. name.*

سودازده * *A. P.* Melancholic.

Enamoured.
سوداگر Trader.
سوداگری Trade; business.
سود آور Profitable.
سودائی A. Atrabilious. Melancholy. Passionate.
سودجو(یی) Profiteer(ing).
سودمند Useful. Profitable.
سودمندی Usefulness - اصالت س. Utilitarianism.
سودن [سای] To rub. To grind.
سوده [P. P. of سودن] a. Pulverized. Rubbed. — n. Dust; powder.
سودیوم Fr. Sodium.
سور Feast; party; junket. - س خوردن or +س.زدن To feast; play a good knife and fork.
سور (sovar) [Pl. of سوره]
سوراخ Hole. Cavity.- س. وسنبه × Nook and corner.- پارچه س است There is a hole in the cloth. - سوراخ بینی Nostril.- سوراخ دعارا گم کردن Met. To get hold of the wrong end of the stick. - سوراخ سوزن Eye of a needle. - س. شدن To be pierced. To spring a leak. - س. کردن To pierce; bore. To prick.
سوراخ سوراخ Full of holes. Perforated. Porous.
سوراخ کن Perforator. Punch.
سورَت (su:-) = سوره
سورَت (sow-) A. = شدت - حمله
سورتمه T. Sledge.
سورچران Sponger; hanger-on.
سورچرانی Sponging; dinner-hunting.
سورچی T. Carriage-driver.
سورسات T. Provisions. - س. تهیه کردن To purvey (articles of food); cater.
سورسات چی T. Purveyor; caterer.
سورکنتر Fr. (C. P.) Redouble.
سورنجان Meadow-saffron; hermodactyl; colchium.
سوره A. [سُوَر] Sura(h): chapter of the Koran.
سوری [For گل س.] Red rose.
سوری Person fond of feasting or dinner-hanging; hanger-on.
سوریه A Syria.
سوز 1) Imp. of سوختن 2) -n. Cold breeze. Smart pain. Anguish. - سوز دل Heartache. Mental vexation. Grudge. - س. زدن To smart.
سوزا 1) سوزان 2) Combustible.
سوزاک or سوزنک Gonorrhœa.- سوزنك غیرمسری زنان Leucorrhœa; the whites.
سوزاکی Gonorrhœal.
سوزان 1) Burning. Smarting. Fervent. 2) Imp. of سوزاندن
سوزاندن To burn. To set on fire. To scorch. F. To worry or fret.
سوزآور 1) Caustic. 2) سوزناك
سوزایی Combustibility.
سوزش Burn(ing); combustion. Scald. Smart pain. Irritation. Prickly sensation.

سوزَك Pimple. Prickly sensation.
سوزَن Needle. — سوزن آبله کوبی Vaccine-point. — یك سر سوزن A little bit. — سوزن دو راهی Switch point. — س. زدن To prick with a needle. To have a shot (*i. e.* injection).
سوزناك Plaintive; touching.
سوزن بان Pointsman.
سوزن بند [*In a sewing-machine*] Clamp.
سوزن‌دان Needlecase.
سوزندگی Consuming power; burning effect. Causticity.
سوزنده Burning. Caustic.
سوزن دوزی Needle-lace.
سوزن زنی Needlework.
سوزن سوزنی شدن To feel pins and needles; have a prickly sensation.
سوزنك *S. u.* سوزاك
سوزنی Needle-like. Worked by a needle. Prickly. [*Of a hole*] Minute. — تفنگ س. Needle-gun. — فتیل س One-way valve. *See* فتیل
سوزنی Small cashmere cloth.
سوزه = سوزك
سوس Liquorice. — ربّ س. Extract of liquorice.
سوس (*sos*) or سس *Fr.* Sauce.
سوسك Beetle. — سوسك غله Zabrus; caraboid beetle. — سوسك طلائی Gold-beetle. Cockchafer. — سوسك گرمابه Cockroach.

سوسمار Lizard. Crocodile.
سوسماری Crocodile-brand.
سوسن Lily (of the valley).
سوسنی Liliaceous.
سوسو زدن + To flicker.
سوسه Weevil. Serration (in a blade). *F.* Flaw. Doubt. — س. در کار آوردن To interpose difficulties. To put a spoke in one's wheel.
سوسی *H.* Susi.
سوسیالیست *Fr.* Socialist.
سوسیالیستی *Fr. P.* Socialistic.
سوسیالیسم *Fr.* Socialism.
سوش *Fr.* Counterfoil; stub.
سوغات *T.* Present sent or brought by a traveller.
سوغان اسبی را گرفتن To pare the hoofs of a horse. To train a h. for the race.
سوف Zander; also, whitefish.
سوفار Notch of an arrow.
سوفال Pantile. *S. a.* سفال
سوفسطائی *A-G.* Sophist.
سوفلور *Fr.* = سخن رسان
سوق ○ *A.* [اسواق] = بازار
سوق (*sowgh*) *A.* Impelling; driving. — س. دادن To lead.
سوق الجیش ○ *A.* = لشکرکشی
سوق الجیشی *A.* Strategic.
سوق الدواب ○ *A.* Livestock market.
سوك = کنج & گوشه
سوکمیسیون *Fr.* Sub-committee
سوگ Sorrow. Mourning.
سوگلی *T.* Favourite (wife).

سوگند Oath. — س. خوردن To take an oath; swear.—س.دادن To administer an o. to; swear. —سوگند دروغ خوردن To perjure oneself.

سوگندشکن Guilty of perjury.

سوگند شکنی Perjury.

سوگند نامه Swearing formula.

سوگوار ○ =عزادار Mournful.

سوگواری Mourning; lamentation. — س. کردن To mourn.

سوگیری ○ = طرفداری Partiality.

سولفات *Fr.* Sulphate.

سولفات دوسود *Fr.* Sodium sulphate; Glauber's salts.

سولفات دومنیزی *Fr.* Sulphate of mangnesium.

سولفور *Fr.* Sulphide.

سوله Saker. — سولهٔ نر Sakeret.

سوّم Third.

سومی The third (one).

سومین The third

سوهان File. — سوهان چوب ساب Rasp. — س. زدن To file.

سوهان خور ○ Allowance for further rasping or filing. — س. ندارد + No margin is allowed for it. It is as sure as a gun.

سوهان کار Filer; filecutter.

سوهان کاری Filing; rasping.

سوی *S. u.* سو

سوی *A.* (*seva*) *S. u.* سوا

سویِ At; tow rd. *See* سو

سوئد *Fr.* Sweden.

سویداء ○ *A.* The heart's core.

سوئدی *Fr. P.* Swedish.

سوئز *Fr.* Suez : ترعهٔ س.

سویس *Fr.* Switzerland.

سویسی *Fr. P.* Swiss(-made).

سَویه *A.* = برابری Equality. — بالسویه *ad.* Equally. —علی‌السویه (*alasaviyeh*) *ad.* Equally. Without distinction. —*a.* Equal; same.

سه Three. — هرسه All three.

سها or سهی *A.* (*soha*) *Name ot a dim star in Ursa.*

سهام [Pl. of سهم]

سهامی *A. P.* Made up of shares; joint-stock.

سه‌آنس *Fr.* Meeting; sitting. .[At cinema] Performance.

سه باله Having 3 (pairs of) wings. — هواپیمای س. Triplane.

سه بری or سه بر Trilateral.

سه برابر Threefold. Three times as many or as much.— س.کردن To triple.

سه برگه 1) *a.* Trifoliate. 2) *n.* Marsh trefoil.

سه پا *a.* Three-legged. —*ad.* In triple time.

سه پایه Tripod. Trivet. Music-stand. Easel.

سه پرچمی *Bot.* Triandrous.

سه پهلو Trilateral.

سه تا Three [*used without a noun*] : او دوقلم دارد من س. دارم

سه تیر Three-loader; three-cartridge magazine rifle.

سه جانبه *P. A.* Tripartite.
سه جمله‌ای *P. A.* Trinomial.
سه چرخه Tricycle ; also, velocipede.
سه چندان Threefold; triple.
سه حرفی *P. A.* Triliteral.
سه‌دوری ○ The three dimensions [Usu. ابعاد سه گانه].
سُهراب *Mas. pr. name.*
سه راه Forked road ; parting of two roads. Y-track. Tee.
سه رنگ Tricolour.
سه رویه Trihedral.
سِهره Goldfinch.
سه ساله Three-year-old.
سه سر 1) *a.* Three-headed. — ماهیچهٔ س. Triceps. 2) *n.* (*C. P.*) Pair royal.
سه‌شاخه *a.* Three-horned ; tricorn. Three-pronged. —*n.* Pitchfork.
سه شنبه Tuesday.
سه‌ضربی *P.A.* (In) triple time.
سه طرفه *P. A.* Tripartite.
سه قاب (Game played with three) knucklebones.
سه قولو *P. T.* [For بچهٔ س.] Triplet.
سه‌کنج Corner; solid angle.
سه‌گوش *a.* Triangular. Tricuspid. —*n.* Triangle.
سه‌گوشه Triangular.
سَهل *A.* Easy [آسان]. — س. کردن To facilitate. — س. گرفتن To take (it) easy. To slight; make light (of). — موسیقی ایرانی که س. است موسیقی فرنگی هم میدانست He not only knew Iranian music, but European m. as well.
سه لا Three-ply. Threefold.
سهل‌الادراك *A.* Easy of apprehension.
سهل‌الاستعمال *A.* Handy ; easy to use.
سهل‌الحصول *A.* = زودیاب
سهل‌العبور *A.* Easy to cross.
سهل‌الوصول *A.* Easy to collect.
سهل‌الهضم *A.* Easy of digestion ; digestible.
سهل انگار *A. P.* Careless; nonchalant.
سهل‌انگاری *A. P.* Nonchalance; carelessness. [In religious matters] Latitudinarianism.
سه لختی Tricuspid.
سَهم *A.* [سِهام] Share; portion. Contribution. Arrow. — س. بردن To share. To partake. — س. کردن To s. or divide. — صاحب س. = سهمدار ‖ سود سهام Dividend. — سهام قرضه Debentures ; debenture bonds.
سَهم = ترس Dread ; awe.
سهم‌الرامی *A.* (*Astr.*) The Arrow or Sagitta.
سه ماهه *a.* Three-month-old. Quarterly : گزارش س. ‖ —*ad.* In three months time.
سهمدار *A P.* Shareholder.
سهمگین Dreadful; formidable.
سهمناك = ترسناك
سهمی *A.* Sagittal. Slyloid. Based on (the number of)

shares.

سهمیه *A.* Quota. Share.

سه نوبت ○ *P. A.* Music anciently played three times a day before the royal pâlace.

سَهو *A.* Error; slip; oversight. — سهو زبان Slip of the tongue; *lapsus linguae.* — سهو قلم S. of the pen; *lapsus calami.* — س. کردن To make an error or mistake.

سهواً (*sahvan*) *A.* By mistake; inadvertently.

سه وجهی *P. A.* Trihedral.

سُهولت *A.* Ease. Fluency. — به آسانی = بسهولت Easily.

سه هجائی *P. A.* Trisyllabic. — کلمهٔ س. Trisyllable.

سَهی * Straight : سرو سهی

سه یك One-third. — نوبهٔ س. Tertian fever.

سُهیل *A.* Canopus.

سَهیم (*A.*) *a.* Having a share or shares; participant. —*n.* Partner. — س. شدن To partake; participate; take part.

سی Thirty. — سی سال × Never in (all) my life.

سیاح *A.* Tourist; traveller.

سیاحت *A.* Touring. — س. کردن To (make a) tour; travel (through). To explore.

سیاحت نامه *A. P.* (Tourist's) itinerary.

سیادت *A.* Lordship; supremacy.

سیار *A.* 1) *a.* Itinerant. 2) *n.* I. traveller. Wanderer.

سیاره *A.* [سیارات] Planet. — سیارهٔ خرد Asteroid. — سیارات صغار Minor planets; planetoids or asteroids.

سیاس *A.* Great politician, statesman, or diplomat.

سیاست *A.* Politics. Policy. Strict administration of justice. Punishment. — س. کردن *vt.* To punish. —*vi.* To exercise politics [also س. راندن].

سیاستمدار *a. p.* 1) *n.* Politician. Statesman. 2) *a.* Versed in politics. Diplomatic.

سیاسنگ Basalt.

سیاسی *A. a.* Political. Diplomatic. —*n.* [Only in the pl. سیاسیون politicians; statesmen]. — مرد سیاسی Statesman; politician. — گفتگوی س. کردن To talk politics.

سیاسیات *A.* Politics; political matters. [Pl. of سیاسیه fem. of سیاسی]

سیاق *A.* Order. Style. Course. Trend. — سیاق عبارت Context. Style of an expression.

سیال *A.* Fluid; flowing.

سیاله ○ *A.* Current. [*Orig. fem. of* سیال]

سی‌ام Thirtieth.

سیام *Geog.* Siam.

سیامی Siamese.

سیانور *Fr.* Cyanide.

سیاوش *Mas. pr. name.* — خون س. Maidenhair. — بر سیاوش or خون‌سیاوشان Dragon's-blood.

سیاه Black. Blackamoor; negro. *Mus.* Quarter-note — س. پوشیدن To wear black. — س شدن To turn b. — س. کردن To blacken. — رویش س. شد He was put to shame. — س. و سفید را (از هم) تشخیص نمیدهد He doesn't know chalk from cheese; he is illiterate.

سیاه آب Marsh; bog.

سیاه بخت = بدبخت

سیاه پوست Dark-skinned.

سیاه پوش Wearing black; clothed in mourning.

سیاه تاوه 1) o Black pan. 2)+ [*Used as an a.*] Dark-coloured; melanoid.

سیاه چال Dungeon; black hole.

سیاه چرده or سیه چرده Dark-coloured; melanoid.

سیاه چشم Black-eyed.

سیاه دانه Nigella seeds. Ergot of rye. [ted conscience.

سیاه دل or سیه دل Of a blun-

سیاهرگ Vein [ورید].

سیاه‌رنگ Black; dark-coloured.

سیاه رو or سیه رو Disgraced put to shame.

سیاه روز or سیه روز Unhappy; whose life is unsuccessful.

سیاه زخم Anthrax; charbon.

سیاه زنگ Wheat rust [*Puccinia graminis*].

سیاه سُرفه Whooping-cough.

سیاه سنگ or سیاسنگ Basalt.

سیاه قلم *P. A.* Niello; inlaid enamel; etching. Black-and-white.

سیاهک Smut: disease affecting cereal grasses; also, brown rust.

سیاه کاج Larch.

سیاه کاری or سیه کاری • Wickedness.

سیاه‌گوش Lynx; also, caracal.

سیاهه Invoice; bill. — س. کردن To make out a b. for. To inventory.

سیاهی Blackness; black colour. — سیاهی، کی هستی؟ Who goes there? — سیاهی‌لشکر Mere numbers; noses; multitude — چشمم س. میرود + My eyes see black.

سیب Apple. — سیب صحرائی. Crab-apple. — یك س. را دو نصف کرده‌اند They are as alike as two peas in a pod.

سیب تراش Apple-grater.

سیبری (-be-) *Fr.* Siberia.

سیب زمینی Potato. *Met.* Nerveless or cowardly (person). — سیب زمینی ترشی Jerusalem artichoke.

سیبك *Bot.* Tuber. — خروج س. Prolapse of the uterus.

سیبی Malaceous; pomaceous.

سیبیا [f. G. *sepia*] Cuttlefish.

سیحون *A.* — سیر دریا

سیخ 1) *n*. Skewer; spit. Broach. — سیخِ بخاری Poker. [Of an opium pipe] Stilette. [Of a cock's leg] Cockspur. 2)*a*. Stiff. Stubby. — س. زدن To stir (by a poker). To goad; prod. To give a shove off (to).— س.شدن To stiffen.— س. کردن To s. To cock. — بسیخ کشیدن To fix on a spit or skewer.

سیخ پَر New-fledged.

سیخچه 1) = سیخك 2) Small spit.

سیخ شدگی Stiffness. [*Of the neck*] Torticollis; stiffneck.

سیخك Spur. Prod; goad. Tail-skid.— س. زدن To prod or g.

سیخ گردان Device for turning a spit, as used in roasting meat. Smokejack.

سید *A*. [Fem. سیده] Sayid: descendant of the Prophet. *OS*. Lord; master. [Pl. سادات which is orig. pl. of سادة pl. of سائد].

سیده *A*. [Fem. of سید] Title of a woman who has descended from the Prophet. *OS*. Lady; princess. — سیدهٔ دریاها Mistress of the Seas.

سیر Full; having had enough; satisfied. [*Of colour*] Deep. *F*. Weary; disgusted.— س. شدم I (have) had enough.— س. کردن To fill; satisfy. To feed (to satiety). To glut. To weary. — س. خوردن To eat until one is full; eat one's fill (of.)

سیر Garlic.

سیر *Old weight almost equal to 75 grammes*.

سیر (*seyr*) *A*. Travelling. Excursion. Sightseeing. Revolution. — سیرقهقرائی Retrogression.— س. کردن To go sightseeing. To travel. To revolve.— خط س. Route; itinerary.

سیر (*siar*) [Pl. of سیرت]

سیراب Drunk to satiety. Thoroughly irrigated. — س. کردن To give to drink to s.; quench the thirst of. To irrigate thoroughly.

سیرابی Tripe; sheep's paunch prepared for food.

سیرت *A*. [سیر *siar*] Character. Conduct Nature.

سیر دریا Jaxartes.

سیرك *Fr*. Circus.

سیرمانی × = سیری ‖ س. ندارد He is insatiable or greedy.

سیره *A*. (*siareh*) 1) = دَیِش 2) Corruption of سیرت. 3) Name of a book on the Prophet's character sketch.

سیروس *Fr*. Cyrus. *Mas. pr. name*.

سیری Fullness: lack of hunger. Satiety. Weariness.

سیری ناپذیر Insatiable.

سیزاب Brooklime.

سیزدَه Thirteen.

سیزده بدر Thirteenth day of

the New Year festival on which people go out for pleasure.
سیزدهم Thirteenth.
سیزدهمی (The) thirteenth.
سیزدهمین The thirteenth.
سیسنبر Wild thyme.
سیسیل *Fr.* Sicily.
سیصد Three-hundred.
سیصدم Three-hundredth.
سیطره ○ *A.* Supremacy; rule.
سیف *A.* [شمشیر = اُسیوف]
سیف *E.* C. I. F.; cif.
سیف‌الجبار (*seyfol-jabar*) *A.* Orion's Belt. (*Astr.*)
سیف‌الغراب *A.* Gladiolus [now usu. known by its Fr. name *glaieul* گلایول].
سیفن *Fr.* Siphon.
سیکران Henbane seeds.
سیگار *Fr.* Cigarette — سیگار برگی Cigar. — س. کشیدن To smoke a cigar(ette). — س. کشیدن ممنوع است "No smoking allowed."
سیگار آتش‌زن *Fr. P.* Cigarette-lighter.
سیگارت *Fr.* Cigarette ○. Small tube or cylinder on which thread is wound.
سیگاری *Fr. P. a.* Cigarette-shaped; tubular. —*n.* C.-seller.
سیل *A.* Flood; torrent; inundation.
سیلاب *A. P.* Flood-water.
سیلابی *A. P.* Torrential.
سیلان *A.* Flowing; flux. — سیلان ابیض Leucorrhea. — سیلان بزاق Salivation. Ptyalism.
سیل آورده *A. P.* Torrential.
سیل برگردان *A. P.* Bund for flood prevention.
سیل خیز *A. P.* Giving rise to inundations; submergible.
سیل‌زده *A. P.* [سیل زدگان] Flood victim.
سیلگیر *A. P.* Submergible.
سیلندر *Fr.* = استوانه Cylinder. — کلاه س. Top hat; chimney-pot hat.
سیلو *Fr.* Silo; store-pit.
سیلی Slap; box on the ear. — س خوردن To be slapped in the face. — سیلی روزگار خوردن To experience a hardship. — س زدن To give a slap (to). — صورت خود را به س سرخ نگهداشتن To keep up appearances.
سیلیس *Fr.* Silica.
سیلیسی *Fr. P.* Silicious; siliceous.
سیلیکات *Fr.* Silicate.
سیم Silver; *by e.* money. Wire; line. *Mus.* String; cord. — ماهی س Bream. — بسازی س انداختن To string an instrument. — س. کشیدن To wire. To be infected by exposure to cold weather. — سیم سفید برای روز سیاه Shining gold for dark days.
سیم (*seyom*) = سوم
سیما Mien. Physiognomy.

سیماب • Quicksilver ; mercury [usu. جیوه].
سیمابی Mercurial.
سیمان *Fr.* Cement.
سیم اندام • Of a silvery or delicate body.
سیمان کار *Fr. P.* Cement layer.
سیمانکاری *Fr. P.* Cement laying. Terrazo-works.
سیمانی *Fr.P.* Made of cement.— پلهٔ س. Precast concrete step.
سیمَبر • Of a silvery bosom.
سیمُبر Wire-cutter.
سیم پرست = زر پرست
سیم پوش Wire insulator.
سیم پیچ *n.* Armature winder. —*a.* Tied by wires.
سیم پیچی Armature winding.
سیمتن • = سیم اندام
سیمدار Wired. Stringed.
سیمرغ *Fabulous bird variously identified.*
سیمکش Wireman; also; lineman.
سیمکشی Wire-extension; wiring. —س. کردن (در) To wire.
سیمگون • Silver-white.
سیمگیر Tailpiece of a violin.
سیمی Made of wire. *Mus.* Stringed : آلات س. ‖ توری یا پارچهٔ س. Wire-gauze; wire cloth.
سیمی (*seyo*-) = سومی
سیمین • Silvery. (Made) of silver. *F.* Silver-white; fair.
سینا *A-Heb.* Sinai. *Mas. pr. name.*
سینرر *Fr.* Cineraria ; fleawort.

سینما *Fr.* Cinema ; pictures.— او عاشق س. است He is a film-fan.
سینماتوگراف *Fr.* Cinematograph.
سینه Breast ; bosom. Chest. [*As joint of meat*] Brisket. [*Of a ship*] Bow. [*Of a mountain*] Slope. — سلّ س Pulmonary tuberculosis. — س.زدن To beat one's breast.— س. سپر کردن To take up the cudgels. — س. صاف کردن To clear the throat; hem; hum and ha(w); hawk.— بسنگ چیز برا سینه زدن To strike a blow for s. t.— س.کردن To ricochet.
سینه ای Pectoral. Thoracic. Pulmonary [ریوی].
سینه بند Breastband. Bib. Poitrel.
سینه پهلو Pneumonia.
سینه چاك • Greatly afflicted.
سینه‌درد Pectoralgia, pneumonalgia, or any other disease connected with the chest.
سینه ریز Necklace with part covering the breast.
سینه زن Member of religious procession of mourners beating their breasts, esp. on the anniversary of the martyrdom of Emam-Hosein.
سینه سوزی Anguish.
سینه‌کش Slope.
سینه مال رفتن To creep; crawl; glide.

سیه‌روز - سیه‌دل - سیه‌چرده etc. *S. u.* سیاه چرده etc.

سیئه o *A.* [سیآت] = گناه Evil act; sin.

سینی Tray. Salver. *M.* Shield or tray.

سی‌وجهی *P.A.* Triacontahedral.

سیورسات *T.* = سورسات

سیه • [Cont. of سیاه]

ش [شان] 1) His or her. Ex. دلش 2) Him or her. Ex. (a) برایش for him or her. (b) دیدمش I met him or her.

شاب o *A*. Young man. *Cf*. جوان

شاباش [Cont. of شادباش] Money strewn about at weddings.

شاپور *Mas. pr. name.*

شاتون *R*. Connecting-rod.

شاخ Horn. Branch. — شاخ‌حجامت Cupping-glass. — شاخ و برگ Foliage; herbage. *F*. Details; enlargement; also, embellishment — ش. بشاخ کسی گذاشتن + To quarrel with, or oppose, s. o ; also, come to grips with him. — ش. درآوردن ×To be struck (*or* knocked) all of a heap. *OS*. To have a horn grow on one's head. — ش. را برداشتن × To cease bothering or bibbling. *OS*. To remove the cupping-glass. — ش. زدن To butt ; gore. — ش. شکستن To break or train, as a horse. — شاخ و شانه کشیدن × To bully s. o. *O.S*. To thrust one's horns and shoulders forward. — اینکه روی‌شاخش‌است + That is taken for granted.

شاخابه Tributary (stream).

شاخ. بزی Resembling a goat's horns [only in طاق ش. Persian or Saracenic arch].

شاخدار Horned. — دروغ ش. Rousing or swingeing lie ; thumper. — مرغ ش. Guinea-fowl. — عینك ش. Spectacles.

شاخسار *a*. Full of branches or trees. —*n*. Thicket; grove.

شاخص Gnomon; sun-dial. Indicator.

شاخك Small horn or branch. Antenna. — شاخك حساس Feeler; tentacle.

شاخه Branch. B.-line. B.-pipe. Tributary. — لوستر سه ش. 3-armed chandelier.

شاخه‌شاخه Branching. — ش. شدن To branch out; ramify.

شاخی Horny; (made) of horn.

شاد Glad ; happy. — ش. شدن To become glad. — ش. کردن To gladden ; make h. — روحش ش. باد Peace (be) to his departed spirit. — ش باشید Cheerio ! Good-bye.

شاداب Juicy; succulent. Fresh.

شادان • = **شاد**

شادباش = تبریك Congratulation. Good wishes. — ش. گفتن To congratulate. To offer one's good w.

شاد بهر o Merry; joyful.
شاد خوار(ه) o 1) Merry; joyful 2) میگسار 3) Easy-going.
شادروان The deceased (whose soul may be happy); the late. *Cf.* مرحوم
شادُروان o Cornice. Eaves. Ornamental tent or carpet. Large curtain. Shady place.
شادکام Happy. Triumphant.
شادکامی Happiness. Success.
شادمان Glad. Joyful.
شادمانی Joy; rejoicing.—ش کردن To rejoice; make merry.
شادی Joy; merry-making. — ش. کردن To rejoice.
شاذّ *A.* = کمیاب Rare.
شارِب *A* [شوارب] Hair of the moustache growing beyond the upper lip.
شارت و شورت ×Fuss; bluster.
شارِح *A.* Commentator; expositor.
شارِع *A.* Legislator; lawgiver. Road [pl. شوارع] — شارع خاص Private road.—شارع عام Public r.; thoroughfare; highway.
شارِق o *A.* = تابان
شارلاتان *Fr.* Charlatan.
شاسی *Fr.* Chassis; frame.
شاش [*Indecent*] Piss; urine.— شاشیدن = ش. کردن
شاش‌بند (Suffering from) retention of the urine. — ش. شدن To suffer from r. of the urine.
شاشدان Chamber-pot. Bladder.
شاشو + Who has the habit of pissing in his clothes or bedclothes.
شاشیدن To piss; urinate. [Not in polite use]. *See* ادرار کردن
شاطِر *A. n.* Footman; outrunner o. Baker. —*a.* o Nimble. Clever.
شاطریون *A.-G.* Satyrium.
شاعِر *A.* [شُعرا] Poet.
شاعرانه *A. P. ad.* Poetically. —*a.* Poetical.
شاعرك *A. P.* Poetaster.
شاعره *A.* [Fem. of شاعر]
شاعری *A. P.* Poetical art.
شاغِل *A.* Having a (specified) business. Occupying.
شاف *S. u.* شیاف
شافع o *A.* 1) = شفیع 2) Preemptor.
شافی *A.* Categorical or satisfactory: جواب ش. ‖ *OS.* Healing.
شاقّ *A.* = سخت Difficult; hard. [Fem. شاقه]. — حبس با اعمال شاقه Imprisonment with h. labour; penal servitude.
شاقول Plumb-line; bob. Plummet.
شاقه *S. u.* شاق
شاکِر *A.* = شکرگزار
شاکی *A.* Complainant.—ش. بودن To complain.
شاگرد Apprentice. Shopboy. Journey-man. Student; pupil. Disciple. — شاگرد شدن To be bound apprentice — ش. آشپز

Cook's mate; also, scullion.– ش. راننده Driver's m.-*Note*. The last two items are also read without the *ezafeh*, being regarded as compound words.

شاگردانه Tip given to shopboy.

شاگردی Apprenticeship. Discipleship.– ش. کردن To serve as an apprentice.

شال Long piece of cloth wound by men as a belt round the waist. Sash. Scarf. Shawl. – شال کشمیر Cashmere (shawl). – شال عماری Pall. – شال گردن Muffler.

شالسنجان Azedarach.

شالنگی o Ropemaker.

شالوده Foundation – شالودهٔ چیزیرا ریختن To lay the foundation of s. t.

شالی Paddy. *By e.* Rice.

شالی Camlet; camleteen.

شام Evening. Supper. – شام جهل Night of ignorance.– ش. خوردن To sup. – شام غریبان گرفتن To pass the night in darkness. *OS.* To do as the forlorn survivors of Emam-Hosein did on the night after the disastrous event of Karbela.

دمشق = شام

شامات [Pl. of شام] Syria.

شاهپانی *Fr.* (-*pan'y*) Champagne.

شامپو *Fr.* Shampoo; hair-wash.

شآمت *A.* Inauspiciousness.

شامخ *A.* Lofty; eminent [بلند].

شامگاه Eventide. *Mil.* Tattoo.

شامِل *A.* Containing; including. Applicable. – ش. بودن To include. – قانون شامل این مورد نیست The law does not apply to this case.

شامه Membrane.

شآمّه *A.* Sense of smell. Scent.– عصب ش. Olfactory nerve.

شامی Damascene; Syrian. Food consisting of pulverized peas minced with meat.

شان [Pl. of ش *or* اش] Their or them.

شان (Honey)comb. *Cf.* شانه

شأن *A.* [شوون] Dignity. Case. Behalf. – شأن او نیست که It is below his dignity to. . .

شانزده Sixteen.

شانزدهم Sixteenth.

شانزدهمی (The) sixteenth.

شانزدهمین The sixteenth.

شانس *Fr.* = 1) بخت 2) Chance.

شانکر *Fr.* Chancre.

شانه Comb. Hackle. Loader (of a magazine-rifle). – ش. زدن *or* ش. کردن To comb. To card, as cotton. To heckle, as flax – شانهٔ عسل Honeycomb.– شانه نکرده [*Compound*] Uncombed; untidy; unkempt.

شانه Shoulder. – ش. بالا انداختن To shrug the shoulders. –

ش. خالی کردن [With از] To shirk; avoid; also, crave at.
شانه بسر Hoopoe.
شانه پهن Broad-shouldered.
شانه‌دان Comb-case.
شانه ساز or شانه تراش Comb-maker.
شاه Shah: King [*esp. at chess*].
شاه‌اندازی Ostentation; vaunting. — ش. کردن To vaunt; brag; boast.
شاهانه 1) *a.* Kingly; royal. 2) *ad.* In a kingly manner.
شاهباز Royal falcon.
شاه بلوط *P. A.* Chestnut.
شاه بلوطی *P. A.* Chestnut (colour).
شاه بوی = عنبر
شاه بیت *P. A.* Best verse of a poem.
شاهپر Quill; pen-feather; pinion.
شاه پرست Royalist.
شاه پرستی Royalism
شاه پسند [For گل ش.] Verbena.
شاهپور Prince
شاه تره Fumitory.
شاه توت Black mulberry.
شاه تیر Main beam; summer (tree).
شاه چین [*Of fruits*] Choice. *OS.* Picked by, or for, the king.
شاهد *A.* [شهود or شواهد] Witness [گواه]. Example مثال Beautiful woman or handsome youth *. — ش. آوردن To cite (as) an example. — ش. گرفتن To call to witness.
شاهدانه Hemp-seed. Main bead in a rosary. — شاهدانه عدسی Nummulite.
شاهدخت Princess.
شاهراه Main road; arterial r.
شاهرخ The great rook. *Mas. pr. name.*
شاهرگ Jugular vein.
شاهزاده Prince.
شاهزاده خانم Princess.
شاهسپرم Sweet basil.
شاه سیم Main line (or wire). Trunk line.
شاه فنر Main spring. Main leaf (in a leaf s.).
شاهق ० *A.* = بلند - شامخ
شاهکار Masterpiece. Feat.
شاه لوله Main pipe(line).
شاه مات *P. A.* (Check)mate.
شاه‌ماهی Red mullet. Herring.
شاهنامه "Book of Kings": epic poetry and legendary history of Iran by *Ferdowsi*.
شاهنده ० = پرهیزکار
شاهنشاه Shahinshah: king of kings; emperor.
شاهنشاهی Imperial: دولت ش.
شاه نشین Dais; alcove; bay.
شاهوار * Kingly; royal: درّ ش.
شاهی Kingship; sovereignty. Reign. *Bot.* Cress — شاهی آبی Watercress.

شاهی اشرفی *P.A. Bot.* Cosmos.

شاهین Royal falcon. [*O' a scale*] 1) Beam; 2) index; tongue; pointer.

شایان Worthy; deserving. — شایان تمجید Praiseworthy.

شائبه *A.* [شوائب] Taint ; stain. Alloy.

شاید [*Usu. with the stress on the 1st. syl.*] Perhaps.

شایستگی Merit. Suitability. Competence.

شایستن [شای o] To befit; become ; suit. To merit ; be worthy of. — چنانکه باید و شاید As one ought; duly.

شایسته 1) Worthy; deserving: شایستهٔ انعام است He deserves a bonus. 2) Suitable. 3) Competent. 4) Decent.

شایع *A.* Prevalent; rife ; spread abroad ; going a.

شایعه *A.* [شایعات] Rumour ; gossip. [Orig. fem. of شایع]

شایق *or* **شائق** *A.* = **مشتاق**

شایگان * Worthy; befitting. Abundant. Immense.

شَب Night. Eve: شبِ عید ‖ شب فردا ‖ **دیشب** = گذشته To-morrow night.—شبِ شنبه Friday n. — شب بشما خوش *or* شب بخیر Good n. ! — شب و روز Day and n. Double tides — همه شب 1) Every n. [also هر شب]. 2) * All n. long. — روز را شب کردن To end (*or* pass) the day. — شب را بسر بردن To pass (*or* stay during) the n. — شب را صبح نکرد *or* شب را بسر نبرد He did not live out the night. — شب زنده داشتن * To stay up all n. ; spend the n. awake.

شَباب *A.* = **جوانی**

شُباط *Jewish and Syriac month* (Jan.-Feb.).

شب تاب = **شب افروز**

شَبان Shepherd.

شبانگاه *n.* Night(fall) ; evening. —*ad.* At night. Overnight

شبانه *a.* Nightly ; nocturnal. —*ad.* By night. Overnight.— آموزشگاه ش. N. school; evening class.

شبانروز *or* **شبانه‌روز** Day and night In one day.

شبانه روزی Boarding-house. — آموزشگاه ش. Boarding-school.

شَبانی *n.* Being a shepherd pastoral occupation. —*a.* Pastoral ; bucolic.— ش. کردن To be a s. ; tend flocks.

شباویز [For مرغ ش.] Screech-owl.

شباهت *A.* Resemblance imilarity. — شباهت خارجی تام Protective mimicry.—باهم ش. دارند They resemble each other.

شباهنگ o Morning-star. Dogstar. Nightingale.

شب بو [For گل ش.] Wallflower;

شبکار Night-shift (worker).
شبکاری Night-shift; -work.
شبکلاه Night-cap.
شبکور *n*. Bat. *–a*. Nyctalopic.
شبکوری Nyctalopia.
شَبَکه *A*. Network. Lattice; grating. Grid. Section. (Electrical) substation. [Of a telescope] Reticle. – شبکهٔ خار دار Wire entanglement.
شبکیه *A*. Retina. – ورم ش. Retinitis.
شبگرد Night-prowler. Thief. Somnambulist. Watchman.
شبگز 1) = کیك Flea. 2) = ساس Bedbug.
شب‌گشا *Bot*. Vespertine.
شبگیر • 1) Nocturnal: دعای ش. 2) Singing or travelling by night.
شب مانده Left over from the preceding night; stale.
شب نشینی 1) Evening party. 2) = شب زنده داری
شَبنم Dew. – شبنم نخود Ciceric acid. – ش زدن To dew.
شبه Black coral. Jet. B. beads.
شَبَه *A*. (-*bah*) [اشباه] Likeness. Analogue; similar thing.
شبه (*shebh*) *A*. [اَشباه] 1) Likeness. *Cf*. شباهت & شبیه ‖ 2) *Rendering the E. suf*. -oid. – شبه‌استوانه Cylindroid. – شبه بلور Crystalloid. – شبه جزیره Peninsula. – شبه‌دایره Cycloid. – شبه ذوزنقه Trapezoid. – شبه ظل

gillyflower; common stock. – شب بوی هراتی Garden rocket; dame's violet.
شب پره *or* **شبپره** Bat.
شب پره‌ای Sphenoid: استخوان ش.
شِبِت Common dill.
شب تاب Shining at night. – کرم ش. Glowworm.
شب چراغ [For گوهر شب چراغ] Kind of gem or pearl said to radiate by night. *L*. Carbuncle.
شب چَره Sweetmeat or dried fruits keeping a person busy during the night or enabling him to stay up.
شَبح *A*. [اشباح] Figure seen from a distance. Phantom.
شبخوان ○ 1) Night singer. 2) = بلبل
شبخیز (One) who rises at midnight. Nocturnal (animal).
شبدَر Clover. – شبدر سگ Cow-grass.
شبدیز *Shabdi:z*: name of the horse of Khosrow Parviz. *OS*. Night-coloured; dark.
شبرو *a*. Going out by night. *–n*. = دزد
شب زنده دار Vigilant during the night.
شب‌زنده‌داری (All-night) vigil.
شبستان 1) = حرم 2) = خوابگاه 3) Part of a mosque designed for sleeping or nocturnal prayers.
شبق ○ *A*. = شهوت Lust.

Penumbra. — شبه فلز Metalloid. — شبه کره Spheroid. — شبه منشور Prismoid.

شُبهه *A*. Doubt. Misgiving. — القای ش. کردن To instil (*or* instill) doubts into one's mind. To misrepresent a case. — ش. را قوی گرفتن To admit for the sake of argument. — دفع ش. کردن To remove all doubts.

شبهه ناك *A*. *P*. Doubtful. Suspicious.

شَبیخون Surprise attack by night. — ش. زدن To surprise by night [*with* بر].

شبیه *A*. = مانند *a*. Similar; alike. —*n*. Portrait. (Religious) representation. — ش. در آوردن To represent a drama; dramatize. — شبیه کسیرا درآوردن To play the part of s. o. — شبیهِ Like; similar to.

شبیه ساز *A*. *P*. Dramatist.

شب پره = شپره

شِپِش Louse. — شپش زهار Pediculus (*or* Phthirius) pubis; crab-louse. — ش. گرفتن To be infested with lice; verminate. — ش. در کلاه داشتن To have a thorn in one's side (*or* flesh). — ش. در کلاهٔ کسی انداختن To give one cause for suspicion.

شپشك 1) = شپشه 2) (Kind of) pediculus.

شپشو Lousy.

شپشه Weevil; plant-louse; acarina. Animal-louse.

شپلاق o *T*. = سیلی Slap.

شَت o *Old title meaning* حضرت *q. v.*

شِتا *A*. = زمستان

شِتاب Hurry. *Ph*. Acceleration. — شتاب منفی Negative or minus acceleration. — بشتاب Quickly; hurriedly. — ش. کردن = شتابیدن

شتابان *ad*. Hastily; quickly. —*a*. Hurrying.

شتابانیدن To hasten. To expedite.

شتاب زدگی Precipitance.

شتاب زده Precipitate; hasty.

شتابکار Rash. Quick in action.

شتابکاری Rashness.

شتاب نما Hodograph.

شتابی *Ph*. Accelerative.

شتابیدن [شتاب] To make haste; hurry (up).

شتابیدن = شتافتن

شُتر Camel. — شتر ماده She-camel. — ش. دیدی؟ نه Say you saw me not (*i. e.* relieve yourself of all commitments). — شتررا کشتند All is quiet (again); nothing doing.

ساربان = شتربان

شتردار Carrier using camels.

شترگاوپلنگ Camelopard. *Met*. Medley; hotchpot(ch).

شترگربه + Contrarieties; incongruous statements. *Cf*.

شترگاو پلنگ

شترگلو Subterranean siphon.

شتر مرغ Ostrich.

شتری Of the colour of camel's hair. — بارشتری Camel's load. — کینهٔ ش. Deep rancour; vindictiveness.

شَتل Handsel given by winners to those present at a game. *F*. Windfall.

شتم *A*. = **بدگویی**

شتوی (*shatvi:*) *A*. = زمستانی Raised in winter. Belonging to w.

شَته Aphis. — شتهٔ مو Phylloxera; vineborer.

شجاع *A*. Brave.

شجاعانه *A*. *P*. Bravely.

شجاعت *A*. Bravery.

شَجر *A* [اشجار] = درخت Tree(s).

شجره *A*. (A single) tree. *S. a.* شجره نامه

شجره نامه *A*. *P*. Genealogical tree; pedigree; family t.

شَحم *A*. [شُحوم] = **چربی**

شَحنه *A*. (*Obsolete*) Chief of the police. Also, policeman or watchman.

شَخ • [*Cont. of* شاخ]

شَخ *or* شق + Stiff. Inelastic. Erect. — شق کردن To erect. To stiffen.

شخار Pearl-ash. — شخار خاکستر Potash.

شخانه ○ Meteor(ite). *See* شهاب

شَخص *A*. [اشخاص] Person. Individual. — شخص وزیر The minister (himself). — خیلی اشخاص Many persons; many people.

شخصاً *A*. Personally.

شخصی *A*. Personal. Private. Individual. Civilian.

شخصیات *A*. Personalities. *Cf. the s.* شخصیت ‖ واردشخصیات شدن To become personal.

شخصیت *A*. Personality. Character.

شُخم Plough(ing). — ش زدن *or* ش. کردن To plough.

شَخیص *A*. Of note : شخص ش.

شِداد ○ *A*. = سخت Severe. [Orig. pl. of شدید] — شدادوغلاظ Hard and fast.

شَدّاد *A*. *Shada:d:* name of a tyrant king who founded the earthly paradise [ارم].

شدائد *A*. = سختی ها Hardships. [Pl. of شدیده ○]

شدّت *A*. Intensity; vehemence. — شدت ناخوشی Paroxysm. — ش. کردن To be intensified or aggravated. — خیلی ش. کند + At the worst; at its highest degree; at most. — بشدت Severely

شدگان • [Pl. of شده] Those who have departed; the dead.

شُدن [شو] To become. To get: خسته ش. ‖ To grow: تاریک ش. ‖ To happen : بعد چه ش. ‖ To go • نمیشود رفت [رفتن] It is impossible to go ; one [illegible] not go. — او را چه میشود [illegible]

the matter with him? What ails him? بردهشد ـ It was carried. ـ خورده میشود It is (*or* will be) eaten.

شدنی Feasible; practicable.

شُده 1) [P. P. of شدن] 2) *S. u.* شدگان

شَدّه *A.* 1) String (of pearls). 2) = تشدید The sign (ّ).

شَدید *A.* = سخت Intense; violent. Severe. [Fem. شدیده]

شدیداً *A.* Severely. Strongly.

شدیداللحن *A.* Strong; rude or abrupt; rough-spoken.

شدیده *S. u.* شدید & شدائد

شرّ . *A.* [شُرور o] Evil. Mischief. ـ ازشرش خلاص شدیم We got rid of him (*or* it). ـ شرش ما را گرفت We had to take the consequences.

شراء *A.* = خرید Purchase.

شَراب *A.* Wine. ـ ش. انداختن *or* ش. ریختن To make (*or* vint) wine.

شرابخور *A. P.* Wine-bibber.

شرابخوری *A. P.* Drinking wine. [For گیلاس ش.] Wine-glass.

شرّابه *A.* Tassel. Sword-knot.

شرابی Vinaceous. ـ گل ش. Carolina anemone.

شرار [A pl. of شراره]

شرارت *A.* Wickedness. Insurgence. Mischief. ـ ش. کردن To do mischief. To act wickedly.

شرارت‌آمیز *A. P.* Evil; wicked.

شراره *A.* [شرار & شرر]. Single spark.

شُراع *A.* = بادبان Sail.

شراع‌الحنك o *A.* Velum; soft palate.

شراعی *A. P.* Furnished with a sail or sails. ـ کشتی ش. Sailboat.

شَرافت *A.* Honour. Nobleness. ـ شرافت نفس Self-respect.

شرافتمند *A. P.* Honourable; of a noble character.

شرافتمندانه *A. P. ad.* Honourably; nobly. —*a.* Honourable.

شراکت *A.* Partnership. Joint action. ـ ش. کردن To enter into partnership. ـ بشراکت = شراکةً

شراکةً *A.* In joint partnership. Jointly.

شراکتی *A.* Joint : سرمایهٔ ش.

شَرایط *A.* Conditions; terms. Qualifications. [Pl. of شریطه but usu. regarded as the pl. of شرط]. ـ واجدشرایط Qualified. ـ واجد شرایط شدن To qualify for s. t. ـ فاقد شرایط Unqualified; disqualified.

شرایع [Pl. of شریعت].

شرایین [Pl. of شریان].

شُرب *A.* Act of drinking. ـ آشامیدنی = قابل ش.

شَرَبت *A.* Cooling drink; sherbet. Syrup; elixir. Medicinal draught. ـ شربت اپیکا Ipecacuahna wine. — شربت آبلیمو Lemon squash. — شربت بنفشه Syrup of violets.— شربت‌خشخاش Diacodion. — شربت سرفه or شربت سینه Cough mixture. — شربت نارنج Orangeade.

شربت خانه *A. P.* 1) Servery. 2) = **آبدارخانه**

شربت‌دار ० *A.P.* = آبدار Butler.

شربین = سیاه کاج Larch.

شرپنل *E.* Shrapnel.

شَرح *A.* [شُروح ०]. Description. Exposition; explanation. Recital. Account; statement; report. Details.— ش. دادن To give an account of. To describe; explain. — شرحی بمن نوشت که He wrote to me to say that.— بشرح زیر As follows.

شرحه ० *A.* Slice.

شِرذِمه ० *A.* Small party or detachment.

شرر [A pl. of شراره]

شرربار • *A. P.* Scintillant. *OS.* Raining sparks.

شرزه • Fierce : شیرِ شرزه

شِرشِر + Murmuring (noise).— ش. کردن To murmur or purl.

شُرشُر + (Noise of) flowing or falling water. Freshet. — ش. کردن To flow or fall, as water.

شُرشُره + Freshet; rapids.

شَرط *A.* [شُروط *S. a.* شرایط]. Condition; term; stipulation. Wager; bet. *Logic.* Protasis.— ش. بستن To b.; lay a wager or b. — ش. کردن To make (it) a condition; stipulate; lay down.— ش. باشد برگردد I b. you (*or* guarantee that) he will return. — آنکار شرط ادب نبود That was not polite. — شرط انصاف نیست Justice forbids. — بشرط امتحان خریدن To buy on trial (*or* approval).— بشرط آنکه *or* بشرطی که On the c. that; provided (that). — بشرط حیات If my life does not fail me.— بیع ش. Revocable sale.

شرط‌بندی *A. P.* Betting; wagering; staking money on s. t.— ش. دراسب‌دوانی Sweepstake(s).— ش. بستن To bet; lay a wager; stake money on s. t.

شُرطه • *A.* Favourable (wind).

شَرطی *A.* Conditional. [Fem. شرطیه]. — وجه ش. Subjunctive mood. — قضیه شرطیه Conditional clause.

شَرع *A.* Religious law; canon.

شرعاً *A.* According to religious law; canonically.

شرعی Lawful; legal. Religious; canonical. [Fem. شرعیه with the pl. شرعیات religious laws; canon law].

شرعیات *S. u.* **شرعی**

شَرَف *A.* Honour; dignity. Moral distinction; superiority. — شرف کسیرا بردن To

شرکت‌نامه *A. P.* Memorandum.

شَرم Shame. Pudency.— شرم‌حضور Shame caused by looking one in the face; coyness. *Cf.* رودربایستی — ش. داشتن *or* ش. کردن To be ashamed. — ازسخن‌گفتن ش. داشت He was a. (*or* too modest) to speak.

شرم‌آور Indecent; shameful.

شرمرو Bashful. Modest.

شرم‌زده = شرمسار

شرمسار Put to shame; ashamed. —ش.شدن To be put to s. —ش. کردن To put to s.

شرمساری Shame; disgrace. — ش. کشیدن *or* ش. بردن To be put to shame; be disgraced.

شرمگاه Privy parts.— استخوان ش. (Os) pubis.

شرمگین *or* **شرمناك** = شرمسار

شرمندگی Shame. Blush.

شرمنده Ashamed. Put to shame.— ش.شدن To be ashamed. To be put to the blush.— ش. کردن To make a. To put to the b. by one's favours or compliments.

شرنگ = • 1) زهر 2) حنظل

شَرور Wicked. Restive. [Fusion of شَریر and شُرور]

شُرور [Pl. of شرّ]

شروط [Pl. of شرط].

شُروع *A.* = آغاز Beginning; start; commencement.—ش.شدن To begin *vi.* — ش. کردن To b. or commence: ش. کرد

cast aspersions on a person's character. — بشرف عرضِ ... رساندن To bring to the attention of (a specified dignitary).

شرف (*shoraf*) *A.* [Usu. pronounced *-rof*] Cornices; merlons o. [Pl. of شرفه]. *F.* Verge; point: در شرفِ رفتن بود He was about to go.

شُرَفاء [Pl. of شریف]

شُرفه *S. u.* شرف (*shoraf*).

شرفیاب شدن *A. P.* [In p. c.] To come (to meet). *OS.* To seek the honour of (the person whom one wishes to meet).

شرفیابی *A. P.* Honour of being received in audience.

شَرق *A.* = خاور The East or Orient. — شمال ش. North-east.

شرقا *A.* On the east.

شرقی *A.* Eastern. Oriental. — ش. غربی Lying east and west.

شِرك *A.* Polytheism.

شُرَكاء [Pl. of شریك]

شِرکت *A.* Company; firm. Part(nership). — شرکت تعاونی Cooperative society. — ش. داشتن To have a share. To participate; take part. To attend, as a member. — ش. کردن To enter into partnership. — در مسابقه‌ای ش. کردن To sit for a selcction (*or* competitive) examination.

شريك‌الارث *A*. Coheir ; joint heir.

شريك‌الملك *A*. Joint owner (of a landed property).

شَست Thumb. Fishing-net ; fishing-hook. Thumbstall.— شست پا Big toe ; great t.— شستم خبردار شد A little bird told me so.

شست etc. = شصت etc.

شُستشو Washing. Bathing. *Med* Irrigation.—ش. دادن To wash; bathe. — ش. کردن To bathe ; wash oneself. To irrigate.

شستن [(شو(ی] To wash. To w. away. *F*. To wipe a. To pay (one) out well ×.

شستنی That is to be washed.— رختهای ش. Laundry; wash.

شسته [P. P. of شستن] Washed.— ش و رُفته Neat ; tidy ; shipshape; clear; explicit.

شَستی Push-button.

شِش Six.

شُش Lung(s).

شِش انداز ○ = نرّاد

شش بر Hexagon(al).

شش پر Mace with six prongs ; knobstick.

ششدانگ *n*. The entire six parts into which a real estate is divided. *Mus*. Highest pitch. *–ad*. + Entirely ; clean.

ششدانگی Entire; whole.

شِشدَر *n*. Position of a piece

بسخن گفتن He began to speak.— ش. به تیر اندازی کردن To open fire. — آتش ش. ! Open f. !

شرو ور × (*sherover*) Balderdash ; rigmarole ; nonsense. [Per. contractions of شِعر and وِرد *q. v.*]

شَره ○ (*-rah*) *A*.= حرص & آز

شَره ○ (*-reh*) *A*.= آزمند

شَریان *A*. [شرائين] Artery. — ورم شریان Arteritis.

شریان بند *A. P*. Tourniquet.

شریانی *A*. Arterial : خون ش.

شَریر *A*. Wicked (person). *Cf. the pl*. اشرار

شریطه *S. u*. شرايط

شَریعت *A*. [شرایع] Religious law.

شریعت‌گزار *A. P*. Lawgiver.

شریعت مدار *a. p*. Versed in religious law. Holy; spiritual.

شَریف *A*. 1) *a*. Noble. Honourable. 2) *n*. Nobleman. Aristocrat. — احوال ش. چطور است [*In p. c.*] How are you ?

شَریك *A*. [شُرکا] Partner. Associate. Accomplice. — لاوی و شرکا Levi & Co. — شریك شدن To join hands. To enter into partnership. — شریك‌ارث Joint heir; coheir.— شریك جرم *Law*. Abettor. — شریك دزد Receiver of stolen goods. — شریك دزد و رفیق قافله Jack-on-both-sides; one who runs with the hare and hunts with the hounds.

that is locked up behind six consecutive points [at backgammons]. *–a.* Blocked.

شش سطحی *P. A.* = شش‌وجهی

ششصد Six-hundred.

ششصدم Six-hundredth.

ششصدمی (The) six-hundredth.

ششصدمین The six-hundredth.

شش ضلعی *A. P.* = شش بر

ششگوش & ششگوشه *n.* Hexagon. *–a.* Six-angled.

ششلول Six-shooter. Revolver.

ششم Sixth. – ش. آنکه Sixthly.

ششماهه Biannual; semi-annual. Six-month-old.

ششمی (The) sixth.

ششمین The sixth.

شش و بش *P. T.* Six and five (*at backgammons*).

شش وجهی *P. A.* Hexahedral. – جسم ش. Hexahedron.

ششی Pulmonary. Light red.

شصت [Orig. شست] Sixty.

شصت تیر Machine-gun.

شصتم Sixtieth.

شصتمی (The) sixtieth.

شصتمین The sixtieth.

شط *A.* [شطوط o]. Large river.

شط العرب *A. Shattel-Arab*: the rivers Tigris and Euphrates united.

شطرنج *A-P.* Chess.

شطرنجی *A. P.* Checkered.

شطوط [Pl. of شط]

شعار *A.* Standard; colour; device. Slogan; motto. Party cry. Battle-cry. Profession + ش. دادن To demonstrate by means of a slogan.

شعاع *A.* [اشعه] Ray; beam [پرتو]. Radius. – شعاع بردار or شعاع حامل Radius vector. – شعاع عمل Cruising-range.

شعاع افکن *A. P.* = پرتو افکن

شعاع گستر *A. P.* Radiant.

شعاعی *A.* Radial.

شعائر *A.* Rites; observances; *mores*. [Pl. of شعیره barley-corn]

شعب (*she'b*) *A.* [شعاب] = گردنه Mountain-pass; defile.

شعب (*sho-ab*) [Pl. of شعبه]

شعبات [Pl. of شعب pl. of شعبه]

شعبان (*A.*) *Eighth lunar month. Mas. pr. name.*

شعبده [*f. Semitic origin*]. Jugglery; legerdemain. – فانوس ش. Magic lantern.

شعبده باز Juggler.

شعبده بازی Jugglery; legerdemain.

شعبه *A.* [شعب] Branch (office.) Section. Tributary stream.

شعر o *A.* = مو Hair.

شعر *A.* [اشعار] Poem. Poetry; verse. – ش. گفتن or ش. ساختن To compose a poem or poems. – بشعر در آوردن To versify.

شعراء [Pl. of شاعر]

شعرباف *A. P.* = نساج & بافنده

شعری *A.* Capillary. [Fem.

[عروق ش. Ex. شعریه
شعری (-ri:) A. P. Poetical.
شعری (she'ra) A. Dog-star. — شعرای شامی Procyon. — شعرای یمانی Sirius.
شعشعه A. Radiance.
شعف A. = خوشی Joy; delight.
شعله A. Flame. Ph. Calorie.— ش. زدن To flame or blaze.
شعله‌ور - شعله‌زن A. P. Flaming.
شعور A. Sense. Intelligence.— شعور حیوانی Instinct.
شعیب A. Jetro, the father-in-law of Moses.
شعیره S. u. شعائر
شغار(ه) Badger.
شغال Jackal.
شغال به Wild quince.
شغب ० A. = غوغا
شغل A. [اشغال] Employment. Vocation. Cf. کار & پیشه
شفاء A. Cure. Remedy.— ش. دادن To cure.— ش. یافتن To be cured.
شفابخش A. P. Curative; health-giving.
شفا خانه A. P. Dispensary (for students).
شفاعت A. Intercession.— اذا و نزد من ش. کردند They interceded for him with me.
شفاعت‌آمیز A. P. Intercessory; mediatory.
شفاف A. Transparent. Limpid.
شفاهاً A. Verbally; orally.
شفاهی A. P. Verbal; oral.

شفت Bot. Drupe.
شفتالو *Variety of peach.*
شفترنگ or + شبرنگ Variety of peach of a dark red colour.
شفته Concrete. — شفتهٔ طبیعی Conglomerate; clastic rock.
شفتین A. [D. of شفه ०]. OS. The two lips.— شفتین صغری Labia minora.— شفتین کبری L. majora.
شفعه A. [For حق ش.] Right of preemption.
شفق A. [اشفاق ०] Aurora. Evening twilight.— شفق جنوبی A. australis. — شفق شمالی A. borealis.
شفقت A. Compassion; pity. — ش. کردن بر To have p. on.
شفوی or شفهی A. = لبی Labial.
شفیع A. Intercessor. Preemptor. *Mas. pr. name.*
شفیق A. Compassionate. Kind.
شق S. u. شخ
شق A. Splitting. Crack.
شق A. [شقوق] Alternative. Possibility. Subdivision. Phase.
شقاق A. Schism Discord. Split.
شقاقل Wild carrot.— شقاقل بری Cow-parsnip. — شقاقل مصری W. parsnip; p. of the desert.
شقاقلوس [f. G. *sphakelos*] Gangrene. — ش. شدن To sphacelate.
شق القمر A. Herculean task. OS. Splitting of the moon.

شقاوَت *A*. Adversity. Villainy.
شَقایِق *A*. Corn-poppy.— شقایق شقایق فرنگی or پُرپَر Peony.— شقایقِ نعمان Anemone.
شقوق [Pl. of شِق]
شَقه *A*. Side (of mutton, etc.).— ش.کردن To cleave lengthwise in two parts.
شقی (*shaghiy*) *A*. [اشقیاء] Wretched (person). Vicious (person).
شقی (*shaghi:*) *A*. Temporal. — صداع ش. Hemicrany.
شَقیقه *A*. 1) Temple. 2) o *Med*. Hemicrany; migrim.
شَك *A*. Doubt. Suspicion. — شك فلسفی Scepsis. — بدون شك Doubtless. — شك بچیزی آوردن To hesitate in believing s. t. — شك کردن To doubt. — بشك افتادن To fall into suspicion.— بشك انداختن To cause to d.; lead into d. — شکی در آن نیست There is no d. about that.— در رفتن اوشك دارم I d. whether he will go.
شِکار Hunting. Prey; game. *F*. Victim. Booty. — ش. شدن + To be upset or disconcerted. *OS*. To be hunted.— ش.کردن To hunt.
شکاربان Game-keeper.
شکارچی *P.T*. Hunter; huntsman.
شکار دُزد Poacher.
شکارگاه Hunting-ground; park.
شکارگردان Huntsman; member of the hunt.
شکاری 1) Used for hunting.— سگ ش. Hunting-dog. 2) Predatory. — ساعت ش. H.-watch; hunter; capped watch. — مرغ ش. Bird of prey. — هواپیمای ش. Chaser.
شکاف 1) *n*. Split; fissure. Gap.— شکاف درجه Hindsight.— ش. خوردن To split (partially). — ش. دادن To s. 2) *Imp. of* شکافتن
شِکافتن [شکاف] *vt*. To split; cleave. To unsew; unstitch; undo. *F*. To analyze. —*vi*. To s. To be unstitched.
شکافته [P. P. of شکافتن] Split; cloven. Forked. Undone.
شکاف دار Having a crack or crevice.— گره ش. Clove-hitch.
شکاك *A*. Doubter. Sceptic(al).
شکاکیون *A*. [Pl. of شکاکی treated as a n.] Sceptics.— مسلك ش. Scepticism.
شکال o *A*. Shackle.
شِکایت *A*. [شِکایات] Complaint. Grievance. *Cf*. گله ‖ ش.کردن To complain. — شکایت مرا پیش رئیس برد He reported me to the director.
شکایت آمیز *A. P*. Plaintive.
شکر (*shekar*) (Granulated) sugar. — شکر خام Moist s.; moscovado.— شکرسرب Acetate of lead; s. of lead.— شکرسرخ Brown s.
شکر (*shokr*) *A*. Thanks(giving).—

خدارا شکر Thank God.— ش. کردن To thank (G.); give thanks to (G.). — ش. گزاردن To give thanks.

شکراب Estrangement; coolness.

شکران *A.* Thankfulness; gratitude.

شکرانه *A.P.* (Sign of) gratitude or thankfulness.— بشکرانهٔ ... As a sign of g. for; in acknowledgment of.

شکر پاره *Variety of apricot.*

شکرپنیر *Kind of confectionery.*

شکرخا • Sweet-spoken.

شکرخنده • (Person with a) sweet smile.

شکردان Sugar-bowl.

شکردن • ο [شکر] 1) = شکستن 2) To drive away.

شکر دهان • Sweet-spoken.

شکر ریز = شیرینی ساز - قناد

شکرك Manna.

شکرگزار *A. P.* Giving thanks (to God); thankful.

شکرگزاری *A. P.* Thanksgiving (to God). — ش. کردن To give thanks

شکرلب • Sweet-lipped. Sweet-[spoken.

شکری Sugared; sugary. Cream-coloured.

شکست Defeat. Failure. Breakage; fracture. *Ph.* Refraction.— ش. خوردن To be defeated. To fail. — ش. دادن To defeat; beat. *F.* To surpass.

شکستگی Breakage; fracture. Breakdown. [*In words*] Contraction.

شکستن [شکن] *vt.* To break. *F.* To infringe. —*vi.* To b. (up). — درهم ش. To b. up. To rout.

شکست ناپذیر Invincible.

شکستنی Breakable.

شکسته [P. P. of شکستن] Broken. B. down. [*Of tunes*] Sad; doleful.— خطش. B. or crooked line. *Kind of cursive writing.*— ش. شدن To be weighed, broken, or bowed down.

شکسته بال *OS.* Broken-winged. *F.* 1) = بیچاره 2) = بدبخت

شکسته بسته Fragmentary.

شکسته بند Bone-setter.

شکسته بندی Bone-setting.

شکسته خاطر *P. A.* & شکسته دل = دل شکسته

شکسته نفسی *P. A.* Modesty; humility. — ش. کردن To be modest; show h.

شکفتگی State of being opened, as a flower. *F.* Cheerfulness.

شکفتن [شکف] To open: غنچه شکفت ‖ *F.* To cheer up. To smile.

شکفته [P. P. of شکفتن] Opened. *F.* Cheerful.

شَکل *A.* [اَشکال] Shape; form. Figure. Syllogism. — بچه ش How? In what manner?

شکلاً *A.* In shape.

شکلات *Fr.* Chocolate.

شکلاتی *Fr.P.* Chocolate brown.

شکل پذیر *A. P.* Plastic.

شکلک *A. P.* Grimace; wry face. — ش. درآوردن To make mouths (at s. o.); pull a wry f.
شکلی *A.* Dealing with forms and procedure.— قانون ش. Law of p.; adjective law.
شِکم Belly. Stomach. Womb. *F.* Interior.— شکم گرسته Hungry belly; hunger.— ش. دادن To sag. To bulge.— شکمش کار نمیکند His bowels do not move. — شکم خود را صابون زدن × To expect a feast; also, whet one's appetite. — شکمی از عزا در آوردن × To play a good knife and fork; do justice to a meal.— سه ش. زائید She gave birth to three children.
شکم بند Corset; stays.
شکم بنده • ○ Glutton.
شکمبه Paunch; rumen.
شکم پا Gastropod.
شکم پائی Gastropodous.
شکم پرست Glutton(ous).
شکم پرستی Gluttony.
شکم چه Cerebral ventricle.
شکم خوار(ه) • = **شکم پرست**
شکم درد 1) = دلدرد 2) Gripes.
شکم رَوِش Diarrhœa [اسهال].
شکم گنده + Big-bellied; gluttonous.
شکمو + Gluttonous.
شکمه Ventricle of the heart.
شکمی Abdominal. Ventral. Uterine. — پیوند ش. (Shield-) budding.— گودال ش. Abdomen.
شکن 1) *Imp. of* شکستن 2) • Curl; ringlet. Fold; crease.
شکنج • Bend; twist. Wrinkle.
شکنجه Torture; rack.— ش. کردن To (put to the) torture; excruciate.
شکنندگی Fragility. Brittleness.
شکننده Brittle. Breakable.
شَکور ○ *A.* Very grateful.
شکوفه Blossom. — ش. کردن To blossom.
شُکوه Splendour; magnificence.
شکوه (*shakveh*) *A.* Complaint.— ش. کردن To complain.
شکیب Patience.
شکیبا *or* **شکیبنده** Patient.
شکیبایی Patience; fortitude.
شکیبیدن ○ = صبر کردن
شکیل [Coined from the A. word شکل] = **خوش ترکیب**
شگرف • Wonderful; great. Excellent.
شِگفت Wonder; astonishment.— درشگفت شدن To be astonished or surprised.
شگفتا • [*With the stress on the 2nd. syl.*] Wonder! How surprising it is!
شگفت انگیز & **شگفت آمیز** Surprising; wonderful.
شگفتن etc. = **شکفتن** etc.
شگفتی Wonder(ful thing).
شُگون Good omen.

شَل Lame. – یك پایش شل است He is lame in (*or* of) one leg. شل کردن To lame; cripple.

شُل Slack. Loose; lax. (Too) soft. *F*. Languid. Too lenient. – شل دادن + To relax one's efforts. – شل شدن To loosen. To be slackened. – شل کردن To 1. To slack(en). To make lax.

شلاق *A*. Whip; lash. – ش. خوردن To be whipped or flogged. – ش. زدن To whip; flog; lash.

شلاق‌خور + *A. P*. Knockabout; durable; tough.

شلاق کش + *A. P*. At full drive; post-haste.

شلاقی *A. P. a*. Flagelliform. –*ad*. (*Mus*.) Fortissimo. – آچار شلاقی Stillson wrench.

شلال Long stitch. – ش. کردن To sew with long stitches.

شل باف *or* **شل بافت** Loosely-woven; of a loose texture.

شَلتوك Paddy; rough rice.

شلجمی *A*. [t. P. شلغمی] Parabolical.

شلخته Slovenly; sluttish; slipshod; untidy.

شَلغم Turnip.

شلغمی 1) o Turnip-like. 2) = شلجمی

شِلم *Fr*. [At bridge] Slam.

شلم شوربا ×Higgledy-piggledy; confused. [Cont. of شلغم‌شوربا "Pottage of turnip"].

شلنگ (*shlang*) *R*. Flexible hose

شلنگ (*shelang*) Stride. – ش. زدن *or* ش. برداشتن To stride.

شلنگ انداز + With rapid (or giant) strides; by leaps and bounds.

شَلوار (Pair of) trousers.

شلوق *T*. and شلوق پلوق + *n*. Confusion; disorder. Bustle; noise. Riot. –*a*. Crowded. Noisy. Disorderly; confused. – ش. کردن *vi*. To make noise. To riot; disturb public peace. –*vt*. To put in disorder.

شله قلمکار & **شُله** *Kinds of soft dish with rice and vegetables*. – آش شله قلمکار + Hodge-podge; medley.

شِله Red twill; Turkey red.

شله‌ای Scarlet (colour).

شَلی Lameness.

شُلی Looseness. Slackness. Softness.

شَلیته Old-fashioned short petticoat worn under the dress.

شِلیك Volley; salvo. Report of a gun. – شلیك پی در پی Fusillade. – شلیك خطر Distress-gun. – ش. کردن To volley. To fire a gun.

شلیل Nectarine.

شَمّ *A*. Flair. *OS*. Smelling. – شم چیزی را داشتن To have a flair for s. t.

شُما You [*pl. of, and polite substitute for* تو]. [*Prece-*

ded by an "ezafeh"] Your. Ex. کتاب ش. Your book. – ش. ها [*Real pl.*] You.

شماتت *A*. Rejoicing at another's misfortune. – ش. کردن To rejoice at another's m. Also, to taunt.

شمار 1) *Imp. of* شمردن ‖ 2) *n*. Reckoning. Number. – بشمار آمدن *or* بشمار رفتن To be reckoned (among). To allow of counting. – بشمار آوردن To reckon (among).

شمارش (Act of) counting.

شمارنده (One) who counts.

شماره 1) Number: شمارهٔ ۵ No. 5 ‖ 2) Issue : درشمارهٔ ... روزنامهٔ اطلاعات ‖ صفت ش. Numeral adjective.

شماره‌گیر (Telephone) dial.

شماس ° *A*. Deacon.

شماطه *A*. Din; uproar. – ساعتِ شماطه‌ای Alarm-clock.

شماع ° *A*. = **شمع ساز**

شمال *A*. North. – شمال شرق N.-east. – شمال غرب N.-west.

شِمال ° *A*. Left (hand). *See* چپ

شمالا *A*. On the north.

شمال‌شرقی *a. p.* North-eastern.

شمال‌غربی *A. P.* North-western.

شمالی *A. P.* Northern. Arctic.

شمائل *A*. (Good) qualities. Portrait; icon. Character sketch. [Pl. of شمیله °.]

شمایل پرست *A. P.* Iconolater.

شمایل پرستی *A. P.* Iconolatry.

شمائم [Pl. of شمیمه]

شمخال *T*. Harquebus.

شمد (Bed)sheet.

شمر [Imp. of شمردن] = **شمار**

شمر *A. Shemr:* general who slew Emam-Hosein. *Met.* Cruel person. – دست ش. را از پشت بستن To out-herod Herod.

شمردگی Distinctness.

شمردن [شمار *or* شمر] To count; compute. *F.* To reckon.

شمرده *a*. Distinct. *OS*. Counted. *–ad*. Distinctly: ش. بخوان ‖ پول نشمرده Immense wealth.

شمس *A*. [شموس] Sun. *Cf.* خورشید & آفتاب ‖ *Mas. pr. name.* – شمس کاذب Parhelion.

شمس الدین *A. Shamsedi:n* : *mas. pr. name. OS*. Sun of the Faith.

شمسه *A*. Frog : ornamental fastening or loop.

شمسی Solar. – منظومهٔ ش. S. system

شمسی قمری *a. p.* or شمسی و قمری Lunisolar.

شمسیه *A. Fem. pr. name:* [Orig. fem. of شمسی]

شِمش Bullion; ingot. Bar.

شِمشاد Box-tree. – چوب ش. Boxwood.

شِمشه Rule used in pointing.

شمشیر Sword; sabre. – ش. زدن To strike with a sword. To use a s. – ش. کشیدن To draw one's s. – ش. پیش ! *Mil*. Present sabre! – ش. کش!

Mil. Draw s.! ش. جا ! —
Mil. Return s.! زخم ش. —
Sword-cut.
شمشیر باز Fencer.
شمشیر بازی Fencing. — ش.کردن To fence.
شمشیر زن Swordsman.
شمشیر ساز Sword-cutler.
شمشیر سازی Sword-cutlery.
شمشیر ماهی Swordfish.
شمشیری Sword-shaped. *Anat.* & *Bot.* Ensiform; gladiate.
شَمع *A.* [شُموع ○] Candle. Shore; prop. Candle-power; *L.* Watt. *M.* Spark plug.— ش.زدن To shore up; support by a shore; prop.
شمعدان *A. P.* Candlestick.
شمعدانی *A. P.* Geranium; cranesbill. — شمعدانی عطر Pelargonium.
شمع ساز *A. P.* Candle-maker.
شمعك *A. P.* Shore; prop. *OS.* Small candle; taper.
شمعون *A-Heb.* Simon. Simeon.
شموس [Pl. of شمس]
شموع [Pl. of شمع]
شُمول *A.* Comprisal; inclusion. Applicability. Scope.
شَمه *A.* Small part; slight notion; short account.
شمیم *A.* [Collective for شمیمه]
شمیمه ○ *A.* [شمائم] (Sweet) odour.
شِن Sand. Gravel. — بشن نشستن To strand; run aground.
شِنا Swimming [also شناو]. — ش.کردن To swim.
شناخت = شناسایی
شناختن [شناس] To recognize. To know (a person).
شناخته [P. P. of شناختن] Known. Recognized.
شناس [Imp. of شناختن]
شناسا *a.* Acquainted. —*n.* Acquaintance.
شناسانیدن To make known; introduce.
شناسایی Recognition. Acquaintance.
شناسنامه Identity card (*or* certificate.)
شناسنده (One) who knows or recognizes.
شناعت & شنعت *A.* Obscenity.
شناگاه Swimming-pool(s); baths.
شناگر Swimmer. Float; buoy.
شناگری Swimming, natation.
شناوَر Floating. Buoyant. — رهنمای ش. Buoy. — ش. ساختن To (cause to) float.— ش. شدن To f. To buoy.
شناوری Buoyancy. Swimming.
شنبلیله = • شنبلید
شنبلیله Fenugreek.
شنبه (*shambeh*) Saturday.
شن پاش Sand-box.
شن پاشی Sandblasting.
شنجار *or* شنگار Alkanet.
شنجرف *A-P.* = شنگرف
شندر غاز × [*With the stress on the 2nd syl.*] Insignificant amount; nothing to

shout about. [Used adverbially or objectively]. Ex. ش. حقوق میگیرد He receives a very small salary.

شن ریزی Ballasting. — ش. کردن To ballast.

شن‌زار *a.* Sandy; beachy. —*n.* S. place; beach; strand.

شنفتن etc. = **شنیدن** etc.

شن‌کش Rake. [a rake.

شن‌کشی Raking; working with

شَنگ + = 1) شوخ 2) قشنگ

شِنگ Salsify.

شنگار *S. u.* شنجار

شنگرف Cinnabar, vermilion.

شنگول + Gay; sportful. Tipsy.

شنگیدن + To be ticklish.

شنل Cape; mantle; cloak.

شنو [Imp. of شنیدن]

شنوا That can hear: گوش ش.

شنوانیدن To cause to hear or to be heard.

شنوایی Hearing. — ازمن ش. دارد He listens to me.

شُنود *or* **شنید** Hearing [only in گفت و شنید conversation].

شنیدن = **شُنودن**

شنونده [شنوندگان] Hearer; listener; auditor.

شِنی Sandy; sand-like.

شنید *S. u.* شنود

شنیدن [شنو] To hear. To listen to. To smell. — ش. کی بود مانند دیدن Seeing is believing.

شنیدنی Interesting; worth hearing. Strange.

شنیده [P. P. of شنیدن]

شَنیع *A.* = زشت Obscene; abominable. *Cf. the fem.* شنیعه

شنیعه *A.* [شنایع] Obscene act. [Orig. fem. of شنیع]

شو *or* **شوی** [Imp. of شستن]

شو *or* **شوی** [Short for شوهر]

شو (*show*) [Imp. of شدن]

شو (,,) = شب [in some dialects].

شوارب [Pl. of شارب].

شوارع [Pl. of شارع]

شوّال *Tenth A. lunar month.*

شوالیه *Fr.* Knight.

شواهد *S. u.* شاهد

شوخ *a.* Gay; jovial. Witty. Saucy. —*n.* (*C. P.*) Joker.

شوخ چشم * Impudent; saucy.

شوخ چشمی Impudence; insolence. [witty nature.

شوخ طبع *P. A.* Of a gay or

شوخی Joke; jest; fun. Witticism. Trick. Sauciness; impudence * — حس درك ش. Sense of humour. — ش. کردن To joke; jest. — شوخیِ بدتر از جدّی Half jest and whole earnest. — ش. بکنار Joking apart.

شود (*sheved*) + = **شبت**

شِوِدی Asparagus. Also, love-in-a-mist.

شور *a.* Salt(y); brackish: ب ش. salt water. —*n.* Sensation; emotion; passion. Fervour; enthusiasm. Anxiety. — ش. درسر

داشتن To be fervent or passionate. To be full of emotions.— شور وشعف نشان دادن To go into rhapsodies. — دلم ش. میزند I am anxious or uneasy (about it). — شورش را درآوردن + To go too far; be outrageous in one's conduct.
شور A. (*showr*) Deliberation; consultation. Reading : شورِ دوم لایحه ‖ ش. کردن To deliberate; consult.
شورا S. u. **شوری** (-*ra*)
شوراب Salt or brackish water.
شورانیدن To cause to revolt.
شور انگیز Sensational.
شوربا Pottage.
شور بخت * etc. = بدبخت etc.
شور چشم etc. = **بد چشم** etc.
شورش Revolution; revolt. — ش. کردن To r.
شورش طلب P. A. a. Revolutionary. —n. Revolutionist.
شورشی Revolutionary.
شور مزه Salt(ish).
شورو (*shevro*) Fr. Kidskin.
شوروی A. Consultative; deliberative. [For دولت ش.] The Soviet Government.
شوره Nitre ; saltpetre. [*Of the head*] Scurf; dandruff; furfur. [*Of the skin*] Pityriasis. — ش. بستن To form scurfs. To effloresce.— علف ش. Saltwort; glasswort.— شورهٔ قلمی Potassium nitrate. — زمین ش. Brackish ground.
شوره پز Saltpetre-maker.
شوره پزی Saltpetre-making.
شوره زار n. Salt-marsh. —a. Brackish; saltish.
شوری Saltiness; salinity.
شوری A. (-*ra*) Council: شورای امنیت The Security C.— مجلسِ شورای ملی The National Consultative Assembly.
شوریدگی Frenzy; (love) madness.
شوریدن [شور] To revolt; rise.
شوریده 1) P. P. *of* شوریدن 2) Frenzied; (love-)mad.
شوریده بخت * = **بد بخت**
شوریده‌حال P. A. = **پریشان‌حال**
شوریده مغز ○ = **دیوانه**
شوسه [f. Fr. *chaussée*] Road; high road ; roadway.
شوشکه R. Circassian sabre.
شوشه Prism. Ingot.
شوفر Fr. Driver. *Chauffeur*.
شوق A. [اشواق ○] Strong desire. Great interest ; enthusiasm. [Often شوق و ذوق] Delight; pleasure.
شوك ○ A. = خار Thorn. — باد آورد = شوك مبارك
شوکا (Roe)buck.
شوکت A. Glory. Power. *Fem. pr. name*.
شوکت‌الیهود ○ A. Acanthus.
شوکران Hemlock. — شوکران آبی Water hemlock ; cowbane ; also, water dropwort.

شولا Quilt-like mantle or cloak.

شوم (*sho'm*) *A*. Bad omen. [Pronounced *shu:m* and treated as an adjective]. Inauspicious.

شومی *A*. *P*. Inauspiciousness.

شومیز = بوشه Folder; flat file. [f. Fr. *chemise*].

شونیز = سیاه دانه Nigella seeds.

شوون (*sho-u:n*) [Pl. of شأن erroneously spelled شئون].

شوونات [Pl. of شوون pl. of شأن erroneously written شئونات]

شوهر Husband. ش. دادن To give in marriage. *F*. To give away. ش. کردن To get married; marry. شوهر مادر Stepmother. شوهردوزن Bigamist.

شوهردار Married : زن ش. married woman; feme covert.

شوی *S*. *u*. شو

شویگاه and شورگاه + = غسال خانه

شه • [*Cont*. *of* شاه]

شهاب *A*. Shooting-star; meteor. کانون ش. *Astr*. Radiant point.

شهادَت *A*. [شهادات] Witness [گواهی]. Martyrdom. ش. دادن To witness; bear w. (to); give evidence (of). To profess (one's faith). بشهادت رسیدن To suffer martyrdom. بشهادت طلبیدن To call to w. کلمهٔ ش. Credo or formula (of the Islamic faith).

شهادتگاه *A*. *P*. Scene or site of martyrdom.

شهادت نامه *A*. *P*. 1) = گواهی نامه 2) ○ Passional; passionary.

شهامت *A*. Moral heroism; the courage of one's opinion; bravery. Greatness. *OS*. Vigour.

شهباز [Cont. of شاهباز]

شهپر Aileron.

شَهد *A*. Honey(comb). Nectar; honey-dew.

شهدا [Pl. of شهید]

شهداب *A*.*P*. Hydromel. Mead.

شهدداز *A*. *P*. Nectariferous.

شهدالله (*shahada*lah) *A*. Indeed; truly. *OS*. May God witness.

شهدخت [Cont. of شاهدخت]

شهدی *A*. [Fem. شهدیه] Nectareous. سعفهٔ شهدیه Honeycomb scall.

شَهر City; town. شهر ِهرت × Place where there is no law or justice; babel; scene of confusion.

شَهر *A*. [شُهور] = ماه Month.

شهرآرا(ی) ○ Officer in charge of town decoration.

شهربانی Police. [For ادارهٔ کل ش.] P. Headquarters.

شهربانو *Fem*. *pr*. *name*.

شُهرَت *A*. Fame; renown. *Cf*. نام ‖ Rumour. Surname. ش. دادن To spread a rumour (about). To give publicity to. ش. یافتن To win fame. ش. دارد که

There is a r. that.
شهرتاش *P. T.* = **همشهری**
شهردار Mayor.
شهرداری Municipality. — انجمن ش. Town council; municipal c.
شهرستان Small province; township. — دادگاه ش. Court of First Instance.
شهرِفرنگ Peep-show. *F.* Medley; *omnium gatherum.*
شهر نشین Burgess.
شهروا ○ Base money with a nominal value.
شُهره [f. A. شهرت] Celebrated (person or thing).
شَهری *a.* Urban. Civic. Municipal. —*n.* Townsman; citizen. *Variety of melon.*
شهریار * Sovereign; monarch.
شهریاری Sovereignty. (His) Majesty.
شهریوَر *Sixth month having 31 days.*
شَهریه *A.* = ماهانه Monthly tuition.
شهزاده [Cont. of شاهزاده]
شهنشاه etc. = **شاهنشاه** etc.
شهوات [Pl. of شهوت]
شهوانی *A.* Sensual; carnal.
شهوانیت *A.* Sensuality.
شَهوَت *A.* [شهوات] Lust; passion. *By e.* Inordinate desire or appetite.
شهوت آمیز *A. P.* Lustful; carnal.
شهوت انگیز *A. P.* Exciting lust. Aphrodisiac.
شهوت پرست *A. P.* Lascivious.
شهوت پرستی *A. P.* Voluptuousness; lasciviousness.
شهوت ران *A. P.* Sensual; voluptuous; libidinous.
شهوت‌رانی *A. P.* Sensuality.— ش.کردن To gratify one's passions. To be sensual.
شُهود *A.* [Pl. of شاهد]
شهود *A.* Witnessing. Presence. Intuition.
شهور [Pl. of شهر]
شهی * [Cont. of شاهی]
شَهید *A.* [شهداء] Martyr.—ش.شدن To suffer martyrdom. — ش.کردن To martyr(ize).
شَهیر *A.* = **مشهور**
شهیق *A.* Inspiration; inhalation.
شیی (*shay'*) *A.* [اشیاء] Thing; object. Affair. *Cf.* چیز
شیاد *A.* Impostor.
شیادی *A. P.* Imposture.
شیار Furrow; groove. Ploughland. — ش.کردن To plough or furrow.
شیار دار Grooved. Ploughed.
شیاطین [Pl. of شیطان].
شیاف *A.* Suppository.
شیب Gradient; grade. Slope
شیب پیما Grad(i)ometer.
شیب سنج 1) = شیب پیما 2) Gradienter.
شیپسی *R.* Small pincers; bodkin.
شیپور Trumpet; bugle. — شیپو.ر

اوستاش Eustachian tube ; syrinx. — شیپور بیداری *Mil.* Reveille. — شیپور جمع *Mil.* Assembly. — شیپور خاموشی *Mil.* Last post. — شیپور خبر *Mil.* First p. — شیپور رحمی Fallopian tube. — ش. زدن To blow a trumpet. — گل شیپوری Trumpet-flower; bignonia.

شیپورچی *P. T.* = **شیپور زن**

شیپور زن Trumpeter; bugler.

شیت + (?) Crushed. Mashed. Squashy. Spread out.

شیخ *A.* [شیوخ] Sheik(h): venerable old man ; elder ; learned man ; chieftain [used as a title. Ex. ش. سعدی] . — شیخ زنگوله بپا Sheikh wearing small bells on his ankles to scare ants and save them from being trodden on. *F.* Hypocritical or prudish person. — شیخی را دیدن × To slip away (*or* off); make oneself scarce.

شیخ السفرا (*sheikhosofara*') *A.* Doyen; dean.

شیخ نشین *A. P.* Sheikhdom.

شیخوخت *A.* Eldership. Old age.

شید *A.* = **فریب** & **مکر**

شیدا • Frenzied (with love).

شیدالله (*shayadalah*) *A.* May God strengthen. . .

شیدایی • Madness. Frenzy (of love).

شیر Lion. Tap; cock; valve. — شیر برفی *Met.* Cardboard cavalier ; man of straw. — شیر ماده Lioness. — ش. یا خط Head or tail. Toss — ش. کردن To brave.

شیر Milk. — ش. دادن To feed or nurse (a child) — ازشیر گرفتن To wean. — شیر خشك Powdered milk ; m. powder. — شیر مادیان *Lac equinum*. — شیر ماك Colostrum; beestings. — شیر مرغ *Met.* Goat's wool; blue diamond. — ش. بشیر زائیدن *or* شیره بشیره زائیدن To be delivered of another child before weaning the one who is being nursed.

شیرازه Headband (of a book). *F.* Order. Tie.

شیربان Lion-keeper.

شیر بچه (Lion's) whelp.

شیر بَر Lactiferous.

شیر برنج Rice-milk ; rice-pudding.

شیر بندی Dairy.

شیر بها Gift to a bride's mother (for having nursed her): now, part of the marriage-portion settled upon the wife, which is paid beforehand in cash.

شیرجه Dive; header. — ش. رفتن To plunge head foremost ; dive.

شیرچای Tea with milk.

شیرچنگ • Having claws like those of a lion.

شیرخانه o Dairy. Lion-cage.
شیرِ خشت Purgative manna. — طبع شیرخشتی Hot liver.
شیرخوار(ه) *or* **شیرخور** At the breast ; b.-fed. — بچهٔ ش. Child at the b.; suckling.
شیرخوارگاه Nursery.
شیرخوری Milk-jug. [For فنجانِ شیرخوری] Milk cup.
شیردان Abomasum.
شیر در قرابه Yellowish or pale green. *See* شیر & قرابه
شیردل Lion-hearted.
شیردوش Breast pump.
شیرده 1) Milch : گاو شیرده 2) Nursing : مادران ش.
شیرزا Galactogogue. — گیاه ش. Milkwort.
شیر زَن Heroine; virago.
شیر زور * Strong, as a lion.
شیرسنج Lacto(densi)meter.
شیر شکری Yellowish-white ; white dotted with yellow.
شیرقلاب *P. A.* (Large) buckle.
شیرقهوه *P.A.* Coffee with milk.
شیرکچی *P. T.* Distiller.
شیرکخانه Distillery. Tavern o.
شیرگرم Milkwarm. — تخم مرغ ش. Soft-boiled egg.
شیرگیاه Milkweed. Milkwort.
شیرمال (Pastry) made with milk.
شیرمرد Lion-heart; hero.
شیرمست *a.* [*Of a child at the breast*] Sufficiently fed with milk. —*n.* Young fatling.
شیروانی Gable roof.
شیره Juice. Sap. Syrup. Molasses. Emulsion; milk: شیرهٔ بادام ‖ Preparation from opium residue.— شیرهٔ کسیرا کشیدن To sap or exhaust a person('s vigour); also, bleed him white. — ش. به ش. زائیدن *Same as* شیر بشیر زائیدن *q. v.*
شیره‌ای 1) *n.* = شیره‌کش 2) *a.* Like sirup ; sirupy; sticky.— دستش شیره ایست He is light-fingered.
شیره‌کش Person addicted to smoking opium residue.
شیری Milky ; milk - white. Lacteal ; lactic. — بچهٔ ش. Child at the breast; b.-fed child. — حباب ش. Opal globe. — دندان ش. Milk-tooth.
شیرین *a.* Sweet. Melodious. —*n. Fem. pr. name.*— آب ش. Fresh water. — ش. شدن To be in demand; have a good market.— ش. کردن To sweeten. To soften, as water. To improve, as land.
شیرین بیان *P. A. a.* Of attractive speech. —*n.* Sweet-root; liquorice [سوس].
شیرین زبان Sweet-spoken: بچهٔ ش.
شیرین سخن Sweet-spoken.
شیرینك Lamb's-lettuce. *Kind of* infantine eczema. [*In plants*] Exanthema.

شیرین‌کاری Feat; achievement; stroke of policy. Masterpiece. *Mus*. Grace; figure.

شیرینی Sweetness. Sweets; confectionery. Tip or bribe.– نان ش. Pastry.

شیرینی فروش & شیرینی پز Confectioner.

شیرینی پزی Confectionery.

شیرینی‌خوران Betrothal party.

شیرینی خوری Sweet-dish.

شیرینی فروشی Confectionery. [For دکان ش.] Confectioner's shop.

شیشك Year-old-lamb; yearling.

شیشکی بستن × To give the raspberry [also ش. در کردن].

شیشه Glass. Glass bottle. [*In a motor car*] Windscreen.– شیشهٔ داروئی Vial. – شیشه ساعت Watch-glass.– شیشه سنگ Plate-glass. – شیشهٔ عدسی Lens.– شیشهٔ عکاسی Plate; negative. – ش. انداختن [with به] To glaze.– خونِ مستأجرین را شیشه میکرد He racked his tenants.

شیشه‌آلات *P. A.* Glassware.

شیشه‌ای (Made) of glass; glass [*used as an a.*]. Vitreous. Vitriform.

شیشه باز *or* **شیشه‌گردان** ○ Juggler.

شیشه بُر Glazier. Glass-cutter.

شیشه بری Glazing; glaziery.

شیشه جان Over-precautious about one's life. *OS*. Whose life is (as brittle as) glass.

شیشه سازی Glass manufacture. [For کارخانهٔ ش.] Glassworks.

شیشه‌گر Glass-blower.

شیشه‌گرخانه Glassworks.

شیشه‌گری Glass-blowing.

شیطان *A. n.* [شیاطین] Satan; Devil. —*a*. Devilish. Naughty. – ازخرسیاه ش. پائین آمدن To come off one's high horse. – ش. را درس میدهد He knows one point more than the Devil.

شیطانك *A. P.* Click; pawl; detent. [*In a guitar or similar instrument*] Nut.

شیطانی *A. a.* Satanic; devilish. —*n*. Devilishness. Naughtiness. – ش. شدن To have a nocturnal pollution.– ش. کردن To be naughty. To do mischief.

شیطنت *A.* Naughtiness. Mischief. *OS*. Devilish acts. – ش. کردن To be naughty or mischievous. To do mischief.

شیعه *A.* Shiite. Sectarian.

شیعی *A.* Shiite. Pertaining to the Shiites.

شیفتگی Infatuation; state of being enamoured.

شیفتن [شیو ○] To enamour. To infatuate.

شیفته [P. P. of شیفتن] Enamoured. Infatuated.– ش. شدن To be enamoured or in-

fatuated.
شیفن *Fr.* Chiffon.
شیك *Fr.* Smart; stylish; fashionable. Pretty+.
شیك پوش *Fr. P.* Smartly dressed.
شیکی *Fr. P.* Smartness. Prettiness+.
شیل [A. pl. شیلات] Fishery.
شیلات *S. u.* شیل
شیلان ○ Royal feast.
شیلنگ + *See* شلنگ (*shlang*).
شیله‌پیله ×Nigger in the woodpile (*or* fence).
شیلینگ *E.* Shilling.
شیمی *Fr.* Chemistry.
شیمیایی *Fr. P.* Chemical.
شیمی‌دان *Fr. P.* Chemist.
شیوا Charming. Eloquent.
شیوخ [Pl. of شیخ]
شُیوع *A.* Outbreak; prevalence. ش. دادن To publish; noise or spread abroad. — ش. یافتن To be s. or published.
شیوَن Wailing; wail; loud mourning. — ش. کردن To w.; mourn loudly.
شئون *S. u.* شأن & شوون
شیوه (Peculiar) style or method. Trick +. — بکسی ش. زدن To play a trick on s. o.
شیهه Neighing. — ش. کشیدن To neigh.

صابر *A*. etc. = شکیبا etc.
صابون *A-G*. Soap.— ص. زدن To soap.— صابون دستشوئی Toilet-soap; wash-ball. — صابون مایع Soft soap.
صابون پز *A. P*. Soap-boiler; soap - maker.
صابون‌پزی *A. P*. Soap-boiling. [For کارخانهٔ ص.] Soapworks.
صابونی *A. P*. Soapy.— ص. کردن To (wash with) soap.— آب ص. Soap-suds.
صابئی *or* صابی *A*. Sabian.
صاحِب *A*. Owner; master. [With or without the *ezafah*] Possessor (of); one endowed (with): صاحب ثروت Wealthy.— صاحب کتابِ . . Author of...— صاحب کرامت (Person) endowed with a miraculous power. Generous. [Pl. اصحاب those e. (with)].
صاحب اختیار *a. p*. (Man) of authority.
صاحب استخوان *A. P*. Of noble birth.
صاحب‌الزمان (*A*.) *Title of the Twelfth Imam*.
صاحب امتیاز *a. p*. Concessioner or concessionaire; grantee. [Of a newspaper] Proprietor.
صاحب جمال *a. p*. = خوبرو
صاحبخانه *A. P*. Proprietor or owner of a house; landlord. Host or hostess [میزبان].
صاحب خیر *a. p*. Benefactor.
صاحبدل *A.P*. Pious or devout person. Wise p.
صاحب کار *A. P*. Client. Employer.
صاحب‌کرم *a. p*. 1) *a*. Beneficent; generous. 2) *n*. Benefactor. Giver; bestower.
صاحب‌کمال *a. p*. Accomplished.
صاحب مال *a. p*. Owner (of a specified property).
صاحب محضر *a. p*. = سر دفتر
صاحب‌مرده *A. P*. Whose owner is dead. Dirt-cheap+.
صاحب ملك *a. p*. Landlord.
صاحب منصب *a. p*. 1) *Mil*. = افسر 2) = پایور 3) Civil official; functionary.
صاحب‌نظر *a. p*. Clear-sighted.
صاحب نفس *a. p*. One whose prayers or curses are effective.
صاحب هنر *A. P*. = هنرمند
صادِر *A*. [Fem. صادره] Issued. Exported. Outgoing: مراسلات صادره ‖ ص. شدن To be issued. To be exported. To emanate. — ص. کردن To issue. To

export.

صادرات A. Exports. [Orig. pl. of صادره fem. of صادر q. v.]

صادرکننده A. P. Exporter.

صادق A. a. Truthful [راستگو] True. —n. Mas. pr. name.

صادق‌القول A. = راستگو

صادقانه A. P. Truthfully. Sincerely.

صارم ○ A. Sharp. Austere. Intrepid.

صاریغ Fr. Opossum.

صاعقه A. [صواعق ○] Thunderbolt. Cf. تندر & آذرخش

صاغرمار T. P. Deaf adder.

صاغری T. Shagreen. Croup or rump of a horse.

صاف A. 1) a. Clear; limpid; pure. Smooth. F. Candid; sincere. 2)+ad. Direct(ly).— ص. کردن To filtrate; clarify; strain; rack. To smooth. F. To clear; settle; square or balance (accounts with s. o.). To pave. Humorous To shave [also صاف و صوف کردن]. ⨯سینه— ص. کردن To c. the throat. — ص. شدن To c. be filtered or clarified. To smooth. — هوا دارد صاف میشود It is clearing up.—صاف و پوست کنده In plain words; frankly. — صاف و ساده Ingenuous; straightforward.

صاف‌کرده A.P. Filtered; clarified. Shaved; smoothfaced.

صاف‌کن A. P. Strainer.

صافن A. [For ورید صافن] Saphena; internal saphenous vein.

صافی A. Clear; pure.

صافی A. P. Strainer. Filtre. Air-cleaner. Clearness; purity. Smoothness. F. Candour.

صالح A. [Fem. صالحه] a. Good; pious. Competent: محاکم صالحه || —n. G. or pious man [pl. صلحاء]. Mas. pr. name.

صامت ○ A. = گنگ Silent; mute.

صانع A. = آفریننده - سازنده

صائب A. = درست Right; correct.

صائم A. = روزه‌دار

صبا A. [For باد صبا] Zephyr. The morning breeze.

صباح A. = صبح & بامداد Morning.—علی‌الصباح In the m.

صباحت A = زیبائی Beauty.

صباغ A. = رنگرز

صباوت A. Childhood. Nonage.

صبایا [Pl. of صبیه]

صبح A. = بامداد Morning.—صبح زود Early (in the) morning.— امروزصبح This m.—فردا صبح To-morrow m. — صبح روز بعد The next m.—صبح شما بخیر Good m.

صبحانه A. P. Breakfast.

صبحدم A. P. n. (Early) morning. —ad. Early in the m.

صبحگاه A. P. = صبحدم

صبحگاهان • A. P. (In the) morning. Early in the m.

صبحگاهی • A. P. Of the morning; matin.

صَبر A. 1) = شکیب & شکیبایی Patience. 2) = عطسه Sneeze.– کاریرا سرصبر انجام دادن To take one's time in doing s. t.– صبرم تمام شد S. u. تمام ‖ ص. آمد There is a sneeze; so we must make a pause: superstitious belief. [For صبر زرد] Juice of aloes. – ص. کردن To wait. To have patience. [With بر] • To tolerate.

صَبوح • A. Morning draught [also **صبوحی**].– صبوحی زدن • To take a morning draught.

صبور A. (Very) patient.

صبورانه A. P. Patiently.

صبوری A. P. = شکیبایی Patience.– ص. کردن To use patience. Cf. صبر کردن

صَبیّ ○ A. [صِبیان] Lad; youth. Cf. the fem. صبیه

صبیان ○ [Pl. of صبی]

صبیح ○ A. = **خوبرو**

صبیه A. [صبایا] = دختر Daughter or + my daughter.

صَحابت A. Companionship; company.– بصحابت In c. with; together w.

صحابه A. [Pl. of صاحب] Companions.

صحاری [Pl. of صحرا]

صحاف A. Bookbinder.

صحافی A. P. Bookbinding. – ص. کردن vt. To bind. –vi. To be a binder.

صحائف [Pl. of صحیفه]

صُحبت A. Conversation [گفتگو] Company •.– ص. کردن To talk. To associate; keep company.– چون ص. از . . . . میان آمد Talking of . . . . – در صحبت را باز کردن To start a conversation.

صِحت A. (Good) health. Cf. تندرستی ‖ Correctness [درستی].– صحت عمل Honesty; integrity.– صحت مزاج G. health.– ص. داشتن To be true.– ص. یافتن To recover from illness. – ص. باشد ! or صحتِ آب گرم I wish you good health [said to one who has just had a bath].– صحت خواب I hope you have had a sound or good sleep.

صحت بخش A. P. Healthful: promoting good health.

صَحرا A. [صَحاری] Desert. Field.

صحرا نشین A. P. Nomadic.

صحرا نورد A. P. (One) who travels in the desert.

صحرایی A. P. Pertaining to the desert; wild. Open air.– توپخانهٔ ص. Field-artillery.

صحف [Pl. of صحیفه]

صَحن A. Court(-yard). Precinct. Large dish.

صَحنه A. P. Stage. Theatre; sphere of operations.

صحنه آرا A. P. Stage-designer.

صحه A. Signature; endorsement. – ص. گذاشتن To endorse; sign. To sanction.– صحهٔ ملوکانه Royal assent or signature.

صحی *A*. Sanitary ; hygienic; health [*used as an a.*].
صحیح *A*. True. Correct; right; proper [درست]. Authentic. Sound. Integral.— ص.است That is right. O. K. Approved. — عدد صحیح Integer.
صحیحاً *A*. Correctly. Intact.
صحیح‌البنیه *A*. = **تندرست**
صحیح العمل *A*. = **درستکار**
صحیح‌المزاج *A*. = **تندرست**
صحیفه *A*. Leaf or page [pl. صحائف]. Book [pl. صحف].
صحیه. *A*. [*Orig. fem. of* صحی] = **بهداری**
صخره *A*. = خاره Rock.
صد Hundred: صدی پنج *or* پنج در صد Five per cent.
صدا *A*. Sound. Voice. Noise. Vowel-sound. — صدای پا Foot-fall. — با صدای آهسته Slowly; with a low voice.— باصدای بلند With a loud v. ; loudly. — ص. بصدا نمیرسد One can hardly hear himself out.— صداشان در آمد They showed discontent ; they began to grumble or complain — ص. در آوردن To make a noise. To produce a sound. — ص. زدن To call. — ص. کردن *vt*. To c.—*vi*. To make a n. To (produce a) s. To ring : گوشم ص. ‖ زنگ ص. میکند میکرد My ears were burning.— بصدا در آمدن To ring. To complain (publicly).— بصدا در آوردن To s. To r.— یك دست ص. ندارد One hand makes no (clapping) noise; i. e. union is strength.
صدا پیچ شدن *A.P*. To resound.
صدا دار *A. P*. Sonorous. Having a vowel(-sound). Phonetic.
صدارت *A*. Premiership ; rank or office of a صدراعظم *q. v.*
صدارس *A. P*. (Within) hearing distance.
صدا سنج *A. P*. Phonometer.
صدا شناس *A. P*. Phonologist.
صدا شناسی *A. P*. Phonology. Acoustics.
صداع *A*. Headache [سردرد].
صداق *A*. = **مهریه**
صداقت *A*. = راستکویی Truthfulness; truth.
صدا کرکن *A. P*. Sourdine.
صدانویس *A.P*. Phonographist.
صدایی *A.P*. Phonetic. Vocal.— حروف ص. The literal vowels; i. e. ا - و - ی
صد برگ Hundred-leaved ; centifolious.— گل ص. Hundred-leaved rose.
صد پا Centipede.
صد تومانی *P. T*. [For گل ص.] Peony. *OS*. Worth 100 *tomans*. *See* تومان
صدد *A*. Plan; design. Neighbourhood o.— در صدد کردن کاری بودن To be planning (*or* about) to do s. t.— درصدد (چیزی) بر آمدن To intend (to). To seek.

صد درجه‌ای *P. A.* Centigrade.
صَدر *A.* 1) Upper part; first p. 2) = سینه ‖ صدر مجلس Seat of honour.
صدر اعظم (*sadra'zam*) *A.* Grand vizier; chancellor.
صدری *A.* = سینه‌ای Pectoral o. Thoracic o. — تکلم ص. Pectoriloqui. [For برنج ص.] *Variety of rice.*
صدغی *A.* (*Anat*). Temporal.
صَدَف *A.* [اصداف o] Mother of pearl; nacre. Shell. Shellfish; (p.-)oyster.— صدف حلزونی Conch. — صدف گوش Cochlea.
صدف‌شناس *A. P.* Conchologist.
صدف شناسی *A. P.* Conchology.
صدفی *A.* (Made) of shell ; shell *a.* Nacreous.
صِدق *A.* Truth. — ص. کردن To hold true. To satisfy the condition.
صَدَقه *A.* [صدقات] Alms.— امین ص. Almoner.— ص. رفع بلااست Alms are the golden key that opens the gate of heaven. *OS.* Alms avert calamity.
صدقه خور *A. P.* Almsman ; eleemosinary.
صدم - صدمی etc. = سدم etc.
صَدمه *A.* [صدَمات] = آسیب Injury. Collision ; shock. Hardship [سختی]. — ص. دیدن To be injured. To experience hardship.— ص. زدن (به) To injure; damage; hurt.
صُدور *A.* Issuance. Export.— ص. یافتن To be issued.
صده [Orig. سده] Century.
صدی چند or سدی چند Percentage.
صَدیق *A.* [اصدقاء o] True or sincere friend. [Pious.
صِدّیق *A.* (Very) truthful.
صِدّیقه *A.* Truthful or pious (woman). [Fem. of صدّیق].
صَدَیك One per cent.
صَراحت *A.* Clearness; explicitness. — صراحت لهجه Frankness.— باصراحت لهجه Frankly.— ص. داشتن To be clear. To be clearly stipulated.
صراحةً *A.* Clearly; explicitly.
صُراحی *A.* Decanter. Flask. Baluster.
صِراط o *A.* Road; way [راه].— پل ص. Bridge which the righteous only can cross on the road to Paradise.
صَرّاف *A.* Money-changer. — صراف سخن * Critic or weigher of words ; also , eloquent speaker.
صرافت *A.* Notion ; thought ; idea. Design. — از صرافت چیزی افتادن To forget s.t.gradually; lose interest in it. - ازصرافت چیزی انداختن To cause to dispense with, or forget s. t.— بصرافت انداختن To set thinking; put it in the mind of.—

صرافت خود بخود Spontaneity.

صرافخانه *A. P.* Money-changer's hall.

صرّافی *A. P.* Money-changing. Testing coins. Agiotage. — ص. کردن To be a money-changer; do banking. *F.* To criticize; also, test.

صرب *Fr.* Serbia(n).

صَرصَر ○ *A.* [صراصر] Hurricane Cold wind.

صَرع *A.* Epilepsy. *Cf.* حمله

صَرف *A.* Spending. Using; consuming; eating. *Gr.* Conjugation; also, inflexion. — صرف برات Agio.—ص. شدن To be used, spent, eaten, or drunk.— ص. کردن *vt.* To spend: وقت ص. کردن ‖ To use (up); consume. To eat or drink. To conjugate. To decline or inflect. —*vi.* To pay : be profitable.— صرف نظر کردن از To dispense with. To waive or relinquish. To abandon or disregard.— صرف نظر از Apart from; irrespective of.

صِرف *A.* Mere ; pure. [*Used also as a n.*] Ex. بصرف گفته شما باور میکنم I believe your bare word.

صِرفاً *A.* Merely; purely.

صرف و نحو (*sarfonahv*) *a. p.* Grammar [now usu. دستورزبان]. *OS.* Inflexions and syntax.

صرف و نحوی *A. P.* Grammatical.

صَرفه *A.* Profit; advantage. Economy. — بصرفه نزدیك است It is economical. — ص. داشتن To be profitable or e.

صرفه جو *A. P.* Thrifty ; saving; economical.

صرفه جویی *A. P.* Economy ; thrift; saving. — ص. کردن To economize. To save.

صَرفی *A.* 1) *a.* Grammatical. 2) *n.* Grammarian [pl. صرفیون].

صُرّه ○ *A.* [صُرَر] Purse of silver or gold (money).

صَریح *A.* Explicit; clear.

صریحا *A.* Explicitly; clearly.

صریح اللهجه *A.* = **رك گو**

صریر ○ *A.* Cry. Grating sound.

صَعب *A.* = **دشوار**

صعب الادراك ○ *A.* Difficult to understand. [obtain.

صعب الحصول *A.* Difficult to

صعب العبور *A.* Difficult to pass; impracticable.

صعب العلاج *A.* Difficult to cure; refractory.

صعوبت *A.* = **سختی - دشواری**

صُعود *A.* Climbing. Ascension. — ص. کردن To ascend ; rise. [With از] To climb ; mount.

صعوه *A.* = **سهره**

صِغار *A.* [Pl. of صغیر] Minors.

صِغر *A.* Childhood. Minority.

صُغری (-*ra*) *A. a.* Lesser; minor [fem. of اصغر]. —*n.* Minor premiss. *Fem. pr. name.*

صغیر *A.* 1) *a.* Small [کوچك]. Young; minor. — آسیای ص. Asia Minor. 2) *n.* [Pl صغار] M. (child); infant.

صغیره *A.* [صغائر] Venial sin.

صَفّ *A.* [صُفوف] Rank. Row; line. — صف آراستن To array troops. — صف بستن or صف کشیدن To line up; marshal. To queue up. — خارج ازصف Out of the ranks; i. e. irregular or non-combatant. — بحالت صف در آوردن *Mil.* To deploy. — درصف آوردن To array; draw up; marshal. — در صفِ . . . قرار گرفتن To rank with. . .

صَفا *A.* Purity. Clearness; limpidity. Pleasantness. Pleasure; enjoyment. — صلح و صفا Peace(ful life); quiet life. — صفای خاطر Sincerity; good heart. — ص. دادن To make pleasant. To reconcile. — ص. کردن To enjoy oneself; have a g. time.

صفا بخش *A. P.* Pleasant; enlivening.

صفات [Pl. of صفت]

صفار o *A.* Worker in brass.

صف آرایی *A. P.* Arrayal of troops.

صفاف o (*safaf*) *A.* Stacker.

صفافی o *A. P.* Stacking.

صِفاق *A.* [Also بردهٔ ص.] Peritoneum. — ورم ص. Peritonitis.

صف بندی *A. P.* Arrayal (of troops). Alignment.

صِفت *A.* [صفات] Quality. Attribute. *Gr.* Adjective.

صفحات [Pl. of صفحه]

صَفحه *A.* [صفحات] **Page. Sheet. Plate. Surface; expanse; area.** — صفحهٔ شطرنج Chess-board. — صفحهٔ شماره گیر Dial (of a telephone). — صفحه گرامافون Gramophone record. — صفحهٔ گردنده Turntable. — ص. گذاشتن × To spin a (long) yarn.

صفحه بندی *A. P.* Make-up; paging; imposition. — ص. کردن To page up; make up; impose pages in type.

صفحه کلید *A. P.* Switch-board.

صفحه گردان *A. P.* Turntable.

صفدر o *A. P.* Valiant.

صفر (*safar*) *Second A. lunar month. Mas. pr. name.*

صِفر *A.* [اَصفار] Zero; cipher.

صَفراء *A.* Bile. Biliousness. *OS.* Yellow [fem. of اصفر].

صفرا شکن or **صفرا بُر** *A. P.* Antibilious.

صفرائی or **صفراوی** *A.* Biliary. Bilious; choleric.

صَفوَت o *A.* Choicest (part).

صُفوف [Pl. of صف]

صُفه o *A.* Platform. Stone-bench.

صَفی o *A. a.* Pure. Choice. —*n.* [Pl. اصفیاء the chosen].

صفی الله *A. Safio*llah: ep. of

Adam. *OS*. God's chosen one.
صفیر *A*. = سوت Whistle.— ص زدن *or* ص. کشیدن To whistle.
صفیری *A*. (*Gr*.) Sibilant.
صَفیه *A*. *Fem. pr. name*. [Orig. fem. of صفی]
صَلا * *A*. Call; invitation. Proclamation. — ص. در دادن *or* ص. زدن To call. To proclaim.
صلابت *A*. Hardness [سختی]. Firmness. Awe.
صُلابه *A*. Gallows; gibbet.
صَلات *A*. = نماز Prayer. *Cf. the pl*. صلوات
صَلاح *A*. Goodness; moral soundness. Advisability. Interest(s). Well-being. [*Used as an a*.]+Advisable; expedient: گفتن این حرف ص. نیست It is not advisable to say this.— ص. دانستن To deem (it) a.
صلاحدید *A. P*. Discretion. Expediency.
صلاحیت *A*. Competence. Jurisdiction. — صلاحیت پرواز Airworthiness.— درصلاحیت او نیست It lies beyond his competence
صلاحیت دار *A. P*. Competent.
صلایه کردن *A. P*. To pulverize; bray; pound.
صُلب *A*. 1) *n*. Loins [کمر]. 2) *a*. Hard: نبض ص.
صلبی *A*. Consanguineous.
صلبیه *A*. Sclerotic (coat).— آماس ص. Scleritis.

صُلح *A*. 1) = آشتی Peace. 2) Compromise. 3) Conveyance. — صلح موقتی Truce.— با هم ص. دادن To reconcile; make it up between. — ص. کردن To make peace. To convey; transfer.— امین ص. Justice of the Peace.
صلحا [Pl. of صالح].
صلح آمیز *A. P*. Conciliatory.
صلح جو *or* **صلح دوست** *A. P*. Peaceable; pacific.
صلح طلب *a. p*. = **صلح جو**
صلح نامه *A. P*. Peace pact. Deed of conveyance.
صلحیه *A*. *See* دادگاه بخش *under* بخش
صلوات (*sala-*) *A*. (Special formula of) praise and greeting to God, Mohammed, and his descendants. [Orig. pl. of صلات]. — ص. فرستادن To utter this f.
صِله *A*. Bond. Relationship. Prize given to a poet. — صلهٔ رحم (Observation of) relationship.
صَلیب *A*. Cross. — ص. کردن = مصلوب کردن
صلیبی *A*. Cruciform. — جنگ ص. Crusade.
صُمّ *A*. [Pl. of اصم] The deaf [کران].
صماء *A*. [Fem. of اصم] = سخت Hard: صخرهٔ ص.
صماخ *A*. Orifice of the ear.— پردهٔ ص. Ear-drum.

صم بکم (*somonbokm*) *A*. (The) deaf and dumb.

صَمد *A*. *a*. Eternal. —*n*. Lord. *Mas*. *pr*. *name*.

صَمصام *A*. *Mas*. *pr*. *name*. *OS*. Finely-tempered (sword).

صَمغ *A*. Gum.— صمغ صنوبر Pine resin. Galipot. Common frankincense.— صمغ عربی Gum arabic. — صمغ کاج (White) resin.— صمغ نشاسته Dexterin(e).

صمغ *A*. Gummy. Gummiferous [also صمغ آور].

صَمیم *A*. Bottom : ازصمیم قلب

صمیمانه *A*. *P*. *ad*. Heartily; sincerely. —*a*. Heartfelt ; sincere : ادعیهٔ ص. s. wishes.

صمیمی *A*. 1) Intimate: دوست ص I. or close friend. 2) Heartfelt ; sincere.

صمیمیت *A*. Sincerity. Cordiality. Close friendship.

صَناعت *A*. [صناعات] Industry. Art ; craft.

صنایِع *A*. [Pl. of صنیعه o] Arts; industries. — صنایع بدیعی Figures of speech.

صَندَل *A-P*. Sandal wood [often چوب ص.]. — جوهر صندل Santalic acid; santaline.

صندل [For کفش ص.] Sandal.

صَندلی Chair. *Cf*. کرسی

صَندوق *A*. Box; chest. Case. [For دایرهٔ ص.] Cash office. — صندوق آراء Ballot-box. — صندوق آهنی Safe. — صندوق زباله Orderly bin. — صندوق عقب اتوموبیل Rear booth.

صندوق بندی *A*. *P*. Packing.

صندوقچه *A*. *P*. Small chest or box. — صندوقچهٔ اسرار One who is faithful to secrets; also, the chest of such a person. [store-room.

صندوق خانه *A*. *P*. Closet ;

صندوق‌دار *A*. *P*. Cashier.

صندوقه *A*. *P*. Box-wall(ing).

صندوقی *A*. *P*. Box-shaped ; coffer-shaped. Carried or sold in cases. — سدّ ص. Coffer-dam.

صِندید o *A*. [صَنادید] Chief; lord.

صُنع *A*. Make; manufacture. Creative power.

صَنعت *A*. Industry; art. Handicraft; trade. Manufacture. Workmanship. [Pl. صنایع which is orig. the pl. of صنیعه].

صنعت کار or **صنعت‌گر** *A*. *P*. Artisan.

صنعتی *A*. *P*. Industrial. Artistic. — آموزشگاه ص. = هنرستان ‖ شهر صنعتی Manufacturing city. — ص. کردن To industrialize.

صِنف *A*. [صنوف & اصناف] Trade; guild. Class. — اتحادیهٔ **صنفی** Trade union.

صَنم *A*. [اصنام]. = بت Idol.

صِنوَبر *A*. Spruce-fir. Also, pine. *Fem*. *pr*. *name*.

صنوف [A pl. of صنف]

صَنیع o *A*. 1) *n*. Work; deed. 2) *a*. Trained; skilful.

صنیعه o *A.* Work ; deed. *Cf. the pl.* صنایع

صَواب *A.* Right action. Pious act. [*Used as an a.*] Right; correct [درست]. ــ ص. کردن To do a pious act.

صوابدید *A. P.* Approbation. Advice.

صواعق [Pl. of صاعقه]

صوامع [Pl. of صومعه]

صوب *A.* Direction : بصوبِ in the direction of.

صوت *A.* [اصوات]=صدا Sound. Voice. *Gr.* Interjection.

صور *A.* Horn or trumpet blown on (روزصور) the Day of Resurrection.

صور *A.* (*Geog.*) Tyre.

صور (*sovar*) [Pl. of صورت]

صورت *A.* [صور *sovar*] Face. Figure. Effigy. Picture. List ; statement. Bill. Circumstance; case. [Of a fraction] Numerator. *C. P.* Coat-card ; court-card. *Astr.* 1) Phase of the moon. 2) = صورت فلکی ‖ صورت حساب Account s. ; bill ; invoice ; debit note . ــ بصورت ظاهر Outwardly; on the outside.ــ صورت خوشی نخواهد داشت It will not look nice or decent. ــ صورت فلکی Constellation. ــ صورت مجلس Procès-verbal. ــ صورت مجلس سیاسی Protocol. ــ صورت موجودی Inventory. ــ ازچیزی ص. برداشتن To inventor or make a list of s. t.ــ ص.دادن 1)=انجام دادن , 2) To render an account (of).ــ سروصورتدادن To get into shape. ــ ص.گرفتن To be accomplished or realized. To take place.ــ درصورت امکان If possible. ــ در صورت لزوم If necessary.ــ در صورتیکه In case ; in the event that. Whereas. Provided (that). ــ در این ص. In this c. ; in the circumstances. ــ در غیر این ص. Otherwise. ــ در هر صورت In any case; at any rate.

صورت پذیر *A. P.* Achievable.

صورت پرست *A. P.* 1) Adorer of (superficial) beauties. 2) = شمایل پرست

صورت ساز *A. P.* Forger of statements and documents *S. a.* صورتگر

صورت سازی *A. P.* Forging statements; forgery.

صورتگر *A. P.* Portraitist.

صورتگری *A P.* Portraitism.

صورتی *A. P.* Light red. Figured [also صورت دار].

صورةً *A.* Outwardly. In the face.ــ ص. زیبا است Her face is pretty; she is p. in the f.

صوری *A.* External ; formal ; apparent. Sham; feigned.

صوف *A.* Camlet or other woollen stuff.

صوفی *A.* Sufi ; mystic.

صوفیه *A.* The Sufi sect. Sufism. *Geog.* Sofia.

صولت • *A.* Attack. Violence. Authority. Awe.

صوم *A.* = روزه Fast(ing).

صومعه *A.* [صوامع] Monk's cell; monastery.

صَهباء • [Fem. of اصهب reddish] Wine.

صَهیونی *A-Heb.* Zionist(ic).

صَیاد *A.* Hunter. Fisherman.– صیادمروارید Pearl-fisher; pearl-diver.

صیادی *A. P.* Hunting; chase. Fishing. *Cf.* شکار

صیام *A.* = روزه Fasting.

صیانت *A.* = نگهداری Protection; preservation.

صیت *A.* Fame; renown. *Cf.* شهرت & آوازه

صیحه *A.* Shout; cry. – ص. زدن or ص.کشیدن To shout or c.

صید *A.* Prey. Hunting. Fishing. *Cf.* شکار ‖ ص.کردن To hunt or fish.

صیدگاه *A. P.* = **شکارگاه**

صیغه *A.* [صیغ *siagh*] Fashion. Formula (of marriage or other contract). Concubine+. *Gr.* Form; model; paradigm.– ص. جاری کردن To pronounce the formula (*i. e.* complete the formalities) of a specified legal transaction.

صیف *A.* = **تابستان**

صیفی *A.* = تابستانی Estival.– محصول ص. Summer crop.

صیفی کاری *A. P.* Cultivation of summer crops.

صیقل *A.* Polish. – ص. زدن or ص. دادن To polish; furbish. To lustre.

صیقل گر *A. P.* Polisher; furbisher.

صیقلی *A. P.* Polished– ص. کردن To polish ; furbish.

ضابط A. 1) n. Bailiff; executive officer. 2) a. Retentive. [Fem. ضابطه]. — قوهٔ ضابطه R. faculty.

ضارب A. = زننده Striker; person guilty of battery.

ضالّ A. Stray. [Fem. ضاله]

ضامن A. Surety; guarantor. Safety-bolt; sere or sear. [*In a knife*] Lock-back. — ضامن کسی شدن To stand g. for a person. — من ض. میشوم که حاضر شود I guarantee his appearance. — ض. دادن To give security. — ضامنِ دست بکیسه Guarantor required to pay at any moment whether the original debtor declines or is ready to pay.

ضامن‌دار A. P. Sponsored by a surety. Guarded. — چاقویِ ض. Clasp-knife (with a lock-back).

ضایع A. Spoiled. Damaged. Lost; futile. — ض. شدن To be decayed. To be lost, as labour. — ض. کردن To spoil. To damage. To render futile.

ضایعات [Pl. of ضایعه]

ضایعه A. [ضایعات] Wastage. Loss.

ضباط A. = بایگان

ضَبط A. Confiscation; forfeiture. Restraint. Retention. Archives. — ضبط دولت Forfeit to the State. — دستگاه ضبط صوت Recorder. Sound recorder. — ض. و ربط Management; control. — ض. کردن To file; keep on f. To confiscate. To restrain. To record (in a gramophone). To manage; govern ○.

ضجور A. = بیزار - تنگدل

ضجه A. = ناله - فریاد

ضِحك ○ A. = خنده

ضحاك *Zahak: tyrant king in Iranian mythological history.*

ضخامت A. = کلفتی Thickness.

ضَخیم A. Thick [کلفت]. Coarse.

ضخیم‌الجلد A. Pachydermatous. Cf. پوست‌کلفت

ضِدّ A. [اَضداد] n. Contrary; opposite. Antagonist. — a. Opposite or opposed. — سفید ضدّ سیاه است White is the opposite of black. — برضدِّ Against; contrary to. — ضد عفونی کردن To disinfect or antisepticize. — ضد و نقیض a. Contradictory. — n. Contrariety. Antithesis. —

ضدّجرب معالجهٔ بضدّ Allopathy.– ضدّ زنگ Antiscorbutic.– ضدّ صفرا Anti-corrosive. – ضدّ ضربه Antibilious. – ضدّ قی Shockproof.– ضدّ قی Antiemetic.– ضدّ ورم Antiphlogistic.

ضدّگویی *A. P.* 1) Contradictory speaking. 2) = بدگویی

ضدّیت *A.* Opposition. – با کسی ض. کردن To oppose s. o.

ضر۳ *A.* = بدبختی Adversity.

ضرابخانه *A. P.* Mint.

ضرائب [Pl. of ضریب]

ضَرب *A.* Beating. (*Law*) Battery [also ایراد ضرب]. Blow; stroke[ضربت]. Bruise. Coining. Pressure ; force. Multiplication. *Mus.* 1) Tempo; time; rythm; measure; 2) = **تنبك** ‖ ض. کردن To multiply: ۲ را در ٤ ض. کنید M. 2 by 4. – ض. گرفتن = با ضرب *or* بضرب ‖ **تنبك** زدن = By f. ; hard. – بضربِ By f. of ; by dint of.

ضربات [Pl. of ضربت *or* ضربه]

ضرب‌الاجل *A.* Grace (period).

ضرب‌المثل *A.* Proverb.– ض. شدن To become a by-word.

ضرَبان *A.* Beating.

ضرَبت *A.* [ضربات] Stroke; blow. Contusion. – ض. وارد آوردن بر To inflict a b. on.

ضرب‌خور *A. P.* Buffer ; also, bumper.

ضرب‌در *A. P.* [For علامت ض.] Sign of multiplication.

ضَربه *A.* [ضربات] Stroke; blow. Shock. – بیست ض. شلاق خورد He was given 20 lashes. – ضربه فنی Knockdown (blow). [Used also figuratively]. – موتور چهار ضربه Four-stroke engine.

ضربه‌خفه‌کن o *A. P.* Shock-absorber.

ضربی *A. P.* Shaped like a ضرب *or* تنبك *q. v.* ; barrel-shaped. – طاق ض. Barrel-vault; barrel-arch.

ضَرَر *A.* = زیان Loss. Harm.– ض. داشتن To be harmful or noxious.– چه ض. دارد What harm will it do ? [phrase meaning 'very well']. – ض. دیدن To sustain or incur a loss . – ض. زدن به To cause to s. a loss. To be noxious to. – ض. دادن *or* ض. کردن To lose; s. a loss . – بضرر فروختن To sell at a l. – بمن ض. خورد I sustained a l.

ضرطه *A.* = **گوز**

ضَرغام o *A.* 1) = شیر Lion. 2) *Mas. pr. name.*

ضَرورَت *A.* Necessity. Exigency. Emergency. Distress.– ض. داشتن To be necessary. – برحسب ض. As occasion arises; if n.

ضرور(ی) *A.* (Very) necessary; essential. – غیر ضروری Unnecessary; non-essential.

ضروريات A. Necessaries.

ضَريب A. [ضرائب] Coefficient. — ضريب انتفاع Efficiency.

ضَريح A. = قبر & گور

ضرير A. = کور Blind.

ضَريع A. [Also ضريع استخوان] Periosteum. — ضريع غضروف Perichondrium. — آماس ض. Periostitis.

ضريعى A. Periosteal.

ضَعف A. Weakness. Swoon. Fainting. — ضعف بنيه Weak health or constitution; adynamia. — ضعف اعصاب Neurasthenia. — ضعف عضله Myasthenia. — ض. رفتن *or* ض. كردن To swoon or faint; fall into a fit. — نقطهٔ ض. Weak point; weak side; foible.

ضِعف A. [اضعاف] Double.

ضعفاء [Pl. of ضعيف]

ضَعيف A.n. Weak; feeble. Faint. Thin. F. Poor. Defenceless. —n. [Pl. ضُعفاء] W. or poor man. — ض. كردن To weaken. — ض. شدن To grow thin; lose flesh. To be weakened.

ضعيف البنيه A. Of a weak constitution; adynamic.

ضعيف الجثه A. Of a weak body. Small in size.

ضعيف الحال A. = عليل - ضعيف

ضعيف العقل A. Weak-minded.

ضعيف المزاج A. Of a poor health; weak.

ضعيف النفس A. Wanting self-reliance. Cowardly.

ضعيفه A. [Orig. fem. of ضعيف] One of the weak sex; i. e. woman [not used by the educated classes].

ضغطه A. Pressure. Shock. — تلمبهٔ ضغطه‌اى Force-pump.

ضفدع A. Ranula. *OS.* = وزغ

ضَفن A. = كيسهٔ خايه Scrotum.

ضلال & **ضلالت** A. Straying. Deviation. Perdition. Error.

ضِلع A. [اضلاع] 1) Rib [دنده]. 2) *Geom.* Side. — پنج ضلعى Pentagonal.

ضلعى o A. Lateral. Costal.

ضَمّ o A. Annexation.

ضماد A. Poultice. — ضماد خردل Mustard poultice; sinapism. — ضماد گرم Fomentation. — ضماد لب Lipsalve.

ضَمان A. = ضمانت

ضمانت A. Guaranty; security; surety(ship). — ض. كردن To guarantee. To warrant. — ضمانت كسيرا كردن To stand guarantor for s. o. — ضمانت اجرائى داشتن To be protected by sanctions. [guaranty.

ضمانت نامه A. P. Surety-bond;

ضمائر [Pl. of ضمير]

ضمائم [Pl. of ضميمه]

ضِمن A. Meantime; interim. — درضمن In the i.; meanwhile. — در ضمنِ Among. While.

ضمناً A. In the meantime;

meanwhile. Incidentally. By the way. Implicitly.

ضمنی A. P. Implicit ; tacit : Incidental. — اشارۀ ض. ‖ رضایت ض Implication ; connotation. — واقعۀ ض. Circumstantial event.

ضمه A. Name of the vowel-point (’), called in P. پیش

ضَمیر A. Heart; mind. Conscience. Gr. Pronoun [pl. ضمائر].

ضمیری A. Pronominal.

ضمیم o A. = پیوسته Annexed. Cf. the fem. ضمیمه

ضَمیمه A. [ضمائم] Enclosure ; annex. Appendix; addendum [pl. addenda] ; supplement. — ورم ضمیمۀ اعور Appendicitis. — ضمیمۀ خایه Epididymis. — ض. کردن To attach; annex — رونوشت نامۀ وی ض. است Copy of his letter is herewith enclosed.

ضوء o & ضیاء A. = روشنایی

ضیاءالدین (A.) Mas. pr. name. OS. Light of the faith.

ضیاع A. Properties ; estates. [Pl. of ضیعه o]

ضیافت A. = مهمانی

ضیغم o A. = شیر Lion.

ضیف o A. = مهمان

ضیق A. = تنگی Tightness. Med. Stricture. — ضیق مجرای بول Coarctate urethra. — ضیق وقت Short time.

ضیق‌النفس A. = تنگه نفس

ضیمران o A. Wild basil.

طابَ ثَراه ० *A.* May his dust (*i. e.* grave) be fragrant.

طابق النعل بالنعل *A.* Word for word; strictly; to the letter.

طاحنه *A.* [طواحن] = اُسیاب دندان

طاحونه *A.* [طواحین] = آسیاب

طارُم ० *A.* [f. P. تارم] Wooden house with a dome. Palisade round a garden. *Met.* The sky.

طارمی *A. P.* Balustrade.

طاس *A.* [f. P. تاس] 1) *n.* Copper bowl used in bath-houses. Die or dice.—طاس لغزنده Ant-hill.—ط. ریختن *or* ط. انداختن To throw d.—ط. گرفتن To cog the d. (*or* a die) 2) *a* Bald

طاس کباب *Kind of dish.*

طاسی *A. P.* 1) *n.* Baldness. 2) *a.* Cuboid : استخوان ط .

طاعات [Pl. of طاعت]

طاعَت *A.* [طاعات] Worship. Obedience.

طاعون *A.* Plague; pestilence.

طاعونی *A.* Pestilential.

طاغی *A.* Rebel(lious).

طاق *A.P.* 1) *n.* Arch; vault. (Arched) roof. 2) *a.* Odd. *F.* Unparalleled. — طاق پیروزی *or* طاق نصرت Arch of triumph.— ط. زدن To construct an arch (over). — طاقتم ط. شد I lost patience.

طاق باز *A. P.* 1) *a.* Supine. 2) *ad.* In a supine position on one's back.

طاقت *A.* Endurance. Fortitude.— طاقت آنرا ندارم I cannot support (*or* endure) that. — دلم ط. نمی آورد که I cannot find it in my heart to.

طاقت فرسا *A. P.* Insupportably tiresome. Intolerable; oppressive.

طاقچه *A. P.* Niche; ledge. Shelf. — طاقچه دیوار کوب Bracket; console.— طاقچهٔ روی بخاری Mantel (shelf).

طاقدار *A. P.* Arched. Roofed.

طاقدیس ० *A. P. a.* Arch-like. —*n.* Anticline. Name of the arched throne of Khosrow.

طاق نما *A. P.* False arch.

طاقه Piece (of cashmere, etc.)

طالار = تالار

طالب *A.* (One) who seeks or demands. *Cf. the plurals* طلاب *or* طلبه & طالبین ‖ طالبِ چیزی بودن To seek s. t. To be fond of s. t. — ط. ندارد There is no demand for it.

طالبی (*A. P.*) *Variety of deep-ribbed melon.*

طالبین *A.* Those interested.

Cf. the s. طالب
طالح *A.* = بدکار Wicked.
طالع *A. a.* Rising; appearing. —*n.* Horoscope. Lucky star. Luck. — ط . دیدن To cast a horoscope. To tell fortunes.
طالع بین *A. P.* Fortune-teller.
طالع بینی *A. P.* Horoscopy; fortune-telling; genethlialogy.
طامات o *A.* Idle talk.
طاوس *or* **طاووس** *A.* Peacock.— طاوس ماده Peahen.
طاول etc. = تاول etc.
طاهر *A.* = پاك Clean; pure; chaste. *Mas. pr. name.*
طاهره (*A.*) *Fem. pr. name.* [Orig. fem. of طاهر]
طایر [f. A. طائر—pl. طیور] 1) = مرغ 2) *Astr.* Altair.— طایر قدس = * فرشته
طائف o *A.* One who performs the rites of circumambulation at Ka'beh.
طایفه [f. A. طائفه—pl. طوائف] Clan; tribe. Sect.
طبّ *A.* Medicine. *Cf.* پزشکی ‖ طب قانونی Medical jurisprudence; forensic medicine; legal m.
طبابت *A.* Medical profession.— ط . کردن To practise medicine.
طباخ etc. *A.* = آشپز etc.
طباطبائی *A.* Descended from the Prophet on both sides.
طباع *A.* 1) *Pl. of* طبع 2) Natural disposition.
طبال *A.* = طبل زن
طبایع [Pl. of طبیعت]
طبخ *A.* Cooking. Batch; bake.
طبری Hyrcanian: native of Tabarestan or Mazanderan.
طبع *A.* Impression; printing. Nature; temper. — طبع شعر Poetic gift (*or* verve). — تحت ط. In the press; in print.— ط . ونشر کردن To publish.
طبعا *A.* Naturally.
طبق (*tabagh*) *A.* [اطباق] Tray. Large dish. *Bot.* Receptacle. *M.* Plate.
طبق (*tebgh*) *A.* Conformity.— برطبق In conformity with; according to.
طبقات *A.* [Pl. of طبقه] Storeys. Categories; classes. Strata; layers. — اختلاف **طبقاتی** Class distinctions.
طبقات الارض *A.* Strata of the earth. [For علم ط] Geology [now زمین شناسی].
طبقات الارضی *A.P.* Geological.
طبق کش *A. P.* Porter using a tray for carrying things.
طبقه *A.* [طبقات] Layer; stratum [چینه]. Class; category. Stage. Grade. Order; group. Storey. — طبقه اول Ground floor.— طبقه دوم First floor.
طبقه بندی *A. P.* Classification. — ط . کردن To classify.
طبل *A.* Drum [کوس].— طبل گوش D. of the ear; tympanum. — طبل وارونه D. of mourning. — ط . زدن To drum; beat a d.—

طبل عقب نشینی زدن To beat a retreat.

طبل زن *A. P.* Drummer.

طبله *A. P.* (Perfumer's) tray ـ ط . کردن To come off.

طبلی *A.* Drum-like. Tympanic. ـ استسقاء ط . Tympanites.

طِبی *A.* Medical. Medicinal.

طَبیب *A.* [اطباء] = پزشك Physician; doctor. [Fem. طبیبه]. ـ طبیب قانونی Medical examiner; medico-legal e.

طَبیعت *A.* [طبایع] Nature. Temper. ـ طبایع چهارگانه The four temperaments.

طبیعةً *A.* Naturally.

طبیعی *A. a.* Natural. Physical. Normal. [Fem. طبیعیه with the pl. طبیعیات natural sciences –also علوم طبیعی]. –*n.* Naturalist [pl. طبیعیون] . ـ غیر طبیعی Unnatural; violent : مرگ غیر طبیعی

طپانچه *T.* = **تپانچه**

طپاندن = **تپانیدن**

طِحال *A.* = اسپرز Spleen. ـ ورم ط . Splenitis.

طحالُ *A.* Splenalgia.

طرّاح *A.* Designer ; modeller ; sketcher. Schemer.

طَراحی *A. P.* Designing; planning; sketching. ـ ط . کردن To sketch ; plan.

طرّار *A.* Impostor. Pickpocket.

طراز *A-P.* = **تراز**

طراوَت *A.* = تازگی Freshness.

طَرَب *A.* = خوشی Joy; mirth. ـ مطرب & خنیاگر = اهل ط .

طرب انگیز *A. P.* Exciting joy ; joyful.

طربناك *A. P.* Joyful.

طَرح *A.* Plan; design; sketch. Rough draft. Scheme. Project. ـ ط . ریختن To make a scheme ; draw a r. plan. ـ ط . کردن To d. or sketch. To p. or project. To propose ; set forth; propound. ـ طرحِ آئین نامه Draft regulation. ـ طرح قانونی Members' bill.

طرح ریزی *A. P.* 1) = طراحی 2) Laying a foundation.

طرداً للباب (*tardan-1e1bab*) *A.* Incidentally.

طَرد کردن *A. P.* To reject. To banish. To excommunicate.

طَرز *A.* Manner; method; mode.

طَرَف *A.* [اَطراف] Side; direction [سو]. End ; extremity [سر]. ـ طرف دعوی Party to a suit ; litigant. ـ باکسی ط . شدن To enter into quarrel with s. o. To oppose s. o. ـ باکه ط هستی Who are you getting at ? ـ بر طرف کردن To eliminate; do away with. To cure (radically) . ـ از طرفِ On behalf of ; for. On the side of. By. ـ از یك ط . On the one hand. On one part. ـ از طرف دیگر On the other h. On the other p. ـ از طرفی هم Moreover. On the o. hand. ـ طرفِ بطرفِ To(ward). At. ـ

غروب Towards evening.– طرف اعتماد Trustworthy.– در اطراف About *ad*. – در اطرافِ About *prep*.– اطراف سافله The lower extremities.– اطراف عالیه The upper e.

طَرف *A. P.* 1) = طَرَف 2) = سود 3) = گوشه ‖ (بر) بستن .ط To gird oneself. *F*. To derive advantage. – طرفی * A portion of; some of.

طرفدار *A. P. n.* Adherent; partisan; advocate. –*a*. Partial. – طرفدارِ کسی بودن To take the part of, or side with s. o.– طرفدار عقیده‌ای بودن To favour an opinion.

طرفداری *A. P.* Partiality. – ازکسی ط . کردن To take the part of, or side with s. o.

طُرفه *A.* Novelty; new or rare (thing). [the eye.

طرفة‌العین *A.* Twinkling of

طرفیت *A.* Being party to a dispute; interest or involvement. Opposition.

طرفین *A.* [D. of طَرف] 1) The two parties; both p. 2) *Math*. The extremes.

طُرُق [Pl. of طریق]

طُرقه [f. T. طورغای] Ouzel.

طُرّه *A.* Lock of hair; tress.

طَریق *A.*[طُرُق] = راه Way; road. Channel. – از طریقِ Via. – بطریقِ By way of.– بچه ط How? In what manner?– ارائهٔ ط . کردن To guide.– مهندس طرق و شوارع Civil engineer. [rule of life.

طریقت *A.* (Religious) way;

طریقه *A.* Method; manner.

طشت etc. *A-P.* = **تشت** etc.

طعام *A.* [اطعمه] = خوراك Food.– ط . گزاردن To serve food.

طَعم *A.* Flavour. *Cf.* مزه

طُعمه *A.* Bait. – طعمهٔ آتش Prey to fire.

طعن *A.* (*Collective for* طعنه)

طَعنه *A.* Taunt(ing); sarcasm; sneering. Irony. – ط . زدن To speak ironically; say one thing and mean another. [*With* به] To taunt; reproach. [Ironical.

طعنه‌آمیز *A. P.* Sarcastic.

طُغری *or* **طغرا** *T.* Piece; No. [used in counting bills, etc., but not rendered in E.]: سه ط . قبض three bills. *OS*. Royal monogram.

طُغیان *A.* Overflowing. Inundation. *F*. Rebellion. Outburst – ط . کردن To overflow (its banks). To rage. To rebel.

طَفره *A.* Evasion; elusion. – ط . زدن To elude; evade; dodge. [جواب ط .]

طفره آمیز *A. P.* Evasive:

طفل *A.* [اطفال] = بچه & کودك

طفلانه *A. P.* = بچگانه

طفلك *A. P.* Little child. [*Used sympathetically*]

Poor boy; poor fellow.

طفولیت *A*. Childhood [بچگی].

طُفیلی *A*. Parasite. *Met*. Uninvited person accompanying a guest. [The Arabic has طفیل with the same meaning].

طلا *or* تلا = زر Gold. — ساعت ط. G. watch. — طلای سفید Platinum.

طلا آلات *P. A*. Gold ware.

طلاب & طلبه *A*. Scholars; templars. *Cf. the s.* طالب

طَلاق *A*. Divorce. — ط. دادن To d. — ط. گرفتن از To be divorced from; be granted a divorce by.

طلاقت *A*. Freedom from impediment. Glibness.

طلاق نامه *A.P*. Bill of divorce (*or* divorcement); legal instrument of divorce.

طلاکوب Gold blocker.

طلاکوبی Gold blocking. Tooling.

طلایع [Pl. of طلیعه]

طلایه • [f. A. طَلایع] Vanguard; advance-guard.

طلایی Golden. Gilt. (Of the colour of) gold. — ماهی ط. Gold fish. — ط. کردن To gild.

طَلب *A*. Search. Request. Begging. Demand. Claim. — دو ریال از من ط. دارد I owe him 3 *rials*; 2 *rials* is due him by me. — ط. کردن 1) To search; seek. 2) = طلبیدن ‖ [*With* از] To ask; request; beg.

طلبکار *A. P*. = بستانکار.

طلبکاری *A. P*. 1) = بستانکاری 2) Pressing for the payment of one's due. — از کسی ط. کردن To press s. o. for payment of a debt; dun him.

طلبه *S. u*. طلاب

طلبیدن *A. P*. [طلب] To call; invite. To summon. To ask. To seek. — طلبیدگان Those invited [pl. of طلبیده p. p.].

طلسم *A-G*. Talisman; charm; spell. Amulet. — ط. شدن To be s.-bound. To become inextricable. — ط. کردن To spell; cast a s. upon. To charm; enchant.

طلسم گر *A. P*. Witch-doctor; medicine-man; exorcist.

طَلعت • *A*. Countenance; face. Mien. *Fem. pr. name*.

طَلق *A*. Mica; isinglass; talc.

طِلق *A*. Free; unconditional.

طَلقی *A. P*. Talcose; talcous. Micaceous.

طُلوع *A*. Rising: طلوع آفتاب ‖ Appearance. — ط. کردن To rise.

طلیسه One-to-three-year-old heifer.

طلیعه *A* [طَلایع] Vanguard. *F*. Van; leader. [greedy.

طماع *A*. Very covetous or

طُمأنینه *A*. = آرامش - وقار

طمث *A*. The menses.

طُمطراق Pomp. Grandiloquence.

طَمع *A*. Covetousness. — طمع فطری Acquisitiveness. — ط. بریدن To give up hope. — ط. کردن

vt. To covet. *–vi*. To be covetous.– چشم ط . بچیزی داشتن To have views upon s. t.

طمعکار *A. P*. Covetous.

طناب *A*. Rope; cord.– ط . انداختن To hang. – یك مو را طناب کردن To make mountains of mole-hills.

طناب پیچ کردن *A. P*. To tie or bind with a rope.

طناب خور *A. P*. Depth measured by a rope. [Used as an a. Ex. چاه ط. Draw-well].

طنابسازی *A. P*. Rope-making. [For کارخانهٔ ط.] Ropery; ropewalk. [rope.

طناب بازی *A. P*. Skipping the

طناب کشی *A. P*. [For مسابقهٔ ط.] Tug of war.

طنابی *A. P*. Rope-like; restiform.– نردبان ط. Rope-ladder.

طناز • *A*. Coquettish.

طنازی *A. P*. Coquettishness.

طنبی *or* **تنبی** o *A. P*. Parlour.

طنز *A*. Scoffing.

طنطنه *A*. Pomp. Fuss. *OS*. Tinkling. Buzz. Din.

طنطور *Fr*. Tincture.

طنین *A*. Tingle (*or* ringing) in the ears. – ط . انداختن To ring; tingle. To resound.

طواحن [Pl. of طاحنه]

طواحین [Pl. of طاحونه]

طواف *A*. Circumambulation (of the Kaaba). – ط . کردن *or* ط . زدن To circumambulate; go round.

طوّاف *A*. Peddling fruiterer; coster(monger).

طوایف [Pl. of طایفه]

طوبی (*-ba*) *A*. *Name of a tree in paradise*. *Fem. pr. name*. *OS*. Blessedness.

طوج o *T*. Bronze.

طور (*tu:r*) *A*. Mount Sinai [often طور سینا *or* کوه ط.].

طور (*towr*) *A*. Manner; method. Kind. *Cf. the pl*. اطوار ‖ چطور *or* چه ط. How? In what m.? احوال شما چطور است How are you? – چطور مگر؟ Why?– اینطور Thus; in this m.; (in) this way.– اینطور اشخاص Such people.– همینطور است Exactly. That is right. –همینطورها So-so. – بطوری So. – بطوریکه So that. As. – بطور کامل Perfectly.– همانطور که (Just) as. – +هر طور شده *or* هر طور هست By all means.

طوسی (?) Dark grey.

طوطی Parrot.– طوطی ماده Hen-p.

طوطیوار 1) *a*. Parrot-like. 2) *ad*. By rote.

طوعا *A*. Willingly; of one's own accord. – طوعاً (و) کرهاً Willy-nilly; nolens volens; whether one wishes or not.

طوفان *A.G*. Deluge; flood. Storm; tempest.

طوفانزاد *A. P*. Diluvian.

طوفان نما *A. P*. Storm-card.

طوفانی *A. P.* Stormy.

طوق *A.* Necklace. Collar. Ruff. Chain; torque. [*Of an officer*] Gorget. *F.* Yoke; tie.—طوق لعنت *Met.* Ball and chain; also, the battleaxe.— ط. درگردن کردن To wear a necklace.

طوقدار *A. P.* Collared; ring-necked. Ruffed.

طوقه *A. P.* Curb; puteal.

طول *A.* Length [درازا]. Longitude [also درجهٔ ط].—طول‌زمان or طول‌مدت L. of time; duration.—پرش بطول Broad jump.— ط. دادن To protract; prolong. To be long (in doing s. t.).— ط. کشیدن To last. — دو سال ط. کشید It took (*or* lasted) two years. — طولی نخواهد کشید که Before long. — طولی نکشید که Soon after. — بطول انجامیدن To take a long time.— بطولِ سه متر 3 metres long.

طولاً *A.* In length; lengthwise.

طولانی *A, P,* = دراز Long.

طولی *A. P.* Linear. Longitudinal. — پرش‌ط. Broad jump.

طومار *A.* Scroll. Roll.

طوماری *A. P. Bot.* Volute. [*In architecture*] Voluted.

طَویل *A.* = دراز Long.

طویل‌العمر *A.* Longeval.

طویل‌القامت *A.* = **قد بلند**

طویل‌المدت *A.* Long-term *a.*

طویله *A. P.* Stable. Shed.

طویله‌دار *A. P.* Livery-man.

طَهارَت *A.* Ceremonious purification after easing nature. *OS.* = پاکی ‖ ط. گرفتن To wash oneself after easing n.

طُهر ○ *A.* Purity of women when not menstruous.

طَیّ *A.* Going or travelling through. — طی کردن To go or travel through; traverse. To fix: قیمت آنرا باید طی کرد ‖ در طیِ In the course of. (Enclosed) with.

طیار *A.* Flying. Volatile. — چرخ ط. Fly-wheel.

طیارات [Pl. of طیاره]

طیاره *A.* [طیارات] = **هواپیما**

طیب *A. a.* Sweet-smelling. —*n.* Sweet smell. — بطیب خاطر With a good will or mind; of one's own free w.

طیب ○ (*tayeb*) *A.* Good. Sweet-smelling. Delightful.

طیبات *A. Tayebat*: poetical work by Sa'di: the «Fine Odes». [Pl. of طیبه fem. of طیب (*tayeb*)].

طینت *A.* = شوخ، خوش طبع، &

طیبه (*tayebeh*) *A.* 1) Good deed. *Cf. the pl.* طیبات ‖ 2) *Fem. of* طیب

طیر *A.* [طیور] = **پرنده**

طَیران *A.* = **پرواز**

طیره ○ *A.* Bad omen.

طیش *A.* Levity. Unsteadiness.

طیف *A.* Spectre. Spectrum.

طیف‌بین *A. P.* Spectroscope.
طیفی *A.* Spectral. [Pall.
طیلسان ٥ *A-P.* Mantle. Hood.
طیموس *A-G.* Thymus (gland).
طین ٥ *A.* = ِگل Clay; mud.
طینت *A.* Nature; inborn disposition. *Cf.* طین
طیور [Pl. of طیر & طایر]

ظالم *A.* [ظلمه] *n.* Oppressor; tyrant. Top dog. *–a.* Cruel.

ظالمانه *A. P. ad.* Tyranically. *–a.* Unjust; oppressive.

ظاهر *A. a.* Apparent. Outward; external. *–n.* [Pl. ظواهر] O. appearance. E. conduct.– درظاهر Outwardly; on the surface. – صورت ظ. Outward a.– وضع ظ. O. appearance; the outer man.– ظ. شدن To become apparent.– ظ. کردن To cause to appear. To develop, as a film.– حکم بظاهر کردن To judge by appearances.

ظاهراً *A.* Apparently. Outwardly; on the face of it.

ظاهر الصلاح *A.* Outwardly good. [observer.

ظاهربین *A. P.* Superficial

ظاهر سازی *A. P.* Simulation.

ظاهری *A. P.* External; outward. [humour.

ظرافت *A.* Elegance. Wit;

ظرائف *A.* Witty sayings; humours. [Pl. of ظریفه o.]

ظربان o *A.* Polecat.

ظرف *A.* [ظروف] Vessel; container. Dish. *Gr.* Adverb of time or place. Duration; course. *F.* Capacity. Forbearance. – نفت با ظرف و بی ظ. Packed and bulk oil.– درظرفِ During; within (a period of). – در ظرفِ دو ماه In two months' time.

ظرفاء [Pl. of ظریف]

ظرف شویی *A. P.* Washing-up. (scullery) sink.

ظرفیت *A.* Capacity. *Chem.* Valency [also واحد ظرفیت].

ظروف [Pl. of ظرف]

ظریف *A.* 1) *a.* Elegant. Nice. Delicate. Miniature. Subtle. Witty. Clever. 2) *n.* [Pl. ظرفاء the w. or elegant].

ظفر *A.* Victory [پیروزی]. – پیروز شدن = ظ. یافتن or ظ. کردن

ظلّ *A.* Shadow [سایه]. *F.* Shelter. *Astr.* Umbra.– ظل تمام Cotangent.– شبه ظل Penumbra.– در ظل توجهاتِ Under the auspices of.

ظل الله (zelolah) *A.* Shadow of God [old title of kings].

ظلام *A* = ظلمت or تاریکی

ظلم *A.* = ستم Oppression; cruelty.– ظ. کردن بر To oppress. To do injustice to.

ظلمات *A.* Deep darkness. Dark region where the 'water of life' was believed to be.

ظلمانی *A. P.* = تاریك Dark.

ظلمت *A.* Darkness.

ظلمه [Pl. of ظالم]

ظَنّ *A.* = گمان Opinion. Suspicion. Conjecture. — ظن بردن به To be suspicious of. — حسن ظن Good, high, or favourable opinion: بمن حسن ظنی داشت He had a good o. of me. — سوء ظن Suspicion; mistrust. — ظن قوی Presumption.

ظنین *A.* = **بدگمان**

ظواهر [Pl. of. ظاهر]

ظَهر *A.* Back; reverse [پشت]. در ظهر ورقه Overleaf.

ظُهر *A.* Noon. — پیش ازظهر 1) Before noon. 2) Forenoon. — سه ساعت پیش از ظهر 9 a. m.

ظَهر نویس etc. *A. P.* = **پشت نویس** etc.

ظُهور *A.* Appearance. Advent. *Med.* Outburst. [*In obstetrics*] Presentation. — بظهور رسیدن To appear. To happen. — ظ. کردن To a.

ظَهیر *A.* Assistant. Supporter.

ظهیرالدین (*A.*) *Mas. pr. name. OS.* Supporter of the faith.

عابِد *A.* [عباد] *n.* Worshipper. —*a.* Pious; devout.

عابر *A.* [عابرین] Passer-by.

عاج *A.* Ivory. — عاج دندان Dentin(e); ivory.

عاج تراش *A. P.* Ivory-turner.

عاجز *A. a.* Disabled; crippled. Unable: از بردن آن ع. بود He was unable to carry it. — قلم از شرح آن ع. است My pen is inadequate to describe it. —*n.* [Pl. عجزه] Cripple. Disabled person. — ع. شدن To be disabled or crippled. To be brought to bay. To be rendered unable. — ع. کردن To harass. To disable. To confound or confute; argue down.

عاجزانه *A. P.* Humbly.

عاجل *A. a.* Immediate. Hasty. Transitory. —*n.* ○ One who makes haste.

عاجلاً *A.* Immediately. With a view to the present.

عاد *A.* Aliquot part.

عادات [Pl. of عادت]

عادَت *A.* [عادات] Habit [خو]. Custom. [For عادت زنانه] The menses.— ع. دادن To accustom. To habituate. — ع. شدن To grow into a habit. — ع. کردن To fall into the h. (of). — برحسب ع. Habitually; as a rule.— حبس ع. Amenorrhoea.— خلاف ع. Unusual (thing); abnormal(ity).

عادِل *A.* 1) Just [دادگر]. 2) Righteous [*Biblical*].

عادلانه *A. P. ad.* Justly. Righteously. —*a.* Just: قضاوت ع.

عادله *A.* Fair; reasonable: قیمت ع. ‖ [Orig. fem. of عادل]

عادةً *A.* Habitually.

عادی *A.* 1) Ordinary; usual.— غیر عادی Unusual. 2) = معتاد

عار *A.* Shame; disgrace. Disdain. — از دروغ گفتن ع. دارم I scorn to lie.

عارِض *A.* 1) Petitioner. 2) ⋆ Face; also, cheek. — ع. شدن 1) To go to law; lodge a complaint in the court. 2) = دخ دادن

عارضه *A.* Accident; event. *Cf. the pl.* عوارض ‖ عارضهٔ کسالت Illness or indisposition.

عارضی *A.* Accidental; non-essential; adventitious.

عارِف *A. a.* Gnostic; learned. —*n.* [Pl. عرفاء] G.; l. person.

عاری *A.* Devoid; destitute. Void. *OS.* Naked [برهنه]. — ع. از حقیقت False; unfounded.

عاریت ⋆ *Same as* **عاریه**

عاریه *A.* Loan. — ع. دادن To

loan or lend. — ع. گرفتن To borrow; have the loan of.

عاریتی • *A. P.* Borrowed. *F.* False ; fictitious.

عازِم *A.* Starting; setting out; on the point of leaving. Resolved ; determined. — عازمِ سفر شدن To start on a journey. — عازمِ آبادان شد He left for Abadan.

عاشِق *A.* [عشاق] *n.* Lover. —*a.* Amorous; fond. — بکسی ع. شدن *or* عاشقِ کسی شدن To fall in love with s. o.

عاشقانه *A. P.* Amorous(ly). — نامهٔ ع. Love-letter.

عاشقی *A. P.* Being in love. *S. a.* عشقبازی

عاشورا *A.* The tenth day of the lunar month, *Moharam*, on which the martyrdom of *Emam Hossein* took place.

عاصی *A.* = 1) گناهکار 2) یاغی

عاطِر *A.* Fragrant [only in خاطرِ عاطرِ . . . The good or noble mind of . . .]

عاطِفه *A.* [عواطف] Feeling. Kind feeling. Sentiment.

عاطل *A.* Idle Useless.

عافیت *A.* Good health. Welfare. — ع. باشد (God) bless you! I wish you good h.

عاق *A.* Disobedient. Anathematized. Disinherited.

عاقبت *A.* [عواقب] *n.* End [انجام]. Consequence. Futurity. —*ad.* = عاقبت‌الامر

عاقبت‌الامر *A.* = سرانجام At last; in the long run.

عاقبت اندیش *A. P.* Provident.

عاقبت اندیشی *A. P.* Foresight; providence.

عاقبت‌بخیر *A. P.* Ending well *or* successfully; successful.

عاقِد *A.* Concluder (of a contract). Priest or notary marrying a couple.

عاقرقرحا *A.* Pellitory of Spain.

عاقِل *A. a.* = خردمند Wise. —*n.* Wise man [pl. عقلاء].

عاقلانه *A. P. ad.* Wisely. —*a.* Wise : کارهای ع.

عاقله *A.* [*Of a woman*] Of ripe years. Elderly. [Orig. fem. of عاقل "wise"].

عاکف *A.* Devotee praying in seclusion.

عالَم *A.* [عوالِم] = جهان World; universe. — او در این عوالم نیست He does not think of these things. — یك ع. + Heaps ; lots (of).

عالِم *A.* = دانشمند *a.* Learned. —*n.* L. man ; scholar. Scientist. *Cf. the pl.* علماء

عالماً *A.* = عمداً & دانسته

عالم تاب • *or* **عالَم افروز** *A. P.* World-illuminating.

عالم‌الغیب *A.* Knowing the invisible or occult ; omniscient.

عالمگیر *A. P.* World-conquering. *F.* Universal.

عالمیان *A. P.* Inhabitants of the world. [Pl. of عالمی o]
عالی *A.* High. Sublime. Grand. Excellent. Of surperior quality. [Fem. عالیه used as a fem. pr. name].
عالیجاه *A.P.* عالی جناب .- *a. p.*- عالی‌مقام *a. p.* High in position.
عالی رتبه *a. p.* = بالا رتبه
عامّ *A.* 1) *a.* Common: اسم ع. ‖ General. Generic. Public. Vulgar. [Fem. عامه]. قوائدعامه – Works of public utility. – دوای عام Panacea; catholicon; heal-all. 2) *n.* [Pl. عوام] One of the common people; commoner. Layman.
عام‌المنفعه *A.* Of public utility.
عامداً *A.* = عمداً & دانسته
عامِل *A.* *n.* Agent. *Math.* Factor. *Cf. the plurals* عمله - عوامل - عمال ‖ *a.* Active. Skilled. Managing; executive: مدیر عامل M. director.
عاملیت *A.* Skill.
عامه *A.* 1) *n.* The public. 2) *a.* [Fem. of عام]
عامی *A.* *a.* Illiterate. Vulgar. Popular. Laic. –*n.* = عام
عامیانه *A. P.* Vulgar.
عانه *A.* = استخوان‌شرمگاه Os pubis.
عایِد [f. A. عائد] *a.* Returning. (Being) earned. –*n.* *Mil.* Counter-recoil mechanism.– ع. داشتن To pay or return; fetch. – ع. شدن To be e. – منافعی که عاید جامعه میشود Advantages accruing to society.
عایدات *A.* [Pl. of عا ِئده the regular pl. of which is عوائد *q. v.*]. Incomes. Revenue.
عایده o *A.* 1) *Fem. of* عاید 2) *S. of* عواید
عایق *A.* Detent; click.– عایقِ گرما Non-conductor.
عایق‌دار *A. P.* Insulated.
عایق کاری *A. P.* Lagging. Water-proofing. [family.
عائله *A.* Wife (and children);
عائله‌مند etc. *A. P.* = عیالمند etc.
عَبا *A.* Men's loose sleeveless cloak open in front.
عِباد [Pl. of عبد]
عُباد (*Obad*) [Pl. of عابد]
عبادَت *A.* Worship. Servitude. *Cf.* پرستش & بندگی ‖ ع. کردن To worship. To serve or obey.
عبادتگاه *A. P.* = پرستشگاه
عبارَت *A.* [عبارات] Expression; phrase; language. Wording. Style.– ع. بودن از To consist of. – بعبارت دیگر In other words. – اصلاحات عبارتی Amendments in wording.
عبارت‌پردازی *A. P.* Speaking in style; (pedantic)phraseology.
عباس (*A.*) *Mas. pr. name.*
عَبث *A.* 1) *a.* Vain; useless. 2) *ad.* In vain; to no avail.
عَبد *A.* [عِباد] = بنده Servant or slave o. Worshipper.
عبدالله (*A.*) *Mas. pr. name.*

OS. Servant of God.
عِبرانی A. Hebrew; Hebraic.
عِبرت A. Example ; lesson ; warning. ـ ع. شدن To serve as an example. ـ ع. گرفتن To take an e. or lesson.
عبرت انگیز A. P. Serving as an example. Surprising.
عبرت بین A. P. That can see (or take) an example.
عبرةً للناظرین (ebratan-lenaze-) A. As a lesson for observers.
عِبری A. Hebrew (language).
عبودیت A. =بندگی Servitude; slavery. Devotion.
عُبور A. Passing ; passage ; crossing. Transit. ـ ع. دادن To cause to pass. To ferry. ـ ع کردن از To p. or cross. ـ غیرقابل ع. Impassable; impracticable. ـ عبور و مرور Traffic ; passage. ـ منع عبور و مرور شب Curfew. ـ عبور و مرور ممنوع (است) "No thoroughfare." ـ عبور و مرور شب را آزاد کردن To lift the curfew.
عبوراً A. In passing; in transit.
عَبوس A. Stern. Grim(-faced).
عبهر o A. n. 1) = نرگس 2) = یاسمن ‖ —a. Elegant.
عَبید o A. [A pl. of عبد]
عبید A. Obeyd: mas. pr. name. OS. Little servant.
عَبیر A. Compound perfume.

عتاب A. Reproof. ـ ع. کردن To reprove. To be angry (with).
عتبه A. [عتبات] Threshold. Round; step [پله] o. By e. Royal court. ـ عتبات عالیات The Holy Shrines.
عته o (atah) A. Insanity [دیوانگی]. ـ عته شیخی Dotage; senility; second childhood.
عتیق A. Old ; antiquated. Cf. کهن & کهنه ‖ عهد عتیق 1) The O. Testament. 2) The old or ancient days.
عتیقه A. [عتیقات] n. Antique ; relic. —a. [Fem. of عتیق] Old or antique. ـ اشیاء عتیقه Antiquities; antiques; relics.
عثمان (A.) Mas. pr. name. ـ عثمان لنگ Met. An old lame rogue.
عثمانی A. Ottoman. Turkish.
عجاله A. Thing hastily done or food h. prepared o. ـ علی العجاله For the time being.
عجالةً A. For the present ; for the time being.
عجان A. Perineum.
عجانی A. Perineal. [Wonders.
عجایِب A. [Pl. of عجیبه o.]
عجب (ajab) A. 1) n. Wonder ـ ع. است It is surprising. ـ ع. داشتن To be surprised. 2) int. Strange !
عُجب (ojb) A. = خود بینی
عجز (ajz) A. Inability; impotence ; weakness. Failure.—

از انجام کاری ع. داشتن To be unable to do a thing.

عجز (*ajoz*) *A*. Hinder part of the body. Buttocks o. Last word of a verse. — استخوان ع. Sacrum.

عجزه [Pl. of عاجز]

عِجل o *A*. = **گوساله**

عَجله *A*. = شتاب Hurry; haste. — ع. کردن To make h.; hurry up. — ع. دارم I am in a h. for it. — با عجله *or* بعجله Hurriedly; hastily.

عَجم *A*. Non-Arabs. Iranians.

عجمی *A*. *a*. Foreign (to the Arabs); barbarian. —*n*. Non-Arab. Iranian.

عجوز(ه) *A*. Old woman; crony.

عَجول *A*. Hasty; rash.

عَجیب *A*. Wonderful; strange. [Fem. عجیبه].

عجیب‌الخلقه *A*. Monstrous; of a queer formation.

عجین o *A*. = **سرشته**

عِداد *A*. = شمار Number. Class; category. — در عِداد Among.

عدالت *A*. 1) Justice. 2) *Biblical use* Righteousness.

عداوَت *A*. Enmity [دشمنی]. Hatred. Grudge. — با کسی ع. داشتن To be an enemy of s. o.; bear him a grudge. — ع. ورزیدن To act like an e.

عَدَد *A*. [اعداد] Number [شماره]. Figure. Piece; No. [word used as a unit in counting objects. Ex. ۳ عدد سیب three apples].

عددکوب *A*. *P*. Figure-punch.

عدد نویسی *A*. *P*. Notation.

عددی *A*. *P*. 1) Sold by the piece. 2) = رقمی

عَدَس *A*. Lentil.

عدسك *A*. *P*. (*Bot*.) Lenticel.

عدسی *A*. Lentiform. [For شیشهٔ ع.] Lens. — عدسی شیئی Object-glass; objective.

عَدل *A*. Justice.

عِدل *A*. Bale. Half a load.

عِدل بندی *A*. *P*. Packing; baling.

عَدل پرور *A*. *P*. Who fosters justice; just. [دادگستری]

عدلیه (*A*.) *Old word for*

عَدَم *A*. Non-existence [نیستی]. Lack; absence; want. — عدم رعایت Non-observance.

عدم‌النفع (*adamonaf'*) *A*. Loss of prospective profits.

عدن (*adn*) *A*. Eden.

عَدَن (*adan*) *A*. (*Geog*.) Aden.

عَدو *A*. [اعداء] = **دشمن**

عُدوانی *A*.*P*. Unjust. Forcible. — تصرف ع. F. (entry and) detainer.

عُدول *A*. Deviation. — ع. کردن To deviate. — از قول خود عدول کردن To go back on one's word; revoke one's promise.

عِدّه *A*. 1) Number [شماره]. 2) *Mil*. Detachment. 3) Period during which a divorced or widowed woman may not be married to another man.

عدید *A.* [Fem. عدیده] Numerous : در موارد عدیده

عدیل *A. n.* Peer; equal. —*a.* Equiponderant; equivalent.

عدیم المثال *A.* = **عدیم النظیر**

عدیم النظیر (*adi:monazi:r*) *A.* Peerless; incomparable[بی مانند]

عذاب *A.* Torture ; torment. Punishment. — ع. دادن (به) 1) To trouble ; give t. 2) [More often ع. کردن] To torture or punish.

عذار • *A.* Cheek or face.

عذب البیان ○ *A.* Of a sweet or agreeable expression.

عذر *A.* Excuse. *Cf.* پوزش ‖ Pretext [بهانه].— ع. آوردن To offer an excuse. — ع. خواستن To apologize; e. oneself. — ع. میخواهم E. me; I beg your pardon.— عذرش خواسته است He has a good e.; he is out [often ironical]. — عذر کسیرا خواستن To dismiss s. o. from service.— عذر بدتر از گناه Lame or pitiful excuse. [Virgin.

عذرا *A. Fem. pr. name. OS.*

عذرخواهی *A. P.* Apologizing; apology. — ع. کردن To offer an apology; apologize.

عرابه [Variation of ارابه].

عراده *A.* (Gun-)carriage. — سه ع. توپ Three guns.

عرایض [Pl. of عریضه]

عرب *A.* The Arabs [pl. of عربی]. *C. E.* Arab(ian).

عربده *A.* Drunken brawl. — ع. کشیدن or ع. کردن To b. from drunkenness ; raise an uproar; paint the town red.

عربده جو *A. P.* Quarrelsome.

عربستان *A. P.* Arabia.

عربی *A.* 1) *a.* Arabic. Arabian.— اسب ع. Arab (horse).— یخه عربی Stand-up collar. 2) *n.* The Arabic language.

عربیت *A.* Arabic literature.

عرش *A.* The empyrean. *OS.* Throne [تخت].

عرشه *A. P.* Deck: عرشهٔ کشتی

عرصات *A.* Open space where the last judgment is carried on. *Cf. the s.* عرصه

عرصه *A.* Open space; square. Arena. *Cf. the pl.* عرصات ‖ Building-site; ground ; land.— عرصهٔ شطرنج Chessboard.

عرض *A.* 1) Width; breadth [پهنا].— بعرض دو متر 2 metres wide.— درعرض During; within; in the course of. 2) *Geog.* Latitude [also ع. درجهٔ]. 3) *Geom.* Abscissa.

عرض *A.* Presentation. [*In p. c.*] Remark [by an inferior to a superior]. Petition. — ع. کردن [*In p. c.*] To say. To present; exhibit. To submit.— بعرض رساندن To have the honour to submit or communicate (to a higher authority). – بعرض . . . رسیدن To hear or consider the case of ; listen to. – چه ع.کنم What shall I say ? [usu. meaning 'I do not know'].

عرض (*araz*) *A*. [اَعراض] Accident; form.

عِرض *A*. = آبرو Reputation; honour. – عرض خود را بردن To damage one's reputation.

عَرضا *A*. In width; breadthwise. Transversally.

عرضحال *a. p.* = دادخواست

عرضه *A*. Presentation. Proposal. – ع. و تقاضا Offer and demand. – ع. داشتن To present ; offer for view. To propose.

عُرضه *A*. Capability ; efficiency.

عرضی *A*. Transversal.

عَرَضی *A*. 1) Accidental. 2) *Bot*. Adventitious.

عَرعَر *A*. Juniper-tree.

عرعر Braying; heehaw. – ع.کردن To bray.

عُرف *A*. Common law. Usage. C. language or parlance. Secular law. [law; commonly.

عرفاً *A*. According to common

عرفاء [Pl. of عارف]

عِرفان *A*. Knowledge. Gnosticism. [cism; gnostic.

عِرفانی *A*. Based on gnosti-

عَرَفه *A*. Day before the Festival of Sacrifices.

عَرَق *A*. Perspiration; sweat [خوی]. Arrack; aqua vitae. – عرق آلوبالو Cherry brandy ; maraschino. – عرق بادیان & عرق زنیان Anisette. – عرق بید Willow-water. – عرق خونی Haematidrosis. – عرق رازیانه Fennel-water. – عرق مرگ Death-damp. – ع. ریختن To perspire (from blushing). – ع. کردن To perspire. To have one's temperature fall by perspiring. *F*. × To shell out; pay, as a bribe. – عرق کسیرا درآوردن + To put s. o. to the blush. – ع.کشیدن To distil [usu. with از].

عِرق *A*. [عُروق] Blood-vessel [رگ]. Root. *F*. Origin. – عروق شعریه Capillary vessels.

عرق‌النساء (*erghonesa'*) *A*. Sciatic nerve. *Med*. Sciatica.

عرق‌آور *A. P*. Sudatory.

عرقچین *A. P*. Skull-cap.

عرق‌سوز *A. P*. Heat-rash.

عرق‌کش ○ *A. P*. Distiller.

عرق‌کشی *A. P*. Distillation. – کارخانهٔ ع. Distillery.

عرق‌گز *A. P*. (Pimples caused by) overheating.

عرق‌گیر *A. P*. Numnah or namda; pad ; saddle-cloth.

عُرقوبی *A. P*. False: مواعید ع.

عرقی *A*. Perspiratory. – غدهٔ ع. Sweat-gland. [To ascend.

عروج *A*. Ascension. – ع.کردن

عَروس A. Bride. Daughter-in-law. — قضیهٔ ع. The Pythagorean theorem.

عروسك A. P. Doll. — عروسكِ پس پرده Alkekenji. — عروسكِ خیمه شب بازی Puppet; marionette. — عروسكِ پای نقاره Mere tool; cat's-paw.

عروسك بازی A. P. Playing with dolls. Childish act.

عروسی A. P. Marriage; wedding. — با کسی ع. کردن To marry s. o.

عَروض A. Prosody. Metre.

عروضی A. P. a. Prosodic(al). —n. Prosodist.

عروق [Pl. of عِرق]

عُروه A. (*Astr.*) Ansa.

عروةالوثقی ○ (*orvatol-vosgha*) A. Firm handle or support. F. True faith.

عُریان A. = برهنه Naked. F. Bare; unvarnished. — ع. کردن = برهنه کردن

عریانی A. P. = برهنگی

عَریض A. Wide; broad. F. Extensive. — ع. کردن To widen.

عریضه A. [عرایض] Petition.

عریضه نگاری A. P. Writing a letter or petition.

عریکه ○ A. [عرائك] = خو

عِزّ A. Honour; glory; power.

عزا A. Mourning. — لباس ع. پوشیدن To wear mourning. — ع. گرفتن To mourn.

عزادار A. P. a. In mourning; mournful. —n. Mourner.

عزاداری A. P. = سوگواری ‖ ع. کردن = سوگواری کردن

عزازیل A. Name of a fallen [angel.

عزایم A. Verses designed to conjure away evil spirits. *Cf. the s.* عزیمت

عزب A. [عزّاب] n. Bachelor; unmarried person. —a. Unmarried; single.

عِزّت A. Honour; glory. — عزت نفس Self-respect. — ع. دادن or ع. نهادن [With بر] To honour or respect.

عزت‌الله (A.) *Mas. pr. name. OS.* Glory of God.

عِزرائیل A. Azrael.

عَزل A. Deposal; removal from office. — ع. کردن To depose; discharge. — قابل ع. Removable. — غیر قابل ع. Irremovable.

عزلت A. Retirement; seclusion. — ع. اختیار کردن To retire or seclude oneself.

عَزم A. Resolution; firm purpose. Intention. *Ph.* Moment [now گشتاور]. — ع. کردن To resolve; determine. To intend. — عزم سفر کردن To start on a journey; set about for a j.

عُزوبت A. Celibacy.

عَزّوجلّ A. May... be honoured and glorified. [*Used as an a.* Ex. خدای ع. The Glorious God].

عَزيز A. a. Dear [گرامی]. Honoured. Powerful. —n. Darling.— عزیزم My dear one; darling. — ع. داشتن To endear or esteem. To take tender care of. — عزیز بیجهت Tin god.

عزيزالله (A.) *Mas. pr. name.* OS. God's dear one.

عزيزدُردانه + A. P. (Spoiled) darling; unique child (who has been spoiled). *See* دردانه

عزيزكرده A. P. Darling. Favourite.

عزيزه A. 1) *Fem. of* عزيز 2) *Fem. pr. name.*

عزيمت A. Starting; leaving. (Firm) resolution. Incantation; also, prayer for the sick [pl. عزایم] o. — ع. کردن To start; leave: برشت ع. کرد He left for Rasht. — فسخ ع. کردن To give up the idea of going; cancel a journey.

عساكر [Pl. of عسکر]

عسرالبول A. Dysuria.

عسرالطمث A. Dysmenorrhoea.

عسرالنفس A. Dyspnoea.

عسرت A. = سختی Hardship.

عسس A. = گزمه & شحنه

عسكر A. [عساکر] = لشکر

عَسل A. = انگبین Honey.— زنبور عسل Bee; honey-bee.

عسلك A. P. Honey-dew.

عسلى A. P. 1) a. Honey-like. Honeyed. Yellow. 2) n. Small tea-table. (Foot)stool.

عَشاء o A. = شام Supper.

عِشاء A. 1) = غروب & شام 2) Evening prayer.

عشاق [Pl. of عاشق]

عشاير A. [Pl. of عشیره o] Tribes.

عُشبه A. Sarsaparilla.

عُشر A. [عشور] = ده يك Tenth.

عشرات A. [Pl. of عشره] Tens [دهگان].

عِشرت A. Pleasure; feasting.— ع. کردن To live in p.

عشره A. [عشرات] = ده(گانه) [dues.

عُشريه A. Tithe; ten per cent

عِشق A. Love. — ع. ورزیدن To make love.— ×وقتی که عشقش بکشد When the humour takes him.

عشق‌انگيز A. P. Exciting love.

عشقبازى A. P. Love-affair; love-intrigue. Gallantry. — ع. کردن To make love.

عشق‌ورزى A. P. Love-making.

عشقه A. Bindweed.

عشور [Pl. of عُشر]

عشوه (eshveh) A. Coquetry; amorous gest. — ع. کردن To coquet.

عشوه‌گر A. P. Coquettish.

عشوه‌گرى A. P. Coquettishness.

عشيره S. u. عشایر

عَصا A. Cane; stick.— عصای چوپانی Shepherd's staff or crook. — عصای زیر بغل Crutch(es). — عصای سلطنتی Sceptre.— عصای موسی Moses' rod.— عصای پیری Prop or stay of one's age.— دست به ع. رفتن To act cautiously.

عصابه o *A*. Headband. Bandage. Turban [عمامه].
عصار *A*. Oil-presser.
عصاری *A*. *P*. Oil-pressing. – دستگاه ع. Oil-press.
عُصاره *A*. Extract; expressed juice. Ooze.
عصاکش *A*. *P*. Leader of a blind man; guide.
عَصب *A*. [اعصاب] Nerve [پی]. – درد اعصاب Neuralgia. – سلسلهٔ اعصاب Nervous system. – ورم اعصاب Neuritis.
عَصبانی *A*. High(ly)-strung; easily excited; excitable. Nervous. Mad. – ع. شدن To get excited or highly strung; fly into a rage. To g. angry or mad. – ع. کردن To make nervous or mad; get on one's nerves.
عصبانیت *A*. Nervousness. Fury.
عصبی *A*. *P*. Nervous: مرض ع.
عصبیت *A*. Party-spirit.
عَصر *A*. (Late) afternoon. Epoch; age [pl. اعصار]. – عصر تازه‌ای در تاریخ باز کرد It made an epoch. – امروز عصر This afternoon.
عصرانه *A*. *P*. Afternoon tea; five o'clock t.
عُصعص *A*. Coccyx.
عِصمت *A*. Chastity. *Fem. pr. name*. – هتك ع. Rape.
عصیان *A*. Sin. Rebellion. – ع. ورزیدن To sin. To rebel.
عَصیر *A*. (Expressed) juice. *Cf*. عصیرمعده ‖ شیره Gastric juice. – جوهرِ عصیر معده Pepsin.
عِضاده *A*. Alidade.
عضد o *A*. Upper arm. *Cf*. بازو ‖ *F*. Aid; support.
عضلات [Pl. of عضله]
عضلانی *A*. *P*. Muscular.
عضله *A*. [عضلات] = ماهیچه Muscle. – آماس ع. Myositis. – انقباض ع. Myonicity. – دردعضله Myalgia.
عضو (*ozv*) *A*. [اعضاء] Member. Limb. Organ. – کشورهای ع. M. countries. – عضوِ انجمنی شدن To join a society (as member). – ع. کردن To admit as a member.
عضویت *A*. Membership.
عطاء *A*. Grant; gift. – ع. کردن To bestow; give [بخشیدن].
عطاءالله (*A*.) *Mas. pr. name*. *OS*. Gift of God. [gifts.
عطا بخش • *A*. *P*. Bestower of
عطار *A*. Grocer (dealing in tea, sugar, spices, and the like). *OS*. Perfumer.
عطارد *A*. = تیر Mercury.
عطاری *A*. *P*. Grocery.
عطایا [Pl. of عطیه]
عطر *A*. Perfume; scent. – عطر گل Attar or otto of roses. – شمعدانی ع. *or* برگ ع. Geranium. – بچیزی ع. زدن To scent s. t. – (بخود) ع. زدن To perfume oneself.
عطرپاش *A*. *P*. Atomizer.
عطر دان *A*. *P*. Scent-box;

scent-bottle [also شیشهٔ عطری].

عطرساز *A. P.* Perfumer.

عطرسازی *or* **عطرکشی** *A. P.* Perfumery; manufacture of perfumes.

عطری *A. P.* Perfumed. Aromatic. *Cf.* معطر ‖ شیشهٔ ع. Scent-bottle.

عطریات *A.* Perfumes; perfumery. [Pl. of عطری regarded as a n.]

عَطسه *A.* Sneeze; sneezing. — ع. زدن *or* ع. کردن To sneeze.

عطسه‌آور *A. P.* Sternutatory.

عَطَش *A.* = تشنگی Thirst. — دفع ع. کردن To quench one's thirst.

عطشان ○ *A.* = **تشنه**

عطش آور *A. P.* Causing thirst; dry.

عَطف *A.* Inclination. Adverting; turning. Connecting. Doubling; bending. [*Of a book*] Backing. — نقطهٔ ع. Turning-point. — ع. کردن *vi.* To refer; advert. —*vt.* To connect. To cause to return. — ع. بماسبق کردن To be retroactive or retrospective. — حرف ع *Gr.* Conjunction.

عُطوفت *A.* = مهربانی Affection; kindness.

عطیه *A.* [عطایا] = بخشش Gift; present.

عظام [Pl. of عظم & عظیم]

عَظم ○ *A.* [عِظام] = **استخوان**

عظمت *A.* = بزرگی Greatness; grandeur. Pomp. Magnificence. Immensity.

عظمی (*ozma*) *A.* [Fem. of اعظم]

عَظیم *A.* 1) *a.* = بزرگ Great. Grand. Magnificent. Immense. 2) *n.* ○ The Highest: ep. of God. [Pl. عِظام usu. in آقایان عظام Honourable gentlemen.]

عظیم‌الجثه *A.* Huge; of enormous size.

عظیم‌الشأن *A.* Great; glorious. *OS.* Of high rank.

عظیمه *A.* 1) *Fem. of* عظیم ‖ 2) *Fem. pr. name.*

عِفاف ○ *A.* = **عفت**

عفت *A.* Chastity; modesty. *Fem. pr. name.*

عِفریت *A.* Demon; afrit. *Met.* Fiendish person. [Fem. عفریته]

عفن ○ (*afan*) *A.* = **عفونت**

عفن (*afen*) *A.* = **گندیده**

عفو (*afv*) *A.* = بخشش Forgiveness. — عفو عمومی Amnesty. — بخشیدن = ع. کردن To pardon; forgive. — قابل ع. Pardonable. — غیرقابل ع. Unpardonable.

عُفونت *A.* Putrefaction. Stink. Infection. — بوی ع. دادن To stink; give off an offensive odour. — دفع ع. Disinfection.

عفونی *A. P.* 1) Infectious: بیماریهای ع. ‖ 2) Infected. — ضد عفونی کردن To disinfect.

عَفیف *A.* [Fem. عفیفه] Chaste.

عِقاب *A.* Punishment. Requital.

عُقاب *A.* = دال Eagle.

عقابی *A*. Aquiline.
عقار o *A*. Landed property.
عقارب [Pl. of عقرب]
عِقال o *A*. Shackle [پابند]. Headband [of the Arabs].
عقاید [Pl. of عقیده]
عقَب *A. n*. Back; rear [پشت]. *OS*. = پاشنه ‖ *C. the pl*. اعقاب ‖ *-a(dv.)* Behind-(hand). Slow. – عقبِ *prep. or* در عقبِ Behind; at the back of. – عقبِ کسی فرستادن To send for s. o. – ازعقبِ (From) behind. After (the death of)*. – ازعقب کسی رفتن To follow s. o. – ع افتادن To be deferred or postponed. To remain behind. To fall into arrears. – ع. انداختن To postpone. To retard. – ع. بردن To set back, as a clock. – ع. زدن *vt*. To push back. To keep b. To withdraw. *–vi*. To recoil. To retreat. – ع. کردن To pursue; follow. To chase. To push back. – ع. کشیدن *vt*. To draw b. To withdraw. *–vi*. To retreat. To flinch. – ع. گذاشتن To leave behind. To outpace; outstrip.
عقب افتادگی *A. P*. Retardation. Lag. Arrearage. Backwarded state.
عقب افتاده *A. P*. Arreared. Lagging behind. Backwarded: کرایهٔ ع. ‖ ملل ع. Backrent.
عقب‌دار *A. P*. Rear-guard.
عقب‌گرد *A. P*. About turn. – ع. کردن To turn about.
عقب نشینی *A. P*. Retreat. – ع. کردن To retreat.
عقَبه *A*. Continuation. Follow-up. Consequence.
عقبی (*aghebi:*) *A P*. Hinder. – درِ ع. Back door. [to come.
عُقبی (-*b*a) *A*. Futurity; life
عقَد *A*. Contract [عقود]. Conclusion (of an agreement). – ع. کردن To conclude a marriage contract with. To marry. To hold; convoke. *OS*. To tie. – ع. بستن To enter into, or conclude, a contract. – عقدِ نماز بستن * To prepare for prayer.
عِقد *A*. [عقود] = **گردن بند**
عقدکنان *A. P*. Party given on the occasion of performing marriage ceremonies.
عقدنامه *A.P*. Marriage contract
عُقده *A*. Knot; node [گره]. Lump (in one's throat). *Anat*. Ganglion. *F*. Problem. Difficulty. Impediment (in speech). Obligation. Pressure. – عقدهٔ دل گشادن To get a thing off one's chest. – عقدهٔ کهتری Inferiority complex.
عقده‌گشا *A. P*. Resolver of difficulties.
عقَدی *A.P*. Married under a contract of unlimited period.

عَقرَب *A.* [عقارب] 1) = کژدم Scorpion. 2) *Astr.* Scorpio. 3) *Old name of* آبان

عقربك *A. P.* Hand (of a watch or clock). Style or gnomon (of a sun-dial). Cramp-iron. *Med.* Whitlow.

عقربه *A. P.* 1) = عقربك Hand (of a timepiece). 2) Pointer.

عَقل *A.* [عُقول] Intellect; reason. Wisdom. — عقل معاش Domestic economy. — عقلش بجائی نرسید He was at his wits' end. — خلاف ع. Injudicious or imprudent. — دندان ع Wisdom-tooth. — عقل کسیرا دزدیدن To throw dust in some one's eyes.

عَقلاً *A.* Rationally; logically.

عُقلاء *A.* [Pl. of عاقل]

عَقلانی *A. P.* = **عقلی**

عُقلائی *A. P.* Reasonable.

عَقلی *A.* Intellectual. Rational. Reasonable. [Fem. عقلیه].

عقلیون *A.* Rationalists. [Pl. of عقلی regarded as a n.]

عُقوبت *A.* Requital; punishment. Torment. — ع. کردن To punish. To torment.

عقود [Pl. of عَقد & عِقد]

عقول [Pl. of عقل]

عَقیده *A.* [عقاید] Belief. Opinion. Idea. — ع. بچیزی داشتن To believe in s. t.; have faith in it. — بعقیدهٔ من In my opinion. — اظهار عقیده کردن To express an o.; make a suggestion.

عقیده مند *A. P.* = **معتقد**

عَقیق *A.* Carnelian; red chalcedony [عقیق سلیمانی]. Agate [عقیق یمانی].

عَقیم *A.* Barren. Abortive; vain. — ع. گذاردن To render abortive. To paralyze. — ع. ماندن To come to nought.

عکا (*Geog.*) Acre.

عکاس *A.* Photographer.

عکاسخانه *A. P.* Photographer's studio.

عکاسی *A. P.* Photography.

عَکس *A.* Photograph; picture. Image. Reverse. — ع. انداختن To take a photograph. To have one's p. taken. — ع. از چیزی برداشتن To p., or take the p. of, s. t. — برعکس On the contrary. Vice versa. — کتاب ع. Picture-book; album.

عکس العمل (*aksol-amal*) *A.* = واکنش Reaction.

عکس برداری *A. P.* Photography. Film-taking. — از چیزی ع. کردن To photograph s. t. To shoot films of s. t.

عکس دار *A. P.* Illustrated. Pictorial. — کارت پستال ع. Picture post-card.

عکسی *A. P.* Photographic. Pictorial. Illustrated.

علاء *A.* = بلندی High rank.

علاءالدین (*A.*) *Mas. pr. name.*

OS. Grandeur of religion.

عِلاج *A*. Remedy. Medical treatment. — ع. کردن To remedy or cure [شفا دادن].

علاج بخش *A. P*. Remedial; medicatory.

علاج پذیر *A. P*. Remediable.

علاج ناپذیر *A. P*. Irremediable.

علاف *A*. Forage-seller. Cornchandler.

عَلاقه *A*. [علائق] Attachment, interest; concern. Tie. *Cf*. دلبستگی ‖ *By e*. Estate; property. *Cf*. ملك

علاقه بند *A.P*. Dealer in thread and trimmings; laceman.

علاقه بندی *A. P*. Dealing in thread or lace; *passementerie*.

علاقه‌مند *A. P*. Interested; concerned. — من بآن ع هستم I am interested in that.

علاقه‌مندی *A. P*. = دلبستگی Interest. Attachment.

علامات [A pl. of علامت]

عَلامَت *A*. [علائم & علامات] Sign; mark [نشان]. Symptom[نشانه]. Signal. Standard; flag[برچم] — ع. گذاشتن To m.

علامه *A*. 1) *a*. Very learned. 2) *n*. Great scholar.

علانیه *A*. Publicity; notoriety.

عَلانِیَةً = آشکارا *ad*.

عِلاوه *A*. Excess; suplus. Addition. — ع. کردن To add. To increase. — ع. بر In addition to. — ع. بر این *or* بعلاوه Furthermore; besides. — بعلاوهٔ In a. to. Plus. — نشان بعلاوه The plus sign.

علائق [Pl. of علاقه]

علائم [A pl. of علامت]

عِلت *A*. [علل] Cause; reason. Defect. Illness. Excessive menstruation. — ذکر علت بجای معلول Metonymy. — ع. بچه *or* چه ع. دارد که Why? — بعلتِ By r. of; because of. — بعلت اینکه Because; for the r. that.

علت‌العلل (*elat-elal*) *A*. First cause. *OS*. Cause of causes.

علت شناسی *A. P*. Aetiology.

عَلف *A*. Grass. Herb. Forage; fodder; provender. — علف تکرگی Star-of-Bethlehem. — علف خشك Dry grass; hay. — علف خنازیر Figwort. — علف شیطان Broomrape; choke-weed. — علف قورباغه Ironwort. — علف ماه Moonwort; lunarium. — علف هرزه Weed. — ع. دادن To feed with fodder. To graze.

علف بُر *A. P*. = **علف چین**

علف چَر *A. P*. Grazer.

علف چین *A. P*. Lawn-mower.

علف‌خوار *A. P*. Herbivorous.

علف‌زار *A.P*. 1) *n*. Grass-plot. 2) *a*. Grassy.

علفی *A. P*. Grassy. Made of hemp or jute fibres.

علقه (*alagheh*) *A*. 1) = زالو 2) Coagulum; grume. 3) ○ Embryo. — علقه مُضغه E. and foetus. *F*. Deformed or misshaped person or creature; also, overweening but mean person.

علقه (*olgheh*) o 1) = علاقه 2) Property.

علك (*alak*) = الك

علك (*elk*) A. Gum or resin. – مصطکی = علك رومی

علل [Pl. of علت]

علم (*alam*) A. [اعلام] Standard; flag [پرچم]. – ع. شدن To signalize oneself. – ع. کردن To erect; raise. To s. To use as a proper noun. – علمای اعلام The distinguished *Ulema*.

علم ِ A. [علوم] Science. Learning. *Cf*. دانش ‖ با علم باینکه In spite of being aware that.

علماً (*elman*) A. Scientifically.

علماء (*olama'*) A. [Pl. of عالم] Scientists. Learned men. The *Ulema* or religious authorities.

علمدار َ A. P. = پرچمدار

علمشناسی ِ A.P. Epistemology.

علم شنگه َ × = غوغا

علم فروش ِ A. P. Pedantic; arrogant; ostentatious.

علمقلم ×(*alamghalam*) Tricky.

علمی ِ A. Scientific. Theoretical. [Fem. علمیه]

علناً (*alanan*) A. – آشکارا *ad*.

علوّ ُ (*olov*) A. = بلندی Elevation; eminence. – علوشأن High rank. – علوطبع Magnanimity. – علو همت H. ambition. Generosity.

علو (*alow*) T. Flame.

علوفه A. Provender; fodder; forage.

علوم [Pl. of علم ِ]

علوی ّ (*ala-*) A. Descendant of Ali. [Fem. علویه]

علوی ُ A. High. Celestial.

علی َ (A.) *Mas. pr. name. OS.* High; eminent. [Fem. علیه]

علی (*ala*) A. = بر Upon; on [used only in A. phrases and compounds.]

علی o (*ola*) A. = بلندی Eminence.

علیا A. [Fem. of اعلی] Higher; greater. – ع. حضرت Her Majesty.

علی الاتصال A. = اتصالاً

علی الاصول A. = اصولاً

علی الاطلاق (*alal-et-*) A. Absolutely. Generally. – حکیم ع. The All-Wise (God).

علی البدل (*alalbadal*) A. Serving as a reserve; appointed as substitute. – عضو علی البدل Substitute; reserve.

علی التحقیق A. = محققاً

علی التوالی A. = متوالیاً

علی الحساب (*alal-hesab*) A. On account; in part payment [Often redundantly برسم ع. or بطور علی الحساب].

علی الخصوص (*alalkho-*) A. = مخصوصاً & بویژه

علی الدوام A. = دائماً

علی السویه (*alasaviyeh*) A.

See سویه [At dawn.

علی الطلوع (*alatolu:*) *A.*

علی الظاهر (*alzaher*) *A.* = ظاهراً

علی العجاله *A. See* عجاله

علی العمیا (*alal-amya*) *A.* = کورکورانه

علی الله *A.* [Short for توکلاً علی الله (*tavakolan-alalah*)] 1) Let us trust on God (and see what will happen). 2) + The hell with it!

علی ای حال (*ala-ayo-*) *A.* In any case.

علیت (*eliyat*) *A.* Causality.

علیحده (*alahedeh*) *A.* = جداگانه Separate(ly).

علی رغم *S. u.* رغم

علیق *A.* Fodder or barley.

علیک *A.* = بر تو Upon thee [in سلام ع. (Peace be upon t.) and ع. السلام (*the reply to it*)].

علیکم (*A.*) *S. u.* سلام [valid.

علیل *A.* Sickly ; infirm ; in-

علیلی *A. P.* Infirmity.

علیم *A.* Omniscient.

علیون & علیین (*eliyi:n*) *A.* The Highest or Seventh Heaven [often اعلی علیین].

علیه (*alayh*) *A.* = براو Upon him. Against him. — برعلیه *or* علیه Against; con.— علیه السلام Peace be upon him; greetings to him.

علیه (*aliyah*) *S. u.* علی (*aliy*)

علیها *A.* (*alay-*) [Fem. of علیه] Upon or against her.

علیهذا (*alahaza*) *A.* = بنا بر این

علیهم (*alayhom*) *A.* = بر ایشان Upon or against them (*the men*).

علیین *S. u.* علیون

عم *A.* Paternal uncle [عمو].

عماد *A.* Pillar [ستون]. Support. *Mas. pr. name* [usu. عمادالدین i. e. Pillar of the Faith].

عمارات [Pl. of عمارت]

عمارت *A.* [عمارات] Building. *Cf.* ساختمان ‖ ع. کردن = 1) ساختن 2) تعمیر کردن

عماری *A.P.* Catafalque; litter.

عماً قریب *A.* (*aman-*) = قریبا

عمال (*omal*) *A.* Agents. Functionaries ; public officers. *Cf. the s.* عامل

عمامه *A.* [عمائم] Turban.

عمد *A.* Intention; design. — عمداً = از روی ع.

عمدا *A.* = دانسته Intentionally.

عمده *A.* 1) *a.* Chief ; main ; leading. 2) *n.* M. subject; chief point = عمدهٔ مطلب ‖ [Used as an ad.]. Ex. ع. فروختن To sell by wholesale.

عمده فروش *A. P.* Wholesaler; wholesale dealer. [trade.

عمده فروشی *A. P.* Wholesale

عمدی *A. P.* Intentional; deliberate.— غیر ع. Unintentional.

عمر (*A.*) *Fictitious name*.— عمر و زید Tom, Dick, and Harry.

عُمر *A*. Life(time). — ع. کردن To live (a specified number of years). — عمرش وفا نکرد His life failed him. — درازیِ ع. Longevity. — عمر دوباره New lease of life.

عمر (*A*.) *Omar: the second successor of the Prophet*.

عِمران *A*. *Amram*: father of Moses.

عُمران *A*. = آبادانی Improvement; reconstruction.

عِمرانی *A*. *P*. Intended for development or improvement; (re)constructive.

عمری (*omra*) *A*. Life-estate. Life-interest.

عُمق *A*. [اعماق] = گودی & ژرفا Depth. — عمق آن چقدر است How deep is it?

عمق پیما *A*. *P*. Sounder. Sounding-instrument; plummet.

عمق پیمایی *A*. *P*. Sounding.

عُمقی o *A*. *P*. 1) Based on depth. 2) = عمیق Deep. — آتش ع *Mil*. File-firing.

عمل *A*. [اعمال] Act; deed. Action. Work. Process. Operation. Practice — (به) ع. آمدن To be manufactured. To be raised or produced. To grow. — خوب ع. نیامده است It has not been properly cooked. — چه اقدامی بعمل آمد؟ What action was taken? — (به) ع. آوردن To produce; manufacture. To raise. To grow. To take: ع. کردن ‖ اقداماتی بعمل آوردم To do; practise; act. To operate on: درکدام بیمارستان او شکمش ع نمیکند ‖ را عمل کردند؟ His bowels do not move. *See* اصالت ع. ‖ کارکردن Pragmatism. — اطاق ع. Operating-room; also, operating-theatre. — حسن ع. Good behaviour or deed. — قابل ع. Operable. — نامهٔ اعمال Record of deeds (*religious term*). — عمل (فلان کس) Sculpsit (such and such a person).

عملاً *A*. In practice.

عملجات *S*. *u*. عمله [tion)

عملکرد *A*. *P*. Revenue (operation)

عملگی *A*. *P*. Work done by a coolie; menial labour. — ع. کردن To work as a c. or labourer.

عمله *A*. 1) Labourers; coolies. *Cf. the s*. عامل ‖ 2) [Treated as singular] Labourer; coolie [pl. عملجات].

عملی *A*. *P*. Practicable. Artificial. Requiring surgical operation. Addicted to smoking opium +. — ع کردن To put in practice; carry out. To render practicable.

عملیات *A*. Operations; activities [used as the pl. of عمل].

عمو *A*. *P*. (Paternal) uncle. — دختر عمو & پسر عمو Cousin.

عمو اقلی *A*. *P*. *T*. Cousin [son

of a paternal uncle].
عمود A. 1) = ستون 2) Perpendicular. 3) o = گرز ‖ خطی را بر خط دیگر عمود کردن To draw a perpendicular to a line.
عموداً A. Perpendicularly; vertically. [dicular.
عمودی A. Vertical; perpen-
عموزاده A.P. Cousin [child of a paternal uncle].
عموم A. The public.— باطلاع ع. رسانیدن To notify the p.
عموما A. Generally; universally. All.
عمومی A. General. Public. Universal. — ع کردن To generalize. To popularize.
عمومیت A. Generality; universality. — ع. دادن To generalize.
عمه A. (Paternal) aunt.— پسرعمه & دختر عمه Cousin.
عمه اقلی A. T. = پسر عمه Cousin [son of a paternal aunt].
عمه زاده A. P. Cousin [child of a paternal aunt].
عمیاء [Fem. of اعمی]
عمید A. 1) o Chief. 2) *Mas. pr. name.*
عمیق A. = گود Deep. Profound.
عمیم o A. General. Comprehensive.
عنا o A. = رنج & محنت
عناب A. = شیلان Jujube.
عناد A. Contumacy. Rebellion.
عناصر [Pl. of عنصر]
عنان A. Rein; bridle [دهنه]. — ع. تافتن * To turn away.
عنانت o A. Impotency.
عناوین [Pl. of عنوان]
عنایات [Pl. of عنایت]
عنایت A. [عنایات] Favour. — ع. کردن To favour (with). To grant.
عنایت‌الله (A.) *Mas. pr. name. OS.* God's favour.
عنبر (*ambar*) A. Ambergris. *Met.* Ringlets; curls.
عنبر بوی * A. P. Fragrant as ambergris.
عنبرچه A. P. Sachel; perfume-cushion; p.-bag. Kind of necklace o.
عنبر ماهی A. P. Sperm-whale.
عنبر نصارا *a. p.* Dung of a she-ass.
عنبری A. Fragrant as ambergris. Perfumed with a. Amber-coloured.— گل ع. Jonquil.
عنبرین * = عنبری
عنبی o A. Grape-like [انگوری]. Vinous.— پردهٔ ع = عنبیه
عنبیه A. Iris of the eye.
عنتر A. [f. G. *entellus*] Barbarian ape; baboon.
عندالاقتضا A. *Same as* لدی‌الاقتضا. *q. v. under* اقتضا
عندالحاجت A. In time of need.
عنداللزوم (*endalozu:m*) A. In case of need.
عندالله (*enda*lah) A. Before God.
عندالمطالبه A. On demand; at call.

عندلیب *A.* [عنادل ٥] = بلبل

عنزوجدین *A.* (*Astr.*) The Kids.

عُنصر *A.* [عناصر] Element. Principle.

عنصری ٥ *A.* 1) *a.* Elemental. 2) *n.* *Name of a poet.*

عنصل *A.* Squill ; sea-onion [usu. پیاز عنصل]. Bulb ٥.

عَنعنات *A.* Series of traditions each beginning with the word عن 'from' (i. e. from such and such a person). Hence, traditions descended from generation to g.

عُنف *A.* = زور Violence.

عنفاً *A.* By violence [بزور].

عُنفوان *A.* Bloom (of youth); prime of life.

عُنق *A.* [اعناق ٥] = گردن

عنقا (*A.*) *Mythical bird of great wisdom, L.* phœnix.

عَنقریب *A.* = بزودی Shortly; soon.

عَنکبوت *A.* [عناکب ٥] = کارتنه

عنکبوتی *A.* Arachnidian. Arachnoid [تنندوبی].

عنن *A* Impotence; impotency.

عِنوان *A.* [عناوین] Title; heading; score. Address ; superscription. *F.* Ground; plea; excuse. — بعناوین مختلف On various grounds ; under v. excuses. — بعنوانِ 1) To (the address of). 2) On the ground of. 3) As : بعنوانِ وام as a loan. — ع. کردن To set forth ; propound. To introduce. To address.

عنیف *A.* = 1) سخت 2) زشت

عِنین *A.* Impotent.

عوا [3] *A.* (*Astr.*) Bootes.

عَوار ٥ *A.* = سوراخ - عیب

عوارض *A.* Charges; taxes. Accidents. *Cf. the s.* عارضه

عواریه [f. Fr. *avarié*] Damaged.

عواطف [Pl. of عاطفه]

عواقب [Pl. of عاقبت]

عوالِم *S. u.* عاَلم

عَوام *A.* The vulgar; the common or illiterate people [often عوام‌الناس *monas*]. *Cf. the s.* مجلس ع. ‖ عام House of Commons. [pular(ly).

عوامانه *A. P.* Vulgar(ly). Popular.

عوام پسند *A. P.* Popular.

عوام فریب *A. P.* Demagogical.

عوام فریبی *A. P.* Demagogy.

عَوامِل *A.* [Pl. of عامل] Agents. Factors. — عوامل مکانیکی Mechanical powers.

عواید *A.* [Pl. of عائده ٥]

عود *A.* Aloes-wood. *Mus.* Lute.

عود (*owd*) *A.* = برگشت Returning. *Med.* Reappearance. — برگشتن = ع. کردن To reappear. To return. [Orpine.

عودالصلیب *A.* [also عود صلیب]

عودت *A.* Returning. *Mil.* Counter-recoil. — ع. دادن To return; give back [برگرداندن].

عود زن *A. P.* Lutist.

عور *A.* (*C. E.*) Naked. [Orig.

pl. of اعور which cf.]. — ع. آمدن × To show flippant moods. To act coquettishly.

عورَت A. 1) = برهنکی 2) *By e.* a) Privy parts. b) = زن ‖ — ستر عورت کردن *S. u.* سَتر

عوَض A. Substitute. Exchange. Reward; compensation. — درعوض Instead. — بعوضِ *or* درعوضِ I. of; in lieu of. For. In exchange for; in return for. — ‖ **پاس بخش** = عوضِ نگهبان ع. دادن To reward. To give in e. — ع. کردن To change. To replace. To relieve.

عوضی A. P. Wrong: ع. کتاب ‖ Changed; exchanged. — ع. گرفتن To mistake (for another person or thing). — ع. گرفته اید I am not the man you are looking for; you have chosen the wrong person.

عوعو + Bowwow. *Cf.* پارس ‖ ع. کردن To bowwow.

عون A. [اعوان] Help; aid. *Cf.* کمك & یاری ‖ بعون‌الله 1) By divine help. 2) = انشاءالله

عهد A. [عُهود] Promise. Covenant; treaty. Testament. Time; era; epoch. — ع. بستن To conclude a treaty. *L.*, to make a promise. — ع. کردن To promise; pledge one's word. — درعهدِ *or* درعهد سلطنتِ In the reign of.

عهد شکن A. P. = **پیمان شکن**

عهد نامه A. P. Treaty.

عهدهُ A. Charge; trust. Responsibility. Undertaking. — از عهدهٔ کاری بر آمدن To be able to do, or succeed in doing, s. t. — برعهده گرفتن To undertake (to do); assume the responsibility of. To guarantee. — بعهدهٔ کسی گذاشتن To charge (*or* entrust) s. o. with (a duty); e. to a person. — بعهدهٔ تعویق افتادن To be postponed or delayed. — عهدهٔ بانک ملی (Drawn) on the National Bank.

عهده‌دار A. P. Responsible. Charged or entrusted. — من عهده‌دارِ آن وظیفه هستم I am charged with that duty. — ع. شدن To undertake.

عهده‌داری A. P. Charge; responsibility; incumbency.

عهدِی A. [*Of a will*] Directive.

عهود [Pl. of عهد]

عیادت A. Visit. — ع. کردن To visit (a sick person).

عیاذ A. = پناه Refuge. — العیاذ بالله God forbid!

عیار (*iar*) A. Fineness; standard (of coins). Criterion. Assay. — طلای ۱۸ ع. Gold 18 carats fine. — ع. گرفتن To assay.

عیار (*ayar*) A. 1) *n.* Impostor 2) *a.* Deceitful; also, sly.

عیارگیر *A. P.* Assayer.

عیاری *A. P.* Imposture. Charlatanry. Slyness.

عیاش *A.* 1) *a.* Pleasure-seeking. 2) *n.* Man of pleasure; luxurious person; reveller.

عیاشی *A. P.* Living in pleasure. Revelry. — ع.کردن To live in p. or voluptuously.

عیال *A.* Wife (and children); family.

عیال‌وار & **عیال مند** *A. P.* Encumbered by a (numerous) family.

عیان *A.* = آشکار Clear; (self-) evident; also, visible. — ع. کردن To clear or explain.

عیب *A.* [عیوب] Defect; fault.— ع. است It is a shame (*or* disgrace). — ع. جستن از *or* ع. گرفتن از To find fault with; cavil. To blame. To criticize. — ع کردن *vi.* To be spoiled or damaged. —*vt.* To blame. — ع. ندارد There is no harm in it. There is nothing wrong with it. — چه ع. دارد All right. It will not h.

عیب پوش *A. P.* Who conceals or palliates others' faults.

عیب پوشی *A. P.* Connivance at others' faults. — ع. کردن To conceal, connive at, or gloss over, a fault.

عیبجو *A. P.* Fault-finder; caviller.

عیبجویی *A. P.* Fault-finding.— ع. کردن [With از] To find fault with; cavil.

عیب‌گیر *A. P.* = **عیبجو**

عیبناك *A. P.* = **معیوب**

عید *A.* [اعیاد] Festival; feast.— ع. گرفتن To celebrate (a festival). — عید شما مبارك (باد) Happy New Year.

عیدی *A. P.* New-Year gift.

عیسو *or* **عیصو** *A-Heb.* Esau.

عیسوی *A.* Christian.

عیسویت o *A.* = **مسیحیت**

عیسی (*i:sa*) *A.* Jesus.

عیش *A.* Pleasure. (Living in) luxury. *OS.* = زندگی ‖ ع.کردن To live in pleasure or luxury. To enjoy oneself. — عیش و نوش Feasting and drinking; luxury; pleasure.

عیش طلب *a. p.* Pleasure-seeking. *Cf.* عیاش

عین *A.* = 1) چشم 2) چشمه 3) ذات *Cf. the plurals* عیون o & اعیان ‖ عینِ نامه The original letter. — در عین حال At the same time. — عین خیالش نیست + He doesn't care a fig; he couldn't care less. — عین مرحمت است It is the greatest favour.— اسم ع. = اسم ذات

عینا (*eynan*) *A.* 1) Exactly; just. 2) In the original form. — نامه ع. پس فرستاده شد

The o. letter was sent back. 3) Literally. 4) In kind [جنساً].

عین الثور *A.* (*Astr.*) Aldebaran. *OS.* The eye of the Taurus.

عین الحیات *A.* Fountain of life.

عین الشمس *A.* Precious opal ; noble o. ; fire o.; girasol(e).

عین الناس *A.* = **اناناس**

عین الهر *A.* = Cat's-eye; opal.

عین الیقین *A.* Positive knowledge.

عینك *A. P.* Glasses. – ع. زدن *or* ع. گذاشتن To wear glasses. – عینك آتشی Burning-glasses. – عینك آفتابی Sun-glasses. – عینك دودی Smoked glasses. – عینك فنری عینك شاخدار Spectacles. – *or* عینك دماغی *Pince-nez* ; eye-glasses. – عینك یك‌چشمه Monocle.

عینك ساز *A. P.* Optician.

عینك سازی *A. P.* Optician's trade.

عینك فروش *A. P.* Dealer in glasses or optical goods.

عینکی *A. P.* Spectacled. – مار عینکی Cobra.

عینه (*eynohu:*) *A.* 1) The thing itself; the original (thing). 2) + Exactly [بعینه].

عینی *A.* (*Law*) Irreplaceable, as a right or property. Identical.

عینیت *A.* Identicalness.

عیوب [Pl. of عیب]

عیوق *A.* (*Astr.*) The Capella.

عیون [A pl. of عین].

غات غات *or* قات قات Cackle.— غ. كردن To cackle.

غار *A.* Cave; cavern. Den. — يارغار *Ep. of Abubakr, who accompanied Mohammed in his flight and on one occasion went with him into a cave. Met.* Bosom friend.

غار *A.* Laurel(-tree).

غارت *A.* Plunder; pillage. — غ. كردن To plunder. — به غ. رفتن To be plundered.

غارت زده *A. P.* Plundered.

غارت گر *A. P.* Plunderer. Robber. [Robbery.

غارتگری *A. P.* Plundering.

غاردانه *A. P.* Laurel berries.

غار غار Croaking; cawing. — غ. كردن To croak.

غارگيلاس *A. P.* Cherry-laurel.

غار نشين *A. P.* Cave-dweller.

غار و غور + Rumbling noise. Croaking. Rumour o.

غاريقون *A.G.* Larch agaric.

غاز [*f. T.* قاز] Goose. — غاز نر Gander.

غاز *or* قاز Money of account worth half a دينار 'dinar'.

غازه *or* غاژه o = سرخاب Rouge.

غازی o *A.* [غزات] Warrior fighting against infidels.

غاشيه *A.* [غواشی] 1) = زين پوش Saddle cover. 2) *Z.* Mantle.— غ. كشيدن * To be submissive.

غاصب *A. n.* Usurper. Extortioner. —*a.* Usurping. Tyrant.

غافث *A.* Agrimony.

غافل *A.* Negligent. Unaware. Heedless. — غ. شدن To take no notice. — غ. از اينكه U. of the fact that; little knowing that.— غ. كردن To deceive the vigilance of. — غ. گرفتن To surprise; seize unawares.

غافل گير كردن *A. P.* To come upon unawares; surprise.

غافلگيری *A. P.* Surprisal; attacking unawares.

غافلی *A. P.* = عفلت - بيخبری

غالب *A. a.* Prevailing. Conquering. —*n.* Most (part); majority.— غ. آمدن *or* غ. شدن [With بر] To prevail upon; p. over. To overcome.

غالباً *A.* Frequently; very often; mostly.

غالبيت *A.* 1) Predominance. 2) o = پيروزی

غاليه o *A.* Perfume composed of musk and ambergris.

غامض *A.* Abstruse. Obscure.

غامضه *A.* [غوامض] Abstruse or difficult problem. [Orig. fem. of غامض]

غانقرایا *A.G.* Gangrene.
غایِب [f. A. غائب] *a.* Absent. Hidden. *–n.* A. person; absentee [pl. غائبین]. – غ. شدن To absent oneself. To be a. To hide o.; abscond. To disappear.– غ. کردن To hide; conceal [usu. pronounced '*ghayem-*].
غایب شدنك *or* **غایب موشك** *A. P.* Hide-and-seek.
غائبی *A. P.* Mark of absence. Absent student, soldier, etc.
غایَت *A.* [غایات] Extreme limit; end. (Desired) object.– بدین غ. To this extent. – بغایت Extremely. – از دوم لغایتِ ششم From the 2 nd. to the 6th. inclusive.
غائر o *A.* Internal. – ورید غائر I. (jugular) vein.
غایط [f. A. غائط] Feces.
غائله *A.* Disturbance; riot. *OS.* Hatred. Evil.
غائی *A.* Final : علت غ.
غِبّ o *A.* Visiting every other day. *Med.* Tertian : نوبهٔ غب T. fever.
غباً o *A.* Every other day [یك روز درمیان]. Alternately.
غُبار *A.* Dust. *Med.* Nebula.
غبار آلود(ه) *A. P.* Dusty; soiled. [Dusty.
غباردار *A. P.* Misty; dim.
غباری *A. P.* Dusty; dust-coloured. Misty. Nebular.

غَبراء o Surface of the earth.
غِبطه خوردن *A. P.* To envy or emulate [with به].
غَبغب *A.* Double chin. [*Of a cow*] Dewlap; jowl.
غَبن *A.* State of being cheated in business. Fraud.
غِثیان *A.* Nausea. – غ. کردن To nauseate. *S. a.* قی کردن
غُدّ × = 1) کله شق 2) خودبین
غَدّار *A.* = **خائن**
غَدّاره *T.* Broadsword; glaive.
غدد [Pl. of غده].
غَدر *A.* = **خیانت** (کردن)
غُدغُد Clucking. – غ. کردن To cluck or chuck.
غدغن etc. *See* **قدغن** etc.
غُدّه *A.* [غُدَد] Gland.
غده‌ای *A. P.* Glandular; glandulous.
غَدیر *A.* Pool; fond. [Only in عید غدیر festival celebrated on the occasion of Ali being appointed successor of Mohammed : so-called because the event took place near a pool called غدیرِ خُم].
غِذاء *A.* [اغذیه] = خوراك Food; meal. Diet.– غ. خوردن To eat; take food. – غ. دادن (به) To feed. To board.– سرِ غذا At table; at mess. – صورت غ. Menu; bill of fare.
غذائی *A.* Alimentary; nutritious. [Fem. غذائیه Ex. موادِ غذائیه Foodstuffs; articles

of food].

غذائیت *A*. Nutritiveness; nutritiousness. [nutritive.

غذائیت دار *A. P*. Nutritious;

غر + Moving of the hips or loins in dancing; shimmy (*near parallel*)– construed with دادن

غُر Ruptured. Depressed; sunk. — غر شدن To contract hernia. To be depressed.

غُر 1) *Imp. of* غریدن 2) Grumble [often غرولند]. — غر زدن *vi*. To grumble or murmur. –*vt*. × To pinch; pick up, or entice away, as a woman.

غَرّاء *A*. Excellent; brilliant; gushing. Fervent.

غُراب *A*. 1) *n*. (a) Raven. (b) *Astr*. Corvus. 2) *a*. + Arrogant and selfish.

غرابالبین • *A*. Kind of raven whose appearance was supposed to forebode separation from friends.

غَرابَت *A*. Strangeness; queerness. Peculiarity. — غرابتی ندارد There is nothing strange about it.

غُرابی *A.P*. Crow-like; corvine. — نان غ. *Kind of* macaroon.

غَرغره کردن *A.P*. To rinse the mouth.

غَرامَت *A*. [غرامات] Indemnity; damages; reparations. Compensation. — غرامت خسارات کسیرا دادن To indemnify s. o. for his losses; compensate his l.

غُرّان Roaring. Thundering.

غَرائب *A*. Strange things; wonders. Freaks. *Cf. the s*. غریبه

غَرب *A*. = باختر West. The W. or Occident.

غربا *A*. On the west. To the w.

غرباء [Pl. of غریب]

غِربال *A*. Coarse sieve; riddle; screen. — غ. کردن To r. or sift.

غربالی *A*. 1) Cribriform. 2) (*Anat*.) Ethmoid.

غُربَت *A*. Being away from one' home (town). Exile. — غ. اختیار کردن To travel abroad. To emigrate.

غربتی *A. P*. (Homeless and vagrant as a) gypsy.

غَربی *A*. = باختری Western.

غربیله Sinuous movement of the body. Coquettish gesture.

غَرس *A*. Planting. — غ. کردن To plant. *Cf*. نشاندن & کاشتن

غُرّش Roar(ing). — غ. کردن To roar. To thunder.

غَرَض *A*. [اغراض] Motive; purpose. Private motive. Grudge; spite. — باس غ. دارد He bears me a grudge. — غ. ورزیدن To bear or entertain a g. To show partiality.

غرض آمیز & غرض آلود *A. P*. Based on private motives or personal interest. Tendentious. Partial. Spiteful.

غرض‌ورزی & غرض‌رانی *A. P.* Act(s) based on private motives; partial behaviour.

غُرغُر *or* **قرقر** Grumbling; murmuring; muttering. – غ. کردن To grumble.

غُرغُرو Given to grumbling. Shrewish : زن غ.

غَرغَره *A.* Gargling. Gargle. – غ. کردن To gargle.

غِرغِره *or* **قرقره** Spool. Pulley. – غرغرهٔ القاء Induction-coil.

غرغشه Wrangle. Fuss. Worry.

غُرفه *A.* [غُرَف & غرفات] Booth. Upper chamber *.

غَرق *A.* Drowning; being drowned. – غ. شدن To be d.; drown. To sink, as a ship. – غ. کردن To d. or sink. – غرقِ افتخارات Laden with honours. – غرق اندیشه Absorbed in thinking. – غرق بدهی Plunged in debt. [Whirlpool.

غرقاب *A. P.* Deep water.

غرقه *A.* Drowned. – غ. بخون Weltering in one's blood.

غُرَماء *A.* [Pl. of غریم o] Creditors o. – غ. کردن + To distribute among the creditors in proportion to their claims, as a bankrupt's estates [short for بغرماء تقسیم کردن]. – داخل در غرماء شدن To rank as creditor in the estates of a bankrupt.

غُرنبیدن To roar. *S. a.* رمبیدن

غرّان = غُرّنده

غُروب *A.* = شام Sunset; evening. – غ. کردن To set.

غُرور *A.* Pride; vanity. – غرورِ جوانی 1) P. or impetuosity of youth. 2) *Med.* Acne.

غُروش *T.* Piaster. [Cocksure.

غَرّه *A.* Deluded. Proud.

غُرّه *A.* [غُرَر o] First day of a lunar month. Blaze. Frontlet of a horse o.

غَریب *A.* 1) *a.* Strange; queer. Foreign [بیگانه]. Lonely. Not feeling at home. [Fem. غریبه]. 2) *n.* [Pl. غُرَباء] Stranger. Foreigner.

غریب‌گز *A. P.* Kind of nettle supposed to bite only strangers. [strangers.

غریب نواز *A. P.* Hospitable to

غریب نوازی *A. P.* Hospitality to strangers. – غ. کردن To show hospitality, or be hospitable, to strangers.

غریبه *A.* [Orig. fem. of غریب]. 1) Strange thing [only in the pl. غرائب *q. v.*]. 2) + Stranger.

غریبی *A. P.* 1) = غربت 2) = بیگانگی 3) Sad verse describing the condition of a lonely stranger [*obsolete*].

غُریدن [غر] 1) To grumble; murmur. 2) [Often غُرّیدن] To roar. To rave. To thunder. [Nature.

غَریزه *A.* [غَرائز] Instinct.
غریزی *A.* Instinctive. Natural.— غ. گرمای N. heat; animal h.
غَریق *A.* Drowned or drowning (person).
غَریو • Clamour; exclamation — غریویدن *or* غ. بر آوردن To clamour or exclaim.
غَزا o *A.* War (against infidels) *Cf.* جنگ & جهاد
غَزال *A.* = آهو Gazelle.
غَزل *A.* Lyric poem; love-p.; ode.— غزلغزلها Song of Songs; Canticles. — غزل خداحافظی را خواندن To prepare for going; say good-bye.
غَزلاغ Lark.
غزل خوان *A. P.* (Person) who sings lyric poems or odes.
غزل سرا *A. P.* 1) = غزل خوان 2) Composer of lyric poems or odes.
غزل سرایی *A. P.* Singing or composing lyrics.
غزلیات *A.* (Collection of) lyric poems or odes.
غزنوی *Ghaznavi* (*Dynasty*). (Founder or member) of the *G. D.*
غَزوه o *A.*·[غَزَوات] (Mohammed's) war against infidels.
غِژ + Ping; whiz.
غِژغِژ + Creaking noise.
غسال *A.* = مرده شوی
غسال خانه *A. P.* = مرده شوی‌خانه
غساله o 1) *a.* Washing or purging. 2) *n.* Woman who washes dead women's bodies.
غُسل *A.* (Ceremonial) washing; ablutions. — غ. دادن To wash (ceremonially). To dip. — غ. کردن To perform one's a.
غَش [f. A. غشی] Swooning; fit. — غش کردن To swoon; fall into a fit; faint. — از خوشی غش کرد He was transported with joy. — برای چیزی غش کردن To be dying (or crazy) for s. t. — نوبهٔ غش Convulsive or comatous malaria.
غِش *A.* Fraud. Counterfeit coin. [Only in بیغش *q. v.*]
غِشاء *A.* [اغشیه] Membrane [now شامه]. Film; coat. Covering.— اغشیهٔ دماغی Meninges.— ورم اغشیهٔ دماغی Meningitis.
غشائی *A.* Membraneous.
غُشه [f. T. قشه] Race.— غ. گذاشتن To run a race.
غَشی *A. P.* Habitually swooning; epileptic. Syncopal.
غَصب *A.* Usurpation.— غ. کردن To usurp. To misappropriate. To extort.
غصباً *A.* Usurpingly.
غَصبی *A. P.* Usurped.
غُصن o *A.* [اغصان] = شاخه
غُصه *A.* Grief; sorrow [اندوه]. Worry. — غ. خوردن To be grieved; become sorrowful.— چه غ. ایست There's no cause

for worry; don't bother.
غصه خور *A. P.* (One) who gives way to grief.
غصه خوری *A. P.* Sorrowing; grieving; worrying.
غصه‌دار *A. P.* Having a worry or worries; sorrow-stricken.
غضب *A.* = خشم Anger; wrath. — غ. کردن *vi.* To get angry. —*vt.* To disfavour. — بغضب آوردن To make a.; provoke; rouse to anger.
غضب آلود(ه) *A. P.* = غضبناك
غضبان *A.* = 1) غضبناك 2) تند خو
غضبناك *A. P.* = خشمگین Angry.
غضروف *A.* Cartilage.
غضروف‌شناسی *A.P.* Chondrology.
غضروفی *A.* Cartilageous; chondroid.
غضنفر *A.* = شیر Lion. *Mas. pr. name.*
غطاء ٥ *A.* = پرده - پوشش
غفار *A.* 1) = بخشنده 2) *Mas. pr. name.*
غفرالله (*ghafara*lah) *A.* May [God forgive.
غفران *A.* = آمرزش - بخشش
غفلت *A.* Neglect; carelessness. — غ. کردن *or* غ. ورزیدن To neglect. [careless.
غفلت کار *A. P.* Neglectful;
غفلة *A.* All of a sudden; unexpectedly.
غفور *A.* = غفار
غفیر *A.* Numerous [only in جم غ. ٥ Large crowd].
غل + Roll(ing). — غل خوردن *vi.* & غل دادن *vt.* To roll.
غل *A.* 1) = کینه 2) = فریب [only in بیغل و غش *q. v.*].
غل + Boiling. — غل زدن To boil [جوشیدن].
غل *A.* Iron collar; chains. Yoke [یوغ].
غلا *A.* Dearth.
غلات [Pl. of غله]
غلاظت *A.* 1) Coarseness. 2) = غلظت
غلاف *A.* Sheath; scabbard [نیام]. Case [جلد]. Cover [پوشش]. Pod. Vagina. — غ. کردن *vt.* To sheathe. To invaginate. —*vi.* × To draw in one's horns.
غلافی *A. P.* Sheath-like. Vaginal. — پیوند غلافی Cleft-grafting; chink-grafting. — لولهٔ غ. Casing [also لولهٔ جداری].
غلام *A.* Slave [بنده]. Page; lad. Servant [نوکر]. *Cf. the pl.* غلمان [Sodomite.
غلام پاره & غلام باره *A. P.*
غلامزاده *A. P.* The child of your slave. [*In p. c.*] My child or son.
غلام سیاه *A. P.* Negro slave.
غلام‌گردش *A. P.* Corridor.
غلامی *A. P.* = بردگی Slavery.
غلبه *A.* Prevalence; predominance. Victory. [In rhetoric] Autonomasia. — غلبهٔ خون Hyperaemia; also, congestion. — غ. کردن [With بر] To prevail (*or* win) over. To overcome; defeat.

غَلت 1) *Imp. of* غلتیدن 2) *n.* Roll(ing). *Mus.* Trill.

غلتان Rolling. [*Of a pearl*] Round and unbored.

غلتاندن To roll *vt.*

غلتبان 1) Cuckold. 2) = بام غلتان

غَلتك Roller. Castor; small wheel. Hoop. Pulley. *F.* + Routine. — غ. زدن To roll; use a roller on (a house-top) — روی غ افتادن + To get into a groove; be set on its feet.

غلت‌گاه Inclined plane.

غلتیدن [غلت] To roll. To wallow. To welter: در خون غ.

غَلط *A.* [اغلاط] 1) Mistake; error.— غلطچاپی Typographical error; misprint. — غلط دستوری Solecism. — غلط مشهور Error allowed by usage; customary error. — غ. کردن To make a mistake. — غ. کردم I made a mistake; I repent. — غ. کردید [*Used as an insult*] You should repent for the silly act (or remark). — غ. گفتم * Nay.— غ. گرفتن بر To correct or criticize [*also with* از]. 2) [*Used as an a.*] Erroneous; incorrect [نادرست]. Wrong: جواب غ. ‖ Wrongful. 3) [*Used as an ad. for* بغلط] Erroneously; improperly; amiss. Wrong: غ. حدس زدن ‖ غ. افتادن * To happen to be in the wrong place. — بغلط افتادن To be led into an error.

غلط انداز *A. P.* Misleading; delusive.

غلطانیدن etc. = غلتانیدن etc.

غلط کاری *A. P.* Wrong-doing; misdeed. Corruption.

غلط گیری *A. P.* Proof-reading. — غ. کردن *vi.* To read a proof. —*vt.* To correct.

غلط نامه *A. P.* Errata.

غلطی + *A. P.* = 1) اشتباهی 2) اشتباهاً

غِلظت *A.* Viscosity. Concentration. Density. *F.* Coarseness.

غُلغُل Gurgle. Bubbling (noise); ebullition. — غ. زدن To bubble; boil. — غ. کردن To gurgle. To uproar.

غُلغُلك Jug (which keeps water cool), goglet.

غِلغِلك +Tickling; titillation.— غ. دادن To tickle. — غلغلکش میشود He is ticklish.

غِلغِلکی + Ticklish.

غُلغُله *A.* Confused noise; hubbub; tumult.

غِلغِلی + = غلغلك. Tickling.

غُلفه or قلفه *A.* Prepuce; foreskin.

غلق [f. T. قِلق] Mood.

غُلك Money-pot; money-box.

غِلمان *A.* Handsome lads dwelling in Paradise. *Cf.* غلام

غُلنبه + 1) *a.* Bombastic; grandiloquent. Pindaric. Protuberant. 2) *n*. Lump. Protuberance.

غلوّ *A*. Exaggeration or hyperbole [in rhetoric]. — غ. کردن To exaggerate.

غلّه *A*. [غلات] Corn; grain; cereals. — انبار غله Granary.

غلیان (*ghala*-) *A*. Boiling; ebullition [جوش]. *F*. Excitement. — غ. کردن To boil. To ferment.

غلیان or قلیان (*ghal*-) Nargileh; hookah. — غ. کشیدن To smoke a nargileh.

غلیظ *A*. Thick; concentrated; viscous. Dense. *F*. * Rude; coarse. — غ. شدن To thicken *vi*. — غ. کردن To thicken *vt*.; concentrate; inspissate.

غلیظی *A*. *P*. = غلظت

غلیواج Kite (*bird*).

غم *A*. [f. A. غمّ —pl. غموم o] Sorrow; grief [اندوه]. Worry; care. — غ. خوردن To worry. — غم کسی را خوردن To care for s. o.; also, sympathize with him. — غمی نیست There is no cause for worry. *Cf*. غصه

غمّاز *A*. Tale-bearer [سخن‌چین]. Slanderer [بدگو]. Eavesdropper.

غمازك *A*. *P*. Cork-float.

غمازی *A*. *P*. Tale-bearing. Slander. Eavesdropping.

غم انگیز *A*. *P*. Sad; doleful.

غمباد *A*.*P*. Swelling (believed to be caused by sorrow).

غمخوار *A*. *P*. *n*. One who looks after a person with tender care. —*a*. Sympathetic.

غمخواری *A*. *P*. Sympathetic care or attendance.

غمخور *A*. *P*. Afflicted; who partakes of others' sorrow.

غمخورك *A*. *P*. = بوتیمار

غمدیده *A*. *P*. Afflicted.

غمز o *A*. Wink. Hint [اشاره]. Tale-bearing. Slander.

غمزدا * *A*. *P*. Removing sorrow; cheering. [afflicted.

غمزده *A*. *P*. Sorrow-stricken;

غمزه *A*. Ogling; amorous glance. *OS*. A wink. *Cf*. غمز ‖ غ. کردن To ogle.

غمض *A*. Connivance; condonation [also غمض عین]. — غمض کلام Reticence; preterition. — غمض‌عین کردن از To connive at.

غم فزا * *A*. *P*. Causing grief.

غمگسار * *A*. *P*. = غمخوار

غمگین *A*.*P*. Sad. Sorry. — غ شدن To feel (*or* become) sad.

غمگینی *A*. *P*. Sorrow.

غمین * *A*. *P*. = غمگین

غنا *A*. = بی نیازی Freedom from want. Riches o. *See* غنی

غِناء *A*. [اغنیه] Singing; song; music.

غنا o (*ghana*) *A*. = خرّم Verdant.

غنائم [Pl. of غنیمت]

غنج *P*-*A*. Amorous jest; leer.

غنج Cutworm; plusia; also,

cabbage butterfly.
غُنچه Bud. – غ کردن To bud; put forth buds. To purse : لب های خود را غنچه کرد
غنچه دهان * With a bud-like (i. e. small) mouth.
غُند a. o Gathered together. n. (Ph.) Mass.
غُنده + Grumbling [غُرغُر]. – غ. زدن To grumble.
غَنم A. [اغنام] Flock.
غُنودن * [غنو o (ghanav)] To sleep; repose; nestle.
غُنه A. Twang; nasal pronunciation. See تو دماغی
غَنی A. 1) a. Free from want [بی نیاز]. Rich [دولتمند&توانگر]. 2) n. [Pl. اَغنیاء] R. man.
غَنیمت A. [غنائم] Booty; spoil. F. Windfall. – غ. دانستن or غ. شمردن To make the most of; avail oneself of.
غو – قو
غواشی [Pl. of غاشیه]
غَوّاص A. Diver. – غواص مروارید Pearl-diver; pearl-fisher. – اسفرود = مرغ غ.
غواصی A. P. Diving. – غ. کردن To dive; be a diver.
غوامض [Pl. of غامضه]
غوچ [f. T. قوچ] Ram. – غوچ زل Merino. – o غوچ قلعه خراب کن Battering-ram. – غوچ وحشی Moufflon; wild sheep.
غور (ghowr) A. Bottom; depth o. – در چیزی غ. کردن – To go deep into s. t.; study it profoundly.
غورت [Also غُرت] Gulp; draught. – غ. انداختن × To talk big; bluff. – غ. دادن To swallow, as food.
غوررسی A. P. Deep investigation. – غ. کردن [With در] To investigate deeply.
غوره Sour grapes; unripe g. – غ. چلاندن + To shed forced tears; also, weep (for no good reason). – غ. نشده مویز شدن To try to run before one has learned to walk (or creep).
غوزك Malleolus.
غوزکی Malleolar.
غوزه or قوزه Boll; cotton-pod. – کرم غ. Bollworm. Cocoon.
غوش or غوشه Birch.
غوص o A. Diving. F. Going deep into a matter [غور].
غوطه A. Plunging; duck. – غ خوردن To plunge; dive. – غ. دادن To p. or dive. To immerse.
غوطه ورشدن A.P. = غوطه خوردن
غوغا A. Uproar; tumult. Disturbance; riot. – غ (بر پا) کردن To raise an uproar or disturbance. To quarrel.
غوك = وزغ Frog.
غول A. [غیلان o] Ghoul; ogre. By e. Giant. – غول بی شاخ و دم Met. Tall or burly rude fellow; huge beast.

غياب *A.* Absence. – **حكم غيابی** Judgment by default.

غياباً *A.* In one's absence. By default.

غياث *A.* Help. Redress of grievances. *Mas. pr. name.*

غيار کردن *A.P.* To pare (a hoof).

غيب *A.* The invisible or mysterious; hidden things. – خزانهٔ غ. God's i. treasure or h. store.– عالم غ. The i. world.– علم غ. Prescience. Divining power. – غ. شدن To vanish; disappear. – غ. گفتن To divine; foretell (events). – غيبش زد + He vanished or disappeared; he slipped off.

غيباندن *A. P.* [غيبان] To palm or conceal, as in jugglery. To cause to vanish.

غيبت *A.* Backbiting; speaking ill of an absent person. Absence. – غ کردن To absent oneself; be absent. [With از] To backbite.

غيب دان *A. P.* Omniscient; prescient.

غيبگو *A. P.* Diviner.

غيبگوئی *A. P.* Divination.

غيبی *A. P.* Occult; invisible. Oracular: صدای غ.

غير *n.* [pl. اغيار] Another (person). Stranger; foreigner [بيگانه] –*a.* (An)other; different. – غيرِ *gheyre* [*used as a prep.*] = جز & بجز Except. Other than. Outside.– در غيرِ ساعات اداری O. the office hours. – غير از *or* بغير از. Except; save; with the exception of. Other than.– بغيرِ Except. Without. –*Note.* غيرِ usu. renders the prefixes *im-*, *in-*, *un-*, and the like, mostly before A. adjectives. Ex. غير ارادی involuntary; غير رسمی unofficial.

غيرت *A.* Zeal; enthusiasm. Jealousy; emulation. – سرِ غيرت آوردن To rouse the jealousy of. To put (s. o.) on his mettle. To defy. To give ardour to. – بالای غيرتتان + I appeal to your sense of honour; be generous enough to. [lous.

غيرت کش *A. P.* Partisan. Jealous.

غيرتی *A. P.* = 1) تعصبی 2) با غيرت

غيره + *A. P.* Stranger.

غيره (*gheyro*h) *A.* Other than that (*or* he). [Only in وغيره 'and so forth; etc.'].

غيظ *A.* Indignation; anger. – غ. کردن To feel indignant; get angry. *Cf.* قهر کردن

غيلان [Pl. of غول]

غيورَ *A.* Zealous. Jealous; intolerant of rivalry.

غيورانه *A. P.* Zealously. Jealously.

فابريك *Fr.* = كارخانه

فاتح *A.* 1) *a.* = پيروز Victorious.– ف. شدن To conquer ; win a victory. 2) *n.* Conqueror. *Mas. pr. name.*

فاتحه *A.* Introduction ; exordium. سورهٔ ف. The opening chapter of the Koran. – فاتحهٔ چيزيرا خواندن To ring the knell of s. t. ; consider it done for.– ف. براى كسى نخواندن To pay no attention to s. o.

فاتحه خوانى *A. P.* Assembly convened to pray for the dead. *OS.* Reciting the فاتحه *q. v.*

فاتر o *A.* Weak; lukewarm.

فاجر *A.* 1) *n.* Debauchee. 2) *a.* Lewd. [Fem. فاجره]

فاجع *A.* Calamitous. Tragic. Unexpected. *Cf.* فاجعه

فاجعه *A.* [فواجع] Calamity ; disaster. Tragic event; tragedy. [Orig. fem. of فاجع]

فاحش *A.* Notorious. Obscene.– شكست ف. Signal defeat. – غبن ف. Gross fraud.

فاحشگى *A. P.* Whoredom.

فاحشه *A.* [فواحش] Prostitute.

فاحشه خانه *A. P.* Brothel.

فاخته *A.* Ringdove.

فاخر *A.* Fine ; sumptuous ; rich; costly : لباس ف.

فادزهر = پادزهر

فارس *Fars* : large province in South Iran. Persia(n).

فارسه Persepolis.

فارسى Persian (language).

فارغ *A.* Free ; disengaged. Through (with one's work) ف. شدن To get through. To be delivered (of a child).. ف. كردن To release. To disburden; disengage.

فارغ البال *A.* = آسوده خاطر

فارغ التحصيل *A.* One who has finished a course of study ; graduate.

فاروق *A.* Discriminating *a.*– ترياق ف. Thebaic electuary.

فاز *Fr.* Phase.– سه ف. 3-phased

فاستونى or فاصتونى Serge. [Per. f. Fr. *façonné*].

فاسد *A.* Corrupt; depraved. Rotten. – ف. شدن To decay. To deteriorate. To be depraved.–ف. كردن To deprave; corrupt. To decay. To vitiate. To eat away; canker.

فاسدالاخلاق *A.* Immoral.

فاسدالعقيده *A.* Heretic.

فاسق *A.* Lewd (person); libertine. Paramour.

فاش Open(ly). Frank(ly). – ف. کردن To reveal; divulge.

فاشیست *Fr.* Fascist.

فاشیسم *Fr.* Fascism.

فاصِل *A.* Separating *a.* – خط ف. Line of demarcation

فاصِله *A.* [فواصل] Space. Distance. Interval. Interruption. – فاصلهٔ کانونی Focal distance or length. – ف. دادن To space. – ف. گرفتن To keep aloof. – بفاصلهٔ دو روز In two days. – بلافاصله Immediately; uninterruptedly.

فاصله زن *A. P.* Space-bar.

فاصله‌گیر *A. P.* Spacer.

فاضِل *A.* 1) *a.* Learned; scholarly. [Fem. فاضله]. Surplus. 2) *n.* L. man; scholar [pl. فضلاء]. Remainder; residue. Surplus.

فاضل آب *A. P.* Sewage; surplus water. – مجرای ف. Sewer.

فاطمه (*A.*) *Fem. pr. name.*

فاعِل *A.* Doer; agent. – فاعل مختار Having free will. – اسم ف. Name of the agent. Active participial adjective.

فاعلیت *A.* Agency o. – حالت ف. Nominative case.

فاق *A.* Split. Notch. – ف. خوردن *vi.* & ف. دادن *vt.* To split.

فاقد *A.* Missing; wanting. – ف. بودن To miss; lack. – فاقدِ شرایط لازمه Lacking necessary qualifications; disqualified.

فاقه *A.* = **تنگدستی**

فاکتور [f. Fr. *facture*] = سیاهه Invoice; bill.

فاکتور [f. Fr. *facteur*] Factor [only in فاکتورگیری Factoring].

فاکهه o *A.* [فواکه] = **میوه**

فال *A.* Omen. Fortune. Lot. – ف. گرفتن To tell fortunes; also, have one's fortune told. To divine. To consult a book. – بفال نیك گرفتن To augur well from; consider as a good omen. – فال ورق Cartomancy. [*S. a.* فالگیر.

فال بین *A. P.* Bibliomancer.

فالِج *A.* Paralyzed (person); paralytic. – ف. شدن To be paralyzed. – ف. کردن To paralyze; maim.

فالگیر *A. P.* Fortune-teller.

فالگیری *A. P.* Soothsaying. – ف. کردن To tell fortunes.

فالوده = **پالوده** *n.*

فام Colour. [*Used as a suf.*]

فامیل [f. Fr. *famille*] = خانواده Family.

فامیلی *Fr. P.* = **خانوادگی**

فانتزی *Fr.* Fancy *a.*: اجناس ف.

فانسقه *or* **فانوسقه** Cartridge-belt. [Corruption of T. بالاسقه]

فانوس *A.* (Paper) lantern. [*Of a camera*] Bellows. – فانوس دریایی Pharos; lighthouse. – فانوس فنری Folding lantern. – فانوس شعبده Magic

1. – فانوس هوائی Fire-balloon.
فانی *A.* Mortal. Transient.
فایده [f. A. فائده –pl. فوائد] Profit [سود]. Use; utility. Moral of a story. – ف. بردن To derive a benefit. To make a profit.– ف. بخشیدن To be useful. – ف. کردن To be profitable; sell at a profit; also, make a p.
فائز شدن *A. P.* To attain. To obtain.
فائض *A.* Abundant. Diffusing. [Liberal.
فائق *A.* Excellent; superior.– ف. آمدن بر To surmount.
فائقه *A.* 1) *a.* [Fem. of فائق].– احترامات ف. را تقدیم میدارد Assuring you of our highest esteem, . . . 2) *n. Fem. pr. name.*
فبها *A* Well Ex اگر بپرداخت ف. وگرنه عارض خواهم شد If he pays it, well; but if not, I will go to law.
فتادن = افتادن
فتان *A. a.* Fascinating. –*n.* Seducer.
فَتح *A.* [فتوح & فتوحات] Conquest; victory [پیروزی]. *OS.* Opening. – ف. کردن *vt.* To conquer. To open. –*vi.* To win a v. – فتح باب کردن To be the first to begin a custom, business, etc.
فتح‌الله (*A.*) *Mas. pr. name. OS.* God's conquest.
فتراك o Saddle-strap.
فَترت *A.* Interval. [For ایام ف.] Interregnum. [rupture.
فَتق *A.* [Also باد فتق] Hernia;
فتق بند *A. P.* Truss.
فتنه *A.* [فتن *fetan* o] Sedition; revolt. Nuisance; trouble.– ف. انگیختن To excite a s.; raise a disturbance.– ف. کردن 1) = ف. انگیختن 2) To make mischief. – گل ف Sweet-scented acacia. [سخنان ف.
فتنه آمیز *A. P.* Seditious
فتنه انگیز *A. P.* Seditious.
فتنه‌جو *A. P.* Seditious.
فتنه‌جویی *A. P.* Seditiousness.
فتوی = فتوا [ness.
فتوّت *A.* Generosity. Manliness.
فُتوح *A.* 1) [Pl. of فتح] 2) Grace. – پر فتوح Bestowed with God's grace.
فتوحات *A.* Conquests. [Pl. of فتوح pl. of فتح]
فُتور *A.* Langour. Tepidity.– ف. کردن To grow weak or lukewarm. *C. E.* To go beyond all bounds; rage.
فَتوی (-*va*) *A.* [فتاوی] Sentence; judgment. – ف. دادن To pronounce a j.; give a s.
فته = پته
فتی o (*tata*) *A.* [فتیان]=جوانمرد
فتیله *A.* Wick. Fuse. Quick-match or slowmatch. [In surgery] Drain. – تفنگ فتیله‌ای Matchlock. – چراغ سه فتیله ای Three-burner cooker. – داغِ

فتیله ای Moxa.
فجاه (*foj-eh*) *A*. Sudden death.
فجایع [Pl. of فجیعه]
فجر *A*. Day-break. Aurora. — فجر جنوبی A. australis. — فجر شمالی A. borealis.
فجور *A*. Debauchery.
فجیع *A*. Tragic. Calamitous.
فجیعه *A*. [فجایع] Tragical event. Atrocious act. [Orig. fem. of فجیع]
فحاش *A*. Abusive ; foul-mouthed.
فحاشی *A*. *P*. Abusiveness. — ف. کردن To use foul language.
فحش *A*. Abusive or foul language. — ف. دادن To use bad language. [With به] To revile.
فحشاء *A*. Obscene act ; fornication.
فحل o *A*. Male animal. Distinguished person [pl. فحول] — ف. آمدن To rut; be in heat.
فحول *S*. *u*. فحل
فحوی (-*va*) *or* **فحوا** Tenor ; purport.
فخار(ی) *A*. *P*. = **کوره پز(ی)**
فخامت *A*. Dignity.
فخذ *A*. Thigh-bone; femur.
فخذین *A*. [D. of فخذ 'thigh']. — فخذین مبدأ نخاع Cerebellar peduncles.
فخر *A*. Honour. Pride. — ف. کردن To p. oneself.
فخرالدین (*A*.) *Mas*. *pr*. *name*. *OS*. Pride of the Faith.
فخیم *A*. Great ; dignified.
فدا *A*. Ransom ; redemption. Sacrifice. — ف. کردن To sacrifice. — فدایت شوم [*Obsolete*] Dear Sir [in addressing dignitaries].
فداکار *A*. *P*. *a*. Devoted; self-sacrificing. —*n*. Devotee.
فداکاری *A*. *P*. Self-sacrifice ; devotion . — ف. کردن To devote oneself to a cause. *OS*. To sacrifice oneself.
فدایی *A*. *P*. Devotee.
فدوی *A*. Devoted servant or friend. [*In* *p*. *c*.] I.
فدیه *A*. Ransom. — کسی را با فدیه آزاد کردن To r. or redeem s. o.
فر Pomp; splendour.
فر Spinning; turn. — ف. خوردن & ف. دادن To spin.
فر [f. Fr. *fer*] Curling-iron; c.-tongs. Cooking-range ; cooking-stove ; oven . — ف. زدن *or* ف. دادن & ف. خوردن To curl ; friz(z) ; frizzle.
فرا *Prefix with opposite sets of meanings, such as* forward and backward ; up and down ; near and far, etc. — ف. تر * Farther up ; higher. — ف. چنگ آوردن * To take hold of. To obtain. — ف. خواندن To summon. To recall. — گوش ف. داشتن * To lend the ear. — ف. رسیدن To come (about). To befall. [With به] To reach or overtake. — ف. گرفتن To acquire. To

envelop. To merge.
فُرات *A.* Euphrates.
فَراخ Wide; broad. Ample. Large: رودهٔ ف.
فراخوانی Summoning. Recalling
فراخور Suitable. — فراخورِ من S. for me. — بفراخورِ In proportion to. According to. Such as suits. [Front sight.
فرادید [*In a firearm*]
فِرار *A.* [*Cf.* گریز] Flight; escape. — ف. دادن To put to flight; cause to e. — ف. کردن To run away; flee.
فَرّار *A.* Volatile. Fugacious.
فِراری *A. P.* Fugitive. Runaway. *F.* Abhorrent. — ف. شدن To be put to flight.
فرّاریت *A.* Volatility.
فَراز [*Word with opposite sets of meanings*] 1) *a.* Open or closed. 2) *ad.* Above or below. Up or down. Near. Behind. 3) *n.* Top; summit. Acclivity. — ف آوردن * To bring back or forward. To collect. To give b. ○
فرازیاب Altimeter.
فراست *A.* Insight. Instinct; sense. Keen guess.
فراسیون True hoarhound. Motherwort.
فِراش *A.* Bed ○. — تجدید فراش کردن To marry a second time.
فَرّاش *A.* Ferash; office-boy; servant; footman; peon; valet. — فراش پست Postman.
فراعنه [Pl. of فرعون]
فراغ *A.* = **فراغت**
فَراغت *A.* Leisure. Ease. Rest. — فراغتِ خاطر Tranquillity; peace of mind.
فَراق *A.* Separation (esp. from a friend or sweetheart).
فراك *E.* Frock(-coat). [party.
فراکسیون *Fr.* Parliamentary
فراماسون *Fr.* Freemason.
فرامرز *Mas. pr. name.*
فَراموش Forgotten. — ف. شدن To be f. — ف. کردن To forget. — فراموشم شد I forgot it. — ف. کرده‌ام I forget; I have forgotten it. — گل مرا فراموش مکن Forget-me-not.
فَراموشخانه Freemason's hall.
فراموشکار Forgetful.
فراموش نشدنی Never-to-be-forgotten.
فراموشی Forgetfulness. Oblivion. — ف. داشتن To have a bad memory.
فرامین [A. pl. of فرمان]
فرانسوی *Fr. A.* French(man). [Pl. فرانسویان 'the French people'].
فرانسه France. French (language). — جنگ ف. و آلمان The Franco-German war.
فرانك *Fr.* Franc.
فَراوان *a.* Abundant; in great supply [also × فت و فراوان]. —*ad.* Much. — پنبه ف. است

There is a great s. (*or* plenty) of cotton.

فراوانی Plenty ; abundance ; great supply.

فَراهم Available. (Gathered) together.— ف. آمدن 1) * To come together ; assemble. 2) = ف. شدن ‖ ف. آوردن * To bring together; collect. To b. about; effect.— ف. شدن To be brought a. To be made available. — ف. کردن To make a. To bring about. To obtain. To collect. — ف. کشیدن * To draw together.

فراياز Progressive.

فرايازی Progression.

فرائد [Pl. of فریده]

فرائض [Pl. of فریضه]

فَربه Fat. — ف. شدن To grow fat; put on weight.— ف. کردن To make f. ; fatten.

فربهی Fatness; obesity.

فرتوت Decrepit (old man).

فرتوتی Decrepitude.

فَرج *A.* [فروج ○] Vulva.

فرج (*faraj*) *A.* Relief.

فُرَج *S. u.* فرجه

فرج‌الله (*A.*) *Mas. pr. name. OS.* Relief from God.

فَرجام ○ End; conclusion. Result. — ف. خواستن To appeal to the Supreme Court. — رسیدگی فرجامی Investigation in the S. Court (*or* C. of Cassation).

فرجام‌خواسته Object of claim in respect of which an appeal is made to the Supreme Court.

فرجام خوانده Person against whom appeal is made to the Supreme Court.

فرجام خواه One who appeals to the Supreme Court.

فُرجه *A.* Respite. [Pl. فُرَج pores (only in خلل و فرج)].

فرچه (?) Shaving-brush.

فَرح *A.* Cheerfulness ; joy. *Cf.* شادی & خوشی

فرح افزا * *A. P.* Exhilarating.

فرح‌بخش * *A.P.* Pleasant; enlivening; exhilarating.

فرحناك *A. P.* = **فرح بخش**

فرّخ Auspicious. *Pr. name.*

فرخندگی Auspiciousness.

فرخنده * *a.* Happy ; auspicious. *–n. Fem. pr. name.*

فَرد *A.* Individual [pl. افراد]. Unit. Single verse. [*Used as an a.*] S. or unique. Odd. Alone.— فرد اعلی + Of superior quality. — راه حلِ منحصر بفرد The only solution. — هر فردی از آنها Each one of them.

فَردا To-morrow. — ف. شب To-m. night. — فردای آنروز On the morrow; the next day.— دوشیزهٔ امروز عروس فردا Present maid, prospective bride.

فرداً *A.* Singly. — ف. فرد One

by one ; singly. Each o. (separately).

فردوس *A.* = 1) باغ 2) بهشت.

فردوسی *Ferdowsi* : author of the *Shahnameh*.

فَردی *A. P.* Individual.

فِرز + Quick; prompt.

فَرزان o Learned; wise.

فرزانگان [Pl. of فرزانه]

فرزانگی Prudence ; wisdom. Learning. Excellence.

فرزانه Wise or learned (person). [Pl. فرزانگان]. [vulva.

فرزجه Suppository for the

فَرزَند Child : son or daughter.

فرزندخوانده Adopted child.

فرزندکش & فرزندکشی Filicide.

فرزندی Filial (relation). — بفرزندی قبول کردن To adopt as one's child.

فَرزین [*In chess*] = وزیر Queen.

فَرَس *A. Astr.* Pegasus. *OS.* = اسب

فُرس Persia. Iran. — فرس قدیم Old Persian (dialect).

فرسا(ی) [Imp. of فرسودن]

فَرسایش Erosion. Wearing out.

فرست [Imp. of فرستادن]

فرستادن [فرست] To send; despatch. To remit. — بیرون ف. To s. out. To export.

فرستاده 1) [P. P. of فرستادن]. 2) *n.* Messenger. Envoy. Apostle [pl. فرستادگان].

فرستنده Sender. — دستگاه ف. Transmitting set; transmitter.

فرسخ *A-P.* = فرسنگ

فرسنگ *Unit of length equal to 6.24 kilometres.*

فرسودگی Wear; tear. Depreciation. Fatigue *.

فرسودن [فرسا] *vt.* To wear (out); rub (off); obliterate. To erode. To tire. To fret. —*vi.* To w.; be worn or torn.

فرسوده [P. P. of فرسودن].

فَرش *A.* [فُروش] Carpet. Pavement. *See* سنگ فرش ‖ ف. کردن To cover with a carpet or carpets ; carpet. To pave.

فُرش (Fine) sand.

فرشتگان [Pl. of فرشته]

فرشته [فرشتگان] Angel.

فُرش کن Dredger; drag.

فُرَصت *A.* Opportunity; leisure. Chance. — ف. یافتن (*or* ف. کردن +) To find an opportunity. — ف. را غنیمت شمردن To seize the o.— ف. را از دست دادن To miss the o. ; lose the chance. — در نخستین (وهلهٔ) ف. آنرا بنویسید Write it at your earliest convenience.

فَرض *A.* Supposition. Assumption. Hypothesis. Duty; obligation. —[*Used as an a.*] Incumbent : بر من ف. است که بروم It is i. on me to go. — ف. کردن To suppose ; assume; grant. — مسلم ف. کردن or فرض ِ مسلم گرفتن To take for granted. — ف. شمردن To consider it one's duty. — برفرض ِ بفرض اینکه or اینکه Supposing that.

فرضاً *A.* Supposedly; supposing (that); let us suppose that.

فرضی *A.* Supposed. Imaginary. Assumed. [Theory.

فرضیه *A.* [فرضیات] Hypothesis.

فَرط *A.* Excess. Intensity. — از فرط محبت From excessive love.

فَرع *A.* [فُروع] Branch [شاخه]. Interest (on money). *F.* Details; minor points. — فرع ِ Consequent on; due to.

فرعاً *A.* Including interest.

فِرعون *A.* [فراعنه] Pharaoh.

فَرعی *A.* Secondary; of s. importance; minor. Tributary. *Gr.* Subordinate. [Fem. فرعیه]. — خط ف. Siding; side-track. — محصول ف. By-product.

فِرفره Top; whirligig.

فِرفری + Curly; wavy.

فَرق *A.* Distinction. Difference. Crown (of the head). Parting of the hair. — باهم ازهم ف. دارند or ف. دارند They differ from each other. — چه ف. میکند What difference does it make? — ف. گذاشتن To make a distinction; discriminate. — ف. باز کردن To part the hair.

فرق (*feragh*) [Pl. of فرقه]

فُرقان *A.* Distinction between truth and falsehood.

فرقد *A.* (*Astr.*) Pointer. [D. فرقدان] [*Cf.* حزب

فِرقه *A.* [فِرَق] Sect. Caste.

فُرم *Fr.* 1) = شکل 2)Forme.

فرما [Imp. of فرمودن]

فرمالیته *Fr.* Formality; ceremony. *Cf.* تشریفات & آئین

فَرمان [A. pl. فرامین] Command; order. Firman. Control. Word of command. *M.* 1) Steering-wheel. 2) Governor. — ف. بردن To obey; execute a c. To go on an errand. — ف. دادن To c.

فرمانبر Obedient.

فرمانبردار Obedient.

فرمانبرداری Obedience.

فرماندار Governor.

فرمانداری Governorship. Governor's office or residence.

فرمانده Commander. [army.

فرماندهی Command of an

فرمانرَوا o Ruler; sovereign.

فرمانروایی Rule; sovereignty.

فَرمانفرما [Old title of a] governor-general.

فَرمایش Order; command. [*In p. c.*] Something said; words; remarks. — ف. کردن To speak; make a remark — چه ف. دارید

1) What do you (want to) say, please ? 2) W. can I do for you, sir ?

فرمایشات *C.E.* [A. pl. of فرمایش]

فرمایشی 1) = سفارشی Made to order. 2) Ordered; inspired.

فرمز *Fr.* Formosa.

فِر مُژه Eyelash curler.

فَرمودَن [فرما(ی)] To bid; order; command. [*In p. c.*] To say. — بفرمایید Please take a seat. Come. Go. Speak, say, or go on, please. Help yourself. There you are.

فرموده 1) [P. P. of فرمودن]. 2) *n.* Commandment; precept.

فرمول *Fr.* Formula.

فرنج *Mil.* Tunic. [f. 'French'; i. e. F. tunic].

فَرنجمشك Common calamint.

فرنسیس European leather.

فرنگستان & فرنگ Europe.

فرنگی European.

فِرنی Pudding made with ground rice, milk, and sugar.

فُرو [*Used in compound verbs*] Down(ward). — ف. بردن To swallow. To dip. To sink. — ف. رفتن To s. ; go down. To plunge. — ف. ریختن * To collapse ; fall down; f. in ; tumble d. — ف.کردن To thrust. To drive, as a nail. To stick. — ف.کشیدن To subside. — ف. کوفتن * To knock down. To give a good beating to. — ف.گذاشتن To omit or leave out. — ف. ماندن از * To be unable to do. — ف. نشاندن * To suppress. To quench ; cause to subside; slake or slack. — ف. نشستن * To subside. To be quenched. To sink ; cave in.

فُروتن Humble; meek.

فروتنی Humility. — ف.کردن To be modest or meek.

فُروختن [فروش] To sell : آنرا ده ریال فروختم I sold it for *10 Rials*.

فروخته [P. P. of فروختن]

فُرود * 1) *ad.* Down; below. 2) *n.* Descent. *Ph.* Cathode. — ف. آمدن To come down ; descend. To land. — ف. آوردن To cause to d.

فرودگاه Aerodrome.

فَروَردین *First month having 31 days.*

فرو رفتگی Depression.

فرو رفته Depressed. Sunken.

فروزان * Luminous; bright.

فروزندگی Luminosity.

فروزنده Luminous; shining.

فُروش Sale. — (به) ف. رفتن To be sold; sell *vi.* — بفروش‌رساندن 1) = فروختن 2) To s. off. — ف. نکردیم We sold nothing ; there was no business.

فروش [Imp. of فروختن].

فروش‌رفتنی Salable ; market-

able. [place.
فروشگاه Stores. *OS*. Selling-
فروشندگی Salesmanship.
فروشنده [فروشندگان] Seller ; vendor ; dealer. Salesman.
فروشـ (Designed) for sale ; on s. ; on offer.
فروع [Pl. of فرع]
فروعات [Pl. of فروع pl. of فرع]
فروغ 1) * Brightness [روشنی]. 2) *Fem. pr. name.*
فروکش کردن To subside.
فروگذار کردن [With از] To omit; neglect.
فروگذاری Omission; neglect.
فروماندگی * Weariness. Failure. Distress. Astonishment.
فرومانده * Weary. Unable (to do any thing). Astonished.
فرومایگی Baseness.
فرومایه * [فرومایگان] Base or ignoble (person).
فَروَند [*Word used in counting ships*]. — ده ف. کشتی 10 ships; 10 sail.
فُروَهر ٥ = 1) جوهر 2) ذات
فَرهاد *Mas. pr. name.*
فَرهَنگ Culture. Education: وزارت ف. ‖ Dictionary. — فرهنگ جغرافیایی Gazeteer.
فرهنگستان Academy.
فرهنگ نویس Lexicographer.
فرهنگی Cultural. Educational.
فَرّهی * = شکوه
فَریاد Shout; cry.— ف. کردن To shout or c. — بفریاد کسی رسیدن To come to a person's rescue.
فریادرس One who comes to another's rescue.
فَریب 1) *n*. Deceit; fraud. — ف. خوردن To be deceived.— ف. دادن To deceive. 2) *Imp. of* فریفتن
فریبا * = فریبنده
فریب‌آمیز Deceitful : سخنان ف.
فریبرز *Mas. pr. name.*
فریبندگی Charm. [Deceitful.
فریبنده Charming. Fallacious.
فَرید *A. a.* Single. Unique. *See* فریده ‖ *—n. Mas. pr. name.*
فریده *A.* [فَرایِد] Unique or precious pearl. *Fem. pr. name.* [Orig. fem. of فرید].
فریدون *Mas. pr. name.*
فریسی *A-Heb.* Pharisee.
فَریضه *A.* [فرایض] Precept (of God); religious duty.
فریفتگی Delusion. Inveiglement. [enamour.
فریفتن [فریب] To deceive. To
فریفته [P. P. of فریفتن]
فریق * *A.* Party; sect. Company.
فزایش * [Cont. of افزایش]
فَزَع * *A.* Fear. Call for help.
فزودن * [Cont. of افزودن]
فزون * [Cont. of افزون]
فساد *A.* Corruption. Deterioration; decay. Sedition. Pus; matter + [چرک]. *Law.* Invalidity; defect.— فساداخلاق

Immorality. — فساد عقیده Heresy. — ف. برپا کردن To excite a sedition.
فسان [For سنگ ف.] Whetstone.
فسانه * [Cont. of افسانه]
فُسحت * A. Space; amplitude. F. Liberty.
فَسخ A. Dissolution. Annulment. — ف. کردن To dissolve, as a partnership. To annul; cancel; terminate. To rescind. — غیرقابل ف. Irrevocable.
فسردن * [Cont. of افسردن]
فسرده * [Cont. of افسرده]
فسفات Fr. Phosphate.
فسفر Fr. Phosphorus.
فسفری Fr. P. Phosphorous or phosphoric.
فِسفس کردن + To tarry; linger; dally.
فِسق A. Debauchery; fornication.
فِسقلی × Tiny; contemptible.
فِسنجان *Kind of dish with ground walnut as its chief ingredient.*
فسوس * [Cont. of افسوس]
فسون * [Cont. of افسون]
فشار Pressure. Stress; strain. — ف. آوردن To bear p.; press; [*with* بر] p. against. — ف. دادن To p. or squeeze. — فشار خون (High) blood pressure. — فشار زندگی Press of life. — فشار فقر Grip of poverty. — ماشین ف. Compressor.
فشار سنج Pressure-gauge; compression-gauge; manometer.
فشار نگار Barograph.
فشاری Pressed: آجر فشاری ‖ دکمهٔ ف. Snap (fastener).
فشردن [فشر - فشار] To tread, as grapes. S. a. فشار دادن & افشردن
فشرده [P. P. of فشردن] Pressed; squeezed. F. Condensed; compressed.
فِش زدن + To squirt. To gush.
فِشفشه (Sky-)rocket; jet.
فشنگ T. Cartridge.
فشنگ پُرکن T. P. Cartridge-filler.
فشنگی T. P. Cartridge-shaped. — فیوز فشنگی Cartridge-fuse. See یاتاقان ف. ‖ فیوز Roller-bearing.
فصاحت A. Eloquence.
فصاد * A. = رگزن [over.
فِصح A. [For عید فصح] Passover.
فصحاء [Pl. of فصیح]
فَصد A. Phlebotomy.
فَصل A. [فُصول] Section; chapter. Season. Settling; deciding. OS. Separation. — قطع و فصل کردن To settle.
فصلی A. Seasonal.
فصول [Pl. of فصل]
فَصیح A. 1) *a*. Eloquent. Clear. Rhetorical. 2) *n*. [Only in the pl. فصحاء Eloquent writers or orators.]
فضاء A. Space. Room.
فضاحت A. Disgrace. — ف. کردن To act disgracefully.
فضاحت آمیز A. P. Disgraceful.
فضادار A. P. Spacious; roomy.

فضائح [Pl. of فضیحت]

فضائلَ [Pl. of فضیلت]

فضائی *A*. [Fem. فضائیه] Dealing with space. — هندسهٔ فضائیه Solid geometry.

فضلَ *A*. Favour ; grace. Excellence; merit. Learning.

فضلاء [Pl. of فاضل].

فضل‌الله (*A*.) *Mas. pr. name. OS*. God's grace.

فضلهَ *A*. Residue. Excrement.

فضولُ *A*. 1) *n*. Meddler. Nosy person. Intruder. Blabber. Know-all. *OS*. Meddling. 2)*a*. *C. E*. Nosy ; meddlesome.

فضولات *A*. Waste matter ; refuse; also, residue.

فضولی *A. P*. Meddling; officiousness. *OS*. (One) who meddles. — معاملات ف. Unauthorized transactions.— ف. کردن To meddle. To blab.

فضیح * *A*. [Fem. فضیحه] Disgraced.

فضیحتَ *or* فضیحه * *A*. [فضائح] Disgrace. Shameful act. — فضیحه کردن To disgrace or betray : « آدمیرا زبان فضیحه کند »

فضیحت آور & فضیحت آمیز *A. P*. Disgraceful ; shameful; scandalous.

فضیلتَ *A*. [فضائل] Virtue; excellence; superiority. Attainment. — ف. داشتن بر To excel; be preferable to. [ty.

فطانت * *A*. Intelligence. Sagaci-

فطرِ *A*. Breaking a fast.

فطرتِ *A*. Nature ; temperament ; constitution.

فطرةً *A*. By nature.

فطریِ *A*. Natural; innate.

فطیرَ *A*. Unleavened (bread).

فعالَ *A*. Active; energetic. — فعال مایشاء One who does what he wishes ; powerful monarch ; dictator.

فعالیت *A*. Activity.

فعلِ *A*. [افعال] Act ; action ; deed. *Cf*. کار ‖ *Gr*. Verb. — بفعل آوردن To put in practice.

فعلاً *A*. At present. Actually.

فعلگیَ *A. P*. (Menial) labour; work done by a coolie. Drudgery. [Coolie(s).

فعله *A*. [Orig. pl. of فاعل]

فعلیِ *A*. Present ; actual. *Gr*. Verbal.— وضع فعلی The status quo ; the existing state of affairs. [2) * Alas !

فغان 1) [Cont. of 1 st. افغان]

فغفوری *a*. Belonging to the Chinese emperors. —*n*. [For چینی ف.] C. porcelaine.

فقار *A*. Vertebræ. *Cf. the s*.فقره

فقاعُ ° *A*. 1) = آبجو 2) Drink made of rice or fruits.

فقدان *A*. Absence; want; lack. Loss. Bereavement.

فقرَ *A*. = تهیدستی Poverty.

فقراء [Pl. of فقیر]

فقرات [Pl. of فقره]

فقرالدم *A*. = **کم خونی**

فقره *A*. [فقرات&فقار] Vertebra ○. Passage. Item; entry. Point; matter. [sole. *Cf.* تنها

فقط *A. ad*. Only. −*a*. Only ;

فقه (*fegh*h) *A*. Religious jurisprudence.

فقها [Pl. of فقیه]

فقید *A*. Lost ; missing. *By e*. Dead ; deceased . − شاه ف. The late Shah.

فقیر *A. a*. Poor [بینوا&تهیدست]. Meek. −*n*. P. fellow [pl. فقراء the p.]. − ف. شدن To be reduced to poverty. − ف. کردن To reduce to p.

فقیری *A. P*. = تهیدستی Poverty.

فقیه *A*. [فقهاء] Jurisconsult (in Mohammedan law).

فك *A*. Separation. Removal. Redemption. − وثیقه ای را فك کردن To redeem a security.

فك *A*. [D. فکین] = آرواره

فکاهت ○ *A*. = شوخی Humour.

فکاهی *A*. Humorous. [Fem. فکاهیه with the pl. فکاهیات Humorous anecdotes ; humours ; also, jokes].

فکر *A* [افکار] Thought ; reflection. *Cf*. اندیشه ‖ Idea. Mind. Care. − ف. کردن To think ; reflect. − بفکر انداختن To set thinking. − توی ف. رفتن + To begin to think. − در فکر چیزی بودن To care for, think about, or look after, s. t. [tion.

فکرت • *A*. Reflection; medita-

فکری *A*. Mental. Melancholic ○. − ف شدن To begin to think.

فکسنی × Tumble-down; dilapidated ; worn-out.

فکل *Fr*. (Detachable) collar. − ف. زدن To wear a c.

فکندن • [Cont. of افکندن]

فکور *A*. Able to think deeply. − آدم ف. Deep thinker; great t.

فکی *A*. Maxillary. Mandibular.

فکیف ○ *A*. How then ? H. much more (or less) ?

فکین *S. u*. فك

فگار • [Cont. of افکار]

فگانه • [Cont. of افگانه]

فلات *A*. [فلوات] Extensive and waterless desert. Plateau. − فلات قاره Continental shelf.

فلاح *A* = رستگاری

فلاح (*fa*lah) *A*. = کشاورز Agriculturist. Peasant, fellah.

فلاحت *A*. = کشاورزی Agriculture. − ف. کردن To farm ; cultivate the ground.

فلاحتی *A. P*. Agricultural.

فلاخن Sling.

فلاسفه [Pl. of فیلسوف]

فلاکت [Word coined in the A. fashion from فلك] = فلك زدگی

فلاکت بار Miserable. Deplorable.

فلامك [f. فلمنك 'Fleming or Holland'] Rose diamond [also الماس ف.]

فلان *A. a*. Such and such; a certain. −*n*. S. and s. a

person. Any one. — ف. و بهمان S. and s. a thing or person. So-and-so. One t. or other.— ای ف. * O what's-your-name!

فلانل *Fr*. Flannel. [person.

فلانی *A. P*. Such and s. a

فلج *A*. Paralysis; palsy.— فلج تام (General) paralysis.— فلج ناقص، عضلات Paresis. — فلج نصف تن Hemiplegia. — ف. کردن To paralyze.

فلز *A*. [فلزات] Metal. *F*. Mettle; nature. — شبه ف. Metalloid.

فلزآلات *A. P*. Hardware; metal ware.

فلزی *A. P*. Metallic; of metal.

فلس *A*. Small copper coin. Scale of a fish. Scab. *Cf. the pl.* فلوس

فلسطین *A*. Palestine.

فلسفه *A-G*. Philosophy.

فلسفی *A*. Philosophic(al).

فلفل *A*. [f. P. پلپل] Pepper.— فلفل آبی Water-pepper; smart-weed. — فلفل برّی (Seed of the) chaste-tree or *Agnus castus*. — فلفل فرنگی Red p. — (گرد) فلفل هندی (Cayenne p. — فلفل فرنگی شیرین Pimento; all-spice. — دانهٔ ف. Peppercorn.

فلفل دان Pepper-box.

فلفل مون Wild peppermint; savoury.

فلفل نمکی Pepper-and-salt *a*. Grizzly.

فلفلی + Tiny but smart; dap-per. Precocious. *OS*. Peppery.

فلق *A*. Morning twilight.

فلك *A*. [افلاك] Firmament. Heavenly sphere. Orbit. *F*. Fortune; also, destiny.

فلك or فلكه *A*. (Wooden instrument used for the) bastinado. — فلك کردن To b.; give the b. (to).

فلك زدگی *A. P*. Adversity. Affliction. [Afflicted.

فلك زده *A. P*. Unfortunate.

فلكه *A*. Belt-pulley. Whirl of a spindle. Traffic circle; roundabout. *S. a. under* فلك ‖ شیر فلكه‌ای Gate-valve.

فلكی *A*. Celestial. Astronomical. [Fem. فلكیه] [buzz off.

فلنگ را بستن × To pack off;

فلوات [Pl. of فلات]

فلوت *Fr*. Flute. — ف. زدن To (play on the) flute.

فلوت‌زن *Fr. P*. Flutist.

فلوس *A*. Small copper coins. Scales. *Med*. Purging cassia; cassia-pods. *Cf. the s.* فلس

فلوکس *E. or Fr*. Phlox.

فم ० *A*. =1) دهن 2) دهانه ‖ *Cf. the pl.* افواه ‖ فم قصبة الريه Glottis. — فم معده Cardia.

فم‌الحوت *A*. Fomalhaut.

فنّ *A*. [فنون] Art. Branch (of knowledge). Technique. Knack; trick +. — فنونِ آزاد Liberal arts.

فنا *A*. Annihilation; destruc-

tion; ruin. — ف. شدن To be annihilated. To be ruined. — ف. کردن To annihilate. — بباد فنادادن To a. To dissipate.
فنا پذیر *A. P.* Destructible. Mortal.
فنا ناپذیر *A. P.* Indestructible.
فُنج *or* **پُنج** Punch. [f. P. پَنج 'five']. [cupful a day
فنجان Cup. — روزی یك ف One
فنجان‌بازی Thimblerig.
فنجانی Cup-shaped. *Anat.* Cotyloid; acetabular. — گل ف. Cup-shaped evening primrose. — گودال ف. Acetabulum.
فندق Hazel-nut; filbert.
فندق شکن Nut-cracker.
فندقك Ivory-nut.
فندقه Achene; akene.
فَندَك Lighter; strike-a-light.
فَندول [*f. Fr.*] Pendulum.
فَنر [*f. G. origin*] Spring. [*Of a watch*] Hair-spring. [*Of hatmakers*] Conformator. [*Of a motor car*] Leaf spring. [*Of a bicycle*] Coil.
فنری Resilient; elastic. Working with a spring; clockwork *a.* — بولك ف. Lock washer.
فَنگ *Word used in military commands, and corresponding to 'arms'. See* دوش فنگ
فنون [Pl. of فن]
فنی *A.* Technical.
فنیقی *A.* Phœnician.
فواحش [Pl. of فاحشه]
فؤاد *A.* 1) o = دل Heart. 2) *Mas. pr. name.*
فوّاره *A.* Jet (of water); *jet-d'eau*; spout; fountain. — فوارهٔ گردان *or* فوارهٔ افشان Girandole.
فواصل [Pl. of فاصله]
فواق *A.* = سکسکه Hiccup.
فواکه [Pl. of فاکهه]
فوائد [Pl. of فائده]
فوب (*fob*) (*E.*) f. o. b. *or* fob (free on board).
فوت Puff; blow. Puffing. Blowing (out). — ف. کردن To blow out; extinguish by blowing. To blow on. — ف. بودن × To have at one's fingers' ends (*or* tongue's end). — فوت کاسه‌گری + Knack. Last touch.
فوت (*fowt*) *A.* Death; dying. — ف. شدن To elapse. To be missed. — ف. کردن To die [مردن]. To miss; allow to escape. — بدون فوت وقت کاریرا کردن To lose no time in doing s. t.
فوتبال *E.* (Game of) football.
فوتبالیست *E. & Fr.* (Good) footballer. [of fife.
فوت فوتك Toy whistle. Kind
فوتوی (*fotoi*) *Fr.* Arm-chair; easy chair.
فوتی + *A. P.* Very urgent.

OS. Liable to lapse.

فوج A. [افواج] 1) = هنگ Regiment. 2) Multitude.

فوراً A. = بیدرنگ At once; immediately.

فوَران A. Eruption. Ebullition. Effervescence.

فوری A. Urgent. Immediate; quick. – عکس ف. Snapshot. – عکس ف. برداشتن از To snap.

فوریت A. Urgency. – بفوریت = فوراً At once. – با قید دو فوریت With a two-starred urgency or priority. – فوریت اول First urgency question.

فوریه Fr. February.

فوز o A. = رستگاری – کامیابی

فوفل Betel-nut; areca-nut.

فوفه o A. Leaf-brass.

فوق A. = بالا Top; upper part. – در فوق Above. – فوقِ Above *prep.*; beyond.

فوقاً A. Above.

فوق‌التصوّر A. Beyond imagination.

فوق‌الجلد A. = روپوست

فوق‌الذکر A. (C. E.) Above-mentioned.

فوق‌الطاقه A. Insupportable.

فوق‌العاده A. a. Extraordinary. –n. Allowance. Extra. – فوق‌العادهٔ خارج از مرکز Out-station allowance; field a.

فوق‌المعده A. Epigastrium.

فوقانی A. = بالایی Upper.

فولاد etc. = پولاد etc.

فونوگراف Fr. Phonograph.

فهرست List. Index. – فهرستِ موجودی Inventory. – فهرستِ مندرجات Table of contents. – ف. کردن To make a list of. To index. To inventory.

فهم A. Understanding; comprehension. – ف. کردن To understand. – قابل ف. Comprehensible; intelligible. – غیرقابل ف. Incomprehensible; unintelligible.

فهماندن A. P. To cause (*or* give) to understand. To explain. – مقصود خود را فهماندن To express oneself.

فهمیدگی A. P. Intelligence. Prudence; judiciousness.

فهمیدن A. P. [فهم] 1) To understand. 2) + = شنیدن

فهمیده A. P. 1) P. P. of فهمیدن 2) a. Having common sense; intelligent; judicious.

فهیم A. Of understanding. Intelligent; wise.

فی A. *prep.* At the rate of; at. By. OS. In [در]. –n. Unit cost. – فی زدن + To estimate.

فیاض A. = 1) بخشنده 2) فراوان

فی‌الجمله (*feljomleh*) A. To sum up. In the abstract.

فی‌الحال o A. At once.

فی‌الحقیقه A. Indeed.

فی‌الفور A. = فوراً

فی‌المثل A. = مثلاً

فی‌المجلس A. On the spot.

فی‌الواقع *A.* = واقعاً
فیبر *Fr.* Fibre(-board).
فیثاغورث *A-G.* Pythagoras.
فیثاغورثی *A.* Pythagorean.
فیروز etc. = پیروز etc.
فیروزه Turquoise.
فیروزه‌ای Turquoise-coloured; azure. Of turquoise.
پیروزی = فیروزی
فیزیك *Fr.* Physics.
فیزیك‌دان *Fr. P.* Physicist.
فیزیولوژی *Fr.* Physiology.
فیس + (Swelling with) pride. — ف. کردن To swell with p.; boast. [fizz or hiss.
فیش Fizz. Hiss. — ف. کردن To
فیش *Fr.* Slip; index card.
فشفشه = فیش فیشه
فیصل‌دادن *A. P.* To settle (by arbitration). To determine.
فیض *A.* Grace; blessing. Bounty. Profusion. Profit +. — فیض حضور [In p. c.] Favour to be in some one's presence.
فیض‌الله (*A.*) *Mas. pr. name. OS.* God's grace.
فیضان *A.* Overflowing; abundance. Emission. — فرضیهٔ فیضان نور E. theory.
فیض بخش *A. P.* Bountiful. Charitable. Fertilizing.
فیف‌کردن + To spit, as a cat.
فیل [A. f. P. پیل] Elephant. [*In chess*] Bishop. — دندان ف. Elephant's tusk; ivory. — گوش ف Kind of confection. — کار حضرت ف. × Herculean task.
پیلبان = فیلبان
پیلتن = فیلتن
فیلد مارشال *E.* Field-marshal.
فیل دوقس (*-doghos*) Lisle thread [f. Fr. *fil d'Ecosse*].
فیلسوف [*A-G.*] [فلاسفه] Philosopher. [cally.
فیلسوفانه *A. P.* Philosophi-
فیلگوش ○ Iris. Nenuphar.
فیلم [*Fr.* & *E.*] Film. — فیلمش خوب میشود + It films well.
فیلم‌برداری *Fr. P.* Film-taking.
فیمابین *A.* (In) between.
فین Snot. — ف. کردن + To blow one's nose.
فین‌فینی + Snotty.
فینه Fez.
فیوز *E.* Fuse(-wire). [In it.
فیه *A.* [Fem. فیها] In him.

قاب *T*. Plate ; dish. Frame. Case. — ق.کردن *or* ق.گرفتن To f. To provide with a case.

قاب Knuckle-bone. — ق. زدن To gamble with knucklebones.— قاب کسیرا دزدیدن × To get round s. o.

قاب بازی (Game played with) knucklebones.

قاب بال *T. P.* Coleopterous.

قاب دستمال *T. P.* Dish-cloth; clout.

قاب ساز *T. P.* Framer.

قابض *A.* Astringent. Styptic. *OS.* Seizer; taker.

قابض‌الارواح *A.* (Ep. of) the Angel of Death. *See* قابض & ارواح

قابضیت *A.* Astringency. Stypticity.

قابِل *A.* Qualified. Capable. Worthy. — ق. نیست Don't mention. — قابلِ W. of. Capable of [*rendering the E. suf.* -able *or* -ible].

قابلگی *A. P.* = مامایی

قابلمه *T.* Steam-tight stew-pan for keeping food hot. Dinner-pail; tiffin-carrier.— تکمهٔ قابلمه‌ای Snap fastener.

قابله *A.* 1) = ماما 2) Receptacle.

قابلیت *A.* Ability ; merit ; worth. Capability [*rendering the E. suf.* –ability *or* –ibility].

قابیل *A.* Cain.

قاپیدن = + **قاپ زدن**

قاپوچی *T.* [*Obsolete*] = دربان

قاپوق *or* **قاپُق** *T.* Pillory.

قاپیدن *T. P.* [قاپ] To snatch.

قاتق *T.* Anything eaten with bread; *L.* spread.

قاتِل *A. n.* Murderer ; homicide [آدمکش] *OS.* Killer. —*a.* Deadly ; fatal [کشنده].

قاتمه *T.* Sackmaker's thread.

قاجاریه *Dynasty preceding the present Pahlavi D.*

قاچاق *T. a.* Contraband; illicit. —*n.* 1) C. or smuggled goods. 2) Smuggling. — ق. شدن +To slip off. To play the truant.— ق.کردن To smuggle.

قاچاقچی *T.* Smuggler.

قاچاقی *T. P.* Contraband; smuggled.

قادِر *A.* 1) Able : ق. برفتن able to go. 2) Powerful. *Cf.* توانا ‖ ق. کردن To enable. — قادر مطلق Omnipotent.

قاذورات *A.* [Pl. of قاذوره] Ordure ; dirt. — جزو قاذورات Taken to no account. Good-for-nothing.

قاصد A. Messenger [بیك]. Ovary of the dandelion flown about by the wind.
قاصر A. Falling short; failing. Defective. OS. Short[کوتاه]. — از انجام آن ق. آمد He failed to do it; he could not do it.
قاضی A. [قضاة] Judge. — تنها نزد قاضی رفتن To reckon without one's host. OS. To go alone to the judge (to have his ear).
قاضی الحاجات A. Provider of needs: ep. of God.
قاطبه A. The whole. — قاطبهٔ اسلام Pan-Islam.
قاطبةً A. = عموماً
قاطر T. = استر Mule.
قاطرچی T. Muleteer.
قاطع A. Decisive; categorical. Geom. Secant. OS. Trenchant. — رأی ق. Casting vote.
قاطع الطریق A. [قطاع الطریق] = راهزن
قاطی T. or قاتی Mixed. — ق. کردن To mix [آمیختن]. To confound.
قاطی پاطی or قاطی واتی × Pell-mell.
قاعدگی A. P. Menstruation.
قاعده A. [قواعد] Rule; method. Formula. Geom. Base. [Used as an a.] Unwell; having her periods. — برحسب ق. According to the rule; as a r. — ق. شدن To menstruate.
قاعدةً A. As a rule.
قاف Fabulous mountain iden-

قارت وقورت × Bragging. Fuss.
قارچ T. Mushroom [سماروغ].
قارچ کش T. P. Fungicide.
قارچی T.P. Fungous; fungoid. — گیاه ق. Fungus.
قارشمیش + T. = درهم برهم
قاروره ○ A. Urinal.
قارون A. Korah. L. Crœsus.
قارّه A. Continent.
قاری A. Reader of the Koran.
قارئین A. = خوانندگان Readers. Cf. the s. قاری
قاز S. u. غاز
قازاَیاغی T. Goosefoot; chenopod.
قاز چران T. P. Gooseherd.
قاز چرانی T. P. Tending geese. Met. Loafing about; also, wool-gathering. [pr. name.
قاسم A. Distributor ○. Mas.
قاسم الصدر A. Mediastinum.
قاسی ○ A. [Fem. قاسیه] = سخت
قاش T. Slice. — ق. کردن To slice; cut (open). To splinter. — ق. خوردن To be split or c. — قاش زین or قاچ زین Pommel of a saddle.
قاشق T. Spoon. — روزی سه ق. Three spoonfuls a day — قاشق چای خوری Teaspoon(ful). — قاشق سوپ خوری Tablespoon(ful).
قاشق تراش T. P. Spoonmaker; horner.
قاشقك T. P. Castanets; clappers.
قاشقی T.P. Spoon-shaped. Measured or sold by the spoon. — آچار قاشقی Ring-spanner.

tified with Mt. Caucasus.
قافله *A.* [قوافل] Caravan. Convoy. [caravan.
قافله سالار *A. P.* Leader of a
قافیه *A.* [قوافی] Rime or rhyme. — با هم ق. شدن To r. with (*or* to) each other. — ق. را باختن To be frustrated and unable to answer; be stuck. — ق.اش تنگ شد He ran short of rimes. *F.* He was driven to extremities.
قافیه‌پرداز * *A.P.* Rimer; poet.
قاق *T.* 1) *n.* Last player. 2) *a.* Dry. Lank.
قاقا Nicy; goody; lollilops.
قاقم *A.* Ermine.
قال *T.* Smelting; refining. — ق.کردن To smelt or refine.— ق. گذاشتن To leave in the lurch; keep waiting too long. — قال چیزیرا کندن + To get s. t. over and finished with. [fully قیل و قال
قال *A.* Speech o. Noise — more
قالَ o *A.* = گفت (He) said.
قالِب *A.* Mould. Model; form; matrix. Centering. Shuttering. [In shoemaking] Last. [*Of a boot*] Tree. [*Of soap*] Cake; tablet. *F.* Body.— ق.کردن To mould; model; shape; form. *F.* To pass off; fob; foist off (s. t. on some one). — ق. تهی کردن * To resign one's life.
قالب ریز *or* قالب گر *A. P.* Moulder; modeller.
قالب ریزی *A. P.* Moulding.
قالبی *A. P.* Moulded. Formed into cakes or bars. Of exact dimensions +.
قالپاق *T.* Hubcap.
قالگر *T. P.* Refiner (*or* smelter) of metals.
قالگری *T. P.* Refining of metals.— کورهٔ ق. Cupola-furnace.
قال مقال + *a. p.* Noise; fuss.
قالی *T.* Carpet.
قالی باف *T. P.* Carpet-weaver.
قالی بافی *T. P.* Carpet-weaving.
قالیچه *T. P.* Rug.
قامَت *A.* Stature. *Cf.* قد
قاموس o *A.* Dictionary [فرهنگ]. *OS.* Ocean. [ing.
قامه [Per. f. A. قائمه] *M.* Bush-
قانِع *A.* Contented. — ق. شدن To be contented, convinced, or satisfied. — ق کردن To satisfy. To give contentment (to). To convince.
قانون *A.G.* [قوانین] Law; statute; (parliamentary) act. Rule. Canun: kind of zither or dulcimer.
قانوناً *A.* Legally. [consult.
قانون‌دان *A. P.* Jurist; juris-
قانون‌گزار *or* قانون‌گذار *A. P.* Legislator. Lawgiver.
قانون‌گذاری *A. P.* Legislation.
قانونی *A.* Legal. Statutory.
قاهِر *A.* Forcible; powerful;

قَبا *A.* Long garment open in front, worn by men. — ق. كردن * To rend (one's shirt).
قَباحت *A.* = زشتى Obscenity. — ق. دارد It is a shame.
قُباد *Mas. pr. name.*
قِبال *A.* Front; face ○. — درقبالِ Alongside of. In f. of. In lieu of. In comparison with.
قباله *A.* [قبالجات] Title-deed. Marriage-contract. — ق. كردن To purchase (by a deed).
قبائح or قبايح [Pl. of قبيحه]
قبائل or قبايل [Pl. of قبيله]
قُبح *A.* Indecency [زشتى] Indecent appearance.
قَبر *A.* [قُبور] = گور Grave; tomb. — ق. كردن To bury.
قِبراغ Nimble. Equipped for action.
قِبرس *A.* Cyprus.
قبرستان *A. P.* = گورستان
قبرسى *A.* Cyprian. Cypriot. — زاج ق. Green vitriol; sulphate of iron. — گلِ ق. Cyprus clay.
قبركن *A. P.* Grave-digger.
قَبض *A.* [قُبوض] Bill; note. Receipt [often قبض رسيد]. — قبض و اقباض Delivery. — قبضِ عندالمطالبه Note of hand; promissory note. — ق. كردن To seize ○. To constipate.
قَبضه *A.* Handle; hilt. Grasp. Fist's length. — سه ق. تفنگ 3 rifles. — يك ق. شمشير One sword. — درقبضهٔ تصرف درآوردن

subduing. [Cairo.
قاهره *A.* [Orig. fem. of قاهر]
قاه قاه 1) *n.* Fit of laughter. 2) *ad.* Loudly; boisterously. — ق. خنديدن To laugh b.
قائد *A.* Leader. General.
قايق *T.* Boat. — قايق موتورى Motor boat; launch.
قايقران *T. P.* Boatman.
قايقرانى *T. P.* Boating; yachting. Boatmanship.
قائل *A. a.* Who believes (in). —*n.* Believer. *OS.* = گوينده ‖ ق. شدن به To believe in. To maintain. — امتيازاتى براى وى ق. شدند They granted certain privileges to him.
قائم *A.* Erect; right; vertical. *F.* Living; existent ○. — ق. بالذات Self-existent. [Fem. قائمه Ex. زاويهٔ قائمه Right angle]
قايم + [f. A. قائم] *a.* Secure; fast; firm. [*Confused with* غائب] Hidden. —*ad.* Firmly; fast. Severely. — ق. شدن To hide (oneself). — ق. كردن To h. To secure; make f.
قائم‌الزاويه *A.* Right-angled. — ق. [illegible] Right triangle.
قائم مقام *a. p.* Successor; locum tenens; substitute.
قايم‌موشك *A. P.* Hide-and-seek.
قائمه *A.* 1) *a.* [Fem. of قائم] 2) *n.* ○ Perpendicular. Side post. Invoice.
قائن *A-Heb.* = قابيل

To take possession of.

قِبطی A. Coptic. Gipsy. Egyptian o.

قَبل A. = پیش Ago: دو سال ق. 2 years ago. ‖ Before; preceding.- شب ق the night before.- از ق. Before: از این ق. b. this; previous to this. - ق. از آنکه شما بیائید B. you came. - دو ساعت ق. از ظهر 10 a. m. - ق. از وقت Ahead of time; beforehand.

قبل (*ghebal*) A. Side; part.- از قبلِ From. Through.

قُبل o (*ghobol*) A. Forepart. Privy parts.

قبل (*ghobol*) T. Holster. - ق (و)منقل [*Obsolete*] Outfit.

قَبلاً A. Beforehand. Previously. First of all. Already. In anticipation. Heretofore.

قبلتین A. [D. of قبله] The Two Kiblahs; *i. e.* Mecca and Jerusalem.

قِبله A. Kiblah: direction to which Mohammedans turn in praying.- قبلهٔ حاجت Centre-point looked to for the attainment of one's ends. - پشت به ق. Facing the north.- رو به ق. F. the south; exposed to the sun.

قبله نما A. P. Compass (showing the Kiblah).

قبلی A.P. Previous; preceding.- با تقدیم تشکرات ق. Thanking you in anticipation, ...

قبور [Pl. of قبر]

قبوض [Pl. of قبض]

قَبول A. Acceptance. Admitting. Agreement; consent. [*Used as an a.*] Accepted.- ق. داشتن To maintain as true; believe (in). - ق. دارم I admit; I agree. - ق. شدن To be accepted or admitted. To be approved. To be granted. - ق. کردن To accept. To believe (in). To admit. To agree to.- جواب ق. [Without the *ezafah*] Reply paid.- عدمِق. Non-acceptance; refusal.

+قبول دارشدن A. P. To accept.

قبولی A. P. 1) *n.* = پذیرش Acceptance. - ق. نوشتن To write one's a.; accept a bill. 2) *a.* Accepted. [Pommel.

قُبه A. Dome; cupola. Knob.

قَبیح A. = زشت Obscene. - از من ق. است It is a shame for me; it is beyond my dignity.

قبیحه o A. [قبائح] Shameful act. [Orig. fem. of قبیح]

قَبیل A. Kind; category. *Cf.* این ق. زنان ‖ جور & نوع Such women. - از قبیلِ S. as.

قبیله A. [قبائل] Tribe. Family.

قپان T. Steelyard. - ق. کردن To weigh by a s.

قپانچه شدن T. P. To swoop.

قپانداری T.P. Weighing charges.

قپلان o T. = ببر Tiger.

قپی آمدن × To bluff.

قِتال o *A.* = جنگ & کارزار

قتال (*gha*tal) *A.* = کشنده Deadly. [*Fem.* قتاله *—only in* آلت قتاله lethal weapon].

قَتل *A.* Killing; murder. — بقتل رساندن = کشتن To m.; kill. — بقتل رسیدن To be murdered or killed. — قتل عام General massacre. — قتل عمدی (Wilful) murder. — قتل غیر عمدی Manslaughter.

قچاق *T.* = 1) چابك 2) خوش بنیه

قحبه *A.* = فاحشه

قَحط *A.* Dearth. Famine.

قحط سال *A. P.* Year of dearth or famine.

قحطی *A. P.* Famine.

قحطی زده or قحط زده *A. P.* Famine-stricken (person).

قَد *A.* Stature. Size. — قد خم کردن To stoop; bend one's back. — بمن ق نمیدهد It is beyond my depth. — قد علم کردن To signalise oneself; attract attention. — ق. کَشیدن To grow tall. To g above one's age. — ق. گرفتن + To measure [اندازه گرفتن]. — دو قدِ من Twice my size. — بچه های قد و نیم قد + Kids of all ages (or sizes).

قداره = غداره

قدامی o *A.* = جلوی & پیشین

قد بلند *A. P.* Tall : آدم ق.

قَدح *A.* = سرزنش & ذم

قَدَح (*-dah*) *A.* Cup; bowl.

قدر (*ghadr*) *A.* Value; worth. Merit. Amount; quantity. — قدر . . . را دانستن To appreciate; know the value of. — آنقدر 1) So. Ex. آنقدر گرسنه بود که 2) As much. 3) That m.; this m. — اینقدر 1) So m.; this m. 2) So [+ اِنقدر]. — بقدرِ As m. as. To the extent of. — قدری *a.* Some; a little. *—ad.* Somewhat. — بقدری 1) So : بقدری گرم بود که . . . ‖ 2) So m.. : بقدری حرف زد که ‖ بقدری که or آنقدر که As m. as; so m. as. To the extent that. — چقدر 1) How m.? 2) H. long? 3) H. ! Ex. ! چقدر مهربان بود H. kind he was! He was so k. 4) Many a. — هر قدر 1) As much as. 2) However. Ex. هر قدر کودن باشد H. stupid he may be.

قَدَر (*-dar*) *A.* Divine decree. Predestination. *S. a.* قدر (*ghadr*). — چه قدر - اینقدر - آنقدر *S. u. the preceding entry.*

قُدرَت *A.* Power; ability [توانایی]. *Mas. or fem. pr. name.*

قدرت‌الله (*A.*) *Mas. pr. name.* *OS.* God's power.

قدرتی *A. P.* Brought about by Providence.

قدردان *A. P.* Appreciative; *L.*; grateful.

قدردانی *A. P.* Appreciation.— ق.کردن To express one's a.; [with از] to appreciate.
قدر شناس *A. P.* = قدردان
قَدَری *S. u.* قدر [fatalist.
قَدَری *A.* Predestinarian; [fatalist.
قُدس *A.* Holiness. — قدس شریف Jerusalem.
قدس‌الاقداس *A.* The Holy of Holies (*Biblical*).
قدس سره (*ghodesa-seroh*) *A.* May his grave be sanctified.
قدسی *A. P. a.* Holy. Celestial. —*n.* [Pl. قدسیان] = فرشته
قدسیه (*A.*) *Fem. pr. name.* [Orig. fem. of قدسی]
قدغن *T.* Prohibition. Order; injunction. [*Used as an a.*] Prohibited; forbidden. — ق.کردن To prohibit. To order.
قَدَك Buckram (used inside garments to keep them in shape). [Short.
قدکوتاه *A. P.* [*Of a person*]
قَدَم *A.* [اقدام] 1) ○ Foot [پا]. 2) Footstep; pace.—ق. برداشتن To take a step.—ق. داشتن To bring good luck. — ق. زدن To walk. To s.; pace. — سرقدم رفتن ق. رفتن To march.— بقدم ق. To go to stool. — ق. بالای چشم Step by s. — You are (*or* will be) most welcome.
قدم (*ghedam*) *A.* = قدمت

قُدَما *A.* = پیشینیان The ancients. *Cf. the s.* قدیم
قِدَمت *A.* Antiquity; oldness. Precedence. [Odograph.
قدم پیما *A. P.* Pedometer.
قدم شمار *A. P.* Pedometer.
قُدّوس *A.* Very holy.
قُدّوسیت *A.* Extreme holiness.
قُدوم *A.* Coming; advent.
قدومه Hedge-mustard.
قدوه ○ *A.* Model. Leader.
قدّی *A. P.* Full-length: آینهٔ ق.
قدیر *A.* Almighty.
قَدیم *A.* 1)*a.*= باستانی Ancient; old. 2) *n.* A. times. *Cf. the pl.* قدما ‖ از قدیم *or* ازقدیم‌الایام From olden times.
قدیماً *A.* Anciently.
قدیمی *A. P.* Old. Primitive.
قدیمی مسلك *a. p.* Fogyish; old-fashioned.
قراء [Pl. of قریه]
قرابادین (?) Pharmacopœia.
قَرابَت *A.* Proximity [نزدیکی]. Affinity. Relationship. — قرابت صلبی Consanguinity.
قرابه Flask. Carboy.
قرابین *or* قرابینه *T-It.* Carbine; carabin(e).
قراچی *T.* Gipsy.
قَرار *A.* Rest; repose. Stability. Arrangement; agreement. Resolution. Stipulation. Ruling; also, order or decree.— ق. دادن To place. To set. To

appoint; fix. To resolve.— ق. شد It was agreed or resolved. — ق. است امروز وارد شود He is due to arrive to-day. — ق. گذاشتن To make an arrangement or appointment; agree. — ق. گرفتن To settle. To be comforted. — رأی ما براین ق. گرفت که We resolved (or decided) to . . . — قرار ملاقات Appointment; rendezvous. — ق. و مدار + Agreement; also; collusion. — ازقرارِ At the rate of. According to. — بقرارِ زیر As follows. — ازقراریکه میگویند It is said (or reported) that. — از این ق. Thus. Then. — از همان ق. Accordingly.

قرارداد *A. P.* Agreement; contract. Convention. Appointment; arrangement.

قراردادی *A. P.* Conventional. Based on a contract.

قراردم *A. P.* (Blacksmith's) fuller. [Headquarters.

قرارگاه *A. P.* Resting-place.

قراسوران *T.* Escort. Road-guard.

قُراص or قُراصه [f. E. *gross*] Gross : 12 dozen.

قُراضه *A. n.* Scrap (metal). Filings. —*a.* Worn-out; dilapidated. [Gnawing.

قَرّاضه *A.* [Fem. of قَرّاض]

قراقر *A.* Grumbling in the stomach; borborygmus.

قراقروت *T.* Dried black curds.

قران *A.* Conjunction. *F.* Crisis.

قُرآن *A.* The Koran.

قراوُل *T.* Sentinel; watchman; patrol. — ق. رفتن To take aim.

قراول‌خانه *T. P.* Guard-house.

قِرائَت *A.* Reading. — ق. کردن To read [خواندن].

قرائت‌خانه *A. P.* Reading-room.

قرائن [Pl. of قرینه] [worth.

قُرب *A.* 1) = قرابت 2) Esteem;

قُربان *A.* Offering; sacrifice. *Mas. pr. name.* — ق. کردن To s. — (به) قربان کسی رفتن To be (ready to be) sacrificed for s. o. To adore s. o.

قربانی *A. P.* 1) *n.* Sacrifice; offering. *F.* Victim. 2) *a.* Set aside for sacrifice. — قربانیِ . . . شدن To fall a victim to . . . . . — ق. کردن To s.; offer a s.

قُرَبت *A.* Proximity [نزدیکی]. Approach; drawing close. Favour; grace.

قربةً الی الله *A.* To win God's favour; to please God.

قرتی × Effeminate beau.

قُرحه *A.* Ulcer. — قرحهٔ آکله Lupus.

قُرص *A.* 1) *n.* Disk or disc. Tablet; lozenge. Round loaf (of bread). — قرص کمر = بلادر ‖ قرص نعناع Peppermint-drop. 2) *a.* + Firm; strong; durable. — ق. کردن To make firm. To

غرغشه = قرقشه
قِرقی (?) Sparrow-hawk.
قِرِمز Red.ـ ق. شدن To become red. To blush. ـ ق.کردن To make r.; redden. To roast brown. ـ قرمزِ or قرمز فرنگی قرمز دانه = کچ کش
قرمزدانه Cochineal; kermes of Poland. ـ جوهرِ ق. Carmine.
قرمزی Redness.
قرمساق T. Pimp to his own wife; also, cuckold.
قُرمه T. Preserved or potted meat; corned beef. ـ ق.کردن To preserve or pot.
قَرن A. [قُرون] Century. Age. Horn o. ـ قرون وُسطی (-ta) Middle Ages.
قرنطینه A-It. Quarantine.
قرنفل A-G. Clove gilliflower.
قرنیه A. Cornea. ـ ورم ق. Keratitis.
قروض [Pl. of قرض]
قرون [Pl. of قرن]
قُرّه A. Coolness; freshness o. Lustre; brightness.ـ قُرّةالعین (ghoratol-eyn) C. of the eye. F. Comfort; joy.
قره قوش T. = دال & عقاب
قره کل T. Caracul.
قره کهر T. Dark bay.
قره مینا T. Blunderbuss.
قره نی T. P. Clarinet.
قَریب A. a. Near. Approximate. —n. Kindred [only in the

secure.
قَرض A. [قروض] Debt [بدهی].ـ ق. دادن To lend or loan. ـ ق.کردن To borrow.ـ ق.گرفتن To b. To have the loan of. ـ ق. بهم or ق. بالا آوردن رساندن To contract a debt.ـ قرض وقوله کردن × To borrow from various sources.
قرض‌الحسنه A. Money loaned without interest.
قرضه A. = وام Loan.
قرطاجنه A. Carthage.
قِرطاس‌بازی A. P. Red-tapism; officialism.
قُرطُبه A. Cordova.
قُرعه A. Lot [بشك]. Ballot.ـ بطریق ق. By drawing lots.ـ ق. انداختن To cast lots. ـ ق.کشیدن To draw l. ـ ق. بنام او اصابت کرد The lot fell upon him.
قرعه‌کشی A. P. Draw; drawing (of lots). Lottery. Balloting.
قُرُق T. n. Preserve; park. —a. Reserved for exclusive use; preserved. ـ ق. کردن To fence; preserve. To exclude outsiders from.
قَرقاوُل T. Pheasant.ـ قرقاول ماده Hen-pheasant. ـ قرقاول نر Cock-pheasant.
قرقر etc. = غرغر etc.
قِرقره S. u. غرغره

pl. اَقرِباء 'relations']. – قریبِ دوسال Nearly two years. – ماضی ق. Present perfect.

قریباً *A.* Presently; shortly.

قریب‌الوُقوع *A.* Imminent.

قَریحه *A.* [قرائح] Inborn disposition. Talent. Verve.

قَرین *A. a.* Coupled. Allied; cognate. Symmetrical. –*n.* [Pl. اقران] Associate; companion. Peer; match. – قرینِ مفتخر = قرین‌افتخار ‖ ممنون = امتنان

قرینه *A.* [قَرائن] Symmetry. Context. Analogy. Indication.

قَریه *A.* [قُراء] = ده Village.

قز *A-P.* = کژ Raw or floss silk.

قَزّاق *T-R.* Cossack.

قِزل *T.* Red. Roan.

قزل‌آلا *T. n.* Trout. –*a.* Shot.

قَزن قفلی *T.A.* Hook and eye.

قساوت *A.* = **سخت دلی**

قِسراق *T.* Filly.

قَسری *A.* [f. قسر 'compelling']. Mechanistic.

قِسط *A.* [اقساط] Instalment. – باقساط By instalments.

قسط بندی *A. P.* (Arrangement for) payment by instalments.

قُسطَنطنیه *A-G.* Constantinople.

قِسطی *A. P.* (Paid or to be paid) by instalments.

قِس‌علی‌هذا (-*a*la-*h*a-) *A.* Infer (the rest) from this. – وقس علی هذا And so forth; etc.

قسم (*ghasam*) *A.* = سوگند Oath. – ق. خوردن *or* ق یادکردن To take an oath; swear. – ق. دادن To administer an o. – قسم دروغ خوردن To s. falsely; perjure oneself. – بخدا قسم (I s.) by God. – بخدا قسمت میدهم For God's sake.

قِسم *A.* [اَقسام] Kind; variety. *Cf.* جور & نوع ‖ چه ق. 1) What k. of? 2) [Also بچه ق.] How? In what manner? – بقسمی که So that. – اقسام کلمه Parts of speech.

قِسمت *A.* Part; portion; share [بخش]. Section. Lot; fortune; destiny. – خارج ق. Quotient. – ق.کردن To divide; distribute. To share. – قابلِ ق. Divisible. – غیر قابل ق. Indivisible.

قَسم نامه *A. P.* Swearing formula. Affidavit.

قسی ° *A.* = سخت Hard. Cruel.

قسی‌القلب *A.* = **سخت دل**

قَسیم ° *A.* 1) *a.* Handsome. 2) *n.* Participant. Distibutor.

قِشر *A.* [قُشور] = پوست Skin. Bark. Husk. Rind. Shell. Crust. – ق. بستن To form an incrustation.

قُشعریره ° *A.* Horripilation; gooseflesh.

قشقون *T.* = **پاردم**

قِشلاق *T.* Winter quarters.

قَشنگ 1) *a.* Pretty. Handsome. 2) *ad.* + Nicely; well.

قشنگی Prettiness.

قشو´ *T.* Currycomb. – ق.کردن To curry or comb.

قشور [Pl. of قشر]

قشون *T.* [Old word for ارتش]

قص ٥ *A.* = سینه ‖ عظم قص [now (جناغ (سینه] Wishing-bone.

قصاب *A.* = گوشت فروش

قصابی *A. P.* = گوشت فروشی

قصابخانه *A. P.* 1) = کشتارگاه 2) Butcher's (shop).

قصار (*gha*sar) *A.* Fuller.

قصار ِ *A.* [Pl. of قصیر ´short'] – کلمات ق. Aphorisms.

قصاص´ *A.* Laburnum.

قصاص ِ *A.* Retaliation; punishment. – ق.کردن To punish. – قصاص قبل از جنایت (Act based on) prejudgment. *OS.* Punishment of a crime not yet committed.

قصائد [Pl. of قصیده]

قصب´ *A.* Reed; cane [نی]. Windpipe. Kind of fine linen.

قصبات [Pl. of قصبه]

قصب‌الحبیب *A.* 1) = نی 2) = نیشکر 3) *F.* Pen. [sweetflag.

قصب‌الذریره *A.* Calamus;

قصبه´ *A.* [قصبات] Borough; small town. Reed; cane ٥.

قصبةالرّیه *A.* Trachea; windpipe [نای]. [Tracheal.

قصبی *A.* Tibial. Fibular.

قصد´ *A.* Intention. Purpose. Attempt. – ق.داشتن To have an i.; intend. To mean. – ق.کردن To i. To determine. – قصد جان ویرا کردند They made an attempt on his life. – بقصد ِ ‖ قصداً = از قصد With the intention of. [purpose.

قصداً *A.* Intentionally; on

قصدی *A. P.* Intentional. – بچهٔ ق. Changeling; elf-child.

قصر´ *A.* [قُصور] = کاخ

قصر ِ دررفتن (-*ser*-) + To go scot-free; save one's skin.

قصص [Pl. of قصه]

قُصور´ *A.* Shortcoming[کوتاهی]. Omission. Defect [عیب] ٥. – ق. ورزیدن To fail; come short; [with از] neglect.

قصور [Pl. of قصر]

قصه ِ *A.* [قصص] = داستان Tale; story. – ق.کردن To narrate. – ق.کوتاه کردن To shorten the story; sum up.

قصیده´ *A.* [قصائد] Elegy; laudatory, elegiac, or satirical poem; "purpose-poem"

قصیر *A.* = کوتاه(قد)

قصیل´ *A.* Green barley for fodder.

قضاء´ *A.* Judgment. Decree. Destiny; fate. Accident; chance. – ق.شدن To lapse. – قضای حاجت کردن To ease nature. – ق. را *or* از قضا By c. It (so) happened that.

قضاو´ت *C. E.* = قضا Judgment. – ق.کردن To judge.

قضاة *or* قضات [Pl. of قاضی]

قضائی *A.* Judicial; juridical;

legal.

قَضیب *A.* [قُضبان] = شاخه ـ میل

قَضیه *A.* [قضایا] Case. Theorem; proposition ; premise or premiss. *Gr.* Clause. ـ قضیهٔ بدیهیه Axiom. ـ بی‌خبر از قضایا Unaware of what is (*or* was) going about.

قُطاب *A.* (*Kind of pastry like*) turnover.

قِطار *A.* Train. Row; file. ـ ق. کردن To set in a row or f. To make a string of.

قِطاع *A.* Sector (of a circle).

قُطاع [Pl. of قاطع]

قَطاعی *A. P.* (Act of) scissoring out. [pivot.

قُطب *A.* [D. قطبین] Pole. Axis;

قطب نما *A. P.* Compass.

قطبی *A.* Polar. ـ ستارهٔ ق. The North Star or pole-star.

قُطر *A.* Diameter. Thickness. Diagonal. *Cf. the pl.* اقطار ـ قطر درونی لوله Calibre. ـ قطرِ ظلّ تمام Cosecant.

قطرات [Pl. of قطره]

قَطران *A.* = قیر Tar. ـ جوهر قطران Creosote. [dance.

قُطرُب *A.* Chorea; St. Vitus's

قَطره *A.* [قطرات] Drop. ـ ق. ق. D. by d. ـ ق. ق. چکیدن To drip; fall in drops.

قطره چکان *A. P.* Dropping-tube; dropper.

قط زن *A. P.* Bone on which pens are nibbed; pen-cutter.

قَطع (*ghat'*) *A.* Cutting; amputation. Interruption. Severance. Settling; fixing. Form; cut; size. ـ ق. کردن = بریدن To cut (off). To break off; interrupt. To fell, as a tree. To settle (upon); fix : قیمت آنرا اول ق. کنید ‖ To decide. To switch off. To ring off. ـ قطع امید کردن To lose hope ; despair. ـ قطع روابط کردن To break off relations ; come to a rupture. ـ قطع رحم o Breaking off ties of relationship. ـ قطع زائد Hyperbola. ـ قطع مکافی Parabola. ـ قطع ناقص Ellipse. ـ قطع نظر از Apart from ; irrespective of . ـ بیع ق. ‖ **قطعاً** = بطور قطع Irrevocable sale.

قِطَع (*gheta'*) [Pl. of قطعه]

قَطعاً *A.* Certainly. Absolutely. *S. a.* اصلاً

قطعات [Pl. of قطعه]

قطع نامه *A. P.* Statement ; manifesto.

قِطعه *A.* [قِطَع *gheta'* & قطعات] Piece. *Cf.* پاره & تیکه ‖ Section ; part . Segment . Tract; plot. Fragment of an elegy —often an independent poem. Continent. ـ ق. ق. کردن To cut to pieces. To parcel.

قَطعی *A.* Final. Definite. Decisive. Positive ; certain.

Outright. Irrevocable. Fixed; last : بطور قطعی = قطعاً ‖ بهای ق.

قطعیت A. Final nature. ـ بچیزی ق. دادن To finalize s. t.

قَطور A. Thick; voluminous.

قَطیفه A. Bath-towel. Bathing-wrap; bath-robe. [Abyss.

قَعر A. Bottom [ته]. Depth.

قعود A. Sitting [نشستن].

قَفا A. Nape of the neck. *By e.* Neck. ـ ق. خوردن * To receive a slap on the neck. ـ ازقفای کسی رفتن To follow s. o.

قفائی Of the colour of lavender; also, mauve. [Per. f. قفا cont. of زبان در قفا *q. v.*].

قفرالیهود A. Jews'-pitch; bitumen of Judea.

قَفس or قفص A. Cage.

قفسه A. P. Cupboard; set of shelves. ـ قفسهٔ سینه Thorax.

قفسه بندی A. P. Arrangement of shelves; shelving.

قفقاز(ی) Caucasia(n).

قفقازیه Caucasia.

قُفل A. Padlock. ـ قفل ابجد or قفل حروفی Combination lock; letter-lock. ـ قفل مغزی Lock. ـ ق. کردن To lock.

قفل ساز A. P. Locksmith.

قَقنس A-G. Phoenix.

قُلاب A. Hook. *Chem.* Valence. ـ ق. کردن To curve like a h. ـ به ق. زدن To hang on, fasten with, a h. ـ دلش ق. شد + He was affected with colic.

قلابدار A. P. Hooked.

قلاب دوز A. P. Crocheter.

قلاب‌دوزی A. P. Crochet work. Crocheting.

قلاب سنگ A. P. = سنگ قلاب

قلابی A. P. Faked; phon(e)y.

قلاج T. Fathom.

قَلاده A. (Dog's) collar. ـ سه ق. سگ Three dogs.

قلاش (?) 1) Rogue. 2) = مفت‌خور 3) = میگسار 4) = لوده

قِلاع [Pl. of قلعه]

قُلاع ه A. = برفك

قلاویز [Per. f. T. غلاغوز 'guide'] Tap. *Cf.* حدیده

قَلب A. [قلوب] = دل Heart. *F.* Mind. Courage. Centre. ـ از ته ق. Most heartily; sincerely. ـ قوت ق. Assurance. Stout heart.

قَلب A. Inversion. Permutation. [*Used as an a.*] Counterfeit; base. ـ ق. کردن To invert. ـ قلب ماهیت Transmutation.

قلباً A. Heartily; cordially.

قلب‌الاسد A. (*Astr.*) Regulus; Alpha Leonis. *By e.* The dog-days.

قلب‌العقرب A. (*Astr.*) Antares; Alpha Scorpio.

قلب ساز & قلب زن A. P. Coiner of base money.

قلبه = قلوه or کلیه

قلبی A. Heartfelt; cordial. ـ خال ق. C. P. Heart.

قلت *A.* = کمی
قلتاق *T.* Saddle-tree.
قَلتبان Cuckold. Effeminate person.
قلچاق ○ *T.* Gauntlet.
قلچماق *T.* Strong; robust.
قُلدُر *T.* Tough guy. Bully. One who, by using violence, imposes his unjust views on others.— حکومت قلدری Sword-law.
قُلزُم *A.* Clysma. — دریای ق. The Red Sea.
قَلع *A.* Tin [also قلعی]. Eradication; evulsion. — ق. وقمع کردن To eradicate.
قَلعه *A.* [قِلاع] Castle. Fort [دژ]. — ق. رفتن To castle.
قلعی *A. P.* Tin [usu. قلع].
قلفه *S. u.* غلفه
قَلق (-lagh) *A.* = اضطراب
قِلق (-legh) *T.* Mood. Habit.— قلق کسیرا بدست آوردن + To get the length of one's shoes.
قلل [Pl. of قله]
قَلم *A.* [اقلام] Pen [خامه]. Item; entry. *F.* Variety. Style; penmanship. — قلم پا Shin; s.-bone. — قلم حجاری Boasting chisel. — قلم حکاکی Engraving-chisel.— قلم گچ Crayon.— قلم نی Reed pen. — ق. خوردن To be crossed out. To be cancelled or altered. — ق. زدن To write off; cross out [also ق. کشیدن]. To chase; engrave.— ق. کردن To break; cut in two, as a bone. — از قلم افتادن To be omitted in writing. — بقلمِ آقای ح. By (*i. e.* written by) Mr. H.
قلم‌انداز × *A. P.* Scribblingly; rapidly.
قلمتراش *A. P.* Penknife.
قلم خوردگی *A. P.* Alteration. Cancellation. *See* قلم خوردن
قلم خورده *A. P.* Crossed out. Cancelled. Altered.
قلمداد کردن *A. P.* To figure. To present; give. To declare.
قلمدان *A. P.* Pen-case.
قلمدوش کردن + *A.P.* To carry astraddle on one's shoulders.
قلمرو *A. P.* Realm; jurisdiction. Area.
قلم زده *A. P.* Crossed out. Engraved. Chased. Etched.
قلمزن ○ *A. P.* Quill driver. Engraver.
قلمستان *A. P.* Nursery for raising trees.
قلمکار *A. P.* (Printed) calico; figured c.; print.
قلم مو *A. P.* Painting-brush.
قلمه *A. P.* Cutting; slip; scion. — ق. زدن To propagate by slips.
قلمی *A. P.* Tapering; slender. Crystallized. Etched. Engraved. Clerical. — شورهٔ ق. Potassium nitrate. — ق. داشتن [*Obsolete*] = نوشتن
قلندر *A.P.* Calender: men-

dicant or wandering dervish. — چادر قلندری Bell-tent; gipsy-tent.
قلنسوه o *A*. Mitre.
قلوب [Pl. of قلب]
قَلّ وَ دَلّ *A*. Concise and expressive; laconic.
قُلوه Kidney. [Per. f. A. کلیه]
قلوه سنگ Rubble-stone.
قلوه کن کردن + To tear (s. t.) so that a piece is cut out of it; tear it in the middle.
قله *A*. [قُلل] Summit. *F*. Climax.
قُلی *T*. = پسر Son [in comb.]. *Mas. pr. name*.
قَلیا *A*. Alkali. — قلیای قمی *or* قلیای صابون پزی Barilla. — جوهرِ قلیا Carbonate of soda. — شبه ق. Alkaloid.
قلیا سنج *A. P*. Alkalimeter.
قَلیان [Per. f. غُلیان] Hookah; nargileh.
قلیائی *A*. Alkaline.
قلیج o *T*. = شمشیر [Only in دست ق. the decisive or odd game at backgammons].
قَلیل *A*. = کم Little; few.
قلیل المدت *A*. = کم مدت
قَلیه (*A*.) *Dish like fricassee*. — قلیهٔ انتظار Barmecide feast.
قُمار *A*. Gambling. — ق. کردن To gamble (away).
قمار باز *A. P*. Gambler.
قمار بازی *A. P*. Gambling. — ق. کردن To gamble.
قمارخانه *A. P*. Gaming-house; gambling-house.
قماری *A. P*. Hazardous; aleatory; speculative.
قُماش *A*. [اقمشه] Piece goods; textile fabrics. *F*. Type.
قُمپز در کردن × To bluff or swagger.
قَمچی *T*. Switch; horse-whip.
قَمر *A*. [اقمار] Moon [ماه]. Satellite. *Fem. pr. name*.
قمر درعقرب *A. P*. Mansion of the moon confronting the Scorpio, and believed by some to have an unlucky consequence.
قَمری *A*. Lunar. *Cf*. شمسی
قُمری *A*. Turtledove; also, ringdove.
قَمع *A*. Suppression. Battering.
قُمقمه *A*. Flask. Thermos-pot.
قَمه Straight poniard. [canal.
قَنات *A*. [قنوات] Subterranean
قَناد *A*. Confectioner.
قنادی *A. P*. Confectionery.
قناره *A*. Butcher's hook; gambrel.
قناری *Fr*. Canary (-bird).
قناص (?) *n*. Angulation. Angular piece of land. —*a*. Angular. Crooked. *F*. Odd-shaped; bizarre. Shabby-lookin[g]
قَناعت *A*. Contentment. — ق. کردن To be contented; content oneself. [name
قنبر *A*. *Ghambar*: mas. pr.
قَند *A. P*. Lump sugar; cube

s. – شیرهٔ ق. Molasses. – مرض ق. Caramel. – قند سوخته Diabetes mellitus. – قند کله Loaf-sugar. – قندکلوخه Lump sugar. – ق. توی دلش آب شد + He was all smiles.

قَنداغ Hot water with sugar.

قُنداق *T.* Swaddling-clothes; -bands. [Of a rifle or gun] Stock. – ق. کردن To swaddle; swathe.

قنداغه *T. P.* Gunstock.

قندان *A. P.* Sugar-bowl.

قَندَران Caoutchouc.

قندگیر *A. P.* Sugar-tongs.

قندی *A. P.* Sugared; candied.

قنوات [Pl. of قنات]

قنوط *R.* Knout.

قو *T. or* **غو** Swan. – پرِ قو Eider-down.

قو (*ghow*) *T.* Amadou; German tinder; touchwood.

قُوا *A.* Forces. Faculties. *Cf. the s.* قوه ‖ تجدید قوا Reinforcement.

قَواره (Dress) length. *F.* Stature; also, figure or cut.

قواره‌کن Quarryman

قواعد [Pl. of قاعده]

قوافی [Pl. of قافیه]

قوّال *A.* = قصه‌گو - خنیاگر

قَوام *A.* Straightness. Stature.

قِوام *A.* Consistency; firmness. Existence. Order. *Mas. pr. name.* – قوام بول Pellicle of the urine – ق. گرفتن To get into shape. To be settled.

قوانین [Pl. of قانون]

قوباء *A.* Tetter. Herpes. – زرد زخم = ○ قوباء اصفر

قوت *A.* Nourishment; food. – قوت لایموت Scanty f. just enough to keep one alive.

قوت (*ghovat*) *A.* Strength; force [زور & نیرو]. Faculty. Authority. [In the last two senses usu. قوه]. – ق. دادن To strengthen. To give nourishment (to). To reinforce. – ق. گرفتن To take vigour; gather strength. – بقوت خود باقی بودن To remain in force; continue to be valid. – قوت قلب Assurance. Courage. Stout heart.

قورباغه *T.* Frog [غوك & وزغ]. – سنگ ق. Toadstone. – علف ق. Ironwort.

قورخانه *T. P.* = زرادخانه

قوری Tea-pot.

قوز 1) *n.* Hump. Protuberance. – قوز بالای ق. Kick in the pants; one difficulty added to another. – سرِ قوز افتادن ✕ To get one's back up; become stubborn. – قوز سینه Chicken-breast. 2) *a.* Humpbacked. Humped. – ق. کردن *vi.* To crouch or squat. –*vt.* To hump.

قوزُ پشت Humpbacked.

قوزدار 1) Protuberant. 2) = قوزپشت

غوزك = قوزك

قوزی Humpback(ed).

قوس *A*. [اقواس o] Bow [کمان]. Arc. *Astr*. Sagittarius. [Old name of آذر]. قوس آورتا— Arch of the aorta. — قوس تربیع Quadratrix. — قوس خارجی Extrados. — قوس داخلی Intrados. — قوس قزح Rainbow.

قوش *T*. Falcon. — قوش جره Male falcon. — قوش طور or قوش ماده Female falcon. — قوش قزل Goshawk.

قوشی *T. P*. Aquiline.

قوطی *T*. Small box. Can; tin. — قوطی چای Tea-caddy. — قوطی سیگار Cigarette-case. — قوطی کبریت Match-b. — در قوطی ریختن To can or tin. [can-o.

قوطی بازکن *T. P*. Tin-opener;

قول *A*. [اقوال] Promise; word. Speech. Saying. — ق. دادن To promise. — ق. گرفتن از To make (s. o.) promise. — قول شرف Word of honour; *parole d'honneur*. — سر قول خود ایستادن To abide by one's word. — زیر قول خود زدن To go back on one's word. — از قول من باو بگو Tell him for me. — حسن از قول علی گفت Hassan, quoting Ali, said. — بقول شما According to you; as you say.

قولنامه *A. P*. Written promise; prelimin:ry agreement.

قولنج *A-G*. Colic. — قولنج امعاء Gripes. — قولنج ایلاوس Ileus; iliac passion. — قولنج سربی Lead colic; painter's c.

قولون *A-G*. (*Anat*.) Colon. — ورم ق. Colonitis.

قوم *A*. [اقوام] People; nation. Tribe. Group of followers. — قوم و خویش Relative(s).

قوم وخویشی *A. P*. = خویشاوندی

قومیت *A*. Racial or national character. Relationship. Clanship.

قوه [قوا] [f. A. قوت] Power; strength; force; energy. Faculty : قوهٔ ناطقه ‖ Authority. Battery. — ق. دادن (به) To strengthen. — از قوه بفعل آوردن To realize. To bring into effect. ... ق. اش نمیرسد که He is not strong enough to...; also, he cannot afford to... — پنج بقوهٔ ۳ 5^3.

قوی *A*. 1) *a*. [Fem. قویه]Strong; powerful [نیرومند]. 2) *n*. [only in the pl. اقویاء the powerful or influential (people)]. — احتمال ق. میرود There is a s. probability.

قویاً *A*. Strongly.

قوی البنیه *A*. or قوی بنیه *a. p*. Physically strong; robust.

قوی القلب *A*. Stout-hearted.

قوی پنجه *A. P*. Of strong claws. *F*. Strong.

قوی هیکل *a. p*. Huge. Formidable; robust. Well-set.

قهوه‌خوری *A.P.* [For فنجان‌ق.] Coffee-cup.

قی *A.* Vomiting. — داروی ضدّ قی Antemetic. — قی خونی Hematemesis. — قی آوردن To provoke vomiting. — قی کردن To vomit. — چشمانش قی گرفته است. He has sleep in the corner of his eyes.

قیاس *A.* Analogy. Deduction. — ق. کردن To infer by a.; analogize. To syllogize. — قیاس بنفس کردن To measure other people's corn by one's own bushel. — قیاس کاذب Paralogism. — بر قیاسِ On the analogy of.

قیاساً *A.* Analogically; by analogy or comparison.

قیاسی *A.* Analogical. Deductive. *Gr.* Regular.

قیاصره [Pl. of قیصر]

قیافه *A.* Physiognomy; mien.

قیافه‌شناس *A.P.* Physiognomist.

قیافه شناسی *A.P.* Physiognomy.

قیام *A.* Rising. *Cf.* نهضت&جنبش ‖ Insurrection; revolt. — ق. کردن To revolt or rise. — تاقیام قیامت + Till doomsday; for ever and a day.

قیاماً *A.* By rising or standing. In a s. posture.

قیامت *A.* = رستاخیز Resurrection. — ق. کردن To do s. t. marvellously well; be a prodigy of s. t. — ق. برپا کردن To kick up a row.

قی‌آور *A. P.* Emetic.

قَهّار *A.* 1) *a.* Very powerful; omnipotent. 2) *n.* Avenger or subduer: ep. of God.

قَهر *A.* Wrath; anger. Violence; force. Sulking. — من با او قهر هستم I am not on speaking terms with him. — ق. کردن To sulk. To walk out in protest. To break off relations. — قهرش گرفت He flew into a rage. — قهر خود را سر کسی خالی کردن To vent one's anger on s. o.; pour out one's fury on him.

قهراً *A.* By force; forcibly. Naturally. Automatically.

قَهرَمان Hero. Champion. — قهرمان رانندگی C. driver.

قهرمانی 1) *n.* Championship. 2) *a.* Promoting c.

قَهری *A.* Forcible. Natural. Automatic. [Fem. قهریه].

قَهقرا *A.* Retrogradation. — به ق. رفتن To retograde.

قهقرائی *A. P.* Retrogressive. — سیر قهقرائی Retrogradation.

قَهقهه *A.* Boisterous laugh. — ق. زدن To roar with laughter.

قَهوه *A.* Coffee. — قهوهٔ بی شیر Black c. — جوهرِ ق. Caffein(e).

قهوه ای *A. P.* Coffee-brown.

قهوه جوش *A. P.* Coffee-pot.

قهوه‌چی *A. T.* Tea-shop keeper. *OS.* Coffee-house k.

قهوه خانه *A. P.* Tea-house; coffee-house; tea-shop.

قیچی T. (Pair of) scissors. — ق.کردن To scissor (out). To cut (up). To shear. — قیچی ِ باغبانی Pruning-shears.

قید A. [قیود] Press; cramp. F. tie; bond; obligation. Stipulation; reservation. Care. Gr. Adverb. — ق. کردن To stipulate. — درقید چیزی بودن To care for, or be particular about, s. t. — قید چیزیرا زدن +To abandon or forget s. t. — بدون ق. و شرط Unconditional-(ly). — درقید حیات بودن To be living.

قیدی A. P. Adverbial.

قیر A. Tar. — ق. زدن or با قیر اندودن To smear with tar; bituminize. — قیر حل شده Cutback. — قیر خیابان Asphalt. — قیر معدنی Bitumen.

قیراط A-G. Carat.

قیر اندود Tarred; smeared with tar. — ق.کردن To smear with tar; bituminize.

قیرگون * Pitch-dark; black.

قیروان o Environs of the earth; horizon. End.

قیری 1) = قیر اندود 2) = قیرگون 3) Bituminous.

قیسی or قیصی [f. T. قایسی apricot] *Variety of apricot.*

قیش T. Thong; strap.

قیصر A. [قیاصره] Caesar.

قیصوم A. — ‖ قیصوم ماده Wormwood. — قیصوم نر Southernwood.

قیطان T. Braid; cord.

قیف Funnel. [Of the brain] Infundibulum.

قیفی Funnel-shaped. — بستنی ق. Cone icecream. — نان ق. Cornet. — کلاه ق. Dunce's cap.

قیقاج T. n. Shooting backward. Parthian shot; P. shaft. —ad. Obliquely. Backwards. —a. Oblique.

قیل و قال a. p. Noise; din; fuss. — ق. کردن To make a noise. To wrangle.

قیلوله o A. Siesta.

قیلی ویلی رفتن × To have a gnawing sensation; turn over: شکمم ق. میرود

قیم (ghayem) A. Guardian; tutor. — دولت ق. Mandatary.

قیماق T. Scum of milk; cream.

قیمت A. = بها Price; cost; value. — ق.کردن 1) = ارزیابی کردن ‖ 2) To inquire the price of.

قیمتی A. P. = پر بها

قیمومت A. Guardianship; tutorship. Mandate.

قیمه T. Minced meat; hashed m. — ق.کردن To mince; hash. — ق. و قرمه کردن × To beat black and blue; make a mince-meat of.

قیود [Pl. of قید]

قیودات [Pl. of قیود pl. of قید]

قیوم A. Self-existent.

کاباره *Fr.* Cabaret.
کابل *Fr.* Cable.
کابوتاژ *Fr.* Cabotage; coasting.
کابوس *A.* = بختك
کابین Marriage-settlement. Dower.
کابینه *Fr.* 1) Cabinet (council). 2) = آبریز
کاپوت *R. or Fr.* Bonnet (of an automobile). French leather.
کاتالوگ *Fr.* Catalogue.
کاتوزی ○ Clergyman.
کاتِ کبود Sulphate of copper.
کاتِب *A.* [کتاب *kotab*]=نویسنده Writer; scribe; amanuensis.
کاتولیك *Fr.* Catholic.
کاج (Scotch or red) pine. — چوب ك. P.-needle. — برگ ك. Deal.
کاجی Pineal. Coniferous.
کاجیره = کافیشه
کاچی Dish of flour, sugar, fat, and spices, given to parturient women.
کاخ Palace. [work.
کادر *Fr.* Staff; *cadre*; frame-
کاذِب *A. a.* 1) = دروغگو 2) False. —*n.* Liar [pl. کَذَبه].
کاذبانه *A. P.* Falsely; untruthfully.
کار Work. Labour. Employment; job; business. Task; duty. Workmanship. Act. Affair. Case. Matter: کار چند دقیقه نیست It is not a matter of a few minutes. — ك. کردن To work. To operate or run, as a machine. To wear: ‖ کفشها یك سال ك. خواهد کرد شکمش ك. نکرد His bowels did not move. — کاری نمیتوان کرد Nothing can be done. — ك. گذاشتن To instal; fix; work in place. — از کار افتادن To be disabled. To be laid up. To be upset: ‖ کابینه از کار افتاد از کار انداختن To disable. To lay up, as a machine. To u. To discharge; remove from office. — بکار آمدن To (prove to) be useful [also (به) ك. افتادن —]. بکار خوردن To start to operate or run (again). — بکار انداختن To commission; operate; work, as a mine. To invest. — بکار بردن To use. — (به) ك. بستن To apply. To put into practice. — بکار رفتن To be used. To be useful. — بکار زدن To find some use for. To use. — بکار گرفتن To employ or exploit. — سر کار At work. — باشما کار دارم I want to have a word with you. — چه ك. دارید What is

Supply Department.

بغچه = کارپیچ

کار پیشَ بر Feed-dog.

کارت Fr. Card. — کارت ویزیت Visiting-card.

کارت ُپستال Fr. Post(al) card.

کارتر Fr. Oil-pan.

کار ِتل Ger. Cartel; Kartel.

کار ُتن Fr. Pasteboard box; carton. Box-file.

کارتنك or کارتنه Spider.

کارچاق کن × Go-between who procures means by influencing or corrupting others.

کارخانجات + [Pl. of کارخانه]

کارخانه Factory; works. Studio. [Of a watch or clock] Mechanism. — کارخانهٔ برق Power station. — کارخانهٔ تعمیر Repairing-shop; repair shop.

کارد (Large) knife — کاردش باستخوان رسید He was on his beam-ends; he was driven to extremities. — ك. و کارد کشی داشتن To be at daggers drawn; be like a bull and a red rag with each other.

کاردار *Chargé-d'affaires.*

کاردان Ingenious. Skilful. Experienced. Sagacious.

کاردانی Ingeniousness. Skill; tact. *Savoir faire.*

کارد ساز Knifesmith; cutler.

کارد سازی Cutlery.

کار آزموده = کار دیده

کارزار * Battle. Cf. نبرد & جنگ

your business (here)? W. can I do for you? — خیلی‌ك. دارم I am very busy. — این کاری بمذهب ندارد That has nothing to do with religion. — کاری به (کار) او نداشته باشید Let him alone. — کاری ندارد There is nothing hard about it; it is every man's work. — کاراو نیست He is not likely to have done this. He is not equal to the task. — کاردستتان خواهدداد It will get you in trouble. — کارش ساخته است It is all over with him. He is done away with. — کارش خراب است He is ruined. It is all over with him. She has fallen; she is spoiled. — ك. از کار گذشته است The die is cast. It is all over. — کاروبار Affair. Business.

کار [Imp. of کاشتن]

کار آزموده Experienced.

کارآگاه Detective.

کارآمد Skilled. Efficient.

کارآموز Trainee.

کارآموزش Training.

کارآموزی Training. Probation.

کارآیی Efficiency.

کار ُبر Efficient.

کار ُبرد Application.

کار ُبن Fr. = کاغذ واکیره Carbon.

کاربنات Fr. Carbonate.

کارپرداز Person in charge of supplies.

کار پردازی [For ادارهٔ ك.]

کارساز Promoting, or promoter of, affairs [ep. of God].
کارسازی Payment. — ك. داشتن To pay [پرداختن].
کارشکنی Obstructionism.
کارشناس Expert.
کارفرما Employer.
کارکرد Earning. Output.
کارکرده Used; second-hand.
کارکشته Veteran. Experienced.
کارکن *a*. Hard-working; toiling. Durable; tough. —*n*. Physic ; purgative.
کارکنان Personnel; employees. *Cf. the s.* کارکن
کارگاه Working-place ; workshop. Loom. Frame (holding canvas for embroidery).
کارگر *n*. Worker ; workman ; labourer. —*a*. Efficacious.
کارگردان Stage-manager.
کارگری *n*. Situation of a worker. —*a*. Fit for a w. — خانه‌های ك. Labour quarters.
کارگزار Agent ; correspondent.
کارگزاری Agency.
کارگزینی [For ادارهٔ ك.] Staff Department.
کارگشائی (Relieving by way of) loaning. — بنگاه ك. Pawnshop ; loan-bank.
کارمزد Piece-work wage. Commission. [ployee.
کارمند Member of staff; employee.
کارمندی Membership of staff.
کارنامه Report card.
کارنده Sower; planter.
کاروان Caravan.
کاروانسرا Carvanserai; inn.
کاروانسرادار Custodian of a caravanserai. Inn-keeper o.
کاروانك *Z*. Crane.
کاروانکش Dog-star; Sirius.
کاروانی Member of a caravan.
کارورز Intern(e).
کارورزی Internship. Training.
کاری Effective. Mortal: زخم ك. ‖ Active; efficient : مرد کاری
کاریابی Procuration of employment. — بنگاه ك. E. agency.
کاریز 1) =قنات 2) Drain; sewer.
کاریکاتور *Fr*. Caricature.
کاریکاتور ساز *Fr. P*. Caricaturist.
کازینو *Fr*. Casino.
کازیه *Fr*. (Letter-)tray.
کاسب *A*. [کسبه] Tradeseman ; business-man.
کاس برگ Sepal.
کاسبی *A. P*. Business; trading.— ك. کردن *vi*. To do b.; trade. —*vt*. + To earn.
کاست *or* **کاستی** * Decrease. Loss.
کاستن [کاه] *vt*. To diminish; decrease [often with از]. To subtract ; deduct. —*vi*. To be decreased. To detract.
کاسته 1) [P. P. of کاستن]. 2) *n*. Subtrahend.
کاسد *A*. Dull, as a market.
کاسك *Fr*. Helmet(-like cap).
کاسکت *Fr*. (Peaked) cap.

کاسنی Chicory.
کاسه Bowl; porringer. Calyx; cup. [Of a guitar] Belly. [Of a tortoise] Carapace. – کاسهٔ زانو ‖ چشمخانه = کاسهٔ چشم Knee-cap ; -pan. – کاسهٔ سر Skull; cranium. – کاسهٔ از آش گرمتر More Catholic than the Pope. – کاسه وکوزه (Poor man's) odds and ends. – کاسه وکوزه را سرِکسی شکستن To lay the blame on s. o. ; b. it on him. – زیر کاسه نیم کاسه‌ای هست There are wheels within wheels. There is s. t. in the wind.
لاك پشت = کاسه پشت
کاسه ترمز *P. R.* Brake-drum.
کاسه ساچمه *P. T.* Ball-bearing race.
کاسه لیس Sycophant. Sponger.
کاسه لیسی Flattery. Sponging on others.
کاسه نمد [In a motor car] Oil seal.
کاش I wish ; O that ! [Also ك. او – . ك. که + *or* ای ك.] ك. او را میدیدم I w. I would (*or* could) see him.
کاشانه • Lodging. Cottage.
کاشتن [کار] To sow. To plant. [*In some games*] To spot. *F*. To leave in the lurch.
کاشته [P. P. of کاشتن]
کاشِف *A*. Discoverer. – ك. بعمل آمد It was found out.
کاشکل *Fr*. Neckerchief. Scarf.
کاشکی *or* **کاش که** + = **کاش**
کاشه *Fr*. Cachet; wafer.
کاشی [For آجر کاشی] Glazed tile.
کاشی‌ساز & کاشی‌پز Tiler : maker of glazed tiles.
کاظِم *A*. 1) *Mas. pr. name*. 2) One who represses his anger.
کاغَذ Paper. Letter. Instrument; document. – پول ك. P.-money.
کاغذبُر Paper-knife. Guillotine; p.-cutting machine.
کاغذ پاره Scrap of paper.
کاغذ سازی Forgery. [For کارخانهٔ ك.] Paper-mill.
کاغذگیر Paper-clip.
کاغذی Of paper. Thin as p. Thin-skinned. – گل ك. Bourgainvillia.
کافر *A*. [کفار] Unbeliever; infidel. Pagan.
کافر ماجرا *a. p.* Recalcitrant (in religious matters).
کافری *A. P.* Infidelity. Heathenism. Blasphemousness.
کافور *A*. Camphor.
کافوری *A. P.* Camphorated. – شمع ك. Spermaceti candle.
کافه *Fr*. Café ; coffee-house.
کافه (*kafah*) *A*. = همگی All.
کافی *A*. [Fem. کافیه] Sufficient; enough.
کافیشه Bastard saffron ; safflower.
کافئین *Fr*. Caffeine.
کاکا 1) (Old) slave. 2) = برادر
کاکاسیاه Negro slave.

کاکائو *Fr*. Cocoa.
کاکل Forelock; topknot.
کاکلی *a*. Crested. *–n*. C. lark.
کاکوتی [*f*. *T*.] Wild thyme.
کال = نارس Unripe; green.
کالا Goods; merchandise; ware.
کالباس *R*. Sausage.
کالبد Frame; skeleton. Mould; form. Body; carcass.
کالبد شکافی Dissection.
کالبد شناس Anatomist.
کالبد شناسی Anatomy.
کالبدگشایی Autopsy.
کالج *Fr*. College. *Cf*. دانشکده
کالسکه *R*. Coach.
کالك *Fr*. Calk; tracing paper.
کام Palate. *By e*. Mouth. Mortise. *F*. Aim. (Object of) gratification or fruition. – ك. جستن To seek f. – کام کسیرا دادن To gratify a person's wishes. – کام دل گرفتن *or* بکام دل رسیدن To enjoy f. To attain one's aim. – بکام * As one wishes.
کامران *or* **کامروا** Successful; enjoying fruition.
کامرانی Fruition. Happy life.
کامل *A*. Perfect; complete; thorough; full. Elderly; of ripe years. [Fem. کامله] – ك. کردن To c.; bring to perfection – ك. شدن To be completed. To attain p.
کاملا *A*. Completely; thoroughly; absolutely; all *ad*.
تمام عیار = کامل العیار
کاملةالوداد *A*. Most-favoured: دوَل ك. [pointed.
کام ناروا Unsuccessful. Disappointed.
کامیاب Successful. – ك. شدن To be successful; succeed.
کامیابی Success(fulness).
کامیون *Fr*. Lorry; truck.
کان Mine. – کان سنگ Quarry.
کاناپه *Fr*. Sofa; settee.
کانال *Fr*. Canal [ترعه]. Duct.
کاندر * [Cont. of که اندر].
کاندید *Fr*. Candidate. – ك. کردن To nominate.
کان شناس Mineralogist.
کان شناسی Mineralogy.
کان کن Miner. – کان کنی Mining.
کانگورو *Fr*. Kangaroo.
کأن لم یکن (*ka an lamyakon*) *A*. Null (and void).
کانوا *R*. Knitting wool.
کانون *A*. Fireplace; hearth o. Society or club. *Ph*. Focus.
کانون *Name of two Jewish and Syriac months*: کانون اول (Nov -Dec.) *and* کانون دوم (Dec. -Jan.).
کانونی *A*. Focal: فاصلهٔ ك.
کانه (*ka-anahu:*) *A*. Exactly.
کانی o Mineral [معدنی].
کاو [Imp. of کاویدن].
کاواك Hollow [پوك].
کاوش Digging. *F*. Deep search. – ك. کردن To investigate.

کاویدن [کاو] To dig. *F.* To search deeply.

کاه Straw. Chaff.– پرِ کاه Blade of straw. – ك. را کوه کردن To make mountains out of mole-hills.

کاه [Imp. of کاهیدن *or* کاستن].

کاهبن Stubble.

کاهدان Straw-rick.

کاهربا etc. = **کهربا** etc.

کاهِش Decrease. Deduction. Subtraction. – ك. یافتن To be decreased or diminished.

کاهش یاب Minuend.

کاهگل Plaster of clay and straw ; cob. – ك کردن To thatch with clay and s.

کاهِل *A.* Indolent ; lazy.

کاهلی *A.* Indolence; laziness.

کاهِن *A.* [کهنه *kaha-*] 1) = فالگیر 2) Jewish priest. [cent.

کاهنده Diminishing. Decrescent.

کاهو Lettuce; romaine. – کاهوی پیچ Curled or cabbage l.

کاهی (Made) of straw. Straw-coloured.– مقوای ك. S.-board.

کای * (*key*) [Cont. of که ای]

کاین *or* **کین** * [Cont. of که این]

کائِنات *A.* [Pl. of کائنه fem. of کائن ○] Beings. Nature. Universe. Circumstances+.

کائوچو *Fr.* Caoutchouc; rubber.

کباب Meat roasted on a skewer ; roast meat. – ك. کردن To grill; cook on a skewer. *F.* To cut to the heart.– گوشت **کبابی** Roast (meat) ; steak.

کبابه *A.* Cubeb.

کباده *A.* Bow-shaped iron instrument used in gymnastics.

کبار [Pl. of کبیر]

کبائر [Pl. of کبیره]

کبد *A.* = جکر سیاه Liver.

کِبر *A.* Haughtiness; pride.

کبر (*kebar*) *A.* Advanced age.– کبرِ سن Senility. Majority.

کبرا *Fr.* Cobra.

کبره Crust. Patina. – ك. بستن To form a c. To indurate.

کُبری (-*ra*) *A.* [Fem. of اکبر] Major (term). *Fem. pr. name.*

کِبریاء *A.* Grandeur. Omnipotence. *By e.* The Great God.

کِبریت *A.* Match. – ك. زدن To strike a m.– کارخانهٔ کبریت سازی Match-factory.– اتوموبیل **کبریتی** Station-waggon. [cumber.

کبست ○ Colocynth. Wild cucumber.

کبك Partridge. – سرِ خود را مثل ك. زیر برف کردن To bury one's head ostrich-like in the sand.

کبوتر Pigeon; dove. [cote.

کبوترخان Pigeon-house; dove-cote.

کبود Dark blue ; black and blue. [*Of the sky*] Azure. [*Of a horse*] Grey.

کبوده Black poplar.

کبودی Dark blue (colour).– ك. زدن To tattoo oneself.

کبیر *A.* 1) *a.* Great [بزرگ]. Elder. *Law.* Major. [*Of a*

crime] Capital; mortal. — داریوش ك. Darius the G. 2) *n*. [Pl. کبار] Major. Elder. Dignitary. — سفیر کبیر [pl. سفرای کبار] Ambassador.
کبیره *A*. [کبائر] Mortal sin; capital crime. [Orig. fem. of کبیر]. [Leap year.
کبیسه *A*. Intercalary. — سال ك.
کپ Demijohn.
کپر Hut; lodge.
کپسول *Fr*. = پوشینه Capsule.
کپك Mould; mustiness.— ك. زدن To mould; get musty.
کپه (*kapeh*) Mortar-board. Pan of a scale. [Per. f. کفه]
کپه (*kopeh*) Heap; pile.
کپیه *Fr*. Copy. — دفتر کپیه Copy letter book. — مداد کپیه Copying pencil; indelible p. — ك. کردن To copy [رو نویس کردن].
کت [Corruption of کتف].—کت کسیرا بستن To pinion s. o.; bind his arms fast. *F*. To make rings round s. o.
کت • (*kel*) = که ات & که ترا
کت [f. E. *coat*] = نیمتنه Jacket.
کتاب *A*. [کتب] Book.
کتاب (*kotab*) [Pl. of کاتب]
کتابت *A*. Writing; inscription.
کتابچه *A*. *P*. Booklet. Blank-book; note-book.
کتابخانه *A*. *P*. Library.
کتابدار *A*. *P*. Librarian.
کتاب فروش *A*. *P*. Bookseller.
کتاب فروشی *A*. *P*. Dealing in books. [For دکان ك.] Bookshop; bookseller's.
کتابی *A*. *P*. Bookish. Biblical.
کتان [f. A. *katan*] Linen. Flax. — کتان صحرائی Dodder. — تخم ك. Linseed.
کتانی *A*. *P*. *a*. Of linen; linen. —*n*. Drill(ing) or duck. Cotton edging or trimming. — کفش ك. Canvas shoe.
کتب (*kotob*) [Pl. of کتاب]
کتبا *A*. In writing.
کتبی *A*. *P*. Written: امتحان ك.
کتره ای × (Said) with no truth or in jest. Thoughtlessly.— ك. میگوید He doesn't know (*or* mean) what he says.
کتری Kettle. Skillet.
کتف [f. A. کتف *katef*] [اکتاف] Shoulder(-blade).
کتك Beating. Cudgel ○.— ك. زدن To beat; thrash. — ك. خوردن To be beaten.
کتل Steep hill. Mountain pass. Led horse.
کتلت *Fr*. Cutlet.
کتمان *A*. Reservation; reticence. — ك. کردن To reserve; refrain from saying frankly.
کته Boiled rice. Meal-tub; coal-bin.
کتیبه *A*. Inscription; epigraph. Frieze. Coping. Epitaph.
کتیرا Gum tragacanth.
کثافات [Pl. of کثافت]

کج *or* **کژ** Raw or floss silk.

کجا Where? — ازکجا Whence? How : ازکجا پولدار شد ‖ کجاتان درد میکند؟ Where do you feel the pain? — کجاش را دیدی ؟ + The worst (*or* best) part of it is behind; it's only the beginning. — اواهل ك است *or* **کجائی** است Where is he from? *i. e.* of what city or country is he a native of? — این ك و آن ك There is no comparison between the two.

کجاغند ○ Cuirass quilted with silk

کژاوه *or* **کجاوه** Pannier used in pairs on camels or mules; camel-litter.

کج بین 1) ○ Squint-eyed. 2) *F.* Of unsound judgment.

کج بینی Cross-eye. *F.* Unsound judgment or reasoning.

کج خلق etc. *P. A.* = **بدخلق** etc.

کج خیال *P. A.* = 1) بد گمان 2) بد اندیش

کجدار و مریز In a middling position; so-so; within judicious bounds. [fingered.

کج دست Thievish; light-

کژ دم = **کجدم**

کجراه Perverted. Deviating.

کجراهی Pervertedness.

کجرفتار = بد رفتار [verseness.

کجروی Misbehaviour. Per-

کج سلیقه *P. A.* Of bad tastes.

کثافت *A.* [کثافات] Impurity; dirt. Density; thickness ○.

کثافت کاری *A. P.* Dirty work; sorry w.; daubing. Making a mess of something.

کثرت *A.* Great number; large quantity. Excess; superfluity. — کثرت استعمال Long usage. — کثرت جمعیت Large crowd; dense population. — کثرت خون Hyperemia. — کثرت وقوع Frequency. [Much.

کثیر *A.* = زیاد Numerous; great.

کثیرالاضلاع *A.* Polygon(al).

کثیرالانتشار *A.* With a wide circulation.

کثیرالتألیف *A.* Voluminous.

کثیرالزوایا *A.* Polygonal.

کثیرالمسافره *A.* Valid for repeated visits or frequent travel : ویزای ك.

کثیرالوجوه *A.* Polyhedron.

کثیرالوقوع *A.* Frequent.

کثیف *A.* = ناپاك & چرك Dirty. Dense; thick ○. — ك کردن To make d.; soil. To pollute.

کج *a.* Crooked. Curved. Inclined. *F.* Ill; wrong; unjust. Dishonest. Perverted. —*ad.* In a crooked manner. In a tilted or oblique position. — کج شدن To slant. To be distorted. — کج کردن To bend; curve. To s. or tilt. — دستش کج است His fingers are lime-twigs.

Awkward.
کج طبع • P. A. Ill-natured.
کج فعل P. A. = بدکردار - بدکار
کج نهاد • Ill-set; ill-natured.
کجی Crookedness. Dishonesty.
کچل Scald-headed; affected by scalp ringworm. — ك. کردن To pester or harass.
کچلك بازی ×Monkey-business.
کچلی Scalp ringworm.
کچوله Nox vomica.
کحال A. — چشم پزشك [sion.
کحالی A. P. Oculist's profes-
کُحل A. — سرمه
کَدّ ○ A. Toil; labour. — کدِّ یمین Manual labour; toil.
کُدام Which (one)? — ك. یك or ك. یکی W. one? — هرکدام Whichever. Any one. Either one. — هیچکدام No one; none; neither.
کدام = • کدامین
کدبانو Mistress of the house; housewife. Thrifty woman.
کدخدا Headman (of a village).
کدخدا منشی Arbitration (such as is practised by the headman of a village).
کَدَر ○ A. Turbidness.
کَدِر A. Turbid. F. Offended. — ك. شدن To be offended. To become turbid. — ك. کردن To tarnish. To offend.
کَدو Squash. Marrow. — کدوی تنبل Pumpkin. — کدوی رشتی Squash. — کدوی or کدوی قلیانی — کشکولی Gourd or calabash. — کدوی مسمایی (Vegetable) marrow. — کرم ك. ـِ Tapeworm.
کدودانه Tapeworm.
کُدورَت A. Displeasure; offence; indignation. Turbidity.
کدیور = کدخدا - باغبان - [برزگر]
کذا A. Sic. OS. Thus; such. — ك. وکذا S. and s. So and so.
کذّاب A. Great liar.
کذائی + A. P. The famous...; such and such a...
کِذب A. = دروغ
کَر Deaf. — کر کردن To deafen. To deaden or stun, as a sound. — کر و لال Deaf-mute.
کَرّات [Pl. of کَرّة]
کُرات [Pl. of کُره]
کَرّار ○ A. Who attacks repea- [tedly.
کِراراً A. Repeatedly.
کرّاسه ○ A. Fascicle. Fragment.
کرام S. u. کریم
کرامات [Pl. of کرامت]
کرامَت A. [کرامات] Generosity [بخشش]. Greatness [بزرگی]. — ك. کردن vi. To show generosity. — vt. To grant [بخشیدن].
کران End. Border. [End ○.
کرانه Shore; littoral. Border.
کراوات Fr. Necktie; tie.
کراهت or کراهیت A. Aversion. Loathsomeness. — ازچیزی ك. داشتن To hate or abominate s. t. — کراهت منظر = زشتی
کراهت انگیز A. P. Repulsive.

Hideous.

کِرایه *A* Fare Freight; transport charges; cost of t. Hire; rent. — ك. دادن To hire out; let out on h. — ك. کردن To h. To r.

کرایه‌ای *A. P.* On hire. Public. Hackney. — منزل کرایه‌ای Lodging(s).

کرایه‌نشین *A. P.* Tenant; renter.

کَرباس Tent-cloth; canvas. Burlap. — از سر (و ته) یك ك. Of the same leaven; tarred with the same brush.

کرباسی Made of canvas or tent-cloth. — متر کرباسی Linear metre. *Cf.* متر مربع

کرباس محله × *P. A.* Necropolis; bone-yard.

کرپ دوشین *Fr.* Crêpe-de-chine.

کرپ‌ژرژت *Fr.* Georgette (crêpe).

کُرپی *T.* = اسکله

کَرجی Boat. — کرجی موتوری Motor boat or launch; barque.

کرجی بان Boatman.

کُرچ Brooding. — مرغ ك. B.-hen; brooder. — ك. شدن To brood.

کَرچك Castor beans. C.-oil plant. — کرچك هندی Croton seeds. — روغن ك. Castor-oil.

کرخ or کَرخت Benumbed. — ك. کردن To benumb.

کُرد [A. pl. اکراد] Kurd.

کِردار Act; deed. — بکردارِ • In the manner of; like.

کردارمه *Fr.* (Army) corps.

کردگار Creator; God.

کَردن [کُن] 1) To do. 2) • To make. 3) Aux. verb used (a) after an abstract noun or an infinitive to change it to a verb. Ex. درمان ك. 'to cure', and فرض ك. 'to suppose'; (b) after a concrete noun where it means 'to change to' or 'to make'. Ex. آب ك. 'to melt' and کسیرا شاه ك. 'to make one a king'; (c) after an adj. where it means 'to render' or 'make'. Ex. سخت‌ك. 'to harden; make hard'; (d) after an ad. to form a transitive verb. Ex. در کردن 'to fire (a gun)'; پائین ك. 'to drop; cause to descend'; (e) as a substitute for certain verbs of vague nature. Ex. دستکش‌دست ك ‖ آتش‌ك. 'to wear gloves'; (f) in impersonal verbs as آفتابك. 'to clear up'.

کَردو Sown plot with a raised bank.

کرده *P. P. of* کردن ‖ —*n.* Act; deed.

کُردی Kurdish.

کرست *Fr.* Corset; stays.

کرسنه o Bitter vetch.

کُرسی Chair [صندلی] •. Throne. Stool. S.-like frame of wood which is covered all about with quilts and blankets, and under which a fire is placed for heating the legs in winter. *Med.* Department; seat. — کرسی خطابه Rostrum; pulpit. — + دندانك Molar tooth. — حرف خود را بکرسی نشاندن To have the last word.

کِرشمه Ogling; amorous gesture. Nod or wink. — بيك ك. دوكار كردن To kill two birds with one stone.

کَرَف Male fern.

کَرَفس *A.* Celery.

کَرَك = بَدبَده & بلدرچين

کُرك *T.* Down. Soft wool; knitting w. Fluff. Nap. — ك. شدن To mat, as the hair.

کُرکُر (?) *Curtain material like monk's cloth.*

کِر کِر خندیدن + To titter.

کِرکِرهای Corrugated. Made of slats. — پنجرهٔ ك. Shutter. Venetian blinds. — درِ کرکرهای Roller shutter.

کُرکُری خواندن × To beat about the bush; evade the main question.

کُرکی *T.P. a.* (Made) of soft wool. Downy. —*n.* Flannel.

کَرگَدَن Rhinoceros.

کرگس or **کرکس** Vulture.

کَرَم *A.* Generosity. Greatness. — ك. كردن To be generous. To deign to ... *Cf.* کرامت

کِرم Worm. *F.* + Inordinate desire. — کرم ابریشم or کرم پیله Silkworm. — کرم پنیر Cheese-mite. — کرم کود or کرمِ بهن Muckworm. — کرم تاك Vine-borer. — کرم جرب Acarid. — کرم حشره Larva. — کرم خاکی Earthworm; rainworm. — کرم درخت or کرم‌صدپا Caterpillar. — کرم روده Ascarid; helminth. — + کرم کار Veteran; past-master. — کرم شب افروز or کرم شب تاب Glowworm. — کرم کدو or کرم یکتا Tapeworm; tænia. — کرم مغز Coenura (in sheep). — ك. خوردن To be worm-eaten. To decay. — ك. ریختن × To grimace. To monkey or dodge. To act coquettishly or pruriently. — جوهر کرم Santonin. — داروی (ضدّ) ك. Vermifuge.

کِرِم *Fr. n.* Crême; cream. Custard. —*a.* Cream(-coloured).

کرم خوردگی Decay. [*Of the teeth*] Caries. [cayed.

کرم خورده Worm-eaten. Decayed.

کرمك Pinworm. *Med.* Oxyuriasis.

کرم کش Vermicidal. [For داروی ك] Vermicide.

کِرمو Worm-eaten; decayed.

کَرموش Musk-rat.

کِرمینه Larva.

کرنا Trumpet; horn.

کُرَند or **کُرَنگ** Sorrel or chestnut (horse).

کُرنش Homage; prostration.— ك کردن To do h. (to); bow down (before).
کرو o (*kerow*) Small sailboat.
کرّوبی *A*. Cherub. [Pl. کروبیان Cherubim]. [crunch.
کُروچ کُروچ کردن + To
کُرور *H*. Half a million.
کَرّ وفرّ *a*. *p*. Pomp. Pride. *OS*. Attack and retreat.
کُروك *T*. Hood (of a vehicle).
کِرّ و کرّ Rumbling noise. — ك. کردن To tarry. To drag.
کُرَوی *A*. Spherical.
کرویات *A*. Spherical geometry.
کرویت *A*. Sphericity.
کَره Butter. — کرهٔ تقلیدی Margarene. — روغن ك. B.-fat; clarified butter; ghee.
کُره *A*. [کرات] Sphere; globe.— کرهٔ زمین or کرهٔ ارض The terrestrial g.; the earth.
کُره *Fr*. Korea.
کرة or کَرّت *A*. [کرّات] Time; turn. — بکرات = بارها Repeatedly; time and again.
کرّه (*koreh*) Young (of certain animals). — کرهٔ اسب Colt. — کرهٔ الاغ Foal. — کرهٔ خر Foal; [without the *ezafah*] silly person; also, impolite child. — کرهٔ دریایی Sea-horse; hippopotamus o.— کرهٔ مادیان Filly.
کَرهاً *A*. Reluctantly.
کَره‌ای Buttery. Containing butter.
کره‌گیری or کره‌سازی Butter-making; churning.
کَری Deafness.
کریاس o = 1) درگاه 2) دربار
کریچه o Cottage; hut.
کریدور *Fr*. Corridor; lobby.
کَریم *A*. 1) *a*. [Fem. کَریمه] Generous [بخشنده]. Great. Noble. — احجار کریمه Precious stones.— آقایان کرام Gentlemen.— اولیای کرام Dignitaries; authorities. 2) *n*. (a) Great or generous person [pl. کِرام]. (b) *Mas*. *pr*. *name*.
کریم‌النفس *A*. Noble-minded.
کریه *A*. Detestable.
کریه‌الصوت *A*. Having an unpleasant voice.
کریه‌المنظر *A*. = زشت
کَز * [Cont. of که از]
کزاز *A*. Tetanus; lockjaw.
کِز دادن + To singe.
کِزکردن + To crouch or squat. To shrink.
کُزَل Culm. Stubble. Half-threshed stalks.
کزو * [Cont. of که از او]
کزین * [Cont. of که از این]
کژ = کج *in all senses*.
کژ دُم Scorpion.
کژ دمه Whitlow [عقربك].
کژی = کجی
کَس Person. Companion or relative (esp. in the pl.

کسان). [*Used as a pron.*] 1) One. 2) * No one. – کسی Some one; somebody; any o. – کسیکه One who; he w.– هر کس Any one. Whoever. Every o. [*usu.* همه ك]. – همه ك. E. one; everybody.– هیچکس No o.; nobody. – ك. و ناکس Noble and ignoble; i. e. everybody. – کس و کار Kith and kin. – کسِ بیکسان He who befriends the forlorn–ep. of God.

کساد *A.* Dullness (of market). [*Used as an a.*] Dull; stagnant.–ك. کردن To make d.

کسادی *A. P.* (*C. E.*) = کساد Dull market. *S. a.* کساد *n.*

کسالت *A.* Indisposition; slight illness. Indolence. – ك. داشتن To be ill; not feel well.

کسالت آور *A. P.* 1) = کسل کننده 2) Causing sickness.

کَسب *A.* Business; trade. Acquisition. – ك. کردن *vt.* To acquire, earn. —*vi.* To do business. – مسائل **کسبی** Business matters.

کسبه [Pl. of کاسب].

کَسر *A.* [کُسور] Fraction. Deduction. Discount. *F.* Detraction. – کسر بها Depreciation; devaluation. – کسر تمبر داشتن To be understamped. –کسرشأن Disdain; detraction from one's dignity. – کسر صندوق Cash deficit; also, cashier's allowance; risk-money. –کسرعمل Deficit. – ك. آمدن To have a deficit. To run short. – ك. شدن To be deducted or depreciated. – ك. کردن To deduct or discount.–ك. گذاردن To deduct; recoup. – کسرش میشودکه . . . He is too proud to . . .; it is below his dignity to . . . ‖ کسور ریال Fractions of a *rial*. – دوهزار و کسری 2000 odd.

کسره *A.* The vowel-point (ِ) called in P. زیر

کسری *A.* 1) *a.* Fractional. Missing.–عدد کسری Mixed number. 2) *n.* Missing portion; balance.

کسری (*kesra*) *A-P.* = **خسرو**

کُسِ شعر × *P. A.* Cock and bull story.

کُسِ گربه Venus's shell.

کسل *A.* Indisposed; (slightly) ill. Sluggish. *F.* Wearied. Losing, or having lost, interest. – ك. کردن To weary.

کسل کننده *A. P.* Tedious. Humdrum.

کسوَت ० *A.* – **پوشاك** & **لباس**

کسور [Pl. of کسر]

کسوف *A.* Eclipse of the sun.

کش [Imp. of کشیدن]

کِش Elastic (ribbon, band, or web). India-rubber. Elasticity. Sash(-window). *F.* Flexibility. – کش جوراب Garter. – کش ران Groin; inguinal region. ـ کش شیروانی Purlin. ـ کش آمدن To stretch ; admit of being drawn out.ـ کش دادن or کش آوردن To s. ; draw out. *F*. To strain. To wrest. To pervert. ـ کش رفتن × To filch ; crib.

کِش * [Cont. of که اش]

کُش [Imp. of کُشتن]

کشاف *A*. Discoverer. *A commentary on the Koran*. ـ شرح ك. Detailed description.

کشاکش Struggle. Contention.

کشاله Trail ; tail. ـ کشالهٔ ران or کش ران Groin. ـ ك. رفتن + To stretch oneself forward, as for an attack.

کشان کشان (By) dragging. ـ ك. بردن To carry by d.; drag.

کشانیدن [کشان] To draw (out). To prolong; protract.

کشاوَرز Agriculturist. Farmer.

کشاورزی Agriculture.

کِشباف *n*. Knitted work; knitwork. —*a*. Knitted.

کِشت Cultivation. Plantation. [Of bacteria] Culture; incubation. ـ ك. کردن To cultivate. To incubate.

کُشت (Act of) killing.

کُشتار Killing. Slaughter. ـ ك. کردن To engage in massacre. To slaughter animals.ـ کشتارِ دسته جمعی Massacre.

کشتارگاه Slaughter-house.

کِشتزار Sown field; plantation.

کشتکار Husbandman; tiller.

کشتکاری Husbandry; farming.

کشتگان [Pl. of کشته]

کاشتن = کِشتن

کُشتن [کُش] To kill. To murder. To put out ; extinuish *. *F*. To suppress.ـ به ك. دادن To cause to be killed. ـ نفس ك. * To mortify one's passions.

کشتنی Deserving execution. Condemned to death.

کِشته 1) [P. P. of کِشتن]. 2) *n*. Anything sown; seed.

کُشته 1) [P. P. of کشتن] 2) *a*. Slaked: آهك ك. ‖ 3) *n*. (Body of a) killed person [pl. کشتگان] ـ ك. شدن To be killed.

کَشتی Ship; vessel ; boat. ـ کشتی بادی Sailing-v. ; sailboat. ـ کشتی باری Cargo ship; freighter.ـ کشتی بازرگانی Merchant - man . ـ کشتی بخار(ی) Steamship. ـ کشتی جنگی Warship ; man-of-war. ـ کشتی نوح Noah's ark. ـ کشتی هوایی Airship. ـ کشتی یدك کش Tugboat.ـ ك. راندن To sail a ship. ـ سوارِ کشتی شدن To embark ; go on board a s. ـ سوار کشتی کردن To e. ; take on b. a ship. [wrestle.

کُشتی Wrestling. ـ ك. گرفتن To

کشتیبان Captain or pilot of a ship.

کشتیران Sailor. Navigator.

کشمیری (Native) of Cashmere. — شال ك. C. shawl.

کشنده ِ a. Attractive. Who draws or smokes. —n. ○ Smoker. Painter. [n. Murderer.

کُشنده a. Fatal. S.a. طاقت‌فرسا ||

کشو ِ Drawer. Slide. [Of a door] Bolt. — درِ کشوی Sliding door. [کشاکش

کش‌واکش Convulsion. S. a.

کشوَر ِ Country. Fem. pr. name. — دیوان ك. Supreme Court; High C. of Cassation. — وزارت ك. Ministry of the Interior; Home Office.

کشورگشائی ∗ Conquest.

کشوری Civil. Pertaining to the State.

کشیدگی Protraction. Tallness.

کشیدن [ِکش] To draw. To drag; pull; haul. To carry: بار کشیدن || To protract. To stretch; extend: سیم ك. || To serve, as food. To extract; express. To smoke: سیگار کشیدن || To weigh: آرد را بکشید || To paint: تصویر کشیدن || To lead: لشکر کشیدن || To last: دو روز بیشتر نکشید || To suffer; endure: سختی ك.

کشیده 1) P. P. of کشیدن 2) a. Protracted. Elongated: صورت ك. || Tall. 3) n. Slap; box on the ear.

کشیش Priest.

کشیشی Priestho

کشتیرانی Navigation. Shipping. — قابل ك. Navigable. — ك. کردن To navigate.

کشتی ساز Shipwright.

کشتی‌سازی Ship-building. [For کارخانهٔ ك.] Shipyard.

کشتی شکستگی Shipwreck.

کشتی شکسته Shipwrecked.

کُشتی گیر Wrestler.

کشتی گیری Wrestling.

کِش‌دار Elastic. F. Flexible.

کشش Draught; haulage; traction. Tension. F. Allure.

کشف A. Discovery; detection. — ك. کردن To discover.

کشف‌الآیات A. Concordance.

کشف‌الابیات A. Index of verses.

کشفیات A. Discoveries.

کشك Dried whey. — کشکت را بساب × Mind your own business.

کشکول Cup suspended by a chain and carried by a dervish. OS. Sea-cocoanut. — کشکول گدایی دست گرفتن To send round the hat.

کشکی 1) = کتره‌ای + 2) Ironical(ly). 3) Phoney or sham.

کِشمش Raisin. — کشمش بیدانه Sultana. — کشمش پلوی Small plums. — کشمش کولی Mistletoe.

کشمشك Mistletoe.

کشمکش Conflict; scuffle. Skirmish. — ك. کردن To s. To struggle or contend

کشیک T. Watch; guard. Post. ـ ك. دادن To be on duty, as a sentinel ; keep w. ـ ك.کشیدن To watch ; keep w. To g.

کشیکچی T. Watchman; sentinel.

کظم ○ A. Restraining; curbing. ـ کظم غیظ کردن To restrain or curb one's anger.

کعب A. Cube-root. Ankle-bone. Die ○. Base; bottom ○.

کعبتین A. [D. of کعبه] The two Kaabas. Pair of dice.

کعبه A. Kaaba. F. Centre-point. Chief aim.

کف Froth ; foam. Scum. [Of soap] Lather. ـ کف دریا Sea-f. Cuttle-bone. Meerscham. ـ کف آوردن To cause to lather. ـ کف کردن To l. To f.

کف [f. A. کفّ] [Of the hand] Palm. [Of the foot] Sole. [Of a shoe] 1) Insole; 2) sock. [Of a room, etc.] Floor. [Of a stocking] Foot. [Of a road] Bed. ـ کف درگاه Sill. ـ کف زدن To clap (the hands). To applaud. ـ ازکف دادن * To give away. ـ مگرکف دست بوکرده بودم ؟ + How was I expected to know ?

کفّ A. Restraining. Denial. ـ کف نفس Self-restraint ; self-control. Cf. خودداری

کفار [Pl. of کافر]

کفاره or **کفارت** A. Expiation; atonement. ـ کفاره دادن To make an atonement; atone. ـ ك.کردن To a. for; expiate.

کفاش (C. E.) = **کفشدوز**

کفاشی (C. E.) = **کفشدوزی**

کفاف A. Sufficiency. Livelihood. ـ ك. دادن To suffice.

کفالت A. (Personal) surety ; guarantee. ـ ك.کردن To act as s.; become (or go) bail. To act for s. o. in a position. ـ کفالت وزارت جنگ‌را داشت He was the Acting Minister of War.

کفایت A. Sufficiency. F. Capability; efficiency. ـ ك.کردن To be sufficient. To suffice. ـ بقدر کفایت Sufficiently; enough. ـ آب بقدر کفایت هست There is e. (or plenty of) water. ـ کفایت مذاکرات Closure; winding up the debate. ـ عدم ك. Insufficiency. Inefficiency.

کف بین A. P. Palmist.

کف بینی A. P. Palmistry.

کفتار Hyena.

کفتر + = کبوتر Pigeon. ـ کفتر پرقیچی Decoy.

کفترباز Pigeon-fancier.

کفچه A. P. Ladle; skimmer.

کفر A. Blasphemy . ـ ك. کفتن To utter b. ; swear; curse. ـ ‖ **کفران** (نعمت) = کفر نعمت ـ کفرکسیرا بالاآوردن + To drive one mad. OS. To cause him to utter b.

کفر آمیز A. P. Blasphemous; profane : سخنان ك.

کفران A. Ingratitude [usu. کفران نعمت]. – کفران نعمت کردن To be guilty of i.

کفش Shoe. – کفش برفی Snow-shoe. – کفش‌چوبی Sabot; clog. – کفش دم پایی or کفش سرپایی Slippers. – کفش کسیرا جفت کردن To show one the door. – هر دو پا را در یك ك. کردن To persist in one's opinion or demand.

کفش‌پاك‌کن Door-mat. Scraper.

کفشدوز Shoemaker. [bug.

کفشدوز(ك) Lady-bird; lady-

کفشدوزی Shoemaking.

کفش‌کن Sill; threshold. – اطاق ك. Anteroom.

کف شناس etc. = **کف بین** etc.

کفشیر Solder; borax.

کفگیر Skimmer. Shallow flat-bladed utensil used for serving food. – کفگیر ماهی گردانی Fish-slice. – کفگیرش به ته دیگ خورد He was at the end of his tether; he was driven to extremities.

کفگیرك Anthrax [per.

کفل A. Buttocks. Rump; crup-

کفن A. Wrapping in a winding-sheet; shrouding.

کفن (kafan) A. Winding-sheet; shroud. – ك. کردن To s.; wrap in a winding-sheet.

کفو (kofv) A. Equal; match.

کف‌و کف + Successively [only in ك. سرفه کردن].

کفه A.P. = کپه Pan of a scale.

کفیل A. Personal surety or bail. One who acts for another in a specified capacity. – کفیل وزارت جنگ Acting Minister of War. – کفیل خرج Supporter of a family; breadwinner. – ك. دادن To give bail. – ك. شدن To stand (or go) b. – بقید کفیل آزاد کردن To release on b.

کك + = کیك Flea. – ککش نمی گزد × He doesn't care a fig.

ککمك Freckles.

کل A. Baldhead or scaldhead.

کل A. Burden. S. a. سربار

کل A. n. = همه The whole; all. –a. Total. Full. Universal. – جمع کل Grand total. – مدیر کل Director general. – مهندس کل Chief engineer; c.-in-chief. – علی کل حال ala-= در هر حال In any case.

کلا A. = تماما

کلابرك Bot. Capitulum.

کلاچ F. Clutch. – ك را گرفتن To take out the clutch. – ك. را ول کردن To let in the c.

کلاس Fr. & E. Class; grade. Classroom. – کتابهای کلاسی School books.

کلاسور (-sor) Fr. Index-file; boxfile. Filing-cabinet. Stationery rack.

کلاسیک *Fr.* Classic(al).
کلاش (?) Sponger. Swindler.
کلاغ Crow; raven. – کلاغ بغدادی Carrion-crow. – کلاغ جاره (Mag)pie. – کلاغ کاکلی Jay.
کلاف Skein; hank. Cradling. [*In machines*] Setting. – ک.کردن To form into a skein or hank. To hobble.
کلافه *n.* Skein; hank. Network. –*a.* + Heat-struck; stifled. *By e.* Harassed; pestered.
کلالةً *A.* Collaterally.
کلام *A.* Speech; word. Commandment. – خلاصهٔ ک. To sum up; in short.
کلان Huge. Enormous. – بازی ک.کردن + To play high.
کلانتر Magistrate. Ship's pilot. Harbour's master. Elder. Headman.
کلانتری Police station. – رئیس ک. Magistrate (of a p. s.).
کلاه Hat; cap. – ک. سر کسی گذاشتن *or* کلاهِ کسیرا بر داشتن To defraud s. o. – کلاه تقی را سر نقی گذاشتن To rob Peter to pay Paul. – کلاه خودرا پیش خود قاضی کردن To judge for, or talk to, oneself. – کلاه خود را بهوا انداختن + To leap for joy; fling up one's cap; thank one's lucky stars. – کلاهش پشم ندارد He carries no weight. – کلاه شرعی سرچیزی گذاشتن To get round the law; play a legal trick. – کلاهمان توی هم رفت + We came to a rupture.
کلاه بردار *a.* Fraudulent; fraudulous. –*n.* Swindler.
کلاه برداری Fraud; swindling.
کلاه خود (*-khu:d*) Helmet.
کلاه دوز Hatter; hatmaker.
کلاه دوزی Hat-making. [For ladies] Millinery.
کلاه فرنگی Pavilion: isolated ornamental building.
کلاه فروش Hatter. Milliner.
کلاهك Chimney's cowl. *Bot* Galea.
کلاه کلاه کردن × To rob Peter to pay Paul; make shifts.
کلاه گیس Wig; periwig.
کلب *A.* = سگ Dog ○. *Astr.* Canis. – کلب اصغر C. Minor. – کلب اکبر C. Major.
کلبتین *A.* Dentists' forceps.
کلبه Cottage; hut.
کلبی *A.* Canine ○. Cynic.
کلپتره × Nonsense; foolish talk.
کلدانی Chaldean. Chaldaic.
کلرات *Fr.* Chlorate.
کلسیوم *Fr.* Calcium.
کلش Stubble.
کلف *A.* Freckle. *Astr.* Flocculus.
کلفت (*kolfat*) *A.* Maidservant. *OS.* 1) زحمت 2) تکلف
کلفت (*koloft*) Thick. – ک. شدن To become thick; thicken. [*Of the voice*] To get hoarse. – ک.کردن To thicken.
کلفتی (*kolof-*) Thickness.

کلفن *Fr.* Rosin; colophony. – ك. زدن To rosin.

کَلَك (*kalak*) Raft or float supported by inflated skins. Clay brazier or chafing-dish.– ك. زدن + To play a trick.– کلك چیزیرا کندن + To make short work of it. – کلك کسیرا کندن + To get rid of, dispatch, or make an end of s. o.

کلك (*kelk*) o = 1) قلم 2) نی

کلکته Calcutta.

کلك رانی Rafting

کلکسیون *Fr.* Collection; set.– يك کلکسیون پروانه A cabinet of butterflies. [carpet.

کلگی Bridle; headstall. Head-

کلم Cabbage. – کلم پیچ White-headed cabbage; savoy c.– کلمِ دکمه‌ای Brussels sprouts.– کلم قمری Turnip c. – کلم گل Cauliflower.

کلمات [Pl. of کلمه]

کلمه *A.* [کلمات] Word. – ك. بکلمه W. for word; w. by w.; verbatim.

کلنجار o – خرچنگ Crab. – ك. رفتن + To come into grips.

کُلنگ Pick. *Z.* Crane. – کلنگ دوسر *or* کلنگ روسی Pickaxe.– ك. زدن To (use a) pick.

کلوب *Fr.* = **باشگاه**

کلوچه *or* **کلیچه** o Cookie.

کلوخ Clod; lump of earth.

کلوخ کوب Clod-crusher; mallet.

کلوخه Clod. Ore. – قند کلوخه Lump sugar.

کلورور *Fr.* Chloride.

کلوروفرم *Fr.* Chloroform.

کلون [*Obsolete*] Wooden bolt.– ك کردن To b., as a door.

کله (*kaleh*) Head; pate. Top. Mind. – ك. ای دو ریال 2 *rials* per head. – ك. زدن To push with the head. *S. a.* سروکله‌زدن

کُله • [Cont. of کلاه]

کله پا شدن × To fall down. To be taken ill.

کله خر × Stupidly obstinate.

کله خشك Brainless. Foolish.

کله شق + Stubborn.

کله شقی + Obstinacy.

کله قند Sugar-loaf. Cone o.

کله قندی Conical. [grandee.

کله‌گنده × Bigwig; swell;

کُلی *Fr.* = بسته Parcel.

کلی (*koli:*) *A.* General. Total. Considerable. – بکلی Totally. Absolutely. Altogether.– بطورکلی As a general rule; generally. On the whole.

کلیات *A.* Generalities. Poetical works; whole works. [Pl. of کلیه which is orig. the fem. of کلی] – کلیات خمس The five predicables.

کلی پستال *Fr.* Post parcel; postal packet.

کلیت (*koliyat*) *A.* Generality.

کلید [f. G. origin] Key. Switch. Bottle-opener; also, tin-opener [often درِ قوطی بازکن].–

ک. انداختن To apply a key to. — ک. شدن To lock, as the teeth. — ک. کردن To (lock with a) key.

کلیددار One entrusted with the keys. Custodian; care-taker.

کلیس or **کولیس** *Fr.* Slide-callipers.

کلیسیا or **کلیسا** *A.-G.* Church.

کلیسایی *A. P.* Ecclesiastic(al).

کلیشه *Fr.* Cliché; stereotype (plate). — ک. کردن To s.

کلیم *A.* Interlocutor. [Short for کلیم‌الله] [Ep. of] Moses.

کلیمی *A.* Jew(ish). [Pl. کلیمیان 'the Jews'].

کلینیك *Fr.* = **درمانگاه**

کلیوی (*kolyavi:*) *A.* Renal.

کلیه (*kol-*) *A.* = گرده Kidney. [D. کلیتین] [totality.

کلیه (*koliyeh*) *A.* All [همه];

کلیةً *A.* In general. As a whole. Altogether; all.

کم 1) *a.* Few; little; insufficient. Slight. Missing. Short: این پول : سنگ کم ‖ Too short: دو ریال کم است ‖ Less. 2) *ad.* Little. Slightly. — من کمتر از او پول دارم I have less money than he. — کم آمدن To run out; r. short. — کم آوردن To r. short of; r. out of. — کم شدن To be diminished or decreased. To grow less. — کم کردن To diminish; decrease; lessen. To deduct or subtract. — زحمت شما را کم میکند It will save you trouble. — کم گرفتن To slight; think nothing of. — بیست فرسخ چیزی کم Nearly 20 farsakhs. — (یك) کمی A little. Somewhat; slightly. — کم و بیش or کم یا بیش More or less [also کمابیش]. — کم ِ [*Used idiomatically.*] Made up for, or compensated by. Ex. کچلیش کم ِ آوازش His good voice makes up for his baldness.

کم Rim; frame.

کما ○ *A.* (Such) as. — ک. اینکه See ک. فی‌السابق ‖ بطوریکه As before. — ک. کان As (it was) b.

کم اب Droughty. Dry; not juicy.

کمابیش More or less.

کماج *Kind of spongy cake.*

کماجدان Stew-pan. Skillet.

کمال *A.* Perfection. Accomplishment. Good breeding. — کمال مطلوب Ideal; ideal perfection. — با کمال درستی Most honestly. — بحد کمال رسیدن To attain p. or maturity.

کمالات *A.* Accomplishments.

کمان Bow. Arc. — ک. کردن To bend ○. — ک. کشیدن To draw a bow. — کمانش را نمیتوان کشید One cannot cope with him.

کمانچه Violin-like instrument

resting on the ground during performance.
کماندو *Fr*. Commando. [chet.
کمانه Rim. Hoop. Tyre. Rico-
کمانی *Anat*. Semilunar.
کمبر Of little breadth.
کم بسامد *Ph*. Low-frequency.
کمبود Shortage. Deficit.
کم بها Of little value. Cheap.
کمپانی *Fr*. = شرکت Company.
کمپرس *Fr*. Compress; packing-sheet. Gauze.
کمپرسور *Fr*. Compressor.
کمپرسی *Fr*. *P*. — ماشین ك Tip-cart; tip-truck; tip-waggon.
کم پشت Thin; of few leaves.
کمپوت *Fr*. = خوشاب
کمتر [Comp. of کم] *a*. Less. —*ad*. L. (often). —*n*. Lesser part. — ك کسی Few persons.
کمترین [Sup. of کم] Least (part). [courage.
کم جرأت *P*. *A*. Of little
کم جمعیت *P*. *A*. Thinly populated.
کمچه Wooden ladle.
کم حافظه *P*. *A*. Of a poor memory. [quiet; taciturn.
کمحرف *P*. *A*. Of few words;
کم حوصله *P*. *A*. Short-tempered; irritable. Impatient.
کم خرج *P*. *A*. Inexpensive.
کم خواب Suffering from insomnia; sleepless. [nia.
کمخوابی Sleeplessness; insom-
کمخور(اك) Eating little; abstemious; frugal.
کم خون Anemic.
کم خونی Anemia.
کمد (*komod*) *Fr*. Wardrobe. Chest of drawers.
کم دل = 1) کم جرأت 2) کم حوصله
کُمدی *Fr*. Comedy.
کَمر Loins; waist. Girdle; belt. Rock. — ك بستن To put on one's g.; gird one's clothes. *F* To resolve upon doing s. t. — کمر کاریرا شکستن To break the neck of a task. — ك سستیِ Impotency. — اسلحهٔ کمری Side-arms.
کمر بسته Wearing a gird. *F* Prepared for service *.
کمربند Belt; girder; waist-band. Sash. *Mil*. Sabot. — [*In architecture*] Cordon.
کمر درد Lumbago.
کمرشکن Onerous; grinding; heart-breaking.
کمرکش + Half-way; middle.
کمرنگ Faint(-coloured); pale. Weak: چای ك.
کمرو Bashful; shy; diffident.
کمرویی Bashfulness. Shyness.
کمری Lumbar ∘. Bent under a burden; knocked up. *S*. *a*. *under* کمر
کم زور Powerless; weak.

کمست o Amethyst.
کم سو Weak; dim :چشمش‌ك. است
کم عرض P. A. Narrow ; of little breadth. Cf. باریك
کم عقل P. A. = بی‌خرد
کم عمر P. A. Short-lived.
کم عمق P. A. Shallow.
کم فرصت P. A. Having little or no opportunity. Rash.
کم فروش (Tradesman) who gives short weight.
کم فروشی Using short weights; selling underweight.
کم قیمت P. A. = کم بها
کمك [f. T. کو َمك] Help; aid.– ك.آشپز Cook's mate; کمك خلبان copilot [read without the *ezafah*].–(به) ك. دادن To help; assist; lend one's assistance.– (به) ك. کردن To help or assist. To contribute (to).
کمك خرج T. A. or کمك هزینه T. P. Allowance ; subsidy. [Also کمك معیشت].
کمك داروساز T. P. Dispenser.
کمك راننده T. P. Driver's mate.
کمك فنر Shock-absorber. *See* کمك & فنر *for origins*.
کم‌کم Little by little; gradually. In small quantities.
کمك مکانیك T. Fr. Fitter ; mechanic's mate.
کمکی T. P. Aid; mate. Auxiliary.
کم حرف = کم‌گفتار

کملین (?) The influential ; the elect; the big shots.
کم مایه Of a small capital. Weak, as a liquid. F. Of little or superficial knowledge; shallow.
کم مدت P. A. Short-term *adj*. Of short duration. – اخطارِ کم مدت Short notice.
کَمند Lasso; running-noose. Rope-ladder. F. Snare. – ك. انداختن To use a r. for scaling a wall. To throw the lasso.
کم نور P. A. Weak: چشمان ك. ‖ Dim. Of little light.
کموتاتور Fr. Commutator.
کم وقوع P. A. Infrequent.
کمون A. 1) = نهفتگی 2) + Interior.
کمونیست Fr. Communist.
کمونیستی Fr. P. Communistic.
کمونیسم Fr. Communism.
کَمی Insufficiency; scantiness; meagreness. Fewness. Shortage. Deficiency.
کمی (*kami:*) A. = چندی Quantitative.
کمیاب Rare; scarce.
کمیابی Scarcity; dearth.
کمیت (*kamiyat*) A. Quantity; magnitude.
کمیت o (*komeyt*) A. Bay horse with a black tail and mane.– کمیتش لنگ است He is hard up for money; he is distressed.
کمیته Fr. Committee; society
کمیسیون Fr. Committee ;

commission.

کمین • Least; smallest. [Sup. of کم = کمترین].

کَمین *A*. Ambush; ambuscade.— ك. كردن To lie in a. (for); lurk. — درکمین نشستن To lie in wait; lie in ambush.

کمینگاه *A. P.* Ambush; ambuscade; lurking-place.

کمینه = کمین Least or smallest; minimum.

کَن [Imp. of کندن].

کُن [Imp. of کردن].

کِنار 1) *n*. Side: درکنارمن by my s. Edge. Shore; coast. 2) *ad*. Aside; apart.— درکنارِ Beside; by the side of. — ك. آمدن To come to terms; c. to an agreement. — ك. كشيدن To draw aside *or* to one s. To withdraw. — ك. گذاشتن To lay a. To abandon. — در کنار گرفتن • To embrace or hug. — از گوشه و کنار From every corner; f. all sides. — شوخی بکنار All joking apart. — بوس و کنار • Kissing and cuddling (or hugging); also, necking.— میز کناری Side-table.

کُنار Lote or lotus (tree).

کنار افتاده Set aside. Laid-up.

کناره Border. Side. Runner; side carpet Sea shore. — ك كردن To keep aloof.

کناره جویی Keeping aloof; shunning. — ك. كردن To withdraw; keep a.; sequester (*or* seclude) oneself.

کناره‌گیر Who keeps aloof from society; stand-offish.

کناره‌گیری Retirement. Resignation. — ك. كردن To retire or withdraw. To hold aloof. [With از] To resign.

کناس *A*. Nightman. Scavenger.

کنام ں *A*. Thicket. Lair; den. Pasture. *Cf.* بیشه

کنایس [Pl. of کَنیسه].

کنایه *A*. Allusion. Metaphor. Symbol. Sarcastic remark. — ك. زدن To speak allusively or sarcastically. [castic.

کنایه‌دار *A. P.* Allusive. Sarcastic.

کُنت *Fr*. Earl; count.

کنتر *Fr*. (*C. P.*) Double.

کنترات *Fr*. Contract. *Cf.* پیمان & مقاطعه || ك. كردن To contract. To employ by c.

کنتراتی *Fr. P.* Employed under a contract [now usu. پیمانی].

کنترل *Fr*. Checking; auditing; verification. Control [نظارت].— ك. كردن To check, audit, or control. [Auditor.

کنترولور *Fr*. Comptroller.

کنتور *Fr*. Meter.— کنتور ساعت‌دار *or* کنتر دو تعرفه ای Double-tariff meter.

کُنج Corner; solid angle.

کنجاره & کنجیده Oil-cake obtained from the sesame.

کنجد Sesame.

کنجدك Freckle. Mole.
کنجکاو Curious ; inquisitive.
کنجکاوی Curiosity ; inquisitiveness. — ك. کردن To be inquisitive; pry; search.
کُند *a.* Blunt; dull : چاقوی ك. ‖ Slow : ساعت ك. است ‖ Stupid. —*ad.* Slowly. —*n.* Stocks. *See* کنده ‖ ك. کردن To blunt To retard. To set on edge.
کند ذهن *P. A.* Stupid; dull.
کند ذهنی *P. A.* Stupidity.
کندر *A-G.* Frankincense. — کندر رومی Mastic.
کندرو Of a slow pace.
کند زبان Slow of speech.
کندش White hellebore. — جوهرِ کندش Veratrine.
کندکار Slow of action; sluggish.
کندن [کَن] To dig; excavate. To pluck; pull off. To take off : کفش خود را کند ‖ To engrave. — از بیخ ك. To root up (*or* out); eradicate. — موی خود را کندن To tear one's hair.
کَندو Beehive.
کَنده 1) *P. P. of* کندن 2) *n.* Engraved or carved work. *S. a.* خندق
کُنده Log; block. Stump; stub.— کندهٔ زانو + Knee-pan. — ك. زدن + To kneel down.
کَنده کار Engraver. Carver.
کنده کاری Carving. Engraving.— ك. کردن To carve; engrave.
کُندی Bluntness; dullness. Slowness. Sluggishness.
کنز اللغات *A.* Repository of words ; thesaurus.
کنس + (*kenes*) Stingy.
کنسرت *Fr.* Concert.
کنسرو *Fr.* Conserve.
کنسرسیوم *Fr.* Consortium.
کنسول *Fr.* Consul.
کنسولگری *Fr. P.* Consulate.
کنسولی *Fr. P.* Consular.
کنسولیار *Fr. P.* Vice-consul.
کَنش Digging.
کُنش o Action ; doing.
کنشت o [f. Heb. origin] Synagogue.
کنش کاو Rabbet.
کنعان *A.* Canaan.
کنف *A.* [اکناف] Wing [بال]. *F.* Shelter.— اکناف زمین Remote parts of the earth.
کنف *A-Lat.* Cannabis. Hemp.
کنفت + Shop-soiled ; dirty. *F.* Disgraced.
کنفرانس *Fr.* 1) Conference. = سخنرانی 2)
کن فیکون کردن + *A. P.* To destroy utterly; annihilate. — *Note.* کن‌فیکون literally means "Be, and so it is" [Creative phrase or command].
کَنگ o = 1) بال 2) بازو
کنگاش o Deliberation.
کنگر Prickly artichoke. Acanthus. — کنگر فرنگی = **انگنار**
کنگرزد Emetic resin.

کنگره Crenation; notch. Milling; milled edge. Turret; pinnacle. Battlement.

کنگره *Fr.* Congress.

کنگره دار Milled. Crenate. — ك.کردن To mill. To crenulate.

کَننده Digger.

کُننده Doer. [Rendering the E. suf. *er* or *or* when the P. verb is construed with کردن .Ex. درست ك. maker].

کنون * [Cont. of اکنون]

کنونه ○ Actual situation.

کنونی Present. Modern.

کَنه Tick. — مثل ك. چسبیدن To stick like a leech.

کنه (*konh*) *A.* Depth; bottom [ته]. *F.* Essence; substance.

کنیاك [f. Fr. *cognac*] Brandy.

کَنیز Bondswoman; female slave. *Cf.* [illegible]

کنیزك Slave-girl; bondsmaid.

کنیسه *A.* [کنایس] Synagogue.

کُنیه *A.* Nickname.

کو Where is? W. are?

کو *or* **کوی** Quarter. *Cf.* کوچه

کو * [Cont. of که او]

کو (*kow*) = شپشه Weevil.

کواکب [Pl. of کوکب]

کوب [Imp. of کوبیدن].

کوبنده Beater; pounder; knocker; rammer.

کوبه Knocker; hammer.

کوفتگی = کوبیدگی

کوبیدن [کوب] To pound or bray. To grind. To mash. To flail; thresh. To drive: میخ ك. ‖ To knock (at); also, k. down or defeat. — آبلهٔ بچه‌ای را کوبیدن To vaccinate a child against smallpox. — رقصیدن = * پای ك.

کوبیده 1) [P. P. of کوبیدن]. 2) *n.* Mashed meat.

کوپال ○ Mace; club.

کوپن *Fr.* Coupon.

کوپه *Fr.* Coupée. Compartment.

کوتاه Short. Brief. [*Of a tree*] Low. — ك. آمدن 1) = قاصر آمدن ‖ 2) To draw in one's horn; lower one's note. — ك. شدن To be shortened; shorten. [*Of days*] To draw in. — ك. کردن To s. To crop, as the hair. To cut short. To abridge. — دست کسی را کوتاه کردن To cut off a person's hand (from doing a specified thing). — سخن را کوتاه کنیم Let us be brief; to be brief.

کوتاهی Shortness. Brevity. Shortcoming. — ك. کردن To be negligent; fail (to do s. t.).

کوت + = کود ‖ ك. کردن To heap up.

کوتوله + Dwarf(ish).

کوته * [Cont. of کوتاه]

کوته بین Short-sighted. *F.* Improvident.

کوته بینی Short-sightedness. [Improvidence.

کوته فکر *P. A.* Lacking fore-

sight. [sight.
کوته فکری. *P. A.* Lack of fore-
کوته نظر *P.A.* Narrow-minded.
کوته نظری *P. A.* Narrow-mindedness. Illiberality.
کوثر (*A.*) *A river in Paradise.*
کوچ Family ○. *Cf.* خانواده ‖ Wandering tribe. — ك. كردن To decamp. To migrate.
کوچانیدن To cause to migrate.
کوچك Small ; little. Short. *F.* Humble. Insignificant.—. جهان ك. Microcosm. — ك. شدن To dwindle in size. *F.* To lose one's dignity [usu. كوچيك شدن]. — ك. كردن To reduce in s. To humiliate.— اينحرف او را كوچك خواهدكرد It would be small of him to say that.— لباس او برايش ك. شده است He has outgrown (*or* grown out of) his clothes.
کوچك ابدال ○ *P. A.* Young disciple ; novitiate.
کوچکی Smallness ; small size. *F.* Humility. — ك.كردن To humble oneself.
کوچ نشین Colony. Immigrant.
کوچولو + *a.* Small ; tiny. —*n.* Little child; kid.
کوچه Lane. Street. Alley. — ك. دادن (به) To open a lane (across). To give way (to).— + خود را بكوچه علی‌چپ زدن To evade the main issue; fence with a question.
کوچه‌گرد ○ Vagrant; walking in the streets.— بچهٔ ك. Street arab. [march; migrate.
کوچیدن [كوچ] To decamp ;
کود Manure ; fertilizer. — كود گياهی Compost. — ك. دادن To fertilize or manure. — ك.كردن To pile or heap.
کودتا *Fr.* Coup d'état.
کودك Infant; baby.
کودکانه Childish(ly).
کودکستان Kindergarten.
کودکش Nightman.
کودکی Infancy; childhood.
کودن Stupid; dull.
کودنی Stupidity; dullness.
کور *a.* Blind. —*n.* Blindman.— گرهِ ك. Hard knot. —ك. شدن To go blind. — ك. كردن To b. ; make b. To fill up ; close or cover up, as a pit. To obscure the light of. — كورِ مادر زاد (One) born blind. — از يك چشم ك. Blind of one eye.
کوراب = سراب Mirage.
کوران *Fr.* Draught.
کوربخت etc. = بدبخت etc.
کورتاژ *Fr.* Curettage.— ك.كردن To curette.
کوردل * Inwardly blind.
کورس *Fr.* Race. Course. Trip or journey (in a bus, etc.) for which a single fare is payable. — دوكورس بايد بدهيد You should pay double fare.

کورش Cyrus.
کورَك Boil.
کورکورانه Blindly. Gropingly.
کورکور کردن + To glimmer. To flare.
کورکوری + Flaring.
کروك = **کوروك**
کورمالی کردن To grope.
کور منجه + Half-blind.
کورموش Mole.
کوره Furnace. Kiln. — کورهٔ آجرپزی Brick-kiln. — کورهٔ آهنگری Forge. — کوره قالگری Cupola (furnace).
کوره پز Kilnman.
کوره‌پزی Brick-burner's or lime-burner's trade.
کوره راه Obscure narrow path.
کوره سواد + *P. A.* Partial ability to read and write.
کوری Blindness. — بکوریِ چشمِ دشمنان In spite of our enemies.
کوزه Jug. Pitcher. Jar. Pot (of wine or flower).
کوزه‌گر Potter.
کوزه‌گری Pottery. — گِلِ ك. or گل کوزه‌گران Potter's clay.
کوژ • = کج Crooked.
کوژ پشت • = قوز پشت
کوس • (Kettle-)drum. Jump; start. — ك. بستن To take off for a spring; give a start. — ك. زدن o To beat the d. — کوس صلح میزنند They claim to have introduced (*or* to be supporting) peace. — کوسِ عقب نشینی زدن To beat a retreat. — کوس رحلت • Signal for departure.
کوسه [*Of a beard*] Thin. [*Of a man*] Thin-bearded. [*Of a gun*] Hammerless. — ماهی ك. Man-eating shark; sea-devil. — ك. و ریش پهن Contradictory (remarks).
کوش [Imp. of کوشیدن]
کوشا Diligent.
کوشاد o Gentiana.
کوشش Effort. — کوشش بیهوده or کوشش بیفایده Lost labour; vain effort. — ك. کردن = کوشیدن
کوشك Villa; mansion; palace.
کوشه *Fr.* Italic. — حروف ك. Italics.
کوشیدن [کوش] To endeavour; try; make an effort.
کوفت Syphilis. — ك. کردن ✕ [Derogatory for خوردن] To eat. — کوفتش باشد ✕ I hope it (*i. e.* what he has eaten) will choke him.
کوفتگی Bruise; contusion. Extreme fatigue.
کوبیدن = **کوفتن**
کوفته [P. P. of کوفتن] 1) *a.* Bruised. Pounded. Exhausted; tired out. 2) *n.* Meat-ball; rissole. One who is worn out by fatigue.
کوفتی Syphilitic.
کوفی *A.* Kufic. — نقشهٔ خط کوفی Greek fret.

کوك Basting. — ك. زدن To baste. To stitch loosely.

کوك *T*. 1) *a*. Tuned; in tune. Wound (up). *F*. Wrought up; high(ly)-strung. — کیفش ك. است × He is in his glory; he is having fun; he is in high feather. 2) *n*. Tuning. — ك. کردن To tune. To key, as a piano. To wind up, as a watch. *F*. To string up; make nervous. — ك. شدن To be tuned. To be wound up. *F*. To be wrought up.

کوك (*kok*) *E*. Coke.

کوکائین *Fr*. Cocaine.

کوکب *A*. [کواکب] = ستاره Star. گل ك. Dahlia.

کوکبه *A*. Pomp. Suite; train.

کوکنار White poppy. Poppy-shell.

کوکو Savoury omelet.

کوکو Cuckoo. C.'s note.

کول Back; shoulder. — ك. کردن *or* ك. گرفتن To carry pickaback. — بسر و کول هم ریختن × To jump on one another.

کولاب 1) Puddle. 2) = آبگیر

کولاك Rough sea; tempest.

کولر *E*. Cooler.

کوله Load carried on the back; pack. [sack.

کوله بار & **کوله پشتی** Knap-

کولی Riding pickaback. — ك. گرفتن To ride p.

کولی [For ماهی ك.] Anchovy.

کولی *n*. Gipsy. —*a*. Shrewish.

کومك *T*. [Origin of کمك *q. v.*]

کومه Heap.

کون (*ku:n*) Anus. — کون خر × • Arrant ass (*or* fool).

کون (*kown*) *A*. Existence. Creation. — کون ومکان Universe.

کونه Root. Counter of a shoe. — ك. کردن To take root.

کونین *A*. This world and the next w. [D. of کون *kown*]

کوه Mountain. [*In pr. names*] Mount [Mt.]. — کوه آتش فشان Volcano. — کوه نور Koh-i-Noor. — کوه یخ Iceberg.

کوهان (Camel's) hump.

کوهاندار Humped.

کوه بر Rock-excavator; rock-piercer. — متهٔ ك. Rock-drill.

کوه پایه (Valley or plain at the) foot a mountain.

کوه پیکر • Of a huge body.

کوهسار Hilly (country).

کوهستان Hilly or mountainous country; highland.

کوهستانی Mountainous; hilly.

کوه گرد Mountaineer. Explorer of mountains.

کوه گردی Exploration of mountains.

کوه نورد Mountaineer. Traveller of mountainous regions. [mountains.

کوه نوردی Travelling in

کوهه Pommel; also, saddle-bow. Hump o.
کوهی 1) = کوهستانی 2) Wild.
کوی *S. u.* کو
کَویر Salt desert; brackish [ground.
که • (*ka*h) [Cont. of کاه].
که • (*ke*h) *a.* Young; little. —*n.* Y. or insignificant fellow.
که • (*ko*h) [Cont. of کوه].
که (*ke*) *inter. pron.* [*Usu. replaced by* کی] Who? — که رفت W. went? — که را دیدید Whom did you see? — برای که For w.? — قلمِ که Whose pen? —*Note.* The pl. of که is کی ها o, که ها +, *or* کیان • (*kia*n).
که (*ke*) *rel. pron.* 1) Who: کسی که He w. 2) That or which. — کتابی که دیدید The book that you saw. — کاغذی که روی آن نوشتید The paper on which you wrote. — شهر هایی که Cities which; such cities as. — من همانقدر خوردم که او خورد I ate as much as he did. 3) [*Used idiomatically*] من که As for me; for my part. Ex. من که آنرا دیده ام As for me, I have seen it; also, I have already seen it. — اینکه کاری ندارد Why, there's nothing difficult about it; as for this, there's nothing...
که (*ke*) *rel. ad.* 1) When در عصری که in an age w. — وقتی که When; the time w. 2) Where: جایی که او می‌خوابید the place w. he slept. 3) [*Used idiomatically*] When; after: شام که خورد میخوابد W. he has eaten his supper (*or* after eating his supper), he goes to bed.
که (*ke*) *conj.* That; in order that. — نمیدانستم (که) او ایرانی است I did not know (t.) he was an Iranian. — رفتم (که) او را به بینم I went to see him. — تا اینکه *or* برای اینکه In o. that; so t. — چنانکه *or* بطوریکه As. — حال که Now t. Since. — + که چه؟ What is the idea? W. for?
کهانت *A.* Priesthood. Divination.
کهتر [Comp. of که *ke*h] Younger; junior. [*See* عقده
کهتری Juniority. Inferiority.
کهترین [Sup. of که] Youngest.
کَهر Bay (horse).
کهرُبا Amber. — کهربای سیاه Jet.
کهربایی Amber-like. Amber-coloured. Electrical. — قوهٔ ك o Electricity.
کُهسار • [Cont. of کُوهسار]
کَهف *A.* = غار Cave.
کَهکشان The Milky Way.
کُهن Old; ancient. [world.
کهن‌دیر • *P. A.* (*Met.*) The old
کهن‌سال Aged; very old.
کهنگی Oldness. Antiquity.
کهنه (*kahanah*) [Pl of کاهن]

کهنه (*koh*-) *a*. Old; used. Worn-out. Archaic. –*n*. Rag. Wadding. Lint. [*For a baby*] Diaper. — ك. کردن To wear out; make old. *F*. + To have experienced.

کهنه (بر) چین Rag-picker.

کهنه پرست Fogyish; old-fashioned.

کهنه پرستی Adherence to the old-fashioned; fogyism.

کهنه سرباز Veteran (soldier).

کهنه کار Past-master; veteran.

کهولت *A*. Ripe years. Indolence.

کهیر Nettle-rash; urticaria.

کهین *or* **کهینه** * Youngest. Least. Smallest. *Cf*. کهترین

کی + (*ki:*) Who? *See* که (*ke*).

کی (*key*) When? — از کی Since when? — تا کی *or* تا بکی How long? Until w.? — او کی راضی خواهد شد He will never agree to that.

کی (*key*) *Title of kings of the Keyan Dynasty* [*used in comb. Ex*. کیخسرو].

کیاست *A*. Ingenuity. Sagacity.

کیان *S. u*. که *inter. pron*.

کیان (*keyan*) *The Keyan Dynasty*. [Pl. of کی]

کیانی Of the *Keyan Dynasty*. Royal.

کیپ + Water-tight. Air-tight.

کیخسرو *A king of the Keyan Dynasty. Mas. pr. name*.

کید *A*. 1) = مکر 2) = خیانت

کیس 1) *n*. Shrink; strain. 2) *a*. Shrunk. Uneven.

کیست [Cont. of که است] Who is it? W. is he? — این کتاب مال ك. Whose book is this?

کیسه *A*. Bag; sack. Purse. Rough glove used by rubbers in a Turkish bath. *Z*. & *Anat*. Pouch. *Med*. Cyst. — کیسهٔ خایه Scrotum. — کیسهٔ صفرا Gall-bladder. — ك. بستن To form a cyst. — ك. دوختن + To have an eye on some one's money; start swindling money out of him. — سر کیسه را شل کردن To loosen the purse strings. — سر (و) ك. کردن × To fleece; strip of money. — (در) ك. کردن To put in a b. or sack. — ك. کشیدن To rub with a glove, as in a bath.

کیسه بر *A. P*. = جیب بر

کیسه دار *A. P*. Pouched; marsupial. Encysted.

کیش Faith; religion [دین].

کیش 1) Shoo! [uttered only when driving away fowls]. 2) Check. — ك. کردن To shoo; drive away. To check. — کیش و مات Checkmate.

کیف (*ki:f*) Purse (of money). Bag Brief-case; brief-bag; attaché-case; portfolio. — کیف بغلی

Pocket-book ; letter - case ; purse ; wallet . ـ کیفِ بندی Satchel. ـ کیف جراحی Surgeon's case. ـ کیف دستی زنانه Handbag. ـ کیف سفری Travelling-bag.

کیف (*keif*) *A*. Intoxicating drug ; opiate. Kick ; pleasurable thrill. *By e*. Enjoyment ; pleasure ; treat. ـ ك. دادن (به) To intoxicate or inebriate. To give pleasure. ـ ك. کردن To enjoy oneself. To go pleasuring. To have fun.

کیف ० *A*. = چگونه How ?

کیفر Punishment. ـ ك. دادن To punish. ـ بکیفرِ . . . رسیدن To be duly punished for.

کیفرخواست Bill of indictment.

کیفری Penal.

کیف ماانفق ० (*keyfamatafagh*) *A*. At random.

کیفی (*key-*) *A*. = چونی Qualitative.

کیفیت *A*. Quality [چگونگی] Circumstances; facts. Manner.

کیفیتی *A. P*. Modal. Circumstantial.

کیقباد *A king of the Keyan Dynasty*.

کیك or کاك + Flea. ـ کیك خاکی Flea - beetle . ـ ك در تنبان *Met* Disquietude.

کیك *E*. Cake.

کیکاوس *A king of the Keyan Dynasty*.

کیل *A*. [اکیال] Measure (for grains). ـ ك. کردن To m. ـ آب دریا به ك. پیمودن To try to m. sea-water by a pint-pot.

کیلو (-*lo*) [Cont. of کیلو گرم]

کیلووات *Fr*. Kilowatt.

کیلوس *A-G*. Chyle.

کیلوگرم *Fr*. Kilogramme.

کیلومتر *Fr*. Kilometre. ـ دریك کیلو متریِ At a distance of 1 kilometre from.

کیلومتر شمار ِ *Fr. P*. Kilometre-post ; milestone ; mile-post. Speedometer.

کیله *A*. (Single) measure.

کیمخت ० Shagreen.

کیموس *A-G*. Chyme.

کیمونو Kimono.

کیمیا *A-G*. Alchemy. Philosopher's stone.

کیمیاگر Alchemist.

کیمیاگری Alchemy; transmutation of metals.

کین Rancour; spite. Revenge. ـ ك. خواستن To take revenge.

کین or کاین • [Cont. of که این]

کینه Rancour; spite; grudge ; hatred. ـ ك. گرفتن or ك. کشیدن To take vengeance. ـ کینهٔ شتری Deep r.; revengeful feeling.

کینه توز • = **کینه‌جو**

کینه‌جو Revengeful (person).

کینه جوئی Revengefulness ; vengeance. ـ ك. کردن از To take v. on.

کینه خواه etc. = **کینه جو** etc.

کینه‌دار Spiteful; revengeful.

کیوان Saturn [زحل].

کیومرث *First king of the Pishdadian Dynasty*.

کیهان • = **جهان**

گاباردین *Fr.* [Often گاواردین] Gabardine.

گار *Fr.* = ایستگاه راه‌آهن Railway [station.

گاراژ *Fr.* Garage.

گارد *Fr.* Guard. Guardsman.

گاردنال *Fr.* Phenobarbital; luminal.

گاردن پارتی *E.* Garden-party.

گارمن *R.* Harmonium.

گاری *H.* Cart; waggon.

گاریچی *H. T.* Carter; cart-driver.

گاز Bite; biting. — گ. گرفتن To bite: سگ او را گ. گرفت

گاز *Fr.* Gas. — گازِ خفه کننده Poison gas. — گاز دستی (*M.*) Throttle. — چراغ گ. Gas-light. — کارخانهٔ گ. G.-works. — نفت گ. G. oil. — گ. دادن To step on the g.; accelerate. — با گاز خفه کردن To gas.

گاز *Fr.* Gauze.

گازانبر (Pair of) pincers.

گازدار *Fr. P.* Gassy; gaseous. Aerated.

گازُر ० Washerman; launderer.

گازسنج *Fr. P.* Gas-meter.

گازسوز *Fr. P.* Gas-burner.

گازویل *E.* Gas oil.

گاسه or گاسِ [f. R. *cassa*] Case [in printing].

گال *Fr.* The itch or scabies.

گالُش *Fr.* Galosh; overshoe.

گالُن *Fr-E.* Gallon.

گاله Wide-mouthed sack.

گام * Pace; step. Gait. — گ. زدن or گ. برداشتن To walk. To p.

گام *Fr.* Gamut; scale.

گامبی *Fr.* Gambit.

گاومیش or گامیش Buffalo.

گاو Cow; ox. — گاو کوهان دار Zebu. — گاو عنبر Sea-cow supposed to produce ambergris. — گاو ماده Cow. — گاو نر Ox; bull. — گاو پیشانی سفید *Met.* (One who is) as well-known as the Devil or village pump; notorious (person). — گوشت گ. Beef.

گاوآهن Plough. Trail.

گاوبازی Bullfight.

گاوبندی Collusion; hitching horses together.

گاوران & گاوچران Cowherd; cowboy; goadsman.

گاودار Cow-keeper; dairyman.

گاودارو Stone in the gall-bladder of an ox.

گاودان Cow-shed; cow-pen.

گاودانه American vetch; buffalo pea.

گاودوشه & گاودوش Milk-pail.
گاوَرس Italian millet; panic grass.
گاو زبان [For گل گ.] Borage. Cowslip. [*As beverage*] C. tea.
گاو سر Two-pronged pole; fork. Mace.
گاوشیر Opopanax.
گاوصندوق *P. A.* Large chest or coffer; safe.
گاومیش *S. u.* گامیش
گاوه *or* گوه Wedge. [pox.
گاوی Bovine. — آبلهٔ گ. Cow-
گاه [Mostly used in comb.] *n.* Time. Place. *—ad.* Sometimes. — گاه و بیگاه At times. Every now and then. — گاهی Sometimes; once in a while.— گاهی گداری × Occasionally. — بگاهِ * At the time of. — گ. میشود *or* گ. است It happens (that).
گاه گاه From time to time.
گاه گاهی Occasional. [*With the stress on the 2nd. syl.*] Occasionally; from time to time.
گاهنامه = سالنامه & تقویم
گاهواره Cradle [usu. گهواره].
گاهی *S. u.* گاه
گائیدن [گای] [*Derogatory*] To lie with. *F.* To do in.
گبر Ghebre; fireworshipper. *Cf.* زرتشتی [idly.
گپ زدن + To chatter. To talk

گتر *Fr.* Gaiter.
گترهای In a lump sum. By the job. As a fixed sum.
گچ Gatch; Iranian plaster. Plaster of Paris. Chalk. — سنگ گچ Gypsum. — قلم گچ Crayon. — گ. گرفتن To dress with plaster cast.
گچ بُر Plaster-moulder.
گچ بری Plaster-moulding.
گچ پزی Gatch-burning.— کورهٔ گ. Gatch kiln; plaster-k.
گچ کار Gatch-plasterer.
گچ کاری Gatchwork. Stucco-work. Parget.
گچی Made of gatch or plaster. Coated with gatch or p.— شمع گ. Stearine candle.
گدا Beggar. — گ. کردن To reduce to beggary. — گدای سامره Importunate beggar. *OS.* B. from Samaria.— گ. ها رامی گیرند × Nothing doing.
گدا بازی Beggarliness; miserliness. *OS.* Playing the beggar
گداختن [گداز] To melt; fuse. To clarify, as butter. *F.* To consume.
گداخته [P. P. of گداختن] Melted. Clarified.— روغن گ. C. butter.
گدار Ford(ing-place). [گداختن
گداز 1) Fusion. 2) *Imp. of*
گدازش Melting. Fusion.
گدازنده Melter
گدازه Lava. [Beggarly.

گدا صفت *P. A.* or **گدا منش**

گدایی Begging; mendicity. — گ. کردن To beg.

گدوک Mountain-pass.

گذار 1) Passage. — گذارم افتاد بر I happened to pass by. 2) *Imp. of* گذاشتن

گذاردن or **گذاشتن** [گذار] 1) To put; lay; place. 2) To leave. 3) To allow or let: بگذارید برود Let him go. 4) To invest. *S. a.* گزاردن

گذاره Passage o. — کشتی گ. Ferry-boat.

گذاشتن *S. u.* **گذاردن**

گذر Passage. Part of a street.

گذر [Imp. of گذشتن]

گذران 1) *a.* Passing. Transient. 2) *n.* Subsistence; means of livelihood. — گ. کردن To subsist; (manage to) live; get along; fare; shift. 3) *Imp. of* گذراندن

گذراندن [گذران] 1) *vt.* To pass; spend. To p. successfully. To (cause to) p.; lead. To transmit. To clear (from the Customs). To p.: get through; cause to be approved, as a bill. To get over (a dispute). — بخیال خود گذراند که It occurred to him that. 2) *vi.* To get along; pass one's time. — بدگذراندن To have a bad time; be ill at ease.

گذرگاه Crossing. Passage-way. Fording-place. — گذرگاه تراز Level crossing.

گذرنامه Passport.

گذشت Generous disposition. Remission. Indulgence. Concession. Ability to do without a thing. — گ. کردن از To overlook or remit; also, waive. To do without. [*Without* از] To make concessions. To waive one's claim.

گذشتگان The deceased. The ancients. *Cf. the s.* گذشته

گذشتن [گذر] To pass. To p. away. [*With* از] To cross. To overlook; spare; forgive. — لایحه (از مجلس) گذشت The bill got through the Majlis. — از نادیده گ. To ignore. — خوش میگذرد It fares well; we are enjoying ourselves. — آب از سرش گذشته است It is all over with him.

گذشته 1) *P. P. of* گذشتن 2) *a.* Past; bygone. Last: سال گ. ‖ 3) *n.* P. time. P. tense [usu. زمان گ.]. P. event. *Cf. the pl.* گذشتگان ‖ گ. ها گذشت Let bygones be bygones. — ازشوخی گ. All joking apart. — از گ. Apart from; besides. — از این گ. Furthermore; besides.

گر • [Cont. of اگر]

گر *n.* Mange; scab. —*a.* = **گردار**

گر [Suf. forming 1) nouns of agency, as in زرگر 'goldsmith'; 2) adjectives from abstract nouns, as in ستمگر 'oppressive'].

گُراز Boar. — گرازِ دریایی Porpoise. — گراز وحشی Wild b.

گرافیت Fr. Graphite.

گرامافون Fr. Gramophone.

گرامی Dear. Honourable. — گ. داشتن To honour. To hold dear.

گِران Expensive; dear. Heavy*. F. Insupportable. — گ. شدن To rise in price. — گ. کردن To raise the p. of. — گ. خریدن To buy d.; pay too much for. — گ. فروختن To sell d.; charge too m. for. — برای من گ. تمام شد I paid d. for it; it cost me dear(ly).

گران بار Heavy-laden; overloaded. S. a. باردار

گرانبها Precious; valuable.

گرانجان ○ Sluggish. Niggardly.

گران فروش One who overcharges; swindler.

گران فروشی Overcharging; swindling.

گران مایه * Precious. F. Serious; grave. Important.

گرانی Dearness; expensiveness. Dearth. Gravity. Heaviness ○. سال گ. Year of dearth.

گرانی گاه Centre of gravity.

گراوور (-vu:r) Fr. Engraving. — گ. کردن To engrave.

گراوورساز Fr. P. Engraver.

گراوورسازی Fr. P. Engraving.

گرا(ی) [Imp. of گراییدن]

گرایش Tendency. [inclined.

گراینده Having a tendency;

گراییدن [گرا(ی)] To be inclined; have a tendency; [with به] have a t. for; also, believe in.

جربزه = گربزه

گُربه Cat. — گربهٔ آبی [also گربهٔ براق — سمور آبی] Otter. — گربهٔ براق S. u. ‖ گربهٔ دشتی or گربهٔ وحشی Wild cat. — گربهٔ زباد See زباد ‖ گربهٔ ماده She-cat. — گربهٔ نر Tom-cat. — بچه گ. Kitten. — گ. رقصاندن To wirepull; lead one a dance. — گ. را نمی تواند پیش کند He can't say "bo" to a goose. — گوشت را بدست گ. سپردن To set the fox to watch the geese.

گربه رقصانی P. A. Wirepulling. Intriguing.

گربه رو Air-drain; gallery.

گربه شور کردن + To give oneself a lick and a promise.

گرجستان Georgia.

گرجی Georgian.

گرچه * [Cont. of اگرچه]

گَرد (Flying) dust. Powder. — گرد دندان Tooth-powder. — گرد گوگرد Flowers of sulphur. — گرد لیمو Powdered dry lime. — گ.کردن *vi*. To make (*or* raise) dust. —*vt*. To reduce to powder. — گ.گرفتن *or* گ. نشاندن To shake off the d. — بگرد کسی رسیدن To overtake or approach s. o.

گَرد [Imp. of گردیدن *or* گشتن]

گِرد *a*. Round ; circular. —*n*. Whole note ; semibreve. — گردِ Round (*prep*.); around. — گ. آمدن • To assemble. To be amassed. — گ. آوردن • To amass; accumulate. To assemble ; rally. — گ. کردن • To accumulate. To make round. To r. off. — گردِ کاری گشتن • To seek to do s. t. — عقلش گ. است + He is a button short.

گُرد • Hero.

گِرداب Whirlpool; eddy.

گَردار Scabbed; mangy.

گرداگرد All round. — گرداگردِ *prep*. All r. ; all around.

گَرد آلود(ه) Dusty.

گَردان 1) *a*. Rotating; revolving. Rolling. — تنخواه گ. Revolving fund ; imprest. 2) *Imp. of* گرداندن

گُردان Battalion.

گرداندن [گردان] To turn (round). To rotate. To take for a walk. To show round. To manage ; run. To ward off. To make : مرا شادگرداند

گردآوری Gathering. Rally.

گِرد باد Whirlwind; cyclone.

گِرد باف Selvage.

گِردُبر = مته Gimlet; auger.

گَرد پاش Pounce box.

گردش Walk(ing). Circulation. Revolution; rotation. Change. گردش بیرونِ شهر Excursion ; outing. — گردش روزگار Vicissitudes of time. — گ. کردن To take a walk. To circulate. To rotate or revolve. To change. — (به) گ. رفتن To go (out) for a w. — (به) گ. بردن To take for a w.

گردشگاه Public walk; public park ; promenade.

گِردَکان = گردو • Walnut. — گ. بر گنبد *Met*. Water off a duck's back.

گردگیر Duster; whisk.

گردگیری Dusting. — گ. کردن To dust. To clean down.

گَردَن Neck. — یك سر و گردن Head and shoulder. — گ.زدن To behead. — ماشین گردن زنی Guillotine. — گ. کشیدن • To rebel. — گ. نهادن • To submit (to). — (به) گردن من On my responsibility. Upon my conscience. — (به)گردن کسی گذاشتن To lay at one's door; hold s. o. responsible for. To bring home to s. o. — گردن کسیرا گرفتن To lie at one's door. — گ.گرفتن To confess;

declare oneself r. for. — (به) گردنش بار شد He had no way out (of his commitment); he was led into doing what he had said.

گردنا *Anat*. Patella.

گردن بند Necklace. Collar.

گردنده Turning (round). Rotating. *F*. Changeable. *Bot*. & *Z*. Versatile.

گردن شمشیری Ewe-necked.

گردن‌فراز • Haughty.

گردن کش Refractory; stubborn.

گردن کشی Refractoriness.

گردن کلفت + *a*. Sturdy; in rude health. —*n*. Roughneck. Bully. Ruffian. — گردن کلفتی کردن To behave as a r. or bully; use violence; push people about.

گردن‌گیرشدن To lie at one's door; lead into doing (a specified act). — گردن گیرش شد *Same as* گردنش بار شد *q. v. under* گردن

گردنه Pass; defile.

گردو Walnut. — پوست گ. Nutshell. — دست کسیرا توی پوست گ. گذاشتن Not to give a person freedom of action.

گردون Celestial sphere; firmament. *F*. Fortune; fate.

گردونه Vehicle. Roulette ○.

گرده Powdery substance. Pounce. *Bot*. Pollen. — از چیزی گ. برداشتن To pounce or stencil s. t. — از روی گردهٔ کسی کار کردن To take a leaf out of a person's book.

گرده Round loaf.

گرده Kidney. Hip. Back or loins +. — از گردهٔ کسی کار کشیدن + To exploit s. o.

گرده فشانی Pollination.

گرده ماهی Convex. Ridged.

گردی Powdery; dust-like. Gossamer; also, flimsy.

گردی Roundness.

گردی • Bravery; heroism.

گردیدن [گرد] To turn; t. round. To revolve; circulate. To walk; ramble. To search. To become [شدن] •.

گردیده [P. P. of گردیدن]

گرز Mace; club.

گر زدن + To burn quickly.

گرزن *Bot*. Cyme.

گرسنگی Hunger. — گ. خوردن *or* گ. کشیدن To starve. — گ. دادن To famish; starve. — از گ. مردن To s. to death.

گرسنه Hungry (person). [Pl. گرسنگان the hungry]. — من گ. ام هست *or* گ. هستم I fool h.; I am h. — گرسنهٔ چیزی بودن To hunger for (*or* after) s. t.

گرشاسب *Mas. pr. name*.

گرفتار Caught; captured. *F*. Preoccupied. Tied up; very busy +. Having a problem or problems. — گرفتار بدهی Encumbered by debts. —

گرفتار عشق او Enamoured of her love. — گ. شدن To get into difficulty. To be captured. — گ. کردن To capture; arrest. To involve. To tie up.

گرفتاری Preoccupation. Embarrassment. Worry; cares; problem(s). Arrest.

گرفتگی Obstruction. Depression. Eclipse [*in comb.*]. — گرفتگی صدا Hoarseness. — گرفتگی هوا Miserable or sultry weather.

گِرفتن [گیر] 1) *vt.* To take. To receive. To obtain. To catch. To arrest; capture. To conquer. To recruit; employ. To extract. To marry or take. To pare or trim: ناخن گ. ‖ To use; occupy; take up: همهٔ وقتم را میگیرد ‖ To cover or veil. To fill up (a crack). To stop (up); clog. To bite. To admit; suppose. To contract, as a disease. — خود را گرفتن To put on a supercilious air. 2) *vi.* To be clogged: بینی‌من گرفت ‖ To be eclipsed. To become close: هوا گرفت ‖ To take fire. To catch on; also, take: آن نمایش نگرفت ‖ شوخی او نگرفت His joke fell flat. — دستِ بگیر *F.* Itching palm; grasping love of money.

گرفته 1) *P. P. of* گرفتن ‖ 2) *a.* Dull; close; miserable: هوای گ. ‖ Clogged. Hoarse. Depressed; dejected.

گُرگ Wolf. — گرگ ماده She-wolf. — گرگ باران دیده *Met.* An old fox who understands a trap; old stager; old veteran. — گ. در لباس میش *Met.* A wolf in sheep's clothing. — هوای گرگ و میش Twilight; gloaming.

گرگاس *Bot.* Tare.

گُرگم بهوا Game of tag.

گرگی 1) *a.* Wolfish. — سگ گ. Wolf-dog. 2) *n.* Wolfishness.

گَرگین • Scabbed.

گَرم Warm; hot. *F.* Ardent; enthusiastic. Fiery. Friendly. Effective. Charming. [Of an entertainment or party] Warm. — چه گ. است How hot it is! — گرمم است I feel warm. — اسلحهٔ گ. Firearms. — بازار گرم Brisk market. — مهمانی گ. بود The party was a success. — گ. شدن To grow hot or w. To w. up. — گ. کردن To heat. *F.* To excite. To make brisk. — باهم گ. گرفتن To get in close connections with each other; become friends. — کله‌اش گ. است He is tipsy (or lit up). — گرمِ کار Absorbed in work. — گرم وسردِ روزگار Ups and downs; vicissitudes of fortune. — گرم ونرم Snug.

گرم *Fr*. Gramme.
گرما Hot weather. Heat.
گرمابه Turkish bath(s); hammam; hot bath-house.
گرمازده Heat-struck.
گرماسنج Thermometer.
گرماگرم Hot and hot. Fresh.
گرمخانه The hot chamber of a Turkish bath. Greenhouse; hothouse; conservatory. Place for keeping the poor during the winter.
گرمسیر Tropical country; warm climate.
گرمسیری Tropical.
گرمك *Kind of early melon*. — باقلا گرمك Boiled beans.
گرمی Heat; warmth. *F*. Ardour; enthusiasm. Attractiveness. Friendly or hospitable attitude.
گرمی دانه Prickly heat; rash.
گرنه • [Cont. of اگر نه]
گرو (*gerow*) Pledge; pawn; security. Mortgage. Wager. — گ. کردن ‖ شرط بستن = گ. بستن = گ. کشیدن ‖ رهن کردن To distrain upon. — گ. گذاشتن To put in pledge; give as a p. To mortgage. — از گرو در آوردن To redeem.
گرو (*gerev*) *Fr*. = اعتصاب
گروانیدن To cause to adhere to or believe in. To make inclined. [Bondman.
گروگان Pledge. Hostage.
گرّ و گر + In torrents. In heaps. Off the reel. Intensely: گ. میسوخت
گروه Crowd; band. Group. — کشور های گروه استرلینگ Sterling block countries.
گروهان *Mil*. Company.
گروهبان *Mil*. Sergeant. — گروهبان اصطبل Farrier. — گ. یکم S. Major.
گروهبانی Sergean(t)cy.
گروهه Clew (of thread). Ball.
گروی *a*. Pledged. —*n*. = گرو
گرائیدن = گرویدن
گره Knot. *Unit of length* = 2.56 + *inches*. *F*. Knotty affair. — گره بشکه Barrel-sling. — گره چار گوش Reef-knot. — گ. خوردن To form a knot. To kink. *F*. To come to a deadlock; also, be entangled. — گ. دادن *or* گ. زدن To tie; knot. — مشت گ. کردن To clench the fist. — گ. برجبین زدن • To knit the brow. — گ. از جبین گشادن • To smooth the b.
گره‌دار Knotted; knotty.
گره‌گره Inch by inch. Gradually. Desultorily; irregularly.
گره‌گشا Resolver of difficulties. [ficulties.
گره‌گشایی Resolving of dif-
گری Scab; mange.
گریان Weeping. Tearful. —

ک. شدن To come to tears.
گریاندن To cause to weep ; move to tears.
گریبان Collar. ـ گریبان کسیرا گرفتن To seize one by the collar. To befall s. o. ـ سرش توی گریبان خودش است He keeps to himself. ـ سر به ک. فرو بردن * To meditate or muse.
گریبانك *Bot.* Involucel.
گریبانه *Bot.* Involucre.
گریپ *Fr.* Influenza; grippe.
گریختن [گریز] To run away ; flee.
گریخته [P. P. of گریختن]
گریز 1) *n.* Flight ; escape. Metabasis. *F.* Evasion; elusion. ـ راه ک. Way or means of escape. Link for transition. ـ ک. زدن To run away ○. To dodge (round). To deviate. [With از] To elude or evade. ـ از مدرسه ک. زدن To play the truant. 2) [Imp. of گریختن]
گریزان Running away. ـ ک. بودن [*With* از] To avoid or abhor.
گریزاندن To cause to escape. To smuggle. To omit.
گریز پا Runaway. Truant.
گریزگاه Refuge. Transition-verse.
گریزنده (One) who escapes or avoids.
گریس *E.* Grease.
گریستن • [گری ger'y] To weep.
گریس کاری *E. P.* Greasing. ـ تلمبهٔ ک. Grease-gun.
گریل *Fr.* Gorilla.
گریم *Fr.* Make up. ـ ک. کردن To make up; paint.
گریندە ○ Weeper.
گریوه * Mound of earth.
گریه (*garyeh*) Weeping; tears. ـ ک. کردن To weep ; cry. ـ به ک. افتادن To be driven to tears. ـ به ک. انداختن To move to tears. ـ زیر گریه خواب رفتن To cry oneself to sleep. ـ گریهٔ زورکی Forced tears. ـ گریهٔ شادی Tears of joy.
گریستن = گرییدن
گز Tamarisk or manna-tree. *Kind of* confectionery made from manna. ـ گزخونسار *Tamarix mannifera.* ـ گز سرخ or گزمازو Gall-bearing tamarisk. ـ گز شوره Species of t. growing in salt marshes. ـ گز علفی The great prickly cupped oak (*Quercus valonica*).
گز Metre ; ell. ـ گز کردن To measure.
گز [Imp. of گزیدن]
گزاردن [گزار] To perform or say : نماز گزاردن ‖ To serve : ناهار گزاردن ‖ *S. a.* گذاردن
گزارش Report; account; return. Interpretation [also گزاره]. ـ ک. دادن To submit a report.
گزاره *S. u.* گزارش
گزاف *a.* Exorbitant. Extrava-

gant. —*n*. = گزاف گویی
گزاف‌گویی Idle talk. Exaggeration. Bragging.
گزانگبین (Manna of the) *Tamarix mannifera.*
گَزر 1) = هویج 2) Pestle.
گزش Bite. Thrilling condition.
گزك = 1) فرصت 2) نوبت or بهانه
گِزگز کردن + To smart, as a wound.
گَزلك Knife-poniard.
گزمه ○ *T*. Night-watch.
گَزند * Injury; harm.—گ. رساندن (به) To h. or injure.—گ. یافتن To be harmed or injured.
گزندگی Mordancy; bite. Causticity.
گزنده 1) *a*. Biting. Caustic. 2) *n*. B. creature; stinger.
گزنه Nettle. [Rabies.
گَزیدگی Bite. گزیدگی سگ هار—
گَزیدَن [گز] To bite [not used of dogs]; sting.
گُزیدَن [گزین] To choose; select. To prefer.
گزیده [P. P. of گزیدن]
گزیر * Remedy; help. — ازآن گ. نیست We cannot help it.
گزین [Imp. of گزیدن.]—گ. کردن * To choose or select.
گزیننده Selector; chooser.
گَس Astringent; acrid.
گُساردن * [گسار] To drink. To absorb. To consume.
گُستاخ Rude; impudent.
گستاخانه Impudently.
گستاخی Impudence; boldness.
گستر [Imp. of گستردن] [to s.
گسترانیدن To spread; cause
گستردن [گستر] To spread.
گسترده [P. P. of گستردن]
گسترش Act of spreading ○. Deployment.
گسیختگی = گسستگی
گسیختن = [گسل] گسستن
گسل [Imp. of گسستن or گسیختن]
گسلانیدن * To (cause to) tear or break.
گسله (*Geology*) Fault.
گُسیختگی Break; interruption. Missing link. Fault. Cancellation. Liberty of action.
گسیختن [گسل] To break (off); tear; disconnect. To cancel or terminate. To annul.
گسیخته 1) [P. P. of گسیختن] 2) *a*. Broken (off); interrupted. Cancelled.
گسیل * Despatched. — گ. داشتن = روانه کردن To despatch; send.
گشا [Imp. of گشودن or گشادن]
گُشاد Wide. Loose-fitting. — گ. کردن To widen. To make loose. — گ. گ. راه رفتن To straddle. — برای سرش گ. است + That is out of his depth.
گشاد بازی [*At backgammons*] Trick of exposing intentionally one's men to be hit. *F*. Extravagance; burning the candle at both ends.

گشودن = **گشادن**
گشاده Open(ed). [liberal.
گشاده دست * Open - handed ;
گشاده دل * Liberal.
گشاده‌رو * Unveiled. Cheerful.
گشادی Wideness. Looseness.
گُشایش Opening ; inaugura - tion. Relief.
گشایشی Inaugural.
گشاینده Opener. Resolver (of difficulties).
گَشت Walk; excursion. Round; tour.— ك. زدن To make one's round. To cruise. [With در] To patrol. [*Shahnameh*.
گشتاسپ *Mas. pr. name in the*
گشتاوَر *Ph*. Moment.
گشتن [گرد]=گردیدن To turn; t. round. To circulate. To walk or ramble. To search. To become * [شدن] .
گشته 1) [P. P. of گشتن] 2) *a*. ○ Changed. Crooked. Squint.
گشتی Patrol(man).
گُشن آمدن To (have a) rut.
گشن گیری Fecundation.
گرسنه = + **گُشنه**
گشنیزِ Coriander. — **گشنیزی** خال C. P. Club(s).
گشودن *or* **گشادن** [(گشا(ی] To open. To conquer ○. *F*. * To disclose. To resolve.
گفت * Thing said ; speech ; word. — گفت و شنید = **گفتگو**
گفتا *v*. [*In poetry*] = **گفت**

گفتار Speech ; word. Topic. Discourse. Chapter *.
گفتگو Conversation ; talk. Dispute — ك.كردن To converse ; talk. — گفتگومان شد + We had words; *i. e.* dispute.
گفتگویی Colloquial ; conversational.
گفتن [(گو(ی] 1) *vt*. To say or tell: گفت نمی آیم He said he was not coming ; he said, "I am not coming". — باو گفتم بیاید * اورا گفتم بیاید *or* I told him to come.—(می)گویند It is said; the story goes.—نمیتوان گفت One can't say ; it is hard to tell. — گوسفند نر را قوچ میگویند A male sheep is called a ram. 2) *vi*. To talk: می گفتیم و می خندیدیم
گفتنی (Word) that must or can be said.
گفته 1) [P. P. of گفتن] 2) *n*. Saying ; maxim . Speech ; word.
گفتی * One would say. *See* گویی
گَل ○ [Cont. of گله "flock"]. — تیر در میان گل زدن To fire into the brown.
گِل Mud. Clay. — گِل شُل *or* + گل و شُل Soft mud; mire. — گل مالیدن To smear or plaster with mud. To roughcast. — گل گرفتن To m. off : چاه ها را گل گرفتند ‖ To conceal with m. — بگل نشستن To strand ; run aground. — حق آب و گل

Priority arising from tenancy of long duration.

گُل Flower. Rose *. Snuff of a candle. *F*. Best or choice part; pick. — یك گل آتش A glowing piece of charcoal; an ember. — گل انداختن To flush, as the face. — گل‌چیدن To pick or pluck flowers. *F*. To enjoy fruition. — گل دادن To flower or blossom. — گل کردن 1) = گل دادن 2) To hang fire. 3) *F*. + To show up; appear; come out. — گلی + از هزار گلش نشگفته است He is in the prime of life (*or* bloom of youth). — از گل گلش می شکفت He was all smiles. — گل گفتی + Hear! Hear! [*ironical*]. — گل شمع را گرفتن To snuff a candle. — گل سر سبد Pick of the basket (*or* the whole lot); flower of the flock. — گلی به (گوشه) جمالت × Well done indeed! [*ironical*]; that was clever of you. — پرورش گل Floriculture.

گُل *E*. Goal.

گلاب (*ge*-) Mire; marsh.

گُلاب Rose-water. — سیب گ. *Variety of sweet-smelling apple*. — گل گ. Damascus rose.

گلاب‌پاش Rose-water sprinkler.

گُلابتون Gold or silver lace. Braid.

گلابدان Rose-water bottle.

گُلابی Pear.

گل‌آذین *Bot*. Inflorescence.

گل افشان *a*. Strewn with flowers. —*n*. Benign scarlet fever.

گلافی [f. Fr. *calfatage*] Caulking. — گ. کردن To caulk.

گِل‌آلود Muddy. Splashed with mud. Turbid. — گ. کردن To make turbid or muddy. — ازآب گ. ماهی گرفتن To fish in troubled waters.

گلاله * Ringlet. *Bot*. Stigma.

گل‌اندام *a*. Of a delicate body. —*n*. *Fem*. *pr*. *name*.

گل انگبین Rose-preserve [orig. made with honey].

گِلاویزشدن To grapple.

گلائیل *Fr*. Sword-lily; gladiolus.

گُلباد Compass-card.

گلباز Flower-fancier.

گلبانگ * Shout. Nightingale's note.

گلبرگ Petal. Rose-leaf.

گلبن Rose-bush.

گلبند Garland.

گِل‌پاك‌کن (Door-) scraper.

گُلپر Marjoram; origan.

گِل تراش (Door-)scraper.

گُلچه *Bot*. Floret.

گلچهره 1) *a*. Rose-cheeked. 2) *n*. *Fem*. *pr*. *name*.

گلچین Gatherer of flowers.

F. Selector. Selection. — گ. کردن To select. To cull.— گلچین ادبی Anthology.
گلچینی Selection; act of selecting. *OS*. Picking flowers.
گلخانه Conservatory; also, greenhouse or glasshouse.
گلخن Stove of a bath.
گلدار Flowered; figured.
گلدان Flower-vase. Flower-pot. — گلدان ادرار Urinal.
گلدسته 1) (Top of a) minaret. 2) = دسته‌گل
گلدوز Embroiderer (of floral [designs).
گلدوزی Embroidery with flower designs.
گلرخ * Rose-cheeked.
گلرنگ Rose-coloured.
گلزار (*gel-*) Bog; marsh.
گلزار Rose-garden.
گلساز Maker of nosegays; [florist.
گلِ سرخی Rosaceous. Having rose patterns or designs.
گلستان Rose-garden.
گلسنگ Lichen.
گلشن o Flower-garden.
گلچهره = *P. A.* * گلعذار
گلف *Fr.* & *E.* Golf.
گل فروش Florist.
گلفروشی Dealing in flowers. [For دکان گ.] Florist's shop.
گلفشان *a*. o Ejecting mud. — کوه گ. Mud volcano.
گلفهشنگ Stalactite.— گلفهشنگِ وارونه Stalagmite.
گلقند or گلشکر Conserve of roses; rose-preserve.
گلکار Floriculturist; gardener expert in layout of flower-beds.
گلکاری Flower-work; flower-[designs.
گلگاس Cockle.
گلگشت Pleasure-ground.
گلگون * Rose-coloured.
گلگیرِ Mudguard; fender; wing.
گلگیر Snuffers.
گلمالیِ Mud-plastering. Rough-[casting.
گل مژه Sty.
گلمیخ Peg. Tent-nail. Boss.
گلنار Pomegranate blossoms. — گلنارفارسی Balaustine flowers.
گلن کیم *T*. Who goes there?
گلنگدن *T*. Breech-block.
گلنم Sprinkle. Gentle rain.
گلو Throat. — گلوی زهدان Neck of the womb. — گ. تر کردن To refresh oneself. — گریه در گلویش گرفت He was choked with tears.
گل و بته Floral pattern; flower [design.
گلو بند Necklace.
گلو بین Pharyngoscope.
گلودرد Sore-throat; also, diphtheria.
گلوگاه 1) Pharynx. 2) = گردنه
گل و گردن × The parts about the neck. [Orig. = گلو و گردن]
گل و گشاد × Quite loose or wide. — گ. نشستن To sprawl.
گلوگیر Sticking in the throat; suffocating.— لقمهٔ گ. Choking bit; an enterprise too big

to cope with.

گُلوله Ball; spherical object. Bullet; shot. — گلولهٔ برف Snowball. — گلولهٔ توپ Cannon ball; c.-shot. — گ. کردن To form into a b.; roll up; conglomerate.

گلوله باران کردن To shell or bombard; open fire on.

گلویی Cornice.

گَله Flock. — گلهٔ گاو Cattle; herd.

گِله (Mild or friendly) complaint; a bone to pick with s. o. — گ. کردن To complain.

گُله + Spot. [complaint.

گِله آمیز Expressive of a

گله بان = چوپان & شبان

گله‌دار Cattle-man.

گِله‌گزار Complainant.

گِله‌گزاری Complaining (in a mild or friendly way).

گله‌مند بودن To have a (mild) complaint; have a bone to pick with s. o.

گِلی Muddy. Earthen. — خانهٔ گ. Mud-house. [pr. name.

گُلی *a*. Rose-coloured. —*n*. Fem.

گلیسیرین *Fr*. Glycerine.

گلیسین *Fr*. Wistaria.

گِلیم Short-napped coarse carpet. — گلیم خود را از آب کشیدن To keep the wolf from the door. — پارا باندازهٔ گ. دراز کردن To cut one's coat according to one's cloth.

گلین *T. Fem. pr. name.*

OS. Bride [عروس].

گُم Lost; missing. Mislaid. Invisible. — گم شدن To be lost or mislaid. To disappear. — گم کردن To lose. To miss. — گم و گور کردن × To misplace or lose; throw out of sight. — خود را گم کردن To be above oneself. — دست و پای خودرا گم کردن To be confused from excitement; lose oneself. — گ. شو Get away! Get out! G. lost [also کورت‌را گم کن ×].

گمار [Imp. of گماشتن]

گماردن = گماشتن

گماشتگی Appointment.

گُماشتن [گمار] To appoint. — بریاست گ. To a. (as) chief.

گماشته [P. P. of گماشتن] 1) *a*. Appointed; delegated. 2) *n*. [pl. گماشتگان] Servant. Agent. Piquet.

گُمان Belief; opinion: بگمان من in my o. ‖ Supposition. — گ. کردن ‖ گ. بردن 1) See 2) To be suspicious. — بمن گ. بردند They were s. of me. — + گمانم باو میرود I suspect him. — گ. کردن To believe or think. To be of the opinion. To imagine. — بگمانم I think; I believe; also, I thought, etc.

گمانه Sounding-line. Divining rod. — گ. زدن To dowse; sound (the depth of).

گمراه Misled. Astray. — گ.شدن To go a. To be m. To be seduced. — گ.کردن To lead a.; mislead. To seduce.
گمراهی State of being misled; aberration. Perversion.
گمرك *T-It*. [A. pl.گمرکات] Customs. C. duties. — گ. بستن To levy duties. — گ.کردن + To assess and levy duties on, or complete the Customs formalities in respect of. — از گمرك درآوردن To clear from the Customs. — حقوق گمرکی C. duties.
گمرك‌چی *T*. Customs' officer. C. appraisor or assessor.
گمرك خانه *T.P*. Custom-house.
گمره * [Cont. of گمراه]
گمشده or **گمگشته** * *a*. Lost; missing. Misled. —*n*. L. person or object.
گملاستیك *Fr*. Gum elastic.
گمنام Obscure; unknown. — قبر سرباز گمنام Cenotaph.
گمنامی Obscurity; want of fame
گناه Sin. Crime. — گ.کردن To sin. — گ. دارد or گ. است It is a sin to.
گناهکار *a*. Sinful. —*n*. Sinner.
گناهکاری Sinfulness. [vault.
گنبد or **گنبذ** Dome; cupola;
گنج Treasure(-trove).—گنج قارون Mine of wealth; tons of money. *See* قارون [گنجیدن
گنج Volume. *S. a. under*
گنجا o Voluminous.
گنجاندن To insert. To include.
گنجایش Capacity; room.
گنجایی o Voluminosity.
گنجشك Sparrow.
گنجشك روزی Who lives from hand to mouth.
گنجفه Playing-cards.
گنجور o Guardian of a treasure. Treasurer. [pantry.
گنجه Larder; cupboard;
گنجیدن [گنج] To be contained. To be inserted. — بعقل گ. To seem reasonable.
گنجینه Treasure. Store; depositary.
گند Stink; fetid smell. — گندش را در آوردن + To be outrageous in one's conduct; go too far (in a notoriously indecent act). To make a mess of it.— گندش بالا آمد It began to stink. *F*. It was publicly known.
گنداب Sewage. Fetid water.
گنداب‌رو Sewer.
گنداندن To (cause to) putrefy.
گند زدا Disinfectant.
گند زدایی Disinfection.
گند زدوده Disinfected.
گندگی + Bigness.
گندم 1) Wheat.— نان گ. W. or wheaten bread. 2) Grain [unit of weight]. — آرد گندم Flour; corn-meal. — گل گ. Corn-flower; blue centaury.

گندم‌کوب Flail.
گندم‌گون Swarthy; tawny.
گندم‌نما Who shows wheat [in جو فروشِ گ. Double-dealer].
گندمه Freckle; lentigo; fleck.
گندمی *Bot*. Graminaceous. *OS*. Wheaten. *S. a.* گندم‌گون
گندنا (Variety of) leek. – گندنای کوهی Horehound.
گنده = گ. شدن ‖ گندیده = گندانیدن = گ. کردن ‖ گندیدن
گنده +Big; huge. Corpulent. – گ. شدن To grow big. – گ.کردن To make big.
گنده آروغ Fetid eructation.
گنده تاول Anthrax; carbuncle.
گندیدگی Fetidness. [decay.
گندیدن [گند] To putrefy or
گندیده Putrefied; fetid; addle.
گنگ Dumb; mute. – گ. کردن To make (or strike) dumb. – ریشهٔ گ. Surd.
گنگ Earthen water-pipe.
گنگی Dumbness.
گنه • [Cont. of گناه]
گنه‌گنه Quinine. – گنه گنهٔ شیرین Ethyl carbonate of quinine.
گو [Cont. of گوی]
گوا • [Cont. of گواه]
گواتر *Fr*. Goitre.
گوارا Digestible. Wholesome. Agreeable.
گوارایی Wholesomeness. Digestibility.
گوارش Digestion.
گوارنده Digestive; promoting digestion; peptic. – جوهر گوارنده Pepsin.
گواریدن ০ [گوار] *vi*. To be digested. –*vt*. To digest.
گواه Witness. – گ. آوردن To w.; give evidence. – گ.خواستن‌از *or* گ. گرفتن To call to w.
گواهی Witness; testimony; evidence. Certification. – گ. دادن To give e. (of); bear w. (to). To certify; attest. – دلم گ. نمیدهد که . . . I do not find it in my heart to. . .
گواهی نامه Certificate. – گواهی‌نامه سهام Share warrant.
کوپال = گوپال
گوجه Greengage. Plum.
گوجه فرنگی Tomato.
گود (*gowd*) 1) *a*. Deep. – گ. شدن To sink. – گ. افتادن & گ. کردن To deepen. 2) *n*. Pit; cockpit. – گود خاك برداری Borrow-pit. – گودزورخانه Gymnasium pit or ground.
گوداب Stain left after a distemper. [Abdomen.
گودال Pit. Cavity. – گودال‌شکمی
گود برداری Excavation.
گودرز *Mas. pr. name*.
گوده Pit or ditch. *Anat*. Acetabulum. – مفصل گلوله و گوده Ball-and-socket joint.
گودی Depth. Hollow; cavity. – گودیِ چاه چقدر است How deep is the well?
گور Grave; tomb. – گ. کردن

To bury. To outlive [also زنده بگور کردن —]. گ. گذاشتن To b. alive. — پایش لب گ. است He has one foot in the grave. — گ. بگور شدن To be refused burial in any graveyard.

گور خر = **گور**

گور اسب Zebra.

گور خر Wild ass; onager.

گور زاد Pygmy; elf. Gnome.

گورستان Cemetery.

گورکن Grave-digger. Body-snatcher. Z. Badger.

گورگیاه Sweet-rush; bogrush; camel's hay; lemon-grass.

گوز [*Indecent*] Fart.

گوزن (*gavazn*) Deer.— گوزن ماده Doe; she-deer; hind.— گوزن نر Stag; hart. — گوزن شمالی Reindeer; also, caribou or elk.— شاخ گ. Hartshorn.

گوساله Calf.— گوسالهٔ اخته Steer.— گوسالهٔ ماده Heifer. — گوسالهٔ نر Bull-calf. — گوشت گ. Veal.

گوساله ماهی Z. Seal.

گوسفند = **گوسپند**

گوسفند (Fat-tailed) sheep. — گوشت گ. Mutton.— کود گوسفندی Sheep's dung.

گوش Ear. — گوش خارجی External ear; auricle; pavilion. — گوش داخلی Internal e. — گوش میانی Tympanum; middle e. — گ. بفرمان کسی بودن To be at one's beck and call. — گ. تا گوش From one end to the other.— گ. ایستادن To eavesdrop. — گ. بفرمان من Attention to orders! گوش کسیرا بریدن To swindle money out of a person; also, fleece him. — سراپا گوش بودن To be all ears. — گ. خوابانیدن To wait silently for an opportunity; lie low. — گ. دادن To listen. To hearken or obey [sometimes with به]. — گ. کردن To listen (to); obey [sometimes گ. گرفتن] To wear, as an earring [short for در گوش کردن]. — آب در گوش ـِ کسی کردن To throw dust in s. o.'s eyes.— چیزیرا بگوش کسی رساندن To inform s. o. of s. t. — بگوش او رسید He heard it. — پشت گ. انداختن To pass by; neglect; disregard. — گوشتان بمن باشد Listen, or pay attention, to me. — گوشش بحرفهای من بدهکار نیست He turns a deaf ear to my words. — گوشش از این حرفها پر است He is callous to such words; he has too often heard these words to be inconvenienced by them. — گوش شیطان کر! Touch wood!

گوش بر Swindler; trickster.

گوش بری Swindling.— گ. کردن To swindle or cheat.

گوش بزنگ + On the alert; on the watch. Expecting

anxiously.
گوش بریده Crop-eared.
گوش بین Auriscope.
گوش پاک کن Earpick; aurilave.
گوش پناه o Ear-cap; ear-tab.
گوشت Meat. Flesh. Pulp (of a fruit). ـ گوشت زیادی Fleshy outgrowth ; excrescence . ـ گوشت کسیرا ریختن To give one a gooseflesh; have a rasping effect on him. ـ گوشت نو بالا آوردن To heal up. ـ گ بدست گربه سپردن To set the fox to watch the geese. ـ روغن گ. Dripping ; fat of meat. ـ گ. گرفتن To put on weight or flesh.
گوشتالو + Plump; fleshy.
گوشت تلخ Grumpy. Morose.
گوشت تلخی Moroseness
گوشتخوار Carnivorous.
گوشت خرد کن Meat-chopper.
گوشتدار Fleshy; plump.
گوشت رُبا o Kite or crow.
گوشت فروش Butcher ; meat-seller. [or trade.
گوشت فروشی Butcher's shop
گوشت کوب (Meat-)masher. *M.* Silent block.
گوشتی Fleshy. Carnal. Consisting of meat. Flesh-coloured.
گوش خیزك Earwig.
گوش درد Earache; otalgia.
گوشزد کردن To notify. To point out.
گوشَك Earlet. Auricle. *Mus.* Peg or key. ـ گوشكِ ماهی 1) Gill; 2) = گوش ماهی
گوشمال *or* **گوشمالی** Slight punishment . Reproof . ـ گ. دادن To give a slight p. to; chastise. To rebuke.
گوش ماهی Earshell; nacre.
گوشوارك *Bot.* Stipule.
گوشوار(ه) Earring.
گوشه Corner. Angle. *F.* Hint; allusion. Sarcastic remark. *Mus.* Figure. ـ گ. زدن To speak sarcastically. ـ گوشهٔ حرفی را گرفتن To second or support a statement; follow it up.
گوشه‌دار Angular ; cornered. *F.* Piquant. Sarcastic.
گوشه نشین = گوشه‌گیر
گوشه نشین *a.* Recluse; secluded. —*n.* Hermit or recluse.
گوشه نشینی Seclusion; sequestered life ; retirement . ـ گ. اختیار کردن To sequester oneself from the world.
گوشی Receiver (of a telephone). Ear-trumpet. *Med.* Stothoscope *Mus. See* گوشك ‖ گ. خدمتتان باشد Hold the line (*or* hold on), please. ـ گ. دستم است I am wise to it ; I am in the know. ـ گ. دستتان باشد Watch out ; be wise to it.
گوگرد Sulphur. ـ گوگرد سرخ Philosopher's stone. ـ جوهرِ گوگرد Sulphuric acid. ـ گ. زدن

To sulphurate.
گوگردانک Tumblebug; tumbledung; scarab. [rous.
گوگردی Sulphuric; sulphu-
گول Fraud; deceit.— (کسیرا) گول خوردن To be deceived (by s. o.). — گ. زدن To deceive.
گول [For ماهی‌کول] Carp.
گول خور Gullible; deceivable.
گول زن Dummy; comforter; pacifier. *OS*. Deceiver.
گون *Suf*. 1) Colour. 2) Kind.
گون (*gavan*) Goat's-thorn; camel's-thorn; milk-vetch.
گوناگون Diverse; various. Miscellaneous. Variegated.
گونه Kind. Manner. Colour. *Bot*. & *Z*. Species. — چگونه How? In what m.? [bone.
گونه Cheek. — استخوان گ. Malar
گونی Gunny (bag).
گونیا *Gr*. Set-square.
گوه (*goveh*) Wedge.
گوهر Gem; jewel. Pearl. *F*. Essence. Origin; descent.
گوهر فشان & **گوهر بار** • Eloquent. Raining.
گوهر فروش • Jeweller; dealer in gems or pearls.
گوهر نشان Studded with gems; inlaid with jewels; gemmed.
گوهری • = **جواهری**
گو(ی) [Imp. of گفتن]. — گو که or گواینکه Although.— گو مباش • Let there not be; I don't want.
گو(ی) Sphere; ball; globe. Bead. — گوی سبقت ربودن از To outstrip or outdo. To excel.
گویا Speaking. *F*. Expressive. *Math*. Rational.
گویا [*Stress on the 1st. syl.*] It seems (that). — گ. خسته هستید You seem to be tired.
گویایی Faculty of speech.
گویج Haw(thorn).
گوی‌چه Small globe; globule.
گوینده [گویندگان] Teller. Announcer. Speaker. Narrator.
گویه Buoy.
گویی • One would say (or think). Indeed.
گوئیا • *Same as* 2*nd*. گویا
گه • (*ga*h) [Cont. of گاه].
گه (*go*h) [*Indecent*] Excrement.
گهر • [Cont. of گوهر]
گهربار • = **گوهربار**
گه‌غلتان = **گوگردانک**
گهگاه • [Cont. of گاهگاه]
گه‌گیجه × Absolute giddiness; confused or puzzled state.
گهگیر Restive. — اسب گ. R. horse; jibber.
گهواره Cradle. — گهوارهٔ هوائی Aerostat.— بچهٔ **گهواره‌ای** Child in cradle. — صندلی **گهواره‌ای** Rocking-chair.
گهی • [Cont. of گاهی] [herb.
گیاه Vegetable; plant. Grass;
گیاه خوار Herbivorous. Vegetarian. — جانور گیاه خوار H.

animal ; herbivore.
گیاه شناس Botanist.
گیاه شناسی Botany.
گیاهك = رویان Embryo.
گیاهی Herbaceous. — غذای گ. Vegetable food.
گیتی * World. *Cf.* جهان & دنیا
گیج Giddy ; absent-minded. Confused. Bewildered : puzzled. Fuddled. — گ. خوردن To feel giddy. To reel. To stagger. — گ. شدن To become g. To get p. To be confused. — گ. کردن To make g. To give the vertigo (to). To bewilder. To stupefy.
گیجگاه + Temple [شقیقه].
گیجی Giddiness ; dizziness. Stupour. Puzzled state.
گیر 1) *Imp. of* گرفتن 2) *n.* Hold ; (power to) grasp. Grip. *F.* Difficulty. Entanglement. — گ. آمدن + To be had ; be obtainable or available. To be caught. — بد جوری گ. آمده‌ام + I am in a bad fix (*or* an awkward situation). — گ. آوردن To catch. To manage to obtain. To corner. — گ. افتادن To be caught or betrayed. — گ. انداختن To betray; give up. To entrap. To corner. — گ. کردن To get caught. To be stuck. To meet with a difficulty. To catch. To stammer : زبانش گ. کرد ‖ To hesitate. To stumble. [With به] To touch or hit : پایش بسنگ بهم گ. کردن ‖ گ. کرد To collide ; fall foul. To engage (*vi.*) or mesh.
گیرا Grasping. Biting. *F.* Effective; granted, as a prayer.
گیراندن To kindle or start.
گیرانك *or* **گیرانه** Kindling.
گیرم [f. گرفتن] Granted (that); suppose or admit (that).
گیرندگی Attractiveness. [*Of a liquor*] Headiness.
گیرنده *n.* Recipient. Payee. —*a.* Receiving. Gripping ; attractive. Heady. — دستگاه گیرنده R. set ; receiver.
گیروانکه *T.* Pound.
گیرودار (-ro-) Conflict; scuffle. Authority; pomp. — در این گ. At this juncture.
گیره Clip. Vise. Hairpin. Clothes-peg; clothes-pin.
گیس (Woman's) hair. Tail of h. — گیس دستی Wig.
گیس بریده Shameless : زن گ.
گیس بند Fillet for binding the hair.
گیس سفید Elderly woman ; [duenna.
گیسو * (Woman's) hair. Ringlet ; tress.
گیسو پوش Mob-cap; coif.
گیشه *Fr.* Ticket-office ; booking-office.

گیلاس Cherry. [goblet.
گیلاس [f. E. *glass*] Glass ;
گیلز *R*. Unstuffed cigarette ; tubular c. - paper.
گیلك Native of *Gilan*, a northern province of Iran.
گیله Bride's ornamental veil.
گین *Suf*. Full of ; having.
گیو *Mas. pr. name in the Shahnameh*. [shoes.
گیوه Light cotton summer
گیه * [Cont. of گیاه]
جهان & کیهان = ٥ گیهان

لا Fold ; ply. Thickness. – تختهٔ سه لا Three-p. board. – طناب چهار لا Rope of four strands. – چندلا Manyfold. – لای ِ prep. 1) In(side) : مداد لای ِ کتاب است ‖ 2) Within. – لاش گذاشتن + To (make a) fuss. To pad it.

لا = لای

لا A. = نه No. – بدون لا و نعم Without saying a word.

لاُ بالی A. Careless; remiss.

لاابالی گری A. P. Carelessness.

لاَ ادری A. "I do not know"-confession of one's ignorance.

لااقلّ A. = دست کم At least.

لاُ بدّ A. ad. Necessarily. Certainly. –a. = ناچار & ناگزیر

لابراتوار Fr. = آزمایشگاه

لابلا n. Inner folds ; whole interior. –a. Of many f. – ازلابلای آنها Between the lines.

لابه A. Entreaty. – ل. کردن To entreat ; supplicate.

لاپه Rafter.

لاپوست = زیر پوست

لات or لاط Ruffian. Hoodlum. Tatterdemalion.

لاتعدّ ولاتحصی (-to-ad'ovala-toh'sa) A. Countless(ly).

لاتکلیف or بلاتکلیف A. At a loss what to do.

لات و لوت + Destitute ; naked. S. a. لات

لاتی Destitution. Roguishness.

لاُ جرعه * A. At one gulp.

لاَ جرَم * A. Necessarily. (It follows) therefore.

لاجواب A. Unable to answer ; mute. Unanswerable.

لاجورد Azure; cobalt-blue. – لاجورد کاشی or لاجورداصل Ultramarine. – لاجوردفرنگی Smalt. – سنگ ل. Lapis lazuli.

لاجوردی Azure. – ل. کردن To azure; colour blue.

لاُجون + Weak; sickly. Thin as a lath ; lean as a rake.

لاِحق A. Coming next ; following. Adjoining.

لاحقه A. 1) Fem. of لاحق ‖ 2) n. [pl. لواحق] Supplement ; annex. – سابقه و لاحقه Context.

لادَن Labdanum; ladanum [usu. لادن عنبری]. – گل ل. Nasturtium; Indian cress.

لاروب Dredger. [dredge.

لاروبی Dredging. – ل. کردن To

لاریز Corbie-step(s).

لازِم A. [Fem. لازمه] Necessary. Inherent; inseparable. Gr. Intransitive. Law. Binding ; enforceable. — ل. شدن or ل. آمدن * To be(come) necessary. [With بر] To become incumbent on.— ل. داشتن To need ; require. — دو روز وقت ل. دارد It takes two days (to be done). — ل. دانستن To deem (it) necessary.— ل. نکرده است [*Uttered in a harsh tone*] It is not necessary at all. — ل. وملزوم Correlative. Interdependent . — غیر لازم Unnecessary.

لازم‌الاجراء *A.* That must be executed ; binding ; enforceable.

لازمه *A.* 1) *Fem. of* لازم ‖ 2) *n.* Requisite ; essential condition. Inevitable result. *Cf. the pl.* لوازم ‖ لازمهٔ Essential to; necessary to; integral to. Incidental to.

لاس Female animal; esp. bitch o. Flirting. — لاس ابریشم Coarse silk; floss-silk.— نر ولاس The good with the bad ; the fat with the lean. — ل. زدن To flirt or spoon.

لاستیك *Fr.* Rubber. Tire or tyre.— لاستیك رویی Pneumatic t. — لاستیك توبی Tube.

لاستیکی *Fr. P.* (Made) of rubber ; rubber *adj.*

لاسی Flirtatious ; flirty.

لاش Carcase ; carcass. Carrion.

لاشخور Carrion-kite. Vulture.

لاشریك *A.* Having no partner; single : ep. of God.

لاشك *A.* = بیشك

لاشه Corpse. Carcass.— لاشهٔ برات Retired draft.

لاشه خوار Necrophagous.

لاشیئی o *A.* Worthless.

لاط etc. = لات etc.

لاطار *or* لاطری [f. E. *or* Fr.] Lottery. Raffle. — ل. گذاشتن To raffle (off). [surd.

لاطائل *A.* Idle. Useless. Absurd.

لاعلاج *A.* = علاج ناپذیر

لاعلاجی *A. P.* = ناچاری

لاغر Thin. Lean. — ل. شدن To grow thin (*or* meagre); lose flesh. — ل. کردن To make thin ; emaciate.

لاغرمیان * Slender(-waisted). [Of a horse] Having thin flanks.

لاغری Thinness. Leanness.

لاغیر *A.* No other. Alone.

لاف Boasting ; vaunting. — ل. زدن To boast ; brag. — لاف دوستی زدن To claim to be a friend.

لافزن Braggart ; boaster.

لاقید *A.* Careless ; remiss.

لاقیدی *A. P.* Carelessness. — ل. کردن To be careless.

لاك Sealing-wax. Lac. — لاك‌الکل Lacquer. — لاك شیشه ای Shellac.— لاك ناخن Nail-varnish.— لاك الکل زدن To lacquer. — ل. ومهر کردن To seal up.

لاك o Wooden cup. Shell ;

carapace. *See* لاك پشت ‖ از توی ل. در آمدن To come out of one's shell. [Turtle.
لاك پشت Tortoise. — لاك پشت آبی
لاكتاب + *a. p.* Irreligious; impious. *OS.* Having no Bible.
لاكردار + *A. P.* Ill-treating. Unprincipled.
لاكی Lac-coloured; crimson.
لال Dumb. — ل. كردن To make *or* strike dumb. To silence.
لالا Bye-bye. — ل. كردن To go to bed. [as a pearl.
لالا * Resplendent; glittering,
لالایی Lullaby. — ل. گفتن To lullaby. — لالایی کسیرا گفتن To sing a l. to s. o.; lull him to sleep.
لال بازی Dumb-show. Dumb gestures. — ل. در آوردن To pretend to be dumb.
لاله Tulip. — لالهٔ گوش Auricle. — لالهٔ نعمان Anemone.
لاله عباسی *P. A.* Marvel-of-Peru; four-o'clock.
لاله‌وش *Z.* Crinoid.
لالی Dumbness.
لآلی [Pl. of لؤلؤ]
لام *A.* 1) *Name of the letter* ل 2) Frisette.
لامپ *Fr.* Electric bulb. [*Of a radio*] Valve; tube [U. S.].
لامپا *R.* Lamp.
لآمت *A.* = پستی
لامح *A.* = درخشنده

لامحاله *A.* 1) Inevitably. 2) + = اقلاً
لامذهب *A.* Irreligious.
لامذهبی *A. P.* Irreligion.
لامسه *A.* Sense of touch.
لامع *A.* = درخشنده
لامكان *A.* Having no abode; illocal: ep. of God.
لامی *A.* Lambdoid. Hyoid.
لانجین Large copper bowl.
لانه Nest. [Of a rabbit] Burrow. [Of a dog or fox] Kennel. [Of a bee] Vespiary. [Of a pigeon] Pigeon-hole; pigeonry. [Of an ant] Ants' nest; ant-hill; formicary. — ل. كردن To nestle; live as in a nest. [*With* در] To make a n. of; choose as a n.
لانه سازی Nidification.
لاوك Wooden pan; buddle. — لاوك خاك شوئی Cradle; gold-washer. [irrecoverable.
لاوصول *A.* [*Of a debt*] Bad;
لاوی *A.-Heb.* Levi(te). — سفر لاویان Leviticus.
لاهوت *A.* Divinity. [For علم ل.] Theology. — لاهوت ادبی Moral t. — لاهوت نظری Dogmatic t. — عالم ل. The spiritual world.
لاهوتی *A.* Divine. Theological.
لاهه *Fr.* The Hague.
لا(ی) Sediment. Lees. — لا افتادن To settle; deposit; clear itself. — لا انداختن To s.
لای [*Imp. of* لاییدن]

لای S. u. لا

لایتجزا A. Indivisible; infinitesimal.

لایتغیر A. = تغییر ناپذیر

لایتناهی A. Infinite.

لایحه A. [لوایح] Bill [usu. لایحهٔ قانونی]. Essay.

لایُدرَك A. Incomprehensible.

لایَزال A. Eternal. Indestructible.

لایَشعر A. Lacking common sense. – ضمیر لایشعر The unconscious mind.

لایَعقل A. = بی‌خرد

لایَعلم A. = نادان

لایِق A. = شایسته Worthy; fit; meritorious. – لایق آن نیست He is not worthy of it; he does not deserve it.

لایُقرا A. Illegible. [S. u. قوت

لایموت A. Immortal. – قوت ل.

لاینحلّ A. Insoluble; insolvable. Inexplicable.

لاینفك A. Inseparable. – جزء ل. Integral part; p. and parcel.

لاینقطع A. Incessantly.

لایه Layer.

لایی Wadding; stuffing; dunnage; padding. Packing.

لاییدن o [لای] To bark.

لَب Lip. Edge; brink. – لب بام E. of a roof. – لب دریا Seashore. – لب بستن To keep silent. – لب ترکردن To refresh oneself (by a drink). – لب زدن To taste. – زیرلب حرف زدن To speak below one's breath. – زیر لب خندیدن To laugh in one's sleeve. – لبش را تو گذاشتن × To curtail one's words; cut it short; also, hold one's tongue; hush. – لبش کلفت شد × See لب و لوچه‌اش آویزان شد under لب و لوچه

لُبّ A. [اَلباب] Pith. Essence. Choice part. OS. Heart.

لباب A. Choice part; pith.

لِباس A. [البسه] = پوشاك Clothing; clothes; dress; garment. F. Garb; appearance. – لباس خانه Dressing-gown; undress. – لباس خواب زنانه Night-gown; pyjamas. – لباس خواب مردانه Pyjamas. – لباس زنانه (Ladies') dress. – لباس کار Overall(s); boiler suit. – لباس مبدّل Disguise. – لباس نظامی Military uniform. – دودست ل. Two suits (of clothing). – ل. پوشیدن To dress (up); put on one's clothes.

لباشه or لواشه Barnacles.

لبالب Filled to the brim.

لُبان A. Olibanum; frankincense. – لبان جاوی = حسن لبه ‖ لبان شامی Pitch-resin.

لب برگردان Turndown.

لب بلب ad. Up to the brim. –a. Brimful.

لب پریده Chipped: چینی ل.

لب تُرش Sourish.

لب تَلخ Somewhat bitter.

لبخند Smile. – ل. زدن To s.

لبدیس *Bot*. Labiate.
لبریز Overflowing. – ل. شدن To overflow; run over. – ل. کردن To cause to overflow.
لب شکری Hare-lipped.
لب طلایی Gilt-edge(d).
لبکی Hem(ming).
لبلاب *A*. Bindweed.
لُبنان *A*. Lebanon.
لبنانی *A*. Lebanese.
لَبنیات *A*. Dairy products. – کارخانهٔ ل (سازی) D. farm.
لبنیات فروش *A. P*. Dairyman.
لَبو Boiled beetroot.
لب و لوچه × Chops. – لب و لوچه‌اش آویزان شد He pulled a long face; his countenance fell.
لبه Edge; hem. Rim. Visor of a hat. Eaves of a roof.
لبه‌دار Edged. Having a visor.
لبه دوزی Edging; hemming.
لَبی Labial.
لبیب ○ *A*. = خردمند
لبیك * *A*. Here am I. Yes.
لُپ + = دهن ‖ لپ لپ خوردن To lap; gobble; guzzle.
لپر [For بازی ل.] Ducks and drakes. [seed-leaf.
لپه Split peas. *Bot*. Cotyledon;
لُپی ×Of the mouth. [Only in اشتباه ل. Slip of the tongue].
لَت Sheet. – دریك لتی One-leaf door.
لت و پار کردن × To smash; beat black and blue. To murder: انگلیسی ل. کردن

لثوی (*lasavi:*) *A*. Gingival.
لثه *A*. Gum of the teeth. – ورم ل. Gingivitis.
لَج *A*. Grudge; spite. – بکسی لج داشتن or با کسی لج بودن To bear one a g. – لج کردن To be obstinate. To get one's back up.
لجاجت *A*. Obstinacy; pertinacity. Grudge. – ل. کردن To be obstinate. To bear a g.
لجاره Virago; shrew.
لِجام *A-P*. = لگام
لجباز *A. P*. Pertinacious; obstinate.
لجبازی *A. P*. = لجاجت
لَجن Black mud; slime; ooze. – لجنِ اسید Acid tar.
لجن مال Covered with mud. *F*. Disgraced. – ل. کردن To fling mud at; disgrace.
لَجوج *A*. Pertinacious; obstinate; mulish. [deep.
لُجه *A*. Depth (of the sea); the
لچر + = 1) چرك 2) پست
لَچك Fichu; triangular shawl.
لچك بسر [Derogatory word for] woman.
لحاظ *A* Point of view; respect. Attention: آنرا از لحاظ مبارك می‌گذرانند We bring it to Your Excellency's attention. *Cf. the s.* لحظه ‖ ازلحاظِ For purposes of. With a view to; in the light of.
لحاف *A*. Eider-down; quilt;

comforter. [pledget.
لحافك o *A. P.* Pad; compress;
لحد ´ *A.* Niche in the side of a tomb ; *L.* tomb.
لحظات [A pl. of لحظه]
لحظه ´ *A.* [لحظات & لحاظ o] Moment. *OS.* Side-glance.
لحمی *A.* Fleshy. Sarcomatous.
لحن ´ *A.* [الحان] Tune; melody. *F.* Tone ; strain.
لحیم ´ *A.* Solder ; also, soldering. – ل. کردن To solder.
لحیم گر *A. P.* Solderer.
لحیم گری *A. P.* Soldering.
لحیه ِ *A.* = ریش Beard. – اظهار ل. کردن To throw in a remark.
لخت ´ 1) *n.* Part; piece [only in لختی *q.v.*]. 2) *a.* Lax. Lean.
لخت ُ Naked ; bare. – ل. شدن To take off one's clothes ; undress (oneself). – ل. کردن To strip (of one's c.) To rob; also, to fleece. – اسب ل. سوار شدن To ride bareback.
لخته ´ Clot (of blood).
لختی ´ • (*lakh'ti:*) For a while. Somewhat. *See* لخت´
لختی ُ Nakedness.
لدانم *Fr.* Laudanum.
لدغه o *A.* = نیش Sting.
لدنی ´ *A.* 1) Divine: علم ل. ‖ 2) Theological. 3) Mystical.
لدی الاقتضاء (*A.*) *S. u.* اقتضاء
لدی الورود *A.* On arrival.
لذا ِ *A.* So; therefore. *Cf.* پس - از اینرو - بنا بر این

لذات [Pl. of لذت]
لذائذ ´ *A.* [Pl. of لذیذه o] Pleasures; enjoyments.
لذت ´ *A.* [لذات] Pleasure; enjoyment. Deliciouness. – ل. بردن [With از] To enjoy or relish. To be delighted in. – ل. دادن To give p. or enjoyment. To be delicious.
لذت بخش *A. P.* Delightful ; delectable. Delicious.
لذیذ ´ *A.* Delicious; dainty.
لر ´ o = **لخت** ´ *a.*
لر ُ *Native of Lorestan.* [A. pl. الوار]. *F.* Dupe. Fool.
لرد ُ *E.* Lord.
لرد ِ Dregs ; lees.
لرز ´ 1) Trembling ; tremor.– لرز شیر Milk-fever. – ل. کردن = لرزیدن ‖ 2) *Imp. of* لرزیدن
لرزان Trembling. Tottering.
لرزاندن [لرزان] To cause to tremble ; shake.
لرزانك Jelly or marmalade.
لرزش Tremor. Vibration.
لرزنده Trembling. Tremulous. Shivering.
لرزه Shudder(ring) ; trembling.– ل. براندامش افتاد He was filled with horror ; he began to shudder.
لرزیدن [لرز] To tremble. To shudder. To shiver.
لری ُ *n. or a.* (The dialect) of the *Lurs.* –*ad.* Frankly or point-blank.

لزج *A*. Viscous; slimy.
لزگی Lesghian (dance).
لزوجت *A*. Viscosity.
لزوم *A*. Need ; necessity. — لزوم‌ذاتی Inherence. — درصورت ل. *or* در موقع ل. In case of n. ; if necessary. — بقدر لزوم As much as n. — لزومی ندارد There is no need of. — ل. پیدا کردن To become necessary.
لزوماً *A*. Necessarily. — ل. تذکر میدهد I deem it necessary to point out; I have to p. out.
لژ *Fr*. Box [in a theatre]. — لژ بالا Gallery.
لس + Flabby. [Language.
لسان *A*. [السنه] = زبان Tongue.
لش *n*. Flesh : inner side of a skin. *S. a*. لاشه ‖ —*a*.+ Nerveless. Good-for-nothing. Wanton. Lumpish.
لشکر Army. *Mil*. Division.
لشکرکشی Military expedition.
لشکری *a*. Belonging to the army. —*n*. Soldier or military [pl. لشکریان •].
لش‌گیری Fleshing. *See* لش
لطافت *A*. Purity. Delicateness ; thinness ; tenderness. Elegance. Wit.
لطائف [Pl. of لطیفه].
لطف *A*. [الطاف] Kindness [مهربانی]. Grace. Amenity. Condescension. Elegance. — لطفی ندارد 1) It is not nice or decent. 2) It lacks point. — ل. کردن To do kindness. [*In p. c.*] To give. — لطف سرکار زیاد Thank you (very much).
لطفاً *A*. Kindly.
لطف‌الله (*A*.) *Mas. pr. name*. *OS*. God's favour.
لطمه *A*. Injury. Damage. Shock. *OS*. Slap. — ل. خوردن To be injured or damaged. — باو لطمه خورد He incurred a loss. — ل. زدن *or* ل. وارد آوردن [With به] To injure or damage. To cause a serious interruption to.
لطیف *A*. Fine ; pure. Delicate; tender; thin. Elegant. Kind; gentle. — جنس ل. The gentle (or fair) sex.
لطیفه *A*. [لطائف] Wit ; humour; jest. Maxim. [tious.
لطیفه‌گو *A. P*. Witty ; facetious.
لطیفه‌گویی *A. P*. Witticism.
لعاب *A*. Mucilage. Glaze; enamel. Lustre. — لعاب عنکبوت Gossamer. — ل. دادن To glaze or e. *F*. To embellish. To enrich with details.
لعابدار *A. P*. Enamelled ; glazed. Mucilaginous.
لعابی *A. P*. Enamelled ; glazed. *S. a*. لعاب دار ‖ رنگ ل. Distemper.
لعب *A*. = **بازی**

لعبت A. Plaything; toy. Puppet; doll [عروسك]. Game o. *Met*. Beautiful woman.

لعل A. Spinel-ruby. Garnet.– لب ل. Ruby (*or* red) lips.

لعل فام & **لعل گون** * A. P. Ruby-coloured; rosy.

لعن A. Ban. Cursing.– ل. كردن To ban; put under the b.

لعنت A. Curse; execration.– ل. كردن To c.; anathematize.– بلعنت خدا نمی ارزد It is not worth a damn.– ل. بر او C. on him! D. him!– عليه اللعنه C. upon him.

لعين A. Cursed. Damned.

لغ *or* **لق** + [Of teeth] Loose. [Of eggs] Addle.

لغ + = 1) بی تربيت 2) پررو

لغات [Pl. of لغت]

لغاز Cheek (of a door).

لغايت S. u. غايت

لغت A. [لغات] Word. *By e.* Language or dialect.– كتاب ل. Dictionary [فرهنگ].

لغت نامه A. P. Dictionary.

لغز Puzzle; riddle. Wisecrack.– ل. خواندن To w.; make sarcastic remarks.

لغزاندن [لغزان] To cause to slip; stumble. To lubricate.

لغزش Slip; stumble. Blunder; error. Offence.– ل.خوردن To s. To b.– سنگ ل. Stumbling-block.

لغزنده Slippery. Rickety.

لغزيدن [لغز] To slip; stumble. To blunder o.

لغو (*laghv*) A. Idle talk; nonsense. Nullification. [*Used as an adj.*] Null. Nonsensical.– ل. كردن To nullify. To cancel.

لغوى (*logha-*) A. 1) Literal. 2) *n*. Lexicographer [usu. in the pl. لغويون] [dities.

لغويات A. Idle talks. Absurdities.

لف A. Wrapping; folding o.– در لف Enclosed with.– لف و نشر Involution and evolution [in rhetoric].

لفا A. Herewith. [(person).

لفاظ A. Verbose or pedantic (person).

لفاظى A. P. Use of mere words and bombastic style [often with chicanery]. Word-splitting.

لفاف A. Wrapper; cover. Folder.– ل. كردن To wrap; c. with burlap.

لفافه A. 1) = لفاف 2) F. Cover; guise; veil.– در لفافه گذاردن To cover; veil; couch.

لفت دادن × 1) To lengthen out with tiresome details [usu. لفتش نده]. *Cf*. لعاب دادن ‖ 2) To fuss. [others.

لفت و ليس × Sponging on others.

لفظ A. [الفاظ] Word.– ل. به ل. W. for word; verbatim.– لفظ لفظمعنى Affix.– لفظ قلم Bookish or written language; also, pedantic language.

لفظاً A. Literally. By mere words. In sound.

لفظی A. Literal. Verbal.

لَق S. u. لغ

لِقاء * A. Countenance; face.

لقاح الزهر A. = گرده Pollen.

لقانطه T-It. Restaurant.

لقب A. [القاب] Title (of honour). — ل. دادن To bestow a title (on). To entitle.

لقلق A-P-T. = لگلگ

لُقمان A. Eastern fabulist often identified with Aesop. — به ل. پند آموختن To teach one's grandmother to suck eggs.

لُقمه A. Morsel. Mouthful. Z. Sting ray; trygon. — لقمهٔ چرب Met. A tidy sum of money; a fortune. — ل. را از پشت سر در دهن گذاشتن To do s. t. in a roundabout way. — ل. کردن To break in morsels. — ل. ل. کردن To make a mince-meat of.

لقمة الصباح A. Breakfast.

لقوه (laghveh) A. Paralysis (of the face).

لَك Spot. Stain. — لك افتادن To stain. To become spotted. — لك کردن or لك انداختن To blot or blur. To stain or soil. — لك زدن To become spotted, as fruit. — جگرش برای . . . لك میزند He is dying for . . .

لَك Lac (100,000).

لُك + Staringly. — لك نگاه کردن To stare.

لکات Face-card of the lowest value in the game of آس q. v.

لکاته = روسپی & فاحشه

لك دار 1) = لك زده 2) Stained.

لك زده Spotted, as fruit.

لکن (laken) A. But. However.

لکنت A. Stammering. — ل. داشتن To stammer; stutter.

لکنتی × Tumbledown; dilapidated.

لکوپلست Fr. Sticking-plaster.

لك و لك کردن (lekolek-) × To scrape along. To hang, or lag, behind.

لوکوموتیو Fr. Locomotive.

لکه (lakeh) Spot. F. Stain. Blemish; stigma.

لکه دار Stained. Blemished. — ل. کردن To stain; blemish; cast aspersions on; stigmatize.

لُکه رفتن (lokeh-) To trot.

لکه گیری Minor repairs. (Dry) cleaning. — ل. کردن To make minor r. (in). To dry-clean or dry-cleanse.

لگاریتم Fr. Logarithm.

لگام * Bridle. Reins.

لگد Kick(ing). — لگد پشه Met. Flea-bite. — ل. انداختن To kick. F. To recalcitrate against rules. — ل. خوردن To be kicked. — ل. زدن vt. To kick. —vi. To recoil. — ل. کردن To tread on; trample.

لگد خور Knockabout; tough;

durable.
لگدزن Kicking. Vicious.
لگدکوب Trampled. Crushed.
لگدمال Trampled; trod (upon).– ل کردن To trample.
لگلگ´ T. Stork [often لقلق].
لگن Basin. Pan. – لگن بیمار Bedpan. – لگن خاصره Pelvis.– لگن زبرین False pelvis. – لگن زیرین True p. – لگن بالای ناودان Rain-water head.
لگن پیما Pelvimeter.
لگنچه Small basin. Pan.
لگنی Pelvic.
للگی´ Tutorship.
لله´ Tutor; mentor. Eunuch taking care of children.
لله A. To God. For God's sake.– للهالحمد (*lelahelhamd*) Thanks (*or* praise) to God.
لم´ [Imp. of لمیدن]. – لم دادن = لمیدن
لِم + Knack; trick; hang. – لم چیزیرا یادگرفتن To get the h. of s. t.; know the ropes.
لُمباندن × To swallow without chewing. To suck like an old man without teeth.
لمحه´ A. Glance; glimpse. Flash; moment.
لمس´ A. 1) *n*. Palpation; touching. – ل. کردن To touch. To feel of. 2) *a*. + Paralyzed. Lax.
لمعات [Pl. of لمعه]
لمعان A. = روشنی & تابش
لمعه´ A. [لمعات] Brightness. Flash. Glance.
لِمی A. Deductive; *a priori*: برهان ل. *a. priori* argument.
لمیدن´ [لم] + To lounge; loll.
لم یزرع A. Barren; arid.
لم یزل A. *or* لم یزلی = ابدی
لنبر *or* لنبه = کفل
لنبر زدن + To lap.
لِنت [In a motor car] Lining. [f. Fr. *lint* or R. *lenta*].
لنتر´ (Hanging) lantern or lamp [f. Fr. *lanterne*].
لن ترانی´ + A. Disappointing or irrelevant answer. *OS*. Thou shalt not see me.
لُندلُند Grumbling; muttering.– ل. کردن To grumble or mutter.
لندن´ London.
لندنی *n*. Londoner. –*a*. Of or pertaining to London.
لندوك´ 1) *a*. × Lanky. 2) *n*. Unfledged young bird.
لُند(ه) = غُرغُر
لندهور´ × Giant(-like person).
لنف´ *Fr*. Lymph.
لنفاوی *or* لنفی *Fr-A*. Lymphatic.
لنگ´ Lame [شل]. *F*. Wanting facilities. – ل. کردن *vt*. To make lame. *F*. To stop; interrupt. To paralyze. –*vi*. To halt. To linger.
لِنگ [*Indecent*] Leg.
لُنگ Loin-cloth; waist-cloth. Apron. – ل. انداختن To throw up the sponge; give in; give

a person best. لنگ ملا نصرالدین ـ *Met.* Article serving various purposes.

لنگان Limping.

لنگاندن To cause to limp.

لنگان لنگان *or* لنگ لنگان Limpingly; haltingly.

لنگر Anchor. *F.* Preponderance. Dignity. ـ ل. انداختن To cast anchor; come to a. *F.* To halt. ـ درجایی ل. انداختن To stay in a place too long; outstay one's welcome. ـ ل. دادن To overbalance. ـ ل. (بالا) کشیدن To weigh anchor. ـ چرخ ل. Fly-wheel.

لنگرگاه Anchorage; harbour.

لنگه Half a load. Bale. Mate; match; fellow: لنگهٔ دستکش ‖ Leaf: لنگهٔ در ‖ یك ل. کفش *or* یك لفش ل. An odd shoe. ـ ل. به ل. Ill-matched; ill-mated. [facilities.

لنگی Lameness. *F.* Want of

لنگیدن [لنگ] To go lame; walk lame, limp. [flag.

لواء *A.* [الویه] = پرچم Banner;

لواحق [Pl. of لاحقه]

لوازم *A.* Equipment. Necessaries; outfit. Essentials. *Cf. the s.* لازمه

لوازم‌التحریر *A.* = نوشت افزار

لواش Kind of thin flat bread.

لواط *A.* = بچه بازی Pederasty.

لواف *A.* Seller (*or* maker) of tent-materials.

لوایح [Pl. of لایحه]

لوبیا Haricot-bean. ـ لوبیای چشم بلبلی Black-eye bean; black-eyed cowpea. ـ لوبیای سبز Runner-beans; French bean. ـ لوبیای قرمز Kidney-bean. ـ لوبیای مرمری *or* لوبیای سفید Navy-bean.

لوت 1) = برهنه 2) *S. u.* لات

لوتو *Fr.* Lotto; also, tombola.

لوث *A.* Pollution; contamination. ـ ل. شدن To be slurred over.

لوچ Squint(-eyed).

لوچی Squint; strabismus.

لوح *A.* [الواح] Table; tablet. Plate. Board. Tomb-stone; grave-stone. ـ لوح سنگ Slate. ـ لوح محفوظ (Person with) divine memory.

لوحش‌الله * *A.* Well done! What a (good) . . .! God forbid!

لوحه *A.* Tablet. Plate. Sign-board. *Cf. the collective* لوح

لوخ ٥ = بردی Papyrus.

لو دادن + To betray.

لودگی Clownery.

لوده Pannier. Clown; buffoon.

لوز *A.* Confectionery cut in the shape of lozenges.

لوزالمعده *A.* Pancreas. ـ شیرهٔ ل. Pancreatic juice.

لوزتین *A.* [D. of لوزه] The tonsils. ـ ورم ل. Tonsillitis.

لوزه *A.* Tonsil. [D. لوزتین].

OS. = بادام ‖ ورم لوزهٔ سوم
Adenoids.

لوزی *A.* Lozenge.

لوزینه *A. P.* Almond-cake.

لوژ *Fr.-Ger.* Luge.

لوس Spoiled : بچهٔ ل. ‖ Insipid; flat : شوخی ل. ‖ Who makes flat jokes. Who ingratiates himself in an insipid manner. Soppy ; corny . — ل. کردن To spoil ; molly-coddle.

لوستر *Fr.* Chandelier ; lustre; electrolier.

لوط *A.-Heb.* Lot. — بحر لوط The Dead Sea.

لوطی *A. P.* Pederast. Rogue.

لوطی خور شدن × *A. P.* To be misappropriated or dissipated. *OS.* To be eaten by rogues.

لوطی گری کردن + *A. P.* To be lavish of one's money; also, be of a forgiving attitude.

لوك Male camel.

لوکس *Fr.* De luxe.

لوکوموتیو = **لکوموتیو**

لول 1) *n.* Stick (of opium). Roll. — تفنگ دو لول Two-barrelled gun. 2) *Imp. of* لولیدن ‖ ل. زدن + To toss, as in bed; fidget.

لول ∘ = 1) سرخوش (2 شوخ چشم

لولا Hinge. — ل فرنگی Butt-h.

لولو Bugbear. — لولوی سر خرمن Scarecrow.

لوء لوء *A.* [لآلی] = **مروارید**

لوله Tube.[*For liquids*] Pipe. [*Of a gun*] Bore. [*Of a kettle*] Spout. — لولهٔ آتش نشانی Fire-hose. — لولهٔ جلد *or* لولهٔ جدار *or* لولهٔ غلافی Casing. — لولهٔ خرطومی Hose (pipe). — لولهٔ دود Exhaust-pipe. — لولهٔ لامپا Lamp-chimney. — ل . کردن To form into a tube ; tubulate. To roll. — ل. کشیدن To lay a pipe(line).

لوله‌ای Tubular. Tubulous. — پیوند لوله‌ای Flute-grafting.

لوله پاك کن Pipe-cleaner. Swab

لوله شو Ductile.

لوله‌کش Pipe-layer. Plumber.

لوله کشی Pipe-laying. Pipe-work. Plumbing; plumbery. Water reticulation. — ل. کردن *vi.* To lay pipes. To do plumbing. —*vt.* To plumb or pipe: supply with pipes.

لولی ∘ Gipsy. Harlot.

لولیدن [لول] To wriggle. To toss, as in bed. To fidget.

لولئین (Earthen) ewer with a spout. — لولئینش خیلی آب برمیدارد + He carries much weight.

لوم *A.* = **ملامت**

لون *A.* [الوان] = **رَنگ**

لوَند Lewd. Shrewish.

لوندی Shrewishness. Lewdness. Coyness +.

لوئی *or* **لویی** Cat-tail ; reed-mace.

لهَ *A.* To him. For h. [Fem. لها]. — له او *or* برلهِ او For

him ; in his favour.
لَه R. Pole ; Polander.
لِه Crushed. Trod. T. upon. [*Of fruit*] Squashy.—له شدن To be crushed or trod. —له كردن To squash. To crush. To squeeze. To mash. *F*. To slur or elide. To tread.
لهات *A*. Uvula.
لهب ○ *A*. = شعله
لَهجه *A*. Dialect. Accent.
لهذا (*lahaza*) *A*. = از اينرو Therefore.
لهراسب *Name of a king*.
لهستان Poland.
لهستانى *a*. Polish. —*n*. Pole.
لهف ○ *A*. = افسوس & تاسف
لَه لَه زدن + To pant To yearn.
لَهو (*lahv*) *A*. Play. Sportiveness. —لهو ولعب Pleasure. Amusements. Debauchery.
لهيب ○ *A*. = ملتهب & مشتعل
لهيدن = له شدن
لياقت *A*. Merit ; worth. Capability; efficiency. لياقت آنرا ندارد He is not worthy of it; he does not deserve it.
ليالى [Pl. of ليل]
ليبى *Fr*. Lybia.
ليت *A*. = اى كاش [Only in بليت واهل گذرانـدن To procrastinate. To gain time by saying "I wish" (كاش) or "perhaps" (شايد)
ليتر *Fr*. Litre.
ليث *A*. Lion [شير]. *Mas. pr. name*.
ليچار or ريچار + Cutting words. Balderdash. *S. a*. متلك
لير *It*. Lira.
ليره *It*. Pound (sterling).
ليز Slippery. —ل. خوردن To slide. To slip.
ليزى Slipperiness. [Lap.
ليس 1) *Imp. of* ليسيدن 2). *n*
ليسانس *Fr*. Licentiate's degree.
ليسانسيه *Fr*. Licentiate.
ليسك Snail [حلزون].
ليسه Scraper. Drawshave ; drawknife.
ليسيدن [ليس]. To lick.
ليطر *S. u*. ليتر
ليف *A*. [الياف] 1) Fibre; filament. 2) *Bot*. Loofah. 3) Flesh-brush. 4) The hem in a pair of pyjamas through which tape is drawn.—ل. زدن To soap with a flesh-brush.
ليفه *A*. = ليف *4th. sense*.
ليفى *A*. Fibrous. Fibriform. — غضروف ل. Fibro-cartilage
ليك * [Cont. of ليكن].
لیکن [f. A. لكن] But.
ليكور (*-kor*) *Fr*. Liqueur.
ليل *A*. [ليالى] = شب Night.
ليلاج *S. u*. لجلاج [night
ليله *A*. = شب (يك) (A single)
ليلى (*leili:*) *Fem. pr. name*.
ليلى (*leilei*) Hopping — ل. كردن To hop. — چرخ ل Scooter.

لئیم - لئیم‌الطبع - لئیم‌النفس *A.* Base; mean. *Cf.* فرومایه & پست

لیموئی Lemon-coloured. Lemon-shaped. Citrous.

لین (*layen*) *A.* Soft. Gentle.

لینت *A.* Laxity ; loose bowels.

لیوان Tumbler ; glass. [*For beer*] Beer-mug. [*Of a laboratory*] Beaker. - لیوان خمره‌ای *S. u.* خمره

لیلی (*li:li:*) (?) - لی‌لی بلالای کسی گذاشتن X To bear a person's airs ; spoil him by giving too much importance to him.

لیمو (Sweet) lemon.

لیمو ترش 1) Lemon. 2) Lime. 3) Citron. - جوهر لیمو ترش Citric acid.

لیمو فشار Lemon-squeezer.

لیموناد *Fr.* Lemonade.

م *a) Pronominal ending for the present and past tenses meaning "I". Ex.* میروم *I go ;* رفتم *I went ; (b) pronominal ending meaning "my", as in* پایم *my foot, or "me", as in* می بیندم *He sees me; (c) suf. changing cardinals to ordinals. Ex.* دَهُم *tenth ; (d) syn. of the negative* ن *in literary styles, as in* مخور *which equals* نخور *'Do not eat.'*

ما 1) We. 2) [After a prep.] Us. Ex. کتاب را بما دادند ‖ 3) [Preceded by an *ezafah*] Our. Ex. شاهِ ما

ماء *A.* [میاه] = آب Water.

مابعد *A.* What comes next.

مابقی *A.* = (مانده) باقی

مابون *A.* 1) *a.* Affected with itching. Prurient. 2) *n.* Catamite.

مابه التفاوت *A.* [Excess. Difference.

مابین *A.* Space between; middle. — مابینِ *prep.* Between.

مات *A.* Checkmated. [*Of glass*] Mat or ground ; opaque ; frosted. — م. شدن To be astonished or stupefied. To be checkmated. — م. کردن To checkmate. To mat. To stupefy. — ماتش برد + He was struck dumb.

مآت *A.* [Pl. of مئه] Hundreds.

ماتحت *A.* Podex. Anus.

ماتَرَك *A.* Estate (of a deceased person).

ماتَم *A.* Mourning. — م. داشتن To be in mourning. — م. گرفتن To mourn (for or over).

ماتم زده & ماتمدار *A.P.* Mournful; in mourning.

ماتیك [Cont. of the Fr. کسمتیك] Lipstick [also ماتیك لب].

مآثر *A.* Memorable deeds ; memorials. [Pl. of مأثره]

ارجمند & محترم = .A مآجد

ماجَرا [f. A. ماجری *majara*] Circumstances ; incidents. Events. Adventure. Dispute.

ماجراجو *A. P.* Adventurous. Quarrelsome.

ماچ etc. + بوسه — etc.

ماچه [*Of a dog or ass*] Female. *Cf.* ماده

ماحَصل *A.* Result. Summary. Average. — ماحصلِ کلام To sum up.

ماحَضر *A.* Ready victuals. Food prepared in haste.

مأخذ *A.* [مآخذ] 1) Basis. — روی مأخذِ or بمأخذِ On the basis of. 2) Origin; source.

ماخلق الله *A.* What God has created. — اول م. Wisdom or intellect. *Cf.* خرد & عقل
مأخوذ *A.* Taken. Derived.
ماد Media ; Medes.
مادام *A.* Duration o. — م. که So long as. Also, while.
مادام *Fr.* = بانو. Madam(e).
مادام الحیات *A.* During one's lifetime.
مادِح o *A.* Praiser. *Cf.* مدّاح
مادَر Mother. — مادر بزرگ Grand-mother. — مادر بزرگ = o • مادرِ مادر
مادر اندر o Step-mother.
مادرانه Motherly; maternal.
مادر بخطا *P. A.* = حرامزاده
مادرزاد Congenital. — کورمادرزاد (One who is) born blind *or* congenitally b.
مادر زن Mother-in-law [wife's mother].
مادر شوهر Mother-in-law [husband's mother].
مادری 1) *n.* Motherhood. — م. کردن To act as a (kind) mother. 2) *a.* Maternal. — زبان م. Mother tongue.
مادگی Buttonhole. *Bot.* Pistil.
مادموازل *Fr.* = دوشیزه. Made-moiselle. Miss.
مادون *A.* (What is) below or inferior. *See* دون
ماده Female. — الاغ م. She-ass. — سگ م Bitch. — گاو ماده Cow.
مادّه *A.* Matter. *F.* Essence. Article [pl. مواد]. Abscess. — م. اش مستعد بود He was disposed to do it. ; he was of that type.
ماده الاغ She-ass.
ماده بز She-goat.
ماده سگ Bitch; female dog.
ماده شیر Lioness.
ماده گاو Cow.
مادی *A. a.* Median. — *n.* Mede.
مادّی *A. a.* Material. — *n.* Mate-rialist [pl. مادّیون].
مادّیات *A.* Material things (*or* concerns). [Orig. pl. of مادّیه fem. of مادّی].
مادیان Mare. — کرهٔ م. Filly.
ماذَریون Spurge-olive; spurge daphne ; mezereon. *Med.* Mezereum.
مأذون *A.* Permitted.
مار Serpent Snake. — مار جرس‌دار *or* مار زنگی *or* مار جلاجل *or* مار زنگوله Rattlesnake.
مارپیچ Spiral; helical.
مارچوبه Asparagus.
مارس *T.* Gammon. — م. کردن [To g.
مارس *Fr.* March
مارسان *Z.* Ophiurian.
مارش *Fr.* March. — م. کردن To [m.
مارشال *E.* & *Fr.* Marshal.
مارك *Fr.* Mark : monetary unit.
مارك *Fr.* Mark; brand [نشان].
مارك‌دار *Fr. P.* Marked ; noto-rious.
مارگزیدگی Snake-bite.
مارگزیده Snake-bitten.
مارگیر Snake-charmer.

مارمالاد *Fr*. Marmalade.
مار ماهی Eel. Also, moray.
مارمولك Lizard. *Met*. Sly person.
مارونی *A*. Maronite.
ماز ○ Maze. Twist. Fold.
مازاد *A*. Surplus; excess. – م. بر S. to : م. براحتیاجات
مازو Gallnut. Harrow. – جوهر مازو Tannic acid; tannin.
مازوت *R*. Mazut.
مازه *or* **مازو** [For گوشت م.] Fillet; undercut.
ماساژ *Fr* Massage *Cf*. مشت‌ومال
ماسبق *A*. What has preceded; i. e. the foregoing.
ماست Yoghurt. – ماست خود را کیسه کردن + To draw in one's horns; settle down; also, put one's tail between one's legs. – م. را نمی برد It's a good knife; it will cut butter when 'tis melted. – علف م. Cleavers; lady's-bedstraw
ماست مالی کردن + To slur over.
ماسك *Fr*. = نقاب Mask. – ماسك ضد گاز Gas-mask.
ماسوا [f. A. ماسوی] What is separate or apart.
ماسوره Bobbin; reel. *Cf*. پیوند **ماسوره‌ای** ‖ غرغره Flute-grafting.
ماسوره پیچ [In a sewing-machine] Cam.
ماسوره نگهدار [In a sewing-machine] Carrier.
ماسه (Fine) sand.
ماسه‌زی *Z*. Arenicolous.
ماسیدن + [Orig. ماستیدن] To be congealed or coagulated. – چیزی نمی ماسد × Nothing doing.
ماش Chickling vetch. – ماشِ هر آش *Met*. One who has a finger in every pie.
ماشاءالله (*mashala*) *A*. Well done! May you be preserved from evil eye! What wonders God has wrought. *OS*. What God has willed. —*Note*. ماشاالله is also used as a mas. pr. name.
ماشرا Canker.
ماشورم Culm; haulm.
ماشه Trigger. Pincers.
ماشی Greenish yellow; moss-green [also ماشی رنگ].
ماشین *Fr*. Machine; plant. Engine. Motor-car. Railway-train – ماشین‌تحریر Typewriter. – ماشین چاپ Printing-press. – ماشین مو زنی Hair-cropper. – ماشین حساب Comptometer. – م. کردن To type. To print. To crop (hair).
ماشین‌آلات *Fr*. *A*. Machinery.
ماشین چی *Fr*. *T*. Machine-operator. Pressman.
ماشین‌خانه *Fr*. *P*. Engine-house.
ماشین‌رو *Fr*. *P*. Carriage-way.
ماشین سوارکن *Fr*. *P*. Erector (of machinery).
ماشین کار *Fr*. *P*. Engine-man;

machinist. Operator. Pressman. [operator.

ماشین گردان *Fr. P.* Machine-

ماشینی *Fr. P.* Machine-made. Engine-driven. Typed.

ماضی *A.* = گذشته Past (tense). [Fem. ماضیه . Ex. قرون ماضیه].

ما عدا *A.* What is outside a sphere or category. – اثباتِ شیئی نفیِ م. نمیکند It does not follow from affirming something as a predicate that other predicates must be negated of the subject on hand.

ماغ *or* **ماق** Mooing; lowing.– م کشیدن To moo or low. *By e.* To moan.

مافات *A.* (What is) bygone or past. – جبران م. کردن To make up for the p.

مافوق *a. p.* Beyond; above. – مافوق طبیعت Hyperphysical ; supernatural.

ماقبل *A.* Preceding (part). – ما قبلِ Before . – ما قبل آخر Penultimate.

ماك *S. u.* شیر

ماکارونی *Fr.* Macaroni.

ماکو Shuttle. [edible.

مأکول *A.* = خوردنی Eatable ;

مأکولات *A.* Eatables. [Pl. of مأکوله o fem. of مأکول]

ماکیان Hen; fowl. *Cf.* مرغ

ماکیانی Gallinacious.

مال *A.* Property; wealth [pl. اموال]. Beast of burden. Riding animal. – مالِ من است It is mine ; it is my property ; it belongs to me. Also, it is for me. – مالِ سر دردش است + It is due to his headache.

مال [Imp. of مالیدن]

مآل (*ma-al*) *A.* Issue ; result; end. Return(ing) o.

مالاً *A.* Financially.

مآلاً *A.* Ultimately. Consequently.

مالاریا *Fr.* Malaria.

مالاریایی *or* **مالاریاخیز** *Fr. P.* Malarial.

مال الاجاره *A.* Rent.

مال التجاره *A.* Merchandise.

مالا مال * *A. P.* Filled to the brim. Heaped up.

مالاندن × To give a good dressing to.

مآل اندیش *A.P.* = **عاقبت اندیش**

مال اندوز (One) who amasses wealth; mammonish (person).

مال بگیری + *A.P.* Requisition of beasts.

مال بند *A. P.* Shaft; thill.

مال پرست *A. P.* Mammonish.

مال پرستی *A. P.* Mammonism.

مالت *Fr.* 1) Malta. – تب م. M. fever. 2) Malt.

مالدار *A. P.* = **توانگر**

مالدُن *Fr.* (*C. P.*) Misdeal.

مالِش Rubbing. Friction. Massage. – م . دادن To give a

rubbing to. To knead or massage. — م. رفتن + [*Of the stomach*] To have a gnawing sensation.

مالك *A.* [مالکین] Owner. Landlord; proprietor. — م. بودن To own. [lord.

مالك‌الرقاب *A.* Suzerain; over-

مالكانه *A. P.* Possessory : سهم م.

مالكيت *A.* Ownership. — حق م. O. right; r. of ownership.

مالوف *A.* Usual. Familiar.

ماله Trowel. — مالهٔ رنگ آمیزی Palette-knife. [*fem.* ماليه

مالى *A.* Financial. *Cf. the*

ماليات *A.* Tax(es). — م. بر درآمد Income tax. — م. برچیزی بستن To levy a tax on s. t.

ماليات بده *A. P.* Taxpayer.

مالياتى *A. P.* Pertaining to taxes or taxation — تحصیلدارِ مالیاتی Tax-collector. — مؤدیِ م. Taxpayer.

ماليخوليا *A-G.* Melancholia.

ماليخوليائى *A. G.* Melancholy *adj.*

ماليدن [مال] To rub. — بدن خود را روغن م. To rub one's body with ointment. — نمد مالیدن To make felts.

ماليدنى (Medicine) designed for external use.

ماليده 1) [P. P. of ماليدن] 2) *a.* Called off. — م. گرفتن or م. حساب کردن To call off; start (at) scratch.

ماليه *A.* Finance. [*Orig. fem. of* مالى] *See* دارایی

مام * = 1) ماما 2) مادر (رضاعی)

ماما Midwife. *S. a.* مامان

ماماچه [*Derogatory for* ماما]

مامان *Fr.* [Often ماما] Mamma.

مامايى Midwifery. — علم م. Obstetrics.

ما مَضى (-za) *A.* = **مافات**

مامن *A.* Safe place; p. of refuge; haven.

مامور *A. n.* [مامورین] Official; functionary. Delegate. —*a.* Commissioned; appointed. Sent on duty. — م. شد آنرا بازرسی کند He was a. (*or* ordered) to inspect it. — به رشت م. شد He was sent on duty to Rasht. — م. کردن To send on duty; commission; appoint; delegate.

ماموريت *A.* Duty; commission. — بقم م. یافت He was sent on duty to Ghom.

مامول *A.* (That which is) hoped or desired. [wort.

ماميران Celandine; swallow-

ماميزه Meconium.

ماميشا Common field scabious.

مان [Pl. of م] Our. Us.

مان [Imp. of ماندن]

ماناكه * As if; as though.

مانحن‌فيه *A.* Subject on hand. *OS.* What we are in.

ماندگار Permanent. Staying. — م. شدن To stay.

ماندن [مان] To remain. To be left. To stay. To last; wear. *S. a.* یك || فرو ماندن ربع مانده بیك It is a quarter to one.—رفتارش خیلی م. است تا... His conduct leaves much to . . . — چیزی نمانده بود که در آن بیفتد He barely missed falling into it ; he came within an inch of falling into it.

ماندنی Permanent. Resident. That can keep, as food.

ماندولین *Fr.* Mandolin(e).

مانده *a.* Left (over); remaining. Tired out. *–n.* Difference; remainder. Balance.

مانستن * [مان] To resemble.—بچه میماند ؟ What does it r. ? W. is it like ?

مانش *Fr.* [For دریای م.] The English Channel.

مانِع *A.* [موانع] Obstacle; impediment. — اسب دوانی با پرش از موانع Hurdle-race ; the hurdles. — م. شدن To prevent; hinder ; keep. — مانعی ندارد There is no objection to it ; it is in order ; there is nothing against it.

مانعةالجمع *A.* Incompatible. Impenetrable.

مانَند *a.* Resembling. *–n.* Like; parallel. — مانندِ *prep.* Like ; as. — مانند هم Alike; similar. — نقاشی و مانند آن Painting and the like.

مانور *Fr.* Manœuvre. Shunting [in railways].

مأنوس *A.* Familiar. — با کسی م. شدن To become familiar with s. o. — باچیزی م. شدن To get used to s. t.

مانَوی *A.* Manichæan.

مأنَویت *A.* Manichæism.

مانی Manes.

مانیکن *Fr.* Mannequin.

مانیکور *Fr.* Manicure.

مأوا [f. A. مأوی *ma'va*] Abode; residence. Shelter. — م. دادن To lodge. To give s. — م. گرفتن To dwell; reside.

ماوَراء *A.* What is beyond. — ماوراءِ *or* ماورایِ B. or besides. — ماوراء اردن Transjordan. — ماوراء بحار Overseas. — ماوراء بنفش Ultra-violet.— ماوراء قرمز Infra-red.

ماوراءالنهر *A.* Transoxania.

ماوَقَع *A.* = رویداد Circumstances; incidents ; event.

مأوی *S. u.* مأوا

ماه 1) Moon. Month. — علف م. Moonwort; lunary. — ماهی صد ریال 100 Rials a month (*or* per mensem). — بچهٔ دوماهه 2-month-old baby. — آبستنِ شش ماهه Six months gone with child. — همه ماهه *or* هر ماهه Every month. 2) [*Used as an adj*] × Out of this world ; exquisite.

ماهانه [also ماهیانه] *a*. Monthly : گزارش م. ‖ *—n*. M. salary, wages, or tuition. *—ad*. M.; per month; per mensem.
ماه‌پیکر * Of a moonlike figure; also, beautiful.
ماهتاب *See* مهتاب
ماهچه ○ Half-moon. Crescent.
ماه دَرد False labour pain.
ماهِر *A*. Skilful; skilled; expert. Dexterous Crack.
ماهرانه *A. P*. Skilfully. Dexterously.
ماهرُخ رفتن To point [said of dogs called pointers]
ماهرو(ی) * Moon-faced.
ماه طلعت * *P. A*. = ماهرو
ماه‌گرفت Lunar eclipse.
ماهوت Broadcloth. Baize.
ماهوت پاك‌كن Brush.
ماهوتی Made of, covered with, broadcloth or baize - توپ م. Tennis-ball.
ماهور 1) Rising ground ○. 2) *Mus*. Kind of melody.
ماهی Fish. - ماهی درشت قنات Bleak. - ماهی ریز قنات Gudgeon. - ماهی روغن Cod; c.-fish. - م. گرفتن To (catch) f. - روغن م. Cod-liver oil.
ماهیانه *S. u*. ماهانه
ماهی پرور Pisciculturist.
ماهی پروری Pisciculture.
ماهیت *A*. Essence; nature; quiddity. [frying-pan.
ماهی تابه P n for frying fish;
ماهیچه Muscle. - ماهیچهٔ پا Calf of the leg.
ماهی خانه ○ Aquarium.
ماهی‌خوار Heron.
ماهی‌خور *a*. Piscivorous; living on fish. *—n*. = ماهی خوار
ماهی خورك Kingfisher.
ماهی درهم In-and-out; suggestive of wriggling fish.
ماهی‌زَهره Indian berry.
ماهی شناس Ichthyologist.
ماهی شناسی Ichthyology.
ماهی فروش Fishmonger.
ماهی گردان Fish-slice.
ماهی گیر Fisher(man). Angler.
ماهی‌گیری Fishing. Angling. - کشتی م. *or* کرجی م. F.-boat.
مایتحلل *A*. What is wasted or assimilated - بدل م. *S. u*. بدل
مایَحتاج *A*. Necessaries.
مائده ○ *A*. (Table with) victuals; food [خوراك].
مایع *A* Liquid. *See* آبکی
مایعات *Pl. of* مایعه ○ *fem. of* مایع
مایِل *A*. Inclined; oblique. *F* Fond; desirous. - مایلِ اوست He is fond of her. - م. برفتن Fond of going. - م. بزردی Yellowish. - مخروط م. Scalene cone. [sions.
مایَملك *A*. Property; possessions.
مایو *Fr*. (Skin-tight) bathing or swimming costume.

مأیوس *A*. Disappointed; h peless [نا امید]. م. شدن – To be disappointed; despair. – م. کردن To disappoint.

مایه Ferment; leaven; yeast. Capital; funds; stock. *F*. Source, cause. Grounding; also, background. *Med*. Vaccine. *Mus*. Key or pitch – مایهٔ آبجو Barm. – مایهٔ پنیر Rennet. – مایهٔ خنده Laughing-stock. – مایهٔ ماست Starter. – او مایهٔ افتخار این آموزشگاه است He is a credit to this school. – م. ای ندارد It is not expensive or difficult. – م. به م. At cost. – م. گذاشتن + To spend; outlay; pay. – برای کسی م. گرفتن + To insinuate against s. o.; also, involve him in trouble by underhand methods.

مایه‌دار Well-grounded. Possessing the necessary funds. [Of solutions] Strong.

مایه سوز Losing, or having lost, one's capital or stock-in-trade.

مایه کوبی Vaccination.

مائی ○ *A*. = آبی Watery. Aqueous. Aquatic. Serous. – خلط م. Lymph.

مُباح *A*. Open to any one. Belonging to no one. Impunible. [*Of acts*] Allowable. – خونش م. است He may be killed with impunity.

مباحات *A*. Rights or properties belonging to no particular person. Religious acts that may or may not be performed. [Pl. of مباحه fem. of مباح]

مباحث [Pl. of مبحث].

مُباحثه *A*. [مباحثات] Controversy. Argument. – م. کردن To enter upon a c. [*With* در] To controvert.

مَباد • 1) = نباشد Let it not be. L. there not be. 2) = **مبادا**

مبادا [*Stress on the 1st. syl.*] Lest. – از برای م. (Just) in c. [*In this sense the stress is on the last syl.*]. – م. آنرا ذکر کنید Be careful you don't mention it. – م. نیائید Do not fail to come.

مُبادرَت *A*. Making haste ○. Embarking; setting. – بکاری م. کردن To embark upon an undertaking.

مبادلات [Pl. of مبادله]

مُبادله *A*. [مبادلات] Exchange. Barter. Truck. – م. کردن To exchange. To bandy. – چیزیرا با چیز دیگر مبادله کردن To e. one thing for another.

مَبادی *A*. Elements; principles; fundamentals. *Cf*. the s. مبدأ

مبادی آداب *a. p.* Of good manners.

مُبارز *A*. Fighter. Champion.
مبارز طلب *a. p*. Challenger (to single combats).
مُبارزه *A*. Fighting together; combat. Campaign.— م. کردن با To fight ; campaign against.
مُبارَك *A*. Blessed. Auspicious.— نوروز بر شما مبارك باشد Happy New Year ! — این‌عروسی م. باشد I congratulate you (*or* wish you good luck) for this wedding.
مبارکباد *A. P*. Good wishes ; congratulation(s).
مبارکی *A. P*. Auspiciousness.
مُباشِر *A*. Supervisor. Overseer. [*Of a train*] Conductor. [*Of labourers*] Foreman.
مباشَرَت *A*. Supervision. Foremanship. — م . کردن (بر) To supervise ; oversee. To manage; conduct.
مَبال *A*. = مستراح
مُبالات *A*. Care. Regard.
مبالغ [Pl. of مَبلغ]
مُبالغه *A*. Exaggeration; hyperbole. — م. کردن To exaggerate.
مبالغه‌آمیز *A. P*. Exaggerated.
مبانی [Pl. of مبنی *or* مبنا].
مُباهات *A*. (Taking) pride ; glorying. — بچیزی م. کردن To take pride in s. t.
مُباهله ○ *A*. Cursing each other.
مُباین *A*. = مغایر
مباینت *A*. Contrast. Separation.
مُبتدا *A*. (*Gr*.) Subject.
مُبتدی *A*. Beginner; novitia
مُبتذَل *A*. Commonplace; tri
مُبتکر *A. n*. Originator; init tor. —*a*. Original : نز مبتکر
مبتکراً *A*. On one's own in tiative.
مبتکرات *A*. Initiated things [in م. کمیسیون Committee initiating proposed legislation].
مُبتلا *A*. Affected. Suffering. Addicted; given. [With به] S. from ; given or addicted to. Enamoured of. — مبتلا کردن To cause to suffer. To addict. To captivate.
مُبتنی *A*. Founded; based.
مَبحث *A*. [مباحث] Subject (of discourse). *S. a*. گفتار
مَبدأ *A*. Origin. Principle. *Geom*. Generatrix. *Cf. the pl*. مبادی ‖ مبدأ نخاع Medulla oblongata.
مُبدع *A*. Innovator. Creator ○.
مبدّل (*mobadal*) *A*. Changed. Transformed. — م . کردن To change. To transform. — با لباس م. In disguise.
مبدّل (*mobadel*) *A*. Transformer. Converter. Reducer.
مُبذّر *A*. Lavish; prodigal.
مَبذول *A*. Given generously. Bestowed. — م. داشتن To give generously. To allow. — سعی وافی م . داشت He spared no effort ; he made every

effort.
مُبرّا A. Innocent. م. کردن To exempt. To exonerate.
مَبرّات A. Charitable deeds. [Pl. of مبرت ○]
مُبرّد A. Refrigerant. Humective.
مَبرَز A. = مستراح
مبرز (mobaraz) A. Distinguished.
مُبرَم A. Confirmed.
مُبرِم A. Importunate. Pressing.
مَبرور ○ A. Pious. Absolved through piety.
مَبروص A. 1) a. Leprous. 2) n. Leper.
مبرهن A. Demonstrated; proved. Clear.
مَبسوط A. Expanded. Detailed.
مبسوطاً A. In detail; fully.
مُبشر A. Harbinger of good news. Forerunner.
مبصر (mobaser) A. One who makes another see or understand; enlightener.
مبصر (mobser) A. Monitor.
مُبطل A. (adj.) Invalidating; rendering null; cancelling.
مُبعد A. Abducting. [Fem. مبعده Ex. عضلهٔ مبعده Abductor].
مَبعوث A. Sent on a mission, as a prophet; appointed. — م. کردن به To appoint as.
مُبل Fr. Furniture. See مبله
مبل‌ساز Fr. P. Furniture-maker.
مَبلغ (-lagh) A. [مَبالِغ] Sum; amount. — چکی بمبلغِ A cheque for (the sum of). — آنرا در چه م. خریدید؟ How much did you pay for it?
مبلغ (mobalegh) A. [مبلغین] Missionary. Propagandist.
مُبله Fr. Furnished. See مبل ‖ م. کردن To furnish.
مَبنا [f. A. مَبنی -na] [مبانی] Basis; foundation. Base. — توپ م. Mil. B. piece; directing p.
مَبنی A. Based. — م. بر B. on.
مُبهم A. Ambiguous; vague. — ضمیر مبهم Indefinite pronoun. [Fem. مبهمه with the pl. مبهمات I. pronouns or adjectives].
مَبهوت A. Astonished; struck dumb. — م. کردن To astonish.
مُبهی A. Aphrodisiac. [Fem. مبهیه].
مَبیض A. = تخمدان
مَبیع A. Object of sale.
مُبین A. Clear. True.
مبین (mobayen) A. Explanatory.
مُتابعت A. = پیروی Following. — م. کردن از To follow or obey.
مُتأثر A. Touched; moved. — م. ساختن To touch or move.
مُتأخر A. a. Recent; modern. —n. [Pl. متأخرین Moderns].
متأذی A. Inconvenienced; troubled; vexed.
مُتارکه A. Discontinuation. Abandonment. — متارکهٔ جنگ Truce; armistice. — م. کردن To abandon. To hold a truce.

مُتأسف *A.* Sorry : متاسفم که نمی توانم بیایم I am sorry I cannot come; I regret not being able to come.

متأسفانه *A. P.* Unfortunately. Regretfully.

متأسی شدن *A. P.* [With به] To take model from; imitate; follow.

مَتاع *A.* [امتعه] Goods. Thing; stuff. Dainty; delicacy.

مُتألم *A.* Grieved; sad. *OS.* م. شدن ‖ درد ناك To feel s. To be grieved.

مَتانت *A.* Self-possession; coolness. Firmness.

مُتأهل *A.* Married [said of a man]. — م. شدن To marry.

مُتبادِر *A.* Making haste to get the start. — م. بذهن That first springs to the mind.

مُتبادِل *A.* [Fem. متبادله] Interchangeable . — زوایای متبادله Alternate angles.

مُتبارَك *A.* Blessed.

مُتباعِد *A.* Divergent [واگرا]

مُتباین *A.* Distinct. Different. *Arith.* Prime : با هم م. هستند They are relatively prime.

مُتبحر *A.* Versed; erudite.

متبرّك *A.* Holy; sacred. [Fem. s. اماکن متبرکه . Ex. متبرکه places ; shrines].

متبسم *A.* Smiling.

مُتبلوِر *A.* Crystallized.—م. کردن To crystallize.

مَتبوع *A.* Followed; obeyed *By e.* Sovereign [Fem. متبوعه . Ex. دولت متبوعه State to which one belongs].

مُتتبع *A.* Researcher.

مُتجاسر *A. a.* Insurgent.—*n.* [pl. متجاسرین the insurgents].

مُتجانس *A.* Homogeneous.

مُتجاوِز *A.* 1) *a.* Aggressive ; offensive. — م. از Exceeding ; more than. 2) *n.* Aggressor; transgressor.

مُتجاهر به *A. P.* Notorious for.

مُتجدِد *A.* Modernized; modern; modern-minded.

متجسس *A.* Researcher.

مُتجلی *A.* Clear. Revealed. Transfigured.

مُتحابّ *A.* [Fem. مُتحابه] (Mutually) amicable.

مُتحارِب *A.* [Fem. متحاربه] Belligerent : دول متحاربه

متحجر *A.* Petrified.

مُتحد *A.* 1) *a.* United; allied. [Fem. متحده Ex. ایالات متحدهٔ امریکا The U. States of America]. 2) *n.* [pl. متحدین] Ally. — م. کردن To unite. — م. شدن To u. ; be united.

متحداً *A.* Unitedly.

متحدالشکل *A.* Uniform.

متحدالمال *A.* = بخشنامه

متحدالمرکز *A.* = هم مرکز

مُتحرّك *A.* Mobile; movable ; moving. *Gr.* Marked with a vowel-point.

مُتحصن A. (One) who takes sanctuary in an inviolable place.— م. شدن See بست نشستن

مُتحمل A. Who supports or suffers. — م. شدن To support. To suffer. To sustain : ضرری م. نشد

مُتحیر A. Astonished; surprised. — م. شدن To be s. — م. کردن To astonish.

مُتخاصم A. Hostile. [Fem. دول م. : متخاصمه H. powers].

مُتخالف A. Mutually discordant.

مُتخذ A. [Fem. متخذه] Adopted; accepted. Taken : تصمیمات متخذه

مُتخصص A. 1) n. Specialist. Expert. Cf. کارشناس ‖ 2) a. Specialized. — متخصص قالی E. in carpets.

متخطی A. Transgressor.

متخلص به A. P. Having a (specified) nom-de-plume or pen-name.— آقای فلان م. به ... Mr. so-and-so whose n.-de-plume is . . .

مُتخلف A. n. [متخلفین] Violator; infringer. —a. Violating.

متخلق به A. P. Endowed with, or possessing (a specified character).

متخیل A. Having a strong imagination. [Fem. متخیله. Ex. قوهٔ م. Imaginative faculty].

مُتداخل A. Of which one is the aliquot part of the other. — ۲ و ٦ م. هستند 2 is an aliquot part of 6.

مُتداعی A. Litigant (party). [D. متداعیین. Ex. طرفین متداعیین the litigants]

مُتداول A. Common ; usual.

مُتدرّجاً A. Gradually.

مُتدین A. Religious. — م. بدین اسلام Professing the Mohammedan religion.

متذکر شدن A. P. 1) OS. To remember. 2) C. E. To point out; also, to remind.

متر Fr. Metre. Tape-measure. — سه م. است It is 3 metres long — م. کردن To measure (in terms of metres).

مُترادف A. 1) a. Synonymous. 2) n. Synonym.

مُتراکم A. Heaped up. Condensed. — م. شدن To be h. up. To be c. — م. ساختن To heap up. To condense.

مترتب A. [With بر] Resulting or derived from. — فایده‌ای بر آن م. نیست It is of no avail.

مُترجم A. [مترجمین] Translator. Interpreter.

مترجمی A. P. Position of a translator. Translation work.

متردّد A. 1) Plying back and forth 2) = مردد [Scarecrow.

مترس (matars) or مترسك

مترس (metres) Fr. Mistress.

مترسل A. = دبیر - نویسنده

مترشح o *A.* Exuding.
مُترِصد *A.* Lying in wait. – مترصد فرصت بودن To look out for an opportunity.
مترقب *A.* E pected. [Fem. مترقبه Ex. مخارج غیر مترقبه unexpected expenses].
مُترقی *A.* Advancing; progressive. [Fem. مترقیه Ex. ملل م.]
مترنم *A.* Singing or trilling. Also, performing.
مِترو (-ro) *Fr.* Underground (railway) ; tube.
مَتروك *A.* [Fem. متروکه] Abandoned. Obsolete [metre.
متری *Fr. P.* (Sold) by the
مُتزلزل *A.* Unstable ; shaky. Uncertain . – م. ساختن To shake. To weaken.
مُتساوی *A.* = مساوی
متساوی‌الاضلاع *A.* Equilateral.
متساوی‌الزوایا *A.* Equiangular.
متساوی‌الساقین *A.* Isosceles.
مُتساهل o *A.* Latitudinarian.
مُتسع *A.* Dilated. – م. کردن To dilate. [mologous.
مُتشابه *A.* = [illegible] Similar. Ho-
متشابه‌الترکیب *A.* Isomeric.
متشبث شدن *A. P.* To resort.
مُتشتت *A.* 1) = پراکنده 2) Divided; also, diversified.
مُتشخص *A.* Dignified; of great personality. [law. Pious.
متشرّع *A.* Versed in religious
مُتشکر *A.* = سپاسگزار Thankful; grateful. – برای . . . از من م. بود He was grateful to me for... ‖ (از شما) متشکرم Thank you.
مُتشکل *A.* Organized. Formed.
مُتشنج *A.* Convulsive. – جلسه م. شد Confusion broke out in the meeting.
مُتصاعد *A.* Ascending; rising. Progressing ; progressive.
متصالح *A.* Donee (by compromise).
مُتصدّی *A.* (Person) in charge.
مُتصرّف *A.* Possessor. Occupier. – م. شدن To take possession of.
متصرَفات *A.* Possessions.
مُتصف *A.* Endowed. – م. به E. with ; possessing.
مُتصل *A.* = پیوسته Connected. Adjoining. Continuous. – ضمیر متصل Inseparable pronoun. – م. شدن To be connected ; join. – م. کردن To connect ; join.
متصلاً *A.* = پیوسته Incessantly.
متصوَر *A.* Conceived ; conceivable; imaginable.
متصوّف *A.* Sufistic. Mystical.
مُتضاد *A. n.* Antithetical. Opposed. –*n.* Antonym.
مُتضامنا *A.* Jointly (and severally). [loss).
مُتضرّر شدن *A. P.* To incur (a
مُتضمن *A.* Comprising ; containing. – م. بودن To comprise. *F.* To entail.
مُتظاهر به *A. P.* Pretending or

professing to be.

متظلم A. a. Having a grievance or complaint. —n. Petitioner.

مُتعارِف A. Known to each other. Given to compliments or gallantry.

متعارفی A. P. Common; ordinary. Vulgar: کسر متعارفی

مُتعاقب A. Subsequent; following immediately. — متعاقبِ S. to; after.

مُتعاقد A. Contracting. [D. متعاقدین. Ex. طرفین م. the contracting parties].

مُتعال A. Exalted: خدای م.

مُتعامل A. Party to a transaction. [D. متعاملین].

مُتعاهد A. Contracting. [D. متعاهدین. Ex. طرفین م. the contracting parties].

متعبد A. Devout (person).

مُتعجب A. Surprised. — م. شدن To be surprised; wonder. — م. ساختن To fill with w.

مُتعدّد A. Numerous.

متعدّی A. Transgressing; aggressive. Gr. Transitive.

مُتعذّر A. Difficult or impossible o. — م. به Resorting to (a specified excuse).

مُتعرّض شدن A. P. To interfere with; prevent. Also, to disturb or molest. — کسی متعرضِ او نمیشد No one prevented him (from doing it).

متعسر A. = 1) دشوار 2) پیچیده

مُتعصب A. 1) a. Bigoted; prejudiced. Fanatical. 2) n. B. person. Fanatic.

متعصبانه A. P. Fanatically. Out of prejudice.

متعظ A. Disposed to being preached to. Accepting advice o. — غیر متعظ Not practising what one preaches.

مُتعفن A. Putrefied; stinking. — م. شدن To be putrefied.

مُتعلق A. Belonging; pertaining. Dependent. — م. بودن To belong. — متعلقان Dependants.

متعلقات A. Appurtenances. Attachments. Cf. the s. متعلقه

متعلقه A. Supported or dependent (woman); i. e. wife. [Orig. fem. of متعلق]

متعلم A. = شاگرد & دانش‌آموز

متعمد A. (One) who does a thing intentionally.

متعند A. = 1) لجوج 2) دشمن

مُتعه A. Concubine [صیغه].

متعهد A. (One) who undertakes. — م. شدن To undertake.

متعهدله (mota-ahedon-lah) A. Obligee; guarantee.

مُتغیر A. Angry; filled with indignation. Changeable. — م. شدن To get angry.

مُتفاوِت A. Different. — م. بودن با To differ from.

متفرّع A. Branching out. [Fem. متفرعه with the pl. متفرعات Derivatives; by-products].

متفرعن *A.* = باد درسر

مُتفرّق *A.* Dispersed [پراکنده] — م. شدن To be d. or scattered. — م. کردن To disperse.

مُتفرّقه *A.* Miscellaneous ; sundry. [Orig. fem. of متفرق].

مُتفق *A. a.* Allied. Agreeing with each other. [Fem. متفقه]. —*n.* [*Usu. in the pl.* متفقین the allies]. — م. شدن To be allied ; form an alliance. — م. بودن بر To agree (up)on.

متفقا *A.* Unanimously. Together. Unitedly.

متفق‌الرای *A.* = همرأی

متفق‌القول *A.* Unanimous.

متفق علیه *A.* (*motafeghon-alay*h) Unanimously agreed upon.

مُتفکر *A.* Reflective. Pensive. — م. شدن To (begin to) think. To reflect.

مُتقابل *A.* [Fem. متقابله] Reciprocal. *Geom.* Corresponding : م. دو زاویهٔ م. ‖ دعوی م. Counterclaim. — معاملهٔ متقابله Reciprocal treatment; reciprocity . — زوایای متقابل برأس Vertical angles.

متقارب *A.* Convergent.

مُتقارن *A.* Symmetrical. Simultaneous . Concurrent . *Ph.* Polar. [multaneously.

متقارناً *A.* Concurrently ; si-

مُتقاضی *A.* Applicant.

متقاطر *A.* Antipodal. Diametrical. — نقاط م. Antipodes.

متقاطراً Diametrically.

متقاطع *A.* Intersecting.

مُتقاعد *A.* 1) Convinced. 2) = باز نشسته ‖ م. شدن To be c. To be pensioned off. — م. کردن To convince. To pension off.

متقال *R.* Unbleached calico; Mexican cloth; grey sheeting. [To support.

متقبل شدن *A. P.* To undertake.

متقدم *A.* Ancient. — متقدمین *n. pl.* The ancients [پیشینیان].

مُتقلب *A.* Dishonest; fraudulent.

مُتقن *A.* = استوار Firm. [pious.

متقی *A.* = پرهیزکار Virtuous ;

مُتکا *A.* = بالش Pillow; bolster.

متکافی *A.* Equal or adequate. — م. فندول Compensation pendulum. [Ionic order.

متکائی *A. P.* Scrolled. — سبك م.

مُتکبر *A.* Proud. [haughtily.

متکبرانه *A. P.* Proudly ;

متکدّی *A.* Begging ; also, of begging habits.

مُتکفل *A.* (One) who undertakes or supports. — متکفل (مخارج) خانواده ای بودن To support a family.

مُتکلم *A.* Speaker. *Gr.* First person. — م. شدن To speak. — متکلم وحده است You can't get a word in edgeway with him; he is the sole speaker.

متکوّن *A.* Coming into exis-

tence.
مُتکی A. Based. Relying. OS. Leaning. — م. شدن بر To rely (up)on; base oneself on.
مُتلاشی A. Decomposed. Scattered. Shattered.
مُتلاطم A. Rough; stormy.
متلذّذ A. Enjoying; taking delight. — م. شدن از To enjoy; relish; take a d. in. [digal.
مُتلف A. n. Waster. —a. Prodigal.
مَتلک × Wisecrack; quib.
مُتلوّن A. 1) = رنگارنگ 2) F. Fickle; capricious [often متلون‌المزاج].
متلهف ० A. = متأسف
مُتمادی A. Long; protracted.
متمایز A. Distinct.
مُتمایل A. Inclined; disposed.
متمتع A. = بهره‌مند
مُتمدّن A. Civilized. [Fem. متمدنه]. — نیم م. or نیمه م. Semi-civilized.
مُتمرّد A. Rebellious; disobedient. — م. شدن To rebel. To disobey.
مُتمرکز A. Concentrated. — م. کردن To concentrate. To centralize. [resort to.
متمسك شدن به A. P. To hold; resort to.
مُتمکن A. Having (pecuniary) power. Resident. Established.
مُتملق A. n. Flatterer; fawner. —a. Flattering. [fawningly.
متملقانه A. P. Flatteringly; fawningly.
مُتمم A. Supplement(ary); complement(ary). — متممِ . . . Supplementary to . . .
مُتمنی A. = خواهشمند Requesting; asking. — م. است [In p. c.] I shall be glad if you will . . .
متموّج Undulating. Floating. Med. Fluttering: نبض م.
مُتموّل A. = توانگر & دولتمند Wealthy.
مَتن A. [مُتون] Text.
مُتنازِع A. Litigant.
متنازع فیه (motanaze-onfi:h) A. Contentious; litigious.
مُتناسِب A. Proportional; proportionate. Symmetrical; well-set. [Fem. متناسبه]. — قاعدهٔ اربعهٔ متناسبه Rule of three.
مُتناقض A. Contradictory.
مُتناوِب A. Alternate. Arith. Recurring. Med. Periodical. — خدمتِ م. Broken service.
متناوباً A. Alternately.
مُتناهی A. Finite. Terminated.
مُتنبه A. Awakened; warned. — م. کردن To give a lesson or warning (to). [prophet.
متنبی A. Pretending to be a prophet.
مُتنجن Roasted or fried meat. Dish with dried fruits.
متنصر ० A. Converted to Christianity.
متنعم A. Enjoying comforts of life; living in pleasure.
مُتنفذ A. Influential. — متنفذین n. pl. I. men.

مُتنفّر A. Disgusted. — از چیزی م. بودن To hate s. t.; be disgusted with it.

متنفس A. 1) a. Breathing o. 2) n. Soul; living being.

متنکر A. Disguised.

متنکراً A. In disguise.

متنوّع A. Various; miscellaneous. [Fem. متنوعه]

متواتر A. Successive. Related by successive witnesses.

متواتراً A. By successive witnesses. Successively.

مُتواری A. Hidden; fled to an unknown destination.

متوازن A. Symmetrical.

مُتوازی A. Parallel.

متوازی الاضلاع A. Paralellogram.

متوازی السطوح A. Parallelepiped.

متواضع A. = فروتن

مُتوافق A. Agreeing; congruous. Commensurable.

مُتوالی = پی‌درپی A. Consecutive; successive.

متوالیاً A. Consecutively; successively [پی‌درپی].

متوّج o A. = تاجدار Crowned.

مُتوجه A. Careful. Taking notice. OS. Turning the face. — م. شدن به To turn to; face; address. To take notice of. — حادثه ای متوجه او شد He met with an accident. — م. ساختن To remind; notify. To aim. — م. نشد م. I didn't notice it. I didn't understand.

متوحش A. Frightened. — م. شدن = ترسیدن To be f. — م. ساختن = ترساندن To frighten.

متورّق A. Laminated.

مُتورّم A. Swollen. F. Inflated. — م. شدن To be inflated. To swell. — م. ساختن To cause to be inflamed. To inflate.

مُتوسط A. 1) a. [Fem. متوسطه]. Intermediate; middle. Mean; average. — دبیرستان = مدرسهٔ متوسطه ‖ موج م. Medium wave. — بطور متوسط On the a. 2) n. Average; mean.

متوسل شدن A. P. [With به] To resort to; have recourse to; take refuge in.

متوطن شدن A. P. To take one's abode; choose as one's home.

متوفی (mɔtavafa) A. Deceased. [Fem. متوفیه (-fiah)].

مُتوقّع A. Expecting. — م. بودن To expect. — ازمن م. نبود He did not e. me to do (or say) that.

مُتوقف A. Halting. Stopped; coming to a standstill. Insolvent; who has ceased payment. — م. شدن To stop; come to a standstill. To stay. To cease payment.

متوکل A. Trusting. — م. شدن به To trust upon.

مُتوکلاً *A.* Resignedly.—م. علی‌الله Trusting on God.

مُتولِّد *A.* Born. —م. شدن To be born. —*n. pl.* متولدین. Ex. متولدین سالِ ... Those born in the year . . .

متولی *A.* Custodian or administrator (of a pious foundation).

مَته Drill; auger; gimlet. [*Of a dentist*] Burr. —متهٔ کوه‌بری Rock-drill. — م. کردن To bore or drill.—م. به‌خشخاش گذاشتن To strain a gnat; split hairs; also, be over stingy.

متهاجم *A.* Attacking; offensive.

متهاوِن *A.* Negligent.

مته قرقره Ratchet-drill.

مته‌کمان [Orig. مته و کمان] Bow-drill.

متهم (*motaham*) *A.* (The) accused.—م. شدن به To be accused of. — م. ساختن To accuse.

متهم (*motahem*) Accuser.

مُتهوّر *A.* Impetuous; rash.

متهورانه *A. P.* Impetuously.

متی (*mata*) *A-G.* Matthew.

مُتیقن Sure; certain. —قدر متیقن آنست که So much is c. that.

مِتیل *or* میتیل Slip; (pillow-)case.

مَتین *A.* Firm. *F.* Sedate. Self-possessed; cool. Sound: فرمایش م.

مَثابه *A.* Position. —بمثابهٔ As; in the p. or manner of.

مِثال *A.* Example [pl. امثله]. Likeness. [nary bladder.

مثانه *A.* = آبدان Vesica; uri-

مثانی ٥ *A.* (Second strings of a) lute. (*Name of certain parts of*) the Koran.

مُثبت (*-bat*) *A.* Affirmative.

مُثبت (*-bet*) *A.* Proving; demonstrative. Constructive.

مِثقال *A.* *Unit of weight nearly = 5 grammes.*

مثل (*masal*) *A.* [اَمثال] Parable. Proverb. Example. — مثلی است مشهور It is a common p. As the saying is. —م. زدن To cite an e. or p.

مثل (*mesl*) *A.* [امثال] Likeness. Peer.—معاملهٔ بمثل با کسی کردن To pay a man back in his own coin.—مثلِ Like. — مثل اینکه [For مثل اینست که] It seems as if. — امثال من People like me; such as I am.— کتاب و امثال آن Books and the like.

مثل (*mosol*) *A.* Ideas: مثل افلاطون ‖ *Cf. the s.* مثال

مَثلاً *A.* For example; for instance; (*exempli gratia*) e. g.

مُثلث *A.* = سه‌گوش 1) *n.* Triangle. 2) *a.* Triangular. Marked with 3 dots, as the letter ث

مثلثات *A.* Trigonometry.

مُثله کردن *A. P.* To mutilate in order to set an example.

مثلی (*masa-*) *A. P.* Proverbial.

مثلی (*mes-*) *A.* Fungible.

مُثمر *A.* Fruit-bearing. *F.* Fruitful; useful [*often*

redundantly [مثمر ثمر].
مُثمّن *A.* Octagon(al)○. Consisting of 8 feet.
مَثنوی *A.* Poetry consisting of distichs riming between themselves; couplet-poems.— م. هفتاد من کاغذ شود That is (*or* will be) a long story.
مثنی *A.* 1) *a*. Double(d). Dual. 2) *n*. Duplicate. *See* المثنی
مُجاب *A.* Confuted; reduced to silence. — م. کردن To confute; defeat (in a controversy).
مُجادِله *A.* [مجادلات] Contention; dispute. — م. کردن To d.
مجار Magyar.
مجارستان Hungary.
مجاری [Pl. of مَجری *or* مجرا]
مَجاز *A.* Trope; metaphor; figure. Allegory.
مُجاز *A.* Authorized. Permissible. Chartered: حسابدار مجاز ‖ پزشك م. Non-graduate licensed physician.
مَجازاً *A.* Figuratively.
مُجازات *A.* = کیفر Punishment. م. کردن To punish.
مجازی *A.* Figurative. Metaphorical. False. — آفتاب م. Mean sun.
مَجاعه *A.* = 1) گرسنگی 2) قحطی
مَجال *A.* Opportunity; leisure. — م. (پیدا) کردن To find an opportunity.
مجالس [Pl. of مجلس].
مُجالست *A.* Sitting together. Companionship.
مجامع [Pl. of مجمع]
مُجامعت *A.* Sexual intercourse.
مُجامله *A.* Flatterous courtesy or kindness.
مَجاناً *A.* Gratuitously; free [of cost.
مجا نِب *A.* Asymptotic.
مُجانبت *A.* Keeping aloof.
مَجانی *A.* Gratuitous.
مجانین [Pl. of مجنون]
مُجاوِر *A.* Adjacent; neighbouring.
مجاورَت *A.* Vicinity; neighbourhood. *Cf.* نزدیکی & همسایگی ‖ در مجاورتِ In the vicinity of; near.
مُجاهد *A.* Soldier of the holy war. Fighter (for liberty, etc.).
مجاهده *or* مجاهدت *A.* Endeavour [کوشش]. Struggle.— م. کردن To e. or strive.
مُجبر *A.* [Fem. مجبره] Coercing.— قوه مجبره ○ Force majeure.
مَجبور *A.* Compelled; forced; obliged. — مجبورم بروم I am o. to go. — م. کردن To force; compel.
مجبوراً *A.* = اجباراً
مُجتبی (-*taba*) *A.* = برگزیده
مجتمع *A.* Convened; assembled. — م. شدن To assemble.
مجتمعاً *A.* = باهم & متحداً
مُجتهد *A.* Clergyman practising religious jurisprudence.
مجد (*majd*) *A.* (Traditional)

honour or greatness.
مُجِدّ (*mojed*) *A*. = کوشا Diligent; striving hard.
مجدّانه *A*. *P*. Diligently.
مُجدّد *A*. Renewed. Further — تا اخطار مجدد Until f. notice.
مجدداً *A*. = دوباره Again.
مجدّر *A*. = آبله رو
مَجذوب *A*. Attracted. Enchanted. — م. کردن To attract. To fascinate.
مجذوبیت *A* Enchantment.
مَجذور *A*. = توان ِ دوم Square.
مجذوم *A*. Leprous.
مجرا [f. A. مجری *majra* —pl. مجاری] Channel. Passage. Duct; canal. — مجرای پیشاب Urethra. — مجرای عصب Nerviduct. — مجرای نخاع Neural c.
مُجرّب *A*. 1) Experienced : م. پزشك. 2) Tried : داروی م.
مُجرّد *A*. Single; unmarried. Naked [برهنه]. Abstract. — حبس مجرد Solitary confinement. — بمجرد Immediately upon. — بمجردی که As soon as.
مجرّدی *A*. *P*. = جرز
مُجرِم *A*. Guilty (person). Criminal.
مجرمیت *A*. Guilt
مَجروح *A*. = زخمی Wounded. — مجروحین *n*. *pl*. The wounded. — م. شدن To be w. — م. کردن To wound. *F*. To injure.
مَجری *S*. *u*. مجرا
مِجری (Small) box. *Bot*. Pixidium.
مُجری *A*. (One) who executes or enforces. [Fem. مُجریه. Ex. قوهٔ مجریه Executive power].
مُجری (-ra) *A*. Enforced. — م. داشتن To carry out; enforce.
مجزا [f. A. مجزی *mojaza*] Distinct; separate. — م. کردن To s. To segregate.
مجزی *S*. *u*. مجزا
مجسطی *A*-*G*. The Almagest.
مُجسّم *A*. Incarnate. Personified. Solid. *Cf*. *the fem*. مجسمه ‖ م. شدن To be p. To be imagined. — م. کردن To incarnate or embody. To personify. To see in one's imagination; imagine.
مجسمات *A*. Solid bodies. Statues o. Ideals o. *Cf*. *the s*. مجسمه
مُجسمه *A*. [Orig. fem. of مجسم] Statue; image. — مجسمهٔ پیاده Pedestrian s. — مجسمهٔ سواره Equestrian s. — مجسمهٔ نیمتنه Bust. [statuary.
مجسمه ساز *A*. *P*. Sculptor;
مجسمه سازی *A*. *P*. Sculpture.
مُجعد *A*. Curly.
مَجعول *A*. = جعلی
مُجلد *A*. *a*. Bound; covered. [Fem. مجلده]. —*n*. Volume; tome. —*Note*. مجلدات the pl. of مجلده has been adopted as the pl. of مجلد *or* جلد
مَجلس *A*. [مجالس] Assembly. House : مجلس عوام ‖ Meeting;

session. Party. Scene. *Cf.* صورت م. ‖ پرده Procès-verbal.

مجلس آرا *A. P. a.* Giving life to a party. —*n.* The life and soul of a party.

مجلسی *A. P.* Fit for a party or assembly; presentable. — مجلسیان *n. pl.* The members of a party or parliament.

مجلسین *A.* [D. of مجلس] The Two Houses (of the Iranian Parliament).

مُجلل *A.* = باشکوه

مَجله *A.* [مجلات] Magazine; review. Gazette.

مَجمر * ○ *A.* Censer.

مَجمع *A.* [مجامع] Assembly. Association. League.

مجمع الجزایر *A.* Archipelago.

مجمع القوانین *A.* Code.

مجمع الکواکب *A.* Constellation.

مَجمعه *A.* (Copper) tray.

مُجمل *A.* 1) *a.* Brief. 2) *n.* Summary; compendium.

مجملاً *A.* = اجمالاً

مجموع *A. n.* Total; whole. —*a.* * Peaceful; tranquil.

مجموعاً *A.* Totally.

مجموعه *A.* Collection; set. Miscellany. Magazine.

مجنون *A.* [مجانین] — دیوانه

مجوز (*mojavez*) *A.* Authorization. Justification; ground.

مجوس *A-G-P.* The Magi. —*Note.* مجوس is collective for مجوسی a magian.

مُجوّف *A.* = پوك & میان‌تهی

مُجهز *A.* Equipped; well-appointed. Mobilized. — م. کردن To equip. To mobilize.

مَجهول *A* Unknown (quantity). Passive (voice). — سلسلهٔ اعصاب م. The sympathetic nervous system. — دو مجهوله With two unknown quantities.

مجهول القوا *A.* Exponential.

مجهول المالك *A.* Of unknown ownership; also, derelict.

مجهول الهویه *A.* Of unknown identity. Fameless.

مُجیب *A.* (One) who grants (a prayer or request).

مَجید *A. a.* Great; honourable. —*n.* *Mas. pr. name.*

مُجیر *A.* = حامی & یاور

مجیز گفتن × To flatter or cajole.

مُچ Wrist [in full مچ‌دست]. — مچ پا Ankle. — مچ کسیرا گرفتن To catch one in the act.

مچ پیچ Puttee.

مُچی Carpal. Tarsal. — ساعت م. Wrist-watch.

مُچاله کردن + To crumple [(up).

مَچل شدن × = بور شدن ـ بکر شدن ـ شکار شدن

مُحابا *A.* Regard; consideration; respect. *See* بی محابا

مُحاجه *A.* Pleading. — م. کردن To plead; reason (together).

مُحاذی *A.* Opposite. Parallel.

مُحارِب A. Combatant. [war.
محاربه A. Fighting (together);
محارم [Pl. of محرم]
مُحاسِب A. = حسابدار
محاسبات A. Accounts. Cf. the s. محاسبه ‖ اشکالات محاسباتی Accounting difficulties.
مُحاسبه A. Calculation; computation. Calling to account o.
مَحاسِن A. Good deeds. Beauties. Beard [ریش].
مُحاصره A. Siege; blockade.— م. کردن To besiege.
محاضر [Pl. of محضر]
مُحاط A. Surrounded. Inscribed.— م. کردن To inscribe.
محافظ A. = نگهدار
مُحافظت A. = نگهداری Protection. — م. کردن از To protect or preserve; look after.
محافظه A. [Orig. = محافظت] 1) = محافظه کاری 2) Sense of modesty and discretion.
محافظه کار A. P. Conservative.
محافظه کاری A. P. Conservativeness. — اصالت م. Conservatism.
محافل [Pl. of محفل]
مَحاق A. Wane of the moon.
محاقی A. Interlunar.
مُحاکا o Talking to, or imitating, each other. Resembling.
محاکم [Pl. of محکمه]
محاکمات [Pl. of محاکمه]
مُحاکمه A. [محاکمات] Trial; court procedure; hearing.— م. کردن To try (judicially).— اصول محاکمات حقوقی Civil procedure. — دیوان محاکمات Tribunal.
مَحال [Pl. of محل]
مُحال A. Impossible. Absurd. [Fem. محاله o with the pl. محالات Impossibilities. Absurdities].
مُحال علیه A. = برات گیر
مَحامِد A. Laudable qualities. [Pl. of محمده o].
محامل [Pl. of محمل]
مُحاوِره A. [محاورات] = گفتگو Conversation.— م. کردن To talk.
محاوره‌ای A. P. Colloquial.
مُحِبّ A. = دوستدار
مَحبت A. Love; kindness; affection.— م. کردن To be kind.
محبت آمیز A. P. Affectionate; kind. سخنان م.
مَحبس A. = زندان
محبوب A. a. Beloved; loved. Favourite. Popular. —n. Friend. Darling. Cf. محبوبه
محبوب القلوب A. Loved by all; popular.
مَحبوبه A. Sweetheart. [Orig. fem. of محبوب q. v.]
محبوبیت A. Popularity.
مَحبوس A. a. Imprisoned. Cf. زندانی ‖ n. pl. محبوسین Prisoners
مُحتاج A. Needy; poor [نیازمند]. [With به] Needing. — م. بذکر نیست It is needless to men-

tion. — م.کردن To reduce to poverty. — محتاج ِ کسی شدن To need some one's help.
مُحتاط A. Cautious.
محتاطانه A. P. Cautiously.
مُحتال A. = حیله‌گر
محترز ○ A. Shunning or shunner. Cautious (person).
محترق [Fem. محترقه] Inflammable. Explosive. — م. شدن To explode. — مواد محترقه Explosives.
مُحتَرَم A. a. [Fem. محترمه] Honourable. —n. Fem. p.r. name. — م. داشتن To honour or respect. —n. pl. محترمین Dignitaries; notables.
محترماً A. Respectfully. — م. آگاهی میدهد I have the honour to inform you.
محترمانه A. P. Respectably; honourably. [officer.
محتسب • A. Municipal or police
محتشم A. Magnificent; pompous.
مُحتضر A. In a dying state; moribund. — م. بودن To be d.; suffer the agony of death.
مُحتکر A. [محتکرین] Hoarder.
محتلم شدن A. P. To have a nocturnal pollution.
مُحتمل A. Probable. — م. است رفته باشد He has probably gone. — م. است ناخوش شود He is likely to get sick.
محتمل الوجهین A. Equivocal verse susceptible of two opposite interpretations.
محتمل الوقوع A. Contingent.
مُحتوی (-tavi:) A. Containing.
محتویات (-tava-) A. Contents. [Pl. of محتوی mohtava]
مَحجر A. Fence; railing; parapet.
محجر (mohajar) A. Petrified.
مَحجوب A. Modest; coy.
محجوبانه A. P. Modestly. Politely.
محجوبیت A. Modesty. Shamefacedness. [Also محجوبی]
محجور A. Interdicted. — م کردن To interdict.
محجوریت A. Interdiction.
مُحدّب A. = کوژ Convex.
محدب الطرفین A. Biconvex.
مَحدود A. Limited. Bounded. — ازشمال م. است به It is bounded on the north by... ‖ م. کردن To limit.
محدودیت A. Limitation.
مَحذور A. 1) a. (Needing to be) avoided. 2) n. Dread ○.
مَحذوف A. Omitted. Eliminated.
مِحراب A. Altar; adytum.
مُحرِز A. = 1) نویسنده 2) سردفتر
مُحرَز A. Established. Confirmed. — م.کردن To establish or confirm. To prove.
محرّف A. 1) a. Tampered with. 2) n. Anagram. — نصف م. Hemihedron.
محرق A. Burning. Caustic.

مُحرِقه *A*. [For حمای م.] Typhus. [Orig. fem. of محرق]

مُحرّك *A*. Motive; motor. Stimulant. Instigator; inciter. [Pl. محرکین & fem. محرکه] — اعصاب محرکه Motor nerves. — قوهٔ محرکه M. power.

مَحرَم *A*. *a*. Of close relationship. With whom marriage is prohibited. —*n*. *pl*. مَحارِم Very near relatives. — زنا با محارم Incest. — محرمِ راز Confidant.

مُحرّم (*A*.) *First A. lunar month*.

محرمانه *A.P*. *a*. Confidential. —*ad*. Confidentially.

محرمیت *A*. Close relationship. Privity.

مَحروس *A*. [Fem. محروسه] Fortified. Guarded.

مَحروم *A*. Deprived. — م. شدن To be d. — م. کردن To deprive; divest; bereave.

محرومیت *A*. Privation. Bereavement. — م. از حقوق مدنی Civil degradation; c. death.

مُحزن *A*. = غم‌انگیز

مَحزون *A*. = غمگین

مُحسن *A*. 1) *a*. Beneficent. [Fem. محسنه]. 2) *n*. Benefactor. *Mas. pr. name*.

محسنات *A*. Virtues; good qualities. Advantages; merits. Good points. Beauties o.

مَحسوب *A*. Carried to account; taken into a. — م. داشتن *or* م. کردن To carry to a. — بهای آنرا ده ریال برای من م. داشت He charged me 10 *rials* for it; also, he debited me 10 *rials* for the price.

مَحسود *A*. Envied.

مَحسوس *A*. [Fem. محسوسه] Perceptible; sensible. Palpable. Marked: تفاوت م.

محسوسات *A*. Perceptible or obvious things. [Pl. of محسوسه fem. of محسوس].

مَحشر *A*. Gathering-place of mankind on the day of judgment. — روز محشر Day of j. — م. کردن + To perform (a specified act) wonderfully well.

مَحشور *A*. Associated. — م. کردن To (cause to) associate.

مُحصل *A*. [محصلین] 1) Student. [Fem. محصله with the pl. **محصلات** female students; school-girls]. 2) = تحصیلدار

مُحصن *A*. 1) *a*. Continent. 2) *n*. Married man. [Fem. محصنه married (woman); (feme) covert]. — زنای محصنه Adultery (with a m. woman). — زنای م. با محصنه Double adultery.

مَحصور *A*. Besieged. Fenced.

مَحصول *A*. Crop. Produce; product. — محصول فرعی By-product.

محصولات *A*. Products. [Pl.

of محصوله fem. of محصول]. - محصولات نفتی Oil products.
مَحض A. Mere. Downright : محض دروغ م. ‖ محضِ prep. For. - محض خاطرِ For the sake of. - بمحض اینکه As soon as.
محضاً A. Merely.
مَحضاً لله (-zanlelah) A. (Merely) for God's sake.
مَحضر A. [Pl. for 3d. sense محاضر] Presence. Disposition; nature. Notary public's office [now usu. دفتر اسناد رسمی].
محضری A. P. Notarial; registered (by a notary public).
مَحظور A. Obstacle. Impediment.
مَحظوظ A. [With از] Delighted in; enchanted by. - م. کردن To delight or please.
مِحفظه A. Case; chest. Compartment.
مَحفل A. [محافل] Assembly. - محافل سیاسی Political circles.
مَحفوظ A. Protected. Secure. Reserved. - م. داشتن To reserve. To protect. - حق طبع م. است "Copyright reserved".
محفوظات A. [Pl. of محفوظه o fem. of محفوظ] Memories. Things learnt by heart.
مُحق A. Entitled; rightful.
مُحقر A. Contemptible. Small; paltry; mean.
محقق (mohaghagh) A. Certain. - م. داشتن To ascertain or verify..
محقق (mohaghegh) A. [محققین]. Researcher ; investigator (of truth); inquirer.
محققاً A. Certainly.
مِحکّ A. Touchstone. F. Test; criterion. - م. زدن To test.
مُحکم A. 1) a. = استوار Firm; strong . Secure. 2) ad. Firmly ; fast ; tightly. - م. کردن To make firm; fasten. To secure. - م. گرفتن To hold fast. F. To observe strictly.
مُحکمات A. [Pl. of مُحکمه fem. of محکم] Verses admitting of no allegorical interpretation.
محکمکاری + A. P. Precautious or preventive measures.
مَحکمه A. Law court [pl. محاکم]. Doctor's "surgery" or practice.
مُحکمی A. P. Firmness.
مَحکوك A. Engraved. Erased; obliterated.
مَحکوم A. 1) Condemned ; sentenced : م. به اعدام s. to death. 2) Adjudged : م. به پرداختِ adjudged to pay... ‖ م. شدن To be c. To be a. (to pay a sum); lose the case. - م. کردن To condemn or stentence. To adjudge.
محکوم به (-mon-beh) A. Judgment debt.
محکوم علیه (-mon-alayh) A. Losing party. [party.

محکوم له (*-mon-lah*) *A.* Winning

محکومیت *A.* Conviction.

مَحل *A.* [محال] Place ; locality [جا]. Post: محل مأموریت ‖ Vacancy ispace. Credit allocation. – " م. ندارد " No effects (N/E). – محل اقامت Residence. – در محل Locally.

مَحل *A.* Heed. – م. گذاشتن To heed or pay attention. – محل سگ باو نگذاشتند × They did not take the least notice of him.

مُحلل *A.* Solvent. Resolvent. One who marries a "thrice-divorced" woman and dismisses her after consummation of marriage so that she may lawfully marry her former husband.

مَحلول *A.* Solution. [rish.

محله *A.* [محلات] Quarter; parish.

محلی (*mahali:*) *A.* Local.

محلی (*mohala*) *A.* = آراسته

محمد *A.* Mohammed. *OS.* Praised or praiseworthy.

محمدی *A.* Mohammedan. – گل م. Damascus rose.

محمر ๐ *A.* Rubefacient.

محمل *A.* [محامل] Camel-litter.

مَحمود (*A.*) *Mas. pr. name.* *OS.* Laudable.

محموده *A.* Scammony.

مَحمول *A.* 1) *a.* Consigned. *Cf. the fem.* محموله 2) *n.* Predicate [*in logic*].

محمولات [Pl. of محموله]

محمول الیه *A.* Consignee.

مَحموله *A.* [محمولات] Consignment. [Orig. fem. of محمول]

مَحمی ๐ *A.* 1) *a.* Protected. 2) *n.* Protégé.

محن [Pl. of محنت]

مِحنت *A.* [محن] Suffering ; affliction; hardship; toil. – م. کشیدن To suffer a h. To be afflicted.

محنت زده *A. P.* Afflicted.

محو (*mahv*) *A.* Effacement. *F.* Abolition. Suppression. – م. شدن To be obliterated. To disappear. To fade. To be eliminated. – م. کردن To wipe out; efface. To eliminate.

مِحوَر *A.* = آسه Axis; pivot.

مِحوری *A.* Axial ; pivoted. – رقص م. *Astr.* Nutation. – مفصل م. Trochoid joint.

مُحوطه *A.* Enclosure; precincts ; yard.

مُحوّل *A.* Turned over; given o. – م. کردن To devolve ; turn o. ; delegate.

محیرالعقول *A.* Stupendous ; wonderful.

مُحیط *A.* 1) *n.* Circumference. Perimeter. *F.* Environment; milieu. Atmosphere ; meridian. – محیط مرئی Contour. Silhouette. – تغییرمحیط Change of scene. 2) *a.* Surrounding. – بحر محیط The Ocean.

محیطی *A*. Circumferential.

مُحیل *A*. Cunning (person).

مُخ Brain. – بی‌مخ + Brainless.

مُخا Mocha.– قهوهٔ م. M. coffee.

مُخابره *A*. [مخابرات] Despatch. Message. Communication; signal. – م. کردن To despatch, as a telegram.

مَخارِج *A*. = هزینه Expenses. *Cf. the s.* مخرج

مخازن [Pl. of مخزن]

مخاصمه *A*. Hostility. [Pl. مخاصمات Hostile activities].

مُخاط *A*. Mucus. – مخاط شیطان ○ Gossamer.

مُخاطَب *A*. Person spoken to. *Gr*. Second person. – م. ساختن To address.

مُخاطِب *A*. Addresser; speaker.

مُخاطره *A*. [مخاطرات] Risk. Adventure.– به م. انداختن To risk or jeopardize.

مخاطره آمیز *A. P*. Perilous; hazardous. Adventurous.

مخاطره‌جو *A. P*. Adventurous. شخص م. A. person; adventurer.

مخاطی *A*. Mucous.

مخافت *A*. = 1) ترس 2) خطر

مخالطت *A*. Intercourse.– م. کردن To associate or mix.

مُخالِف *A*. Opposed. Contrary. Disagreeing. – مخالفِ صلح O. to peace. – با رفتن من م. است He does not agree to my going. – مخالفین *n. pl*. Opponents. The opposition; those against; the cons.

مخالفت *A*. Opposition.– م. کردن با To oppose; disagree with.

مخالف خوانی *A. P*. (Showing signs of) opposition.

مُخبر *A*. [مخبرین] Reporter; *rapporteur* : مخبر کمیسیون ‖ Informer.

مُخبط *A*. Affected with a mental disorder; idiotic.

مختار *A*. Free in one's action. Empowered. – فاعل م. (One) having free will; f. agent.– وزیر مختار Minister plenipotentiary.

مُخترع *A*. [مخترعین] Inventor.

مُختص *A*. Special; allocated. [Fem. مختصه]

مختصات *A*. Special features; characteristics. *Math*. Coordinates. [Pl. of مختصه fem. of مختص].

مُختصر *A*. 1) *a*. Brief; short [کوتاه]. Slight: تب م. ‖ Small: مبلغ م. ‖ 2) *n*. Summary; résumé. 3) *ad*. [For مختصر کلام] To sum up; to be brief. – م. کردن To abridge. To abbreviate.

مختصراً *A*. Briefly.

مختفی *A*. = مخفی & پنهان

مُختل *A*. Deranged; disordered. Confused.

مُختلج *A*. 1) Convulsive. 2) *Med*. Thrilling : نبض م.

مُختلس *A*. Embezzler.

مخروطی *A.* Conic(al). — م. مقاطع *or* مخروطیات Conic sections.

مَخزَن *A.* [مخازن] Magazine. Store(house) ; warehouse [انبار]. Tank. Treasure o.

مخزن‌دار *A. P.* Provided with a tank. — م. ماشین Tank-lorry.

مَخصوص *A.* Special; particular. Specific. *Cf.* ویژه ‖ Proper. — مخصوصِ Specially adapted (*or* designed) for. Peculiar to.

مخصوصاً *A.* = بویژه Especially. Particularly.

مُخطط *A.* Striped.

مخطوبه o *A.* = نامزد Fiancée.

مُخفف (*mokhafaf*) *A.* *a.* Abbreviated. —*n.* Abbreviation.

مُخفف (*mokhafef*) *A.* Extenuating. [Fem. مخففه . Ex. جهات مخففه E. circumstances].

مَخفی *A.* = پنهان Hidden. Secret. — م. کردن & م. شدن To hide. — م. نماند Be it known to all.

مخفیانه *A. P.* In secret.

مُخل *A.* Disturbing; interrupting. — مخل آسایش کسی شدن To disturb s. o. ; intrude upon him (*or* his privacy).

مُخلد *A.* = جاودانی

مُخلص *A.* 1) Devoted (friend). 2) + Your d. f.; *i. e.* I.

مخلصانه *A. P. ad.* Devotedly; sincerely. —*a.* Sincere.

مُخلفات *A.* Sundries. [Pl. of

مختلط *A.* = آمیخته Mixed.

مُختلف *A.* Different; various. Sundry. [Fem. مختلفه]

مختلف‌الاضلاع *A.* Scalene.

مختلف‌الشکل *A.* Heteromorphic.

مختلف‌المرکز *A.* Eccentric.

مُختنق *A.* Strangulated: فتق م.

مَختوم *A.* Sealed. Finished. — گلِ م. Sealing-clay.

مَختون *A.* Circumcised.

مُخچه Cerebellum.

مُخدر (*mokhadar*) *A.* Chaste [only in the fem. مخدره C. (woman) —pl. مخدرات].

مُخدر (-*der*) *A* Narcotic ; opiate. [Fem. مخدره Ex. ادویهٔ م. N. or dangerous drugs ; narcotics].

مَخدوش *A.* Having signs of alteration; altered; not clear and concise.

مَخدوم *A.* *a.* Served ; waited on. —*n.* Master. [Pl. مخادیم o]

مُخدّه *A.* Cushion for the back.

مُخرّب *A.* Destructive. — مخربِ اخلاق D. to morality.

مَخرج *A.* Outlet ; egress; issue. *Math.* Denominator. *Cf. the pl.* مخارج

مَخروب *A.* = ویران Ruined. *Cf. the fem.* مخروبه

مخروبه *A.* Ruined (place). [Orig. fem. of مخروب]

مَخروط *A* Cone. — مخروط ناقص Truncated cone ; frustum (of a c.).

مخلفه fem. of مخلف ○ 'left behind, as heritage'].
مَخلوط A. a. Mixed; blended [آمیخته]. Complex. —n. Mixture.— م. شدن To be mixed. — م. کردن To mix or blend.
مَخلوع A. Deposed.
مَخلوق A. a. Created [آفریده]. —n. C. being; creature. People.
مخلوقات A. Created beings; creatures. [Pl. of مخلوقه fem. of مخلوق].
مخلی ○ (*mokhala*) A. 1) = خالی 2) Set free. — م. بطبع Free from intrusion. Unceremonious; easy.
مخمر (*mokhamar*) A. Fermented. Kneaded. F. Inbred. — م. کردن To ferment or leaven.
مخمر (*mokhamer*) A. Fermentative. [Fem. مخمره]. — مادهٔ مخمره Ferment.
مخمس A. Fivesome (poem). Geom. = پنج گوش
مَخمصه A. = 1) ○ گرسنگی 2) اشکال & دردسر
مَخمل A. Velvet. — مخمل نخ و ابریشم Velveteen; plush. — م. گل Globe amaranth.
مخملك A. P. Scarlet fever.
مخملی A. P. Velvety. Soft.
مَخمور * Half-drunk. Languishing : چشم م.
مُخنث * A. 1) a. Effeminate. 2) n. E. man. Catamite.
مَخوف A. = **ترسناك**

مُخیر A. Having the option or choice (to . . .) : در رفتن یا ماندن م. است. He has the option to go or stay.
مخیله A. Imaginative faculty.
مَد A. 1) Flow.— جزرومد Tide. 2) The vowel placed over the "consonant alef", as in آسمان ‖ در مد نظر داشتن To To have in mind.
مد Fr. = ماد Media.
مُد Fr. 1) n. Fashion. 2) a. Fashionable; in fashion.— مد نبودن To be out of f. — از مد افتادن To go out of f.
مَداح A. Panegyrist.
مداحی A.P. Eulogy. — م. کردن To panegyrize.
مَداخل A. Earning; also, perquisite. *Cf. the s.* مدخل
مُداخله A. Intervention.— عدم م. Non-intervention. — م. کردن To intervene. [tionist.
مداخله طلب a. p. Interven-
مداد A. Pencil.— م. به ابرو کشیدن To pencil one's eyebrow.
مداد پاك كن A. P. Rubber; eraser. [sharpener.
مداد تراش A. P. Pencil-
مَدار A. Orbit. Pivot; axis. — مدار قطب شمال Arctic Circle.— مدار قطب جنوب Antarctic C. — مدار نصف النهار Meridian.— مدارات یومیه Parallels of latitude.
مُدارا A. Moderateness. Leniency. Caution. Fellowship. —

م. کردن To act moderately.

مدارِج A. Degrees; steps. [Pl. of مدرج o]

مدارس [Pl. of مدرسه].

مدارك [Pl. of مدرك].

مدارین A. [D. of مدار] The two tropics.

مُدافع A. Defender. — وکیل م De-fending attorney; barrister.

مدافعه A. [مدافعات] Defence. — دفاع کردن = م. کردن

مدال Fr. (Prize-)medal.

مُدام A. Continual(ly).

مُداوا [f. A. مُداوی -va] Medi-cal treatment. — م. کردن To treat medically.

مُداوِم A. Continuous; con-tinued. Persevering.

مداومت A. Continuance. Per-severance [پشت کار]. — م. کردن To persevere.

مُداهنه A. Flattery. — م. کردن To flatter; oil the tongue.

مدائح [Pl. of مدیحه]

مدائن A. Ctesiphon. [Orig. pl. of مدینه]

مُدَبر A. Swivel.

مدبر (modaber) A. Efficient or prudent (person).

مدبرانه A. P. Prudently. Efficiently.

مُدّت A. Period; duration. Term. — در مدت سه روز Within a p. of 3 days. — مدت مدیدی است که It is a long time since. — مدتی For some t.; also, for a long t.

مدت‌دار A. P. Due at a speci-fied date after sight; payable at maturity : برات م.

مَدح A. Praise; eulogy. — م. کردن To praise; eulogize.

مدحت A. = تمجید & ستایش

مَدخل A. Entrance. By e. Prelude. Cf. the pl. مداخل

مَدخول بها (-lonbeha) A. (Woman) lain with.

مَدد A. Aid; assistance [کمك]. — م. خواستن To seek help. — م. کردن To h.; give aid. — مددمعاش Allowance; monetary aid—now usu. کمك هزینه.

مُدِرّ A. Diuretic. [Fem. مدرّه]. — مدرّ صفرا Cholagogic. — ادویهٔ مدرّه طمث Emmenagogues.

مُدرّب o A. Trained.

مُدرّج A. Graduated. Scaled.

مُدرّس A. Teacher (esp. of theology). Cf. معلم & آموزگار

مَدرسه A. [مدارس] = آموزشگاه School.

مَدرَك A. [مَدارِك] Document; evidence.

مُدرِك A. Perceptive. [Fem. مدرکه. Ex. قوهٔ مدرکه].

مُدعا A. Claim; pretension.

مدعابه = خواسته Object of claim. — تامین م. کردن To levy a sum on a person's property.

مَدعوّ A. Invited. — مدعوین n. pl. The i.; the guests.

مُدعی A. Claimant. Pretender. Law. Plaintiff [خواهان].

مدعی‌العموم *A.* = **دادستان**
مدعی‌علیه (*moda-a-alayh*) *A.* Defendant [خوانده].
مدفن *A.* = **آرامگاه - گور**
مدفوع *A.* Excrement; feces.
مدفوعات Excrements. [Pl. of مدفوعه fem. of مدفوع]
مَدفون *A.* Buried.
مدقق *A.* Scrutinizer.
مُدِل *Fr.* Model. Design.
مُدِلّ *A.* Guiding or demonstrating: that guides, etc.
مُدلل *A.* Demonstrated; proved. – م. کردن To prove.
مَدلول *A.* Purport; sense.
مُدّمغ × *A.* Sniffy. Foolishly proud.
مُدُن [Pl. of مدینه] [Medina.
مدنی *A.* Civil [کشوری]. Of
مدنیت *A.* Civilization.
مُدوّر *A.* = **گرد** *gerd.*
مُدوّن *A.* Collected into a book; compiled. Codified.
مُدهش *A.* = **ترسناك**
مَدهوش *A.* Unconscious; senseless [بیهوش]. – م. کردن To make unconscious. To stupefy.
مدیترانه *Fr.* Mediterranean.
مَدیحه *A.* [مدائح or مدایح] Eulogy; praise.
مَدید *A.* Long. – مدت مدیدی است که It is a long time since.
مُدیر *A.* Director; manager. [*Of a school*] Headmaster. [*Of a newspaper*] Editor. [Fem. مدیره Directress. Headmistress]. – مدیر تصفیه Liquidator. – مدیر دروس Registrar. – مدیر کل Director general. – مدیرعامل Managing director. – هیئت‌مدیره Board of directors. – مدیرهٔ بیمارستان Matron of a hospital. [nagement.
مدیریت *A.* Directorship; ma-
مَدینه *A.* [مَدائن & مُدُن] = شهر City. *Geog.* Medina.
مَدیون *A.* Debtor [بدهکار]. – م. بودن To owe. – مدیونِ Indebted to.
مُذاب *A.* = گداخته Melted.
مذابح [Pl. of مذبح]
مَذاق *A.* Taste; palate. – بمذاقش خوش نیامد It did not suit his taste.
مذاکرات [Pl. of مذاکره]
مُذاکره *A.* [مذاکرات] Conversation; discussion [گفتگو]. – م. کردن To hold a c.; talk. – مذاکرات مجلس Proceedings of the Parliament. – داخل مذاکرات شدن To enter into negotiations. – خلاصهٔ مذاکرات Minutes; proceedings.
مذاهب [Pl. of مَذهَب]
مذبح *A.* [مذابح] Altar.
مُذبذب *A.* = **دو دل**
مَذبوح *A.* Slaughtered.
مذبوحانه *A. P.* Like a slaughtered animal. *F.* Passively. With resignation.

مُذَکَر A. Masculine.
مَذکور A. [Fem. مذکوره] Mentioned. — مذکور (در) فوق M. above; aforesaid.
مذلت A. = ذلت & خواری
مَذمت A. Reproach. Slander.— م. کردن To r. To s.
مَذموم A. = زشت & ناپسند
مذهب (*maz-hab*) A. [مذاهب] Religion. *Cf.* آئین - کیش - دین
مذهب (*mozahab*) A. Gilt. Illuminated, as a book.
مَذهبی A. Religious.
مُذیل ○ A. Having a specified appendix.

مَر Counter ○. *By e.* Number [only in بیمر *q. v.*]
مَر Blowfly.
مَر *Pleonastic or emphatic particle used in old styles before the objective case.*
مُرّ 1) *a.* ○ = تلخ Bitter. 2) *n.* Myrrh. — مرّ قانون The letter of the law.
مَرا 1) Me. 2) To me; for me.

مُرابحه A. Percentage.
مُرابطه A. (Inter)communication; (inter)relation.
مِرآت A. = آئینه Mirror. *Cf. the pl.* مرایا
مَرّات *S. u.* مره
مَراتب A. Circumstances; facts; case. *Cf. the s.* مرتبه ‖ بمراتب By far; out and away; infinitely.

مراتع [Pl. of مرتع]
مراثی [Pl. of مرثیه]
مراجع [Pl. of مرجع]
مُراجعات A. References. Business orders. *See* مراجعه
مُراجعت A. Return. — م. کردن = برگشتن To return. — در مراجعت ازرشت On my r. from Rasht.
مُراجعه A. Reference. Recourse. *Cf. the pl.* مراجعات ‖ م. کردن به To refer to; approach; call on. To consult به پزشك م. کردن
مراحل [Pl. of مرحله]
مراحم [Pl. of مرحمت]
مُراد A. 1) *n.* Desire; wish. Intention. *Mas. pr. name.*— ازآن چه م. دارید What do you mean by that?— بمراد خود رسید He attained his aim. 2) *a.* Intended; looked for.
مُرادف A. = مترادف
مَرارت A. [مرارات] Hardship; suffering. *OS.* = تلخی ‖ م. کشیدن To suffer hardship.
مَراره A. = زَهره & صفرا
مُراسله A. [مراسلات] = نامه Letter. — دفتر ارسال مراسلات *See* دفتر نامه رسانی
مَراسم A. Ceremonies; formalities. Customs. [Pl. of مرسوم but regarded often as the pl. of رسم]
مُراعات A. Observance. Regard. Assistance. — م. کردن To observe. To regard.
مرا فراموش مکن Forget-me-not.

مُرافعه *A*. [مرافعات] Litigation; lawsuit. Quarrel +. — م. کردن To carry on a l. To quarrel.

مرافعه‌جو *A. P*. Litigious.

مُرافقت *A*. Comradeship; companionship.

مَراق *A*. Hypochondria.

مُراقب *A*. Attentive; watchful. — م. باشید که . . . See that . . . — پلیس مراقب او بود The police was on his track.

مُراقبت *A*. Attention; supervision; control. Contemplation *. — م. کردن To supervise; look after. To watch; observe. — م. کنید که . . . Ensure that . . . ; see that . . .

مراقد [Pl. of مرقد]

مراکب [Pl. of مرکب]

مراکز [Pl. of مرکز]

مَراکش Morocco.

مراکشی Moroccan.

مَرال = **بزکوهی** & **شکار**

مَرام *A*. Aim; object. Platform (of a party).

مرامنامه *A. P*. "Aims" [part of a society's constitution describing its aims].

مُراوده *A*. Intercourse. Frequentation.

مَرایا *A*. [Pl. of مرآت] Mirrors o. — (علم) مناظر و مرایا Perspective.

مُربّا *A*. Jam.

مربائی *A. P*. Containing jam. — کیك م. J. tart. — نان م. Kind of swiss-roll.

مُربع *A*. Square. — متر مربع S. [meter.

مَربوط *A*. [Fem. مربوطه] Connected; related. Relevant; also, concerned. — م. بودن To pertain. To be connected. To depend. — م. بمن نیست It does not concern me. — م. ساختن To connect. To link.

مُربی *A*. Educator; preceptor; tutor. Tamer (of animals).

مُرتاض *A*. [مرتاضین] (Indian) fakir; yogi.

مُرتب *A*. In good shape; regular; proper. — م. کردن To give a good s. to; arrange.

مرتباً *A*. Regularly.

مُرتبط *A*. Connected. [Fem. مرتبطه]. — ظروف مرتبطه Communicating vessels.

مَرتبت * *A*. Rank; degree. *Cf*. رتبه & مرتبه

مَرتبه *A*. [*Cf. the pl*. مراتب] 1) Degree; rank. 2) اشکوب ‖ 3) دفعه *or* بار Time. — سه م. Thrice. 4) *Arith*. Place.

مُرتجع *A*. [مرتجعین] Reactionary.

مُرتَدّ *A*. Apostate; backslider. — م. شدن To apostatize.

مُرتشی *A*. Bribee.

مُرتضوی *A*. Descended from Morteza(-Ali).

مُرتضی (*-taza*) *A*. *Mas. pr. name*. *OS*. Approvable.

مَرتع *A*. [مراتع] = **چراگاه**

مُرتعش *A*. Trembling *adj*. —

مَرحله *A.* [مراحل] Stage. Phase. Process. Remove. — ازمر-له پرت است He is off the track; he is all abroad.

مَرحمت *A.* [مراحم] Favour. Mercy. — م. کردن To do favour; To be kind. [In p. c.] To give. — مرحمت سرکار زیاد Thank you (very much).

مرحمةً *A.* By way of favour; as a f.; kindly.

مرحمتی *A. P.* 1) *a.* Given. 2) *n.* Present.

مَرحوم *A.* Deceased; defunct; of blessed memory. *OS.* Pitied or b. — مرحومِ فروغی The late *Forughi*. — م. شدن To pass away; die [مردن].

مُرخص *A.* Dismissed. Excused. Released. — م. شدن To be d. or released. To go. — م. کردن To dismiss; send away. To release: جنس را ازگمرك م. کردم ‖ To excuse. To relieve. — م. بفرمائید [In p. c.] May I take my leave?

مرخصی *A. P.* Leave of absence. — درمرخصی On leave. — به م. رفتن To go (*or* proceed) on l. — م. با (استفاده از) حقوق Leave with pay. — م. بابتِ ناخوشی Sick leave.

مُرَخم *A.* Apocopated.

مَرد Man. Partner; playmate. — او مرد این کار نیست He is not equal, or adequate, to the task; he is not the man

— [لرزیدن] م. شدن To tremble — م. ساختن To cause to tremble.

مُرتَفِع (*-fe'*) *A.* = بلند High; elevated. Overhead.

مُرتَفَع (*-fa'*) *A.* Removed or eliminated. — م. ساختن *or* م کردن To eliminate or remove.

مُرتکب *A.* [مرتکبین] Perpetrator. — مرتکبِ جنایتی شدن To commit a crime.

مُرتَهَن (*-han*) *A.* Mortgaged.

مُرتَهِن (*-hen*) *A.* Mortgagee.

مَرثیه *A.* [مراثی] Elegy; lamentation; threnody.

مَرجان *A.* Coral. — مرجان سیاه Black coral; jet. — سنگ م. Corallite. — شبه م. Coralloid.

مرجان آور *or* **مرجان دار** *A.P* Coralliferous.

مرجانی *A.* Coral(ine); coralloid. — جزیرهٔ م. Coral island.

مُرَجّح *A.* Preferred; preferable. — ترجیح بلامرجح Distinction without a difference.

مَرجع *A.* [مراجع] 1) *OS.* Place to return or refer to. 2) *F.* Authority: مراجع قانونی ‖ 3) *Gr.* Antecedent.

مَرجُمك Lentil [عدس]

مَرجوع *A.* Returned. Brought back. — م. داشتن = پس دادن ‖ سهو و نسیان م. است Errors and omissions excepted [E. & O. E.].

مَرحبا *A.* 1) Well done! 2) o Hail! Welcome!

for it.
مُرداب Lagoon. Marsh. [dine.
مردابی Marshy. Paludal; palu-
مُرداد *Fifth month having 31 days.* [*Cf.* لاشه
مُردار Carrion ; dead corpse.
مرد افگن * Valiant.
مردانگی Manliness ; courage. Generosity. – م. کردن To be generous or manly.
مَردانه *a*. Manly. Courageous. Men's. م. کفش ‖ –*ad*. As a man; bravely. Generously.
مُرَدَّد *A*. Uncertain; wavering.
مردِرند + *a*. Cheaply clever or smart. –*n*. Smart alec(k).
مردك [Dim. of مرد] Little fellow. [gun; sirrah.
مردِکه × Fellow ; son of a
مردگان [Pl. of مرده]
مَردُم People; men. Man(kind).
مردمك (چشم) = مردم چشم
مردمآزار *a*. Man-tormenting; inhumane (to mankind). –*n*. Oppressor ; tyrant.
مردم آزاری Inhumanity (to mankind). Oppression.
مردم خوار * Man-eating ; cannibal.
مردمدار Possessing tact, address, and civility. [tact.
مردم داری Address ; civility;
مردم دَر = * درنده
مردم شناس ○ Anthropologist.
مردم شناسی Anthropology.

مَردمك Pupil (of the eye).
مهر گیاه = مردم گیاه
مردم َنوازی Courtesy; civility.
مردمی Humanity ; courtesy.
مُردَن [میر] To die. – ازسرما مردن To freeze to death. – از گرسنگی م. To starve to d.
باکره & دوشیزه = ○ مرد نادیده
مَردنگی *H*. Globe; shade. Bell-jar. [Worn-out.
مُردنی Dying ; moribund.
مَردوار 1) *a*. Manly. Sexless: زن م. ‖ 2) *ad*. Like a man.
مَردود *A*. Rejected. Banned. – م. شدن To be r. To fail (in the examinations). – م. کردن To reject. To ban. [*At school*] To turn down.
مُرده [*P. P. of* مردن] 1) *a*. Dead. *Med*. Necrosed ; necrotic. – م. باد . . . Down with. . . ! 2) *n*. [pl. مردگان] D. person. *C. P.* Dummy. – م . را پاك شستن *Met*. To give full measure.
مَرَدَه *A*. [Pl. of مارد ، 'stubborn', but erroneously adopted as the pl. of مرید].
مرده پرستی Necrolatry ○ . *F*. Praising of the dead.
مرده خور & مردهخوار Necrophagous. [heritage.
میراث = مردهریگ Patrimony ;
مردار سنگ *or* مرده سنگ Litharge.

+ مرده شور or مرده شوی Washer of the dead. - مرده‌شورش ببرد ! Confound him !

مرده شوی خانه Place where the dead are washed ; *L.*, mortuary.

مرده وار As dead. - م. شنا کردن To swim on the back.

مَردی Manhood; manliness. Virility.

مَرز Frontier. *By e.* Land. - نقاط مرزی F. localities.

مَرزبان or مرزدار Frontier official; f. controller. - ادارهٔ مرزبانی Frontier Control Department.

مرزنجوش [Arabicized form of مرزنگوش] Mouse-ear; myosotis. Sweet marjoram.

مَرزنشین Frontiersman. Marcher.

مرز و بوم (Native) country.

مَرزه Sweet fennel; origany.

مَرس Leash; couple.

مِرس Beech.

مرسریزه *Fr.* Mercerized.

مُرسل *A.* Sent on a mission, as a prophet.

مِرسله *A.* Thing sent ; i. e. letter or consignment.

مَرسول *A.* Dispatched; mailed. [Fem. مرسوله with the pl. مرسولات letters ; mail].

مَرسوم *A.* Custom(ary).

مِرسی *Fr.* Thank you. [Better say متشکرم or سپاسگزارم].

مُرشد *A.* Spiritual guide or preceptor ; father ; sheikh.

مُرصع *A.* = گوهر نشان Studded (*or* inlaid) with jewels.

مَرَض *A.* [امراض] Disease; illness [ناخوشی]. - + غرض و مرض (Private) motive. - علم امراض Pathology.

مرضا *S. u.* مریض

مرض شناس *A. P.* Pathologist.

مرض شناسی *A. P.* Pathology.

مَرضی (-za) [Pl. of مریض]

مَرضی *A.* [Fem. مَرضیه used as a fem. pr. name] Agreeable. Laudable.

مَرَضی *A.* Morbid. Pathological

مَرضی الطرفین *A.* Mutually agreed to.

مَرطوب *A.* = نمسار Damp; moist. Humid. - م. ساختن To moisten.

مَرعوب *A.* Terrified.

مَرعی *A.* Observed; regarded. - م. داشتن To observe.

مَرغ Meadow. *S. a.* چمن

مُرغ Bird. Hen; fowl. - مرغ و خروس or مرغان خانگی Poultry; domestic fowls.

مُرغابی Duck. - مرغابی جره Teal. - مرغابی نر Drake.

مُرغباز Bird-fancier.

مَرغزار Meadow.

مُرغ شناسی Ornithology.

مرغ فروش Poulterer.

مُرغك Birdie. Gusset; gore. Chuck; dog; mandrel.

مُرغوا ○ Bad omen.
مَرغوب A. Of good quality; in demand. OS. Desirable.
مرغوبیت A. Desirability ; good quality.
مَرغوله ○ Ringlet .
مِرفَق ○ A. = آرنج
مُرفه(الحال) A. = آسوده‌حال
مرفین Fr. Morphine.
مَرَق A. Gravy; dripping.
مَرقد A. [مراقد] Sepulchre.
مَرقُس A-G. Mark : انجیل م.
مُرقع A. 1) a. Ragged. 2) n. R. garment . Scrap-book ; album. Patchwork.
مَرقوم A. Written. — م. داشتن [Polite substitute for نوشتن]
مرقومه A. 1) Fem. of مرقوم. 2) Letter [نامه].
مَرکب A. [مراکب] Animal for riding; mount. Ship ○.
مرکب (morakab) A. 1) a. Composed; consisting; made up. Compound. [Fem. مرکبه]. 2) n. Ink. [For جسم م.] Compound. — جهل م. Double ignorance ; i. of one's i. — ماهی م. Cuttlefish.
مرکبات A. Citrous fruits. Compound words. [Pl. of مرکبه fem. of مرکب].
مرکب پاك‌کن A. P. Ink eraser.
مرکب خشك‌کن A.P. Blotting-paper. Blotter.
مَرکز A. [مراکز] Centre. Head-office ; headquarters. Principal seat.
مرکزجو A. P. Centripetal.
مرکزگریز A. P. Centrifugal.
مرکزی A. Central.
مرکزیت A. Centrality. — م. دادن To centralize.
مَرکب A. = مرکوب
مرکورکرم Fr. Mercurochrome.
مَرکوز A. Implanted. — مفصل م. Gomphosis. — ذهنی = مرکوزِ ذهن
مَرگ Death. — مرگ موش Rat's-bane ; white arsenic. — مرگِ ماهی Indian berry. — در دمِ م. On the point of death — شهرت پس‌ازمرگ Posthumous fame. — معاینه پس از مرگ Postmortem examination . — بمرگ خودم On my l. ; (I swear) by my life. — آمارمرگ‌ومیر Mortality.
مَرگبار Deathful; deathly.
مرگی (Cattle-)pest.
مَرمت A. Repair. — م کردن To r.
مَرمر Marble. — مرمر سبز Malachite . — مرمر سفید White marble; alabaster. — مرمر سیاه Basalt. — مرمر مصری Ophite.
مرمرنما Marbled ; marble-veined; marmoreal.
مرمری Marbly. Marmoreal . Polished. — م. کردن To polish or smooth , as marble.
مَرموز A. Mysterious; secret.
مرموك Garden clary.
مِرنگ Fr. Meringue.

مرو (*marv*) Marram; marum.– مرو خوشبو Marum-germander.
مُروا ٥ Good omen. –م. زدن To wish one good luck.
مَرمی ٥ *A*. Missile; projectile.
مُروارید Pearl. – صید مروارید P.-fishing. – گُل م. Daisy.
مُروّت *A*. (*OS*.) Manliness. *F*. Compassion. Generosity.
مُروّج *A*. Promoter.
مُرور *A*. Passing ; passage. Lapse.–م. کردن To pass ٥ [گذشتن] To go over; review.–مرور زمان Statutory limitation ; also, prescription. – قانون مرور زمان Statute of limitations. – مشمول مرور زمان Time-barred ; barred by statute. – بمرور *or* بمرور زمان In course of time.
مَروَزی *A*. (Native) of Merv.
مروّق *A*. = صاف & ناب
مَرّة *or* مرّه [مرّات] = بار & دفعه (Single) time.
مَرهم *A*. (Cooling) ointment. *F*. Balm. – م. گذاشتن To apply an o. (to).
مرهم‌کش *A*. *P*. Spatula; slice.
مرهم نه • *A*. *P*. One who applies an ointment to a wound; dresser. [I. to.
مَرهون *A*. Indebted. – مرهونِ
مَری Oesophagus; gullet.
مِرّیخ *A*. = بهرام Mars.
مُرید *A*. Disciple. Devotee.
مَریض *A*. *a*. 1) = بیمار Ill ; sick. 2) Morbid; diseased.– م شدن To fall ill. –*n*. Patient [pl. مرضی –*za* *or* مرضا]
مریضخانه *A*. *P*. = بیمارستان
مَریم *A-Heb*. 1) Mary. 2) Miriam. – گُل م. Tuberose.
مریم گلی *A*. *P*. Garden sage.
مریم نخودی Water germander.
مَرئوس *A*. Subordinate.
مَرئی *A*. = پدیدار Visible.–افق م. Sensitive horizon.
مِزاج *A*. [امزجه] (Condition of) health ; physical constitution. Temperament. – استعداد مزاج *Med*. Predisposition; diathesis. –مزاج شریف چطور است ؟ How is your h. ?
مزاج‌گویی *A*. *P*. Obsequiousness; flattery.
مزاجی *A*. Constitutional. – حالت م. (Condition of) health.
مِزاح *A*. = شوخی
مزاح (*mazah*) *A*. Jester.
مُزاحِم *A*. Obtrusive.–پیشکشی م. White elephant . – ببخشید مزاحم شدم I am sorry to interrupt (*or* inconvenience) you.
مُزاحمت *A*. Inconvenience. – (اسباب) مزاحمت کسیرا فراهم کردن To inconvenience s. o.
مَزار *A*. = 1) زیارت گاه 2) قبر
مَزارع [Pl. of مزرعه]
مُزارع *A*. Farm lessor.

مُزارعه *A.* Contract of farm-letting.
مزامیر [Pl. of مزمور *or* مزمار]
مُزاوجت *A.* Marrying. *Cf.* عروسی ‖ باکسی م. کردن To marry s. o.
مزایا [Pl. of مزیت]
مُزایده *A.* Auction. — به م. گذاشتن To put up to auction. — به م. فروختن To sell by a. — پیشنهاد مزایده Bid (at auction). — حائز حد اکثر مزایده شدن To be the highest bidder.
مَزبله *A.* [مَزابل] Rubbish-heap.
مَزبور *A.* Aforesaid; above-mentioned. [Fem. مزبوره].
مَزج o *A.* Mixing.
مُزجات o *A.* Small; insignificant; of little value.
مُزخرف *A.* 1) *a.* Absurd; nonsensical. 2) *n.* Nonsense; absurd or silly talk. Offensive language. [Fem. مزخرفه o with the pl. مزخرفات 's. talks'].
مُزد Wage(s). Reward. [gate.
مُزدَوَج o *A.* Coupled. Conjugate.
مُزدور *n.* Wage-earner; hired worker. [In a bad sense] Hireling. —*a.* Hired. Mercenary. — م. کردن To hire; employ for wages.
مزدیسنی Mazdaism.
مِزراق o *A.* = زوبین
مَزرع [Collective for مزرعه]
مَزرعه *A.* [مزارع] Farm.
مَزروع *A.* 1) *a.* Cultivated. 2) *n.* C. land. Crop. [vated.
مزروعی *A. P.* Arable. Culti-
مُزعفر o *A.* (Rice dish) flavoured with saffron.
مَزغل *A.* Gun-port.
مزکی (*mozaka*) *A.* = پاك
مزلف [Of a young gigolot] Wearing a head of hair. [Coined from زلف in the A. fashion].
مِزمار *A.* 1) = نی Pipe; flute. 2) = چاك صوت
مزمزه کردن To sip; taste a little at a time.
مُزمِن *A.* Chronic.
مَزمور *A.* [مزامیر] Psalm.
مُزوِّر *A.* 1) *n.* Dissimulator; impostor. 2) *a.* Deceitful; guilty of fraud.
مَزه Taste. Snack; chips. *F.* Interest. — م کردن 1) *vt.* To taste. 2) *vi.* To be eaten with relish. *F.* To be interesting. — م. انداختن + To crack a joke. — مزه دهن کسیرا چشیدن *Met.* To feel a person's pulse.
مَزیت *A.* [مزایا] Preference. Merit. Advantage; benefit. Privilege; prerogative.
مَزید *A.* Increase. — مزید تشکر خواهد بود اگر ... I shall be (ever more) grateful if ... ‖ م. کردن To increase; add to. — مزید برعلت شدن To aggravate the condition.

چشیدن = [مز] o مزیدن
مُزیّن A. Adorned; decorated. — م. کردن To decorate; adorn. — م. فرمودن [In p. c.] To seal or sign : خواهشمند است م. فرمائید
مژدگانی (Reward for bringing) good news.
مُژده Good news or tidings. — م. دادن To give glad tidings.
مُژکدار Z. Ciliate.
مُژگان [Pl. of مژه] Eyelashes. — م. بهم زدن To twinkle. To bat an eyelid.
مژه Eyelash. *See* مژگان
مَسّ A. Touching. — مس کردن To touch or feel. [dishes.
مِس Copper. C. vessels or
مَساء A. = غروب & شام
مُسابقه A. [مسابقات] Competition. [For امتحان م.] Selection examination; competitive e. — مسابقهٔ دو Race. — مسابقهٔ میدانی و صحرائی Track-and-field sport (*or* event). — مسابقهٔ فوتبال Football match. — با کسی م. گذاشتن To have a m. or competition with s. o. To race with s. o. — در مسابقه شرکت کردن To sit for a competitive (*or* selection) examination.
مساجد [Pl. of مسجد]
مَسّاح A. = زمین پیما
مَساحت A. 1) Area. 2) = مساحی
مَساحی A. P. Land-measurement; surveying. — م. کردن *vt.* To measure or survey. —*vi.* To do surveying; be a surveyor.
مُساعِد A. Favourable.
مُساعدت A. Assistance; aid. — با کسی م. کردن To assist or aid s. o. To favour s. o.
مُساعده [f. A. مساعدة] Advance (money). — بکسی م. دادن To make an advance to s. o. — بطور مساعده In a.
مَساعی A. Efforts. (Good) offices. [Pl. of مسعاة o]
مَسافت A. [مسافات] Distance.
مسافت پیما A. P. Odometer.
مسافت سنج A. P. Speedometer.
مسافت یاب A. P. Range-finder.
مُسافِر A. [مسافرین] Traveller. Passenger.
مُسافربَر A. P. Fit for carrying passengers. — بنگاهِ مسافربر(ی) Passenger service.
مُسافرت A. Travel(ling); journey; visit. — مسافرت دریا Voyage. — م. کردن To travel.
مسافرخانه A. P. Inn; hotel.
مسافری A. P. Fit for travelling. — اتوموبیل م. Passenger car.
مساکن [Pl. of مسکن]
مساکین [Pl. of مسکین]
مسالك [Pl. of مسلك]
مُسالِمت A. Peacefulness.
مسالمت آمیز A. P. Peaceful.
مسامّ [Often مسامات] A. Pores. [Pl. of مسمّ o]
مُسامحه A. Negligence. Non-

chalance. Forbearance. — م. کردن To be indulgent. To neglect. [careless.
مسامحه کار A. P. Negligent ;
مُساوات A. = برابری Equality.
مُساوی A. = برابر Equal. — م. با E. to ; same as. — م. کردن To equalize — بطورمساوی Equally.
مُساهله A. Indulgence; leniency. Carelessness.
مَسائل A. Problems ; questions; affairs ; matters. *Cf. the s.* مسئله
مِسبار (Tombac, bronze, or other alloy) containing copper.
مُسبب A. [مسببین] Cause ; one who occasions s. t. — قمارمسبب بدبختی است Gambling causes (or brings about) adversity.
مُسبع A. (Stanza) composed of seven lines. Heptagon(al).
مَسبوق A. = آگاه Aware ; informed. — م. بسابقه Precedented. — م. کردن To inform; let know.
مست a. Drunk(en); intoxicated. *F* Ravished. Furious. —*n*. Drunkard. — م. شدن To get drunk. — م. کردن *vt*. To make d. *F*. To elate. —*vi*. + To brawl, as a drunkard. — مست لایعقل *or* مست خراب Dead drunk ; blind d.
مُستأجر A. [مستاجرین] Tenant; lessee ; also, lodger. Farmer.
مستاجره A. Object of lease.
مُستأصل A. Driven to extremities; helpless. — م. کردن To render h. ; drive to e.
مستأنف A. = پژوهش خواه
مستانف علیه A. = پژوهش خوانده
مستانف عنه A. = پژوهش خواسته
مَستانه Drunken. Languishing: نگاه م.
مُستبد A. Despotic; arbitrary.
مستبدانه A. P. *ad*. Despotically. —*a*. Despotic(al) ; arbitrary.
مستبعد A. Improbable.
مُستتر A. Hidden. Elliptical. *Gr*. Understood.
مستثنیات A. Exceptions. — مستثنیات دین Properties not liable to distraint for debt. [Pl. fem. of مستثنی].
مُستثنی (-*tasn*a) A. Exceptional. Excepted. — م. کردن To except; exclude.
مُستجاب A. Granted, as prayer. — م. شدن To be g. or accepted. — م. کردن To hear or grant.
مستجاب‌الدعوه A. Whose prayers are accepted. [Fossil.
مستحاثه A. [مستحاثات] = سنگواره
مُستحب A. [Of certain religious precepts.] Recommended.
مستحسن A. = پسندیده
مُستحضر A. Informed ; aware. — خاطر آن جناب را مستحضر میدارد که I beg to inform Your Excellency that.

مُستحفظ *A.* [مستحفظین] Guardian. Caretaker.
مُستحقّ *A.* Deserving; entitled [سزاوار]. Needy; poor [نیازمند]. — مستحق E. to...
مستحکم *A.* = استوار & محکم
مُستخدم *A.* [مستخدمین] Employee. Servant. [Extracted.
مستخرَج *A.* [Fem. مستخرجه].
مستخرِج ○ *A.* Extractor.
مُستخلص *A.* Released ; set free. — م.کردن = رها کردن
مُستدام *A.* 1) = مدام & دائمی 2) ○ Assiduous.
مُستدعی *A.* = خواهشمند (One) who requests or asks. — م هستم I request you to . . .
مُستدعی (*-tad-*a) *A.* (Thing) asked for. (Object) wished. [Pl. مُستدعیات *-ayat* 'wishes ; requests'].
مُستدلّ *A.* Proved or convinced by reasoning. Documentary.
مستدیر *A.* = گرد Round.
مستدیم ○ *A.* = 1) دائمی 2) ابدی
مُستراح *A.* = آبریز Lavatory; water-closet.
مُستردّ *A.* Restored ; refunded. — م. داشتن To return ; refund. To ask to be returned; take back.
مسترق ○ *A.* = دزدیده Stolen. [Fem. مسترقه only in خمسهٔ م. the five intercalary days; *L.* the five d. of epact].
مُستزاد *A.* [Of some verses] Having an additional part.— شعر مستزاد Complemented . poem ; *L.* echo verse.
مُستسقی (*-tasgha*) *A.* Dropsied or dropsical (person).
مُستشار *A.* Advisor.
مُستشرق *A.* [مستشرقین] = خاورشناس
مستشعر *A.* Apprehensive. — ضمیر مستشعر ○ Conscience.
مُستطاب *A.* Excellent; great. — جناب مستطاب آقایِ (*Obsolete*) His Excellency . . .
مُستطیل *A.* Rectangular [usu. in مربع م. Rectangle].
مُستظرف *A.* Fine.[Fem. مستظرفه Ex. صنایع م. 'the fine arts'].
مستظهر *A.* Relying or relier.
مُستعار *A.* Fictitious. Metaphorical. Transient ○. *OS.* Borrowed. — نام م. F. name ; pseudonym.
مُستعان *A.* Whose aid is asked for : ep. of God.
مُستعجَل (*-ta'jal*) *A.* Hurried.
مُستعجِل (*-ta'jel*) *A.* Hasty ; precipitate.
مُستعدّ *A.* Fit ; talented; apt. Disposed ; ready [آماده]. Susceptible. — مستعد تغییر S. of change . — مستعد ناخوش شدن Liable to become sick. — م. کردن To prepare; dispose; incline .
مستعرب ○ *A.* One who adopts Arabian customs. Mozarab.
مستعصم ○ *A.* Holding fast.

مُستعفی A. Resigned or resigning. — م. شدن To resign.
مستعمراتی A. P. Colonial.
مستعمره A. [مستعمرات] Colony.
مُستعمل A. Used; also, second-hand. Current ; in common use. [Fem. مستعمله]
مستغاث A. Implored to for help : ep. of God.
مستغرب ○ A. Occidentalist.
مُستغرَق A. Drowned ○. F. Absorbed ; overwhelmed ; plunged. [giveness.
مستغفر ○ A. (One) who asks for-
مُستغل A. Real estate; landed property. Cf. مستغلات
مستغلات A. [Pl. of مستغله fem. of مستغل] Real estates. [For مالیات م.] Rental tax.
مُستغنی A. Able to do without. — م. ازتوصیف Not needing description; beyond d.
مُستفاد A. Understood ; gathered.
مستفسر ○ A. Inquirer.
مستفید ○ A. (One) who profits by s. t. [delighted.
مُستفیض A. Benefited ; L. ,
مُستقبل (-bal) A. = آینده
مستقبل (-bel) A. (One) who goes out to meet s. o.
مُستقر A. Settled; firmly fixed; established.
مُستقل A. Independent.
مستقلاً A. Independently (of others) ; separately.
مُستقیم A. Direct adj. Straight.
مستقیماً A. Direct ad.
مُستلزم بودن A. P. To necessitate or require
مُستمر (-ta-mar) A. Continued.
مُستمر (-ta-mer) A. = دائمی
مستمراً A. Continually.
مستمرّی A. (Life-)pension.
مستمسك A. Pretext. Ground.
مُستمع A. [مستمعین] Hearer; listener. — مستمع آزاد Observer.
مستملك ○ A. Possessed.
مستملکات A. Possessions ; colonies. [Pl. of مستملکه fem. of مستملك]
مُستمند = بیچاره Afflicted. Needy.
مُستند A. Based; supported. [With بر] B. on; s. by.
مستنسخ A. Transcriber; copyist.
مستنطق A. = بازپرس
مستنکف A. Refuser.
مستوجب A. = سزاوار Deserving.
مَستور A. Covered [پوشیده]. Veiled; chaste. [Fem. مستوره c. woman]. — م. داشتن To hide. To cover or veil.
مستوری A. P. Being veiled. Concealment. By e. Chastity.
مُستوفی A. [Old title of a] state accountant.
مستولی A. Predominant. Seizing. — ترس بر او مستولی شد He was filled with terror.
مُستوی A. 1) Plane : سطح م. ‖ 2) = برابر 3) = راست [dest.

مستهجن *A*. Obscene; immo-

مُستهلك *A*. Amortized. Absorbed. — م کردن To amortize.

مستی Drunkenness; intoxication. Rut.

مسجد *A*. [مساجد] Mosque.

مسجع *A*. Rimed (prose).

مُسجل *A*. Confirmed. Registered. — م. کردن To confirm.

مَسح *A*. Anointing. — م. کشیدن To wet one's forehead and toes in performing one's ablutions.

مسحور *A*. Fascinated.

مسحوق *A*. Pulverized.

مَسخ *A*. Metamorphosis. — م شدن To be metamorphosed. — م. کردن To metamorphose.

مُسخر *A*. Conquered. — م. کردن To conquer; take.

مسخرگی *A. P*. Buffoonery; mockery; drollery. — م. کردن To play the buffoon.

مَسخره *A*. Buffoon; clown. Mockery; ridicule. Laughing-stock. — م کردن To mock or r.; make a fool of.

مسخره آمیز *A. P*. Ridiculous.

مسخره بازی *A. P*. Buffoonery. Monkey business.

مِسدار Cupriferous.

مسدّد *A*. Obstructing; stopping. [Fem. مسدده]. — پردهٔ مسدده Obturator.

مسدّس *A*. 1) *a*. Composed of six parts. Hexagonal. 2) *n*. Verse composed of six lines. Hexameter. Hexagon.

مَسدود *A*. Closed; obstructed. — م. کردن = بستن To close.

مَسرّت *A*. = خوشی Joy; pleasure.

مسرت آمیز & مسرت بخش *A.P*. Joyful.

مُسرِف *A*. Lavish; prodigal.

مسرفانه *A. P. ad*. Prodigally. —*a*. Prodigal; extravagant.

مسرودیطوس *A-G*. Mithridates. [For م. معجون] Mithridate.

مَسرور *A*. = شادمان & خوشحال

مُسروق *A*. [Fem. مسروقه]. Stolen [دزدیده شده].

مُسری *A*. [Fem. مُسریه] = واگیره دار Contagious.

مُسطح *A*. Flat. Level; plane. [Fem. مسطحه. Ex. هندسهٔ م. Plane geometry].

مِسطر *A*. = سطر آرا

مَسطور *A*. Written [نوشته]. Aforesaid; above-mentioned.

مسطوره *A*. = نمونه Sample. [Orig. fem. of مسطور]

مَسعود *A. a*. Happy; prosperous. —*n*. *Mas. pr. name*.

مُسقط *A*. [Fem. مسقطه] Causing to lapse. — مرور زمان م Negative prescription. — ادویهٔ مسقطهٔ جنین Abortive medicines.

مَسقط الرأس (-*ghato*ra's) *A*. Birthplace.

مُسقف *A*. Roofed.

مَسك *A*. Restraining. — مسكِ نفس Self-restraint; self-control.

مسکت *A*. Silencing; convincing
مُسکر *A*. Intoxicating (drink).
مسکرات *A*. Intoxicating drinks. [Pl. of مسکره fem. of مسکر].
مَسکن (*-kan*) *A*. [مساکن] Dwelling; abode.
مُسکن (*mosaken*) *A*. Calmative.
مسکنت *A*. = فقر & تهیدستی
مَسکوت *A*. [Also مسکوت عنه *-ton-anh*] Left unsaid. — م. گذاردن To leave u. To put in abeyance. — م ماندن To fall into a. To be left u.
مَسکوك *A*. 1) *a*. Coined. 2) *n*. Coin [سکه]
مسکوکات *A*. Coins. [Pl. of مسکوکه fem. of مسکوك]
مَسکون *A*. Habitable; inhabited. — ربع م The i. portion of the earth.
مسکونی *A. P*. Residential.
مسکه Fresh butter.
مِسکین *A*. *a*. Indigent; poor. —*n*. [مساکین] I. person; beggar.
مِسگر Coppersmith.
مسگرخانه Copperworks.
مسگری Coppersmithing.
مُسلح *A*. Armed. [Fem. مسلحه]. — بتن م. Reinforced concrete [f. Fr. *béton armé*]. — م. شدن To take up arms; arm oneself. — م. کردن To arm.
مسلحانه *A. P. ad*. With arms or weapons; in a. —*a*. Armed.
مَسلخ *A*. = کشتارگاه

مُسلسل *A*. *a*. Chained or linked together. Consecutive. Fluent; flowing. —*n*. Machine-gun. — به م. بستن To machine-gun.
مُسلط *A*. Predominant; overruling. — م. شدن [With بر] To rule over. To get mastery of. — م. کردن To give predominance; set (over).
مِسلفه *A*. = مازو Harrow.
مَسلك *A*. [مسالك] Principle. Course; policy. Method; way.
مسلم (*mosallam*) *A*. Certain; indisputable. [Fem. مسلمه]. — م گرفتن or م. فرض کردن To take for granted. — م. کردن To prove or establish. — قدر مسلم اینست که So much is certain that.
مُسلم (*-lem*) *A*. [مسلمین] Moslem [fem. مسلمه]. *Mas. pr. name*.
مسلماً (*mosallaman*) *A*. Certainly; undoubtedly.
مُسلمان *A. P*. Mussulman; Mohammedan [Pl. مسلمانان]
مسلمانی *A. P*. Mohammedanism; Moslem life.
مسلوب‌المنفعه *A*. Non-productive; unutilized.
مَسلول *A*. [مسلولین] Tuberculous (person); consumptive.
مسما *Dish of brinjal, marrow (or other vegetables), and meat*.
مُسمط *A*. Multiple poem.

مسمن *A.* = فربه & سمین
مَسموع *A.* Heard. *F.* Justifiable. – از قرار مسموع It is rumoured that ; we understand that. [Fem. مسموعه with the pl. مسموعات Rumours; reports].
مَسموم *A.* Poisoned. – م. شدن To be p. – م کردن To poison. To infect.
مسمومیت *A.* Poisoning : morbid condition due to poison.– م. از جیوه Mercurialism; hydrargyrism. – م. از سرب Plumbism.
مسمی (*mosa*ma) *A.* Named ; called [with به].
مُسِنّ *A* Advanced in years ; aged; also, rather old.
مَسند *A.* Seat. Throne [تخت]. *F.* Dignity ; position.
مُسند *A.* Predicate [خبر]. – فعل مسندی Finite verb.
مُسنداليه (*-nadon-elay*h) *A.* (*Gr.*) Subject.
مسنن *A.* = دندانساز
مِسوار 1) o Resembling copper. 2) = مسبار
مِسواك *A.* Tooth-brush.
مُسوّده *A.* Rough copy; draft.– م. کردن To make a rough c. of; draft.
مُسهل *A.* Purgative; physic. – مسهل بلغم Phlegmagogue. – مسهل سودا Melanagogue. – مسهلِ صفرا Cholagogue.

مِسی *or* مِسین Made of copper : م. ظروف c. vessels.
مَسیح *A.* Messiah; Christ. *OS.* Anointed.
مَسیحا • *A.* Christ.
مسیحی *A.* Christian.
مسیحیت *A.* Christianity.
مَسیر *A.* Course; route ; itinerary. Line; direction. [*Of a bullet*] Trajectory.
مَسیل *A.* Dry river. *S. a.* آبراهه
مسئلت *A.* Asking. Request. – م. کردن To ask or r.
مسئله *A.* [مسائل] Problem. Question; affair. [f. مسئلت]
مَسئول *A.* 1) Responsible : پیش‌من م. است He is r. to me. 2) Liable : مسئول خسارات L. for damages. ‖ م. دانستن To hold responsible.
مسئولیت *A.* Responsibility. – بمسئولیت خودم On my own responsibility.
مُشابه *A.* = مانند *or* همانند Similar; analogous ; resembling.
مشابهت *A.* = شباهت
مُشاجره *A.* [مشاجرات] Dispute; quarrel. – م. کردن To q. or d.
مُشار *A.* Indicated. Pointed to.
مشاراليه (*-ron-elay*h) *A.* = او He. *OS.* (Man) referred to. [Fem. مشاراليها She].
مشار(اليه)بالبنان *A.* Pointed to by the finger ; i. e. notable or influential .
مشارق [Pl. of مشرق]

مُشارکت *or* **مشارکه** *A.* Partnership — م. کردن To participate or join. To cooperate. — بالمشارکه Jointly.

مشاطه *A.* Bride-dresser; tire-[woman.

مُشاع *A.* Held in undivided shares; held in common. — مالکین م Joint owners.

مشاعاً *A.* Jointly; in common.

مشاعر [Pl. of مشعر]

مُشاعره *A.* Capping verses; poetical contest.

مشاغل [Pl. of مشغله]

مُشافهه ○ *A.* Mouth to mouth conversation.

مَشاق *A.* Instructor or teacher (of music or writing).

مَشام *A.* (Organ of) smelling. (Sense of) smell.

مُشاور *A.* 1) *n.* Advisor; counsellor. 2) *a.* Consulting. — وزیر مشاور Minister without portfolio.

مُشاوره *A.* Consulting together; deliberation. — م. کردن To consult together; deliberate.

مُشاهده *A.* [مشاهدات] Observation. — م. کردن To observe; see [دیدن]; perceive.

مشاهیر [Pl. of مشهور]

مشایخ *A.* [A pl. of شیخ] Elders; sheiks. Learned men.

مُشایعت *A.* Seeing a person home. — م. کردن To see h.; see to the door. To accompany or escort.

مشائین *A.* Peripatetics. [Pl. of مشاء '(good) walker'].

مُشبك *A.* Netted; reticular Latticed. — م. کردن To form into a net(work); reticulate.

مُشبه *A.* 1) *a.* Likened; compared. 2) *n.* [*In a simile*] The thing likened.

مشبه به *A.* [In a simile] That unto which a thing is likened.

مُشت Fist. Blow with the f. Handful. *L.* A number. — م. زدن To strike with the f. To box. — م کردن To take a handful of. To take up by handfuls. — م. بدرفش زدن To run against the point of a spear; kick against the pricks. — مشتِ در کونی × A kick to the fallen; a k. in the pants.

مُشتاق *A.* 1) Eager; anxious. — مشتاقِ دیدار او E. to see him. 2) Loving; amorous.

مشتاقانه *A. P.* Eagerly.

مشت زن *S. a.* **مشت باز** Boxer.

مُشتبه *A.* Dubious; obscure. Confused. Confusing. — امر بر من م. شد I was under the wrong impression. I was led into error. — م. ساختن To misrepresent. To render d.

مشت پر کن × Tangible. *OS.* That can fill one's hand.

مُشتوك [f.. R. *moondshtook*] Hollow stem of a cigarette.

مشتمال *or* مشت ومال Massage; kneading. — م. دادن To knead; give a massage to.

مُشته Muller. Wooden instrument with which a cotton-beater strikes his bow. Shoemaker's mallet.

مُشتهیات *A*. Desires. Appetites. *F*. Temptations. [Pl. of مشتهیه fem. of مشتهی 'desired'].

مُشجر *A*. Planted with trees. Figured with t. and leaves.— م. کردن To plant with trees.

مَشحون *A*. = پُر & مملو

مُشخص (*-shakhas*) *A*. Distinguished; marked. Specified; defined. [Fem. مشخصه]. — م. کردن To specify or define. To distinguish.

مُشخص (*-shakhes*) *A*. (One) who distinguishes or specifies. *Med*. Diagnostic. *Gr*. Diacritical. [Fem. مشخصه. Ex. صفات م. Characteristics].

مُشخصات *A*. Specifications; particulars. [Pl. of مشخصه fem. of مشخص *-shakhas*].

مُشدّد (-d*ad*) *A*. Aggravated. Corroborated. Marked with the sign of تشدید *q. v*.

مشدّد (-d*ed*) *A*. Aggravating. Intensifying. [Fem. مشدده. Ex. شرایط م. A. circumstances].

مَشرب *A*. Natural disposition.

مُشترك (*-tarak*) *A*. Common. Joint. Held in common. — دیوار مشترك Party wall.

مُشترك (*-tarek*) *A*. [مشترکین] Subscriber. Participator. — م. شدن To subscribe (to).

مشتركاً *A*. Jointly. In common. In partnership.

مشترك‌المقیاس *A*. Commensurable.

مشترك‌المنافع *A*. Having common interests. — کشور های م. Commonwealth.

مُشت رَنده Hand-plane.

مُشتری *A*. 1) Customer. *Cf*. خریدار ‖ 2) *Astr*. Jupiter.

مشت زن • Pugilist; athlete.

مُشتعل *A*. Aflame; in flames; ablaze. *F*. Inflamed; excited. — م شدن To take fire; be inflamed. — م. ساختن To inflame; set on f.

مشتغل ○ *A*. = مشغول

مُشتقّ *A*. 1) *a*. Derived. Derivative. [Fem. مشتقه]. 2) *n*. Differential coefficient.

مشتقات *A*. Derivatives. Derivations. [Pl. of مشتقه fem. of مشتق].

مشتق گیری *A*. *P*. Differentiation.

مشتلق *T*. Reward to one who gives tidings that a lost object has been found.

مشتمال *S. u*. مشت و مال

مُشتمل *A*. [With بر] Consisting of; containing.

مُشرف (*-sharaf*) *A*. Honoured (because of having visited a person or a holy place).— م فرمودید [In p. c.] It was nice having you. *OS*. You have honoured us by your visit.

مشرِف *A*. Imminent. Overlooking. — م بودن To be imminent. [With بر] To overlook or command. — م بموت At the point of death.

مَشرق *A*. [مشارق] = خاور East. — در مشرقِ On the east of.

مشرق زمین *A*. *P*. The Orient.

مشرقین *A*. [D. of مشرق] East and West.

مُشرك *A*. Polytheist or dualist.

مَشروب *A*. 1) *n*. Alcoholic liquor or drink. [Pl. **مشروبات** orig. pl. of مشروبه fem. of مشروب]. 2) *a*. Drinkable. Irrigated. — م شدن To be irrigated. — م کردن To irrigate; supply with water.

مشروب فروش *A*. *P*. Seller of alcoholic liquors; saloon-keeper — جایگاه مشروب فروشی Saloon; public house.

مَشروح *A*. Detailed; comprehensive. Amplified. [Used also as a n. Ex. مشروح اخبار News in detail].

مشروحاً *A*. In detail.

مَشروط *A*. Conditioned; conditional. — م براینکه On condition that; provided (that).

مشروطه *A*. Constitutional government; constitution.

مشروطه خواه *A*. *P*. Constitutionalist.

مشروطیت *A*. Constitution. [For اصول م] Constitutionalism.

مَشروع *A*. Lawful; legitimate. [Fem. مشروعه]. — غیر مشروع Unlawful; illegitimate.

مُشطِ پا *A*. *P*. Metatarsus.

مشطِ دست *A*. *P*. Metacarpus.

مَشعر (*-ar*) *A*. [مشاعر] External sense. Wit; intelligence.

مُشعر (*-er*) *A*. Indicating; stating. — م براینکه To the effect that; s. that.

مُشعشع *A*. Brilliant.

مَشعل *A*. [مشاعل] Torch.

مشعلدار *A*. *P*. Torch-bearer, link-boy. *F*. Pioneer.

مَشعوف *A*. Delighted; pleased. *Cf*. خوشنود ‖ م شدن To be d.; become glad. — م ساختن To delight; give pleasure (to).

مشغله *A*. [مشاغل] Occupation; work. *Cf*. کار & شغل

مَشغول *A*. Busy; occupied. — مشغولِ خواندن B. reading. — م شدن To get busy; employ oneself. — مشغولِ درس خود شوید Get b. with your lesson. — م کردن To make (*or* keep) b. To amuse.

مشغول الذمه *A*. Under an obligation; indebted.

مشغولیت *A*. Employment. Amusement.

مُشفق *A*. Kind; tender.

مَشق *A*. Exercise; drill; training. — م. دادن To d. or exercise. To train.— م. کردن To e. or drill. — م. گرفتن To take a lesson or model.

مَشقت *A*. [مشقات] = سختی Hardship. Difficulty.

مشقی *A. P*. Under training. Designed for sporting or exercising. — تفنگ م. Target rifle. [water-skin.

مَشك Large leathern bottle;

مُشك Musk.

مشکوة - مشکاة - مِشکات (-*kat*) *A*. (Niche for a) lamp.

مُشکبو Musk-scented.

مشکك Salad burnet.

مُشکل *A*. 1) *a*. = سخت Difficult; hard. [Fem. مشکله] م. کردن *or* م. ساختن To render difficult. 2) *n*. D. question; problem.— م. دوتا شد You have made it more d.; it is no clearer than it was. 3) *ad*. Hardly: م. بتواند آنرا بخواند He can h. read it; I don't believe he can read it.

مشکلات *A*. Difficulties; problems. [Pl. of مشکله fem. of مشکل].

مشکل‌پسند *A. P*. Hard to please; fastidious; fussy; dainty.

مشکل‌گشا(ی) *A. P*. Resolver of difficulties.

مَشکوك *A*. Doubtful.

مشکو(ی) o = 1) حرم سرا 2) کوشك

مشکی Black. Musk-coloured.

مشکیجه [For گل م.] Musk-rose.

مشکین * Musk-scented. Musk-coloured; jet-black. *Cf*. مشکی || گل م. Jonquil.

مِشمش White book muslin.

مشمشه Glanders.

مشمشه‌ای Glanderous.

مُشمع *A*. Oil-cloth; floor-c.; linoleum. *Med*. Plaster. — مشمع خردل Mustard-plaster. — مشمع ذراریح Vesicatory. — مشمع سریشمی Court-plaster; sticking-plaster.

مَشمول *A*. 1) *a*. Included; covered. — مشمولِ خدمتِ وظیفه Liable to military service.— مشمول مالیات Taxable.— او مشمول قانون نمیشود The law does not apply to him. 2) *n*. Conscript(able person).[Pl. مشمولین]

مشمولیت *A*. Liability (to military service, etc.).

مُشمئز *A*. Shrunk. *F*. Horrified.— م. شدن To shrink. To be h.

مَشوب *A*. Tainted. *OS*. Mixed (with an alloy). — م. کردن To poison; taint: ذهن او را مشوب کردند.

مَشوَرت *A*. Counsel. Consultation; deliberation. — م. دادن To give a counsel (to). — باکسی م. کردن To consult s. o. — بامشورتِ In consultation with

مُشوَّش *A*. Disturbed; agitated. — م. کردن To disturb.

مُشوّق A. Encourager. Patron.

مَشهد A. Place where a martyr has been buried.

مَشهود A. Obvious; clear. OS. Witnessed. [Fem. مشهوده with the pl. مشهودات 'observations; things observed or experienced].

مَشهور A. Celebrated; well-known. — م. شدن To become famous; celebrate oneself. —n. pl. مشاهیر 'celebrated or f. men'.

مُشهی A. Appetitive. Aphrodisiac.

مشی (mash'y) A. Walking *. Gait. — م. خط = رویه Policy.

مَشیت A. = خواست Will. — مشیت الهی Divine w. or decree.

مُشیر A. Counsellor. OS. One who points to s. t.

مَشیمه A. Amnion. — مشیمهٔ چشم Choroid coat. — مشیمهٔ خارجی جنین Chorion.

مشئوم A. = شوم

مُصاحب A. Companion.

مُصاحبت A. Companionship; society. — م. کردن To associate.

مصاحبه [f. A. مصاحب] Interview. — باکسی م. کردن To intervi w s. o.

مَصاحف [Pl. of مُصحف]

مصادر [Pl. of مصدر]

مصادره or مصادرت A. Requisition. Fine [جریمه]. — به م گرفتن To call into r.; put in r. — م. کردن To fine. To confiscate.

مُصادِف A. Coincident; concurrent. — نوروز با . . . م. شد The New Year's day fell on . . .

مُصادم A. Colliding.

مصادمت A. Collision. Concussion.

مصارعت A. = کُشتی

مَصارف A. Expenses. Cf. the s. مصرف

مصافّ A. Battle(-field). — م. کردن = جنگیدن

مُصافحه A. Shaking hands. — دست دادن = م. کردن To shake h. (with each other).

مَصالح A. 1) Interests: مصالح کشور ‖ 2) Materials: مصالحِ ساختمانی ‖ 3) Seasonings. 4) o Affairs. Cf. the s. مصلحت

مُصالح A. Donor.

مُصالحه A. Compromise. Exchange. — م. کردن To compromise. To agree to exchange.

مصائب [Pl. of مصیبت]

مَصبّ A. Mouth: مصبِ رود

مِصباح A. [مَصابیح] = چراغ

مُصحح A. Corrector. Proof-reader.

مُصحف (-haf) A. [مَصاحِف] Book; esp. the Koran.

مُصحف o (-sahaf) A. Misread or misspelled.

مُصحف (-sahef) A. One who misreads s. t.

مَصحوب o. A. Accompanied.

مِصداق A. Meaning; sense. Proof; evidence. Applicability. — بمصداقِ According to (the sense of).—م. پیدا کردن To prove applicable.

مَصدر *A.* [مَصادِر] Infinitive. *Mil.* Orderly. — مصادر امور The authorities (*or* high functionaries) of the State.— مصدرِ کار (One) appointed to some position.— اسم م. Verbal noun (having the nature of an infinitive). — وجه مصدری The i. mood.

مُصدّع *A.* Obtrusive; troublesome. — مصدعِ کسی شدن To inconvenience or trouble s. o.

مصدق (*mosadagh*) *A.* Certified.— رو نوشت م. C. or true copy.

مصدق (*mosadegh*) *A.* Arbitrator [داور]. *OS.* One who confirms or certifies.

مِصر (*mesr*) *A.* Egypt. *OS.* Large city [pl. اَمصار].

مُصرّ (*moser*) *A.* Insistent. Importunate. — در عقیده ای م. بودن To insist on, or hold to, an opinion.

مصراع *or* مصرع *A.* [مصاریع o] Hemistich.

مصرّانه *A. P.* Persistently; urgingly; importunately [also مصراً].

مُصرّح *A.* Stipulated; specified. [Fem. مصرحه with the pl. مصرحات 'stipulations'].

مَصرف *A.* Consumption; use. *Cf. the pl.* مصارف ‖ م. کردن *or* بمصرف رسانیدن To consume or use. To dispose of.

مصرفی *A. P.* Used; consumed. [*As a n.*] Consumption.

مَصروع *A.* Epileptic.

مَصروف *A.* Spent. Used. — م. داشتن To spend; use.

مِصری *A.* Egyptian. — روغن م. Balsam oil.

مصطبه o *A.* Stone bench or platform. Inn.

مُصطفوی *A.* Related to, or descended from مصطفی *q. v.*

مُصطفی (*-tafa*) *A. Mas. pr. name. OS.* Chosen: ep. of Mohammed.

مصطکی *A-G.* Mastic.

مُصطلح *A.* In common use. Idiomatic. [Fem. مصطلحه with the pl. مصطلحات Idioms; expressions in c. use]. — غیر مصطلح Not in common use; barbarous.

مُصعّد *A.* Sublimated.

مُصغّر *A.* Diminutive.

مُصفا [f. A. مصفی *mosafa*] Refined. Pleasant: باغِ م. ‖ م. کردن To make p. To refine.

مصقل *A.* Polishing-tool.

مُصلا [f. A. مصلی] Place for public prayer outside the town.

مُصلح *A. n.* Peacemaker; accommodator. Reformer. *—a.* Of a conciliating disposition.

مصلحانه *A. P. ad.* Peacefully. *—a.* Conciliatory.

مَصلحت *A.* Policy. Best thing

to do. Good purpose. Interest [usu. in the pl. مصالح]. Good intention. Affair [امر]. [Short for م. مقرون به] Advisable ; expedient. — م. دانستن or م. دیدن To think it advisable.

مصلحت آمیز *A. P.* Directed to a good purpose; justified by its motive. Politic; expedient. — م. دروغ Lie j. by its motive; also, pious fraud.

مصلحةً *A.* Conveniently. For some motive.

مصلحتی *A. P.* Based on convenience. — م. ازدواج Marriage of c. — کر مصلحتی Conveniently deaf.

مصلوب کردن *A. P.* To crucify ; *L.* to hang.

مصلی (*mosa*la) *S. u.* مصلا

مُصمت *A.* Consonant.

مُصمم *A.* Determined ; resolved. — م. شدن To determine; make up one's mind.

مُصنف *A.* [مصنفین] Author. Composer.

مَصنوع *A.* Manufactured; made. Created. [Fem. مصنوعه with the pl. مصنوعات Manufactures ; industrial products]. [ساختگی

مصنوعی *A. P.* Artificial. *Cf.*

مُصوّب *A.* Approved. [Fem. مصوبه with the pl. مصوبات sanctioned laws or regulations].

مُصوّت *A.* Vowel. *OS.* Causing (a consonant) to be sounded. [ted.

مُصوَّر (*-savar*) *A.* Illustra-

مُصوِّر (*-saver*) *A.* Portraitist. Painter. — م. خط Projection of a point.

مَصون *A.* Immune. Inviolable. — م. از خطا Infallible.

مصونیت *A.* Immunity. — مصونیت پارلمانی Privilege of Parliament.

مصیب ٥ *A.* = درست Just; right. *OS.* Hitting the mark.

مُصیبت *A.* [مصائب] Tragical event ; disaster ; calamity. Hardship; suffering.

مصیبت زده *A. P.* Afflicted ; overtaken by a calamity.

مَضارّ [Pl of مضرت]

مضارِب ٥ Bailee investor. Sleeping partner.

مُضاربه *A.* Bailment of a capital. Limited partnership.

مُضاعَف *A.* Doubled. Multiplied. [*Of a pump*] Double-acting. — م کردن To double. To multiply.

مُضاف *A.* Noun governing the genitive, as خواست in خواستِ خدا 'God's will'.

مضافاً *A.* In addition.

مضافات *A.* [Pl. of مضافه ٥ fem. of مضاف] Appurtenances ; additions. Appendages.

مضاف الیه (*-fon-elay-*h) *A.*

Noun in the genitive case.
مضامین [Pl. of مضمون]
مُضایقه A. (Act of) sparing. – از چیزی م. کردن To spare or withhold s. t. – از کردن کاری م. کردن To refuse to do s. t.
مَضبوط ○ A. Confiscated. Committed to memory. Kept (on file).
مُضحك A. Laughable; comic. Funny; ridiculous.
مَضحکه A. Laughing-stock.
مُضِرّ A. = زیان‌آور Harmful; injurious; noxious.
مِضراب A. Plectrum.
مَضرَب A. Multiple. – کوچکترین مضرب مشترك Least common m.
مَضرّت A. [مضرات & مضارّ] Noxiousness; harmful effect. *By e.* Disadvantage.
مَضروب A. 1) *a.* Beaten. Multiplied. 2) *n.* Multiplicand. B. person.
مَضروب فیه (-*bonfi*:h) A. Multiplier.
مُضطَرّ A. Reduced to extremity; rendered helpless.
مُضطرب A. Disturbed; agitated. – م. کردن To agitate; disturb.
مُضعِف A. Weakening *adj.*
مَضغ A. Mastication.
مُضغه ○ A. Lump of flesh. Foetus.
مُضِلّ A. Leading astray *adj.*
مُضمحل A. Overthrown. – م کردن To overthrow; overset.
مُضمر A. 1) = پنهان 2) Understood; implied.
مضمضه کردن A. P. To rinse the mouth with.
مَضمون A. 1) *a.* Guaranteed. 2) *n.* a) G. sum. b) Contents; subject-matter. c) = متلك Wisecrack; quib.[Pl. مَضامین] – م. کوك کردن × *See* متلك گفتن
مَضمون له (-*nonla*h) A. Person to whom a guaranty is made or given; guarantee.
مضمون عنه (-*non-an*h) A. Person on whose behalf a guarantee is made; principal.
مَضیقه A. Difficulty; distress; pinch. – از بی‌پولی در مضیقه هستم I am hard up (*or* pushed) for money.
مُطابق A. Conforming; conformable. Corresponding. – مطابقِ According to; conformably to. Similar to; like. – م. بودن با To conform to; be similar to. To correspond to. – رونوشت مطابقِ اصل است "True copy." – م. کردن To (cause to) conform. To compare.
مطابقت A. Conformity. Concordance. *Gr.* Agreement.
مطابقه [f. A. مطابقت] 1) Act of comparing. 2) = مطابقت ‖ م. کردن *vi.* To correspond; tally –*vt.* To compare or check.

مُطاع A. 1) a. Obeyed; also, worthy of obedience. 2) n. One who is (to be) obeyed.
مَطالب [Pl. of مطلب]
مُطالب A. = طلبکار or بستانکار
مُطالبات A. Claims; sums due to a person. Cf. the s. مطالبه
مُطالبه A. Claiming; demanding. — م کردن To claim or demand; also, dun.
مطالعات [Pl. of مطالعه]
مُطالعه A. [مطالعات] Study. Studying; perusal. Consideration. — اطاق م. Study. — م. کردن To study; peruse; consider.
مطامح [Pl. of مطمح]
مطامع [Pl. of مطمع]
مُطاوعت A. = بیروی & اطاعت
مطایبات [Pl. of مطایبه]
مُطایبه A. [مطایبات] Jest(ing); pleasantry; joke [شوخی].
مَطَبّ A. Doctor's "surgery" (or practice).
مَطبخ A. [مطابخ] = آشپزخانه
مَطبعه A. [مَطابع] = چاپخانه
مُطبِقَة A. Typhoid (fever).
مَطبوخ A. Cooked (food).
مَطبوع A. 1) a. Agreeable; pleasant. Printed. [Fem. مطبوعه] 2) n. P. matter.
مَطبوعات A. Publications; printed matter. The press. [Pl. of مطبوعه fem. of مطبوع]
مَطران A-G. Metropolitan.
مُطرب A. = خنیاگر Hired musician; minstrel.
مَطرح A. Under consideration; on the carpet; propounded. — م. کردن To set forth for discussion; propound.
مِطرَقی A. Dicrotic : نبض م
مطرود A. Rejected.
مطلا or مطلی (motala) A. Gilt. — م. کردن To gild.
مَطلب A. [مَطالب] Subject; s.-matter. Question; affair. Case. — مطلبی نیست It does not matter; it is a trifling m. — مطلب ویرا برآورد She granted his request.
مطلع (matla') A. [مطالع] Opening verse. (Place of) rising of the sun.○ — حسن م Beauty of exordium.
مطلع (motale') A. Informed; aware [آگاه]. Well-informed.— م. شدن To be informed; come to know. — م. کردن To inform. —n. pl. مطلعین Well-informed persons.
مُطلق A. Absolute. Unconditional. Independent. [Fem. مطلقه] — حکومت مطلقه A. or despotic rule. — عدد مطلق Abstract number.— قادر مطلق (The) Almighty.
مطلقاً A. Absolutely. Invariably.
مطلق العنان A. = خودسر
مطلقه A. (motalagheh) Divorced (woman).
مَطلوب A. Desired; desirable.

Sought (after) ; demanded. [Fem. مطلوبه]

مطلوبيت *A.* Desirability.

مطلی *S. u.* مطلا

مَطمح *A.* [مطامح] Place looked at [usu. مطمح نظر]. Object of desire.

مَطمع *A.* [مطامع] Thing coveted ; object of desire.

مُطمئن *A.* Assured; confident; certain. Secure; safe. —م. شدن To be assured ; persuade oneself. — م. ساختن To assure.

مطمئناً *A.* Certainly.

مُطوّل *A.* = دراز & مفصل

مُطهر *A.* Pure [پاك] ; holy [مقدس]. [Fem. مطهره].

مُطيب *A.* Perfumed o. [Fem. مطيبه : attribute of the holy city of Medinah].

مُطيع = فرمانبردار Obedient. — م. شدن To be reduced to obedience. To submit. — م. كردن To reduce to o. ; cause to obey ; subjugate.

مَظالم [Pl. of مظلمه] Oppressions. Grievances. — ديوان م. [*Obsolete*] Court for the hearing of grievances.

مظانّ *A. S. u.* مظنه

مظاهر [Pl. of مظهر]

مَظروف *A.* 1) *n*. Contents (of a vessel). — ذكر ظرف بجای م. Metonymy (consisting of the use of the container for the contained). 2) *a*. Packed.

مُظفر *A. a.* Victorious [پيروز]. —*n. Mas. pr. name.*

مظفريت *A.* = **پيروزی**

مُظلم *A.* 1) = تاريك 2) Gloomy. 3) Disastrous.

مَظلمه [f. A. مظلمت] [مظالم] = 1) ستم & ظلم 2) دادخواهی o

مَظلوم *A. a.* 1) Oppressed ; wronged . 2) + Meek ; submissive. —*n*. [Pl. مظلومين] One who is oppressed or w.; the underdog.

مظلومانه *A. P.* 1) *ad*. As one who is oppressed or wronged. 2) + *a*. Meekly.

مظلوميت *A.* State of one who is oppressed or wronged.

مَظنون *A.* 1) *a*. Suspected. 2) *n*. S. person ; suspect.

مَظنه *A.* Market-price ; p. ruling; p. quoted ; quotation. Conjecture . Place where anything is likely to be [pl. مظانّ]. — م. دادن To quote prices.— م. كردن + To obtain quotations , inquire about prices. — درمظان تهمت Exposed or liable to accusation.

مَظهر *A.* [مظاهر] Manifestation. Object of view.

مِعاء *A.* [امعاء] = **روده**

معابد [Pl. of معبد]

معابر [Pl. of معبر]

مَعاد *A.* Future life. Resurrection (day). *See* رستاخيز

مُعادِل *A.* Equivalent.

معادله *A.* [معادلات]. Equation. — معادلات درجه دوم Quadratics.

معادن [Pl. of معدن]

مَعاذَالله *A.* God forbid! Far from it! *See* نعوذبالله

معاذیر *S. u.* **معذرت**

مُعارِض *A.* Interrupter. Opponent. *S. a. under* تصرف ‖ م. شدن To interfere with; molest. To oppose.

معارضه *A.* [معارضات] Opposition. Contention; dispute. — م. کردن To oppose (each other.)

مَعارِف *A.* Learnings o. Education. *Cf. the s.* معرفت

معارف‌پرور *A.P.* 1) *a.* Fostering education. 2) *n.* Patron of e.

مُعارفه *A.* (Ceremonial) introduction of persons to each other. — م. مجلس Party given for this purpose.

مَعاریف *A.* Famous persons. [Pl. of معروف which is used only as an adj.]

مَعاش *A.* Livelihood; subsistence; living. — مدد معاش L. allowance; subsidy.

مُعاشر *A. n.* Companion; associate. —*a.* Sociable.

مُعاشرت *A.* Association; society; company; social (*or* enjoyable) intercourse. — م. کردن To associate; keep c. — م. حسن Sociability. — قابل م. Sociable; companionable.

مُعاشقه *A.* Making love to each other.

مُعاصر *A.* Contemporary; contemporaneous.

معاصی [Pl. of معصیت]

معاضد o *A.* Assistant; aid.

معاضدت *A.* Mutual aid or assistance; cooperation.

مَعاف *A.* = بخشوده Exempt. Excused. — م. کردن To exempt or excuse. To dismiss.

معافیت *A.* Exemption.

مع‌التاسف *A.* = متاسفانه

مُعالج *A.* 1) *a.* Treating. — پزشك م. Treating physician; p. in attendance. 2) o *n.* = پزشك معالج

معالجه *A.* [معالجات] Medical treatment. — م. کردن To treat; give medical treatment to; also, cure.

معالجه پذیر *A. P.* = درمان پذیر

معالجه ناپذیر *A. P.* = درمان ناپذیر

مع‌الوصف *A.* = باوجوداین Nevertheless.

مُعامل *A.* One who transacts business with another.

معاملات [Pl. of معامله]

مُعامله *A.* [معاملات] Transaction. Dealing; treatment. — معاملهٔ معاملهٔ بمثل *S. u.* متقابل ‖ با متقابله *S.u.* مثل ‖ م. کردن کسی کردن To transact; do business; negotiate. To deal. To trade in for. *Cf.* فروختن

معاند A. 1) Obstinate (person). 2) = دشمن [دشمنی

معاندت A. 1) Obstinacy. 2) =

معانقه A. Hugging or embracing (each other).

معانی A. Meanings. Semantics. F. Graces. *See the s.* معنی ‖ م. و بیان Rhetoric. [برگشت

معاودت A. Return(ing). *Cf.*

معاوضه A. [معاوضات] Exchange.- (با هم) م. کردن To exchange with each other.

معاون A. Assistant. A. director (*or* chief). [Of a ministry] Under-secretary. - معاون جرم Accessory to a crime

معاونت A. (Mutual) assistance. *Cf.* کمک ‖ Office of an assistant or under-secretary. - معاونت عمومی Public relief. - م. کردن To assist or help (each other).

معاهده A. [معاهدات] = پیمان Treaty; pact. - م. بستن To conclude a treaty.

معایب A. = عیوب Defects; faults. [Pl. of معابه o].

معاینه A. [معاینات] Examination; inspection. - م. کردن To examine (medically). To inspect.

معبد A. [معابد] Place of worship [پرستشگاه]. Temple.

معبر (*ma'bar*) A. [معابر] = گذرگاه Passage; thoroughfare. Ford. Road o. [of dreams.

معبر (*mo-aber*) A. Interpreter

معبود A. Object of worship; deity. *OS.* Worshipped.

معتاد A. Addicted. Accustomed. - بچیزی م. شدن To be accustomed, addicted, or given (over) to, s. t.; get the habit of it.

معتبر A. Creditable; of good standing. Authentic; reliable. Valid; good. Considerable; great +.

معتدل A. Temperate; moderate. [Fem. معتدله. Ex. منطقهٔ معتدلهٔ شمالی North T. Zone].

معتدلانه A. P. Moderately.

معتذر o A. One who excuses himself; apologizer.

معترض A. Objector; protester. Opposer. - بچیزی م. بودن To object to s. t.; oppose it.

معترضه A. 1) *Fem. of* معترض ‖ 2) Coming in or between; parenthetical : جملهٔ م.

معترف A. (One) who confesses or acknowledges. - بچیزی م. بودن To confess s. t.

معتزل A. Schismatic(al).

معتصم o A. Holding fast. Abstaining from sin.

معتضد o A. P. Who seeks به: assistance from.

معتقد (*mo'taghed*) A. *a.* Believing. *—n.* Believer. - بچیزی م. بودن To believe in s. t.- من معتقدم (به این) که I b. that; I am convinced that.

معتقد (*mo'taghad*) A. Believed. Persuaded [Fem. معتقده with the pl. معتقدات Beliefs; articles of faith].

معتکف *A*. (Person) retiring for prayer.

مُعتمد *A*. *a*. Reliable; trustworthy. —*n*. *pl*. معتمدین R. persons.

معتنی به (-*nabeh*) *or* مُعتنابه *A*. Considerable: یك مبلغ م.

مُعجب *A*. = خودبین

مُعجز *A*. *a*. Rendering unable; disabling. —*n*. Miracle.

معجزآسا *A*. *P*. Miraculous.

معجزه *A*. [معجزات] Miracle. [Orig. fem. of معجز]. م. کردن— To perform (*or* do) a m.

معجل *A*. Hurried. — مَهر معجل Marriage-portion payable at any time after marriage; prompt dower.

معجلاً *A*. Hurriedly.

مُعجم o *A*. Dotted, as a letter. [Fem. معجمه].

مَعجون *A*. Electuary.

مُعدّ o *A*. = مستعد - آماده

مُعدّل *A*. Adjuster; rectifier. Average (mark).

مَعدلت *A*. = عدالت

مَعدن *A*. [معادن] Mine [کان]. Ore; mineral.—معدن زغال سنگ Coal-mine; coal-pit.—معدن‌سنگ Quarry. — معدن نمك Salt-pit; salt-mine; s.-marsh.

معدنچی *A*. *T*. Miner.

معدن شناس *A*. *P*. Mineralogist.

معدن شناسی *A*. *P*. Mineralogy

معدنی *A*. *P*. Mineral.

مَعدود *A*. Computed. Limited; few. — معدودی از آنها A few of them.

مَعدوم *A*. Non-existent. Lost. — م. شدن To be annihilated. To disappear. — م. کردن To annihilate. To destroy.

مِعده *A*. Stomach.

معده بین *or* معده نما *A*. *P*. Gastroscope.

مِعدی *A*. Gastric; stomachic.

مُعذّب *A*. Tormented o. Inconvenienced; uneasy. — م. داشتن To inconvenience.

مَعذرت *A*. [مَعاذِر —also معاذیر which is the pl. of مِعذار o]. Apology, excuse. *Cf*. پوزش & عذر ‖ م. خواستن To apologize. —م. میخواهم = ببخشید I beg your pardon. [theless.

معذلك (*ma'zalek*) *A*. Never-

مَعذور *A*. Excused. — م. داشتن To excuse. — از رفتن معذورم I (am sorry I) cannot go.

مِعراج *A*. Ascension (to heaven).

معرّب *A*. Arabicized (form of a word).

مَعرض *A*. Place of exposure.— در معرض Exposed to.

مُعرّف *A*. Introducer. Recommender. *Chem*. Reagent. — معرف مایه *Mus*. Keynote.

مَعرفت *A* Knowledge [دانش] Acquaintance. Insight. Wisdom.

Cf. the pl. معارف

معرفت‌الارض *A.* = زمین شناسی

مُعرّفی *A. P.* Introduction; presentation. *Chem.* Reaction. — م. کردن To introduce; present. — فوراً خودتان‌را بمن م. کنید Report to me at once.

معرفی نامه *A. P.* Letter of introduction.

معرّق *A.* Sudorific; diaphoretic.

مَعرکه *A.* 1) = میدان جنگ 2) = جنگ 3) Open space where jugglers display their art. 4) + *a*) Row; quarrel. *b*) A prodigy of . . . Ex. در ویولن م. است He is a p. violinist. — م. میکند He does it wonderfully well.

مَعروض *A.* Presented; offered. — م. داشتن [In p. c.] To say; state. *See* عرض کردن & گفتن ‖ عریضه ای م. داشت He submitted a petition. — محترماً م. میدارد I have the honour to state.

مَعروف *A.* Famous. *Cf.* معاریف ‖ م. به پرخوری Notorious for gluttony. — م. به روحی Known as *Ruhi*.

معروفه *A.* Public (woman). [Orig. fem. of معروف].

معروفیت *A.* Fame.

مُعزّز *A.* Honoured. Dearly esteemed.

مَعزول *A.* Deposed; dismissed or removed from office. — م. کردن To depose; dismiss. To discharge, as an attorney.

مُعزّی‌الیه *A.* [Polite substitute for او] He. [Fem. معزی الیها She].

مُعسر *A.* Insolvent.

مَعشر o *A.* Assembly; crowd.

مَعشوق *A.* Man who is loved by a woman. *Cf.* معشوقه

معشوقه *A.* [Fem. of معشوق] Sweetheart; lady-love.

مِعصره *A.* (*Anat.*) Sinus.

مَعصوم *A.* Innocent; immaculate; chaste; impeccable.

معصومه *A.* *Fem. pr. name.* *OS.* Innocent (*or* impeccable) woman. [Fem. of معصوم]

معصومیت *A.* Innocence. Impeccability.

مَعصیت *A.* [معاصی] = **گناه**

مُعضل *A.* Difficult. Intricate. [Fem. معضله with the pl. **معضلات** Intricate questions. Difficulties].

معطر *A.* Fragrant; perfumed; sweet-smelling. — م. کردن To perfume.

مُعطل *A.* Kept waiting. Detained. — م. شدن To be kept w. To be detained. — م. کردن *vt.* To keep w.; detain. —*vi.* To linger or delay. — م. ماندن To be at a loss (as to what course one should pursue). To be pinched for money.

معطلی *A. P.* Delay ; retardation. Datainment. Cause for delay. — بدون م. Promptly. — کرایهٔ م. Demurrage.

مَعطوف *A.* Inclined. — م. داشتن To turn; draw : خاطر عالی را معطوف میدارد I beg to d. your attention.

معطوفاً به *A. P.* Adverting to; with reference to.

معظم (*mo'zam*) *A.* — بزرگ Great ; large; considerable. [Fem. معظمه]

معظم (*mo-azam*) *A.* Honourable or honoured ; dignified; great [بزرگ]. [Fem. معظمه] — دول معظمه The great powers.

معظم‌له (*mo-azamonlah*) *A.* He [Used as a substitute for او for men of high position].

معفو (*ma'fov*) *A.* Pardoned ; excused. — م. داشتن = بخشیدن

معقود ○ *A.* Concluded. Tied.

معقوده *A.* 1) [Fem. of معقود] 2) ○ Married, as a woman.

مَعقول *A.* [Fem. معقوله] Rational ; reasonable. Contemplative : علوم معقوله ‖ Polite+.

معقولات *A.* Rational ideas. [Pl. of معقوله fem. of معقول]

مَعکوس *A. a.* Reversed. Inverted. Contrary. —*n.* Reverse. Reciprocal. — ترقی م. Retrogradation; retrogression.

معکوساً *A.* Inversely.

معلا *S. u.* معلی

مُعلق *A.* 1) *a.* Hanging ; suspended. *F.* Undecided. Conditional. — بین زمین و آسمان م. On tenter-hooks; in a state of suspense or anxiety. — م کردن To suspend (from service). 2) *n.* Somersault.— م. زدن To turn a s.

معلقی *A. P.* Sudden or unexpected : اجل م.

مُعلم *A.* [معلمین] = آموزگار Teacher. [Fem. معلمه School-mistress or governess (pl. معلمات)]

معلمی *A. P.* Teaching. — م. کردن To teach ; be a teacher.

مَعلول *A. n.* Effect. — علت و معلول Cause and effect. — معلولِ Caused by; due to.

مَعلوم *A.* Known. Evident; obvious; clear. — بنای م. Active voice. — م. نیست It is not certain. Nobody knows ; one can't tell. — از قرار معلوم Evidently. We understand (that) . — م. شد از آن آگاه است It was revealed that he knew it ; he proved to be aware of it. — م. کردن To make known. To ascertain or fix. To prove.

معلومات *A.* Qualifications ; knowledge. [Pl. of معلومه ○ fem. of معلوم]

معلی (*mo-ala*) *A. or* معلا Exalted : ep. of کربلا

مُعما *A.* = چیستان Riddle; puzzle. *L.* Problem. — م. را حل کرد He guessed the riddle.

معمارِ *A.* Architect.

معمارساز + *A. P.* Jerry-built.

معماری *A. P.* Architecture.

مُعمر *A.* Aged. Longeval.

مُعمم *A.* Wearing a turban.

مَعمور *A.* [Fem. معموره] = آباد

مَعمول *A. a.* Usual; customary. [Fem. معموله]. —*n.* Usage custom. — مطابق م. As usual.— م. داشتن (1 = م. کردن (2 To do; effect. — م. کردن To intro-duce. To put into practice.

مَعمولاً *A.* Usually; ordinarily.

معمول به (*-lonbeh*) *A.* Prac-tice; usage.

معمولی *A. P.* Ordinary; usual. Commonplace.

معنا *See Note under* معنی

مَعناً *A.* Virtually.

معنبر ○ *A.* Perfumed with ambergris (عنبر) .

معنعن *A.* Descended by suc-cessive hearsay. *See* عنعنات

مَعنوی *A.* Intellectual. Moral. Spiritual. Contemplative. Ideal(istic). [Fem. معنویه].

معنویت *A.* Intellectuality. Spirituality. Ideality.

مَعنی *A.* Meaning; sense. Spirit. Reality. *Cf. the pl.* معانی ‖ م. کردن To explain. To define. *L.* to translate or interpret — م. ندارد It has no meaning. It is nonsense. The idea ! [In this sense also چه م. دارد]. — بدین م. که That is to say; thus. To the effect that.— بمعنیِ به + ور نداشتن To take in good part . — بتمام م. Par excellence ; in the fullest sense of the word ; with a vengeance.—درمعنی In reality; virtually . —*Note.* معنی is also spelled معنا esp. in such cases as معنای این کلمه 'the meaning of this word'.

مُعوّج *A.* = کج

مُعوّض *A.* Replaced. [Only in صلح م. Gift made for a consideration].

مُعوّق *A.* Delayed. Postponed. Outstanding. Delinquent . [Fem معوقه]. — م. گذاردن To delay ; postpone. — م. ماندن To be delayed. To fall into arrears.

مَعهذا (*-ha-*) *A.* = با وجود این

مَعهود *A.* Promised ; agreed. Usual; customary. — بعادت م. As usual.

معیارِ *A.* Standard; criterion.

مَعیت *A.* Company. —بمعیتِ In company with [با *or* همراهِ].

مَعیشت *A.* Livelihood; living. Means of livelihood.

مُعیل *A.* Encumbered by a (numerous) family.

معین (*mo-i:n*) *A.* Assistant.

Adjutant. – فعل م. Auxiliary verb. – معین فعل Adverb (modifying a verb).

معین (*mo-ayan*) *A*. 1) *a*. Fixed; specified. Certain. Given. [Fem. معینه]. – م. کردن To fix; specify. To appoint – غیرِ معین Undetermined; uncertain. 2) *n*. Rhomb; lozenge. – شبه م. Rhomboid.

معین‌التجاری *A. P.* [For گُلِ م.] Dwarf rose-bay; rhododendron.

مَعیوب *A*. Defective; faulty. Damaged; injured.

مُغ Magician; fire-worshipper. Tavern-keeper *.

مُغار or **مقار** (?) Gouge.

مَغاره *A*. Cave. Den.

مغاری *A*. Cavernous.

مُغازله *A*. Reciting amorous verses to each other.

مَغازه Store; shop. [f. Fr. *magasin* f. A. مخزن]

مَغاك Pit. Abyss. *Met*. Grave.

مغاکی Abyssal.

مُغالطه *A*. Sophistry; chicanery. – م. کردن To sophisticate; reason fallaciously.

مُغایر *A*. Contrary; adverse. Inconsistent. – مغایرِ I. with; contrary to.

مغایرت *A*. Contradiction; disagreement. – م. داشتن [With با] To be contrary to; be inconsistent with.

مُغبچه * Young tavern-keeper. *OS*. Y. magician. *See* مغ

مَغبون *A*. Cheated (in business). – م. کردن To cheat.

مَغبونیت *A*. State of being cheated. – م. دارم I am c.

مُغتنم *A*. Regarded as a booty. *Met*. Valued. – م. شمردن = غنیمت شمردن

مُغذّی *A*. Nutritive.

مَغرب *A*. = باختر West. – درمغربِ On the west of.

مغربی *A. P.* = **باختری**

مُغرض *A. a*. Self-interested; having a private motive. Spiteful. –*n*. Self-interested person. [Pl. مغرضین].

مغرضانه *A.P.* From self-interest; with a private motive.

مَغرور *A*. Proud; haughty. Deluded. – م. شدن To be deluded. To become proud or h. – م. کردن To elate; make p.

مغز Pith. Pulp. Brain [مخ]. – مغز قلم or مغز استخوان Marrow. – مغز بادام Shelled almond. – مغز حرام or مغز تیره Spinal cord. – مغز نان Crumb. – مغزِ هسته Kernel. – م. بستن To k.; ripen into, or produce, kernels. – م. کردن To shell; peel. – مغز خر خورده است He is a perfect ass. – مغز مرا برد He talked my head off.

مغز پرده Pia mater [نرم شامه].

مغزِ پسته‌ای Yellowish-green.
مغزدار Pithy. Marrowy. Pulpy. Kernelled.
مَغزی 1) *n*. Nipple ; also, adapter. [In a shoe] Welt ; also, piping. 2) *a*. Cerebral.
مَغشوش *A*. Disorderly; confused. Falsified. Aberrant.— م. کردن To confuse ; confound . To disorder . To adulterate.
مَغضوب *A*. Disfavoured; blacklisted ; in one's black list.
مِغفر o *A*. (Head covering worn under the) helmet.
مَغفرت *A*. = بخشش & آمرزش
مَغفور *A*. Forgiven [بخشیده]. — مرحومِ مغفورِ نصیری The late *Nassiri* of blessed memory.
مَغفول *A*. Neglected. [Fem. مغفوله]. — ضمیرِ *or* حافظه مغفوله مغفول The unconscious.
مَغلطه *A*. Misleading question. Sophistical statement.— م. کردن To confuse different subjects. To sophisticate.
مُغلق *A*. Abstruse.
مُغلم o *A*. = 1) شهوت انگیز 2) بچه باز
مَغلوب *A*. Overcome ; defeated. [Fem o مغلوبه] — م. کردن = شکست دادن ‖ جنگ مغلوبه بود It was the thick of the fight
مغلوبیت *A*. Defeat.
مَغلوط *A*. Wrong; erroneous. Containing mistakes ; foul.
مغموم *A*. = غمگین
مغناطیس *A-G*. Magnet.
مغناطیسی *A-P*. Magnetic.
مُغنّی *A*. Singer. *By e*. Musical performer. [*Fem*. مغنیه female singer; cantatrice].
مغول Mogul (tribe).
مغولستان Mongolia.
مغولی Mogul.
مغیث o *A*. (One) who helps.
مغیلان *A*. Kind of thorny bush.
مُف Snot.
مفاتیح [Pl. of مفتاح]
مُفاجات *A*. Unexpected attack.— مرگِ م. Sudden death.
مفاخر [Pl. of مفخرت]
مُفاخرت *A*. Priding oneself; self - glorying. — م. کردن To pride oneself; glory.
مُفاد *A*. Purport; substance.
مُفارقت *A*. = جدائی Separation. Parting with each other. — م. کردن از To separate from ; part with.
مفاسد [Pl of مفسده]
مُفاصا *A* Clearance; release; certificate of liquidation.
مفاصل [Pl. of مَفصل]
مفاهیم [Pl. of مفهوم]
مُفاوضه *A*. [مفاوضات] Conversation ; table-talk ; exchange of views.
مُفت *ad*. Gratis ; free of cost. —*a*. Gratuitous. *By e*. Dirt-cheap. — جان م. بدر بردن To have a narrow escape.— حرفِ م.

Nonsense. Bad language. - (به) م. هم نمی‌ارزد I would not have it at a gift. - م. از دست دادن To lose unluckily; give away for no good cause. - م. جستن To have a narrow escape. To go scot-free. - مفت شما + So much the better for you. - م. و مسلم + For nothing. Dirt-cheap.

مفتاح A. [مفاتیح] = کلید

مُفتّح A. (*Med*). Deobstruent.

مفتح‌الابواب A. The opener of doors : ep. of God

مُفتخَر (-*takhar*) A. Honoured.

مُفتخِر (-*takher*) A. Proud. *S. a. the preceding entry.*

مفتخراً A. Honourably.

مُفت‌خور *a.* Parasitic; parasitical. —*n*. Parasite; sponger.

مفت‌خوری Sponging on others; parasitic life.

مُفتری A. = افترا زننده Calumniator; slanderer.

مُفتش A. [مفتشین] Inspector [بازرس]. Detector [کارآگاه].

مُفتضح A. = رسوا Disgraced.- م. کردن To disgrace.

مفتقر ○ A. = نیازمند

مُفتن A. 1) *a*. Seditious. 2) *n*. S. person; mischief-maker.

مَفتوح A. Open(ed). Conquered.

مَفتول A. Wire (staple). - ماشینِ مفتول‌دوزی Stapling machine; stapler.

مَفتون A. Fascinated. - م. شدن To be fascinated. - م. کردن To fascinate ; charm.

مُفتی A. Mufti: expounder of the (Mohammedan) law.

مفتی C. E. = مفت

مفخر A. = مفخرت

مَفخرت A. [مفاخر] (Object or cause of) glory or honour.

مُفخم A. Glorious; great.

مَفرّ A. Refuge. *OS*. Place to escape to [گریزگاه].

مُفرّح A. Exhilarating ; refreshing. Enlivening.

مُفرد A. Singular. Single. Simple. [Fem. مفرده with the pl مفردات Simple substances. Elements. S. distichs].

مَفرش A. Travelling-bag.

مُفرط A. Excessive.

مفرغ A. Admiralty-metal.

مَفروز A. Divided. Partitioned. - م. کردن = افراز کردن

مَفروش A. Covered with carpets. Spread, as a carpet.

مَفروض A. Supposed. Given; granted. [Fem. مفروضه with the pl. مفروضات Things granted or supposed; data].

مَفروغ A. Liquidated ; settled. - م. کردن To liquidate.

مفروق A. Subtrahend.

مَفروق منه (-*ghon-menh*) A. Minuend.

مُفسد A. Seditious (person).

مَفسده A. [مفاسد] Mischief. Evil.

مفسده جو A. P. = مفسد

مُفسر A. [مفسرین] Commentator. Exegetist.
مَفصل A [مفاصل] Joint [بند]. — مفصل خرگوشی Hock; gambrel. — مفصل غیرمتحرك Synarthrosis. — مفصل متحرك Diarthrosis. — بادِ مفاصل + Articular rheumatism.
مُفصّل (-fasal) A. a. Detailed; lengthy. —ad. + = مفصلاً
مفصلاً A. In detail; at (full) length; fully. [jointed.
مَفصل‌دار A. P. Articulate;
مفصلةالاسامی (mofasalatol-asami:) A Mentioned or named (above or below).
مَفصلی A. P. Articular.
مُفضض A. Coated with silver; electroplated. — م. کردن To electroplate [آب نقره دادن].
مَفعول A. Object (of a verb). — اسم م. Passive participial adjective used as a noun.
مفعولی A. P. (Gr.) Objective. — حالت مفعولیت Objective case.
مَفقود A. [Fem. مفقوده] Lost or missing. = گمشده ‖ م. شدن = گم شدن ‖ م. کردن = گم کردن
مفقودالاثر A. Missing; untraceable. [ورشکسته
مُفلس A. 1) Indigent. 2) =
مفلوج A. = فالج
مَفلوك A. = فلك‌زده
مُفنگی × Weakly or sickly; soft; timorous of pain; also, raw-boned. [over.
مُفوّض A. Entrusted; turned

مَفهوم A. 1) n. [Pl. مفاهیم] Purport; sense; tenor. Concept. — مفهوم ما اینست که It is our understanding that. 2) a. Intelligible.
مُفید A. Useful [سودمند]. — م واقع شدن To (prove to) be useful. — مفید معنی Conveying a sense.
مفیدیت A. = سودمندی
مقابر [Pl. of مقبره]
مُقابل A. a. Opposite [روبرو]. Corresponding. Equivalent. —n. E. amount. — مقابلِ Opposite (to); vis-à-vis. C. to. — درمقابلِ Opposite. Against. Versus. — سه م. Thrice as much (or as many). — م. شدن با To encounter; confront.
مقابله A. Comparison; collation; checking; verifying. — م. کردن To compare; collate; check. To confront. — جبر و مقابله Algebra.
مُقاتله o A. Killing, or fighting with, each other.
مقادیر [Pl. of مقدار].
مُقاربت A. Sexual intercourse. — م. کردن To have s. i.; lie.
مقاربتی A. P. Venereal: مرض م.
مُقارن A. Simultaneous. Near. Connected. — مقارنِ ظهر About noon. — مقارن این احوال About this time.
مقاصد [Pl. of مقصد]
مقاطع [Pl. of مَقطع]
مُقاطعه A. Contract — م. کردن

To c. (for). (به) م. دادن – To put out to c.; award to a contractor. [Contractor.

مقاطعه کار A. P. = پیمانکار

مقاطعه کاری A. P. Contract work.

مَقال A. = گفتار - گفتگو - بحث

مَقاله A. [مقالات] Article. Essay. Discourse.

مَقام A. Place; position; office. *Mus.* Tune or mode.

مَقامات A. [Pl. of مقام or مقامه] Positions. Modes or tunes. – مقامات صلاحیت دار Competent authorities.

مُقامر ○A. Gambler.

مُقاوِله A. = گفتگو. S. a. مقاوله نامه

مقاوله نامه A. P. Written agreement; protocol.

مُقاومت A. Resistance. – م. کردن با To resist. To oppose.

مُقایسه A. Comparison – م. کردن To compare.

مَقبره A. [مقابر] = 1) گورستان 2) قبر or گور [مساجد]

مُقبل A. 1) Fortunate. 2) –

مَقبول A. Accepted. Granted, as a prayer. Pretty +. – م. افتادن or م. واقع شدن To be accepted or heard.

مُقتبس A. Extracted; borrowed; excerpted.

مُقتدا [f. A. مقتدی -tada] *a.* Imitated; followed. —*n.* Leader.

مقتدر A. = قادر & توانا

مقتدرانه A. P. Powerfully.

مقترح ○ A. Improvisator.

مقترن ○ A. Associated; united.

مقتصد A. Economical; thrifty.

مقتضا [f. A. مُقتضی -za] Exigency; necessity. [Pl. مُقتضیات Circumstances. Exigencies].

مُقتضی A. Appropriate. Advisable. Fit. – م. دانستن To think fit; deem advisable.

مقتضیات S. u. مقتضا

مَقتول A. [مقتولین] Killed (person). – م. شدن To be killed. – م. ساختن = کشتن To kill.

مِقدار A. [مقادیر] 1) Quantity; amount; also, number. – مقدار کمی آرد A small quantity of flour. – یك م. کتاب A n. of books. – بمقادیر زیاد In large quantities. – بر آورد کنندهٔ مقادیر Q. surveyor. 2) *F.* • Worth; value.

مقداری A. P. Quantitative.

مُقدّر A. Destined. *Gr.* Understood; implied. – م. کردن To predestinate. – وارث م. Heir presumptive.

مقدرات A. Destinies. Divine decrees. [Pl. of مقدره fem. of مقدر].

مَقدَس A. Holy place.

مُقدس (-*ghadas*) A. [Fem. مقدسه] Holy. – کتاب م. Bible.

مقدسات A. All that is sacred. [Pl. of مقدسه fem. of مقدس]. – بی احترامی به م. Profanity.

مَقدَم A. Arrival. – خیر مقدم Address of welcome.

مُقدّم A. *a.* 1) Prior. – م. بر P. to.

مُقرّر A. Prescribed; specified; laid down; enjoined. Appointed; arranged; agreed (upon). Regular. [Fem. مقرره]. م. داشتن ـ To prescribe, ordain. To appoint; fix. To arrange. To resolve.

2) Preferred : م. داشتن ‖ سهام م. To give priority (to). To prefer. —n. Antecedent.

مقدمات A. Preliminaries; first steps. Elements. Cf. the s. مقدمه

مقدماتی A. P. Preliminary.

مقدم‌السفراء (moghadamosofara') A. Doyen.

مُقدمه A. [Orig. fem. of مقدم]. Introduction; preface. Preamble. Premiss. Cf. the pl. مقدمات ‖ م. چیدن To set forth an introductory statement serving as an excuse; build up a case or argument.

مقدمةً A. First of all; before everything else.

مقدمةالجیش A. (Mil.) = جلودار

مَقدور A. a. Possible; within one's power.ـ برای‌من م. نیست که I am not in a position to... —n. What is in one's power; ability.

مقدونی A. Macedonian.

مقرّ (maghar) A. Domicile; residence. Seat.

مقرّ (mogher) A. (One) who confesses. ـ م. آمدن To be reduced to confession. ـ م. شدن (به) To confess.

مِقراض A. Scissors [قیچی].ـ یك م. A pair of scissors.

مُقرّب A. Admitted to be near F. Favourite; esteemed.

مقرح A. Epispastic.

مُقررات A. Provisions; requirements; dispositions; regulation(s). [Pl. of مقرره fem. of مقرر].

مقرراتی A. P. Adhering to hard and fast rules; also, advocating red-tapism.

مُقرری A. P. Regular salary or pension.

مُقرنس A. Vaulted or arched (building). (Place) decorated with paintings.

مَقروض A. Having a (specified amount of) debt; indebted. Cf. بدهکار ‖ ده ریال بمن م. است He owes me 10 Rials. ـ م. شدن To run into a debt; contract a d.

مَقرون A. Connected. Allied.ـ م. بحقیقت True. ـ م. بصرفه Economical.

مَقرّه A. Insulator.

مَقسم A. Place of partition. ـ مقسم آب Divide or watershed.

مُقسم (.ghasem) A. Divider; distributor.

مَقسوم A. a. Distributed. Apportioned (by Fate). —n. (Arith.) Dividend [بخشی].

مَقسوم علیه (-mon-alayh) A.

Divisor [بخش یاب].
مُقشّر A. Hulled; shelled.
مَقصد A. [مقاصد] 1) Destination. F. Aim. 2) + = مقصود
مُقصّر A. Guilty (person); culpable (p.). — مقصرین سیاسی State criminals.
مَقصود A. Purpose; intention. Aim; object (of desire). Moral. — م. از این کلمه چیست What is meant by this word?— مقصودم اینست که I mean. . . . — مقصودی ندارم I don't m. it. I have no particular motive.
مَقضی‌المرام A. = کامیاب
مُقطّر A. Distilled.
مَقطع (-ta') A. [مقاطع] Section. Closing verse of a poem. — مقطع طولی Longitudinal section; profile.— حسن م. Beauty of peroration.
مقطع (moghata') A. Interrupted. Separate(d). OS. Cut to pieces. [Fem. مقطعه].
مُقطّعات A. Fragments. [Pl. of مقطعه fem. of مُقطع].
مَقطعی A. P. Showing the section. — نقشهٔ م Profile.
مَقطوع A. Cut off. Interrupted. Fixed, as a price.
مقطوعاً A. As a fixed sum. At a f. price. — صد ریال م. A f. sum of 100 *rials*.
مَقعد A. = کون Anus.
مُقعّر A. Concave [کاو].
مقعرالطرفین A. Biconcave; concavo-concave.
مُقفل A. Locked. [rimed.
مُقفّی A. or مقفا Rhymed or
مُقل A. Bdellium.
مقلد A. 1) Imitator; mimic. F. Follower. 2) Buffoon.
مَقلوب A. *a*. Inverted; reversed. —*n*. Anagram. [چشم
مُقله A. = تخم چشم *q. v. under*
مقناطیس A-G. Magnet.
مقناطیسی A. P. Magnetic.
مُقنع A. Convincing.
مِقنعه o A. = چادر Veil.
مُقنن A. 1) *n*. Legislator. 2) *a*. Legislative. [Fem. مقننه . Ex. قوهٔ م. The L. Power].
مقنی A. = چاه‌کن
مُقوّا or مقوی (-ghava) A. Cardboard or pasteboard.
مُقوّائی A. P. Of cardboard or pasteboard. F. + Flimsy.— جعبهٔ م. Carton; bandbox.
مقوّس A. Arched. [Topic.
مقوله A. [مقولات] Category.
مُقوّم A. = ارزیاب
مُقوّی A. Strengthening; fortifying; tonic. [Fem. مُقوّیه]
مَقهور A. Subdued. — م. کردن or م. ساختن To subdue or vanquish.
مُقی A. = قی‌آور Emetic.
مِقیاس A. Scale. — بمقیاس یك اینچ در یك میل On a scale of one inch to the mile.
مُقیّد A. Tied. F. Bound. Stipulated. Particular.— عددِ مقید

Concrete number.
مُقیم *A*. Resident; residing: مقیم ایران r. in Iran; resident of I. — م. بودن To reside.
مِك [Imp. of مکیدن]. — مك زدن To suck. To twinge slightly.
مُك × Neither more nor less.
مُکابره *A*. Contention. — م. کردن To contend or dispute (saucily).
مکاتب [Pl. of مکتب]
مُکاتبه *A*. Correspondence; communicating with each other by letters. [Pl. **مکاتبات** Correspondence]. — م. کردن To correspond.
مکاتیب [Pl. of مکتوب]
مکار *A*. [Fem. مکاره] Deceitful. Also, sly.
مکارم [Pl. of مکرمت]
مکاره *R*. Makariev. — بازار مکاره Fair.
مُکاری *A*. Common carrier.
مَکاسب *A*. Earnings; acquisitions. [Pl. of مکسب ٥]
مُکاشفه [f. A. مکاشفت]. Revelation. Divine presence. Spiritual contemplation. [Pl. مکاشفات]. [liation.
مکافات *A*. Retribution; reta-
مُکافی *A*. Parabolic. — قطع م. P. section; parabola. — شبه قطع م. Paraboloid.
مُکالمه *A*. [مکالمات] = گفتگو Conversation; dialogue. — م. کردن To converse.

مَکان *A*. [امکنه & اماکن] = جا Place; locality. Dwelling. — مکان هندسی *Geom*. Locus.
مکانی *A*. (*Geom*) Local.
مِکانیزه *Fr*. Mechanized. — م. کردن To mechanize.
مکانیك *Fr*. 1) Mechanics. 2) + Mechanic.
مکانیك‌دان *Fr*. *P*. Mechanic.
مکانیکی *Fr*. *P*. Mechanical. — آدم م: 1) Robot. 2) Automaton.
مَکائد *A*. [Pl. of مکیده ٥] Deceits. Snares.
مُکِبّ ٥ *A*. Prostrating. Humiliating. [Fem. مکبه]. — عضلهٔ مکبه Pronator.
مَکتب *A*. [مکاتب] Old-fashioned primary school. *By e*. School.
مکتب‌گریز ٥ *A*. *P*. Truant.
مکتسب ٥ *A*. Acquired.
مَکتوب *A*. [مکاتیب] Letter [نامه]. *OS*. Written [نوشته].
مکتوم *A*. = پوشیده & پنهان
مَکث *A*. Pause. Halt(ing). — م. کردن To make a p. To stay.
مَکتَف *A*. Waste basket
مُکدَّر *A*. Offended. — از کسی م. شدن To take offence at s. o. — م. کردن To offend.
مَکر *A*. Trick. Deceit.
مکرآمیز *A*. *P*. Deceitful.
مُکرَّر *A*. Repeated. — م. کردن To repeat [Fem. مکرره with the pl **مکررات** Repetitions].

مکرراً *A.* Repeatedly ; also, again [دوباره].

مُکرَّم *A.* [Fem. مکرمه] Honoured; honourable.

مَکرمت *A.* [مکارم] Generosity. Greatness; noble act. — مکارمِ اخلاق Good morals.

مَکروه *A.* Abominable. Disapproved but not absolutely unlawful.

مَکشوف *A.* Discovered; revealed. — م. شدن To be r. — م. کردن To reveal; discover.

مُکعب *A. a.* Cubic. —*n.* Cube.

مَکفول *A.* One whose presence must be produced by a person who has undertaken to do so.

مَکفولٌ‌له (*-lon-lah*) *A.* One to whom it has been undertaken to produce the presence of a person.

مکلس *A.* Calcined. — م. کردن To calcine.

مُکلف *A.* Bound ; required. Charged with a duty. Having attained puberty. — م کردن To bind ; charge with a (specified) duty.

مکمل (*mokamal*) *A.* Completed ; perfect.

مکمل (*mokamel*) *A.* Complementary. Supplementary.

مَکمن ｏ *A.* = کمینگاه

مُکنت *A.* Pecuniary ability. *L.* Wealth.

مَکنون *A.* = پوشیده

مکنونات *A.* Hidden things ; secrets. [Pl. of مکنونه fem. of مکنون 'hidden'].

مَکه *A.* Mecca.

مکی *A.* Meccan. [Fem. مکیه] — سورهٔ مکیه *Surah* revealed at Mecca.

مکیدن [مك] To suck. To [absorb.

مکیده [P. P. fo مکیدن]

مُکیف *A. n.* Inebriant; intoxicant. —*a.* Intoxicating.

مَکین ｏ *A. a.* Fixed or dwelling in a place. —*n.* Dweller. Occupier of a place.

مَکینه ｏ Sucker [pipe through which water, etc. is drawn by suction].

مگر [*Stress on the 1st. syl.*]

1) Except.— م. اینکه *or* م. آنکه [*Idiomatic use*] Unless — م. شما بمن کمك کنید (وگرنه دیگری نمیکند) It is only you who could help me (and no one else). *OS.* Unless you hplp me, there is no one else . . . 2) [Interrogative word used by one who hears a remark contrary to his previous supposition] Ex م. شما نمیدانید ؟ You know, don't you ? — چطور مگر ؟ Why (i. e. why do you ask) ?

مگرمج ｏ Crocodile.

مَگس Fly. ـ م. پراندن To idle away one's time. ـ م. در هوا رگك زدن To beat the air. ـ م. درآنجا پر نمیزند There is not a soul there.
مگس پران Fly-net ; fly-flap.
مگس پرانی Idleness; loafing.
مگس‌خوار Feeding on flies. ـ مرغ م. Humming-bird.
مگس‌کش Killing flies o. ـ کاغذ مگس کش Fly-paper. ـ گَرد مگس کش Fly-powder.
مگس‌گیر Fly-trap. Catch-fly.
مگس وَزن P. A. Fly-weight.
مگسی Flea-bitten : اسب م.
مَگو Unutterable : سرّ مگو
مُل • = باده - شراب
مُلا [f. A. مولی] Mullah : person versed in theology and sacred law.
ملاء (mala') A. Fullness. Crowd; assembly. ـ ملاء اعلی Heavenly court; assembly of angels. ـ درملاء عام In the public view; in p.
ملاج or ملازگ (?) Fontanelle.
مَلاح A. = ملوان
مَلاحت A. Charm; attractiveness.
ملاخده [Pl. of ملحد].
ملاحظات S. u. ملاحظه
مُلاحظه A. Observation; notice. Consideration; regard. Remark [pl. ملاحظات]. ـ م. کردن To observe or n. ; consider. To have regard for. [In p. c.] To see [often م. فرمودن]. ـ ملاحظهٔ اطراف کار Circumspection. ـ بملاحظهٔ Considering. In view of. ـ بدون ملاحظهٔ Irrespective of. ـ قابل م. Noteworthy; remarkable.
ملاحظه کار A. P. Cautious ; reserved ; circumspective ; wary.
ملاحی A P. = ملوانی
مَلاذ A. = پناهگاه
مُلازم A. a. Attending; accompanying. Attached; inherent. —n pl. ملازمین Attendants.
ملازمت A. Attendance. Assiduity. ـ م. داشتن با To attend o. To involve necessarily.
ملاز(ه) = زبان کوچك Uvula.
مِلاس Fr. Molasses.
مَلاست A. Softness [نرمی]. ـ ملاست استخوان Med. Rickets.
مَلاط A. 1) Cement o. 2) Mortar [for گِل م.].
مُلاطفت A. = مهربانی
ملاعب [Pl. of ملعبه]
مُلاعبه A. 1) Playing together. 2) = شوخی
ملاعین [Pl. of ملعون].
ملافه [f. A. ملحفه] Bedsheet; cover.
مُلاقات A. Meeting; visit; interview. ـ م. کردن To meet or v.
مَلاقه [f. A. ملعقه] Ladle; dipper
مِلاك A. Basis. Criterion.
ملاك (ma1ak) A. [ملاکین] Landowner.
مُلاکتابی +a. p. Pedantic.

مَلال (A.) S. u. ملالت

ملال انگیز A. P. Wearisome ; annoying.

ملالت or ملال [its collective] Weariness. Vexation. Sadness.

مَلامت A. = سرزنش

مُلامسه A. Feeling, or flirting, with the hand.

ملانتربوق × A. P. Misshapen, rough-hewn, or shabby-looking person.

ملا نقطی + a. p. 1) Who searches for dots and strokes. See نقط ‖ 2) = ملاکتابی

مَلاهی A. Unlawful sports; profane delights.

مَلائت A. Pecuniary ability to justify bail.

مَلائك or ملائکه [Pl. of ملك malak].

مُلایم A. Mild; gentle. Temperate. Soft. Lenient. — م. شدن To grow mild. — م. کردن To milden. To temper. To soften. To tone down.

مُلایمت A. Mildness; gentleness; softness. Moderateness. Leniency.

مُلبس A. Clothed ; dressed ; [with به] d. with; wearing.

مَلبوس A. = پوشاك & لباس

ملت A. [ملل] Nation; people.

مُلتجی A. (One) who takes refuge or seeks protection. — م. شدن To take r. ; seek p.

ملتحمه A. Conjunctiva. [Orig. fem. of ملتحم 'healing or connective']. — ورم م. Conjunctivitis.

مُلتزم A. a. Bound over. — م. شدن To be bound o. ; undertake. — م. کردن To bind o. —n. Attendant [pl. ملتزمین]. — ملتزمینِ رکاب Suite ; retinue.

ملتفت A. Aware; sensible. — م. شدن To take notice (of). To understand. — م. باشید Take n. ; look out. — ملتفتِ پله باشید Mind the step.

ملتقا [f. A. مُلتقی -tagha] Confluence. Junction.

مُلتمس A. Request(ed).

مُلتوی A. Sigmoid : غضروف م. ‖ OS. = پیچیده q. v.

مُلتهب A. Inflamed. F. Enthusiastic; fervent.

مَلجا A. = پناه (گاه)

مَلچ و مُلوچ کردن × To smack one's lips; lick one's chops.

ملِح A. [املاح] Chem. = نمك

مُلحد A. [مَلاحده] Atheist.

ملحفه S. u. ملافه

مُلحق A. Joined. — م. شدن To be joined ; join vi. — م. کردن To j. To annex.

مُلحقات A. Additions; supplements. [Pl. of ملحقه fem. of ملحق].

مَلحوظ A. Observed; seen. — م. شدن or م. افتادن To be s. or observed.

ملحوظات A. Observations.

Thoughts. [Pl. of ملحوظه fem. of ملحوظ].

مَلَخ Locust; grasshopper. [Of a plane] Airscrew; propeller.

مُلَخَّص A. a. Summarized. —n. Summary; extract.

مُلزَم A. Bound. — م. شدن To be bound. — م. کردن To bind; oblige. To convince.

مَلزوم A. Attached. Insepa-rable. [Fem. ملزومه with the pl. ملزومات Supplies; necessaries]. S. a. under لازم

مَلَس A. = میخوش Subacid.

مُلصَق A. Fastened; pinned. Attached.

ملعبه A. [ملاعب] = بازیچه

ملعقه S. u. ملاقه

مَلعَنت o A. 1) = لعنت 2) Abo-minable deed

مَلعون A. a. Accursed; damned. —n. [Pl. ملاعین] A. person. The Devil.— م. کردن To curse; anathematize.

مُلغی (-gha) A. Cancelled. — م. کردن To annul; cancel.

مَلفوظ A. Pronounced. Gr. Aspirate. [Fem. ملفوظه]. — غیر ملفوظه Gr. Mute.

مَلفوفه A. Enclosure. (Annex of a) firman.

ملفه A. See ملحفه & ملافه

ملقب به A. P. Entitled; sur-named .

ملك (malak) A. [ملائك & ملائکه] Angel [فرشته]

ملك (malek) A. [ملوك] = پادشاه King.

ملك (molk) A. [املاك] Landed property; estate. Possession. Kingdom *.

ملکات [Pl. of ملکه malakah]

ملك‌الحارس A. Guardian angel.

ملك‌الشعراء A. Prince of poets; poet laureate.

ملك‌الموت (malakolmowt) A. Angel of death.

ملك المورّخین A. Prince of historians.

ملکزاده * A. P. = شاهزاده

مَلَکوت A. Kingdom (of heaven).

ملکوتی A. Heavenly; celes-tial. Spiritual.

مَلَکوك A. = لکه‌دار

ملکه (malakah) A. [مَلَکات] Habit; second nature Auto-matism. — م. اش شد He mas-tered it.

ملکه (malekah) A. Queen. [Fem. of ملك malek]. — ملکهٔ مادر Q. mother.

مُلکی A. P. Privately-owned. Landed. — م. دلال معاملات Real estate broker; land-agent.

ملکیت A. Ownership.

ملل [Pl. of ملت].

مُلَمَّع A. Macaronic verse; bilingual poem.

ململ Variety of muslin; mull.

مَلَنگ Gay. Tipsy. Ecstasied o. [Of a stone] Irregularly shaped; i. cubical.

مَلوان Sailor.
ملوانی Sailorship; seamanship.
مُلوَّث A. Polluted. Contaminated. م . کردن ـ To defile. To contaminate.
ملوس +Lovable; pet. Mignon.
ملوط o A. Catamite.
مُلوك A. 1) [Pl. of ملك *malek*]. 2) *Fem. pr. name.*
ملوك الطوايفی A. P. Feudal (system).
ملوکانه A. P. *a.* Kingly; royal. *-ad.* In a k. manner.
مَلول A. Wearied. Fed up. Dejected. Tepid. Indisposed.
مُلوَّن A. [Fem. ملونه] Colouring [*persicus*).
مَله Species of tick (*Argas*
مُلهم A. Inspired.
ملی (*meli:*) A. National. Popular. م . آموزشگاه ـ Private school. باغ م ـ Public garden. حکومت م ـ Democratic government. م . کردن ـ To nationalize.
ملی (*mali:y*) Able to justify bail; pecuniarily qualified.
مِلیت A. Nationality.
مَلیح A. Charming; of attractive beauty. Melodious.
مَلیحه A. 1) *Fem. of* ملیح 2) *Fem. pr. name.*
ملیله دوزی Filigree(d) work.
مُلین A. Laxative.
مِلیون A. Nationalists. [Pl. of ملی used as a n.]

مَمات A. = موت & مرگ
مُمارست A. Assiduity; application. Practice. م . کردن ـ To practise; exercise.
مُماس A. Tangent.
مُماشات A. Condescension. Pretended concordance. م. کردن ـ To condescend (flatteringly). To comply or agree.
ممالك [Pl. of مملکت]
مُمانعت A. Prevention [جلوگیری]. ـ م. کردن To prevent.
مُمتاز A. Distinguished; excellent. [Fem. ممتازه]. سهام ـ ممتاز(ه) Preference shares; gilt-edged s. ـ دیون ممتاز(ه) Preferential debts.
مُمتحِن (*-tahen*) A. 1) *n.* Examiner [pl. ممتحنین]. 2) *a.* Examining. [Fem. ممتحنه. Ex. هیئتِ ممتحنه Examining board; examiners].
مُمتحَن o (*-tahan*) A. 1) *a.* Examined. 2) *n.* Examinee.
مُمتد A. 1) Prolonged; extended. 2) *F.* = زیاد
مُمتنع A. 1) *a.* Impossible. ـ سهل وممتنع Easy but difficult to imitate, as a poem. 2) *n.* Abstainer [pl. ممتنعین]. ـ دو نفر ممتنع بودند There were two abstentions.
مُمثل A. 1) *a.* Likened; compared. ـ غیرممثل Far-fetched. 2) *n.* Object of comparison.
مُمد A. Helping; promoting.

ممدوح A. 1) *a*. Praised. 2) *n*. Object of praise.

ممدود o A. Extended. Marked with the sign (ٓ).

ممرّ A. Pass(age). Outlet. F. Means. Source. Respect.

ممرز Blue beech.

ممزوج A. = آميخته

ممسك A. Parsimonious.

ممسك الاعنه A. (*Astr.*) The Auriga or Charioteer.

ممضى (-za) A. Signed.

ممكن A. Possible. [*Fem.* ممكنه]. — غيرممكن Impossible. — م. است بيايد He may come. — آيا ممكن است بروم ؟ May I go? — تا آنجا كه م. است As much as possible; so far as p.

ممكنه o A. [ممكنات] Possible thing; possibility. [Orig. fem. of ممكن]

ممل o A. Wearisome. Disgusting.

مملك o A. Acquisitive.— مرور زمان م. A. or positive prescription.

مملكت A. [ممالك] = كشور Country. — امور مملكتى State affairs. [م. از Full of.

مملو A. = پر Full; filled.—

مملوك o A. [مماليك] Slave.

ممنوع A. Prohibited; forbidden. Debarred. [Fem. ممنوعه with the pl. ممنوعات forbidden things]. — م. كردن or م. داشتن To prohibit; forbid. To debar.

ممنوع الورود A. The import of which is prohibited.

ممنوعيت A. Prohibition.

ممنون A. Obliged; grateful.— (ازشما) ممنونم I am g. to you; thank you. — ازمساعدت شماممنونم T. you for your assistance. — خيلى م. شدم I was (*or* am) much obliged (*or* pleased).— م. كردن To oblige; make g.

ممنونيت A. = امتنان

ممه + = پستان Breast.

ممهد o A. Arranged; prepared.

ممهور A. Sealed. — م. كردن = مهر كردن To seal. —*Note*. This word is coined from the P. مهر 'seal'.

مميز (*momayaz*) Distinguished. Investigated by the Supreme Court.

مميز (*momayez*) A. 1) *n*. Auditor; controller. Surveyor. [Pl. مميزين]. Decimal point. 2) *a*. Discerning; discriminative. [Fem. مميزه Ex. قوه م. The d. faculty].

مميزعنه A. Person against whom appeal has been made to the Supreme Court.

مميزى A. P. Audit; control. Survey. — م. كردن To audit. To survey.

من 1) I : من رفتم I went. 2) [Governed by a prep.] Me : آنرا بمن گفت ‖ 3) [Preceded by an *ezafah*] My : برادرِ من My brother.

مَناط *A*. Basis; example.
مناطق [Pl. of منطقه]
مناظر *A*. [Pl. of منظر(ه)]
مُناظره *A*. [مُناظرات] Debate, dispute. — م. کردن To debate.
مَناعت *A*. Inaccessibility. Magnanimity. Proper pride.
مناف *A*. *Name of an idol*.
مُنافات *A*. Incompatibility; inconsistency. — م. داشتن با To be inconsistent with.
منافذ [Pl. of منفذ]
مَنافع *A*. Interests. Profits. *Cf. the s*. منفعت
مُنافق *A*. *a*. Hypocritical. Seditious. —*n*. Mischief-maker. Hypocrite. [Pl. منافقين]
منافقت *A*. = دو بهمزنی - دورویی
مُنافی *A*. Inconsistent. [With the *ezafah*] I. with; repugnant to. — عملِ منافیِ عفت Unchaste act; criminal conversation.
مناقب [Pl. of منقبت]
مُناقشه *A*. [مناقشات] Dispute. — م. کردن To dispute.
مُناقصه *A*. Calling for tenders.— آگهی م. دادن To call for tenders. — با م. گذاهس To put out to tender; invite bids for. — حائز حداقل م. شدن To be the lowest bidder.
مَنال ○ *A*. Profit or share. — منال دیوانی Government's s. of the proceeds of a ceded crown land. — مال و منال = ثروت

مَن Unit of weight approximately — 3 kilogrammes.
مَنّ *A*. Grace; favour.
مَنّ *A-Heb*. Manna.
مَنابر [Pl. of منبر]
منابع [Pl. of منبع]
منات *R*. Rouble.
مُناجات *A*. Fervent prayer (often chanted).
مُنادِم *A*. Companion. *S. a*. نديم
منادمت *A*. Companionship.
مُنادی *A*. Proclaimer; herald Public crier [جارچی].
مُنادی (-*da*) *A*. Addressed.— اسم م. Nominative independent.
منار *A*. = مناره
مَناره *A*. Minaret. Lighthouse ○.
مُنازعه *A*. Litigation. Quarrel.— م. کردن = نزاع کردن
منازل [Pl. of منزل]
مُناسب *A*. 1) Suitable; fit : مناسبِ موقع f. for the occasion. 2) (Rather) cheap.
مُناسبات *A*. Relations. *Cf. the s*. مناسبت
مُناسبت *A*. Suitability; fitness. Relation. Occasion. *Cf. the pl*. مناسبات ‖ م. داشتن To be fit or opportune. To be based on some reason. — بمناسبتِ On the occasion of. Due to.— بچه م. For what r.? What is the o.? [مراسم
مناسك ○ *A*. [Pl. of منسك] =
مناصب [Pl. of منصب]
مُناصفه *A*. Dividing in halves.

مَنام o A. =1) خواب 2) خوابگاه

مَنان A. Munificent or beneficent : ep. of God.

مَناهی A. [Pl. of منهی] Prohibited acts; sins.

مِنبابِ A. By way of.

مُنبت A. Inlaid. Fretted.

منبت کاری A. P. Fretwork Inlaid work.

منبر (membar) A. [منابر] Raised structure for a preacher; pulpit. Baker's board on which bread is exhibited. — قبل از قاضی به م. رفتن To prejudge.

مُنبسط A. Expanded. [Fem. منبسطه]. — م. کردن To expand. — عضلهٔ منبسطه Extensor-muscle.

منبع (mamba') A. [منابع] Source. Cistern. F. Origin. — منبع موثق Reliable source; authority. — منابع طبیعی Natural resources.

مِنبعدِ A. Henceforth.

منبه o A. Awakening adj.

مِنت A. Obligation ; indebtedness. Praise. Grace; favour. [Pl. منن]. — ازکسی م. داشتن To hold oneself indebted to s. o. for his favour. — م. برسر کسی گذاشتن To remind s. o. of a f. done to him ; not let him forget it; also, reproach him for it. — م. از کسی کشیدن To put oneself under a person's obligation for his favour; be beholden to s. o. for a favour. — به منتش نمی‌ارزد It is not worth asking for the favour.

مَن‌تبع A. Follower(s).

مُنتج (-taj) A. Resulting. Inferred ; deduced. — م. شدن To result. S. a. منجر شدن

مُنتج (-tej) A. Producing a result [often redundantly منتجِ نتیجه].

مُنتحل o A. Plagiarist.

مُنتخب (-takhab) A. Elected. [Fem. منتخبه]. —n. pl. منتخبین Those elected.

مُنتخب (-takheb) A. [منتخبین] Elector. Chooser.

مُنتخبات A. Selections. [Pl. of منتخبه fem. of منتخب -takhab].

مَنتر کردن To enchant by animal magnetism; magnetize. By e. To influence; cause to follow or obey.

مُنتزع A. (Being) wrested. — م. شدن To be w. — م. کردن To wrest.

مُنتسب A. Related.

مُنتشر A. Published. Circulated. — م. شدن To be p. — م. کردن To publish. To spread. To circulate or issue.

مُنتصر A. = پیروز

مُنتظر (-tazar) A. Expected. [Fem. منتظره]. — غیر منتظر(ه) Unexpected.

منتظر (-tazer) A. Waiting. — منتظرِ...شدن To wait for... —

منتظر فرصت بودن To look for an opportunity. — م. کردن To keep waiting.

منتظر الوکاله *A.* (*Humorous*) Would-be deputy; aspirant to the position of M. P.

مُنتظم *A.* Regular : نبض م.

مُنتفع *A.* Deriving a benefit.— م. شدن از To profit by ; be benefited by.

مُنتفی شدن *A. P.* To cease to exist; lose its point.

منتقد *A.* Criticizer.

مُنتقل *A.* Transferred. Made to understand. — م. شدن To u. or grasp. To be transferred. — م. کردن To transfer.

مُنتقل الیه (*montaghalon-elay*h) *A.* = **انتقال گیرنده**

مُنتقم *A.* Revenger.

منت‌گذار *A. P.* Obliging

مُنتها [f. A. منتهی *-taha*] Maximum; utmost (extent). — منتهای آرزوی وی His u. desire. [*Used adverbially*] At the most. At (the) latest. Except that ; only ; the thing is.

مُنتهی (*-taha*) (*A.*) *S. u.* منتها

مُنتهی (*-tahi:*) *A.P.* Ending.— م. شدن به To end or culminate in.

منتهی الیه (*-taha-elay*h) *or* **منتها الیه** *A.* End; extremity. Farthest end.

مُنتهی درجه (*-taha-*) *a.p.* Highest degree.— م. به To the highest d. ; extremely.

مَنثور *A.* Written in prose.— شعر منثور Blank verse.

منجانبِ *A.* From; on the part of; by. — منجانبُ الله From God.

مُنجذب ᴑ *A.* Attracted; drawn.

مُنجر *A.* Leading. Terminating; resulting. — م. شدن به To culminate in. To result in.

منجز *A.* Unconditional.

منجزاً *A.* Unconditionally.

مَنجلاب Voidance water.

مُنجلی *A.* Clear; conspicuous.

منجم *A.* [منجمین] = **اختر شناس**

مُنجمد *A.* Frozen. [Fem . منجمده]. — م. شدن To freeze. — م. کردن To cause to f. ; congeal . — اقیانوس منجمد شمالی Arctic Ocean. — اقیانوس منجمدِ جنوبی Antarctic O. — منطقهٔ منجمده Frigid Zone.

منجملهِ *A.* Among others. Including. Such as. S. is ; such are .

مَنجنیق *A.-G.* Catapult; ballista; mangonel. War engine.

منجوق Glass beads.

مُنجی *A.* = رهاننده Saviour.

مُنحرف *A.* Deviated. — م. ساختن To cause to deviate. To pervert. — م. شدن To d. or turn.

مُنحصر *A.* Confined; limited. Exclusive. — م. کردن To restrict ; confine ; limit. — م. بفرد Unique; single in kind.

منحصراً *A.* Exclusively.

مُنحَلّ *A*. Dissolved; disbanded Wound up. [Fem. منحله]. — م. شدن To be dissolved. To break up. To wind up, as a company. — م. کردن To dissolve; disorganize. To w. up.

مُنحنی *A*. Curve(d). — منحنیِ تراز Contour.

منحوس *A*. Sinister. Wretched.

مِن‌حیث‌المجموع *A*. = روی‌همرفته On the whole.

مَنخرین *A*. Nostrils [D. of منخر ○]

مَنداب Wild rocket.

مَن‌درآوردی × Self-invented Immethodical. Eccentric.

مُندَرَج *A*. Inserted. [Fem. مندرجه with the pl. مندرجات Contents].

مُندرس *A*. Worn out. Obliterated. — م. شدن To be worn out; wear out.

مُندفع ○ *A*. Repulsed.

مُنزجر *A*. = بیزار Disgusted.

مَنزِل *A*. [منازل] Lodging; accommodation; house; quarters. *Cf*. خانه ‖ Halting-place. A day's journey. *F*. Stage; degree. Goal. — منزل‌اجاره‌ای Lodging; diggings; digs. — (به) م. دادن To lodge; accommodate. — م. کردن To l.

مُنزَل *A*. [Fem. منزله] Sent down (from Heaven).

مَنزلت *A*. Rank. Esteem.

منزلگاه *A.P*. Halting-place. Goal.

مَنزله *A*. [Orig. same as منزلت]. — بمنزلهٔ As; in the rank of. Tantamount to.

مُنزَوی *A. n*. Hermit; recluse. —*a*. Secluded. — م. شدن To retire; live in seclusion.

مُنزّه *A*. Pure; guiltless. Infallible. Transcendent. — م. از Free from. Superior to.

مَنسوب *A. a*. Related; allied. Imputed; ascribed. —*n. pl*. منسوبین Relatives [خویشاوندان]. — م. کردن به To charge with.

مَنسوج *A. n*. Textile; tissue. —*a*. = بافته Woven. [Fem. منسوجه with the pl. منسوجات textile or woven fabrics].

مَنسوخ *A*. Abolished. — م. کردن To abolish.

مَنش Nature; disposition. Relish [رغبت].

مَنشأ *A*. Source. — منشأ اثر Effective. Valid. — منشأ اثر نیست It is null and void.

مُنشآت *A*. Epistolary writings. Compositions. [Pl. of منشأه fem. of منشأ ○]

مِنشاری ○ *A*. Saw-like; serrated. Denticulate. Zigzag.

مُنشعب *A*. Branching. Forked. — م. شدن To branch out (*or* off). — م. کردن To divide into branches.

مُنشقّ *A*. Split; forked.

مَنشور *A*. Charter. Firman; patent. Prism.

مُنشی A. = نویسنده & دبیر

مَنصب A. [مناصب] Office; post.

مُنصرف A. Dispensing or having dispensed (with); abandoning or having abandoned the idea. — م. شدن To change one's mind; give up the i.; [with از] to dispense with. — م. کردن To dissuade.

منصعق ○ A. Thunder-struck.

مُنصف (-sef) A. [منصفه] Just; equitable. — هیئت منصفه Jury.

منصف (monasef) A. = نیمساز Bisector.

منصفانه A. P. ad. Equitably; justly. —a. Fair; just.

مَنصوب A. Appointed. — بریاست م. شد He was appointed chief. — م. کردن به To appoint (as).

مَنصور A. 1) = پیروز 2) Mas pr. name.

مَنصه A. Place of exhibition○. — بمنصهٔ ظهور آوردن To cause to appear.

مُنضم A. Annexed; joined. [Fem. منضمه with the pl. **منضمات** annexes; appurtenances]. — م. کردن To annex or join.

مُنطبق A. Conforming. Applicable. Coincident. — م. بودن با To conform, or be applicable, to. — م. کردن To c. or apply. *Geom*. To superpose.

مَنطق A. Logic. — منطق ارسطو The Organon or Organum. — منطق نوین The Novum O. — م. بافتن + To chop logic.

مُنطق A. (*Math.*) = گویا Rational.

مَنطقا A. Logically.

منطق‌دان A. P. Logician.

مَنطقه A. [مناطق] Zone; area. *Med*. Shingles. — مناطق نفت خیز Oil-producing regions; oil-field areas; oil-fields.

منطقةالبروج A. Zodiac.

منطقی A. Logical. [منطقی s.]

منطقیون A. Logicians. *Cf. the*

مَنظر A. [مناظر] Appearance. Aspect. — دیدن مناظر Sight-seeing. — (علم) مناظر و مرایا (Art of) perspective.

مَنظره A. [مناظر] View; sight; landscape. Spectacle. Scenery. Appearance.

مُنظم A. Regular. — م. کردن To put in good order; give good shape to; arrange.

منظما A. Regularly.

مَنظور A. n. Aim; object. Intention. Expectation. —a. Provided for. Considered. Intended. — م. داشتن To appreciate or remember; be grateful for. — م. کردن 1) To allow for; make allowance for; provide for. 2) To carry (into an account). — منظور نظر Aimed at. Accepted. Favourite.

مَنظوم A. Versified. — حکایت م. Story in verse. *See* منظومه

مَنظومه A. [منظومات] Versified story; poem. System : منظومهٔ شمسی ‖ [Orig. fem. of منظوم].

مَنع A. Prohibition. Forbidding. Prevention. م. کردن To prohibit. To check ; prevent. — قرار منع تعقیب Verdict for staying the proceedings.

منعدم A. = معدوم

منعزل A. = معزول

مُنعقد A. Concluded. In session. Coagulated. — م. کردن 1) To conclude : قراردادی م. کردند ‖ 2) To hold : جلسه‌ای م. کردند ‖ 3) To coagulate : م. کردنِ خون

مُنعکس A. Reflected. — م. شدن To be reflected. To resound. — م. کردن To reflect. To reverberate. L. To show or mention.

مُنعِم • A. a. Beneficent. Rich. —n. Rich man.

مِن‌درآوردی × a. p. = مِن‌عِندی

منغص A. Disturbed. — م. کردن To disturb. To mar. To damp.

منغمز A. Serrated : نبض م.

مِن‌غیرِ رسم A. Unofficially.

مُنفجر A. Exploding; exploded ; detonating ; bursting out. [Fem. منفجره . Ex. موادِ م. explosives] . — م. شدن To explode. — م. کردن or م. ساختن To explode.

مَنفذ A. [منافذ] Hole. Pore.

مُنفرج A. [Fem. منفرجه]. Obtuse : زاویهٔ منفرجه

منفرج‌الزاویه A. Obtuse-angled.

مُنفرد A. Single. Solitary. Isolated.

منفرداً A. Severally. Alone.

مَنفس A. Air-hole; vent. Breathing-hole. Cf. منفذ

منفسخ ٥ A. Dissolved. Cancelled.

منفصل A. [Fem. منفصله] Separate. Detached. Discharged or dismissed. Detachable ; separable. — قطعات منفصله D. parts; accesories. — ضمیر منفصل S. pronoun (as من in دست های من). — م. کردن To discharge. — م. شدن To be discharged.

مَنفعت A. [منافع] Profit. Benefit. Interest. — منافع دولت The Government's interests. — م. بردن To make a p. To derive a b. — م. کردن To make a p. ; gain. To bring or yield a p. — بمنفعتِ For the benefit of.

مُنفعل A. (C. E.) = شرمنده Ashamed. — م. شدن To be ashamed ; also, be put to shame. — م. کردن To put to s.

مُنفق A. (One) who readily gives away his money. Almsgiver.

مُنفك A. Separated. Removed.

مَنفور A. Hated ; detested. — منفورِ همه Hated by all.

مَنفی A. Negative.

منفی باف A. P. Negativist.

منفی بافی A. P. Negativism.

مُنقاد A. = مطیع
مِنقار A. = نوك Beak; bill.
منقارالغرابی A. Coracoid.
منقاری A. Rostral; rostriform.— بینی م. Aquiline nose.
مِنقاش A. = موچینه
مَنقبت A. [مناقب] Virtue; merit; talent.
مُنقبض A. Contracted. [Fem. منقبضه] . — م. شدن To be contracted; contract; shrink.— م. کردن To contract.
مُنقرض A. Overthrown; extinct. — م. شدن To be o. — م. کردن To overthrow.
مُنقسم A. Divided. — م. کردن To divide.
مُنقش A. Painted; illuminated. — م. کردن To paint or illuminate.
مَنقصت o A. Deficiency; loss.
مُنقضی A. Expired; elapsed. Overdue. —م. شدن To elapse or expire. — موعد آن م. شد It came to maturity.
مُنقطع A. Cut off. Interrupted. — م. ساختن To cut off. To interrupt.
مَنقل A. Brazier; chafing-dish.— منقل فرنگی Stove.
مُنقلب A. Turned. Upset. Fundamentally changed. Stormy.— م. شدن To be upset. To be deeply moved. To be changed. — م. کردن To turn; change; transform. To upset. To revolutionize.

مَنقوش A. Engraved; carved.— م. کردن To engrave; carve.
مَنقوط A. [Fem. منقوطه] Dotted, as the letter ت
مَنقول A. Movable. Narrated; quoted. Traditional.— غیرمنقول Immovable. — م. از صفحهٔ قبل Brought forward.— م. بصفحهٔ بعد Carried forward.
منقی o (*mona*gha) A. Cleaned; purged. — بادام م. or بادام منقا Kind of thin-shelled almond; Jordan a.
مُنکر (*-kar*) A. 1) *a*. Prohibited; unlawful. *OS*. Denied. 2) *n*. Sin of commission.
مُنکر (*-ker*) A. 1) *n*. Denier. 2) *a*. Denying. Disowning. — م شدن To deny; repudiate.
مُنکسر A. Broken. Refracted, as light. *F*. B.-spirited; depressed.
منکشف A. = مکشوف
مَنکوب A. Vanquished. Afflicted.—م. ساختن To vanquish.
مَنکوحه A. Married (woman).
مَنگ + Fuddled; confused.
مَنگل Subterranean siphon.
مَنگله or منگوله Tassel; tuft.
مَنگنه Press. Perforator. Eyelet-ring. — م. کردن To press. To perforate. — منگنهٔ آبی Hydrostatic press.
منم زدن + To be egotistic. To praise oneself. *OS*. To say, "I am," or "It is I."
مِن‌مِن کردن + To mutter.

مِنوال *A* Manner.
مَنوچهر *Mas. pr. name.*
مُنوَّر 1) *a.* = روشن Illuminated; bright. — روشن. کردن = م. کردن
2) *n. Fem. pr. name.*
منورالفکر *A.* = **روشن فکر**
مَنوط *A.* Depending; subject.— م. بتصویب او است It depends on, or is s. to, his approval.
مُنوِّم *A.* = خواب‌آور Soporific.— جوهر منوم افیون o Morphine.
مَنوی *A.* Intended. [Fem. منویه with the pl. **منویات** intentions].
مِنها *A.* [Usu. منهایِ] Minus; less. — منها کردن To subtract.
مِنهاج o *A.* [مناهج] = راه Way; manner.
مُنهدم *A.* Destroyed; demolished. Overthrown.— م. شدن To be d. or destroyed. — م. ساختن To destroy or demolish [خراب کردن].
مُنهزم *A.* Routed; put to flight — م. کردن To rout; put to f.; defeat.
مَنهی *A.* Forbidden. [Fem. منهیه with the pl. **منهیات** *or* مناهی forbidden acts; sins of commission].
مَنی *A.* [Usu. آب م.] Sperm.
مُنیر *A.* Shining; bright.
منیره (*A.*) *Fem. pr. name.* [Orig. fem. of منیر *q. v.*]
مَنیزی (*-ye-*) *Fr.* Magnesium.
مَنیژه *Fem. pr. name.*

مَنیع *A.* Inaccessible. Lofty.— مقام منیعِ... His Highness *or* His Excellency...
مُنیف o *A.* = بلند Eminent.
منم زدن = • **منی** کردن
مو *or* **موی** Hair. Flaw. — مویِ دماغ *Met.* Nuisance; bore; intruder; also, gooseberry.— مو بمو In detail; to a hair.— مو بر بدنم راست شد My hair stood on end. — مثل موئی که از ماست بکشند As easy as shelling peas; as e. as winking.— سرِ مو Hair-breadth.
مو (*mow*) Vine. [(land).
مَوات *A.* Waste or unutilized
مَوّاج *A.* Swelling; rough; stormy. *F.* Fluctuating.
مَواجب *A.* Salary.
مُواجه *A.* Confronting; facing; encountering. — م. شدن با To meet; encounter.
مواجهه *A.* (Act of) confronting. — م. کردن با To meet; confront; encounter.
مواخذ (*mo-akhez*) *A.* Who calls (another) to account or takes him to task. [Pronounced *-khaz*] Liable to be called to account or taken to task.
مواخذه *A.* Calling to account. Taking to task; remonstrance. —(از) م. کردن To take to task. To bring to book; call to account .

مَوادّ *A*. Materials. Articles. Products. *Cf. the s.* مادّه

مَوارد [Pl. of مورد]

موازات (*mova*-) *A*. Parallelism; being parallel. — بموازاتِ Parallel or equivalent to. In a parallel direction with.

موازنه (*mova*-) *A*. Balance; equilibrium. — م. کردن To balance. — موازنهٔ خود را از دست دادن To be off one's b.; lose one's equilibrium.

موازی ('') *A*. Parallel. — م. با *or* موازیِ P. to; (*or* with).

مَوازین [Pl. of میزان]

مَواشی *A*. Quadrupeds; cattle. [Pl. of ماشیه o walking (animal)].

مواصلت (*mova*-) *A*. Coming together; union. Interview o. Communication [pl. مواصلات].

مَواضع [Pl. of موضع]

مواضعه (*mova*-) *A*. Agreement [قرارداد]. Connivance [تبانی].

مواظب ('') *A*. Careful; attentive. — مواظب کسی بودن 1) To take care of s. o. 2) To mind s. o.; watch over him.

مواظبه *A*. [Fem. of مواظب only in م. نوبهٔ Quotidian fever].

مواظبت (*mova*-) *A*. Attention; care. Assiduity; application. — م. کردن To take c. of; watch (over); mind.

مواعد [Pl. of موعد]

مواعظ [Pl. of موعظه]

مواعید *S. u.* موعود & وعده

موافق (*mova*-) *A*. Agreeable; agreeing. Conformable. Favourable. — باپیشنهادی م. بودن To agree to a proposal. — با کسی م. بودن To agree with s.o. — موافقِ According to.

موافقت *A*. Agreement; consent. — باکسی م. کردن To agree with s. o. — باچیزی م. کردن To a with s. t. — موردموافقت واقع‌شد It was approved; it was agreed to.

موافقت نامه *A. P.* Written agreement; letter of a.

مواقع [Pl. of موقع]

مواقعه (*mova*-) o *A*. Fight(ing) [جنگ]. Sexual intercourse.

مَوالید *A*. 1) [Pl. of مولود]. 2) Natality. 3) Kingdoms: موالید سه‌گانه

موانست (*mo-anesat*) *A*. Familiarity.

موانع [Pl. of مانع]

مواهب [Pl. of موهبت]

مو َبد Zoroastrian priest.

مؤبد o (*mo-abad*) *A*. = ابدی

موت (*mowt*) *A*. = مرگ Death. — موت کاذب Lethargy.

مؤتلف (*mo'talef*) *A*. Joining in a coalition; also, united. — م. شدن To coalesce or unite.

مؤتمن *A*. Trusted; trustworthy.

موتو Sardine.

موتور *Fr*. Engine; motor.

موتورسیکلت *Fr*. Motor cycle.

موتوری *Fr. P*. Engine-driven —

م. دوچرخهٔ Motor bicycle. — م. قایق M.-boat ; launch.

موتوریزه *Fr.* Motorized. — م. کردن To motorize.

مؤثر (*mo-aser*) *A.* Effective. Efficacious. Touching. Forcible. [Fem. مؤثره].

موثق (*movasagh*) *A.* Reliable; authentic. [Fem. موثقه]. — منبع م. R. source.

موثقیت *A.* Authenticity; reliability.

موج *A.* [امواج] Wave. — م. زدن To swell (with waves); roll; surge. To have a wavy appearance. To undulate.

موجب *A. n.* Cause; motive. —*a.* Causing. Affirmative. [Fem. موجبه]. — م. شدن To cause; occasion; bring about. — بموجب According to; by virtue of.

موجبات *A.* [Pl. of موجبه fem. of موجب] Causes. Means.

موجد *A.* 1) *a.* Causing. 2) *n.* Cause. Inventor.

موجدار *A. P.* Wavy. Watered: حریر موجدار

موجر *A.* Lessor; landlord.

موجز *A.* Brief; laconic.

موج شکن *A. P.* Breakwater.

موجگیر *A. P.* Antenna; aerial.

مؤجل (*mo-ajal*) *A.* Ultimate. Not yet due; not matured. — مهرمؤجل Deferred dower.

موجود *A.* Existing. Available. [Fem. موجوده with the pl. موجودات Beings; creatures]. — م. داشتن To have in stock. — + م. نداریم We are sold out (of this commodity).

موجودی *A. P.* Stock; inventory. Cash on hand. — ازموجودی Out of stock; ex s. — م. را رسیدگی کردن To take s. or i.

موجودیت *A.* 1) Existence. 2) Entity. — موجودیت ایران را ثابت کرد He proved that Iran was an entity. 3) Existentionalism.

موجه (*movajah*) *A.* [Fem. موجهه] Good; acceptable; well-founded: عذر موجه good excuse. — دلائل م. Adequate reasons. — غیر موجه Poor; unfounded; lame.

موجه‌نما *A. P.* Plausible; glossy.

موجی *A. P.* Wavy. Corrugated.

موج یاب *A. P.* (*Ph.*) Detector.

موچینه & **موچین** Tweezers.

موحد (*movahed*) *A. n.* Monotheist [pl. موحدین]. —*a.* Monotheistic.

موحش *A.* [Fem. موحشه] = [ترسناك]

مؤخر (*mo-akhar*) *A.* Hinder. Latter. Delayed. Postponed. — مقدم م. کردن To put the first last; reverse the order of.

مؤخره ○ *A.* Hinder part. Consequent.

مودار Hairy. Flawy; crazed.

مؤدب (*mo-adab*) *A.* Polite.

مؤدِب *A.* Chastiser. Educator.

مؤدَبانه *A. P.* Politely.
مودّت (*mavadat*) *A.* Cordiality. Friendship [دوستی].
مودت‌آمیز *A. P.* Cordial.
مؤدی (*mo-adi:*) *A.* Payer. ـ مؤدی‌مالیاتی *or* مالیات Taxpayer.
مؤذن *A.* Muezzin : one who calls people to prayer.
موذی *A.* 1) = زبان آور ‖ 2) + Sly; crafty.
موذیگری *A. P.* Slyness.
مور * Ant. [Usu. مورچه]. ـ مثل مور و ملخ (Swarming) like locusts; numerous.
مورّب *A.* Oblique. Diagonal.
مورِث *A.* Causing. ـ م. شدن To cause; occasion.
مورّث (*movares*) *A.* Legator or devisor; bequeather.
مورچال Ant-hill *By e.* Rifle-pit.
مورچه Ant [مورچگان *] *Cf.* مور ‖ سوار مورچه شدن To go at a snail's pace (*or* gallop).
مورچه خوار 1) *n.* Ant-eater. 2) *a.* Ant-eating.
مورچه سواری Large (species of) ant.
مورَخ (*movarakh*) *A.* [Fem. مورخه] Dated : نامهٔ مورخ . . . letter dated . . .
مورِخ *A.* [مورخین] Historian.
مورد (*mu:rd*) Myrtle.
مورد (*mowred*) *A.* [موارد] Instance. Case. Proper occasion or place. —[*Used as an adj.*] Exposed. Liable. ـ مورد تعقیب L. to prosecution. ـ مورد معامله Object of transaction. ـ مورد بازرسی قرار دادن To inspect. ـ بسته است بهم. As the case may be. ـ در مواردی که In cases when.
مورد دانه Myrtle-berry.
مور شناسی Myrmecology.
مورمور + Creeping sensation; horror; shivers. ـ مورمورم‌میشود I have a creeping sensation; I have the shivers.
موروث *A.* Inherited : ملك م.
موروثی *A. P.* Inherited. Hereditary : ناخوشی م.
موریانه Termite.
موز Banana. Also, plantain.
موزائیك *Fr.* Mosaic. ـ آجر م. Terrazzo tile.
موزر *Fr.* Mauser.
موزّع (*movaze'*) *A.* Distributor.
موزَنی Cutting (*or* cropping) the hair [chiefly in ماشین م. Cropper].
موزون *A.* Rhythmical. Well-proportioned. Elegant.
موزه *Fr.* Museum.
موزیك *Fr.* Music; also, setting.
مؤسس (*mo-asas*) *A.* Established; founded. *Cf. the fem.* مؤسسه
مؤسس (*mo-ases*) *A.* [Fem. مؤسسه] Founder; promoter (of a company). Constituent. [Pl. مؤسسان *or* مؤسسین] ـ اعضای م. F. members. ـ مجلس مؤسسان C. Assembly.

موشکافی Thorough analysis; minute investigation. *OS.* Hair-splitting. — م. کردن To make a thorough analysis.
موشك دوانی Making mischief; setting intrigues of foot.
موشکور Bat. — موشکور زیر زمینی Mole.
موشور *A.* = منشور or شوشه
موصوف *A.* 1) *a.* Qualified. Characterized. — م. بصفات حمیده Endowed with laudable qualities. 2) *n.* Substantive.
موصول *A.* Joined. *Gr.* Relative: ضمیر موصول
موصی *A.* Testator. [Fem. موصیه testatrix].
موصی به (-*sabeh*) *A.* Legacy.
موصی له (-*salah*) *A.* Legatee or devisee.
موضع *A.* [مواضع] Place; locality. Position. [داروی م.]
موضعی *A.* Local. Topical:
موضوع *A.* [موضوعات & o مواضیع] which is properly the pl. of موضوعه fem. of موضوع]. Subject(-matter). Object. Case. — موضوع بحث Matter on hand. — مالیات موضوع بحث The tax in question. — کالای موضوع پروانه Goods covered by the permit. — خارج از موضوع Out of question; not to the point. — ازموضوع خارج شدن To digress; deviate from the main subject. — در موضوعِ On

مؤسسات [Pl. of مؤسسه]
مؤسسه *A.* [مؤسسات] = بنگاه Establishment; institution. [Orig. fem. of مؤَسس]
موسم *A.* Season. Time.
موسمی *A. P.* Seasonal.
موسوم به *A. P.* Named. — به علی م. شد He was n. Ali.
موسَوی *A. a.* Mosaic. Jewish. Descended from *Emam Moosa*. —*n.* Jew.
موسی (-*sa*) *A.* Moses.
موسیر Shallot.
موسیقی *A.-G.* Music.
موسیقی‌دان *A. P.* Musician.
موسیو *Fr.* 1) Mr. [Better say آقایِ]. 2) = آقا Sir.
موش Mouse. — موش دو پا Jerboa. — مثل موش آب کشیده Wet to the skin; dripping wet. — موش‌صحرائی Rat. Field-mouse. — دو موش با هم دعوا کنند خفه میشوند There is no room to swing a cat in.
موشح (*movashah*) *A. a.* Adorned. — م. کردن To adorn. —*n.* Acrostic. To give (royal) assent to.
موش ُخرما Ferret; Asiatic marmot.
موَشك [Dim. of موش] Rocket. Flare. Missile. — موشكِ هدایت شونده Guided missile. — موشك هوائی Sky-rocket. — م. دواندن To set intrigues on foot; lay a train. To make mischief. To queer one's pitch.

occasion.— (در) موقعی که When; at the moment that. — م. را مغتنم شمردن To avail oneself of the opportunity.

موقع طلب *a. p.* Opportunist.

موقعیت *A.* Situation; position. Footing. — م. ندارد که The circumstances do not allow to.

موقف o *A. See* جا - مقام - ایستگاه - توقفگاه

موقوف *A.* 1) Depending; subject. — م. بتصویب اوست It depends on his approval. 2) Suspended. 3) Abolished; also cancelled. — م. شدن To be cancelled or abolished. — م. کردن To cancel. To abolish. To stop. 4) Endowed, as a pious foundation.

موقوف‌علیه (*mowghu:fon-alayh*) *A.* Beneficiary (of an endowment).

موقوفه *A.* [موقوفات] Pious foundation; endowed property. [Orig. fem. of موقوف]

موکب *A.* [مواکب] Retinue. Cavalcade. [strict.

مؤکد (*mo-akad*) *A.* Emphatic;

مؤکداً *A.* Emphatically.

مُوکل (*movakal*) *A.* Delegated; appointed. — م. کردن To appoint or delegate.

موکل (*movakel*) *A.* Client; principal.

موکن = موچینه Tweezers.

موکول *A.* Depending; subject.

the s. of; concerning. — م. کردن To deduct.

موطلائی Golden-tressed.

موطن *A.* (Place adopted as one's) motherland or home.

موظف (*movazaf*) *A.* 1) Bound. — م. به مراجعت است He is bound to return. 2) Stipendiary; paid; salaried. — غیر موظف Unpaid. — م. کردن To charge (with a duty).

موعد *A.* [مواعد] (Fixed) time. Date on which a bill falls due; maturity.

موعظه *A.* [مواعظ] Sermon. Preaching. — م. کردن = وعظ کردن To preach.

موعود *A.* 1) *a.* Promised. 2) *n.* [pl. مواعید]. = وعده

موفق (*movafagh*) *A.* Successful. *Cf.* کامیاب ‖ من م. شدم بلیط بگیرم I succeeded in obtaining, or managed to obtain, a ticket.

موفقیت *A.* Success. — م. پیدا کردن To succeed.

موقت (*movaghat*) *A.* Temporary.

موقتاً *A.* Temporarily.

موقتی *A. P.* Temporary.

موقر *A.* Grave; dignified; demure. Serious.

موقع *A.* [مواقع] Occasion; (proper) time. Opportunity. — در موقعِ At the time of; in t. of. During. — در موقعِ لزوم In t. of need. On

ceti.– مومِ معدنی Paraffin wax.– در دست من مثل م. است I have him in my pocket; also, I can mould him like wax.

موم اندر آب o Gluten.

موم اندود Coated with wax. Cerated. – کاغذ موم اندود Wax-paper.

مؤمن (mo'men) A. [مؤمنین] Believer. Pious man. [Fem. مؤمنه pl. مؤمنات].

مومی Waxen. Waxy.

مومی‌الیه o (mu:ma-elayh) A. Above-mentioned (person). OS. (Person) hinted at.

مومیائی Mummy. Kind of mineral asphalt used as a panacea. – م. کردن To mummify.

مؤَنت or مؤونت o (ma-u:-) A. Allowance; alimony; money for expenditure.

مؤنث (mo-anas) A. Feminine.

مونس A. Companion.

موهبت A. [مواهب] Gift. Talent.

موهوب A. Given; made a gift of. [Donee.

موهوب له (mowhu: bonlah) A.

موهوم A. Imaginary. Fictitious: م. منافع ‖ Superstitious.

موهومات A. Superstitions. [Pl. of موهومه fem. of موهوم]

موهوم پرست A. P. Superstitious. [tiousness.

موهوم پرستی A. P. Supersti-

موهون o A. Weakened.

Trusted o.– م. است به ... It depends on . . . ; it is s. to...– م. کردن To leave. To trust. – م. بیعد کردن To postpone. To adjourn.

مول o Paramour.

مولا S. u. مولی

مولانا A. Our master or lord [used as a title].

مولد (mowled) A. [موالد] Birthplace.

مولد (movalad) A. Born o. [Fem. مولده with the pl. مولدات those b.; births].

مولد (movaled) A. a. Producing –n. Generator; producer.

مؤلف (mo-alaf) Compiled o. [Fem. مؤلفه with the pl. مؤلفات compilations; works].

مؤلف (mo-alef) A. [مؤلفین] Compiler; author.

مولع o (-le') A. = حریص

مؤلم (mo'lem) A. [Fem. مؤلمه] Painful. Sad; tragic.

مولود A. 1) a. Born. 2) n. Male child [pl. موالید]. Birth(day).– م. شدن To be born. – موالید سه‌گانه The three kingdoms.

مولی (mowla) A. Master; lord [written also مولا esp. when it is followed by the ezafah. Ex. مولای ما].

مولی‌علیه (movala-alayh) A. Pupil (law term); ward.

موم Wax. – موم کافوری Sperma-

موی S. u. مو
مؤید (*mo-ayad*) *A*. Assisted (by God); gifted.
مؤید (*-ayed*) *A. n*. Confirmer. One who assists or favours. *—a*. Confirmatory. — مؤیدِ اظهارات من است It confirms my statements.
مَویز Large raisins. Currant. — یك م. و چهل قلندر A single bone and a hundred dogs. *—Note*. This E. translation has been coined to serve as a parallel for the P. *See* قلندر
مویزك Lousewort.
مویه • Lamentation. Weeping. Sad or mournful verses.
مویی *or* موبین • Hair-like ; hairy. Capillary.
موئیدن ○ To mourn or weep.
مَه • [Cont. of ماه]
مِه (*meh*) Fog; mist. — هوا (را) مه گرفته است It is foggy.
مِه ('') Great [بزرگ]. Elderly.
مِه (*me*) *Fr*. May.
مَهابت *A*. =1) ترس 2) حرمت
مُهاجر *A n*. Emigrant or immigrant [depending on the standpoint of the speaker]. *—a*. Migratory.
مهاجرَت *A*. Emigration. — م. کردن To emigrate.
مهاجر نشین *A P*. Colony.
مُهاجم *A*. Invader.
مَهار Halter; leading rope. Moorings; stays; guy. —م. کردن To halter. To moor. To cap, as a well. *F*. To control.
مَهارَت *A*. Skill. Dexterity.
مِه‌آلود Foggy.
مَهامّ *A*. [Pl. of مهمه fem. of مُهم] Important affairs.
مهبط ○ *A*. Place of descent.
مَهبِل *A*. Vagina. — ورم م. Vaginitis.
مهبلی *A*. Vaginal.
مَهتاب [Cont. of ماهتاب] Moonlight.
مهتابی 1) *a*. Moonlit. Fluorescent: لامپ م. ‖ 2) *n*. Terrace ; belvedere .
مُهتدی *A*. Directed to the right path.
مِهتر • [Comp. of مه] = بزرگتر Greater ; elder.
مِهتر Groom.
مهتری Greatness. Eldership.
مهتری Groom's office.—م. کردن To groom horses; work as a g.
مَه‌جبین • *P.A*. Of a silvery or moonlike brow.
مَهجور *A*. [Fem. مهجوره] Separated. Excluded. Forlorn Obsolete : واژه های م.
مَهجوری • *A*. Separation. Forlorn state.
مَهد *A*. = گهواره Cradle. —مهدِ آزادی Nurse of liberty.
مه‌گرفته = مِه‌دار
مَهدورالدم (*-rodam*) *A*. Whose blood may be shed with

immunity.

مَهدی (*A.*) *Mas. pr. name.*

مُهذب *A.* Refined; polished. Accomplished. [portion.

مَهر & مَهریه *A.* Marriage-

مِهر 1) • Sun [خورشید]. 2) Affection. *Cf.* محبت & مهربانی

مِهر *Seventh month having 30 days.*

مُهر Seal; stamp. Impression. — م. زدن To seal. — م. کردن To s. (up). — مهر (و) موم کردن To s. up with (sealing-) wax. To keep under lock and key. — مهر چیزیرا برداشتن To remove the seal from s. t. — مهر انگشت Fingerprint.

مِهربان Kind; affectionate.

مهربانانه Kindly.

مِهربانی Kindness. — باکسی م. کردن To do k., or be kind to, s. o.

مِهرداد Mithridates. [For معجون م.] Mithridate.

مُهردار Keeper of a seal; chancellor.

مِهر دارو ○ • Love-potion.

مُهر ساز Engraver of seals. Counterfeiter. [*festival.*

مهرگان *Ancient autumnal*

مِهرگیاه *or* مردم‌گیاه Mandrake; mandragora.

مَهرو • [Cont. of ماهرو]

مُهره Marble. Bead. [In games] Piece; man; also, die [pl. dice]. Vertebra. Nut: پیچ و مهره Bolt and nut. — م. کشیدن To glaze; gloss; mangle.

مُهره‌ای Beady: چشمان م.

مُهره بازی Playing marbles. Thimblerig. *F.* Deceitfulness. — مهره (و) ماسوره *M.* Union; nut and union.

مَهریه *S. u.* مَهر

مه طلعت • [Cont. of ماه طلعت]

مِه‌گرفتگی Fogginess.

مِه‌گرفته Foggy.

مُهلت *A.* Respite; extension of time; grace; g. period. Reprieve. Moratorium.

مَهلقا • *P. A.* 1) *a.* Moon-faced. 2) *n. Fem. pr. name.*

مُهلك *A.* = کُشنده Fatal.

مَهلکه *A.* [مهالك] Dangerous place; perilous situation.

مُهِمّ *A.* 1) *a.* Important. 2) *n.* I. or serious affair.

مُهمات *A.* Munitions; ammunitions. [Orig. pl. of مهمه fem. of مهم].

مِهمان Guest. Also, visitor. — م. کردن To treat: مرا به سینما مهمان کرد

مهمانخانه Hotel. Drawing-room [now usu. اطاق پذیرائی].

مهمانخانه‌دار Hotel-keeper; innkeeper.

مهماندار 1) = میزبان 2) Officer in charge of entertaining foreign visitors, etc.

مهمان سرا Guest-house.

مهمان نَواز Hospitable

مهمان نوازی Hospitality.

مِیادین [A. pl. of میدان]

مِیان Middle; centre. Interior; inside. Waist; loin. *Math.* Mean. – میانِ [For در میانِ] In the middle of. Between. Among. – میان آب و آتش B. the devil and the deep sea.– از میانِ From among(st); out of.–ازمیان برداشتن To eliminate. – بمیان آوردن To put up for discussion; raise (a question).–میان کلام شما شکر + 1) (I am) sorry to interrupt you. 2) By the way.– میان دعوا نرخ طی کردن To fish in troubled waters.–یك‌درمیان Every other one.–یك‌روزدرمیان E. o. day. – دو روز در میان E. third day.

میان بُر *n.* Short cut. –*a.* Cut across.–م. کردن To cut across; crosscut. To take a short cut; cut off a corner.

میان پرده Interlude.

میان تُهی • Hollow.

میانجی Mediator.

میانجی گری Mediation. – م. کردن To mediate. To arbitrate.

میان چوب Heartwood.

میان سال Middle-aged.

میان قد *P. A.* Middle-sized.

میان گیری *Mil.* Bracket; ladder. *S. a.* میانه روی

میانگین Average [متوسط].

میان منزل *P. A.* Intermediate stage; link.

مهمانیِ Banquet; feast; party; entertainment; reception.– م. کردن To give a party.

مُهمل *A. a.* Nonsensical. Neglected. Obsolete. Undotted; as a letter ه. –*n.* Nonsense; idle talk.– م. گذاشتن To abandon; neglect.

مهملات *A.* Idle talks; balderdash. [Pl. of مهمله fem. of مهمل].

مِهمیز Spur.– م. زدن [With به] [To spur.

مُهندس *A.* Engineer.–مهندس برق Electrical engineer. – مهندسِ مکانیك [With or without the *ezafah*] Mechanical e.

مهندسی *A. P.* Engineering.

مهو ش • [Cont. of ماهوش 'moon-like']. *Fem. pr. name.*

مُهوّع *A.* Nauseating.

مِهی • = بزرگی Greatness.

مُهیا *A.* = آماده Prepared; ready. – م. شدن To get r.; prepare (oneself). – م. کردن To p.; make r.

مُهیب *A.* Dreadful; formidable.

مَهیبت ه *A.* Cause of fear.

مهیج (*mohayej*) *A.* Exciting; fiery. [ep. of God.

مُهیمن *A.* Protector; watcher:

مهین 1) *a.* = بزرگترین Greatest. 2) *n.* *Fem. pr. name.*

مهینه • = بزرگترین Greatest.

می • (*mey*) Wine.

مئات or مآت *A.* Hundreds. [Pl. of مئه].

میان‌وَزن *P. A.* Middle weight.

میانه 1) *n*. Middle. *F*. a) Relations. b) Liaison [in a bad sense]. — میانهٔ دو کس را گرفتن To make it up, or judge, between two persons. — میانهٔ دو نفر را بهم زدن To set two persons at variance; embroil a person with another. — میانهٔ ایشان بهم خورد They came to a rupture. 2) *a*. Middling; mediocre. *Math*. Mean — خاور میانه Middle East. — قرنهای م. Mediæval ages.

میانه آج Bastard: سوهان م.

میانه‌رو Moderate. Economical.

میانه‌رَوی Moderation; the golden mean. Economy ○.

میانه‌گیر = 1) میانه‌رو 2) میانجی

میانی Middle; central.

میانین Perineum [عجان].

میاه *A*. [Pl. of ماء] Waters.

می‌پرست * (One) who is excessively fond of wine; wine-bibber.

می‌پرستی * Excessive fondness of wine; wine-worship.

میت *A*. [اموات] = مرده Dead (person).

میتیل *S. u*. متیل

میثاق *A*. [مواثیق] = عهد & پیمان

میخ Nail. — میخ چوبی Peg. — م. زدن To nail. — م. کوبیدن To drive (*or* hammer) a nail.

میخانه * Tavern.

میخچه Small nail. *Med*. Corn.

میخ‌چین Nippers.

میخك Clove. — گل م. Carnation.

میخکوب *a*. Nailed (up). Studded with nails. —*n*. Mallet. — م. کردن To stud with n. To nail (up). *F*. To ensure.

میخکوبی Staking. Pile-driving. Driving nails. Stud crossing. [also میخکوب].

میگسار(ی) = **میخوار(گی)**

میخوش Subacid.

میخی Nail-shaped. Cuneiform.

میدان [A. pl. میادین] Square; open space. Field: میدانِ مغناطیسی ‖ Furlong. *F*. Range. Liberty of action. — میدانِ اسب دوانی Race-course. — میدان جنگ Battlefield. — میدانِ سان Parade-ground. — میدان‌طیاره Aerodrome [usu. فرودگاه]. — میدان نوَسان *Ph*. Amplitude. — روز میدان * Field-day; day of battle. — از میدان در رفتن To show the white feather.

میدانگاه Open space; square.

میده Fine flour.

میر [Imp. of مردن]. *S. a. under* مرگ

میر [Cont. of امیر].

میراب Water distributor.

میراث *A*. Inheritance. — (به) م. بردن To inherit.

میراث‌بَر *A. P.* = **وارث**

میراخور Head-groom; master of the horse; equerry.

میراندن ○ To cause to die;

deprive of life. *Cf.* کشتن

میرزا 1) *Abolished title used before a gentleman's or after a prince's name.* [Orig. = میرزاده son of a prince]. 2) = دبیر *or* منشی

میرزا بنویس + Clerk who writes only what is dictated to him; yesman. Also, hack or drudge.

میرشکار Master of the hunt

میرغضب *P. A.* Executioner.

میز Table – میز با تختی Side-table [also میز با دیواری]. – میز تحریر Desk. – سر میز At table – میزی فرهنگ D. dictionary.

میزاب 1) = ناودان 2) Urethra.

میزان *A.* 1) o = ترازو 2) *Astr.* Libra. 3) Seventh month of the year now called [مهر ماه]. 4) Measure ; metre. 5) Amount. – بمیزانِ Amounting to. 6) Basis; standard. [Pl. موازین]. 7) + [*Used as an adj.*] Round, as a sum. – م. کردن To set, as a watch. To adjust or regulate; focus. To tune up (an engine)

میزان‌الحراره *A.* = گرماسنج

میزان‌الهوا *A.* = هواسنج

میزانه *A. P.* Measure ; time ; tempo.– چوب م. Baton.

میزانه شمار *A. P.* Metronome.

میزبان Host(ess).

میزبانی Duty of a host(ess) ; entertainment.

میزه = پیشاب Urine.

میزه راه Urethra.

میزه شناسی o Urinology.

میزه نای Ureter.

میسر (*moyasar*) *A.* Possible. *Cf.* شدنی & ممکن ‖ Procurable. Easy.

میسره *A.* Left wing. *Mil.*

میسور o *A.* Successfully accomplished.

میش Ewe. *S. a. under* کرگ

میشن [f. T. میشین] Sheep leather; basil or basan.

میشوم *A.* Inauspicious.

میشی [Of the eyes] Hazel ; also, maroon.

میعاد *A.* & میعادگاه *A. P.* Rendezvous o.

میعان *A.* Liquidity.

میغ Fog [مه]. Cloud [ابر].

میفروش * Tavern-keeper. *OS.* Wine-seller.

میکائیل *A-Heb.* Michael.

میخانه = * میکده

میکروب *Fr.* Microbe ; bacteria ; germ. [logist.

میکروب‌شناس *Fr. P.* Bacterio-

میکروب شناسی *Fr. P.* Bacteriology.

میکروب‌کش *Fr. P.* Microbicide.

میکروسکوپ *Fr.* Microscope.

میکروفون *Fr.* Microphone.

میگسار * Wine-bibber.

میگساری * Wine-drinking.

میگو Prawn; also, shrimp.

میل (*meyl*) *A*. [امیال] Desire; wish. Inclination. *Astr*. Celestial latitude.—میل ترکیبی *Chem*. Affinity. — م. داشتن To like. To w. or desire. *OS*. To be inclined (toward). —م. دارم (که) بروم I like to go; I wish to go.— م. فرمودن [Polite substitute for خوردن or آشامیدن] To eat or drink; take. — با کمال م. Most willingly. — هرطور میل شما است Just as you like. Suit yourself.—میلم کشید +I felt like it. I fancied it.

میل (*mi:l*) *A*. Rod; bar; shaft. Pin. — میل بافندگی Knitting-needle.— میل بولوس Axleshaft; halfshaft.—*Note*. بولوس is a Russian word. — میل جراحی Probe; bougie. — میل حلقوم Probang. — میل سگدست King-pin. — میل فرمان Tie-rod. —میلِ میل لنگ قامه فنر Shackle-pin. — Crankshaft. — میل مجرای بول Catheter. — میل ورزش Indian club. — م. زدن To probe. To catheterize.

میل *Fr*. Mile.

میلاد *A*. Birth. Christian era.— پیش ازمیلاد B. C. [before the birth of Christ].—پس از میلاد A. D. [Anno Domini] — عیدِ میلاد مسیح Christmas.

میلادی *A. P*. Of the Christian era. — در سال شصت م. In the year 60 A. D.

میل‌میلی *A. P*. Corded; ribbed.

میله *A. P*. Bar; shaft; rod [in a piston, etc.]. Rib (of an umbrella). *Bot*. Filament. — میلهٔ اهرم Tommy bar. — یاتاقان میله‌ای Roller-bearing.

میلی + *A. P. a*. Facultative. —*ad*. Of one's free will.

میلیار(د) *Fr*. Milliard.

میلیگرم *Fr*. Milligramme.

میلیمتر *Fr*. Millimetre.

میلیون *Fr*. Million.

میلیونر *Fr*. Millionaire.

میمنه *A*. Right wing. *Mil*.

مَیمون *A*. Auspicious; happy.

مِیمون = بوزینه Monkey; ape. — گل م. Snapdragon.

مین *Fr*. (*Mil*.) Mine.

مینا Enamel. Blue glass; b. decanter). Azure.— گل م. Aster.

میناکار or میناگر Enameller.

میناکاری or میناگری Enamel-work; enamelling. [Azure.

مینایی Enamelled. Glazed.

مین‌جمع‌کن *Fr. A. P*. = مین‌روب

مین‌روب *Fr. P*. Mine-sweeper.

مین‌گذار *Fr. P*. Mine-layer.

مین‌گذاری *Fr. P*. Mine-laying.

مینو ० = بهشت

مینوت *Fr*. = پیش نویس

مینو.رشت • Of a heavenly nature.

مینوی • ० = بهشتی

میناتور *Fr*. Miniature.

میناتورساز *Fr. P*. Miniaturist.

میو (*miow*) Miaou; mewing. – میو (میو) کردن To mew.

میوجات *S. u.* میوه

میوه [میوجات pl. formed in the A. fashion] Fruit. – باغ م. Orchard . – پرورش م. Pomiculture. – درخت م. Fruit-tree ; fruiterer . – قند میوه Fructose. – میوهٔ دل * (Beloved) child. Fruit of the womb. – م. دادن To bear fruit; fructify.

میوه‌خوار Frugivorous.

میوه خوری Fruit-bowl.

میوه‌دار Fruit-bearing ; fructiferous.

میوه فروش Fruitmonger.

مئه (*me-ah*) *A.* = سده Century. *Cf. the pl.* مئات

میهمان etc. = **مهمان** etc.

میهن Native land ; mother-land; native country.

میهن پرست Patriot(ic).

میهن پرستانه *ad.* Patriotically. –*a.* Patriotic: احساسات م.

میهن پرستی Patriotism.

میهن دوست = **میهن پرست**

میهن فروش Traitor to one's country.

ن [Cont. of نه used in making negative verbs. Ex. نمیروم *I do not go*, and نرو *Do not go*].
نا *Prefix equivalent to the E.* in-, un-, etc. Ex. نادرست incorrect ; ناگفته unsaid.
ناآزموده Inexperienced.
نااستوار Unstable; unsteady.
ناامن *P. A.* Insecure.
ناامنی *P. A.* Insecurity.
نااُمید Hopeless; desperate. – ن. شدن To despair; give up hope. – ن. کردن To disappoint. – امیدکسیرا ناامیدکردن + To dash one's hopes.
ناامیدی Hopelessness ; despair.
نا اهل *P. A.* Unworthy.
ناب 1) Pure : زرِ ناب ‖ 2) Clear : شراب ن.
ناباب Unsuitable; unfit.
نابالغ *P. A.* Under age.
نابجا 1) Inopportune. 2) *Bot.* Adventitious.
نا برجا Movable [منقول].
نابغه *A.* [نوابغ] Genius.
نابکار ○ * Wicked. Useless.
نابلد *P. A.* Unacquainted.
نابود Non-existent . Annihilated. – ن. شدن To disappear. To be annihilated. – ن. کردن To annihilate or destroy.
نابهنگام Untimely ; inopportune.
نابینا = کور Blind.
نابینایی = کوری Blindness.
ناپاك Unclean.
ناپاکی Uncleanness. Pollution.
ناپایدار 1) Transient. 2) *Ph.* Unstable.
ناپایداری Transience. Instability.
ناپخته *or* + نپخته = 1) خام 2) نارس 3) ناآزموده
ناپدری Step-father.
ناپدید Invisible. Disappeared. – ن. شدن To disappear or vanish. – ن. کردن To cause to d.
ناپرهیزگار Incontinent.
ناپرهیزی Inattention to diet ; intemperance. *See* پرهیز
ناپسری Step-son.
ناپسند *or* ناپسندیده Indecent. Disagreeable.
ناپیدا Invisible.
ناتمام *P. A.* Incomplete. – ن. گذاردن To leave unfinished.
ناتنی Of half blood: برادر ناتنی half-brother.
ناتو + Awkward. Hard to deal with. – آدم ن. A. customer ; hard nut to crack.
ناتوان Weak. Infirm.

ناتوانی Weakness ; debility.
ناجنس P. A. = بد جنس
ناجوانمرد Coward(ly).
ناجوانمردانه As a coward. Foul(ly). ـ ن. رفتار کردن To play foul. [play.
ناجوانمردی Cowardice. Foul
ناجور Ill-matched ; odd. Incongruous. Uncongenial. ـ وضع ن. + Bad fix; awkward situation.
ناجی o A. One who escapes or is saved. Cf. منجی
ناچار a. Compelled ; forced. Helpless. —ad. Necessarily ; of necessity [also بناچار]. ـ ن. شدن To be compelled or f.
ناچاری Distress ; helplessness.
ناچیز Insignificant. Worthless.
ناحق P. A. a. Unjustified; unlawful. Undue. False. —ad. [Also بناحق] Unlawfully. Unjustly. Unduly.
ناحیه A. [نواحی] District ; region. Area. Ward [now بخش].
ناخدا Captain (of a ship).
ناخدا دو Lieutenant colonel [in the Navy].
ناخدا سه Major [in the Navy].
ناخلف P. A. Not worthy of his (or her) father.
ناخن (Finger-)nail. ـ ن. گرفتن To pare (or trim) one's nails. [خسیس & جوکی
ناخن خشك + Close-fisted. Cf.
ناخنك Melilot. Med. Pterygium. OS. Small nail. ـ ن. زدن To pick (and steal); pilfer.
ناخنك‌زن or ناخنکی (One) who habitually picks or pilfers.
ناخن‌گیر Nail-scissors ; nail primmer.
ناخنی Ungual : استخوان ن
ناخواسته Unwished.
ناخوانده Uninvited.
ناخوش a. Ill; sick. Unpleasant; harsh. —n. I. person ; patient. ـ ن. شدن To fall ill.
ناخوش‌آواز o Having an unpleasant voice.
ناخوشی Illness. Disease.
نادار or ندار = تهیدست
ناداری or نداری = تهیدستی
نادان 1) a. Ignorant. Foolish. 2) n. I. person. Fool.
نادانی Ignorance. Foolishness.
نادختری Step-daughter.
نادِر A. 1) a. = کمیاب Rare. 2) n. Mas. pr. name.
نادرست Incorrect. Untrue ; false. Dishonest. [ness.
نادرستی Dishonesty. Incorrect-
نادره A. [نوادر] Rarity; curiosity. (Witty) anecdote. [Orig. fem. of نادر].
نادِم A. = پشیمان
نادیده Unseen. ـ ن. پنداشتن or ن. گرفتن To ignore; wink or connive at. To be indifferent to.
نار • [Cont. of انار]
نار o A. = 1) آتش 2) دوزخ

ناراحت *P. A.* Uncomfortable. Uneasy. Inclined to make trouble or mischief. — ن. کردن To inconvenience; disturb. To worry. — ن. شدن To w. To be inconvenienced.

ناراحتی *P. A.* Inconvenience; uneasiness; annoyance. Worry.

ناراست = 1) نادرست 2) دروغ

ناراسته Indirect [غیر مستقیم].

ناراستی Falsehood. Dishonesty.

ناراضی *P. A.* Dissatisfied; displeased; discontent(ed).

ناردان Dried pomegranate seeds.

نارَس Unripe; green.

نارَسا Inaudible. Inexpressive.

نارضایتی *P. A.* Dissatisfaction; discontent.

نارفته Unpassed, as a road.

نارگیل 1) Cocoa-nut. 2) ○ [Also نارکیله] Nargile; hookah. *Cf.* غلیان ‖ درخت ن. Cocoa-nut palm.

نارَنج (Sour) orange.

نارنجستان Orangery.

نارنجك Grenade; shell.

نارنجی Orange(-coloured).

نارنگی Tangerine.

نارو + Foul play; nasty trick. — ن. بکسی زدن To play s. o. a nasty trick; p. him false. [Undue.

نارَوا Inadmissible; unjust.

نارو َن Elm-tree.

ناز Love-airs. Mincing air; affected or lackadaisical manners. Also, coquetry. — ناز شست Tribute of praise; prize; credit. — ن. کردن To put on airs. To play hard to get. To be coaxed. To make a fuss. To mince. To feign disdain. — ناز کسیرا کشیدن To bear some one's airs. — ن گل ُ Humble plant.

نازا Barren: زنش ن. بود

نازایی Barrenness.

نازبالش Small cushion.

ناز پرو َرده Delicately brought up; pampered.

نازدار Affected; lackadaisical. Mincing. Coquettish.

نازُك Thin. Delicate; tender. — ن. کردن To make thin(ner). To soften, as one's voice.

نازك بدن * *P. A.* Of a delicate body.

نازك دل Tender-hearted.

نازك كارى Elaborate work; delicate touch; hair-stroke.

نازك نارنجی + Hard to please; fastidious.

نازك نی Fibula.

نازكی Thinness. Delicateness.

نازِل *A.* Low; reduced: قیمتهای ن. Descending ○. — ن. شدن = پایین آمدن

نازنین Nice; fine; lovely. Tender. Precious: اوقات ن. زشت = **نازیبا**

نازیدن [ناز] To boast. To

exult; [with به] b. of ; plume oneself on.

ناس A. = مردم

ناس Snuff [انفیه].

ناساز Out of tune ; discordant. Unhealthy.

ناسازگار Unwholesome. Unsuitable. Unsociable. Incompatible.

ناسازگاری Unsociability. Incompatibility.

ناسپاس Unthankful ; ungrateful.

ناسپاسی Ingratitude.

ناسِخ A. 1) a. Abrogating. 2) n. Abolisher. Order superseding previous one. Verse abrogating another.

ناسره Base; bad.

ناسزا Abusive (language).

ناسزاوار Undeserving.

ناسُفته • Unbored. F. Virgin.

ناسك o A. Ascetic or devout (man).

ناسوت o A. Human nature. – عالم ن. The earthly world.

ناسور A. [نواسیر] Fistula; sinus.

نسوز = ناسوز

ناشاد = غمگین

ناشایسته Indecent. Undeserving.

ناشتا Fasting; hungry.

ناشتایی 1) o Hunger; fast. 2) = صبحانه Breakfast.

ناشر A. [ناشرین] Publisher.

ناشُکر P. A. Ungrateful (to God).

ناشکری P. A. Unthankfulness or ingratitude (toward God).

ناشکیب & ناشکیبا Impatient.

ناشکیبائی Impatience.

ناشمرده Indistinct. Uncounted or countless. Cf. نشمرده

ناشناخت Disguised; incognito.

ناشناس Unacquainted. Disguised; incognito.

ناشنیده Unheard(-of).

ناشور Wool in the grease. Unbleached sheeting.

ناشی A. [Fem. ناشیه] Arising; resulting . – ن. شدن از To arise or spring from ; be prompted by. To issue.

ناشی (?) Inexpert; unskilful.

ناشی‌گری Lack of skill.

ناصاف P. A. Uneven. Impure.

ناشکیبا(ئی) = P. A. ناصبور(ی)

ناصِح A. Admonitor; adviser. [Pl. نصحا o & ناصحین]

ناصِر A. Assister ; friend. Defender. *Mas. pr. name.*

ناصرالدین (A.) *Mas. pr. name.* OS. Defender of the faith

ناصَواب P.A. = نادرست Incorrect.

ناصیه A. [نواصی] 1) = پیشانی 2) F. Mien ; appearance.

ناطِق A. 1) a. Talking. Rational. – حیوان ن. R. being; i. e. man. – فیلم ن. T. film. 2) n. Speaker; orator.

ناطقه A. 1) a. [Fem. of ناطق]. 2) n. [For قوة ناطقه]. Faculty of speech.

ناطلبیده P. A. = **ناخوانده**

ناظِر A. 1) *a*. Seeing; watching. Controlling. — عضو ناظر (*Law*) Official receiver. 2) *n*. Spectator. Observer. Controller; overseer. [Pl. ناظرین & *Cf*. نظار]. — ناظر خرج Steward. — ن. بودن [With به] To see or watch. To govern or order; be applicable to.

ناظم A. 1) *n*. Superintendent. Regulator. 2) *a*. [Of a line] Normal.

ناف Navel. *F*. Centre.

نافذ A. 1) *OS*. Penetrating. 2) *F*. *a*) Binding. *b*) Valid.

نافِر • A. = **بیزار - بیمیل**

نافرمان Disobedient.

نافرمانی Disobedience. — ن. کردن To be disobedient.

نافع A. = **سودمند**

نافله A. [نوافل] Supererogatory (prayer).

نافه A. Bag of musk.

نافَهم or + نفهم P. A. Stupid; unintelligent, foolish.

نافهمی P. A. Silliness; dullness of understanding.

نا قابل P. A. Insignificant; trifling [ناچیز]. Unworthy; undeserving [ناشایسته].

ناقِص A. Defective: فعل ن. ‖ Deficient. Also, imperfect — قطع ن. Ellipsis. — مخروط ن Truncated cone. — هرم ن T. pyramid. — ن. شدن To be mutilated or deformed. To be badly hurt +. — ن. کردن To mutilate. To render defective.

ناقص الخلقه A. Deformed; malformed.

ناقص العقل A. = کم‌عقل & بی‌خرد

ناقِض A. 1) *a*. Violating. Cancelling. Contradicting. 2) *n*. Violator.

ناقِل A. Conductor. Transmitter. Narrator. Vehicle. [Fem. ناقله. Ex. نواقل = آلات ن. means of conveyance; transport means].

ناقُلا + Naughty. Cagey; shrewd cunning; sly.

ناقله A. 1) *a*. [Fem. of ناقل]. 2) *n*. [For آلت ن.] Means of transport. *Cf*. *the pl*. نواقل

ناقوس A. Gong; bell. — برج ن. Belfry.

ناك *Suf*. *meaning* full of. Ex. ترسناك Dreadful.

ناك × Cleaned out; penniless.

ناکار کردن To knock out [in boxing]. — *Note*. ناکار is per. a corruption of the E. "knockout".

ناکام Unsuccessful; disappointed.

ناکامی Disappointment; failure.

ناکرده کار o Inexperienced.

ناکس Ignoble (person). Coward(ly).

ناکسی Meanness. Cowardice.

ناکوك Out of tune.

ناگاه Suddenly.
ناگزیر Having no alternative. Inevitable. — ن. بود از اینکه حرف بزند He could not help speaking. [manent.
ناگسستنی • Inseperable. Permanent.
ناگشا *Bot*. Indehiscent.
ناگفتنی *or* **نگفتنی** Unspeakable; inexpressible; ineffable.
ناگفته Unsaid. — ن. نماند که Let it not remain unsaid that.
ناگوار *or* **ناگوارا** Unpleasant. Unwholesome. Indigestible.
ناگه • [Cont. of ناگاه].
ناگهان Sudden(ly).
ناگهانی Sudden; unexpected.
نالان Groaning. Complaining.
نالایق *P. A.* Incapable. Unworthy. [strain.
نالش 1) = ناله 2) Plaintive strain.
ناله Groan(ing). Complaint. — آه و ناله ‖ **نالیدن** = ن. کردن G. and cursing.
نالیدن [نال] To groan; moan. To lament. To complain. [With از] To g. under.

نام Name. *Cf*. اسم ‖ *By e*. Fame.— ن. بردن To name or mention.— ن. نهادن To n. or call.— نام و نشان Name and particulars (*or* address). — بنامِ In the n. of. On behalf of. By the name of — شخصی حسن ن. A man named Hassan. — بحسن نامی آنرا فروختم I sold it to one Hassan.

نامادری Step-mother.
نامدار — • نام آور
نامبرده *a*. Above-named; above-mentioned. —*n*. The above-named person; he *or* she [pl. نامبردگان the above-named persons; they].
نامتناهی *P. A.* Infinite.
نامجو Who seeks fame.
نامحدود *P. A.* Unlimited. *Math*. Indeterminate.
نامحرم *P. A.* Not intimate (enough to have access to the women's apartment).
نامدار Celebrated; famous; illustrated.
نامرادی *P. A.* = **ناکامی**
نامربوط *P. A.* 1) *a*. Irrelevant. Incoherent. 2) *n*. Abusive language. I. speech.
نامرتب *P. A.* Irregular. Untidy. Muddled up.
نامرد Coward(ly).
نامردی Cowardliness; dastardliness; foul play. — ن. کردن To play f.; be cowardly.
نامرضی *P A* = **ناپسند(یده)**
نامرغوب *P. A.* Of inferior quality; undesirable.
نامرغوبی *P. A.* Undesirability; inferior quality.
نامرئی *P. A.* = **ناپیدا**
نامزد *a*. Engaged; betrothed. —*n*. Candidate. Fiancé(e). — ن. شدن To be betrothed. To

be nominated. ـ ن. کردن To engage. To nominate.

نامزدی Engagement.

نامزروع *P. A.* Uncultivated.

نا مُساعد *P. A.* Unfavourable.

نا مُساوی *P. A.* Unequal.

نا مستعد *P. A.* Untalented.

نا مَشروع *P. A.* Unlawful; illegal. ـ درآمد نامشروع Illicit (*or* immoral) earning.

نامطبوع *P. A.* Unpleasant; disagreeable. [bad.

نامطلوب *P. A.* Undesirable;

نا مُعتبر *P. A.* Wanting good reputation. Unreliable; spurious.

نامعتمد *P. A.* Unreliable.

نا مَعروف *P. A.* Unknown. Fameless.

نامعقول *P. A.* Irrational.

نامعلوم *P. A.* Unknown. Uncertain; undecided.

نامعین *P. A.* Indefinite. Uncertain.

نامفهوم *P. A.* Unintelligible.

نا مُلایم *P. A.* Rough; harsh.

نامُلایمات + *P. A.* [f. نامُلایم regarded as a noun and pluralized in the A fashion]. Disagreeables.

ناممنون *P. A.* Ungrateful.

نا مُناسب *P. A.* Unsuitable; unfit [*Of price*] Unreasonable.

نا مُنظم *P. A.* Irregular. Fitful.

نام نویسی Enlistment; enrolment. Registration. ـ ن. کردن To enrol. To register.

نا مُوافق *P. A.* Averse. Unfavourable.

نا مُوجه *P. A.* [*Of an excuse*] Poor; unfounded; lame.

ناموَر • = نامدار

ناموزون *P. A.* Unrythmical.

ناموس *A.* [نوامیس] Principle; law. Chastity. *By e.* One's wife and daughters.

نامه 1) Letter. 2) Book [in comb.]. 3) [Short for روزنامه]. 4) Deed; certificate.

نامه بَر Letter-carrier. ـ کبوتر نامه بر Carrier-pigeon.

نامه رَسان Postman; post-boy. ـ دفتر نامه رسانی Peon-book; dispatch-book.

نامهربان Unkind.

نامهربانی Unkindness.

نامه نگاری Letter-writing.

نامی = نامدار & معروف

نامیدن [نام] To name; call.

نامیده [P. P. of نامیدن]

نامیسر *P. A.* Impossible.

نان Bread. ـ نان بستنی Wafer. ـ نان شیرینی Pastry. ـ ن. دادن (به) To give daily bread (to); support. ـ ن. بهم قرض دادن *Met.* To "claw each other" [adapted from the E. proverb "Claw me, and I'll claw thee"]; "honour each other like thieves"; assist each other by dishonest means. ن. را بنرخ روز خوردن – *Met*. To go with the tide; be a time-server. – نانش توی روغن است *Met*. His bread is buttered on both sides. – ن. پیدا کردن *or* ن. درآوردن To earn one's bread. – ن. توش درمیاد + It brings grist to the mill; it is lucrative. – با کسی نان و نمك خوردن To eat salt with a person. – درختن ن. Breadfruit.

نان‌آور Bread-winner; supporter.

نانوا = نان پز

نانجیب *P. A*. Unchaste; lewd.

نانخور Dependant; dependent.

نان‌دانی + [Vulgarly نون‌دونی] Means of earning bread or (illegal) profit.

نانوا Baker.

نانواخانه Bakery. Bakers collectively.

نانوایی Baking bread. [For دکان ن.] Bakery.

ناو (War)ship.

ناو استوار [In the Navy] Warrant officer.

ناوبان [In the Navy] Lieutenant.

ناوبر Navigator.

ناوبری Navigation. – ناو بری هوائی Aeronavigation.

ناوتیپ Naval brigade.

ناوچه Small battleship. Vedette-boat; picket-boat; scout.

ناودان Downpipe; rain-(water) pipe. [Of a mill] Hopper; feeder.

ناودیس Synclinal.

ناو سروان Naval captain.

ناوسمان Aqueduct.

ناوشکن Destroyer.

ناوك * Small arrow.

ناوگروه 1) Brigade [in the Navy]. 2) Flotilla.

ناوه Hod.

ناوه کش Hodman.

ناوی 1) *a*. Boat-like. *Anat*. Scaphoid. 2) *n*. Soldier (in the Navy); sailor.

ناویژه Gross: سود ناویژه

ناه Mustiness. – بوی ن. Musty smell.

ناهار 1) Luncheon. 2) ناشتا = o [Orig = ناآهار ‖ *See* آهار]

ناهارخوری Dining-room.

ناه کش Air-drain.

ناهمرنگ Ill-matched.

ناهموار Uneven. *F*. Disagreeable.

ناهمواری Unevenness.

ناهنجار Rough. Crooked. Abnormal.

ناهید Venus [زهره]. *Fem. pr. name*.

نای 1) = نی 2) Windpipe. – دریچهٔ ن. Epiglottis.

نایاب Unobtainable; rare.

نایب *A*. [نوءاب] 1) Deputy. 2) = ستوان ‖ 3) [Of a legation] Secretary.

نایب‌الحکومه *A*. = بخشدار

نایب السلطنه *A*. Regent; vi-

ceroy.
نایب رئیس *a. p.* Vice-president. Deputy-chairman.
نایب مناب *a. p.* Locum-tenens; vicegerent; deputy.
نائبه o *A.* [نوائب] Calamity.
نایچه *or* **نایژه** Bronchus. *OS.* Small reed or pipe. — ورم ن *or* نزلهٔ ن. o Bronchitis.
نایره *A.* = شعله - آتش
نائِل *A. or* **نایل** Attaining. — ن. شدن به To attain or obtain.
نائم *A.* = خواب & خوابیده
نباتˊ *A.* 1) = گیاه Plant; vegetable. 2) Sugar-candy.
نباتی *A. P.* 1) = گیاهی 2) Light buff.
نباداˊ = مبادا
نبردˊ Battle. — ن. کردن = جنگیدن
نبردگاه • Battlefield.
نبردناو Battle cruiser.
نبشˊ *A.* Exhumation. Corner; angle; edge. — خانه اش نبشِ خیابان است His house stands at an angle to the street. — آهن نبشی Angle-iron.
نبضˊ *A.* Pulse. — نبض کسیرا گرفتن To feel a person's pulse.
نبض سنج *A. P.* Pulsimeter; pulsometer.
نبض‌شناسی *A. P.* Sphygmology.
نبض نگار *A.P.* Sphygmograph.
نبوّت *A.* Prophecy. Prophetic mission.
نُبوغ *A.* Genius.
نبویˊ *A.* Prophetic. Descended from the Prophet.
نبی *A.* [انبیاء] = پیغمبر
نبید o = 1) نوید 2) نبیذ
نبیذ o *A.* (Date) wine.
نبیرهˊ Great great grandchild.
نبیلˊ o *A.* Noble. Generous.
نبیه *A.* [Fem. of نبی] Prophetess.
نپخته = 1) خام 2) نارس
نُت *Fr.* (*Mus.*) Note.
نِتاج *A.* Breed. Progeny.
نتایج [Pl. of نتیجه]
نتراشیده و نخراشیده + *or* × Rough-hewn; unlicked; uncultivated.
نتربوق [*Usu.* ملانتربوق *q. v.*]
نترس + Fearless [usu. in سرِ نترس intrepidity; boldness].
نتیجهˊ *A.* [نتایج] Result. Conclusion. Issue. Great grandchild. — ن. دادن To produce a result. To be efficacious. — ن. گرفتن To conclude. To infer. To get a good r. — ن. آنکه To sum up. — در نتیجه Consequently. — در نتیجهٔ As a (*or* the) result of.
نتیجةًˊ *A.* Consequently.
نتیجه بخش *A. P.* Efficacious; useful.
نثار *A.* Money scattered at a wedding or feast. Garnish. — ن. کردن To scatter or strew.

To offer or sacrifice.
نثر´ *A.* Prose.
نثراً *A.* In prose.
نجابت *A.* Noble character ; gentleness ; chastity.
نجات *A.* = رستگاری Deliverance; salvation. – ن. دادن = رهانیدن To save; deliver. – کرجی ن. Life-boat.
نجات‌الله (*A.*) *Mas. pr. name. OS.* Deliverance from God.
نجات دهنده *A. P.* Saviour ; deliverer; redeemer.
نجار´ *A.* Carpenter. Joiner. – نجارشیروانی Roof-truss maker.
نجاری *A.P.* Carpentry. Joinery.
نجاست *A.*' Uncleanness. Excrement.
نجاشی *A.* Negus.
نُجباء *A.* The nobles; the nobility. *Cf. the s.* نجیب
نجس´ *A.* (Ceremonially) unclean. *Cf.* ناپاك & پلید.
نجم´ *A.* [انجم & نجوم] = ستاره
نجوا´ or نجوی (*-va*) *A.* Whisper. – ن. کردن To whisper.
نجوم [A pl. of نجم]
نجوم‌بین *A. P.* = ستاره شناس
نجوم بینی *A. P.* = ستاره شناسی
نُجومی *A. P.* Astronomical ; also, astrological. – تقویم ن. Almanach.
نجیب´ *A.* Noble; gentle; chaste. [*Of colour*] Soft ; sober ; quiet. *Cf. the pl.* نجبا
نحریر *A.* = دانشمند - زبردست

نحس´ *A. a.* Unlucky; sinister. Miserable. *–n.* = نحوست
نحسان´ or نحسین *A.* [D. of نحس] The two unlucky stars; i. e. Mars and Saturn.
نحسی = + نحوست ‖ ن. کردن To be miserable, as a child.
نحل´ o *A.* = زنبور عسل
نحو (*nahv*) *A.* [انحاء] 1) Manner ; way. – بچه ن. How ? In what m. ? 2) Syntax.
نُحوست *A.* Inauspiciousness ; unlucky effect.
نحوه´ *A.* Special manner of doing something. *Cf.* نحو
نحوی *A.* 1) *a.* Syntactic. 2) *n.* Grammarian [usu. in the pl. نحویون].
نحیف´ *A.* = لاغر & ضعیف
نخ´ Thread; string. Yarn. (Sewing-)cotton. – نخ پشم Worsted. – نخ کردن To thread. To string.
نُخاع *A.* Spinal cord. Marrow.
نُخاعی *A.* [Fem. نخاعیه] Medullary. – اشعهٔ نخاعیه M. rays.
نُخاله *A.* Siftings; bran. Rubbish. – نخالهٔ بنائی Rubble.
نُخبه *A.* Best part; choice p.
نخ ریس = نخ تاب
نخجیر = شکار Prey. Hunting. – ن. کردن To hunt.
نخ ریس Spinner. Spinning-jenny.
نخ ریسی Spinning.
نخست *a.* First. *–ad.* At f.

نخست زاده First-born (child).
نخست وزیر *P. A.* Prime Minister; Premier.
نخستین First.
نَخشب City in Torkestan; famous for a well near it from which a magician or sage was said to have raised an imitation of the moon.
نخ کوك Basting(s).
نخ گیر [In a sewing-machine] Thread eyelet.
نَخل *A.* [Collective for نخله] = درخت خرما Date-palm.
نخلستان *A. P.* Palm-grove.
نخلی *A.* Palmaceous.
نخ نما Threadbare.
نَخوت (-*vat*) *A.* = خودبینی & [غرور
نُخود Pea. — داغ ن. Issue-pea. — نخود همه آشی بودن To have a finger in every pie. — بی نخود سیاه فرستادن To send for yard-wide pack-thread; also, send on a fool's errand. *OS.* To keep (a child) out of the way, or get rid of him, by sending him to fetch black peas.
نخود آب Broth with peas and lean meat; pea-soup. Decoction of peas.
نخودچی Chick-pea.
نخودی Pea-shaped. Buff (colour). *Anat.* Pisiform. — ن. خندیدن To giggle.

نَخی Cotton *adj.* : قماش ن.
نَخیل *A.* (Date-)palm.
نِدا *A.* Proclamation. Voice. — حالت ن. Vocative case. — حرف ن. Interjection.
نَدار *S. u.* نادار
نداری or **ناداری** Poverty; indigence.
ندّاف o *A.* = **پنبه زن**
ندامت *A.* = **پشیمانی**
ندانسته Unknowingly.
ندانم کار + Tactless. Inexperienced.
ندانم کاری + Lack of experience or tact.
نُدبه *A.* = **سوگواری - گریه**
نُدرَت *A.* Rareness. — بندرت Seldom; rarely.
ندما [Pl. of ندیم].
ندید بدید + Parvenu; sordid.
ندیده 1) Unseen. 2) *n.* + Great great great grandchild.
ندیم *A.* [ندماء] Boon companion. King's jester.
نَذر *A.* Vow. Oblation. — ن. بستن ن. داشتن ‖ **شرط** بستن = + To be under a vow. — ن. کردن To vow; dedicate by a v. To distribute charitably
نَذری *A.P.* 1) Vowed. Votive; oblatory. 2) + = **مجانی**
نذیر o *A.* Nazarite.
نَر Male.
نَرّاد *A.* (Great) dicer.
نِرخ Rate; price. — بنرخِ At the rate of. — بنرخ روز At

the current price. – ن. بستن
To fix prices. [With بر]
To rate or tariff.
نرخ بندی Rating; fixing rates; tariffication.
نَرد Backgammons.
نَردبان Ladder. – نردبان دو طرفه
Pair (*or* set) of steps. –
مثل نردبان دزد ها *F*. Lanky.
نَرده Hand - rail; palisade.
S. a. نورد [*name*.
نَرگس Narcissus. *Fem. pr*.
نرگسی Kind of dish with eggs and vegetables.
نَرم Soft. Smooth. Fine. *F*.
Mild ; gentle. – ن. کردن To
reduce to powder ; pulverize. To soften. To tame.
To mollify. [نر & ماده
نر ماده Hermaphrodite. See
نرم بالك Malacopterygian.
نرم تن Molluscan. *OS*. Of
a soft or delicate body.–
نرم تنان *npl*. Mollusks.
نرم دل Tender-hearted; soft.
نرمش Suppleness; softness.
نرم شامه Pia mater.
نرم‌نرم Softly; gently.
نرم نرمك (1 = نرم نرم
2) Gradually.
نر ماده = نرموك
نَرمه Soft part. Fontanel.– نرمهٔ
ساق پا Calf. – نرمهٔ گوش Ear-lap ; lobe of the ear.
نرمه استخوان Cartilage[غضروف].
نَرمی Softness; gentleness.
Fineness. Mildness. Leniency. – ن. کردن To behave
softly, gently, or leniently.–
بنرمی Gently or softly.
نروژ *Fr*. Norway.
نروژی *Fr. P*. Norwegian.
نرّه خر + = خرِ نر He-ass.
F. Burly, coarse fellow.
نرّه گاو + = گاوِ نر Bull; ox.
نرّه غول + Giant. *OS*. Male ghoul.
نری Maleness. Virility.
نریان Stallion.
نریمان *Mas. pr. name*.
نَزار • Thin; lean.
نِزاع *A*. Quarrel ; dispute. –
ن.کردن To quarrel or d.
نزاکت Elegance. Courtesy.
[Word coined from نازك
in the A. fashion].
نَزدِ Near ; by the side of.
With : کتاب نزد من است ‖ In
the opinion of •.
نَزدیك Near Neighbouring.
At hand. Close ; approximate. Related. – نزدیكِ *prep*.
Near; close to; by. – نزدیكِ
دوسال Nearly 2 years.– ن. شدن
To come near(er). To draw
near ; approach. – ن. کردن
To bring n. ; cause to a. –
راه را نزدیك کردن To take a
short cut. *Met*. To meet
one's end ; go to one's last
home. – از نزدیك دیدن To see
for oneself.

نزدیکان Relatives [pl. of نزدیك which is only an adj.].

نزدیك بین 1) *a*. Near-sighted ; myopic. 2) *n*. Myope.

نزدیك بینی Short-sightedness; near-sightedness ; myopia.

نزدیکی Nearness ; proximity. Vicinity ; neighbourhood . Relationship . — در این ن. In the vicinity; nearby.— درهمین ن. ها Shortly ; presently. — ن. کردن To lie; have sexual intercourse.

نزع *A*. Agony of death.

نزف الدم *A*. = خون رَوی

نزله *A*. Catarrh; rheum. — نزلهٔ و بائی همه جاگیر ○ Influenza.

نزول *A* Descending. Revelation. Interest (on money).— نزول آب سبز Glaucoma . — نزولِ آب سیاه Amaurosis. — ن. کردن *vi*. To come down ; descend. To arrive or lodge [in speaking of a king نزولِ اجلال فرمودن]. —*vt*.+To borrow on interest.

نزهت *A*. Pleasure; recreation.— نزهت خاطر • Enlivening of the mind.

نژاد Race. Breed : نژاد اسب

نژاد شناس Ethnologist.

نژاد شناسی Ethnology.

نژادی Racial.

نژند = 1) غمگین 2) ترسناك 3) خشمگین

نساء *A*. = زن Woman.

نساج *A*. = بافنده Weaver.

نساجی *A*. *P*. = بافندگی

نسار Place not exposed to the sun.

نسب *A*. [انساب] Lineage; parentage.— علم انساب Genealogy.

نسبت *A*. Relation. Consanguinity. Ratio or proportion. Regard ; respect. — به ن. As compared with. Than. With r. to. Relative to; concerning. To(ward). — به ن. Proportionally.— به نسبتِ In the proportion of. On a scale of. — ن. دادن To attribute, impute, or ascribe.

نسب نامه *A*. *P*. Genealogy ; genealogical tree.

نسبةً *A*. Comparatively; relatively.

نسبی (*nasa-*) *A*. Consanguineous. - قرابت ن. Consanguinity.

نسبی (*nes-*) *A*. Relative. Proportional. — شرکت ن. P. liability partnership.

نسبیت *A*. Relativity.

نسترن Sweetbrier ; eglantine.

نستعلیق *a*. *p*. Style of writing used in lithography.

نسج *A*. Tissue; texture.

نسخ (*naskh*) *A*. Abrogation ; abolition. Style of writing used in typography . — ن. کردن To annul ; abolish.

نسخ (*nosakh*) [Pl. of نسخه]

نسختین *A*. [D. of نسخه] Two copies ; duplicate.

نسخه *A*. [نسخ (*nosakh*)]

Copy. *Med.* Recipe; prescription. — ن. برداشتن از To copy or transcribe; make a copy of. — در دو نسخه In duplicate. — در سه ن. In triplicate.

نسخه بدل *a. p.* Variant.

نَسر *A.* 1) o = دال Eagle. 2) o = کرکس Vulture. — نسر طایر *Astr.* E. or Aquila. — نسر واقع *Astr.* Lyra.

نَسرین [For گل ن.] Jonquil.

نسطوری *A.* [نساطره] Nestorian.

نَسق *A.* Mode; manner; style. Order. Arrangement. *Astr.* [In full النسق (*anasagh*)] Orion. — کسیرا نسق کردن To torture s. o. by mutilating some part of his body. — بر این ن. In this manner. — وحدتِ ن Coordination.

نَسل *A.* Offspring; seed. Generation. — نسلاً بعدِ نسلٍ From generation to g.

نَسناس *A.* Orang-outang.

نِسوان *A.* = زنان Women.

نسوز or **ناسوز** Fireproof. — آجرِ نسوز Fire-brick; refractory brick. — پنبهٔ ن. Asbestos.

نِسیان *A.* = **فراموشی**

نَسیم Breeze. Zephyr *.

نِسیه *A.* 1) *a.* Credit transaction; credit sale. 2) *ad.* On credit; on tick. — ن. فروختن To sell on credit.

نِشا Seedling. — ن. کردن To plant out.

نِشادُر Sal-ammoniac; ammonium chloride. — جوهر نشادر Aqua ammonia.

نشاسته Starch.

نشاسته‌ای Starchy. Amylaceous.

نِشاط *A.* = خوشی Joy; mirth. — ن. کردن = o **خوشی کردن**

نشاط آور *A. P.* = **نشاط انگیز**

نشاط انگیز *A. P.* Exhilarating. Lively; gay; allegro.

نشاف o *A.* Absorbing *adj.*

نِشان Mark; trace; sign; token. Symptom. Decoration; badge; insignia. Aim; target. — نشان شیروخورشید Order of the Lion and Sun. — ن. دادن To show. — ن. زدن To wear a decoration. — ن. کردن To mark (out); m. off. To select. To aim at. To sight (a gun). — با یك تیر دو نشان زدن To kill two birds with one shot.

نشان [Imp. of نشاندن] [pared.

نشاندار Marked. *C. P.* Pre-

نِشاندن or **نشانیدن** [نشان] To seat. To settle. To set; plant. To shake off, as dust *. To wash away *. To suppress *. To extinguish * [خاموش کردن]. — آن زن را نشانده بودند That woman was in keeping.

نشانده [P. P. of نشاندن]

نشانگاه Butt; target.

نشانه Indication; sign; token. Symptom. Aim. Butt; target. Memento; reminder. — ن رفتن To (take) aim.

نشانه رَوی Aiming; sighting.— ن.دستگاه Sighting instrument; sight.

نشانی Address. Indication. Token; proof. —بنشانی «فلان‌چیز» And the proof or password is "such and s. a thing."

نشت or **نشد** (?) Leakage. — ن.کردن To leak or ooze.

نِشتر S. u. نیشتر [Leakage.

نشتی or **نشدی** a. Leaky. —n.

نُشخوارکردن To chew the cud.

نشخوارکننده [نشخوار کنندگان] Ruminant; cud-chewer.

نشدنی Impossible.

نَشر A. Publication. Spreading about. —حشر و نشر Associating together. — ن.کردن = **انتشار**دادن

نشریه A. [نشریات] Publication. Leaflet.

نِشست Act of sitting. Session. Subsidence; sinking.— ن.کردن To subside; settle. — ن. و برخاست Association.

نِشستن [نشین] To sit; take a seat. To reside [ساکن‌شدن]. To be quelled; cease •. — ته ن. To settle.—آب باین‌زمین نمی‌نشیند This land is too high to be irrigated.

نشسته 1) [P. P. of نشستن] (Having) sat. 2) a. Sitting. 3) ad. In a sitting posture. 4) n. pl. نشستگان Those sitting; sitters.

نیشگان = **نشکنج** [knife.

نشگرده Cobbler's or saddler's

نشمرده Uncounted. F. Countless. Cf. ناشمرده

نشمه (?) = **فاحشه**

نشمیدن ○ To feast and drink; live in luxury.

نشنیدنی Unfit to be heard; shocking.

نشنیده = **ناشنیده**

نشو (nashv) A. Growth.— نشوو نماکردن To grow up; thrive.

نُشور A. = **رستاخیز**

نُشوق A. Errhine. [Ecstasy.

نشوه (nashveh) A. Inebrity.

نشیب Declivity; descent.

نَشید ○ A. = **سرود**

نشیمن Dwelling. Seat.— ن.کردن To dwell. To sit. — اطاق ن. Sitting-room.

نشیمن‌گاه Dwelling-place. [Of a bird] Roost.

نشین 1) [Imp. of نشستن] 2) n. Anus or podex.

نشئه [Corruption of نشوه]

نصّ A. [نُصوص] Text.

نِصاب A. Taxable limit. Estate; dignity. An Arabic vocabulary with Persian translations in rime.— حد نصاب Quorum.

نصارا A. [Pl. of نصرانی]

نصایح [Pl. of نصیحت]

نَصب A. Erection; installation. Appointment. — ن. کردن To

erect; instal. To appoint.
نصب‌العین *A*. Set before the eyes. — ن. قراردادن To set b. the eyes; *i. e*. observe.
نُصحا [Pl. of ناصح]
نَصر *A*. = 1) یاری 2) پیروزی
نصرالله *A. Mas. pr. name*. *OS*. Help from God.
نَصرانی *A*. [نصارا] Christian. *OS*. Nazarene.
نُصرت *A*. 1) = پیروزی 2) = یاری 3) *Fem. pr. name*. — طاق ن. Arch of triumph.
نصرت‌الله (*A*.) *Mas. pr. name*. *OS*. God's help or triumph.
نِصف *A*. (One-) half. — ن. کردن To cut in two equal parts; divide in halves. To reduce to half. — نصف‌شب Midnight — درد نصف سر Hemicrany; migraine. — فلج نصف بدن Hemiplegia.
نصف‌النهار *A*. Midday. *Cf*. دایرهٔ ن. ‖ ظهر Meridian.
نِصفه *A*. Half. H.-done.
نصفه‌کاره *A. P*. Half-finished.
نصفه کاری *A. P*. Dividing of profits in equal shares.
نَصوح *A*. Name of a man proverbial for his sincere repentance.
نصوص [Pl. of نص]
نَصیب *A*. Portion; share; lot. *F*. Destiny. — نصیبِ . . . شدن To fall to the lot of. — موفقیت هایی که نصیب ما شد Successes won by us. — خدا نصیب کند God grant.
نَصیحت *A*. [نصایح] Advice; exhortation; admonition. — ن. کردن To admonish.
نصیحت‌آمیز *A. P*. Exhortative; admonitory.
نَصیر *A*. [انصار] Helper; aid. Defender. *Mas. pr. name*.
نُضج *A*. Ripening. Suppuration. — ن. گرفتن To ripen. To develop. To flourish or thrive. [Of a boil] To come to a head.
نَطّاق *A*. Great talker. Orator.
نطاقی *A. P*. Oratory.
نَطع *A*. Leathern (table-) cloth.
نُطفه *A*. Sperm. *By e*. Seed.
نُطق *A*. Speech. *Cf*. سخن & سخنرانی ‖ Power of speech. — ن. (ایراد) کردن To deliver a s.
نُظّار *A*. [Pl. of ناظر] Spectators. Controllers. — انجمن ن. Election supervisory council.
نِظارت *A*. Control. — ن. کردن To control or supervise. — انجمن ن. Election supervisory council.
نَظاره *A*. Looking; watching. *S. a*. نظارت ‖ ن. کردن = دیدن To see; watch.
نظاره (*naza-*) *A*. [نظارگان] Spectator.
نظافت *A*. = پاکیزگی Cleanliness.
نِظام *A*. Order. Discipline. The military. *Mas. pr. name*. —

خدمت ن. Military service. — ن. گرفتن To get into line; line up. To be restored to order *. — نظام‌وظیفه Compulsory military s. — چهار نظام – سه نظام M. Three-jawed; four-jawed.

نظامات A. Regulations; rules.

نظامنامه A. P. Regulation(s). Constitution (of a society). Cf. آئین نامه

نظامی A. P. Military. — آجر ِ نظامی Kind of brick 40 centimetres by 40 c. — حکومت ن. M. government. — قانون حکومت ن. Martial law. — دادگاه ن. Court martial; military court.

نظائر A. Similar cases [pl. of نظیره]. — مطبقه و نظائر آن Typhoid and the like.

نظر A. [انظار] Sight. Look. View. Opinion: بنظر من in my o. ‖ Mind. Viewpoint. Consideration. Intention. Discretion. (Good or evil) eye. — نظر اجمالی Glance. — * ن. افکندن or ن. انداختن To look; cast a glance. — ن. دادن To express one's opinion; make a comment. — ن. زدن = ن. کردن بر ‖ چشم زدن To look at; see. To regard. — بنظر آمدن To seem; appear; look. — بنظرم رسید که In occurred to me to. — در نظر داشتن To have in mind; bear in m.; remember. To propose. — در نظر گرفتن To take into consideration. To bear in m. To take into account. — با در نظر گرفتن ِ Taking into c.; with due regard to. — صرف ن. کردن از To dispense with. To waive; relinquish. — تجدید نظر کردن (در) To revise. — جلب ن. کردن To attract notice or attention. — ن. باینکه In view of the fact that; considering that — از نظر اقتصادی From an economic point of v. — با نظر مساعد نگریستن To v. favourably. — تحت ِ ن. Under police surveillance. — تحت ِ نظر ِ Under the supervision of; sponsored by. — حسن ن. Good opinion; favourable attitude. — ن. بچپ Mil. Eyes left!

نظراً A. Apparently. By sight.

نظر باز A. P. Ogler.

نظر بازی A. P. Ogling.

نظر بلند A. P. Liberal; magnanimous; high-minded.

نظر تنگ A. P. Illiberal; narrow-minded. [insularity.

نظر تنگی A. P. Illiberality;

نظرکرده A. P. Favoured or favourite.

نظرگاه A. P. Viewpoint.

نظری A. P. Theoretical. Speculative. — لاهوت ن. Dogmatic theology.

نظریات [Pl. of نظریه]
نظریه ´A. [نظریات] View; recommendation; suggestion. — ن. دادن To express one's views; make a comment.
نظم ´A. Good order. Verse; poetry. — ن. دادن (به) To restore o. in; give good shape to. — بنظم در آوردن To versify.
نظیر ´A. = مانند Equal; like; parallel: ن. ندارد It is unparalleled. — نظیر قضیهٔ شما است It is similar (or analogous) to your case. — مراعات ن. Poetical congruity.
نظیرالسمت A. (*Astr.*) Nadir.
نظیره o A. Example. Similar thing. [Usu. in the pl نظائر *q. v.*].
نظیف ´A. = پاك Clean.
نعال [Pl. of نعل]
نعت ´A. Epithet. Description. [Praise.
نعره ´A. Cry; clamour; roar. (Applauding) shout. — ن. زدن To cry or r.
نعش ´A. Corpse. Coffin. Dummy [in a theatre].
نعش کش A. P. Hearse.
نعل ´A. [ن نعال] Horseshoe. — نعل درگاه Lintel. — نعل کفش Shoe plate. — نعل وارونه *Met.* False colours. — ن. وارونه زدن To show false c.; misrepresent facts (by deceitful means). — ن. کردن To shoe. To calk [also ن. زدن]. — یکی بمیخ و یکی به ن. زدن To run with the hare and hunt with the hounds.
نعلبکی (?) Saucer.
نعلبند ´A.P. Shoesmith; farrier.
نعلبندی A. P. Farriery.
نعلکی A. P. Heel (-piece); heel-tap. [babooches.
نعلین A. [D. of نعل] *Kind of*
نعم o (*na'am*) = بله Yes.
نعم (*ne'am*) & نعمات [Plurals of نعمت]
نعم البدل ِA. An excellent or better substitute.
نعم المطلوب A. So much the better.
نعمت ِA. [نعم & نعمات] Affluence; riches. Easy life. Blessing; gift; favour. Talent.
نعمت الله (A.) *Mas. pr. name. OS.* God's gift.
نعنا(ع) ´A. Spearmint. — نعناع آبی Dittany. — جوهر نعناع فلفل Menthol.
نعوذ بالله ´A. God forbid. Save us, Good Lord! *OS.* We seek refuge in God.
نعوظ ´A. Erection. — ن. با شدت شبق o Satyriasis.
نعوظی A. Erectile. — عضلهٔ ن. E. muscle; erector.
نعیب ´o A. = غارغار
نعیم ´A. Luxury; pleasure. Blessing *Mas. pr. name.* — جنات ن. = **بهشت**.
نغز ´ Excellent. Marvellous.

نَفَر A. Individual ; person [*placed between a numeral and a noun denoting the name of a person. Ex.* سه ن. محصل 3 students]. – سه ن. از آنها *or* سه نفرِ آنها Three of them. – نفر اول The first or the best one. – من یك ن. I for one. – ماشین ۷ نفره Seven-seater.

نفرات A. Soldiers ; militaries. *Cf. the s.* نفر

نفرت A. Aversion ; disgust. – ن. داشتن از To hate.

نفرت انگیز A. P. Disgusting.

نفرین Curse. *Cf.* دشنام ‖ ن. کردن To curse ; imprecate.

نفس (*nafas*) A. Breath. B. of air ; breeze [pl. انفاس]. *F.* Moment. – ن. برآوردن • 1) To open one's lips ; breathe; speak. 2) • ○ To heave a sigh . – ن. زدن To breathe. – ن. کشیدن To b. – ن. ن. زدن To pant or gasp for breath. – نفسش از جای گرم بلند میشود He is blind to the difficulties. – از نفس افتادن To get out of breath. – ن. تازه کردن To get a fresh b. of air ; rest (and refresh oneself). – نفست در بیاد × Spit it out – ن. کشیدن از یادش رفت × He resigned his breath.

نفس (*nafs*) A. 1) Self. 2) Soul;

نَغمه A. [نغمات] Melody. – نغمه تازه ای ساز کردن To say a different thing or offer a new excuse – باز نغمه تازه‌ای ساز کرد There he goes again! *See* ساز کردن

نغمه پرداز • A. P Musician.

نغمه سرا • A. P. Singer.

نغمه سرایی A. P. Singing.

نِفاس ○ A. = زایمان Childbirth. *Med.* Lochia.

نفاست ○ A. Preciousness.

نِفاسی A. Lochial. Puerperal.

نِفاق A. Discord. Hypocrisy.– ن. انداختن To sow discord.

نفائس S. u. نفیس

نَفت Oil; petroleum. – نفت سفید *or* نفت لامپا Kerosene. – نفتِ سوختی Fuel oil.

نفتالین Fr Naphthaline.

نفت اندازی ○ Game of lighting the two ends of a stick, which is then turned rapidly round the finger.

نفت سوز Oil-burner.

نفت کش [For اتومبیل ن.] Tanker lorry; oil tank car. [For کشتی ن] Oil tanker.

نفتی Oily ○. Produced from petroleum. – مواد ن. *or* محصولات ن. Oil products.

نَفخ A. Blowing. Swelling. – نفخ شکم Tympanites; meteorism. – ن. کردن To swell. To be flatulent.

نفخه A. A blowing or blast.

person. *Cf. the pl.* نفوس ‖ 3) Essence. 4) Passions.—ن. کشتن* To mortify one's passions. — بنفسه (*benafse*h) Personally; in person. —فی نفسه In itself; intrinsically.

نفس الأمر *A.* Essence of a thing; the thing itself.

نفسانی *A.* Sensual; carnal.

نفسانیت Sensuality.

نفس پرست *A. P.* 1) Sensual; carnal. 2) = خودپرست

نفس پرستی *A.P.* = 1) شهوت پرستی 2) خودپرستی

نفس تنگه *or* **نفس تنگی** *A. P.* Asthma.

نفس کش *A. P.* Vent. Stairhead; landing. Living being; soul+.

نفع *A.* Profit. Benefit. Interest. *Cf.* سود ‖ بنفعِ In the interests of. For the benefit of. — ن. بردن To b. To make a profit [also ن. کردن] — ن. رساندن To do good. To be useful. [With به] To benefit.

نفقه *A.* Alimony. Subsistence.

نفلهِ شدن + To be wasted or spoiled. To die pitifully.

نفوذ *A.* Penetration. *F.* Influence. — تحت ن. قراردادن To influence.— ن. کردن To penetrate. — اِعمال ن کردن To use one's influence; exercise i. — اعمال نفوذ ناروا Undue i.

نفور *A.* = متنفر & بیزار ○

نفوس *A.* Population.— نفوسِ بد زدن +To forebode an evil. *Cf. the s.* نفس (*nafs*).

نفی (*naf'y*) *A.* Negation. *Gr.* Negative.—ن. کردن To negate; deny. — نفی بلد کردن = تبعید ‖ نفیِ در نفی کردن Double negative; two negatives.

نفیر *A.* (Sound of a) trumpet.— ن. کشیدن To snore. To blow a trumpet.

نفیس *A.* Precious. *Cf.* پر بها & گرانبها ‖ Exquisite. [Fem. نفیسه with the pl. نفائس precious articles].

نِقاب *A.* Mask. Black veil. — ن. زدن To wear a mask.

نقابت *A.* = ریاست - بزرگی

نقاب‌دار *A. P.* Masked. Veiled.

نقاد *A.* Critic. Assayer.

نقادی *A. P.* Criticism. Critique. Assay. — ن. کردن To act as critic.

نِقار *A.* = 1) دشمنی 2) کینه

نقاره *A.* Kettledrum. —ن. زدن To beat the kettledrum.

نقاره خانه *A. P.* Place where the drums are beaten at fixed intervals.

نقاش *A.* Painter. Portraitist.

نقاشخانه *A. P.* Painter's studio. Picture-gallery.

نقاشی *A. P.* Painting. Drawing. Picture. — ن. کردن To paint. To draw.

نقاط [Pl. of نقطه]

نقال *A*. Narrator. Conveyor o.

نقاله *A*. [Orig. fem. of نقال] Protractor. — سیم ن. Aerial ropeway. — سیم نقالهٔ الکتریکی Telpher line.

نقاهت *A*. Convalescence.

نقائص [Pl. of نقیصه]

نقب *A*. Burrow. Tunnel. Mine. — نقب‌افقی Gallery [in mining]. — ن. زدن To burrow or mine. — از زیر ن. زدن To undermine.

نقب زن *A. P. a*. Burrowing. —*n*. Burrower. House-breaker.

نقد *A*. 1) *n*. [نقود] Cash. 2) *ad*. For c.: ن. فروختن to sell for c. — ن.کردن To c. 3) *a*. [only in پول ن.] Cash; ready money]. — بنقد *a*) Already; at present. *b*) = نقداً

نقداً *A*. In cash; for c. For the time being. On the spot.

نقدی *A.P*. Cash *adj*.: paid, or to be p. for, in cash. Pecuniary: مجازات ن. ‖ Monetary. — غیر نقدی Non-monetary; non-peçuniary.

نقدینه *A. P*. Cash; also, precious articles.

نقرس *A*. Gout. — نقرس دست Chiragra.

نقرسی *A*. or *A. P*. Gouty.

نقره *A*. = سیم Silver.

نقره آبی *A. P*. Bluish-white.

نقره آلات *a. p*. Silverware.

نقره ای *A. P*. Silver(y); argentine. Silver-white.

نقره داغ کردن +*A. P*. To fine; also, blackmail. *OS*. To cauterize by silver (money).

نق زدن ×To nag and murmur.

نقش *A*. [نقوش] Design; drawing. Trace. Painting. Impression; print. Part; rôle. — چه نقشی ایفا کرد What part did he play? — ن. آوردن +To have a lucky hand or throw. *By e*. To have a l. hit; be l. — در نقشِ As; playing the part of. — ن. بستن To be imprinted. To be formed or designed. — ن.کردن To draw; paint. — نقشِ برآب کردن To bring to nought; knock on the head; frustrate. — نقشِ زمین شدن To measure one's length; come a cropper.

نقش بند o * *A. P*. = **نقاش**

نقشه *A*. Plan; drawing. Map. — نقشهٔ دریایی Chart. — ن. کشیدن To draw a map or plan. *F*. To design.

نقشه بردار *A. P*. Topographer. Surveyor. [Survey.

نقشه برداری *A.P*. Topography

نقشه‌کش *A. P*. Draftsman.

نقشه‌کشی *A. P*. Drawing.

نقص *A*. Deficiency; defect. Decrease.

نقصان *A*. Deficiency. Decrease. Shortage; deficit. — کم شدن = ن. پذیرفتن To be decreased . ـ رو به ن. گذاردن To be in decrease ; begin to decline.

نقض´ A. Breach; violation. ـ نقض عهد Perjury. ـ ن.کردن To violate. To reverse.

نقط (*noghat*) A. Points or dots. [A pl. of نقطه & Cf. نقاط]. *See* ملا نقطی

نقطه´ A. [نقاط & Cf. نقط] Point; dot. Spot; locality. ـ نقطهٔ اتکاء Fulcrum . ـ نقطهٔ مقابل Reverse ; opposite . ـ نقطهٔ نظر P. of view. ـ ن.گذاشتن To point or dot. ـ در بعضی نقاط In certain parts.

نقطه‌چین A.P. Dotted. ـ ن.کردن To dot; mark with dots.

نقطه‌دار A. P. Dotted; pointed.

نقطه گذاری A. P. Dotting . Punctuation. ـ ن . کردن To dot or point. To punctuate.

نقل´ A. Conveying ; transport. Transfer . Transmission. Quotation. Narration. ـ ن. کردن To narrate. To convey. To quote. ـ نقل قول کردن To q. or cite. ـ نقل مکان کردن To remove ; shift to a new place. ـ او خیلی ن . دارد + There is much to tell about this man. ـ نقلی ندارد + It doesn't matter; don't worry.

نقل´ A. Sugar-plum; comfit. ـ نقل مجلس The life and soul of a party.

نقلاً´ A. Traditionally. According to the Scriptures.

نقلی´ A. Traditional. Scriptural. ـ ماضی ن. Historic past ; C. E. present perfect.

نقلیه´ A. [Orig. fem. of نقلی] Transport (service). [For وسائط ن. T. means [now وسائلِ بارکشی].

نقود [Pl. of نقد].

نقوش [Pl. of نقش].

نقوعی ٥ A. = نمرو

نقی´ (A.) *Mas. pr. name.* OS. = پاك

نقیب ٥ A. [نقباء] Chief; leader. Apostle.

نقیصه´ A. [نقائص] Defect or deficiency; lacuna.

نقیض´ A. Contradictory (remark) ; contrary; opposite.

نقیضه´ A. [نقائض´] Contradictory remark or judgment.

نك´ • = انك

نکات [Pl. of نکته´].

نکاح A. Marriage. ـ عقد نکاح M. contract . ـ زنیرا بعقد نکاح در آوردن To marry a woman.

نکبت A. Adversity. Abomination. [adversity.

نکبت زده A P. Stricken by

نکته´ A. [نکات] Point. Witticism. Epigram. ـ ن. گرفتن To cavil. To make a nice distinction.

نکته سنج A. P. Witty ; sagacious. Ingenious.

نکته‌گیر A.P. Caviller. Critic.

نکته‌گیری *A. P.* Cavilling.
نَکث ○ *A.* Breaking a promise.
ناکرده کار = + نکرده کار
نَکِره *A.* Indeterminate noun.— یاءِ ن. The indefinite article ی as in مردی '*a* man'.
نَکِره ×Thick-set and clumsy; lumpish. [Per f. نکره in the preceding entry].
نُکس *A.* Relapse. Decline.
نِکو * [Cont. of نیکو]
نُکول کردن *A. P.* To dishonour (a bill). To abstain. — از حرف خود نکول کردن To go back on one's word ; back out .
نِك و نال ×Nagging and complaining (*or* groaning).
نیکنام = * نکو نام
نِکوهش Blame; reproach — ن. کردن To blame or r.
نکوهیدن ○ To blame. To despise.
نکوهیده Blameworthy.
نَکهت * *A.* Breath Odour
نَکیر *A.* Name of an angel who, with his companion angel منکر (*monkar*), interrogates the dead person in his tomb.
نِگار * 1) Picture ; painting. 2) Sweetheart or mistress.— ن. کردن To paint, depict.
نِگار [Imp. of نگاشتن]
نگارخانه * Picture-gallery . *S. a.* نقاشخانه

نِگارِش Writing. Painting.— نگارشِ حییم Written or compiled by Haim. — ادارهٔ ن. Department of Publications.
نگارنده Writer; I, the present writer. Painter ○.
نِگاره Figure [شکل].
نِگاری Reticulum. Pipe used for smoking شیره juice prepared from opium residue.
نگارین * Beautiful mistress. *OS.* Painted or dyed.
نگاشتن * ○ [نگار] To write. To paint or draw.
نگاشته 1) [P. P. of نگاشتن]. 2) *n.* ○ Writing. Letter.
نِگاه Look. — ن. داشتن [Often نگهداشتن] To hold. To keep. To support. To observe. To prevent. To preserve . To retain. — ن. کردن *vi.* To look : بمن ن. کنید L. at me. —*vt.* To see; observe — ن. کن *or* ن. کنید +L. here! I say. Be careful.
نگاهبان Watchman; sentinel.
نگاهبانی Watch; guard.
نگاهداری *or* **نگهداری** Keeping. Maintenance . Safe custody. Observance.— ن. کردن To keep ; have c: of. To support; sustain.
نگر [*Imp. of* نگریستن]
نِگران Anxious; uneasy; exercised. *OS.* Looking.
نگرانی Anxiety. — ن. داشتن To

be anxious or concerned.

نِگریستن • [نگر] To look; see. To view.

نگفتنی S. u. ناگفتنی

نِگون • Turned upside down. F. Adverse. — ن. کردن To turn upside down.

نگون بخت • = بد بخت

نگون‌سار • Turned upside down.

نگه • [Cont. of نگاه] — ن. داشتن or نگهداشتن S. u. نگاه.

نِگهبان Guard(sman). Watchman. Half-back.

نگهبانی Watch ; guard. — ن. کردن To watch or g. — افسرِ ن. Orderly officer.

نگهدار Keeper ; preserver ; protector. Custodian. — خدا نگهدار Good-bye !

نگهداری S. u. نگاهداری

نگهداشت 1) = نگهداری 2) Maintenance.

نِگین Stone ; bezel ; signet. Bot. Key fruit — زیر نگین درآوردن To subdue.

نم´ n. Moisture ; humidity. [For شبنم] Dew. —a. = نمسار ‖ نم کردن 1) To moisten; make damp 2) × To reserve ; prepare beforehand. — نم کشیدن To be damaged by moisture — × فرانسه‌اش کمی نم کشیده است His French is a little rusty. — نم پس‌دادن To infiltrate moisture. — نم پس ندادن × To be close-fisted.

نما (no-;na-) 1) n. Facing; façade. Outward appearance. Chart. Math. Exponent. F. Look; aspect. — نمای بخاری Mantelpiece. 2) Imp. of نمودن

نماء´ A. 1) Growth. S. a. under نشو ‖ 2) Product. — ن. تملك Law. Accession.

نماز´ Prayer. — ن. خواندن or ن گزاردن or ن. کردن To pray; say one's prayers.

نمازخانه Church.

نمام´ A. etc. = سخن‌چین etc.

نمایان Visible ; apparent.

نمایاندن To show ; indicate.

نمایش Representation ; exhibition ; show ; play. Appearance. — نمایش هندسی Graphic representation; graph. — درمعرض ن. On view; open to public inspection. — ن. دادن To show; exhibit; represent. To s. off. To give a s. — بمعرض ن. گذاشتن To present ; show; exhibit.

نمایشگاه Fair; place of exhibition ; display room. — نمایشگاه جراحی Operation-theatre.

نمایش نامه Play(-book).

نمایندگان [Pl. of نماینده]

نمایندگی Agency. Representation; delegation. — بنمایندگیِ 1) Representing ; (acting) on behalf of. 2) C. E. Represented by.

نمس ِ o *A.* Ichneumon.
نمسار َ Damp; moist.
نم سنج َ Hygrometer
نمسه َ *T.-R.* Austria or Germany. – چای ن. Javanese tea.
نمط َ • *A.* Manner: . بدین ن. or بر این ن. in this manner.
نمك َ Salt. *F.* Charm. –ِ نمك ترکی Rock-salt. – نمك تیزاب Nitrate. – نمك میوه • Fruit-salt. – جوهر نمك Hydrochloric acid. – ن. بر زخم کسی باشیدن To put one's finger in another's sore; rub it in; aggravate one's sad condition. – حق ن. Ties of hospitality. *Cf.* نمك خوارگی ‖ نان و نمك خوردن To eat salt; break bread. – ن. زدن or ن. کردن To salt.
نمك نشناس = *P. A.* **نمك بحرام**
نمك پاش Salt-sprinkler.
نمك پرورده Brought up or fed by another.
نمك خوارگی Gratitude due to hospitality received.
نمك دان 1) Salt-cellar. 2) [*Humorous*] One who makes flat jokes; also, one who has inelegant habits.
نمك زار Salt-marsh.
نمك زده Salted.
نمك سوز + or **نمك سود** Pickled with salt; preserved in brine.
نمك شناس Grateful.

نماینده [نمایندگان] Representative. Agent. Indicator. *Math.* Exponent. Index. – نمایندهٔ مجلس Deputy (of the Parliament); member of p. [M. P.]. – هیئت نمایندگان سیاسی Diplomatic body (or corps); *c. diplomatique.*
نمد َ 1) Felt. 2) F. carpet. – ن. مالیدن To make felts. – کلاه ن. Felt hat. – ما را هم از این ن. کلاهی Where is our cut? [Often referring to a share in illicit gains].
نمدار Moist; wet.
نمد زین Woollen saddle-cloth.
نمد مال Felt-maker.
نمدی 1) *a.* (made of) felt. 2) *n.* Kind of felt jacket worn by shepherds. – ن آفتاب کردن + To be allowed a chance to look after one's own interest. [Moist.
نمدیده Damaged by moisture.
نمرو َ Infusorial.
نمره ُ [f. Fr. *numéro*]. Number. No. Private cubicle in a public bath (حمام نمره) *q.v. below.* [*At school*] Mark. [A. pl. نمرات]. – ن. زدن To number. – حمام ن. Public bath with private cubicles.
نمره‌دار *Fr. P.* Numbered.
نمره زنی *F. P.* Numbering. – ماشین ن. N. machine.
نمره‌گذاری *Fr. P.* Numbering.

نمك شناسی Gratitude.
نمك فرنگی [also نمكِ فرنگی] Sulphate of sodium or sulphate of magnesium. — *Note*. The former was known as نمك فرنگیِ مصنوعی and the latter as نمك فرنگی اصل
نمك‌گیر Bound by ties of hospitality. [Ungrateful.
نمك نشناس or نمك ناشناس
نمك نشناسی Ingratitude.
نمکین Salty; saline *S. a.* بانمك
نمناك´ Damp; humid.
نم نم In fine drops. — نم نمِ باران Drizzling-rain.
نموّ *A.* = رشد Growth. Development. — ن. كردن To grow (up).
نمود (*no-*; *na-*) Appearance.
نمودار *a* Apparent; visible — ن.شدن To appear. — *n.* Graph — نمودار بارزی است از . . . It represents a graphic picture of, or speaks volumes for ...
نمودن [نما] *Auxiliary verb* — كردن ‖ (*Original meanings*) 1) • To show. 2) To appear; seem : چنین مینماید كه It appears that
نموده [P. P. of نمودن].
نمور´ + = نمناك
نمونه Sample; specimen. Model. [For نمونهٔ غلطگیری] Proof. — نمونهٔ ستونی Galley-proof.
نمونه‌گیر Sample-thief; sampler.

نمونه‌گیری Sampling.
نمیر´ Undying; immortal.
نُنر × 1) = لوس 2) Foolishly selfish.
ننگ´ Shame; disgrace Disdain. — ... مرا ننگ آید كه • I disdain to ...
ننگین Shameful.
ننو´ Hammock (for children).
ننه´ Mamma; mummy.
نو (*now*) New — نوِ نو Brand-new — نوكردن. To change for a new one. To renew. — از نو or از سرنو Anew; over again.
نوا´ Tune; air. — نوای كسیرا در آوردن To mimic s. o. — بنوائی رسیدن To reap profit from s. t.; come into money, etc.
نوّاب´ *A.* [Pl. of نایب —used as a title of honour].
نواحی [Pl. of ناحیه]
نواختن [نواز] To play (on) To strike; beat. To caress.
نواخوان o Singer Mimic; imitator.
نوادر [Pl. of نادره]
نواده 1) Descendant. 2) = نوه Grandchild.
نوار´ Ribbon. Band.
نوار پیچ Bandage(d). — ن. كردن To (tie up with) bandage.
نوار چسب Banderole.
نواز [Imp. of نواختن]
نوازش´ Caress; fondling. — ن. كردن To caress; fondle.
نوازندگی Musical perfor-

mance ; playing. Musical profession.

نوازنده [نوازندگان] Player ; performer; musician.

نواسیر [Pl. of ناسور]

نواقص *A.* Deficiencies. Defects. [Pl. of ناقصه o fem. of ناقص].

نواله *A. P.* Mess; victual ; morsel. Grub. Draft; gulp.

نوامبر *Fr.* November.

نوان o Oscillating. Invalid.

نوآموز Beginner. Apprentice.

نوامیس [Pl. of ناموس]

نوان‌خانه Asylum for invalids.

نواهی [Pl. of ناهیه o] Forbidden things or acts.

نوآئین o Convert.

نوباوه First-fruits. *Cf.* نوبر ‖ نوباوگان *npl.* Young men; new generation.

نوبت *A.* Turn. Time. *Gam.* Lead. — نوبت مرض Paroxysm; period of a disease. — بنوبت In turn. — در نوبت های معین Periodically. — ن. گرفتن To reserve one's turn ; also, queue up ; line up ; wait one's turn.

نوبت‌کار *A. P.* Shift (worker).

نوبت‌کاری *A. P.* Shift (work).

نوبتی *A. P.* Periodical. Working by shift. Operating by turn.

نوبر First-fruits. —[*Used as an adj.*] New or strange. — ن. کردن To eat for the first time.

نوبنیاد Newly-established.

نوبه *A.* Paludal fever ; malaria. [For تب ن.] Intermittent fever .

نوبهار Early spring.

نوبه‌خیز *A. P.* Malarious ; malarial.

نوجوان Lad; stripling; youth.

نوجوانی Youth; adolescence.

نوچه Beginner ; novice ; neophyte; tyro. Chrysalis.

نوح *A.Heb.* Noah. — عمر نوح Methuselah's life.

نوحه *A.* Wailing. Mournful songs.

نوخاسته • Youthful (person); youth; lad.

نوَد Ninety.

نوداماد Young husband ; also, bridegroom.

نوَدُم Ninetieth.

نودمین - نودمی (The) ninetieth

نو دولت *P. A.* = **نوکیسه**

نو دیده = **نوکیسه**

نور *A.* [انوار] = روشنائی Light. Lustre. — نور چشم *or* نور دیده Darling; dear child; acushla. *Cf.* نورعلی نور ‖ نورچشمی 1) *ad.* So much the better. 2) *n.* A much b. condition.— ن دادن *vi.* To emit or give light. —*vt.* To expose, as a film.

نور افشان *A. P.* Luminous ; diffusing light.

نور افکن *A. P.* Searchlight.

Floodlight. Flash - light. Projector.

نوراللّه (*A.*) *Mas. pr. name OS.* Light of God.

نورانی *A. P.* Luminous. Of a holy aspect. Transfigured.

نورانیت *A.P.* Luminosity. Holy aspect or appearance.

نور بخش *A. P.* 1) = نور افشان 2) Illuminating; enlightening.

نور چشمی *A.P.* (My) child or darling. Favourite.

نوَرد Rolling - pin ; beam ; cloth-beam. Carriage (of a typewriter).

نَوردیدن [نورد] * To travel over; traverse. To roll up.

نورَس Just ripened. *F.* Young; fresh.

نورُسته Newly sprung up. Young; tender. *Cf.* نوخاسته

نو رسیده *a.* Newly arrived. —*n.* New-born child.

نوروز New Year's Day. *Mas. pr. name.* — عید نوروز New-Year festival.

نوروزی New Year's. Vernal. — مرغ ن. Gull.

نوره *A.* Depilatory (paste).

نوزاد = 1) نوزاده 2) Larva.

نوزاده [نوزادگان] New-born (child).

نوزده Nineteen.

نوزدهم & نوزدهمین Nineteenth.

نوزدهمی (The) nineteenth.

نوساز - نوساخت New-built.

نَوَسان *A.* Vacillation. Oscillation. — ن. کردن To vacillate.

نو سفر *P. A.* Traveller for the first time.

نوسنگی Neolithic.

نوش 1) [*Imp. of* نوشیدن] 2) Act of drinking. Wholesome drink. *F.* Enjoyment. — نیش بیش از نوش More kicks than halfpence. — ن. کردن = نوشیدن To drink. — نوش‌جان ! 1) [Reply to one who says, " To your health "] Cheero ! Drink-hail ! D. good health ! 2) [Reply to one who, while eating, says to another, "Please share with me"] Thank you. *OS.* May it prove wholesome to you! — نوش جان کردن To eat or drink heartily. — کتك خوبی نوش جان کرد He received a good beating (which he deserved).

نوشابه (Alcoholic) drink ; beverage.

نوشانیدن To give to drink.

نوش‌آور Nectariferous.

نوشت افزار Stationery.

نوشتن [نویس] To write. — پدرم نوشت که . . . My father wrote to say that . . . — مثنوی می نویسد که It is written in the *Masnavi* that . . .

نوشتنی (That must be) written . — مسائل ن. Written problems. *Cf.* کتبی

نوشته 1) *P. P.* of نوشتن ‖ 2) *a*. Written. 3) *n*. Writing. Document. [Pl. نوشتجات writings].

نوشدارو Antidote.

نوشگفته New-blown.

نوشیدن [نوش] To drink.

نوشیدنی 1) *a*. Drinkable. 2) *n*. Drink; beverage.

نوشین * Sweet : خواب ن.

نوظهور *P. A*. New; new-fangled; new-fashioned.

نوع *A*. [انواع] 1) Kind : چه ن. پرنده‌ایست What kind of a bird is it? 2) Manner. 3) Species. — نوع بشر Mankind. — بنوعی که So that. — بانواعِ ... In a variety of; by various ...

نوعاً *A*. In a generic manner.

نوع پرست *A. P*. Philanthropic. — شخص ن. Philanthropist; altruist.

نوع پرستی *A.P*. Philanthropy.

نوع خواه etc. *A. P*. = **نوع پرست** etc.

نوعی *A. P*. Representing the kind. — «شما»ی ن. را میگویم I mean not "you in particular", but "you in general"; any one.

نوغان Silkworm (seeds). First crop.

نوك Point; tip. Bill; beak. — نوك قلم Pen-nib. — (با) نوك پنجه Tiptoe. — ن. زدن To peck. — نوك کسیرا چیدن To snub s. o.; give him a rebuff.

نوكار Externe; non-resident medical student.

نوك تیز Sharp-pointed.

نوك‌دار Pointed. Nibbed.

نوك دراز Snipe; longbill.

نوكر Servant; domestic.

نوكری Service as a domestic. — ن. کردن To be a servant.

نوكیسه Upstart; parvenu.

نوگل Newly-blown flower.

نوم ○ *A*. = **خواب** Sleep.

نومید * etc. = **نا امید** etc.

نوَنوار Wearing new clothes.

نونهال Sapling. *F*. Youth.

نوه Grandchild. *Cf*. نواده

نوی New state; newness.

نوید 1) Glad tidings. 2) = وعده

نویس [Imp. of نوشتن]

نویسندگی Writing; literary compo ition. [For شیوهٔ ن.] Penmanship. Clerkship.

نویسنده [نویسندگان] Writer; author. Penman. Clerk.

نوئل *Fr*. Christmas.

نوین New. Modern.

نه 1) No. [Often نه خیر or simply خیر]. 2) Not : نه ایستاد or نایستاد He did not stand. — نه سفید نه سیاه Neither white nor black. — نه، بابا + You don't say so!

نه (*ne*h) [Imp. of نهادن]

نه (*no*h) Nine.

نهاد Nature. Habit. Heart. Position. Structure; composition.

نهادن * [نه] To put ; place ; also, lay [گذاشتن]. To put by ; store ; save. — بنا نهادن To build; found. To begin.
نهاده 1) [*P. P. of* نهادن] 2) = اندوخته *n.*
نهار *A.* = روز
نهار *C. E.* = ناهار
نهال Sapling. Twig. Young tree
نهالی ○ = تشك *or* دوشك
نهان *a.* Hidden. *Ph.* Latent.—*n.* Concealment. — در نهان Secretly. — ن. کردن = پنهان کردن
نهان دانه Angiospermatous.
نهان زا Cryptogam(ous).
نهانی *ad.* Secretly; privately. —*a.* Secret ; hidden.
نهایت *A. n.* Extremity; end. Limit. —*ad.* Extremely. At the most. Except that — الی غیر نهایت To infinity.
نهب *A.* = غارت
نهج *A.* Manner. - بدین ن In this manner.
نهر *A.* [انهار] Stream; river. Canal. *Cf.* نهرسر پوشیده ‖ رودخانه Culvert.
نهصد Nine-hundred.
نهصدم Nine-hundredth.
نهضت *A.* Movement.
نه ضلعی *P. A.* Enneagon.
نهفتگی Concealment. — دورهٔ ن. Period of incubation. [نهادن
نهفتن * 1) = پنهان کردن 2) =
نهفته * = پنهان & پوشیده
نهق ○ *A.* = عرعر Braying.

نهم Ninth.
نهمی (The) ninth.
نهمین Ninth.
نهنج *Bot.* Receptacle.
نهنگ Crocodile.
نهی (*na*h'y) *A.* Prohibition. Inhibition. Negative command ; n. imperative. — ن کردن To prohibit.
نهیب Dread. — ن دادن To terrify. To browbeat.
نی (*ney*) Reed ; cane. Straw. Flute; pipe.—نی قلیان Tube of a hookah ; h.-snake.—مثل نی قلیان Barebone ; thin as a lath ; lean as a rake. — نی بوریا Rush (used in mat-making). — نی نهاوندی Sweetrush; sweet-flag ; calamus. — وقت گل نی When two Sundays meet. — نی زدن To (play on a) pipe.
نی * = نه No; not; nay.
نیا (*ni*a) [نیاگان] Grandfather. Ancestor.
نیابت *A.* Vicegerency; succession. — نیابت سلطنت Regency.— ن. کردن To act on behalf of another. — به نیابت or نیابهً ازطرفِ On behalf of
نیابتی *A. P.* Vicarious.
نیات [Pl. of نیت]
نیاز Need; necessity.— ن. آوردن * To supplicate or pray. *OS.* To enumerate one's needs (before God).— ن کردن ○ To give; offer.

نیازمند Needy; necessitous. — بچیزی ن. بودن To need s. t.

نیازمندی Need; indigence.

نیاگان [Pl. of نیا]

نیام Sheath ; scabbard. *Bot*. Ocrea — نیام‌ماهیچه Aponeurosis.

نیام بال Coleopterous.

نیامك *Bot*. Pod.

نی‌انبان (*neyamban*) Bagpipe.

نیایش Benediction ; praise.

نیت *A*. [نیات] Purpose; aim. Wish. Heart; mind. — ن. کردن To intend ; design. To decide. To concentrate on one's wishes (before consulting a book or doing a religious act). — بنیتِ With the intention (*or* idea) of. — با حسن ن. With good faith ; bona fides. — سوء ن. Bad faith.

نیچه Blowtube. Pipette.

نیر (*nayer*) *A*. Luminary.

نیران [Pl. of نار]

نیرنگ Deceit. Trick. Magic.— ن. کردن *or* ن. زدن To play a trick.

نیرنگ ساز *a*. Tricky; deceitful. —*n*. T. person. Juggler ○

نیرو Force ; power; strength.— نیروی دریایی Naval f. ; navy.— نیروی هوائی Air force.

نیروَبر Troop-carrying.— کشتی ن. Troopship.— هواپیمای ن. Troop-carrier.

نیروسنج Dynamometer.

نیرومند Powerful.

نیرومندی Power(fulness).

نیز Also; too. Besides. *Cf*. هم

نیزار *n*. Reed-bed; reed-brake; rushbrake. —*a*. Reedy.

نیزك Shooting star.

نیزه Spear ; lance ; javelin. — پرش با نیزه Pole-vault.— پرتاب ن. Throwing the j. — ن. زدن To lance; thrust with a spear.

نیزه بازی Combat with lances. — نیزه بازیِ سواره Jousting.

نیزه‌دار Lancer ; spearman.

نیزه فنگ *Mil*. Fix bayonets !

نیسان *A*. *Jewish and Syriac month* (March-April).

نیسانی *A*. Pertaining to نیسان (March-April) ; vernal.

نیست 1) [Negative of است *or* هست] (He, she, it) is not. 2) *a*. Non existent. 3) *n*. Non-existence [نیستی] . — ن. شدن To be annihilated. To disappear. — ن. کردن To annihilate. To squander.

نیستان (*neyas-*) = **نیزار** *n*.

نیستی Non-existence.

نیش Sting. Canine(-tooth). — [Of a snake] Fang.— نیش قلم ○ The (sharp) point of a pen. — نیش وجدان Prick (*or* twinge) of conscience.— ن. زدن To sting. — ن. وا کردن × To grin. Also, [derogatory for خندیدن] to laugh.

نیشتر *or* **نشتر** Lancet. — ن. زدن

To lance. [grin.
نیشخند Grin(ning). – ن. زدن To
نیشدار Stinged. *F*. Pungent.
نیش‌زن Stinging ; biting.
F. Pungent. [cane.
نیشکر Cane-sugar. Also, sugar-
نیشگان Pinch(ing). – ن. گرفتن To pinch.
نیشو + Who grins habitually.
نیك *a*. Good. *–ad*. * Well. Very. – نیکان *n. pl*. the good (people).
نیك اختر * Fortunate.
نیك اختری Good luck.
نیك انجام Prosperous; ending well.
خوشبخت = نیك بخت
نیك‌پی Prosperous. Auspicious. Of a good consequence.
نیکتین *Fr*. Nicotine.
نیکخواه Benevolent.
نیکخواهی Benevolence.
نیك سرشت Of a good nature.
نیك سیرت *P. A.* Of a good character; moral.
نیك انجام = نیك فرجام
نیکل *Fr*. Nickel.
نیك محضر *P. A*. 1) Of a good disposition. 2) = خوش محضر
نیکمردی Manliness; generosity.
نیك‌منظر * *P.A*. Good-looking; handsome.
نیکنام Of a good reputation
نیکنامی Good name.
نیك نفس (*-nafs*) *P. A*. Of a noble spirit; inwardly good.
نیك سرشت = نیك نهاد

نیك & خوب = نیکو
نیکوکار Beneficent; righteous.
نیکوکاری Beneficence ; charitable acts.
نیکی - خوبی = نیکویی
احسان - خوبی = نیکی
نیل (*neil*) *A*. Attainment; obtaining . – نیل بمقصود A. of one's end.
نیل (*ni:l*) *A*. Nile (River). Indigo-plant. (Indigo) blue. – نیل‌فرنگی Prussian b. – ن. زدن To b. ; dye with b.
نی‌لبك *Mus*. (Wooden) pipe.
نیلگون * Blue ; cerulean.
نیلوفر Nenuphar; water-lily. – نیلوفر پیچ Morning-glory.
نیلوفری * Azure.
نیله Grey horse.
نیلی *A. P*. Azure ; cerulean. Dyed with blue.
نیم Half. – ن. ساعت H. an hour. – ساعت دو و نیم H. past two.
نیم * (*niam*) = نیستم I am not.
نیم باز Half-open ; ajar.
نیم بال Hemipteral.
نیم بسمل * *P. A*. Half-slaughtered. [Half-cock.
نیم پا Partly raised. – حالت ن.
نیم پایه Abutment of a bridge.
نیم پرده Semitone.
نیمتاج Diadem. [Sofa.
نیم تخت Tap; half-sole; clamp
نیمتنه Jacket. – مجسمهٔ ن. Bust.
نیم چکمه *P. T*. Half-boot.
نیمچه 1) *a*. Half-size. 2) *n*.

Pullet; fat chicken.
نیمخورده Leavings; orts.
نیم خیز Half-raised.
نیمدار Second-hand; used.
نیم دایره *P. A.* Semicircle.
نیم دور *P. A.* Semi-rotary.
نیم راه *S. u.* نیمه راه
نیمرخ Profile.
نیم‌رس Half-ripe.
نیم رسمی *P. A.* Semi-official.
نیمرو Fried eggs. — ن. کردن To fry (on one side).
نیمروز ○ Midday.
نیمساز Bisector.
نیم ستون Engaged column.
نیم سنگین Light-heavy. Semi-portable.
نیمسوز Fire-brand.
نیم سیر Not quite-satisfied; half-full; half-hungry.
نیمشب Midnight.
نیم شلواری Knee-breeches.
نیم قد Half-size. — قد و نیم قد *S. u* قد
نیم‌کاسه Small bowl or porrin- [ger.
نیمکت Bench; sofa. [*In a motor car*] Seat.

نیمکره Hemisphere.
نیم کوب Half-crushed.
نیمگرد *n.* Half-note; minim. —*a.* Half-round ‖ سوهان ن.
نیمگرم Tepid; lukewarm.
نیم وزن *P. A.* Light-heavy weight.
نیمه *a.* Half. H.-done. Half-size. —*n.* One-half. Half-brick. — ن. افراشتن To (hang at) halfmast.
نیمه آگاه Subconscious.
نیمه‌افراشته At half-mast (high).
نیمه جان Half-dead.
نیم راه *or* نیمه راه Half-way.— رفیق ن. Fair-weather friend.
نیمه‌کاره Incomplete; half-finished.
نینوا Ninevah.
نی نی Baby [childish word]
نی نی کوچولو + (Cry-)baby.
نیوشیدن * [نیوش] To listen; hearken.
نِئون *Fr.* Neon (light).
نئی *or* نیی Made of reeds or rushes.
نئین *or* نیین * = نئی

و

وَ And. [Pronounced also *o* (1) in poetry and (2) in cases when he coordinate members are very closely related Ex. زن و بچه (*zano-bacheh*) 'wife and children', i e. family].
وا [*Only in comb.*] = باز
وا اَسفا • *A.* = افسوس
وا افتادن To cease. To be relaxed.
وا ایستادن To stand. To cease. [Imp. وا ایستا + or وا ایست]
وابستگی Relationship. Connection.
وابستن ○ To collude.
وابسته *a.* Related. Attached. Depending.— اعضای و Adherents. —*n.* Attaché. Relative; also, dependent [pl. وابستگان].
واپس Back, again. — و آمدن To come back. — و. دادن To give b. ; return.
واپسین • 1) = بازپسین 2) آخرین
وات *Fr.* Watt.
وات سنج *Fr. P.* Wattmeter.
واثِق *A.* Firm; sure. — رجاء و. Confident hope
واجِب *A.* (Very) necessary; essential; indispensable; also, due.— واجب‌الاحترام Worthy of respect; honourable.— واجب‌الادا Due; payable. — واجب‌الرعایه That must be observed; binding.— واجب‌القتل Who must be punished by death. — • بواجب Condign(ly).
واجبات *A.* Duties. Things necessary to be done. [Pl. of واجبه fem. of واجب].
واجب‌النفقه *A.* Entitled to an alimony.
واجب‌الوجود *A.* Self-existent.
واجبی *A.P.* Depilatory paste.
واجِد *A.* Possessing. — واجد شرایط لازمه P. the necessary qualifications; qualified.
واچُرتیدن × To be taken aback.
واحد *A.* Single; unique. [Fem. واحده . Ex. مادهٔ و. S. article]. —*n.* Unit.
واحسرتا *A.* = وا اسفا
واحه *A.* [واحات] Oasis.
واخ Ouch! Ah! [واخواستن]
واخواست Protest. — و. دادن =
واخواستن To (lodge a) protest.
واخواسته Object of protest.
واخواندن To read over.
واخوانده Party against whom a protest is made.
واخواه Protester.

واخواهی Protest(ing).

واخوردن + To be refused or rejected. *Cf.* وازدن ‖ To be shocked. To be disillusioned.

وادادن To give in. To be relaxed. To be soothed. To be disintegrated.

وادارکردن To persuade. Also, to oblige.

واداشتن *vt*. To set up; (cause to) stand . To detain. To persuade. *–vi*. To abate. To cease.

وادنگ + Repudiation of one's [word.

وادی *A*. Valley [دره] . – **گورستان** = ٭ وادی خاموشان

وار [*Suf. meaning* 1) Resembling; like; 2) Full of; having; 3) Befitting.

وارث *A*. [ورثه & وُرّاث] Heir. [Fem. وارثه] . – وارث مسلم H. apparent . – وارث مقدر H. presumptive . – و. شدن To inherit. To succeed.

وارد *A*. [Fem. وارده]. Arriving; entering. Entered; registered. Incoming : مراسلات وارده ‖ Imported: اجناس وارده ‖ *F*. Justified; justifiable. Acquainted; in touch. – و. شدن To arrive. To be imported; [with در] arrive at; enter; come in; join. – «شاه و. میشود» '*Enter* King'.– و. کردن To import. To enter or register. *F*. To initiate. To involve.

واردات *A*. [Pl. of وارده fem. of وارد] Imports. Incoming letters.

واردین *A*. [Pl. of وارد regarded as a n.] Incomers. Visitors.

وارستگی Deliverance. Freedom.

وارستن = رَستن

وارسته Free. Delivered.

وارَسی Investigation; search. Verification. – و. کردن To search. To verify; audit.

وارفتگی Relaxation.

وارفتن + To be relaxed. To become loose.

وارفته Relaxed. Washed out.

وارو + = وارونه ‖ حروف و. [In printing] Turn.

وارون ٭ Inverted. *F*. Adverse.

وارونه *a*. Inverted; turned upside down or inside out. *F*. Contrary. Queer. *–ad*. Upside d. Inside out.– و جلوه دادن To distort or misrepresent. – و. کردن To turn inside out or upside d.

واریته *Fr*. Variety; music-hall entertainment; vaudeville [U. S.]. – سالن و. Music-hall.

واریز کردن = **واریختن**

واریخته [Of an account] Settled. [Of a roof] Sloping. [Orig. p. p. of واریختن]

واریز *a*. Settled. *n*. (C. E.)

Settlement. و. کردن To settle; liquidate; clear up.
واریزی or **واریخت** Settlement.
وازدن *vt*. To reject. To refuse. *–vi*. [Of an engine] To fail; knock or pink.
وازده Rejected. Refused.
وازلین *Fr*. Vaseline; petroleum jelly. – وازلین زرد Amber p. jelly.
وارنش Repulsion.
واژگون 1) = وارونه 2) Overturned; upset. 3) Reversed. – و. کردن 1) = وارونه کردن 2) To overturn or upset.
واژه Word. *Cf*. لغت & کلمه
واسطه *A*. Intermediator. Medium. Go-between; agent; middleman. Cause. Means [pl. وسائط Ex. وسائط نقلیه M. of transport]. – مفعول بیواسطه Direct object. – مفعول بواسطه Indirect o. – بواسطهٔ Due to; on account of. By. For the sake of. – بواسطهٔ اینکه Because. – باین و. For this reason. – و. شدن To act as an intermediary or agent.
واسع *A*. 1) = وسیع 2) Liberal.
واسکازین *R* Gear oil.
واشدن + = باز شدن
واشر *E*. Washer; gasket. *Cf*. پولك ‖ واشر کلویی Packing oil pan.
واصف *A*. Describer. Praiser.
واصل *A*. Arrived or arriving. Connected. [Fem. واصله. Ex. اطلاعات و. Information obtained or received]. و. شدن To be r. To reach; [with به] to join. – نامهٔ شما واصل شد I am in receipt of your letter.
واضح *A*. [Fem. واضحه] Clear; plain. – و. کردن To (make) clear; elucidate; explain.
واضحات *A*. [Pl. of واضحه fem. of واضح] (Self-)evident matters. – توضیح و. Explaining the self-evident; superfluous explanation.
واضع (-ze') *A*. Founder; onactor. – واضع قانون = **قانون‌گزار**
واعظ *A*. [واعظین & وعاظ] Preacher. – کتاب و. Ecclesiastes. *See* جامعه [To b.
واغ واغ + Bowwow. – و. کردن
وافر *A*. = **زیاد & فراوان**
وافور Opium-smoker's pipe.
وافوری *a*. Addicted to smoking opium. *–n*. Opium-smoker. *Cf*. تریاکی
وافی *A*. Sufficient; ample. *OS*. Faithful to a promise. [Fem. وافیه].
واقع *A*. *a*. Situated; located. Happening. *–n*. Reality; fact. *Cf*. *the fem*. واقعه ‖ در واقع In reality; indeed. – رخ دادن = و. شدن To happen; occur; take place.
واقعاً *A*. Really. [alist.
واقع بین *A*. *P*. Realist. Actu-

واقعه *A*. [وَقايِع & واقعات] 1) Event; incident. 2) ٥=نبرد

واقعی *A. P*. Real; actual; true. — كسر واقعى Proper fraction. — مخارج و. Actual or out-of-pocket expenses

واقعيت *A*. Reality.

واقف *A*. 1) *a*. Aware [آگاه].—و به A. of. 2) *n*. Settler or bequeather of a pious foundation; benefactor.

واقوليدن ×*P. A*. To go back on one's word.

واكردن + = باز كردن

واكس *R*. Shoe-polish. —و. زدن To polish.

واكسن *Fr*. Vaccine.

واكسى *R. P*. Shoe-black.

واكسيل بند *R*. Aiguillette.

واكنش Reaction.

واگذار Left; given over. — و. كردن To leave; give, make, or turn over; transfer.

واگذاردن *or* **واگذاشتن** 1) = واگذار كردن 2) To abandon.

واگذارنده Transferor; assignor.

واگذارى 1) *n*. Transfer. 2) *a*. Made over; transferred.

واگذاشتن *S. u*. واگذاردن

واگرا(ى) Divergent.

واگرايى Divergence.

واگراييدن To diverge.

واگردان Designed for changing. — جامهٔ و. Change of clothes.

واگرداندن To turn back. To invert. To change.

واگرفتن To put by (*or* aside). To catch (by contagion).

واگفتن + = بازگو كردن

واگن *or* **واگون** *Fr*. Waggon; railway car. Tramcar.

واگير Catching by contagion. *C. E*. = واگير(ه)دار

واگيره Contagion. Copy(ing).— و.كردن To catch; be infected by. To copy.

واگير(ه)دار Contagious.

وال *or* **بال** Whale.

وال *Fr*. Voile.

والا Eminent. — حضرت و His Excellency [used for princes].

وَالّا (*-e*la) *A*. = وگرنه Otherwise; or (else); if not. — و. فلا Otherwise, no.

والاتبار • Of a noble descent.

والاحضرت *P. A*. His Royal Highness.

والان Valance.

والاهمت • *P. A*. Of high ambitions. Magnanimous.

والد ٥ *A*. Male parent. *Cf*. پدر

والده *A*. Female parent; mother [مادر]. [Fem. of والد]. — والدهٔ آقا مصطفى× The missus (or missis); the old woman.

والدين *A*. [D. of والد] Parents.

والس *Fr*. Waltz.

والسلام (*vasa-*) *A*. There is nothing else to say; and there

is an end of it. *OS*. And peace (be upon you).
والله (*va*lah) *A*. By God.
واله * Enamoured; distracted.
والی *A*. [وُلات] استاندار
والی بال *E*. Volley-ball.
وام Loan. — و. دادن To make a loan; lend. — و. گرفتن To borrow; have the loan (of).
واماندگی Fatigue. Lag. [lag.
واماندن To be tired out. To
وامانده *a*. 1) Tired out; fatigued. 2) Lagging. 3) Disabled. 4) + Damned; cursed. —*n*. Leavings; residue.
وام خواه One who asks for a loan.
وام ده Lender.
وام فرسایی Amortization of a debt in instalments.
وام گیر Borrower.
وان *R*. Bath; bathing-tub.
وانگهی Furthermore.
وانمود کردن To pretend; make believe; feign.
وانیل *Fr*. Vanilla.
واویلا *A*. Woe. — و. برمن W. betide me! W. is me.
واهب *A*. Donor.
واهمه *A*. 1) Fear [ترس & بیم]. 2) Imagination. — قوهٔ و. Imaginative faculty.
واهی *A*. [Fem. واهیه] Chimerical. Vain.
وای Woe! Alas! Ah! — و. برمن W. is me! — و بحال 1) Woe is . . . ; woe betide . . . 2) Heaven save us from. . . 3) It is an ill . . . (that).
وَبا *A*. Cholera. — وبای پائیزه Sporadic cholera.
وَبال *A*. Trouble; inconvenience. (Responsibility arising from) sin; evil result.
وبائی *A*, *P*. Choleraic. Suffering from cholera.
وَتد *A*. [اوتاد] *OS*. Tent-peg ○. [In prosody] Foot. — وتدِ مجموع Iambus.
وَتر *A*. [اوتار] Chord. Hypotenuse. Tendon.
وِتو *Fr*. Veto. — از حق و. استفاده کردند They exercised their v.
وتیره * *A*. = 1) راه 2) طریقه
وِثاق * *A*. Alliance. Covenant.
وُثوق *A*. Confidence; reliance.
وثیق ○ *A*. Firm; sure.
وثیقه *A*. [وثائق] Security.
وجاهت *A*. Beauty. — وجاهت ملی Popularity. — ملکهٔ و. Queen of beauty; reigning b.
وَجب *A*. Span. — و. کردن To s.
وَجد *A*. Ecstasy. Joy. — و. کردن To be in an e. To rejoice. — به و. آوردن To enrapture.
وِجدان *A*. Conscience.
وجداناً *A*. In all conscience.
وجدانی *A*. Conscientious. Moral; inward.
وَجع ○ *A*. [اوجاع] = دَرد
وَجنات *A*. Indications; outward

appearance. *Cf. the s.* وجنه

وجنه *A.* = گونه Cheek. *S. a.* & *cf. the pl.* وجنات

وَجنی *A.* Malar; jugal.

وُجوب *A.* Indispensableness; necessity.

وُجود *A.* Existence [هستی]. Presence. Essence. Human body. Personality; influence.— و. داشتن To exist.—بوجود آمدن To come into existence. — بوجود آوردن To bring into e. — باوجودِ In spite of; notwithstanding. — باوجود اینکه In spite of the fact that.

وُجوه *A.* Funds. Phases. Modes. *OS.* Faces. *Cf. the s.* وجوه اهالی ‖ وجه Notables; influential citizens.

وجوهات *A.* 1) [Pl. of وجوه pl. of وجه]. 2) + =Money.

وَجه *A.* [وُجوه] (Sum of) money; payment Fee. Phase. Manner; way. Justification; cause. *Gr.* Mood. *Geom.* Surface. *OS.* Face.—به بهترین و. *or* بوجه احسن In the best manner. — بهیچوجه By no means; at all [with a negative context]. — وجه تسمیهٔ آن اینست که It is so-called because. — در وجه To the order of.

وجه‌الضمانه *A.* Guaranty; caution money; bond.

وجه المصالحه *A.* Scapegoat.

وجه خالی *a. p.* [Of a cheque] For which sufficient funds are not available in the bank. *See* چك بیمحل

وجهه *A.* 1) Popularity [usu. وجههٔ ملی]. — وجههٔ خود را از دست دادن To lose caste; fall. 2) Mode; manner.

وَجهی *A.* Facial. [Fem. وجهیه Ex. زاویهٔ وجهیه facial angle].

وجین کردن To weed out.

وَجیه *A.* = زیبا & خوشگل

وجیه‌المله *A.* Popular.

وجیهه *A.* 1) *Fem. of* وجیه 2) *Fem. pr. name.*

وَحدانیت *A.* Unity (of God).

وَحدت *A.* Unity. Solitary state. Singularity. Sameness; identity. — وحدت وجود 1) Monism or unitism. 2) Pantheism.

وَحش *A.* [وُحوش] Wild beast. — باغ وحش Zoo(logical garden).

وَحشت *A.* Fear (caused by loneliness). —و. کردن To be frightened (usu. by loneliness). *Cf.* ترسیدن

وحشت ناك & **وحشت انگیز** *A. P.* = **ترسناك**

وَحشی *A. P.* Savage; wild.

وحشیانه *A. P. ad.* Savagely; wildly. —*a.* Savage: اعمال و.

وحشی‌گری *A. P.* Savagery.

وَحل ○ *A.* = گِل Mud.

وحوش [Pl. of وحش]

وحی (*vah'y*) *A.* Inspiration; revelation. Voice.

وَحید A. = واحد & یگانه
وَخامت A. Seriousness. Dangerousness. — وخامت اوضاع Serious state of affairs.
وَخیم A. Serious; dangerous; grave; critical. Noxious.
وداج A. Jugular vein.
وِداد A. = دوستی Friendship.
وِداع A. Farewell. Cf. بدرود & و. کردن ‖ خداحافظی To bid f.
وداعی A. Valedictory. — نطق و. Farewell speech.
ودایع [Pl. of ودیعه]
ودکا R. Vodka.
ودود ○ A. Very affectionate.
وَدیعه A. [ودایع] = سپرده Deposit. — در بانك و. گذاردن To d. in (or with) the bank.
ودیعه‌گذار A. P. Depositor.
ور * [Cont. of واگر] And if. Even if; even though.
وَر Suf. = endowed with; versed in.
وَر = بر - طرف - سو Side.
وِرا * [Cont. of او را]
وَراء A = پشت Back. — وراءِ Beyond. Besides; other than. See ماوراء [cession.
وراثت A. Inheritance. Suc-
وِراج + Chatty; talkative. Also, given to gabbling.
وراجی Talkativeness. Babbling or gabbling. — و. کردن To talk too much. To babble.
وَرادید [In a firearm] Rear sight.
ورآمدن + To come off; come loose. To peel off. To flake; scale off. To be leavened.
ورآمده Leavened. See ور نیامده
ورافتادن + To go out of fashion. To be abolished.
ورپاشیدن + To dredge or sift.
ورپریدن + To drop off; d. away; go out like snuff of of a candle; hop the twig.
ورثه [A pl. of وارث].
ورجه فروجه + Gambol; frolic [more often ورجه ورجه]. — و. کردن To gambol or f.
وَرد * ○ = گل سرخ
وِرد A. [اوراد] Incantation. Prayer recited by rote; formula. — ورد زبان Habitual phrase. — و. خواندن To tell one's bids; bid beads.
وُردار و وَرمال (-ro-) × [Orig. بردار و برمال] Light-fingered. [Used as a n.] Grab-all; snatcher.
ورداشتن + = برداشتن
وَردَنه Rolling-pin. [fool.
ور رفتن + To dally; play;
وَرز [Imp. of ورزیدن].
وَرزَدن + To grizzle, as a baby. [chatter.
وِرزدن + To gabble or
وَرزش (Physical) exercise; gymnastics. Training. — و. دادن To train or e. — و. کردن To e.
ورزش خوبی Acrobatism.
ورزشکار One who takes phy-

sical exercises ; athlete.

ورزشی Athletic; gymnastic.

وَرزگاو Ploughing-ox.

ورزیدگی Experience; training.

ورزیدن [ورز] To knead. *F.* To cultivate. To train. To exercise. To commit : گناه و.

ورزیده Trained. Experienced.

وَرس *A.* Dyer's (green) weed; dyer's woad ; dye-weed.

وِرساد *R.* Composing-stick.

و رست *R.* Verst.

وَرَش • [Cont. of واگرش] *See* اگر *and* ش *(2 nd. sense).*

ورشکست Bankrupt. – و. شدن To go bankrupt ; fail.

ورشکستگی Bankruptcy. – ورشکستگی به تقصیر Culpable bankruptcy.– ورشکستگی به تقلب Fraudulent b.

ورشکستن To go bankrupt; fail.

ورشکسته Bankrupt. *See* ورشکست

ورشو *R.* Warsaw. W. silver; German s.

وَرطه • *A.* Abyss; gulf.

وَرَع ٥ *A.* = پرهیزکاری

وَرغلپیدن × To heave.

وَرَق *A.* Leaf. Sheet. Playing-card. *Cf. the pl.* اوراق ‖ آهن و. S. iron. [For و. بازیِ] Game of cards. – و. زدن To turn over (a leaf). – و. برگشت The tide has turned. – و. و. کردن To run over the leaves of (a book). To cut into layers or sheets.

ورق بازی *A. P.* Card-playing.

ورق بزرگ *A. P.* Folio. – کاغذ ورق بزرگ Fool's-cap.

ورق‌پاره *A. P.* Scrap of paper. *F.* Worthless document.

ورق زن *A. P.* Card-sharper.

ورق شماری *A. P.* Counting the leaves of a book; foliation.

ورقه *A.* [اوراق] Sheet ; leaf. Paper ; document . Form . Coat. Layer. Card: ورقهٔ دعوت ‖ Foil : ورقهٔ قلع

ورقه ورقه *a. p.* Laminate ; consisting of layers. Foliate.– و. و. شدن To laminate or foliate.– و. و. کردن To laminate.

ورك *A.* [For استخوان و.] Ischium.

وَرَم *A.* [اورام] Swelling; also, inflammation. *L.* tumour.

ورمالیدن × To slip off (*or* away).

وَرنام Surname.

وَرنه • [Cont. of واگرنه] Otherwise. *OS.* And if not.

وِرنی *Fr.* Varnish; polish. – و. زدن To varnish or p.

ورنیامده Unleavened.

وِرنیه *Fr.* Vernier.

وُرود *A.* 1) Arrival.– لدی‌الورود (*ladalvoru:d*) On arrival. 2) Entrance.– و. ممنوع است 'No e.; no admittance'. 3) *C. E.* Import. – زاویهٔ و. Angle of incidence. – و. کردن To enter.

ورودی *A. P.* (To be) imported . ـ گمرک و. Import duties. ـ دَرِ ورودی Entrance-door; entry. [mission fee.

ورودیه A. Entrance-fee; ad-

وِرور + Jabbering. Muttering. ـ و کردن To jabber. To mutter (the formula of incantation. ـ وروِر جادو Formula of i. By e. Witch.

وَرید A. [اورده] ـ سیاهرگ Vein. ـ ورم و. Phlebitis.

وریدی A. Venous.

وَز * [Cont. of و از 'and of' or 'and from'].

وزارت A. Ministry.

وزارتخانه A. P. Ministry.

وزارتی A. P. Ministerial.

وَزان Blowing [f. وزیدن].

وزان * [Cont. of و از آن] And of (or from) that.

وِزر ○ A. = 1) بار 2) گناه

وزراء [Pl. of وزیر]

وَزَغ A. Frog. Cf. قورباغه & بچه و. or بچهٔ و. ‖ غوك Tadpole. ـ سنگ و. Toadstone.

وِز کردن + To frizzle up. S. a. وزوزکردن

وِزکرده + Frizzly.

وَزن A. [اوزان] Weight. Measure; rhythm. ـ و.داشتن & و.کردن To weigh : دوکیلو وزن دارد It weighs two kilo-grammes. ـ وزن ظرف Tare. ـ وزن مخصوص Specific gravity.

وَزنه A. [اوزان] Weight.

وزنه برداری A. P. Weight-lifting.

وزنه پرانی A. P. Shot-put.

وِز وِز کردن + To buzz; hum; drone.

وِز وِزی + Fuzzy; frizz(l)y.

وزیدن [وَز] To blow.

وَزیر A. [وُزراء] 1) Minister. ـ وزیرِ مختار M. plenipotentiary. 2) [At chess] Queen.

وزیری A. P. 1) n. ـ وزارت 2) a. [in کاغذ وزیری Fool's-cap paper].

وَزین A. Heavy [سنگین]. F. Of weight or influence : مردان و.

وساده ○ A. Cushion; pillow.

وساطت A. Mediation; inter-cession. ـ و کردن To mediate; act as an intermediary.

وساوس [Pl. of وسوسه]

وسائط [Pl. of واسطه].

وسائل [Pl. of وسیله].

وسخ ○ A. = چرك & پلیدی

وَسط A. 1) n. Middle (part); centre. Interior. 2) a. Average; middling. Situated in the middle.

وَسطی A. P = میانی

وُسطی (-ta) A. Middle; central. [Fem. of اوسط]

وَسطین A. The two means. [D. of وسط].

وُسع A. Ability. Capacity. ـ وسعم نمیرسد آنرا بخرم I cannot afford to buy that.

وُسعت A. Extent; space. Capa-

وصایا [Pl. of وصیت]
وصایت A. Executorship.
وَصف A. Description. Quality [pl. اوصاف]. — و. کردن To describe. To praise. — بوصف در نمی آید It is indescribable.
وصف‌ناپذیر A.P. Indescribable.
وصفی A. Qualitative ; descriptive. — عدد وصفی Ordinal number. — قید وصفی Adverb of manner. — وجه و. Participial mood; participle. — وجه وصفیِ مجهول Past participle. — وجهِ وصفی معلوم Present participle.
وَصل A. Joining; union; connection. — و. شدن To be joined or connected. — و. کردن To unite; connect.
وَصلت A. Conjugal or matrimonial union ; marriage. — باکسی و. کردن To marry s. o. — و. دادن To become available (*or* be ready) by a specified time [usu. with a negative context]. Ex. برای شام و. نمیدهد
وَصله A. Patch. — وصلهٔ تن One's own flesh and blood ; kinsman; relative. — و. کردن To patch (up).
وُصول A. Collection. Recovery. — و. شدن To be collected or recovered. — و. کردن To collect; receive. To recover. — قابل و. Recoverable. — غیرقابل و. Irrecoverable; bad, as a debt.
وصولی A.P. 1) *a.* (That is to city. *F.* Ease (of life). — و. دادن To widen. To expand.
وَسمه A. Woad(-leaves). — و. کشیدن To dye with woad or indigo.
وَسواس A. Scruple. Freak; vagary. Whim. Obsession.
وسواسی A. P. Scrupulous. Whimsical. Irresolute.
وَسوسه A. [وَساوِس] (Satanic) temptation. — و. کردن To inspire evil suggestions.
وَسیع A. Vast ; extensive. — و. کردن To widen. To extend or expand.
وَسیله A. Means. Resort. Facility. [Pl. وسائل facilities]. — بچه و. By what means ? — بدین و. 1) In this manner ; thus. 2) Hereby. — بوسیلهٔ By means of; through. — باتمامِ وسائل جدید With all modern conveniences (or facilities).
وَسیم ○ A. = خوبرو & زیبا
وَش *Suf.* = -like-; ful.
وِشگون = + نیشگان
وُشم ○ = بلدرچین & بدبده
وَصاف ○ A. Good describer.
وصال (*vasal*) A. Patcher. Tinker.
وِصال A. Union. Fruition. — به و. رسیدن To succeed in uniting (again) with a sweetheart. To enjoy fruition.
وَصالی A.P. Patching; patchery. Rebinding.

be) collected. 2) *n*. Receipt.
وَصیّ *A*. [اوصیاء] Executor. [Fem. وصیه executrix].
وَصیت *A*. [وصایا] (Last) will. Precept. Injunction.— و. کردن 1) To make one's w. 2) ○ To command.
وصیت نامه *A.P*. Testament; will
وَضع *A*. [اوضاع] Situation; status; condition; position. Shape; posture. Manner. Disposition. Enactment: وضع قانون ‖ Levying: وضع مالیات ‖ Deduction: پس از وضع ۵ دلار After deducting $ 5. — و. کردن To enact. To levy. To deduct. To invent or coin, as a word. — وضع حمل کردن To have a baby; be delivered of a child. — وضع فعلی The status quo; the existing state of affairs.
وَضعیت *A*. (*C. E.*) Situation; condition; position. State of affairs.
وُضو *A*. Ablution before prayer. Water for a.— و. گرفتن To perform one's ablutions.
وُضوح *A*. Clearness; clarity.— با کمال و. Most clearly.
وَضیع *A*. = پست Mean.
وَطن *A*. [اوطان] = میهن Mother country; fatherland; home.— در مکانی و. کردن To choose a place as one's home.
وطن پرست *A. P*. = میهن پرست
وطن پرستی *A. P*. = میهن پرستی
وطن فروش *A. P*. Traitor to one's country.
وطنی *A. P*. Home-made. Homespun: پارچهٔ و.
وطواط ○ *A*. = شب پره
وظائف [Pl. of وظیفه]
وظائف الاعضاء *A*. [For علم و.] Physiology ○. *OS*. Functions of the (bodily) organs.
وَظیفه *A*. [وَظائِف] Duty. Function. Pension. — و. خوردن To receive a pension or ration.— نظام و. Compulsory military service. [pensioner.
وظیفه خور *A. P*. Stipendiary;
وظیفه دار *A. P*. Having a (specified) duty. *Cf*. موظف
وظیفه شناس *A. P*. Conscientious; dutiful.
وظیفه شناسی *A. P*. Sense of duty; conscientiousness.
وُعاظ [Pl. of واعظ]
وَعائی *A*. = آوندی
وعد *A*. [Collective for وعده]
وَعده *A*. Promise. Due date; term; maturity. — و. دادن *or* و. کردن To promise. To make an appointment. — و. گرفتن To invite. — با سه ماه و. At 3 months' date. — وعدهٔ آن هنوز نرسیده است It is not yet due.— سی روز وعده At 30 days' usance. — بی و. Payable at sight.
وعده دار *A. P*. Due at a spe-

cified date after sight ; payable at maturity.

وعده خلافی +a. p. = خلف وعده

وَعظ A. Preaching. Sermon. — و. کردن To preach.

وَعید A. = تهدید

وغ کردن + To yelp.

وَغ وَغ etc. = واغ واغ etc.

وغیره S. u. غیره

وَفا A. Fidelity; (good) faith. — و. کردن To be faithful to (one's promise). — عمرش و. نکرد His life failed him.

وَفات A. Death [درگذشت & مرگ]. — و. کردن To die [مردن & درگذشتن].

وفادار A. P. Loyal; constant ; faithful.

وفا داری A. P. Constance ; loyalty; fidelity; faithfulness; also, gratitude. — و. کردن To be constant or faithful.

وِفاق A = توافق & همآهنگی

وَفق or + **وِفق** A. Conformity. — و. دادن To adapt. — بر وفقِ In accordance with ; in conformity with.

وُفور A. Abundance; plenty ; affluence. Cf. فراوانی & زیادی ‖ و. داشتن To be abundant.

وَقاحت A. = بیشرمی

وَقار A. Dignity ; gravity.

وَقایع A. [Pl. of واقعه] Events; incidents. Proceedings . — دفتر وقایع Minute-book.

وقایع نگار A. P. Minute-writer; secretary. Annalist.

وَقایه o A. = نگهداری - دفاع

وَقت A. [اوقات] Time. — و. کردن To find a leisure or opportunity ; afford time. — وقتی Once; at one time.[For وقتی که] When. — تا وقتی که As long as. By the time that. — یك وقتی Once upon a time. Some time or other. — چه و. When ? — چندوقت است(که) At what t. ? — چندوقت How long is it since? — چند پیش از این Some t. ago. — آن و. وقت یك بار ؛ How often? — Then. Afterwards. — هر وقت Whenever. — همه و. = همیشه ‖ وقت آنست که ‖ هرگز = هیچوقت It is time to. — وقت و بی‌وقت +From time to time. OS. In season and out of s. — بوقت In (good) time ; in season. — بوقت خود In due (course of) t. — سر وقت کسی رفتن To beat up one's quarters ; visit him . — آقای جم وزیردارایی و. Mr. Jam, then Minister of Finance.

وقت شناس A. P. Punctual.

وقت شناسی A. P. Punctuality.

وقس علی‌هذا S. u. قِس

وَقع A. Dignity . Regard ; esteem. — و. گذاشتن [With به]

To heed; pay attention to.

وَقعه o A. = 1) واقعه 2) جنگ

وَقف A. [اوقاف] Pious foundation. — و. کردن To endow

(for pious purposes). To dedicate. To entail.

وقف نامه *A. P.* Deed of endowment.

وَقفه *A.* Pause. Standstill. Interruption.

وُقوع *A.* Occurring; happening; taking place. Incidence. — وقوع جنگ Outbreak of war. — و. یافتن To take p.; happen.

وُقوف *A.* = 1) آگاهی 2) خبرگی

وَقیح *A.* = 1) بی شرم 2) زشت

وَقیه *A-G.* Ounce.

وَکالت *A.* Power (of attorney); procuration; proxy. Attorneyship. Lawyer's or barrister's profession. Membership of the Parliament. — وکالتِ انتخابی Referred brief. — بکسی و. دادن To give s. o. powers; appoint him as one's attorney (or proxy). — و. کردن To be a lawyer; go to the bar; act as counsel. To act in another's right. To be a deputy (of the Parliament).

وکالت نامه *A. P.* Power of attorney.

وکالةً *A* In another's right; as a proxy.

وُکَلاء [Pl. of وکیل]

وُك وُك وُك وُك کردن + To throb.

وَکیل *A.* [وکلاء] Counsel; lawyer. Attorney. Proxy. Agent. — وکیل مرافعه Barrister-at-law. — وکیل خرج Steward. — وکیل مجلس Member of the Parliament; deputy. — وکیل عمومی =

و. کردن || دادیار To elect for the P. To appoint as one's counsel; brief. To empower.

وگر * [Cont. of و اگر]

وِل Hanging loose Detached. Free. *F.* Unrestrained — ول شدن To hang l. To be d. To drop. *F.* To become dissolute; go astray. — ول کردن To let go. To drop; let fall. To abandon; give up. — ول گشتن To rove. To go about unemployed.

ولاء o *A.* = دوستی

وُلات [Pl. of والی]

وِلادت *A.* Birth. — روز و. Birthday.

وُلان *Fr.* Flounce.

وِلایت *A.* Province [pl. ولایات]. Guardianship. — ولایت عهد = ولیعهد(ی)

ولایتی *A. P.* Provincial.

ولتاژ *Fr.* Voltage.

وُلت سنج *Fr. P.* Voltmeter.

وِلخرج *P. A.* Lavish of one's money; profligate; prodigal.

ولخرجی *P. A.* Prodigality; lavishness; profligacy.

وَلد *A.* Son [پسر]. Child [فرزند]. *Cf. the pl.* اولاد

ولدالزناء *A.* Illegitimate child; bastard. *Cf.* حرامزاده [ملد ل

وِلرم + Tepid. *Cf.* نیمگرم &

ولع *A.* = 1) اشتیاق 2) حرص

ولکن (*valaken*) *A.* = **ولیکن**

وِلکن (*-kon*) [often ولکن معامله] +Ready to leave the matter [usu. in the negative. Ex. ولکن معامله نیست He is persistent on that matter].

وِلگرد Vagrant. Idle wanderer. Loafer. [cy. Roving.

وِلگردی Vagabondage; vagrancy.

وِلگو Loose talker.

وِلنگار + Gossipy; slanderous. Having no sense of responsibility.

ولنگ وباز× (Left) wide open. F. Careless; easy-going.

ولو (val'ow) A. Though; even t.

وُلوج ० A. = ورود - دخول

وَلود A. 1) Prolific [برزا]. 2) Viviparous [بچه‌زا]. غیرِ ـ ولود Oviparous.

وِلو کردن + To spread or stretch out. To scatter about. To unroll or unfold.

وِلوله A. Clamour; tumult. Wailing. Clang. Reverberation.

وله (valahu:) A. Idem; by the same poet or author.

ولی (valiy) A. Guardian; warden. Tutor. Saint. Friend. Master. Cf. the pl. اولیاء

ولی (val'i:) P. A. But.

ولیّ‌الله A. Mas. pr. name: title of the Prophet's son-in-law. OS. God's friend.

ولی‌النعم A. Benefactor. See نعمت - نعم - ولی

ولیعهد a. p. Crown prince.

ولیعهدی A. P. Succession to the throne. State or rank of a crown prince.

ولیکن A. = لیکن

وَلیمه A. Feast. Housewarming.

ولینعمت a. p. Benefactor.

وَند Suf. = 1) possessing; 2) resembling.

ونك (vanak) Cony; coney.

وَنگ ونگ کردن (vango-vung-) To grizzle or cry, as a baby.

ونیزی Fr. P. Venetian.

وول زدن + (vul-) To toss, as in bed [also لول زدن].

وَه * Oh! Alas! O that!

وَهاب A. Bestower; giver: ep. of God. Mas. pr. name.

وهابی A. Wahhabi.

وَهله A. Instance. در وهلهٔ اول ـ In the first instance. By priority.

وَهم A. [اوهام] Imagination. Groundless fear.

وَهمناك A.P. = 1) ترسناك 2) بیمناك

وَهمی A. P. Imaginary. Illusive. Groundless.

وی (vei) = او He or she.

وی * ('') [Cont. of وَای]

ویار Longing of pregnant women; pica.

ویتامین Fr. Vitamin.

ویتامینی or ویتامین دار Fr. P. Vitaminous.

ویترین Fr. Shop-window.

ویر ० = 1) هوش 2) حافظه

ویران Desolate; ruined. و. کردن ـ To ruin. To lay waste.

ویرانه Ruined place; ruin.

چاه و. Bottomless pit. *Met.* Oblivion.

ويلا *Fr.* Villa.

ويلان Vagrant ; wandering . Helpless. – ويلان و سيلان × Vagrant; at a loose end.

ويلانی = 1) سرگردانی 2) بیچارگی

وين *Fr* Vienna.

وينی *Fr. P.* Viennese.

ويولن (*violon*) *Fr.* Violin.

ويولن زن *Fr. P.* Violinist.

ويولن سل *Fr.* Violoncello.

ويرانی Ruined state; desolation.

ويزا *Fr.* = روادید Visa ; visé. – و. کردن To v.

ويزر *Fr.* View-finder.

ويزيت *Fr.* 1) Visit. 2) +: = کارت و. ‖ پایمزد Visiting-card.

ويژه Special. – سود ویژه Net profit. – بویژه Especially.

ويسکی *E.* Whisky.

ويسکی سودا *E.* High-ball [U. S.].

ويشه Woodbine; honeysuckle.

ويل ० (*veil*) *A.* Calamity. Woe.-

ها [pl. ending. Ex. مداد ها]
ها Behold! Be careful! Here you are! I see!
هاتف • A. Voice of an invisible speaker; mysterious voice. [name.
هاجر A. Hagar. Fem. pr.
هاج و واج × Flabbergasted.
هادی A. 1) = راهنما Guide. — خطه. Directrix. — منحنیه. Quadratrix. 2) Mas. pr. name.
هار Rabid; mad. — گزیدگیِ سگ ه. Rabies; hydrophobia.
هارون A-Heb. Aaron.
هاری Rabidness; madness.
هاشم (A.) Mas. pr. name.
هاشور Fr. Hatching.
هاضمه A. [Orig. fem. of هاضم]. Digestive power [short for قوهٔ ه.]. — جهازِ ه. D. organs
هاف کردن + To yap or yelp.
هاگ Spore.
هاگچه Sporule.
هال [In football] = دروازه Goal.
هالو + Nincompoop; dupe; greenhorn.
هالو E. Hullo.
هاله A. Halo. Med. Areola.
هامن Plane surface.
هامون Plain. Desert.
هان • Behold! Beware!

هاون Mortar. — دستهٔ ه Pestle. — آب در هاون سائیدن To carry water in a sieve.
هاویه A. 1) Abyss. 2) = دوزخ ‖ 3) Soldering-iron.
هائل A. = ترسناك Terrible.
هائله A. Frightful event. [Orig. fem. of هائل].
های وهوی + Tumult; uproar
های های n. Cry of weeping. — ad. With a loud cry; also; bitterly: ه. گریه کرد
هبوط • A. Descent; fall. — ه. کردن To descend or f.
هِبه A. Gift (inter vivos); donation. — ه. کردن To make a d. of; donate.
هبه نامه A. P. Deed of gift.
هپلی هپو × Harum scarum; unprincipled; lawless.
هتاك A. Asperser (of another's reputation); defamer.
هتاکی A. P. Aspersion; revilement. — بکسی ه. کردن To cast aspersions on a person's reputation.
هتك A. (OS.) Tearing o. — هتكِ شرف Aspersion of another's character or reputation. — هتك ناموس Violation; assault.
هِجاء A. 1) Syllable. 2) Spelling. — حروف ه. Alphabet.

3) = هجو [betical.
هجائی A. Satiric(al). Alpha-
هِجدَه Eighteen.
هجدهم Eighteenth.
هجدهمی (The) eighteenth.
هِجران * A. Separation; being away from friends.
هجرَت A. Departure. Hegira.— ه . کردن To emigrate.
هجری A. Reckoned from the Hegira ; A. H. (i. e. *anno Hejiræ*).
هجو (*hajv*) A. 1) *n*. Satire.— ه . کردن To lampoon ; libel. 2) *a*. + Good-for-nothing.
هُجوم A. Rush; attack. Crowding; swarming. — ه . کردن To rush ; make an attack. To crowd ; swarm.
هَجویه A. [هجویات] Satirical poem ; satire. [spell.
هِجی A. Spelling.— ه . کردن To
هَخامنشی Achæmenian.
هدایا [Pl. of هدیه]
هِدایت A. Guidance [راهنمایی]. Conduction : هدایت گرما ‖ *Mas. pr. name*. — ه . کردن To guide ; load.
هدایت‌الله (A.) *Mas. pr. name*. *OS*. Guidance by God.
هَدَر A. Useless effort.— به ه . رفتن or ه . شدن To become useless ; come to nothing. To be shed with impunity : خون وی به ه . رفت [purpose.
هَدَف A. Target [آماج]. Aim;
نشانه روی = A. P. هدف گیری
شانه بسر = هُدهُد
هدیه (*hadiyeh* or + *had-yeh*) A. [هدایا] Present [پیشکشی].— ه . کردن To offer ; make a present of. To dedicate.
هذا (*haza*) A. = این This [only in A. words or phrases].
هُذلولی A. 1) *a*. Hyperbolic. 2) *n*. Hyperbola.
هَذیان A. Delirium. — ه . گفتن To rave. To be delirious.
هذیانی A. Delirious.
هَر Every; each. Any. — هرآنچه ‖ هرکه = هرآنکه = هرچه = هرجا Everywhere. Wherever. — هر کجا Wherever . Anywhere.
هَراس Alarm ; fear [ترس].
هراسان Alarmed ; frightened.
هراسانیدن To frighten.
ترسیدن = [هراس] * هراسیدن
هرآینه * Indeed; verily; also, certainly. — ه . اگر If indeed; if peradventure.
هَرج A. Confusion; riot.
ولگرد = هرجاگرد
هرجایی Gadabout; loose.
هَرج و مَرج + (-*jo*-) A.P. 1) *n*. Anarchy. Disorder ; chaos. 2) *a*. Chaotic; anarchical.
هرج‌ومرج‌طلب P. A. Anarchist.
هرچ * [Cont. of هرچه]
هرچقدر or هر قدر P. A. However ; no matter how

much (or how many) هر قدر هم فقیر باشد However poor he may be.
هرچند Although. However
هرچه Whatever. — ه. بادا باد Come what may. — ه. زودتر بهتر: The sooner the better.
هردمبیل × Unprincipled (person). Harum-scarum.
هردم خیال + *P. A.* Capricious; fickle.
هردو Both. — هردوی آنها They both; b. of them.
هَرز 1) Loose : این پیچ ه. است 2) Wasted; gone (or run) to waste. 3) = پوچ ‖ ه. رفتن To go (or run) to waste. — ه. شدن To work loose.
هرزگی 1) Lewdness; debauchery. 2) Abusive language. 3) × The genital organ. — ه. کردن To give up oneself to d. To use bad l.
هرزه Profligate ; dissolute. Abusive. — علف ه. Weed.
هرزه خند • (One) who laughs without reason.
هرزه‌درای • 1) *n*. Idle talker. 2) *a*. Given to babbling.
هرزه‌گرد = ولگرد
هرزه‌گو = هرزه درای
هر ساله 1) Every year [often همه ساله]. 2) = سالیانه
هَرَس کردن To prune.
هرکاره = 1) همه کاره 2) دیگ
هرکجا or هرجا Wherever.
هرکدام Each (one) ; every one ; any one.
هرکه Whoever ; he who. — ه. را Whomsoever.
هرکه هرکه + Anarchical ; disorderly.
هرگاه In the event that ; in case. Whenever.
هرگز 1) Never [used with a negative verb. Ex. ه. او را ندیده بودم I had never seen him]. 2) Ever : آیا هرگز سفر کرده اید ؟
هِرَم *A*. [اهرام] Pyramid.
هُرمز *Mas. pr. name.*
هرمزد = اهورمزدا & اورمزد
هِرمی *A*. Pyramid(ic)al.
هِرّه Brick-on-edge course; string-course.
هِرهِر خندیدن + To giggle.
هُرهُری + Irreligious (person). (One) who has no firm belief.
هرّی × Go away; move on. [*Derogatory*].
هَریسه *Kind of porridge.*
هریك Each (one) ; every o.; any one.
هَزار Thousand. — هزار هزار One-million. — ه. میلیون One milliard. — در هزار Per mille.
هزار دستان = • هزار آوا
هزارپا Myriapod or centipede.
هزار پیشه Work-box with many compartments.
هزار چشان White bryony.
هزار دانه Designating a kind

of rosary (تسبیح هزار دانه) with 1000 beads.

هزار دستان = 1) بلبل 2) سار

هزار فامیل The upper ten-thousand. *See* فامیل

هزارفن *P. A.* Jack-of-all-trades

هزارلا Manyplies; omasum.

هزارم & هزارمین Thousandth.

هزارمی (The) thousandth.

هزاره Group of 1000 persons or things Thousandth anniversary. – گل ه Double-poppy.

هزال o *A.* Emaciation.

هزّال *A.* = هزل‌گو [شوخی

هزل *A.* Facetious saying. *Cf.*

هزل‌گو *A. P.* Facetious (person); wag(gish).

هزلیات *A.* Facetiæ.

هزیمت *A.* = شکست Rout; defeat.

هزینه Expense(s).

هژیر o Praiseworthy. Clever. Dignified.

هست 1) = هستی 2) Is [Third person s. present of بودن].

هستو = 1) هسته 2) Nucleus.

هست و نیست (-*to*-) All one has; one's all.

هستویه Nucleolus.

هسته (Fruit-) stone. Nucleus.

هستی Existence. Possession; property. – از هستی ساقط شد He was bereaved of his possession. *S. a. under* ساقط

هسر Glazed frost; silver thaw.

هش * [Cont. of هوش]

هشت Eight. – هشتش گرو نه است + He cannot make both ends meet.

هشتاد Eighty.

هشتادم & هشتادمین Eightieth.

هشتادمی (The) eightieth.

هشت پا Octopus.

هشت وجهی *or* هشت سطحی *P. A.* Octahedral. – جسم ه Octahedron.

هشت صد *or* هشتصد Eight-hundred.

هشتصدم *or* هشتصدمین Eight-hundredth.

هشتصدمی (The) eight-hundredth. [هشت‌گوش

هشت ضلعی *P. A.* = هشت گوشه & هشت گوش Octagon(al).

هشتم & هشتمین Eighth.

هشتمی (The) eighth.

هشتن o [هل] = گذاشتن

هشت و نه (Game like) baccarat.

هشتی Vestibule (originally having eight sides).

هشدار * Be careful ! Beware ! Look out ! *See* هش

هشلهف X Meaningless; incoherent; silly. Confused.

هشیار * [Cont. of هوشیار]

هضم *A.* Digestion. *Cf.* گوارش ‖ – ه . کردن To digest. *Cf.* گواریدن ‖ قابل ه . Digestible. – غیرقابل ه . Indigestible.

هفت Seven.

هفتاد Seventy.

هفتادمین & هفتادم Seventieth.
هفتادمی (The) seventieth.
هفت‌برابر Sevenfold; septuple.
هفت بند Knotgrass.
هفت پهلو + Very equivocal. *OS*. Septilateral.
هفت تن The Seven Sleepers of Ephesus. The seven planets.
هفت جوش Alloy of iron, lead, copper, tin, gold, silver, and antimony.
هفت خط × *P. A.* Extremely sly or leery.
هفتخوان The Seven Adventures (of *Rostam*). *See* خوان
هفت سطحی *or* هفت وجهی *P. A.* Heptahedral.— جسم ه. Heptahedron.
هفتصد Seven-hundred.
هفتصدمین & هفتصدم Seven-hundredth. [dredth.
هفتصدمی (The) seven-hun-
هفت ضلعی *P. A.* = هفت گوش
هفت قلم *P.A.* To the nines.— ه. آرایش کردن To dress up to the n.
هفت گوشه & هفت گوش Heptagon(al).
هفتگی Weekly.
هفتمین & هفتم Seventh.
هفتمی (The) seventh.
هفته´ Week. [ساعت ه.
هفته کوك Eight-day *adj.*:
هفته‌وار Weekly.
هفته‌واری + Weekly (payment).
هفده Seventeen. [teenth.

هفدهمین & هفدهم Seven-
هفدهمی (The) seventeenth.
هفهفو´ × Wrinkled with age; decrepit.
هکتار *Fr.* Hectare
هکذا (*hakaza*) *A.* Thus; such. Likewise. *Cf.* همچنین & همینطور
هکهك، Hiccup.— ه. کردن To h.
هِل، Cardamom(s).
هِل، [Imp. of هشتن *or* هلیدن]
هُل Push. Jostle. — هل دادن To push. To jostle (against).
هلا´ Oh! Hey! Beware!
هلاك´ *A.* Perdition; death. Ruin. — ه. شدن To perish; die. — ه. کردن = کُشتن
هلاکت *A.* Perdition; destruction. [*king*.
هلاکو *Name of a Mogul*
هلال´ *A.* [اهله o] New moon; crescent.
هلالی *A.* Crescent.
هلالین *A.* [D. of هلال] Round brackets; parentheses.
هلاهل (Fabulous creature with a) deadly poison. [*Used as an adj.*] Deadly: زهر هلاهل
هُلدان *or* هلدانی [Usu. هلدونی] × *S. u.* هول
هُلفدان *or* هلفدانی × Black hole. [Per. corruption of هولدان *q. v.*]
هلند´ *Fr.* Holland; Netherlands.
هلندی 1) *a.* Dutch. 2) *n.* Dutchman or Dutchwoman.

هُلو Peach. – هلوی پوست کنده *Met*. 1) Marriageable girl with ruddy cheeks. 2) Peach : beauty.

هَلهله *A-P*. Applause. Cry of exultation. – ه . کردن To c. for joy. To applaud.

هله هوله × Bits and pieces (of eatables). [رها کردن

هلیدن = 1) هشتن *or* گذاشتن 2)

هلیله Myrobalan. – هلیلهٔ کابلی Chebulic myrobalan.

هَلیم *Kind of dish with wheat groats and meat.*

هلیوم *Fr*. Helium.

هَم *ad*. Also ; too : او هم رفت He also went. 2) Even : در خواب هم آواز می‌خواند ‖ 3) Either ; [with a neg] neither : من هم آنرا ندیدم I did not see him either; neither did I see him. – هم کاغذ هم مرکب Both paper and ink. – آنهم And . . . at that : فرصت ‖ از دستش رفت آنهم چه فرصتی ! –*pron*. Each other ; one another : با هم حرف نمی زنند They are not on speaking terms with eachother. – باهم Together; with each o ; with one another. – بهم Together. To each other; to one a. Against each other. – برهم 1) =بهم 2) Over or upon e. other. – بهم آمدن To macth (with) e. other. To heal up. To be closed or stopped, as a hole [vulgarly هم آمدن]. – بهم زدن To cancel. To render null.

هَمّ • *A*. [هُموم] Care ; grief.

هُما 1) = همایون & همای 2) *Fem. pr. name.*

هم ارز Equivalent.

همار • [Cont. of همواره].

هم اسم *P. A.* = **همنام**

هم آغوش = **همخواب**

همال ○ Peer ; equal ; like. *See* بیهمال

هَمان (The) same. That very. – همانَدم That v. moment; immediately. – ه . بهتر Nothing better than. – همانطورکه Just as. – ه . است که گفتم There is no more to it ; I will not change what I have said. – خوردنش ه . و مردنش ه . بود He no sooner ate it than he died. – ه . آش (است) وهمان کاسه (It is) the same old story in the s. old way.

همانا • Indeed; verily.

همانند Similar; like.

همانندی Similarity ; resemblance.

هم‌آواز Concordant ; harmonious.

هم‌آهنگ Harmonious ; concordant. – ه . کردن To harmonize . To coordinate ; bring in line.

هم‌آهنگی Harmony ; perfect agreement. Coordination.

Mus. Symphony.
هم‌اکنون Already. Even now.
(هما(ی 1) Osprey. 2) *Fabulous bird of good omen*. 3) [only هما]. *Fem. pr. name*.
همایون Auspicious; fortunate. — اعلیحضرت همایون‌شاهنشاهی His Imperial Majesty. — همای = * مرغ ه
همایونی Imperial [only in اعلیحضرت ه. His I. Majesty].
همبازی Playmate.
همخواب = **هم بستر**
همبستگی Correlation.
هم بسته Correlated.
همپا Going with, or at the same pace as (another). — همپای من آمد He came (*or* went) along with me.
همپایه Of the same grade or rank; coordinate.
هم پیاله Pot-companion.
هم پیشه Fellow-workman; fellow-tradesman. *Cf*. همکار
هم پیمان Confederate.
هم پیمانی Confederacy.
همت *A*. [هم] Ambition. Aspiration; lofty purpose. Magnanimous spirit. Good offices; effort. — ه. ورزیدن To take efforts. [peer.
همتا Mate; fellow. Equal;
هم تراز = . **همپایه**
هم‌ترازو • — 1) همپایه 2) هم‌وزن
همجنس *P. A*. Homogeneous; congeneric. *S. a*. همنوع
همجوار *P. A*. Neighbouring.
همجواری *P. A*. = **همسایگی**
هم چشمی *or* + چشم و هم چشمی Emulation; vying with each other. Competition. — ه. کردن To vie or compete (with one another.). To keep up with the Joneses.
همچنان *ad*. In that manner; so; thus. Ever; continuously; consistently. —*a*. Such. — ه. که S. that; so that.
همچند Equivalent.
همچندی Equation.
همچنین *ad*. In this manner; thus; so. Also, as well (as). Likewise. So do I; the same to you [usu. بنده ه.]. —*a*. Such. [as.
همچو & **همچون** Such. Like;
همچین [Cont. of همچنین].
همخانه *a*. Living in the same house. —*n*. Cohabitant.
همخو Of the same habits; congenial.
همخواب Bed-fellow; spouse; also, cohabitant.
همخوابه = **همخواب**
همخویی Congeniality.
همداستان *or* **همدستان** • 1) *a*. = متفق 2)*n*. Accomplice. Companion. — ه. شدن To agree with each other. To conspire.
همدرد *n*. Fellow-sufferer. —*a*. Sympathetic.
همدردی Fellow-feeling; sym-

pathy. Condolence. — ه . کردن To sympathize. To condole.

همدرس *P. A.* Fellow-student.

همدست Collaborator ; aid . Accomplice. Companion. — ه . شدن To collaborate; join hands. To conspire.

همدستی Collaboration. Com - plicity

همدل 1) = همفکر 2) = همرأی

همدلی 1) = همفکری 2) Unanimity.

همدم Companion ; confident. *Fem. pr. name* [liarity.

همدمی Companionship. Fami-

همدوش Of the same rank ; equal.

همدیگر One another ; each other. — با همدیگر With one a.; with e. other. Together.

همدین *P. A.* = **همکیش**

همراز *a.* Of common secrets. Intimate. —*n.* Confidant.

همراهٔ Fellow-traveller; companion in the way. Attendant. Escort. — همراه من بیائید Come along with me.— ه . با 1) Inclined to assist : با من ه. است 2) *Mus.* Accompanied by. — خدا بهمراه Bon voyage; pleasant journey.

همراهی Accompaniment ; escort. *F.* Assistance. — ه. کردن [With با] To accompany ; escort. To assist. To fa - vour. — تا دم در او را ه. کنید See him to the door. — بهمراهیِ In company with ; accompanied by.

همرأی *P. A.* Unanimous ; of the same opinion.

همرتبه *P. A.* Of the same grade or rank. Coordinate.

همردیف *P. A.* Civil employee enjoying the privileges of a specified military rank. [gent.

همرس Concurrent. Conver -

همرکاب *P. A.* Fellow-rider.

همرنگ Of the same colour. *F.* Similar. — همرنگ جماعت شدن To go with the stream ; "do as the Romans do" .

همرنگی Similarity (in colour); resemblance.

همرو Opposite o. Parallel.

هم روزگار Contemporary.

همریش = + **باجناغ**

همریشه Cognate.

همزاد Twin. Co-walker; also, wraith or double.

همزبان Speaking the same language. *F.* Unanimous.

همزمان *P. A.* Contempora - neous. Synchronous.

همزهٔ The Arabic "consonant *alef*", marked thus (ء).

همزیستی Symbiosis. Coexis - tence. [eval.

همسال Of the same age; co-

همسایگان [Pl of همسایه].

همسایگی Neighbourhood ; vicinity. ـ قیود ِ ه . Ties of n.
همسایه [همسایگان] Neighbour.
همسر َ Spouse; consort. ـ سروهمسر Fellowmen; equals.
همسری Fellowship ; companionship. Emulation. Marriage. ـ ه . کردن To emulate. To be a match.
همسفر P.A. Fellow-traveller. ـ ه . شدن To travel together.
همسفره P. A. Who eats at the same table; commensal.
همسن ُ P. A. = همسال
همسنگ َ • Of the same weight. Equal. Coordinate.
همسوگند = 1) هم پیمان 2) هم ِ قَسم
همشاگردی Fellow-student.
همشهری Fellow-citizen.
همشیره Sister [خواهر].
همشیره زاده Nephew or niece (by a sister).
هم صحبت P. A. Companion in conversation; interlocutor.
هم صدا P. A. Of the same voice or opinion.
هم طویله P. A. Of the same stable (or string). (*Humorous or* •) Companion.
هم عصر P. A. = معاصر
هم عهد P. A. = هم پیمان
هم فکر P. A. Of the same mind. Sympathetic.
هم فکری P . A . Thinking alike; knowing each other's mind. Sympathy.

هم قدم P. A. Fellow-traveller. Companion. Cooperator.
هم َقسم P. A. Confederate by oath; united by oath.
همقطار P. A. Colleague. Fellow-soldier ; companion-in-arms.
همقطاری P. A. Colleagueship. Companionship.
همکار Fellow-tradesman ; fellow-workman . Colleague . Collaborator. Competitor.
همکاری Cooperation ; collaboration . Competition . ـ ه . کردن To cooperate. To compete.
هم کاسه One who eats from the same dish.
هم کفو P. A. 1) *a*. Equal in family rank. 2) *n*. Match.
همکلاس P. Fr. [Also همکلاسی] Classmate. *Cf*. همشاگردی
هم کلام P. A. = هم صحبت
هم کیش Coreligionist [همدین].
همگان [Pl. of همه]
همگانی = عمومی Public. General.
همگرا(ی) Convergent.
همگرایی Convergence.
همگنان • Fellowmen. Rivals. The company present.
همگی *pron*. All. *Cf*. همه
همگیر [In machines] Collar.
همگیس [*Obs*]. Of the same age : said of women.
همم [Pl. of همت]
هم مذهب P. A. = همکیش

هم مَرز Having a common frontier ; neighbouring ; conterminous.
هم مرکز P. A. Concentric.
هم مسلك P. A. 1) a. Of the same principles. 2) n. Colleague in a party.
هم مشرب P. A. Of the same disposition; congenial.
هم معنی P. A. Synonymous.
هم میهن Fellow-countryman ; compatriot.
همنام a. Of the same name. Homonymous. —n. Namesake.
همنفس P. A. = 1) همدم 2) همسر
همنشین One sitting with another. Companion; associate.
همنگار Synoptic(al).
همنوع P. A. Fellow-creature.— حس ّ همنوعی Fellow-feeling
همَوار Even; level; smooth. F. Gentle. — برخود هموار کردن To tolerate. [sistently.
همواره Always ; ever ; con-
همواری Evenness; levelness.
هم وزن P. A. Of the same weight.
هموطن P. A. = هم میهن
هموم [Pl. of همّ]
همَه pron. & a. All; the whole. همهٔ ایشان رفتند A. of them went; they all went.— ه. جا Everywhere. — ه. روز(ه) Every day. — ه. روز • All day long. — همه کس Every one. — آنهمه So many ; so much. A. that. — اینهمه So many ; so much; this m. — با این ه. • In spite of all that. — از همهٔ اینها گذشته Apart from all that. Furthermore.
همه‌جاگیر Epidemic. [S.a. مبتذل
هرجائی or همه‌جایی Gadabout.
همه فن حریف P. A. All-round; factotum ; "of all trades".
همه‌کاره (One) who can do anything; all-round (person).— ه. وهیچکاره Jack of all trades and master of none.
همه‌گوشه یکی Equiangular.
همَهمه Tumult ; uproar. Rumour. — ه. کردن To u.
همی Particle denoting progression. Ex. همیرفت • 1) He was going. 2) He kept on g.
همیان Scrip; wallet.
همیدون • 1) Likewise. 2) = اکنون
همیشگی n. Perpetuity. —a. Permanent. Usual. [good.
همیشه Always. — برای ه. For
همیشه بهار n. [For گل ه.] Marigold. —a. o Evergreen.
همین This same ; this very. Only +. — ه. بود That was all; that is all. — همینطور S. u. طور ‖ همینکه As soon as ; just as.
همینطوری +P. A. Just like that. Gratuitously; ex gratia. At random. In one lot.
همینقدر P. A. Simply; only.— ه. که معالجه شود فرق نمیکند بدست

کی معالجه شده است So he is cured, it matters not by whose hand.

هَنجار o Mason's rule or plumb-line. *F.* Manner; custom. *See* بهنجار & ناهنجار

هندَباء o *A.* Endive.

هند(ستان) [Cont. of هندوستان]

هِندسه *A.* [Per. f. P. اندازه] Geometry.

هندسه‌دان *A. P.* Geometrician.

هندسی *A.* Geometrical. — ارقام ه . Arabic figures.

هندل Crank. [Apparently f. E. 'handle']. — ه . زدن To crank (up).

هِندو Hindu. Indian.

هندوانه Water-melon. — ه. زیرِ بغل کسی گذاشتن To lay it on thick (*or* with a trowel); brave s. o. by praising him too much. — دو هندوانه در یك دست گرفتن To have two strings to one bow.

هندوچین Indo-China.

هندوستان India. [dustani.

هندوستانی 1) = هندی 2) Hin-

هندی [A. pl. هُنود] Indian.

هُنر 1) Art: هنرهای زیبا fine arts. *Cf.* صنعت ‖ 2) Virtue; excellence; merit. 3) Skill. 4) Feat; exploit.

هنراموز Student of an industrial school.

هنر پیشه [.هنرپیشگان] Artist; esp. actor or actress.

هنرجو Scholar in arts.

هنرستان Industrial school. S. of art. Conservatory.

هنرسرا Technical school; institute of technology.

هنرکار Technician. [arts.

هنرمند Ingenious. Skilful in

هنرمند = • **هنروَر**

هنری Artistic. Skilful.

هِنزر پنزر × [Per. corruption of خنصر & بنصر *q. v.*] Odds and ends; stray articles.

هَنگ Regiment.

هَنگام Time; season. *Mus.* 1) Gamut; scale. 2) = آهنگ ‖ هنگامِ At the time of; while. — هنگامی که When. — سیکل دو هنگام *Fr. P.* Two-stroke cycle.

هنگامه 1) *n.* Uproar. Scene. Great crowd. — ه . بر پا کردن To make a s. 2) + *a.* [In the phrase ه : است He does such and s. a thing wonderfully well; he is a prodigy of...]. *Cf.* معرکه

هَنگفت Enormous; excessive.

هُنود [A. pl. of هندی]

هَنوز 1) Yet: ه . زیادسرد نیست ‖ 2) Still: ه . سرد است

هو (*hu:*) Exclamation uttered by dervishes as a curse or good wish.

هو (*hu:*) = **هو** (*hovah*)

هو (*how*) Hoot; hiss. False

rumour. — هو انداختن × = هـ.کردن ‖ چو انداختن To boo(h); cry down; give a bird to.— هو و جنجال راه انداختن + To start a big row.

هو (*hovah*) *A.* = او He. [Fem. هی (*hiah*) 'she']. — هوَ به هوَ Word for word ; verbatim.

هوا [f. A. هواء or هوَی] Air; atmosphere. Weather. Air ; tune. *F.* Hope. Intention. Desire. — هـ . خوردن To breathe (pure) air ; take the a. ; take a breath of fresh air.— هـ . پس است + Things don't look well . — هـ . دادن To air. To aerate. To expose to air. — هـ . کردن To fly, as a kite. — هوای چیزیرا داشتن To watch s. t. ; keep the equilibrium of it. — هوای چیزیرا در سر داشتن To have the intention of doing s. t. — هـ . و هوس Carnal desire(s). — یك هـ . A thought ; slightly.

هوا پرست = نفس پرست

هواپیما Aeroplane ; aircraft.

هواپیما بَر Aircraft carrier.

هواپیما زن Anti aircraft

هواپیمایی Aviation ; aeronautics . — شرکت هواپیمایی ایران The Iranian Airways.

هواخواه Partisan ; adherent ; votary .

هواخواهی Partisanship. Support. — ازکسی هـ . کردن To take the part of s. o. ; side with him; support him.

هواخوردگی Slight cold.

هواخوری Recreation in the open air; airing; blow.

هوا دار 1) Well-ventilated. 2) = هوا خواه

هواداری = **هوا خواهی**

هوار + 1) = آوار 2) Cry for help; shout. — هـ . کشیدن To cry for h. — هـ . شدن To gate-crash; hang (on s. o.).

هوا سنج Barometer.

هواشناس Meteorologist. Aerologist.

هواشناسی Aerology. Meteorology.

هوا کش 1) Air-cleaner. 2) = بادکش

هواگیر Air-chamber.

هوامّ ٥ *A.* Insects or reptiles. [Pl. of هامه *hamah*].

هوانوَرد Aviator.

هوانوردی = هواپیمایی Aviation.

هوائی *A. P.* 1) *a.* Aerial. Atmospheric . Overhead : سیم هـ . ‖ *F.* Vain. Idle. Casual +. — پست هـ. Air mail.— خط هـ . Air-line. — توپ هـ . High ball. — هـ . زدن To fly (a b.); hit it high. 2) *ad.* As a windfall.

هوبره Bustard.

هوچی + *P.T.* Hooligan. Gossip.

هوچی گری + Hooliganism.

هودج *A.* [هوادج] Camel-litter.

هور ٥ = **خورشید**

هول‌هولکی × [also هُل‌هُلکی]
Hurry-scurry; helter-skelter.
هوو (*havu:*) Rival wife.
هَوه چوبه Alkanet.
هوی (*hav*a) *A*. Passion ; desire. – ه . و هوس Carnal desires. *Cf*. هوا
هُویت *A*. Identity. Individuality. – هویتِ . . . . را تعیین کردن To identify...
هَویج Carrot. – هویج فرنگی Reddish short variety of carrot.
هُویدا 1) = آشکار & پیدا 2) Indisputable.
هَویزه Curb.
هِی *int*. Hey ! Alas ! Bravo ! –*ad*. + Consistently. On and on. Time and again; every now and then. – هی حرف (می)زد He kept on speaking. – هی کردن To urge on.
هی [Fem. of هو (*hovah*)]
هیئت = **هیأت**
هیاکل [Pl. of هیکل]
هَیاهو Tumult ; uproar. – ه . کردن To raise an u.
هیبت *A*. Appalling presence; awe ; reverence. Majesty. Formidableness.
هیپنوتیست *Fr*. Hypnotist.
هیپنوتیسم *Fr*. Hypnotism.
هیجا • ٥ *A*. = **جَنگ**
هیجان (*haya-*) *A*. Excitement; tension. – به ه . آمدن To be excited . – به ه . آوردن To excite; animate.

اورمزد = هورمزد
هورا *Fr*. Hurrah ; cheer. – ه . کشیدن To c. ; shout h.
هَوَس *A*. (Passing) fancy; fad; whimsy. Shallow or temporary love. Aspiration or desire. – ه . راندن To indulge in one's desires or passions. – ه . کردن To take a fancy to. To aspire (at *or* after).
هوس ران *A. P*. Sensual.
هوس رانی *A. P*. Indulgence in one's desires ; sensuality.
هوسناك • *A. P*. Fanciful. Desirous.
هوش Intelligence. Memory. Consciousness. Sense. – هوشِ اختراع Ingenuity . – بهوش آمدن To come to, or recover, one's senses; c. round. – بهوش آوردن To bring round. – از هوش رفتن To become unconscious.
هوشمند Intelligent. Wise.
هوشمندی Intelligence.
هوشنگ *Mas. pr. name.*
هوشیار Sober. *Cf*. مست ‖ Vigilant; cautious. Intelligent. – ه . شدن To become sober. To come to one's senses.
هوشیاری Soberness. Vigilance.
هول *A*. Sudden fear; shock. – ه . خوردن To have a s. – ه . دادن (به) To give a sudden fear to; terrify.
هولناك *A. P*. = **ترسناك**

هیجان آور & هیجان آمیز *A. P.* Exciting.

هیچ *n*. Nothing [with a negative context]. — ه . نگفت He said nothing; he did not say a word. —*a*. 1) No : ه . پول ندارم I have no money. 2) Any [in an interrogative sentence] : آیا هیچ کاغذ دارید ‖ —*ad*. a) At all [with a negative context] : ه . او را ندیدم I did not see him at all. b) Never [with a negative context] : ه . به آلمان مسافرت نکرده ام I have never visited Germany. c) Ever : آیا هیچ عقاب دیده اید Have you ever seen an eagle? — ه . چیز [usu. هیچ] Nothing. — ه . دیگر No longer; no more; nothing else [with negative contexts]. — ه . کار برای من نکرد He did nothing for me. — هیچ و پوچ *n*. Nothing. Trifle. Vanity. —*a*. Null and void. Vain.

هیچ کاره Good-for-nothing. Idle; jobless.

هیچکدام No one; neither [with negative contexts].

هیچکس Nobody; no one; none [with negative contexts] : ه . نرفت Nobody went.

هیچگاه = هرگز Never.

هیچگونه No... whatsoever : ه . کالائی نداشت He had no goods w.

هیچ مدان *a*. Perfectly ignorant. —*n*. Know-nothing.

هیچیك = هیچکدام

هیربد Magian or Zoroastrian [priest.

هیز Infamous. Effeminate.

هیزم Firewood.

هیزم شکن Woodcutter.

هیزم کش Wood-carrier.

هیزی Infamy. Effeminacy.

هیضه ○ *A*. Flux and vomiting. *Cf*. وبا

هیکل *A*. [هیاکل] Image; figure. (Frame of) the body. (*Biblical term*) Temple.

هیکل تراش *A. P.* Sculptor.

هیکل تراشی *A. P.* Sculpture.

هیمه = هیزم

هین 1) = اینك 2) Hurry up.

هیولا *A-G*. Matter; chaos. Monster.

هیون Dromedary; also, two-[humped camel.

هیهات *A*. 1) = افسوس 2) Not in the least.

هی هی Hey! Alas! Oh!

هیئت *A*. Figure; form; aspect. Body of men; board; council. [For علم ه .] Astronomy. — هیئت اعزامی Mission. — هیئت رئیسه Executive committee; managing c.; officers (of a society); [*of a university*] senate. — هیئت مدیره Board of directors. Managing c. — هیئت ممتحنه Examining c.; (board

وزیران Council of Ministers.
هیئت دان *A. P.* **Astronomer.**
هیئتی *A. P.* **Astronomical.**

of) examiners. **ـِ** هیئت نمایندگان سیاسی Diplomatic body ; *corps diplomatique*. **ـ** هیئت

ی

ی [Verbal ending equivalent to هستی 'thou art']. Ex. (a) اگر مردی If thou art a man; (b) تورفته ای Thou art gone.

یا 1) Or. 2) Either: یاشما یامن E. you or I.

یا *A*. = ای O: Ex. یاخدا [often ای خدا or خدایا] O God!

یا الله (-*a*lah) *A*. O God! [used (1) in invocations and prayers; (2) on meeting a person after his journey or long absence, in which case it means 'hallo(a)'; (3) in various senses such as 'Hurry up! Go on! Up with you!', in which cases it is vulgarly pronounced *yal'a*; (4) in token of respect while rising before a guest who comes in; (5) upon entering a house as an announcement to the women inside that a man has come: an obsolescent custom].

یاب [Imp. of یافتن]

یابس o *A*. = خشک Dry.

یابنده Finder. — جوینده ی. است He who seeks will find.

یابو Pack-horse; nag; sumpter. — یابوی تاتو Pony or nag.

یاتاقان *T*. (*M*.) Bearing.

یأجوج *A-Heb*. Gog. — ی. ومأجوج Gog and Magog.

یاحق *A*. Cheerio! So long! *OS*. O God!

یاخته Cell.

یاخته شناسی Cytology.

یاد Memory; remembrance; commemoration. — بیادِ In m. of; in r. of. — (به) ی. آمدن To be remembered. — (به) ی. آوردن To remember; call to mind. — بیاد او آوردم که I reminded him that. — یادم افتاد I remembered; it occurred to me. — ی. دادن To instruct; teach how to do. — ی. دارم - + یادم می‌آید or یادم هست To remember. — ی. کردن To r. or commemorate. To mention. — ی. گرفتن To learn. — از یاد بردن To forget. — از یاد رفتن To escape the memory [usu. (از) یادم رفت I forgot it. — بیاد انداختن To remind. — یادم نیست I do not remember it; I cannot think of it. — یادم نماند It escaped my memory]. — یادش باد May he be ever remembered. — یادش بخیر May he be always remembered or highly spoken of [used in speaking of , or quoting from, an absent friend].

یاد آوَر شدن To remind. To notify.

یادآوری Reminding. Commemoration. Remembrance ; recollection.— ی. کردن To remind. To commemorate.

یادبود Reminiscence. Commemoration. *S. a.* یادگار ‖ بیادبودِ In commemoration of. (Sacred) to the memory of.

یاد داشت Memorandum ; note. Memoire. —ی. برداشتن To take notes. — ی. کردن To note (down).—یادداشت پرداخت یادریافت Debit or credit note.—دسته ی. Block n. paper. —دفترِ یادداشت Note-book.

یادکرد Mention [ذکر].

یادگار 1) Commemoration ; memory. Memorial. — بیادگارِ In memory of. For remembrance of. — به ی. گذاشتن To leave as a memorial. To hand down. 2) Monument. 3) [Also یادگاری] Keepsake; souvenir; memento. — برسم ی. As a s.; for a k.; for keeps.

یادگاری *S. u.* یادگار

یار Friend; companion. Partner. Aid; mate. Sweetheart*.

یارا *or* + **یارایی** Ability or power. Courage. *See* یارستن

یارَب *A.* = خدایا O Lord!

یارد *E.* Yard. Yardstick.

یارَستن ○ [یار] To have the power or courage.

یارو × 1) That fellow. 2) Mate! Sirrah ! [Used as a nominative independent].

یاری Assistance; help. Friendship; companionship.—ی. کردن [often with با] To assist.

یاریار Kind of refrain in popular songs. *OS.* O sweetheart!— + ی. نمی‌خواند؟ What is wrong with it ? Do you want bells on it ?

یازدَه Eleven.

یازده‌گوشه Hendecagon(al).

یازدهم & **یازدهمین** Eleventh.

یازدهمی (The) eleventh.

یاس Jasmin.—یاس‌درختی - یاس کبود *or* یاس‌شیروانی Lilac; syringa.—یاس شامپا White j. — یاس کرنایی *or* یاس‌شیپوری Trumpet-flower.

یأس (*ya's*) *A.* = نومیدی Despair; disappointment ; hopelessness. — آیهٔ ی. Wet blanket; damper. — آیهٔ ی. نخواندن To be a wet b ; make disappointing remarks. — سنّ ی. Decline of life.

یاسا ○ [f. Mongolion origin] = 1) قانون 2) رسم

یاس‌آور *A. P.* Disappointing.

یاسمن Jessamine; jasmin(e).

یاسین *A.* Title of a *Surah* (*or* chapter) of the *Koran*. — ی. بگوش خر خواندن To play a lyre (in vain) to an ass.

یاعو Gull (*bird*).

یاغی [Per. f. T. origin] Rebel; insurgent. —بکسی ی. شدن To rebel against s. o.

یاغی گری Rebellion; mutiny.

یافت‌شدن • To be found or obtained; be available or obtainable. [tain.

یافتن • [یاب] To find. To ob-

یافته [P. P. of یافتن]

یافث *A-Heb.* Japheth.

یاقوت *A.* Ruby. — یاقوت ارغوانی Amethyst. — یاقوت رمانی or یاقوت آتشی Carbuncle.— یاقوت زرد Topaz. — یاقوت کبود Sapphire.

یاقوت لب • *A. P.* Ruby-lipped.

یاقوتی *A. P.* Resembling a ruby. Ruby-coloured; red.— انگور یاقوتی *Kind of grapes resembling rubies.*

یال Mane. [*By e.* Care-free.

یالغوز *T.* Single; unmarried.

یالیت ○ *A.* = **(ای) کاش**

یاور Assistant or supporter. [Old word for سرگرد].

یاوری — **یاری** & **کمك**

یاوه Idle talk; nonsense.

یاوه‌سرا or **یاوه‌گو** (One) who speaks nonsense; (person) given to babbling or idle talking.

یاوه‌گویی or **یاوه‌سرائی** Speaking nonsense; idle talk.

یاهو *A.* (O) God. *Cf.* یارب

یائسه *A.* Woman on the decline (of life); w. on the wane. [Fem. of یائس ○]

یباب *A.* Ruined; desolate [usu. خراب ویباب].

یبروج or **یبروح** ○ *A.* = **مهرگیاه**

یبس *A.* 1) = خشکی ‖ 2) = یبوست ‖ معده‌اش ی. است *C. E.* He is constipated.

یبوست *A.* Constipation. — دچار یبوست Constipated.

یتیم *A.* 1) Orphan (child). [Pl. ایتام]. 2) *F.* • Unique.

یتیمچه (*A. P.*) *Kind of dish with brinjal.*

یتیم خانه *A. P.* Orphanage; orphan asylum.

یتیمی *A. P.* Orphanhood.

یحتمل *A.* Probably; perhaps.

یحیی (*yahya*) *A.* John.

یخ Ice. — یخ بستن To freeze. — یخ زدن To f. To be freezing.— یخ کردن To freeze; feel very cold. To get cold.— یخش نگرفت × His joke fell flat; the glue did not take. — کلاه یخ or کیسهٔ یخ Ice-bag.— تودهٔ یخ‌غلتان Glacier [also رودخانهٔ یخ] — تودهٔ یخ شناور Iceberg [also کوه یخ]. — گل یخ Chimonanthus fragrans.

یخ باز Skater. [Skate.

یخ بازی Skating. — کفش ی.

یخ بسته Frozen. Ice-bound.

یخ بندان Freezing-weather; (white) frost.

یخچال Ice-house. Refrigerator.

یخچه Hail-stone. *Cf.* تگرگ

یخدان ´ Chest. Ice-chest; ice-box. Earthen vessel from which ice-water was drunk.

یخ دربهشت. *Starch pudding (when cooled).*

یخ زده Frozen.

یخ شکن Ice-pick; ice-chopper.- کرجی ی. Ice-breaker; ice-boat.

یخ کرده Cooled. Frozen.

یخنی *Name of various dishes.* *OS.* Stored away; reserved.

یخه = یقه

ید ´ *A.* Hand [دست]. *F.* Power; authority. Right. – یدِ طولی (-*la*) Profound knowledge; great skill. *OS.* Long hand.

ید ´ *Fr.* Iodine.

یدالله (*A.*) *Mas. pr. name.* *OS.* God's hand.

ید فرم ´ *Fr.* Iodoform.

یدك ´ Led horse.

یدك كش Groom leading a horse. – کشتی ی. Tug-boat.

یدکی Spare. – اسباب ی. [also اشیاء ی.] S. parts; spares.

یدی ´ *A. P.* = دستی Manual. – صنایع ی. M. arts; handwork.

یِر *T.* Kitty; pool; stake.

یراغ *or* **یراق** *T.* Galloon. Harness. *By e.* Fittings – ی. کردن To harness.

یِرالماسی *T.* Jerusalem artichoke

یرتمه *or* **یورتمه** *T.* Trot. – ی. رفتن To trot.

یُرغه ´ *or* **یورغه** *T.* Amble. – ی. رفتن To amble.

یرقان ´ *A.* 1) = زردیان ‖ 2) Blight or mildew.– یرقان سفید Chlorosis; green sickness. – یرقان کبود Cyanosis.

یرقانی *A. P.* Chlorotic. Icteric.

یرلیغ ○ *T.* Royal firman. Safe-conduct.

یزدان ´ 1) = ایزد & خدا God. 2) *Yazdan*: originator of good; the Good Principle.

یزدانی = خدائی - الهی

یسار ´ *A.* = چپ Left. [bearer.

یساول ○ *T.* Mounted mace-

یُسر ´ Easy (circumstances) ○. Black coral; jet.

یشم ´ Jasper. – یشم ختائی Blood-stone.– یشم شیری رنگ Galactite.– یشم سبز Jade.

یشمی Jaspery; jasper-green.

یعقوب ´ *A-Heb.* Jacob. [In the New Testament] James.

یعنی ´ *A.* 1) (It) means.– ی. چه ؟ What does. . . mean? It is surprising. There is no sense in it. The idea! 2) Namely; that is (to say); i. e. (*id est*); viz. (*videlicet*).

یغلا ´ Small frying-pan. *S. a.* یغلاوی

یغلاوی Mess-tin. *S. a.* یغلا

یغما ´ Plunder. –ی. کردن *or* به ی. بردن To plunder.

یغماگر Plunderer.

یُقر ´ × Stout or sturdy.

یقنعلی بقال × Person of low, social rank. (Any) Tom,

Dick, or Harry. —*Note*. یقنلی is per. a cont. of یقین‌علی —typical mas. name.

یقه *T*. *or* + **یخه** Collar. — یقهٔ کسیرا گرفتن To seize some one by the collar. — یقهٔ برگردان Turndown collar. *See* یقه برگردان ‖ یقهٔ عربی Stand-up collar. *See* یقه‌عربی

یقه باز *or* **یخه باز** *T. P.* Low-necked; *décolleté*. [Of men's shirts] Open-necked.

یقه‌برگردان *T.P.* With a turn-down collar. [up collar.

یقه عربی *T. A.* With a stand-

یقین *A. a.* Sure. —*n.* Positive knowledge; certainty. —*ad.* + = یقیناً ‖ ی. داشتن To be sure or certain. — ی. کردن To make s.; become s. — یقینم شد I became s.; I was convinced. — یقیناً = بیقین

یقینا *A.* Certainly; surely.

یك 1) One: یك اطاق ‖ 2) A; an: یك شخصی a (certain) person. 3) Single. خدا یك است ‖ یك‌بیك One by one.

یك انگشتی Monodactyllous.

یکایك One by one.

یکباره & **یکبارگی** All at once. At a single instance.

یك‌بَر Tilted. [Of a ship] Heeled. — ی. کردن To tilt (over); tip; cant; heel.

یك بردو Double; twice as many or as much. [petalous.

یك برگه Monophyllous. Mono-

پیوسته = + **یك بند**

یك پارچه *a.* Concrete; solid. Well-knit. —*ad.* + Sheer; absolutely. — خر یك پارچه *or* ی. خر A blithering ass.

یك پهلو 1) One-sided. 2) = یك دنده

یکتا Single; unique. Incomparable. [ness.

یکتایی Oneness. Incomparable-

یك تخمه Monospermous.

یك‌تَنه Alone. [at once.

یك تیر دو نشان With two aims

یکجا In a lump sum. All together; *en masse*. — ی. کردن To consolidate. — سودا را یکجا کردن To put all one's eggs in one basket.

یك جانبه *P. A.* Unilateral.

یك جمله‌ای *P. A.* Monomial.

یك چشم One-eyed.

یك‌چشمه Monocular. One-eyed. Single-spanned. — عینك ی. Monocle. [while. A few.

یکچند For some time; for a

یك دانه Unique (pearl). [only.

یکدر Obtainable in one shop

یك درمیان Every other one; alternate(ly). — درخت ها را ی. علامت گذاشت He marked every other tree.

یکدست Pure; unmixed. Entire; whole. Single-armed. — قرمز یکدست Full red.

یکدستی زدن + To fish for information (in a roundabout way or by means of a false statement).

یك دفعه *P. A.* = ناگهان

یکدگر * [Cont. of یکدیگر]

یکدل Unanimous.

یکدلی Unanimity; accord.

یك دنده Holding to one's opinion; persistent; adamant; inflexible. [ther.

یکدیگر Each other; one another.

یك راست + Direct : ی. رفت بقم

یك رای *P. A.* = همرای

یك رنگی Sincerity. *S. a.* یکانکی

یك رو or یکرنگ Sincere; guileless

یك روز در میان *ad.* Every other day. *–a.* Tertian: تب ی.

یك زبان Of one voice; unanimous. – ی. شدن To agree.

یك زبانی Unanimity.

یکساله *a.* One-year-old; year-old. *Bot.* Annual. *–ad.* In one year.

یکسان Alike; similar. Uniform. – ی. کردن To unify. – باخاك ی. کردن To level to (*or* with) the ground; raze to the ground.

یکسانی Uniformity. Similarity.

یکسر Totally; entirely. Direct; straight.

یك سرو دوگوش Raw head and bloody bones.

یکسره One-session : خدمت ی. ‖ Through : بلیط ی. ‖ Single trip; travelling one way only. – ی. تا برلین پرواز کرد He flew non-stop to Berlin.– ی. کردن To settle; have it out.

یکشبه *a.* Of one night's duration. *–ad.* 1) In one night. 2) Overnight.

یکشنبه Sunday. [Unilateral.

یك طرفه *P. A.* or یك طرفی

یك قلم *P. A.* In the lump; entirely; all at once.

یك کاره + What a silly idea (to do such a thing particularly)! *–Note.* یك کاره means "particularly (but not for any good reason)".

یك کاسه *a.* Consolidated. Global. – ی. کردن To consolidate. *–ad.* In a lump sum.

یك کلام *P.A.* Fixed, as prices.

یك لا One-fold. Thin. Of a single width; narrow.

یك لتی Single-leaf : درِ یك لتی

یکم First. – بیست ویکم Twenty-first.

یکماهه A month old. – آبستن ی. One m. pregnant; one m. gone (with child).

یکمرتبه *P. A.* Suddenly.

یکمی & یکمین (The) first.

یك نفره & یك نفری *P. A.* 1) Single : رختخواب ی. ‖ Done by one person. 2) *ad.* = تنها

یك نواخت Monotonous; hum-